MORAL ISSUES IN BUSINESS

MORAL ISSUES IN BUSINESS
Fifth Edition

William H. Shaw
San Jose State University
Vincent Barry
Bakersfield College

Wadsworth Publishing Company
Belmont, California
A Division of Wadsworth, Inc.

Philosophy Editor: Kenneth King
Editorial Assistant: Cynthia Campbell
Production: Del Mar Associates
Print Buyer: Randy Hurst
Permissions Editor: Robert Kauser
Designer: Cynthia Bogue
Copy Editor: Karen Bierstedt
Cover Designer: MaryEllen Podgorski
Compositor: TypeLink

This book is printed on acid-free paper that meets Environmental Protection Agency standards for recycled paper.

1 2 3 4 5 6 7 8 9 10 — 96 95 94 93 92

Library of Congress Cataloging in Publication Data

Shaw, William H., 1948–
    Moral issues in business / William H. Shaw, Vincent Barry. — 5th
ed.
        p.   cm.
    Includes bibliographical references and index.
    ISBN 0-534-16704-7
    1. Business ethics.   2. Business ethics — Case studies.   I. Barry,
Vincent E.   II. Title.
HF5387.B35 1992   174′.4 — dc20   91-11719
                                                        CIP

PREFACE

As *Moral Issues in Business* enters its fifth edition, business ethics is now a well-established academic subject. Most colleges and universities offer courses in it, and scholarly interest in the field continues to grow. This is all to the good: It is hard to imagine an area of study that has greater importance to society or greater relevance to students.

Yet some people still scoff at the idea of business ethics, jesting that the very concept is an oxymoron. To be sure, recent years have seen the newspapers filled with lurid stories of corporate misconduct and felonious behavior by individual businesspeople. And many suspect that what the newspapers report represents only the tip of the proverbial iceberg. Yet these reports should push the reflective person, not to make fun of business ethics, but rather to think more deeply about the nature and purpose of business in our society and about the ethical choices individuals must inevitably make in their business and professional lives.

Business ethics has an interdisciplinary character. Questions of economic policy and business practice intertwine with issues in politics, sociology, and organizational theory. Although business ethics remains anchored in philosophy, even here abstract questions in normative ethics and political philosophy mingle with analysis of practical problems and concrete moral dilemmas. Furthermore, business ethics is not just an academic study but also an invitation to reflect on our own values and on our own responses to the moral choices that people face in the world of business. Accordingly, this book sticks to the four main objectives of previous editions: to expose students to the important moral issues that arise in various business contexts; to provide them with an understanding of the moral, social, and economic environments within which those problems occur; to introduce them to the ethical concepts that are relevant for resolving those moral problems; and to assist them in developing the necessary reasoning and analytical skills for doing so. Although the book's primary emphasis is on business, its scope extends to related moral issues in other organizational and professional contexts.

Moral Issues in Business has four parts. Part I, "Moral Philosophy and Business," discusses the nature of morality and presents the main theories of normative ethics and the leading approaches to questions of economic justice. Part II, "American Business and Its Basis," examines the institutional foundations of business, focusing on capitalism as an economic system and the nature and role of corporations in our society. Part III, "The Organization and the People in It," identifies a variety of ethical issues and moral challenges that arise out of the interplay of employers and employees within an organization, including the problem of discrimination. Part IV, "Business and Society," concerns moral problems involving business, consumers, and the natural environment.

Changes in This Edition

Although instructors who have used the previous edition will find the organization and content of the book familiar, the book has been thoroughly revised, and there are significant changes throughout. In revising, we have updated material and tried to enhance the clarity of our discussions and the accuracy of our treatment of both philosophical and empirical issues. We remain committed to providing students with a book that they will find clear, understandable, and engaging. With two chapters on moral problems in the workplace, the book now gives expanded treatment to the many ethical issues facing real people in the world of work: civil liberties on the job, personnel policies and procedures, union issues, drug testing, job satisfaction, worker participation, day care and maternity leave, the "mommy track," and employee health and safety, among other issues.

We have increased the number of case studies to forty-four, adding nine new ones and revising and updating many of the others. The case studies vary in kind and in length, but they are designed to enable instructors and students to pursue further some of the issues discussed in the text and to analyze them in more specific contexts. The case studies should provide a lively springboard for classroom discussions and the application of ethical concepts.

We have also expanded the number of readings to thirty-three, fourteen of which are new. These include essays on drug testing, sexual harassment, employee rights, unions, multinational corporations, the ethics of sales, and much more. The readings are intended to supplement the text by permitting selected topics to be studied in more detail and by exposing students to alternative perspectives and analyses. In selecting and editing the readings, we have sought to provide philosophically interesting essays that will engage students and lend themselves well to class discussion. Although we have added some fresh and timely essays, we have retained those readings that previous users report work well in the classroom.

Ways of Using the Book

A course in business ethics can be taught in a variety of ways. Instructors have different approaches to the subject, different intellectual and pedagogical goals, and different classroom styles. They emphasize different themes and start at different places. No textbook can be all things to all instructors. In any case, were a textbook to succeed in this goal, it would lose its individual voice. Nevertheless, because of the range of topics covered, because of the three types of material in the book—text, cases, and readings—and because of the increased amount of material we have provided, teachers have greater flexibility than ever in how they use *Moral Issues in Business* and in how they organize their courses.

Naturally, the book can be taught cover to cover just as it is, but in a semester course this will require a brisk pace. Many instructors will wish to linger on certain topics, touch briefly on others, and skip some altogether. Assigning all the cases and extra readings as well as the text of a chapter obviously provides for the greatest depth of coverage, but the text can easily be taught by itself or with only some of the cases or readings. The book readily permits topics to be dealt with briefly by assigning only selections from the case studies, the readings, or the text itself, instead of the chapter as a whole. Depending on the instructor's approach, it is even possible to focus the course on the case studies themselves or the readings, with the text assigned only as background.

The chapters themselves are quite self-contained, allowing them to be taught in various orders without loss of coherence. Instructors eager to get to the more specific moral issues discussed in later chapters could skip Parts I and II (perhaps assigning only Solomon and Hanson's "It's Good Business") and begin with the topics that interest them. Other instructors may choose to start with the analysis of capitalism in Chapter 4 or with the discussion of corporate responsibility in Chapter 5, then spend the bulk of the term on the chapters devoted to particular moral topics in business, returning later to some of the issues of Part I. Still other teachers will wish to devote much of a semester to the foundational concerns of Parts I and II and deal more briefly and selectively with later matters.

Acknowledgments

We wish to acknowledge our great debt to the many people whose ideas and writings have influenced us over the years. Philosophy is widely recognized to involve a process of ongoing dialogue. This is nowhere more evident than in the writing of textbooks, whose authors can rarely claim that the ideas being synthesized, organized, and presented are theirs alone. Without our colleagues, without our students, and without a larger philosophical community concerned with business and ethics, this book would not have been possible. We would especially like to thank Sterling Harwood for his help and the reviewers of this and the previous edition for their thoughtful suggestions and useful criticisms: George E. Derfer, Salvatore DeSimone, Robert Winslow Faaborg, Frank Fair, Ralph Forsberg, Leslie Francis, Steven Jay Gold, Samuel Gomez, Michael Harrington, Robert M. Johnson, Dinah Marie Payne, Christine Pierce, Brian Steverson, and Robert Sweet.

BRIEF CONTENTS

CONTENTS

PART III: THE ORGANIZATION AND THE PEOPLE IN IT   261

Chapter 6: The Workplace (1): Basic Issues   261

Chapter 7: The Workplace (2): Today's Challenges   307

Chapter 8: Moral Choices Facing Employees   365

Chapter 9: Job Discrimination   425

MORAL ISSUES IN BUSINESS

PART I

MORAL PHILOSOPHY AND BUSINESS ☐

CHAPTER 1

THE NATURE OF MORALITY ☐

Sometimes the rich and mighty fall. Ivan F. Boesky's world began crumbling in the last months of 1986. On April 23, 1987, he formally pleaded guilty in federal court to a felony charge of stock manipulation. Although everyone in the courtroom realized that he had been involved in a wide range of criminal activities, Boesky was not charged on any further counts because he was cooperating with the authorities in their investigations. But a brilliant career had nose-dived and crashed.

Boesky had been Wall Street's best-known speculator in corporate takeovers. During the boom months in the stock market, as various corporate wars of merger and acquisition were fought, Boesky was often behind the scenes as the institutional fates of billion-dollar organizations were decided. He became rich in the process, but he was also a symbol of the new breed of corporate raiders and Wall Street financiers. *Time* had put him on its cover. Now everybody knew that he was crooked.

When word of Boesky's impending indictment was first made public, Wall Street was awash in rumors. Boesky was a big fish; if he did time for illegal insider trading, it seemed clear that other giants of commerce would too. And Boesky was soon telling authorities shocking tales of corruption on Wall Street and disclosing wrongdoing by a number of major securities firms. When the extraordinarily sustained bull market led to an

equally spectacular crash in October 1987, some business writers drew comparisons with the shady characters who had dominated the stock market before the great crash of 1929 and who were later jailed for their illegal activities. Nor was Wall Street's reputation helped much by the well-publicized 1987 drug bust of some of its top brokers, caught by a federal sting operation in the act of offering cocaine to their clients along with the usual array of stock options.

Against this backdrop, Federal Judge Morris Lasker decided that Boesky should go to jail as a warning to others, despite his having cooperated with authorities. On December 18, 1987, Lasker sentenced the former arbitrageur to three years in jail. In addition, Boesky had already paid a $100 million civil penalty and still faced scores of lawsuits.

Boesky implicated a number of friends and associates, including a flamboyant stock speculator who was arrested in possession of an Israeli assault rifle after threatening the life of Boesky and Boesky's chief trader. Boesky also led investigators to Wall Street's biggest behind-the-scenes player, Michael R. Milken, junk-bond chief at Drexel Burnham Lambert.

Milken was Wall Street's whiz kid, who in a few years almost single-handedly built junk-bond financing into the tool of choice for corporate raiders. In charge of the 150 people who worked at Drexel's junk-bond operation and working twelve to thirteen hours a day, seven days a week, Milken helped transform the world of American business and finance. He also made himself fantastically wealthy and turned Drexel from a second-rank firm into a Wall Street powerhouse.

In 1988 the Securities and Exchange Commission (SEC) brought a 184-page civil complaint and criminal charges against Drexel. Among other things, the company had "parked" stocks with Boesky. To manipulate the market, Boesky would hold stocks secretly owned by Drexel and carry out its buy and sell instructions. He and the company would then divide the profits and destroy the records to keep investigators from finding out about the transactions. Drexel quickly pleaded guilty to six felonies related to market fraud and agreed to pay $650 million in fines and penalties. This and the collapse of the junk-bond market forced Drexel out of business in 1990.

Milken himself was involved in these illegal deals and much, much more. In 1989 the government brought the full force of the federal racketeering law against him for illegal insider trading and various fraudulent activities, and a federal grand jury returned a ninety-eight-count indictment. As a result of intense negotiation, Milken pleaded guilty in April 1990 to six felonies—including conspiracy, securities fraud, mail fraud, and filing false tax forms—and agreed to pay a record $600 million in penalties in return for federal prosecutors dropping the remaining ninety-two charges. Seven months later, Federal District Judge Kimba M. Wood sentenced Milken to ten years in prison for those six crimes. After Milken serves his time, he faces a three-year period of probation, during which he will be required to serve 5,400 hours of community service.

Although the topic of business ethics has long interested the popular media, the Boesky, Milken, and other Wall Street scandals have combined with the crash of the savings and loan industry—where federal au-

thorities estimate that fraud contributed to more than 40 percent of thrift failures[1]—to keep it almost continuously in the headlines. In the newspapers and on television, commentators worry that greed is running rampant in the business world—that its leaders are more interested in fast profits through corporate takeovers, stock maneuvers, and financial legerdemain than in making money through the more time-honored practice of actually producing goods and competing with them in the marketplace. The nation's recent crop of MBAs has also come in for a drubbing, with various pundits alleging that our future captains of finance and industry are devoid of any sense of social responsibility and uniquely single-minded in their pursuit of personal gain.[2]

Although business ethics makes good copy for the media, not all moral issues in business involve the giants of Wall Street or cocaine sales, and few cases of business ethics gain wide publicity. The vast majority of them involve the mundane, uncelebrated moral challenges that working men and women meet daily. The topic of business ethics includes not just the question of the moral or immoral motivations of businesspeople, but also a whole range of problems that arise in the context of business. These issues are too numerous to compile, but consider these typical questions:

> Is passing a personality or honesty test a justifiable pre-employment condition? Are drug tests? What rights do employees have on the job? How should business respond to employees who have AIDS? What, if anything, must it do to improve work conditions?

> Should manufacturers reveal all product defects? At what point does "acceptable exaggeration" become lying about a product or service? When does aggressive marketing become consumer manipulation?

Is a corporation obliged to help combat social problems such as poverty, pollution, and urban decay? Must business fight sexism and racism? How far must it go to ensure equality of opportunity? How should organizations respond to the problem of sexual harassment?

May employees ever use their positions inside an organization to advance their own interests? Is insider trading or the use of privileged information immoral? How much loyalty do workers owe their companies? What say should a business have over the off-the-job activities of its employees?

What obligations does a worker have to outside parties, such as customers, competitors, or society generally? When, if ever, is an employee morally required to "blow the whistle"?

These questions typify business issues with moral significance. The answers we give are determined largely by our moral standards, principles, and values. What these standards and principles are, where they come from, and how they can be assessed are some of the concerns of this opening chapter. In particular, you will encounter the following topics:

1. The nature, scope, and purpose of business ethics

2. The distinguishing features of morality and how it differs from etiquette, law, and professional codes of conduct

3. The relation between morality and religion

4. The doctrine of ethical relativism and its difficulties

5. What it means to have moral principles, the nature of conscience, and the relationship between morality and self-interest

6. The place of values and ideals in a person's life

7. The social and psychological factors that sometimes jeopardize an individual's integrity

8. The characteristics of sound moral reasoning

ETHICS

"The word *ethics* comes from the Greek word *ethos*, meaning character or custom," writes philosophy professor Robert C. Solomon.[3] Today we use the word *ethos* to refer to the distinguishing disposition, character, or attitude of a specific people, culture, or group (as in, for example, "the American ethos" or "the business ethos"). According to Solomon, the etymology of *ethics* suggests its basic concerns: (1) individual character, including what it means to be "a good person," and (2) the social rules that govern and limit our conduct, especially the ultimate rules concerning right and wrong, which we call *morality*.

Some philosophers like to distinguish ethics from morality, such that "morality" refers to human conduct and values and "ethics" refers to the study of those areas. "Ethics" does, of course, denote an academic subject, but in everyday parlance, we interchange "ethical" and "moral" to describe people we consider good and actions we consider right. And we interchange "unethical" and "immoral" to describe what we consider bad people and wrong actions. This book follows that common usage.

Business and Organizational Ethics

The primary focus of this book is ethics as it applies to business. *Business ethics* is the study of what constitutes right and wrong, or good and bad, human conduct in a business context. For example, is a worker ever right in "blowing the whistle"? Under what conditions, if any, can such an act be justified? Is a worker ever morally obliged to blow the whistle?

One difficulty in talking about business ethics is that "business" and "businessperson" have various meanings. "Business" may denote a corner hamburger stand or a corporation that does business in several nations. A "businessperson" may be a gardener engaged in a one-person operation or a corporation president responsible for thousands of workers and enormous corporate investments. Accordingly, the word *business* will be used here simply to mean any organization whose objective is to provide goods or services for profit. *Businesspeople* are those who participate in planning, organizing, or directing the work of business.

But this book takes a broader view as well. It is concerned with moral issues that arise anywhere that employers and employees come together. Thus, it is as much about organizational ethics as business ethics. An *organization* is a group of people working together to achieve a common purpose. The purpose may be to offer a product or service primarily for profit, as in business. But the purpose may be health care, as in medical organizations; public safety and order, as in law-enforcement organizations; education, as in academic organizations; and so on. The cases and illustrations you will come across in this book deal with moral issues and dilemmas in both business and nonbusiness organizational settings.

People occasionally poke fun at the idea of business ethics, declaring that the term is a contradiction or that business has no ethics. Such people take themselves to be worldly and realistic. They think they have a down-to-earth idea of how things really work. In fact, despite its pretense of sophistication, this attitude is embarrassingly naive. People who express it have little grasp of the nature of ethics and only a superficial understanding of the real world of business. After you have read this book, you will perhaps see the truth of this judgment.

Because the study of business and organizational ethics is part of the broader study of ethics, this book discusses basic ethical concepts and general theories of right and wrong. If, for instance, you are to discover guidelines for moral decision making within an organization, you must first explore guidelines for making moral decisions generally. The intimacy between ethics in general and ethics as applied to business contexts implies that one's personal ethics cannot be neatly divorced from one's organizational ethics. In fact, it is safe to say that those who have studied and thought seriously about ethics in general have a more useful basis for making moral decisions in an organizational setting than those who have not.

Perhaps recognition of the intimacy between personal and organizational ethics was what prompted a number of chief executive officers of top American companies and the deans and alumni of prestigious business schools to suggest in an important study that the ideal graduate program in business administration should include a sound grounding in ethics. In the words of Roger L. Jenkins, dean for graduate business programs at the University of Tennessee and the study's conductor: "Today's marketplace calls for a business executive who is bold enough to build his [or her] reputation on integrity and who has a keen sensitivity to the ethical ramifications of his [or her] decision making."[4]

If people within business and nonbusiness organizations are to have "keen sensitivity to the ethical ramifications" of their decision making, they must have moral standards. Moral standards are the basis for moral behavior and differ significantly from nonmoral standards.

MORAL VERSUS NONMORAL STANDARDS

What falls outside the sphere of moral concern is termed *nonmoral*. Whether your new sports car will "top out" at 120 or 130 miles per hour is a nonmoral question. Whether you should top it out on Main Street on a Wednesday at high noon (or even at 3 A.M., for that matter) is a moral question. To see why requires an understanding of the difference between moral standards and other kinds of standards.

Wearing shorts to a formal dinner party is boorish behavior. Murdering the "King's English" with double negatives violates the basic conventions of proper language usage. Photographing the finish of a horse race with low-speed film is poor photographic technique. In each case a standard is violated — fashion, grammatical, artistic — but the violation does not pose a serious threat to human well-being.

One characteristic of *moral standards* that distinguishes them from others is that they concern behavior that can be of serious consequence to human welfare, that can profoundly injure or benefit people.[5] The conventional moral norms against lying, stealing, and murdering deal with actions that can hurt people. And the moral principle that human beings should be treated with dignity and respect uplifts the human personality. Whether products are healthful or harmful, work conditions safe or dangerous, personnel procedures biased or fair, privacy respected or invaded are also matters that seriously affect human well-being. The standards that govern our conduct in these areas are moral standards.

A second characteristic follows from the first. Moral standards take priority over other standards, including self-interest. Something that morality condemns, for instance, the burglary of your neighbor's home, cannot be justified on the nonmoral grounds that it would be a thrill to do it or that it would pay off handsomely. We take moral standards to be more important than other considerations in guiding our actions.

A third characteristic of moral standards is that their soundness depends on the adequacy of the reasons that support or justify them. For the most part, fashion standards are set by clothing designers, merchandisers, and consumers; grammatical standards by grammarians and students of language; artistic standards by art critics and academics. Legislators make laws, boards of directors make organizational policy, and licensing boards establish standards for professionals. In every case, some authoritative body is the ultimate validating source of the standards and thus can change the standards if it wishes. Moral standards are not made by such bodies, although they are often endorsed or rejected by them. More precisely, the validity of moral standards depends not on authoritative fiat but on the adequacy of the reasons that support or justify them. Precisely what constitutes adequate reasons for moral standards is problematic and, as you will see, underlies disagreement about the legitimacy of specific moral principles.

Although these three features set moral standards apart from others, it is useful to distinguish morality more specifically from three areas with which it is sometimes confused: etiquette, law, and so-called professional codes of ethics.

Morality and Etiquette

Etiquette refers to any special code of behavior or courtesy. In our society, for example, it is usually considered bad etiquette to chew with your mouth open or to use obscene language in public; it is considered good etiquette to say "please" when requesting and "thank you" when receiving and to hold a door open for someone entering immediately behind us. Good business etiquette typically calls for writing follow-up letters after meetings, returning phone calls, and dressing appropriately. It is commonplace to judge people's manners as "good" or "bad" and the conduct that reflects them as "right" or "wrong." "Good," "bad," "right," and "wrong" here simply mean socially appropriate or socially inappropriate. In these contexts, such words express judgments about manners, not ethics.

So-called rules of etiquette that you might learn in an etiquette book are prescriptions for socially acceptable behavior. If you want to "fit in," get along with others, and be thought well of by them, you should observe common rules of etiquette. If you violate the rules, then you're rightly considered ill-mannered, impolite, or even uncivilized, but not necessarily immoral.

Rules of etiquette are generally nonmoral in character: "Say 'congratulations' to the groom but 'best wishes' to the bride"; "Push your chair back into place upon leaving a dinner table." But violations of etiquette can have moral implications. The male boss who refers to female subordinates as "honey" and "doll" shows bad manners. If such epithets diminish the worth of female employees or perpetuate sexism, then they also raise moral issues concerning equal treatment and denial of dignity to human beings.

Scrupulous observance of rules of etiquette does not make one moral. In fact, it can camouflage moral issues. Not too long ago in some parts of the United States, it was thought bad manners for blacks and whites to eat together. Those who obeyed the convention and were thus judged well-mannered certainly had no grounds for feeling moral. The only way to dramatize the injustice underlying this practice was to violate the rule and be judged ill-mannered. For those in the civil rights movement of the 1960s, being considered boorish was a small price to pay for exposing the unequal treatment and human degradation that underlay this rule of etiquette.

Morality and Law

Before distinguishing between morality and law, you should understand the term *law*. Basically, there are four kinds of law: statutes, regulations, common law, and constitutional law.

Statutes are laws enacted by legislative bodies. The law that prohibits theft is a statute. Congress and state legislatures enact statutes. (Laws enacted by local governing bodies like city councils usually are termed *ordinances*.) Statutes make up a large part of the law and are what many of us mean when we speak of laws.

Limited in their knowledge, legislatures often set up boards or agencies whose functions include issuing detailed regulations of certain kinds of conduct—*administrative regulations*. For example, state legislatures establish licensing boards to formulate regulations for the licensing of physicians and nurses. As long as these regulations do not exceed the board's statutory powers and do not conflict with other kinds of law, they are legally binding.

Common law refers to laws applied in the English-speaking world before there were any statutes. Courts frequently wrote opinions explaining the bases of their decisions in specific cases, including the legal principles they deemed appropriate. Each of these options became a precedent for later decisions in similar cases. Over the years, a massive body of legal principles accumulated that is collectively referred to as common law. Like administrative regulations, common law is valid if it harmonizes with statutory law and with still another kind, constitutional law.

Constitutional law refers to court rulings on the constitutionality of any law. The courts are empowered under the U.S. Constitution to decide whether laws are compatible with the Constitution. State courts may also rule on the constitutionality of state laws under state constitutions. Although the courts cannot make laws, they have far-reaching powers to rule on the constitutionality of laws and to declare them invalid. The U.S. Supreme Court has the greatest judiciary power and rules on an array of cases, some of which bear directly on the study of ethics.

The legality of an action, however, does not guarantee that the action is morally right. Consider an actual case of a four-month-old baby suffering from diarrhea and fever.[6] The family physician prescribed medication on the second day of the child's illness and saw him during office hours on the third day. On the fourth day, the child's condition worsened. Knowing that the doctor was not in the office that day, the parents whisked the child to the emergency room of a nearby hospital, where they were told that hospital policy forbade treating anyone already under a doctor's care without first contacting the doctor. Unable to reach the doctor and thus denied emergency treatment, the parents took their child home, where he died later that day of bronchial pneumonia.

There was a time when hospitals had a legal right to accept for emergency treatment only those they chose to accept. Under such a rule, then, the hospital would have been exercising its legal right. But would the hospital have been morally justified in exercising that right, when by so doing it would deny the child life-saving care? Philosophers might disagree in their answers. But they would agree that the issue cannot be satisfactorily resolved by appeal to law alone. (As it happened, the case went to court and set a precedent by repudiating the traditional discretionary powers given a hospital in operating its emergency facility. But even if the court had upheld the institution's legal right, the hospital's policy would still be open to moral assessment and possible criticism.)

Consider a second case. Suppose that you're driving to work one day and see an accident victim on the side of the road, blood oozing from his leg. He is clearly in need of immediate medical attention, which you can provide since you just completed a first-aid course.

Legally speaking, you have no obligation to stop and offer aid. Under the common law, the prudent thing would be to drive on, since by stopping you would bind yourself to use reasonable care and thus incur legal liability if you fail to do so and the victim thereby suffers injury. Most states have enacted so-called "Good Samaritan laws" to provide immunity from damages to those rendering aid (except for gross negligence or serious misconduct). But the law does not oblige people to render such aid or even (in most states) to call an ambulance. Moral theorists would agree, however, that if you sped away without rendering aid or even calling for help, your action might be perfectly legal but would be morally suspect. Regardless of the law, such conduct would almost certainly be wrong.

What then may we say of the relationship between law and morality? In theory and practice, law codifies customs, ideals, beliefs, and a society's moral values. Law undoubtedly reflects changes in a society's outlook in its view of right and wrong, good and bad. But it is a mistake to see law as sufficient to establish the moral standards that should guide an individual, a profession, an organization, or a society. Law simply cannot cover the variety of individual and group conduct. The law does prohibit egregious affronts to a society's moral standards and in that sense is the "floor" of moral conduct. But breaches of moral conduct can fall through the cracks in that floor.

Conformity with law is not sufficient for moral conduct any more than conformity with etiquette is. By the same token, nonconformity with law is not necessarily immoral, for the law disobeyed may be unjust. Probably no one in the modern era has expressed this point more eloquently than Dr. Martin Luther King, Jr. Confined in the Birmingham, Alabama, city jail on charges of parading without a permit, King penned his now famous "Letter from Birmingham Jail" to eight of his fellow clergymen who had published a statement attacking King's unauthorized protest of racial segregation as unwise and untimely. King wrote:

> All segregation statutes are unjust because segregation distorts the soul and damages the personality. It gives the segregator a false sense of superiority and the segregated a false sense of inferiority.

Segregation, to use the terminology of the Jewish philosopher Martin Buber, substitutes an "I-it" relationship for an "I-thou" relationship and ends up relegating persons to the status of things. Hence segregation is not only politically, economically, and sociologically unsound, it is morally wrong and sinful. . . . Thus it is that I can urge men to obey the 1954 decision of the Supreme Court,* for it is morally right; and I can urge them to disobey segregation ordinances, for they are morally wrong.[7]

Professional Codes

Somewhere between etiquette and law lie *professional codes of ethics*. These are the rules that are supposed to govern the conduct of members of a given profession. Generally speaking, the members of a profession are understood to have agreed to abide by those rules as a condition of their engaging in that profession. Violation of the professional code may result in the disapproval of one's professional peers and, in serious cases, loss of one's license to practice that profession. Sometimes these codes are unwritten and are part of the common understanding of members of a profession — for example, that professors should not date students in their classes. In other instances, these codes or portions of them may be written down by an authoritative body so they may be better taught and more efficiently enforced.

These written rules are sometimes so vague and general as to be of little value, and often they amount to little more than self-promotion by the professional organization. The same is frequently true when industries or corporations publish statements of their ethical standards. In other cases, for example

with attorneys, professional codes can be very specific and detailed. It is hard to generalize about the content of professional codes of ethics, however, since they frequently involve a mix of purely moral rules (for example, client confidentiality), of professional etiquette (for example, the billing of services to other professionals), and of restrictions intended to benefit the group's economic interests (for example, prohibition of price competition).

Given their nature, professional codes of ethics are neither a complete nor a completely reliable guide to one's moral obligations. First, not all the rules of a professional code are purely moral in character, and even where they are, the fact that a rule is officially enshrined as part of the code of a profession does not guarantee that it is a sound moral principle. As a professional, you must take seriously the injunctions of your profession, but you still have the responsibility to critically assess those rules for yourself.

Regarding those parts of the code that concern etiquette or financial matters, bear in mind that by joining a profession you are probably agreeing, explicitly or implicitly, to abide by those standards. Assuming that those rules don't require morally impermissible conduct, then consenting to them gives you some moral obligation to follow them. In addition, for many, living up to the standards of one's chosen profession is an important source of personal satisfaction. Still, you must be alert to situations in which professional standards or customary professional practice conflicts with the ordinary demands of morality. Adherence to a professional code does not exempt your conduct from scrutiny from the broader perspective of morality.

Where Do Moral Standards Come From?

So far you have seen how moral standards are different from various nonmoral standards, but you are probably concerned to

---

* In *Brown* v. *Board of Education of Topeka* (1954), the Supreme Court struck down the half-century-old "separate but equal doctrine," which permitted racially segregated schools as long as comparable quality was maintained.

know the source of those moral standards. Most, if not all, people have certain moral principles or a moral code that they explicitly or implicitly accept. Because the moral principles of different people in the same society overlap, at least in part, we can also talk about the moral code of a society, meaning the moral standards shared in common by its members. How do we come to have certain moral principles and not others? Obviously, many things influence us in the moral principles we accept: our early upbringing, the behavior of those around us, the explicit and implicit standards of our culture, our own experiences, and our critical reflections on those experiences.

For philosophers, though, the important question is not how in fact we came to have the particular principles we have. The philosophical issue is whether the principles we have can be justified. Do we simply take for granted the values of those around us? Or like Martin Luther King, Jr., are we able to think independently about moral matters? By analogy, we pick up our nonmoral beliefs from all sorts of sources: books, conversations with friends, movies, various experiences we've had. The philosopher's concern is not so much with how we actually got the beliefs we have, but whether or to what extent those beliefs—for example, that women are more emotional than men or that telekinesis is possible—can withstand critical scrutiny. Likewise, ethical theories attempt to justify moral standards and ethical beliefs. The next chapter examines some of the major theories of normative ethics. That is, it looks at what some of the major thinkers in human history have argued to be the best-justified standards of right and wrong.

But first the relationship between morality and religion on the one hand and morality and society on the other needs to be discussed. Some people maintain that morality just boils down to religion. Others have argued for the doctrine of *ethical relativism*, which says that right and wrong are only a function of what a particular society takes to be right and wrong. Both these views are mistaken.

RELIGION AND MORALITY

Any religion provides its believers with a world view, part of which involves certain moral instructions, values, and commitments. The Jewish and Christian traditions, to name just two, offer a view of humans as unique products of a divine intervention that has endowed them with consciousness and an ability to love. Both these traditions posit creatures who stand midway between nature and spirit. On the one hand, we are finite, bound to earth, and capable of sin. On the other, we can transcend nature and realize infinite possibilities.

Primarily because of the influence of Western religion, many Americans and others view themselves as beings with a supernatural destiny, as possessing a life after death, as being immortal. One's purpose in life is found in serving and loving God. For the Christian, the way to serve and love God is by emulating the life of Jesus of Nazareth. In the life of Jesus, Christians find an expression of the highest virtue—love. They love when they perform selfless acts, develop a keen social conscience, and realize that human beings are creatures of God and therefore intrinsically worthwhile. For the Jew, one serves and loves God chiefly through expressions of justice and righteousness. Jews also develop a sense of honor derived from a commitment to truth, humility, fidelity, and kindness. This commitment hones their sense of responsibility to family and community.

Religion, then, involves not only a formal system of worship but prescriptions for social relationships. One example is the mandate "Do unto others as you would have them do unto you." Termed "the Golden Rule," this injunction represents one of humankind's highest moral ideals and can be found in essence in all the great religions of the world.

> Good people proceed while considering that what is best for others is best for themselves. (*Hitopadesa*, Hinduism)

> Thou shalt love thy neighbor as thyself. (*Leviticus* 19:18, Judaism)

> Therefore all things whatsoever ye would that men should do to you, do ye even so to them. (*Matthew* 7:12, Christianity)

> Hurt not others with that which pains yourself. (*Udanavarga* 5:18, Buddhism)

> What you do not want done to your-self, do not do to others. (*Analects* 15:23, Confucianism)

> No one of you is a believer until he loves for his brother what he loves for himself. (*Traditions*, Islam)

Although inspiring, such religious ideals are very general and can be difficult to translate into precise policy injunctions. Religious bodies, nevertheless, occasionally articulate positions on more specific political, educational, economic, and medical issues, which help mold public opinion on matters as diverse as abortion, euthanasia, nuclear weapons, and national defense. Roman Catholicism has a rich tradition of formally applying its core values to the moral aspects of industrial relations. The National Conference of Catholic Bishops' pastoral letter, *Economic Justice for All*, on Catholic social teaching and the U.S. economy, stands in this tradition. Having gone through several drafts over more than two years before its final approval by the Conference in November 1986, the pastoral letter is really a book-length reflection on the moral dimensions and human consequences of American economic life. It examines specific policy questions and is intended to help shape a national discussion of these issues.

Morality Needn't Rest on Religion

Many people believe that morality must be based on religion, either in the sense that without religion people would have no incentive to be moral or in the sense that only religion can provide us guidance. Others contend that morality is based on the commands of God. None of these claims is very plausible.

First, although a desire to avoid hell and to go to heaven may prompt some of us to act morally, this is not the only reason or even the most common reason that people behave morally. Often we act morally out of habit or simply because that is the kind of person we are. It would just not occur to most of us to swipe an elderly lady's purse. And if the idea did occur to us, we wouldn't do it because such an act simply doesn't fit with our personal standards or with our concept of ourselves. We are often motivated to do what is morally right out of concern for others or just because it is right. In addition, the approval of our peers, the need to appease our consciences, and the desire to avoid earthly punishment, all may motivate us to act morally. And it is worth noting that many atheists—like the philosopher Bertrand Russell—have led morally admirable lives.

Second, the moral instructions of the world's great religions are general and somewhat vague: They do not relieve us of the necessity to engage in moral reasoning ourselves. For example, the Bible says, "Thou shall not kill." Yet Christians disagree among themselves over the morality of fighting in wars, of capital punishment, of killing in self-defense, of slaughtering animals, of abortion and euthanasia, and of allowing foreigners to die from famine because we have not provided them with as much food as we might have. The Bible does not give unambiguous answers to these moral problems. So even believers must engage in moral philosophy if they are to have intelligent answers. On the other hand, there are lots of reasons for believing that, say, a cold-blooded murder motivated by greed is immoral; you do not have to believe in a religion to figure that out.

Third, although some theologians have advocated the *divine command theory*—that if something is wrong (like killing an innocent person for fun), then the only reason it is wrong is that God commands us not to do it—many theologians and certainly most philosophers would reject this view. They would contend that if God commands human beings not to do something, like commit rape, it is because God sees that rape is wrong, but it is not God's forbidding rape that makes it wrong. The fact that rape is wrong is independent of God's decrees.

Most believers think not only that God gives us moral instructions or rules but also that God has moral reasons for giving them to us. According to the divine command theory, this would make no sense. In this view, there is no reason that something is right or wrong, other than it being God's will. All believers, of course, believe that God is good and that He commands us to do what is right and forbids us to do what is wrong. But this doesn't mean, say critics of the divine command theory, that God's saying so makes a thing wrong, any more than it is your mother's telling you not to steal that makes it wrong to steal.

All this is simply to argue that morality is not necessarily based on religion in any of the three senses distinguished above. That religion influences the moral standards and values of most of us is beyond doubt. But given that religions differ in their moral principles and that even members of the same faith often disagree among themselves on moral matters, practically speaking you cannot justify a moral principle simply by appealing to religion—for that will only persuade those who already agree with your particular interpretation of your particular religion. Besides, most religions hold that human reason is capable of understanding what is right and wrong, so it is human reason to which you will have to appeal in order to support your ethical principle.

ETHICAL RELATIVISM

Some people do not believe that morality boils down to religion but rather that it is just a function of what a particular society happens to believe. This view is called *ethical relativism*. It is the theory that what is right is determined by what a culture or society says is right. What is right in one place may be wrong in another, because the only criterion for distinguishing right from wrong—and so the only ethical standard for judging an action—is the moral system of the society in which the act occurs.

Abortion, for example, is condemned as immoral in Catholic Spain but is practiced as a morally neutral form of birth control in Japan. According to the ethical relativist, then, abortion is wrong in Spain but morally permissible in Japan. The relativist is not saying merely that the Spanish believe abortion is abominable and the Japanese do not; that is acknowledged by everyone. Rather, the ethical relativist contends that abortion is immoral in Spain because the Spanish believe it to be immoral and morally permissible in Japan because the Japanese believe it to be so. Thus, for the ethical relativist there is no absolute ethical standard independent of cultural context, no criterion of right and wrong by which to judge other than that of particular societies. In short, what morality requires is relative to society.

Those who endorse ethical relativism point to the apparent diverseness of human values and the multiformity of moral codes to support their case. From our own cultural perspective, some seemingly "immoral" moralities have been adopted; polygamy, homosexuality, stealing, slavery, infanticide, and cannibalism have all been tolerated or even encouraged by the moral system of one society or another. In light of this fact, the ethical relativist believes that there can be no non-ethnocentric standard by which to judge actions.

Contrary to the relativist, some argue that the moral differences between societies are not as great or as significant as they appear. They contend that variations in moral standards reflect differing factual beliefs and differing circumstances rather than fundamental differences in values. But suppose the relativist is right about this matter. His conclusion still does not follow. As Allan Bloom writes, "The fact that there have been different opinions about good and bad in different times and places in no way proves that none is true or superior to others. To say that it does so prove is as absurd as to say that the diversity of points of view expressed in a college bull session proves there is no truth."[8] Disagreement in ethical matters does not imply that all opinions are equally correct.

Moreover, ethical relativism has some unpleasant implications. First, it undermines any moral criticism of the practices of other societies as long as their actions conform to their own standards. We cannot say that slavery in a slave society like that of the American South of the last century was immoral and unjust as long as that society held it to be morally permissible.

Second, and closely related, is the fact that for the relativist there is no such thing as ethical progress. While moralities may change, they cannot get better or worse. Thus, we cannot say that our moral standards today are any more enlightened than they were in the Middle Ages.

Third, it makes no sense from the relativist's point of view for people to criticize principles or practices accepted by their own society. People can be censured for not living up to their society's moral code, but that is all; the moral code itself cannot be criticized. Whatever a society takes to be right really is right for it. Reformers who campaign against the "injustices" of their society are only encouraging people to be immoral—that is, to depart from the moral standards of their society—unless or until the majority of the society agrees with the reformers. The minority can never be right in moral matters; to be right it must become the majority.

The ethical relativist is right to emphasize that in viewing other cultures we should keep an open mind and not simply dismiss alien social practices on the basis of our own cultural prejudices. But the relativist's theory of morality doesn't hold up. The more carefully we examine it, the less plausible it becomes. There is no good reason for saying that the majority view on moral issues is automatically right, and the belief that it is automatically right has unacceptable consequences.

Relativism and the "Game" of Business

In his well-known and influential essay "Is Business Bluffing Ethical?" Albert Carr argues that business, as practiced by individuals as well as by corporations, has the impersonal character of a game—a game that demands both special strategy and an understanding of its special ethical standards.[9] Business has its own norms and rules, differing from those of the rest of society. Thus according to Carr, a number of things that we normally think of as wrong are really permissible in a business context. His examples include conscious misstatement and concealment of pertinent facts in negotiation, lying about your age on a résumé, deceptive packaging, automobile companies' neglect of car safety, and utility companies' manipulation of regulators and overcharging of electricity users. He draws an analogy with poker:

Poker's own brand of ethics is different from the ethical ideals of civilized human relationships. The game calls for distrust of the other fellow. It ignores the claim of friendship. Cunning deception and concealment of one's strength and intentions, not kindness and openheartedness, are vital in poker. No one thinks any the worse of poker on that account. And no one should think any the worse of the game of business because its standards of right and wrong differ from the prevailing traditions of morality in our society.

What Carr is defending here is a kind of ethical relativism: Business has its own moral standards, and business actions should be evaluated only by those standards.

One can argue whether Carr has accurately identified the implicit rules of the business world (for example, is misrepresentation on one's résumé really a permissible move in the business game?), but let's put that issue aside. The basic question is whether business is a separate world to which ordinary moral standards don't apply. Carr's thesis implies that any special activity following its own rules is exempt from external moral evaluation, but as a general thesis this is unacceptable. The Mafia, for example, has an elaborate code of conduct, accepted by the members of the rival "families." For them, gunning down a competitor or terrorizing a local shopkeeper may be strategic moves in a competitive environment. Yet we rightly refuse to say that gangsters cannot be criticized for following their own standards. Normal business activity is a world away from gangsterism, but the point still holds. Any specialized activity or practice will have its own distinctive rules and procedures, but those rules and procedures can still be morally evaluated.

Moreover, Carr's poker analogy is itself weak. For one thing, business activity can affect those—like consumers—who have not consciously and freely chosen to play the "game." Business is indeed an activity involving distinctive rules and customary ways of doing things, but it is not really a game. It is the economic basis of our society, and we all have an interest in the goals of business (in productivity and consumer satisfaction, for instance) and in the rules business follows. Why should these be exempt from public evaluation and assessment? Later chapters return to the question of what these goals and rules should be. But to take one simple point, notice that a business/economic system that permits, encourages, or tolerates deception will be less efficient (that is, work less well) than one in which the participants have fuller knowledge about the goods and services being exchanged.

In sum, by divorcing business from morality, Carr misrepresents both. He incorrectly treats the standards and rules of everyday business activity as if they had nothing to do with the standards and rules of ordinary morality. And he treats morality as something that we give lip service to on Sundays but that otherwise has no influence on our lives.

HAVING MORAL PRINCIPLES

Most people at some time in their lives pause to reflect on what moral principles they have or should have and on what moral standards are the best justified. (Moral philosophers themselves have defended different moral standards, and Chapter 2 discusses these various theories.) When a person accepts a moral principle, when that principle is part of his or her personal moral code, then naturally the person believes the principle is important and that it is well justified. But there is more to moral principles than that, as Professor Richard Brandt of the University of Michigan has emphasized. When a principle is part of a person's moral code, that person is strongly motivated toward the conduct required by the principle and against behavior that conflicts with that principle. The person will tend to feel guilty when his or her own conduct violates that principle and to disapprove of others whose behavior conflicts with it. Likewise, the person will tend to hold in esteem those whose conduct shows an abundance of the motivation required by the principle.[10]

Other philosophers have, in different ways, reinforced Brandt's point. To accept a moral principle is not a purely intellectual act like accepting a scientific hypothesis or a mathematical theorem. Rather, it involves also a desire to follow that principle for its own sake, the likelihood of feeling guilty about not doing so, and a tendency to evaluate the conduct of others according to the principle in question. We would find it very strange, for example, if Sally claimed to be morally opposed to cruelty to animals yet abused her own pets and felt no inclination to protest when some ruffians down the street lit a cat on fire.

Conscience

People can and, unfortunately, sometimes do go against their moral principles. But we would doubt that they sincerely held the principle in question if violating it did not bother their conscience. We have all felt the pangs of conscience, but what exactly is conscience and how reliable a guide is it? Our conscience, of course, is not literally a little voice inside of us. To oversimplify a complex story in developmental psychology, our conscience evolved as we internalized the moral instructions of the parents or other authority figures who raised us as children.

When you were very young, you were probably told to tell the truth and to return something you liked to its proper owner. If you were caught lying or being dishonest, you were probably punished—scolded, spanked, sent to bed without dinner, denied a privilege. On the other hand, truth telling and honesty were probably rewarded—with approval, praise, maybe even hugs or candy. Seeking reward and avoiding punishment motivate small children to do what is expected of them. Gradually, children come to internalize those parental commands. Thus, they feel vaguely that their parents know what they are doing even when the parents are not around. When children do something forbidden, they experience the same feelings as when scolded by their parents—the first stirrings of guilt. By the same token, even in the absence of explicit parental reward, children feel a sense of self-approval about having done what they were supposed to have done.

As we grow older, of course, our motivations are not so simple and our self-understanding is greater. We are able to reflect on and understand the moral lessons we were taught, as well as to refine and modify those principles. As adults we are morally independent agents. Yet however much our consciences have evolved and however much our adult moral code differs from the moral perspective of our childhood, those pangs of guilt we occasionally feel still stem from that early internalization of parental demands.

The Limits of Conscience

Something like this is the psychological story of conscience, but how reliable a guide is it? People often say, "Follow your conscience" or "You should never go against your conscience," but not only is such advice not very helpful, it may sometimes be bad advice. First, when we are genuinely perplexed over what we ought to do, we are trying to figure out what our conscience ought to be saying to us. When it is not possible to do both, should we keep our promise to a colleague or come to the aid of an old friend? To be told that we should follow our conscience is no help at all.

Second, it may not always be good for us to follow our conscience. It all depends on what our conscience says. Our conscience might reflect moral motivations that cannot withstand critical scrutiny. Consider an episode in Chapter 16 of Mark Twain's *The Adventures of Huckleberry Finn*. Huck has taken off down the Mississippi on a raft with his friend, the runaway slave Jim. But as they get nearer to the place where Jim will become legally free, Huck starts feeling guilty about helping him run away:

> It hadn't ever come home to me, before, what this thing was that I was doing. But now it did; and it stayed with me, and scorched me more and more. I tried to make out to myself that *I* warn't to blame, because I didn't run Jim off from his rightful owner; but it warn't no use, conscience up and say, every time: "But you knowed he was running for his freedom, and you could a paddled ashore and told somebody." That was so — I couldn't get around that, no way. That was where it pinched. Conscience says to me: "What had poor Miss Watson done to you, that you could see her nigger go off right under your eyes and never say one single word? What did that poor old woman do to you, that you could treat her so mean? . . ." I got to feeling so mean and miserable I most wished I was dead.

Here Huck is feeling guilty about doing what we would all agree is the morally right thing to do. But Huck is only a boy, and his pangs of conscience reflect the principles that he has picked up uncritically from the slave-owning society around him. Unable to think independently about matters of right and wrong, Huck in the end decides to disregard his conscience. He follows his instincts and sticks by his friend Jim.

The point here is not that you should ignore your conscience but that the voice of conscience is itself something that can be critically examined. A pang of conscience is like a warning. When you feel one, you should definitely stop and reflect on the rightness of what you are doing. On the other hand, you cannot justify your actions simply by saying you were following your conscience. Terrible crimes have occasionally been committed in the name of conscience.

Moral Principles and Self-Interest

Sometimes doing what you believe would be morally right and doing what would best satisfy your own interests may be two different things. Imagine that you are in your car hurrying home along a quiet road, trying hard to get there in time to see the kickoff of an important football game. You pass an acquaintance who is having car trouble. He doesn't recognize you. As a dedicated fan, you would much prefer to keep on going than to stop and help him, thus missing at least part of the game. You might rationalize that someone else will eventually come along and help him if you don't, but deep down you know that you really ought to stop. On the other hand, self-interest seems to say, "Keep going."

Or consider an example suggested by Baruch Brody.[11] You have applied for a new job, and if you land it, it will be an enormous break for you: It is exactly the kind of position you want and have been trying to get for some time. It pays well and will settle you into a desirable career for the rest of your life. The competition has come down to just you and one other person, and you believe correctly that she has a slight edge on you. Now imagine that you could spread a nasty rumor about her that would guarantee that she wouldn't get the job and that you could do this in a way that wouldn't come back to you. Presumably, circulating this lie would violate your moral code; on the other hand, doing it would clearly benefit old "number one."

Some people argue that moral action and self-interest can never genuinely be in conflict, and some philosophers have gone to great lengths to try to prove this, but they are almost certainly mistaken. They maintain that if you do the wrong thing, then you will be caught, your conscience will bother you, or in some way "what goes around comes around," so that your misdeed will come back to haunt you. This is often correct. But unfortunate as it may be, sometimes—viewed just in terms of personal self-interest—it may pay off for you to do what you know to be wrong. People sometimes get away with their wrongdoings, and if their conscience bothers them at all, it may not bother them that much. To believe otherwise not only is wishful thinking but also shows a lack of understanding of morality.

Morality serves to restrain our purely self-interested desires so we can all live together. The moral standards of a society provide the basic guidelines for cooperative social existence and allow conflicts to be resolved by appeal to shared principles of justification. If our interests never came into conflict—that is, if it were never advantageous for one person to deceive or cheat another—then there would be little need for morality. We would already be in heaven. Both a system of law that punishes people for hurting others and a system of morality that encourages people to refrain from pursuing their self-interest at a great expense to others help to make social existence possible.

Usually, following our moral principles is in our best interest. This idea is particularly worth noting in the business context. Several recent writers have argued persuasively not only that moral behavior is consistent with profitability but also that the most morally responsible companies are among the most profitable.[12] Apparently, respecting the rights of employees, treating suppliers fairly, and being straightforward with customers pay off.

But notice one thing. If you do the right thing only because you think it will pay off, you are not really motivated by moral concerns. Having a moral principle involves having a desire to follow the principle for its own sake—just because it is the right thing to do. If you do the right thing only because you believe it will pay off, you might just as easily not do it if it looks as if it is not going to pay off.

In addition, there is no guarantee that moral behavior will always pay off in strictly selfish terms. As argued above, there will be exceptions. From the moral point of view, you ought to stop and help your colleague, and you shouldn't lie about competitors. From the selfish point of view, you should do exactly the opposite. Should you follow your self-interest or your moral principles? There's no final answer to this question. From the moral point of view, you should, of course, follow your moral principles. But from the selfish point of view, you should look out solely for "number one."

Which option you choose will depend on the strength of your self-interested or "self-regarding" desires in comparison with the strength of your "other-regarding" desires (that is, your moral motivations and your concern for others). In other words, your choice will depend on the kind of person you are, which depends in large part on how you were raised. A person who is basically selfish will pass by the acquaintance in distress and will spread the rumor, while a person who has a stronger concern for others, or a stronger desire to do what is right just because it is right, will not.

Although it may be impossible to prove to selfish persons that they should not do the thing that best advances their self-interest (since, if they are selfish, that is all they care about), there are considerations that suggest it is not in a person's overall self-interest to be a selfish person. People who are exclusively concerned with their own interests tend to have less happy and less satisfying lives than those whose desires extend beyond themselves. This is sometimes called the "paradox of hedonism." Individuals who care only about their own happiness will generally be less happy than those who care about others. And people often find greater satisfaction in a life lived according to moral principle, and in being the kind of person that entails, than in a life devoted solely to immediate self-interest. Thus, or so many philosophers have argued, people have self-interested reasons not to be so self-interested. How do selfish people make themselves less so? Not overnight, obviously, but by involving themselves in the concerns and cares of others, they can in time come to care sincerely about those persons.

MORALITY AND PERSONAL VALUES

Some philosophers distinguish between morality in a narrow sense and morality in a broad sense. In a narrow sense, morality is the moral code of an individual or a society (insofar as the moral codes of the individuals making up that society overlap). While the principles that make up our code may not be explicitly formulated, as laws are, they do guide us in our conduct. They function as internal monitors of our own behavior and as a basis for assessing the actions of others. Morality in the narrow sense concerns the principles that do or should regulate people's conduct and relations with others. These principles can be debated, however. (Take, for example, John Stuart Mill's contention that society ought not to interfere with people's liberty when their actions affect only themselves.) And a large part of moral philosophy involves assessing rival moral principles. This discussion is part of the ongoing development in our moral culture. What is at stake are the basic standards that ought to govern our behavior—that is, the basic framework or ground rules that make coexistence possible. If there were not already fairly widespread agreement about these principles, our social order would not be possible.

But in addition we can talk about our morality in a broader sense, meaning not just the principles of conduct that we embrace but also the values, ideals, and aspirations that shape our lives. Many different ways of living our lives would meet our basic moral obligations. The type of life each of us seeks to live reflects our individual values—whether following a profession, devoting ourselves to community service, raising a family, seeking solitude, pursuing scientific truth, striving for athletic excellence, amassing political power, cultivating glamorous people as friends, or some combination of these and many other possible ways of living. The life that each of us forges and the way we understand that life are part of our morality in the broad sense of the term.

It is important to bear this in mind throughout your study of business ethics. While the usual concern is with the principles that ought to govern conduct in certain situations—for example, whether a hiring officer may take the race of applicants into account, whether employees may be forced to take an AIDS test, or whether corporate bribery is permissible in countries where people turn a blind eye to it—your choices in the business world will also reflect your other values and ideals—or in other words, the kind of person you are striving to be. What sort of ideal do you have of yourself as a businessperson? How much weight do you put on profitability, for instance, as against the quality of your product or the socially beneficial character of your service?

Many of the decisions you make in your career and much of the way you shape your working life will depend not just on your moral code but also on the understanding you have of yourself in certain roles and relationships. Your "morality"—in the sense of your ideals, values, and aspirations—involves, among other things, your understanding of human nature, tradition, and society; your proper relationship to the natural environment; and your place in the cosmos. Professionals in various fields, for example, will invariably be guided not just by rules but also by their understanding of what "being a professional" involves. And a businessperson's conception of the ideal or model relationship to have with clients will greatly influence his or her day-to-day conduct.

But there is more to living a morally good life than being a good businessperson or being good at your job, as Aristotle (384–322 B.C.) argued long ago. He underscored the necessity of our trying to achieve virtue or excellence, not just in some particular field of endeavor but as human beings. Aristotle thought that things have functions. The function of a piano, for instance, is to make certain sounds, and a piano that performs this function well is a good or excellent piano. Likewise, we have an idea of what it is for a person to be an excellent athlete, an excellent manager, or an excellent professor — it is to do well the types of things that athletes, managers, or professors are supposed to do.

But Aristotle also thought that, just as there is an ideal of excellence for any particular craft or occupation, similarly there must be an excellence that we can achieve simply as human beings. That is, he thought that we can live our lives as a whole in such a way that they can be judged not just as excellent in this respect or in that occupation, but as excellent, period. Aristotle thought that only when we develop our truly human capacities sufficiently to achieve this human excellence will we have lives blessed with happiness. Philosophers since Aristotle's time have been skeptical of his apparent belief that this human excellence would come in just one form, but many would underscore the importance of developing our various potential capacities and striving to achieve a kind of excellence in our lives. How we understand this excellence is a function of our values, ideals, and world view — our morality in a broad sense.

INDIVIDUAL INTEGRITY AND RESPONSIBILITY

Previous sections discussed what it is for a person to have a moral code, as well as the sometimes conflicting pulls of moral con-science and self-interest. In addition, you have seen that people have values and ideals above and beyond their moral principles, narrowly understood, that also influence the lives they lead. And you have seen the importance of reflecting critically on both moral principles and moral ideals and values as we seek to live morally good and worthwhile lives. None of us, however, lives in a vacuum, and social pressures of various sorts always affect us. Sometimes these pressures make it difficult to stick with our principles and to be the kind of person we wish to be. Corporations are a particularly relevant example of an environment that can potentially damage individual integrity and responsibility.

The Individual Inside the Corporation

Corporations exact a price for the many benefits they offer their members — jobs, status, money, friendship, personal fulfillment. Sometimes the price of corporate membership amounts to individual conscience, as the experience of David A. Frew, professor of behavioral science, indicates.[13]

As a case-working theorist, Frew interviewed a number of workers at various levels of a corporation known to be a substantial polluter. Frew discovered that, although each person recognized and deplored the organization's pollution activities, each was willing to continue daily activities that contributed to the problem. One respondent even volunteered that it wouldn't be long before the company despoiled the surrounding area. When pressed further about his feelings, he said that he could do nothing but move to a cleaner environment.

Frew was frightened by the "ecologically schizophrenic" behavior he witnessed. But this schizophrenia goes beyond ecological issues. On many fronts — marketing, pricing, competition, contract fulfillment, management practices — the man or woman inside the organization can find it difficult, at times perhaps impossible, to reconcile the dictates of conscience with organizational policy.

You need not study the corporate scene long before observing the bind that people can experience from trying to reconcile two basic roles. The first role is that of the private individual: a decent, responsible person who readily admits the need for moral principles. The second role is that of the organization member: a human being who rarely exhibits, or is expected or encouraged to exhibit, any of the moral sensitivity of the private person. These Jekyll-and-Hyde personalities share little moral ground, and Hyde can often brutalize Jekyll when personal and organizational values collide.

About a century ago, Dan Drew, church builder and founder of Drew Theological Seminary, made a distinction between one's private life and one's business life that can be viewed as a philosophical basis for the subordination of the individual to organizational interests. Addressing a group of businessmen in the late nineteenth century, Drew said:

> Sentiment is all right up in that part of the city where your home is. But downtown, no. Down there the dog that snaps the quickest gets the bone. Friendship is very nice for a Sunday afternoon when you're sitting around the dinner table with your relations, talking about the sermon that morning. But nine o'clock Monday morning, [such] notions should be brushed aside like cobwebs from a machine. I never took any stock in a man who mixed up business with anything else. He can go into other things outside of business hours, but when he's in the office he ought not to have a relation in the world—and least of all a poor relation.[14]

The many recent cases of corporate misconduct suggest that corporate organizations have frequently embraced Drew's exhortation. "Downtown," the dominant businessperson personality, Mr. Hyde, often is expected to repress the values that the private individual, Dr. Jekyll, lives by at home. In conflicts, the decent personality is to be sacrificed on the altar of expedience with a prayerful "that's business."

But don't assume that members of corporations would not prefer it otherwise. A basic assumption of this book is that people would rather be Dr. Jekyll than Mr. Hyde, would rather be morally responsible individuals than conscienceless "team players." And yet the structure and function of organizations in general, and corporate organizations in particular, require that their members adhere to organizational norms and, in fact, force commitment and conformity to them.

Organizational Norms

One of the major characteristics of an organization, indeed any group, is the shared acceptance of organizational rules by its members. The acceptance may be conscious or unconscious, take one form or another, be overt or subtle, but it is almost always present.

The corporation's goal is profit. To achieve this goal, top management sets goals for return on equity, sales, market share, and so forth. For the most part, the norms or rules that govern corporate existence are derived from these goals. But clearly there's nothing in either the norms or goals that encourages moral behavior, and in fact they may discourage it.

There is mounting evidence that managers at every level experience role conflicts between what is expected of them as efficient, profit-minded managers and what is expected of them as ethical persons. The most frequent role conflicts experienced today center around honesty in communication; gifts, entertainment, and kickbacks; fairness and discrimination; contract honesty; and firings and layoffs. One survey discovered that managers at all levels experience such role conflicts primarily because of "pressure from the top" to meet corporate goals and comply with corporate norms. Of the managers interviewed, 50 percent of top managers, 65 percent of middle managers, and 84 percent of lower managers agreed that "managers today feel under pressure to compromise personal standards to achieve company goals."[15]

At the very least, this study and others show that although corporate goals and norms may not be objectionable, they frequently put in a moral pressure cooker corporate members who must implement them. Meeting corporate objectives and playing by the "rules of the game" may call for unethical behavior.

Commitment

Like any group, an organization can survive only if it holds its members together. Organizations accomplish group cohesiveness by getting members to "commit" themselves—that is, to relinquish some of their own personal freedom in order to further organizational goals. One's degree of commitment—the extent to which one will subordinate self to organizational goals—is a measure of one's loyalty to "the team."

In most instances, the freedom one surrenders is trivial: I must wear a jacket and tie rather than my own preference, jeans and an open-neck shirt; or I must accept periodic reassignment rather than stay in one place, which I'd prefer. But in some cases, the freedom lost may amount to freedom of conscience. Acting on moral principle may be viewed as lack of commitment—disloyalty.

Professor Albert Carr recounts the experience of an executive who wrote several memoranda to superiors detailing instances of the company's environmental pollution.[16] Rather than being lauded for his sense of social responsibility, the executive was reprimanded for a "negative attitude." Another executive of Carr's acquaintance realized his company was involved in political corruption. As far as he could determine, he had only three choices: (1) argue for unprofitable change and thus

jeopardize his job by being labeled unrealistic or idealistic; (2) remain silent and lose self-respect; or (3) move to another company and swap one set of moral misgivings for another.

Carr's examples suggest that the commitment organizations exact for self-maintenance can so constrain choice as to make individual acts of moral responsibility exceedingly difficult. And it is safe to assume that many more men and women silently suffer such intrapsychic conflict, conflict that results from being forced to choose between fidelity to one's own conscience and loyalty to organization.

Conformity

It is no secret that organizations exert pressures on their members to conform to norms and goals. What may not be so widely known is how easily individuals can be induced to behave similarly to others. A dramatic example is provided in the early conformity studies by social psychologist Solomon Asch.[17]

In a classic experiment, Asch asked groups of seven to nine college students to say which of three lines on a card (right, below) matched the length of a standard line on a second card (left, below):

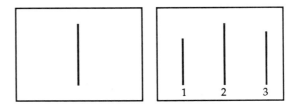

Only one of the subjects in each group was "naive," or unaware of the nature of the experiment. The others were stooges of the experimenter, who had instructed them to make incorrect judgments in about two-thirds of the cases and in this way to pressure the dissenting naive subjects to alter their correct judgments.

The results were revealing. When subjects were not exposed to pressure, they inevitably judged correctly. But when the stooges gave false answers, the subjects changed their responses to conform with the unanimous majority judgments. When one stooge differed from the majority and gave the correct answers, naive subjects maintained their position three-fourths of the time. But when the honest stooge switched to the majority view in later trials, the errors made by naive subjects rose to about the same level as that of subjects who stood alone against a unanimous majority.

Why did they yield? Some respondents said they didn't want to seem different, even though they continued to believe their judgments were correct. Others said that, although their perceptions seemed correct, the majority couldn't be wrong. Still other subjects didn't even seem aware that they had caved in to group pressure. Even those who held their ground tended to be profoundly disturbed by being out of step with the majority and confessed to being sorely tempted to alter their judgments. Indeed, a later study found that students who stood firm in their judgments suffered more anxiety than those who switched. One student with the strength of his correct convictions was literally dripping with perspiration by the end of the experiment.[18]

It's worth noting that in these experiments, which cumulatively included several hundred students, the subjects were not exposed to the authority symbols that people inside an organization face: bosses, boards, presidents, peer groups, established policy, and so on. Nor would their responses entail the serious long-range impact that "bucking the system" can carry for members of an organization: being transferred, dismissed, "frozen" in a position, or made an organizational pariah. And of course the students did not bring to these experiments the financial, educational, and other personal investments that individuals bring with them into jobs, which they can jeopardize by not going along with the majority. In short, men and women within the organization are under greater pressures to conform than the students in Asch's studies. Conformity can mean the surrender of moral autonomy. It can also result in what social psychologists term "bystander apathy."

Bystander Apathy.   Back in the 1960s a tragic event leaped off the front pages of the newspapers. A young woman named Kitty Genovese was stabbed to death in New York City. The murder was not in itself so unusual. What was particularly distressing was that thirty-eight of Kitty Genovese's neighbors witnessed her brutal slaying. In answer to her pitiful screams of terror at 3 A.M., they came to their windows and remained there for the 30 minutes it took her assailant to brutalize her. Of the thirty-eight, not one attempted to intervene in any way; no one even phoned the police.

So distressed by this shocking behavior were scientists John M. Darley and Bibb Latané that they began a study to find out why people refuse to help others in similar situations. Darley and Latané believe their findings support the conclusion that the individual's sense of personal responsibility is inversely proportional to the number of people witnessing the event.[19] Thus, the more people who are observing an event, the less likely any of them will feel obliged to do anything. In emergency situations, we seem naturally to let the behavior of those around us dictate our response. Faced with a conflict between what we believe is the right thing to do and fear of violating group norms and expectations, most of us — about two-thirds, according to researchers — will yield to the group.

Bystander apathy appears to result in part from diffusion of responsibility. Submerged in the group, the individual can lose any sense of individuality. Deindividualization can occur in a group of strangers or large crowds, when pursuing a "great cause" or following orders. In such situations, the individual may not only feel anonymous, and thus not responsible, but in fact may not even question the morality of his or her actions.

Is there anything about the corporate organization that encourages diffusion of responsibility and thus bystander apathy? Viewed as a massive group, corporations certainly encourage these phenomena as much as, and perhaps more than, most groups. Moreover, organizational pressure to produce, make profit, and conform can cultivate, or at least do nothing to inhibit, these propensities. Beyond this, many corporations fail to institutionalize ethics. They don't articulate or communicate ethical standards to their members; they don't actively enforce them; and they retain structures and policies that thwart individual integrity.

Although what is expected of members of a corporation sometimes clashes with their own moral values, they are rarely encouraged to deal with the conflict in an open, mature way. In fact, the more one suppresses individual moral urges in the cause of organizational interests, the more "mature," committed, and loyal one is considered to be. Conversely, the less willing the individual, the less "mature" and the more suspect. Thus, it should come as no surprise that employees frequently have to fight hard to maintain their moral integrity in a showdown with organizational priorities.

Often, of course, the problem facing us is not that of doing what we know to be right but rather of deciding what the right thing to do is. In business and organizational contexts, many difficult and puzzling moral questions need to be answered. How do we go about doing that? Is there a single "right way" or method for answering moral questions? In science, the scientific method tells us what steps to take if we seek to answer a scientific question, but there is no comparable "moral method" for engaging moral questions. There is, however, general agreement about what constitutes good moral reasoning.

MORAL REASONING

It is useful to view moral reasoning at first in the context of *argument*. An argument is a group of statements, one of which (called the *conclusion*) is claimed to follow from the others (called the *premises*) Here's an example of an argument:

Argument 1:

If a person is a mother, the person is a female.

Fran is a mother.

Therefore, Fran is a female.

The first two statements (the premises) of this argument happen to entail the third (the conclusion), which means that if I accept the first two as true, then I must accept the third as also true. Not to accept the conclusion while accepting the premises would result in a contradiction — holding two beliefs that cannot both be true at the same time. In other words, if I believe that all mothers are females and Fran is a mother (the premises), I cannot deny that Fran is a female (the conclusion) without contradicting myself. An argument like this one, whose premises logically entail its conclusion, is termed *valid*

An *invalid* argument is one whose premises do not entail its conclusion. In an invalid argument, I can accept the premises as true and reject the conclusion without any contradiction. Thus:

Argument 2:

If a person is a mother, the person is a female.

Fran is a female.

Therefore, Fran is a mother.

The conclusion of this argument does not necessarily follow from the true premises. I can believe that every mother is a female and that Fran is a female and deny that Fran is a mother without contradicting myself.

One way to show this is by means of a *counterexample*, an example that is consistent with the premises but is inconsistent with the conclusion. Let's suppose Fran is a two-year-old, a premise that is perfectly consistent with the two stated premises. If she is, she can't possibly be a mother. Or let's suppose Fran is an adult female who happens to be childless, another premise that is perfectly consistent with the stated premises but obviously at odds with the conclusion. If an argument is valid (such as Argument 1), then no counter-examples are possible.

A valid argument can have untrue premises, as in the following:

Argument 3:

If a person is a female, she must be a mother.

Fran is a female.

Therefore, Fran must be a mother.

Like Argument 1, this one is *valid*. If I accept its premises as true, I must accept its conclusion as true; otherwise I will contradict myself. Although valid, this argument is unsound because one of its premises is false—namely, "If a person is a female, she must be a mother." Realizing the patent absurdity of one of its premises, no sensible person would accept this argument's conclusion. But notice why the argument is unsound—not because the reasoning procedure is invalid but because one of the premises is false. *Sound arguments*, like Argument 1, have true premises and valid reasoning. *Unsound arguments* have at least one false premise, as in Argument 3, or invalid reasoning, as in Argument 2.

Now let's consider some *moral arguments*, which can be defined simply as arguments whose conclusions are moral judgments, as-sertions about the moral worth of a person, action, activity, policy, or organization. Here are some examples that deal with affirma-tive action for women and minorities in the workplace:

Argument 4:

If an action violates the law, it is morally wrong.

Affirmative action on behalf of women and minorities in personnel matters vio-lates the law.

Therefore, affirmative action on behalf of women and minorities in personnel mat-ters is morally wrong.

Argument 5:

If an action violates the will of the major-ity, it is morally wrong.

Affirmative action on behalf of women and minorities in personnel matters vio-lates the will of the majority.

Therefore, affirmative action on behalf of women and minorities in personnel mat-ters is morally wrong.

Argument 6:

If an action redresses past injuries to special groups, it is morally permissible.

Affirmative action on behalf of women and minorities in personnel matters re-dresses injuries done to special groups.

Therefore, affirmative action on behalf of women and minorities in personnel mat-ters is morally permissible.

Argument 7:

If an action is the only practical way to remedy a social problem, then it is mor-ally permissible.

Affirmative action on behalf of women and minorities in personnel matters is the only practical way to remedy the social problem of unequal employment opportunity.

Therefore, affirmative action on behalf of women and minorities in personnel matters is morally permissible.

The first premise in each of these arguments is a moral standard, the second an alleged fact, and the conclusion a moral judgment. *Moral reasoning* or argument typically moves from a moral standard; through one or more factual judgments about some person, action, or policy related to that standard; to a moral judgment about that person, action, or policy. Good moral reasoning will frequently be more complicated than the examples above; often it will involve an appeal to more than one standard as well as to various appropriate factual claims. But the above examples illustrate its most basic form.

Defensible Moral Judgments

If a moral judgment or conclusion is defensible, then it must be supportable by a defensible moral standard, together with relevant facts. A moral standard supports a moral judgment if the standard, taken together with the relevant facts, logically entails the moral judgment and if the moral standard itself is a sound standard. If someone argues that affirmative action for minorities and women is right (or wrong) but cannot produce a supporting principle when asked, then the person's position is considerably weakened. And if the person does not see any need to support the judgment by appeal to a moral standard, then he or she simply does not understand how moral concepts are used or is using moral words like ''right'' or ''wrong'' differently from the way they are commonly used.

Keeping this in mind—that moral judgments must be supportable by moral standards and facts—will aid your understanding of moral discourse, which can be highly complex and sophisticated. It will also sharpen your own critical faculties and improve your moral reasoning and ability to formulate relevant moral arguments.

Patterns of Defense and Challenge

In assessing arguments, one must be careful to clarify the meanings of their key terms and phrases. Often premises can be understood in more than one way, and this ambiguity may lead people to accept (or reject) arguments that they shouldn't. For example, ''affirmative action'' seems to mean different things to different people (see Chapter 9 on job discrimination). Before we can profitably assess Arguments 4 through 7, we have to agree on how we understand ''affirmative action.'' Similarly, Argument 5 relies on the idea of ''violating the will of the majority,'' but this idea has to be clarified before we can evaluate either the moral principle that it is wrong to violate the will of the majority or the factual claim that affirmative action does violate the majority's will.

Assuming that the arguments are logically valid in their form (as Arguments 4 through 7 are) and that their terms have been clarified and possible ambiguities eliminated, then we must turn our attention to assessing the premises of the arguments. Should we accept or reject their premises? Remember that if an argument is valid and you accept the premises, you must accept the conclusion.

Let's look at some further aspects of this assessment process:

1. *Evaluating the factual claims.* If the parties to an ethical discussion are willing to accept the moral standard (or standards) in

question, then they can concentrate on the factual claims. Thus, for example, in Argument 4 they will focus on whether affirmative action on behalf of women and minorities is in fact illegal. In Argument 7 they will need to determine if affirmative action is really the only practical way to remedy the social problem of unequal employment opportunity. Analogous questions can be asked about the factual claims of Arguments 5 and 6. Answering them in the affirmative would require considerable supporting data.

2. *Challenging the moral standard.* Moral arguments generally involve more than factual disputes. The moral standards they appeal to may be controversial. One party might challenge the moral standard on which the argument relies, contending that it is not a plausible one and that we should not accept it. The critic might do this in several different ways — for example, by showing that there are exceptions to the standard, that the standard leads to unacceptable consequences, or that it is inconsistent with the arguer's other moral beliefs.

In the following dialogue, for example, Lynn is attacking Sam's advocacy of the standard "If an action redresses past injuries to special groups, it is morally permissible."

Lynn: What would you think of affirmative action for Jews in the workplace?
Sam: I'd be against it.
Lynn: What about Catholics?
Sam: No.
Lynn: People of Irish extraction?
Sam: They should be treated the same as anybody else.
Lynn: But each of these groups and more I could mention were victimized in the past by unfair discrimination and probably in some cases continue to be.
Sam: So?
Lynn: So the standard you're defending leads to a judgment you reject: Jews, Catholics, and Irish, although wronged in the past, should not be compensated. How do you account for this inconsistency?

At this point Sam, or any rational person in a similar position, has three alternatives: abandon or modify the standard, alter his moral judgment, or show how women and minorities fit the original principle even though the other groups do not.

3. *Defending the moral standard.* When the standard is criticized, then its advocate must defend it. Often this requires invoking an even more general principle. A defender of Argument 6, for example, might defend the redress principle by appealing to some more general conception of social justice. Or defenders might try to show how the standard in question entails other moral judgments that both the critic and the defender accept, thereby enhancing the plausibility of the standard. In the following exchange, Lynn is defending the standard of Argument 5: "If an action violates the will of the majority, it's wrong":

Lynn: Okay, do you think the government should impose a national religion on all Americans?
Sam: Of course not.
Lynn: What about requiring people to register their handguns?
Sam: I'm all for it.
Lynn: And using kids in pornography?
Sam: There rightly are laws against it.
Lynn: But the principle you're objecting to — that an action violating the will of the majority is wrong — leads to these judgments that you accept.

Of course, Lynn's argument is by no means a conclusive defense for her moral standard. Other moral standards could just as easily entail the judgments she cites, as Sam is quick to point out:

Sam: Now wait a minute. I oppose a state religion on constitutional grounds, not because it violates majority will. As for gun control, I'm for it because I think it will reduce violent crimes. And using kids in pornography is wrong because it exploits and endangers children.

Although Lynn's strategy for defending the standard about majority rule proved inconclusive, it does illustrate a common and often persuasive way of arguing for a moral principle.

4. *Revision and modification.* Arguments 1 through 7 are only illustrations, and all the moral principles they mention are very simple—too simple to accept without qualification. (The principle that it is immoral to break the law in all circumstances, for example, is implausible. Nazi Germany furnishes an obvious counterexample to it.) But once the standard has been effectively challenged, the defender of the argument, rather than abandon the argument altogether, might try to reformulate it. That is, the defender might replace the original, contested premise with a better and more plausible one that still supports the conclusion. For example, Premise 1 of Argument 4 might be replaced by: "If an action violates a law that is democratically decided and that is not morally unjust, then the action is immoral."

In this way, the discussion continues, the arguments on both sides of an issue improve, and we make progress in the analysis and resolution of ethical issues. In general, in philosophy we study logic and criticize arguments not in order to be able to score quick debating points but rather to be able to think better and more deeply about moral and other problems. Our goal as moral philosophers is not to "win" arguments but to arrive at the truth—or, put less grandly, to find the most reasonable answer to an ethical question.

Notwithstanding these basic features of moral reasoning and argumentation, moral discussion and the analysis of ethical issues can take various, often complicated, paths. Nevertheless, the preceding discussion implies certain minimum adequacy requirements for moral judgments.

Minimum Adequacy Requirements for Moral Judgments

Although there is no complete list of adequacy criteria for moral judgments, moral judgments should be (1) logical, (2) based on facts, and (3) based on sound or defensible moral principles.[20] A moral judgment that is weak on any of these grounds is open to criticism.

Moral Judgments Should Be Logical. To say that moral judgments should be logical implies several things. First, as indicated in the discussion of moral reasoning, our moral judgments should follow logically from their premises. The connection between (1) the standard, (2) the conduct or policy, and (3) the moral judgment should be such that 1 and 2 logically entail 3. Our goal is to be able to support our moral judgments with reasons and evidence, rather than basing them solely on emotion, sentiment, or social or personal preference.

Forming logical moral judgments also means ensuring that any particular moral judgment of ours is compatible with our other moral and nonmoral beliefs. We must avoid inconsistency. Most philosophers agree that if we make a moral judgment—for example, that it was wrong of Smith to alter the figures she gave to the outside auditors—then we must be willing to make the same judgment in any similar set of circumstances—that is, if our friend Brown, our spouse, or our father had altered the figures. In particular, we cannot make an exception for ourselves, judging something permissible for us to do while condemning others for doing the same thing.

Moral Judgments Should Be Based on the Facts.   Adequate moral judgments cannot be made in a vacuum. We must gather as much relevant information as possible before making them. For example, an intelligent assessment of the morality of insider trading would require an understanding of, among other things, the different circumstances in which it can occur and the effect it has on the market and on other traders. The information supporting a moral judgment, the facts, should be relevant—that is, the information should actually relate to the judgment; it should be complete, or inclusive of all significant data; and it should be accurate or true.

Moral Judgments Should Be Based on Acceptable Moral Principles.   We know that moral judgments are based on moral standards. At the highest level of moral reasoning, these standards embody and express very general moral principles. Reliable moral judgments must be based on sound moral principles—principles that can withstand critical scrutiny and rational criticism. What, precisely, makes a moral principle sound or acceptable is one of the most difficult questions that the study of ethics raises and is beyond the scope of this book. But one criterion is worth mentioning, what philosophers call our "considered moral beliefs."

These beliefs contrast with beliefs we just happen to hold, perhaps because of ignorance or prejudice. As professor of philosophy Tom Regan puts it, "Our considered beliefs are those we hold *only after* we have made a conscientious effort (a) to attain maximum conceptual clarity, (b) to acquire all relevant information, (c) to think about the belief and its implications rationally, (d) impartially, and with the benefit of reflection, (e) coolly."[21] We have grounds to doubt a moral principle when it clashes with not one but many such beliefs. Conversely, conformity with not one but many considered beliefs is good reason for regarding it as provisionally established.

This does not mean that conformity with our considered beliefs is the sole or even basic test of a moral principle, any more than conformity with well-established beliefs is the exclusive or even fundamental test of a scientific hypothesis. (Copernicus's heliocentric hypothesis, for example, did not conform with what passed in the medieval world as a well-considered belief, the Ptolemaic view that the earth was the center of the universe.) But conformity with our considered beliefs seemingly must play some part in evaluating the many alternative moral principles that are explored in the next chapter.

SUMMARY

1. Ethics deals with (1) individual character and (2) the moral rules that govern and limit our conduct. It investigates questions of moral right and wrong, duty and obligation, and moral responsibility.

2. Business ethics is the study of what constitutes right and wrong, good and bad human conduct in a business context. Closely related moral questions arise in other organizational contexts.

3. Moral standards, as opposed to nonmoral standards, concern behavior that has serious consequences for human well-being. Their soundness depends on the adequacy of the reasons that support or justify them.

4. Morality must be distinguished from etiquette (which concerns rules for well-mannered behavior), from law (statutes, regulations, common law, and constitutional law), and from professional codes of ethics (which are the special rules governing the members of a profession).

5. Morality is not necessarily based on religion. Although we draw our moral beliefs from many sources, for philosophers the issue is whether those beliefs can be justified.

6. Ethical relativism is the theory that right and wrong are determined by what your society says is right and wrong. There are many problems with this theory. Also dubious is the theory that business has its own morality, divorced from ordinary ideas of right and wrong.

7. Accepting a moral principle involves a motivation to conform one's conduct to that principle. Violating the principle will bother one's conscience. But conscience is not a perfectly reliable guide to right and wrong.

8. Part of the point of morality is to make social existence possible by restraining self-interested behavior. Sometimes doing what is morally right can conflict with our personal interests. In general, though, following your moral principles will enable you to live a more satisfying life.

9. Morality as a code of conduct can be distinguished from morality, in the broader sense, as the values, ideals, and aspirations that shape a person's life.

10. Several aspects of corporate structure and function work to undermine individual moral responsibility. Organizational norms, group commitment, pressure to conform, and diffusion of responsibility (sometimes leading to bystander apathy)

can all make the exercise of individual integrity difficult.

11. Moral reasoning consists of forming moral judgments, assessments of the moral worth of persons, actions, activities, policies, or organizations. Moral reasoning and argument typically appeal both to moral standards and to relevant facts. Moral judgments should be entailed by the relevant moral standards and the facts, and they should not contradict our other beliefs. Both standards and facts must be assessed when moral arguments are being evaluated.

12. Philosophical discussion generally involves the revision and modification of arguments; in this way progress is made in the analysis and resolution of moral and other issues.

13. Conformity with our "considered moral beliefs" is an important consideration in evaluating moral principles. A considered moral belief is one held only after we have made a conscientious effort to be conceptually clear, to acquire all relevant information, and to think rationally, impartially, and dispassionately about the belief and its implications. We should doubt any moral principle that clashes with many of our considered beliefs.

CASE 1.1

Made in the U.S.A. — "Dumped" in Brazil, Africa, Iraq . . .

When it comes to the safety of young children, fire is a parent's nightmare. Just the thought of their young ones trapped in their cribs and beds by a raging nocturnal blaze is enough to make most mothers and fathers take every precaution to ensure their chil-

dren's safety. Little wonder that when fire-retardant children's pajamas hit the market in the mid-1970s, they proved an overnight success. Within a few short years more than 200 million pairs were sold, and the sales of millions more were all but guaranteed. For their manufacturers, the future could not have been brighter. Then, like a bolt from the blue, came word that the pajamas were killers.

In June 1977, the U.S. Consumer Product Safety Commission (CPSC) banned the sale of these pajamas and ordered the recall of millions of pairs. Reason: The pajamas contained the flame-retardant chemical Tris (2,3-dibromoprophyl), which had been found to cause kidney cancer in children.

Whereas just months earlier the 100 medium- and small-garment manufacturers of the Tris-impregnated pajamas couldn't fill orders fast enough, suddenly they were worrying about how to get rid of the millions of pairs now sitting in warehouses. Because of its toxicity, the sleepwear couldn't even be thrown away, let alone sold. Indeed, the CPSC left no doubt about how the pajamas were to be disposed of — buried or burned or used as industrial wiping cloths. All meant millions of dollars in losses for manufacturers.

The companies affected — mostly small, family-run operations employing fewer than 100 workers — immediately attempted to shift blame to the mills that made the cloth. When that attempt failed, they tried to get the big department stores that sold the pajamas and the chemical companies that produced Tris to share the financial losses. Again, no sale. Finally, in desperation, the companies lobbied in Washington for a bill making the federal government partially responsible for the losses. It was the government, they argued, that originally had required the companies to add Tris to pajamas and then had prohibited their sale. Congress was sympathetic; it passed a bill granting companies relief. But President Carter vetoed it.

While the small firms were waging their political battle in the halls of Congress, ads began appearing in the classified pages of *Women's Wear Daily*. "Tris-Tris-Tris . . . We will buy any fabric containing Tris," read one. Another said, "Tris — we will purchase any large quantities of garments containing Tris."[22] The

ads had been placed by exporters, who began buying up the pajamas, usually at 10 to 30 percent of the normal wholesale price. Their intent was clear: to dump* the carcinogenic pajamas on overseas markets.[23]

Tris is not the only example of dumping. In 1972, 400 Iraqis died and 5,000 were hospitalized after eating wheat and barley treated with a U.S.-banned organic mercury fungicide. Winstrol, a synthetic male hormone that had been found to stunt the growth of American children, was made available in Brazil as an appetite stimulant for children. Depo-Provera, an injectable contraceptive known to cause malignant tumors in animals, was shipped overseas to seventy countries where it was used in U.S.-sponsored population control programs. And 450,000 baby pacifiers, of the type known to have caused choking deaths, were exported for sale overseas.

Manufacturers that dump products abroad clearly are motivated by profit or at least by the hope of avoiding financial losses resulting from having to withdraw a product from the market. For government and health agencies that cooperate in the exporting of dangerous products, the motives are more complex.

For example, as early as 1971 the dangers of the Dalkon Shield intrauterine device were well documented.[24] Among the adverse reactions were pelvic inflammation, blood poisoning, pregnancies resulting in spontaneous abortions, tubal pregnancies, and uterine perforations. A number of deaths were even attributed to the device. Faced with losing its domestic market, A. H. Robins Co., manufacturer of the Dalkon Shield, worked out a deal with the Office of Population within the U.S. Agency for International Development (AID),

---

* "Dumping" is a term apparently coined by *Mother Jones* magazine to refer to the practice of exporting to overseas countries products that have been banned or declared hazardous in the United States.

whereby AID bought thousands of the devices at a reduced price for use in population-control programs in forty-two countries.

Why do governmental and population-control agencies approve for sale and use overseas birth control devices proved dangerous in the United States? They say their motives are humanitarian. Since the rate of dying in childbirth is high in Third World countries, almost any birth control device is preferable to none. Third World scientists and government officials frequently support this argument. They insist that denying their countries access to the contraceptives of their choice is tantamount to violating their countries' national sovereignty.

Apparently this argument has found a sympathetic ear in Washington, for it turns up in the "notification" system that regulates the export of banned or dangerous products overseas. Based on the principles of national sovereignty, self-determination, and free trade, the notification system requires that foreign governments be notified whenever a product is banned, deregulated, suspended, or canceled by an American regulatory agency. The State Department, which implements the system, has a policy statement on the subject that reads in part: "No country should establish itself as the arbiter of others' health and safety standards. Individual governments are generally in the best position to establish standards of public health and safety."

Critics of the system claim that notifying foreign health officials is virtually useless. For one thing, other governments rarely can establish health standards or even control imports into their countries. Indeed, most of the Third World countries where banned or dangerous products are dumped lack regulatory agencies, adequate testing facilities, and well-staffed customs departments.

Then there's the problem of getting the word out about hazardous products. In theory, when a government agency such as the Environmental Protection Agency or the Food and Drug Administration (FDA) finds a product hazardous, it is supposed to inform the State Department, which is to notify local health officials. But agencies often fail to inform the State Department of the product they have banned or found harmful. And when it is notified, its communiqués typically go no further than the U.S. embassies abroad. One embassy official even told the General Accounting Office that he "did not routinely forward notification of chemicals not registered in the host country because it may adversely affect U.S. exporting." When foreign officials are notified by U.S. embassies, they sometimes find the communiqués vague or ambiguous or too technical to understand.

In an effort to remedy these problems, at the end of his term in office, President Jimmy Carter issued an executive order that (1) improved export notice procedures; (2) called for publishing an annual summary of substances banned or severely restricted for domestic use in the United States; (3) directed the State Department and other federal agencies to participate in the development of international hazards alert systems; and (4) established procedures for placing formal export licensing controls on a limited number of extremely hazardous substances. In one of his first acts as president, however, Ronald Reagan rescinded the order. Later in his administration, the law that formerly prohibited U.S. pharmaceutical companies from exporting drugs that are banned or not registered in this country was weakened to allow the export to twenty-one countries of drugs not yet approved for use in the United States.

But even if communication procedures were improved or the export of dangerous products forbidden, there are ways that companies can circumvent these threats to their profits — for example, by simply changing the name of the product or by exporting the individual ingredients of a product to a plant in a foreign country. Once there, the ingredients can be reassembled and the product dumped.[25] Upjohn, for example, through its Belgian subsidiary, continues to produce Depo-Provera, which the FDA has consistently refused to approve for use in this country. And the prohibition on the export of dangerous drugs is not that hard to sidestep. "Unless the package bursts open on the dock," one drug company executive observes, "you have no chance of being caught."

Unfortunately for us, in the case of pesticides the effects of overseas dumping are now coming home. The Environmental Protection Agency bans from the United States all crop uses of DDT and Dieldrin, which kill fish, cause tumors in animals, and build up in the fatty tissue of humans. It also bans heptachlor, chlordane, leptophos, endrin, and many other pesticides, including 2,4,5-T (which contains the deadly poison dioxin, the active ingredient in Agent Orange, the notorious defoliant used in Vietnam) because they are dangerous to human beings. No law, however, prohibits the sale of DDT and these other U.S.-banned pesticides overseas, where thanks to corporate dumping they are routinely used in agriculture. The FDA now estimates, through spot checks, that 10 percent of our imported food is contaminated with illegal residues of banned pesticides. And the FDA's most commonly used testing procedure does not even check for 70 percent of the pesticides known to cause cancer.

Discussion Questions

1. Do you think dumping involves any moral issues? What are they?

2. Complete the following statements by filling in the blanks with either "moral" or "nonmoral":
   a. That the Dalkon Shield was dumped overseas is a _____ issue.
   b. Whether or not dumping should be permitted is a _____ question.
   c. "Are dangerous products of any use in the Third World?" is a _____ question.
   d. "Is it proper for the U.S. government to sponsor the export of dangerous products overseas?" is a _____ question.
   e. Whether or not the notification system will protect the health and safety of people in foreign lands is a _____ matter.

3. Can a moral argument be made in favor of dumping, when doing so does not violate U.S. law? Do any moral considerations support illegal dumping? Speculate on why dumpers dump. Do you think they believe that what they are doing is morally permissible?

4. Defend or challenge the present notification system by appeal to moral principles and facts.

5. What moral arguments can be made against legal and illegal dumping? Should we have laws prohibiting more types of dumping? What is your position on dumping, and what principles and values do you base it on?

CASE 1.2
The A7D Affair

Kermit Vandivier could not have predicted the impact on his life of purchase order P-23718, issued on June 18, 1967, by LTV Aerospace Corporation. The order was for 202 brake assemblies for a new Air Force light attack plane, the A7D, a project Vandivier didn't become personally involved in until April 11, 1968, the day of the thirteenth test on the brakes—and the thirteenth failure. Six months later, on October 25, Vandivier was told by his boss, H. C. Sunderman, to clean out his desk and immediately leave the B. F. Goodrich plant at Troy, Ohio, where he'd worked for six years.[26]

Back in June 1967, news of the LTV contract had been cause for uncorking the champagne at the Troy plant. Everyone agreed, including Vandivier, that Goodrich had carried off a real coup. Although the LTV order was a small one — the total price for the 202 assemblies was $69,417, a paltry sum in an industry where brake contracts can run into the millions — it signaled that Goodrich was back in LTV's good graces after ten years living under a cloud of disrepute. Back in the mid-1950s Goodrich had built a brake for LTV that, to put it kindly, hadn't met expectations. As a result, LTV had written off Goodrich as a reliable source of brakes. So although modest, the LTV contract was a chance for Goodrich to redeem itself, one that the people at the Troy plant were determined to make good.

LTV's unexpected change of heart after ten years was easily explained. Goodrich made LTV an offer it couldn't refuse — a ridiculously low bid for making the four-disk brake. Had Goodrich taken leave of its financial senses? Hardly. Since aircraft brakes are custom-made for a particular aircraft, only the brakes' manufacturer has replacement parts. Thus, even if it took a loss on the job, Goodrich figured it could more than make up for it in the sale of replacement parts. Of course, if Goodrich bungled the job, there wouldn't be a third chance.

John Warren, a seven-year veteran and one of Goodrich's most capable engineers, was made project engineer and lost no time in working up a preliminary design for the brake. Perhaps because the design was faultless or perhaps because Warren was given to temper tantrums when criticized, co-workers accepted the engineer's plan without question. So there was no reason to suspect that young Searle Lawson, one year out of college and six months with Goodrich, would come to think Warren's design was fundamentally flawed.

Lawson was assigned by Warren to produce the final production design. He had to determine the best materials for brake linings and any needed adjustments in the brake design. This process called for extensive testing to meet military specifications. If the brakes passed the grueling tests, they would then be flight-tested by the Air Force.

Lawson was under pressure to meet LTV's target date for flight tests, the last two weeks of June 1968, so he lost no time in getting down to work. Since he hadn't received the brake housing and some other parts yet, he used a housing from a brake similar to the A7D's and built a prototype of the four-disk design. What Lawson particularly wanted to learn was whether the brake could withstand the extreme internal temperatures, in excess of 1,000 degrees F, when the aircraft landed.

When the brake linings disintegrated in the first test, Lawson thought the problem might be defective parts or an unsuitable lining. But after two more consecutive failures, he decided the problem lay in the design: The four-disk design was simply too small to stop the aircraft without generating heat enough to melt the brake linings. In Lawson's view, a larger, five-disk brake was needed.

Lawson knew well the implications of his conclusion. The four-disk brake assemblies that finally had begun to arrive at the plant would have to be junked, and more tests would have to be conducted. The accompanying delays would preclude delivery of the first production brakes in the few short weeks that LTV anticipated.

Lawson reported his findings and recommendations to John Warren. Going to a five-disk design was impossible, Warren told him. Officials at Goodrich, he said, were already boasting to LTV about how well the tests were going. Besides, Warren was confident that the problem lay not in the four-disk design but in the brake linings themselves.

Unconvinced, Lawson went to Robert Sink, who supervised engineers on projects.

Sink was, to say the least, in a tight spot. If he agreed with Lawson, he would be indicting his own professional judgment: He was the man who had assigned Warren to the job. What's more, he had accepted Warren's design without reservation and had assured LTV more than once that there was little left to do but ship them the brakes. To recant now would mean explaining the reversal not only to LTV but also to the Goodrich hierarchy. In the end, Sink, who was not an engineer, deferred to the seasoned judgment of Warren and instructed Lawson to continue the tests.

His own professional judgment overridden, Lawson could do little but bash on with the tests. Since all the parts for the brake had by this time arrived, he was able to build up a production model of the brake with new linings and subject it to the rigorous qualification tests. Thirteen more tests were conducted, and thirteen more failures resulted. It was at this point that data analyst and technical writer Kermit Vandivier entered the picture.

On April 11, Vandivier was looking over the data of the latest A7D test when he noticed an irregularity: The instrument recording some of the stops had been deliberately miscalibrated to indicate that less pressure was required to stop the aircraft than actually was the case. Vandivier immediately showed the test logs to test lab supervisor Ralph Gretzinger. Gretzinger said he'd learned from the technician who miscalibrated the instrument that Lawson had requested that he miscalibrate it. Later, while confirming this account, Lawson said he was simply following the orders of Sink and Russell Van Horn, manager of the design engineering section, who according to Lawson were intent on qualifying the brakes at whatever cost. For his part, Gretzinger vowed he would never permit deliberately falsified data or reports to leave his lab.

On May 2 the brake was again tested, and again it failed. Nevertheless, Lawson asked Vandivier to start preparing the various graph and chart displays for qualification. Vandivier refused and told Gretzinger what he'd been asked to do. Gretzinger was livid. He again vowed that his lab would not be part of a conspiracy to defraud. Then, bent on getting to the bottom of the matter, Gretzinger rushed off to see Russell Line, manager of the Goodrich Technical Services Section.

An hour later, Gretzinger returned to his desk looking like a beaten man. He knew he had only two choices: defy his superiors or do their bidding.

"You know," he said to Vandivier, "I've been an engineer for a long time, and I've always believed that ethics and integrity were every bit as important as theorems and formulas, and never once has anything happened to change my beliefs. Now this. . . . Hell, I've got two sons I've got to put through school and I just . . ." When his voice trailed off, it was clear that he would in fact knuckle under. He and Vandivier would prepare the qualifying data, then someone "upstairs" would actually write the report. Their part, Gretzinger rationalized, wasn't really so bad. "After all," he said, "we're just drawing some curves, and what happens to them after they leave here, well, we're not responsible for that." Vandivier knew Gretzinger didn't believe what he was saying about not being responsible. Both of them knew that they were about to become principal characters in a plot to defraud.

Unwilling to play his part, Vandivier decided that he too would confer with Line. Line was sympathetic; he said he understood what Vandivier was going through. But in the end he said he would not refer the matter to chief engineer H. C. "Bud" Sunderman, as Vandivier had suggested. Why not? Vandivier wanted to know.

"Because it's none of my business, and it's none of yours," Line told him. "I learned a long time ago not to worry about things over which I had no control. I have no control over this."

Vandivier pressed the point. What about the test pilots who might get injured because of the faulty brakes? Didn't their uncertain fate prick Line's conscience?

"Look," said Line, growing impatient with Vandivier's moral needling. "I just told you I have no control over this thing. Why should my conscience bother me?" Then he added, "You're just getting all upset over this thing for nothing. I just do what I'm told, and I'd advise you to do the same."

Vandivier made his decision that night. He knew, of course, he was on the horns of a dilemma. If he wrote the report, he would save his job at the expense of his conscience. If he refused, he would honor his moral code and, he was convinced, lose his job—an ugly prospect for anyone, let alone a forty-two-year-old man with a wife and seven children. The next day, Vandivier phoned Lawson and told him he was ready to begin on the qualification report.

Lawson shot over to Vandivier's office with all the speed of one who knows that, swallowed fast, a bitter pill doesn't taste so bad. Before they started on the report, though, Vandivier, still uneasy with his decision, asked Lawson if he fully understood what they were about to do.

"Yeah," Lawson said acidly, "we're going to screw LTV. And speaking of screwing," he continued, "I know now how a whore feels, because that's exactly what I've become, an engineering whore. I've sold myself. It's all I can do to look at myself in the mirror when I shave. I make me sick."

For someone like Vandivier who had written dozens of them, the qualification report was a snap. It took about a month, during which time the brake failed still another final qualification test and the two men talked almost exclusively about the enormity of what they were doing. In the Nuremberg trials they found a historical analogy to their own complicity and culpability in the A7D affair. More

than once, Lawson opined that the brakes were downright dangerous, that anything could happen during the flight tests. His opinion proved prophetic.

On June 5, 1968, the report was published and copies went to the Air Force and LTV. Within a week test flights were begun at Edwards Air Force Base in California. Goodrich dispatched Lawson to Edwards as its representative, but he wasn't there long. Several "unusual incidents" brought the flight tests literally to a screeching halt. Lawson returned to the Troy plant, full of talk about several near crashes caused by brake trouble during landings. That was enough to send Vandivier to his attorney, to whom he told the whole sorry tale.

Although the attorney didn't think Vandivier was guilty of fraud, he was convinced that the analyst/writer was guilty of participating in a conspiracy to defraud. Vandivier's only hope, the attorney counseled, was to make a clean breast of the matter to the FBI. Vandivier did.

Evidently the FBI informed the Air Force of Vandivier's disclosure, for within days the Air Force, which had previously accepted the qualification report, demanded to see some of the raw data compiled during the tests.

Lawson resigned from Goodrich in October. Vandivier submitted his own resignation on October 18, to take effect November 1. In his letter of resignation, addressed to Russell Line, Vandivier cited the A7D report and stated: "As you are aware, this report contained numerous deliberate and willful misrepresentations which, according to legal counsel, constitute fraud and expose both myself and others to criminal charges of conspiracy to defraud. . . . The events of the past seven months have created an atmosphere of deceit and distrust in which it is impossible to work. . . ."

On October 25, Vandivier was summoned to the office of Bud Sunderman, who scolded him mercilessly. Among other things, Sunderman accused Vandivier of making irresponsible charges and of arch disloyalty. It would be best, said Sunderman, if Vandivier cleared out immediately.

Within minutes, Vandivier had cleaned out his desk and left the plant. Two days later Goodrich announced it was recalling the qualification report and replacing the old brake with a new five-disk brake at no cost to LTV.

Aftermath:
On August 13, 1969, a congressional committee reviewed the A7D affair. Vandivier and Lawson testified as government witnesses, together with Air Force officers and a General Accounting Office team. All testified that the brake was dangerous.

Robert Sink, representing the Troy plant, depicted Vandivier as a mere high school graduate with no technical training, who preferred to follow his own lights rather than organizational guidance. R. G. Jeter, vice president and general counsel of Goodrich, dismissed as ludicrous even the possibility that some thirty engineers at the Troy plant would stand idly by and see reports changed and falsified.

The congressional committee adjourned after four hours with no real conclusion. The following day the Department of Defense, citing the A7D episode, made major changes in its inspection, testing, and reporting procedures.

The A7D eventually went into service with the Goodrich-made five-disk brake.

Searle Lawson went to work as an engineer for LTV assigned to the A7D project.

Russell Line was promoted to production superintendent.

Robert Sink moved up into Line's old job.

Kermit Vandivier became a newspaper reporter for the *Daily News* in Troy, Ohio.

Discussion Questions

1. To what extent did Lawson, Vandivier, and Gretzinger consider the relevant moral issues before deciding to participate in the fraud? What was their reasoning? What led Vandivier to seek legal counsel and then to become a government witness?

2. How did Sink and Line look at the matter? How would you evaluate their conduct?

3. Do you think Vandivier was wrong to work up the qualification report? What moral principle or principles underlie your judgment?

4. Do you think Vandivier was right in "blowing the whistle"? Was he morally required to do so? Again, explain the moral principles on which your judgment is based.

5. Identify and discuss the pressure to conform evident in the A7D episode. Explain the effect of diffusion of responsibility in this case.

6. Do you think the existence of a corporate ethical code, a high-ranking ethics committee, or in-house ethical training might have altered events? What steps could Goodrich take to ensure more ethical behavior in the future?

7. In your opinion, can Goodrich in any way be held morally responsible for the A7D affair, or does the responsibility fall solely on individuals?

NOTES

1. "Probe Shows Fraud Key in S & L Failures," *San Francisco Chronicle*, October 31, 1990, C1. Cf. "Behind the S & L Debacle," *Wall Street Journal*, November 5, 1990.

2. A visiting professor at the Harvard Business School, for instance, has bemoaned the difficulty of getting MBA students to "see that there is more to life than money, power, fame, and self-interest."

See Amitai Etzioni, "Money, Power, and Fame," *Newsweek*, September 18, 1989, 10.

3. Robert C. Solomon, *Morality and the Good Life* (New York: McGraw-Hill, 1984), 3.

4. Beverly T. Watkins, "Business Schools Told They Should Produce Generalists, Not Specialists," *The Chronicle of Higher Education*, April 25, 1984, 13.

5. On this and the following two characteristics, see Manuel G. Velasquez, *Business Ethics*, 2nd ed. (Englewood Cliffs, N.J.: Prentice-Hall, 1988), 14.

6. *Wilmington General Hospital* v. *Manlove*, 54 Delaware 15, 174 A. 2nd 135 (1961).

7. Martin Luther King, Jr., "Letter from Birmingham Jail," in *Why We Can't Wait* (New York: Harper & Row, 1963), 85.

8. Allan Bloom, *The Closing of the American Mind* (New York: Simon & Schuster, 1987), 39.

9. Albert Z. Carr, "Is Business Bluffing Ethical?" *Harvard Business Review* 46 (January–February 1968).

10. Richard B. Brandt, *A Theory of the Good and the Right* (New York: Oxford University Press, 1979), 165–170.

11. Baruch Brody, *Beginning Philosophy* (Englewood Cliffs, N.J.: Prentice-Hall, 1977), 33.

12. See, in particular, Tad Tuleja, *Beyond the Bottom Line* (New York: Penguin Books, 1987).

13. See David A. Frew, "Pollution: Can the People Be Innocent While Their Systems Are Guilty?" *Academy of Management Review*, March 1973.

14. Quoted in Robert Bartels, ed., *Ethics in Business* (Columbus: Ohio State University Press, 1963), 35.

15. See Milton Snoeyenbos, Robert Almeder, and James Humber, eds., *Business Ethics* (Buffalo, N.Y.: Prometheus Books, 1983), 99.

16. Albert Z. Carr, "Can an Executive Afford a Conscience?" *Harvard Business Review* 48 (July–August 1970).

17. See Solomon E. Asch, "Opinion and Social Pressure," *Scientific American*, November 1955, 31–35.

18. M. D. Bogdanoff et al., "The Modifying Effect of Conforming Behavior Upon Lipid Responses Accompanying CNS Arousal," *Clinical Research 9* (1961): 135.

19. J. Darley and B. Latané, "When Will People Help in a Crisis?" in *Readings in Psychology Today* (Del Mar, Calif.: CRM Books, 1969).

20. For additional criteria, see Tom Regan, ed., *Just Business: New Introductory Essays in Business Ethics* (New York: Random House, 1984), 13–18.

21. Ibid., 17.

22. Mark Hosenball, "Karl Marx and the Pajama Game," *Mother Jones*, November 1979, 47.

23. Unless otherwise noted, the facts and quotations reported in this case are based on Mark Dowie, "The Corporate Crime of the Century," *Mother Jones*, November 1979, and Russell Mokhiber, *Corporate Crime and Violence* (San Francisco: Sierra Club Books, 1988), 181–195. See also Jane Kay, "Global Dumping of U.S. Toxics Is Big Business," *San Francisco Examiner*, September 23, 1990, A2.

24. See Mark Dowie and Tracy Johnston, "A Case of Corporate Malpractice," *Mother Jones*, November 1976.

25. Mark Dowie, "A Dumper's Guide to Tricks of the Trade," *Mother Jones*, November 1979, 25.

26. The material for this case has been drawn from Kermit Vandivier, "Why Should My Conscience Bother Me?" in Robert Heilbroner, ed., *In the Name of Profit* (New York: Doubleday, 1972). For a discussion skeptical of Vandivier's version of these events, see John H. Fielder, "Give Goodrich a Break," *Business and Professional Ethics Journal 7* (Spring 1988).

It's Good Business

Robert C. Solomon and Kristine Hanson

Solomon and Hanson argue for the immediate, practical relevance of ethics for our business lives. They debunk the idea that business is fundamentally amoral or immoral. Business is not a blind scramble for profits and survival. It is an established practice with firmly fixed rules and expectations, and *people in business are professionals. Although unethical business, like crime, sometimes pays, there is no conflict between ethical business behavior and success. Solomon and Hanson conclude with eight crucial rules for ethical thinking in business.*

Why Ethics?

Our seminars in business ethics . . . almost always begin with and are periodically brought back around to such practical questions as "What does this have to do with my job?" or "Will understanding ethics help me do my job better?"

Such questions deserve and demand three immediate, practical answers.

1. Ethical errors end careers more quickly and more definitively than any other mistake in judgment or accounting. To err is human, perhaps, but to be caught lying, cheating, stealing, or reneging on contracts is not easily forgotten or forgiven in the business world. And for good reason: Such actions undermine the ethical foundation on which the business world thrives. Almost everyone can have compassion for someone caught in an ethical dilemma. No one can excuse immorality.

For every glaring case of known unethical conduct that goes unpunished, a dozen once-promising careers silently hit a dead end or quietly go down the tubes. On relatively rare occasions, an unhappy executive or employee is singled out and forced to pay public penance for conduct that everyone knows — he or she and the attorney will loudly protest — "goes on all the time." But much more often, unethical behavior, though unearthed, will go unannounced; indeed, the executive or employee in question will keep his or her job and may not even find out that he or she has been found out — may never even realize the unethical nature of his or her behavior. A career will just go nowhere. Responsibilities will remain routine, promotions elusive.

What makes such career calamities so pathetic is that they are not the product of greed or immorality or wickedness. They are the result of ethical naiveté.

They happen because an employee unthinkingly "did what he was told to do" — and became the scapegoat as well.

They happen because a casual public comment was ill-considered and had clearly unethical implications — though nothing of the kind may have been intended.

They happen because a middle manager, pressed from above for results, tragically believed the adolescent clichés that pervade the mid-regions of the business world, such as "In business, you do whatever you have to do to survive." (It is both revealing and instructive that although we often hear such sentiments expressed in seminars for middle managers, we virtually never hear them in similar seminars for upper-level executives.)

They happen because upper management wasn't clear about standards, priorities, and limits, or wasn't reasonable in its expectations, or wasn't available for appeal at the critical moment.

They happen because an anonymous employee or middle manager hidden in the complexity of a large organization foolishly believed that such safe anonymity would continue, whatever his or her behavior.

They happen, most of all, because a person in business is typically trained and pressured to "think business," without regard for the larger context in which business decisions are made and legitimized.

Unethical thinking isn't just "bad business"; it is an invitation to disaster in business, however rarely (it might sometimes seem) unethical behavior is actually found out and punished.

2. Ethics provides the broader framework within which business life must be understood. There may be a few people for whom business is all of life, for whom family and friendship are irrelevant, for whom money means only more investment potential and has nothing to do with respect or status or enjoying the good life. But most successful executives understand that *business is part of life.* Corporations are part of a society that consists of something more than a market. Executives and employees do not disappear into their jobs as if into a well, only to reappear in "real life" at the end of the business day.

Successful managers, we now all know, stay close to their subordinates — and not just as subordinates. The best corporations in their "search for excellence" begin and remain close to their customers, and not just in their narrowest role as consumers. Money may be a scorecard, a measure of status and accomplishment, but it is not the ultimate end. Business success, like happiness, often comes most readily to those who do not aim at it directly.

Executives are most effective and successful when they retain their "real life" view of themselves, their position, and the human world outside as well as inside the corporation. Business ethics, ultimately, is just business in its larger human context. . . .

3. *Nothing is more dangerous to a business — or to business in general — than a tarnished public image.* A few years ago, *Business and Society Review* reported the results of a Harris Poll — one among many — that showed that public confidence in the executives running major corporations had declined "drastically" from 55% in 1966 to 16% in 1976; 87% of the respondents in a parallel poll agreed that most businessmen were more interested in profits than in the public interest. Whether or not such suspicions seriously affect sales, they indisputably hurt the bottom line in a dozen other hurtful ways — not least among them the pressure for government regulation. The fact is that a tarnished image has direct consequences, for sales, for profits, for morale, for the day-to-day running of the business. Distrust of an industry ("big oil," "the insurance racket") can hurt every company, and distrust of an individual company can quickly drive it to bankruptcy. . . .

The Myth of Amoral Business

Business people have not always been their own best friends. John D. Rockefeller once boasted that he was quite willing to pay a man an annual salary of a million dollars, if the man had certain qualities:

> [He] must know how to glide over every moral restraint with almost childlike disregard . . . [and have], besides other positive qualities, no scruples whatsoever, and [be] ready to kill off thousands of victims — without a murmur.
>
> Robert Warshow, *Jay Gould* (1928)

Such talk is unusually ruthless, but it exemplifies horribly a myth that has often clouded business thinking — what University of Kansas business ethicist Richard De George calls the "myth of amoral business." According to the myth, business and ethics don't mix. People in business are concerned with profits, with producing goods and services, with buying and selling. They may not be immoral, but they are amoral — that is, not concerned with morals. Moralizing is out of place in business. Indeed, even good acts are to be praised not in moral terms but only in the cost/benefit language of "good business."

The myth of amoral business has a macho, mock-heroic corollary that makes ethical paralysis almost inevitable. It is the dog-eat-dog rhetoric of the Darwinian jungle — "survival of the fittest." In fact, almost everybody and most companies manage to survive without being the "fittest." The anxiety of switching jobs, of not getting promotions, of losing an investment, or of going bankrupt, however upsetting, is rarely a "matter of life and death." In *The Right Stuff*, Tom Wolfe sympathetically quotes the wife of one of the Air Force test pilots. She mentions a friend's complaint about her husband's dog-eat-dog existence on Madison Avenue and reflects, "What if her husband went into a meeting with a one-in-four chance of survival?"

If the myth of amoral business and its Darwinian corollary were nothing but a way of talking on the way to the office, it would not be worth attention or criticism. But the fact is that it does enter into business thinking, and often at exactly the critical moment when an ethical decision is to be made. Worse, the amoral rhetoric of business quickly feeds public suspicion of business and easily becomes part of the condemnation of business. A handful of scandals and accidents that might otherwise be viewed as the unfortunate byproducts of any enterprise become "proof" of what the businessmen themselves have been saying all along — that there is no interest in ethics in business, only the pursuit of profits. . . .

Business people who do not talk about ethics often complain a great deal about "regulation" without realizing that the two are intimately connected. Legal regulation is the natural response of both society and government to the practice of amorality, however nobly that practice is couched in the rhetoric of "free enterprise." If a business scandal or tragedy is quickly and convincingly chastized by business people, there is neither time nor pressure for regulation. But when scandal and tragedy are at the same time surrounded by ethical neglect or silence or, worse, yet another appeal to "the market" as the long-term corrective, government regulation becomes inevitable. In case anyone still wants to ask why ethics should be relevant to the bottom line, one might simply reply that regulation is the price business pays for bad ethical strategy.

The Three Cs of Business Ethics

. . . Business ethics is not an attack on business but rather its first line of defense. Adam Smith knew this well enough: Business has prospered because business has dramatically improved the quality of life for all of us. Moreover, the emphasis on freedom and individuality in a business society has done more than any conceivable socialist revolution to break down traditional inequities in power and wealth, even if it inevitably creates some inequities of its own. Business ethics begins with consumer demand and productivity, with the freedom to engage in business as one wishes, and with the hope — inconceivable in most parts of the world — that one can better one's life considerably through one's own hard work and intelligence. These are the values of business ethics, and the whole point of business ethics is to define and defend the basic goals of prosperity, freedom, fairness, and individual dignity.

Many critics of business are trained in the rhetoric of ethics, but most business people are not. Those in business naturally prefer to stick with what they know and sidestep the ethical issues — which is ruinous. It is one thing to know that product Z costs $0.14 to make and retails for $1.59, that raising the price to $1.79 would increase profits and not dampen demand, that cheaper materials or foreign labor could lower the cost of manufacturing to $0.09, although sales would eventually diminish as consumer expectations went unsatisfied. But it is something more to think about the quality of product Z, the contribution it makes to American life (even if only by way of amusement or novelty). Not incidentally, these ethical virtues may be essential to the bottom line as well.

Business ethics is nothing less than the full awareness of what one is doing, its consequences and complications. Thinking about ethics in business is no more than acknowledging that one has taken these into account and is willing to be responsible for them. It is being aware of

1. the need for *compliance* with the rules, including the laws of the land, the principles of morality, the customs and expectations of the community, the policies of the company, and such general concerns as fairness;
2. the *contributions* business can make to society, through the value and quality of one's products or services, by way of the jobs one provides for workers and managers, through the prosperity and usefulness of one's activities to the surrounding community;
3. the *consequences* of business activity, both inside and outside the company, both intended and unintended, including the reputation of one's own company and industry. . . .

Part of the problem for business ethics is the image of business as "big" business, as a world of impersonal corporations in which the individual is submerged and ethics is inevitably sacrificed to bureaucratic objectives. To set the image straight, therefore, let us remind ourselves of a single vital statistic: Half of American business is family business; 50% of the GNP; 50% of the employees. Some of these family businesses are among the Fortune 500. Others are Mom and Pop groceries and Sally and Lou's Restaurant. But it is essential to remember that however much our focus may be on corporations and corporate life, business in America is not a monolithic, inhuman enterprise. As the great French philosopher Rousseau once said of society, we might say of American business life that its origins are in the family, that its "natural" model *is* the family. Business is ultimately about relationships between people — our compliance with the rules we all form together, our contributions to the well-being of others as well as to our own, the consequences of our activities, for good and otherwise. There is nothing amoral or unethical about it.

Business Scum

The most powerful argument for ethics in business is success. Ethical businesses are successful businesses; excellence is also ethical. But ethics is no guarantee of success. To say so on our part would be — unethical. The fact is that there are, as we all know, business scum — those shifty, snatch-a-buck operations that give business a bad name. And some of them, ethics be damned, are profitable.

Brake Breakers, Inc., is a small franchise in the Midwest that specializes in brake, suspension, and wheel repairs. Company policy includes hiring men with little education and working them long hours at a single semiskilled job. Wages are accordingly minimal, and employee turnover is more often a matter of burnout than of leaving for another job. (This saves a lot on fringe benefits and pensions; no one has ever collected on them.) Foremost among the employee's skills, however, is the delivery of a prepackaged sermon designed to convince all but the most cautious customer that the $149.25 brake-rebuilding special is far preferable to the mere replacement of the brake shoes, which is all that is usually required (and often all that is actually done).

Managers are rewarded on the basis of the success of these little speeches by their employees. Their job is first and foremost to make sure that the minimum is never enough—not hard given the level of mechanical know-how of most of the customers. But even with the $149.25 special, extra costs are almost always included, sometimes for some other (unnecessary) part but more often than not because of the "unexpected difficulty" of this particular repair. When a customer insists on the minimum repair, it is up to the manager to see to it that more absolutely necessary work is "discovered" in the middle of the job. (This is called the "step method.") Few customers are in a position to do more than complain and curse for the moment, but no one ever expects them to come back anyway.

Managers are expected to keep actual costs down. Used parts are sold in place of new parts. (Sometimes, the car's original part is cleaned or polished and simply reinstalled.) A few miles down the road, who can tell?

Within the company, employees are reminded daily, "There are fifty people waiting for your job." Everyone is hired with the promise "Within three years, you can work up to a managerial position." In fact, managers are always hired from outside—typically friends of the boss. (It is understood that they will supplement their salaries by skimming within the shop.) Managerial turnover, accordingly, is low. Brake Breakers is not the sort of company that can afford to have a disgruntled manager quit in disgust, although any charges he might bring against the company could dependably be turned against him as well.

Brake Breakers, Inc., is everyone's stereotypical image of unethical business in action. Its people sell a shoddy product to customers who don't need it, and they don't always sell what they say they are selling. Employees are treated like serfs, and accounting procedures at every level of the company are, to put it politely, suspect. The customer is virtually never satisfied, but it is the nature of the business that people who need brake repairs need them fast and do not know what has to be done or

how much it should cost. They are ripe for the taking, and they are taken. The price is still low enough and the job near enough adequate that no one sues. The "lifetime guarantee" isn't worth the paper it's printed on, but it is a fact about brake jobs that there is only so much that can go wrong, and a disgruntled customer usually doesn't bother coming back anyway. It's a perfect setup. At least half of the profits, even on a modest system of objective ethical accounting, are obtained by cheating the customer and the employees.

How does Brake Breakers, Inc., stack up according to our three Cs of business ethics? Not very well.

Compliance: Minimal; just enough to avoid legal penalties and major lawsuits but far below the level of concern for ethics that we all expect of every business.

Contributions: Well, they do fix brakes, even if some of them aren't broken. But a dozen more dependable businesses—both national franchises and local service stations—would do a better job with less flimflam. To provide a service is not in itself a contribution. We also want to know if it is a service that would otherwise be performed as well and as cheaply by other firms.

Consequences: Disgruntled customers, hesitation among motorists to have their brakes checked when they ought to, occasional accidents, a notoriously bad reputation for car-repair shops in general (hurting those that do good, honest work), and an exemplary case of unethical business to turn consumers and congressional investigators against business in general.

It is too often supposed that the business of business ethics is to prove to the management of such unethical enterprises as Brake Breakers, Inc., that crime does not pay. That is too much to ask for.

Show them, perhaps, that they are setting themselves up for lawsuits.

In fact, it just hasn't happened.

Show them, then, that they are losing customers.

In fact, it is a business with a regular supply of customers, no repeat customers in any case and little dependence on word of mouth. (In fact, they depend on the absence of word of mouth, since people are often too ashamed at having been "taken" to tell their friends about it.)

Show them how well Midas and Meineke have been doing because of their reputation for dependability.

But, the manager at Brake Breakers tells us with a laugh, "We ain't Midas."

Argue, then, that unethical business practices cannot possibly pay off in the long run.

"In the long run," the amused manager tells us, unknowingly echoing the economist John Maynard Keynes, "we're all dead."

The fact—sad, perhaps—is that unethical business, like crime, sometimes pays. In any system based on trust, a few deceivers will prosper. There is no guarantee that ethics is good for the bottom line. There is no guarantee that those who do wrong will get caught or feel guilty. There is no guarantee—in business or elsewhere—that the wicked will suffer and the virtuous will be rewarded (at least, not in this life). But, that said, we can nonetheless insist without apology that good ethics is good business. Where immorality is so easily identified, we can be sure that morality is the general rule, not merely an accessory or an exception. The *point* of doing business is to do well by providing the best service or product at a reasonable cost. Those businesses that exploit the *possibility* of getting away with less are merely parasitic on the overwhelming number of businesses that are doing what they are supposed to.

Practices Make Perfect: A Better Way to Look at Business

A practice is any association of definitely patterned human behavior wherein the description and meaning of kinds of behavior involved and the kinds of expectations involved are dependent upon those rules which define the practice.

John Rawls
(professor of philosophy, Harvard University)

Business is not a scramble for profits and survival. It is a way of life, an established and proven *practice* whose prosperity and survival depend on the participation of its practitioners. Business ethics is not ethics applied to business. It is the foundation of business. Business life thrives on competition, but it survives on the basis of its ethics.

Business is first of all a cooperative enterprise with firmly fixed rules and expectations. A view from a visitor's gallery down to the floor of the New York Stock Exchange may not look very much like a cooperative enterprise with fixed rules and expectations, but beneath the apparent chaos is a carefully orchestrated set of agreements and rituals without which the Exchange could not operate at all. There can be no bogus orders, and bid ranges are carefully controlled. The use of information is restricted, but traders trade information as well as securities. The rules of the exchange, contrary to superficial appearances, are uncompromising. Break them and you're off the floor for good. Right there at the busy heart of capitalism, there is no question that *business is a practice*, and people in business are *professionals*.

In business ethics, it is often profitable to compare business with a game. Games are also practices. Baseball, for instance, is a practice. It has its own language, its own gestures with their own meanings, its own way of giving significance to activities that, apart from the game, might very well mean nothing at all. (Imagine a person who suddenly runs and slides into a canvas bag filled with sand on the sidewalk, declaring himself "safe" as he does so.) The practice is defined by certain sorts of behavior—"pitching" the ball in a certain way (if, that is, the practice designates you as the "pitcher"), trying to hit the ball with a certain well-defined implement (the "bat"), running a certain sequence of "bases" in a certain order subject to certain complex restrictions (one of which is that one not be "tagged" by another person holding the ball). Anyone who has tried to explain what is happening in a baseball game to a visitor from another country with a different "national pastime" can attest to the complexity of these rules and definitions, though most Americans feel quite familiar with them and can focus their attention—as players or as spectators—on such simple-sounding concerns as "Who's up?" and "Who's on first?"

Business is like baseball in that it is a practice. A day at the stock exchange makes it quite clear just how many rituals, rules, and restrictions are involved in every buy-and-sell transaction. . . . The business world is far more open to extra "players" and to alternative courses of action than is baseball, but within the institutions that make up the practice of business, roles and alternatives are clearly specified—as "jobs" and "positions," as obligations and options. Strategic ethics begins by emphasizing business as a practice with strict rules and expectations that acceptable players honor implicitly—*or they are out of the game.* To throw out players who cheat is as important to a healthy enterprise as is the inevitable exit of players who can't play well. Bad business is much more damaging to business than are badly run businesses.

Business, like baseball, is defined by its rules. Some of these have to do with the nature of contracts. Many have to do with *fairness* in dealing with employees, customers, and government agents (hence the existence of such policing bodies as the IRS, the SEC, the FDA, etc., etc.). Indeed, the notion of fairness in exchanges is more central to business than to any other practice—whether in terms of work and salary, price and product, or public services and subsidies. Without fairness as the central expectation, there are few people who would enter into the market at all. (Consider the chill on the market following dramatic "insider trading" cases.) Without the recognition of fair play, the phrase "free enterprise" would be something of a joke. The rules of business, accordingly, have mainly to do with fairness. Some of these rules ensure that the market will remain open to everyone. Some of the rules protect those who are not players in the practice but whose health, jobs, or careers are affected by it. Some of the rules have to do with serving the needs or wishes of the community (the law of supply and demand can be interpreted not only as an economic mechanism but as an ethical imperative). Some have to do with "impact"—the effects of a business on its surrounding communities and environment. If business had no effects on the surrounding community but was rather a self-enclosed game, there would be no more public cry for business ethics than for "hopscotch ethics" (which is not to say that there is no ethics to hopscotch).

It is within this description of a practice that we can also define the terms "virtue" and "vice" in business ethics. Some virtues and vices go far beyond the bounds of business, of course; they are matters of morality (honesty, for instance). But in business ethics there are virtues and vices that are particular to business and to certain business roles. Close accounting and "watching every penny" are virtues in a shipping clerk but not in someone who is entertaining a client. Keeping a polite distance is a virtue in a stockholder but not in a general manager. Tenaciousness may be a virtue in a salesman but not in a consultant. Outspokenness may be a virtue in a board member but not in the assistant to the president. Being tough-minded is a virtue in some managerial roles but not in others.

In general, we can say this: A virtue sustains and improves a practice. A virtue in business is an ethical trait that makes business in general possible, and this necessarily includes such virtues as respect for contracts as well as concern for product quality, consumer satisfaction, and the bottom line. A vice, on the other hand, degrades and undermines the practice. Shady dealing and reneging on contracts are vices and unethical not because of an absolute moral law but because they undermine the very practice that makes doing business possible.

Thinking about business as a practice and business people as professionals gives us a set of persuasive responses to the Brake Breakers case:

1. Business in general depends on the acceptance of rules and expectations, on mutual trust and a sense of fairness, even if—as in any such practice—a few unscrupulous participants can take advantage of that trust and betray that concern for fairness.

2. Brake Breakers, Inc., can continue to prosper in their scummy ways only so long as they remain relatively insignificant, with a small enough market share not to bring down the wrath of major competitors and sufficiently little publicity not to inspire a class-action suit. Unethical behavior may bring profits, but only limited profits.

3. It is clearly in the interest of business in general and other firms in that particular industry to warn consumers about Brake Breakers, even to put them out of business. The success and strength of a profession and its independence from externally imposed regulations depends on the internal "policing" of unethical behavior. Doctors have never doubted this; lawyers are learning. But so long as business thinks of itself as unregulated competition where "anything goes" rather than as a profession to be protected from abuse, this vital policing for survival will go unattended, or it will be attended to by the government.

4. The practice of business is a small world. Fly-by-Night Enterprises Ltd. and Brake Breakers, Inc., may succeed for a while, but, in general,

people catch on—fast. Irate customers tell their friends—and their lawyers. They also get even. They sue, for triple damages. They write the newspapers, or "60 Minutes." They drop a note to the IRS, or they call the Better Business Bureau. The banker's kid who was cheated on the job complains to his father the month before the lease has to be renewed. Or the victim happens to be a litigious lawyer with time on his hands. But the effects of unethical business practices are not always so obvious as a dip in the bottom line or a subpoena waiting at the office. They are often slow and insidious, the bottom of a career eaten out from under, or a company that is doing "OK" but could and should be doing much better. There are no guarantees that unethical behavior will be punished, but the odds are pretty impressive.

5. In any profession, it's hard to get clean again. Suppliers tighten their terms; priority status disappears. The hardheaded businessman is supposed to say "Who cares?" But if so, there are few hardheaded businessmen, only a small number of bottom-line-minded sociopaths. Character is who you are, the thing you are trying to prove by making money in the first place. One of the classic movie lines is "My money's as good as anyone else's." Perhaps. But are *you* as good? That isn't just a matter of money.

Why should Brake Breakers, Inc., get ethical? Let's ask another question: How would you feel about yourself if you spent your working days as a manager of Brake Breakers? What would you tell your kids? . . .

Thinking Ethics: The Rules of the Game

Ethics is, first of all, a way of thinking.

Being ethical is also—of course—*doing* the right thing, but what one does is hardly separable from how one thinks. Most people in business who do wrong do so not because they are wicked but because they think they are trapped and do not even consider the ethical significance or implications of their actions.

What is thinking ethically? It is thinking in terms of *compliance* with the rules, implicit as well as explicit, thinking in terms of the *contributions* one can make as well as one's own possible gains, thinking in terms of avoiding harmful *consequences*

to others as well as to oneself. Accordingly, we have constructed eight crucial rules for ethical thinking in business.

Rule No. 1: Consider other people's well-being, including the well-being of nonparticipants. In virtually every major religion this is the golden rule: "Do unto others as you would have them do unto you"; or, negatively, "Do not do unto others as you would not have them do unto you." Ideally, this might mean that one should try to maximize everyone's interests, but this is unreasonable. First of all, no one really expects that a businessman (or anyone else) would or should sacrifice his own interests for everyone else's. Second, it is impossible to take everyone into account; indeed, for any major transaction, the number of people who will be affected—some unpredictably—may run into the tens or hundreds of thousands. But we can readily accept a minimum version of this rule, which is to make a *contribution* where it is reasonable to do so and to avoid *consequences* that are harmful to others. There is nothing in the golden rule that demands that one deny one's own interests or make sacrifices to the public good. It says only that one must take into account human effects beyond one's own bottom line and weigh one's own gain against the losses of others.

Rule No. 2: Think as a member of the business community and not as an isolated individual. Business has its own rules of propriety and fairness. These are not just matters of courtesy and protocol; they are the conditions that make business possible. Respect for contracts, paying one's debts, and selling decent products at a reasonable price are not only to one's own advantage; they are necessary for the very existence of the business community.

Rule No. 3: Obey, but do not depend solely on, the law. It goes without saying, as a matter of prudence if not of morality, that businesses and business people ought to obey the law—the most obvious meaning of *compliance*. But what needs to be added is that ethical thinking is not limited to legal obedience. There is much unethical behavior that is not illegal, and the question of what is right is not always defined by the law. The fact is that many things that are not immoral or illegal are repulsive, disgusting, unfair, and unethical—belching aloud in elevators, throwing a disappointing dish at one's host at dinner, paying debts only after the "final notice" and the threat of a lawsuit arrives, fleecing the feebleminded, taking advantage of trust and good faith, selling faulty if not dangerous merchandise under the rubric "Buyer beware." Check the law — but don't stop there.

Rule No. 4: Think of yourself—and your company—as part of society. Business people and businesses are citizens in society. They share the fabric of feelings that make up society and, in fact, contribute much of that feeling themselves. Business is not a closed community. It exists and thrives because it serves and does not harm society. It is sometimes suggested that business has its own ethical rules and that they are decidedly different from those of the larger society. Several years ago business writer Albert Carr raised a major storm in the *Harvard Business Review* by arguing that business, like poker, had its own rules and that these were not to be confused with the moral rules of the larger society. The comparison with poker has its own problems, but, leaving those aside for now, we can see how such a view not only invites but *demands* the most rigorous regulation of business. Business is subject to the same ethical rules as everyone else because businessmen do *not* think of themselves as separate from society. A few years ago, the then chairman of the Ford Foundation put it bluntly: "Either we have a social fabric that embraces us all, or we're in real trouble." So too with ethics.

Rule No. 5: Obey moral rules. This is the most obvious and unavoidable rule of ethical thinking and the most important single sense of *compliance*. There may be room for debate about whether a moral rule applies. There may be questions of interpretation. But there can be no excuse of ignorance ("Oh, I didn't know that one isn't supposed to lie and cheat"), and there can be no unexcused exceptions ("Well, it would be all right to steal in *this* case"). The German philosopher Immanuel Kant called moral rules "categorical imperatives," meaning that they are absolute and unqualified commands for everyone, in every walk of life, without exception, not even for harried executives. This is, perhaps, too extreme to be practical, but moral rules are the heart of ethics, and there can be no ethics — and no business — without them.

Rule No. 6: Think objectively. Ethics is not a science, but it does have one feature in common with science: The rules apply equally to everyone, and being able to be "disinterested" — that is, to think for a moment from other people's perspectives — is essential. Whether an action is *right* is a matter quite distinct from whether or not it is in *your* interest. For that matter, it is quite independent of your personal opinions as well.

Rule No. 7: Ask the question "What sort of person would do such a thing?" Our word "ethics" comes from the Greek word *ethos*, meaning "character." Accordingly, ethics is not just obedience to rules so much as it is the concern for your personal (and company) character — your reputation and "good name" — and, more important, how you feel about yourself. Peter Drucker summarizes the whole of business ethics as "being able to look at your face in the mirror in the morning."

Rule No. 8: Respect the customs of others, but not at the expense of your own ethics. The most difficult kind of ethical thinking that people in business have to do concerns not a conflict between ethics and profits but rather the conflict between two ethical systems. In general, it is an apt rule of thumb that one should follow the customs and ethics of the community. But suppose there is a conflict not only of mores but of morals, as in the apartheid policies of South Africa. Then the rule to obey (and support) one's own moral principles takes priority. What is even more difficult is what one should do when the moral issue is not clear and moral categories vary from culture to culture. A much debated example is the question of giving money to expedite a transaction in many third-world countries. It is "bribery" in our system, "supporting public servants" in theirs. Bribery is illegal and unethical here because it contradicts our notion of a free and open market. But does the same apply in the third world, where business (and social life) have very different presuppositions? . . .

Ethical thinking is ultimately no more than considering oneself and one's company as citizens of the business community and of the larger society, with some concern for the well-being of others and — the mirror image of this — respect for oneself and one's character. Nothing in ethics excludes financially sound thinking, and there is nothing about ethics that requires sacrificing the bottom line. In both the long and the short run, ethical thinking is essential to strategic planning. There is nothing unethical about making money, but money is not the currency of ethical thinking in business.

Review and Discussion Questions

1. Solomon and Hanson describe the view that business and ethics don't mix as the "myth of amoral business." Why do they think it is a myth? Do you agree?

2. Do most business people respect the "Three Cs"? In your opinion, how much unethical be- havior is there in business today? What happens to companies like Brake Breakers? Can they be successful?

3. Does the existence of "business scum" under- mine Solomon and Hanson's claim that busi- nesspeople are professionals and that business is a practice with definite rules?

4. What are the "rules of the game" in business today? Should those rules be changed in any way?

5. Assess Solomon and Hanson's claim that "there is nothing about ethics that requires sacrificing the bottom line" (p. 44). Is it com- patible with their statement that "there is no guarantee that ethics is good for the bottom line" (p. 41)?

Explaining Wrongdoing

Michael Davis

Why do businesspeople and professionals act wrongly? In this essay Michael Davis examines the General Electric price-fixing scandal, insider trading, and the ill-fated Challenger *launch decision and argues that weakness of the will, self-deception, ignorance, and moral immaturity do not suffice to explain why the wrongdoers acted as they did. Rather he sees "micro- scopic vision" as the key to explaining business and profes- sional misconduct, and he discusses what can be done to combat it.*

> How often is a man, looking back at his past actions, astonished at finding himself dishonest!
>
> Cesare Beccaria,
> *On Crimes and Punishments,* Chapter 39

What first interested me in professional ethics were the social questions: the problems faced by those trying to act as members of a profession, the op- tions available, the reasons relevant to deciding be- tween those options, and the methods of assessing those reasons. I thought of myself as advising deci- sion makers within a complex institution. I could, it seemed to me, contribute to right action in the pro- fessions simply by applying skills developed in po- litical and legal philosophy to this new domain. But, like many others who began to do applied ethics in this way, I soon learned that matters are not that simple.

Part of studying professional ethics is reading the newspaper accounts, congressional testimony, and court cases that wrongdoing in the professions generates. I read such documents to identify new problems. But, in the course of reading so much about wrongdoing, I began to wonder how much use my advice could be. Though the wrongdoers were usually well-educated and otherwise decent, much of what they did seemed obviously wrong. Surely, they did not need a philosopher to tell them so. I also began to wonder at how little the wrong- doers themselves had to say about why they did what they did. They seemed far less articulate about that than many an illiterate criminal.[1]

Having begun to wonder about the motivation of the wrongdoers I was studying, I turned to the philosophical literature explaining wrongdoing. I was surprised at how little there was—and at how unhelpful. My wrongdoers did not seem to have done what they did simply because they were weak-willed, self-deceiving, evil-willed, ignorant, or morally immature—or even because they com- bined several of these failings. At most, those fail- ings seemed to have played a subsidiary part in what my wrongdoers did. Yet the philosophical lit- erature offered no sustained discussion of anything

Reprinted by permission from the *Journal of Social Philosophy* 20 (Spring/Fall 1989).

else. Only when I turned to the more practical literature of organization analysis did I find more. And, even there, I did not find enough. I still did not have a satisfactory explanation of the wrongdoing I was studying. I concluded that we lack an adequate psychology of wrongdoing.

This paper has three objectives: first, to provide some evidence for the claim that evil will, weakness of will, self-deception, ignorance, and moral immaturity, even together, will not explain much wrongdoing of concern to students of professional (or business) ethics; second, to add one interesting alternative to the explanations now available; and third, to suggest the practical importance of that alternative. Ultimately, though, this paper has only one objective: to invite others to pick up where I leave off. We need a better psychology of wrongdoing.

I. Three Examples of Wrongdoing

Let's begin with the testimony of a minor figure in the General Electric price-fixing scandal of the 1950s. No longer facing criminal or civil charges, he described how he got into trouble in this way: "I got into it . . . when I was young. I probably was impressed by the manager of marketing asking me to go to a meeting with him [where price-fixing discussions took place]. I probably was naive."[2]

This explanation of our price fixer's wrongdoing is more interesting for what is missing than for what is actually there. We hear nothing about greed, temptation, fooling oneself, or anything else we tend to associate with those destined to do wrong. What we do hear about is *ordinary* socialization. Having worked nine years at GE as an engineer, our price fixer (at age 32) was promoted to "trainee in sales." His superior then showed him how things were done. Yet, something is wrong. Our witness twice indicates that this is only "probably" what happened. Though the acts in question are his, he talks about them like a scholar analyzing someone else's. A screen has come down between him and the person he was only a few years before.

An inability to understand their own past wrongdoing is, I think, not uncommon in wrongdoers like our witness. But I can give only one more example here, just enough to show that he is not unique. *The Wall Street Journal* recently carried a follow-up on the fifty people convicted of inside trading over the last ten years. Here is a part of what we learn from one of them: "When it all started, I didn't even know what inside information was." But around 1979, he says, he began reading about people being arrested for inside trading—yet he continued trading even though he knew it was illegal. It's a decision he wouldn't repeat. "In the long run," he says, "you are going to get caught."[3]

This testimony comes from a small investor, not a broker, analyst, arbitrageur, or the like. Unlike our price fixer, this inside trader was never really inside the relevant organization. He simply received information from inside that he had no right to. Yet, for our purposes, that doesn't matter. What matters is that he knew early on that he was doing something illegal and stood a fair chance of being arrested. He went on trading nonetheless. Why? He doesn't say and, more important, he doesn't seem to know. He does not report greed, temptation, or evil will. What he reports is that he would not have done it if he had known *then* what he knows *now*. What has changed? What does he know now that he did not know then? It cannot be what he says, that is, "In the long run, you are going to get caught." He has no way to know that every inside trader will get caught in the long run. Statistics on the occurrence of illegal inside trading do not exist; but, if inside trading is like other crimes, a substantial percentage of those engaged in it will never be caught.

Our witness's overstatement of the risks of being caught is, I think, better understood as a way of calling attention to *what* he risked and would not risk again. He now regrets doing what he did because he now appreciates what was at stake in a way he did not at the time. He does not so much have new information as a new perspective on the information he had all along. It is this new perspective that makes it hard for him to understand how he could have done what he did. The person we are listening to differs in an important way from the person who engaged in inside trading a few years before, even if he does not know anything he did not know before. It is as if he sees the world with new eyes.

These two wrongdoers are minor figures in major scandals. One may therefore wonder whether the major figures differ in some significant way. I don't think they do. Consider the now familiar events on the night before the *Challenger* exploded:

The Space Center was counting down for a launch the next morning. Robert Lund, vice president for engineering at Morton Thiokol, had earlier presided at a meeting of engineers that unanimously recommended *against* the launch. He had concurred and informed his boss, Jerald Mason. Mason informed the Space Center. Lund had expected the flight to be postponed. The Center's safety record was good. It was good because the Center would not allow a launch unless the technical people approved.

Lund had not approved. He had not approved because the temperature at the launch site would be close to freezing at lift-off. The Space Center was worried about the ice forming here and there on the boosters, but Lund's worry was the "O-rings" that sealed the booster's segments. Data from previous flights indicated that they tended to erode in flight, with the worst erosion occurring on the coldest preceding lift-off. Experimental evidence was sketchy but ominous. Erosion seemed to increase as the rings lost their resiliency and resiliency decreased with temperature. At some temperature, the rings could lose so much resiliency that one would fail to seal properly. If a ring failed in flight, the shuttle could explode.

Unfortunately, almost no testing had been done below 40°F and no lift-off had occurred after a night as cold as this one. The engineers had had to extrapolate. But, with the lives of seven astronauts at stake, the decision seemed clear enough: Safety first.

Or so it had seemed earlier in the day. Now Lund was not so sure. The Space Center had been "appalled" by the sketchy evidence on which the no-launch recommendation had been based. They wanted to launch. They didn't say why, but the reasons were obvious. Previous delays had put them well behind schedule already. The State of the Union message was only a day away. Everyone supposed the President was anxious to announce the first teacher in space. If the Space Center did not launch tonight, they would have to wait at least a month.

The Space Center wanted to launch, but they would not launch without Thiokol's approval. They urged Mason to reconsider. He reexamined the evidence and decided the O-rings should hold at the expected temperature. Joseph Kilminster, Thio-

kol's vice president for shuttle programs, was ready to sign a launch approval, but only if Lund approved. Lund was now all that stood in the way of launching.

Lund's first response was to repeat his objections. Nothing had happened to change his no-launch recommendation. Then Mason had drawn the managers to one side of the meeting room and said something that made Lund think again. Mason had urged Lund to "take off [your] engineering hat and put on [your] management hat." Lund did and changed his mind. The next morning the shuttle exploded during lift-off, killing all aboard. An O-ring had failed.[4]

II. Explaining Lund's Decision

The story of the *Challenger* resembles many cases discussed in professional (and business) ethics. While no one broke the law, as many did in the General Electric price-fixing scandal, there was wrongdoing. And, in retrospect, everyone recognized that—or at least sensed it. Mason quickly took early retirement. Kilminster and Lund were moved to new offices, told they would be "reassigned," and left to read the handwriting on the wall. Morton Thiokol didn't treat them as if their errors were merely technical; nor did it defend their decision in the way we would expect a company to defend a decision it believes in. Thiokol's defense consisted largely of lame excuses, attempts to suppress embarrassing information, and similar self-convicting maneuvers.

What had gone wrong? Well, from the perspective of engineering ethics, it seems obvious. Lund, an engineer who held his position in part because he was an engineer, had a professional duty to act like an engineer. He was not free to take off his engineering hat (though he could wear other hats in addition). For an engineer, safety is the paramount consideration. The engineers could not say the launch would be safe. So, Lund should have delayed the launch. Seven people died, in part at least, because he did not do what, as an engineer, he was supposed to do.[5]

One of the features of the *Challenger* disaster that made it an instant classic is that it has what seems to be a clear clash of legitimate perspectives. Lund was not just an engineer. He was also a manager. Managers are *not*, by definition, evil doers in the way that even price fixers or inside traders are. Government openly supports institutions to train managers. Most of us want people to wear "management hats" now and then. Very few would want to forbid managers to practice their trade. As a vice president of Morton Thiokol, part of Lund's job was to wear a management hat. What then was wrong with his giving approval after putting on that hat?

The answer must be that, in the decision procedure he was part of, his job was to stand up for engineering. He was supposed to represent engineering judgment in management decision. He was vice president *for* engineering. When he took off his engineering hat, he simply became another manager. He ceased to perform the job he was needed for. That, in retrospect, is why, even from management's perspective, he had done something wrong.

Why then did he take off his engineering hat that night? Lund's explanation for deciding as he did was, and remains, that he had "no choice" given the Space Center's demand. Self-interest will not explain what he means by "no choice." To approve the launch was in effect to bet his career that the *Challenger* would not explode, to bet it against the best technical advice he could get. Had he refused to approve the launch, he would *at worst* have been eased out of his position to make way for someone less risk averse. He would have had no disaster on his record and a good chance for another good job either within Thiokol or outside. Self-interest would seem to support Lund's decision not to launch.

What about moral immaturity?[6] This is a possibility, but only that. The records we have tell nothing about anyone's moral development. Participants said nothing about social pressure, law, ordinary morality, or professional ethics. They spoke entirely in the bland technical language engineers and managers use to communicate with one another. Whatever we say about Lund's moral development as of that night would be mere speculation. Something similar is true of the hypothesis that Lund acted with evil intent. By all reports, Lund was too decent a person for that.

What about carelessness, ignorance, or incompetence?[7] I think none of these explanations will do. Too much time went into the decision to dismiss it as simply careless. Since Lund had the same training as his engineers and all the information they had, we can hardly suppose him to be ignorant in any obvious sense. Nor can we declare him to be incompetent. Too many experienced people—both at Thiokol and at NASA—concurred in Lund's decision for it to be incompetent. Lund may well have been operating at the limit of his ability or beyond. But that is not necessarily incompetence. We generally speak of "incompetence" only when we have competent alternatives. Here we have no reason to believe that anyone who could have occupied Lund's place that night would have done better.

Can we then explain Lund's decision by weakness of will?[8] Did he know better but yield to temptation, give in to pressure, or otherwise knowingly do what he considered wrong because he lacked the will to do better? The evidence seems against this explanation too. Mason's advice, "Take off [your] engineering hat and put on [your] management hat," does not sound like tempting Lund to act against his better judgment. It sounds much more like an appeal *to* his better judgment, an appeal from engineering instinct to management rationality.

Lund did, of course, give in to pressure. But to say that is not to explain his decision, only to describe it on the model of a physical process (for example, the collapse of a beer can when we stamp on it). We still need to explain why the appeal to management rationality was so convincing when nothing else was. (We need something like the physical theory that allows us to understand why the beer can collapses under our weight but not under the weight of, say, a cat.) Well, you will say, that's easy enough. The appeal to management rationality allowed Lund to fool himself into thinking he was doing the right thing.

Explaining Lund's decision in this way, that is, as a result of self-deception, is, I think, much closer to the mark. Mike Martin, coauthor of a good text in engineering ethics, recently published a book on self-deception. Among his many examples of self-deceivers are participants in the GE price-fixing scandal. So, I have no doubt that he could find some self-deception in Lund as well.[9]

Yet, if we can, we should avoid explaining what Lund did by self-deception. Self-deception, though common, is an abnormal process. It is something you *do*, not simply something that happens to you. You must knowingly fail to think about a question in the way you believe most likely to give the right answer. You must then not think about the unreliability of the answer you get even, or especially, when you must act on it. In its extreme form, self-deception may involve believing something while being aware that the evidence decisively supports the opposite belief. Self-deception is, as such, a conscious flight from reality.[10]

We should, I think, not explain the conduct of responsible people in this way unless the evidence requires it. The evidence hardly requires it in Lund's case. We can explain why Lund did what he did by a process which, though similar to self-deception, is normal, familiar, and at least as probable on the evidence we have as any of the explanations we have considered so far. For lack of a better name, let's call the process "microscopic vision."

III. Microscopic Vision Examined

What is microscopic vision? Perhaps the first thing to say about it is that it is *not* "tunnel vision." Tunnel vision is a narrowing of one's field of vision without any compensating advantage. Tunnel vision is literally a defect in vision and figuratively a defect in our ability to use the information we have available. Tunnel vision is often associated with self-deception. Microscopic vision resembles tunnel vision only insofar as both involve a narrowing of our field of vision. But, whereas tunnel vision reduces the information we have available below what we could effectively use, microscopic vision does not. Microscopic vision narrows our field of vision only because that is necessary to increase what we can see in what remains. Microscopic vision is enhanced vision, a giving up of information not likely to be useful under the circumstances for information more likely to be useful. If tunnel vision is like looking through a long tunnel to a point of light at the other end, microscopic vision is like looking into a microscope at things otherwise too small to see. Hence, my name for this mental process.

Microscopic vision is also not nearsightedness or myopia. A nearsighted person has lost the ability to see things far off. His acuity close up is what it always was. But when he looks into the distance, he sees only a blur. Like tunnel vision, myopia is partial blindness; microscopic vision is, in contrast, a kind of insight. The nearsighted person needs glasses or some other aid to regain normal vision. A person with microscopic vision need only cease using his special powers to see what others see. He need only look up from the microscope.

Every skill involves microscopic vision of some sort. A shoemaker, for example, can tell more about a shoe in a few seconds than I could tell if I had a week to examine it. He can see that the shoe is well or poorly made, that the materials are good or bad, and so on. I can't see any of that. But the shoemaker's insight has its price. While he is paying attention to people's shoes, he may be missing what the people in them are saying or doing. Microscopic vision is a power, not a handicap, but even power has its price. You cannot both look into the microscope and see what you would see if you did not.

Though every skill involves what I am calling microscopic vision, the professions provide the most dramatic examples. In part, the professions provide these because the insight they give is relatively general. The microscopic vision of a lawyer, engineer, doctor, minister, or accountant concerns central features of social life as the microscopic vision of a shoemaker does not. In part, though, professions provide the most dramatic examples of microscopic vision because both the long training required to become a professional and the long hours characteristic of professional work make the professional's microscopic vision more central to his life. A profession is a way of life in a way shoemaking is not (or, at least, is not anymore).

Consider, for example, the stereotypes we have of professionals—the pushy lawyer, the comforting doctor, the quiet accountant, and so on. We do not, I think, have similar stereotypes of the shoemaker, the carpenter, or the personnel director. These skills don't seem to shape character as much. We joke about professional myopia—for example, the surgeon who thinks the operation a success even though the patient died. Behind the joke is an appreciation of the power a profession has to shape, and therefore, misshape, the consciousness of its members. Real professional myopia is probably rare. Few professionals seem to lose altogether the ability to see the world as ordinary people do. Common, however, is a tendency not to look up from the microscope, a tendency unthinkingly to extend the profession's perspective to every aspect of life.

Managers are not professionals in the strict sense. Though managing now has schools like those of the professions, managers lack two features essential to professionals strictly so called: first, a formal commitment to public service; *and* second, a common code of ethics. Indeed, managers seem to me to lack even a clear sense of themselves as *managers*, that is, as *custodians* of other people's wealth, organization, and reputation. I am surprised by the number of managers who think of themselves as entrepreneurs or capitalists, that is to say, business people who risk their own money, not someone else's.

Nonetheless, managing does today have many of the characteristics of a profession, including distinctive skills and a corresponding perspective, but — most important — a way of life that can make their microscopic vision seem all that matters. We have the stereotype of the manager who can't see the toxic wastes beyond the end of his budget. Behind that stereotype is a certain reality. Managers, especially senior managers, work almost entirely with other managers. Their days are spent ''in the office'' doing the things that managers do. Often, those days are quite long, not 9 to 5 but 8 to 7 or even 7 to 8. They read management magazines and go to management meetings. They come to see the world from the perspective of a manager.

There is a natural process by which people are made into managers. But most companies are not satisfied with ''normal acculturation.'' They have special programs to train managers in a certain style of management. Roger Boisjoly, one of the engineers who tried to get Lund to stick to his no-launch recommendation, was himself briefly a manager. He went back to being an engineer because he wanted to be closer to work on the shuttle. Though he has mocked the programs Thiokol had for managers as ''charm schools,'' he has also pointed out that they helped to make the managers at Thiokol a cohesive team. They helped to give the engineer-turned-manager a clear sense of the priority of the manager's way of looking at things.[11]

What is the difference between the way an engineer might look at a decision and the way a manager might? For our purposes, what is important is the way engineers and managers approach risk. I think engineers and managers differ in at least two ways:

First, engineers would not normally include in their calculations certain risks, for example, the risk of losing the shuttle contract if the launch schedule was not kept. Such risks are not their professional concern. But such risks are properly a manager's normal concern.

Second, engineers are trained to be conservative in their assessment of permissible risk. Often they work from tables approved by the appropriate professional association or other standard-setting agency. When they do not have such tables, they try not to go substantially beyond what experience has shown to be safe. Engineers do not, in general, balance risk against benefit. They reduce risk to permissible levels and only then proceed. Managers, on the other hand, generally do balance risk against benefit. That is one of the things they are trained to do.

We have then two perspectives that might be brought to the same problem, the engineer's and the manager's. Which is better? The answer is: Neither. The engineer's perspective is generally better for making engineering decisions while the manager's perspective is generally better for making management decisions. Either perspective has a tendency to yield a bad result only if applied to the wrong kind of decision. Indeed, that is nearly a tautology. If, for example, we thought a certain decision better made by managers than engineers, we would describe it as (properly) a management, rather than an engineering, decision.

If that is so, it's not too hard to understand why Lund changed his mind the night before the *Challenger* exploded (and why he might still claim that he had ''no choice''). Once he began thinking about the launch as an ordinary management decision, he could rationally conclude that the risk of explosion was small enough to tolerate given the demands of NASA and how much was at stake for Morton Thiokol. But why *would* Lund think about the launch like a manager rather than an engineer?

As I described the difference between the engineer's perspective and the manager's, the two approaches to risk are inconsistent. Lund had to choose. In a way, Mason's plea to Lund to take off his engineering hat and put on his management hat accurately stated the choice Lund faced. In another way, however, it did not. Mason's plea assumed that the decision to launch was an ordinary management decision. This would be just what any manager would normally assume, especially a manager who had himself been an engineer. For an engineer to be made a manager is a promotion, an opening of new horizons. Managers are in charge of engineers. They regularly receive engineering recommendations and then act on them, taking into account more than the engineers did. Engineers generally defer to managers. Anyone who thought of relations between engineers and managers in this way would, I think, have succumbed to Mason's plea — *unless* he had a clear understanding of what made him different from other managers.

Lund seems to have had no such understanding. Indeed, Mason's plea probably shows that no one in the senior management at Morton Thiokol did. Mason could hardly have urged Lund to take off his engineering hat in front of so many managers if it had been common knowledge that Lund had a duty to keep his engineering hat on. Perhaps those who originally organized the decision procedure at Thiokol understood things better. If so, they failed to institutionalize their understanding. Without some way to preserve that understanding, ordinary management understanding would eventually take over. The *Challenger* explosion was the natural outcome of ordinary management.

My purpose here is not to defend Lund's decision but simply to understand how he might have made it without being careless, ignorant, incompetent, evil-willed, weak-willed, morally immature, or self-deceiving. I have explained his decision as rational from a particular perspective, that of an ordinary manager, and then explained why that perspective might seem the right one at the decisive moment. Earlier, I pointed out that, in retrospect, everyone seemed to see not only that Lund made an unfortunate decision but that the decision he made was wrong. I have now explained why. Lund was not an ordinary manager; he was supposed to be an engineer among managers.

I should now like to generalize what we have learned from Lund. We have a tendency to suppose that doing the right thing is normal, that doing the wrong thing is abnormal, and that when something goes wrong the cause must be something abnormal, usually a moral failing in the wrongdoer. What the analysis so far suggests is that sometimes at least the wrong may be the result of normal processes.

The analysis also suggests something more. Managers sometimes say of obeying the law, of doing what's morally right, or of maintaining professional standards, "That should go without saying" — or, in other words, that the importance of

such things is so obvious that pointing it out is unnecessary. The truth, I think, is almost the reverse. I shall come back to this point later.

IV. Price Fixing and Inside Trading

Lund may be taken to represent one category of wrongdoer, those whose conduct was merely unprofessional. There is another, those whose wrongdoing is illegal. Could what I said of Lund apply to this other category as well? Let's try to answer that question by briefly examining the two lawbreakers with whom we began. We are, I think, now ready to understand how they might have done what they did.

First, the price fixer at General Electric. Arriving at his new job eager to learn, he found that much he had learned as an engineer did not quite fit. Every day was a struggle to get "up to speed," as they say. One day his superior invited him to go to a meeting. He went. The meeting consisted of sales managers from the other two major turbine manufacturers, clearly respectable people and clearly engaged in fixing market prices. There was no question that the meeting was secret. But what conclusion should he have drawn from that? A company like GE has many secrets. The meeting did not take long and soon our future price fixer was doing other things. After a few more meetings like this, he would be allowed to go without his superior. Soon the meetings would be routine.

He may initially have had qualms about the meetings. We often have qualms about a practice with which we are unfamiliar. But we have learned to suspend judgment for a decent interval. Often the qualms disappear as understanding increases. Of course, our price fixer may have had more than the usual reasons for qualms. He may have received in the mail a copy of a GE policy that forbade what he was doing ("policy 20.5"). But the policy would have come from the law department, not from anyone in his chain of command. Nothing would have made that mailing seem more important than other mailings from law or other non-line departments managers routinely ignore. What filled our price fixer's time, his field of vision, as we might say, was learning to be a manager. He had little time to think about matters that seemed to matter to no one with whom he dealt. Eventually, he would stop thinking about the price-fixing as price-fixing at all.[12]

I have now told the price fixer's story in terms appropriate to microscopic vision. I have described him as developing in a normal way a sense for what matters and what does not matter in a certain environment. The process is similar to the "desensitizing" that a surgeon must undergo before she can calmly cut off a human limb or put a knife into a still-beating heart. Though the process I have described does *not* require learning to block anything out, only failing to use some information because one is busy using other information, it does share at least one important feature with self-deception (something ordinary desensitizing does not): The price fixer was misled. The process nonetheless differs from self-deception in at least two ways:

First, while self-deception presupposes in the self-deceiver some sense for the unreliability of the procedure he is using to learn about the world, the process I have described presupposes no such thing. Our price fixer might well have believed his procedure would yield an accurate, albeit incomplete, picture of the world in which he worked.

Second, while self-deception presupposes that the procedure used is in fact generally unreliable, we need not presuppose that either. The procedure I have described might well be *generally* reliable. The problem is that the price-fixer's procedure was not "designed" to distinguish legal from illegal management. That design may well have made sense in the 1950s. Who then would have thought that the managers of a company like GE would have engaged in extensive illegal conduct? The discovery must have astonished many people, including our price fixer.

Now consider our inside trader. He did get warnings of a sort our price fixer did not. He actually read about indictments of people for inside trading. Yet, he continued to trade on inside information. Why? Perhaps he deceived himself about the chances of being caught. A more interesting possibility, though, is that he never thought about being caught. Consider: He began inside trading with a clear conscience. He read of its illegality only after he had grown used to inside trading. Perhaps those with whom he cooperated showed no fear. Busy with many things beside inside trading, normal prudence would have told him that, if he feared everything the newspapers invited him to fear, he would live with numberless terrors. We must use the judgment developed in daily life to put newspaper stories in perspective. His immediate environment seemed as safe as ever. So, why should he worry about what he read in the newspaper? Again, we have a normal process leading to an abnormal result.

I do not, of course, claim that this is how it was. What is important here is not that I have the story of these two right, but that what I say about them seems a plausible description of many of those who engage in wrongdoing of the sort that concerns us, even if it happens not to be true of these two. I am suggesting a hypothesis, not demonstrating it.

Though that is all I claim for these two stories, I should, I think, point out one piece of evidence suggesting that I have got both at least partly right. Remember that neither of these wrongdoers seemed to understand how he came to do what he did. That is what we should expect if my version of their stories is more or less right. As I have told their stories, each did wrong in part at least because he did not use certain facts—policy 20.5 in one case, arrests of inside traders in the other—in a way that would have led him to a true understanding of what he was doing or to the conduct such an understanding would normally lead to. The facts did not trigger the fear of punishment or concern about having done wrong that seems normal outside the environment in which they were working. The facts seemed to have been pushed from consciousness by other facts, as most of the world is pushed aside when we look into a microscope.

Once our two wrongdoers were pulled from the microscope, they would cease to see the world as they had. They would not, however, have that sense of having "known it all along" so characteristic of coming out of self-deception (since they could not have known it until they looked at the world somewhat differently). They would instead be aware of seeing something that—on the evidence now before them—*must* have been there all along. Microscopic vision is a metaphor for a mental process, a "mind set" or "cognitive map." Because the mechanics of such mental processes are no more visible to the person whose mind it is than it is to an outside observer, our two wrongdoers need not have been aware of what made them attend to other things until now. They could honestly be perplexed about how they could have missed for so long what is now as plain as day.

V. Some Practical Lessons

What I have tried to do so far is describe wrongdoing as the outcome of a social process the literature on wrongdoing seems to have overlooked. I have tried to avoid assuming such serious moral failings as weakness of will or self-deception. I have, of course, not described my wrongdoers as paragons of rationality or virtue. The price fixer and inside trader were certainly naive, that is, lacking enough insight into the way the world works to recognize signs of trouble a more experienced person would have. Lund, however, seems no more naive than the rest of us. I can imagine myself doing what he did. I assume many of you can too.

If the process I have described in fact explains much wrongdoing in large organizations, we may draw some interesting conclusions about how to prevent wrongdoing. The most obvious, perhaps, is that screening out potential wrongdoers of the sort we have been discussing is probably impractical. Who would be let in by a procedure that would screen out the wrongdoers we have been discussing? We must instead consider how to prevent wrongdoing by the relatively decent people an organization must employ.

The problem as I have described it is that normal processes can lead to important information going unused at a decisive moment. Lund's training as a manager would not prepare him to see how special his role was. The future price-fixer's way of learning his job would not alert him to the risks of illegality, much less to any moral objections to fixing prices. The inside-trader's experience would make him discount the warning signs in the newspaper. Though microscopic vision is not a flight from reality, it does involve a sacrifice of one part of reality for another. Usually, the sacrifice is worth it. Sometimes it is not. When it is not, we need to change the microscopic vision of those working in the environment in question or change the environment. Sometimes we need to change both. Often, changing one changes the other too.

How might we change the environment? One way is simply to talk openly and often about what we want to have people notice. Lund would, for example, probably have refused to do as Mason suggested if the people back at Morton Thiokol's headquarters in Chicago had regularly reminded him that he was no ordinary manager: "We are counting on you to stand up for engineering considerations whatever anyone else does." Indeed, had *Mason* heard headquarters say that to Lund even a few times, he could hardly have said what he did say. He might well have deferred to Lund's judgment, even though NASA was pressuring him. "Sorry," he could have said, "my hands are tied."

Business professors especially, but ordinary managers as well, often decline to talk about what they call "ethics" because, as they say, they do not want to "sermonize." Sermons, they say, cannot lead people to do the right thing. If adults haven't learned to be ethical by now, or don't want to, what can a sermon do?

These professors and managers seem to use the word "ethics" as a catch-all for whatever "value" considerations seem so obvious to them that they would be embarrassed to raise the matter. I must admit to some doubts about their consistency here. These same people regularly sermonize about profit. They do not seem to find mention of "profit" embarrassing though we might suppose that, for them, profit would be the most obvious value consideration of all.

Still, whatever doubts I have about their consistency, I can easily respond to their concern about the ineffectiveness of sermonizing. However obvious the sermon's content, the sermon itself can help to keep legal, moral, and professional considerations in an organization's collective field of vision. That, I think, is why both business professors and ordinary managers talk so much about profit. That is how they keep profit a primary concern. So, doing the same for ethical considerations should, by itself, be a significant contribution to getting decent people to do the right thing.

Sermons are, of course, hardly the best way to do that. Better than sermons are such familiar devices as a code of ethics, ethics audits, ethics seminars for managers, discussion of ethics in the course of ordinary decision making, and reward of those who go out of their way to do the right thing ("reward" including not only praise but also the other valuables that normally go to those who serve their employer well, especially, money and promotion). But, whatever the merits of these particular devices in themselves, they all have this important characteristic in common. They help to keep employees alert to wrongdoing. They help to maintain a certain way of seeing the world.

Now, about teaching. Part of teaching is getting people used to thinking in a certain way. What academics call "disciplines" are in fact forms of "microscopic vision." We should, therefore, pay as much attention to what we don't teach as to what we do teach. If we limit ourselves to teaching technical aspects of a discipline, those we teach will tend to develop a perspective including *only* those technical aspects. They will not automatically include what we do not teach. Indeed, they would have to be quite unusual students even to see how to include such extras. If, then, we teach engineering without teaching engineering ethics, our graduates will begin work thinking about the technical aspects of engineering without thinking of the ethical aspects. They will not dismiss the ethical aspects. They will not even see them.

The same is true of business ethics. Business professors who limit themselves to technical matters do not simply fail to do good. However unintentionally, they *actively* contribute to the wrong their students do, if they eventually do wrong. They help to blind their students to something they might otherwise see.

Of course, we can teach what we should and still do little good. Good conduct in business or a profession presupposes a suitable social context. If a morally sensitive graduate goes to work in a company where ethics is ignored, he will, if he stays, slowly lose his sense of the ethical dimension of what he does. His field of vision will narrow. Eventually, he may be as blind as if we had taught him nothing. This is — I should stress — not a claim about moral development (as that term is now commonly understood). Our graduate may well score no worse on a Kohlberg test than he did before. He will simply have ceased to think of a certain range of decisions as raising questions to which moral categories are important. The questions will seem "merely technical," "an ordinary business decision," or in some other respect "merely routine."

That organizations can in this way make the teaching of ethics ineffective is, I think, no reason not to teach ethics. But it is good reason to conceive ethics teaching as part of a larger process; and good reason too, to try to transmit that conception to our students. Caroline Whitbeck of MIT has, I think, provided a good example of what I have in mind. As part of a course in Engineering Design, she has her students contact companies in the Boston area to find out how an engineer in the company could raise an issue of professional ethics related to design. Her students thus learn to think of their future employers as in part "ethics environments." But that is not all her students do. Their inquiries make it more likely that their future employers will think about how an engineer could raise an ethics issue. So, Professor Whitbeck may also be helping to improve the ethics environment in which her students will some day work.[13]

Notes

1. My wrongdoers, for example, are not much like the "hard men" in Jack Katz, *Seductions of Crime: Moral and Sensual Attractions of Doing Evil* (New York: Basic Books, 1988). Katz's criminals do indeed seem to will evil.

2. "Price Fixing and Bid Rigging in the Electrical Manufacturing Industry," *Administered Prices*, Hearings Before the Subcommittee on Antitrust and Monopoly of the Committee on the Judiciary, United States Senate, Part 27, 1961: p. 16652.

3. "After the Fall: Fates are Disparate for those Charged with Inside Trading," *Wall Street Journal* 210 (November 18, 1987): 22.

4. This description is derived from *The Presidential Commission on the Space Shuttle Challenger Disaster* (Washington, D.C.: June 6, 1986), esp. v. I, pp. 82–103. The quotation is on p. 93.

5. For the full defense of this claim, see Heinz Luegenbiehl and Michael Davis, *Engineering Codes of Ethics: Analysis and Applications*, forthcoming. For a shorter version, see "Why Engineers Should Support their Profession's Code" (Chicago: Center for the Study of Ethics in the Professions, 1987).

6. Compare Lawrence Kohlberg, *Essays on Moral Development* (San Francisco: Harper & Row, 1981).

7. Compare Chester A. Barnes, *The Functions of the Executive* (Cambridge, Mass.: Harvard University Press, 1938), p. 276. . . .

8. See, for example, Jan Elster, *Ulysses and the Sirens*, Revised Edition (New York: Cambridge University Press, 1984) for a good treatment of weakness of will.

9. Mike W. Martin, *Self-Deception and Morality* (Lawrence, Kansas: University Press of Kansas, 1986).

10. For a convenient survey of the literature on self-deception that brings out the range of mental state that might be included within that capacious term, see Alfred Mele, "Recent Work on Self-Deception," *American Philosophical Quarterly* 24 (January 1987): 1–17. For discussion of the related phenomenon of shifting responsibility, see Stanley Milgram, *Obedience to Authority: An Experimental View* (New York: Harper & Row, 1974). . . .

11. I derive this information from a video of Boisjoly's appearance before Caroline Whitbeck's engineering design course, "Company Loyalty and Whistleblowing: Ethical Decisions and the Space Shuttle Disaster" (7 January 1987), especially his answers to student questions.

12. In fact, our price fixer has no memory of ever seeing the policy. "Price Fixing," p. 16152. For a somewhat different version of this story (including the claim that he must have seen the policy), see James A. Waters' excellent "Catch 20.5: Corporate Morality as an Organizational Phenomenon," *Organizational Dynamics* 6 (Spring 1978): 3–19. Waters emphasizes "organizational blocks" to proper conduct rather than the normal processes that concern me. But I believe nothing I have said is inconsistent with what he says. Wrongdoing in a complex organization is likely to have many contributing causes. Waters and I differ only in being interested in different contributing causes. It is, of course, an empirical question whether either of us is even partly right (though one very hard decisively to test with the information we have or are likely to get).

13. Caroline Whitbeck, unpublished paper, "The Engineer's Responsibility for Safety: Integrating Ethics Teaching into Courses in Engineering Design."

Review and Discussion Questions

1. Explain what Davis means by "microscopic vision." How does this differ from tunnel vision and nearsightedness?

2. Describe how the concept of microscopic vision applies to each of the three cases of wrongdoing Davis discusses. Do you agree that this concept is the key to understanding these cases?

3. Are any other factors important for understanding these or other cases of business and professional misconduct? What, in your opinion, leads basically good people to do wrong?

4. What can be done to correct microscopic vision? How can moral conduct in business and the professions be encouraged? How much good do courses in business and professional ethics do?

For Further Reading

On Ethics

John Arthur, ed., *Morality and Moral Controversies*, 2nd ed. (Englewood Cliffs, N.J.: Prentice-Hall, 1986) contains essays in both theoretical and applied ethics.

James Rachels, *Elements of Moral Philosophy* (New York: Random House, 1986) is an excellent, clear introduction.

George Sher, ed., *Moral Philosophy* (San Diego: Harcourt Brace Jovanovich, 1986) and **Louis P. Pojman**, ed., *Ethical Theory* (Belmont, Calif.: Wadsworth, 1989) offer more advanced readings on various topics in moral philosophy.

Robert C. Solomon, *Ethics: A Brief Introduction* (New York: McGraw-Hill, 1984) is a brief, useful guide.

Moral Reasoning

Vincent Barry, *Invitation to Critical Thinking* (New York: Holt, Rinehart & Winston, 1984), especially Chapter 7, provides a guide to argument assessment.

Patrick Hurley, *A Concise Introduction to Logic*, 4th ed. (Belmont, Calif.: Wadsworth, 1991) is a good introduction to all the main areas of logic.

Business and Morality

Both **Richard T. De George**, *Business Ethics*, 3rd ed. (New York: Macmillan, 1990) and **Manuel G. Velasquez**, *Business Ethics*, 2nd ed. (Englewood Cliffs, N.J.: Prentice-Hall, 1988) contain useful introductions to moral philosophy in relation to business.

Barbara Ley Toffler, *Tough Choices: Managers Talk Ethics* (New York: John Wiley & Sons, 1986) presents interviews with twenty-one managers who discuss ethical situations at work.

CHAPTER 2

NORMATIVE THEORIES OF ETHICS

Captain Frank Furillo, in an Emmy-award-winning episode of the television drama "Hill Street Blues," firmly believes that the two toughs just brought in by his officers are guilty of the rape-murder of a nun earlier that morning inside the parish church. But the evidence is only circumstantial. As word of the crime spreads, the community is aghast and angry. From all sides—the press, local citizens, city hall, the police commissioner—pressure mounts on Furillo and his department for a speedy resolution of the matter. Outside the Hill Street station, a mob is growing frenzied, hoping to get their hands on the two young men and administer "street justice" to them. One of its members has even taken a shot at the suspects inside the police station!

The police, however, have only enough evidence to arraign the suspects on the relatively minor charge of being in possession of goods stolen from the church. Furillo and his colleagues could demand a high bail, thus keeping the defendants in custody, while the police try to turn up evidence that will convict the men of murder. But in a surprise move at the arraignment, the district attorney, acting in conjunction with Furillo, declines to ask the judge for bail. The men are free to go. But they and their outraged public defender, Joyce Davenport, know that their lives will be worthless once they hit the streets: Community members have sworn to revenge the much-loved sister if the police are unable to do their job. To remain in police custody, and thus safe, their only choice is to confess to murder. So the two men confess.

Davenport argues passionately but unsuccessfully against what she considers to be a police-state tactic. Anyone in that circumstance, guilty or innocent, would confess. It is an affront to the very idea of the rule of law, she contends: police coercion by way of mob pressure. No system of justice can permit such conduct from its public officials. Yet the confession allows the police to locate the murder weapon, thus bringing independent confirmation of the culprits' guilt. Furillo's tactic, nevertheless, does not rest easily on his own conscience, and the screenplay closes with him entering the church confessional later that night: "Forgive me, Father, for I have sinned . . ."

Furillo is understandably worried about whether he did the morally right thing. His action was successful, and it was for a good cause. But does the end always justify the means? Did the police and district attorney behave in a way that accords with due process and the rights of defendants? Should community pressure influence one's professional decisions? Did Furillo act in accordance with some principle that he could defend publicly? In a tough and controversial situation like this, the issue does not concern the moral sincerity of either Furillo or Davenport. Both can be assumed to want to do what is right, but what exactly is the morally justified thing to do? How are we to judge Furillo's tactics? These are the questions.

Chapter 1 noted that a defensible moral judgment must be supportable by a sound moral principle. Moral principles provide the confirmatory standard for moral judgments.

The use of these principles, however, is not a mechanical process in which one cranks in data and out pops an automatic moral judgment. Rather, the principles provide a conceptual framework that guides us in making moral decisions. Careful thought and open-minded reflection are always necessary to work from one's moral principles to a considered moral judgment.

But what are the appropriate principles to rely on when making moral judgments? The truth is that there is no consensus among people who have studied ethics and reflected on these matters. Different theories exist as to the proper standard of right and wrong. As Professor Bernard Williams has put it, we are heirs to a rich and complex ethical tradition, in which a variety of different moral principles and ethical considerations intertwine and sometimes compete.[1]

This chapter discusses the different normative perspectives and rival ethical principles that are our heritage. After distinguishing between what are called consequentialist and nonconsequentialist normative theories, it looks in detail at several ethical approaches, discussing their pros and cons and their relevance to moral decision making in an organizational context:

1. Egoism, both as an ethical theory and as a psychological theory

2. Utilitarianism, the theory that the morally right action is the one that achieves the greatest total amount of happiness for everyone

3. Kant's ethics, with his categorical imperative and his emphasis on moral motivation and respect for persons

4. Other nonconsequentialist normative themes: duties, moral rights, and *prima facie* principles

The chapter concludes with an attempt to tie together the major concerns of the different normative theories and suggests a general way of approaching moral decision making.

CONSEQUENTIALIST AND NONCONSEQUENTIALIST THEORIES

In ethics, *normative theories* propose some principle or principles for distinguishing right actions from wrong actions. These theories can, for convenience, be divided into consequentialist and nonconsequentialist approaches.

Many philosophers have argued that the moral rightness of an action is determined solely by its results. If its consequences are good, then the act is right; if they are bad, the act is wrong. Moral theorists who adopt this approach are therefore called *consequentialists*. They determine what is right by weighing the ratio of good to bad that an action is likely to produce. The right act is the one that produces, will probably produce, or is intended to produce at least as great a ratio of good to evil as any other course of action.

One question that arises here is consequences for whom? Should one consider the consequences only for oneself? Or the consequences for everyone affected? The two most important consequentialist theories, *egoism* and *utilitarianism*, are distinguished by their different answers to this question. Egoism advocates individual self-interest as its guiding principle, while utilitarianism holds that one must take into account everyone affected by the action. But both theories agree that rightness and wrongness are solely a function of an action's results.

By contrast, *nonconsequentialist* (or *deontological*) theories contend that right and wrong are determined by more than the likely consequences of an action. Nonconsequentialists do not necessarily deny that consequences are morally significant, but they believe that other factors are also relevant to the moral assessment of an action. For example, a nonconsequentialist would hold that for Tom to break his promise to Fred is wrong not simply because it has bad results (Fred's hurt feelings, Tom's damaged reputation, and so on) but because of the inherent character of the act itself. Even if more good than bad were to come from Tom's breaking the promise, a nonconsequentialist might still view it as wrong. What matters is the nature of the act in question, not just its results. This concept will become clearer later in the chapter with the discussion of some specific nonconsequentialist theories.

EGOISM

In January 1977, the Firestone Tire and Rubber Company announced that it was discontinuing its controversial "500" steel-belted radial, which according to a House subcommittee had been associated with fifteen deaths and thirty-one injuries. Newspapers interpreted the Firestone announcement as an immediate removal of the tires from the market, whereas Firestone intended a "rolling phase-out."

In the spring of 1978, a House subcommittee found that Firestone had in fact continued making the steel-belted "500" radial, despite earlier media reports to the contrary. Immediately thereafter, newspapers reported a Firestone spokesperson as denying that Firestone had misled the public. Asked why Firestone had not corrected the media misinterpretation of the company's intent, the spokesperson said that Firestone's policy was to ask for corrections only when it was beneficial to the company to do so — in other words, when it was in the company's self-interest.

The view that associates morality with self-interest is referred to as *egoism*. Egoism contends that an act is morally right if and only if it best promotes the individual's long-term interests. ("Individual" can refer to a single person or to a particular group or organization.) Egoists use their best long-term ad-

vantage as the standard for measuring an action's rightness. If an action produces, will probably produce, or is intended to produce for the individual a greater ratio of good to evil in the long run than any other alternative, then that action is the right one to perform, and the individual should take that course to be moral.

Moral philosophers distinguish between two kinds of egoism: personal and impersonal. Personal egoists claim they should pursue their own best long-term interests, but they do not say what others should do. Impersonal egoists claim that everyone should follow his or her best long-term interests.

Misconceptions about Egoism

Several misconceptions haunt both versions of egoism. One is that egoists only do what they like, that they are believers in "eat, drink, and be merry." Not so. Undergoing unpleasant, even painful experience meshes with egoism, provided such temporary sacrifice is necessary for the advancement of our long-term interests.

Another misconception is that all egoists endorse *hedonism*, the view that only pleasure (or happiness) is of intrinsic value, the only good in life worth pursuing. Although some egoists are hedonistic — as was the ancient Greek philosopher Epicurus (341–270 B.C.) — other egoists have a broader view of what constitutes self-interest. They identify the good with knowledge, power, or what some modern psychologists call self-actualization. Egoists may, in fact, hold any theory of what is good.

A final but very important misconception is that egoists cannot act honestly, be gracious and helpful to others, or otherwise promote others' interests. Egoism, however, requires us to do whatever will best further our own interests, and doing this sometimes requires us to advance the interests of others. In particular, egoism tells us to benefit others when we expect that our "generosity" will be reciprocated or when the act will bring us pleasure or in some way promote our own good. For example, egoism might recommend to the chair of the board that she hire as a vice president her nephew, who is not the best candidate for the job but whom the chair is very fond of. Hiring the nephew might bring her more satisfaction than any other course of action, even if the nephew doesn't perform his job as well as someone else might.

Or consider those U.S. companies doing business in racist South Africa that seek the approval of Reverend Leon H. Sullivan and management consultant D. Reid Weedon in order to shield themselves against increasingly harsh criticism from political activists. Weedon and Sullivan want corporations to fight racial discrimination in South Africa, and they administer the Sullivan Code, a system for grading corporate conduct there. Many American companies scramble annually to sponsor "socially responsible" programs in return for passing scores from Weedon and Sullivan. These companies are doing good for other people, but they are thereby advancing their own self-interest—by improving their public relations, fending off legislative interference, and blunting emotional stockholder resolutions. They are thus doing what egoism advises.

Psychological Egoism

So egoism does not preach that we should never assist others but rather that we have no basic moral duty to do so. An egoist would recommend that Ford, Coca-Cola, Monsanto, and other companies only support policies of political and social reform in South Africa to the extent that this furthers their own self-interest. According to egoism, these companies have no obligations toward others. If they do have a moral duty, it is to themselves. The same applies, of course, to individual persons. You and I are not required to act in the interests of others, but we should if that is the only way to promote our own self-interest. In short: Always look out for "number one."

Proponents of the ethical theory of egoism generally attempt to derive their basic moral principle from the alleged fact that humans are by nature selfish creatures. According to this doctrine, termed *psychological egoism*, human beings are, as a matter of fact, so constructed that they must behave selfishly. Psychological egoists claim that all actions are in fact selfishly motivated and that unselfish actions are therefore impossible. Even such apparently self-sacrificial acts as giving up your own life to save the lives of your children or "blowing the whistle" on your organization's misdeeds at great personal expense, say psychological egoists, are selfishly motivated. They are done to satisfy the parents' desires to benefit themselves—for example, to perpetuate their family line or avoid unbearable guilt—or the workers' desires for celebrity or revenge.

Problems with Egoism

Although egoism as an ethical doctrine has always had its adherents, the theory is open to very strong objections. And it is safe to say that few, if any, philosophers today would advocate it either as a personal or an organizational morality. Consider these objections:

1. *Psychological egoism is not a sound theory.* Of course, everyone is motivated to some extent by self-interest, and we all know of situations in which someone pretended to be acting altruistically or morally but was really only motivated by self-interest. The theory of psychological egoism contends, however, that people are always motivated only by self-interested concerns.

Now this claim seems open to many counterexamples. Take the actual case of a man who, while driving eastbound in a company truck, spotted smoke coming from inside a parked car and a child trying to escape from the vehicle. The man quickly made a U-turn, drove over to the burning vehicle, and found a one-year-old girl trapped in the back seat, restrained by a seat belt. Flames raged in the front seat as heavy smoke billowed from the car. Disregarding his own safety, the man entered the car and removed the infant, who authorities said would otherwise have died from the poisonous fumes and the flames.

Or take a more mundane example. It's Saturday, and you feel like having a beer with a couple of pals and watching the ball game. On the other hand, you believe you ought to take your two children to the zoo, as you had earlier suggested to them you might. Going to the zoo would bring them a lot of pleasure—and besides, you haven't done much with them recently. Of course, you love your children and it will bring you some pleasure to go to the zoo with them, but—let's face it—they've been rather cranky lately and you'd prefer to watch the ball game. Nonetheless, you feel an obligation and so you go to the zoo.

These appear to be cases in which people are acting for reasons other than self-interested ones. Of course, the reasons that lead you to take your children to the zoo—a sense of obligation, a desire to promote their happiness—are your reasons, but that by itself does not make them self-interested reasons. Still less does it show that you are selfish. Anything that you do is a result of your desires, but that fact doesn't establish what the believer in psychological egoism claims—namely, that the only desires you have, or the only desires that ultimately move you, are self-interested desires.

Psychological egoists (that is, advocates of the theory of psychological egoism) will claim that deep down both the heroic man who saved the girl and the unheroic parent taking the children to the zoo were really motivated by self-interest in some way or another. Maybe the hero was hoping to win praise or the parent to advance his or her own pleasure

by enhancing the children's affection for the parent. Or maybe some other self-interested consideration motivated them. Psychological egoists can always claim that some yet-to-be-identified subconscious egoistic motivation is the main impulse behind any action.

At this point, though, the psychological egoists' claims sound a little farfetched. And we may suspect them of trying to make their theory true by definition. Whatever example we come up with, they will simply claim that the person is really motivated by self-interest. One may well wonder how scientific this theory is, or how much content it has, when both the hero and the coward, both the parent who goes to the zoo and the parent who stays home, are equally selfish in their motivations.

An egoist could concede that people are not fully egoistic by nature and yet continue to maintain egoism as an ethical doctrine—that is, to insist that people ought morally to pursue only their own interests. Yet without the doctrine of psychological egoism, the ethical thesis of egoism becomes less attractive. Other types of ethical principles are possible. We all care about ourselves, but how much sense does it make to see self-interest as the basis of right and wrong? Do we really want to say that someone acting altruistically is behaving immorally?

2. *Egoism is not really a moral theory at all.* Many critics of egoism contend that the theory misunderstands the nature and point of morality. As Chapter 1 explained, morality serves to restrain our purely self-interested desires so we can all live together. If our interests never came into conflict—that is, if it were never advantageous for one person to deceive or cheat another—then we would have no need of morality. The moral standards of a society provide the basic guidelines for cooperative social existence and allow conflicts to be resolved by appeal to shared principles of justification.

It is hard to see how egoism could perform this function. In a society of egoists, people might publicly agree to follow certain rules so their lives would run more smoothly. But it would be a very unstable world, because people would not hesitate to break the rules if they thought they could get away with it. Nor can egoism provide a means for settling conflicts and disputes, since it simply tells each party to do whatever is necessary to promote effectively his or her interests.

Many moral theorists maintain that moral principles apply equally to the conduct of all persons and that their application requires us to be objective and impartial. Moral agents are seen as those who, despite their own involvement in an issue, can be reasonably disinterested and objective — those who try to see all sides of an issue without being committed to the interests of a particular individual or group, including themselves. If we accept this attitude of detachment and impartiality as at least part of what it means to take a moral point of view, then we must look for it in any proposed moral principle.

Ethical egoists are anything but objective, for they are always influenced by their own best interests, regardless of the issue or circumstances. Egoists should not even attempt to be impartial, except insofar as impartiality furthers their own interests. And any third person offering advice must represent his or her own interest.

3. *Egoism ignores blatant wrongs*. The most common objection to egoism is that by reducing everything to the standard of best long-term self-interest, egoism takes no stand against seemingly outrageous acts like stealing, murder, racial and sexual discrimination, deliberately false advertising, and wanton pollution. All such actions are morally neutral until the test of self-interest is applied.

Of course, the egoist might call this objection a case of question begging: assuming that such acts are immoral as grounds for repudiating egoism when, in fact, their morality is the very issue that moral principles such as egoism are meant to evaluate. Still, egoism must respond to the widely observed human desire to be fair or just, a desire that at least

sometimes seems stronger than competing selfish desires. A moral principle that allows the possibility of murder in the cause of self-interest offends our basic moral intuitions about justice and noninjury; it clashes with many of our "considered beliefs."

UTILITARIANISM

Utilitarianism is the moral doctrine that we should always act to produce the greatest possible balance of good over bad for everyone affected by our action. By "good," utilitarians understand happiness or pleasure. Thus, they answer the question "What makes a moral act right?" by asserting: the greatest happiness of all. Although the basic theme of utilitarianism is present in the writings of many earlier thinkers, Jeremy Bentham (1748–1832) and John Stuart Mill (1806–1873) were the first to develop the theory explicitly and in detail. Both Bentham and Mill were philosophers with a strong interest in legal and social reform. They used the utilitarian standard to evaluate and criticize the social and political institutions of their day — for example, the prison system. As a result, utilitarianism has long been associated with social improvement.

Bentham viewed a community as no more than the individual persons who compose it. The interests of the community are simply the sum of the interests of its members. An action promotes the interests of an individual when it adds to the individual's pleasure or diminishes the person's pain. Correspondingly, an action augments the happiness of a community only insofar as it increases the total amount of individual happiness. In this way, Bentham argued for the utilitarian principle that actions are right if they promote the greatest human welfare, wrong if they do not.

For Bentham, pleasure and pain are merely types of sensations, which differ only in number, intensity, and duration. He offered a "hedonic calculus" of six criteria for evaluating pleasure and pain exclusively by their quantitative differences. This calculus, he believed, makes possible an objective determination of the morality of anyone's conduct, individual or collective, on any occasion.

Bentham rejected any distinctions based on quality of pleasure except insofar as they might indicate differences in quantity. Thus, where equal amounts of pleasure are involved, throwing darts is as good as writing poetry and baking a cake as good as composing a symphony; reading Mickey Spillane is of no less value than reading Shakespeare. Although he himself was an intelligent, cultivated man, Bentham maintained there is nothing intrinsically better about cultivated and intellectual pleasures than about crude and prosaic ones. The only issue is which yields the greater amount of enjoyment.

John Stuart Mill thought Bentham's concept of pleasure was too simple. He viewed human beings as having elevated faculties that allow them to pursue various kinds of pleasure. The pleasures of the intellect and imagination, in particular, have a higher value than those of mere sensation. Thus, for Mill the utility principle allows consideration of the relative quality of pleasure and pain.

Although Bentham and Mill had different conceptions of pleasure, both men identified pleasure and happiness and considered pleasure the ultimate value. In this sense they are hedonists: Pleasure, in their view, is the one thing that is intrinsically good or worthwhile. Anything that is good is good only because it brings about pleasure (or happiness), directly or indirectly. Take education, for example. The learning process itself might be pleasurable to us; reflecting on or working with what we have learned might bring us satisfaction at some later time; or by making possible a career and life that we could not have had otherwise, education might bring us happiness indirectly. By contrast, critics of Bentham and Mill have contended that things other than happiness are or can be also inherently good — for example, knowledge, friendship,

and aesthetic satisfaction. The implication is that these things are valuable even if they do not lead to happiness.

Some moral theorists have modified utilitarianism so it aims at other consequences in addition to happiness. Other utilitarians, wary of trying to compare one person's happiness with another's, have interpreted their theory as requiring us not to maximize happiness but rather to maximize the satisfaction of people's preferences (or desires). The focus here will be utilitarianism in its standard form, in which the good to be aimed at is human happiness or welfare. But what will be said about standard or classical utilitarianism applies, with the appropriate modifications, to other versions as well.

Although this chapter considers later another form of utilitarianism, known as *rule utilitarianism*, utilitarianism in its most basic version, often called *act utilitarianism*, states that we must ask ourselves what the consequences of a particular act in a particular situation will be for all those affected. If its consequences bring more total good than those of any alternative course of action, then this action is the right one and the one we should perform. Thus a utilitarian could defend Frank Furillo's decision not to request bail, thereby coercing a confession from the suspects.

Consider another example: In 1956, medical researchers initiated a long-range study of viral hepatitis at Willowbrook State Hospital, a New York institution for mentally retarded children. The researchers were interested in determining the natural history of viral hepatitis and the effectiveness of gamma globulin as an agent for inoculating against hepatitis. Willowbrook seemed like a good choice for investigation because the disease was rampant there. To get the kind of precise data they considered most useful, the researchers decided to deliberately infect some of the incoming children with the strain of hepatitis virus epidemic at the institution.

The value of the Willowbrook research is well documented. As a direct result, we have increased our scientific understanding of viral hepatitis and how to treat it. But nagging moral questions persist. Should retarded children have been used as experimental subjects in experiments that were not directly therapeutic? Supporters of the research insist that the free and informed consent of the children's parents was obtained. But even if the facts warranted another conclusion, some people would still defend the Willowbrook experiments on the grounds that they produced the most good for the whole society. In other words, the suffering of some individuals was justified because it maximized the total happiness produced.

Six Points about Utilitarianism

Before evaluating utilitarianism, you should understand some points that might lead to confusion and misapplication. First, when a utilitarian like Bentham advocates "the greatest happiness for the greatest number," we must consider unhappiness or pain as well as happiness. Suppose, for example, an action produces eight units of happiness and four units of unhappiness. Its net worth is four units of happiness. An opposed action produces ten units of happiness and seven units of unhappiness; its net worth is three units. In this case we should choose the first action over the second. In the event that both lead not to happiness but to unhappiness, and there is no third option, we should choose the one that brings fewer units of unhappiness.

Second, actions affect people to different degrees. Your playing your radio loudly might enhance two persons' pleasure a little, cause significant discomfort to two others, and leave a fifth person indifferent. The utilitarian theory is not that each person votes on the basis of his or her pleasure or pain, with the majority ruling, but that we add up the various pleasures and pains, however large or small, and go with the action that brings about the greatest total amount of happiness.

Third, since utilitarians evaluate actions according to their consequences and actions produce different results in different circumstances, almost anything might, in principle, be morally right in some particular circumstance. For example, while breaking a promise generally produces unhappiness, there can be circumstances in which, on balance, more happiness would be produced by breaking a promise than by keeping it. In those circumstances, utilitarianism would require us to break the promise.

Fourth, utilitarians wish to maximize happiness not simply immediately but in the long run as well. All the indirect ramifications of an act have to be taken into account. Lying might seem a good way out of a tough situation, but if and when the people we deceive find out, not only will they be unhappy, but our reputations and our relationships with them will be damaged. This is a serious risk that a utilitarian cannot ignore.

Fifth, utilitarians acknowledge that we often do not know with certainty what the future consequences of our actions will be. Accordingly, we must act so that the expected or likely happiness is as great as possible. If I take my friend's money, unbeknownst to him, and buy lottery tickets with it, there is a chance that we will end up millionaires and that my action will have maximized happiness all around. But the odds are definitely against it; the most likely result is loss of money (and probably of a friendship, too). Therefore, no utilitarian could justify gambling with purloined funds on the grounds that it might maximize happiness.

Sometimes it is hard to determine the likely results of alternative actions, and no modern utilitarian really believes that we can assign precise units of happiness and unhappiness to people. But as Mill reminds us, we really do have quite a lot of experience as to what typically makes people happy or unhappy. In any case, as utilitarians our duty is to strive to maximize total happiness, even where it may seem difficult to know what action is likely to promote the good effectively.

Finally, when choosing among possible actions, utilitarianism does not require us to disregard our own pleasure. Nor should we give it added weight. Rather, our own pleasure and pain enter into the calculus equally with the pleasures and pains of others. Even if we are sincere in our utilitarianism, we must guard against the possibility of being biased in our calculations when our own interests are at stake. For this reason, and because it would be time consuming to do a utilitarian calculation before every action, utilitarians encourage us to rely on "rules of thumb" in ordinary moral circumstances. We can make it a rule of thumb, for example, to tell the truth and keep our promises, rather than to calculate possible pleasures and pains in every routine case, because we know that in general telling the truth and keeping promises result in more happiness than lying and breaking promises.

Utilitarianism in an Organizational Context

Several features about utilitarianism make it appealing as a standard for moral decisions in business and nonbusiness organizations.

First, utilitarianism provides a clear and straightforward basis for formulating and testing policies. By utilitarian standards, an organizational policy decision or action is good if it promotes the general welfare more than any other alternative. To show that a policy is wrong (or needs modification) requires only that it not promote total utility as well as some alternative would. Utilitarians do not ask us to accept rules, policies, or principles blindly. Rather, they require us to test their worth against the standard of utility.

Second, utilitarianism provides an objective and attractive way of resolving conflicts of self-interest. This feature of utilitarianism dramatically contrasts with egoism, which seems incapable of resolving conflicts of self-interest. By proposing a standard outside self-interest, utilitarianism greatly minimizes and may actually eliminate such disputes. Thus, individuals within organizations make moral decisions and evaluate their actions by appealing to a uniform standard: the general good.

Third, utilitarianism provides a flexible, result-oriented approach to moral decision making. By recognizing no actions of a general kind as inherently right or wrong, utilitarianism encourages organizations to focus on the results of different actions and policies, and it allows them to tailor their decisions to suit the complexities of their situations. This facet of utilitarianism enables organizations to make realistic and workable moral decisions.

Critical Inquiries

1. *Is utilitarianism really workable?* Utilitarianism instructs us to maximize happiness, but in hard cases we may be very uncertain about the likely results of the alternative courses of action open to us. Furthermore, comparing your level of happiness or unhappiness with mine is at best tricky, at worst impossible — and when many people are involved, the matter may get hopelessly complex. Even if we assume that it is possible to make comparisons and to calculate the various possible consequences of each course of action that a person might take (and the odds of each happening), is it realistic to expect people to take the time to make those calculations and, if they do, to make them accurately? Some critics of act utilitarianism have contended that teaching people to follow the basic utilitarian principle would not in fact promote happiness because of the difficulties in applying utilitarianism accurately.

2. *Are some actions wrong, even if they produce good?* Like egoism, utilitarianism focuses

on the results of an action, not on the character of the action itself. For utilitarians, no action is in itself objectionable. It is objectionable only when it leads to a lesser amount of total good than could otherwise have been brought about. Critics of utilitarianism, by contrast, contend that some actions can be immoral and thus things we must not do, even if doing them would maximize happiness.

Suppose a dying woman has asked you to promise to send the $25,000 under her bed to her nephew in another part of the country. She dies without anyone else knowing of the money or of the promise that you made. Now suppose, too, that you know the nephew is a spendthrift and a drunkard and, were the money delivered to him, it would be wasted in a week of outrageous partying. On the other hand, a very fine orphanage in your town needs such a sum to improve and expand its recreational facilities, something that would provide happiness to many children for years to come. It seems clear that on utilitarian grounds you should give the money to the orphanage, because this action would result in more total happiness.

Many people would balk at this conclusion, contending that it would be wrong to break your promise, even if doing so would bring about more good than keeping it. Having made a promise, you have an obligation to keep it, and a death-bed promise is particularly serious. Furthermore, the deceased woman had a right to do with her money as she wished; it is not for you to decide how to spend it. Likewise, having been bequeathed the money, the nephew has a right to it, regardless of how wisely or foolishly he might spend it. Defenders of utilitarianism, however, would insist that promoting happiness is all that really matters and warn you not to be blinded by moral prejudice.

Critics of utilitarianism, on the other hand, maintain that utilitarianism is morally blind in not just permitting, but requiring, immoral actions in order to maximize happiness.

Philosopher Richard Brandt states the case against act utilitarianism this way:

> Act-utilitarianism . . . implies that if you have employed a boy to mow your lawn and he has finished the job and asks for his pay, you should pay him what you promised only if you cannot find a better use for your money. . . . It implies that if your father is ill and has no prospect of good in his life, and maintaining him is a drain on the energy and enjoyment of others, then, if you can end his life without provoking any public scandal or setting a bad example, it is your positive duty to take matters into your own hands and bring his life to a close.[2]

In the same vein, ethicist A. C. Ewing concludes that "act utilitarian principles, logically carried, would result in far more cheating, lying, and unfair action than any good person would tolerate."[3]

Defenders of act utilitarianism would reply that these charges are exaggerated. While theoretically possible, for example, that not paying the boy for his work might maximize happiness, this is extremely unlikely. Utilitarians contend that only in very unusual circumstances will pursuit of the good conflict with our ordinary ideas of right and wrong, and in those cases—like the death-bed promise—we should put aside those ordinary ideas. The antiutilitarian replies that the theoretical possibility of utilitarianism requiring immoral conduct shows it to be an unsatisfactory moral theory.

3. *Is utilitarianism unjust?* Utilitarianism concerns itself with the total sum of happiness produced, not with how that happiness is distributed. If policy X brings two units of happiness to each of five people and policy Y brings nine units of happiness to one person, one unit each to two others, and none to the remaining two, then Y is to be preferred (eleven units of happiness versus ten), even though it distributes that happiness very unequally.

Worse still from the critic's point of view, utilitarianism may even require that some people's happiness be sacrificed in order to achieve the greatest overall amount of happiness. Sometimes the general utility may be served only at the expense of a single individual or group. Under the right of eminent domain, for example, the government may appropriate private property for public use, usually with compensation to the owner. Thus, the government may legally purchase your house from you to widen a highway — even if you don't want to sell the house or want more money than the government is willing to pay. The public interest is served at your private expense. Is this just?

Or consider the Dan River experiment, which is a recent entry in the long-term controversy over the cause of brown lung disease. Claiming that the disease is caused by the inhalation of microscopic fibers in cotton dust, textile unions have fought for tough regulations to protect their workers. The Occupational Safety and Health Administration (OSHA) responded by proposing cotton dust standards, which would require firms to install expensive new equipment. A few months before the March 27, 1984, deadline for installing the equipment, officials at Dan River textile plants in Virginia asked the state to waive the requirements for six months so the company could conduct an experiment to determine the precise cause of brown lung disease. Both the state and the Department of Labor allowed the extension. In response, the Amalgamated Clothing and Textile Workers Union asked OSHA to stop the proposed project, charging, "It is simply unconscionable to allow hundreds of cotton mill workers to continue to face a high risk of developing brown lung disease."[4]

Suppose that the Dan River project in fact does expose workers to a "high risk" of contracting lung disease. If so, then a small group of individuals — 633 textile workers at ten locations in Danville, Virginia — are being compelled to carry the burden of isolating the cause of brown lung disease. Is this just?

It is, utilitarians would respond, if the experiment maximizes the total good of society. Does it? If the project succeeds in identifying the exact cause of the disease, then thousands of textile workers across the country and perhaps around the world will benefit. Also researchers might discover a more economical way to ensure worker safety, which in turn would yield a consumer benefit: more economical textiles than the ones produced if the industry installs expensive new equipment. Certainly, utilitarians would introduce the potential negative impact on workers at Dan River, but merely as one effect among many others. After the interests of all affected parties are equally weighed, if the extension of the deadline would likely yield the greatest net utility, then it is just to make workers at Dan River carry the main burden of isolating the cause of brown lung disease — even if by so doing those workers may be injured. (This sketch is not intended to justify the project or to foreclose a fuller utilitarian analysis of the case but merely to illustrate generally the utilitarian approach.)

The Interplay Between Self-Interest and Utility

Both self-interest and utility play important roles in organizational decisions, and the views of many businesspersons blend these two theories. To the extent that each business pursues its own interests and each businessperson tries to maximize personal success, business practice can be called egoistic. But business practice is also utilitarian in that pursuing self-interest is thought to maximize the total good, and playing by the established rules of the competitive game is seen as advancing the good of society as a whole. The classical capitalist economist Adam Smith (1723–1790) held such a view. He argued that if business is left to pursue its self-interest, the good of society will be served. Indeed, Smith believed that only through egoistic pursuits could the greatest economic good for the whole society be produced. The essence of Smith's position can be seen in the following passage from *The Wealth of Nations* (1776), where Smith underscores the interplay between self-interest and the social good and between egoism and utilitarianism.

> Every individual is continually exerting himself to find out the most advantageous employment for whatever capital he can command. It is his own advantage, indeed, and not that of the society, which he has in view. But the study of his own advantage, naturally, or rather necessarily, leads him to prefer that employment which is most advantageous to the society. . . .
>
> As every individual, therefore, endeavours as much as he can . . . to employ his capital . . . [so] that its produce may be of the greatest value, every individual necessarily labors to render the annual revenue of the society as great as he can. He generally, indeed, neither intends to promote the public interest, nor knows how much he is promoting it. . . . He intends only his own security; and by directing that industry in such a manner as its produce may be of the greatest value, he intends only his own gain, and he is in this, as in many other cases, led by an invisible hand to promote an end which was no part of his intention. Nor is it always the worse for the society that it was no part of it. By pursuing his own interest he frequently promotes that of the society more effectually than when he really intends to promote it. I have never known much good done by those who affected to trade for the public good. It is an affectation, indeed, not very common among merchants, and very few words need be employed in dissuading them from it.[5]

Many today would agree with Smith, conceding that business is part of a social system, that cooperation is necessary, and that certain competitive ground rules are needed and should be followed. At the same time, they would argue that the social system is best served by the active pursuit of self-interest within the context of established rules. Thus, these individuals might be said to favor viewing the business world as practicing the ethics of "restrained egoism." Such a position is egoistic because it recommends the pursuit of self-interest; it is restrained because it permits pursuit of self-interest only within the rules of business practice.[6]

Chapter 4 examines Smith's position in more detail.

KANT'S ETHICS

Most of us find the ideal of promoting human happiness and well-being an attractive one and, as a result, admire greatly a woman like Mother Teresa, who has devoted her life to working with the poor. Despite the attractiveness of this ideal, many moral philosophers are critical of utilitarianism — particularly because, like egoism, it reduces all morality to a concern with consequences. Although nonconsequentialist normative theories vary significantly, adopting different approaches and stressing different themes, the writings of the preeminent German philosopher Immanuel Kant (1724–1804) provide an excellent example of a thoroughly nonconsequentialist approach. Perhaps few thinkers today would endorse Kant's theory on every point, but his work has greatly influenced philosophers and has helped to shape our general moral culture.

Kant sought moral principles that do not rest on contingencies and that define actions as inherently right or wrong apart from any particular circumstances. He believed that moral rules can, in principle, be known as a result of reason alone and are not based on observation (as are, for example, scientific judgments). In contrast to utilitarianism or other consequentialist theories, Kant's ethics contend that we do not have to know any-thing about the likely results of, say, my tell-ing a lie to my boss in order to know that it is immoral. "The basis of obligation," Kant wrote, "must not be sought in human nature, [nor] in the circumstances of the world." Rather it is *a priori*, by which he meant that moral reasoning is not based on factual knowl-edge and that reason by itself can reveal the ba-sic principles of morality.

Good Will

Chapter 1 mentioned Good Samaritan laws, which shield from lawsuits those ren-dering emergency aid. Such laws, in effect, give legal protection to the humanitarian im-pulse behind emergency interventions. They formally recognize that the interventionist's heart was in the right place, that the person's intention was irreproachable. And because the person acted from right intention, he or she should not be held culpable, except for grievous negligence. The widely observable human tendency to introduce a person's in-tentions in assigning blame or praise is a good springboard for engaging Kant's ethics.

Nothing, said Kant, is good in itself ex-cept a good will. This does not mean that in-telligence, courage, self-control, health, hap-piness, and other things are not good and desirable. But Kant believed that their good-ness depends on the will that makes use of them. Intelligence, for instance, is not good when used by an evil person.

By *will* Kant meant the uniquely human capacity to act from principle. Contained in the notion of good will is the concept of duty: Only when we act from duty does our action have moral worth. When we act only out of feeling, inclination, or self-interest, our ac-tions—although they may be otherwise iden-tical with ones that spring from the sense of duty—have no true moral worth.

Suppose that you're a clerk in a small stop-and-go store. Late one night a customer pays for his five-dollar purchase with a twenty-dollar bill, which you mistake for a ten. It's only after the customer leaves that you realize you shortchanged him. You race out the front door and find him lingering by a vending machine. You give him the ten dol-lars with your apologies, and he thanks you profusely.

Can we say with certainty that you acted from a good will? Not necessarily. You may have acted from a desire to promote business or to avoid legal entanglement. If so, you would have acted in accordance with but not from duty. Your apparently virtuous gesture just happened to coincide with duty. Accord-ing to Kant, if you do not will the action from a sense of your duty to be fair and honest, your action does not have true moral worth. Ac-tions have true moral worth only when they spring from a recognition of duty and a choice to discharge it.

But then what determines our duty? How do we know what morality requires of us? Kant answered these questions by formulat-ing what he called the "categorical impera-tive." This extraordinarily significant moral concept provides Kant's answer to the ques-tion, "What makes a moral act right?"

The Categorical Imperative

You have seen that egoists and utilitarians allow factual circumstances or empirical data to determine moral judgments. In contrast, Kant believed that reason alone can yield a moral law. We do not have to rely on empirical evidence relating to consequences and to sim-ilar situations. Just as we know, seemingly through reason alone, such abstract truths as "Every change must have a cause," so we can arrive at absolute moral truth through nonem-pirical reasoning. And we can thereby dis-cover our duty.

For Kant, an absolute moral truth must be logically consistent, free from internal con-tradiction. For example, it is a contradiction to say that an effect does not have a cause. Kant aimed to ensure that his absolute moral law would avoid such contradictions. If he could formulate such a rule, he maintained, it would oblige everyone to follow it without exception.

Kant believed that there is just one command (imperative) that is categorical—that is necessarily binding on all rational agents, regardless of any other considerations. From this one categorical imperative, this universal command, we can derive all commands of duty. Kant's *categorical imperative* says that we should act in such a way that we can will the maxim of our action to become a universal law. So Kant's answer to the question "What makes a moral act right?" is that a moral act is right if and only if we can will it to become a universal law of conduct.

The obvious and crucial question that arises here is: When are we justified in saying that the maxim of our action can become a universal law of conduct?

By "maxim," Kant meant the subjective principle of an action, the principle (or rule) that people in effect formulate in determining their conduct. For example, suppose building contractor Martin promises to install a sprinkler system in a project but is willing to break that promise to suit his purposes. His maxim can be expressed this way: "I'll make promises that I'll break whenever keeping them no longer suits my purposes." This is the subjective principle, the maxim, that directs his action.

Kant insisted that the morality of any maxim depends on whether we can logically will it to become a universal law. Could Martin's maxim be universally acted on? That depends on whether the maxim as law would involve a contradiction. The maxim "I'll make promises that I'll break whenever keeping them no longer suits my purposes" could not be universally acted on because it involves a contradiction of will. On the one hand, Martin is willing that it be possible to make promises and have them honored. On the other, if everyone intended to break promises when they so desired, then promises could not be honored in the first place, because it is in the nature of promises that they be believed. A law that allowed promise breaking would contradict the very nature of a promise. Similarly, a law that allowed lying would contradict the very nature of serious communication, for the activity of serious communication (as opposed to joking) requires that participants intend to speak the truth. I cannot, without contradiction, will both serious conversation and lying. By contrast, there is no problem, Kant thinks, with willing promise keeping or truth telling to be universal laws.

Consider, as another example, Kant's account of a man who, in despair after suffering a series of major setbacks, contemplates suicide. While still rational, the man asks whether it would be contrary to his duty to take his own life. Could the maxim of his action become a universal law of nature? Kant thinks not:

> His maxim . . . is: For love of myself, I make it my principle to shorten my life when by a longer duration it threatens more evils than satisfaction. But it is questionable whether this principle of self-love could become a universal law of nature. One immediately sees a contradiction in a system of nature whose law would be to destroy life by the feeling whose special office is to impel the improvement of life. In this case, it would not exist as nature: hence the maxim cannot obtain as a law of nature, and thus it wholly contradicts the supreme principle of all duty.[7]

When Kant insists that a moral rule be consistently universalizable, he is saying that moral rules prescribe categorically, not hypothetically. A hypothetical prescription tells us what to do if we desire a particular outcome. Thus, "If I want people to like me, I should be nice to them" and "If you want to go to medical school, you must take biology" are hypothetical imperatives. They tell us what we must do on the assumption that we have some particular goal. If that is what we want, then this is what we must do. On the other hand, if we don't want to go to medical school, then the command to take biology does not apply to us. In contrast, Kant's imperative is categorical—it commands unconditionally. That is, it is necessarily binding on everyone, regardless of his or her specific goals or desires, regardless of consequences. A categorical imperative takes the form of "Do this" or "Don't do that"—no ifs, ands, or buts.

Universal Acceptability. There is another way of looking at the categorical imperative. Each person, through his or her own acts of will, legislates the moral law. The moral rules that we obey are not imposed on us from the outside. They are self-imposed and self-recognized, fully internalized principles. The sense of duty that we obey comes from within; it is an expression of our own higher selves.

Thus, moral beings give themselves the moral law and accept its demands on themselves. But that is not to say we can prescribe anything we want, for we are bound by reason and its demands. Since reason is the same for all rational beings, we all give ourselves the same moral law. In other words, when you answer the question "What should I do?" you must consider what all rational beings should do. If the moral law is valid for you, it must be valid for all other rational beings.

To see whether a rule or principle is a moral law, we can thus ask if what the rule commands would be acceptable to all rational beings acting rationally. In considering lying, theft, or murder, for example, you must consider the act not only from your own viewpoint but from the perspective of the person lied to, robbed, or murdered. Presumably, rational beings do not want to be lied to, robbed, or murdered. The test of the morality of a rule, then, is not whether people in fact

accept it but whether all rational beings thinking rationally would accept it regardless of whether they are the doers or the receivers of the actions. This is an important moral insight, and most philosophers see it as implicit in Kant's discussion of the categorical imperative, even though Kant (who is a difficult writer to understand) did not make the point in this form.

The principle of universal acceptability has important applications. Suppose a man advocates a hiring policy that discriminates against women. For this rule to be universally acceptable, the man would have to be willing to accept it if he were a woman, something he would presumably be unwilling to do. Or suppose the manufacturer of a product decides to market it even though the manufacturer knows that the product is unsafe when used in a certain common way and that consumers are ignorant of this fact. Applying the universal acceptability principle, the company's decision makers would have to be willing to advocate marketing the product even if they were themselves in the position of uninformed consumers. Presumably they would be unwilling to do this. So the rule that would allow the product to be marketed would fail the test of universal acceptability.

Humanity as an End, Never as Merely a Means. In addition to the principle of universal acceptability, Kant explicitly offered another, very famous way of formulating the core idea of his categorical imperative. According to this formulation, rational creatures should always treat other rational creatures as ends in themselves and never as only means to ends. This formulation underscores Kant's belief that every human being has an inherent worth resulting from the sheer possession of rationality. We must always act in a way that respects this humanity in others and in ourselves.

As rational beings, humans would act inconsistently if they did not treat everyone else the way they themselves would want to be treated. Here we see shades of the Golden Rule. Indeed, Kant's moral philosophy can be viewed as a profound reconsideration of this basic nonconsequentialist principle. Because rational beings recognize their own inner worth, they would never wish to be used as entities possessing worth only as means to an end.

Thus, when brokers encourage unnecessary buying and selling of stocks in order to reap a commission (a practice called "churning"), they are treating their clients simply as a means and not respecting them as persons, as ends in themselves. Likewise, Kant would object to using patients as subjects in a medical experiment without their consent. Even though great social benefit might result, the researchers would be intentionally using the patients solely as a means to the researchers' own goals and thus failing to respect the patients' basic humanity.

Kant maintained, as explained first, that what makes an action morally right is that we can will it to be a universal law. We now have two ways of reformulating his categorical imperative that may be easier to grasp and apply:

> *First reformulation:* What makes an action right is that the agent would be willing to be so treated were the positions of the parties reversed.

> *Second reformulation:* What makes an action right is that the agent treats human beings as ends in themselves.

Kant in an Organizational Context

Like utilitarianism, Kant's moral theory has application for organizations.

First, the categorical imperative gives us firm rules to follow in moral decision making, rules that do not depend on circumstances or results and that do not permit individual exceptions. No matter what the consequences may be or who does it, some actions are always wrong. Lying is an example; no matter how much good may come from misrepresenting a product, such deliberate misrepresentation is always wrong. Similarly, exposing uninformed workers to the risk of lung disease could not be justified in order to advance medical knowledge.

Second, Kant introduces a needed humanistic dimension into business decisions. One of the principal objections to egoism and utilitarianism is that they permit us to treat humans as means to ends. Kant's principles clearly forbid this. Many would say that respect for the inherent worth and dignity of human beings is much needed today in business, where encroaching technology and computerization tend to dehumanize people under the guise of efficiency. Kant's theory puts the emphasis of organizational decision making where it belongs: on individuals. Organizations, after all, involve individuals working in concert to provide goods and services for other individuals. The primacy Kant gives the individual reflects this essential function of business.

Third, Kant stresses the importance of motivation and of acting on principle. According to Kant, it is not just enough to do the right thing; an action has moral worth only if it is done from a sense of duty — that is, from a desire to do the right thing for its own sake. The importance of this point is too often forgotten. Sometimes when individuals and organizations believe that an action promotes not only their own interests but those of others as well, they are actually rationalizing — doing what is best for themselves and only imagining that somehow it will promote happiness in general. Worse still, they may defend their actions as morally praiseworthy when, in fact, they are only behaving egoistically. They wouldn't do the morally justifiable thing if they didn't think it would pay off for them. By stressing the importance of motivation, a Kantian approach serves as a corrective to this. Even an action that helps others has moral value for Kant only if the person doing it is morally motivated — that is, acting on principle or out of moral conviction.

Critical Inquiries

1. *What has moral worth?* According to Kant, the clerk who returns the ten dollars to the customer is doing the right thing. But if his action is motivated by self-interest (perhaps he wants to get a reputation for honesty), then it does not have moral worth. That seems plausible. But Kant also held that if the clerk does the right thing out of instinct, habit, or sympathy for the other person, then the act still does not have moral worth. Only if it is done out of a sense of duty does the clerk's action have moral value. Many moral theorists have felt that Kant was too severe on this point. Do we really want to say that giving money to famine relief efforts has no moral worth if one is emotionally moved to do so by pictures of starving children rather than by a sense of duty? We might, to the contrary, find a person with strong human sympathies morally superior to someone who gives solely out of an abstract sense of duty.

2. *Is the categorical imperative an adequate test of right?* Kant said that a moral rule must function without exception. Critics wonder why the prohibition against such actions as lying, promise breaking, suicide, and so on must be exceptionless. They say that Kant failed to distinguish between saying that a person should not except himself or herself from a rule and that the rule itself has no exceptions.

If stealing is wrong, it's wrong for me as well as for you. "Stealing is wrong, except if I do it" is not universalizable, for then stealing would be right for all to do, which contradicts the assertion that stealing is wrong. But because no one may make of oneself an exception to a rule, it does not follow that the rule itself has no exceptions.

Suppose, for example, we decide that stealing is sometimes right, perhaps in the case of a person who is starving. Thus, the rule becomes "Never steal except when starving." This rule seems just as universalizable as "Never steal." The phrase "except . . . " can be viewed not as justifying a violation of the rule but as building a qualification into it. Critics in effect are asking why a qualified rule is not just as good as an unqualified one. If it is, then we no longer need to state rules in the simple, direct, unqualified manner that Kant did.

In fairness to Kant, it could be argued that his universalization formula can be interpreted flexibly enough to meet common-sense objections. For example, perhaps we could universalize the principle that individuals should steal rather than starve to death or that it is permissible to take one's own life to extinguish unspeakable pain. And yet to qualify the rules against stealing, lying, and taking one's life seems to invite a non-Kantian empirical analysis to justify morally the exceptions. One could, it seems, universalize more than one moral rule in a given situation: "Do not lie unless a life is at stake" versus "Lying is wrong unless necessary to avoid the suffering of innocent people." If so, then the categorical imperative would supply at best a necessary, but not a sufficient, test of right. But once we start choosing among various alternative rules, then we are adopting an approach to ethics that Kant would have rejected.

3. *What does it mean to treat people as means?* Kant's mandate that individuals must always be considered as ends in themselves and never merely as means expresses our sense of the intrinsic value of the human spirit and has profound moral appeal. Yet it is not always clear when people are being treated as ends and when as means. For example, Kant believed that prostitution was immoral because, by selling their sexual services, prostitutes allow themselves to be treated as means. Prostitutes, however, are not the only ones to sell their services. Anyone who works for a wage does so. Does that mean that we are all being treated immorally, since our employers are

presumably hiring us as a means to advance their own ends? Perhaps not, because we freely agreed to do the work. But then the prostitute might have freely chosen that line of work too.

OTHER NONCONSEQUENTIALIST PERSPECTIVES

For Kant, the categorical imperative provides the basic test of right and wrong, and he is resolutely nonconsequentialist in his application of it. You know now what he would say about the case of the death-bed promise: The maxim permitting you to break your promise cannot be universalized, and hence it would be immoral of you to give the money to the orphanage, despite the happiness that doing so would bring. But nonconsequentialists are not necessarily Kantians, and several different nonutilitarian moral concerns emerged in the discussion of the death-bed promise example.

Critics of act utilitarianism believe that it is faulty for maintaining that we have one and only one moral duty. A utilitarian might follow various principles as rules of thumb, but they are only calculation substitutes. All that matters morally to utilitarians is the maximization of happiness. Yet this idea, many philosophers think, fails to do justice to the richness and complexity of our moral lives.

Prima Facie Principles

One influential philosopher who argued this way was the British scholar W. D. Ross (1877–1971).[8] Ross complained that utilitarianism is too simple and is untrue to the way we ordinarily think about morality and about our moral obligations. We see ourselves, Ross and others contend, as being under various moral obligations that cannot be reduced to the single obligation of maximizing happiness. Often these obligations grow out of special relationships that we enter or out of determinate

roles that we undertake. We are intertwined with other people in very specific contexts and have, as a result, certain moral obligations.

For example, as a professor, Jones is obligated to assist her students in the learning process, evaluate their work in a fair and educationally productive way, and so on—obligations to the specific people in her classroom that she does not have to other people. As a spouse, Jones must maintain a certain emotional and sexual fidelity to her partner. As a parent, she must provide for the specific human beings who are her children. As a friend to Smith, she may have a moral responsibility to help him out in a time of crisis. Having borrowed money from Brown, Smith has a moral obligation to pay it back. And so on: Different relationships and different circumstances generate a variety of specific moral obligations.

In addition, we have certain moral obligations that do not arise from our unique interactions and relationships with other people. For example, we ought to treat people justly, to remedy injustices, and to promote human welfare. The latter obligation is important, but it is for the nonconsequentialist one among many obligations that we may have.

At any given time, we are likely to be under more than one obligation. Sometimes, unfortunately, these obligations may conflict. That is, we may have an obligation to do *A* and a distinct obligation to do *B*, where it is not possible to do both *A* and *B*. For example, I promised to meet a friend on an urgent matter and now, as I am hurrying there, I pass an injured person who is obviously in need of some assistance. Yet stopping to aid him will make it impossible for me to fulfill my promise. What should I do?

For moral philosophers like Ross, there is no single answer for all cases. What I ought to do will depend on the circumstances and the relative importance of the conflicting obligations. I have an obligation to keep my promise, and I have an obligation to assist people in distress. What I must decide is, in the given circumstance, which of these obligations is more important. I must weigh the moral significance of the promise against the comparative moral urgency of assisting the injured person.

Philosophers like Ross believe that most, or even all, of our moral obligations are *prima facie* ones. A *prima facie* obligation is simply an obligation that can be overridden by a more important obligation. For example, we take promise keeping seriously, but almost everyone would agree that in some circumstances—for example, when a life is at stake—it would not only be permissible but morally required to break a promise. Our obligation to keep a promise is a real one, and if there is no conflicting obligation, then we must keep the promise. But that obligation is not absolute or categorical; it could in principle be outweighed by a more stringent moral obligation. That is foreign to Kant's way of looking at things.

Consider an example that Kant himself discussed. Imagine that a murderer comes to your door, wanting to know where your friend is so he can kill him. Your friend is in fact hiding in your attic. Most people would probably agree that your obligation to your friend outweighs your general obligation to tell the truth: You should lie to throw the murderer off your friend's trail. You have a genuine obligation to tell the truth, but it is a *prima facie* obligation, one that can be outweighed by other moral factors. Kant disagreed. He maintained that you must tell the truth in all circumstances without exception. For him, telling the truth is an absolute or categorical obligation, not a *prima facie* one.

A perspective like Ross's, unlike utilitarianism, is pluralistic in recognizing a variety of genuine moral obligations. But contrary to Kant, these obligations are not seen as absolute and exceptionless. On both points, Ross contended that his view of morality fits more closely our actual moral experience and the way we view our moral obligations.

Ross also sided with common sense morality in thinking that our *prima facie* obliga-

tions are obvious. What we should do when two or more *prima facie* obligations conflict, all things considered, is often difficult to judge. But telling the truth, keeping our promises, and aiding people in distress—these are obligations that any person who has reached the age of reason can discern. We can no more deny that it is wrong to injure people needlessly, Ross thought, than that $2 + 2 = 4$.

Assisting Others

Nonconsequentialists believe that utilitarianism presents too simple a picture of our moral world. In addition, they worry that utilitarianism risks making us all slaves to the maximization of total happiness. Stop and think about it: Isn't there something that you could be doing—for instance, volunteering at the local hospital or orphanage, collecting money for Third World development, helping the homeless—that would do more for the general good than what you are doing now or are planning to do tonight or tomorrow? Sure, working with the homeless might not bring you quite as much pleasure as what you would otherwise be doing, but if it would nonetheless maximize total happiness, then you are morally required to do it. However, by following this reasoning, you could end up working around the clock, sacrificing yourself for the greater good. This notion seems mistaken.

Most nonutilitarian philosophers, like Ross, believe that we have some obligation to promote the general welfare, but they typically view this obligation as less stringent than, for example, the obligation not to injure people. They see us as having a much stronger obligation to refrain from violating people's rights than to promote their happiness or well-being.

From this perspective, a manufacturing company's obligation not to violate OSHA regulations and thereby endanger the safety of its employees is stronger than its obligation to open up day-care facilities for their children, even though the cost of both is the same. The company, in other words, has a stronger duty to respect its contractual and legal employment-related obligations than it does to promote its employees' happiness in other ways. Likewise, for a company to violate people's rights by despoiling the environment through the discharge of pollutants would be morally worse than for it to decide not to expand a job training program in the inner city, even if expanding the program would bring about more total good.

Different nonutilitarian philosophers may weight these particular obligations differently, depending on their particular moral theory. But they typically believe that we have a stronger duty not to violate people's rights or in some other way injure them than we do simply to assist people or otherwise promote their well-being. A utilitarian, concerned solely with what will maximize happiness, is less inclined to draw such a distinction.

Many moral philosophers draw a related distinction between actions that we are morally required to take and charitable or *supererogatory* acts—that is, actions that would be good to take but not immoral not to take. Act utilitarianism does not make this distinction. While we admire Mother Teresa and Albert Schweitzer for devoting their lives to doing good works among the poor, we see them as acting above and beyond the call of duty. We do not expect so much from ordinary people. Yet people who are not moral heroes or who fall short of sainthood may nonetheless be living morally satisfactory lives.

Nonutilitarian theorists see the distinction between morally obligatory actions and supererogatory actions not so much as a realistic concession to human weakness but as a necessary demarcation if we are to avoid becoming enslaved to the maximization of the general welfare. The idea here is that each of us should have a sphere in which to pursue our own plans and goals, to carve out a distinctive life plan. These plans and goals are limited by various moral obligations, in particular by other people's rights, but the demands of morality are not all-encompassing.

Moral Rights

What, then, are rights, and what rights do people have? Broadly defined, a *right* is an entitlement to act or have others act in a certain way. The connection between rights and duties is that, generally speaking, if you have a right to do something, then someone else has a correlative duty to act in a certain way. For example, if you claim a "right" to drive, you mean that you are entitled to drive or that others should—that is, have a duty to—permit you to drive. Your right to drive under certain conditions is derived from our legal system and is thus considered a *legal right*.

In addition to rights that are derived from some specific legal system, we also have *moral rights*. Some of these moral rights derive from special relationships, roles, or circumstances in which we happen to be. For example, if Tom has an obligation to return Bob's car to him on Saturday morning, then Bob has a right to have Tom return his car. If I have agreed to water your plants while you are on vacation, you have a right to expect me to look after them in your absence. As a student, you have a right to be graded fairly, and so on. In these cases the rights in question derive not from legal rules but from moral rules or from our moral obligations.

Even more important are rights that do not rest on special relationships, roles, or situations. For example, the rights to life, free speech, and unhampered religious affiliation are widely accepted, not just as the entitlements of some specific political or legal system but as fundamental moral rights. More controversial, but often championed as moral rights, are the "rights" to medical care, decent housing, education, and work. Moral rights that are not the result of particular roles, special relationships, or specific circumstances are called *human rights*. They have several important characteristics.

First, human rights are universal. Everyone has human rights, just by virtue of their being human, not because they live in a certain legal system and not because they have done something special. If the right to life is a human right, as most of us believe it is, then everyone, everywhere and at all times, has that right. By contrast, there is nothing universal about your right that I keep my promise to you or about my right to drive 65 miles per hour on certain roads.

Second, and closely related, human rights are equal rights. If the right to free speech is a human right, then everyone has this right equally. No one has a greater right to free speech than anyone else. By contrast, your daughter has a greater right than do the daughters of other people to your emotional and financial support.

Third, human rights are not transferable. If we have a fundamental human right, we cannot give, lend, or sell it to someone else. That is what is meant in the Declaration of Independence when certain rights—namely, life, liberty, and the pursuit of happiness— are described as "inalienable." By contrast, legal rights can be transferred, as when one party sells another a house or a business.

Fourth, human rights are "natural" rights, not in the sense that they can be derived from a study of human nature but in the sense that they do not depend on human institutions the way legal rights do. If people have human rights, they have them simply because they are human beings and not because some authoritative body has assigned them these rights. The law may attempt to protect human rights, to make them safe and explicit, but law is not their source. Human rights derive from the assumption that all human beings, merely by virtue of their being human, have certain entitlements.

Rights, and in particular human rights, can be divided into two broad categories: neg-

ative rights and positive rights. *Negative rights* are vital interests that human beings have in being free from outside interference. The rights guaranteed in the Bill of Rights—freedom of speech, assembly, religion, and so on—fall within this category, as do the rights to freedom from injury and to privacy. Correlating with these are duties that we all have not to interfere with others' pursuit of these interests and activities. *Positive rights* are vital interests that human beings have in receiving certain benefits. They are rights to have others provide us with certain goods, services, or opportunities. Today, positive rights often are taken to include the rights to education, medical care, a decent neighborhood, equal job opportunity, comparable pay, and so on. Correlating with these are positive duties for appropriate parties to assist individuals in their pursuit of these interests.

Thus a child's right to education implies not just that no one should interfere with the child's education but also that the necessary resources for that education ought to be provided. In the case of some positive rights—for example, the right to a decent standard of living, as proclaimed by the United Nations' 1948 Human Rights Charter—who exactly has the duty to fulfill those rights is unclear. Also, interpreting a right as negative or positive is sometimes controversial. For example, is my right to liberty simply the right not to be interfered with as I live my own life, or does it also imply a duty to provide me with the means to make the exercise of that liberty meaningful?

The significance of positing moral rights is that they provide grounds for making moral judgments that radically differ from utilitarianism's grounds. Once moral rights are asserted, the locus of moral judgment becomes the individual, not society. For example, if every potential human subject has a moral right to be fully informed about the nature of a medical experiment and the moral right to decide freely for himself or herself whether to participate, then it is wrong to violate these rights—even if, by so doing, the common good will be served. Again, if workers have a right to compensation equal to what others receive for doing comparable work, then they cannot be paid less on grounds of the greatest good for the greatest number. And if everyone has a right to equal consideration for a job regardless of color or sex, then sex and color cannot be introduced merely because so doing will result in greater net utility.

Utilitarianism, in effect, treats all such "entitlements" as subordinate to the general welfare. Thus, individuals are entitled to act in a certain way and entitled to have others allow or aid them to so act only insofar as the greatest good is effected. The assertion of moral rights, therefore, decisively sets nonconsequentialists apart from utilitarians.

Nonconsequentialism in an Organizational Context

You have already looked at Kant's ethics in an organizational context, but the themes of the other nonconsequentialist approaches also have important implications for moral decision making in business and nonbusiness organizations.

First, in its non-Kantian forms nonconsequentialism stresses that moral decision making involves the weighing of different moral factors and considerations. Unlike utilitarianism, nonconsequentialism does not reduce morality solely to the calculation of consequences, but it recognizes that an organization must usually take into account other equally important moral concerns. Theorists like Ross emphasize that, contrary to Kant, there can often be rival and even conflicting obligations on an organization. For example, obligations to employees, stockholders, and consumers may pull the corporation in different directions, and determining the organization's proper moral course may not be easy.

Second, nonconsequentialism acknowledges that the organization has its own legitimate goals to pursue. There are limits to the demands of morality, and an organization

that fulfills its moral obligations and respects the relevant rights of individuals is morally free to advance whatever (morally permissible) ends it has — public service, profit, government administration, and so on. Contrary to utilitarianism, organizations and the people in them need not see themselves as under an overarching obligation to seek continually to enhance the general welfare.

Third, nonconsequentialism stresses the importance of moral rights. Moral rights, and in particular human rights, are a crucial factor in most moral deliberations, including those of organizations. Before it acts, any morally responsible business or nonbusiness organization must consider carefully how its actions will impinge on the rights of individuals — not just the rights of its members, such as stockholders and employees, but also the rights of others, such as consumers. Moral rights place distinct and firm constraints on what sorts of things an organization can do to fulfill its own ends.

Critical Inquiries

1. *How well justified are these nonconsequentialist principles and moral rights?* Ross maintained that we have immediate intuitive knowledge of the basic *prima facie* moral principles, and indeed it would seem absurd to try to deny that it is wrong to cause needless suffering or that making a promise imposes some obligation to keep it. Only someone the moral equivalent of colorblind could fail to see the truth of these statements; to reject them would seem as preposterous as denying some obvious fact of arithmetic — for example, that 12 + 4 = 16. Likewise, it appears obvious — indeed, as Thomas Jefferson wrote, "self-evident" — that human beings have certain basic and inalienable rights, unconditional rights that do not depend on the decrees of any particular government.

Yet we must be careful. What seems obvious, even self-evident, to one culture or at one time in human history may turn out to be not only not self-evident but actually false. That the earth is flat and that heavier objects fall faster than lighter ones were two "truths" taken as obvious in former centuries. Likewise, the inferiority of women and of various nonwhite races was long taken for granted; this supposed fact was so "obvious" that it was hardly even commented on. The idea that people have a right to practice a religion that the majority "knows" to be false — or, indeed, to practice no religion whatsoever — would have seemed morally scandalous to many of our forebears and is still not embraced in all countries today. Today, many vegetarians eschew meat eating on moral grounds and contend that future generations will think our treatment of animals, factory farming in particular, is as morally benighted as slavery. So what seems "obvious," "self-evident," or simple "common sense" may not be the most reliable guide to morally sound principles.

2. *Can nonconsequentialists satisfactorily handle conflicting rights and principles?* People today disagree among themselves about the correctness of certain moral principles. Claims of right, as we have seen, are often controversial. For example, do employees have a moral right to their jobs — an entitlement to be fired only with just cause? To some of us, it may seem obvious that they do; to others perhaps not. And how are we to settle various conflicting claims of right? Jones, for instance, claims a right to her property, which she has acquired honestly through her labors; that is, she claims a right to do with it as she wishes. Smith is ill and claims adequate medical care as a human right. Since he cannot afford the care himself, acknowledging his right will probably involve taxing people like Jones and thus limiting their property rights.

To sum up these two critical points: First, even the deliverances of moral common sense have to be examined critically; and second, nonconsequentialists should not rest content until they find a way of resolving disputes among conflicting *prima facie* principles or

rights. This is not to suggest that nonconsequentialists cannot find deeper and theoretically more satisfactory ways of grounding moral claims and of handling disputes between them. The point to be underscored here is simply the necessity of doing so.

UTILITARIANISM ONCE MORE

Until now, the discussion of utilitarianism has focused on its most classic and straightforward form, called act utilitarianism. According to *act utilitarianism*, we have one and only one moral obligation, the maximization of happiness for everyone concerned, and every action is to be judged according to how well it lives up to this principle. But a different utilitarian approach, called rule utilitarianism, is relevant to the discussion of the moral concerns characteristic of nonconsequentialism — in particular, relevant to the nonconsequentialist's criticisms of act utilitarianism. The rule utilitarian would, in fact, agree with many of the criticisms. (Rule utilitarianism has been formulated in different ways, but this discussion follows the version defended by Professor Richard Brandt of the University of Michigan.)

Rule utilitarianism maintains that the utilitarian standard should be applied not to individual actions but to moral codes as a whole. The rule utilitarian asks what moral code (that is, what set of moral rules) a society should adopt in order to maximize happiness. The principles that make up that code would then be the basis for distinguishing right actions from wrong actions. As Brandt explains:

> A rule-utilitarian thinks that right actions are the kind permitted by the moral code optimal for the society of which the agent is a member. An optimal code is one designed to maximize welfare or what is good (thus, utility). This leaves open the possibility that a particular right action may not maximize benefit. . . . On the rule-utilitarian view, then,

to find what is morally right or wrong we need to find which actions would be permitted by a moral system that is "optimal" for the agent's society.[9]

The "optimal" moral code does not refer to the set of rules that would do the most good if everyone conformed to them all the time. The meaning is more complex. The optimal moral code must take into account what rules can reasonably be taught and obeyed, as well as the costs of inculcating those rules in people. Recall from Chapter 1 that if a principle or rule is part of a person's moral code, then it will influence the person's behavior. The person will tend to follow that principle, to feel guilty when he or she does not follow it, and to disapprove of others who fail to conform to it. Rule utilitarians must consider not just the benefits of having people motivated to act in certain ways but also the costs of instilling those motivations in them. As Brandt writes:

> The more intense and widespread an aversion to a certain sort of behavior, the less frequent the behavior is apt to be. But the more intense and widespread, the greater the cost of teaching the rule and keeping it alive, the greater the burden on the individual, and so on.[10]

Thus, the "optimality" of a moral code encompasses both the benefits of reduced objectionable behavior and the long-term costs. Perfect compliance is not a realistic goal. "Like the law," Brandt continues, "the optimal moral code will not produce 100 percent compliance with all its rules; that would be too costly."

Elements of the rule-utilitarian approach were clearly suggested by Mill himself, although he did not draw the distinction between act and rule utilitarianism. According to the rule-utilitarian perspective, we should apply the utilitarian standard only to the assessment of alternative moral codes; we should not try to apply it to individual actions. We should seek, that is, to determine the specific set of principles that would in fact best promote total happiness for society. Those are the rules we should promulgate, instill in ourselves, and teach to the next generation.

What Will the Ideal Code Look Like?

Rule utilitarians like Brandt argue strenuously that the ideal moral code would not be the single act-utilitarian command to maximize happiness. They contend that teaching people that their only obligation is to maximize happiness would not in fact maximize happiness.

First, people will make mistakes if they always try to promote total happiness. Second, if all of us were act utilitarians, such practices as keeping promises and telling the truth would be rather shaky, because we would expect others to keep promises or tell the truth only when they believed that doing so would maximize happiness. Third, the act-utilitarian principle is too demanding, since it seems to imply that each person should continually be striving to promote total well-being.

For these reasons, rule utilitarians believe that more happiness will come from instilling in people a pluralistic moral code, one with a number of different principles. By analogy, imagine a traffic system with just one rule: Drive your car in a way that maximizes happiness. Such a system would be counterproductive; we do much better in terms of total human well-being to have a variety of traffic regulations—for example, obey stop signs and pass only on the left. In such a pluralistic system we could not justify cruising through a red light with the argument that doing so maximizes total happiness by getting us home more quickly.

The principles of the ideal code would presumably be *prima facie* in Ross's sense—that is, capable of being overridden by other principles. Different principles would also have different moral weights. It would make sense, for example, to instill in people an aversion to killing that is stronger than the aversion to telling "white lies." In addition, the ideal code would acknowledge moral rights. Teaching people to respect moral rights maximizes human welfare in the long run.

The rules of the ideal code provide the sole basis for determining right and wrong. An action is not necessarily wrong if it fails to maximize happiness; it is wrong only if it conflicts with the ideal moral code. Rule utilitarianism thus gets around many of the problems that plague act utilitarianism. At the same time, it provides a plausible basis for deciding which moral principles and rights we should acknowledge and how much weight we should attach to them. We try to determine those principles and rights that, generally adhered to, would best promote human happiness.

Still, rule utilitarianism has its critics. There are two possible objections. First, act utilitarians maintain that a utilitarian who cares about happiness should be willing to violate rules in order to maximize happiness. Why make a fetish out of the rules?

Second, nonconsequentialists, while presumably viewing rule utilitarianism more favorably than act utilitarianism, still balk at seeing moral principles determined by their consequences. They contend, in particular, that rule utilitarians ultimately subordinate rights to utilitarian calculation and therefore fail to treat rights as fundamental and independent moral factors.

MORAL DECISION MAKING: TOWARD A SYNTHESIS

Theoretical controversies permeate the subject of ethics, and as you have seen, philosophers have proposed rival ways of understanding right and wrong. These philosophical differences of perspective, emphasis, and theory are significant and can have profound practical consequences. This chapter has surveyed some of these issues, but obviously it cannot resolve all of the questions that divide moral philosophers. Fortunately, however, many problems of business and organizational ethics can be intelligently discussed and even resolved by people whose fundamental moral theories differ (or who have not yet worked out their own moral ideas in some systematic way). This section discusses some important points to keep in mind when analyzing and discussing business ethics and offers, as a kind of model, one possible procedure for making moral decisions.

In the abstract, it might seem impossible for people to reach agreement on controversial ethical issues, given that ethical theories differ so much and that people themselves place moral value on different things. Yet in practice moral problems are rarely so intractable that open-minded and thoughtful people cannot, by discussing matters calmly, rationally, and thoroughly, make significant progress toward resolving them. Chapter 1 stressed that moral judgments should be logical, should be based on facts, and should appeal to valid moral principles. Bearing this in mind can often help, especially when various people are discussing an issue and proposing rival answers.

First, in any moral discussion, make sure participants agree about the relevant facts. Often moral disputes hinge not on matters of moral principle but on differing assessments of what the facts of the situation are, what alternatives are open, and what the probable results of different courses of action will be. For instance, the directors of an international firm might acrimoniously dispute the moral permissibility of a new overseas investment. The conflict might appear to involve some fundamental clash of moral principles and perspectives and yet, in fact, be the result of some underlying disagreement as to what effects the proposed investment will have on the lives of the local population. Until this factual disagreement is acknowledged and dealt with, little is apt to be resolved.

Second, once there is general agreement on factual matters, try to spell out the moral principles to which different people are, at least implicitly, appealing. Seeking to determine these principles will often help people clarify their own thinking enough to reach a solution. Sometimes they will agree on what moral principles are relevant and yet disagree over how to balance them. But identifying this discrepancy can itself be useful. Bear in mind, too, that skepticism is in order when someone's moral stance on an issue appears to rest simply on a hunch or intuition and cannot be related to some more general moral principle. As moral decision makers, we are seeking not just an "answer" to a moral issue but an answer that can be publicly defended. And the public defense of a moral judgment usually requires an appeal to general principle. By analogy, judges do not hand down judgments simply based on what strikes them as fair in a particular case. They must relate their decisions to general legal principles or statutes.

A reluctance to defend our moral decisions in public is almost always a warning sign. If we are unwilling to account for our actions publicly, chances are that we are doing something we cannot really justify morally. In addition, Kant's point that we must be willing to universalize our moral judgments is relevant here. We cannot sincerely endorse a principle if we are not willing to see it applied generally. Unfortunately, we occasionally do make judgments — for example, that Alfred's being late to work is a satisfactory reason for firing him — that rest on a principle we would be unwilling to apply to our own situations. Hence, the moral relevance of the familiar question: "How would you like it if . . . ?" Looking at an issue from the other person's point of view can cure moral myopia.

Obligations, Ideals, Effects

As a practical basis for discussing moral issues in organizations, it is useful to try to approach those issues in a way that is acceptable to individuals of diverse moral viewpoints. We want to avoid as much as possible presupposing the truth of one particular theoretical perspective. By emphasizing factors that are relevant to various theories, both consequentialist and nonconsequentialist, we can find some common ground on which moral decision making can proceed. Moral dialogue can thus take place in an objective and analytical way, even if the participants do not fully agree on all philosophical issues.

What concerns, then, seem common to most ethical systems? Following Professor V. R. Ruggiero, three common concerns suggest themselves.[11] A first concern is with *obligations*. Every significant human action — personal and professional — arises in the context of human relationships. These relationships can be the source of rather specific duties and rights. Obligations bind us. In their presence, morality requires us, at least *prima facie*, to do certain things and to avoid doing others.

A second concern common to most ethical systems is the impact of our actions on important *ideals*. An ideal is some morally important goal, virtue, or notion of excellence worth striving for. Clearly, different cultures impart different ideals and, equally important, different ways of pursuing them. Our culture respects virtues like tolerance, compassion, and loyalty, as well as more abstract ideals like peace, justice, fairness, and respect for persons. In addition to these moral ideals, there are institutional or organizational ones: efficiency, productivity, quality, stability, and so forth. Does a particular act serve or violate these ideals? Both consequentialists and nonconsequentialists can agree that this is an important concern in determining the moral quality of actions.

A third common consideration regards the *effects* of actions. Although nonconsequentialists maintain that things other than consequences or effects determine the rightness or wrongness of actions, few if any of them would ignore consequences entirely. Concern with consequences generally finds a place in ethical theories and certainly in business.

Ruggiero isolated, then, three concerns common to almost all ethical systems: obligations, ideals, and effects. In so doing he provided a kind of practical synthesis of consequentialist and nonconsequentialist thought, which seems appropriate for our concerns. A useful approach to moral questions in an organizational context will therefore reflect these considerations: the obligations that derive from organizational relationships, the ideals involved, and the effects or consequences of alternative actions. Any action that honors obligations while advancing ideals and benefiting people can be presumed to be moral. An action that does not pass scrutiny in these respects will be morally suspect.

This view leads to what is essentially a two-step procedure for evaluating actions and choices. The first step is to identify the important considerations involved: obligations, ideals, and effects. Accordingly, we should ask if any basic obligations are involved. If so, what are they and who has them? What ideals does the action respect or promote? What ideals does it neglect or thwart? Who is affected by the action and how? How do these effects compare with those of the alternatives open to us? The second step is to decide which of the three considerations deserves emphasis. Sometimes the issue may be largely a matter of obligations; other times, some ideal may predominate; still other times, consideration of effects may be the overriding concern.

Keep the following rough guidelines in mind when handling cases of conflicting obligations, ideals, and effects:

1. When two or more moral obligations conflict, choose the stronger one.

2. When two or more ideals conflict, or when ideals conflict with obligations, honor the more important one.

3. When rival actions will have different results, choose the action that produces the greater good or the lesser harm.

These guidelines suggest that we know (1) which one of the conflicting obligations is greater, (2) which of the conflicting ideals is higher, and (3) which of the actions will achieve the greater good or the lesser harm. They also presuppose that we have some definite way of balancing obligations, ideals, and effects when these considerations pull in different directions.

The fact is that we have no sure procedure for making such comparative determinations, which involve assessing worth and assigning relative priorities to our assessments. In large part, the chapters that follow attempt to sort out the values and principles embedded in the tangled web of frequently subtle, ill-defined problems we meet in business and organizational life. It is hoped that examining these issues will help you (1) identify the obligations, ideals, and effects involved in specific moral issues and (2) decide where the emphasis should lie among the competing considerations.

SUMMARY

1. Consequentialist moral theories see the moral rightness or wrongness of actions as a function of their results. If the consequences are good, the action is right; if they are bad, the action is wrong. Nonconsequentialist theories see other factors as also relevant to the determination of right and wrong.

2. Egoism is the consequentialist theory that an action is right when it promotes the individual's best interests. Proponents of this theory base their view on the alleged fact that human beings are, by nature, selfish (the doctrine of psychological egoism). Critics of egoism argue that (1) psychological egoism is implausible, (2) ego-

ism is not really a moral principle, and (3) egoism ignores blatant wrongs.

3. Utilitarianism, another consequentialist theory, maintains that the morally right action is the one that provides the greatest happiness for all those affected. In an organizational context, utilitarianism provides an objective way to resolve conflicts of self-interest and encourages a realistic and result-oriented approach to moral decision making. But critics contend that (1) utilitarianism is not really workable, (2) some actions are wrong even if they produce good results, and (3) utilitarianism incorrectly overlooks considerations of justice and the distribution of happiness.

4. Kant's theory is an important example of a purely nonconsequentialist approach to ethics. Kant held that only when we act from duty does our action have moral worth. Good will is the only thing that is good in itself.

5. Kant's categorical imperative states that an action is morally right if and only if we can will that the maxim (or principle) represented by the action be a universal law. For example, a person making a promise with no intention of keeping it cannot universalize the maxim governing his action, because if everyone followed this principle, promising would make no sense. Kant's categorical imperative is binding on all rational creatures, regardless of their specific goals or desires and regardless of the consequences.

6. There are two alternative formulations of the categorical imperative. The first is that an act is right only if the actor would be willing to be so treated if the positions of the parties were reversed. The second is that one must always act so as to treat other people as ends, never merely as means.

7. Kant's ethics gives us firm standards that do not depend on results; it injects a hu-

manistic element and stresses the importance of acting on principle and from a sense of duty. Critics, however, worry that (1) Kant's view of moral worth is too restrictive, (2) the categorical imperative is not a sufficient test of right and wrong, and (3) the distinction between treating people as means and respecting them as ends in themselves may be hard to identify in practice.

8. Other nonconsequentialist theories stress other moral themes. Philosophers like Ross argue, against both Kant and consequentialists, that we are under a variety of distinct moral obligations. These are *prima facie*, meaning that any one of them may be outweighed in some circumstances by other, more important moral considerations. Nonconsequentialists believe that a duty to assist others and to promote total happiness is only one of a number of duties incumbent on us.

9. Nonconsequentialists typically emphasize moral rights—entitlements to act in a certain way or to have others act in a certain way. These rights can rest on special relationships and roles, or they can be general human rights. Rights can be negative, protecting us from outside interference, or they can be positive, requiring others to provide us with certain benefits or opportunities.

10. In an organizational context, nonconsequentialism (in its non-Kantian forms) stresses the plurality of moral considerations to be weighed. While emphasizing the importance of respecting moral rights, it acknowledges that morality has limits and that organizations have legitimate goals to pursue. Critics question whether (1) nonconsequentialist principles are adequately justified and (2) nonconsequentialism can satisfactorily handle conflicting rights and principles.

11. Rule utilitarianism is a hybrid theory. It maintains that the proper principles of right and wrong are those that would maximize happiness if society adopted them. Thus, the utilitarian standard does not apply directly to individual actions but rather to the adoption of the moral principles that guide individual action. Rule utilitarianism avoids many of the standard criticisms of act utilitarianism.

12. Despite disagreements on controversial theoretical issues, people can make significant progress in resolving practical moral problems through open-minded and reflective discussion. One useful approach is to identify the (possibly conflicting) obligations, ideals, and effects in a given situation and then to identify where the emphasis should lie among these different considerations.

CASE 2.1
Baby M

In 1985 Mary Beth Whitehead of Brick Town, New Jersey, agreed to be impregnated by artificial insemination with the sperm of a stranger and to carry his child. In other words, she agreed, like hundreds of other women in the past decade, to be a "surrogate mother." She was twenty-nine years old, happily married, with a son and a daughter of her own. Why did she decide to do it? Mary Beth called it "the most loving gift of happiness," but she also saw the practical side. The $10,000 she would earn would help to pay for her children's education.[12]

The man who was to become the sperm-donating father of Mary Beth's child was William Stern, a forty-year-old biochemist. Both he and his wife, Elizabeth, a pediatrician, longed to have children of their own. But Elizabeth was diagnosed as having a mild form of multiple sclerosis, and pregnancy was felt to be risky for her. Not only is there a shortage of healthy, white babies available for adoption, but also the couple was too old to be acceptable to most adoption agencies. In any case, Stern wanted a child that was his own flesh and blood. Noel Keane, a Dearborn, Michigan, lawyer who specializes in surrogacy cases, brought the Sterns together with Whitehead and her husband. They signed a contract, which Keane had drawn up.

The six-page contract was strictly business. In addition to Whitehead's fee, which was put in escrow until Stern received the baby, the Sterns paid over $10,000 in nonrefundable fees and expenses to Keane. In the contract Stern agreed to assume all legal responsibility for the baby, even if it was born with serious defects. On the other hand, Whitehead was required to undergo amniocentesis; if the test indicated problems, she agreed to have an abortion if Stern requested it. In the contract Mary Beth Whitehead acknowledged that the child would be conceived "for the sole purpose of giving said child to William Stern."

Noel Keane's law firm and the Infertility Center of New York (which he partly owns) have arranged more than 150 commercial surrogate births since 1976. Whitehead later claimed that Keane did not give her proper counseling, while he maintains that the standard psychological tests she took gave little reason to anticipate any special problems. In only two cases handled by Keane had the surrogate mothers changed their minds. This was to be the third time.

On March 27, 1986, Mary Beth Whitehead gave birth to a healthy, blond, blue-eyed little girl—called Sara by her, Melissa by the Sterns, and "Baby M" by the courts. Mary

Beth's first moments with the baby were intensely emotional. "Seeing her, holding her. She was my child," Whitehead remembers. "It overpowered me. I had no control. I had to keep her."

Whitehead gave the child to the Sterns as agreed, but her first night without the baby was miserable. The next day she begged the Sterns to let her have the child for just one week. They agreed, but at the end of the week, Whitehead didn't want to return the child. She asked if the Sterns would agree to let her have the child one weekend a month and two weeks during the summer. They insisted on the original contract and went to court to enforce it. The money due Whitehead was still in the escrow account. On May 5, a family court judge awarded the Sterns temporary custody. But the next day the Whiteheads ran off with the baby. The Sterns paid more than $20,000 for a private investigator, who spent three months tracing the Whiteheads to the home of Mary Beth's mother in Florida. He and the FBI visited the home, grabbed the baby, and took her away, returning her to the Sterns.

Four days after Baby M's first birthday, New Jersey Judge Harvey Sorkow called Mary Beth Whitehead a "woman without empathy," and most of the world agreed that she was an unfit mother when it learned of a tape recording that Bill Stern had secretly made of a desperate phone call from her when she was on the run. "I'd rather see me and her dead before you can get her," Mary Beth had said. "I gave her life and I can take her life away." Ruling that the Sterns were better able, emotionally and financially, to be Baby M's parents, Judge Sorkow awarded the child to them and performed an adoption ceremony in his chambers that made Elizabeth Stern the legal mother of Melissa.

A three-judge panel upheld Sorkow's decision, but Whitehead promised to continue the legal battle, claiming that she didn't mean what she had said on the phone. "It was such a stressful time. It was like they were crucifying me. I felt like Jesus Christ, I really did. I would never have hurt Melissa." Months went by. Finally, on February 3, 1988, the New Jersey State Supreme Court ruled that the surrogacy agreement was "illegal, perhaps criminal, and potentially degrading to women." William Stern retained custody, but Whitehead won maternal visitation rights, and adoption by Mrs. Stern (who has no parental rights) was voided.

The court's decision, however, is binding only in New Jersey. Immediately after the Baby M case, measures addressing surrogacy were introduced in every state legislature, but few were adopted. Michigan and Florida now forbid paid surrogacy arrangements, while five other states have deemed surrogacy contracts legally unenforceable. Meanwhile, technology has given a new twist to the continuing moral and legal controversy.

In California in October 1990, Superior Court Judge Richard Parslow denied parental rights to a surrogate mother named Anna L. Johnson. In this case, Johnson had no genetic connection to the baby boy she carried in her womb and gave birth to. He had been conceived by *in vitro* (or laboratory) fertilization from the sperm and egg of Mark and Crispina Calvert and then implanted in Johnson's womb. Declining to follow California law, which defines the mother as the woman who gives birth to the child, Judge Parslow ruled, in effect, that genes make the mom: Anna Johnson's womb was little more than a home in which she had sheltered and fed the legal offspring of the genetic parents.

A few days later, newspapers reported that medical researchers had succeeded in making six prematurely menopausal women pregnant by implanting them with donated eggs fertilized *in vitro* with their husband's sperm. In these cases, though, it was the donor of the fertilized egg—the genetic mother—who relinquished her claim to motherhood, not the gestational mother.

Discussion Questions

1. Is the Baby M case a case of "baby selling," as critics charge, or are surrogate agencies correct to claim that they are simply selling a woman's services? Under either description, is there anything morally questionable about surrogate-mother agreements? How would such agreements be analyzed from the point of view of each of the major theories discussed in this chapter?

2. Discuss the motivations of the various parties to this dispute. To what moral principle(s) could Mary Beth Whitehead appeal to justify her subsequent actions? How could the Sterns defend their response?

3. Lawyers like Noel Keane are in the business of arranging surrogate births. How should their role be morally evaluated?

4. Who should keep Baby M? In your opinion, did the New Jersey State Supreme Court make the right decision? Identify and weigh the relevant moral principles.

5. Is genetic motherhood relevant to your assessment of the Baby M case? Was Mary Beth Whitehead's situation significantly different from Anna L. Johnson's? Should Johnson have been granted visitation rights by Judge Parslow?

6. Should surrogate motherhood be legal? If so, how (if at all) should the law regulate it? What legislative provisions would be best?

CASE 2.2
Ford's Pinto

There was a time when the "made in Japan" label brought a predictable smirk of superiority to the face of most Americans. The quality of most Japanese products usually was as low as their price. In fact, few imports could match their domestic counterparts, the proud products of "Yankee know-how." But by the late 1960s, an invasion of foreign-made goods chiseled a few worry lines into the countenance of American industry. And in Detroit, worry was fast fading to panic as the Japanese, not to mention the Germans, began to gobble up more and more of the subcompact auto market.

Never one to take a back seat to the competition, Ford Motor Company decided to meet the threat from abroad head-on. In 1968, Ford executives decided to produce the Pinto. Known inside the company as "Lee's car," after Ford president Lee Iacocca, the Pinto was

to weigh no more than 2,000 pounds and cost no more than $2,000.

Eager to have its subcompact ready for the 1971 model year, Ford decided to compress the normal drafting-board-to-showroom time of about three-and-a-half years into two. The compressed schedule meant that any design changes typically made before production-line tooling would have to be made during it.

Before producing the Pinto, Ford crash-tested eleven of them, in part to learn if they met the National Highway Traffic Safety Administration (NHTSA) proposed safety standard that all autos be able to withstand a fixed-barrier impact of 20 miles per hour without fuel loss. Eight standard-design Pintos failed the tests. The three cars that passed the test all had some kind of gas-tank modification. One had a plastic baffle between the front of the tank and the differential housing; the second had a piece of steel between the tank and the rear bumper; and the third had a rubber-lined gas tank.

Ford officials faced a tough decision. Should they go ahead with the standard design, thereby meeting the production time table but possibly jeopardizing consumer safety? Or should they delay production of the Pinto by redesigning the gas tank to make it safer and thus concede another year of subcompact dominance to foreign companies?

To determine whether to proceed with the original design of the Pinto fuel tank, Ford decided to do a cost-benefit study, which is an analysis of the expected costs and the social benefits of doing something. Would the social benefits of a new tank design outweigh design costs, or would they not?

To find the answer, Ford had to assign specific values to the variables involved. For some factors in the equation, this posed no problem. The costs of design improvement, for example, could be estimated at eleven dollars per vehicle. But what about human life? Could a dollar-and-cents figure be assigned to a human being?

NHTSA thought it could. It had estimated that society loses $200,725 every time a person is killed in an auto accident. It broke down the costs as follows:

Future productivity losses	
Direct	$132,000
Indirect	41,300
Medical costs	
Hospital	700
Other	425
Property damage	1,500
Insurance administration	4,700
Legal and court expenses	3,000
Employer losses	1,000
Victim's pain and suffering	10,000
Funeral	900
Assets (lost consumption)	5,000
Miscellaneous accident costs	200
Total per fatality	$200,725[13]

Ford used NHTSA and other statistical studies in its cost-benefit analysis, which yielded the following estimates:

Benefits

Savings:	180 burn deaths, 180 serious burn injuries, 2,100 burned vehicles
Unit cost:	$200,000 per death, $67,000 per injury, $700 per vehicle
Total benefit:	(180 × $200,000) + (180 × $67,000) + (2,100 × $700) = $49.5 million

Costs

Sales:	11 million cars, 1.5 million light trucks
Unit cost:	$11 per car, $11 per truck
Total cost:	12.5 million × $11 = $137.5 million[14]

Since the costs of the safety improvement outweighed its benefits, Ford decided to push ahead with the original design.

Here is what happened after Ford made this decision:

Between 700 and 2,500 persons died in accidents involving Pinto fires between 1971 and 1978. According to sworn testimony of Ford engineer Harley Copp, 95 percent of them would have survived if Ford had located the fuel tank over the axle (as it had done on its Capri automobiles).

NHTSA's standard was adopted in 1977. The Pinto then acquired a rupture-proof fuel tank. The following year Ford was obliged to recall all 1971–1976 Pintos for fuel-tank modifications.

Between 1971 and 1978, approximately fifty lawsuits were brought against Ford in connection with rear-end accidents in the Pinto. In the Richard Grimshaw case, in addition to awarding over $3 million in compensatory damages to the victims of a Pinto crash, the jury awarded a landmark $125 million in punitive damages against Ford. The judge reduced punitive damages to $3.5 million.

On August 10, 1978, eighteen-year-old Judy Ulrich, her sixteen-year-old sister

Lynn, and their eighteen-year-old cousin Donna, in their 1973 Ford Pinto, were struck from the rear by a van near Elkhart, Indiana. The gas tank of the Pinto exploded on impact. In the fire that resulted, the three teenagers were burned to death. Ford was charged with criminal homicide. The judge presiding over the twenty-week trial advised jurors that Ford should be convicted if it had clearly disregarded the harm that might result from its actions and that disregard represented a substantial deviation from acceptable standards of conduct. On March 13, 1980, the jury found Ford not guilty of criminal homicide.

For its part, Ford has always denied that the Pinto is unsafe compared with other cars of its type and era. The company also points out that in every model year the Pinto met or surpassed the government's own standards. But what the company doesn't say is that successful lobbying by it and its industry associates was responsible for delaying for nine years the adoption of NHTSA's 20 miles per hour crash standard. And Ford critics claim that there were more than forty European and Japanese models in the Pinto price and weight range with safer gas-tank position. "Ford made an extremely irresponsible decision," concludes auto safety expert Byron Bloch, "when they placed such a weak tank in such a ridiculous location in such a soft rear end."

Discussion Questions

1. Suppose Ford officials were asked, "What makes your moral decision right?" What moral principles do you think they would invoke? Explain.

2. Utilitarians would say that jeopardizing motorists by itself does not make Ford's action morally objectionable. The only morally relevant matter is whether Ford gave each affected party equal consideration and gave their pleasures and preferences equal weight in reaching its decision. Do you think Ford did this?

3. Could Ford's cost-benefit analysis have been improved? How legitimate are such analyses in general? What role should they play in moral deliberation?

4. Speculate about Kant's response to the NHTSA's placing a financial value on a human life.

5. What responsibilities to its customers do you think Ford had? What would you say are the most important moral rights, if any, operating in this case?

6. Would it have made a moral difference if the eleven-dollar savings had been passed on to Ford's customers? Could a rational consumer have chosen to save eleven dollars and risk the more dangerous gas tank? What if Ford had told potential customers about its decision?

7. The maxim of Ford's action might be stated: "When it would cost more to make a safety improvement than not, it's all right not to make it." Can this maxim be universalized? Does it treat humans as ends in themselves? Would manufacturers likely be willing to abide by it were the positions reversed, if they were in the role of unsuspecting consumers?

8. Should Ford have been found guilty of criminal homicide in the Ulrich case?

CASE 2.3
Blood for Sale

Sol Levin was a successful stockbroker in Tampa, Florida, when he recognized the potentially profitable market for safe and uncontaminated blood and, with some colleagues, founded Plasma International. Not everybody is willing to make money by selling his or her own blood, and in the beginning Plasma International bought blood from people addicted to wine. Although innovative marketing increased Plasma International's sales dramatically, several cases of hepatitis were reported in recipients. The company then began looking for new sources of blood.[15]

Plasma International searched worldwide and, with the advice of a qualified team of medical consultants, did extensive testing. Eventually they found that the blood profiles of several rural West African tribes made them ideal prospective donors. After negotiations with the local government, Plasma International signed an agreement with several tribal chieftains to purchase blood.

Business went smoothly and profitably for Plasma International until a Tampa paper charged that Plasma was purchasing blood for as little as fifteen cents a pint and then reselling it to hospitals in the United States and South America for $25 per pint. In one recent disaster, the newspaper alleged, Plasma International had sold 10,000 pints, netting nearly a quarter of a million dollars.

The newspaper story stirred up controversy in Tampa, but the existence of commercialized blood marketing systems in the United States is nothing new. Approximately half the blood and plasma obtained in the United States is bought and sold like any other commodity. About 40 percent is given to avoid having to pay for blood received or to build up credit so blood will be available without charge if needed. By contrast, the National Health Service in Britain relies entirely on a voluntary system of blood donation. Blood is neither bought nor sold. It is available to anyone who needs it without charge or obligation, and donors gain no preference over nondonors.

In an important study, economist Richard Titmuss showed that the British system works better than the American one in terms of economic efficiency, administrative efficiency, price, and blood quality. The commercialized blood market, Titmuss argued, is wasteful of blood and plagued by shortages. Bureaucratization, paperwork, and administrative overhead result in a cost per unit of blood that is five to fifteen times higher than in Britain. Hemophiliacs, in particular, are disadvantaged by the American system and have enormous bills to pay. In addition, commercial markets are much more likely to distribute contaminated blood.

Titmuss also argued that the existence of a commercialized system discourages voluntary donors. People are less apt to give blood if they know that others are selling it. Philosopher Peter Singer has elaborated on this point:

> If blood is a commodity with a price, to give blood means merely to save someone money. Blood has a cash value of a certain number of dollars, and the importance of the gift will vary with the wealth of the recipient. If blood cannot be bought, however, the gift's value depends upon the need of the recipient. Often, it will be worth life itself. Under these circumstances blood becomes a very special kind of gift, and giving it means providing for strangers, without hope of reward, something they cannot buy and without which they may die. The gift relates strangers in a manner that is not possible when blood is a commodity.

This may sound like a philosopher's abstraction, far removed from the thoughts of ordinary people. On the contrary, it is an idea spontaneously expressed by British donors in response to Titmuss's questionnaire. As one woman, a machine operator, wrote in reply to the question why she first decided to become a blood donor: "You can't get blood from supermarkets and chain stores. People themselves must come forward; sick people can't get out of bed to ask you for a pint to save their life, so I came forward in hopes to help somebody who needs blood."

The implication of this answer, and others like it, is that even if the formal right to give blood can coexist with commercialized blood banks, the respondent's action would have lost much of its significance to her, and the blood would probably not have been given at all. When blood is a commodity, and can be purchased if it is not given, altruism becomes unnecessary, and so loosens the bonds that can otherwise exist between strangers in a community. The existence of a market in blood does not threaten the formal right to give blood, but it does away with the right to give blood which cannot be bought, has no cash value, and must be given freely if it is to be obtained at all. If there is such a right, it is incompatible with the right to sell blood, and we cannot avoid violating one of these rights when we grant the other.[16]

Both Titmuss and Singer believe that the weakening of the spirit of altruism in this sphere has important repercussions. It marks, they think, the increasing commercialization of our lives and makes similar changes in attitude, motive, and relationships more likely in other fields.

Discussion Questions

1. Is Sol Levin running a business "just like any other business," or is his company open to moral criticism? Defend your answer by appeal to moral principle.

2. What are the contrasting ideals of the British and American blood systems? Which system, in your opinion, best promotes human freedom and respect for persons?

3. Examine the pros and cons of commercial transactions in blood from the egoistic, the utilitarian, and the Kantian perspectives.

4. Are Titmuss and Singer right to suggest that the buying and selling of blood reduces altruism? Does knowing that you can sell your blood (and that others are selling theirs) make you less inclined to donate your blood? Do we have a right to give blood that cannot be bought?

5. Many believe that commercialization is increasing in all areas of modern life. If this is so, is it something to be applauded or condemned? Is it wrong to treat certain things—like human organs—as commodities?

6. Did Plasma International strike a fair bargain with the West Africans who supplied their blood to the company? Or is Plasma guilty of exploiting them in some way? Explain your answer.

7. Do you believe that we have a moral duty to donate blood? If so, why and under what circumstances? If not, why not?

NOTES

1. Bernard Williams, *Ethics and the Limits of Philosophy* (Cambridge, Mass.: Harvard University Press, 1985), 16.

2. Richard B. Brandt, "Toward a Credible Form of Utilitarianism," in Hector-Neri Castañeda and George Nakhnikian, eds., *Morality and the Language of Conduct* (Detroit: Wayne State University, 1963), 109–110.

3. A. C. Ewing, *Ethics* (New York: Free Press, 1965), 41.

4. Molly Moore, "Did the Experts Really Approve the 'Brown Lung' Experiment?" *The Washington Post National Weekly Edition*, June 4, 1984, 31.

5. Adam Smith, *The Wealth of Nations* (New York: Modern Library, 1985), 223–225.

6. Tom L. Beauchamp and Norman E. Bowie, eds., *Ethical Theory and Business*, 2nd ed. (Englewood Cliffs, N.J.: Prentice-Hall, 1988), 20.

7. Immanuel Kant, *Foundations of the Metaphysics of Morals*, 6th ed., trans. T. K. Abbott (London: Longman's Green, 1909), 15.

8. See, in particular, W. D. Ross, *The Right and the Good* (London: Oxford University Press, 1930).

9. Richard B. Brandt, "The Real and Alleged Problems of Utilitarianism," *The Hastings Center Report* (April 1983): 38.

10. Ibid., 42.

11. Vincent Ryan Ruggiero, *The Moral Imperative* (Port Washington, N.Y.: Alfred Publishers, 1973).

12. The facts of this case are based on articles in *Newsweek*, January 19 and April 13, 1987; *The Economist*, March 21, 1987; *The Los Angeles Times*, March 6, 1989; *The New York Times*, November 4, 1990; and *The Nation*, December 31, 1990.

13. Ralph Drayton, "One Manufacturer's Approach to Automobile Safety Standards," *CTLA News* 8 (February 1968): 11.

14. Mark Dowie, "Pinto Madness," *Mother Jones*, September–October 1977, 20. See also Russell Mokhiber, *Corporate Crime and Violence* (San Francisco: Sierra Club Books, 1988), 373–382, and Francis T. Cullen, William J. Maakestad, and Gray Cavender, *Corporate Crime Under Attack: The Ford Pinto Case and Beyond* (Cincinnati: Anderson Publishing, 1987).

15. This and the following three paragraphs are based on a case prepared by T. W. Zimmerer and P. L. Preston in R. D. Hay, E. R. Gray, and J. E. Gates, eds., *Business and Society* (Cincinnati: South-Western, 1976). The remainder of the case draws on Peter Singer, "Rights and the Market," in J. Arthur and W. H. Shaw, eds., *Justice and Economic Distribution*, 2nd ed. (Englewood Cliffs, N.J.: Prentice-Hall, 1991), and Richard M. Titmuss, *The Gift Relationship* (London: George Allen & Unwin, 1972).

16. Singer, "Rights and the Market." Reprinted by permission of the author.

What Would a Satisfactory Moral Theory Be Like?

James Rachels

After studying various moral theories, one is bound to be left wondering what to believe. In this selection from The Elements of Moral Theory, *James Rachels sketches what he thinks would be a satisfactory ethical theory. Although his theory has much in common with utilitarianism, it takes seriously people's right to choose and the moral importance of treating people as they deserve to be treated. In this way Rachels follows Kant's emphasis on respect for persons.*

> Some people believe that there cannot be progress in Ethics, since everything has already been said. . . . I believe the opposite. . . . Compared with the other sciences, Non-Religious Ethics is the youngest and least advanced.
>
> Derek Parfit, *Reasons and Persons* (1984)

Morality Without Hubris

Moral philosophy has a rich and fascinating history. A great many thinkers have approached the subject from a wide variety of perspectives and have produced theories that both attract and repel the thoughtful reader. Almost all the classical theories contain plausible elements, which is hardly surprising, considering that they were devised by philosophers of undoubted genius. Yet the various theories are not consistent with one another, and most are vulnerable to crippling objections. After reviewing them, one is left wondering what to believe. What, in the final analysis, is the truth? Of course, different philosophers would answer this question in different ways. Some might refuse to answer at all, on the grounds that we do not yet know enough to have reached the "final analysis." (In this, moral philosophy is not much worse off than any other subject of human inquiry—we do not know the final truth about almost anything.) But we do know a lot, and it may not be unduly rash to venture a guess as to what a satisfactory moral theory might be like.

A satisfactory theory would, first of all, be sensitive to the facts about human nature, and it would be appropriately modest about the place of human beings in the scheme of things. The universe is some 18 billion years old — that is the time elapsed since the "big bang" — and the earth itself was formed about 4.6 billion years ago. The evolution of life on the planet was a slow process, guided not by design but (largely) by random mutation and natural selection. The first humans appeared quite recently. The extinction of the great dinosaurs 65 million years ago (possibly as the result of a catastrophic collision between the earth and an asteroid) left ecological room for the evolution of the few little mammals that were about, and after 63 or 64 million *more* years, one line of that evolution finally produced us. In geological time, we arrived only yesterday.

But no sooner did our ancestors arrive than they began to think of themselves as the most important things in all creation. Some of them even imagined that the whole universe had been made for their benefit. Thus, when they began to develop theories of right and wrong, they had held that the protection of their own interests had a kind of ultimate and objective value. The rest of creation, they reasoned, was intended for their use. We now know better. We now know that we exist by evolutionary accident, as one species among many, on a small and insignificant world in one little corner of the cosmos.

Hume, who knew only a little of this story, nevertheless realized that human *hubris* is largely unjustified. "The life of a man," he wrote, "is of no greater importance to the universe than that of an oyster." But he also recognized that our lives are important to *us*. We are creatures with desires, needs, plans, and hopes; and even if "the universe" does not care about those things, we do. Our theory of morality may begin from this point. In order to have a convenient name for it, let us call this theory *Morality Without Hubris* — or *MWH* for short. MWH incorporates some elements of the various classical theories while rejecting others.

Human *hubris* is largely unjustified, but it is not *entirely* unjustified. Compared to the other creatures on earth, we do have impressive intellectual capacities. We have evolved as rational beings.

This fact gives some point to our inflated opinion of ourselves; and, as it turns out, it is also what makes us capable of having a morality. Because we are rational, we are able to take some facts as *reasons* for behaving one way rather than another. We can articulate those reasons and think about them. Thus we take the fact that an action would help satisfy our desires, needs, and so on — in short, the fact that an action would *promote our interests* — as a reason in favor of doing that action. And of course we take the fact that an action would frustrate our interests as a reason against doing it.

The origin of our concept of "ought" may be found in these facts. If we were not capable of considering reasons for and against actions, we would have no use for such a notion. Like the lower animals, we would simply act from impulse or habit, or as Kant put it, from "inclination." But the consideration of reasons introduces a new factor. Now we find ourselves impelled to act in certain ways as a result of deliberation, as a result of thinking about our behavior and its consequences. We use the word "ought" to mark this new element of the situation: we *ought* to do the act supported by the weightiest reasons.

Once we consider morality as a matter of acting on reason, another important point emerges. In reasoning about what to do, we can be consistent or inconsistent. One way of being inconsistent is to accept a fact as a reason for action on one occasion, while refusing to accept a similar fact as a reason on another occasion, even though there is no difference between the two occasions that would justify distinguishing them. (This is the legitimate point made by Kant's Categorical Imperative. . . .) This happens, for example, when a person unjustifiably places the interests of his own race or social group above the comparable interests of other races and social groups. Racism means counting the interests of the members of the other races as less important than the interests of the members of one's own race, despite the fact that there is no general difference between the races that would justify it. It is an offense against morality because it is first an offense against reason. Similar remarks could be made about other doctrines that divide humanity into the morally favored and disfavored, such as egoism, sexism, and (some forms of) nationalism. The upshot is that reason requires impartiality: we ought to act so as to promote the interests of everyone alike.

If Psychological Egoism were true, this would mean that reason demands more of us than we can manage. But Psychological Egoism is not true; it gives an altogether false picture of human nature and the human condition. We have evolved as social creatures, living together in groups, wanting one another's company, needing one another's cooperation, and capable of caring about one another's welfare. So there is a pleasing theoretical "fit" between (a) what reason requires, namely impartiality; (b) the requirements of social living, namely adherence to a set of rules that, if fairly applied, would serve everyone's interests; and (c) our natural inclination to care about others, at least to a modest degree. All three work together to make morality not only possible, but in an important sense natural, for us.

So far, MWH sounds very much like Utilitarianism. However, there is one other fact about human beings that must be taken into account, and doing so will give the theory a decidedly nonutilitarian twist. As rational agents, humans have the power of choice: they may choose to do what they see to be right, or they may choose to do wrong. Thus they are *responsible* for their freely chosen actions, and they are judged morally good if they choose well or wicked if they choose badly. This, I think, has two consequences. First, it helps to explain why freedom is among the most cherished human values. A person who is denied the right to choose his or her own actions is thereby denied the possibility of achieving any kind of personal moral worth. Second, the way a person may be treated by others depends, to some extent, on the way he or she has chosen to treat them. One who treats others well deserves to be treated well in return, while one who treats others badly deserves to be treated badly in return.

This last point is liable to sound a little strange, so let me elaborate it just a bit. Suppose Smith has always been generous to others, helping them whenever he could; now he is in trouble and needs help in return. There is now a *special* reason *he* should be helped, above the general obligation we have to promote the interests of everyone alike. He is not just another member of the crowd. He is a particular person who, by his own previous conduct, has *earned* our respect and gratitude. But now consider someone with the opposite history: suppose Jones is your neighbor, and he has always *refused* to help you when you needed it. One day

your car wouldn't start, for example, and Jones wouldn't give you a lift to work — he had no particular excuse, he just wouldn't be bothered. Imagine that, after this episode, Jones has car trouble and he has the nerve to ask you for a ride. Perhaps you think you should help him anyway, despite his own lack of helpfulness. (You might think that this will teach him generosity.) Nevertheless, if we concentrate on what he *deserves*, we must conclude that he deserves to be left to fend for himself.

Adjusting our treatment of individuals to match how they themselves have chosen to treat others is not just a matter of rewarding friends and holding grudges against enemies. It is a matter of treating people as *responsible agents*, who by their own choices show themselves to be deserving of particular responses, and toward whom such emotions as gratitude and resentment are appropriate. There is an important difference between Smith and Jones; why shouldn't that be reflected in the way we respond to them? What would it be like if we did *not* tailor our responses to people in this way? For one thing, we would be denying people (including ourselves) the ability to earn good treatment at the hands of others. Morally speaking, we would all become simply members of the great crowd of humanity, rather than individuals with particular personalities and deserts. Respecting people's right to choose their own conduct, and then adjusting our treatment of them according to how they choose, is ultimately a matter of "respect for persons" in a sense somewhat like Kant's.

We are now in a position to summarize the outline of what, in my judgment, a satisfactory moral theory would be like. Such a theory would see morality as based on facts about our nature and interests, rather than on some exaggerated conception of our "importance." As for the principles on which we ought to act, the theory is a combination of two ideas: first, that *we ought to act so as to promote the interests of everyone alike*; and second, that *we should treat people as they deserve to be treated, considering how they have themselves chosen to behave*.

But now the key question is: How are these two ideas related? How do they fit together to form a unified principle of conduct? They are not to be understood as entirely independent of one another. The first establishes a general presumption in favor of promoting everyone's interests, impartially; and the second specifies grounds on which this presumption may be overridden. Thus the second thought functions as a qualification to the first; it specifies that we may sometimes *depart from a policy of "equal treatment"* on the grounds that a person has shown by his past behavior that he deserves some particular response. We may therefore combine them into a single principle. The primary rule of morality, according to MWH, is:

> We ought to act so as to promote impartially the interests of everyone alike, except when individuals deserve particular responses as a result of their own past behavior.

This principle combines the best elements of both Utilitarianism and Kantian "respect for persons," but it is not produced simply by stitching those two philosophies together. Rather, it springs naturally from a consideration of the main facts of the human condition—that we are perishable beings with interests that may be promoted or frustrated, and that we are rational beings responsible for our conduct. Although more needs to be said about the theoretical basis of this view, I will say no more about it here. Instead I will turn to some of its practical implications. Like every moral theory, MWH implies that we should behave in certain ways; and in some cases, it implies that commonly accepted patterns of behavior are wrong and should be changed. The plausibility of the theory will depend in part on how successful it is in convincing us that our behavior should conform to its directives.

The Moral Community

When we are deciding what to do, whose interests should we take into account? People have answered this question in different ways at different times: egoists have said that one's own interests are all-important; racists have restricted moral concern to their own race; and nationalists have held that moral concern stops at the borders of one's country. The answer given by MWH is that *we ought to give equal consideration to the interests of everyone who will be affected by our conduct.* In principle, the community with which we should be concerned is limited only by the number of individuals who have interests, and that, as we shall see, is a very large number indeed.

This may seem a pious platitude, but in reality it can be a hard doctrine. As this is being written, for example, there is famine in Ethiopia and millions of people are starving. People in the affluent countries have not responded very well. There has

been some aid given, but relatively few people have felt personally obligated to help by sending contributions to famine-relief agencies. People would no doubt feel a greater sense of obligation if it were their neighbors starving, rather than strangers in a foreign country. But on the theory we are considering, the location of the starving people makes no difference; *everyone* is included in the community of moral concern. This has radical consequences: for example, when a person is faced with the choice between spending ten dollars on a trip to the movies or contributing it for famine relief, he should ask himself which action would most effectively promote human welfare, with each person's interests counted as equally important. Would he benefit more from seeing the movie than a starving person would from getting food? Clearly, he would not. So he should contribute the money for famine relief. If this sort of reasoning were taken seriously, it would make an enormous difference in our responses to such emergencies.

If the moral community is not limited to people in one place, neither is it limited to people at any one *time.* Whether people will be affected by our actions now or in the distant future makes no difference. Our obligation is to consider all their interests equally. This is an important point because, with the development of nuclear weapons, we now have the capacity to alter the course of history in an especially dramatic way. Some argue that a full-scale nuclear exchange between the superpowers would result in the extinction of the human race. The prediction of "nuclear winter" supports this conclusion. The idea is that the detonation of so many nuclear devices would send millions of tons of dust and ash into the stratosphere, where it would block the sun's rays. The surface of the earth would become cold. This condition would persist for years, and the ecology would collapse. Those who were "lucky" enough to escape death earlier would nevertheless perish in the nuclear winter. Other theorists contend that this estimate is too pessimistic. Civilization might come to an end, they say, and most people might die, but a few will survive, and the long upward struggle will begin again.

Considering this, it is difficult to imagine *any* circumstances in which the large-scale use of nuclear weapons would be morally justified. Some political analysts seem to think that *our* interests are served by policies that run the risk of nuclear war.

Let us suppose this is so. To make the best possible case, let us grant that (a) the United States has vital interests that can be protected only by maintaining a nuclear arsenal as a balance against Soviet threats; (b) it is in the best interests of the rest of the world for the United States to pursue this course; and (c) the United States is "in the right" in its conflict with the Soviet Union. In other words, we will grant every point the defenders of our nuclear policy want to make. But then suppose a situation arises in which the Soviet Union, despite America's nuclear strength, acts against the very interests our arsenal is supposed to protect. Would we then be justified in using our strategic weapons? Suppose we did. In executing a policy designed to protect our interests, we would not only have destroyed ourselves; we would have violated the interests of all the people yet to come (assuming, of course, that there were at least some survivors who could try to rebuild civilization). In the larger historical context, our interests are of only passing importance, certainly not worth the price of condemning countless future generations to the miseries of a post–nuclear war age. History would not judge the Nazis to have been the pre-eminent villains of our time. That distinction would be reserved for us.

There is one other way in which our conception of the moral community must be expanded. Humans, as we have noted, are only one species of animal inhabiting this planet. Like humans, the other animals also have interests that are affected by what we do. When we kill or torture them, they are harmed, just as humans are harmed when treated in those ways. The utilitarians were right to insist that the interests of nonhuman animals must be given weight in our moral calculations. As Bentham pointed out, excluding creatures from moral consideration because of their species is no more justified than excluding them because of race, nationality, or sex. . . . Impartiality requires the expansion of the moral community — not only across space and time but across the boundaries of species as well.

Justice and Fairness

MWH has much in common with Utilitarianism, especially in what I called MWH's "first idea." But . . . Utilitarianism has been severely criticized for failing to account for the values of justice and fairness. Can MWH do any better in this re-

gard? It does, because it makes a person's past behavior relevant to how he or she should be treated. This introduces into the theory an acknowledgment of personal merit that is lacking in unqualified Utilitarianism.

One specific criticism of Utilitarianism [has] to do with its implications for the institution of punishment. We can imagine cases in which it promotes the general welfare to frame an innocent person, which is blatantly unjust; and taking the Principle of Utility as our ultimate standard, it is hard to explain why this is so. More generally, as Kant pointed out, the basic utilitarian "justification" of punishment is in terms of treating individuals as mere "means." MWH provides a different view of the matter. In punishing someone, we are treating him differently from the way we treat others — punishment involves a failure of impartiality. But this is justified, on our account, by the person's own past deeds. It is a response to what he has done. That is why it is not right to frame an innocent person; the innocent person has not done anything to deserve being singled out for such treatment. The account of punishment suggested by MWH is very close to Kant's.

The theory of punishment, however, is only one small part of the subject of justice. Questions of justice arise any time one person is treated differently from another. Suppose an employer must choose which of two employees to promote, when he can promote only one of them. The first candidate has worked hard for the company, taking on extra work when it was needed, giving up her vacation to help out, and so on. The second candidate, on the other hand, has always done only the minimum required of him. (And we will assume he has no excuse; he has simply *chosen* not to work very hard for the company.) Obviously, the two employees will be treated very differently: one will get the promotion; the other will not. But this is all right, according to our theory, because the first employee deserves to be advanced over the second, considering the past performance of each. The first employee has earned the promotion, the second has not.

This is an easy case, in that it is obvious what the employer should do. But it illustrates an important difference between our theory and Utilitarianism. Utilitarians might argue that their theory also yields the right decision in this case. They might observe that it promotes the general welfare for companies to reward hard work; therefore the Principle of Utility, unsupplemented by any further consideration, would also say that the first employee, but not the second, should be promoted. Perhaps this is so. Nevertheless, this is unsatisfactory because it has the first employee being promoted for the *wrong reason*. She has a claim on the promotion because of her own hard work, and not simply because promoting her would be better for us all. MWH accommodates this vital point, whereas Utilitarianism does not.

MWH holds that a person's voluntary actions can justify departures from the basic policy of "equal treatment," but *nothing else can*. This goes against a common view of the matter. Often, people think it is right for individuals to be rewarded for physical beauty, superior intelligence, or other native endowments. (In practice, people often get better jobs and a greater share of life's good things just because they were born with greater natural gifts.) But on reflection, this does not seem right. People do not deserve their native endowments; they have them as a result of what John Rawls has called "the natural lottery." Suppose the first employee in our example was passed over for the promotion, despite her hard work, because the second employee had some native talent that was more useful in the new position. Even if the employer could justify this decision in terms of the company's needs, the first employee would rightly feel that there is something unfair going on. She has worked harder, yet he is now getting the promotion, and the benefits that go with it, because of something he did nothing to merit. That is not fair. A just society, according to MWH, would be one in which people may improve their positions through work (with the opportunity for work available to everyone), but they would not enjoy superior positions simply because they were born lucky. . . .

As I said at the outset, MWH represents my best guess about what an ultimately satisfactory moral theory might be like. I say "guess" not to indicate any lack of confidence; in my opinion, MWH *is* a satisfactory moral theory. However, it is instructive to remember that a great many thinkers have tried to devise such a theory, and history has judged them to have been only partially successful. This suggests that it would be wise not to make too grandiose a claim for one's own view. Moreover, as the Oxford philosopher Derek Parfit has observed, the earth will remain habitable for another billion years, and civilization is now only a few thousand years old. If we do not destroy ourselves, moral philosophy, along with all the other human inquiries, may yet have a long way to go.

Review and Discussion Questions

1. Why does Rachels call his theory "morality without hubris"?

2. According to him, what important implications does the fact of human rationality have for ethics?

3. How and why does Rachels modify the utilitarian approach? Would you agree that Rachels successfully combines the best elements of utilitarianism and Kantianism?

4. According to Rachels, who is in "the moral community"? How would adopting his perspective cause people to change their moral attitudes and conduct?

Virtues and Business Ethics _____

Joseph R. DesJardins

Philosophers concerned with business ethics have generally followed the strategy of identifying and defending certain general principles of ethics and then applying them to specific situations in business. DesJardins is skeptical of this approach on both practical and theoretical grounds. Drawing on Aristotle and the contemporary philosopher Alasdair MacIntyre, DesJardins recommends an alternative approach to business ethics, one which focuses on moral virtue and being a good person rather than on formal ethical principles.

Reprinted by permission of the publisher from W. Michael Hoffman, Jennifer Mills Moore, and David A. Fredo, eds., *Corporate Governance and Institutionalizing Ethics.* Copyright © 1984 by D. C. Heath and Company.

Much of the work done by philosophers in business ethics has been structured by an overly narrow understanding of ethical theory. This understanding is characterized by an almost total reliance upon moral rules and principles and an almost total disregard of virtues and the ethics of character. As understood by many philosophers working in business ethics, the goal of ethical theory is to identify and defend some fundamental principle that can serve as the foundation for all morality. Such a principle will provide this foundation if it can, first, be defended as categorically binding on all rational agents and, second, be capable of moving such agents to specific acts that are required by the principle. Generally, this second goal is achieved if the principle can function as a major premise from which specific practical conclusions can be deduced.

Much of the first-order writing done by philosophers in business ethics has involved the second goal: applying general ethical principles to specific situations in business and from these principles deriving what one ought to do in that situation. Moral philosophers less interested in "applied ethics" have been content in pursuing the first goal. Thus, moral philosophy today is often divided into two areas: Those working in ethical theory are charged with justifying certain principles (for example, utility, the categorical imperative) as binding on all persons, while those working in applied ethics attempt to show how these principles commit one to accepting certain specific conclusions about whistle-blowing, employee rights, and so on. Thus applied ethics stands in the same relationship to ethical theory as engineering stands to physics. The theorist defends the general principle while the practitioner applies that principle to solve particular practical problems.

Given this principle-based understanding of ethical theory, the means for institutionalizing ethical responsibility within corporations is clear. The task is to get the corporation to accept some ethical principle as the guide for the activities of its members. A number of different strategies have been proposed to meet this goal. Milton Friedman, for example, suggests that corporations ought to adopt the principle of profit maximization as their guide. This principle, through the functioning of a free and competitive market, will lead the corporation to fulfill its social responsibility. Others have argued for a utilitarian principle broader than profit maximization, claiming that corporations ought to

be guided by a more general understanding of social goods and by the recognition of a responsibility to bring about such goods.

Still others argue for nonutilitarian principles. Tom Donaldson, for example, defends a version of social contract theory of corporate social responsibility.[1] In this view, a corporation institutionalizes its ethical responsibility by obeying the implicit contract that exists between it and society.

These and many other similar strategies share a belief that the road to ethical responsibility lies with the internalization of some independently justified principle. In what follows, I suggest that there are good reasons for thinking that any such approach will fail. I then go on to consider an alternative strategy for institutionalizing ethical behavior.

The Flaw in Principle-Based Ethics

What, then, is wrong with principle-based ethics? Why do I suppose that attempts to institutionalize ethical responsibility within corporations that rely upon principles will fail? There are both practical and theoretical reasons for this skepticism.

First, we should take seriously that fact that in practice, ethical principles seldom give any unambiguous practical advice. Adopting a principle-based approach in business ethics leads to numerous practical difficulties. A seemingly endless series of problems arises when one attempts to derive from such principles as the categorical imperative or the principle of utility, solutions to ethical problems faced by businesspeople. Hopeless ambiguity in application, apparent counterexamples, ad hoc rebuttals, counterintuitive conclusions, and apparently contradictory prescriptions create an overwhelming morass in the discussion of particular moral situations. The confusion is compounded even further when recommendations from competing principles are added to the discussion. Those of us who have tried to teach business ethics in this way can attest that ethics is not engineering: Unambiguously correct or even generally accepted answers occur very seldom. This radical inconclusiveness of ethical debates should at least suggest that something is wrong with our approaches to moral problems.

Beyond these practical problems, and partly explaining them, lie additional conceptual difficulties. By far the most significant is the fact that no ethical principle has yet been established in any plausible fashion as categorically binding upon all people. Philosophers have simply failed to justify the principles they apply in business ethics. Principle-based ethical theories are committed to the view that without the prior independent justification of the principle, attempts to institutionalize ethical responsibility by appeal to a principle will fail. Since we must admit the outright failure of the project of justifying moral principles, we should be skeptical of attempts to ground business responsibility upon moral principles.

Two further problems with the emphasis upon principles can lead us into a discussion of the alternative approach. First, principle-based ethics tends to identify particular actions as the core of morality and tends to ignore the character of the person who performs those acts. Ethical principles, whether they be called rules, maxims, laws, or action guides, inevitably conceive of moral judgments in terms of the question What should I do? and disregard the equally practical question of What [kind of person] should I be? Consequently, business ethics often labors under the inadequate assumption that every particular act can, once and for all, be determined as obligatory, prohibited, or permissible. . . .

Of course, this conviction can be seriously questioned. Why should we assume that the moral world is unambiguous? In light of the vast number of experiences that have given rise to the rapid recent growth of applied ethics, should we not assume just the opposite? I suggest that we recognize the moral life to be often fundamentally ambiguous. Ethics is not like problem solving in science or technology: There just may not *be* clear moral answers "out there" waiting to be discovered if only we use the right method. Principle-based ethics encourages us to think that there are such answers. If only we apply the right principle carefully enough, we can determine the moral status of each individual action.

A second, not unrelated, problem concerns the impersonal nature of principles. Principles are distinct from the people who are to use them: They are external rules to be internalized, adopted, accepted as one's own, and applied. This creates a gap between person and principle, a gap that un-

derlies some of the most serious problems in ethics. Even if moral principles were plausibly justified as binding on all rational agents (a goal that, I suggested above, has yet to be approached), the motivation question remains. Why should I do what is required by this principle? As a motivational question, this remains open. Even if the principle could give us unambiguous advice, we can (and do) sensibly ask Why should *I* do this? Principle-based ethics leaves us with an unbridgable motivational gap between the applied principle and the action. (On the face of it, it seems that the closer a principle comes to the goal of being rationally justified — for example, the categorical imperative — the more formal it is and the more empty it is of motivational content. On the other hand, the closer a principle is to providing a motive to act — for example, the utilitarian happiness principles — the farther it is from being rationally binding on all rational agents.)

An Alternative Approach

Let us suppose that, unlike technical or scientific problems, moral problems have no answers or solutions just waiting to be discovered. What if there were no single right answer to many of the moral problems confronting us? I would like to suggest that there is, and that we can be guided to this alternative by Aristotle.

The Aristotelian Good

Aristotle characterizes good acts as those acts performed by the good man. Although this often is thought to be circular, it seems to me to contain a wealth of truth. Imagine that you are lost deep in a jungle. There is no *one* way out of this predicament and indeed you may never get out. What would you hope for? I would want neither a map nor a survival handbook. Since I don't know where I am to begin with, a map will be of little help. Since the handbook cannot hope to cover every situation that might be encountered, it can be only marginally helpful. Rather, I would like a person who is experienced in the ways of the jungle to act as my guide. I think that Aristotle saw moral problems in much the same way. Deciding how we should live our lives is like deciding what to do in the jungle. Principles and rules will be of little help since, like maps, they can be helpful only when you already know where you are (have already established that the rule is morally justified) and, like handbooks, they cannot hope to cover all situations. What we need is a person experienced in the ways of life.

Accordingly, the Aristotelian good world is not one that conforms to some preestablished principle. Rather, it is a world populated by good people. I suggest that the good business also is not one that conforms to some preestablished principle, but one that is populated by good people. A morally responsible business is not one that measures its actions against some external principle, but is one in which good people are making the decisions.

Such a good person would be a person of character, disciplined to avoid the temptations of immediate, short-term pleasures. She would recognize that much of what is worthwhile in life is not easily and immediately achievable. This person would not be overcommitted to rules and regulations; she would have the courage to be creative, to encourage and entertain new ideas, to sometimes go on intuition. (The good person certainly would not be a bureaucrat!) The good person would also enjoy others, recognizing that solitude in a social world will result in the loss of great good. This might imply that the good person have a sense of humor. The good person would also foster her intellectual abilities. Reason and intelligence can contribute much (but not all) to the good life. Above all else, the good person possesses *phronesis*, or practical wisdom. Following Aristotle, since ethics is not a demonstrative science and since there are no unambiguous answers in ethics, a type of reasoning different from scientific reasoning will be required of the good person. The ability to make reasonable decisions in situations in which there is no right answer is the mark of phronesis: It is to possess practical wisdom.

It is the nature of phronesis that one cannot specify, a priori, what it will amount to in practice. In general, it is the ability to apply lessons learned in the past to new situations in the present. It is to be able to make appropriate adjustments so that general lessons fit the specific situation. Phronesis requires us to fit our reasoning to the situation and to avoid forcing present situations into preconceived categories. In this sense, phronesis is the antithesis of bureaucratic reasoning. It is the ability to adapt to changing situations without losing sight of one's ultimate goal. A business seeking to foster the development of good persons will be well advised to encourage the development of phronesis.[2]

The Nature of Virtues

I would now like to pursue some suggestions about the nature of the virtues that are found in Alasdair MacIntyre's book *After Virtue*.

Traditionally, the virtues have been conceptually tied to some *telos*, or some "good life" for man. The virtues were those character traits that promoted the attainment of the good life. The good man, in turn, was that person who possessed these virtues. The history of moral philosophy from at least the seventeenth century essentially ignores the role of the virtues in ethical theory. At best, the virtues were given a position alongside sentiments and feelings as being part of the noncognitive, and therefore arbitrary and subjective, side of morality. The most compelling explanation for this view centers on the fact that modern philosophy has, by and large, rejected the notion that there is any single, nonarbitrary *telos* for man. Some writers would trace this to the individualism of post-Hobbesian liberalism. The focus of that liberalism is upon man as atomistic individual and away from man as social. Since individual men have different ends, it becomes folly to try to identify some one end for all men. Other writers of a Marxist bent trace this loss of a human telos to the alienation that results from the modern industrial-capitalist society. Still other commentators trace the rejection of a human telos to the rejection of teleology in general during the scientific revolution that took place during the sixteenth and seventeenth centuries. Whatever the cause, the lack of some one telos for all people prevented the development of anything but a subjective, variable account of virtues.

I am not prepared to defend some conception of the good life for man. Nevertheless, some suggestions we find in MacIntyre might start us in the right direction. In regard to the good life, MacIntyre says:

> To ask "What is the good for me?" is to ask how best I might live out that unity [of an individual life] and bring it to completion. To ask "What is the good life for man?" is to ask what all answers to the former question have in common. (p. 203)

What all answers to the first question have in common involves what is necessary to live a unified, whole life. The unity of a life can emerge only when that life is situated in a social and historical context, a "narrative" in MacIntyre's phrase, that gives meaning to that life. Individuals do not exist as solipsists, our every action — indeed, our every thought — can be meaningful only within a complex social, historical, and linguistic context. Thus, to try and live our life in isolation from others will undermine the very context that gives meaning to and ultimately unifies our lives. It will effectively prevent us from attaining our own good, the fulfillment of our life story or narrative.

What does this have to do with business ethics? It seems to me that there are two ways in which the roles people play in business can be understood. Only one of these will contribute to that unity of the human life by situating the person within a social and historical context.

In what I call the *instrumental view*, individuals fill roles that are simply means to some other end (profit for the employer, wages for the employee). In this view, an individual fills a position in much the same way that components are plugged into a stereo system. Individuals are interchangeable parts, and as such they are denied any intrinsic value or meaning of their own. This essentially is the bureaucratic view of business in which an organizational chart gives meaning to each position. The position itself and the individual who fills it have value only so long as they are efficient means to some external end. In this view, individuals are encouraged to think of themselves as role-players. Like the manager in Albert Carr's "Business Bluffing" article, individuals play a variety of roles: managers, spouses, parents, religious believers, political constituents. When stripped of these roles, however, the individual means little or nothing. As a result, individuals are denied the unity of life that is essential to the pursuit of their good life.

On the other hand, there is what I call the *professional view* in which the positions individuals occupy are valuable in themselves and not just as means to some other end. Like the medical or teaching profession, these positions derive their value from those goods (what MacIntyre calls "internal goods") that can be achieved only through the practice of that activity. Individuals occupying these positions derive meaning and value from the pursuit and attainment of goods that are internal to those positions. These goods are essentially social, having developed during a long social history and, in turn, contributing to the future good of that society. As such, these positions are more likely to fos-

ter the unity (or integrity) that is necessary to live out one's life and bring it to completion. Unlike jobs, professions do not ask the individual participant to suspend the pursuit of the good life while at work.

In the instrumental view, work is what one does to earn the money needed to pursue what is valuable. Since value is therefore determined by money, the individual is left to assign her own value to anything at all. In the professional view, one pursues what has been established as valuable in itself by the social history of that profession. This pursuit of the objective social good is an intrinsic part of the profession. I would suggest that we develop the professional conception of business management by recognizing the intrinsic value of business as the supplier of goods and services. In this view the function of business (indeed, its social responsibility) is to produce goods and services that contribute to the good of society. Moral philosophers are encouraged to examine the character traits necessary to attain these goods in the attempt to describe the virtues of business management.

Tying some of these suggestions together, let us say that the "good life" for man lies in the pursuit of excellence. Let us say that excellence for business is the pursuit of goods and services that contribute to and advance the social good. This social good, ultimately, is a decision that should be made in the political arena. (This calls for an approach to business ethics in terms of social and political philosophy rather than in terms of ethical theory.) Nevertheless, we can say that a business can institutionalize ethics by fostering the development of good people within its ranks. Ways of doing this include closely identifying employee positions with the pursuit of business excellence. In part, this requires avoiding the instrumental view of employee roles. It would also include the encouragement of phronesis as its decision procedure and the avoidance of bureaucratic formalism.

Notes

1. See his *Corporations and Morality* (Englewood Cliffs, N.J.: Prentice-Hall, 1981).
2. For an interesting parallel to this account of phronesis in business, see *In Search of Excellence* by Thomas Peters and Robert Waterman (New York: Harper & Row, 1982).

Review and Discussion Questions

1. What does DesJardins mean by "principle-based ethics"? Explain what he sees as its practical and theoretical problems. Do you agree with DesJardins's criticisms? Can we do without principle-based ethics?

2. Explain the significance of Aristotle's concept of *phronesis*. How does Aristotle's approach to ethics differ from those described in this chapter and from that developed by James Rachels in the previous essay?

3. What implications does MacIntyre's discussion of virtues and the good life have for business ethics? Explain the difference between the "instrumental" and the "professional" view of the roles people play in business.

4. What do you think is the best way of doing business ethics? Why? Is it possible to combine principle-based ethics with the approach recommended by DesJardins?

For Further Reading

Tom L. Beauchamp, *Philosophical Ethics*, 2nd ed. (New York: McGraw-Hill, 1991) is an introductory text with selected readings covering classical ethical theories, rights, and the nature of morality.

Richard Norman, *The Moral Philosophers* (New York: Oxford University Press, 1983) discusses the thoughts of several key thinkers in the history of ethics.

J. J. C. Smart and **B. Williams,** *Utilitarianism: For and Against* (New York: Cambridge University Press, 1973) debates the merits of act utilitarianism in clear and accessible essays.

C. H. Sommers, ed., *Right and Wrong* (New York: Harcourt Brace Jovanovich, 1986) provides a good selection of readings on egoism, utilitarianism, and Kantianism.

(Consult also the readings suggested at the end of Chapter 1.)

CHAPTER 3

JUSTICE AND ECONOMIC DISTRIBUTION

It seems strange to recall that until the early years of this century, there was no federal tax on personal income. Only with the passing of the Sixteenth Amendment to the United States Constitution in 1913 was Congress granted the right to collect tax on the income of its citizens. Since then, the income tax laws have grown enormously complex. Lawyers study for years to master the intricacies of the system, and most people with middle incomes or better require professional assistance to file their annual tax forms. Over the years, the tax rules have encouraged our economy to develop in specific directions by rewarding investment in some areas but not in others. Most of us have heard stories of wealthy individuals who manage, legally, to pay little or no income tax, and many of us doubt the fairness of the tax rules.

Yet the exemptions and supposed loopholes in the tax laws, which have done so much to shape the character of our economy as well as the distribution of income across the land, do not affect just so-called special interests. For instance, millions of American families are homeowners, a fact of profound sociological and economic importance and one that has been encouraged by decades of tax deductions for home-mortgage payments.

In 1986 President Ronald Reagan achieved what most Washington pundits had long said was an impossibility: He managed to coax, goad, and pressure Congress into a comprehensive overhaul of the federal income tax code. Traditionally, our income tax has been "progressive," in the sense that wealthy people pay taxes at a higher rate than poor people. President Reagan slashed the top rates substantially during his first term in office,

and the new law further lowered the percentage rate of taxation for the wealthiest income group to well under half what it had once been. On the other hand, by eliminating many pet exemptions and closing numerous loopholes in the previous tax system, the overall result may not have favored the rich as much as the percentages alone suggest. It is hard to measure the exact economic and distributive effects of the recent changes, which were phased in over several years. Only as people adjust themselves to the new system will we be able to see who the winners and losers are and how much they have won or lost.[1] But whatever the results, and despite minor modification of income tax rates in 1990, the principle of "progressivity" — namely, that fairness requires the wealthy to pay more tax than others — has suffered a heavy blow.

President Reagan's overhaul of the tax laws came at a time when economists started reporting "a surge in inequality" in the distribution of income in the United States. Between 1977 and 1990, for example, the wealthiest 1 percent of the nation, those with an average household income of $548,969, increased their share of the country's total income from 8.7 percent to 13.3 percent. As their tax bill decreased by $50 billion, their annual income climbed 86.2 percent.[2] Meanwhile, the poorest fifth of American families became 8 percent poorer.[3] In 1986 the people in the 18 million poorest families had to get by on $93 billion, while the 18 million families at the top pulled in $903 billion — almost ten times as much.[4] According to the U.S. Bureau of the Census, the families that make up the top 20 percent income group now take home

The Growing Gap Between CEO Pay and What Others Make[10]

	1960	1970	1980	1990
Engineer	$ 9,828	$ 14,695	$ 28,486	$ 49,365
Schoolteacher	4,995	8,635	15,970	31,166
Factory worker	4,667	6,944	15,022	22,998
CEO	190,383	548,787	624,996	1,952,806

43.5 percent of the total national income, their highest level since figures were first collected in 1947. The income share of the bottom 60 percent, on the other hand, has fallen to its lowest ever: 32.4 percent. Federal Reserve Board data on income distribution, which include such items as capital gains that are not counted in the Census Bureau's definition of income, show that since 1969 people in the top 10 percent of the population have raised their income share from 29 percent to 33 percent of the national total. Meanwhile, the bottom 60 percent's income has slumped from 32 percent to 28 percent.[5]

To be sure, our nation has long had significant income inequalities. Some years ago, the Nobel Prize–winning economist Paul Samuelson used this metaphor: If we were to make an income pyramid out of child's blocks, with each layer representing $1000 of income, the peak would be far higher than the Eiffel Tower, but most of us would be within a yard of the ground.[6] Since the 1970s, however, inequality in the distribution of income in the United States has, disturbingly, increased even further. Put briefly, the rich are getting richer, the poor are increasing in number, and the middle class is having trouble holding its own.

By the end of the 1980s the average hourly earnings of nonsupervisory workers, adjusted for inflation, were lower than in any year since the mid-1960s. Middle-level managers have fared much better, and top executives have done spectacularly well. In 1988 alone, CEOs of the hundred largest publicly held industrial corporations received raises averaging almost 12 percent.[7] In 1989 *Business Week*'s thirty-ninth annual survey of the two highest-paid executives at 354 companies showed the average salary and bonus for the previous year topping the $1 million mark for the first time, with average total compensation jumping to more than $2 million. Michael Eisner, chairman of the Walt Disney Company, and Frank Wells, president of Disney, led the pack; Eisner earned $40,094,000 and Wells $32,135,000, counting salary, bonuses, and long-term compensation.[8]

In the past few years, CEOs' total compensation has jumped from forty-one times that of a skilled production worker to fifty-five times greater. Lee Iacocca's salary in 1987, for instance, translated into an hourly wage of $8,608; the average assembly line worker at Chrysler made $14 an hour.[9] The disparity between the average income of CEOs and the average incomes of engineers, schoolteachers, and factory workers has been steadily increasing as shown in the accompanying table. The disparity is even greater when one looks at take-home pay. In 1960 the maximum tax rate was 91 percent; in 1990 it was only 28 percent. As a result, the CEO brought home eleven times more than the schoolteacher in 1960 but sixty-six times more in 1990. And this disparity continues to increase. In 1991 the pay of the nation's top executives was again reported to have risen by larger percentages than the wages of any other group of salaried American workers.[11]

Another study of CEO pay, of all companies in the United States with annual sales levels of $100 million or more, shows CEO pay (not including stock options) to be 13.2 times the pay of factory workers, a far higher ratio than other developed capitalist countries. Japan and the United Kingdom, for example, have a multiple of 9.4, France 8.5, Canada 8.4, Italy 8.2, Germany 6.7, Australia 5.9, and Sweden 4.4. The United States leads the world in executive pay, and when stock options are included, the comparative compensation of American CEOs skyrockets.[12]

By contrast with the top CEOs, the Teacher of the Year, Mary V. Bicouvaris of Bethel High School in Hampton, Virginia, received $34,888 in 1989, and the president of the United States was paid only $200,000. Even the income of the best paid CEOs was dwarfed, however, by the $550 million in salary and bonuses that Michael R. Milken, junk-bond wizard and felon, pulled in during 1987 at Drexel Burnham Lambert (which does not count how much he made trading stocks and bonds for his personal account). For that matter, Britain's entire royal family—the queen, her husband, mother, sister, three children, and three cousins—receives only $10 million per year; the price of the Louisiana Purchase in today's dollars would be $122 million; the gross national product of the Republic of Guyana is $460 million; and the annual budget of the Securities Exchange Commission, which is supposed to regulate Wall Street hustlers like Milken, is $137 million. Assuming Milken worked fourteen hours a day, seven days a week, in the time it took him to brush his teeth he could easily have earned enough money to pay his Social Security withholding taxes for the entire year. In the time it took him to get to his office, he could have earned more than the average American would earn all year.[13]

Milken and our well-heeled CEOs are symbols of the well-documented increase in income inequality in the United States. This chapter will not speculate on the causes of this income shift, but we can see the evidence of it all around us. Our economy has created millions of new jobs in the last decade, but these have been predominantly in low-income sectors of the economy, like the fast-food industry. Half of these new jobs pay wages below the official poverty level for a family of four.[14] Good, well-paying middle-income jobs—especially in industries like steel, automotives, and machine tools—are scarcer than ever. More and more families require two incomes just to get by; those with only one income frequently find themselves unable to sustain a middle-class lifestyle. Discount department stores like K mart prosper, as do upscale department stores like Bloomingdale's, while stores in the middle, like Gimbel's, go out of business.[15]

These shifts of income distribution are more dramatic when set against the background of an even more unequal distribution of wealth in this country. Not only does the top 2 percent receive a disproportionate share of the total income, but they already own 28 percent of the nation's total net worth. The top 10 percent has 57 percent of the nation's wealth in its hands, leaving the bottom 50 percent of the population with 4.5 percent. If one leaves out homes and real estate, the top 2 percent of all families owns 54 percent of the nation's net financial assets (stocks, bonds, pension funds, and so on). The top 10 percent controls 86 percent, while those making up the bottom 55 percent have zero or negative financial assets. About half of the country's top wealth holders inherited their wealth; half got to the top through their own efforts. In the wealthiest group, 98 percent are white.[16]

There is nothing inevitable about such great inequalities in income and wealth. The distribution of income in Japan and Germany is far more equal than that in the United States, and both nations are just as thoroughly capitalist as we are. The United States, which has the highest child poverty rate of any industrial country, with 20 percent of its children growing up poor, chooses to spend only 0.6 percent of its gross national product on basic income support for children; Canada spends 1.6 percent.[17] Inequality of income is not some brute fact of nature, even in market-oriented societies. Rather, political choices determine how income is ultimately distributed. How much inequality a society is willing to accept reflects both its moral values and the relative strength of its contending social and political forces.

Arguments can be made for and against different degrees of income inequality, for and against progressivity in taxation, and for and against more specific tax regulations. But whatever one's position on these issues, it probably relies on some theory of economic justice for evaluating a particular tax regulation, the tax system as a whole, or even the society's economic system. The topic of economic justice deals with that constellation of moral issues raised by a society's distribution of wealth, income, status, and power.

Ethical questions arise daily about how wealth and goods should be allocated. Given the relative scarcity of a society's resources, deciding how these resources should be distributed is an important moral task. Should everyone receive roughly the same amount? Or should people be rewarded according to how hard they work or how much they contribute to society? To what extent should economic distribution take need into account? For example, with modern technology at their disposal, today's hospitals are able to perform life-prolonging feats of medicine that were undreamed of only a couple of decades ago. But these services are often extraordinarily costly. Who, then, should have access to them? Those who can afford them? Any who need them? Those who are most likely to benefit?

Chapter 2 discussed several basic moral theories and the general principles of right and wrong associated with them. This chapter focuses on the more specific topic of justice and economic distribution—that is, on the principles that are relevant to the moral assessment of society's distribution of economic goods and services. Although the topic is an abstract one, it is particularly relevant to the study of business ethics, because it concerns the moral standards to be used in evaluating the institutional frameworks within which both business and nonbusiness organizations operate. Specifically, this chapter will examine

1. The concept of justice in general and some basic principles that have been proposed as standards of economic distribution

2. The utilitarian approach to justice in general and economic justice in particular

3. The libertarian theory, which places a moral priority on liberty and free exchange

4. The contractarian and egalitarian theory of John Rawls

THE NATURE OF JUSTICE

Justice is an old concept with a rich history, a concept that is fundamental to any discussion of how society ought to be organized. Philosophical concern with justice goes back at least to ancient Greece. For Plato and some of his contemporaries, justice seems to have been the paramount virtue or, more precisely, the sum of virtue with regard to our relations with others. Philosophers today, however, generally distinguish justice from the whole of morality. To claim something is "unjust" is a more specific complaint than to say it is "bad" or "immoral."

What, then, makes an act unjust? Talk of justice or injustice focuses on at least one of several related ideas. First, a claim that one is treated unjustly often suggests that one's moral *rights* have been violated—in particular, that one has been made to suffer some burden that one had a right to avoid or that one has been denied some benefit that one had a right to possess. If, for example, we agree to go into business together and you back out without justification, costing me time and money, then you have violated a right of mine, and I may well claim that you have treated me unjustly.

Second, justice is often used to mean *fairness*. Justice frequently concerns the fair treatment of members of groups of people or else looks backward to the fair compensation of prior injuries. Exactly what fairness requires is hard to say, and different standards may well be applied to the same case. If corporate manager Smith commits bribery, he is justly punished under our laws. If other managers commit equally serious crimes but escape punishment, then Smith suffers a comparative injustice, since he was singled out. On the other hand, our treatment of Smith and other white-collar lawbreakers is unjust, although this time for the opposite reason, when compared to the stiffer sentences meted out to "common" criminals for less grave offenses.

Injustice in one sense of unfairness occurs when like cases are not treated in the same fashion. Following Aristotle, many philosophers believe that we are required, as a formal principle of justice, to treat similar cases alike except where there is some relevant difference. This principle emphasizes the role of impartiality and consistency in justice, but it is a purely formal principle because it does not tell us which differences are relevant and which are not. Satisfying this formal requirement, furthermore, does not guarantee that justice is done. For example, by treating like cases similarly, a judge can nonarbitrarily administer a law (like an apartheid regulation in South Africa) that is itself unjust. (Similarly, a fair procedure can lead to unjust results, as when a guilty man is mistakenly acquitted by an honest jury.)

Related to Aristotle's fairness requirement is a third idea commonly bound up with the concept of justice, namely that of *equality*. Justice is frequently held to require that our treatment of people reflect their fundamental moral equality. While Aristotle's formal principle of justice does not say whether we are to assume equality of treatment until some difference between cases is shown or to assume the opposite until some relevant similarities

are demonstrated, a claim of injustice based on equality is meant to place the burden of proof on those who would endorse unequal treatment. Still, to claim that all persons are equal is not to establish a direct relationship between justice and economic distribution. We all believe that some differences in the treatment of persons are consistent with equality (punishment, for example), and neither respect for equality nor the requirement of equal treatment necessarily implies an equal distribution of economic goods.

Despite equality, then, individual circumstances—in particular, what a person has done—make a difference. We think it is unjust, for example, when a guilty person goes free or an innocent person hangs, regardless of how others have been treated. This suggests that justice sometimes involves, as a fourth aspect, something in addition to equal or impartial treatment. Justice also requires that people get what they *deserve*.

Rival Principles of Distribution

Justice, then, is an important subclass of morality in general, a subclass that generally involves appeals to the overlapping notions of rights, fairness, equality, and desert. Justice is not the only virtue an individual or social institution can pursue, and difficult dilemmas arise when the requirements of justice conflict with other moral goals or obligations.

On the topic of distributive justice—that is, the proper distribution of social benefits and burdens (in particular, of economic benefits and burdens)—five principles might be used as a basis for distribution. The first possible principle: *To each an equal share.* Accordingly, when a company distributes end-of-year bonuses, it should ensure that each eligible party receives a share equal to every other eligible party. A second possible principle: *To each according to individual need.* Thus, in assigning overtime, the company should distribute work on the basis of the individual needs of the workers, with the more needy getting priority. A third candidate for a principle of distributive justice: *To each according to individual effort*. Using this guideline, the company should promote workers according to the effort put forth by each party eligible for the promotion. A fourth possible principle: *To each according to social contribution*. If the company is making a particularly valuable contribution to the welfare of society (for example, locating in the inner city and training the hard-core unemployed), it should get tax incentives denied a company that is not making a comparable contribution. Finally, a fifth possible principle: *To each according to merit*. This would mean that the company should hire, promote, and distribute bonuses strictly on the basis of individual merit.

Each of these five possible principles of economic distribution—pure equality, need, effort, social contribution, merit—has its advocates, and to be sure, each seems plausible in some circumstances. But only in some. There are problems with each. For example, if equality of income were guaranteed, then the lazy would receive as much as the industrious. On the other hand, effort is hard to measure and compare, and what one is able to contribute to society may depend on being at the right place at the right time. And so on: None of the principles seems to work in enough circumstances to be defended successfully as the one principle of justice in distribution.

It seems, in fact, that we simply apply different principles of justice at different times. For example, the opportunity to vote is distributed *equally* to all citizens above a certain age; each has one vote, and nobody more than one. Welfare programs like those providing food stamps or aiding poor people with children operate on the basis of *need*. At the lower levels of schooling, teachers commonly give grades, in part, on the basis of student *effort*. Corporations in certain industries may be given tax breaks on the basis of *social contri-*

bution. And promotions are usually awarded (distributed) on the basis of *merit*.

Multiple principles, however, may often be relevant to a single situation. Sometimes they may pull in the same direction, as when wealthy professionals like doctors defend their high incomes simultaneously on grounds of superior effort, merit, social contribution, and even (because of the high cost of malpractice insurance) need. Or the principles may pull in different directions, as when a teacher must balance effort against merit in assigning grades to pupils. Many philosophers are content to leave the situation here. They say simply that there are various *prima facie* principles of just distribution and one must find that which best applies to the given situation. If several principles seem to apply, then one must simply weigh them the best one can.

This weighing need not be done uncritically, of course. For example, we can discuss intelligently whether effort or merit (or even need) is the most appropriate basis for assigning grades and why, and we can examine whether doctors really do, as they allege, make a greater social contribution than nurses. But many writers have found themselves discontent philosophically with this sort of situation, in which a great many different commonsense principles seem to be floating about without precise guidelines for balancing them against one another or employing them in specific cases. These moral philosophers have undertaken, instead, to develop more fully some theory of justice in economic distribution, from the perspective of which these principles can be assessed and then modified, discarded, or defended. Three such approaches are the utilitarian, the libertarian, and the Rawlsian (egalitarian).

THE UTILITARIAN VIEW

For utilitarians, as the previous chapter explained, happiness is the overarching value. Whether you assess the rightness and wrongness of actions in terms of how much happiness they produce, as an act utilitarian does, or use happiness as the standard for deciding what moral principles a society should accept as the basis for determining right and wrong, as a rule utilitarian does, happiness is the only thing that is good in and of itself. On that utilitarians are agreed.

For utilitarians, justice is not an independent moral standard, distinct from their general principle. Rather, the maximization of happiness ultimately determines what is just and unjust. Critics of utilitarianism contend that knowing what will promote happiness is always difficult. People are bound to estimate consequences differently, thus making the standard of utility an inexact and unreliable principle for determining what is just. John Stuart Mill, however, did not see much merit in this criticism. For one thing, it presupposes that we all agree about what the principles of justice are and how to apply them. This is far from the case, Mill argued in his famous work *Utilitarianism*. Indeed, without utilitarianism to provide a determinate standard of justice, one is always left with a plethora of competing principles, all of which seem to have some plausibility but are mutually incompatible.

As an example, Mill considered the conflict among principles of justice that occurs in the realm of economic distribution.[18] Is it just or not, he asked, that more talented workers should receive a greater remuneration? There are two possible answers to this question:

> On the negative side of the question it is argued that whoever does the best he can deserves equally well, and ought not in justice be put in a position of inferiority for no fault of his own; that superior abilities have already advantages more than enough . . . without adding to these a superior share of the world's goods; and that society is bound in justice rather to make compensation to the less favored for this unmerited inequality of advantages than to aggravate it.

This argument sounds plausible, but then so does the alternative answer:

> On the contrary side it is contended that society receives more from the more efficient laborer; that, his services being more useful, society owes him a larger return for them; that a greater share of the joint result is actually his work, and not to allow his claim to it is a kind of robbery; that, if he is only to receive as much as others, he can only be justly required to produce as much.

Here we have two conflicting principles of justice. How are we to decide between them? The problem, Mill said, is that both principles seem plausible:

> Justice has in this case two sides to it, which it is impossible to bring into harmony, and the two disputants have chosen opposite sides; the one looks to what it is just that the individual should receive, the other to what it is just that the community should give.

Each disputant is, from his or her own point of view, unanswerable. "Any choice between them on grounds of justice," Mill continued, "must be perfectly arbitrary." What then is the solution? For Mill, the utilitarian, it was straightforward: "Social utility alone can decide the preference." The utilitarian standard must be the ultimate court of appeal in such cases. Only the utilitarian standard can provide an intelligent and satisfactory way of handling controversial questions of justice and of resolving conflicts between competing principles of justice. To understand this better, we must look at Mill's concept of justice.

Mill's Theory of Justice

Most moral theorists agree that the demands of justice are only a subset of the general class of moral obligations. What then is the relation between justice and other moral obligations? Mill's answer was that injustice involves the violation of the rights of some identifiable individual. This distinguishes it from other types of immoral behavior.

> Whether the injustice consists in depriving a person of a possession, or in breaking faith with him, or in treating him worse than he deserves, or worse than other people who have no greater claims—in each case the supposition implies two things: a wrong done, and some assignable person who is wronged. . . . It seems to me that this feature in the case—a right in some person, correlative to the moral obligation—constitutes the specific difference between justice and generosity or beneficence. Justice implies something which is not only right to do, and wrong not to do, but which some individual person can claim from us as his moral right.[19]

But if injustice involves the violation of moral rights, the question arises of how a utilitarian like Mill understands talk of rights. Mill's position was that saying I have a right to something is saying I have a valid claim on society to protect me in the possession of that thing, either by the force of law or through education and opinion. And I have that valid claim in the first place because society's protection of my possession of that thing is warranted on utilitarian grounds. "To have a right, then, is . . . to have something which society ought to defend me in the possession of. If the objector goes on to ask why it ought, I can give him no other reason than general utility."[20] What utilitarianism identifies as "rights" are certain moral rules, the observance of which is of the utmost importance for the long-run, overall maximization of happiness.

Accordingly, Mill summed up his view of justice as follows:

> Justice is the name for certain classes of moral rules which concern the essentials of human well-being more nearly, and

are therefore of more absolute obligation, than any other rules for the guidance of life; and the notion that we have found to be of the essence of the idea of justice—that of a right residing in an individual—implies and testifies to this more binding obligation.

> The moral rules which forbid mankind to hurt one another (in which we must never forget to include wrongful interference with each other's freedom) are more vital to human well-being than any maxims, however important, which only point out the best mode of managing some department of human affairs.[21]

Thus, while justice for Mill was ultimately a matter of promoting social well-being, not every issue of social utility was a matter of justice. The concept of justice identifies certain important social utilities, on which society puts great stake. The importance of these social utilities is marked by the strong feelings that typically attach to them. A perception of injustice causes feelings of resentment, Mill believed, feelings that are absent (or at least much weaker) in other cases where someone has failed to maximize human happiness.

Utilitarianism and Economic Distribution

The utilitarian theory of justice ties the question of economic distribution to the promotion of social well-being or happiness. Utilitarians want an economic system that will bring more good to society than any other system. But what system is that? Utilitarianism itself, as a normative theory, provides no answer. The answer depends on the relevant social, economic, and political facts. A utilitarian must understand the various possibilities, determine their consequences, and assess the available options. Obviously, this is not a simple task. Deciding what sort of economic arrangements would best promote human happiness requires the utilitarian to consider many things, including (1) the type of economic ownership (private, public, mixed); (2) the way of organizing production and distribution in general (pure laissez-faire, markets with government planning and regulation, fully centralized planning); (3) the type of authority arrangements within the units of production (worker control versus managerial prerogative); (4) the range and character of material incentives; and (5) the nature and extent of social security and welfare provisions.

As a matter of historical fact, utilitarians in the early nineteenth century were advocates of laissez-faire capitalism, endorsing the view of Adam Smith that unregulated market relations and free competition best promote the total social good.[22] Today it is probably fair to say that few, if any, utilitarians believe happiness would be maximized by a pure nineteenth-century-style capitalism, without any welfare arrangements. But they are not in agreement on the question of what economic arrangements would in fact maximize happiness. Nonetheless, many utilitarians would view favorably increased worker participation in industrial life and more equal distribution of income.

Worker Participation.   In his *Principles of Political Economy*, originally published in 1848, Mill argued for the desirability of breaking down the sharp and hostile division between the producers, or workers, on the one hand, and the capitalists, or owners, on the other hand.[23] Not only would this be a good thing, it was also something that the advance of civilization was tending naturally to bring about: "The relation of masters and workpeople will be gradually superseded by partnership, in one or two forms: in some cases, association of the labourers with the capitalist; in others, and perhaps finally in all, association of labourers among themselves." These developments would not only enhance productivity but—more importantly—promote the fuller development and well-being of the people involved. The aim, Mill thought, should be to

enable people "to work with or for one another in relations not involving dependence."

By the association of labor and capital, Mill had in mind different schemes of profit sharing. For example, "in the American ships trading to China, it has long been the custom for every sailor to have an interest in the profits of the voyage; and to this has been ascribed the general good conduct of those seamen." This sort of association, however, would eventually give way to a more complete system of worker cooperatives:

> The form of association, however, which if mankind continue to improve, must be expected in the end to predominate, is not that which can exist between a capitalist as chief, and workpeople without a voice in management, but the association of the labourers themselves on terms of equality, collectively owning the capital with which they carry on their operations, and working under managers elected and removable by themselves.[24]

In *Principles* Mill discussed several examples of successful cooperative associations and viewed optimistically the future of the cooperative movement:

> Eventually, and in perhaps a less remote future than may be supposed, we may, through the co-operative principle, see our way to a change in society, which would combine the freedom and independence of the individual, with the moral, intellectual, and economical advantages of aggregate production; and which . . . would realize, at least in the industrial department, the best aspirations of the democratic spirit.

What that transformation implied for Mill was nothing less than "the nearest approach to social justice, and the most beneficial ordering of industrial affairs for the universal good, which it is possible at present to foresee."[25]

Greater Equality of Income.   Utilitarians are likely to be sympathetic to the argument that steps should be taken to reduce the great disparities in income that characterize our society. That is, they are likely to believe that making the distribution of income more equal is a good strategy for maximizing happiness. The reason for this goes back to what economists would call "the declining marginal utility of money." This phrase simply means that successive additions to one's income produce, on average, less happiness or welfare than did earlier additions.

The declining utility of money follows from the fact, as Professor Richard Brandt explains it, that the outcomes we want are preferentially ordered, some being more strongly wanted than others:

> So a person, when deciding how to spend his resources, picks a basket of shopping which is at least as appealing as any other he can purchase with the money he has. The things he does not buy are omitted because other things are wanted more. If we double a person's income, he will spend the extra money on items he wants less (some special cases aside), and which will give less enjoyment than will the original income. The more one's income, the fewer preferred items one buys and the more preferred items one already has. On the whole, then, when the necessities of life have been purchased and the individual is spending on luxury items, he is buying items which will give less enjoyment. . . . This conclusion corresponds well with common-sense reflection and practice.[26]

The obvious implication is that a more egalitarian allocation of income—that is, an allocation that increases the income of those who now earn less—would boost total happiness. Brandt, for one, therefore defends equality of after-tax income on utilitarian grounds, subject to the following exceptions: supplements to meet special needs, supplements necessary for incentives or to allocate resources efficiently, and variations to achieve other socially desirable ends, such as population control.[27] Brandt states that this guiding principle of distribution is of only *prima facie* force and may have to be balanced against other principles and considerations. But it illustrates the point that utilitarians today are likely to advocate increased economic equality.

THE LIBERTARIAN APPROACH

While utilitarians associate justice with social utility, philosophers who endorse what is called *libertarianism* identify justice with an ideal of liberty. For them, liberty is the prime value, and justice consists in permitting each to live as he or she pleases, free from the interference of others. Accordingly, one libertarian asserts: "We are concerned with the condition of men in which coercion of some by others is reduced as much as possible in society."[28] Another maintains that libertarianism is "a philosophy of personal liberty—the liberty of each person to live according to his own choices, provided he does not attempt to coerce others and thus prevent them from living according to their choices."[29] Such views show clearly the libertarian's association of justice with liberty and of liberty itself with the absence of interference by other persons.

Libertarians firmly reject utilitarianism's concern for total social well-being. Utilitarians are willing to restrict the liberty of some, to interfere with their choices, if doing so will promote greater net happiness than not doing so. Libertarians cannot stomach this approach. As long as you are not doing something that interferes with anyone else's liberty, then no person, group, or government should disturb you in living the life you choose—not even if its doing so would maximize social happiness.

Although individual liberty is something that all of us value, it may not be the only thing we value. For the libertarian, however, liberty takes priority over other moral concerns. In particular, justice consists solely of respect for individual liberty. A libertarian world, with a complete commitment to individual liberty, would be a very different world from the one we now live in. Consider the following: In 1986, in the case of *Bowers* v. *Hardwick*, the Supreme Court upheld a Georgia law forbidding sodomy between consenting male homosexuals; the government registers young men for military service and can, if it chooses, draft them; laws prevent adults from ingesting substances that the legislature deems harmful or immoral (like marijuana and cocaine); and the state imposes taxes on our income to, among many other things, support needy citizens, provide loans to college students, and fund various projects for the common good. None of these policies is just from a libertarian perspective.

Given the assumption that liberty means noninterference, libertarians generally agree that liberty allows only a minimal or "nightwatchman" state. Such a state is limited to the narrow functions of protecting against force, theft, and fraud; enforcing contracts; and performing other such basic maintenance functions. In this view, a more extensive state — in particular, one that taxes its better-off citizens to support the less fortunate ones — violates the liberty of individuals by forcing them to support projects, policies, or persons they have not freely chosen to support.

Nozick's Theory of Justice

Although libertarians differ in how they formulate their theory, Harvard professor Robert Nozick's *Anarchy, State, and Utopia* is a very influential statement of the libertarian case.[30] Nozick's challenging and powerful advocacy of libertarianism has stimulated much debate, obliging philosophers of all political persuasions to take the libertarian theory seriously. His views are thus worth presenting in detail.

Nozick begins from the premise that we have certain basic moral rights (for example,

life and liberty). He calls these "Lockean rights," referring to the famous seventeenth-century British philosopher John Locke (1632–1704). By alluding to Locke's political philosophy, Nozick wishes to underscore that these rights are both negative and natural. They are negative because they require only that we refrain from acting in certain ways — in particular, that we refrain from interfering with others. Beyond this, we are not obliged to do anything positive for anyone else, nor is anyone else obliged to do anything positive for us. We have no right, for example, to be provided with satisfying work or with any material goods we might need. These negative rights, according to Nozick, are natural in the sense that we possess them independently of any social or political institutions.

These individual rights impose firm, virtually absolute restrictions (or, in Nozick's phrase, "side constraints") on how we may act. That is, we cannot morally infringe someone's rights for any purpose. Not only may we not interfere with a person's liberty in order to promote the general welfare, we are forbidden to do so even if violating that individual's rights would reduce the total number of rights violations. Each individual is autonomous and responsible and should be left to fashion his or her own life free from the interference of others — as long as this individual course is compatible with the rights of others to do the same. Only the acknowledgment of this almost absolute right to be free from coercion, Nozick argues, fully respects the distinctiveness of persons, each with a unique life to lead.

A belief in these rights shapes Nozick's specific theory of economic justice, which he calls the "entitlement theory." Essentially, Nozick believes that we are entitled to our holdings (that is, goods, money, and property) as long as we have acquired them fairly. Stated another way, if you have acquired your possessions without violating anyone's Lockean rights, then you are entitled to them and may dispose of them however you choose. No one else has a legitimate claim on them. If you have obtained a vast fortune without injuring anyone else, violating their rights, or defrauding them, then you are entitled to do with your fortune whatever you wish — bequeath it to a relative, endow a university, invest it wisely or foolishly, or squander it in riotous living. Even though other people may be going hungry, justice imposes no obligation on you to help them.

Nozick presents his entitlement theory as a function of three basic principles, but he doesn't attempt to specify them in detail. The first of these principles concerns the original acquisition of holdings — that is, the appropriation of unheld goods or the creation of new goods. If a person has acquired a holding in accordance with this principle, then he or she is entitled to that holding. If, for example, you retrieve minerals from the wilderness or make something out of materials you already possess, then you have justly acquired this new holding. Nozick does not spell out this principle or specify fully what constitutes a just original acquisition, but the basic idea is clear and reflects again the thinking of John Locke.

Property is a moral right, said Locke, by virtue of a human's labor. Individuals are morally entitled to the products of their labor. When they mix their labor with the natural world, they are entitled to the resulting product. Thus, if a man works the land, then he is entitled to the land and its products because through his labor he has put something of himself into them. This investment of self through labor is the moral basis of ownership. Locke expressed the case for the moral right to property this way:

> In the beginning . . . men had a right to appropriate, by their labour, each one of himself, as much of the things of nature, as he could use. . . . The same *measures* governed the *possession of land* too: Whatsoever he tilled and reaped, laid up and made use of, before it spoiled, that was

his peculiar right; whatsoever he enclosed, and could feed, and make use of, the cattle and product was also his. But if either the grass of his inclosure rotted on the ground, or the fruit of his planting perished without gathering, and laying up, this part of the earth, notwithstanding his inclosure, was still to be looked on as waste, and might be the possession of any other.[31]

In this early "state of nature" prior to the formation of government, property rights were limited not just by the requirement that one not waste what one claimed but also by the restriction that "enough and as good" be left for others — that is, others must not be made worse off by one's appropriation. Later, however, with the introduction of money, Locke thought that both these restrictions were overcome. You can, for example, pile up money beyond your needs without it spoiling; and by using your property productively and offering the proceeds for sale, others are not made worse off by your appropriation.

Nozick's second principle concerns transfers of already-owned goods from one person to another: how people may legitimately transfer holdings and how they may legitimately acquire holdings from others. If a person comes into possession of a holding through a legitimate transfer, then he or she is entitled to it. Again, Nozick does not formulate the guidelines in detail, but it is clear that acquiring something by purchase, as a gift, or through exchange would constitute a legitimate acquisition. Acquiring it through theft, force, or fraud would violate the principle of justice in transfer.

The third principle rectifies injustice — that is, violations of a person's rights. Nozick holds that a person who has come by a holding in any way other than by applying the first two principles simply is not entitled to it.

In sum, Nozick believes that a distribution is just if all are entitled to the holdings they possess under the distribution and that the following three principles completely cover the subject of distributive justice:

1. A person who acquires a holding in accordance with the principle of justice in acquisition is entitled to that holding.

2. A person who acquires a holding in accordance with the principle of justice in transfer, from someone else entitled to the holding, is entitled to the holding.

3. No one is entitled to a holding except by (repeated) applications of 1 and 2.

Nozick believes that his entitlement principles have decided advantages over other formulations of distributive justice. Other theories hold that justice is determined by the structure of the present distribution of goods (Is it equal? Does it maximize social utility?), or they require that distribution fit some formula, like "To each according to his _____," where the blank is filled in with something like "need," "merit," or "effort." For these theories, what counts is the shape or pattern of economic distribution; what matters for Nozick is how people came to have what they have. If people are entitled to their possessions, then the distribution of economic holdings is just, regardless of what the actual distribution happens to look like (for instance, how far people are above or below the average income). The entitlement theory is historical: Whether a distribution is just depends on how it came about; aside from that, the actual nature of the distribution is irrelevant.

The Wilt Chamberlain Story

In arguing his case for an entitlement approach, Nozick offers some ingenious examples, the most memorable of which concerns Wilt Chamberlain. In the following very famous passage, he argues that a respect for liberty inevitably leads one to repudiate other conceptions of economic justice in favor of his entitlement approach:[32]

It is not clear how those holding alternative conceptions of distributive justice can reject the entitlement conception of justice in holdings. For suppose a distribution favored by one of these nonentitlement conceptions is realized. Let us suppose it is your favorite one and let us call this distribution D_1; perhaps everyone has an equal share, perhaps shares vary in accordance with some dimension you treasure. Now suppose that Wilt Chamberlain is greatly in demand by basketball teams, being a great gate attraction. . . . He signs the following sort of contract with a team: In each home game, twenty-five cents from the price of each ticket of admission goes to him. . . . The season starts, and people cheerfully attend his team's games; they buy their tickets, each time dropping a separate twenty-five cents of their admission price into a special box with Chamberlain's name on it. They are excited about seeing him play; it is worth the total admission price to them. Let us suppose that in one season one million persons attend his home games, and Wilt Chamberlain winds up with $250,000, a much larger sum than the average income and larger even than anyone else has.

So Wilt Chamberlain has become wealthy, and the initial distributional pattern (D_1) has been upset. Can the proponent of D_1 complain about this? Nozick thinks not.

Is [Chamberlain] entitled to this income? Is this new distribution, D_2, unjust? If so, why? There is *no* question about whether each of the people was entitled to the control over the resources they held in D_1, because that was the distribution (your favorite) that (for the purposes of argument) we assumed was acceptable. Each of these persons *chose* to give twenty-five cents of their money to Chamberlain. They could have spent it on going to the movies, or on candy bars, or on copies of *Dissent* magazine, or of *Monthly Review*. But they all, at least one million of them, converged on giving it to Wilt Chamberlain in exchange for watching him play basketball. If D_1 was a just distribution, and people voluntarily moved from it to D_2, transferring parts of their shares they were given under D_1 (what was it for if not to do something with?), isn't D_2 also just? If the people were entitled to dispose of the resources to which they were entitled (under D_1), didn't this include their being entitled to give it to, or exchange it with, Wilt Chamberlain? Can anyone else complain on grounds of justice? . . . To cut off objections irrelevant here, we might imagine the exchanges occurring in a socialist society, after hours. After playing whatever basketball he does in his daily work, or doing whatever other daily work he does, Wilt Chamberlain decides to put in *overtime* to earn additional money. (First his work quota is set; he works time over that.) Or imagine it is a skilled juggler people like to see, who puts on shows after hours.

Having defended the legitimacy of Chamberlain's new wealth, Nozick pursues his case further, arguing that any effort to maintain some initial distributional arrangement like D_1 will interfere with people's liberty to use their resources (to which they are entitled under D_1) as they wish. To preserve this original distribution, society would have to "forbid capitalist acts between consenting adults."

Why might someone work overtime in a society in which it is assumed their needs are satisfied? Perhaps because they care about things other than needs. I like to write in books that I read, and to have easy access to books for browsing at odd hours. It would be very pleasant and convenient to have the resources of Widener Library in my back yard. No society, I assume, will provide such resources close to each person who would like them as part of his regular allotment (under D_1). Thus, persons either must do without some extra things that they want, or be allowed to do something extra to get some of these things. On what basis could the inequalities that would eventuate be forbidden? Notice also that small factories would spring up in a socialist society, unless forbidden. I melt down some of my personal possessions (under D_1) and build a machine out of the material. I offer you, and others, a philosophy lecture once a week in exchange for your cranking the handle on my machine, whose products I exchange for yet other things, and so on. . . . I wish merely to note how private property even in means of production would occur in a socialist society that did not forbid people to use as they wished some of the resources they are given under the socialist distribution D_1. The socialist society would have to forbid capitalist acts between consenting adults.

Nozick argues that any theory of justice other than his inevitably fails to respect people's liberty. The effort to maintain any specific structure of economic distribution involves a sacrifice of liberty, which Nozick finds unacceptable.

The general point illustrated by the Wilt Chamberlain example and the example of the entrepreneur in a socialist society is that no end-state principle or distributional patterned principle of justice can be continuously realized without continuous interference with people's lives. Any favored pattern would be transformed into one unfavored by the principle, by people choosing to act in various ways; for example, by people exchanging goods and services with other people, or giving things to other people, things the transferrers are entitled to under the favored distributional pattern. To maintain a pattern one must either continually interfere to stop people from transferring resources as they wish to, or continually (or periodically) interfere to take from some persons resources that others for some reason chose to transfer to them.

The Libertarian View of Liberty

The next chapter examines the nature of market economies in general and capitalism in particular, but libertarianism clearly involves a commitment to leaving market relations — buying, selling, and other exchanges — totally unrestricted. Force and fraud are forbidden, of course. But there should be no interference with the uncoerced exchanges of consenting individuals. Not only is the market morally legitimate, but any attempt to interfere with consenting and nonfraudulent transactions between adults will be unacceptable. Thus, libertarians are for economic laissez-faire and against any governmental economic activity that interferes with the marketplace, even if the point of the interference is to enhance the performance of the economy.

It is important to emphasize that libertarianism's enthusiasm for the market rests on this commitment to liberty. By contrast, utilitarian defenders of the market defend it on the ground that an unregulated market works better than either a planned, socialist economy or the sort of regulated capitalism with some welfare benefits that we in fact have in the United States. That is, if a utilitarian defends laissez-faire, he or she does so because of its consequences. Convince a utilitarian that some other form of economic organization better promotes human well-being, and the utilitarian will advocate that instead. With libertarians this is definitely not the case. As a matter of fact, libertarians typically agree with Adam Smith that unregulated capitalist behavior best promotes everyone's interests. But even if, hypothetically, someone like Nozick were convinced that some sort of socialism or welfare capitalism outperforms laissez-faire

capitalism economically — greater productivity, shorter working day, higher standard of living — he or she would still reject this alternative as morally unacceptable. To tinker with the market, however beneficial it might be, would involve violating someone's liberty.

This libertarian conviction reflects the priority that the theory puts on liberty over all other values. In addition, it reflects the way the theory understands liberty. Libertarians believe that we have certain natural, Lockean rights not to be interfered with. But we have no basic rights to assistance from others or to be provided with anything by society, not even an equal opportunity to compete with others. Libertarians understand liberty in terms of their conception of rights and thus operate with a distinctive and controversial definition of liberty. Consider a couple of examples.

Suppose, first, that Horace lives in a poor country and has fallen into desperate financial circumstances, perhaps because a natural disaster has destroyed his small farm. His only alternative is to accept your offer of long, hard work on your plantation in return for just enough food to keep him alive. Normally, one might say that Horace was coerced by circumstances and even that your wage offer was exploitative, but a libertarian would disagree on both counts. No one has violated Horace's rights; therefore, he has been neither coerced nor exploited. The agreement was a free and voluntary one.

Or suppose that I want to take a boat out for a spin on the lake. Having none, I attempt to take yours, which is sitting moored and idle. If the harbor police stop me, they have prevented me from doing what I want to do. But according to libertarianism, they have not interfered with my liberty. Why not? Because my "borrowing" the boat would have violated your rights, as the owner of the boat.

In both cases, libertarians seem driven to an unusual and controversial use of familiar terminology, but they have no choice. Libertarianism does not value liberty simply in the sense of people doing what they want. One has liberty only to do that which does not violate someone else's Lockean rights; likewise, one is coerced only when one's rights are violated. If libertarians admit that Horace has been coerced or that allowing me to use the boat would expand my liberty, then their theory would be in jeopardy. They would have to acknowledge that restricting some people's liberty could enhance the liberty of others. In other words, if their theory committed them simply to promoting as much as possible the goal of people doing what they want to do, then libertarians would be in the position of balancing the freedom of one against the freedom of another. For instance, restrictions on the market behavior of some might make it possible for others to do more effectively the things they want to do. But this sort of balancing and trading off is just what libertarians dislike about utilitarianism and want to avoid at all costs.

Markets and Free Exchange

Libertarians defend market relations, then, as necessary to respect human liberty (as their theory defines liberty). But they do not maintain that, morally speaking, people deserve what they receive from others through gift or exchange, only that they are entitled to that which they receive. The market tends generally, libertarians believe, to reward people for skill, diligence, and successful performance. Yet luck plays a role, too. Tom makes a fortune from having been in the right place at the right time with his Hula Hoops, while Karen loses her investment because the market for designer jeans collapses. Nozick is quite clear that the libertarian position is not that Tom deserves to be wealthy and Karen does not. Rather, it is that Tom is entitled to his holdings if he has acquired them in accordance with the principles of justice.

The same point comes up with regard to gifts in general and inheritance in particular. Critics of libertarianism sometimes contend that inheritance is patently unfair. Is it just, they ask, that one child at birth should inherit a vast fortune, the best schooling, and social, political, and business connections that will ensure its future, while another child inherits indigence, inferior schooling, and connections with crime? At birth neither baby deserves anything—a fact suggesting that an equal division of holdings and opportunities is the only fair allocation. For his part, Nozick contends that deserving has no bearing on the justice of inherited wealth; people are simply entitled to it as long as it was not ill-gotten. Or looking at it the other way, if one is entitled to one's holdings, then one is permitted to do with them what one wishes, including using them to benefit one's children.

According to libertarians, totally free market relations are necessary if people are to be allowed to exercise their fundamental rights. In certain circumstances, however, market relations can lead to disastrous results. Unfortunately, this is not just a theoretical possibility. In an important study of several of this century's worst famines, Professor Amartya Sen of Oxford University shows how, in certain circumstances, changing market entitlements, the economic dynamics of which he attempts to unravel, have led to mass starvation.[33] Although the average person thinks of famine as caused simply by a shortage of food, Sen and other experts have pointed out that famines are frequently accompanied by no shortfall of food in absolute terms. Indeed, even more food may be available during a famine than in nonfamine years—if one has the money to buy it. Famine occurs because large numbers of people lack the financial wherewithal to obtain the necessary food.

For example, given the interconnectedness of nations, people in underdeveloped countries can be seriously hurt through fluctuation in commodity prices. So reliant are some of these countries on one or another commodity (for example, tobacco, coffee, cocoa, sugar) that a sharp drop in its price can result in mass starvation. Plummeting prices are not always the result of acts of nature, such as floods or droughts. At least sometimes they result from the profit-motivated manipulation of investors and brokers. A case in point was the 1974 famine in the Sahelian region of Africa and the Indian subcontinent.

Experts attribute the famine partly to climatic shifts and partly to increased oil prices that raised the price of human necessities, fertilizer, and grains such as wheat. Here is how two agronomists accounted for the human loss: "The recent doubling in international prices of essential foodstuffs will, of necessity, be reflected in high death rates among the world's lowest income groups, who lack the income to increase their food expenditures proportionately, but live on diets near the subsistence level to begin with."[34] Philosopher Onora O'Neill called the resulting deaths "killings." "To the extent that the raising of oil prices is an achievement of Arab diplomacy and oil company management rather than a windfall," she writes, "the consequent deaths are killings."[35]

Libertarians would find it immoral and unjust to coerce people to give food or money to the starving. Nor does justice require that a wealthy merchant assist the hungry children in his community to stay alive. And it would certainly violate the merchant's property rights for the children to help themselves to his excess food. Nevertheless, while justice does not require that one assist those in need, libertarians would generally acknowledge that we have some humanitarian obligations toward others. Accordingly, they would not only permit but also presumably encourage people voluntarily to assist others. Justice does not require the merchant to donate, and it forbids us from forcing him to do so, but charity on his part would be a good thing. This reflects the libertarian's firm commit-ment to property rights: What you have legitimately acquired is yours to do with as you will.

Property Rights

Nozick's theory makes property rights virtually sacrosanct. From the perspective of libertarianism, property rights grow out of one's basic moral rights, either reflecting one's initial creation or appropriation of the product, some sort of exchange or transfer between consenting persons, or a combination of these. Property rights exist prior to any social arrangements and are morally antecedent to any legislative decisions that a society might make. Because of this, Nozick believes, for instance, that justice forbids taxation for redistributive purposes. "Taxation of earnings from labor," he writes, "is on a par with forced labor."

In speaking of ownership and of property rights, however, we must avoid oversimplification. We should not assume that property is merely a physical object. In the popular mind, "property" is synonymous with some thing: a car, a watch, a house, a piece of land. But property is not so much a thing as a bundle of rights and corresponding interests. The set of rights implied in the concept of property includes, among other rights, the rights to possess, use, manage, dispose of, and restrict others' access to something.

It is true, of course, that property rights and interests often relate to physical objects. But in developed societies, ownership may involve more abstract goods, interests, and claims. For instance, property may include the right to pay debts with the balance in our bank account, the right to dividends from our corporate investments, and the right to collect from a pension plan we have joined. In fact, the courts have counted as property a wide range of "things," including new life forms, the news, a job, and a place on the welfare rolls.[36]

Thus, it is mistaken to think of property as involving some simple relationship between a person and a thing. Rather, ownership involves all the rules and regulations governing the legal acquisition and transfer of various goods, interests, and claims. Accordingly, many nonlibertarian social and political theorists maintain that property rights are a function of the particular institutions of a given society. Ownership involves a bundle of different rights, and the nature of this bundle differs, as do the types of things that can be owned, between societies. The nature of ownership can also change over time in any given society. As a general trend, the social restrictions on property ownership in the United States have increased dramatically during our history (much to the displeasure of libertarians). This is not to say a society's property arrangements cannot be criticized. On the contrary, they can be morally assessed just as any other institution can.

RAWLS'S THEORY OF JUSTICE

A Theory of Justice by Harvard University's John Rawls is generally thought to be the single most influential work of the postwar period in social and political philosophy, at least in the English language.[37] Not only has Rawls's elegant theory touched a responsive chord in many readers, but also his book has helped to rejuvenate serious work in normative theory. Even those who are not persuaded by Rawls find themselves obliged to come to terms with his thinking. Although Rawls's basic approach is not difficult to explain (and Rawls himself had sketched out his key concepts in earlier articles), *A Theory of Justice* elaborates Rawls's ideas with such painstaking care and philosophical thoroughness that even vigorous critics of the book (like his colleague Robert Nozick) pay sincere tribute to its many virtues.

By his own account, Rawls presents his theory as a modern alternative to utilitarianism, one that he hopes will be compatible with the belief that justice must be associated with fairness and the moral equality of persons. Rawls firmly wishes to avoid reducing justice to a matter of social utility. At the same time, his approach differs fundamentally from that of Nozick. Rawls conceives of society as a cooperative venture among its members, and he elaborates a conception of justice that is thoroughly social. He does not base his theory, as Nozick does, on the postulate that individuals possess certain natural rights prior to any political or social organization.

Two main features of Rawls's theory are particularly important: his hypothetical-contract approach and the principles of justice that he derives with it. Rawls's strategy is to ask what we would choose as the fundamental principles to govern society if, hypothetically, we were to meet for this purpose in what he calls the "original position." He then elaborates the nature of this original position, the constraints on the choice facing us, and the reasoning that he thinks people in the original position would follow. In this way, Rawls offers a modern variant of *social contract* theory, in the tradition of Hobbes, Locke, Rousseau, and other earlier philosophers. Rawls argues that people in the original position would agree on two principles as the basic governing principles of their society, and that these principles are, accordingly, the principles of justice. These principles are examined at some length in a later section. But briefly, the first is a guarantee of certain familiar and fundamental liberties to each person, and the second—more controversial—holds in part that social and economic inequalities are justified only if those inequalities benefit the least advantaged members of society.

The Original Position

Various principles of economic justice have been proposed, but an important question for philosophers is whether, and how, any such principles can be justified. Thinking of possible principles of economic distribution is not all that difficult, but proving the soundness of such a principle, or at least showing it to be more plausible than its rivals, is a challenging task. After all, people seem to differ in their intuitions about what is just and unjust, and their sentiments are bound to be influenced by their social position. Nozick's entitlement theory, for example, with its priority on property rights, is bound to seem more plausible to a corporate executive than to a migrant farm worker. The justice of some children being born into wealth while other children struggle by on welfare does not seem as obvious to the poor as it may to the well-to-do.

The strategy Rawls employs to identify and justify some basic principles of justice is to imagine that people come together for the purpose of deciding on the ground rules for their society, in particular on the rules governing economic distribution. While groups of people have in the past written down constitutions and similar political documents, never have the members of a society decided from scratch on the basic principles of justice that should govern them. Nor is it even remotely likely that people will do this in the future. What Rawls imagines is a thought experiment. The question is hypothetical: What principles would people choose in this sort of original position? If we can identify these principles, Rawls contends, then we will have identified the principles of justice just because they are the principles that we would all have agreed to.

The Nature of the Choice.   On what basis are we to choose these principles? The most obvious answer is that we should select principles that strike us as just. But this won't work. Even if we are all agreed on what is just and unjust, we would be relying on our already existing ideas about justice as a basis for choosing the principles to govern our society.

Philosophically, this approach doesn't accomplish anything. We would simply be going in a circle, using our existing conception of justice to "prove" the principles of justice.

Rawls suggests instead that we imagine people in the original position choosing solely on the basis of self-interest. That is, each individual chooses the set of principles for governing society that will be best for himself or herself (and loved ones). We don't have to imagine that people are antagonistic or that outside of the original position they are selfish; we just imagine that they hope to get the group to choose those principles that will, more than any other possible principles, benefit them. If people in the original position can agree on some governing principles on the basis of mutual self-interest, then these principles will be, Rawls thinks, the principles of justice. Why? Because the principles are agreed to under conditions of equality and free choice. By analogy, if we make up a game and all agree ahead of time, freely and equally, on how the game is to be played, nobody can later complain that the rules are unfair.

The Veil of Ignorance.   If people in the original position are supposed to choose principles on the basis of self-interest, agreement seems unlikely. If Carolyn has vast real estate holdings, she will certainly want rules that guarantee her extensive property rights, while her tenants are likely to support rules that permit, say, rent control. Likewise, the wealthy will tend to advocate rules rather like Nozick's entitlement theory, while those without property will, on the basis of their self-interest, desire a redistribution of property. Conflicts of self-interest seem bound to create totally irreconcilable demands. For instance, artists may contend that they should be rewarded more than professional people, men that they should earn more than women, and laborers that they merit more than people with desk jobs.

Agreement seems unlikely, given that some rules would benefit one group while other rules would benefit another. As a way around this problem, Rawls asks us to imagine that people in the original position do not know what social position or status they hold in society. They do not know whether they are rich or poor, and they do not know their personal talents and characteristics — whether, for example, they are athletic or sedentary, artistic or tone-deaf, intelligent or not very bright, physically sound or handicapped in some way. They do not know their race or even their sex. Behind what Rawls calls "the veil of ignorance," people in the original position know nothing about themselves personally or about what their individual situation will be once the rules are chosen and the veil is lifted. They do, however, have a general knowledge of history, sociology, and psychology — although no specific information about the society they will be in once the veil is lifted.

Under the veil of ignorance, the people in Rawls's original position have no knowledge about themselves or their situation that would lead them to argue from a partial or biased point of view. No individual is likely to argue that some particular group — such as white men, property owners, star athletes, philosophers — should receive special social and economic privileges when, for all that individual knows, he or she will be nonwhite, propertyless, unathletic, and bored by philosophy when the veil is lifted. Because individuals in the original position are all equally ignorant of their personal predicament and they are all trying to advance their self-interest, agreement is possible. The reasoning of any one person will be the same as the reasoning of each of the others, for each is in identical circumstances and each has the same motivation. As a result, no actual group has to perform Rawls's thought experiment. People who read Rawls's book can imagine that they are in the original position and then decide whether they would choose the principles Rawls thinks they would.

The veil of ignorance, in effect, forces people in the original position to be objective and impartial and makes agreement possible. Also, according to Rawls, the fact that people have no special knowledge that would allow them to argue in a biased way accords with our sense of fairness. The circumstances of the original position are genuinely equal and fair, and because of this, the principles agreed to under these conditions have a good claim to be considered the principles of justice.

Choosing the Principles

Although people in the original position are ignorant of their individual circumstances, they know that whatever their particular goals, interests, and talents turn out to be, they will want more, rather than less, of what Rawls calls the "primary social goods." These include not just income and wealth but also rights, liberties, opportunities, status, and self-respect. Of course, once people are outside of the veil of ignorance, they will have more specific ideas about what is good for them — they may choose a life built around religion, one spent in commerce and industry, or one devoted to academic study. But whatever these particular individual goals, interests, and plans turn out to be, they will almost certainly be furthered, and definitely never limited, by the fact that people in the original position secured for themselves more rather than less in the way of primary goods.

How, then, will people in the original position choose their principles? *A Theory of Justice* explores in depth the reasoning that Rawls thinks would guide their choice. At the heart of Rawls's argument is the contention that people in the original position will be conservative, in the sense that they will not wish to gamble with their futures. In setting up the ground rules for their society, they are determining their own fate and that of their children. This exercise is not something to be taken lightly, a game to be played and re-played. Rather, with so much at stake, people will reason cautiously.

Consider, for example, the possibility that people in the original position will set up a feudal society: 10 percent of the population will be nobles, living a life of incredible wealth, privilege, and leisure; the other 90 percent will be serfs, toiling away long hours to support the extravagant lifestyles of the aristocracy. Perhaps some people would consider the joy of being a pampered noble so great that they would vote for such an arrangement behind the veil of ignorance. But they would be banking on a long shot. When the veil of ignorance is lifted, the odds are nine to one that they will be poor and miserable serfs, not lords. Rawls thinks that people in the original position will not, in fact, gamble with their futures. They will not agree to rules that make it overwhelmingly likely that they will have to face a grim life of hardship.

Rawls argues that for similar reasons people in the original position will not adopt the utilitarian standard to govern their society, since the utilitarian principle might sacrifice the well-being of some to enhance society's total happiness. People in the original position, Rawls argues, will not be willing to risk sacrificing their own happiness, once the veil of ignorance is lifted, for the greater good.

What people in the original position would actually do, Rawls believes, is follow what game strategists call the *maximin rule* for making decisions. This rule says that you should select the alternative under which the worst that could happen to you is better than the worst that could happen to you under any other alternative. That is, you should try to *maxi*mize the *mini*mum that you will receive. This rule makes sense when you care much more about avoiding an unacceptable or disastrous result (such as being a serf) than about getting the best possible result (being a noble) and when you have no real idea what

odds you are facing. It is a conservative decision principle, but Rawls thinks that people in the original position will find it a rational and appropriate guideline for their deliberations.

Rawls's Two Principles

Rawls argues that people in the original position considering various alternatives will eventually endorse two principles as the most basic governing principles of their society. These principles, because they are agreed to in an initial situation of equality and fairness, will be the principles of justice. Once these two principles of justice have been decided, the people in the original position can gradually be given more information about their specific society. They can then go on to design their basic social and political institutions in more detail.

Rawls states the two basic principles of justice as follows:

> 1. Each person has an equal right to the most extensive scheme of equal basic liberties compatible with a similar scheme of liberties for all.
> 2. Social and economic inequalities are to meet two conditions: they must be (a) to the greatest expected benefit of the least advantaged; and (b) attached to offices and positions open to all under conditions of fair equality of opportunity.[38]

According to Rawls, the first principle takes priority over the second, at least for societies that have attained a moderate level of affluence. The liberties Rawls has in mind are the traditional democratic ones of freedom of thought, conscience, and religious worship, as well as freedom of the person and political liberty. Explicitly absent are "the right to own certain kinds of property (e.g., means of production), and freedom of contract as understood by the doctrine of laissez-faire." The first principle guarantees not only equal liberty to individuals but also as much liberty to individuals as possible, compatible with others having the same amount of liberty. There is no reason why people in the original position would settle for anything less.

All regulations could be seen as infringing on personal liberty, since they limit what a person may do. The law that requires you to drive on the right-hand side of the road denies you the freedom to drive on either side whenever you wish. Some would argue that justice requires only an equal liberty. For example, as long as every motorist is required to drive on the right-hand side of the road, justice is being served; or if everyone in a dictatorial society is forbidden to criticize the leader's decisions, then all are equal in their liberty. But Rawls argues that if a more extensive liberty were possible, without inhibiting the liberty of others, then it would be irrational to settle for a lesser degree of liberty. In the case of driving, permitting me to drive on either side of the road would only interfere with the liberty of others to drive efficiently to their various destinations, but introducing right-turn-on-red laws would enhance everyone's liberty. In the dictatorship example, free speech could be more extensive without limiting anyone's liberty.

The second principle concerns social and economic inequalities. Regarding inequalities, Rawls writes:

> It is best to understand not *any* differences between offices and positions, but differences in the benefits and burdens attached to them either directly or indirectly, such as prestige and wealth, or liability to taxation and compulsory services. Players in a game do not protest against there being different positions, such as batter, pitcher, catcher, and the like, nor to there being various privileges and powers as specified by the rules; nor do the citizens of a country object to there being the different offices of government such as president, senator, governor, judge, and so on, each with their special rights and duties.[39]

Rather, at issue are differences in wealth and power, honors and rewards, privileges and salaries that attach to different roles in society.

Rawls's second principle states that insofar as inequalities are permitted — that is, insofar as it is compatible with justice for some jobs or positions to bring greater rewards than others — these positions must be open to all. In other words, there must be meaningful equality of opportunity in the competition among individuals for those positions in society that bring greater economic and social rewards. This, of course, is a familiar ideal, but what exactly a society must do to achieve not just legal but full and fair equality of opportunity will be a matter of debate .

The first part of the second principle is less familiar and more controversial. Called the *difference principle*, it is the distinctive core of Rawls's theory. It states that inequalities are justified only if they work to the benefit of the least advantaged group in society. By "least advantaged," Rawls simply means those who are least well off. But what does it mean to require that inequalities work to the benefit of this group?

Imagine that we are back in the original position. We wish to make sure that, under the principles we choose, the worst that can happen to us once the veil of ignorance is lifted is still better than the worst that might have happened under some other arrangement. We might, therefore, choose strict social and economic equality. With an equal division of goods, there's no risk of doing worse than anyone else, no danger of being sacrificed to increase the total happiness of society. And in the case of liberty, people in the original position do insist on full equality. But with social and economic inequality, the matter is a little different.

Suppose, for instance, that as a result of dividing things up equally, people lack an incentive to undertake some of the more difficult work that society needs done. It might then be the case that allowing certain inequalities—for example, paying people more for being particularly productive or for undertaking the necessary training to perform some socially useful task—would work to everyone's benefit, including those who would be earning less. If so, then why not permit those inequalities? Compare the two diagrams:

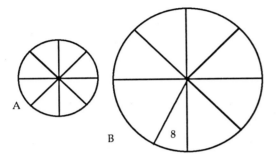

Each pie represents a possible social and economic distribution among eight basic groups (the number eight is arbitrary) in society. In Figure A, things are divided equally; in Figure B, unequally. Imagine that if a society permits inequalities as an incentive to get people to work harder or to do work that they would not have wanted to do otherwise, then the overall amount to be distributed among its members will be greater. That is, the economic pie will increase in size from A to B, and the people with the thinnest slice of B will be better off than they would have been with an equal slice of A.

Which society will people in the original position prefer? Obviously the one represented by Figure B, because the minimum they can attain in B (the slice labeled 8) is bigger than any of the eight equal slices in A. People in the original position do not care about equality of distribution as a value in and of itself; they want the social and economic arrangement that will provide them with the highest minimum.

Rawls is not trying to prove that economic inequalities will always, or even usually, "trickle down" to the least advantaged (although, of course, some people believe that).

Rather, his point is simply that people in the original position would not insist on social and economic equality at all costs. If permitting some people to be better off than the average resulted in the least-well-off segment of society being better off than it would have been under a strictly equal division, then this is what people in the original position will want. Rawls's difference principle is intended to capture this idea. Rawls's principles permit economic inequalities only if they do in fact benefit the least advantaged.

Consider President Bush's proposal to lower the income tax on capital gains (that is, on personal income from the sale of assets like stocks, bonds, and real estate). He claims that the tax break will spur trading in financial assets, which will in turn lead to growth in tax revenues, and that the cut will trigger more long-term investment, helping to revitalize the economy. Critics contest both claims. But everyone agrees that the tax break would certainly increase the income of the rich. The richest 0.7 percent of taxpayers receive 70 percent of capital-gains income, and the wealthiest 5 percent receive 85 percent of capital gains.[40] Will lowering taxes on the rich benefit the least advantaged members of society more in the long run than any alternative tax policy?

This question illustrates the application of Rawls's difference principle in a practical context, but we must remember that Rawls intends his principles to be used not as a direct guide to day-to-day policy decisions but rather as the basis for determining what form society's primary social, political, and economic institutions should take in the first place. What will these institutions look like? More specifically, what sort of economic system will best satisfy Rawls's difference principle? Rawls himself does not answer this question. He sees it as primarily a question for economists and other social scientists, while the task of philosophers like himself is the preliminary one of working out a satisfactory conception of justice. Rawls does appear to believe, however, that a liberal form of capitalism, with sufficient welfare provisions, would satisfy his principles. But he does not rule out the possibility that a democratic socialist system could as well.

Fairness and the Basic Structure

Rawls intends his theory as a fundamental alternative to utilitarianism, which he rejects on the grounds that maximizing the total well-being of society could permit an unfair distribution of burdens and benefits. Utilitarianism, in Rawls's view, treats people's pleasures and pains as completely interchangeable: A decrease of happiness here is justified by greater happiness there. Within a person's own life, such trade-offs are sensible. An increase of pain now (as the dentist fills a cavity in my tooth) is justified in terms of greater happiness later (no painful, rotted tooth). But between individuals, as when Jack's happiness is decreased to provide Jill with a more-than-compensating gain, such trade-offs are morally problematic.

Thus Rawls stresses that, in his view,

> each person possesses an inviolability founded on justice that even the welfare of society as a whole cannot override. . . . Therefore, . . . the rights secured by justice are not subject to political bargaining or to the calculus of social interests.[41]

And he emphasizes that the difference principle

> excludes, therefore, the justification of inequalities on the grounds that the disadvantages of those in one position are outweighed by the greater advantages of those in another position. This rather simple restriction is the main modification I wish to make in the utilitarian principle as usually understood.[42]

On the other hand, Rawls is equally unsympathetic to the approach adopted by Nozick. Contrary to the entitlement theory, he argues that the primary subject of justice is not, in the first instance, transactions between individuals but rather "the basic structure, the fundamental social institutions and their arrangement into one scheme." Why?

> Suppose we begin with the initially attractive idea that the social process should be allowed to develop over time as free agreements fairly arrived at and fully honored require. Straightaway we need an account of when agreements are free and the conditions under which they are reached are fair. In addition, while these conditions may be satisfied at an earlier time, the accumulated results of agreements in conjunction with social and historical contingencies are likely to change institutions and opportunities so that the conditions for free and fair agreements no longer hold. The basic structure specifies the background conditions against which the actions of individuals, groups, and associations take place. Unless this structure is regulated and corrected so as to be just over time, the social process with its procedures and outcomes is no longer just, however free and fair particular transactions may look to us when viewed by themselves. We recognise this principle when we say that the distribution resulting from voluntary market transactions will not in general be fair unless the antecedent distribution of income and wealth and the structure of the market is fair. Thus we seem forced to start with an account of a just basic structure.[43]

Additional considerations support taking the basic structure of society as the primary subject of justice, in particular the fact that the basic structure shapes the wants, desires, hopes, and ambitions of individuals. Thus, Rawls continues,

> it has always been recognised that the social system shapes the desires and aspirations of its members; it determines in large part the kind of persons they want

to be as well as the kind of persons they are. Thus an economic system is not only an institutional device for satisfying existing wants and desires but a way of fashioning wants and desires in the future.

Rawls concludes his discussion by stressing that because the basic structure is the proper focus of a theory of justice, we cannot expect the principles that apply to it to be simply an extension of the principles that govern everyday individual transactions:

> The justice of the basic structure is, then, of predominant importance. The first problem of justice is to determine the principles to regulate inequalities and to adjust the profound and long-lasting effects of social, natural, and historical contingencies, particularly since these contingencies combined with inequalities generate tendencies that, when left to themselves, are sharply at odds with the freedom and equality appropriate for a well-ordered society. In view of the special role of the basic structure, we cannot assume that the principles suitable to it are natural applications, or even extensions, of the familiar principles governing the actions of individuals and associations in everyday life which take place within its framework. Most likely we shall have to loosen ourselves from our ordinary perspective and take a more comprehensive viewpoint.

Benefits and Burdens

The passages quoted here touch on a theme that is central to Rawls's theory. Inevitably, there will be natural differences between human beings—in terms of physical prowess, mental agility, and so on. But there is nothing natural or inevitable about the weight attached by society to those differences. For Rawls, a desirable feature of any account of justice is that it strives to minimize the social consequences of purely arbitrary, natural differences. He stresses that no one deserves his or her particular natural characteristics. We cannot say that Robert Redford deserves to be handsome or that Albert Einstein deserved to be blessed with an excellent mind any more than we can say that Fred merits his shortness or Pamela her nearsightedness. Their attributes are simply the result of a genetic lottery. But Rawls goes beyond this to argue that even personal characteristics like diligence and perseverance reflect the environment in which one was raised:

> It seems to be one of the fixed points of our considered judgments that no one deserves his place in the distribution of native endowments, any more than one deserves one's initial starting place in society. The assertion that a man deserves the superior character that enables him to make the effort to cultivate his abilities is equally problematic; for his character depends in large part upon fortunate family and social circumstances for which he can claim no credit. The notion of desert seems not to apply to these cases.[44]

Accordingly, Rawls thinks we cannot really claim moral credit for our special talents or even our virtuous character. In Rawls's view, then, if our personal characteristics are not something that we deserve, we have no strong claim to the economic rewards they might bring. On the contrary, justice requires that the social and economic consequences of these arbitrarily distributed assets be minimized.

> We see then that the difference principle represents, in effect, an agreement to regard the distribution of natural talents as a common asset and to share in the benefits of this distribution whatever it turns out to be. Those who have been favored by nature, whoever they are, may gain from their good fortune only on terms that improve the situation of those who have lost out. The naturally advantaged are not to gain merely because they are

more gifted, but only to cover the costs of training and education and for using their endowments in ways that help the less fortunate as well. No one deserves his greater natural capacity nor merits a more favorable starting place in society. But it does not follow that one should eliminate these distinctions. There is another way to deal with them. The basic structure can be arranged so that these contingencies work for the good of the least fortunate. Thus we are led to the difference principle if we wish to set up the social system so that no one gains or loses from his arbitrary place in the distribution of natural assets or his initial position in society without giving or receiving compensating advantages in return.[45]

This important passage from *A Theory of Justice* reflects well Rawls's vision of society as a cooperative project for mutual benefit.

SUMMARY

1. Justice is one important aspect of morality. Talk of justice and injustice generally involves appeals to the related notions of rights, fairness, equality, and desert. Economic or distributive justice concerns the principles appropriate for assessing society's distribution of social benefits and burdens, particularly wealth, income, status, and power.

2. Economic distribution might be based on pure equality, need, effort, social contribution, or merit. Each of these principles is plausible in some circumstances but not in others. In some situations, the principles pull us in different directions. Dissatisfied with this fact, some moral philosophers have sought to develop more general theories of justice.

3. Utilitarianism holds that the maximization of happiness ultimately determines what is just and unjust. Mill contended, more specifically, that the concept of justice identifies certain very important social utilities and that injustice involves the violation of the rights of some specific individual.

4. Utilitarians must examine a number of factual issues in order to determine for themselves which economic system and principles will best promote social well-being or happiness. Many utilitarians favor increased worker participation and a more equal distribution of income.

5. The libertarian theory identifies justice with liberty, which libertarians understand as living according to our own choices, free from the interference of others. They reject utilitarianism's concern for total social well-being.

6. The libertarian philosopher Robert Nozick defends the "entitlement theory." His theory holds that the distribution of goods, money, and property is just if people are entitled to what they have — that is, if they have acquired their possessions without violating the rights of anyone else.

7. In the story of Wilt Chamberlain, Nozick argues that theories of economic justice not in accord with his inevitably fail to respect people's liberty.

8. Libertarians operate with a distinctive concept of liberty, defend free exchange and laissez-faire markets without regard to results, put a priority on liberty over all other values, and see property rights as existing prior to any social arrangements. Critics contest each of these features of libertarianism.

9. John Rawls's approach lies within the social-contract tradition. He asks us to imagine people meeting in the "original position" to choose the basic principles that are to govern their society. Although in this original position people choose on

the basis of self-interest, we are to imagine that they are behind a "veil of ignorance," with no personal information about themselves. Rawls contends that any principles agreed to under these circumstances have a strong claim to be considered the principles of justice.

10. Rawls argues that people in the original position would follow the maximin rule for making decisions. They would choose principles guaranteeing that the worst that could happen to them is better than the worst that could happen to them under any rival principles. Rawls argues that they would agree on two principles. The first states that each person has a right to the most extensive scheme of liberties compatible with others having the same amount of liberty. The second principle states that any inequalities must be to the greatest expected benefit of the least advantaged and open to all under conditions of fair equality of opportunity.

11. Rawls rejects utilitarianism because it might permit an unfair distribution of burdens and benefits. Contrary to the entitlement theory, he argues that the primary focus of justice should be the basic social structure, not transactions between individuals. He contends that society is a cooperative project for mutual benefit and that justice requires the social and economic consequences of arbitrary natural differences among people to be minimized.

CASE 3.1
Whatever Happened to the Steel Industry?

Steel was the core of American industry, the heavy metal basis for a productive system that was the envy of the world. Pittsburgh, Youngstown, and other communities in our industrial heartland symbolized that productive system. Built around the steel industry, they were hard working, tough, proud, and patriotic—the home turf of athletes like Joe Namath and Stan Musial. Steel was good for those cities, the people who made it, and the country.

For generations, an implicit social contract had existed in those steel towns. Since the early 1940s, the companies had recognized the union; the union had left investment decisions to the companies; and steelworker families had bought homes, sent children to college for the first time, and retired on pensions.[46] But now, sadly, that world has come to an end. The steel industry has collapsed.

As recently as the 1970s, Youngstown, Ohio, and neighboring Pittsburgh employed more than 100,000 steelworkers, but by the late 1980s little or no steel was being made in either community. (Nationwide, more than 337,500 steel jobs disappeared between 1974 and 1986.)[47] The steel communities were traumatized; their life-support system had been ripped out. As one local union president remarked, "You felt as if the mill would always be there." But now it was all over. The vice president of another local union said: "Most people couldn't believe it. It was so huge and had operated so long and so many people depended on it for their livelihood." More than one steelworker in Youngstown indicated that the only similar upheaval they had experienced was Pearl Harbor.

From 1977 to 1986, the steel companies presented an unchanging public message: They were eager to modernize their mills and continue making steel. But they lacked capital. Through no fault of their own, the steel companies claimed, but as the result of restrictive environmental regulation, high union wages and benefits, and unfair dumping in American markets of foreign, government-subsidized steel, they found themselves unable to make steel profitably. They were therefore unable to accumulate the necessary capital for updating American steel mills.

Initially, communities like Youngstown and Pittsburgh accepted this message and threw their political support behind the companies. When the first major mill closed in 1977, union leaders petitioned Congress to impose emergency quotas on foreign steel. But the attitude of the communities and the workers gradually changed. A string of broken promises led them to doubt the sincerity of the steel industry's claim that it sought to invest in steel. As lawyer and community activist Staughton Lynd reported:

> Painfully it was learned that the problem went beyond the companies' lack of commitment to existing mills. The companies were not even committed to steel. They would "flow" investment capital to whatever investment opportunity was most profitable. They would take money created by steelworkers and use it to buy real estate, chemical companies, savings and loan associations, insurance companies and oil fields.

The steel companies were abandoning steel. Symbolically, in 1986 U.S. Steel changed its name to USX. It was getting out of the steel business.

In the fight against the plant shutdowns that were destroying their communities, local activists and union members came to two conclusions. First, because the steel industry was basing its investment decisions on the effort to maximize profits in the short run, steel companies were postponing needed modernization; they were investing outside the steel industry, where the rate of profit was higher. Second, because of its capital-intensive character, the steel business would probably continue to yield a lower rate of profit than other investment opportunities. Tinkering with external factors (environmental regulation, depreciation allowances, import quotas, currency exchange rates, and so on) to induce the steel companies to make a socially desirable investment in steel was a policy that had failed.

Lots of new, even radical, ideas began to circulate in the traditionally conservative steel towns. One response was the emergence of the idea of "eminent domain," championed by Lynd and others. Legally, eminent domain is the sovereign's power to take private property for public use against the owner's will, subject to the constitutional requirement that "just compensation" be paid. Applied to the crisis in steel, a state or local government could take, or threaten to take, a closed or closing plant from the company that owned it and then operate the plant or sell it to a new owner. In effect, the community says, "If USX (or whatever company) still wants to run the Homestead Works (or whatever facility is threatened with closure), God bless it. But if it refuses to run it any longer, then we, the people, will have to find another way."

In 1985 nine municipalities in the Monongahela Valley joined to incorporate the Steel Valley Authority (SVA), a regional development agency organized under the Pennsylvania Municipal Authorities Act. The SVA has the power to take property by eminent domain for the purpose of retaining and developing existing industries. Armed with eminent domain power, a community could acquire an abandoned steel mill without the consent of its owner and so bring about its continued use. Underlying this, Lynd suggested, is the concept of a generalized trust that a community extends to enterprises within its border to operate for the common good. As Long as the enterprise exercises such stewardship, it can and should remain in private hands. But if the enterprise is permitted to stand idle, or if capital earned there is taken out of the community for other purposes, then the community can rightfully intervene by eminent domain.

Discussion Questions

1. The steel companies blamed the decline of their industry on restrictive environmental regulations, high wages, and unfair foreign competition. Steelworkers argued that the companies were too absorbed with short-run profits, that they failed to anticipate and respond to foreign competition, and that they lacked a sense of social responsibility. Evaluate these claims and counterclaims.

2. What social obligation, if any, does a company have to continue producing an important commodity when it can invest more profitably elsewhere? Union members and activists believe that renewed investment in steel is socially desirable. Assess that assumption.

3. Can the steel companies be accused of acting unjustly? What responsibilities, if any, does a company have to the community and to its work force to continue operating?

4. Does justice require that companies exercise a kind of "stewardship" for the common good, as Lynd suggested?

5. Assess the idea of eminent domain as a response to the crisis in the steel industry. Is it morally defensible?

6. How would the utilitarian, libertarian, and Rawlsian theories of justice evaluate the use of eminent domain, both in general and in this particular case?

CASE 3.2
Poverty in America

According to our government's official definition, 35 million Americans — about one in every seven people in our nation — live below the poverty level. Since 1973 the poverty rate has increased by a third; today it stands at a level higher than any time in the past two decades. An additional 40 million or more live on incomes estimated as below a "low standard adequacy" by the Department of Labor. One out of every four Americans lives in substandard housing. One out of every five adults is functionally illiterate.[48] In the United States today one can see people roaming the streets in tattered clothing, picking their food out of garbage cans. Homeless people — many of them former mental patients released from state hospitals, others jobless individuals and families unable to afford housing — live in abandoned cars and shacks or simply sleep in doorways and on subway grates. The government acknowledges 400,000 homeless, but the National Coalition for the Homeless places the figure at 3 million.[49]

Most people think that those described as "poor" in the United States are pretty well off by world standards. The truth is, in life expectancy twenty-year-old American males rank thirty-sixth among the world's nations, and twenty-year-old American females rank twenty-first. Our infant mortality rate is worse than that in twenty other Western nations. In 1990 the New England Journal of Medicine reported that the life expectancy of black men in Harlem is lower than that of men in

Bangladesh, and the leading cause of high mortality in Harlem is not homicide or drugs, but cardiovascular disease.[50]

One study found that 20 million Americans go hungry each month. Some 50 percent of children from the poorest families grow up with impaired learning ability, and 5 percent are born mentally retarded because of prenatal malnourishment. The Physicians Task Force on Hunger reports that "hunger is a problem of epidemic proportions across the nation," with growing frequency of "third world diseases of advanced malnutrition" like "stunting," "wasting," kwashiorkor, and marasmus. Malnutrition from extreme poverty has caused brain damage in an estimated 1 million babies and young children. Yet less than half the American poor receives either food stamps or free food, and in New York State alone an estimated million people who need food stamps are not getting them. Food stamp benefits have dropped 13 percent in real terms since 1981.[51]

People in different walks of life and in different circumstances experience poverty. Some work but are unable to pull themselves out of poverty. The percentage of "working poor" in the United States—that is, those who work full-time, year-round while earning an income below the poverty line—is at its highest since 1974.[52] Others live on the edge of poverty; although not officially classified as poor, they are continually in danger of falling into poverty. Although job loss precipitates many into poverty, *The Wall Street Journal* reported in 1989 that only 31.5 percent of all unemployed people collect jobless benefits, the lowest level in the thirty-three years for which data are available.[53]

Many poor people are unable to work and depend on outside assistance. Investigation shows, however, that most people do not stay for years on the welfare rolls. They move on and off, and fewer than 1 percent obtain welfare for ten years. Contrary to popular mythology, the majority of those who receive Aid

to Families with Dependent Children (AFDC) are young children whose mothers must remain at home. They are not able-bodied adults, unwilling to work. About 70 percent of AFDC families have only one or two children, and there is little financial incentive to have more. Half of the families who receive AFDC include an adult who works full- or part-time, and research consistently demonstrates that poor people have the same strong desire to work that the rest of the population does.

The number of welfare recipients since 1970 has remained relatively constant at 10 million people, despite an enormous increase in the number of poor people.[54] Since 1968, welfare benefits to families with children have declined by 35 percent in real dollars.[55] There is no way to live well on welfare. Even in the most generous states, stipends fall well below what the government defines as the poverty level. In 1986 annual cash allowances for a family with two children ranged from $1,380 in Alabama to $5,970 in Wisconsin, with the national average at $4,320. In the same year it took an income of $8,740 for a family of three to escape the poverty category.[56] As the following table shows, the typical AFDC stipend amounts to a seventh of the average American family income.

Ratio of Average AFDC Stipend to Median Family Income[57]

Vermont	19.3%
Minnesota	19.0
New York	18.3
United States	14.0
Nevada	8.3
Louisiana	7.6
Mississippi	5.8

Poverty is not an isolated problem, nor is it limited to specific groups. Still, poverty strikes some groups more severely than others. Children are one example. Today in every four children under six, and one in every two black children under six, are poor. Millions of children live in poverty, and their ranks are steadily growing. The problem is particularly serious among female-headed families, where half of all children are poor.

The past twenty years have also seen a dramatic increase in the number of women in poverty. This includes women with inadequate income following divorce, widowhood, or retirement, as well as women raising children alone. Wage discrimination against women is one factor. Women who work full-time, year-round earn only 61 percent of what men earn. Hundreds of thousands of women who hold full-time jobs are still poor. More than 2 million women are working full-time in jobs that pay wages below the poverty line.[58]

Women's responsibilities for child rearing are another important factor. Despite many changes in recent years, women continue to have primary responsibility in this area. When marriages break up, mothers typically take custody and bear the major financial burden. Fewer than half the women raising children alone are awarded child support, and fewer than half of those entitled to it receive the full amount. In 1985 two-thirds of all women were either the sole support of their families or relying on husbands who earned $15,000 or less per year.[59] This table shows the incomes of women who headed households in 1986:

Incomes of Women Who Head Households[60]

Income	Number	Percentage
$50,000 and over	104,000	1.6
$35,000 to $50,000	283,000	4.5
$20,000 to $35,000	1,081,000	17.2
$10,000 to $20,000	1,717,000	27.3
Under $10,000	3,112,000	49.4
	6,297,000	100.0

Most poor people in our nation, about two-thirds of them, are white. But blacks are about three times more likely to be poor. While one out of every nine white Americans is poor, one of every three blacks and Native Americans and more than one of every four Hispanics are below the poverty line. Many members of the minority communities have succeeded in moving up the economic ladder, but the overall picture is bleak. Black family income, for instance, is only 55 percent that of white family income, a gap that is wider than any time in the last eighteen years.

Discussion Questions

1. Does the existence of poverty imply that our socioeconomic system is unjust? Does the concentration of poverty in certain groups make it more unjust than it would be otherwise?

2. What moral obligation, if any, do we have individually and as a society to reduce poverty? What steps could be taken? What role should business play?

3. How would a utilitarian view the facts about poverty? What are the implications for our society of the concept of the "declining marginal utility of money"?

4. How would a libertarian like Nozick view poverty in the United States? How plausible do you find the libertarian's preference for private charity over public welfare?

5. How would our economy be assessed from the point of view of Rawls's difference principle? Can it be plausibly maintained that, despite poverty, our system works to "the greatest expected benefit of the least advantaged"? Is this an appropriate standard?

NOTES

1. See Hilary Stout, "Day of Reckoning," *Wall Street Journal*, April 17, 1989, A1, and "Tax Reform Follies," *St. Louis Post-Dispatch*, January 23, 1989, 15BP.

2. Brendan Boyd, "By the Numbers," *San Francisco Chronicle*, September 30, 1990, B5.

3. Robert B. Reich, "As the World Turns," *New Republic*, May 1, 1989, 23. See also "America's Income Gap: The Closer You Look, the Worse It Gets," *Business Week*, April 17, 1989, 78.

4. Anna DeCormis, "Income Gap Widened Under Reagan," *Guardian* (New York), May 31, 1989, 2.

5. Lester C. Thurow, "A Surge in Inequality," *Scientific American*, May 1987.

6. Ibid.

7. Reich, "As the World Turns," 23.

8. "Is the Boss Getting Paid Too Much?" *Business Week*, May 1, 1989, 46–52.

9. John Eckhouse, "Pay Disparity Threatens U.S.," *San Francisco Chronicle*, June 5, 1989, C1; *Guardian* (New York), May 25, 1988, 2; and *San Francisco Chronicle*, April 8, 1989, B2.

10. "Is the Boss Getting Paid Too Much?" 52, and "The Flap over Executive Pay," *Business Week*, May 6, 1991, 96.

11. "Executives Got Best Pay Boosts," *San Francisco Chronicle*, March 10, 1991, B1.

12. Eckhouse, "Pay Disparity Threatens U.S." and "U.S. Still Tops in Executive Pay," *San Francisco Chronicle*, November 5, 1990, C1.

13. Steve Swartz, "Why Mike Milken Stands to Qualify for Guinness Book," *Wall Street Journal*, March 31, 1989, A1.

14. Robert Reno, "Trump and His Ilk Aren't Helping the Little Guy," *San Francisco Chronicle*, October 15, 1988, B3.

15. Thurow, "A Surge in Inequality."

16. Ibid.

17. Leonard Silk, "Rich-Poor Gap Gets Wider in U.S.," *San Francisco Chronicle*, May 12, 1989, C5, and "America's Income Gap," 79.

18. John Stuart Mill, *Utilitarianism* (Indianapolis: Bobbs-Merrill, 1957), 71.

19. Ibid., 62.

20. Ibid., 66.

21. Ibid., 73.

22. Smith's ideas are discussed further in Chapter 4.

23. John Stuart Mill, *Principles of Political Economy*, edited by Donald Winch (Harmondsworth, Middlesex: Penguin, 1970), 129–141.

24. Ibid., 133.

25. Ibid., 139–141.

26. Richard Brandt, *A Theory of the Good and the Right* (New York: Oxford University Press, 1979), 312–313.

27. Ibid., 310.

28. F. A. Hayek, *The Constitution of Liberty* (Chicago: University of Chicago Press, 1960), 11.

29. John Hospers, *Libertarianism* (Los Angeles: Nash, 1971), 5.

30. Robert Nozick, *Anarchy, State, and Utopia*, (New York: Basic Books, 1974).

31. John Locke, *Second Treatise of Government* (Indianapolis: Hackett Publishing, 1980), 23–24.

32. From *Anarchy, State, and Utopia* by Robert Nozick. Copyright © 1974 by Basic Books, Inc. Reprinted by permission of the publisher.

33. A. K. Sen, *Poverty and Famines* (New York: Oxford University Press, 1981).

34. Lester R. Brown and Erik P. Eckhol, "The Empty Breadbasket," *Ceres*, March–April 1974, 59.

35. Onora O'Neill, "Lifeboat Earth," *Philosophy and Public Affairs* 4 (1975): 288.

36. Lawrence C. Becker and Kenneth Kipnis, eds., *Property: Cases, Concepts, Critiques* (Englewood Cliffs, N.J.: Prentice-Hall, 1984), 3–5.

37. John Rawls, *A Theory of Justice* (Cambridge, Mass.: Harvard University Press, 1971).

38. John Rawls, "A Kantian Conception of Equality," *Cambridge Review* 96 (February 1975): 96; *A Theory of Justice*, 83.

39. John Rawls, "Justice as Fairness," *Philosophical Review* 67 (April 1958): 167.

40. John Miller, "Helping the Rich Help Themselves," *Dollars & Sense* 147 (June 1989): 17.

41. Rawls, *A Theory of Justice*, 4.

42. Rawls, "Justice as Fairness," 168.

43. Rawls, "A Kantian Conception of Equality," 95.

44. Rawls, *A Theory of Justice*, 104.

45. Ibid., 101–102.

46. See Staughton Lynd, "Towards a Not-for-Profit Economy: Public Development Authorities for Acquisition and Use of Industrial Property," *Harvard Civil Rights Civil Liberties Law Review* (Winter 1987), from which this case study is drawn. See also Charles F. Sabel, "Left Behind at the Forge," *New York Times Book Review*, February 5, 1989.

47. Ruth Ruttenberg, "The Death of Steel," *Business and Society Review* 67 (Fall 1988): 77.

48. See Michael Parenti, *Democracy for the Few*, 5th ed. (New York: St. Martin's, 1988), 30–32, and National Council of Catholic Bishops, *Economic Justice for All* (Washington, D.C.: U.S. Catholic Conference, 1986), 83–106, for all figures not cited to other sources and for further references. On the homeless, see Jonathan Kozol, *Rachel and Her Children:*

Homeless Families in America (New York: Ballantine, 1988).

49. Abe Mellinkoff, "Taxpayers Say Tax Us More for Homeless," *San Francisco Chronicle*, January 27, 1989, A32.

50. See Melvin Konner, "Dying of Neglect," *San Francisco Chronicle*, March 11, 1990 in "This World," 3.

51. Reich, "As the World Turns." See also "Study Finds Widespread Hunger of Children Under 12 in U.S.," *San Francisco Chronicle*, March 27, 1991, A3.

52. Ramon G. McLeod, "A Prosperous America Is Still Plagued by Severe Poverty," *San Francisco Chronicle*, August 22, 1988, A4.

53. *Wall Street Journal*, April 17, 1989, A1.

54. Teresa Amott, "War of Attrition," *Dollars & Sense* 143 (January–February 1989): 20.

55. Jonathan Kozol, "Are the Homeless Crazy?" *Harper's*, September 1988, 17.

56. Andrew Hacker, "Getting Rough on the Poor," *New York Review of Books*, October 13, 1988, 12.

57. Ibid., 13.

58. Ann Hornaday, "Pay Dirt," *San Francisco Chronicle*, November 22, 1988, in "This World," 11.

59. Ibid.

60. Hacker, "Getting Rough on the Poor," 13.

Rich and Poor

Peter Singer

After reviewing the seriousness and extensiveness of world poverty, Singer argues that we have a duty to provide far more aid to those in need than we now give. The principle to which he appeals is one that, he argues, we already implicitly acknowledge in everyday life. Singer rejects Nozick's theory of rights and argues against the view that we should simply write certain countries off as "hopeless" and allow famine, disease, and natural disaster to reduce their populations.

Consider these facts: by the most cautious estimates, 400 million people lack the calories, protein, vitamins and minerals needed for a normally healthy life. Millions are constantly hungry; others suffer from deficiency diseases and from infections they would be able to resist on a better diet. Children are worst affected. According to one estimate, 15 million children under five die every year from the combined effects of malnutrition and infection. In some areas, half the children born can be expected to die before their fifth birthday.

Nor is lack of food the only hardship of the poor. To give a broader picture, Robert McNamara, President of the World Bank, has suggested the term 'absolute poverty.' The poverty we are familiar with in industrialized nations is relative poverty — meaning that some citizens are poor, relative to the wealth enjoyed by their neighbours. People living in relative poverty in Australia might be quite comfortably off by comparison with old-age pensioners in Britain, and British old-age pensioners are not poor in comparison with the poverty that exists in Mali or Ethiopia. Absolute poverty, on the other hand, is poverty by any standard. In McNamara's words:

> Poverty at the absolute level . . . is life at the very margin of existence.
>
> The absolute poor are severely deprived human beings struggling to survive in a set of squalid and degraded circumstances almost beyond the power of our sophisticated imaginations and privileged circumstances to conceive.
>
> Compared to those fortunate enough to live in developed countries, individuals in the poorest nations have:
>
> An infant mortality rate eight times higher
> A life expectancy one-third lower
> An adult literacy rate 60% less
> A nutritional level, for one out of every two in the population, below acceptable standards; and for millions of infants, less protein than is sufficient to permit optimum development of the brain.

And McNamara has summed up absolute poverty as:

> a condition of life so characterized by malnutrition, illiteracy, disease, squalid surroundings, high infant mortality and low life expectancy as to be beneath any reasonable definition of human decency. . . .

Death and disease apart, absolute poverty remains a miserable condition of life, with inadequate food, shelter, clothing, sanitation, health services and education. According to World Bank estimates which define absolute poverty in terms of income levels insufficient to provide adequate nutrition, something like 800 million people — almost 40% of the people of developing countries — live in absolute poverty. Absolute poverty is probably the principle cause of human misery today. . . .

The problem is not that the world cannot produce enough to feed and shelter its people. People in the poor countries consume, on average, 400 lbs of grain a year, while North Americans average more than 2000 lbs. The difference is caused by the fact that in the rich countries we feed most of our grain to animals, converting it into meat, milk and eggs. Because this is an inefficient process, wasting up to 95% of the food value of the animal feed, people in rich countries are responsible for the consumption of far more food than those in poor countries who eat few animal products. If we stopped feeding animals on grains, soybeans and fishmeal the amount of food saved would — if distributed to those who need it — be more than enough to end hunger throughout the world.

These facts about animal food do not mean that we can easily solve the world food problem by cutting down on animal products, but they show that the problem is essentially one of distribution rather than production. The world does produce enough food. Moreover the poorer nations themselves could produce far more if they made more use of improved agricultural techniques.

So why are people hungry? Poor people cannot afford to buy grain grown by American farmers. Poor farmers cannot afford to buy improved seeds, or fertilizers, or the machinery needed for drilling wells and pumping water. Only by transferring some of the wealth of the developed nations to the poor of the undeveloped nations can the situation be changed.

That this wealth exists is clear. Against the picture of absolute poverty that McNamara has painted, one might pose a picture of 'absolute affluence.' Those who are absolutely affluent are not necessarily affluent by comparison with their neighbours, but they are affluent by any reasonable definition of human needs. This means that they have more income than they need to provide themselves adequately with all the basic necessities of life. After buying food, shelter, clothing, necessary health services and education, the absolutely affluent are still able to spend money on luxuries. The absolutely affluent choose their food for the pleasures of the palate, not to stop hunger; they buy new clothes to look fashionable, not to keep warm; they move house to be in a better neighbourhood or have a play room for the children, not to keep out the rain; and after all this there is still money to spend on books and records, colour television, and overseas holidays.

At this stage I am making no ethical judgments about absolute affluence, merely pointing out that it exists. Its defining characteristic is a significant amount of income above the level necessary to provide for the basic human needs of oneself and one's dependents. By this standard Western Europe, North America, Japan, Australia, New Zealand and the oil-rich Middle Eastern states are all absolutely affluent, and so are many, if not all, of their citizens. The USSR and Eastern Europe might also be included on this list. To quote McNamara once more:

> The average citizen of a developed country enjoys wealth beyond the wildest dreams of the one billion people in countries with per capita incomes under $200 . . .

These, therefore, are the countries — and individuals — who have wealth which they could, without threatening their own basic welfare, transfer to the absolutely poor.

At present, very little is being transferred. Members of the Organization of Petroleum Exporting Countries lead the way, giving an average of 2.1% of their Gross National Product. Apart from them, only Sweden, The Netherlands and Norway have reached the modest UN target of 0.7% of GNP. Britain gives 0.38% of its GNP in official development assistance and a small additional amount in unofficial aid from voluntary organizations. The total comes to less than £1 per month per person, and compares with 5.5% of GNP spent on alcohol, and 3% on tobacco. Other, even wealthier nations, give still less: Germany gives 0.27%, the United States 0.22% and Japan 0.21% . . .

The Obligation to Assist

The Argument for an Obligation to Assist

The path from the library at my university to the Humanities lecture theatre passes a shallow ornamental pond. Suppose that on my way to give a lecture I notice that a small child has fallen in and is in danger of drowning. Would anyone deny that I ought to wade in and pull the child out? This will mean getting my clothes muddy, and either cancelling my lecture or delaying it until I can find something dry to change into; but compared with the avoidable death of a child this is insignificant.

A plausible principle that would support the judgment that I ought to pull the child out is this: if it is in our power to prevent something very bad happening, without thereby sacrificing anything of comparable moral significance, we ought to do it. This principle seems uncontroversial. It will obviously win the assent of consequentialists; but non-consequentialists should accept it too, because the injunction to prevent what is bad applies only when nothing comparably significant is at stake. Thus the principle cannot lead to the kinds of actions of which non-consequentialists strongly disapprove—serious violations of individual rights, injustice, broken promises, and so on. If a non-consequentialist regards any of these as comparable in moral significance to the bad thing that is to be prevented, he will automatically regard the principle as not applying in those cases in which the bad thing can only be prevented by violating rights, doing injustice, breaking promises, or whatever else is at stake. Most non-consequentialists hold that we ought to prevent what is bad and promote what is good. Their dispute with consequentialists lies in their insistence that this is not the sole ultimate ethical principle: that it is *an* ethical principle is not denied by any plausible ethical theory.

Nevertheless the uncontroversial appearance of the principle that we ought to prevent what is bad when we can do so without sacrificing anything of comparable moral significance is decep-

tive. If it were taken seriously and acted upon, our lives and our world would be fundamentally changed. For the principle applies, not just to rare situations in which one can save a child from a pond, but to the everyday situation in which we can assist those living in absolute poverty. In saying this I assume that absolute poverty, with its hunger and malnutrition, lack of shelter, illiteracy, disease, high infant mortality and low life expectancy, is a bad thing. And I assume that it is within the power of the affluent to reduce absolute poverty, without sacrificing anything of comparable moral significance. If these two assumptions and the principle we have been discussing are correct, we have an obligation to help those in absolute poverty which is no less strong than our obligation to rescue a drowning child from a pond. Not to help would be wrong, whether or not it is intrinsically equivalent to killing. Helping is not, as conventionally thought, a charitable act which it is praiseworthy to do, but not wrong to omit; it is something that everyone ought to do.

This is the argument for an obligation to assist. Set out more formally, it would look like this.

First premise: If we can prevent something bad without sacrificing anything of comparable significance, we ought to do it.
Second premise: Absolute poverty is bad.
Third premise: There is some absolute poverty we can prevent without sacrificing anything of comparable moral significance.
Conclusion: We ought to prevent some absolute poverty.

The first premise is the substantive moral premise on which the argument rests, and I have tried to show that it can be accepted by people who hold a variety of ethical positions.

The second premise is unlikely to be challenged. Absolute poverty is, as McNamara put it, 'beneath any reasonable definition of human decency' and it would be hard to find a plausible ethical view which did not regard it as a bad thing.

The third premise is more controversial, even though it is cautiously framed. It claims only that some absolute poverty can be prevented without the sacrifice of anything of comparable moral significance. It thus avoids the objection that any aid I can give is just 'drops in the ocean' for the point is not whether my personal contribution will make any noticeable impression on world poverty as a whole (of course it won't) but whether it will prevent some poverty. This is all the argument needs to sustain its conclusion, since the second premise says that any absolute poverty is bad, and not merely the total amount of absolute poverty. If without sacrificing anything of comparable moral significance we can provide just one family with the means to raise itself out of absolute poverty, the third premise is vindicated.

I have left the notion of moral significance unexamined in order to show that the argument does not depend on any specific values or ethical principles. I think the third premise is true for most people living in industrialized nations, on any defensible view of what is morally significant. Our affluence means that we have income we can dispose of without giving up the basic necessities of life, and we can use this income to reduce absolute poverty. Just how much we will think ourselves obliged to give up will depend on what we consider to be of comparable moral significance to the poverty we could prevent: colour television, stylish clothes, expensive dinners, a sophisticated stereo system, overseas holidays, a (second?) car, a larger house, private schools for our children . . . For a utilitarian, none of these is likely to be of comparable significance to the reduction of absolute poverty; and those who are not utilitarians surely must, if they subscribe to the principle of universalizability, accept that at least *some* of these things are of far less moral significance than the absolute poverty that could be prevented by the money they cost. So the third premise seems to be true on any plausible ethical view — although the precise amount of absolute poverty that can be prevented before anything of moral significance is sacrificed will vary according to the ethical view one accepts.

Objections to the Argument

Taking Care of Our Own.   Anyone who has worked to increase overseas aid will have come across the argument that we should look after those near us, our families and then the poor in our own country, before we think about poverty in distant places.

No doubt we do instinctively prefer to help those who are close to us. Few could stand by and watch a child drown; many can ignore a famine in Africa. But the question is not what we usually do, but what we ought to do, and it is difficult to see any sound moral justification for the view that distance, or community membership, makes a crucial difference to our obligations.

Consider, for instance, racial affinities. Should whites help poor whites before helping poor blacks? Most of us would reject such a suggestion out of hand: . . . people's need for food has nothing to do with their race, and if blacks need food more than whites, it would be a violation of the principle of equal consideration to give preference to whites.

The same point applies to citizenship or nationhood. Every affluent nation has some relatively poor citizens, but absolute poverty is limited largely to the poor nations. Those living on the streets of Calcutta, or in a drought-stricken region of the Sahel, are experiencing poverty unknown in the West. Under these circumstances it would be wrong to decide that only those fortunate enough to be citizens of our own community will share our abundance.

We feel obligations of kinship more strongly than those of citizenship. Which parents could give away their last bowl of rice if their own children were starving? To do so would seem unnatural, contrary to our nature as biologically evolved beings — although whether it would be wrong is another question altogether. In any case, we are not faced with that situation, but with one in which our own children are well-fed, well-clothed, well-educated, and would now like new bikes, a stereo set, or their own car. In these circumstances any special obligations we might have to our children have been fulfilled, and the needs of strangers make a stronger claim upon us.

The element of truth in the view that we should first take care of our own, lies in the advantage of a recognized system of responsibilities. When families and local communities look after their own poorer members, ties of affection and personal relationships achieve ends that would otherwise require a large, impersonal bureaucracy. Hence it would be absurd to propose that from now on we all regard ourselves as equally responsible for the welfare of everyone in the world; but the argument for an obligation to assist does not propose that. It applies only when some are in absolute poverty, and others can help without sacrificing anything of comparable moral significance. To allow one's own kin to sink into absolute poverty would be to sacrifice something of comparable significance; and before that point had been reached, the breakdown of the system of family and community responsibility would be a factor to weigh the balance in favour of a small degree of preference for family and community. This small degree of preference is, however, decisively outweighed by existing discrepancies in wealth and property.

Property Rights.   Do people have a right to private property, a right which contradicts the view that they are under an obligation to give some of their wealth away to those in absolute poverty? According to some theories of rights (for instance, Robert Nozick's) provided one has acquired one's property without the use of unjust means like force and fraud, one may be entitled to enormous wealth while others starve. This individualistic conception of rights is in contrast to other views, like the early Christian doctrine to be found in the works of Thomas Aquinas, which holds that since property exists for the satisfaction of human needs, 'whatever a man has in superabundance is owed, of natural right, to the poor for their sustenance.' A socialist would also, of course, see wealth as belonging to the community rather than the individual, while utilitarians, whether socialist or not, would be prepared to override property rights to prevent great evils.

Does the argument for an obligation to assist others therefore presuppose one of these other theories of property rights, and not an individualist theory like Nozick's? Not necessarily. A theory of property rights can insist on our *right* to retain wealth without pronouncing on whether the rich *ought* to give to the poor. Nozick, for example, rejects the use of compulsory means like taxation to redistribute income, but suggests that we can achieve the ends we deem morally desirable by voluntary means. So Nozick would reject the claim that rich people have an 'obligation' to give to the poor, in so far as this implies that the poor have a right to our aid, but might accept that giving is something we ought to do and failing to give, though within one's rights, is wrong—for rights is not all there is to ethics.

The argument for an obligation to assist can survive, with only minor modifications, even if we accept an individualistic theory of property rights. In any case, however, I do not think we should ac-

cept such a theory. It leaves too much to chance to be an acceptable ethical view. For instance, those whose forefathers happened to inhabit some sandy wastes around the Persian Gulf are now fabulously wealthy, because oil lay under those sands; while those whose forefathers settled on better land south of the Sahara live in absolute poverty, because of drought and bad harvests. Can this distribution be acceptable from an impartial point of view? If we imagine ourselves about to begin life as a citizen of either Kuwait or Chad—but we do not know which—would we accept the principle that citizens of Kuwait are under no obligation to assist people living in Chad?

Population and the Ethics of Triage.   Perhaps the most serious objection to the argument that we have an obligation to assist is that since the major cause of absolute poverty is overpopulation, helping those now in poverty will only ensure that yet more people are born to live in poverty in the future.

In its most extreme form, this objection is taken to show that we should adopt a policy of 'triage'. The term comes from medical policies adopted in wartime. With too few doctors to cope with all the casualties, the wounded were divided into three categories: those who would probably survive without medical assistance, those who might survive if they received assistance, but otherwise probably would not, and those who even with medical assistance probably would not survive. Only those in the middle category were given medical assistance. The idea, of course, was to use limited medical resources as effectively as possible. For those in the first category, medical treatment was not strictly necessary; for those in the third category, it was likely to be useless. It has been suggested that we should apply the same policies to countries, according to their prospects of becoming self-sustaining. We would not aid countries which even without our help will soon be able to feed their populations. We would not aid countries which, even with our help, will not be able to limit their population to a level they can feed. We would aid those countries where our help might make the difference between success and failure in bringing food and population into balance.

Advocates of this theory are understandably reluctant to give a complete list of the countries they would place into the 'hopeless' category; but

Bangladesh is often cited as an example. Adopting the policy of triage would, then, mean cutting off assistance to Bangladesh and allowing famine, disease and natural disasters to reduce the population of that country (now around 80 million) to the level at which it can provide adequately for all.

In support of this view Garrett Hardin has offered a metaphor: we in the rich nations are like the occupants of a crowded lifeboat adrift in a sea full of drowning people. If we try to save the drowning by bringing them aboard our boat will be overloaded and we shall all drown. Since it is better that some survive than none, we should leave the others to drown. In the world today, according to Hardin, 'lifeboat ethics' apply. The rich should leave the poor to starve, for otherwise the poor will drag the rich down with them. . . .

Anyone whose initial reaction to triage was not one of repugnance would be an unpleasant sort of person. Yet initial reactions based on strong feelings are not always reliable guides. Advocates of triage are rightly concerned with the long-term consequences of our actions. They say that helping the poor and starving now merely ensures more poor and starving in the future. When our capacity to help is finally unable to cope — as one day it must be — the suffering will be greater than it would be if we stopped helping now. If this is correct, there is nothing we can do to prevent absolute starvation and poverty, in the long run, and so we have no obligation to assist. Nor does it seem reasonable to hold that under these circumstances people have a right to our assistance. If we do accept such a right, irrespective of the consequences, we are saying that, in Hardin's metaphor, we would continue to haul the drowning into our lifeboat until the boat sank and we all drowned.

If triage is to be rejected it must be tackled on its own ground, within the framework of consequentialist ethics. Here it is vulnerable. Any consequentialist ethics must take probability of outcome into account. A course of action that will certainly produce some benefit is to be preferred to an alternative course that may lead to a slightly larger benefit, but is equally likely to result in no benefit at all. Only if the greater magnitude of the uncertain benefit outweighs its uncertainty should we choose it. Better one certain unit of benefit than a 10% chance of 5 units; but better a 50% chance of 3 units than a single certain unit. The same principle applies when we are trying to avoid evils.

The policy of triage involves a certain, very great evil: population control by famine and disease. Tens of millions would die slowly. Hundreds of millions would continue to live in absolute poverty, at the very margin of existence. Against this prospect, advocates of the policy place a possible evil which is greater still: the same process of famine and disease, taking place in, say, fifty years time, when the world's population may be three times its present level, and the number who will die from famine, or struggle on in absolute poverty, will be that much greater. The question is: how probable is this forecast that continued assistance now will lead to greater disasters in the future?

Forecasts of population growth are notoriously fallible, and theories about the factors which affect it remain speculative. One theory, at least as plausible as any other, is that countries pass through a 'demographic transition' as their standard of living rises. When people are very poor and have no access to modern medicine their fertility is high, but population is kept in check by high death rates. The introduction of sanitation, modern medical techniques and other improvements reduces the death rate, but initially has little effect on the birth rate. Then population grows rapidly. Most poor countries are now in this phase. If standards of living continue to rise, however, couples begin to realize that to have the same number of children surviving to maturity as in the past, they do not need to give birth to as many children as their parents did. The need for children to provide economic support in old age diminishes. Improved education and the emancipation and employment of women also reduce the birthrate, and so population growth begins to level off. Most rich nations have reached this stage, and their populations are growing only very slowly.

If this theory is right, there is an alternative to the disasters accepted as inevitable by supporters of triage. We can assist poor countries to raise the living standards of the poorest members of their population. We can encourage the governments of these countries to enact land reform measures, improve education, and liberate women from a purely child-bearing role. We can also help other countries to make contraception and sterilization widely available. There is a fair chance that these measures will hasten the onset of the demographic transition and bring population growth down to a manageable level. Success cannot be guaranteed; but the evidence that improved economic security and education reduce population growth is strong enough to make triage ethically unacceptable. We cannot allow millions to die from starvation and disease when there is a reasonable probability that population can be brought under control without such horrors.

Population growth is therefore not a reason against giving overseas aid, although it should make us think about the kind of aid to give. Instead of food handouts, it may be better to give aid that hastens the demographic transition. This may mean agricultural assistance for the rural poor, or assistance with education, or the provision of contraceptive services. Whatever kind of aid proves most effective in specific circumstances, the obligation to assist is not reduced.

One awkward question remains. What should we do about a poor and already overpopulated country which, for religious or nationalistic reasons, restricts the use of contraceptives and refuses to slow its population growth? Should we nevertheless offer development assistance? Or should we make our offer conditional on effective steps being taken to reduce the birthrate? To the latter course, some would object that putting conditions on aid is an attempt to impose our own ideas on independent sovereign nations. So it is—but is this imposition unjustifiable? If the argument for an obligation to assist is sound, we have an obligation to reduce absolute poverty; but we have no obligation to make sacrifices that, to the best of our knowledge, have no prospect of reducing poverty in the long run. Hence we have no obligation to assist countries whose governments have policies which will make our aid ineffective. This could be very harsh on poor citizens of these countries—for they may have no say in the government's policies—but

we will help more people in the long run by using our resources where they are most effective. (The same principles may apply, incidentally, to countries that refuse to take other steps that could make assistance effective—like refusing to reform systems of land holding that impose intolerable burdens on poor tenant farmers.)

Review and Discussion Questions

1. What's the difference between absolute and relative poverty? Do we have absolute poverty in the United States?

2. Describe the analogy Singer uses to develop his argument for an obligation to assist. What is the key moral premise in this argument? Is Singer's principle as uncontroversial as he thinks?

3. How large a sacrifice do you think Singer's principle would require of us? What is "of comparable moral significance" to the reduction of absolute poverty?

4. How would a libertarian respond to Singer's argument? Do you think Singer is correct in maintaining that his argument can survive, even if we accept Nozick's theory?

5. Describe triage and its relevance to Singer's position. On what grounds does Singer reject the triage argument?

6. Do you see any possible objections to Singer's argument that he has overlooked or failed to answer satisfactorily? Do you think that our obligation to assist people in other lands who are in serious distress is a matter of *justice*?

Is Inheritance Justified?

D. W. Haslett

Many people support inheritance because they believe it is essential to capitalism. After reviewing some facts about wealth distribution and inheritance in the United States today, D. W. Haslett argues against this view. He contends not only that inheritance is not essential to capitalism, but that it is inconsistent with the fundamental values that underlie capitalism— in particular, with "distribution according to productivity," "equal opportunity," and "freedom." Haslett maintains, accordingly, that the practice of inheritance, as it exists today, should be abolished.

D. W. Haslett, "Is Inheritance Justified?" *Philosophy and Public Affairs* 15 (Spring 1986). Copyright © 1986 by Princeton University Press. Reprinted by permission of Princeton University Press.

I. Background Information

Family income in the United States today is not distributed very evenly. The top fifth of American families receives 57.3 percent of all family income, while the bottom fifth receives only 7.2 percent.[1]

But, for obvious reasons, a family's financial well-being does not depend upon its income nearly as much as it does upon its wealth, just as the strength of an army does not depend upon how many people joined it during the year as much as it does upon how many people are in it altogether. So if we really want to know how unevenly economic well-being is distributed in the United States today, we must look at the distribution not of income, but of wealth.

Although — quite surprisingly — the government does not regularly collect information on the distribution of wealth, it has occasionally done so. The results are startling. One to two percent of American families own from around 20 to 30 percent of the (net) family wealth in the United States; 5 to 10 percent own from around 40 to 60 percent.[2] The top fifth owns almost 80 percent of the wealth, while the bottom fifth owns only 0.2 percent.[3] So while the top fifth has, as we saw, about eight times the income of the bottom fifth, it has about 400 times the wealth. Whether deliberately or not, by regularly gathering monumental amounts of information on the distribution of income, but not on the distribution of wealth, the government succeeds in directing attention away from how enormously unequal the distribution of wealth is, and directing it instead upon the less unequal distribution of income. But two things are clear: wealth is distributed far more unequally in the United States today than is income, and this inequality in the distribution of wealth is enormous. These are the first two things to keep in mind throughout our discussion of inheritance.

The next thing to keep in mind is that, although estate and gift taxes in the United States are supposed to redistribute wealth, and thereby lessen this inequality, they do not do so. Before 1981 estates were taxed, on an average, at a rate of only 0.2 percent — 0.8 percent for estates over $500,000 — hardly an amount sufficient to cause any significant redistribution of wealth.[4] And, incredibly, the Economic Recovery Act of 1981 *lowered* estate and gift taxes.

Of course the top rate at which estates and gifts are *allegedly* taxed is far greater than the 0.2 percent rate, on the average, at which they are *really* taxed. Prior to 1981, the top rate was 70 percent, which in 1981 was lowered to 50 percent. Because of this relatively high top rate, the average person is led to believe that estate and gift taxes succeed in breaking up the huge financial empires of the very rich, thereby distributing wealth more evenly. What the average person fails to realize is that what the government takes with one hand, through high nominal rates, it gives back with the other hand, through loopholes in the law. . . . Indeed, as George Cooper shows, estate and gift taxes can, with the help of a good attorney, be avoided so easily they amount to little more than "voluntary" taxes.[5] As such, it is not surprising that, contrary to popular opinion, these taxes do virtually nothing to reduce the vast inequality in the distribution of wealth that exists today.

Once we know that estate and gift taxes do virtually nothing to reduce this vast inequality, what I am about to say next should come as no surprise. This vast inequality in the distribution of wealth is (according to the best estimates) due at least as much to inheritance as to any other factor. Once again, because of the surprising lack of information about these matters, the extent to which this inequality is due to inheritance is not known exactly. One estimate, based upon a series of articles appearing in *Fortune* magazine, is that 50 percent of the large fortunes in the United States were derived basically from inheritance.[6] But by far the most careful and thorough study of this matter to date is that of John A. Brittain. Brittain shows that the estimate based upon the *Fortune* articles actually is too low;[7] that a more accurate estimate of the amount contributed by inheritance to the wealth of "ultra-rich" males is 67 percent.[8] In any case, it is clear that, in the United States today, inheritance plays a large role indeed in perpetuating a vastly unequal distribution of wealth. This is the final thing to keep in mind throughout the discussion which follows.

II. Inheritance and Capitalism

Capitalism (roughly speaking) is an economic system where (1) what to produce, and in what quantities, is determined essentially by supply and demand — that is, by people's "dollar votes" — rather than by central planning, and (2) capital goods are, for the most part, privately owned. In the minds of many today, capitalism goes hand in hand with the practice of inheritance; capitalism without inheritance, they would say, is absurd. But, if I am right, the exact opposite is closer to the truth. Since, as I shall try to show in this section, the practice of inheritance is incompatible with basic values or ideals that underlie capitalism, what is absurd, if anything, is capitalism *with* inheritance. . . .

I do not try to show here that the ideals underlying capitalism are worthy of support; I only try to show that inheritance is contrary to these ideals. And if it is, then from this it follows that, *if* these ideals are worthy of support (as, incidentally, I think they are), then we have prima facie reason for concluding that inheritance is unjustified. What then are these ideals? For an answer, we can do no better than turn to one of capitalism's most eloquent and uncompromising defenders: Milton Friedman.

Distribution According to Productivity

The point of any economic system is, of course, to produce goods and services. But, as Friedman tells us, society cannot very well *compel* people to be productive and, even if it could, out of respect for personal freedom, probably it should not do so. Therefore, he concludes, in order to get people to be productive, society needs instead to *entice* them to produce, and the most effective way of enticing people to produce is to distribute income and wealth according to productivity. Thus we arrive at the first ideal underlying capitalism: "To each according to what he and the instruments he owns produces."[9]

Obviously, inheritance contravenes this ideal. For certain purposes, this ideal would require further interpretation; we would need to know more about what was meant by "productivity." For our purposes, no further clarification is necessary. According to *any* reasonable interpretation of "productivity," the wealth people get through inheritance has nothing to do with their productivity. And one need not be an adherent of this ideal of distribution to be moved by the apparent injustice of one person working eight hours a day all his life at a miserable job, and accumulating nothing, while another person does little more all his life than enjoy his parents' wealth, and inherits a fortune.

Equal Opportunity

But for people to be productive it is necessary not just that they be *motivated* to be productive, but that they have the *opportunity* to be productive. This brings us to the second ideal underlying capitalism: equal opportunity — that is, equal opportunity for all to pursue, successfully, the occupation of their choice.[10] According to capitalist ethic, it is OK if, in the economic game, there are winners and losers, provided everyone has an "equal start." As Friedman puts it, the ideal of equality compatible with capitalism is not equality of outcome, which would *discourage* people from realizing their full productive potential, but equality of opportunity, which *encourages* people to do so.[11]

Naturally this ideal, like the others we are considering, neither could, nor should, be realized fully; to do so would require, among other things, no less than abolishing the family and engaging in extensive genetic engineering.[12] But the fact that this ideal cannot and should not be realized fully in no way detracts from its importance. Not only is equal opportunity itself an elementary requirement of justice but, significantly, progress in realizing this ideal could bring with it progress in at least two other crucial areas as well: those of productivity and income distribution. First, the closer we come to equal opportunity for all, the more people there will be who, as a result of increased opportunity, will come to realize their productive potential. And, of course, the more people there are who come to realize their productive potential, the greater overall productivity will be. Second, the closer we come to equal opportunity for all, the more people there will be with an excellent opportunity to become something other than an ordinary worker, to become a professional or an entrepreneur of sorts. And the more people there are with an excellent opportunity to become something other than an ordinary worker, the more people there will be who in fact become something other than an ordinary worker or, in other words, the less people there will be available for doing ordinary work. As elementary economic theory tells us, with a decrease in the supply of something comes an increase in the demand for it, and with an increase in the demand for it comes an increase in the price paid for it. An increase in the price paid for it would, in this case, mean an increase in the income of the ordinary worker vis-à-vis that of the professional and the entrepreneur, which, surely, would be a step in the direction of income being distributed more justly.

And here I mean "more justly" even according to the ideals of capitalism itself. As we have seen, the capitalist ideal of distributive justice is "to each according to his or her productivity." But, under capitalism, we can say a person's income from some occupation reflects his or her productivity only to the extent there are no unnecessary limitations upon people's opportunity to pursue, successfully, this occupation — and by "unnecessary limitations" I mean ones that either *cannot* or (because doing so would cause more harm than good) *should not* be removed. According to the law of supply and demand, the more limited the supply of people in some occupation, then (assuming a healthy demand to begin with) the higher will be the income of those pursuing the occupation. Now if the limited supply of people in some high-paying occupation . . . is the result of unnecessary limitations upon people's opportunity to pursue that occupation, then the scarcity is an "artificial" one, and the high pay can by no means be said to reflect productivity. The remedy is to remove these limitations; in other words, to increase equality of opportunity. To what extent the relative scarcity of professionals and entrepreneurs in capitalist countries today is due to natural scarcity, and to what extent to artificial scarcity, no one really knows. I strongly suspect, however, that a dramatic increase in equality of opportunity will reveal that the scarcity is far more artificial than most professionals and entrepreneurs today care to think — *far* more artificial. . . .

That inheritance violates the (crucial) second ideal of capitalism, equal opportunity, is, once again, obvious. Wealth *is* opportunity, and inheritance distributes it very unevenly indeed. Wealth is opportunity for realizing one's potential, for a career, for success, for income. There are few, if any, desirable occupations that great wealth does not, in one way or another, increase — sometimes dramatically — one's chances of being able to pursue, and to pursue successfully. And to the extent that one's success is to be measured in terms of one's income, nothing else, neither intelligence, nor education, nor skills, provides a more secure opportunity for "success" than does wealth. Say one inherits a million dollars. All one then need do is purchase long-term bonds yielding a guaranteed interest of ten percent and (presto!) one has a yearly income of

$100,000, an income far greater than anyone who toils eight hours a day in a factory will probably ever have. If working in the factory pays, relatively, so little, then why, it might be asked, do not all these workers become big-time investors themselves? The answer is that they are, their entire lives, barred from doing so by a lack of initial capital which others, through inheritance, are simply handed. With inheritance, the old adage is only too true: "The rich get richer, and the poor get poorer." Without inheritance, the vast fortunes in America today, these enormous concentrations of economic power, would be broken up, allowing wealth, and therefore opportunity, to become distributed far more evenly.

Freedom

But so far I have not mentioned what many, including no doubt Friedman himself, consider to be the most important ideal underlying capitalism: that of liberty or, in other words, freedom. This ideal, however, takes different forms. One form it takes for Friedman is that of being able to engage in economic transactions free from governmental or other types of human coercion. The rationale for this conception of freedom — let us call it freedom in the "narrow" sense — is clear. As Friedman explains it, assuming only that people are informed about what is good for them, this form of freedom guarantees that ". . . no exchange will take place unless both parties benefit from it."[13] If at least the parties themselves benefit from the transaction, and it does not harm anyone, then, it is fair to say, the transaction has been socially valuable. So people with freedom of exchange will, in doing what is in their own best interests, generally be doing what is socially valuable as well. In other words, with this form of freedom, the fabled "invisible hand" actually works.

All of this is a great oversimplification. For one thing, a transaction that benefits both parties may have side effects, such as pollution, which harm others and, therefore, the transaction may not be socially valuable after all. So freedom, in the narrow sense, should certainly not be absolute. But the fact that freedom, in this sense, should not be absolute does not prevent it from serving as a useful ideal. . . .

There are others whose conception of freedom is that of not being subject to any governmental coercion (or other forms of human coercion) for any purposes whatsoever—a conception sometimes referred to as "negative" freedom. It is true that governmental (or other) coercion for purposes of enforcing the abolition of inheritance violates this ideal, but then, of course, so does any such coercion for purposes of *maintaining* inheritance. So this "anticoercion" ideal . . . neither supports nor opposes the practice of inheritance, and therefore this conception of freedom need not concern us further here either.

A very popular variation of the anticoercion conception of freedom is one where freedom is, once again, the absence of all governmental (or other human) coercion, *except for any coercion necessary for enforcing our fundamental rights.* Prominent among our fundamental rights, most of those who espouse such a conception of freedom will tell us, is our right to property. So whether this conception of freedom supports the practice of inheritance depends entirely upon whether our "right to property" should be viewed as incorporating the practice of inheritance. But whether our right to property should be viewed as incorporating the practice of inheritance is just another way of stating the very point at issue in this investigation. . . . Consequently, this popular conception of freedom cannot be used here in support of the practice of inheritance without begging the question.

But there is still another conception of freedom espoused by many: that which we might call freedom in the "broad" sense. According to this conception of freedom, to be free means to have the ability, or the opportunity, to do what one wants. For example, according to this conception of freedom, rich people are, other things being equal, freer than poor people, since their wealth provides them with opportunities to do things that the poor can only dream about. . . .

Let us now see whether inheritance and freedom are inconsistent. Consider, first, freedom in the narrow sense. Although inheritance may not be inconsistent with this ideal, neither is the *abolishment* of inheritance. This ideal forbids governmental interference with free exchanges between people; it does not necessarily forbid governmental interference with *gifts* or *bequests* (which, of course, are not *exchanges*). Remember, Friedman's rationale for this ideal is, as we saw, that free exchange promotes the "invisible hand"; that is, it promotes the healthy functioning of supply and demand, which is at the very heart of capitalism. Supply and demand hardly require gifts, as opposed to exchanges, in order to function well.

If anything, gifts and bequests, and the enormous concentrations of economic power resulting from them, hinder the healthy functioning of supply and demand. First of all, gifts and bequests, and the enormous concentrations of economic power resulting from them, create such great differences in people's "dollar votes" that the economy's demand curves do not accurately reflect the needs of the population as a whole, but are distorted in favor of the "votes" of the rich. And inheritance hinders the healthy functioning of supply and demand even more, perhaps, by interfering with supply. As we have seen, inheritance (which, as I am using the term, encompasses large gifts) is responsible for some starting out in life with a vast advantage over others; it is, in other words, a major source of unequal opportunity. As we have also seen, the further we are from equal opportunity, the less people there will be who come to realize their productive potential. And, of course, the less people there are who come to realize their productive potential, the less overall productivity there will be or, in other words, the less healthy will be the economy's *supply* curves. So, while inheritance may not be *literally* inconsistent with freedom in the narrow sense, it does, by hindering indirectly both supply and demand, appear to be inconsistent with the "spirit" of this ideal. . . .

So we may conclude that, at best, inheritance receives no support from freedom in the narrow sense. But it remains for us to consider whether inheritance receives any support from the other relevant ideal of freedom, an ideal many, including myself, would consider to be the more fundamental of the two: freedom in the broad sense—being able to do, or having the opportunity to do, what one wants. So we must now ask whether, everything considered, there is more overall opportunity throughout the country for people to do what they want with inheritance, or without it.

On the one hand, without inheritance people are no longer free to leave their fortunes to whomever they want and, of course, those who otherwise would have received these fortunes are, without them, less free to do what they want also.

But to offset these losses in freedom are at least the following gains in freedom. First, as is well known, wealth has, generally speaking, a diminishing marginal utility. What this means is that, generally speaking, the more wealth one already has, the less urgent are the needs which any given increment of wealth will go to satisfy and, therefore, the less utility the additional wealth will have for one. This, in turn, means that the more evenly wealth is distributed, the more overall utility it will have.[14] And since we may assume that, generally speaking, the more utility some amount of wealth has for someone, the more freedom in the broad sense it allows that person to enjoy, we may conclude that the more evenly wealth is distributed, the more overall freedom to which it will give rise. Now assuming that abolishing inheritance would not lessen *overall* wealth . . . and that it would indeed distribute wealth more evenly, it follows that, by abolishing inheritance, there would be some gain in freedom in the broad sense attributable to the diminishing marginal utility of wealth. Next, abolishing inheritance would also increase freedom by increasing equality of opportunity. Certainly those who do not start life having inherited significant funds (through either gift or bequest) start life, relative to those who do, with what amounts to a significant handicap. Abolishing inheritance, and thereby starting everyone at a more equal level, would obviously leave those who otherwise would have suffered this handicap (which would be the great majority of people) more free in the broad sense.

I, for one, believe these gains in freedom — that is, those attributable to the diminishing marginal utility of wealth and more equality of opportunity — would *more* than offset the loss in freedom resulting from the inability to give one's fortune to whom one wants. Abolishing inheritance is, I suggest, analogous to abolishing discrimination against blacks in restaurants and other commercial establishments. By abolishing discrimination, the owners of these establishments lose the freedom to choose the skin color of the people they do business with, but the gain in freedom for blacks is obviously greater and more significant than this loss. Likewise, by abolishing inheritance the gain in freedom for the poor is greater and more significant than the loss in freedom for the rich. So to the list of ideals that inheritance is inconsistent with, we can, if I am right, add freedom in the broad sense.

To recapitulate: three ideals that underlie capitalism are "distribution according to productivity," "equal opportunity," and "freedom," the latter being, for our purposes, subject to either a narrow or a broad interpretation. I do not claim these are the *only* ideals that may be said to underlie capitalism; I do claim, however, that they are among the most important. Inheritance is inconsistent with both "distribution according to productivity," and "equal opportunity." Perhaps it is not, strictly speaking, inconsistent with the ideal of freedom in the narrow sense, but neither is the abolishment of inheritance. On the other hand, it probably *is* inconsistent with what many would take to be the more fundamental of the two relevant ideals of freedom: freedom in the broad sense. Since these are among the most important ideals that underlie capitalism, I conclude that inheritance not only is not essential to capitalism, but is probably inconsistent with it. . . .

[III. A Proposal for Abolishing Inheritance]

First, my proposal for abolishing inheritance includes the abolishment of all large gifts as well — gifts of the sort, that is, which might serve as alternatives to bequests. Obviously, if such gifts were not abolished as well, any law abolishing inheritance could be avoided all too easily.

Of course we would not want to abolish along with these large gifts such harmless gifts as ordinary birthday and Christmas presents. This, however, raises the problem of where to draw the line. I do not know the best solution to this problem. The amount that current law allows a person to give each year tax free ($10,000) is too large a figure at which to draw the line for purposes of a law abolishing inheritance. We might experiment with drawing the line, in part at least, by means of the distinction between, on the one hand, consumer goods that can be expected to be, within ten years, either consumed or worth less than half their current value and, on the other hand, all other goods. We can be more lenient in allowing gifts of goods falling within the former category since, as they are consumed or quickly lose their value, they cannot, themselves, become part of a large, unearned fortune. The same can be said about gifts of services. But we need not pursue these technicalities further here. The general point is simply that, so as to avoid an obvious loophole, gifts (other than ordinary birthday presents, etc.) are to be abolished along with bequests.

Next, according to my proposal, a person's estate would pass to the government, to be used for the general welfare. If, however, the government were to take over people's property upon their death then, obviously, after just a few generations the government would own virtually everything — which would certainly not be very compatible with capitalism. Since this proposal for abolishing inheritance *is* supposed to be compatible with capitalism, it must therefore include a requirement that the government sell on the open market, to the highest bidder, any real property, including any shares in a corporation, that it receives from anyone's estate, and that it do so within a certain period of time, within, say, one year from the decedent's death. This requirement is, however, to be subject to one qualification: any person specified by the decedent in his will shall be given a chance to *buy* any property specified by the decedent in his will before it is put on the market (a qualification designed to alleviate slightly the family heirloom/business/farm problem discussed below). The price to be paid by this person shall be whatever the property is worth (as determined by governmental appraisers, subject to appeal) and any credit terms shall be rather lenient (perhaps 10 percent down, with the balance, plus interest, due over the next 30 years).

Finally, the abolishment of inheritance proposed here is to be subject to three important exceptions. First, there shall be no limitations at all upon the amount a person can leave to his or her spouse. A marriage, it seems to me, should be viewed as a joint venture in which both members, whether or not one stays home tending to children while the other earns money, have an *equally* important role to play; and neither, therefore, should be deprived of enjoying fully any of the material rewards of this venture by having them taken away at the spouse's death. And unlimited inheritance between spouses eliminates one serious objection to abolishing inheritance: namely, that it is not right for a person suddenly to be deprived, not only of his or her spouse, but also of most of the wealth upon which he or she has come to depend — especially in those cases where the spouse has, for the sake of the marriage, given up, once and for all, any realistic prospects of a career.

The second exception to be built into this proposal is one for children who are orphaned, and any other people who have been genuinely dependent upon the decedent, such as any who are mentally incompetent, or too elderly to have any significant earning power of their own. A person shall be able to leave funds (perhaps in the form of a trust) sufficient to take care of such dependents. These funds should be used only for the dependent's living expenses, which would include any educational or institutional expenses no matter how much. They should not, of course, be used to provide children with a "nest egg" of the sort others are prohibited from leaving their children. And at a certain age, say twenty-one (if the child's formal education has been completed), or upon removal of whatever disability has caused dependency, the funds should cease. This exception eliminates another objection to abolishing inheritance — the objection that it would leave orphaned children, and other dependents, without the support they needed.

The third and final exception to be built into this proposal is one for charitable organizations — ones created not for purposes of making a profit, but for charitable, religious, scientific, or educational purposes. And, in order to prevent these organizations from eventually controlling the economy, they must, generally, be under the same constraint as is the government with respect to any real property they are given, such as an operating factory: they must, generally, sell it on the open market within a year. . . .

[IV. An Objection]

We turn next to what is, I suppose, the most common objection to abolishing inheritance: the objection that, if people were not allowed to leave their wealth to their children, they would lose their incentive to continue working hard, and national productivity would therefore fall. In spite of the popularity of this objection, all the available evidence seems to indicate the contrary. For example, people who do not intend to have children, and therefore are obviously not motivated by the desire to leave their children a fortune, do not seem to work any less hard than anyone else. And evidence of a more technical nature leads to the same conclusion: people, typically, do not need to be motivated by a desire to leave their children (or someone else) great wealth in order to be motivated to work hard.[15]

Common sense tells us the same thing. The prospect of being able to leave one's fortune to one's children is, no doubt, for some people one factor motivating them to be productive. But even for these people, this is only *one* factor; there are usually other factors motivating them as well, and motivating them to such an extent that, even if inheritance were abolished, their productivity would be unaffected. Take, for example, professional athletes. If inheritance were abolished, would they try any less hard to win? I doubt it. For one thing, abolishing inheritance would not, in any way, affect the amount of money they would be able to earn for use during their lives. So they would still have the prospect of a large income to motivate them. But there is something else which motivates them to do their best that is, I think, even more important, and is not dependent on money: the desire to win or, in other words, to achieve that which entitles them to the respect of their colleagues, the general public, and themselves. Because of the desire to win, amateur athletes compete just as fiercely as professionals. Abolishing inheritance would in no way affect this reason for doing one's best either. Athletes would still have the prospect of winning to motivate them. Businessmen, doctors, lawyers, engineers, artists, researchers — in general, those who contribute most to society — are not, with respect to what in the most general sense motivates them, really very different from professional athletes. Without inheritance, these people would still be motivated by the prospect of a sizable income for themselves and, probably even more so, by the prospect of "winning"; that is, by the prospect of achieving, or continuing to achieve, that which entitles them to the respect of their colleagues, the general public, and themselves.

Notes

1. Lester C. Thurow, "Tax Wealth, Not Income," *New York Times Magazine*, 11 April 1976, p. 33. . . .

2. The latest governmental study of the distribution of wealth, carried out in 1983, estimates the amount of net wealth held by the top 2 percent to be 28 percent, and that held by the top 10 percent to be 57 percent. R. Avery, G. Elliehausen, G. Canner, and T. Gustafson, "Survey of Consumer Finances, 1983: Second Report," *Federal Reserve Bulletin* 70 (December 1984): 865. These estimates "account for all financial assets, and equity in homes and other real property as well as consumer credit and other debts. [They] exclude the value of consumer durables such as automobiles and home furnishings, the cash value of life insurance, equity in small businesses and farms, and the present value of expected future benefits from pensions or social security" (p. 861). . . .

3. Thurow, "Tax Wealth, Not Income," p. 33.

4. Lester C. Thurow, *The Impact of Taxes on the American Economy* (New York: Praeger Publishers, 1971), p. 127.

5. George A. Cooper, *A Voluntary Tax? New Perspectives on Sophisticated Estate Tax Avoidance* (Washington, D.C.: Brookings Institution, 1979).

6. Richard A. Smith, "The Fifty-Million Dollar Man," *Fortune* (November 1957); Arthur M. Louis, "America's Centimillionaires," *Fortune* (May 1968); and Arthur M. Louis, "The New Rich of the Seventies," *Fortune* (September 1973).

7. John A. Brittain, *Inheritance and the Inequality of National Wealth* (Washington, D.C.: Brookings Institution, 1978), pp. 14–16.

8. Ibid., p. 99.

9. Milton Friedman, *Capitalism & Freedom* (Chicago: University of Chicago Press, 1962), pp. 161–162.

10. For a useful analysis of the concept of "equal opportunity," see Douglas Rae, *Equalities* (Cambridge, Mass.: Harvard University Press, 1981), ch. 4. . . .

11. Milton & Rose Friedman, *Freedom to Choose* (New York: Harcourt Brace Jovanovich, 1979), pp. 131–140. . . .

12. See, for example, Bernard Williams, "The Idea of Equality," *Philosophy, Politics and Society*, ser. 2, edited by Peter Laslett and W. G. Runciman (Oxford: Basil Blackwell, 1962).

13. Friedman, *Capitalism & Freedom*, p. 13.

14. The more evenly wealth is distributed, the more overall utility it will have since any wealth that "goes" from the rich to the poor, thereby making the distribution more even, will (given the diminishing marginal utility of wealth) have more utility for these poor than it would have had for the rich, thus increasing overall utility.

15. See, for example, D. C. McClelland, *The Achieving Society* (Princeton: Van Nostrand, 1961), pp. 234–235; and Seymour Fiekowsky, *On the Economic Effects of Death Taxation in the United States* (unpublished doctoral dissertation, Harvard University, 1959), pp. 370–371.

Review and Discussion Questions

1. Has Haslett correctly identified the fundamental ideals underlying capitalism? Would you

agree that inheritance is contrary to capitalism's fundamental values?

2. Distinguish freedom in the narrow sense from freedom in the broad sense. Which is the more useful concept? What are the implications of freedom (in both senses) for inheritance?

3. How would a utilitarian, a libertarian, and a Rawlsian evaluate inheritance?

4. How feasible do you find Haslett's proposal for abolishing inheritance? Would it be just?

For Further Reading

John Arthur and **William H. Shaw,** eds., *Justice and Economic Distribution*, 2nd ed. (Englewood Cliffs, N.J.: Prentice-Hall, 1991) contains substantial extracts from Rawls's *A Theory of Justice* and Nozick's *Anarchy, State, and Utopia*, contemporary presentations of the utilitarian approach, and various recent essays discussing the topic of economic justice.

Joel Feinberg, *Social Philosophy* (Englewood Cliffs, N.J.: Prentice-Hall, 1973), Chapter 7, discusses the different types of justice and injustice.

Will Kymlicka, *Contemporary Political Philosophy* (Oxford: Oxford University Press, 1990) covers the major schools of contemporary political thought and their competing views of justice and community.

Philip Pettit, *Judging Justice* (London: Routledge & Kegan Paul, 1980) presents a useful account of the major rival theories of justice.

Robert M. Stewart, ed., *Readings in Social and Political Philosophy* (New York: Oxford University Press, 1986), Part III, provides a number of important essays on justice and equality, including contributions from Rawls and Nozick.

PART II

AMERICAN BUSINESS AND ITS BASIS □□

CHAPTER 4

THE NATURE OF CAPITALISM □□□

The floor of the New York Stock Exchange, the heart of American capitalism, is a noisy and often chaotic place. Now, suddenly, it was becoming eerily quiet, as if someone had turned down the volume on a television set. The hustle and bustle of traders, brokers, and clerks scurrying across the massive floor practically ceased. All eyes were glued to the computer screens hanging above the floor's seventeen trading kiosks, some of which were suddenly and inexplicably going blank. It was Monday morning, October 19, 1987, and those on the stock market floor were witnessing the beginning of what was to be called the "panic of '87," the "market meltdown," or simply "black Monday."[1]

From 10:30 A.M. until 12:30 P.M., the Dow Jones industrial average fell as fast as anyone ever thought it could. Down 50 points in fifteen minutes. Down 100 in forty-five minutes. Down 167 in an hour. Down 200 in an hour and a half. A few traders left, unable to watch. "Holy sh———," someone said softly, "I just lost a million." "There was absolute terror," reported one broker, "things were collapsing all around you." Others simply described it as a "bloodbath." It was like "looking into the abyss," said Michael Starkman, a stockbroker for thirty years, as he recalled watching the plunging figures flicker across the Quotron machine in his Beverly Hills office.

By the end of the day stocks had lost almost a quarter of their value, twice as much as

in the famous crash of October 1929, which had helped pave the way for the Great Depression. The loss of market value of U.S. securities was staggering. An incredible $500 billion blown in a single day. How did it happen? What did it mean? In the aftermath, experts debated the causes of the crash and its likely economic repercussions. Lots of opinions were aired, but nobody seemed to agree. One thing was clear, though. Wall Street's bust had quickly reverberated around the globe, with stocks tumbling in markets as far away as London, Tokyo, Australia, and Hong Kong.

That is not surprising. Capitalism is a worldwide system. Multinational firms operate without regard for traditional political boundaries, and the economies of capitalist nations are intricately interconnected. But what exactly is the nature of the economic system called capitalism? What is its underlying economic philosophy? What has it accomplished and what are its prospects for the future? This chapter examines these and related questions.

Looking back in history, one must definitely credit capitalism with helping to break the constraints of medieval feudalism, which had severely limited individual possibilities for improvement. In place of a stifling economic system, capitalism offered opportunities for those blessed with imagination, an ability to plan, and a willingness to work. In short, capitalism increased the possibilities for individualism and, many would argue, continues to do so.

Capitalism must also be credited with enhancing the numbers and diversity of goods beyond Adam Smith's wildest dreams. It has increased our ownership of material goods and our standard of living and has converted our cities from modest bazaars into treasure troves of dazzling merchandise.

In the light of such accomplishments and the acculturation process that tends to glorify them, it is possible to overlook capitalism's theoretical and operational problems, which have serious moral import. This chapter attempts to identify some of these problems and their moral implications. It provides some basic historical and conceptual categories for understanding the socioeconomic framework within which business transactions occur and moral issues arise. In particular, this chapter addresses the following topics:

1. The definition of capitalism and its major historical stages

2. Four of the key features of capitalism: companies, profit motive, competition, and private property

3. Two classical moral justifications of capitalism—first, in terms of the right to property, and second, by means of the "invisible hand" of Adam Smith

4. Fundamental criticisms of capitalism—in particular, the persistence of inequality and poverty, capitalism's implicit view of human nature, the rise of economic oligarchies, the decline of price competition, and the employee's experience of alienation and exploitation on the job

5. The problem of stagnating productivity and lack of competitiveness that American capitalism faces today—in particular the fixation on short-term performance, the declining interest in the actual manufacturing of goods, and our changing attitudes toward work

CAPITALISM

Capitalism can be defined ideally as an economic system in which the major portion of production and distribution is in private hands, operating under what is termed a profit or market system. The U.S. economy is the world's leading capitalistic economy. All manufacturing firms are privately owned, including those that produce military hardware for the government. The same applies to banks, insurance companies, and most transportation companies. All businesses—small, medium, and large—are also privately owned, as are power companies. With the exception of government expenditures for such things as health, education, welfare, highways, and military equipment, no central governing body dictates to these private owners what or how much of anything will be produced. For example, officials at Ford, Chrysler, and General Motors set their own production goals according to anticipated consumer demand.

The private ownership and market aspects of capitalism contrast with its polar opposite, socialism. Ideally, *socialism* is an economic system characterized by public ownership of property and a planned economy. Under socialism, a society's equipment is not owned by individuals (capitalists) but by public bodies. Socialism depends primarily on centralized planning rather than on the market system for both its overall allocation of resources and its distribution of income; crucial economic decisions are made not by individuals but by government. In the Soviet Union, for example, government agencies traditionally decided the number of automobiles—including models, styles, and colors—to be produced each year. Top levels of government formulated production and cost objectives, which were then converted to specific production quotas and budgets that individual plant managers had to follow.

A hybrid economic system, advocated by some socialists and approximated by Yugoslavia, is *worker control socialism*.[2] Individual firms respond to a market in acquiring the necessary factors of production and in deciding what to produce. The work force of each enterprise controls the enterprise (although it may elect or hire managers to oversee day-to-day operations), and the profits accrue to the workers as a group to divide in whatever manner they agree upon. But although the workers manage their factories, the capital assets of each enterprise are owned by society as a whole and not by private individuals.

Historical Background of Capitalism

What we call capitalism did not fully emerge until the Renaissance in Europe during the fifteenth and sixteenth centuries. Before the Renaissance, business exchanges in medieval Europe were organized through guilds, which were associations of persons of the same trade, pursuit, or interests. People joined guilds for much the same reasons they have always joined clubs, groups, and organizations: for self-protection, mutual aid, maintenance of standards, furtherance of common goals.

Today if you want a pair of shoes, you head for a shoe store. There you find an array of shoes. If nothing strikes your fancy, you set out for another shop, and perhaps another, until at last you find what you want. Or still disappointed, you might tell the store clerk to order you a pair from "the manufacturer." You certainly wouldn't tell the clerk to have someone make you a pair of shoes.

Under the guild organization, shoemakers, who were also shoe sellers, made shoes only to fill orders. If they had no orders, they made no shoes. The shoemaker's sole economic function was to make shoes for people when they wanted them. His labor allowed him to maintain himself, not advance his station in life. When the shoemaker died, his business went with him—unless he had a son to inherit and carry on the enterprise. As for shoe quality and cost, the medieval shopper could

generally count on getting a good pair of shoes at a fair price, since the cobblers' guild strictly controlled quality and price.

Weaving was another big medieval trade. In fact, in the fourteenth century weaving was the leading industry in the German town of Augsburg. Little wonder, then, that an enterprising young man named Anton Fugger became a weaver when he settled there in 1380. But young Anton had ambitions that stretched far beyond the limits of the weaving trade and the handicraft guild system. And they were grandly realized, for within three short generations a family of simple weavers was transformed into a great German banking dynasty.[3]

Discontent with being a weaver, Anton Fugger began collecting and selling the products of other weavers. Soon he was employing lots of weavers, paying them for their labor, and selling their products as his own. His son, Jacob Fugger I, continued the business, which was expanded by Jacob Fugger II, the foremost capitalist of the Renaissance. Under his direction, the family's interests expanded into metals and textiles. Jacob Fugger II also lent large sums of money to the Hapsburg emperors to finance their wars, among other things. In return, he obtained monopoly rights on silver and copper ores, which he then traded. When Fugger bought the mines themselves, he had acquired all the props necessary to erect an extraordinary financial dynasty.

Like latter-day titans of American industry, Fugger employed thousands of workers and paid them wages, controlled all his products from raw material to market, set his own quality standards, and charged whatever the traffic would bear. In one brief century, what was once a handicraft inseparable from the craftsperson had become a company that existed outside any family members. What had once motivated Anton Fugger—maintenance of his station in life—had given way to gain for gain's sake, the so-called *profit motive*. Under Jacob Fugger II, the company amassed profits, a novel concept, that well exceeded the needs of the Fuggers. And the profits were measured not in goods or in land but in money.

Capitalism has undergone changes since then.[4] For example, the kind of capitalism that emerged in the Fuggers' time is often termed *mercantile capitalism*, which was based on mutual dependence between state and commercial interests. Implicit in mercantile capitalism are the beliefs that national wealth and power are best served by increasing exports and collecting precious metals in return and that the role of government is to provide laws and economic policies designed to encourage production for foreign trade, keep out imports, and promote national supremacy.

In America in the period after the Civil War, *industrial capitalism* emerged, which is associated with the development of large-scale industry. The confluence of many postwar factors produced industrial expansion in America, including a sound financial base, the technology for mass production, expanding markets for cheaply manufactured goods, and a large and willing labor force. Exploiting these fortuitous conditions was a group of hard-driving, visionary entrepreneurs called robber barons by their critics and captains of industry by their supporters: Cornelius Vanderbilt, Cyrus McCormick, Andrew Carnegie, John D. Rockefeller, John Gates, and others.

As industrialization increased, so did the size and power of business. The private fortunes of a few individuals could no longer underwrite the accelerated growth of business activity. The large sums of capital necessary could be raised only through a corporate form of business, in which risk and potential profit were distributed among numerous investors.

As competition intensified, an industry's survival came to depend on its financial strength to reduce prices and either eliminate or absorb competition. To shore up their assets, industries engaged in *financial capitalism*, characterized by pools, trusts, holding companies, and an interpenetration of banking, insurance, and industrial interests. Hand in hand with this development, the trend continued toward larger and larger corporations, controlling more and more of the country's economic capacity.

The economic and political challenges of the Great Depression of the 1930s helped to usher in still another phase of capitalism, often called *state welfare capitalism*, in which government plays an active role in regulating economic activities in an effort to smooth out the boom-and-bust pattern of the business cycle. In addition, government programs like Social Security and unemployment insurance seek to enhance the welfare of the work force, and legislation legitimizes the existence of trade unions. Today state welfare capitalism prevails. Conservative politicians sometimes advocate less government control of business, but in reality the governments of all capitalist countries are deeply involved in the management of their economies.

While the study of capitalism's evolution is best left to economic historians, it is important to keep in mind capitalism's dynamic nature. There is nothing fixed and immutable about this or any other economic system; it is as susceptible to the social forces of change as any other institution. Nevertheless, the capitalism we know does have some prominent features that were evident in the earliest capitalistic businesses.

KEY FEATURES OF CAPITALISM

Complete coverage of capitalism's features has filled many a book. Four features of particular significance here—the existence of companies, profit motive, competition, and private property—should be discussed briefly.

Companies

Chapter 2 mentioned the Firestone case, in which a media misrepresentation was left uncorrected. When asked why Firestone officials had not corrected the error, a Firestone spokesperson said that Firestone's policy was to ask for corrections only when it was beneficial to the company to do so. Expressions like "Firestone's policy" and "beneficial to the company" reflect one key feature of capitalism: the existence of companies separate from the human beings who work for and within them.

"It's not in the company's interests," "The company thinks that," "From the company's viewpoint," "As far as the company is concerned" — all of us have heard, perhaps even used, expressions that treat the business organization like a person or at least like a separate and distinct entity. Such personifications are not mere lapses into the figurative but bespeak a basic characteristic of capitalism: Capitalism permits the creation of companies or business organizations that exist separately from the people associated with them.

Today the big companies we're familiar with — Exxon, AT&T, Ford, IBM — are, in fact, incorporated businesses, or corporations. The next chapter inspects the nature of the modern corporation, including its historical evolution and its social responsibilities. Here it's enough to observe that, in the nineteenth century, Chief Justice John Marshall defined a *corporation* as "an artificial being, invisible, intangible, and existing only in the contemplation of law." Although a corporation is not something that can be seen or touched, it does have prescribed rights and legal obligations within the community. Like you or me, a corporation may enter into contracts and may sue or be sued in courts of law. It may even do things that the corporation's members disapprove of. The corporations that loom large on our economic landscape harken back to a feature of capitalism evident as early as the Fugger dynasty: the existence of the company.

Profit Motive

A second characteristic of capitalism lies in the motive of the company: to make profit. As dollar-directed and gain-motivated as our society is, most of us take for granted that the human being is by nature an acquisitive creature who, left to his or her own devices, will pursue profit with all the instinctual vigor of a cat chasing a mouse. In fact, as economist Robert Heilbroner points out, the "profit motive, as we understand it, is a very recent phenomenon. It was foreign to the lower and middle classes of Egyptian, Greek, Roman, and medieval cultures, only scattered throughout the Renaissance times, and largely absent in most Eastern civilizations." The medieval Church taught that no Christian ought to be a merchant. "Even to our Pilgrim forefathers," Heilbroner writes, "the idea that gain ought to be a tolerable — even a useful — goal in life would have appeared as nothing short of a doctrine of the devil." Heilbroner concludes: "As a ubiquitous characteristic of society, the profit motive is as modern an invention as printing."[5]

Modern or not, *profit* in the form of money is the lifeblood of the capitalist system. Companies and capitalists alike are motivated by an insatiable appetite for more and more money profit. Indeed, the profit motive implies and reflects a critical assumption about human nature: that human beings are basically economic creatures, who recognize and are motivated by their own economic self-interests.

Competition

If self-interest and an appetite for money profit drive individuals and companies, then what stops them short of holding up society for exorbitant ransom? What stops capitalists from bleeding society dry?

Adam Smith provided an answer in his monumental treatise on commercial capitalism, *An Inquiry into the Nature and Causes of the Wealth of Nations* (1776). Free competition, said Smith, is the regulator that keeps a community activated only by self-interest from degenerating into a mob of ruthless profiteers. When traditional restraints are removed from the sale of goods and from wages, when all individuals have equal access to raw materials and markets (the doctrine of *laissez-faire*, from the French meaning "leave alone"), all of us are free to pursue our own interests. In pursuing our own interests, however, we come smack up against others similarly motivated. If any of us allows blind self-interest to dictate our actions — for example, by price gouging or employee exploitation — we will quickly find ourselves beaten out by a competitor who, let's say, charges less and pays a better wage. Competition thus regulates individual economic activity.

To sample the flavor of Smith's argument, imagine an acquisitive young woman who wants to pile up as much wealth as possible. She looks about her and sees that people need and want strong, twilled cotton trousers. So she takes her investment capital and sets up a jeans factory. She charges $45 for a pair and soon realizes handsome profits. The woman's success is not lost on other business minds, especially manufacturers of formal slacks and dresses, who observe a sharp decline in those markets. Wanting a piece of the jeans action, numerous enterprises start up jeans factories. Many of these start selling jeans for $40 a pair. No longer alone in the market, our hypothetical businesswoman must either check her appetite for profit by lowering her price or risk folding. As the number of jeans on the market increases, their supply eventually overtakes demand, and the price of jeans declines further and further. Inefficient manufacturers start dropping like flies. As the competition thins out, the demand for jeans slowly catches up with the supply, and the price regulates itself. Ultimately, a balance is reached between supply and demand, and the price of jeans stabilizes, yielding a normal profit to the efficient producer.

In much this way, Adam Smith tried to explain how economic competition steers individuals pursuing self-interest in a socially beneficial direction. By appealing to their self-interest, society can induce producers to pro-

vide it with what it wants — just as manufacturers of formal slacks and dresses were enticed into jeans production. But competition keeps prices for desired goods from escalating. High prices are self-correcting, because they call forth an increased supply.

Private Property

In its discussion of the libertarian theory of justice, the previous chapter emphasized that "property" should not be identified only with physical objects like houses, cars, and video recorders. Nor should "ownership" be thought of as a simple relationship between the owner and the thing owned. First, one can have property rights over things that are not simple physical objects, as when one owns stock in a company. Second, property ownership involves a generally complex bundle of rights and rules governing how, under what circumstances, and in what ways both the "owner" and others can use, possess, dispose of, and have access to the thing in question.

Private property is central to capitalism. To put it another way, capitalism as a socioeconomic system is a specific form of private property. What matters for capitalism is not private property simply in the sense of personal possessions, because a socialist society can certainly permit people to own houses, television sets, and jogging shoes. Rather capitalism requires private ownership of the major means of production and distribution. The means of production and distribution include factories, warehouses, offices, machines, computer networks, trucking fleets, agricultural land, and whatever else makes up the economic resources of a nation. Under capitalism, private hands control these basic economic assets and productive resources. Thus, the major economic decisions are made by individuals or groups acting on their own in pursuit of profit. These decisions are not directly coordinated with those of other producers, nor are they the result of some overall plan. Any profits (or losses) that result from these decisions about production are those of the owners.

Capital, as an economic concept, is closely related to private property. Putting it simply, capital is money that is invested for the purpose of making more money. Individuals or corporations purchase various means of production or other related assets and use them to produce goods or provide services, which are then sold. They do this not for the purpose of being nice or of helping people out but rather in order to make money—more money, hopefully, than they spent to make the goods or provide the services in the first place. Using money to make money is at the heart of the definition of capitalism.

MORAL JUSTIFICATIONS OF CAPITALISM

People tend to take for granted the desirability and moral legitimacy of the political and economic system within which they live. Americans are no exception. We are raised in a society that encourages individual competition, praises capitalism, promotes the acquisition of material goods, and worships economic wealth. Newspapers, television, records, movies, and other forms of popular culture celebrate these values, and rarely are we presented with fundamental criticisms of or possible alternatives to our socioeconomic order. Small wonder, then, that most of us blithely assume, without ever bothering to question, that our capitalist economic system is a morally justifiable one.

Yet as thinking people and moral agents, it is important that we reflect on the nature and justifiability of our social institutions. The proposition that capitalism is a morally acceptable system is very much open to debate. Whether or not we decide that capitalism is morally justified will depend, at least in part, on which general theory of justice turns out to be the soundest. Chapter 3 explored in detail

the utilitarian approach, the libertarian alternative, and the theory of John Rawls. Now, against that background, this chapter looks at two basic ways defenders of capitalism have sought to justify their system: first, the argument that the moral right to property guarantees the legitimacy of capitalism and, second, the utilitarian-based economic argument of Adam Smith. The chapter then considers some criticisms of capitalism.

The Natural Right to Property

As Americans, we live in a socioeconomic system that guarantees us certain property rights. Although we are no longer permitted to own other people, we are certainly free to own a variety of other things, from livestock to stock certificates, from our own homes to whole blocks of apartment buildings. A common defense of capitalism is the argument that people have a fundamental moral right to property and that our capitalist system is simply the outcome of this natural right.

In Chapter 3, you saw how Locke attempted to base the right to property in human labor. When individuals mix their labor with the natural world, they are entitled to the results. And this idea seems plausible in many cases. For example, if Carl diligently harvests coconuts on the island he shares with Adam, while Adam himself idles away his days, then most of us would agree that Carl has an entitlement to those coconuts that Adam lacks. But property ownership as it actually exists in the real world today is a very complex, socially shaped phenomenon. This is especially true in the case of sophisticated forms of corporate and financial property—for example, bonds or stock options.

One could, of course, reject the whole idea of a natural right to property as a fiction, as, for example, utilitarians do. In their view, although various property systems exist, there is no natural right that things be owned privately, collectively, or in any particular way whatsoever. The moral task is to find that property system, that way of organizing production and distribution, with the greatest utility. Yet even if one believes that there is a natural right to property, at least under some circumstances, one need not believe that this right leads to capitalism or that it is a right to have a system of property rules and regulations just like the one we now have in the United States. That is, even if Carl has a natural right to his coconuts, there may still be moral limits on how many coconuts he can rightfully amass and what he can use them for. When he takes his coconuts to the coconut bank and receives further coconuts as interest, his newly acquired coconuts are not the result of any new labor on his part. When we look at capitalistic property — that is, at socioeconomic environments in which people profit from ownership alone — then we have left Locke's world far behind.

A defender of capitalism may reply, "Certainly, there's nothing unfair about Carl's accruing these extra coconuts through his investment; after all, he could have eaten his original coconuts instead." And, indeed, within our system this reasoning seems perfectly correct. It is the way things work in our society. But this fact doesn't prove that Carl has some natural right to use his coconuts to make more coconuts — that is, that it would be unfair or unjust to set up a different economic system (for example, one in which he had a right to consume his coconuts but no right to use them to earn more coconuts). The argument here is simply that the issue is not an all-or-nothing one. There may be certain fundamental moral rights to property, without those rights being unlimited and without them guaranteeing capitalism as we know it.

The Invisible Hand of Adam Smith

Relying on the idea of a natural right to property is not the only way and probably not the best way to defend capitalism. Another,

very important argument defends capitalism in terms of the many economic benefits the system brings, claiming that a free and unrestrained market system, which exists under capitalism, is more efficient and more productive than any other possible system and is thus to be preferred on moral grounds. Essentially, this is a utilitarian argument, but one doesn't have to be a utilitarian to take it seriously. As mentioned in Chapter 2, almost every normative theory puts some moral weight on the consequences of actions. Thus if capitalism does indeed work better than other ways of organizing economic life, then this will be a very relevant moral fact — one that will be important, for instance, for Rawlsians.

This section sketches Adam Smith's economic case for capitalism, as presented in *The Wealth of Nations*. Smith argues that when people are left to pursue their own interests, they will, without intending it, produce the greatest good for all. Each person's individual and private pursuit of wealth results — as if, in Smith's famous phrase, "an invisible hand" were at work — in the most beneficial overall organization and distribution of economic resources. Although the academic study of economics has developed greatly since Smith's times, his classic arguments remain extraordinarily influential.

Smith took it for granted that human beings are acquisitive creatures. Self-interest and personal advantage, specifically in an economic sense, may not be all that motivate people, but they do seem to motivate most people much of the time. At any rate, they are powerful enough forces that any successful economic system must strive to harness them. We are, Smith thought, strongly inclined to act so as to acquire more and more wealth.

In addition, humans have a natural propensity for trading — "to truck, barter, and exchange." Unlike other species, we have an almost constant need for the assistance of others. Yet being creatures of self-interest, it is folly for us to expect others to act benevolently toward us. We can secure what we need from others only by offering them something they need from us:

> Whoever offers to another a bargain of any kind, proposes to do this. Give me that which I want, and you shall have this which you want, is the meaning of every such offer; and it is in this manner that we obtain from one another the far greater part of those good offices which we stand in need of. It is not from the benevolence of the butcher, the brewer, or the baker that we expect our dinner, but from their regard to their own interest. We address ourselves, not to their humanity but to their self love, and never talk to them of our own necessities but of their advantages.[6]

This disposition to trade, said Smith, gives occasion to the division of labor—dividing the labor and production process into areas of specialization, which is the prime means of increasing economic productivity.

Thus, Smith was led to claim that the greatest utility will result from unfettered pursuit of self-interest. Individuals should be allowed unrestricted access to raw materials, markets, and labor. Government interference in private enterprise should be eliminated, free competition encouraged, and economic self-interest made the rule of the day. Because human beings are acquisitive creatures, we will, if left free, engage in labor and exchange goods in a way that results in the greatest benefit to society. In our efforts to advance our own economic interests, we inevitably act so as to promote the economic well-being of society generally.

> Every individual is continually exerting himself to find the most advantageous employment for whatever capital he can command. It is his own advantage, indeed, and not that of the society, which he has in view. . . . [But] by directing that industry in such a manner as its produce may be of the greatest value, he [is] . . . led by an invisible hand to promote an end that was no part of his intention.

> . . . By pursuing his own interest he frequently promotes that of society more effectually than when he really intends to promote it.[7]

To explain why pursuit of self-interest necessarily leads to the greatest social benefit, Smith invoked the law of supply and demand, which was alluded to in discussing competition. The law of supply and demand tempers the pursuit of self-interest exactly as competition keeps the enterprising capitalist from becoming a ruthless profiteer. The law of supply and demand similarly solves the problems of adequate goods and fair prices.

The law of supply and demand even, some think, solves the problem of fair wages, for labor is another commodity up for sale like shoes or jeans. Just as the price of a new product at first is high, like the jeans in the hypothetical example, so too are the wages of labor in a new field. But as labor becomes more plentiful, wages decline. Eventually they fall to a point at which inefficient laborers are eliminated and forced to seek other work, just as the inefficient manufacturers of jeans were forced out of that business and into others. And like the price of jeans, the price of labor then stabilizes at a fair level. As for the inefficient laborers, they find work and a living wage elsewhere. In seeking new fields of labor, they help maximize the majority's opportunities to enjoy the necessities, conveniences, and trifles of human life.

Some modern capitalists claim that capitalism operates as Smith envisioned and can be justified on the same utilitarian grounds. But not everyone agrees.

CRITICISMS OF CAPITALISM

The two major defenses of capitalism have not persuaded critics that it is a morally justifiable system. Their objections to capitalism generally fall into two categories, which are not mutually exclusive: theoretical and operational. Theoretical criticisms challenge capitalism's fundamental values, basic assumptions, or inherent economic tendencies. Operational criticisms focus more on capitalism's alleged deficiencies in actual practice (as opposed to theory) — in particular, on its failure to live up to its own economic ideals.

The following criticisms are a mix of both theoretical and operational concerns. They raise political, economic, and philosophical issues that cannot be fully assessed here. The debate over capitalism is a large and important one; the presentation that follows should be viewed as a stimulus to further discussion and not as the last word on the pros and cons of capitalism.

Inequality

Chapter 3 and Case 3.2 documented the profound economic inequality that exists in our capitalist society. The disparity in personal incomes is enormous; a minority of the population owns the vast majority of the country's productive assets; and in the last decade of the twentieth century, our society continues to be marred by poverty and homelessness. With divisions of social and economic class comes inequality of opportunity. A child born to a working-class family, let alone to an unwed teenager in an inner-city ghetto, has life prospects and possibilities that pale beside those of children born to wealthy, stock-owning parents. This reality challenges capitalism's claim of fairness, and the persistence of poverty and economic misfortune provides the basis for a utilitarian objection to it.

Few doubt that poverty and inequality are bad things, but defenders of capitalism make several responses to those who criticize it on these grounds:

1. A few extreme supporters of capitalism simply deny that it is responsible for poverty and inequality. Rather, they say, government interference with the market causes these problems. Left to itself, the market would eliminate unemployment and poverty, while ultimately lessening inequality. But neither theoretical economics nor the study of history supports this reply. Most economists and social theorists would agree that in this century activist government policies have done much, in all the Western capitalist countries, to reduce poverty and (to a lesser extent) inequality.

2. More moderate defenders of capitalism concede that, in its pure laissez-faire form, capitalism does nothing to prevent and may even foster inequality and poverty. But they argue that the system can be modified or its inherent tendencies corrected by political action, so that inequality and poverty are reduced or even eliminated. Critics of capitalism reply that the policies necessary to reduce seriously inequality and poverty are either impossible within a basically capitalist economic framework or unlikely to be carried out in any political system based on capitalism.

3. Finally, defenders of capitalism argue that the benefits of the system outweigh this weak point. Inequality is not so important if living standards are rising and even the poor have better lives than they did in previous times. This contention rests on an implicit comparison with what things would be like if society were organized differently and is, accordingly, hard to assess. Naturally, it seems more plausible to those who are relatively favored by, and content with, the present economic system than it does to those who are disadvantaged by it.

Some critics of capitalism go on to maintain that, aside from inequalities of income and ownership, the inequality inherent in the worker-capitalist relationship is itself morally undesirable. John Stuart Mill was one who found capitalism inferior in this respect to more cooperative and egalitarian economic arrangements. "To work at the bidding and for the profit of another," he wrote, "is not . . . a satisfactory state to human beings of educated intelligence, who have ceased to think themselves inferior to those whom they serve."[8] The ideal of escaping from a system of "superiors" and "subordinates" was well expressed by the great German playwright and poet Bertolt Brecht when he wrote that "He wants no servants under him/And no boss over his head."[9]

Human Beings as Economic Creatures

The theory of capitalism rests on a view of human beings as rational economic creatures, individuals who recognize and are motivated largely by their own economic self-interests. Adam Smith's defense of capitalism, for instance, assumes that consumers have full knowledge of the diverse choices available to them in the marketplace. They are supposed to know the price structures of similar products, to be fully aware of product differences, and to be able to make the optimal choice regarding price and quality.

But the key choices facing today's consumers are rarely simple. From foods to drugs, automobiles to appliances, fertilizers to air conditioners, the modern marketplace is a cornucopia of products whose nature and nuances require a high level of consumer literacy. Even with government agencies and public interest groups to aid them, today's consumers are rarely an equal match for powerful industries that can influence prices and create and shape markets. The effectiveness of advertising, in particular, is hard to reconcile with the picture of consumers as the autonomous, rational, and perfectly informed economic maximizers that economics textbooks presuppose when they attempt to demonstrate the benefits of capitalism. Consumers frequently seem to be pawns of social and economic forces beyond their control.

According to some critics of capitalism, however, what is objectionable about capitalism's view of human beings as essentially economic creatures is not this gap between theory and reality but rather the fact that it

presents little in the way of an ideal to which either individuals or societies may aspire. Not only does capitalism rest on the premise that people are basically acquisitive, individualistic, and materialistic; in practice, capitalism strongly reinforces those human tendencies. Capitalism, its critics charge, presents no higher sense of human mission or purpose, whereas other views of society and human nature do.

Christianity, for example, has long aspired to the ideal of a truly religious community united in *agape*, selfless love. And socialism, because it views human nature as malleable, hopes to see people transformed from the "competitive, acquisitive beings that they are (and that they are *encouraged* to be) under all property-dominated, market-oriented systems." In the more "benign environment of a propertyless, non-market social system," socialists believe that more cooperative and less selfish human beings will emerge.[10] Such positive ideals and aspirations are lacking in capitalism — or so its critics charge.

Capitalism Breeds Oligopolies

As early as the middle of the nineteenth century, the German philosopher and political economist Karl Marx (1818–1883) argued that capitalism leads to a concentration of property and thus a concentration of resources and power in relatively few hands. Exorbitant costs, complex machinery, increasing demand, and intense competition all work against the survival of small firms, said Marx. Many see proof of Marx's argument in today's economy.

The earlier economy of the Industrial Revolution was characterized by comparatively free and open competition, but today's is made up largely of a handful of enormous companies that can, to a distressing extent, conspire to fix prices, eliminate competition, and monopolize an industry. The food industry is a perfect example. According to Jim

Hightower, former Texas Commissioner of Agriculture, the merger activity of giant firms has produced a series of shared monopolies in the food industry, with four or fewer firms controlling a majority of sales of a given product. Here are the levels of market control by just the top three brands in various categories:

Share of Market Held by Top Three Brands

Product	Percentage of Market
Table salt	91.7
Flour	80.4
Catsup	86.1
Mustard	76.2
Peanut butter	78.6
Salad and cooking oil	85.5
Vinegar	84.1
Gelatin desserts	98.4
Whipped toppings	85.6
Canned evaporated milk	82.3
Marshmallows	98.2
Instant puddings	96.0
Shortenings	81.0
Jams and jellies	75.2
Nuts	80.7
Honey	82.2
Frozen potato products	82.2
Frostings	97.7
Spaghetti sauce	85.9
Pickle relish	79.2
Instant tea	86.0
Frozen dinners	92.8
Corn and tortilla chips	86.7
Canned spaghetti and noodles	96.0
Ready-to-serve dips	81.5
Nondairy cream substitutes	86.1
Pretzels	85.6
Dry milk	80.1
Add-meat dinner mixes	90.7
Canned stews	83.6
Instant potatoes	83.9
Pizza mix	86.6
Instant breakfast products	90.8

Why is this kind of market control significant? When there is little competition, the "natural" regulator of prices is lost, and the consumer pays. "Once a few firms gain a mo-

nopoly position in a product category," says Hightower, "the market for the category is considered to be 'mature,' . . . and the companies are able to 'harvest' it, meaning that they can push up prices. Taking one product at a time, such artificial inflation doesn't make a dramatic impression on shoppers—a few cents more on shortening, a little extra for the pizza mix. But when the whole market basket is pushed to the cash register, consumers have been nickle-and-dimed to death."[11]

It is true that antitrust actions have sometimes fostered competition and broken up monopolies, as in the cases of such corporate behemoths as Standard Oil and AT&T. But on the whole, such actions have proved largely ineffectual in halting the concentration of economic power in large, oligopolistic firms. In some cases, corporate giants have spawned even larger offspring, firms called multinationals that do business in several countries. And it is no secret that the cumulative power of business resulting from greater and greater profits has placed it in the position of a kind of industrial corporate state, an economic colossus that can negotiate independently with governments, solicit favorable franchises and tariffs, and influence self-serving legislation.

Robert Heilbroner suggests that the rise of such giant enterprises is changing the face of capitalism. Unable to function in the highly irrational system of ruthless competition, guided by some metaphysical "invisible hand," the big corporations attempt to alter the market setting through a system of public and private planning. The planning takes the form of efforts to create an atmosphere orderly and stable enough to allow the pursuit of profitable growth. Heilbroner says the planning assumes many guises, from union contracts that eliminate uncertainties in the labor market to sophisticated advertising calculated to create dependable product markets to cozy relationships with government in order to create programs that will ensure continuing high levels of demand. "At its worst," he writes, "we find it in the military-industrial complex — the very epitome of the new symbiotic business-government relations."[12]

True Competition Is Rare

As previously noted, free competition is theoretically the lifeblood of capitalism. Unfettered competition supposedly serves the collective interest while offering the richest opportunities for the individual. And yet some of the same true believers who rabidly preach the doctrine of competition at home balk at applying it to international trade. There they want protection, not competition. Indeed, Robert Reich, for one, claims that America's basic industries lost the "habit of competing" over twenty years ago.[13]

Reich says that by the mid-1960s the industries forming the U.S. industrial base (for example, steel and auto) had become "stable oligopolies of three or four major firms, led by the largest and most entrenched." Woefully unprepared to compete in technology and price, American producers were quick to seek government protection from the influx of low-priced Japanese steel, autos, and televisions. The next twenty years witnessed a variety of protective measures. One of the most publicized are the restrictions that the United States forced Japan to impose on its auto exports. Among the lesser known, though not trivial, protections:

Duties on $3.8 billion worth of imports from Southeast Asia and Latin America, which had the effect of protecting domestic manufacturers of car parts, electrical goods, fertilizers, and chemicals

Special duties on 132 products, ranging from South Korean bicycles to Italian shoes, and including the lowly clothespin

Special tax credits and tax depreciation allowances for specific industries threatened by foreign competition (total cost:

$62.4 billion, or about 3 percent of the GNP)

Federal loan guarantees for specific industries totaling $221.6 billion[14]

A Congressional Budget Office study estimated that business collects more than $60 billion annually through subsidy and credit programs.[15] And at least one writer has contended that corporate America receives more in direct and indirect subsidies than it pays in taxes.[16]

Perhaps "free competition" is nice in theory but ultimately unworkable; government intervention is necessary to protect vital economic interests (as with protective tariffs). Or maybe latter-day capitalists have not kept the faith: They have abandoned or perverted the doctrine of free competition because it has become inconvenient or unprofitable to maintain it. Whatever the explanation, myriad indicators point to the fact that, insofar as competition is concerned, capitalism functions differently from how it was conceived to work. Business professor Robert B. Carson makes the point as follows:

> In surveying the American business system it is obvious that competition still exists; however, it is not a perfect competition. Often it is not price competition at all. With the possible exception of some farm markets where there are still large numbers of producers of similar and undifferentiated products (wheat, for instance), virtually every producer of goods and services has some control over price. The degree of control varies from industry to industry and between firms within an industry. Nevertheless, it does exist and it amounts to an important modification in our model of a free-enterprise economy.[17]

Exploitation and Alienation

Marx argued that as the means of production become concentrated in the hands of the few, the balance of power between capitalists (bourgeoisie) and laborers (proletariat) tips further in favor of the bourgeoisie. Because workers have nothing to sell but their labor, said Marx, the bourgeoisie is able to exploit them by paying them less than the true value created by their labor. In fact, Marx thought, it is only through such an exploitative arrangement that capitalists make a profit and increase their capital. And the more capital they accumulate, the more they can exploit workers. Marx predicted that eventually workers would revolt. Unwilling to be exploited further, they would rise and overthrow their oppressors and set up an economic system that would truly benefit all.

The development of capitalist systems since Marx's time belies his forecast. Legal, political, and other institutions have tempered many of the greedy, exploitative dispositions of capitalism. The twentieth century has witnessed legislation curbing egregious worker abuse, guaranteeing a minimum wage, and ensuring a safer and more healthful work environment. The emergence of labor unions and their subsequent victories have significantly enlarged the worker's share of the economic pie. Indeed, many of the specific measures proposed by Marx and his collaborator Friedrich Engels in the *Communist Manifesto* (1848) have been implemented in capitalist countries: a program of graduated income tax, free education for all children in public schools, investiture of significant economic control in the state, and so on.

Still, many would say that, although democratic institutions may have curbed some of the excesses of capitalism, they can do nothing to prevent the alienation of workers that results from having to do unfulfilling work. Again, because of the unequal positions of capitalist and worker, laborers must work for someone else—they must do work imposed on them as a means of satisfying the needs of others. As a result, they must eventually feel exploited and debased.

But what about workers who are paid handsomely for their efforts? They, too, said Marx, remain alienated, for as the fruits of their labor are enjoyed by someone else, their work ultimately proves meaningless to them. The following selection from Marx's "Economic and Philosophic Manuscripts" (1844) summarizes his notion of alienation as the separation of individuals from the objects they create, which in turn results in one's separation from other people, from oneself, and ultimately from one's human nature:

> The worker is related to the *product of his labor* as to an *alien* object. For it is clear on this presupposition that the more the worker expends himself in work the more powerful becomes the world of objects which he creates in face of himself, the poorer he becomes in his inner life, and the less he belongs to himself. . . . The worker puts his life into the object, and his life then belongs no longer to himself but to the object. The greater his activity, therefore, the less he possesses. What is embodied in the product of his labor is no longer his own. The greater this product is, therefore, the more he is diminished. The *alienation* of the worker in his product means not only that his labor becomes an object, assumes an *external* existence, but that it exists independently, *outside himself*, and alien to him, and that it stands opposed to him as an autonomous power. The life which he has given to the object sets itself against him as an alien and hostile force. . . .
>
> What constitutes the alienation of labor? First, that the work is *external* to the worker, that it is not part of his nature; and that, consequently, he does not fulfill himself in his work but denies himself, has a feeling of misery rather than well-being, does not develop freely his mental and physical energies but is physically exhausted and mentally debased. The worker, therefore, feels himself at home only during his leisure time,

whereas at work he feels homeless. His work is not voluntary but imposed, *forced labor*. It is not the satisfaction of a need, but only a *means* for satisfying other needs. Its alien character is clearly shown by the fact that as soon as there is no physical or other compulsion it is avoided like the plague. External labor, labor in which man alienates himself, is a labor of self-sacrifice, of mortification. Finally, the external character of work for the worker is shown by the fact that it is not his own work but work for someone else, that in work he does not belong to himself but to another person. . . .

We arrive at the result that man (the worker) feels himself to be freely active only in his animal functions—eating, drinking and procreating, or at most also in his dwelling and in personal adornment—while in his human functions he is reduced to an animal. The animal becomes human and the human becomes animal.

Eating, drinking and procreating are of course also genuine human functions. But abstractly considered, apart from the environment of human activities, and turned into final and sole ends, they are animal functions.

We have now considered the act of alienation of practical human activity, labor, from two aspects: (1) the relationship of the worker to the *product of labor* as an alien object which dominates him . . . [and] (2) the relationship of labor to the *act of production* within *labor*. This is the relationship of the worker to his own activity as something alien and not belonging to him. . . . This is *self-alienation* as against the above-mentioned alienation of the *thing*.[18]

In Marx's view, when workers are alienated they cannot be free. They may have the political and social freedoms of speech, religion, and governance, but even with these freedoms, individuals still are not fully free. Freedom from government interference and persecution does not necessarily guarantee freedom from economic exploitation. And it is for this kind of freedom, freedom from alienation, that Marx and Engels felt such passion.

Some would say that one need not wade through Marxist philosophy to get a feel for what he and others mean by worker alienation. Just talk to workers themselves, as writer Studs Terkel has done. In different ways the hundreds of workers from diverse occupations that Terkel has interviewed speak of the same thing: dehumanization.

> Mike Fitzgerald . . . is a laborer in a steel mill. "I feel like the guys who built the pyramids. Somebody built 'em. Somebody built the Empire State Building, too. There's hard work behind it. I would like to see a building, say the Empire State, with a footwide strip from top to bottom and the name of every bricklayer on it, the name of every electrician. So when a guy walked by, he could take his son and say, 'See, that's me over there on the 45th floor. I put that steel beam in.' . . . Everybody should have something to point to."
>
> Sharon Atkins is 24 years old. She's been to college and acidly observes, "The first myth that blew up in my face is that a college education will get you a worthwhile job." For the last two years she's been a receptionist at an advertising agency. "I didn't look at myself as 'just a dumb broad' at the front desk, who took phone calls and messages. I thought I was something else. The office taught me differently."
>
> . . . Harry Stallings, 27, is a spot welder on the assembly line at an auto plant. "They'll give better care to that machine than they will to you. If it breaks down, there's somebody out there to fix it right away. If I break down, I'm just pushed over to the other side till another man takes my place. The only thing the company has in mind is to keep that machine running. A man would be more eager to do a better job if he were given proper respect and the time to do it."[19]

TODAY'S ECONOMIC CHALLENGES

Capitalism, as you have just seen, gives rise to a number of important critical questions, both theoretical and operational. These criticisms are a powerful challenge to capitalism, especially in its pure laissez-faire form. But the capitalism that we know today is a long way from the laissez-faire model. Corporate behemoths able to control markets and sway governments have replaced the small-scale entrepreneurs and free-wheeling competition of an earlier day. And governments in all capitalist countries actively intervene in the economic realm; they endeavor to assist or modify Adam Smith's invisible hand; and over the years they have reformed or supplemented capitalism with programs intended to enhance the security of the work force and increase the welfare of their citizens.

This reality complicates the debate over capitalism. Its defenders may be advocating either the pure laissez-faire ideal or the modified state welfare capitalism that we in fact have. Likewise, those who attack the laissez-faire ideal may do so on behalf of a modified, welfarist capitalism, or they may criticize both forms of capitalism and defend some kind of socialism, in which private property and the pursuit of profit are no longer governing economic principles. We thus have a three-way debate over the respective strengths and weaknesses of laissez-faire capitalism, state welfare capitalism, and socialism.

The rest of this chapter leaves this fundamental debate behind. Instead of looking at criticisms of capitalism in general and at issues relevant to any capitalist society, it examines some of the more specific socioeconomic challenges facing the United States as we enter the last decade of the century.

At the beginning of Chapter 3, the trend toward a more inequitable distribution of national income was discussed. To many experts, it seems that the problem begins with a decreasing rate of growth in the country's gross national product, which has essentially fallen by half in the past two decades, from 3.8 percent per year in the 1960s to 2 percent per year or less in the 1980s. This slowdown reflects a declining rate of growth in productivity, from 2.7 percent per year between 1960 and 1970 to 0.9 percent in the 1980s — the worst productivity showing for any decade of the century. Economists do not agree about the causes of this slowdown, but it is clearly not an international problem. The growth of productivity in countries like Germany and Japan is three to five times the U.S. rate.[20]

If slow growth is not reversed, Americans will become poorer, and their standard of living will sink. By some measures this decline is already happening. The rate of home ownership in the United States fell in the 1980s for the first time since the Depression.[21] Adjusted for inflation, wages of nonsupervisory workers — some four-fifths of the work force — have decreased steadily since their peak in 1972 and have now slumped to the level of 1961. Median family income is only barely above that of 1973, even though twice as many women work as did thirty years ago. Had the economy and living standards grown after 1973 at the same pace as before, real incomes today would be 50 percent higher than they are.[22]

To make matters worse, in the last quarter century the United States has been steadily losing it share of both foreign and domestic markets. The nation's huge balance of trade deficit is only the most visible sign of this. It is now down from its all-time high of $170 billion in 1987, but no one anticipates a return to the lower levels of the 1970s, let alone a closing of the trade gap, in the foreseeable future. The key to enhanced international competitiveness and, thus, to an American economic recovery is increased productivity.

The many complex causes of feeble productivity growth and declining competitiveness go beyond the scope of this book. But recent commentators have drawn attention to three that deserve discussion here because they suggest new areas of business responsibility: (1) a fixation with short-term performance over long-term strategies, (2) an abandonment of the traditional capitalist orientation toward manufacturing goods, and (3) changes in attitude toward work, which may foreshadow a whole new era of employer–employee relations.

Short-Term Performance

Long before his well-publicized trial for selling cocaine, John DeLorean ran General Motors' Pontiac Division and then Chevrolet. He quit GM in 1973 and subsequently started manufacturing his own stainless steel cars. Shortly after leaving GM, DeLorean wrote *On a Clear Day You Can See General Motors*, an inside look at the prototypical well-run American business. At one point in the book, DeLorean writes:

> Never once while I was in GM's management did I hear substantial concern raised about the impact of our business on America, its consumers, or the economy. When we should have been planning switches to smaller, more fuel-efficient, lighter cars in the late 1960s, in response to a growing demand in the market place, GM refused because "we make more money on big cars." It mattered not that customers wanted the smaller cars, or that a national balance-of-payments deficit was being built in large part because of the burgeoning sales of foreign cars in the American market.
>
> Refusal to enter the small car market when the profits were better on bigger cars, despite the needs of the public and the national economy, was not an isolated case of corporate insensitivity. It

was typical. And what disturbed me is that it was indicative of fundamental problems with the system.[23]

One of the "fundamental problems" explicit in DeLorean's observation is American industry's preoccupation with short-term planning. The auto industry, as DeLorean suggests, is a perfect example. In part as a result of such planning, by 1980 imported cars had captured 28.4 percent of the U.S. market, up from about 15 percent in 1970. This erosion contributed to Chrysler Corporation's struggle for survival and to GM's, Ford's, and American Motors's scramble to retain their crumbling shares of the market.

But preoccupation with short-term performance at the expense of long-term strategies is hardly confined to the automotive industry. The same mentality characterizes most corporate executives and managers of industries that grew up together with the rising U.S. population and affluence in the 1950s and 1960s. For these businesspeople, planning consisted largely of increasing productive capacity at the right times in the right places and using short-term profit as the exclusive measure of success. Today's economic realities are far different. As a result, many planning strategists say that U.S. companies must become more visionary, that they must define long-term goals and be willing to stick to them even at the expense of short-term profit. The problem, of course, is how to get businesspeople to do this when they have been trained to think and do otherwise.[24]

A focus on short-term results often goes hand in hand with an effort to avoid genuine economic competition. This attitude was illustrated by Donald Petersen, chairman of the Ford Motor Company, at the end of 1987.[25] Ford was then the world's most profitable auto company, with $9 billion in spare cash. Its cars were once again popular, and its plants were operating at nearly full capacity. Against this backdrop one might suppose that Ford would be ready to drop the "temporary" quotas on Japanese imports in effect since 1980. Wrong. Petersen instead proposed sharp new limits on Japanese imports (the first cutback would be 600,000 cars).

The problem from Petersen's point of view was that the auto industry's total sales were declining. In part, however, high prices were to blame. In 1987 the average car buyer paid $13,520 for a new car, an increase of nearly 80 percent over the 1980 price tag of $7,574, only a small part of which reflects consumers buying bigger cars or selecting more options. Normally in this situation, supply-and-demand pressure would push prices down. Ford could still sell all its cars but at a lower profit margin. But Petersen and Ford were not interested in this aspect of capitalism. They preferred to avoid competition, restrict supply, keep prices and profits high — and let the consumer pick up the tab.

This attitude contrasts sharply with the competitive mentality at Toyota. In 1987 the value of the dollar against the yen was 50 percent of what it had been two years earlier. Normally, a less valuable dollar would greatly increase the price of foreign imports like Japanese cars and make American products more competitive (a 50 percent fall in the dollar is like doubling the price of Japanese products). Toyota's response, however, was to sacrifice profit and increase productivity in order to hold price increases to a minimum. Toyota successfully pursued a long-term strategy of keeping its sales and market share high, even at the cost of lower short-term profit margins.[26]

Lack of Interest in Production

Traditionally, capitalists have made money by producing goods. Manufacturing was the backbone of the American economy and the basis of our prosperity. Yet today, in industry after industry, American manufacturers are closing up shop or curtailing their operations and becoming marketing organizations for other producers, usually foreign. The result is the evolution of a new kind of company: manufacturers that do little or no manufacturing. They may perform a host of profit-making functions — from design to distribution — but they lack their own production base. Companies long identified with making goods of all sorts now often produce only the package and the label. In contrast to traditional manufacturers, they have become "hollow corporations."[27]

Many U.S. manufacturers are now pursuing a strategy of "outsourcing" — that is, buying parts or whole products from other producers, both at home and abroad. The manufacturer's traditional vertical structure, in which it makes virtually all critical parts, is thereby being replaced by a network of small suppliers. Proponents of the new system describe it as flexible and efficient, a logical outcome of the drive to lower the costs of doing business. But critics doubt that the United States can prosper without a strong manufacturing base. As Tsutomu Ohshima, a senior managing director of Toyota Motor Corporation, puts it: "You can't survive with just a service industry." In terms of wages, productivity, and innovation, the service sector fails to compare with basic industry. Nor can the service economy thrive if manufacturing is allowed to wither.

Closely related to the "hollowing" of corporations is the increase in corporate mergers and acquisitions. Although slowed by recession in the early 1990s, the most exciting action in town and the best opportunity for making quick, enormous profits still lies in taking over — or threatening to take over — existing corporations. The players include the nation's large *Fortune 500* corporations, the big Wall Street investment banks, corporate raiders like Carl Icahn and Sir James Goldsmith, and risk arbitrageurs like the fallen Ivan Boesky. With them has come a whole new vocabulary: mergers, hostile takeovers, greenmail, stock buybacks, poison pills, divestitures, leveraged buyouts, junk bonds. When the corporate raiders are successful, the result is usually retrenchment, sale of subsidiaries, and elimination of jobs (both middle management and factory positions), as the raiders ruthlessly cut costs to drive up the value of their new stock.[28]

Takeovers, and the vast "corporate restructuring" that has resulted, made up one of the most visible economic trends of the 1980s. Between 1983 and 1987, for example, no fewer than 12,000 companies and corporate divisions were bought and sold in deals worth $490 billion. The value of mergers and acquisitions jumped from below $40 billion in 1980 to nearly $170 billion in 1986. In 1987 alone, the amount spent on takeovers was greater than the combined profits of America's top 500 companies. Take the oil industry as an example: In 1984 Chevron bought Gulf for $13.4 billion, Texaco bought Getty Oil for $10.2 billion, and Mobil shelled out $5.7 billion for Superior Oil.[29] Yet all this activity is directed toward making money through the manipulation of existing assets rather than the actual production of new or better goods. Many American entrepreneurs and capitalists seem to have found better and easier ways to make profit than the time-honored technique of competing in the manufacture and production of goods.

In their defense, corporate raiders claim that takeovers oust incompetent managers, eliminate useless bureaucracy, and liquidate unproductive assets. Corporate managers, however, claim the opposite. Takeovers force them to waste time trying to keep their stock price high, to cut back on research and development, and to close plants to pay for stock repurchases. Chrysler chairman Lee Iacocca asserts:

> I see billions of dollars tied up in new corporate debt to keep the raiders at bay while research and development go begging. I see billions going for greenmail

that ought to be building new high-tech factories. I also see a huge share of America's best management talent wasted on takeover games when it should be devoted to strengthening the industrial base of the country.[30]

Changes in Attitudes Toward Work

The decline in U.S. productivity growth is rooted in more than a short-term performance mentality, outsourcing, and takeovers. It is also rooted in attitudes toward government, social institutions, business, and especially work.

As American productivity growth, once the high-performance engine of national wealth, has sputtered to an embarrassingly uncompetitive low, management is apt to lament: "Nobody wants to work anymore." What management probably means is that the work ethic is dead. Is it?

The so-called work ethic stresses the value of work for its sake as something necessary for every person. It also emphasizes the belief that hard work pays off in the end. "If you work hard enough," the expression goes, "you'll make it." The work ethic, although not dead, is certainly altered today, because the attitudes toward work are different. As painful memories of the Great Depression have waned, so has the disciplined and docile approach to work that it produced. As financial support systems have been welded into society (unemployment insurance, union benefits, welfare payments, food stamps, and the like), job loss is not the catastrophe it once was. As young people have become increasingly educated, they have rearranged their ideas about what they want out of life. For these and other reasons, the long-held and widely cherished work ethic has indeed changed.

The evidence of this change can be seen in the workplace itself. For example, it is not uncommon for operative workers to balk at doing the monotonous tasks their ancestors once accepted, albeit grudgingly. Loyalty to employers seems on the decline, and loyalty to fellow workers seems on the rise. Turnover rates in many industries are enough to make discontinuity an expensive problem. Organizational plans, schedules, and demands no longer carry the authoritative clout they once did; workers today often subordinate them to personal needs, which results in rampant absenteeism. Moreover, employee sabotage and violence, once unheard of, occur frequently enough today to worry management. Adding to industry's woes, drug use at the office is increasingly the cause of employee theft, absenteeism, and low productivity.

According to a recent international survey about what matters most to different cultures, Americans placed work eighth in importance behind values like their children's education and a satisfactory love life. (In Japan, by contrast, work ranks second only to good health.)[31] Although it is impossible to pin down precisely workers' attitudes toward work today, basically they seem willing to work hard on a job they find interesting and rewarding as long as they have the freedom to influence the nature of their jobs and pursue their own lifestyles. They have a growing expectation that work will provide self-respect, nonmaterial rewards, and substantial opportunities for personal growth. And they have a growing willingness to demand individual rights, justice, and equality on the job.[32]

If industry is to improve productive capacity and be more competitive, it must confront seriously these changing social attitudes. As Paul Bernstein argues, it is counterproductive to compare the contemporary worker with an idealized worker of yesteryear. Rather, we must acknowledge that we have a new work ethic, which in Bernstein's words

> is unrelated to religious demands of ministers and manufacturer's representatives, but is part and parcel of the

individual desire for meaningful and challenging labor in which some autonomy is an integral feature. An increasingly professionalized work force will not accept a golden embrace unless it is accompanied by fulfilling jobs that have been designed for a labor force that sees work in relation to family, friends, leisure and self-development. Work, for most of us, continues as an important part of our lives, but only in relation to our total experience.[33]

SUMMARY

1. Capitalism is an economic system in which the major portion of production and distribution is in private hands, operating under a profit or market system. Socialism is an economic system characterized by public ownership of property and a planned economy.

2. Capitalism has gone through several stages: mercantile, industrial, financial, and state welfare.

3. Four key features of capitalism are the existence of companies, profit motive, competition, and private property.

4. One basic defense of capitalism rests on a supposed natural moral right to property. Utilitarians deny the existence of such rights. Other critics doubt that this right entitles one to have a system of property rules and regulations identical to the one we now have in the United States.

5. Utilitarian defense of capitalism is associated with the classical economic arguments of Adam Smith. Smith believed that human beings are acquisitive and that they have a natural propensity for trading, and he insisted that when people are left free to pursue their own economic interests, they will, without intending it, produce the greatest good for all.

6. Critics question the basic assumptions of capitalism (theoretical challenges) and

whether it has delivered on its promises (operational challenges). Specifically, they raise the following issues: Can capitalism eliminate poverty and reduce inequality? Are humans basically economic creatures? Does capitalism breed oligopolies? Does it promote competition? Does capitalism exploit and alienate?

7. As we enter the last decade of the century, our capitalist socioeconomic system faces a number of challenges. Among the problems that must be overcome are a fixation on short-term performance at the expense of long-term strategies and a lack of interest in the actual manufacturing of goods. In addition, we must come to grips with our society's changing attitudes toward work.

CASE 4.1
Frayed Blue Collars

On January 31, 1980, the press release hit the mayor's desk and the mayor hit the ceiling. "This is devastating!" he shouted. "It's a clear case of corporate bad faith!"

Some months earlier, General Motors chairman Thomas A. Murphy had come to St. Louis and announced plans to invest $100 million in expanding and renovating its 175-acre St. Louis plant. But that was before gasoline shortages persuaded GM to change its manufacturing plans. The city hadn't anticipated the gas crunch either. City officials were so pleased with Murphy's news that they jumped at a GM request for more land to assist in the expansion. In fact, before the January 31 announcement that GM was moving, the city committed $2 million in public funds to acquire a 44-acre site adjacent to the plant.

"Not only were we misled," fumed the mayor, "we're left holding the bag for $2 million."

What happened in St. Louis is happening with alarming frequency in the industrial heartland of America. Old industrial cities, their economies intertwined with the economic health of aging and obsolete manufacturing plants, are ailing as those plants are being forced to close, cut back, or relocate in more modern but sometimes remote locales. Such dislocations devastate the lives of individuals and the well-being of communities.[34]

These plant closings and relocations especially dominate the headlines throughout the industrial crescent of the North and Midwest. Among the areas hardest hit has been Akron, Ohio, once an industrial center for the production of rubber products. Today most of Akron's factories, which once employed nearly 100,000 workers, are maintained by skeleton crews. Mismanagement, foreign competition, the recession, and labor demands have all conspired to cripple the once-vibrant industry.

For the thousands of displaced workers in Akron and the tens of thousands nationwide, the "American Dream" has turned into a nightmare. What once appeared to be a never-ending ascent to higher and higher levels of the "good life" has suddenly turned into a downward spiral in income and self-esteem. In the resulting struggle for survival, some make it, some don't—but nobody succeeds as easily as before.

When Frank Burton was in high school in 1960, he had a part-time job at an Akron convenience store, stocking shelves and ringing the register. Like so many local youngsters his age, Burton eagerly awaited the day he'd graduate and "hire on" at the nearby Firestone tire factory. Burton did just that, and for the next twenty years he worked in the plant from dawn until dusk, just as his father and grandfather had before him. But all that ended in 1981 when the plant shut down.

After he was laid off, Burton tried to get other jobs. He studied 980 hours of computer science. But no one in Akron needed his new skills. He finally landed a job at the old convenience store, doing what he did when he was in high school.

"I got my heart torn out," he says. "At forty-two I should be reaching my top income potential." In fact, he makes $7,000 at the convenience store, a fraction of the $30,000 he earned at the plant. To pay off debts, he has been forced to sell his pension rights.

Professor of industrial relations Dennis Ahlburg has a cold, hard message for people like Frank Burton: "They're lucky they did so well for so long. . . . For a lot of these people it really *is* over." There's some basis for this grim outlook. In 1980 Japan produced 11 million vehicles worldwide, exceeding U.S. production by about 40 percent. That made Japan the world's premiere automaker, a claim it still holds. Many believe the United States will never regain its top spot and thus never be able to reemploy the thousands of Frank Burtons in their old jobs.

Social forecaster John Naisbitt, writing in his best-selling *Megatrends*, even doubts that Japan or any single nation can maintain the top position long, because the world auto industry is undergoing "globalization." Naisbitt explains what he means:

> Half the American population owns a car already, and in Europe, where public transportation is superior to that of the United States, the demand is satisfied with one-third of the people owning cars. The replacement market in automobiles that's left will fall far short of the dynamic growth market that we've known for the past thirty years.
>
> Furthermore, if we think we are going to supply automobiles to satisfy the Third World's growing demand, we had better think again.

There are eighty-six countries in the world that have automobile assembly lines. Mexico, for example, is fast becoming a major auto producer. Volkswagen, Nissan, Ford, GM, and others operate plants in Mexico, which produced nearly 300,000 autos in 1979. Countries with their own auto plants will be in the best position to meet the local demand for automobiles as the developing world becomes rich enough to purchase them. Furthermore, many developing countries have clearly indicated they will act to protect their own growing auto industries from any invasion by big auto makers.

Incredible though it seems, it's in this environment that the United States government bailed out Chrysler. If we continue in that direction, this country will turn its automobile industry into an employment program. . . .[35]

Indeed, the government not only bailed out Chrysler but propped up the entire auto industry by pressuring Japan to impose "voluntary" quotas on the number of autos it sent to the United States. Detroit argued that the quotas were needed to buy time to regain its competitiveness. Labor organizations agreed, adding that the quotas were the only way to protect American jobs and offer people like Frank Burton any hope of reemployment in the industry. Both automakers and workers insisted that Japan must be forced to "play on a level playing field." By this they meant that Japan's remarkable success could be explained largely in terms of the advantages enjoyed by its automakers (for example, tax breaks) but denied its U.S. counterparts. Overlooked in the emotion-charged atmosphere were studies that showed an effective corporate tax rate of about 50 percent for Japanese companies, compared with about 27 percent for U.S. manufacturers. Also disregarded were studies that attributed the Japanese advantage to superior management and production-line techniques. And while automakers and labor leaders lobbied government for protectionist legislation, car buyers who would be denied the Japanese auto alternative were effectively ignored.

Those opposing quotas on auto imports point out that despite such protection in the recent past, the auto industry continues to deteriorate—Chrysler's resurrection notwithstanding. High wages, antiquated plants and equipment, inappropriate management techniques, corporate short-sightedness, superior imports—none of these causes of the industry's malaise, they argue, will be remedied by "voluntary" quotas. Moreover, some claim that the quotas are unfair to consumers because they push up the prices of cars and auto-related products.

These same people do admit, however, that avoiding the protectionist reflex will not come cheaply. The costs in terms of human suffering and social upheaval will be high, perhaps higher than some can pay. Thousands like Frank Burton already are feeling the psychological toll exacted by a forced move to a low-status, poor-paying job.

"We define ourselves in terms of our jobs," says Walter Nord, a professor of organizational psychology, "and that identity permeates our families, especially in towns where one industry is prominent. . . . When you're suddenly working at a hamburger joint instead of Bethlehem Steel, that's a blow to your self-esteem. And the loss of health and other benefits has to have family-life consequences."

Experts fear that as more and more blue-collar workers are laid off and find themselves on a downward spiral, the personal and social problems associated with a diminishing blue-collar work force will worsen. Although the problem already is grave, not much is being done about it.

"We stand last among the major industrial and post-industrial nations in public expenditures on job training and retraining," says urban historian Stanley Schultz. "Because of trends in the economy, we must make a genuine national commitment to education and job retraining for many of our working-class citizens."

As politicians, economists, and academics debate the need for a new industrial policy, General Motors has begun formulating one of its own. Seizing the new technologies of robots, lasers, and computers, GM is innovating in the work its employees do and how they do it.[36] Take, for example, GM's computer-programmed automated guided vehicle (AGV), which tracks wires in a plant floor to tirelessly and correctly deliver parts to various points on the assembly line. The AGV is only one of many pieces of computer-guided equipment GM uses, including more than a hundred welding robots and a score of painting robots, bar-coded gates and computer-equipped gatekeepers, and data banks that make information instantly available to workers on the plant floor.

While admitting it's inevitable, organized labor has mixed feelings about the introduction of high technology into the workplace. For if high-tech means better products that ultimately make jobs more secure, it also means fewer workers and only ones who are trainable. At full production, an auto plant using the new technology requires one-third fewer workers to produce the same number of cars as a conventional plant. And workers lacking basic computational and language skills have about as much chance of getting a job in a computerized plant as a tone-deaf horn blower has of playing with the Boston Pops.

For those still employed, new technology represents their last, best chance to keep their jobs. "We don't look at automation as job elimination," says the head of a United Auto Workers local. "We look at it as a way of making cars of much higher quality. If you don't get the quality at the right price, you don't get the sales. You don't get the sales, you don't get any jobs."[37] The local this man heads represents 14,500 workers, 3,000 on indefinite layoff, at two GM plants in Lansing,

Michigan. At an adjacent plant, which together with the other two constitutes the largest GM assembly complex in the country, 1,400 of its 42,000 workers are on indefinite layoff. As increasingly sophisticated instruments intrude into the automotive workplace, the odds dwindle that many of these laid-off workers will ever return to their jobs. And those still working fear that high-tech manufacturing may salvage the automotive companies at their expense. They're scared for their jobs and are demanding to be protected — not merely by protectionist legislation but by the companies that they and their predecessors helped make big and rich and powerful.

Under the terms of a ground-breaking agreement between GM and the United Auto Workers in October 1984, GM agreed to invest $100 million in new business ventures designed to employ laid-off UAW members and to allow GM workers an equal voice in how the money should be invested. Moreover, the company agreed at a cost of $1 billion to protect 100 percent of the workers' pay and fringe benefits for six years, if jobs are eliminated, work is transferred to other companies here or abroad, operations are consolidated, or new technology eliminates positions. Displaced workers would continue to get their regular pay and could be assigned other jobs at GM, be trained for a new job with GM or someone else, or get work in one of the new ventures that the union and company plan to start with the $100 million fund.

Both management and labor have praised the innovative provisions as potential models for other industries. They consider it a fair and just response to economically stressful conditions. They hope that it will ease the transitions that thousands of workers like Frank Burton will have to make in the years to come.

Discussion Questions

1. How do you assess the future of American manufacturing? Will it be able to increase productivity and meet the challenge of foreign competition?

2. Do you find anything in the current plight of America's blue-collar workers that confirms the Marxist view of capitalism?

3. Do you think that the government bailout of Chrysler and such protectionist legislation as "voluntary" quotas on auto imports are fair? Do they make economic sense? What would Adam Smith say?

4. Do corporations like General Motors have a responsibility to retain workers laid off as a result of foreign competition or new technologies?

5. How do you assess the GM-UAW pact? Should it be a model for other companies? Explain.

6. The costs incurred by GM's 1984 agreement with the UAW are reflected in the price of its products and thus borne by consumers. Do you think this is right?

CASE 4.2
Hucksters in the Classroom

Increased student loads, myriad professional obligations, and shrinking school budgets have sent many public school teachers scurrying for teaching materials to facilitate their teaching.

They don't have to look far. Into the breach has stepped business, which is ready, willing, and able to provide current print and audiovisual materials for classroom use. These activities and industry-supplied teaching aids are advertised in educational journals, distributed to school boards, and showcased at educational conventions. The Dr Pepper Company, for example, displays at such conventions a recipe booklet titled *Cooking with Dr Pepper*. Each recipe includes sugarfilled Dr Pepper soda.

One collective tack taken by the business community has been the ABC Education Program of American Industry, whose annual publication, *Resourcebook*, consists of productspecific "sponsored pages" or ads with accompanying teacher guide sheets. Food and toiletry products are featured, as in the following:

A is for AGREE: the Creme Rinse and Conditioner that helps the greasies.

C is for COCONUT: a tantalizing tropical treat from Peter Paul candies.

E is for EFFECTIVE double deodorant system in Irish Spring (soap).[38]

Advertising space in *Resourcebook* doesn't come cheap: A single ad can run as much as $30,000. But ABC official Art Sylvie thinks it's worth it. After all, he asks, where else are manufacturers going to get such widespread and in-depth product exposure? He has a point: About 2.7 million or 35 percent of all junior high school students in the United States participate in the ABC program, not to mention their 95,000 teachers.

An integral part of the ABC program is an annual essay-writing contest. Essays must deal with some aspect of a product in *Resourcebook* — its production and marketing, the history or importance of an industry to a community or nation, and so on. To be eligible, entries must be signed by a teacher and include a product label or reasonable facsimile. Student writers can earn up to $50 for entering.

The people at ABC say they want to reflect the positive aspects of the world outside the classroom. And they're convinced that the way to do it is through depicting the wonders and genius of industry. "Thus," says re-

searcher Sheila Harty, "history is taught in terms of 'innovative industrial genius,' as students write their essays on the value of soft drinks (C is for Canada Dry) or the production of tires (G is for Goodyear)."[39]

Evidently teachers go for corporate freebies with all the gusto of a softball player at a company picnic. In a survey of its members, the National Educational Association found that about half its members were using industry audiovisual materials and the ten resource guides published annually by Educators Progress Services (EPS). A cursory look at the guides suggests that the offerings are comprehensive and impartial. A closer look reveals that most are privately, not publicly, sponsored.

Some people think corporate-sponsored teaching materials do more than fill curriculum needs. They are also public relations gambits. Thus, in his book *Corporate Response to Urban Crisis*, professor of sociology Ken Neubeck writes:

> Corporations must continually respond to problems which they had a hand in creating in the first place. From this perspective, corporate social responsibility becomes a defensive strategy to be employed whenever the social and political climate become hostile to the active pursuit of corporate economic goals. It is a strategy of "enlightened self-interest."[40]

Corporate America's latest and most dramatic venture into the classroom, however, goes beyond a defensive public relations strategy.[41] In 1989, Whittle Communications began beaming into high schools in six cities its controversial Channel One, a television newscast for high school students, and by June 1991 the number of schools receiving Channel One had grown to 8,600. Although Whittle has grander plans for the future, the broadcasts at present are twelve minutes long — ten minutes of news digest with slick graphics and two minutes of commercials for Levi's jeans, Gillette razor blades, Head & Shoulders shampoo, Snickers candy bars, and other familiar products.

The schools in the program receive thousands of dollars worth of free electronic gadgetry, including television monitors, satellite dishes, and video recorders. And students seem to like the program. "It was very interesting and it appeals to our age group," says student Angelique Williams. "One thing I really liked was the reporters were our own age. They kept our attention."

But Whittle Communications, and interested competitors like Turner Broadcasting and the Discovery Channel, formed in Maryland by four large cable operators, have more in mind than simply making the news interesting to students like Angelique. The prospect of being able to deliver a captive and narrowly targeted audience to its customers promises to be breathtakingly profitable—so profitable, in fact, that advertisers on Channel One pay $150,000 for each thirty seconds of commercial time.

That captive audience is just what worries the critics. Peggy Charren of Action for Children's Television calls the project a "great big, gorgeous Trojan horse. . . . You're selling the children to the advertisers. You might as well auction off the rest of the school day to the highest bidders." This development worries many educators, and New York and New Jersey have banned Channel One and its potential clones from public classrooms.

On the other hand, Principal Rex Stooksbury of Central High School in Knoxville, which receives Channel One, takes a different view. "This is something we see as very, very positive for the school," he says. And as student Danny Diaz adds, "we're always watching commercials" anyway.

Discussion Questions

1. What explains industry's thrust into education? Is it consistent with the basic features of capitalism?

2. What moral issues, if any, are involved in the affiliation between education and commercial interests?

3. Do you think students have a "moral right" to an education free of commercial indoctrination?

4. If you were a member of a school board contemplating the use of either industry-sponsored materials or Channel One, what would you recommend?

5. Do you think industry in general and Channel One in particular are intentionally using teachers and students as a means to profit? Or do they have a genuine concern for the education process? On the other hand, if teachers and students benefit from these educational materials or from viewing Channel One, is there any ground for concern?

6. The materials that industry provides teachers for classroom use fall predominantly into four subject areas: nutrition, energy, the environment, and economics. Rarely is the subject of English addressed. How do you account for this bias, and what are its implications?

CASE 4.3
Licensing and Laissez-Faire

The United States is a capitalist country, and our system of medical care is, to a significant extent, organized for profit. True, many hospitals are nonprofit, but the same cannot be said of doctors, who, judged as a whole, form an extremely affluent and privileged occupational group.

Sometimes physicians themselves seem a little uncomfortable about the business aspect of their professional lives or worry that outsiders will misinterpret their attention to economic matters. For example, the professional journal *Medical Economics*, which discusses such pocketbook issues as malpractice insurance, taxes, fees, and money management (a recent cover story was titled "Are You Overpaying Your Staff?"), works hard at not being available to the general public. When a subscriber left his copy on a commercial airliner, another reader found it and sent the mailing label to the magazine; the magazine's editor sent a cautionary note to the subscriber. The editor advises readers to "do your part by restricting access to your personal copies of the magazine. Don't put them in the waiting room, don't leave them lying about in the examination rooms, and don't abandon them in public places."[42]

Medical Economics probably suspects that even in our capitalist society many people, including probably most doctors, would not like to think of doctors simply as medical entrepreneurs who are in it for the money. And, indeed, many people here and many more in other countries criticize our medical system for being profit oriented. They think medical care should be based on need and that ability to pay should not affect the quality of medical treatment one receives. Interestingly, though, there are those who criticize medical practice in the United States as being insufficiently market oriented. University of Chicago professor of economics, Milton Friedman, is one of those.

Friedman has been a longstanding critic of occupational licensure in all fields. His reasoning is straightforward: Licensure — the requirement that one obtain a license from a recognized authority in order to engage in an occupation — restricts entry into the field. Licensure thus permits the occupational or professional group to enjoy a monopoly in the provision of services. In Friedman's view, this contravenes the principles of a free market to the disadvantage of us all.

Friedman has no objection to certification; that is, to public or private agencies certifying

that an individual has certain skills. But he rejects the policy of preventing people who do not have such a certificate from practicing the occupation of their choice. Such a policy restricts freedom and keeps the price of the services in question artificially high. When one reads the long lists of occupations for which some states require a license — librarians, tree surgeons, pest controllers, well diggers, barbers, even potato growers, among many others — Friedman's case gains plausibility. But Friedman pushes his argument to include all occupations and professions.

Does this mean we should let incompetent physicians practice? Friedman's answer is yes.[43] In his view the American Medical Association (AMA) is simply a trade union, though probably the strongest one in the United States. It keeps the wages of its members high by restricting the number of those who can practice medicine.

The AMA does this not just through licensure but also, even more effectively, through controlling the number of medical schools and the number of students admitted to them. The medical profession, Friedman charges, limits entry into the field by turning down applicants to medical school and making standards for admission and licensure so difficult as to discourage many young people from ever trying to gain admission.

Viewed as a trade union, the AMA has been singularly effective. As recently as the 1920s, physicians were far down the list of professions in terms of income; the average doctor made less than the average accountant. Today, doctors constitute what is probably the profession with the highest status and the best pay in the country. In 1984 the average doctor made $108,000, and the average specialist considerably more. But the AMA is still worried. In July 1987 it predicted a "surplus" of doctors by the year 2000, warning that this "could lower the quality and raise the cost of physicians' services."[44]

Critics of the AMA believe that its real worry is the prospect of stabilizing or declining incomes. Its proposed remedy, in any case, is the familiar one: restrict the size of medical school classes. The problem for the AMA, however, is that would-be doctors have been evading this bottleneck by going to medical school abroad. The AMA is responding to this by attempting to make it harder for the graduates of foreign medical schools to practice here — supposedly out of "concern . . . about the quality of medical training."[45]

Medical licensure restricts the freedom of people to practice medicine and prevents the public from buying the medical care it wants. Nonetheless, most people would probably defend the principle of licensure on the grounds that it raises the standards of competence and the quality of care. Friedman contests this. By reducing the amount of care available, he contends, licensure also reduces the average quality of care people receive. (By analogy, suppose that automobile manufacturers were forbidden to sell any car that did not have the quality of a Mercedes Benz. As a result, people who owned cars would have cars of higher average quality than they do now. But because fewer people could afford cars and more of them would, therefore, have to walk or ride bicycles, such a regulation would not raise the quality of transportation enjoyed by the average person.) Friedman charges, furthermore, that the monopoly created by the licensing of physicians has reduced the incentive for research, development, and experimentation, both in medicine and in the organization and provision of services.

Since Friedman initially presented his argument thirty years ago, some of the alternatives to traditional practice that he proposed have come to pass; prepaid services have emerged, and group and clinic-based practices are on the increase. But what about his main contention that, instead of licensure, we should allow the marketplace to sort out the competent from the incompetent providers of medical services?

Friedman's critics contend that even if the licensing of professionals "involves violating a moral rule" against restricting individuals' "freedom of opportunity," it is still immoral to allow an unqualified person to engage in potentially harmful activities without having subjected the person to adequate tests of competence.[46] Despite the appeal of Friedman's arguments on behalf of free choice, the danger still remains, they say, that people will be victimized by the incompetent.

Consider, for example, the quack remedies and treatments that are being peddled to AIDS patients here and abroad. Twenty-dollar bottles of processed pond scum and eight-dollar concoctions of herbs, injections of hydrogen peroxide or of cells from the glands of unborn calves, the eating of bee pollen and garlic, $800 pills containing substances from mice inoculated with the AIDS virus, and even whacking the thymus gland of patients to stimulate the body's immune system — all these are among the treatments offered to desperate people by the unscrupulous and eccentric.[47] Deregulation of the medical field seems most unlikely to diminish such exploitation.

Discussion Questions

1. What explains the fact that licenses are required for so many occupations? What do you see as the pros and cons of occupational licensure in general? Does it have benefits that Friedman has overlooked?

2. Do you believe that licensure in medicine or any other field is desirable? In which fields and under what circumstances? What standards would you use to determine where licensure is needed?

3. Is occupational licensure consistent with the basic principles and values of capitalism? Is it a violation of the free-market ideal? How would you respond to the argument that licensure illegitimately restricts individual freedom to pursue a career or a trade?

4. Does licensure make the market work more or less effectively? Would you agree that as long as consumers are provided accurate information, then they should be permitted to make their own choices with regard to the services and products they purchase—even when it comes to medical care? Or is licensing necessary to protect them from making incorrect choices?

5. Friedman and others view the AMA as a trade union, and they believe that the high incomes of doctors are due more to artificial restrictions on the free market than to the inherent value of their services. Is this an accurate or fair picture of the medical profession?

6. Is licensing an all-or-nothing issue, or is it possible that while there are certain services that we should permit only licensed practitioners to perform, there are other services now monopolized by the same practitioners that could be performed less expensively but equally competently by paraprofessionals or laypersons?

CASE 4.4
A New Work Ethic?

You would think that employees would do something if they discovered that a customer had died on the premises. But that's not necessarily so, according to the Associated Press, which reported that police discovered the body of a trucker in a tractor trailer rig that had sat—with its engine running—in the parking lot of a fast-food restaurant for nine days. Employees swept the parking lot around the truck but ignored the situation for over a week until the stench got so bad that someone finally called the police.

That lack of response doesn't surprise James Sheehy, a human resources manager in Houston, who spent his summer vacation working "undercover" at a fast-food restaurant owned by a relative.[48] Introduced to co-workers as a management trainee from another franchise location who was being brought in to learn the ropes, Sheehy was initially viewed with some suspicion, but by the third day the group had accepted him as just another employee. Sheehy started out as a maintenance person and gradually rotated through various cooking and cleaning assignments before ending up as a cashier behind the front counter.

Most of Sheehy's fellow employees were teen-agers and college students who were home for the summer and earning additional spending money. Almost half came from upper-income families and the rest from middle-income neighborhoods. More than half were women, and a third were minorities. What Sheehy reports is a whole generation of workers with a frightening new work ethic: contempt for customers, indifference to quality and service, unrealistic expectations about the world of work, and a get-away-with-what-you-can attitude.

A survey released in 1990 shows that employee theft accounts for seven times more revenue loss for retailers than shoplifting.[49] Sheehy's experience was in line with this. He writes that the basic work ethic at his place of employment was a type of gamesmanship that focused on milking the place dry. Theft was rampant, and younger employees were subject to peer pressure to steal as a way of becoming part of the group. "It don't mean nothing," he says, was the basic rationale for dishonesty. "Getting on with getting mine" was another common phrase, as co-workers carefully avoided hard work or dragged out tasks like sweeping to avoid additional assignments.

All that customer service meant, on the other hand, was getting rid of people as fast as possible and with the least possible effort. Sometimes, however, service was deliberately slowed or drive-through orders intentionally switched in order to cause customers to demand to see a manager. This was called "baiting the man," or purposely trying to provoke a response from management. In fact, the general attitude toward managers was one of disdain and contempt. In the eyes of the employees, supervisors were only paper-pushing functionaries who got in the way.

Sheehy's co-workers rejected the very idea of hard work and long hours. "Scamming" was their ideal. Treated as a kind of art form and as an accepted way of doing business, scamming meant taking shortcuts or getting something done without much effort, usually by having someone else do it. "You only put in the time and effort for the big score" is how one fellow worker characterized the work ethic he shared with his peers. "You got to just cruise through the job stuff and wait to make the big score," said another. "Then you can hustle. The office stuff is for buying time or paying for the groceries."

By contrast, they looked forward to working "at a real job where you don't have to put up with hassles." "Get out of school and you can leave this to the real dummies." "Get an office and a computer and a secretary and you can scam your way through anything." On the other hand, these young employees believed that most jobs were like the fast-food industry: automated, boring, undemanding and unsatisfying, and dominated by difficult people. But they dreamed of an action-packed business world, an image shaped by a culture of video games and action movies. The college students in particular, reports Sheehy, identified with the Michael Douglas character in the movie *Wall Street* and believed that a no-holds-barred, trample-over-anybody, get-what-you-want approach is the necessary and glamorous road to success.

Discussion Questions

1. How typical are the attitudes that Sheehy reports? Does his description of a new work ethic tally with your own experiences?

2. What are the implications of the work ethic that Sheehy describes for the future of American business?

3. Some might discount Sheehy's experiences either as being the product of one particular industry or as simply reflecting the immaturity of young employees. Would you agree?

4. Is it reasonable to expect workers, especially in a capitalist society, to be more devoted to their jobs, more concerned with quality and customer service, than Sheehy's co-workers were? What explains employee theft?

5. In what ways does the culture of our capitalist society encourage attitudes like those Sheehy describes?

NOTES

1. See *Newsweek* (international edition), November 2, 1987, from which the details that follow are taken.
2. See David Schweickart, *Capitalism or Worker Control?* (New York: Praeger, 1980).
3. For a succinct treatment of the rise of the Fugger dynasty, see Ned M. Cross, Robert C. Lamm, and Rudy H. Turk, *The Search for Personal Freedom* (Dubuque, Iowa: William C. Brown Company, 1972), 12.
4. Ibid., 13. See also Robert B. Carson, *Business Issues Today: Alternative Perspectives* (New York: St. Martin's Press, 1982), 3–30.
5. Robert Heilbroner, *The Worldly Philosophers*, 5th ed. (New York: Simon & Schuster, Touchstone edition, 1980), 22–23.
6. Adam Smith, *The Wealth of Nations* (New York: Modern Library, 1985), 16.
7. Ibid., 223–225.

8. As quoted by G. A. Cohen, *History, Labour, and Freedom* (Oxford: Oxford University Press, 1988), 273.

9. Ibid., 265.

10. Robert Heilbroner, *The Economic Problem* (Englewood Cliffs, N.J.: Prentice-Hall, 1972), 725.

11. Jim Hightower, "Food Monopoly: Who's Who in the Thanksgiving Business?" *Texas Observer*, November 17, 1978.

12. Heilbroner, *Worldly Philosophers*, 302.

13. Robert Reich, *The Next American Frontier* (New York: Penguin Books, 1983), 174.

14. Ibid., 178. See also Benjamin M. Friedman, *Day of Reckoning* (New York: Vintage Books, 1989), 57–58.

15. Doug Brandon, "Corporate America: Uncle Sam's Favorite Welfare Client," *Business and Society Review* 55 (Fall 1985): 48.

16. Martin Carnoy, *The State and Political Theory* (Princeton, N.J.: Princeton University Press, 1984), 246.

17. Carson, *Business Issues Today*, 29.

18. This entire extract is from *Karl Marx: Early Writings*, translated by T. B. Bottomore, 1963. Used with permission of McGraw-Hill Book Company.

19. Studs Terkel, "Here I Am a Worker," in Leonard Silk, ed., *Capitalism: The Moving Target* (New York: Quadrangle, 1974), 68–69.

20. Lester C. Thurow, "A Surge in Inequality," *Scientific American*, May 1987. See also "Slower Pace for Productivity Gains," *New York Times*, February 5, 1988; "Raising Productivity Will Be Tough in '90s," *Wall Street Journal*, December 10, 1990, A1; and Friedman, *Day of Reckoning*, Chapter 8.

21. *Los Angeles Times*, December 22, 1990, A1.

22. "Can America Compete?" *Business Week*, April 20, 1987, and "Running to Stand Still," *The Economist*, November 10, 1990. See also "U.S. Standard of Living Under Pressure," *International Herald Tribune*, February 20–21, 1988; *San Francisco Chronicle*, February 3, 1989, B6; and *New York Times*, December 16, 1990, 4-1.

23. John DeLorean and J. Patrick Wright, *On a Clear Day You Can See General Motors: John Z. DeLorean's Look Inside the Automobile Giant* (New York: Wright Enterprises, 1979), 132.

24. See Richard T. Wise and Stephan W. McDaniel, "American Competitiveness and the CEO — Who's Minding Shop?" *Sloan Management Review* 29 (Winter 1988); and "Managers Need Milestones," *The Economist*, January 23, 1988.

25. This paragraph and the next are based on Robert J. Samuelson, "Clobbering Car Buyers," *Newsweek* (international edition), December 14, 1987, 43.

26. John Burgess and Fred Hiatt, "How Toyota Clung to Its U.S. Sales," *International Herald Tribune*, February 17, 1988, 1.

27. "The Hollow Corporation," *Business Week*, March 3, 1986, on which this and the following paragraph draw.

28. "The Raiding Game," *Dollars and Sense*, March 1987. See also the film *Wall Street* for a dramatic portrayal of the world of corporate raiders.

29. *Business and Society Review* 53 (Spring 1985): 76; and *Mother Jones*, May 1988, 39.

30. "The Raiding Game," 14.

31. See *New York Times*, May 14, 1989, 3-1.

32. Thomas A. Kochan, Harry C. Katz, and Robert B. McKersie, *The Transformation of American Industrial Relations* (New York: Basic Books, 1986), 209.

33. Paul Bernstein, "The Work Ethic That Never Was," *Wharton Magazine* 4 (1980).

34. Unless otherwise noted, the facts and quotations reported in this case are based on Richard Manning and John McCormick, "The Blue-Collar Blues," *Newsweek*, June 4, 1984.

35. John Naisbitt, *Megatrends* (New York: Warner Books, 1982), 64.

36. See Warren Brown and Michael Schrage, "An Industrial Policy, Built by G.M.," *Washington Post National Weekly Edition*, August 20, 1984, 6–8.

37. Ibid., 7.

38. Sheila Harty, *Hucksters in the Classroom: A Review of Industry Propaganda in Schools* (Washington, D.C.: Center for Study of Responsive Law, 1979), 5.

39. Ibid., 11.

40. Ken Neubeck, *Corporate Response to Urban Crisis* (New York: D. C. Heath, 1974), 117. Quoted in Harty, *Hucksters in the Classroom*, 11–12.

41. As discussed on the "MacNeil/Lehrer News Hour," June 8, 1989. "Mixed Reviews on Classroom Commercials," *San Francisco Chronicle*, March 8, 1989, A1, is the source of the quotations that follow. See also *Wall Street Journal*, May 17, 1989, B6, and November 26, 1990, B5.

42. "Memo from the Editor," *Medical Economics*, November 7, 1988.

43. See the chapter on "Occupational Licensure" in Milton Friedman, *Capitalism and Freedom* (Chicago: University of Chicago Press, 1962), in particular page 149. See also De George, *Business Ethics*, 3rd ed. (New York: Macmillan, 1990) 351; and Doug Bandon, "Doctors Operate to Cut Out Competition," *Business and Society Review* 58 (Spring 1986).

44. TRB, "Doctors Overdose," *The New Republic*, July 7, 1986, 4.

45. Ibid.

46. Bernard Gert, "Licensing Professions: Preliminary Considerations," *Business and Professional Ethics Journal* 1 (Summer 1982): 52, and Donald Weinert, "Commentary," *Business and Professional Ethics Journal* 1 (Summer 1982): 62.

47. "Preying on AIDS Patients," *Newsweek*, June 1, 1987.

48. James W. Sheehy, "New Work Ethic Is Frightening," *Personnel Journal*, June 1990, is the source of this case.

49. "Workers Out-Stealing Shoplifters," *San Francisco Chronicle*, November 24, 1990, B3.

Buddhist Economics

E. F. Schumacher

When thinking about economic matters, people in our society make a number of assumptions. These assumptions have important theoretical and practical consequences, but we simply take their truth for granted. Author and economist E. F. Schumacher exposes several of these implicit dogmas simply by showing how the thinking of a Buddhist economist would differ from that of a modern Western economist on some basic issues: the nature of work, the benefits of mechanization, the relation between material wealth and human well-being, and the use of natural resources.

'Right Livelihood' is one of the requirements of the Buddha's Noble Eightfold Path. It is clear, therefore, that there must be such a thing as Buddhist economics.

Buddhist countries have often stated that they wish to remain faithful to their heritage. So Burma: "The New Burma sees no conflict between religious values and economic progress. Spiritual health and material wellbeing are not enemies: they are natural allies." Or: "We can blend successfully the religious and spiritual values of our heritage with the benefits of modern technology." Or: "We Burmans have a sacred duty to conform both our dreams and our acts to our faith. This we shall ever do."

All the same, such countries invariably assume that they can model their economic development plans in accordance with modern economics, and they call upon modern economists from so-called advanced countries to advise them, to formulate the policies to be pursued, and to construct the grand design for development, the Five-Year Plan or whatever it may be called. No one seems to think that a Buddhist way of life would call for Buddhist economics, just as the modern materialist way of life has brought forth modern economics.

Economists themselves, like most specialists, normally suffer from a kind of metaphysical blindness, assuming that theirs is a science of absolute and invariable truths, without any presuppositions. Some go as far as to claim that economic laws are as free from 'metaphysics' or 'values' as the law of gravitation. We need not, however, get involved in arguments of methodology. Instead, let us take some fundamentals and see what they look like when viewed by a modern economist and a Buddhist economist.

There is universal agreement that a fundamental source of wealth is human labour. Now, the modern economist has been brought up to consider 'labour' or work as little more than a necessary evil. From the point of view of the employer, it is in any case simply an item of cost, to be reduced to a minimum if it cannot be eliminated altogether, say, by automation. From the point of view of the workman, it is a 'disutility'; to work is to make a sacrifice of one's leisure and comfort, and wages are a kind of compensation for the sacrifice. Hence the ideal from the point of view of the employer is to have output without employees, and the ideal from the point of view of the employee is to have income without employment.

The consequences of these attitudes both in theory and in practice are, of course, extremely far-reaching. If the ideal with regard to work is to get rid of it, every method that 'reduces the work load' is a good thing. The most potent method, short of automation, is the so-called 'division of labour' and the classical example is the pin factory eulogised in Adam Smith's *Wealth of Nations*. Here it is not a matter of ordinary specialisation, which mankind has practised from time immemorial, but of dividing up every complete process of production into minute parts, so that the final product can be produced at great speed without anyone having had to contribute more than a totally insignificant and, in most cases, unskilled movement of his limbs.

The Buddhist point of view takes the function of work to be at least threefold: to give a man a chance to utilise and develop his faculties; to enable him to overcome his ego-centredness by joining with other people in a common task; and to bring forth the goods and services needed for a becoming existence. Again, the consequences that flow from this view are endless. To organise work in such a manner that it becomes meaningless, boring, stultifying, or nerve-racking for the worker would be little short of criminal; it would indicate a greater concern with goods than with people, an evil lack of compassion and a soul-destroying degree of attachment to the most primitive side of this worldly existence. Equally, to strive for leisure as an alternative to work would be considered a complete misunderstanding of one of the basic truths of human existence, namely that work and leisure are complementary parts of the same living process and cannot be separated without destroying the joy of work and the bliss of leisure.

From the Buddhist point of view, there are therefore two types of mechanisation which must be clearly distinguished: one that enhances a man's skill and power and one that turns the work of man over to a mechanical slave, leaving man in a position of having to serve the slave. How to tell the one from the other? "The craftsman himself," says Ananda Coomaraswamy, a man equally competent to talk about the modern west as the ancient east, "can always, if allowed to, draw the delicate distinction between the machine and the tool. The carpet loom is a tool, a contrivance for holding warp threads at a stretch for the pile to be woven round them by the craftsmen's fingers; but the power loom is a machine, and its significance as a destroyer of culture lies in the fact that it does the essentially human part of the work." It is clear, therefore, that Buddhist economics must be very

different from the economics of modern materialism, since the Buddhist sees the essence of civilisation not in a multiplication of wants but in the purification of human character. Character, at the same time, is formed primarily by a man's work. And work, properly conducted in conditions of human dignity and freedom, blesses those who do it and equally their products. The Indian philosopher and economist J. C. Kumarappa sums the matter up as follows:

"If the nature of the work is properly appreciated and applied, it will stand in the same relation to the higher faculties as food is to the physical body. It nourishes and enlivens the higher man and urges him to produce the best he is capable of. It directs his free will along the proper course and disciplines the animal in him into progressive channels. It furnishes an excellent background for man to display his scale of values and develop his personality."

If a man has no chance of obtaining work he is in a desperate position, not simply because he lacks an income but because he lacks this nourishing and enlivening factor of disciplined work which nothing can replace. A modern economist may engage in highly sophisticated calculations on whether full employment 'pays' or whether it might be more 'economic' to run an economy at less than full employment so as to ensure a greater mobility of labour, a better stability of wages, and so forth. His fundamental criterion of success is simply the total quantity of goods produced during a given period of time. "If the marginal urgency of goods is low," says Professor Galbraith in *The Affluent Society*, "then so is the urgency of employing the last man or the last million men in the labour force." And again: "If . . . we can afford some unemployment in the interest of stability — a proposition, incidentally, of impeccably conservative antecedents — then we can afford to give those who are unemployed the goods that enable them to sustain their accustomed standard of living."

From a Buddhist point of view, this is standing the truth on its head by considering goods as more important than people and consumption as more important than creative activity. It means shifting the emphasis from the worker to the product of work, that is, from the human to the subhuman, a surrender to the forces of evil. The very start of Buddhist economic planning would be a planning for full employment, and the primary purpose of this would in fact be employment for everyone who needs an 'outside' job: it would not be the maximisation of employment nor the maximisation of production. Women, on the whole, do not need an 'outside' job, and the large-scale employment of women in offices or factories would be considered a sign of serious economic failure. In particular, to let mothers of young children work in factories while the children run wild would be as uneconomic in the eyes of a Buddhist economist as the employment of a skilled worker as a soldier in the eyes of a modern economist.

While the materialist is mainly interested in goods, the Buddhist is mainly interested in liberation. But Buddhism is 'The Middle Way' and therefore in no way antagonistic to physical well-being. It is not wealth that stands in the way of liberation but the attachment to wealth; not the enjoyment of pleasurable things but the craving for them. The keynote of Buddhist economics, therefore, is simplicity and non-violence. From an economist's point of view, the marvel of the Buddhist way of life is the utter rationality of its pattern—amazingly small means leading to extraordinarily satisfactory results.

For the modern economist this is very difficult to understand. He is used to measuring the 'standard of living' by the amount of annual consumption, assuming all the time that a man who consumes more is 'better off' than a man who consumes less. A Buddhist economist would consider this approach excessively irrational: since consumption is merely a means to human well-being, the aim should be to obtain the maximum of well-being with the minimum of consumption. Thus, if the purpose of clothing is a certain amount of temperature comfort and an attractive appearance, the task is to attain this purpose with the smallest possible effort, that is, with the smallest annual destruction of cloth and with the help of designs that involve the smallest possible input of toil. The less toil there is, the more time and strength is left for artistic creativity. It would be highly uneconomic, for instance to go in for complicated tailoring, like the modern west, when a much more beautiful effect can be achieved by the skillful draping of uncut material. It would be the height of folly to make material so that it should wear out quickly and the height of barbarity to make anything ugly, shabby or mean. What has just been said about clothing applies equally to all other human requirements. The ownership and the consumption of goods is a means to an end, and Buddhist economics is the systematic study of how to attain given ends with the minimum means.

Modern economics, on the other hand, considers consumption to be the sole end and purpose of all economic activity, taking the factors of production—land, labour, and capital—as the means. The former, in short, tries to maximise human satisfactions by the optimal pattern of consumption, while the latter tries to maximise consumption by the optimal pattern of productive effort. It is easy to see that the effort needed to sustain a way of life which seeks to attain the optimal pattern of consumption is likely to be much smaller than the effort needed to sustain a drive for maximum consumption. We need not be surprised, therefore, that the pressure and strain of living is very much less in, say, Burma than it is in the United States, in spite of the fact that the amount of labour-saving machinery used in the former country is only a minute fraction of the amount used in the latter.

Simplicity and non-violence are obviously closely related. The optimal pattern of consumption, producing a high degree of human satisfaction by means of a relatively low rate of consumption, allows people to live without great pressure and strain and to fulfill the primary injunction of Buddhist teaching: 'Cease to do evil; try to do good.' As physical resources are everywhere limited, people satisfying their needs by means of a modest use of resources are obviously less likely to be at each other's throats than people depending upon a high rate of use. Equally, people who live in highly self-sufficient local communities are less likely to get involved in large-scale violence than people whose existence depends on world-wide systems of trade.

From the point of view of Buddhist economics, therefore, production from local resources for local needs is the most rational way of economic life, while dependence on imports from afar and the consequent need to produce for export to unknown and distant peoples is highly uneconomic and justifiable only in exceptional cases and on a small scale. Just as the modern economist would admit that a high rate of consumption of transport services between a man's home and his place of work signifies a misfortune and not a high standard of life, so the Buddhist economist would hold that to satisfy human wants from faraway sources rather than from sources nearby signifies failure rather than success. The former tends to take statistics showing an increase in the number of ton/miles per head of the population carried by a country's transport system as proof of economic progress, while to the latter — the Buddhist economist — the same statistics would indicate a highly undesirable deterioration in the *pattern* of consumption.

Another striking difference between modern economics and Buddhist economics arises over the use of natural resources. Bertrand de Jouvenel, the eminent French political philosopher, has characterised 'western man' in words which may be taken as a fair description of the modern economist.

"He tends to count nothing as an expenditure, other than human effort; he does not seem to mind how much mineral matter he wastes and, far worse, how much living matter he destroys. He does not seem to realise at all that human life is a dependent part of an ecosystem of many different forms of life. As the world is ruled from towns where men are cut off from any form of life other than human, the feeling of belonging to an ecosystem is not revived. This results in a harsh and improvident treatment of things upon which we ultimately depend, such as water and trees."

The teaching of the Buddha, on the other hand, enjoins a reverent and non-violent attitude not only to all sentient beings but also, with great emphasis, to trees. Every follower of the Buddha ought to plant a tree every few years and look after it until it is safely established, and the Buddhist economist can demonstrate without difficulty that the universal observation of this rule would result in a high rate of genuine economic development independent of any foreign aid. Much of the economic decay of south-east Asia (as of many other parts of the world) is undoubtedly due to a heedless and shameful neglect of trees.

Modern economics does not distinguish between renewable and non-renewable materials, as its very method is to equalise and quantify everything by means of a money price. Thus, taking various alternative fuels, like coal, oil, wood, or water-power: the only difference between them recognised by modern economics is relative cost per equivalent unit. The cheapest is automatically the one to be preferred, as to do otherwise would be irrational and 'uneconomic.' From a Buddhist point of view, of course, this will not do; the essential difference between non-renewable fuels like coal and oil on the one hand and renewable fuels like wood and water-power on the other cannot be simply overlooked. Non-renewable goods must be used only if they are indispensable, and then only with the greatest care and the most meticulous concern for conservation. To use them heedlessly or extravagantly is an act of violence, and while complete non-violence may not be attainable on this earth, there is nonetheless an ineluctable duty on man to aim at the ideal of non-violence in all he does.

Just as a modern European economist would not consider it a great economic achievement if all European art treasures were sold to America at attractive prices, so the Buddhist economist would insist that a population basing its economic life on non-renewable fuels is living parasitically, on capital instead of income. Such a way of life could have no permanence and could therefore be justified only as a purely temporary expedient. As the world's resources of non-renewable fuels — coal, oil and natural gas — are exceedingly unevenly distributed over the globe and undoubtedly limited in quantity, it is clear that their exploitation at an ever-increasing rate is an act of violence against nature which must almost inevitably lead to violence between men.

This fact alone might give food for thought even to those people in Buddhist countries who care nothing for the religious and spiritual values of their heritage and ardently desire to embrace the materialism of modern economics at the fastest possible speed. Before they dismiss Buddhist economics as nothing better than a nostalgic dream, they might wish to consider whether the path of economic development outlined by modern economics is likely to lead them to places where they really want to be. Towards the end of his courageous book *The Challenge of Man's Future*, Professor Harrison Brown of the California Institute of Technology gives the following appraisal:

"Thus we see that, just as industrial society is fundamentally unstable and subject to reversion to agrarian existence, so within it the conditions which offer individual freedom are unstable in their ability to avoid the conditions which impose rigid organisation and totalitarian control. Indeed, when we examine all of the foreseeable difficulties which threaten the survival of industrial civilisation, it is difficult to see how the achievement of stability and the maintenance of individual liberty can be made compatible."

Even if this were dismissed as a long-term view there is the immediate question of whether 'modernisation,' as currently practised without regard to religious and spiritual values, is actually producing agreeable results. As far as the masses are concerned, the results appear to be disastrous — a collapse of the rural economy, a rising tide of unemployment in town and country, and the growth of a city proletariat without nourishment for either body or soul.

It is in the light of both immediate experience and long-term prospects that the study of Buddhist economics could be recommended even to those who believe that economic growth is more important than any spiritual or religious values. For it is not a question of choosing between 'modern growth' and 'traditional stagnation.' It is a question of finding the right path of development, the Middle Way between materialist heedlessness and traditionalist immobility, in short, of finding 'Right Livelihood.'

Review and Discussion Questions

1. From the Buddhist point of view, what is the function of work? What do you see as the main social and economic implications of the Buddhist perspective?

2. Schumacher sees simplicity as a keynote of Buddhist economics. What's the connection between simplicity and nonviolence? Why does Buddhism value simplicity? Does capitalism promote needless complexity?

3. How do Buddhism and capitalism differ in their understanding of the nature and purpose of human existence? Is the Buddhist view of the role of women sexist?

4. What distinguishes Buddhist economics from modern economics in its approach to material wealth? To natural resources? With which approach are you more sympathetic and why?

5. Is a capitalist economic system compatible with a Buddhist perspective? Is any other economic system?

6. Would you agree that Buddhism has something to teach us about economics?

Reflections on the Triumph of Capitalism _____

Robert Heilbroner

With the collapse of centralized planning in the Soviet Union and Eastern Europe, capitalism appears to have triumphed and the socialist project to have been collapsed. But what are capitalism's prospects for the future? This is the topic of Robert Heilbroner's essay. After reviewing some of the classical economists' doubts about capitalism, Heilbroner analyzes the nature of capitalism and describes the dynamic relation — and current tensions — between the economic and political realms under capitalism, and the implications of this relation for capitalism's continued evolution. He concludes with some reflections on the future of both capitalism and socialism.

Less than seventy-five years after it officially began, the contest between capitalism and socialism is over: capitalism has won. The Soviet Union, China, and Eastern Europe have given us the clear-est possible proof that capitalism organizes the material affairs of humankind more satisfactorily than socialism: that however inequitably or irresponsibly the marketplace may distribute goods, it does so better than the queues of a planned economy; however mindless the culture of commercialism, it is more attractive than state moralism; and however deceptive the ideology of a business civilization, it is more believable than that of a socialist one. . . .

Yet I doubt whether the historic drama will conclude, like a great morality play, in the unequivocal victory of one side and the ignominious defeat of the other. The economic enemy of capitalism has always been its own self-generated dynamics, not the presence of an alternative economic system. Socialism, in its embodiments in the Soviet Union and, to a lesser degree, China, has been a military and political competitor but never an economic threat. Thus, despite the route of centralized planning — to judge by the stories coming from Moscow, it has the proportions of a rout — one would have to be very incautious to assume that capitalism will now find itself rid of its propensity to generate both inflation and recession, cured of its intermittent speculative fevers, or free of threatening international economic problems. Nevertheless, in one very important respect the triumph of capitalism alters the manner in which we must assess its prospects. The old question "Can capitalism work?" to which endless doubting answers have been given by its critics, becomes "Can capitalism work well enough?" which is quite another thing.

Even such hedged speculations are regarded with suspicion by most of the members of my profession. Modern-day economists sedulously avoid scenarios of long-term capitalist development — a caution that was not shared by the great economists of the past, virtually all of whom wrote boldly about prospects for the system. What is perhaps more surprising is that, although they disagreed about many things, those economic thinkers were near-unanimous in depicting the prospects as gloomy. Adam Smith, for example, believed that the society of his time, which had not yet been named capitalism, would have a long run but would end up in decline. Marx, of course, expected the demise of the system, but so did John Stuart Mill, whose "Principles of Political Economy" was published in 1848, the year of Marx's "Manifesto." The most important Victorian economist, Alfred Marshall, warned against socialism and unconsidered changes, but his very Victorianism — he called for "economic chivalry" — makes us squirm a little as we read the exhortative concluding words of his "Principles." His pupil and protégé, John Maynard Keynes, was of a different mind. Only a "somewhat comprehensive socialization" of investment, he wrote, would rescue the system from intolerable levels of unemployment. Even Joseph Schumpeter, the most conservative (and the least publicly known) of these magisterial economists, asked in his famous "Capitalism, Socialism and Democracy," in 1942, "Can capitalism survive?" and answered, "No. I do not think it can." . . .

Keynes . . . based his prognosis not on material limitations of the system but on economic ones — not on the intrinsic lack of any need for a second line from London to York but on the lack of enough purchasing power to buy all the tickets on the first line and thereby establish a possible demand for a second. Quixotically, this lack of purchasing power was itself the result of a failure on the part of business to undertake enough investment projects — railways and others. A pessimistic appraisal of the investment outlook led to insufficient employment on investment projects; and this, in turn, resulted in an insufficiency of the purchasing power needed to make such projects profitable. Given this catch-22, which is one of Keynes' enduring contributions to economic theory, it is not surprising that he looked to the "socialization" of investment as necessary to avoid economic stagnation.

Marx's scenario was not hobbled by a static view of the capacity of the system for inventing new technologies and developing new commodity wants, but it, too, had its catch-22s. These were based on inherent conflicts — contradictions, Marx called them — between the needs of individual enterprises and the working requirements for the system as a whole. One of them was the tendency of capitalism to undercut the buying power of the working class by the continuous introduction of labor-saving machinery, to which business was driven by the pressures of competition. Each enterprise thereby sought to steal a march on its competitors, but instead all enterprises found themselves facing a condition of underconsumption. It is summed up in the perhaps apocryphal story of Henry Ford II walking through a newly automated engine factory with Walter Reuther, the legendary organizing figure of the United Automobile Workers, and asking, "Walter, how are you going to organize these machines?" — to which Reuther is supposed to have answered, "Henry, how are you going to sell them cars?" Another contradiction foreseen by Marx was the erosion of profit rates — not purchasing power — which stemmed from this same substitution of machinery for labor. According to Marx's analysis, labor power was the goose that laid the golden eggs of profits, because employers were able to extract more value from their workers than they paid out as wages. The replacement of living labor by machinery constricted the base from which profit arose, and thus ultimately reduced the rate of return on capital. And well before Marx,

Thomas Robert Malthus (whose fame as a demographer has obscured the fact that he was the first "professional" economist, employed by the East India Company) worried about the possibility of a general glut—a general insufficiency of purchasing power. From the moment Malthus's fears were voiced, they were the subject of refutation and ridicule and, because they were not very cogently put, were easily dismissed. But every time a depression has come, the spectre of a general glut has re-emerged. Indeed, it can be argued, I think, that the lurking question of economics, certainly during the present century, has been whether a capitalist economy will experience general gluts, under whatever name.

An immense body of theory has been built on, about, and against the master theories of Marx and Keynes and their distant predecessor Malthus, and a vast amount of research has sought to produce evidence that profit rates have indeed fallen or that inadequate purchasing power has acted as an undertow against growth. It is fair to say that the debate remains unsettled. . . .

This [suggests] . . . that the decisive factor in determining the fate of capitalism must be political, not economic. Schumpeter, for example, expected capitalism to disappear, but not because of any strictly economic difficulties. The stumbling block was cultural. "Capitalism," he wrote, "creates a critical frame of mind which, after having destroyed the moral authority of so many other institutions, in the end turns against its own; the bourgeois finds to his amazement that the rationalist attitude does not stop at the credentials of kings and popes but goes on to attack private property and the whole scheme of bourgeois values." Schumpeter anticipated a painless metamorphosis of capitalism into socialism, by which he meant a presumably democratic, planned economy run by the former managers of capitalism. Marx would have scoffed at Schumpeter's low appraisal of capitalism's self-esteem, but he, too, laid its ultimate downfall on the doorstep of political, not economic, events. Capitalism would be progressively weakened by its economic crises, but, in the famous words of "Capital," the "knell of capitalist private property" would not sound or the "expropriators" be "expropriated" until the working class arose to take things into its own hands.

Schumpeter obviously did not anticipate the present-day resurgence of conservative self-confidence, nor did Marx expect that working-class attitudes and politics would become middle class. Despite their recognition of the importance of mustering and holding the faith of its participants, neither man fully grasped the capacity of the system to do so. This is so, I believe, because neither sufficiently appreciated that capitalism is a social order built upon a deeply embedded and widely believed principle expressed in the actions and beliefs of its most important representatives. From such a viewpoint it is comparable to imperial or aristocratic or Communist regimes, with their universally accepted principle of kingship or aristocracy or socialism, embodied in the personages of monarchs or lords or sacred texts. Capitalism is not normally thought of as possessing such a principle, but its largely uncritical worship of the idea of economic growth is as central to its nature as the similar veneration of the idea of divine kingship or blue blood or doctrinal orthodoxy has been for other regimes. Suggesting that capitalism can be likened to a "regime" rubs our sensibilities the wrong way, but the word is useful in forcing us to consider capitalism as an order of social life, with distinctive hierarchies, imperatives, loyalties, and beliefs. It is this regimelike aspect of capitalism·that turns Schumpeter's feared rational skepticism of its privileges into a rationalization of its rights, and makes the working class, far from the opposition that Marx hoped it would become, into stalwart supporters.

The idea of a regime also illumines the nature of its central, dominant, "ruling" class. Immanuel Wallerstein, one of the most influential modern economic historians, has suggested that regimes are, save in moments of convulsion, characterized by the presence of one standard-bearing, "universal" class. I have always pictured such a class as regarded by all, including itself, as the living and legitimate embodiment of the aims and sentiments of the entire society. Thus, it is not only lords and monarchs who believe in their intrinsic superiority but the peasants, who throw their caps in the air. If we ask what group in Western societies occupies this position of untroubled self-regard supported by the general esteem of the people at large, I think the answer would be its capitalists, under their workaday title of businessmen. Individual figures in government may be revered, military leaders admired, but neither politicians nor generals put their own group's interests forward as those of the larger society. With due recognition given its well-publicized villains and its occasional bad repute—the counterpart of bad kings and outbreaks of anti-monarchism—it must be conceded that the class of businessmen is the only group that naturally thinks of itself, and is generally thought of, as speaking for the social order as a whole. In this un-complicated sense, business is the universal class of the regime of capitalism.

Although most businessmen would bridle at these terms, recognition of the regimelike character of capitalism and the "universality" of its business class seems to me indispensable in understanding the capacity of the system for withstanding critical assaults and for disarming political disaffection. People in business never think of themselves as the equivalents of kings or lords or commissars, for the very good reason that they are not. And the reason they are not is that capitalism is unique in history in having not one but two centers of authority, one built around the "economic" prerogatives of the business system, the other around the "political" prerogatives of the governmental system. In all other societies, from primitive to socialist, a single source of authority—village council, king, priest-hood, party—makes both the determinations of war, law, and public ceremony, which we recog-nize as political, and the decisions on what shall be produced and how it shall be distributed, which we call economic. A seamless cloak of authority thus extends over the entire social structure, endowing every aspect of it with the aims of whatever group makes up its universal class. Under capitalism, this cloak is torn in two, and the realm of activities hav-ing to do with material life is removed from the reach of political authority. Capitalist governments still make fateful decisions of war and peace, or law and order, but are excluded from what is elsewhere a first prerogative of rulership—direct command over the material resources on which rulership must depend. When we look at the economic realm, we discover an even more astonishing con-striction of authority. Capitalists, in whose name the system is organized, no longer possess the ba-sic powers that accrue to persons of similar impor-tance under earlier systems; unlike the most minor feudal lords, for instance, they cannot try, im-prison, or forcibly muster "their" work forces, or enjoy the privileges of a legal code different from that applicable to other groups, much less promul-gate laws or command military forces within their own bailiwicks. Thus, the two realms of authority

help us understand why, unlike lords and kings and commissars, capitalists genuinely feel them-selves to be without power.

It is not surprising that the establishment of two realms of authority sets the stage for what has always been and will always be the most difficult problem of capitalism—managing the relationship between the two realms. To judge by the talk that occasionally comes from the business community, that relationship is one of opposition and hostility; at times, one might think the government to be a foreign force that has temporarily occupied the capital, like the British in the War of 1812. I think it better to start from the opposite perspective—that ordinarily the government endorses the aims and objectives of the business community and bends a great deal of its efforts toward creating a framework within which business can operate smoothly. This business-oriented cast of mind is partly a conse-quence of the fact that the political realm, having surrendered authority over the workings of the economy, is now dependent on its smooth running to provide the wherewithal to carry out govern-ment programs, but on a deeper level it simply re-flects the fact that the political realm and the eco-nomic realm are both parts of a single regime. Calvin Coolidge spoke the truth, however naïvely, when he said that "the business of America is busi-ness." . . .

Looking back, one sees that the boundary be-tween the realms has moved in two directions. From the eleventh century, when the mercantile es-tate began to establish its place within the feudal hierarchy, through the seventeenth and eighteenth centuries, the authority of the economic realm ex-panded at the expense of that of the political realm. By 1776, "The Wealth of Nations" was able to de-limit the proper economic reach of "the sovereign" to only three functions: "first, the duty of protect-ing the society from the violence and invasion of other independent societies; secondly, the duty of protecting, as far as possible, every member of the society from the injustice or oppression of every other member of it, or the duty of establishing an exact administration of justice; and, thirdly, the duty of erecting and maintaining certain public works and certain public institutions, which it can never be for the interest of any individual, or small number of individuals, to erect or maintain; be-cause the profit could never repay the expense to any individual or small number of individuals, though it may frequently do much more than repay it to a great society."

Although it was certainly not Smith's intent, this minimalist prescription would actually permit a very large government sector—defense, the entire system of law and order, and the provision of what has come to be known as "infrastructure," including (with Smith's explicit approval) public education. What is conspicuously missing from Smith's list is any license for government to carry on or regulate or otherwise become involved in the workings of the market system. Yet, as the examples of the two Roosevelts and the passage of the Federal Reserve Act illustrate, the boundary has moved in precisely that direction since Smith's time, starting with the English Factory Act of 1833, on whose inspectors' reports Marx was to rely heavily for his indictment of the factory system. Since then, of course, the boundaries have extended the reach of government into the economic realm both through the enactment of various entitlements to income, from workmen's compensation to social security in its various forms, and by the more or less official assumption of government responsibility for the over-all level of performance of the system—the latter perhaps first reaching its present-day form in the efforts of the New Deal to "pump up" the economy.

From the beginning, these reassertions of the ancient extent of the public realm have been fiercely debated. Conservative economists, fully as much as businessmen, have feared that the redrawing of the line in favor of the government would cause the goose to lay fewer golden eggs; liberals have feared that a failure to exercise public regulatory or supportive power would threaten the life of the goose. Although the terrain is still contested, I think it is by now abundantly clear that there exists no divinely, or even rationally, ordained division of responsibilities between the realms. At least in the post-Second World War era, the United States has tended to take a somewhat more hands-off attitude than have other capitalist nations, but it is difficult to draw lessons from a comparison of the two policies in practice. During the nineteen-seventies, it seemed that the European style, which featured a good deal of talk and some action toward "concerting" or even "planning" national action, was better suited to promoting economic growth and high employment than the American: European nations enjoyed almost twice

the growth of the United States and suffered only about one-half its unemployment. Recent experience, however, has led to a different conclusion. During the nineteen-eighties, United States growth outstripped European growth, and the American employment record—nineteen million jobs created in a decade—is the envy of the Common Market nations. In similar fashion, Great Britain, virtually the only strict constructionist across the Atlantic, seemed to be paying a high economic price for Margaret Thatcher's determination to dismantle the government-supported economy in the first years of her Prime Ministership, only to emerge in the last two years as the fastest-growing economy in Europe. On the other side of the fence is Japan, where the line of demarcation is drawn in a fashion that bewilders Western observers, blurring the government-enterprise border in ways that have led to its characterization as Japan, Incorporated.

This latitude of workable configuration does not mean, I should add, that it is still possible to relocate the economic-political boundary where Adam Smith placed it. The map has been redrawn in all capitalist nations, not just some, and although the specific elements of the terrain which are allowed to remain on one or the other side differ from one country to the next, all reflect a common enlargement of the political realm. This common movement suggests that the division of authority is affected by forces that override idiosyncrasies of individual place and history. One of these forces is surely the increasing power of industrial technology to puncture the protective mantle of the environment—a development that has moved all governments to intervene in the productive process to safeguard the human habitat against the disturbances caused by industrial processes and products. As an illustration, about five percent of all state and local government employment in the United States exists just to cope with the automobile. A second force must be the growing urbanization of society. Cities have always been the seats of government, and the proportion of American citizens living in cities has increased from about a third in 1900 to over three-quarters today, a trend duplicated in all nations. Yet another force pushing for larger government has to be the increased concatenation of the economic realm itself. The economy of Adam Smith's day, with its many small farms and workshops, could be likened to a pile of sand, composed of innumerable small units of enterprise, each rubbing up against similar small units. Today's economy can best be compared to a girdered assemblage where miscalculations or shocks affect or threaten the entire system. Smith did not write about large-scale economic breakdowns, as Marx or Keynes did, because a sandpile economy does not manifest the instability of a girdered one.

Thus, a central cause of the century-long and universally apparent movement of the public-private boundary toward the side of government reflects the conservative political nature of capitalism much more than it does any emerging economic radicalism within it. Government extends its reach into the economic realm to cushion, restrain, or offset disruptions that emerge from the shuddering industrial machine in the basement. To the degree that the growing visibility and importance of government is due to these self-generated forces, the outlook is certainly for a continuation, and probably an extension, of the long historical trend toward the enlargement of the governmental realm. The disruptive power of technology, the complexity of urban life, the concatenation of the economy are all likely to increase — perhaps dramatically, in the case of technology — bringing with them the need for the government to mount more repair efforts, which usually get blamed after a while for creating the damage they are trying to repair.

This likely development would, however, be no more than an extension of a long-term trend in the division of authority. More significant is the growing encroachment of the economic realm upon the very core principle of the political realm, its sovereignty. Here the threatened salient lies along the boundary line that divides the international concerns of the economy and the state. . . . By the eighteenth century, the aims of government were generally conceived as congruent with those of the economic community. . . . Free trade was then everywhere defended as the logical extension into the world market of the competitive discipline of the domestic market — a process that would ultimately enrich, and therefore strengthen, the nation-states whose economies would be subjected to this Darwinian winnowing process. . . . The internationalization of economic relationships was [seen as] unquestionably in the interests of the capitalist nations themselves. Hence no one perceived

the international extension of the economic realm as a threat to political sovereignty. The reason, we can now see, was that the international economy was itself still in its formative stages. Enterprises were still mainly situated in and entirely identified with their mother countries. International finance linked stock exchanges, but modern international banking was still in its infancy — one travelled abroad with letters of credit. An enterprise in Hamburg or Dayton could not possibly exercise continuous supervision over production flows of manufacturing subsidiaries in Bangkok or Mexico City, and, in fact, had no such subsidiaries. The enlargement of the international exchange of currencies to a level at which it exceeded by tenfold the entire value of the goods and services that crossed national boundaries was beyond the dreams of any banker and certainly beyond the technical capacities of the world's hand-operated banking system. The possibility that corporations in one country could clone themselves in the poorer regions, whence they would export automobiles, cassettes, high-density computer disks and synthetic fabrics to their home markets was never discussed, because it was never remotely realistic.

All these developments are, of course, commonplaces of modern economic life, and a great deal of anxious attention is currently being paid to them. What is not so much discussed is that this movement represents a remarkable change in the complexion of capitalism itself, a change that threatens a considerable part — though, of course, not all — of the prerogatives of the political realm. Can a nation-state still effectively control its own currency, whatever its constitution may say, if currency flows into and out of its banks in volumes that vastly overshadow the size of "its own" money supply? Can it accurately assess the condition of its balance of trade if a significant fraction of its imports comes from its own companies situated abroad? Can the Darwinian process be counted on to strengthen national power if the outcome of the process is that companies situate their productive capacity outside the boundaries of the home country? I have avoided using American names and examples, because the questions apply to Germany and Switzerland as much as to the United States. The multinational corporation and the growth of a vast network of international finance affect the political independence of all capitalist governments.

In the same way, the nascent transplantation of capitalism to parts of Asia and South America — symbolized in the meteoric rise of South Korea — affects the political hegemony that has until now belonged to the capitalisms of North America, Europe, and (more recently) Japan.

These deep-seated changes, present and latent, suggests that the boundaries of the two realms will be further readjusted in the foreseeable future, as the political realms within the older capitalist nations seek to protect their sovereignty against an unexpected threat from their own economic bases. In the emerging contest between the two realms — a contest in which the imperatives of expansion, efficiency, and profitable growth are pitted against those of inviolability, integrity, and independence — I will place my chips on the political side. The economy energizes people to work; the polity inspires them to work together. Men and women will not only salute a flag but fight and die for it — something they will not do for any corporation. The ultimate mobilizing power of capitalism lies in its political, not its economic, half, even though its dynamism and drive derive from the latter. The boundary of the realms is therefore very likely to move again toward an enlargement of state prerogatives with respect to the compartmentalization, quarantine, or buffering of the international reach of capital. The forms and the successes and failures of this reassertion of political prerogative cannot be foretold in particular, but the general movement can, I think, already be discerned under the name "protectionism."

It must seem like a major oversight that I have left until now any discussion of the role of democracy within capitalism. I have done so for two reasons. The first is that capitalism, unlike all other major regimes in history, tolerates democracy but is not itself indissolubly dependent on it, as Nazi Germany, Fascist Italy, apartheid South Africa, and, until recently, dictatorial Chile amply illustrate. The second reason is that the democratic aspect of capitalism appears both as a source of strength and as a problem. The strength lies in the active involvement of citizens in the determination of their collective political life — a counterpart of their personal involvement in the achievement of their collective economic advancement. The problem is that this selfsame political involvement generates a tension within the larger regime, in that the economy kowtows to wealth and income but the polity bows to the general electorate. Because the distribution of wealth and income is highly skewed, the economic realm is inherently a plutocracy, the eager servant of the rich, the deaf servant of the poor. Because the political realm is organized in democratic fashion, it caters to voters, and the vote of the millionaire counts for no more than that of the beggar. The conservative friends of democracy in every capitalist country have worried about the possibility that the masses might take advantage of their voting strength to undo the economic framework of inequality, but the shrewdest among them — starting with Adam Smith — have seen that the regime acquires political cohesion, because it is in "human nature" to admire one's superiors, not resent them.

Nonetheless, there is an inherent pulling apart in a social order composed of two realms — one built on the verticality of wealth, the other on the horizontality of democracy. In this remarkable joining of dissimilars, the political function of the governmental realm is not merely to protect, guide, and superintend the economic process but to prevent it from delegitimatizing itself with the voting public. This has been a motivation of the political sphere which has gained importance as democratic forces have gained strength. The history of every democratic capitalist nation is one of a widening provision of "entitlements," over the nearly universal opposition of business, because from the viewpoint of government these measures have seemed necessary to retain and strengthen the fealty of its citizens.

The political commitment to entitlements, especially in the United States and Great Britain, has waned in recent years, and what seems a fierce debate surrounds the question of whether it should move backward or forward. Nonetheless, the bone of contention is no longer the principle of entitlements but their reach and level, much as the quarrel over the government's responsibility to sustain the economy concerns ways and means rather than whether or not. I suspect, therefore, that political logic will tend to prevail over economic, which is to say that considerations of solidarity of the regime will take precedence over those of sheer efficiency. In all this, the touchstone remains whether the politico-economic system as a whole will work well enough — that is, well enough to maintain the businessman in his position as the representative of the universal class. That depends, of course, not only on the severity of the economic contradictions that capitalism is certain to generate but also on the nonbusiness classes' enthusiasm for— or, at least, acquiescence in— the continued "universal" status of business values. At the risk of sounding banal, I do not see how one can answer the question other than by suggesting that there are likely to be successful and unsuccessful capitalisms, the former maintaining the "animal spirits" (as Keynes called them) of its economic life and the general liberties of its political realm, and the latter moving slowly or abruptly toward something like Schumpeter's anticipated managerial "socialism," only uglier. The characteristics that will sort out capitalisms into one or the other of these categories are apt to be institutional adaptability, ideological pragmatism, and common decency, the international distribution of all of which appears to be as uneven as the distribution of natural resources, although much, much more important.

Even such a relatively open-ended assessment leaves unasked the difficult question of whether captialism could long continue, even in its most successful instances, if shattering explosions of technology or massive relocations of industrial power should alter the present technical and geographical framework of power. That is a question we leave for our grandchildren. The question for our children is whether the capitalism in this country will be one of the successful examples. Given our lack of a national labor or employers' federation to work out a policy on wages and industrial management essential to the control of inflation, our timid and disorganized view of what government's guiding role might be, and our indifference, bordering on hostility, to the large and wretched underclass that has appeared in recent years, I do not see how one can offer bland assurances in answer. Yet candor leads me to recognize that the national performance has been adjudged good enough by the electorate. History is no doubt the final arbiter in these matters, but history does not vote.

And, finally, what of socialism? As I said at the outset, I do not think that the triumph of capitalism means its assured long and happy life or that the defeat of socialism means its ignominious exit from history. The collapse of centralized planning shows that at this moment socialism has no plausible economic framework, but the word has always meant more than a system of economic organization. At its core, it has stood for a commitment to social goals that have seemed incompatible with, or at least unattainable under, capitalism — above all, the moral, not just the material, elevation of humankind. However battered that conception may be from the designation of bloody and cruel regimes as "socialist," the vision has retained its inspirational potential, just as that of Christianity has survived countless autos-da-fé and vicious persecutions. At a more down-to-earth level, the great question seems to be whether the still centralized economies can duplicate the remarkable coexistence of realms which has provided so much of the success of capitalism. As the Soviet Union, China, and Eastern Europe allow an increased autonomy to their managerial cadres and encourage the growth of entrepreneurial activity in the crevices of their economies, we find the ingredients of a new universal class; but if socialism is truly to make way for such a class, more will have to be ceded than the capacity for acting without consultation with the authorities. What is crucially at issue is whether socialism can accept a second republic within its own borders — a republic of economic affairs with its own rewards, punishments, imperatives, and ideology, without which the republic of political affairs seems unlikely to acquiesce in the all-important limitation of its powers.

Would this mean, in effect, the transformation of socialism into capitalism? This is to ask how closely capitalism, under its most democratic impulse, could approach socialism, under its most economically open arrangements. Sweden has always been the living example, real or slightly imaginary, of a system whose economic realm is unmistakably capitalist but whose political leaders have often declared their admiration for socialism, and sought — successfully, on the whole — to move toward its egalitarian standards. This raises the vision, once popular with political scientists and economists, of a historic "convergence" of systems that has grown increasingly less plausible in the light of the immense gulf between the performances of the two social orders. Perhaps the vision will again become a matter for serious consideration if the extraordinarily difficult movement of centralized socialism toward economic and political liberation is not derailed, and if the drift of capitalism toward a more responsible amalgam of economic freedom and political responsibility continues its slow historical advance. Mutterings of both right and left to the contrary, there is no evidence that at least some capitalisms could not progress in this direction. Whether that will be possible for centralized socialism we simply do not know. Meanwhile, for both sides the immediate aim is to create systems that will work well enough. Despite the triumph of capitalism, that is not a matter to be taken for granted, least of all by us.

REVIEW AND DISCUSSION QUESTIONS

1. Heilbroner suggests that "capitalism can be likened to a 'regime.'" What does he mean? Would you agree with him that businesspeople are the universal class of our system, the "group that naturally thinks of itself, and is generally thought of, as speaking for the social order as a whole"?

2. Compare Schumpeter's doubts about capitalism's future with those of Keynes, Marx, and Malthus. Why does Heilbroner believe that politics, not economics, will determine the fate of capitalism?

3. Do you agree with Heilbroner's statement "that capitalism is unique in history in having not one but two centers of authority"—one economic, the other political? What is the relation between the two today, and how has it evolved? What changes, if any, do you think the future will bring?

4. Heilbroner talks about capitalisms in the plural. What different forms of capitalism do you see? Which is likely to work the best in the future?

5. What do you see as the future of capitalism as an economic system? Will it survive? Will it "work well enough"? Will it continue to hold people's allegiance? What value, if any, do the ideals and goals of socialism continue to have?

The Hostile Takeover

Lisa Newton

As mentioned in the text, in recent years takeovers and mergers have become a recurrent feature of our capitalistic business environment, and the drama of corporate raids and junk bonds has frequently held the public spellbound. Yet as Lisa Newton argues, because they regularly throw people out of work, hostile corporate takeovers deserve close ethical scrutiny. Rejecting the usual defenses of takeovers, she argues on a variety of grounds that hostile takeovers are harmful to corporate stakeholders, the economy, and the general public and that the law should restrict or prohibit them. In additon, Newton contends that the right of association means that managers of corporations threatened with takeover have a right and sometimes a duty to defend them.

I. Rights and Consequences

Given the nature and prestige of the players, we might be tempted to think that the *hostile takeover* is just one more game businessmen play. But the business literature on the subject sounds atypically harsh notes, describing this activity in the unbusinesslike language of threat and attacks, followed by occasionally desperate and increasingly sophisticated defenses—the junk-bond bust-up takeover versus the Pac-Man, Poison Pill, Crown Jewel Option defense ranged against the two-tier tender offer and finally the launching of the golden parachutes.

In this colorful literature, the most noticeable feature of a corporate takeover is its terrible human cost. *Fortune* magazine entitled a 1984 article, "Help! My Company Has Just Been Taken Over," and began the article with the story of the suicide of a corporate executive precipitated by his termination following a takeover. "There are more mergers

Reprinted by permission of the author from Tom L. Beauchamp and Norman E. Bowie, eds., *Ethical Theory and Business*, 3rd ed. (Englewood Cliffs, N.J.: Prentice-Hall, 1988).

than ever these days," the author warns, "and their human toll is higher than ever too."[1] A more recent *New York Times* article, entitled "'People Trauma' in Mergers" documents the anxiety and feelings of betrayal experienced by employees — increasingly, down to the hourly level — when the prospect of takeover looms into view. Trust is broken, loyalty ebbs, and, if none of the above is of any interest to managers, productivity plummets.[2] The fact that these alarms come from publications inside the business world is significant; outsiders might be expected to see human effects more clearly than the economic realities that underlie the takeover activity, yet here are the insiders suddenly concluding that the realities of profit may actually be less important than the injuries to the people caught up in it against their will. The hostile corporate takeover is simply *not* business as usual. It is assault with a deadly weapon; and the question seems to be, how can it be right?

Let us backtrack for the moment. A practice requires moral scrutiny if it regularly derogates from human dignity, causes human pain, or with no apparent reason treats one class of human beings less well than another. Any practice that regularly throws people out of work does at least the first two of those (work being possibly the largest factor in self-worth and the major instrument to creature satisfactions), and unless we find the raider's urgent need for self-aggrandizement as a worthy reason for dismembering working units, it probably does the third also. To be sure, all manner of evil things can happen to people in non-takeover situations; part of the fun of being alive is the risk, and part of being in business is knowing that your livelihood may depend on the next quarter's earnings. But as a general moral principle, if I, by my voluntary act and for my own profit, increase the riskiness of your life, no matter how high the base risk and no matter how small the increment by which I raise it for you, then I owe you an explanation. The hostile takeover regularly disemploys at least some people who would not have been unemployed absent the takeover; that makes it, by the above, a proper candidate for moral scrutiny, without presumption one way or another on the results of the scrutiny.

A further problem, if it is a problem, is that a takeover deliberately destroys something — a company, corporation, an instance of human associa-

tion. In the other cases, it can be said that the association itself "decided" to do something to make itself better, or more efficient. But when it is taken over, it does nothing — it is killed, and the atmosphere of the threat of death hangs over the entire proceeding, from the raider's first phone call to the final resolution (usually the acquisition of the company by some party other than the raider). Does it make any difference, that a company is destroyed? Is that an evil over and above all the other disruptions that takeovers occasion? Or is it, strictly speaking, meaningless, beyond the sufferings of the individuals?

We have, in short, two very separate and distinct questions. First, does the hostile corporate takeover serve some ordinary and necessary role in the economy? Whatever the present injuries, is the practice justified in the long run as improving the economic condition of the greatest number? That very pragmatic question is accompanied by a second, metaphysical one: Is the corporation the type of thing whose demise could or should be regretted? Could it have some right to live, to persevere in existence — a right appropriately exercised in management's series of "defenses"? Ordinarily we assume that only individual human beings have dignity, worth, or rights (beyond the uninteresting legal "rights" bestowed on the corporation to permit it to conduct business). But that assumption fits poorly with the fact that people will willingly die for their associations when they will not willingly sacrifice their lives for personal interests; that fact needs further examination before we dismiss the association as a merely instrumental good. We will pursue, then, two separate and logically independent lines of inquiry: First, on straightforward utilitarian reasoning, does the business practice that we know as the *hostile takeover* serve the public interest by performing some useful role in the economy, or are there good utilitarian reasons for limiting or prohibiting it? Second, does the corporation have some right to exist that is violated by any business practice that ends its existence without the consent of its present governors? Along the line of the first inquiry, we will argue, first, that the hostile takeover is damaging to the economy (and the people in it) in the short and middle run and, second, that this practice is a deadly symptom of a long-term process in our relation to material goods, a loss of "ownership," which ought to be noted and, as far as possible, reversed. On the line of the second inquiry, we will argue that "the association," usually the political association, has been invested with dignity since Aristotle's day, and that its right to self-defense is firmly grounded in the individual rights of undisputed worth. Therefore the corporation, acting through its present management, has the right and (sometimes) the duty to defend itself when its existence is threatened, apart from any arguments about immediate effects on the wealth of individuals.

II. Responsible Ownership Profits

Takeovers are generally defended on the utilitarian grounds that they are in the public interest. The "takeover" is simply capital flowing from one sector of the economy to a more profitable one, in this instance, to buy up the stock of a company the value of whose assets is significantly greater than the value of its outstanding stock. Where stock is undervalued, an inefficiency exists in the economy; whether through management ineptness or other market conditions, the return on the shareholder's investment is not as high as it could be. It would be maximized by selling off the assets and distributing the proceeds among the owners; but then, by the above, it is management's duty to do that. The takeover merely does the job that the managers were supposed to do, and the prospect of a takeover, should the stock become undervalued, is an excellent incentive to management to keep the shareholders' interest in mind.

Moreover, defenses against takeovers often involve managers in apparent conflicts of interest. They are protecting their jobs rather than meeting their fiduciary obligations to stockholders. Theory in this instance concurs with current case law; there should be no regulation of takeovers beyond (not very rigorous) anti-trust scrutiny, and defensive moves on the part of management are morally and probably legally illegitimate. To be sure, people get hurt in takeovers, but the shareholders profit, and control of the corporation belongs by statute to them. Against these considerations, what arguments can be raised that unregulated takeover activity is harmful, wrong, contrary to the public interest, and ought to be stopped by new legislation?

The best approach to a response may be to peel an onion: All of the evils seem to be related, differing primarily in the level of analysis suited to elicit them. Beginning with the surface, then, we may note the simple disruption caused by hostile takeover activity: The raider's announcement that a certain percentage of shares of a company have been purchased, more to follow, immediately puts the company in play in a deadly game from which it will not emerge intact. Productive activity, at least at the upper levels of the target (where salaries are highest), stops. Blitzkrieg raider tactics are met with poison pills, sales of crown jewels and other defenses—often of questionable legality. Orderly planning disappears. Employees, terrified for their jobs, spend their days in speculation and the search for another job.[3] Other bidders emerge from the Midwest, from abroad, from next door. Nobody sleeps. All the players hire lawyers, financiers, banks, and start paying them incredible amounts of money. (In the takeover of Revlon by Pantry Pride in the fall of 1985, the investment bankers' share alone came to over $100 million, legal fees to over $10 million, and the negotiated "golden parachutes" to $40 million. Added up, the costs of the takeover—not one penny of which went to shareholders—came to close to 9 percent of the $1.83 billion deal.)[4] However the game ends, people are exhausted, betrayed, out of work, and demoralized. The huge debt incurred by the acquiring company, secured by the assets of the target (by the infamous *junk bonds*), requires the immediate dismemberment of the company for financial survival (more on this later), and financial health, under those circumstances, is out of the question. And all this to what end?

"Hostile takeovers create no new wealth," Andrew Sigler pointed out to the House Committee on Energy and Commerce, "They merely shift ownership, and replace equity with large amounts of debt." He continues:

> More and more companies are being pushed—either in a self-defense against the raiders or by the raiders once they achieve control—into unhealthy recapitalizations that run contrary to the concepts of sound management I have learned over thirty years. This type of leveraging exposes companies to inordinate risks in the event of recession, unanticipated reverses, or significant increases in

interest rates. . . . Generation after generation of American managers have believed that there *must* be a solid equity basis for an enterprise to be successful in the long term. This long-term equity base absorbs — in exchange for the expectation of higher returns — the perils of depression, product failure, strikes and all the other dangers that characterize business in a free economy. That healthy conservatism is now being replaced by a new game in which the object is to see how far that equity base can be squeezed down by layers of debt. And too much of this debt is carrying interest rates far in excess of those a prudent manager can possibly be comfortable with.[5]

At a second level, then, the takeover has two deleterious effects on the management of corporations: First, when the takeover materializes, equity is inevitably transformed into debt, leaving the company terribly vulnerable to foreseeable reverses; second, anticipating takeover attempts, management may well be tempted to aim for short-term profits and engage in aggressive accounting practices to show higher current earnings. These practices may weaken the company and deceive long-term investors, but they will be reflected in a higher stock price and thus one more resistant to attack.[6] As Peter Drucker put it, "Fear of the raider and his unfriendly takeover bid is increasingly distorting business judgment and decisions. In company after company the first question is no longer: Is this decision best for the business? But, will it encourage or discourage the raider?"[7] Fear of the raider may encourage the managers of a company to put up their own money as well as to incur debts well beyond prudence, to take the company privately in a "leveraged buyout." All the same risks, including bankruptcy in the event of any reversal, attend the buyout as attend the takeover.[8] Nor is it clear that the damaging effects of these maneuvers are limited to the domestic scene: As Harold Williams (chairman of the Securities and Exchange Commission during the Carter administration) points out,

> The pursuit of constantly higher earnings can compel managers to avoid needed write-downs, capital programs, research projects, and other bets on the long term. The competitiveness of U.S. corporations has already been impaired by the failure to make long-

term commitments. To compound the problem because of fears of takeovers is a gift to foreign competitors that we cannot afford.[9]

The alarms, confusions, and pains first noted as the result of hostile takeover activity, are then compounded by what seems to be very imprudent business practice. But imprudent for whom? Do the target shareholders, at least, get some profit from the takeover — and if they do, does that not justify it? Michael Jensen, one of a new breed of scholar known as the "shark defenders," argues that they do and that does. He dismisses worries about shareholders' welfare as "folklore," and insists that "science" shows otherwise.[10] His evidence for this claim is interesting:

> More than a dozen studies have painstakingly gathered evidence on the stock price effect of successful takeovers. . . . According to these studies, companies involved in takeovers experience abnormal increases in their stock prices for approximately one month surrounding the initial announcement of the takeover. . . . The evidence shows that target company shareholders gain 30% from tender offers and 20% from mergers.[11]

But isn't the raider's effect pure artifice? Let his initiative be withdrawn — because of government opposition, or because he has agreed to purchase no more stock for whatever reason — and the same studies show that the stock immediately reverts to its previous value.[12] So it was not, really, that the company's stock was too low. It was rather that the flurry of activity, leading to speculation that the stock might be purchased at an enormous premium, fueled the price rise all by itself. Or could it be that certain professional investors find out about the raid before the public does, buy the target's stock at the lowest point, sending it up before the announcement, wait for the announcement, ride the stock to the top, then sell off before the defense moves, government action, or "targeted repurchase" (see the section on "greenmail," below) stop the takeover bid and send the stock back down to its true market value? As Jensen's figures confirm,[13] that value is often a bit *lower* than the starting value of the stock; after all those payouts we are dealing with a much poorer company. Nothing but evil, for all concerned except professional fund managers and investment bankers, seems to come of this takeover activity.

Hence, at the first level there is disruption and tens of millions of dollars' worth of unproductive expense; at the second level there is very dubious business practice. At a third, there is the betrayal of the stakeholders. Current laws, as discussed earlier, force the directors of the target company to consider only shareholder rights and interests, to the probable disadvantage of the other stakeholders: employees, retirees, creditors, host communities, customers, and suppliers. But each of these has helped to build the company to its present state, relying on the company's character and credit-worthiness; the employees and retirees, especially, have worked in expectation of future benefits that may depend in part on the good faith of management, good faith that can hardly be presumed in a raider.[14] The mid-career, upper middle-level managers are especially vulnerable to redundancy and the least likely to be able to transfer their acquired skills and knowledge elsewhere.

Some elimination of positions resulting from duplication is inevitable in any merger, of course, hostile or otherwise, and when carried out under normal conditions succeeds at least in making the company more efficient, even if the cost to the individual is very high. But only some of the people cutting in these extravagant takeovers stems from real redundancy. Companies are paying such high takeover prices that they have to engage in deep cost-cutting immediately, even to the elimination of personnel crucial to continued operations. The "efficiency" achieved may not serve the company well in the long run, but the raider's calculations rarely run very long. As a consequence, middle-management employees (who are, on the whole, not stupid, and read the same business publications as we do) seem to have taken all this into account and reoriented their work lives accordingly:

> Management turnover at all levels is on the rise and employee loyalty is at a low, according to consultants, executive recruiters and the companies themselves. And there is growing evidence, they say, that merger mania is an important reason for both problems, spreading fear about layoffs and dissatisfaction with other changes in the corporate environment. These problems, in turn, promise to make it harder for companies to realize the anticipated efficiencies that many of them pointed to in justifying their acquisitions. . . . Critics of the takeover binge maintain that the

short shrift given to 'people issues' . . . [is] one reason why perhaps half to two-thirds of mergers and acquisitions ultimately fail.[15]

Do we owe anything to people who have worked for a company and who may actually love the company and may be devastated by its dismemberment or transformation? At present, our law does not recognize, or even have any language to describe, the rights possessed by those who have contributed to the growth of an association, have participated in it and loved it, and now see it threatened. The fact that such rights are by no means absolute does not mean they are not there. Classical political theory has the vocabulary to discuss them, under the rubric of the "just war"; discussion of the implications of that doctrine for the hostile takeover issue will occupy the final section of this paper. Rights or no rights, and prudential considerations (as discussed earlier) aside, the condition of the stakeholders ought not, in charity, to be ignored; yet our institutions make no provision for them. Here we have, in the center of the most civilized sector of the civilized world, an open wound, a gap of institutional protection most needed by those who have worked hardest, which we struggle to paper over with the "unemployment benefits" fashioned for different people in different circumstances. Law and business practice seem to require a callousness toward human need and human desert that is incompatible with our notions of justice.

Inevitable disruption, mandated imprudence, and legally required injustice are the first three levels of palpable wrong in the hostile takeover phenomenon. It may be that the fourth layer, the last under consideration in this section, has more worrisome implications than all of the above. The thesis is simple: At primary risk in all of this is our concept of ownership. For all of human history, we have been able to trust property owners (individuals or groups) to take care of their property, because it was in their interest to do so, and outside of military and government property, that was how the property of the world was cared for. With the corporate takeover, that may no longer be the case for the kind of property that looms so large in Western economies, the publicly held corporation. And this development is very alarming.

To begin with the concepts: Ordinarily we use the concepts of *ownership* and *property* interchangeably; even etymologically, they are indistinguishable. But the concept does have two distinct aspects: the primary aspect of a legally protected complex of rights and duties obtaining between the owner and other *persons* and the less prominent aspect of a diffuse set of nonlegal duties, or imperatives, incumbent upon the owner to take care of the *owned thing*, itself. This duty of care has a history of its own; the duty to the thing, analogous to the duty of *stewardship* when the property of others is in question, attaches naturally to the legal owner.

Ownership has the longest history of any concept still extant in the West, certainly longer than its ultimate derivative, *personhood*. Aristotle assumed that the union of man and property, along with the union of man and woman, lay at the foundation of the household and hence of all society. Ownership is presupposed, and discussed, throughout the earliest books of the Bible. The list of *what* was owned was very short: animals, people (slaves), land, tools, buildings, and personal effects. Except for the last item, all were essential to survival, and all required care. The duty arises from that fact.

Whether ownership is single or shared, the duty corresponds to personal interest. If I own a sheep, it is very much in my interest, and incumbent upon me, to take care of the beast and see that it thrives. If you and I together own a sheep, the same interest applies to both of us, the same imperative follows, and we shall divide up the responsibilities of caring for it. If you and I and 998 others own it, enormous practical difficulties attend that care. But however small my interest in that sheep, it is still in my interest that the animal should thrive. Similarly, partial ownership in a whole herd of sheep, or a farm, or a factory, or a business that owns several factories, does not necessitate a change in the notion of *ownership*.

Liquidation consumes something that is owned, or turns it into money that can be spent on consumption. The easiest way to liquidate a sheep is to eat it. The way to liquidate most owned things is to sell them. Then you no longer own the thing, and your responsibilities terminate; but so, of course, does all future good you might have gotten of the thing. Part of the cultural evolution of ownership has been the elaboration of a tension between retention and liquidation, saving and spending, with the moral weight of the most successful cultures on the side of thrift and preservation. The business system probably depends as much on Ben Franklin's "A penny saved is a penny earned" as it does

on Adam Smith's "invisible hand." The foreseen result of the *hand*, we may remember, was to increase the wealth, the assets, of a nation. For the herdsman it is self-evident that if you slaughter or sell all your sheep, you will starve in the next year; for Smith, it was equally self-evident that it is in a businessman's interest, whatever business he may be in, to save his money and invest it in clearing more land, breeding more beasts, or building more plants, to make more money in the future. Hence the cleared land, the herds, and the factories — the assets of the nation — increase without limit, and all persons, no matter how they participate in the economy, in fact share in this increased wealth. Presupposed is the willingness of all players in the free enterprise game to acquire things that need care if they are to yield profit, hence to render that care, and to accept that responsibility, over the long run. Should that willingness disappear, and the population suddenly show a preference for liquidation, all bets are off for the wealth of the nation.

And the problem is, of course, that the developments of ownership made possible in the last century create excess tendencies toward liquidation. If several thousand of us jointly own several thousand shares of stock, we may in theory bear the traditional responsibilities of owners for those companies, but we shall surely not *feel* them. And if we purchased those shares not for the sake of investing in the companies, but for the sake of having money available to us at some future time (say, in a pension fund), we will have acquired them for a purpose that is directly contrary to our concerns as owners. We will be involved in a conflict of interest and obligation with ourselves: On the one hand, we should be protecting and nurturing the company(s) we (partially) own, plowing profit back into improvements in plant on occasion, even if that means no profit this year; on the other, if it seems we could get more money if the company were liquidated and the proceeds shared around, we should work toward that end. Suppose that we several thousand owners hire a fund manager to make sure our pension fund provides us with as much pension as possible. That manager, hired with those instructions, is not an owner, and has *no* responsibility toward the companies. On the contrary, his entire obligation is to us and the increase of our money. Where liquidation serves that purpose, it is his job to bring it about. Ownership, for such a manager, is no more than present legal title to property, a way station between sums of money, and its whole moral framework has become totally irrelevant. To complete the picture, let only the tax structure subsidize that liquidation in cases of takeover:

> Accounting procedures and tax laws . . . shift much of the cost of acquisitions to taxpayers through the deductibility of interest payments and the revaluation of assets in ways that reduce taxes . . . I suspect that many of the acquisitions that proved profitable for acquirers did so largely because of tax benefits and the proceeds from busting up the target company. If liquidation is subsidized by the tax system, are we getting more liquidations than good business would dictate?[16]

The answer is probably yes.

Institutional investors—those gargantuan funds—now own up to 70 percent of the stock of the publicly owned corporations. It must be unprecedented in human history that majority ownership of such entities lies with "owners" whose interests may be best served by the destruction of the object owned. In the case of companies that own large holdings of natural resources, forests, or oil reserves, it is usually the case that the assets sold separately will yield more than the companies' stock. (As Minow and Sawyier grimly put it, under current practices such companies "are worth more dead than alive.")[17] Any company, in fact, that regularly works for the long term (funding research and development, for example), can be profitably liquidated: Whatever those raiders may be, they do not need to be geniuses to figure out which companies to attack. The only limits on the process of liquidation of the country's assets by the managers hired by those investors, or by the raiders that cater to their own interests, might be the success of new and inventive defenses.

The evils of the takeover market, then, go to the philosophical base of our market system, striking at the root of moral habits evolved over 2500 years. The corporate raiders have yet to make their first widget, grow their first carrot, or deliver their first lunch. *All* they do is turn money into money, cantilevering the profit off the shell of responsible ownership. No doubt capital is more productively lodged in some places than others, but it follows from no known economic theory that it is more beneficial to the world when lodged in T. Boone

Pickens's bank account than when lodged wherever it was before he got it. Possibly it will end up facilitating some industrial projects—he has no intention of keeping it in a mattress, after all—but only in those that promise quick profits. We need not look to him to revitalize our smokestack industries and make them competitive on the world markets. The whole productive capacity of the American economy seems at the mercy of moneymen on the rampage, with all productive companies under threat of being taken over, taken apart, and eradicated. Surely this condition cannot be healthy or good.

In sum: This section has tried to provide a series of pragmatic arguments that the present rash of corporate takeover activity is harmful to the stakeholders, to the economy, and to the general public, from all of which it would follow that regulation is justified. In the next section we attempt to provide a defense for the proposition that a corporation has a real right to exist, hence to resist takeover.

III. The Association as Worth Keeping

Individuals may be hurt by the corporate takeover. The corporation, on the other hand, is usually killed. Does this fact add anything to the list of injuries, or is it simply a shorthand way of saying that the individuals are no longer part of it? Does the corporation have a right to life—a right to persevere in existence, as itself, under its own laws and practices, at least to the extent that would give it a presumptive right to mount a defense against hostile takeover?

The disutility of unregulated takeover activity, implying the desirability of some regulation in the public interest, was the theme of the last section. In this section we ask a different question: Can the corporation be seen as an entity analogous to an individual human being, with rights, including the right to defend itself (through the actions of its officers) regardless of the utilities involved in each case? The law is unsympathetic to defensive moves in takeover situations, suggesting that the right in question here is not derivable from any acknowledged legal rights or present powers of the corporation. It must be found, if it is to be found anywhere, as a logical derivation from other recognized rights of the corporation or, more likely, of the individuals who make it up.

We may begin the inquiry by noting that over the last decade, philosophical students of the corporation have been moving cautiously in the direction of grounding their moral discourse, in the assumption that the corporation is a moral individual like other moral individuals.

It is possible, however, that a corporation may be capable of assuming moral responsibility and still not have rights, but it is not likely. Our attribution of rights rests heavily on the attribution of moral agency, which alone confers worth or dignity on the human, and moral agency is the condition for attribution of moral responsibility. In the literature, the development continues, and recent work (e.g., Patricia Werhane's *Persons, Rights, and Corporations*) accepts that corporations have, indeed, moral rights, even if only "secondarily."[18]

There is, however, one body of literature precisely on the point of our question, albeit not one that deals with "the corporation" as this paper understands the corporation. Since Saint Augustine, the right of a nation to defend itself against foreign aggression has been recognized. While the political association, as Aristotle and Augustine understood it, may seem an odd model for Phillips Petroleum and Continental Group, it is possible that the literature articulating any collectivity's right of defense may help us formulate one for the modern corporation.

The queerness of attributing a "right" to a collectivity rather than to an individual was not generally noticed in discussions of the Just War, most likely because its recognition predates the theory of individual rights by several centuries; nations had rights long before we did. But if we are to make sense of this right in a modern political context, it must be restated in terms compatible with individual rights theory. Michael Walzer undertakes this task in *Just and Unjust Wars*. For Walzer, the right of the political association to exist comes from the general right of *social contract* — the right of people to join together in any voluntary association, preeminently the state, the association charged with the whole governance of a people. (This is the right primarily challenged in *aggression*, which threatens to abrogate it permanently.) Like Burke before him, Walzer does not understand the agreement that binds the state as a set of real "contracts."

What actually happens is harder to describe. Over a long period of time, shared experiences and cooperative activity of many different kinds shape a common life. . . . The moral standing of any particular state depends on the reality of the common life it protects and the extent to which the sacrifices required by that protection are willingly accepted and thought worthwhile.[19]

Again,

The rights of a nation or people not to be invaded derives from the common life its members have made . . . and not from the legal title they hold or don't hold.[20]

So the fact of the common life, which has been made by the participants in it, is the immediate source of the right to defend it, presumably necessarily mediated by the desire of participants to defend it. Walzer is likely correct that the right of the state to defend itself stems from the right of a people to create a common life, to adorn and embellish it, to examine and reform it, and by spending themselves on it, to make it valuable — a variety of the rather prosaic right of association. And the reason why people exercise that right in the formation of permanent associations, which build up a history for themselves, is that associations extend individual life in dimensions that the individual otherwise cannot control — in time, in space, in power. To the limited and partial individual, participation in an association provides immortality, global reach, and collective power. The individual needs the association for these benefits, and in this way the right of association is grounded in human nature. When my association is attacked, my basic security in these insecurity-ridden areas is very much endangered, and that is why I so justifiably resent any attacks on it.

Has this argument any validity for the corporation? Here the relatively recent moves to articulate the internal order of a corporation precisely as a historical culture, with a set of values and commitments all its own, may have some relevance. It would be tempting to argue that a corporation that has, as have the best companies of the recent literature, earnestly pursued excellence in all respects, taken care of its employees, stayed close to its customers, produced the highest quality product, and really cared about its communities, has somehow earned the right to exist, while the others have not.[21] Temptation must be resisted: the difficulties of discerning the "excellent" companies from the others are insurmountable. But maybe we don't have to make that judgment: If a corporation, even in theory, can be the kind of collectivity that the state is, and can serve the purposes in human life that a state can serve, then good or bad, it shares in the state's presumptive right to defend itself.

To summarize this section: The association provides those individuals who voluntarily and fully participate in it with goods they can not get elsewhere—social recognition, material reward, and above all the extension of the limited self in space, time, and power. These are the reasons why the right of association exists and is exercised, and why the result of that exercise has, derived from that right, the right to stay in being and to expect its officers to mount a defense for it should that turn out to be necessary. But that is all we need to establish the right to defend itself against hostile takeover attempts.

That conclusion does not entail, of course, that present officers may do anything they like in the course of a defense; as Walzer points out, there are standards of justice in war as well as standards to determine if a war as a whole is just. (At present, for instance, the payment of greenmail to a raider— a premium price to obtain his stock and only his stock, to persuade him to go away and leave the company alone—raises questions of acceptable practice in the event of a takeover, more than the poison pills, ESOPs, and Crown Jewel Options designed to make a company significantly poorer in the event of takeover.)

Conclusion

We have argued that as a matter of right, and as a matter of utility, the takeover game should be ended. Capital is not unlimited; in a country rapidly losing out to foreign competition in part because of outdated plant, and declining in its quality of urban life in part because of obsolete and crumbling infrastructure, there are plenty of worthwhile uses for capital. Law that turns the attentions of the restless rich away from cannibalizing productive corporations, toward investing in the undercapitalized areas of the economy, would be a great public service.[22]

Notes

1. Myron Magnet, "Help! My Company Has Just Been Taken Over," *Fortune*, July 9, 1984, pp. 44–51. See also Joel Lang, "Aftermath of a Merger," *Northeast Magazine*, April 21, 1985, pp. 10–17.

2. Steven Prokesch, "'People Trauma' in Mergers," *New York Times*, November 19, 1985.

3. *Ibid*.

4. *Wall Street Journal*, November 8, 1985.

5. Testimony of Andrew C. Sigler, Chairman and Chief Executive Officer of Champion International Corporation, representing the Business Roundtable, before hearings of the Subcommittee on Telecommunications, Consumer Protection and Finance of the House Committee on Energy and Commerce, Thursday, May 23, 1985.

6. Some of these considerations I owe to conversations and correspondence with S. Bruce Smart, Jr.

7. Drucker, *Wall Street Journal*, January 5, 1983.

8. Leslie Wayne, "Buyouts Altering Face of Corporate America," *New York Times*, November 23, 1985.

9. Harold M. Williams, "It's Time for a Takeover Moratorium," *Fortune*, July 22, 1985, pp. 133–136.

10. Michael Jensen, "Takeovers: Folklore and Science," *Harvard Business Review* 62 (November–December 1984): 109–121.

11. P. 112. The footnote on the studies cites, for a summary of these studies, Michael C. Jensen and Richard S. Ruback, "The Market for Corporate Control: The Scientific Evidence," *Journal of Financial Economics* (April 1983). The studies are cited individually in the same footnote; *ibid.*, p. 120.

12. *Ibid.*, p. 116.

13. *Ibid*.

14. Another point owed to conversations and correspondence with S. Bruce Smart, Jr.

15. Prokesch, "'People Trauma' in Mergers."

16. Williams, "It's Time for a Takeover Moratorium," pp. 133–136.

17. Newton Minow and David Sawyier, "The Free Market Blather Behind Takeovers" Op-ed, *The New York Times*, December 10, 1985.

18. Patricia H. Werhane, *Persons, Rights, and Corporations* (Englewood Cliffs, N.J.: Prentice-Hall, 1985), p. 61.

19. Michael Walzer, *Just and Unjust Wars* (New York: Basic Books, 1977), p. 54.

20. *Ibid.*, p. 55.

21. Criteria freely adapted from Thomas J. Peters and Robert H. Waterman, Jr., *In Search of Excellence* (New York: Harper and Row, 1982).

22. In developing the ideas for this paper, I have profited enormously from conversations with Lucy Katz, Philip O'Connell, Stuart Richardson, Mark Shanley, Andrew Sigler, S. Bruce Smart, Jr., and C. Roger Williams.

Review and Discussion Questions

1. Section II of Newton's essay argues against hostile takeovers on utilitarian or pragmatic grounds. She sees them having negative effects at four different levels. What are these effects?

2. In your view, what are the most significant negative economic results of hostile takeovers? Do they have any positive economic benefits? Are there arguments in favor of takeovers that Newton has not answered?

3. Would you agree with Newton that takeovers are also unjust?

4. Newton argues that takeovers have worrisome implications for our concept of ownership. What does she mean? Do you agree with her that changes in ownership have created an excessive tendency toward liquidation?

5. Should the law prohibit hostile takeovers altogether? Should it restrict them in some way? What legal policy would be effective and sensible?

6. Do you believe that a corporation has a moral right to defend itself against a hostile takeover? Why?

7. What, if anything, do hostile takeovers reveal about the nature of capitalism? What do they spell for the future of American business?

For Further Reading

R. C. Edwards, M. Reich, and **T. E. Weisskopf**, eds., *The Capitalist System*, 3rd ed. (Englewood Cliffs, N.J.: Prentice-Hall, 1986) contains critical essays on capitalism, with an emphasis on economic issues.

Robert L. Heilbroner and **Lester C. Thurow**, *Economics Explained* (New York: Simon & Schuster, 1987) is two respected economists' analysis of how our economy works, what its current difficulties are, and where it is headed.

Tibor R. Machan, ed., *The Main Debate: Communism versus Capitalism* (New York: Random House, 1986) is a collection of accessible essays that debate the relative merits of capitalism and socialism.

"Punters or Proprietors? A Survey of Capitalism," in *The Economist*, May 5, 1990, is an intelligent analysis of contemporary capitalism and the problems that face it.

David Schweickart, *Capitalism or Worker Control?* (New York: Praeger, 1980) is an argument for worker-control socialism.

CHAPTER 5

CORPORATIONS

Forty years ago the vice president of Ford Motor Company described the corporation as the dominant institution of American society. Today that dominance is more obvious than ever: Not only do corporations produce most of the goods and services we buy, but they and their ethos permeate everything from politics and communications to athletics and religion.

As an aggregate, corporations wield awesome economic clout, but some are so vast that individually they exercise influence over the whole of American society. Hundreds of corporate organizations employ thousands of people, and the largest have hundreds of thousands in their ranks. Exxon Corporation, for example, employs about 170,000, a figure that pales beside General Motors's approximately 764,000 and General Electric's 405,000.

And corporations are getting bigger. In 1960 the nation's 200 largest manufacturing firms owned just 54 percent of U.S. industrial equipment and assets. But by the early 1980s, even before the great merger wave of that decade was really under way, their share had jumped to 66 percent. Today the figure is even higher. The Philip Morris Company exemplifies this lust for largeness. In 1985, it ranked twenty-seventh on *Fortune* magazine's list of the biggest U.S. companies. Then it bought out General Foods — owner of Maxwell House, Sanka, Oscar Mayer, and other brands — and vaulted to twelfth place. In 1989 Philip Morris took over Kraft and made itself the ninth largest corporation in America.

By any measure, the biggest corporations are colossi that dominate the earth. In 1989 General Motors had revenues of more than $121 billion, Ford $92 billion, Exxon almost $80 billion,

and IBM $60 billion. By comparison, the gross national product of Sweden (that is, the total market value of all the goods and services produced there) was around $100 billion; that of Portugal was less than $30 billion. The state of California has far and away the largest annual revenue of any American state, but it makes only a little more than half what General Motors makes. Kansas takes in only around $4 billion a year and Montana less than half of that.

Exxon is a typical corporate giant. Like the hundred or so corporations with assets of at least $1 billion and, in combination, the lion's share of America's industrial profits and earnings, Exxon does not really sell the products that produce its mind-boggling revenues. Its oil, chemicals, electronic typewriters, and motors are actually sold by an array of companies that Exxon owns. Business analyst Anthony J. Parisi thus describes Exxon as "a fabulously wealthy investment club with a limited portfolio."[1] It invests in thirteen affiliate companies, whose heads, says Parisi, "oversee their territories like provincial governors, sovereigns in their own lands but with an authority stemming from the power center in New York. The management committee exacts its tribute (the affiliate's profits from current operations) and issues doles (the money needed to sustain and expand those operations)." Most remarkable about Exxon's empire, however, is its scope. It operates in nearly 100 countries. "Its 195 ocean going tankers, owned and chartered, constitute a private navy as big as Britain's."[2]

Like all modern corporations, Exxon is a three-part organization, made up of stockholders, who provide the capital, own the corporation, and enjoy liability limited to the amount of their investments; managers, who run the business operations; and employees, who produce the goods and services. In the best-run organizations the management system is highly structured and impersonal. It provides the corporation's overall framework, the formal chain of command, that ensures the company's profit objectives.

The emergence of corporate giants like Exxon is one of the more intriguing chapters in the evolution of capitalism. Certainly the political theory of John Locke and the economic theory of Adam Smith admitted no such conglomerates of capital as those that originated in the nineteenth century and today dominate America's, even the world's, economic, political, and social life. This book isn't the place to analyze why a people committed to an individualistic social philosophy and a free-competition market economy allowed vast oligopolistic organizations to develop. Rather, the concern here is with the problem of applying moral standards to corporate organizations and with understanding their social responsibilities. After a brief review of the history of the corporation, this chapter looks at the following specific topics:

1. The meaning of "responsibility" and the debate over whether corporations can be meaningfully said to have moral responsibility

2. The controversy between the "narrow" and the "broad" views of corporate social responsibility

3. Four key arguments in this debate: the "invisible hand" argument, the "hand of government" argument, the "inept custodian" argument, and the "materialization of society" argument

4. The importance of institutionalizing ethics within corporations and how this may be done

THE LIMITED-LIABILITY COMPANY

If you ask a lawyer for a definition of "corporation," you will probably get something like the following: A corporation is a thing that can endure beyond the natural lives of its members and that has incorporators who may sue and be sued as a unit and who are able to consign part of their property to the corporation for ventures of limited liability.[3] *Limited liability* is a key feature of the modern corporation. It means that the members of the corporation are financially liable for corporate debts only up to the extent of their investments.

In addition, limited-liability companies, or corporations, differ from partnerships and other forms of business association in two ways. First, a corporation is not formed simply by an agreement entered into among its first members. It becomes incorporated by being publicly registered or in some other way having its existence officially acknowledged by the law. Second, while a partner is automatically entitled to his share of the profits as soon as they are ascertained, the shareholder in a corporation is entitled only to a dividend from the company's profits when it has been "declared." Under American law, dividends are usually declared by the directors of a corporation.

When we think of corporations, we naturally think of giants like General Motors, Exxon, AT&T, General Electric, and IBM, which exert enormous influence over our economy and society. But the local independently owned convenience store may be a corporation, and historically the concept of a corporation has been broad enough to encompass churches, trade guilds, and local governments. Corporations may also be profit making or nonprofit making. Princeton University, for example, is a nonprofit corporation. Companies like Eastman Kodak, by contrast, aim to make money for shareholders. Corporations may be privately owned or owned (in part or whole) by the government. American corporations are almost entirely privately owned, but Renault of France is an example of a publicly owned corporation. A small group of investors may own all the outstanding shares of a privately owned, profit-making corporation (a "privately held" corporation), or its stock may be traded among the general public (a "publicly held" corporation). All companies whose stocks are listed on the New York and other stock exchanges are publicly held corporations.

Several stages mark the evolution of the corporation. The corporate form itself developed during the early Middle Ages, and the first corporations were towns, universities, and ecclesiastical orders. They were chartered by government and regulated by public statute. As corporate bodies, they existed independently of any particular membership. By the fifteenth century, the courts of England had evolved the principle of limited liability — thus setting limits, for example, on how much an alderman of the Liverpool Corporation might be required to pay if the city went bankrupt. During the medieval period, however, the law did not grant corporate status to purely profit-making associations. In those days, something besides economic self-interest had to be seen as uniting the members of the corporation: religion, a trade, shared political responsibilities.

This state of affairs changed during the Elizabethan era, as the actual incorporation of business enterprises began. European entrepreneurs were busy organizing trading voyages to the East and to North America. The East India Company, which symbolizes the great trading companies of this period, was formed in 1600, when Queen Elizabeth I granted to the Earl of Sunderland and a group of investors the right to be "one body corporate" and bestowed on it a trading monopoly to the East Indies. In the following decades,

numerous other incorporated firms were granted trading monopolies and colonial charters. Much of North America's settlement, in fact, was initially underwritten as a business venture.

Although the earliest corporations typically held special trading rights from the government, their members did not pool capital. Rather, they individually financed voyages using the corporate name and absorbed the loss individually if a vessel sank or was robbed by pirates. But as ships became larger and more expensive, no single buyer could afford to purchase and outfit one. Similarly, the loss of a ship would have been ruinous to any one individual. The solution was to pool capital and share liability. Thus emerged the prototype of today's corporations.[4]

The loosening of government restrictions on corporate chartering procedures in the nineteenth century marks the final stage of corporate evolution. Until the mid-1800s, prospective corporations had to apply for charters — in England to the Crown, and in the United States to state governments. Government officials carefully studied applications, rejecting some and burdening others with special conditions (for example, limits on the amount of property that might be owned or restrictions on where it might be held) in order to promote the public good. Critics of the incorporation system charged that it really promoted favoritism, corruption, and unfair monopolies. Gradually, the old system of incorporation was replaced by the system we know today, in which corporate status is essentially granted to any organization that fills out the forms and pays the fees.

Lurking behind this change were two important theoretical shifts. First, underlying the old system was the mercantilist idea that a corporation's activities should advance some specific public purpose. But Adam Smith and, following him, Alexander Hamilton, the first U.S. Secretary of the Treasury, challenged the desirability of a direct tie between business enterprise and public policy. Their idea was that businesspeople should be encouraged to explore their own avenues of enterprise. The "invisible hand" of the market would direct their activities in a socially beneficial direction more effectively than any public official could.

Second, when nineteenth-century reformers argued for changes in incorporation procedures, they talked not only about government favoritism and the advantages of a laissez-faire approach but also about the principle of a corporation's right to exist.[5] Any petitioning body with the minimal qualifications, they asserted, has the right to receive a corporate charter. By contrast, the early Crown-chartered corporations were clearly creations of the state, in accordance with the legal-political doctrine that all corporate status was a privilege bestowed by the state as it saw fit. According to the reformers, however, incorporation is a by-product of the people's right of association, not a gift from the state.

Even though the right of association supports relaxed incorporation procedures, the state must still incorporate companies and guarantee their legal status. Corporations must be recognized by the law as a single agent in order for them to enjoy their rights and privileges. To a large extent, then, the corporation remains, as Chief Justice Marshall put it in 1819, "an artificial being, invisible, intangible, and existing only in the contemplation of the law."[6] Thus corporations are clearly legal agents. But are they also moral agents? And while corporations have definite legal responsibilities, what, if any, social and moral responsibilities do they have?

CORPORATE MORAL AGENCY

In 1976 the citizens of Massachusetts were asked in a referendum whether they wanted to amend the state constitution to allow the legislature to enact a graduated personal income tax. Predictably enough, they said no.

What made an otherwise unremarkable exercise of the initiative process noteworthy was that the First National Bank of Boston and four other businesses in the state wanted to spend money to express opposition to the referendum. The Massachusetts Supreme Judicial Court said they could not, that banks and business corporations are prohibited by law from spending corporate funds to publicize political views that do not materially affect their property, business, or assets. In 1978, however, the U.S. Supreme Court in a 5 to 4 decision (*First National Bank of Boston* v. *Bellotti*) struck down the Massachusetts court's decision and thereby defined the free-speech rights of corporations for the first time.

Writing for the majority, Justice Lewis Powell said: "If the speakers here were not corporations, no one would suggest that the state could silence their proposed speech. It is the type of speech indispensable to decision making in a democracy, and this is no less true because the speech comes from a corporation rather than from an individual." In a dissenting opinion, Justice Byron R. White said that states should be permitted to distinguish between individuals and corporations. "Ideas which were not a product of individual choice," said White, "are entitled to less First Amendment protection."

Immediately some viewed the decision as a major blow to consumers and citizens, although the Court seems to have moderated its position since then.[7] Whatever its precise legal ramifications, *First National Bank of Boston* v. *Bellotti* did have the effect of blurring the distinction between corporations and individuals. For in deciding that corporations enjoy protection under the First Amendment, the Court laid a basis for claiming that corporations should be treated as individuals in every way — that is, that they enjoy the same moral and political rights and bear the same responsibilities as individual human beings. Thus, if corporations are moral agents, then like individuals they can be held morally responsible for particular actions.

The problem, of course, is that corporations are not individuals but artificial persons created by the law. They are collections of individuals who set goals and policies and perform specific actions. Since corporations are not actual persons, in what sense can they be held morally responsible for their actions?

At this point, it may help to understand what is meant by individual "moral responsibility." Often, of course, people are simply said to have a moral responsibility to do whatever it is that morality requires of them. Thus, I may have a moral responsibility to help my neighbor, to keep my promise to Peter, to tell the truth to my colleagues, and to return a misplaced squash racquet to its rightful owner. But reference to an individual's moral responsibility may also have other meanings. Three further senses of "moral responsibility" (or "morally responsible") are relevant here.

Meanings of "Moral Responsibility"

In the first sense, "moral responsibility" refers to holding people morally accountable for some past action. If you leap into a river and rescue a drowning child, you are responsible for the child's being saved and deserve to be praised. If you are playing with your car's radio while you drive and, as a result, cruise through a stop sign, you are responsible for the accident that results. You deserve to be blamed. On the other hand, if the accident resulted from your having suffered a heart attack, you would not be seen as morally responsible (as opposed to legally liable) for it. Morally speaking, the accident was not your fault; we would not criticize you for it. Responsibility in this sense of accountability for actions, therefore, refers to assigning people

blame or praise for particular actions they have performed. Determining responsibility in this sense requires an assessment of causes and various moral considerations.

In the second sense, "moral responsibility" refers to one's accountability, not for a particular past action, but for the care, welfare, or treatment of others as derived from the specific social role that one plays. Thus, parents are responsible for seeing that their children go to school; teachers are responsible for what occurs in their classrooms; doctors are responsible for the treatment of their hospital patients. These specific role responsibilities are typically set by social or organizational conventions.

The third sense of "moral responsibility" refers to one's capacity for making moral or rational decisions on one's own. When parents hire a babysitter for their young children, they implicitly recognize that their children lack the mental and emotional maturity to make informed decisions. Likewise, when the law grants parents almost complete legal control over their young children, it implicitly asserts that children cannot be trusted to make important decisions regarding their own welfare. They are not yet mature enough to be deemed fully responsible for their actions. On the other hand, the babysitter and the parents presumably are morally responsible agents. They have the capacity to make autonomous, informed, and rational moral decisions.

The three senses of "moral responsibility" can be further illustrated. Take the statement "Claire Robinson is morally responsible." If "morally responsible" carries the first sense, then Robinson is said to deserve praise or blame for some action. If "morally responsible" carries the second sense, then Robinson is being designated as ethically accountable for the care or welfare of another. If "morally responsible" carries the third sense, then Robinson is being described as a moral agent, as having the ability to make genuine moral decisions.

If a person is not morally responsible in the third sense, he or she cannot be considered morally responsible in either of the other two senses. If Robinson cannot make rational or moral decisions on her own, she cannot be held accountable for her actions or for the welfare of anyone else. On the other hand, if she can make such decisions, then in theory she can be held accountable for her actions and for the welfare of others. The relationship between the third sense of "morally responsible" and the other two, then, is that it is a necessary, although not a sufficient, condition for the others.

The importance of recognizing the logical priority of moral responsibility in the third sense is that, once it is established, it is theoretically possible to hold the agent responsible in the other senses. This in turn simplifies the issue of corporate moral responsibility. If corporations, like individuals, can make rational and moral decisions on their own—if they are moral agents—then in theory they can have genuine moral responsibilities to others and can be praised or blamed for their actions.

Although this point seems simple, the task of determining whether corporations can make such decisions remains anything but simple. Immediately, we must ponder whether it makes sense to say that any entity other than individual persons can make decisions in the first place, moral or otherwise.

Can Corporations Make Moral Decisions?

Corporate internal decision (CID) structures amount to established procedures for accomplishing specific goals. For example, consider Exxon's system, as depicted by Anthony J. Parisi:

> All through the Exxon system, checks and balances are built in. Each fall, the presidents of the 13 affiliates take their plan for the coming year and beyond to New York for review at a meeting with the management committee and the staff vice presidents. The goal is to get a perfect corporate fit. Some imaginary examples: The committee might decide that Exxon is becoming too concentrated in Australia and recommend that Esso Eastern move more slowly on that continent. Or it might conclude that if the affiliates were to build all the refineries they are proposing, they would create more capacity than the company could profitably use. One of the affiliates would be asked to hold off, even though, from its particular point of view, a new refinery was needed to serve its market.[8]

The implication here is that any decisions coming out of Exxon's annual sessions are formed and shaped to effect corporate goals, "to get a perfect corporate fit." Metaphorically, all data pass through the filter of corporate procedures and objectives. The remaining distillation constitutes "the decision." Certainly the participants actively engage in decision making. But in addition to individual persons, the other major component of corporate decision making consists of the framework in which policies and activities are determined.

The CID structure lays out lines of authority and stipulates under what conditions personal actions become official corporate actions. Some philosophers have compared the corporation to a machine or have argued that because of its structure it is bound to pursue single-mindedly its profit goals. As a result, they claim, it is a mistake to see a corporation as being morally responsible or to expect it to display such moral characteristics as honesty, considerateness, and sympathy. Only the individuals within a corporation can act morally or immorally; only they can be held responsible for what it does.[9]

Others have argued the contrary. The CID structure, like an individual person, collects data about the impact of its actions. It monitors work conditions, employee efficiency and productivity, and environmental impacts. Professors Kenneth E. Goodpaster (philosophy) and John B. Matthews (business administration) argue that, as a result, there is no reason a corporation cannot show the same kind of rationality and respect for persons that individual human beings can. By analogy, they contend, it makes just as much sense to speak of corporate moral responsibility as it does to speak of individual moral responsibility.[10] Thomas Donaldson agrees. He argues that a corporation can be a moral agent if moral reasons enter into its decision making and if its decision-making process controls not just the company's actions but also its structure of policies and rules.[11]

Philosopher Peter French arrives at the same conclusion in a slightly different way.[12] The CID structure, says French, in effect absorbs the intentions and acts of individual persons into a "corporate decision." Perhaps no corporate official intended the course or objective charted by the CID structure. But, says French, the corporation did. And he believes that these corporate intentions are enough to make corporate acts "intentional" and thus make corporations "morally responsible."

Professor of philosophy Manuel Velasquez demurs. "Even if its CID structure shows that a corporation per se can have intentions," he writes, "it does not establish intentionality."[13] An act is intentional, says Velasquez, only if the entity that formed the intention brings about the act through its bodily movements. "The intentions French attributes to corporations, then, do not mark out corporate acts as intentional because the intentions are attributed to one entity (the corporation) whereas the acts are carried out by another entity (the corporate members)." In Velasquez's view, then, the corporation's members and not the corporation bring about the acts of the corporation. Velasquez concludes that only corporate members, not the corporation itself, can be held morally responsible.

Vanishing Individual Responsibility

Some might argue that whether or not corporations as artificial entities can properly be held morally responsible, the nature and structure of modern corporate organizations allow virtually everyone to share moral accountability for an action—"moral responsibility" in the first sense. But in practice this diffusion of responsibility can mean that no person is held morally responsible. The masking of moral accountability, while worrisome, isn't so unusual: In and outside corporations, assigning praise and blame can be problematic. But what the masking phenomenon may reflect is of significant concern. Perhaps the impersonality of the corporate entity so envelops its members that they in effect lose their moral agency. It may be that, for all practical purposes, members of corporate organizations cannot be considered capable of making moral decisions ("moral responsibility" in the third sense) in a corporate context. A case in point is National Semiconductor Corporation.

In 1984 National Semiconductor, California's largest maker of microelectronic circuits, pleaded guilty to a forty-count indictment and was fined $1.75 million for selling parts between 1978 and 1981 that were not subjected to the tests prescribed by the contracting party, the Defense Department. In June 1984, the Pentagon proposed to suspend National Semiconductor from military sales, a ban that it subsequently lifted after the company promised to conduct such tests in the future. What really rankled the defense agency was that Semiconductor refused to identify the company employees responsible for the incomplete testing. Why the refusal? National Semiconductor president Charles Sporch said that no individuals should be singled out for punishment because the incomplete testing was "an industry pattern beyond any one individual's responsibility."[14]

This incident points up the inherent difficulties of assigning personal responsibility to members of corporations. For argument's sake, assume that Sporch is correct: It's virtually impossible to assign moral responsibility to any single individual for the incomplete testing. But why couldn't we rightly expect the appropriate parties to have acted differently? Sporch suggests an explanation: An industry-wide pattern placed the acts of noncompliance outside the realm of personal responsibility. If he's right, then CIDs not only gave rise to the industry pattern but effectively paralyzed, if not usurped, the moral agency of corporate members. From here it is an easy step to the conclusion that, not only does it make no sense to speak of corporate moral agency, it is equally vacuous to speak of individual moral agency in a corporate context. This conclusion in turn raises the specter of actions without actors in any moral sense — of flouted contracts, as in the case of National Semiconductor, without any morally responsible parties.

There are at least two ways to escape the intellectual discomfort posed by morally actorless actions. One would be to attribute moral agency to corporations, to follow the lead of the Supreme Court's decision in *First National Bank of Boston* v. *Bellotti* and assign responsibilities to corporations just as we do to individual persons. The other choice, not necessarily incompatible with the first, is to conclude that explanations like Sporch's are nothing but lame excuses to protect the blameworthy. It may well be that cases like National Semiconductor really dramatize how easy and automatic it has become to conveniently submerge personal responsibility in the protoplasmic CID structures of modern corporate organizations. Perhaps until CID structures are reconstituted to deal with noneconomic matters, we can expect more of the same evasion of personal responsibility.

The issue of corporate moral agency undoubtedly will continue to exercise scholars.

Meanwhile, the inescapable fact is that corporations are increasingly being accorded the status of biological persons, with all the rights and responsibilities implied by that status. Indeed, recent criminal prosecutions, such as the case of Ford's Pinto gas tanks (see Case 2.2), suggest that society accepts in principle the notion of corporate moral responsibility. And corporate officials themselves are gradually moving to this position. Continental Oil Company's in-house booklet on moral standards expresses the public perception and its implications as follows:

> No one can deny that in the public's mind a corporation can break the law and be guilty of unethical and amoral conduct. Events of the early 1970s, such as corporate violation of federal laws and failure of full disclosure, confirmed that both our government and our citizenry expect *corporations* to act lawfully, ethically, and responsibly.
>
> Perhaps it is then appropriate in today's context to think of Conoco as a *living corporation*; a sentient being whose conduct and personality are the collective effort and responsibility of its employees, officers, directors, and shareholders.[15]

If, then, it makes sense to talk about the social and moral responsibilities of corporations, either in a literal sense or as a shorthand way of referring to the obligations of the individuals that make up the corporation, what are these responsibilities?

CORPORATE RESPONSIBILITY

In 1963 Tennessee Iron & Steel, a subsidiary of United States Steel, was by far the largest employer, purchaser, and taxpayer in Birmingham, Alabama. In the same city at the same time, racial tensions exploded in the bombing of a black church, killing four black children. The ugly incident led some to blame U.S. Steel for not doing more to improve race relations. But Roger Blough, chairman of U.S. Steel, defended his company:

> I do not either believe that it would be a wise thing for United States Steel to be other than a good citizen in a community, or to attempt to have its ideas of what is right for the community enforced upon the community by some sort of economic means. . . .
>
> When we as individuals are citizens in a community we can exercise what small influence we may have as citizens, but for a corporation to attempt to exert any kind of economic compulsion to achieve a particular end in the racial area seems to me quite beyond what a corporation can do.[16]

Not long afterward, Sol M. Linowitz, chairman of the board of Xerox Corporation, declared in an address to the National Industrial Conference Board: "To realize its full promise in the world of tomorrow, American business and industry—or, at least, the vast portion of it—will have to make social goals as central to its decisions as economic goals; and leadership in our corporations will increasingly recognize this responsibility and accept it."[17] Thus, the issue of business's corporate responsibility was joined. Just what responsibilities does a corporation have? Is its responsibility to be construed narrowly as merely profit making? Or more broadly to include refraining from harming society and even contributing actively and directly to the public good?

Narrow View: Profit Maximization

As it happened, the year preceding the Birmingham incident had seen the publication of *Capitalism and Freedom*, in which author Milton Friedman forcefully argued that business has no social responsibilities other than to maximize profits:

> The view has been gaining widespread acceptance that corporate officials and labor leaders have a social responsibility that goes beyond serving the interest of their stockholders or their members. This view shows a fundamental misconception of the character and nature of a free economy. In such an economy, there is one and only one social responsibility of business—to use its resources and engage in activities designed to increase its profits so long as it stays within the rules of the game, which is to say, engages in open and free competition, without deception or fraud. . . . Few trends could so thoroughly undermine the very foundations of our free society as the acceptance by corporate officials of a social responsibility other than to make as much money for their stockholders as possible.[18]

Although from Friedman's perspective the only responsibility of business is to make money for its owners, obviously a business may not do literally anything whatsoever to increase its profits. Gangsters pursue profit maximization when they ruthlessly rub out their rivals, but such activity falls outside what Friedman referred to as "the rules of the game." Harvard professor Theodore Levitt echoed this point when he wrote, "In the end business has only two responsibilities—to obey the elementary canons of face-to-face civility (honesty, good faith, and so on) and to seek material gain."[19]

What, then, are the rules of the game? Obviously, elementary morality rules out deception, force, and fraud, and the rules of the game are intended to promote open and free competition. The system of rules in which business is to pursue profit is, in Friedman's view, one that is conducive to the laissez-faire operation of Adam Smith's invisible hand (which was discussed in Chapter 4). Friedman is a conservative economist who believes that, by allowing the market to operate with only the minimal restrictions necessary to prevent fraud and force, society will maximize its overall economic well-being. Pursuit of profit is what makes our system go. Anything that dampens this incentive or inhibits its operation will weaken the ability of Smith's invisible hand to deliver the economic goods.

Because the function of a business organization is to make money, the owners of corporations employ executives to accomplish this goal, thereby obligating these managers always to act in the interests of the owners. According to Friedman, to say that executives have social responsibilities means that at least sometimes they must subordinate owner interests to some social objective, such as controlling pollution or fighting inflation. They must then spend stockholder money for general social interests — in effect, taxing the owners and spending these taxes on social causes. But taxation is a function of government, not private enterprise; executives are not public employees but employees of private enterprise. The doctrine of social responsibility thus transforms executives into civil servants and business corporations into government agencies, thereby diverting business from its proper function in the social system.

Friedman is critical of those who would impose on business any duty other than that of making money, and he is particularly harsh with those business leaders who themselves take a broader view of their social responsibilities — that is, those who

> believe that they are defending free enterprise when they declaim that business is not concerned "merely" with profit but also with promoting desirable "social" ends; that business has a "social conscience" and takes seriously its responsibilities for providing employment, eliminating discrimination, avoiding pollution and whatever else may be the catchwords of the contemporary crop of reformers. . . . Businessmen who talk this way are unwitting puppets of the intellectual forces that have been under-

mining the basis of a free society these past decades. . . .

> [This] short-sightedness is also exemplified in speeches by businessmen on social responsibility. This may gain them kudos in the short run. But it helps to strengthen the already too prevalent view that the pursuit of profits is wicked and immoral and must be curbed and controlled by external forces.[20]

Friedman believes that, by conceding the necessity for a broader view of corporate social responsibility, businesspeople are helping to propagate ideas damaging to capitalism. He acknowledges, however, that often corporate activities are described as an exercise of "social responsibility" when, in fact, they are intended simply to advance a corporation's self-interest:

> To illustrate, it may well be in the long-run interest of a corporation that is a major employer in a small community to devote resources to providing amenities to that community or to improving its government. That may make it easier to attract desirable employees, it may reduce the wage bill or lessen losses from pilferage and sabotage or have other worthwhile effects. . . .
>
> In each of these — and many similar — cases, there is a strong temptation to rationalize these actions as an exercise of "social responsibility." In the present climate of opinion, with its widespread aversion to "capitalism," "profits," the "soulless corporation," and so on, this is one way for a corporation to generate goodwill as a by-product of expenditures that are entirely justified in its own self-interest.[21]

Friedman has no problem with a company pursuing its self-interest by these means, although he rues the fact that "the attitudes of the public make it in [corporations'] self-interest to cloak their actions in this way." Friedman's bottom line is that the bottom line is all that counts. And he rejects any notion of corporate social responsibility that would hinder a corporation's profit maximization.

The Broader View of Corporate Social Responsibility

The rival position to that of Friedman and Levitt is simply that business has other obligations in addition to pursuing profits. The phrase "in addition to" is important. Critics of the narrow view do not as a rule believe there is anything wrong with corporate profit. They maintain, rather, that corporations have other responsibilities as well—to consumers, to their employees, and to society at large. If the adherents of the broader view share one belief, it is that corporations have responsibilities beyond simply enhancing their profits because, as a matter of fact, they have such great social and economic power in our society. With that power must come social responsibility. As professor of business administration Keith Davis puts it:

> One basic proposition is that *social responsibility arises from social power*. Modern business has immense social power in such areas as minority employment and environmental pollution. If business has the power, then a just relationship demands that business also bear responsibility for its actions in these areas. Social responsibility arises from concern about the consequences of business's acts as they affect the interests of others. Business decisions do have social consequences. Businessmen cannot make decisions that are solely economic decisions, because they are interrelated with the whole social system. This situation requires that businessmen's thinking be broadened beyond the company gate to the whole social system. Systems thinking is required.
>
> Social responsibility implies that a business decision maker in the process of serving his own business interests is obliged to take actions that also protect and enhance society's interests. The net effect is to improve the quality of life in the broadest possible way, however quality of life is defined by society. In this manner, harmony is achieved between business's actions and the larger social system. The businessman becomes concerned with social as well as economic outputs and with the total effect of his institutional actions on society.[22]

Adherents of the broader view, like Davis, stress that modern business is intimately integrated with the rest of society. Business is not some self-enclosed world, like a private poker party. Rather, business activities have profound ramifications throughout society. As a result, although society expects business to pursue its economic interests, business has other responsibilities as well.

Melvin Anshen has cast the case for the broader view in a historical perspective.[23] He maintains that there is always a kind of "social contract" between business and society. This contract is, of course, only implicit, but it represents a tacit understanding within society about the proper goals and responsibilities of business. In effect, in Anshen's view, society always structures the guidelines within which business is permitted to operate in order to derive certain benefits from business activity. For instance, in the nineteenth century society's prime interest was rapid economic growth, which was viewed as the source of all progress, and the engine of economic growth was identified as the drive for profits by unfettered, competitive, private enterprise. This attitude was reflected in the then-existing social contract.

Today, however, society has concerns and interests other than rapid economic growth—in particular, a concern for the quality of life and for the preservation of the environment. Accordingly, the social contract is in the process of being modified. In particular, Anshen writes, "it will no longer be acceptable for corporations to manage their affairs solely in terms of the traditional internal costs of doing business, while thrusting external costs on the public."

In recent years we have grown more aware of the possible deleterious side effects of business activity, or what economists call *externalities*. Externalities are the unintended negative (or in some cases positive) consequences that an economic transaction between two parties can have on some third party. Industrial pollution provides the clearest illustration. Suppose, for example, that a factory makes widgets and sells them to your firm. A by-product of this economic transaction is the waste that the rains wash from the factory yard into the local river, waste that damages recreational and commercial fishing interests downstream. This damage to third parties is an unintended side effect of the economic transaction between the seller and buyer of widgets.

Defenders of the new social contract, like Anshen, maintain that externalities should no longer be overlooked. In the jargon of economists, externalities must be "internalized." That is, the factory should be made to absorb the cost, either by disposing of its waste in an environmentally safe (and presumably more expensive) way or by paying for the damage the waste does downstream. On the one hand, basic fairness requires that the factory's waste no longer be dumped onto third parties. On the other hand, from the economic point of view, requiring the factory to internalize the externalities makes sense, for only when it does so will the price of the widgets it sells reflect their true social cost. The real production cost of the widgets includes not just labor, raw materials, machinery, and so on but also the damage done to the fisheries downstream. Unless the price of widgets is raised sufficiently to reimburse the fisheries for their losses or to dispose of the waste in some other way, then the buyer of widgets is paying less than their true cost. Part of the cost is being paid by the fishing interests downstream.

Some advocates of the broader view go beyond requiring business to internalize its externalities in a narrow economic sense.

Keith Davis maintains that, in addition to considering potential profitability, a business must weigh the long-range social costs of its activities as well. Only if the overall benefit to society is positive should business act.

> For example, a firm that builds row upon row of look-alike houses may be saving $500 on each house and passing along $400 of the saving to each buyer, thus serving consumer interests. In the long run, however, this kind of construction may encourage the rapid development of a city slum. In this instance, the lack of long-range outlook may result in serious social costs. . . .
>
> In sum, the expectation of the social responsibility model is that a detailed cost/benefit analysis will be made prior to determining whether to proceed with an activity and that social costs will be given significant weight in the decision-making process. Almost any business action will entail some social costs. The basic question is whether the benefits outweigh the costs so that there is a net social benefit. Many questions of judgment arise, and there is no precise mathematical measures in the social field, but rational and wise judgments can be made if the issues are first thoroughly explored.[24]

Corporations, Stockholders, and the Promissory Relationship

Advocates of the narrow view argue that Davis and others do not understand the proper relationship between management and the owners (or stockholders) of a corporation. This relationship is a *promissory* relationship, and it imposes an obligation on management that is inconsistent with any social responsibility other than profit maximization. In effect, management agrees to maximize stockholder wealth in return for specific compensation. It's as if you turned $10,000 over to an investment manager and told her: "Make me as much money with this as you can. In return, I'll give you 10 percent of the earnings."

If the consultant agrees to the terms, then you would properly consider any whimsical investment of your capital immoral and probably illegal. Of course, she could refuse your offer, thus precluding any such obligation.

Law professor Christopher D. Stone, however, has argued that the relationship between corporate management and its shareholders is not the same as between you and an investment adviser.[25] For one thing, rarely if ever is the purchase of stock in a corporation couched in such explicitly promissory terms. Would-be investors pick companies that look profitable or are likely to grow or whose policies appeal to them, and they buy shares in those firms. Or they ask their stockbrokers simply to purchase what "looks good." Either way, shares are purchased through a broker from current shareholders, who have acquired their shares the same way. Very few investors put their money directly into a corporation; rather, they buy shares that were initially issued years ago.

Other factors further weaken the analogy between holding stock and entrusting money to a financial manager: (1) Most shareholders aren't even aware who the managers of "their" corporations are; (2) most shareholders never have direct contact with management; (3) the complexity of management systems in most modern corporations makes it impossible to pinpoint a single manager or group of managers directly responsible for "keeping the promise"; (4) the managers were never given a choice, as your adviser was, of refusing to maximize your profits as a shareholder.

But even if a promissory agreement exists between shareholder and management obligating management to make the most possible money for shareholders, must such a promise always be kept? Promises create obligations, but few people would claim that the existence of a promise automatically settles all the moral issues. For example, if I promise to meet you on the corner of Main and State at noon, I have an obligation to keep that promise. But that obligation is not absolute. For ex-

ample, we wouldn't regard the promise to meet at a certain time and place as justification for refusing to give cardiopulmonary resuscitation to a heart attack victim. Better to break the promise and save a life than keep the promise and lose a life. The point is that, even if a promise to maximize profits runs from management to shareholders, it's doubtful that the typical shareholder interprets this promise as a mandate for management to maximize profits at all social costs.

Even if such a promise is so construed, we can still ask: Is such an agreement morally binding? After all, a contract to do evil—for example, to kill someone—is invalid. By the same token, a promise that requires management to subordinate all moral considerations—for example, a healthful environment or safe products—to the end of stockholder profits would be immoral. Management, therefore, would not be obliged to honor it and, in fact, should break it.

But then precisely what is the nature of and the basis for the relationship between shareholder and corporate executive? For whom are managers working and to whom are they responsible: shareholders, society, both? Friedman raises this point:

> The whole justification for permitting the corporate executive to be selected by the shareholders is that the executive is an agent serving the interest of his principal. This justification disappears when the corporate executive imposes taxes and spends the proceeds for "social" purposes. He becomes in effect a public employee, a civil servant, even though he remains in name an employee of a private enterprise.[26]

But is it true that stockholders actually select corporate executives? Corporate watchdogs like Ralph Nader and Mark Green make the point that, in modern corporate governance, management in fact selects its board of directors by controlling proxy votes. And the board typically rubber-stamps the policies and executive-officer recommendations of management. Furthermore, corporate boards often are ignorant of the activities of chief executive officers. For well over a year after disclosure of multimillion-dollar bribes by Gulf Oil executives, the board of directors claimed it didn't know that the company's chief executive officer and chairman of the board had been personally involved.[27]

But even if stockholders do select corporate executives, it doesn't follow that the executives are therefore bound to act solely in the interest of stockholder profits. Some stockholders, for example, might expect executives to act in an environmentally responsible manner, even if that means less profit. And why shouldn't stockholders who want to expand the notion of corporate responsibility fight for just that? Friedman dismisses such cases as "some stockholders trying to get other stockholders . . . to contribute against their will to 'social' causes. . . ." But why couldn't it be a case of the activists trying to open debate about the nature of their corporation's social responsibility? Besides, if activist stockholders wish to make their corporations more socially responsible, why don't they have a right to do that as owners?

Friedman believes that, if executives "impose taxes on stockholders and spend the proceeds for 'social' purposes, they then become 'civil servants,' and thus should be selected through a political process." He considers such a proposition absurd, or at best socialistic. And yet others contend that corporations are too focused on profits and fear the damage to society when firms are willing to sacrifice all other values on the altar of the bottom line. They don't think it absurd at all that corporations should take a broader view of their social role and responsibilities. They see nothing in the management-stockholder relationship that would morally forbid corporations from doing so.

Even if Friedman's critics are correct and broadening the notion of corporate social responsibility does not violate a promissory relationship between stockholder and manage-

ment, the discussion is not over. One question must still be asked: Should the notion of corporation responsibility be broadened?

THE ADVISABILITY OF BROADENING CORPORATE RESPONSIBILITY

Four powerful arguments against broadening corporate responsibility can be conveniently termed the "invisible hand" argument, the "hand of government" argument, the "inept custodian" argument, and the "materialization of society" argument.[28] Advocates of broadened corporate responsibility base their case in part on a rejection of these arguments.

The "Invisible Hand" Argument

Adam Smith claimed that when each of us acts in a free-market environment to promote our own economic interests we are led by an "invisible hand" to promote the general good. Like-minded contemporary thinkers like Friedman agree. They point out that corporations, in fact, were chartered by states precisely with utility in mind. If businesses are permitted to seek self-interest, their activities will inevitably yield the greatest good for society as a whole. To invite corporations to base their policies and activities on anything other than profit making is to politicize business's unique economic function and to hamper its ability to satisfy our material needs. Accordingly, corporations should not be invited to fight racial injustice, poverty, or pollution, to broaden competition, or to help reduce prices or increase accessibility to products, except insofar as these activities are a natural outgrowth of improved corporate efficiency.

Yet this argument allows that corporations may still be held accountable for their actions. To the degree that they fulfill or fail to fulfill their economic role, they can be praised or blamed. But corporations should not be held morally responsible for noneconomic matters. To do so would distort the economic mission of business in society and undermine the foundations of the free-enterprise system.

Perhaps within a very restricted area of economic exchange, where parties to the exchange are roughly equal, each pursuing self-interest can result in the greatest net good. But when economic exchanges involve giant corporations, the concept of an "invisible hand" orchestrating the common good stretches credulity.

Modern corporations bear about as much resemblance to Smith's self-sufficient farmers and craftspersons as today's military complex bears to the Continental militia. Today's modern corporation, notes Professor Virginia Held, is "an almost feudal institution in its hierarchical structure and lack of democratic organization."[29] Moreover, corporations are no more "private" in their ability to control our lives than are state governments. If an "invisible hand" has been operating, its movements have been decidedly clumsy. The United States is not becoming more egalitarian. The percentages of rich and poor have not materially changed over the years, although the disparity between them has widened. And whereas large corporations generally can escape the ravages of economic downturns, the unskilled, members of minority groups, women, the aged, and the infirm often cannot find work or even lose the jobs they had.

The "Hand of Government" Argument

Others, like economist and social critic John Kenneth Galbraith, agree that business's social role is purely economic and that corporations should not be considered moral agents.[30] But they reject the assumption that Smith's "invisible hand" will have the effect of "moralizing corporate activities." Left to their own self-serving devices, they warn, modern corporations will enrich themselves while impoverishing society. They will pol-

lute, allow racial and sexual inequalities to fester, deceive consumers, strive to eliminate competition, and keep prices high through oligopolistic practices. And they will use their abundant resources to pressure legislators into enacting legislation that is favorable to them but not necessarily to the rest of us. They will do these things, the argument continues, because being economic institutions they are quite naturally and properly profit-motivated. But what is profitable is not necessarily socially useful or desirable; and what is socially useful and desirable is not always profitable.

Then how is the corporation's natural and insatiable appetite for profit to be controlled? Through government regulation. The strong hand of government, through a system of laws and incentives, can and should bring corporations to heel.

As Kenneth Goodpaster and John Matthews point out, these two views obviously differ in identifying the locus of moral force: For one it is the invisible hand of the market; for the other it is the visible hand of government. Both positions, however, agree that corporate social responsibility should not be expanded.[31]

Critics respond that the "hand of government" view is a blueprint for big, intrusive government. Besides, they wonder if government can control any but the most egregious corporate immorality. Necessarily overlooked, they fear, will be many questionable activities that can be safely hidden within the labyrinth of corporate structure. Moreover, lacking intimate knowledge of the goals and subgoals of specific corporations, as well as of their daily operations, government simply can't anticipate a specific corporation's moral challenges. Rather, it can prescribe behavior only for broad, cross-sectional issues, such as bribery, price fixing, unfair competition, and the like.

Finally, is government a credible custodian of morality? If recent experience has taught anything, it is that government officials are not always paragons of virtue. Looked at as another organization, government manifests many of the same structural characteristics that test moral behavior inside the corporation. Furthermore, given the awesome clout of political action committees (PACs), one wonders whether, as moral police, government officials will do anything more than impose the value systems of their most generous financiers. Since business and corporate interests number among the most influential of PACs, can we seriously expect politicians to bite the hand that feeds them?

The "Inept Custodian" Argument

Some who argue against broadening corporate responsibility say that corporate executives lack the moral and social expertise to make other than economic decisions. To charge them with noneconomic responsibilities would be to put social welfare in the hands of inept custodians. Thus, business analyst Walter Goodman writes: "I don't know of any investment adviser whom I would care to act in my behalf in any matter except turning a profit. . . . The value of these specialists . . . lies in their limitations; they ought not allow themselves to see so much of the world that they become distracted."[32]

It may be true, as Goodman suggests, that corporate members lack the moral or social expertise that a broader view of corporate responsibility would seem to require of them. But more or less the same can be said of most people in organizations: They are not trained moral philosophers or social scientists. And yet we don't ordinarily restrict the activities of these parties, individually or collectively, to carefully circumscribed organizational goals. Physicians, for example, are to provide health care. Is it therefore objectionable for them as physicians to protest nuclear war and campaign for an end to the nuclear arms race — indeed, to conceive of their social responsi-

bility in such terms? Is it beyond the role of pediatricians to publicly support legislation requiring seat belts and other restraining devices in automobiles? Again, every year the Committee on Public Doublespeak of the National Council of Teachers of English gives a "Doublespeak Award," usually to a business or political leader, for flagrant use of language that pretends to communicate but really does not. Should the committee's members, all of whom are teachers of English, confine their language instruction to the classroom and avoid trying to attract public attention to good, clear, solid language usage?

Of course, the analogy between physicians and English teachers on the one hand and corporate executives on the other is imperfect. For one thing, English teachers know proper language usage. And physicians are qualified to address the health aspects of nuclear war and the health hazards of driving without restraining devices. Furthermore, the social activism of these professionals does not threaten the earnings of their employers. Nevertheless, such comparisons do make the larger point that "responsibility" is not always limited to narrow professional or occupational concerns. If we consider physician and teacher activities like the aforementioned defensible, then it seems fair to ask: What, if anything, makes the social role of the corporation unique, so that its responsibility and that of those it employs should be confined solely to profit making?

The "Materialization of Society" Argument

Related to the "inept custodian" argument is one expressing the fear that, permitted to stray from strictly economic matters, corporate officials will impose their materialistic values on all of society. Thus, broadening corporate responsibility will "materialize" society instead of "moralizing" corporate activity.

More than thirty years ago, Harvard professor Theodore Levitt expressed this concern:

> The danger is that all these things [resulting from having business pursue social goals other than profit making] will turn the corporation into a twentieth century equivalent of the medieval church. . . . For while the corporation also transforms itself in the process, at bottom its outlook will always remain materialistic. What we have then is the frightening spectacle of a powerful economic functional group whose future and perception are shaped in a tight materialistic context of money and things but which imposes its narrow ideas about a broad spectrum of unrelated noneconomic subjects on the mass of man and society. Even if its outlook were the purest kind of good will, that would not recommend the corporation as an arbiter of our lives.[33]

This argument seems to assume that corporations do not already exercise enormous discretionary power over us. But as Keith Davis points out, business already has immense social power. "Society has entrusted to business large amounts of society's resources," says Davis, "and business is expected to manage these resources as a wise trustee for society. In addition to the traditional role of economic enterpreneurship, business now has a new social role of trusteeship. As trustee for society's resources, it serves the interests of all claimants on the organization, rather than only those of owners, or consumers, or labor."[34]

As Paul Camenisch points out, business is already using its privileged position to propagate, consciously or unconsciously, a view of humanity and the good life.[35] Implicit in the barrage of advertisements to which we are subjected daily are assumptions about happiness, success, and human fulfillment. Sometimes corporations speak out in unvarnished terms about social issues. For a number of

years, Mobil Corporation has run advertisements in the form of essays on industry-related social issues. One appeared right after William Ruckelshaus, administrator of the Environmental Protection Agency during the Reagan-Bush administration, called on scientists to help the EPA formulate a public policy free from politics. Mobil seized on the opportunity to divide the population into two categories: scientists, who best know what constitutes pollution and hazardous waste, and the rest of us well-intentioned but dangerously benighted souls. In praising Ruckelshaus's emphasis on the central position of scientists in setting standards, Mobil in effect was making industry scientists custodians of the environment.

The point here is that business already promotes consumerism and materialistic values. It doesn't hesitate to use its resources to express its views and influence our political system on issues that affect its economic interests. If corporations take a broader view of their social responsibilities, are they really likely to have a more materialistic effect on society, as Levitt suggests, than they do now? It's hard to believe they could. Levitt's view implies that there is some threat to society's values when corporations engage in philanthropy or use their economic and political muscle for other than purely self-interested ends. But where is the "materialization of society" if, instead of advertising on a silly situation comedy that reaches a large audience, a corporation spends the same amount underwriting a science program with a more limited number of viewers solely out of a sense of social responsibility?

INSTITUTIONALIZING ETHICS WITHIN CORPORATIONS

The criticisms of the four arguments against corporate responsibility have led many people inside and outside business to adopt the broader view of corporate responsibility—

that the obligations of the modern business corporation extend beyond simply making money for itself. Society grants corporations the right to exist, gives them legal status as separate entities, and permits them to use natural resources. It does this not to indulge the profit appetites of owners and managers but, as Camenisch says, because it needs "the available raw materials transformed into needed goods and services, and because business in its contemporary form has been conspicuously successful in doing just that."[36] In return for its sufferance of corporations, society has the right to expect that, at the very least, corporate activities will not cause harm.

Some argue further that the list of corporate responsibilities goes beyond such negative injunctions as "Don't pollute," "Don't misrepresent products," "Don't bribe." Included also are affirmative duties: "Hire the hard-core unemployed," "Give special consideration to members of historically disadvantaged groups," "Contribute to the arts and education," "Locate plants in economically depressed areas," "Improve working conditions." This class of affirmative responsibilities includes activities that are not intrinsically related to the operations of the corporation — responsibilities that each of us, whether individuals or institutions, has simply by virtue of our being members of society.[37] Precisely how far each of us must go to meet these responsibilities depends largely on our capacity to fulfill them, which, of course, varies from person to person, institution to institution. But given their considerable power and resources, corporations seem better able to promote the common good than individuals or small businesses.

How corporations are to promote the common good cannot be answered very specifically; methods will depend on the type of firm and its particular circumstances. Proponents of broadening corporate responsibility probably would agree that the first step is to create an ethical atmosphere within the corporation.

This means making ethical behavior a high priority. How to do this? At least four actions seem called for:

1. Corporations should acknowledge the importance, even necessity, of conducting business morally. Their commitment to ethical behavior should be unequivocal and highly visible, from top management down.

2. Corporations should make a real effort to encourage their members to take moral responsibilities seriously. This commitment would mean ending all forms of retaliation against those who "buck the system" and rewarding employees for evaluating corporate decisions in their broader social and moral contexts.

3. Corporations should end their defensiveness in the face of public discussion. They should stop responding with righteous indignation to external criticism and refrain from automatically wrapping themselves in the red-white-and-blue of free enterprise, thereby reducing legitimate inquiry to some sort of political subversion. Instead, corporations should actively solicit other views from stockholders, managers, employees, customers, and society as a whole. Corporations should invite outside opinions instead of waiting until dissenters are storming the citadel.

4. Corporations must recognize the pluralistic nature of the social system of which they are a part. Society consists of diverse, interlocked groups, all vying to maintain their autonomy and advance their interests. These groups are so related that the actions of one inevitably affect the standing of another on a variety of levels: economic, political, educational, cultural. As part of society, corporations affect many groups, and these groups affect corporations. Failing to realize this or to act on it,

corporations lose sight of the social framework that governs their relationship with the external environment.

Undoubtedly, other general directives could be added to this list. Still, if corporate responsibility should be expanded, then something like the preceding approach seems basic.

Limits to What the Law Can Do

Critics of the "hand of government" argument question Galbraith's view that society should not expect business to behave morally but rather should simply use government to direct business's pursuit of profit in socially acceptable directions. This issue is worth returning to in the present context. All defenders of the broad view of corporate social responsibility believe that more than laissez-faire is necessary to ensure that business behavior is socially and morally acceptable. But there is a tendency to believe that law is a fully adequate vehicle for this purpose.

Law professor Christopher Stone has argued, however, that there are limits on what the law can be expected to achieve.[38] Three of his points are particularly important. First, many laws, like controls on the disposal of toxic waste, are passed only after there is general awareness of the problem; in the meantime, damage has already been done. The proverbial barn door has been shut only after the horse has left.

Second, formulating appropriate laws and designing effective regulations are difficult. It is hard to achieve consensus on the relevant facts, to determine what remedies will work, and to decide how to weigh conflicting values. In addition, our political system gives corporations and their lobbyists significant input into the writing of laws. Not only that, but the specific working regulations and day-to-day interpretation of the law require the continual input of industry experts. This is not a

conspiracy but a fact of life. Government bureaus generally have limited time, staffing, and expertise, so they must rely on the cooperation and assistance of those they regulate.

Third, enforcing the law is often cumbersome. Legal actions against corporations are expensive and can drag on for years. And often the judicial process is too blunt an instrument to use as a way of managing complex social and business issues. In fact, recourse to the courts can be counterproductive, and Stone argues that sometimes the benefits of doing so may not be worth the costs. Legal action may simply make corporations more furtive, breeding distrust, destruction of documents, and an attitude that "I won't do anything more than I am absolutely required to do."

What conclusion should be drawn? Stone's argument is not intended to show that regulation of business is hopeless. Rather, what he wants to stress is that the law cannot do it alone. We do not want a system in which businesspeople believe that their only obligation is to obey the law and that it is morally permissible for them to do anything not (yet) illegal. With that attitude, disaster is just around the corner. More socially responsible business behavior requires, instead, that corporations and the people within them not just respond to the requirements of the law but hold high moral standards—and that they themselves monitor their own behavior.

Ethical Codes and Economic Efficiency

It is, therefore, important that corporations examine their own implicit and explicit codes of conduct and the moral standards that are being propagated to their employees. Yet ethical behavior in the business world is often assumed to come at the expense of economic efficiency. Defenders of the broader view, like Anshen, as well as defenders of the narrow view, like Friedman, seem to make this assumption. Anshen believes that other values should take priority over economic efficiency, while Friedman contends business should only concern itself with profit and, in this way, maximize economic well-being. In his essay "Social Responsibility and Economic Efficiency," Nobel prize–winning economist Kenneth Arrow has challenged this assumption.[39]

First, any kind of settled economic life requires a certain degree of ethical behavior, some element of trust and confidence. Much business, for instance, is conducted on the basis of oral agreements. In addition, says Arrow, "there are two types of situation in which the simple rule of maximizing profits is socially inefficient: the case in which costs are not paid for, as in pollution, and the case in which the seller has considerably more knowledge about his product than the buyer. . . ."

The first type of situation relates to the demand that corporations "internalize" their "externalities." In the second situation, where the buyer lacks the expertise and knowledge of the seller, an effective moral code, either requiring full disclosure or setting minimal standards of performance (for example, the braking ability of a new automobile), enhances rather than diminishes economic efficiency. Without such a code, buyers may purchase products or services they don't need. Or because they don't trust the seller, they may refrain from purchasing products and services they do need. Either way, from the economist's point of view the situation is inefficient.

An effective professional or business moral code — as well as the public's awareness of this code — is good for business. Most of us, for example, have little medical knowledge and are thus at the mercy of doctors. Over hundreds of years, however, a firm code of ethical conduct has developed in the medical profession. As a result, people generally presume that their physician will perform with their welfare in mind. They rarely worry that their doctor might be taking advantage of them or exploiting them with unnecessary treatment. By contrast, used-car companies have historically suffered from a lack of public trust.

For a code to be effective it must be realistic, Arrow argues, in the sense of connecting with the collective self-interest of business. And it must become part of the corporate culture, "accepted by the significant operating institutions and transmitted from one generation of executives to the next through standard operating procedures [and] through education in business schools."

For both Arrow and Stone, then, the development of feasible and effective business and professional codes of ethics must be a central focus of any effort to enhance or expand corporate responsibility. The question is how to create a corporate atmosphere conducive to moral decision making.

Corporate Moral Codes

What can be done to improve the organizational climate so individual members can reasonably be expected to act ethically? If those inside the corporation are to behave morally, they need clearly stated and communicated ethical standards that are equitable and enforced. This development seems possible only if the standards of expected behavior are institutionalized — that is, only if they become a fixture in the corporate organization. To institutionalize ethics within corporations, professors Milton Snoeyenbos and David Jewell suggest that corporations adopt a corporate ethical code, set up a high-ranking ethics committee, and include ethics training in their management development programs.

The code should not be window dressing or so general as to be useless. It should set reasonable goals and subgoals, with an eye on blunting unethical pressures on subordinates. In formulating the code, the top-level ethics committee should solicit the views of corporate members at all levels regarding goals and subgoals, so that the final product articulates "a fine-grained ethical code that addresses ethical issues likely to arise at the level of subgoals."[40] Moreover, the committee should have full authority and responsibility to communicate the code and decisions based on it to all corporate members, clarify and interpret the code when the need arises, facilitate the code's use, investigate grievances and violations of the code, discipline violators and reward compliance, and review, update, and upgrade the code.

The institutionalization of ethics within the corporation can be further aided by devoting part of all employee-training programs to ethics. Such indoctrination could include, but need not be limited to, the study of the code, orientation to the ethics committee, and discussion of employer and employee responsibilities. Snoeyenbos and Jewell believe that institutionalizing ethics within the corporation, while developing industry-wide codes of ethics to address issues beyond a particular firm, will go far toward establishing a corporate climate conducive to individual moral decision making.

Corporate Culture

During the past two decades, organizational theorists and writers on business management have increasingly emphasized "corporate culture" as the factor that makes one company succeed while another languishes. Although intangible in comparison with things like sales revenue and price-earnings ratios, corporate culture is often the key to a firm's success.

What is corporate culture? One writer describes it as "the shared beliefs top managers have in a company about how they should manage themselves and other employees, and how they should conduct their business(es). These beliefs are often invisible to the top managers but have a major impact on their thoughts and actions."[41] Another writer puts it this way: "Culture is the pattern of shared values and beliefs that gives members of an institution meaning and provides them with rules for behavior in their organization."[42] W. Brooke Tunstall, an assistant vice president of AT&T, provides a fuller definition. He describes corporate culture as "a general constellation of beliefs, mores, customs, value systems and behavioral norms, and ways of doing business that are unique to each corporation, that set a pattern for corporate activities and actions, and that describe the implicit and emergent patterns of behavior and emotions characterizing life in the organization."[43]

Corporate culture may be both explicit and implicit. The formal culture of a corporation, as expressed in idealized statements of values and norms, should also be distinguished from the informal culture that shapes beliefs, values, and behavior. In addition, there may be multiple and overlapping cultures within an organization because employees have different backgrounds, work in different divisions of the organization, and may be subject to different systems of rewards and sanctions.[44]

Organizational theorists emphasize the importance of monitoring and managing corporate culture—beginning with an attempt to understand each corporation's distinctive culture—to prevent dysfunctional behavior and processes. If management does not make explicit the values and behavior it desires, the culture will typically develop its own norms, usually based on the types of behavior that lead to success within the organization. Thus, the desired values must be communicated and transmitted throughout the organization. Conduct congruent with them must be rewarded and conduct inconsistent with them sanctioned. Overlooking behavior that contradicts the desired norms can have the effect of encouraging and even rewarding it. At Southern Methodist University, for example, when university officials turned a blind eye to early evidence of cheating by the athletic department, the problem simply grew worse.[45]

These points are crucial when it comes to corporate social responsibility. Management needs to understand the real dynamics of its own organization. For example, how do people get ahead in the company? What conduct is actually rewarded, what values are really being instilled in employees? Andrew C. Sigler, chairman of Champion International, stresses this point: "Sitting up here in Stamford, there's no way I can affect what an employee is doing today in Texas, Montana, or Maine. Making speeches and sending letters just doesn't do it. You need a culture and peer pressure that spells out what is acceptable and isn't and why. It involves training, education, and follow-up."[46]

Strict enforcement of codes is one aspect of follow-up. Chemical Bank, for instance, has fired employees for violations of the company's code of ethics even when nothing illegal was done. Xerox has dismissed people for minor manipulation of records and the padding of expense accounts. Executives at both Xerox and General Mills also emphasize that civic involvement is a crucial part of corporate ethics. As one General Mills executive puts it: "It's hard to imagine that a person who reads to the blind at night would cheat. . . ."[47]

Johnson & Johnson is widely seen as a model of corporate responsibility, especially because of its decisive handling of the Tylenol crisis of 1982, when seven people died in the Chicago area from cyanide-laced Extra-Strength Tylenol capsules. The company immediately recalled 31 million bottles of Tylenol from store shelves across the nation, and it notified 500,000 doctors and hospitals about the contaminated capsules. A toll-free consumer hotline was set up the first week of the crisis, and consumers were offered the opportunity to replace Tylenol capsules with a free bottle of Tylenol tablets. Johnson & Johnson was also open with the public instead of being defensive about the deaths. Accurate information was promptly released, and domestic employees and retirees were kept updated on developments. The chairman of the company appeared on "Donahue" and "60 Minutes" to answer questions about the crisis, and other executives were interviewed by *Fortune* and *The Wall Street Journal*.

Despite the setback — the recall alone cost Johnson & Johnson $50 million after taxes — Tylenol rebounded within a year, in large part because the public never lost faith in Johnson & Johnson. The company itself credits its forty-five-year-old, one-page statement of values, known as the Credo, with enabling it to build the employee trust necessary for maintaining a firm corporate value system. The Credo acknowledges the company's need to make a sound profit while addressing its obligations to provide a quality product, to treat its employees fairly and with respect, and to be a good corporate citizen, supporting the community of which it is a member. These are lofty goals, perhaps, but ones that Johnson & Johnson seems to have succeeded in integrating into its corporate culture.

SUMMARY

1. What we know as the modern business corporation has evolved over several centuries, and incorporation is no longer the special privilege it once was.

2. Corporations are legal entities, with legal rights and responsibilities similar but not identical to those enjoyed by individuals. Business corporations are "limited-liability" companies—that is, their owners or stockholders are only liable for corporate debts up to the extent of their investments.

3. The question of corporate moral agency is whether corporations are the kind of entity that can have moral responsibilities. There are at least three senses of "morally responsible." If corporations can make rational and moral decisions, then they can be held morally blameworthy or praiseworthy for their actions. Philosophers disagree about whether the corporate internal decision (CID) structure makes it reasonable to assign moral responsibility to corporations.

4. This problem is compounded by the difficulty of assigning moral responsibility to individuals inside corporations.

5. Despite these controversies, the courts and the general public find the notion of corporate responsibility useful and intelligible — either in a literal sense or as shorthand for the obligations of individuals in the corporation.

6. The debate over corporate responsibility is whether it should be construed narrowly to cover only profit maximization or more broadly to include refraining from socially undesirable behavior and contributing actively and directly to the public good.

7. Proponents of the narrow view, like Milton Friedman, contend that diverting corporations from the pursuit of profit makes our economic system less efficient. Business's only social responsibility is to make money within the "rules of the game." Private enterprise should not be forced to undertake public responsibilities that properly belong to government.

8. Defenders of the broader view maintain that corporations have additional responsibilities because of their great social and economic power. Business is governed by an implicit "social contract," which requires it to operate in ways that benefit society. In particular, corporations must take responsibility for the unintended side effects of their business transactions (externalities) and weigh the full social costs of their activities.

9. Advocates of the narrow view stress that management has a promissory relation with the owners (stockholders) of a corporation, which obligates it to focus on profit maximization alone. Critics challenge this argument.

10. Should corporate responsibility be broadened? Four arguments against doing so are the "invisible hand" argument, the "hand of government" argument, the "inept custodian" argument, and the "materialization of society" argument. Finding flaws with each of these arguments, critics claim there is no solid basis for restricting corporate responsibility to profit making.

11. Those proposing broader corporate responsibilities see the creation of an ethical atmosphere within the corporation as an important first step. Essential to this atmosphere are corporate acknowledgment of the critical importance of ethics, corporate encouragement of morally responsible conduct by its members, an end to corporate defensiveness in the face of criticism, and corporate recognition of the pluralistic nature of our social system.

12. Corporations and the people who make them up must have high moral standards and monitor their own behavior because there are limits to what the law can do to ensure that business behavior is socially and morally acceptable.

13. All settled economic life requires trust and confidence. The adoption of realistic and workable codes of ethics in the business world can actually enhance business efficiency. This is particularly true when there is an imbalance of knowledge between the buyer and the seller.

14. To improve the organizational climate so individuals can reasonably be expected to act ethically, some writers recommend that, in addition to adopting a corporate ethical code, corporations set up a high-ranking ethics committee and include ethics training in their management development programs. Attention to ''corporate culture'' is also crucial to the successful institutionalization of ethics inside an organization.

CASE 5.1
Exxon and Captain Hazelwood

On the dark night of March 23–24, 1989, an Exxon Corporation supertanker, named the *Exxon Valdez*, ran aground on Bligh Reef in Alaska's Prince William Sound. It ruptured and began emptying its 11 million gallons of oil into the sea, despoiling a coastline the length of California's and creating the worst oil spill the nation has ever seen.[48] More than 36,000 migratory birds, including 100 or more bald eagles, and many other species of wildlife died as a result.[49]

Many of the *Exxon Valdez*'s crew members that night were exhausted from working an average of 140 hours of overtime a month, a routine experience on Exxon ships. The ship itself carried a crew of only twenty, a third smaller than on older tankers. The Coast Guard had approved this reduction after oil companies convinced it that ships in the class of the *Exxon Valdez* did not need larger crews. But modern instruments did not prevent the crew and officers from going long stretches with little or no sleep and from working extensive overtime.

Exxon policy and federal regulations forbid officers from drinking any alcoholic beverage within four hours of embarking or from having drugs or alcohol on board. Exxon relies on the captains of its ships to enforce these regulations, but the captain of the *Exxon Valdez*, Joseph J. Hazelwood, may not have been the best person for this job. He was treated for alcohol abuse in 1985, and he was not licensed to drive a car in his home state of New York because of a conviction for drunken driving. Witnesses report his drinking on voyages. And before the ship departed late on March 23, Captain Hazelwood and several of the ship's officers allegedly spent much of the day boozing in town. He and the ship's chief engineer admit to having drinks up until an hour and a half before departure. (A year later, however, an Anchorage, Alaska, jury acquitted Hazelwood of the criminal charge of operating a watercraft while under the influence of alcohol.)

The *Exxon Valdez* departed at 11:06 P.M. It was initially under the command of an independent harbor pilot, Captain William Murphy. His job done, he left the ship at 11:24 P.M., returning control of it to Hazelwood. He later said that he smelled liquor on Captain Hazelwood's breath, but Murphy did not report it. Hazelwood took command and radioed the Coast Guard that he was turning southeast into the incoming shipping lane to avoid ice. The ship was then put on automatic pilot, something that Coast Guard regulations and Exxon policy say should only be done in the open sea.

A little later, after Third Mate Gregory T. Cousins plotted the ship's course, Hazelwood ordered him to change direction, take the ship off automatic pilot, and steer it due south through the incoming shipping lane into the shallower waters around Busby Island (a few miles before Bligh Reef). When the ship neared a lighted buoy by the island, Cousins was then to turn it back into the inbound shipping lane. The Coast Guard was not notified of this change of course. Meanwhile, Coast Guard radar, although capable of tracking the ship that far, lost touch with the ship when it temporarily went off the screen. With that visual link cut, the Exxon crew and the Coast Guardsmen on duty failed to stay in radio contact.

At this point, half an hour before the ship ran aground, Hazelwood went to his cabin, turning the *Exxon Valdez* over to the third mate. Cousins did not have a license to pilot the tanker, but turning the wheel over to unqualified officers appears to have been a common practice on Exxon tankers. Third Mate Cousins later testified that he ordered the ship to turn in the area of the buoy, as instructed by Hazelwood, at 11:55 P.M. But the ship's recorder shows that the turn was not made until about six minutes later, around the time that a lookout (posted on the bridge instead of 800 feet farther forward on the bow) reported a flashing light. That was the light marking Bligh Reef. Cousins ordered a hard right rudder to avoid the reef. But it was too late. At 12:04 A.M., the *Exxon Valdez* ran aground.

Nearly a quarter of our domestic oil comes through the glaciers surrounding Prince William Sound, but twelve uneventful years of tanker traffic had numbed state regulators, oil company executives, and federal officials to the possibility of an environmental disaster at the edge of the last American wilderness. The Alyeska Pipeline Service Company, a consortium of seven oil companies that includes Exxon, had estimated that a spill of this magnitude could happen only once every twenty-four years. In 1981, the consortium dismissed its oil-spill response team, the only unit set up exclusively to clean up spills in Prince William Sound. Since 1984, the Coast Guard, which watches over marine traffic carrying oil, had also been scaling back.

Alyeska was obligated to have a specific amount of cleanup equipment at the dock and to have any large spill contained within five hours of the accident. But it took fourteen hours for a barge carrying cleanup equipment to arrive at the accident site, and even then an Exxon official turned down a request to circle the tanker with a containment boom. Exxon's elaborate oil-spill response plan is twenty-eight volumes thick, but Dennis Kelso, Alaska's environment commissioner, calls this document "the biggest piece of maritime fiction since *Moby Dick*." Yet it was Kelso's office that had approved it.

Instead of attempting, during the calm weather of the first two days, to encircle the oil with booms and scoop it up with skimmers (as called for in its plan), Exxon decided to use chemical dispersants to break the oil into tiny droplets that would easily dissolve. But it was very slow in doing so. Later, the chairman of Exxon, Lawrence Rawl, contended that the company was not granted permission to use the dispersants during the first two days, when up to half of the spilled oil could have been taken care of. But Exxon never had an adequate supply of chemicals on hand in Alaska. Only 69 barrels were available for a job that called for nearly 10,000, and even six days after the spill Exxon still had only a fraction of the number of barrels needed. And contrary to Rawl's claim that the government had failed to approve the deployment of these chemicals, the records and testimony at a federal inquiry establish that their use had, in fact, been approved in advance.

In March 1991, two years after the accident and with only an estimated 8 percent of the oil spilled by the *Valdez* removed from the environment, Exxon agreed to pay $900 million in civil damages and a $100 million criminal fine in order to settle federal and state claims against it and to avoid going to trial on criminal charges related to the oil disaster. The settlement with the state of Alaska and the federal government called for Exxon, which has an annual revenue of $100 billion, to make payments over a ten-year period. Although Attorney General Dick Thornburgh hailed the settlement as "by far the largest amount ever paid as a result of environmental violation," it falls far short of what confidential government studies have estimated to be the dollar value of the intangible losses suffered by the American public as a result of injury to Alaska's wildlife and coastline. Those studies put the "social cost" of the spill at $3 billion.[50] Persuaded that Exxon was getting off too easy, U.S. District Judge Russel Holland rejected the criminal portion of the settlement a month after it was signed. Prompted by this, the Alaska House of Representatives killed the rest of the deal a few days later. It now looks as if Exxon's legal difficulties will drag on for years.

Discussion Questions

1. Describe the actions, decisions, and policies that contributed to the *Exxon Valdez*'s despoiling of Alaska's coastline. How would you compare the roles played by Captain Hazelwood and by Chairman Rawl?

2. Is Exxon as a corporate agent morally responsible for what happened, or are individuals inside the company responsible? Should a specific person or persons be singled out for blame, or should the entire organization be held accountable?

3. Who or what, in your view, bears prime responsibility for this disaster?

4. What, if anything, does this episode reveal about Exxon's sense of social responsibility? Do you think the company has a narrow or a broad view of its corporate responsibility?

5. Are there specific organizational policies, attitudes, goals, or norms at Exxon that may have contributed to this disaster? If you were the CEO at Exxon, what changes, if any, would you make?

6. How might such environmental catastrophes be avoided in the future? Is greater government regulation called for?

7. In your view, what should Exxon pay for the damage it caused? How could a fair legal settlement be determined. Should the corporation or its officers be subject to criminal punishment? What should this be?

CASE 5.2
Living and Dying with Asbestos

Asbestos is a fibrous mineral used for fireproofing, electrical insulation, building materials, brake linings, and chemical filters. If you are exposed long enough to asbestos particles — usually ten or more years — you can develop a chronic lung inflammation called asbestosis, which makes breathing difficult and infection easy. Also linked to asbestos exposure is mesethelioma, a cancer of the chest lining that sometimes doesn't develop until forty years after the first exposure. Although the first major scientific conference on the dangers of asbestos was not held until 1964, the asbestos industry knew of its dangers more than fifty years ago.

As early as 1932, the British documented the occupational hazards of asbestos dust inhalation.[51] Indeed, on September 25, 1935, the editors of the trade journal *Asbestos* wrote to Sumner Simpson, president of Raybestos-Manhattan, a leading asbestos company, asking permission to publish an article on the dangers of asbestos. Simpson refused and later praised the magazine for not printing the article. In a letter to Vandivar Brown, secretary of Johns-Manville, another asbestos manufacturer, Simpson observed: "The less said about asbestos the better off we are." Brown agreed, adding that any article on asbestosis should reflect American, not English, data.

In fact, American data were available, and Brown, as one of the editors of the journal, knew it. Working on behalf of Raybestos-Manhattan and Johns-Manville and their insurance carrier, Metropolitan Life Insurance Company, Anthony Lanza had conducted research between 1929 and 1931 on 126 workers with three or more years of asbestos exposure. But Brown and others were not pleased with the paper Lanza submitted to them for editorial review. Lanza, said Brown, had failed to portray asbestosis as milder than silicosis, a lung disease caused by long-term inhalation of silica dust and resulting in chronic shortness of breath. Under the then-pending Workmen's Compensation law, silicosis was categorized as a compensable disease. If asbestosis was worse than silicosis or indistinguishable from it, then it too would have to be covered. Apparently Brown didn't want this and thus requested that Lanza depict asbestosis as less serious than silicosis. Lanza complied and also omitted from his published report the fact that more than half the workers examined — 67 of 126 — were suffering from asbestosis.

Meanwhile, Sumner Simpson was writing F.H. Schulter, president of Thermoid Rubber Company, to suggest that several manufacturers sponsor further asbestos experiments. The sponsors, said Simpson, could exercise oversight prerogatives; they "could determine from time to time after the findings are made whether we wish any publication or not." Added Simpson: "It would be a good idea to distribute the information to the medical fraternity, providing it is of the right type and would not injure our companies." Lest there should be any question about the arbiter of publication, Brown wrote to officials at the laboratory conducting the tests:

It is our further understanding that the results obtained will be considered the property of those who are advancing the required funds, who will determine whether, to what extent and in what manner they shall be made public. In the event it is deemed desirable that the results be made public, the manuscript of your study will be submitted to us for approval prior to publication.

Industry officials were concerned with more than controlling information flow. They also sought to deny workers early evidence of their asbestosis. Dr. Kenneth Smith, medical director of a Johns-Manville plant in Canada, explained why seven workers he found to have asbestosis should not be informed of their disease:

It must be remembered that although these men have the X-ray evidence of asbestosis, they are working today and definitely are not disabled from asbestosis. They have not been told of this diagnosis, for it is felt that as long as the man feels well, is happy at home and at work, and his physical condition remains good, nothing should be said. When he becomes disabled and sick, then the diagnosis should be made and the claim submitted *by the Company*. The fibrosis of this disease is irreversible and permanent so that eventually compensation will be paid to each of these men. But as long as the man is not disabled, it is felt that he should not be told of his condition so that he can live and work in peace and the Company can benefit by his many years of experience. Should the man be told of his condition today there is a very definite possibility that he would become mentally and physically ill, simply through the knowledge that he has asbestosis.

When lawsuits filed by asbestos workers who had developed cancer reached the industry in the 1950s, Dr. Smith suggested that the industry retain the Industrial Health Foundation to conduct a cancer study that would, in effect, squelch the asbestos-cancer connection. The asbestos companies refused, claiming that such a study would only bring further unfavorable publicity to the industry and that there wasn't enough evidence linking asbestos and cancer industry-wide to warrant it.

Shortly before his death in 1977, Dr. Smith was asked whether he had ever recommended to Johns-Manville officials that warning labels be placed on insulation products containing asbestos. He provided the following testimony:

> The reasons why the caution labels were not implemented immediately, it was a business decision as far as I could understand. Here was a recommendation, the corporation is in business to make, to provide jobs for people and make money for stockholders and they had to take into consideration the effects of everything they did, and if the application of a caution label identifying a product as hazardous would cut out sales, there would be serious financial implications. And the powers that be had to make some effort to judge the necessity of the label vs. the consequences of placing the label on the product.

Dr. Smith's testimony and related documents have figured prominently in hundreds of asbestos-related lawsuits, totaling more than $1 billion. In March 1981, a settlement was reached in nine separate lawsuits brought by 680 New Jersey asbestos workers at a Raybestos-Manhattan plant. Several asbestos manufacturers, as well as Metropolitan Life Insurance, were named as defendants. Under the terms of the settlement, the workers affected will share in a $9.4 million court-administered compensation fund. Each worker will be paid compensation according to the length of exposure to asbestos and the severity of the disease contracted.

By 1982, an average of 500 new asbestos cases were being filed each month against Manville (as Johns-Manville was now called), and the company was losing more than half the cases that went to trial. In ten separate cases, juries had also awarded punitive damages, averaging $616,000 a case. By August, 20,000 claims had been filed against the company, and Manville filed for bankruptcy in federal court. This action froze the lawsuits in their place and forced asbestos victims to stand in line with other Manville creditors. After more than three years of legal haggling, Manville's reorganization plan was finally approved by the bankruptcy court. The agreement set up a trust fund valued at approximately $2.5 billion to pay Manville's asbestos claimants. To fund the trust, shareholders were required to surrender half the value of their stock, and the company had to give up much of its projected earnings over the next twenty-five years.[52]

Claims, however, soon overwhelmed the trust, which ran out of money in 1990. With many victims still waiting for payment, federal Judge Jack B. Weinstein ordered the trust to restructure its payments and renegotiate Manville's contributions to the fund. As a result, the most seriously ill victims will now be paid first, but average payments to victims have been lowered significantly—from $145,000 to $43,000. Meanwhile, the trust's stake in Manville has been increased to 80 percent, and Manville has been required to pay $300 million to it in additional dividends.[53]

Discussion Questions

1. Should the asbestos companies be held morally responsible in the sense of being capable of making a moral decision about the ill effects of asbestos exposure? Or does it make sense to consider only the principal people involved as morally responsible—for example, Simpson and Brown?

2. Simpson and Brown presumably acted in what they thought were the best profit interests of their companies. Nothing they did was illegal. On what grounds, if any, are their actions open to criticism?

3. Suppose that Simpson and Brown reasoned this way: "While it may be in our firms' short-term interests to suppress data about the ill effects of asbestos exposure, in the long run it may ruin our companies. We could be sued for millions, and the reputation of the entire industry could be destroyed. So we should reveal the true results of the asbestos-exposure research and let the chips fall where they may." Would this kind of reasoning reflect a broad or narrow view of corporate responsibility? Explain.

4. If you were a stockholder in Raybestos-Manhattan or Johns-Manville, would you approve of Simpson and Brown's conduct? If not, why not?

5. "Hands of government" proponents would say that it's the responsibility of government, not the asbestos industry, to ensure health and safety with respect to asbestos. In the absence of appropriate government regulations, asbestos manufacturers have no responsibility other than to operate efficiently. Do you agree?

6. Does Dr. Smith's explanation for concealing from workers the nature of their health problems illustrate how adherence to industry and corporate goals can militate against individual moral behavior? Or do you think Dr. Smith did all he was morally obliged to do as an employee of an asbestos firm? What about Lanza's suppression of data in his report?

7. Do you think a corporate ethical code, together with an industry-wide code, a corporate ethics committee, and training in ethics for management personnel would have encouraged more ethical behavior in this case?

8. It's been shown that spouses of asbestos workers can develop lung damage and cancer simply by breathing the fibers carried home on work clothes and that people living near asbestos plants experience higher rates of cancer than the general population does. Would it be possible to assign responsibility for these effects to individual members of asbestos companies? Should the companies themselves be held responsible?

CASE 5.3
Selling Infant Formula Abroad

In 1860 Henry Nestlé developed infant formula to save the life of an infant who couldn't be breast-fed. According to officials at Nestlé, a Swiss-based corporation that is now the world's largest food company, with annual sales of $24 billion, the Frenchman's concoction has been saving lives ever since, especially in developing countries. They point to relief organizations like the International Red Cross, which has used the formula to feed thousands of starving infants in refugee camps, for example. Without its infant formula, the Nestlé people say, Third World mothers considering use of a breast-milk substitute would use less nutritious local alternatives. Maybe so. But a hundred years after it was first developed, Henry Nestlé's sweet idea turned sour, threatening the Nestlé Corporation's dominant share of the $5–6 billion international market for infant formula.

The infant formula controversy began to heat up in November 1970 at a United Nations–sponsored meeting on infant feeding in Bogota, Colombia. Meeting to discuss different aspects of world hunger, the Protein Advisory Group (PAG) — made up of nutritionists, pediatricians, and food-industry representatives — hammered out a broad framework for cooperation among business, health care, and government. They were especially concerned about the world-wide decline in breast-feeding, despite the demonstrated superiority of mother's milk over infant formula. But some PAG members bristled at what they thought was PAG's failure to engage a critical issue: the implications of marketing infant formula in Third World countries.

Straightaway the media began reporting some of the common marketing practices of formula companies:

Item — Dressed as health-care professionals, representatives of formula companies visited villages to promote the use of infant formula.

Item — While interned in clinics and hospitals, new mothers were given free samples of infant formula.

Item — Free or low-cost supplies of infant formula were given to health institutions, thus routinizing bottle feeding within the hospitals and discouraging breast-feeding.

Item — Product labels failed to warn of potential dangers from incorrect use of infant formula.

Most damaging from the industry's viewpoint was infant formula's alleged complicity in the death of Third World infants. Dr. Derrick B. Jelliffe, then director of the Caribbean Food and Nutrition Institute, claimed that millions of infants suffered and died as a result of bottle feeding. A major reason was that Third World mothers could not take sterilization and storage precautions commonplace in homes with modern kitchens.

Outraged by these allegations, the Infant Formula Action Coalition (INFACT) was formed in 1977. It focused its indignation on Nestlé, the largest producer of infant formula world-wide. Chaired by Douglas A. Johnson and joined by a hundred other religious and health organizations, INFACT instituted an international boycott against the Nestlé Company, charging it with aggressive marketing tactics designed to pressure mothers in underdeveloped countries to switch from breast-feeding to bottle feeding, thus contributing to high infant-mortality rates.

In May 1981, the World Health Organization (WHO) adopted a "Code of Marketing of Breastmilk Substitutes," which called on governments to prohibit advertising of infant formula that discourages breast-feeding. The code would prohibit, for example, sending women dressed as nurses to rural villages or paying local health workers to push infant formula. Of the 119 WHO members who voted, 118 voted for adoption.

The sole opposition vote was cast by the United States, which invoked the principles of free trade and free speech. At the White House, President Reagan's deputy press secretary, James Speakes, said in effect that WHO had no business telling private business how to sell its products, that the United States didn't want to make WHO an international Federal Trade Commission. American officials of WHO resigned in protest of U.S. opposition to the code. Dr. Stephen Joseph, a senior executive of the Agency for International Development (AID), charged that the Reagan administration had been swayed by the self-serving arguments of the infant-formula lobby. Condemnation of the U.S. vote roared through the international community like a prairie fire. The United States, said its harshest critics, preferred profits to babies.

Speaking in his capacity as president of the International Council of Infant Food Industries, E. W. Saunders, a Nestlé vice president, branded the code unacceptably ambiguous. Nevertheless, Nestlé officials announced that Nestlé would support the code. INFACT and others identified four areas for Nestlé to review: educational materials dealing with infant formula, hazard warnings and labels, gifts to health professionals, and free supplies to hospitals. Until Nestlé complied, INFACT threatened to pursue its campaign against the company. Nestlé said it already was complying, that the charges of noncompliance were based on subjective interpretations of the code. To safeguard its reputation, as well as its infant-formula market, Nestlé dipped into its war chest to fight the boycott—to the tune, some say, of $40 million.

While on one front Nestlé was waging a battle to preserve its reputation, on another it was moving toward a more constructive resolution to the problem. Since WHO had no enforcement authority, there was no neutral party to monitor compliance with its "Code of Marketing of Breastmilk Substitutes." So Nestlé formed the Nestlé Infant Formula Audit Commission (NIFAC). NIFAC, which was chaired by former Senator Edmund S. Muskie, was asked to review Nestlé's instructions to field personnel to see if they could be improved. This novel approach to the seemingly intractable situation was like hiring a private judge to arbitrate a personal dispute. At the same time, Nestlé continued to meet with officials at WHO and the United Nations International Children's Emergency Fund (UNICEF) to obtain the most accurate interpretation of the code.

NIFAC labored for eighteen months, issuing quarterly reports to the public and requesting from WHO/UNICEF several clarifications of the code. Its efforts eventually bore fruit. On January 26, 1984, the international boycott against Nestlé was suspended when Nestlé developed procedures for dealing with the four specific points of the code in dispute.

Regarding educational material, Nestlé agreed to include in all materials dealing with the feeding of infants information on (1) the benefits and superiority of breast-feeding, (2) maternal nutrition and preparation for main-tenance of breast-feeding, (3) the negative effect on breast-feeding of introducing partial bottle feeding, (4) the difficulty of reversing the decision not to breast-feed, (5) possible health hazards of inappropriate food or feeding methods, and (6) the social and financial consequences of the decision to use infant formula.

Regarding hazard warning labels, Nestlé agreed to test different statements in Third World countries, with the help of specialized consultants recommended by WHO and UNICEF. It specifically promised to ensure that product users fully understood the consequences of inappropriate or incorrect use arising from unclean water, dirty utensils, improper dilution, and storage of prepared foods without refrigeration.

Regarding gifts to health professionals, Nestlé agreed not to give gifts such as chocolate, key rings, and pens to health professionals. It also agreed to avoid product advertising in technical and scientific publications.

Regarding low-cost supplies of infant formula to health institutions, Nestlé recognized that this might inadvertently discourage breast-feeding. So it agreed to restrict the distribution of supplies to situations in which infants had to be fed on breast-milk substitutes and to help specify the conditions that would warrant such substitutes.

In announcing that a truce had been reached, Nestlé officials and protestors literally broke candy together—Nestlé chocolate, naturally—to celebrate the end of the six-and-a-half-year conflict. Douglas A. Johnson praised Nestlé for moving forward to become a model for the entire industry. The WHO code, said Johnson, has changed from "an urgent moral mandate to the accepted business practice of the largest and singly most important factor in the world." Nestlé officials viewed the settlement as "proof that its efforts" to comply with the WHO code "have finally been recognized." They boasted that Nestlé was the first company to "unilaterally apply the code in developing countries" and to "submit its activities in this area to examination by an independent commission. . . . The time has now come for all interested parties to concentrate their effort on solutions to the fundamental cause of infant mortality and malnutrition in the Third World."[54]

After a verification period of eight months, boycott leaders were satisfied that Nestlé had begun to put into place the agreed-upon changes, and the "suspended" boycott was officially ended. Unfortunately, the story of Nestlé and infant formula does not come to a happy end there. Four years later, in October 1988, Douglas A. Johnson and his Minneapolis-based organization Action for Corporate Accountability charged Nestlé with noncompliance. They urged a resumption of the boycott against Nestlé as well as an expansion of the boycott to include American Home Products (AHP), the second-largest distributor of infant formula in developing nations. Nestlé's Taster's Choice Instant Coffee and Carnation Coffeemate became targets of the boycott, along with AHP's Anacin and Advil pain relievers. Action for Corporate Responsibility accused both companies of violating at least the spirit — and, according to Johnson, also the letter — of the WHO code.

Specifically, Nestlé and AHP are accused of continuing to dump free supplies of formula on hospitals to induce mothers to bottle feed their infants. The code permits donations of formula for infants needing breast-milk substitutes, but it prohibits distributing free formula solely for sales promotion. The effectiveness of free samples is well known in the advertising world. Mothers who receive free samples are far more likely to bottle feed than those who do not. By the time the mother and baby have been discharged from the hospital, the mother's milk will have begun to dry up. She and the baby will have become hooked on the formula, Action for Corporate Responsibility argues, just when the companies' donations stop and profit making begins.

Thad Jackson, a Washington spokesperson for Nestlé, insists that the company is in

"total compliance" with national and international codes. He also says that the company never gives the product directly to mothers. "We do not dump supplies in hospitals," he states. Carol Emerling, an official of AHP, also challenges the boycott. "This whole activity is based on allegations that we violate the WHO code — and we flat out deny that."[55]

Monitoring by the United Methodist Church, however, concludes that the industry continues to violate restrictions on supplies to hospitals. One study of forty-five hospitals in four Asian countries found that Nestlé was supplying formula to 80 percent of them — in enough quantity to feed over 110 percent of their infants. AHP supplied formula to 64 percent of the hospitals. And the companies' own data suggest that the practice is designed to produce sales. In Brazil, for instance, where Nestlé has a monopoly on infant formula, it distributes no free supplies to hospitals. When the government of the Ivory Coast conducted a campaign to promote breast-feeding, Nestlé stepped up its donations of formula to that nation's hospitals.

Nor is this strictly a Third World problem. To secure a contract allowing it to be the only company to provide free formula samples to all mothers giving birth in New York City hospitals, AHP paid $1 million to the New York City Health and Hospital Corporation. New York's plan is to spend the entire sum on promoting breast-feeding. Will this counteract the influence of those free samples to mothers? AHP was willing to gamble $1 million that it won't.[56]

Discussion Questions

1. In light of this case, do you think it makes sense to talk of a corporation like Nestlé as a moral agent, or is it only the people in it who can be properly described as having moral responsibility?

2. Identify the views of corporate social responsibility held by the different actors

and organizations in this case. In what ways does this case raise questions about the social and moral responsibility of corporations?

3. Appraise Nestlé's actions from the perspective of both the narrow and the broader view of corporate social responsibility.

4. How would you assess Nestlé's conduct throughout the whole controversy? Has Nestlé acted in good faith? Do you think it is sincerely concerned about the drawbacks and dangers of using infant formula?

5. Throughout the dispute, Nestlé has insisted that the WHO code is ambiguous and that the company's critics are holding Nestlé accountable to their own subjective interpretation of the code. Does this point have merit? How might the problem be dealt with?

6. What moral issues are raised by the controversy over infant formula? What moral rights, if any, are at stake in this controversy? Do you find anything objectionable in the marketing techniques used to sell infant formula?

7. Can boycotts be effective in pressuring corporations to exercise social responsibility? Do you as an individual have a moral obligation to participate in the boycott against Nestlé and AHP or in any similar boycotts?

8. Do you think the United States was justified in voting against the WHO code? Was the United States preferring profits to babies, as critics charged? If you had been a U.S. official at WHO, would you have resigned in protest of the U.S. vote?

CASE 5.4
Layoffs at Levi

Juvenile Manufacturing of San Antonio, Texas, began making infants' and children's garments in a plant on South Zarzamora Street in 1923; in the 1930s, the company switched to boys' and men's clothing and changed its name to Santone Industries. During the 1970s Santone manufactured sports jackets for Levi Strauss & Co., which eventually decided to buy out the company. In 1981 Levi paid $10 million and took over operations on South Zarzamora Street.

While the garmet industry had been struggling in some parts of the country, it had prospered in San Antonio—not least on South Zarzamora Street. One of three Levi's plants in the city, in the late 1980s the plant was slowly converted from making sports jackets to manufacturing Levi's popular Dockers trousers, which have now surpassed Levi's 501 jeans as the company's top selling

line. And despite the sweatshop image that the industry brings to people's minds, many of San Antonio's semiskilled workers were happy to be employed at Levi Strauss. They thought that pay at the plant—which averaged about $11,480 per year—was good, and the company gave them a turkey every Thanksgiving and a small gift every Christmas. Benefits were respectable, too: paid maternity leave for qualified employees, health insurance, and ten days of paid vacation at Christmas and ten during the summer.

Then in 1990, Levi Strauss decided to close the plant—the largest layoff in San Antonio's history—and move its operations to Costa Rica and the Dominican Republic. This was the course of action that had been recommended the previous year by Bruce Stallworth, Levi's operations controller. Closing the plant would cost $13.5 million, Stallworth calculated, but transferring its production abroad would "achieve significant cost savings," enabling the company to recover its closing costs within two years. In 1989, it cost $6.70 to make a pair of Dockers at the South Zarzamora plant. Plant management had hoped to reduce that to $6.39 per unit in 1990, but even that would be significantly higher than the per unit cost of $5.88 at the Dockers plant in Powell, Tennessee — not to mention the $3.76 per unit cost Levi could get by using Third World contractors.

Stallworth attributed the San Antonio plant's high costs to workers' compensation expenses, to a less-than-full-capacity plant operation, and to the fact that "conversion from sports coats to Dockers has not been totally successful." Retraining workers who have spent years sewing jackets to sew trousers, it seems, is not that easy. Furthermore, running the San Antonio plant efficiently would mean running it at full capacity. But operating at full capacity on South Zarzamora Street with 1,115 workers — compared to 366 and 746 employees, respectively, at Levi's other two U.S. Dockers plants — meant too many pairs of trousers produced by high-priced American labor. Workers at San Antonio averaged $6 an hour, which is about a day's pay for workers in the Caribbean and Central America with the same level of skill.

Bob Dunn, Levi vice president of community affairs and corporate communications, denies that the company did anything it shouldn't have done with regard to closing the plant. "We didn't see any way to bring costs in line." And he adds: "As much as people like Dockers, our research shows people are not willing to pay $5 or $10 more for a pair of pants just because the label says 'Made in the U.S.A.'"

Closing plants is nothing new for Levi Strauss, however. Since 1981 it has closed 58 plants and put 10,400 Americans out of work. The company now has eleven foreign production plants, but most of its overseas produc-

tion is done by contractors, which saves Levi even more money, because in addition to lower wages the company avoids paying directly for benefits like health insurance and workers' compensation. This time, though, Levi's decision to close a domestic plant and move its production abroad prompted local labor activists to fight back. They have filed a $1.6 billion class-action lawsuit and organized a boycott of Levi products.

Despite a 72-hour hunger strike by protesters at Levi headquarters in San Francisco in November 1990, the boycott has gained little publicity outside of San Antonio and doesn't seem to have dampened sales. But it has embarrassed the company, which has long prided itself on being a benevolent employer and a good corporate citizen. In what some see as a damage control operation, Levi has donated nearly $100,000 to help local agencies retrain its former employees and has given San Antonio an additional $340,000 to provide them with extra job counseling and training services. The city, on the other hand, will spend an estimated $10 million on unemployment benefits and retraining and finding jobs for former Levi workers. Despite the city's efforts, though, the results have not been encouraging. Ten months after the plant closing was announced, the tax-funded retraining system had found jobs for just fourteen workers.

Meanwhile, the lawsuit filed on behalf of the laid-off Levi workers threatens to drag on for years, and most politicians have kept a low profile on the issue, praising Levi for offering its workers more than it was legally required to and promising to try to recruit a new company to use the empty factory. U.S. Representative Henry B. Gonzales, however, has spoken out harshly: "When a company is so irresponsible — a company that has been making money and then willy-nilly removes a plant to get further profit based on greed and on cheaper labor costs in the Caribbean — I say you have a bad citizen for a company."

To this, Bob Dunn responds, "our sense is we do more than anyone in our industry and more than almost anyone in American industry." He is proud of the way Levi treats people when it closes plants. "We try to stress the right values," he says. "It's not easy. There isn't always one right answer."[57]

Discussion Questions

1. In a case like this, does it make sense to talk about the company as a morally responsible agent whose actions can be critically assessed, or can we assess only the actions and decisions of individual human beings inside the company?

2. Evaluate the pros and cons of Levi's decision to close its South Zarzamora Street plant. Was it a sound business decision? Was it a socially responsible decision? Could Levi Strauss have reasonably been expected to keep the plant running?

3. Having decided to close the plant, was there more that Levi could and should have done for its laid-off workers?

4. How, if at all, is your assessment of Levi's responsibilities affected by the fact that Levi bought the plant and then closed it nine years later?

5. Are critics of the decision justified in organizing a consumer boycott? When are such boycotts likely to be effective? Under what circumstances would you participate in a consumer boycott?

6. How would you feel if you had been an employee at the plant? Bob Dunn says, "My hope is that as time passes and people have a chance to reflect on what we've done, [people who have lost jobs] will judge us to have been responsible and fair." Do you think Levi's former employees will judge it that way?

7. Clothing imports were virtually unknown until the 1950s, when Japanese manufacturers began exporting into this country. Now, nearly 60 percent of the clothes sold in the United States were sewn somewhere else, and that percentage is growing. Is this cause for concern? What, if anything, can and should be done about it? Are you willing to pay more for products with a "Made in the U.S.A." label?

NOTES

1. Anthony J. Parisi, "How Exxon Rules Its Great Empire," *San Francisco Chronicle*, August 5, 1980, 27.

2. Ibid.

3. Thomas Donaldson, *Corporations and Morality* (Englewood Cliffs, N.J.: Prentice-Hall, 1982), 2.

4. Ibid., 4.

5. Ibid., 5.

6. Ibid., 3.

7. In 1986, for example, the Court upheld the Puerto Rican government ban on casino-gambling advertising, even though casino gambling is legal there.

8. Parisi, "How Exxon Rules," 38.

9. See John R. Danley, "Corporate Moral Agency: The Case for Anthropological Bigotry," in W. Michael Moore and Jennifer M. Moore, eds., *Business Ethics: Readings and Cases in Corporate Morality* (New York: McGraw-Hill, 1984); and John Ladd, "Morality and the Ideal of Rationality in Formal Organizations," in Thomas Donaldson and Patricia Werhane, eds., *Ethical Issues in Business: A Philosophical Approach*, 2nd ed. (Englewood Cliffs, N.J.: Prentice-Hall, 1983).

10. See Kenneth Goodpaster and John B. Matthews, Jr., "Can a Corporation Have a Conscience?" *Harvard Business Review* 60 (January–February 1982): 132–141.

11. Donaldson, *Corporations and Morality*, 10.

12. See Peter French, "The Corporations as a Moral Person," *American Philosophical Quarterly* 16 (July 1979): 207–215. J. Angelo Corlett, "Corporate Responsibility and Punishment," *Public Affairs Quarterly* 2 (January 1988) criticizes French's theory.

13. Manuel G. Velasquez, "Why Corporations Are Not Morally Responsible for Anything They Do," *Business and Professional Ethics Journal* 2 (Spring 1983): 8.

14. Paul Richter, "Pentagon Lifts Threat to Ban National Semi," *Los Angeles Times*, August 8, 1984, IV–1.

15. "The Conoco Conscience," Continental Oil Company, 1976, quoted in Goodpaster and Matthews, "Can a Corporation Have a Conscience?" 141.

16. Quoted in Clarence C. Walton, *Corporate Social Responsibilities* (Belmont, Calif.: Wadsworth, 1967), 169–170.

17. Quoted in Bernard D. Nossiter, *The Mythmakers: An Essay on Power and Wealth* (Boston: Houghton Mifflin, 1964), 100.

18. Milton Friedman, *Capitalism and Freedom* (Chicago: University of Chicago Press, 1962), 133.

19. Theodore Levitt, "The Dangers of Social Responsibility," *Harvard Business Review* 36 (September–October 1958).

20. Milton Friedman, "The Social Responsibility of Business Is to Increase Its Profits," *New York Times Magazine*, September 13, 1970, 33, 126. Copyright © 1970 by The New York Times Company. Reprinted by permission.

21. Ibid., 124.

22. Reprinted from Keith Davis, "Five Propositions for Social Responsibility," *Business Horizons* 18 (June 1975): 20. Copyright © 1975 by the Foundation for the School of Business at Indiana University. Used with permission.

23. Melvin Anshen, "Changing the Social Contract: A Role for Business," *Columbia Journal of World Business* 5 (November–December 1970).

24. Davis, "Five Propositions for Social Responsibility," 22.

25. See Christopher D. Stone, *Where the Law Ends* (New York: Harper & Row, 1975), 80–87.

26. Friedman, "The Social Responsibility of Business," 122.

27. See Michael Hoffman and Jennifer Mills Moore, *Business Ethics* (New York: McGraw-Hill, 1984), 113.

28. See Goodpaster and Matthews, "Can a Corporation Have a Conscience?" 136.

29. Virginia Held, *Property, Profits, and Economic Justice* (Belmont, Calif.: Wadsworth, 1980), 11.

30. Goodpaster and Matthews, "Can a Corporation Have a Conscience?" 137.

31. Ibid.

32. Walter Goodman, "Stocks Without Sin," *Harper's*, August 1971, 66.

33. Levitt, "The Dangers of Social Responsibility," 44.

34. Davis, "Five Propositions for Social Responsibility," 20.

35. Paul F. Camenisch, "Business Ethics: On Getting to the Heart of the Matter," *Business and Professional Ethics Journal* 1 (Fall 1981). Reprinted here on page 253.

36. Ibid., 256 in this book.

37. See Robert C. Solomon and Kristine R. Hanson, *Above the Bottom Line: An Introduction to Business Ethics* (New York: Harcourt Brace Jovanovich, 1983), 238.

38. See Stone, *Where the Law Ends*, Chapter 11.

39. Kenneth J. Arrow, "Social Responsibility and Economic Efficiency," *Public Policy* 21 (Summer 1973). Reprinted here on page 238.

40. Milton Snoeyenbos and Donald Jewell, "Morals, Management, and Codes," in Milton Snoeyenbos, Robert Almeder, and James Humber, eds., *Business Ethics* (Buffalo, N.Y.: Prometheus Books, 1983), 107.

41. Jay W. Lorsch, "Managing Culture: The Invisible Barrier to Strategic Change," *California Management Review* 28, no. 2 (Winter 1986). Quoted by Donald P. Robin and R. Eric Reidenbach, *Business Ethics: Where Profits Meet Value Systems* (Englewood Cliffs, N.J.: Prentice-Hall, 1989), 59.

42. Alyse Lynn Booth, "Who Are We?" *Public Relations Journal* (July 1985). Quoted by Robin and Reidenbach, *Business Ethics*, 59.

43. W. Brooke Tunstall, "Cultural Transition at AT&T," *Sloan Management Review* (Fall 1983). Quoted by Robin and Reidenbach, *Business Ethics*, 59.

44. Robin and Reidenbach, *Business Ethics*, Chapter 4.

45. Ibid., 72.

46. "Businesses Are Signing Up for Ethics 101," *Business Week*, February 15, 1988, 56.

47. Ibid.

48. This case study is based on Timothy Egan, "Elements of Alaska Oil Spill Disaster," *New York Times*, May 22, 1989, A10.

49. "Exxon Agrees to Pay $1 Billion for Oil Spill," *San Jose Mercury*, March 14, 1991, 2A.

50. Ibid.; "Harper's Index," *Harper's*, April 1991, 15; John Lancaster, "Exxon Spill's 'Social Cost' Put at $3 Billion," *San Francisco Chronicle*, March 20, 1991, A8; and *New York Times*, March 21, 1991, A15.

51. See Samuel S. Epstein, "The Asbestos 'Pentagon Papers,'" in Mark Green and Robert Massie, Jr., eds., *The Big Business Reader: Essays on Corporate America* (New York: Pilgrim Press, 1980), 154–165. This article is the primary source of the facts and quotations reported here.

52. See Robert Mokhiber, *Corporate Crime and Violence* (San Francisco: Sierra Club Books, 1988), 285–286; and Arthur Sharplin, "Manville Lives On as Victims Continue to Die," *Business and Society Review* 65 (Spring 1988): 27–28.

53. "Asbestos Claims to Be Reduced Under New Plan," *Wall Street Journal*, November 20, 1990, A4, and "MacNeil-Lehrer Newshour," December 18, 1990.

54. "Boycott Against Nestlé Over Infant Formula to End Next Month," *Wall Street Journal*, January 27, 1984, 1.

55. "New Boycott Plea in Infant Formula Fight," *San Francisco Chronicle*, October 5, 1988, A9.

56. For more on the Nestlé boycott and the infant-formula controversy, see Mokhiber, *Corporate Crime*

and Violence, 307–317; and Carol-Linnea Salmon, "Milking Deadly Dollars from the Third World," *Business and Society Review* 68 (Winter 1989).

57. This case study is based on Jeannie Kever, "What Price Layoffs?" *San Francisco Examiner*, November 18, 1990, D-1.

Social Responsibility and Economic Efficiency

Kenneth J. Arrow

As an economist, Arrow examines and rejects the argument that firms ought only to pursue profit maximization, an argument that ignores the fact of imperfect competition, the unequal distribution of income resulting from unrestrained profit maximization, and the decline in altruism that profit-maximizing, self-centered economic behavior encourages. In addition, profit maximization is socially inefficient in two important cases: where costs are not paid for (externalities) and where there is an imbalance of knowledge between the seller and the buyer. Arrow concludes by discussing ways of institutionalizing the social responsibility of firms through the establishment of stable ethical codes.

Let us first consider the case against social responsibility: the assumption that the firms should aim simply to maximize their profits. One strand of that argument is empirical rather than ethical or normative. It simply states that firms *will* maximize their profits. The impulse to gain, it is argued, is very strong and the incentives for selfish behavior are so great that any kind of control is likely to be utterly ineffectual. This argument has some force but is by no means conclusive. Any mechanism for enforcing or urging social responsibility upon firms must of course reckon with a profit motive, with a desire to evade whatever response of controls are imposed. But it does not mean that we cannot expect any degree of responsibility at all.

One finds a rather different argument, frequently stated by some economists. It will probably strike the noneconomist as rather strange, at least at first hearing. The assertion is that firms *ought* to maximize profits; not merely do they like to do so but there is practically a social obligation to do so. Let me briefly sketch the argument:

Firms buy the goods and services they need for production. What they buy they pay for and there-

fore they are paying for whatever costs they impose upon others. What they receive in payment by selling their goods, they receive because the purchaser considers it worthwhile. This is a world of voluntary contracts; nobody *has* to buy the goods. If he chooses to buy it, it must be that he is getting a benefit measured by the price he pays. Hence, it is argued, profit really represents the net contribution that the firm makes to the social good, and the profits should therefore be made as large as possible. When firms compete with each other, in selling their goods or in buying labor or other services, they may have to lower their selling prices in order to get more of the market for themselves or raise their wages; in either case the benefits which the firm is deriving are in some respects shared with the population at large. The forces of competition prevent the firms from engrossing too large a share of the social benefit. For example, if a firm tries to reduce the quality of its goods, it will sooner or later have to lower the price which it charges because the purchaser will no longer find it worthwhile to pay the high price. Hence, the consumers will gain from price reduction at the same time as they are losing through quality deterioration. On detailed analysis it appears the firm will find it privately profitable to reduce quality under these circumstances only if, in fact, quality reduction is a net social benefit, that is, if the saving in cost is worth more to the consumer than the quality reduction. Now, as far as it goes this argument is sound. The problem is that it may not go far enough.

Under the proper assumptions profit maximization is indeed efficient in the sense that it can

Kenneth J. Arrow, "Social Responsibility and Economic Efficiency," *Public Policy* 21 (Summer 1973). Reprinted by permission.

achieve as high a level of satisfaction as possible for any one consumer without reducing the levels of satisfaction of other consumers or using more resources than society is endowed with. But the limits of the argument must be stressed. I want to mention two well-known points in passing without making them the principal focus of discussion. First of all, the argument assumes that the forces of competition are sufficiently vigorous. But there is no social justification for profit maximization by monopolies. This is an important and well-known qualification. Second, the distribution of income that results from unrestrained profit maximization is very unequal. The competitive maximizing economy is indeed efficient — this shows up in high average incomes — but the high average is accompanied by widespread poverty on the one hand and vast riches, at least for a few, on the other. To many of us this is a very undesirable consequence.

Profit maximization has yet another effect on society. It tends to point away from the expression of altruistic motives. Altruistic motives are motives whose gratification is just as legitimate as selfish motives, and the expression of those motives is something we probably wish to encourage. A profit-maximizing, self-centered form of economic behavior does not provide any room for the expression of such motives.

[Even] if the three problems above were set aside . . . there are [still] two categories of effects where the arguments for profit maximization break down: The first is illustrated by pollution or congestion. Here it is no longer true (and this is the key to these issues) that the firm in fact does pay for the harm it imposes on others. When it takes a person's time and uses it at work, the firm is paying for this, and therefore the transaction can be regarded as a beneficial exchange from the point of view of both parties. We have no similar mechanism by which the pollution which a firm imposes upon its neighborhood is paid for. Therefore the firm will have a tendency to pollute more than is desirable. That is, the benefit to it or to its customers from the expanded activity is really not as great, or may not be as great, as the cost it is imposing upon the neighborhood. But since it does not pay that cost, there is no profit incentive to refrain.

The same argument applies to traffic congestion when no change is made for the addition of cars or trucks on the highway. It makes everybody less comfortable. It delays others and increases the probability of accidents; in short, it imposes a cost upon a large number of members of the society, a cost which is not paid for by the imposer of the cost, at least not in full. The person congesting is also congested, but the costs he is imposing on others are much greater than those he suffers himself. Therefore there will be a tendency to overutilize those goods for which no price is charged, particularly scarce highway space.

There are many other examples of this kind, but these two will serve to illustrate the point in question: some effort must be made to alter the profit-maximizing behavior of firms in those cases where it is imposing costs on others which are not easily compensated through an appropriate set of prices.

The second category of effects where profit maximization is not socially desirable is that in which there are quality effects about which the firm knows more than the buyer. In my examples I will cite primarily the case of quality in the product sold, but actually very much the same considerations apply to the quality of working conditions. The firm is frequently in a better position to know the consequences (the health hazards, for example) involved in working conditions than the worker is, and the considerations I am about to discuss in the case of sale of goods have a direct parallel in the analysis of working conditions in the relation of a firm to its workers. Let me illustrate by considering the sale of a used car. (Similar considerations apply to the sale of new cars.) A used car has potential defects and typically the seller knows more about the defects than the buyer. The buyer is not in a position to distinguish among used cars, and therefore he will be willing to pay the same amount for two used cars of differing quality because he cannot tell the difference between them. As a result, there is an inefficiency in the sale of used cars. If somehow or other the cars were distinguished as to their quality, there would be some buyers who would prefer a cheaper car with more defects because they intend to use it very little or they only want it for a short period, while others will want a better car at a higher price. In fact, however, the two kinds of car are sold indiscriminately to the two groups of buyers at the same price, so that we can argue that there is a distinct loss of consumer satisfaction imposed by the failure to convey information that is available to the seller. The buyers are not necessarily being cheated. They may be, but the problem of inefficiency would remain if they weren't. One can imagine a situation where, from past experience, buyers of used cars are aware that cars that look alike may turn out to be quite different. Without knowing whether a particular car is good or bad, they do know that there are good and bad cars, and of course their willingness to pay for the cars is influenced accordingly. The main loser from a monetary viewpoint may not be the customer, but rather the seller of the good car. The buyer will pay a price which is only appropriate to a lottery that gives him a good car or a bad car with varying probabilities, and therefore the seller of the good car gets less than the value of the car. The seller of the bad car is, of course, the beneficiary. Clearly then, if one could arrange to transmit the truth from the sellers to the buyers, the efficiency of the market would be greatly improved. The used-car illustration is an example of a very general phenomenon. . . .

Defenders of unrestricted profit maximization usually assume that the consumer is well informed or at least that he becomes so by his own experience, in repeated purchases, or by information about what has happened to other people like him. This argument is empirically shaky; even the ability of individuals to analyze the effects of their own past purchases may be limited, particularly with respect to complicated mechanisms. But there are two further defects. The risks, including death, may be so great that even one misleading experience is bad enough, and the opportunity to learn from repeated trials is not of much use. Also, in a world where the products are continually changing, the possibility of learning from experience is greatly reduced. Automobile companies are continually introducing new models which at least purport to differ from what they were in the past, though doubtless the change is more external than internal. New drugs are being introduced all the time; the fact that one has had bad experiences with one drug may provide very little information about the next one.

Thus there are two types of situation in which the simple rule of maximizing profits is socially inefficient: the case in which costs are not paid for, as in pollution, and the case in which the seller has considerably more knowledge about his product than the buyer, particularly with regard to safety. In these situations it is clearly desirable to have

some idea of social responsibility, that is, to experience an obligation, whether ethical, moral, or legal. Now we cannot expect such an obligation to be created out of thin air. To be meaningful, any obligation of this kind, any feeling or rule of behavior has to be embodied in some definite social institution. I use that term broadly: a legal code is a social institution in a sense. Exhortation to do good must be made specific in some external form, a steady reminder and perhaps enforcer of desirable values. Part of the need is simply for factual information as a guide to individual behavior. A firm may need to be told what is right and what is wrong when in fact it is polluting, or which safety requirements are reasonable and which are too extreme or too costly to be worth consideration. Institutionalization of the social responsibility of firms also serves another very important function. It provides some assurance to any one firm that the firms with which it is in competition will also accept the same responsibility. If a firm has some code imposed from the outside, there is some expectation that other firms will obey it too and therefore there is some assurance that it need not fear any excessive cost to its good behavior.

Let me turn to some alternative kinds of institutions that can be considered as embodying the possible social responsibilities of firms. First, we have legal regulation, as in the case of pollution where laws are passed about the kind of burning that may take place, and about setting maximum standards for emissions. A second category is that of taxes. Economists, with good reason, like to preach taxation as opposed to regulation. The movement to tax polluting emissions is getting under way and there is a fairly widely backed proposal in Congress to tax sulfur dioxide emissions from industrial smokestacks. That is an example of the second kind of institutionalization of social responsibility. The responsibility is made very clear: the violator pays for violations.

A third very old remedy or institution is that of legal liability — the liability of the civil law. One can be sued for damages. Such cases apparently go back to the Middle Ages. Regulation also extends back very far. There was an ordinance in London about the year 1300 prohibiting the burning of coal, because of the smoke nuisance.

The fourth class of institutions is represented by ethical codes. Restraint is achieved not by appealing to each individual's conscience but rather by having some generally understood definition of appropriate behavior. . . .

Let me turn to the fourth possibility, ethical codes. This may seem to be a strange possibility for an economist to raise. But when there is a wide difference in knowledge between the two sides of the market, recognized ethical codes can be, as has already been suggested, a great contribution to economic efficiency. Actually we do have examples of this in our everyday lives, but in very limited areas. The case of medical ethics is the most striking. By its very nature there is a very large difference in knowledge between the buyer and the seller. One is, in fact, buying precisely the service of someone with much more knowledge than you have. To make this relationship a viable one, ethical codes have grown up over the centuries, both to avoid the possibility of exploitation by the physician and to assure the buyer of medical services that he is not being exploited. I am not suggesting that these are universally obeyed, but there is a strong presumption that the doctor is going to perform to a large extent with your welfare in mind. Unnecessary medical expenses or other abuses are perceived as violations of ethics. There is a powerful ethical background against which we make this judgment. Behavior that we would regard as highly reprehensible in a physician is judged less harshly when found among businessmen. The medical profession is typical of professions in general. All professions involve a situation in which knowledge is unequal on two sides of the market by the very definition of the profession, and therefore there have grown up ethical principles that afford some protection to the client. Notice there is a mutual benefit in this. The fact is that if you had sufficient distrust of a doctor's services, you wouldn't buy them. Therefore the physician wants an ethical code to act as assurance to the buyer, and he certainly wants his competitors to obey this same code, partly because any violation may put him at a disadvantage but more especially because the violation will reflect on him, since the buyer of the medical services may not be able to distinguish one doctor from another. A close look reveals that a great deal of economic life depends for its viability on a certain limited degree of ethical commitment. Purely selfish behavior of individuals is really incompatible with any kind of settled economic life.

There is almost invariably some element of trust and confidence. Much business is done on the basis of verbal assurance. It would be too elaborate to try to get written commitments on every possible point. Every contract depends for its observance on a mass of unspecified conditions which suggest that the performance will be carried out in good faith without insistence on sticking literally to its wording. To put the matter in its simplest form, in almost every economic transaction, in any exchange of goods for money, somebody gives up his valuable asset before he gets the other's; either the goods are given before the money or the money is given before the goods. Moreover there is a general confidence that there won't be any violation of the implicit agreement. Another example in daily life of this kind of ethics is the observance of queue discipline. People line up; there are people who try to break in ahead of you, but there is an ethic which holds that this is bad. It is clearly an ethic which is in everybody's interest to preserve; one waits at the end of the line this time, and one is protected against somebody's coming in ahead of him.

In the context of product safety, efficiency would be greatly enhanced by accepted ethical rules. Sometimes it may be enough to have an ethical compulsion to reveal all the information available and let the buyer choose. This is not necessarily always the best. It can be argued that under some circumstances setting minimum safety standards and simply not putting out products that do not meet them would be desirable and should be felt by the businessman to be an obligation.

Now I've said that ethical codes are desirable. It doesn't follow from that that they will come about. An ethical code is useful only if it is widely accepted. Its implications for specific behavior must be moderately clear, and above all it must be clearly perceived that the acceptance of these ethical obligations by everybody does involve mutual gain. Ethical codes that lack the latter property are unlikely to be viable. How do such codes develop? They may develop as a consensus out of lengthy public discussion of obligations, discussion which will take place in legislatures, lecture halls, business journals, and other public forums. The codes are communicated by the very process of coming to an agreement. A more formal alternative would be to have some highly prestigious group discuss ethical codes for safety standards. In either case to become and to remain a part of the economic environment, the codes have to be accepted by the significant operating institutions and transmitted from one generation of executives to the next through standard operating procedures, through education in business schools, and through indoctrination of one kind or another. If we seriously expect such codes to develop and to be maintained, we might ask how the agreements develop and above all, how the codes remain stable. After all, an ethical code, however much it may be in the interest of all, is, as we remarked earlier, not in the interest of any one firm. The code may be of value to the running of the system as a whole, it may be of value to all firms if all firms maintain it, and yet it will be to the advantage of any one firm to cheat — in fact the more so, the more other firms are sticking to it. But there are some reasons for thinking that ethical codes can develop and be stable. These codes will not develop completely without institutional support. That is to say, there will be need for focal organizations, such as government agencies, trade associations, and consumer defense groups, or all combined to make the codes explicit, to iterate their doctrine and to make their presence felt. Given that help, I think the emergence of ethical codes on matters such as safety at least, is possible. One positive factor here is something that is a negative factor in other contexts, namely that our economic organization is to such a large extent composed of large firms. The corporation is no longer a single individual; it is a social organization with internal social ties and internal pressures for acceptability and esteem. The individual members of the corporation are not only parts of the corporation but also members of a larger society whose esteem is desired. Power in a large corporation is necessarily diffused; not many individuals in such organizations feel so thoroughly identified with the corporation that other kinds of social pressures become irrelevant. Furthermore, in a large, complex firm where many people have to participate in any decision, there are likely to be some who are motivated to call attention to violations of the code. This kind of check has been conspicuous in government in recent years. The Pentagon Papers are an outstanding illustration of the fact that within the organization there are those who recognize moral guilt and take occasion to blow the whistle. I expect the same sort of behavior to occur in any large organization when there are well-defined ethical rules whose violation can be observed.

One can still ask if the codes are likely to be stable. Since it may well be possible and profitable for a minority to cheat, will it not be true that the whole system may break down? In fact, however, some of the pressures work in the other direction. It is clearly in the interest of those who are obeying the codes to enforce them, to call attention to violations, to use the ethical and social pressures of the society at large against their less scrupulous rivals. At the same time the value of maintaining the system may well be apparent to all, and no doubt ways will be found to use the assurance of quality generated by the system as a positive asset in attracting consumers and workers.

One must not expect miraculous transformations in human behavior. Ethical codes, if they are to be viable, should be limited to their scope. They are not a universal substitute for the weapons mentioned earlier, the institutions, taxes, regulations, and legal remedies. Further, we should expect the codes to apply only in situations where the firm has superior knowledge of the situation. I would not want the firm to act in accordance with some ethical principles in regard to matters of which it has little knowledge. For example, with quality standards which consumers can observe, it may not be desirable that the firm decide for itself, at least on ethical grounds, because it is depriving the consumer of the freedom of choice between high-quality, high-cost and low-quality, low-cost products. It is in areas where someone is typically misinformed or imperfectly informed that ethical codes can contribute to economic efficiency.

Review and Discussion Questions

1. Explain the economic argument that firms ought to maximize profits. What shortcomings does Arrow see in this argument?

2. Explain how Arrow's used-car example illustrates his claim that unrestricted profit maximization can be socially inefficient. How does this differ from the case of pollution or highway congestion?

3. What are the four ways in which social responsibility can be institutionalized?

4. What characteristics must an ethical code have to be useful? How do such codes develop? Can they be enforced? Why does Arrow think that the existence of large firms is a positive factor in this context?

5. Do you think business today sees itself as governed by an ethical code? If so, is this code something that is explicitly discussed and thought about, or is it only implicit in business behavior? In your opinion, do business courses and business schools do enough to develop and transmit a sense of social responsibility among future businesspersons?

Ethical Issues in Plant Relocation

John P. Kavanagh

When a company or plant operates in a community, a web of relationships and interdependencies develop among it, its employees, and the community in general. Its shutdown or relocation can seriously hurt the community in which it has operated and the people who have worked for it and have built their lives around it. Kavanagh argues that companies are responsible for the unintended (although foreseeable) results of their business activities. Accordingly, fairness requires that they avoid moving, if possible, and, if they must move, that they take steps to reduce the harm their relocation causes.

The location of a major new manufacturing plant in a community is often the occasion of great rejoicing. City fathers welcome the enterprise as a vital addition to the town's economy. Visions of augmented tax base to support municipal services, jobs for the unemployed and for entrants into the work force, opportunities for local entrepreneurs to expand markets for goods and services, additional sources of support for civic and charitable endeavors, new challenges for educators to provide education and training—all these contribute to the euphoria of a new plant in the community.

Contrast this picture with that of a community experiencing the shutdown or relocation of a major plant, particularly one which has operated in the community for many years. Many people are hurt. For some it means actual hardship; others find their future expectations diminished to the point of despair. The community as a whole feels a shock to its economic vitality and perhaps to its fiscal stability as well. . . .[1]

The thesis which I would like to establish is simple, but it has relatively far-reaching implications. In its basic form it may be stated:

In deciding whether or not to relocate a manufacturing operation, a company has moral obligations to its employees and to the community in which the operation is located which require that the company

1. take into account the impact of the proposed move on employees and the community;

2. avoid the move if reasonably possible;

3. notify the affected parties as soon as possible if the decision is to make the move; and

4. take positive measures to ameliorate the effects of the move.[2]

In making a decision whether or not to move, companies often do not take into account the impact on employees and the community. The management weighs economic reasons very carefully. It considers the effect on production, sales, public relations and, ultimately, profit. On the basis of reasonable assumptions, it projects the outcomes expected to result from each of the options under consideration. Too often, however, there is no place in the economic calculus for any recognition of the effect the move will have on the work force or the community. Our thesis asserts that the company is not morally free to ignore this impact, since employees and members of the community are not mere things but people, whom the company has an obligation not to harm.[3] This moral fact not only deserves consideration along with economic facts but should be the overriding consideration unless there are countervailing moral reasons.

Reprinted by permission of the author from Tom L.Beauchamp and Norman E. Bowie, eds., *Ethical Theory and Business* 2nd ed. (Englewood Cliffs, N.J.: Prentice-Hall, 1983).

If the company takes this obligation seriously, it ought to start with a strong presumption that the move should be avoided if at all reasonably possible. It should consider every reasonable alternative: rehabilitation of the existing facility, construction of a new plant within the same community, renegotiation of the labor contract, financial assistance from civic or governmental sources, negotiation of special tax incentives, even acceptance of less than maximum profit return. Only after ruling out other available options should the company decide in favor of the move.[4]

After giving serious consideration to other alternatives, the company may still decide it has no reasonable choice but to move. In that case, two obligations remain: the company should notify the affected parties as soon as possible, and it should do whatever is necessary to ameliorate the effects of the move.

Timely notification is important. If given before the final decision is taken, it might provide the opportunity for labor organizations, civic groups, or government agencies to offer options which would enable the company to continue operations. In any event, notification is essential to permit planning for an orderly transition and preparation of programs to accommodate the change.

Ameliorating the effects of the move is not likely to be easy. Companies often offer employees the opportunity to transfer to the new location; for some this might be acceptable, but for others it would be a real hardship. Alternatively, the company might provide effective out-placement efforts as well as income maintenance for displaced workers, at least during a transition period.

To offset adverse effects on the community, the company should make a serious attempt to find a new employer to replace the lost job opportunities. A large corporation might be able to find a replacement within its own organization. Another approach would be to seek another employer among customers, vendors, competitors, or other companies who could utilize the facilities and work force being abandoned. The departing company might donate its plant, if still usable, to the community or local development organization. In some cases the better offer might be to demolish existing facilities and make the improved site available, along with financial help to the local agency concerned with promoting the location of new industries.[5]

These steps may help to make the community whole again, but some situations may require additional effort. In close consultation and cooperation with municipal officials, the company may have to work out a plan to relieve the community of financial burdens of infrastructure improvements, for instance, which were made to serve the company's special needs.

Argument in Support of Thesis

It should be a little clearer now what the proposed thesis means. Before proceeding to argue directly in favor of this position, however, I would like first to establish the following "Externalities Lemma":

> By locating and operating a manufacturing plant (or similar job-creating operation) in a community, a company produces certain externalities, affecting both workers and the community, which are pertinent to the relocation issue.

The term "externalities" is common enough in the literature of economics. It refers to unintended side effects—good or bad—which an operation produces along with its intended product. In recent years environmentalists have emphasized externalities which affect the quality of the air or water in the vicinity of manufacturing plants. A firm really interested in producing paper, for example, also produces physical and chemical waste products which may affect the surrounding environment adversely if not properly controlled. The company has no interest in producing these products nor any direct intention of doing so, but in doing what it does intend—making paper—it also perforce produces these unwanted products.[6] . . .

The "Externalities Lemma" asserts that the operation of a plant results in certain externalities pertinent to the issue of plant relocation. Although the company's intention is simply to manufacture and distribute its product, the act of doing so produces unintended results which seriously affect its workers and the community in which the company operates.

When a person agrees to work for a company, her pay is a return for effort expended to produce the product. These wages, however, do not take into account the myriad relationships which the employee builds up as a result of accepting the job.

In addition to providing labor for the company, the worker adopts a life style which contributes to the work. Many people move their place of residence, enroll children in school, join local churches, become members of clubs, take interest in civil affairs — in short, make a total commitment of their lives to the community and the company. They build up a whole network of relationships based on their association with the company.

These life style commitments are advantageous to the worker, to be sure. They enable him to live a fully rounded life. But the advantage is not one-sided. The company benefits from having an employee involved in these relationships. The situation enhances the worker's ability to do his job, encourages loyalty to the company, and facilitates the employee's continuing progress in learning to do his job effectively.

The stable relationships developed benefit the community as well, but the company's presence also affects the community in other ways. City engineers adjust traffic patterns to accommodate traffic generated by workers going to or leaving the plant as well as incoming and outgoing freight movements. The municipality may have to plan, build, and maintain water and sewerage facilities on a much larger scale to serve the company's needs. Police and fire departments may require more personnel and equipment because of the plant's presence.

Assuming an equitable tax structure, the company will pay its fair share for services provided. Other taxpayers are usually willing to contribute as well because of the indirect benefits they receive. The whole system can work smoothly because of the symbiotic relationship between the plant, its workers, and the community. Merchants, purveyors of services, schools, and private support agencies of all kinds prosper so long as the relationship continues.

When a major plant discontinues operations, however, it becomes evident that an unintended situation has been created. Not only are employees out of work, deprived of their livelihood or dependent on others for it, but the community itself suffers. Businesses dependent on the company or its employees feel the impact. The municipality and its taxpayers are left with more employees and infrastructure than they need, with continuing cost burdens far out of proportion with revenue. Schools, churches, and private associations all find themselves overbuilt as people leave or are unable to contribute to their support.

Results of the kind described are especially obvious in a small community with a single major employer. In such circumstances it is easy to isolate the phenomenon. The same effects occur, however, in larger communities with more complex economies, only they tend to be less easily observed. In the larger setting the impact on the total community may be somewhat less, but it is no less real on those affected. What remains in any case is the whole web of relationships built up which would not exist if the company had not started the operation and particularly if it had not continued over a relatively long period. The company did not intend to create this web, but it is there nevertheless because of the plant — and the operation could not have survived without it.

In light of what we can observe, the "Externalities Lemma" seems to be inescapably true. If that is indeed the case, it is not difficult to establish our thesis. One of the accepted dicta in the law of property, clearly grounded in basic ethical principles of fairness and justice, is the maxim *sic utere tuo ut alienum non laedas* — use that which is yours in such a way that you do not injure another. A company which has established a plant in a community, particularly when it had continued the operation over a long period, would clearly be injuring others if it closed or moved that operation without taking into account — in a significant way — the impact of that move on its workers and the community. By its presence the plant has created the externalities described. It is the company's moral obligation to internalize them — to replace its divot, so to speak. It can move toward meeting this obligation by undertaking the kind of actions discussed above. . . .

Almost any moral system recognizes that every moral agent has an obligation to treat human beings as persons rather than as things. Hiring a person creates a special kind of relationship. For the employer it is not like buying a piece of material or a machine: these are things, which the buyer is free to use as a means of achieving an end, with no moral responsibility owed to the purchased objects. But the employer is not free, morally speaking, to use an employee as a thing, as simply a means to an end. Since the employee is a person, the employer has an obligation to respect her integrity as a person: her feelings, values, goals, emotional relationships, cultural attachments, self-regard. As an autonomous living entity the employee is the center of a complex web of relationships and it is this whole composite with which the employer becomes involved. Obviously, the employer is not responsible for everything which happens to or within this web; but he is responsible for whatever his actions change or otherwise affect. The relationships mentioned in discussing the "Externalities Lemma" are ones which the employer's actions affect adversely in (unmitigated) plant closure decisions. Even though the company no longer needs its workers as a means to its end of profitable production, it may not with moral impunity treat them like excess material or machines, but has an obligation to protect them from the adverse consequences brought about by the company's use of them.

A company which closes or relocates a plant without ameliorating actions is acting unfairly toward its employees and the community. The general idea of fairness is that anyone who chooses to get involved with others in a cooperative activity has to do his share and is entitled to expect others involved to do likewise.[7]

In the kind of situation we are concerned with there is a reasonably just cooperative arrangement under which a person agrees to work for a company; the primary *quid pro quo* is the employer's fair day's pay for the employee's fair day's work. But each party to the agreement has additional legitimate expectations about the other. The employer expects the worker to make a commitment to the job; one of the largest corporations has this to say:

> . . . The challenges of the workplace impose strong mutual responsibilities upon General Motors and its employees. . . .
>
> An employee's most basic responsibility is to work consistently to the best of his or her ability—not just to follow instructions, but to ask questions, think independently, and make constructive suggestions for improvement.
>
> A first-rate job requires employees to maintain their good health and mental alertness, to be prompt and present on the job, to cooperate with fellow workers, and to be loyal to the Corporation—its people and products. Because GM people *are* General Motors—in the eyes of their friends and neighbors—employees also are encouraged to take interest in

the basic goals, problems, and public positions of the Corporation.

> . . . General Motors encourages employees as individual citizens to involve themselves in community service and politics. . . .[8]

The employee, in turn, expects the company to do somewhat more than simply pay agreed-on wages. For example, no one would question that being provided a safe and at least tolerably pleasant workplace is within the worker's legitimate expectations. Beyond that, if it is fair for the company to expect that employees will take all the actions and have all the attitudes which a company like General Motors encourages and considers requisite to "a first-rate job" it also seems reasonable for workers to expect that the employer will not suddenly shut up shop and leave them high and dry with unpaid mortgages (on houses bought so they could be "prompt and present on the job" and involved in "community service and politics"), children in school, and commitments to various people or organizations; all this is part of a lifestyle to which they committed themselves when they entered into their agreement to work for the company—the kind of agreement which the GM statement calls a "partnership which can help assure the Corporation's success in the years to come, as well as contribute to an improved quality of life for the men and women of General Motors."[9]

There is nothing extraordinary in all this. In most social relationships the parties involved in an agreement have legitimate expectations which are often not expressed in the agreement itself. Fairness requires that a company either avoid a move which would cause grave hardship to workers or at least take action which would render the action harmless, since this is a legitimate expectation of the implicit "partnership" agreement between employer and employee.

Objections to the Thesis

. . . [One] objection rests on the notion of the risks inherent in the capitalistic system. It is essential to "free enterprise" that entrepreneurs freely undertake the risk of losing the time and money they invest in a venture in return for the opportunity of gain. In the nature of things there are inherent risks in establishing a manufacturing operation and everybody knows they don't last forever.

These employees didn't have to go to work for us, the company may argue. They know, or should have known, the risk involved. It was their free choice when they agreed to accept the job.

All this is true so far as it goes, but it doesn't wipe out the company's moral obligations. The workers are not free to the same extent as the employer; the way the system works, they have to accept some job just to stay alive and support their families and in most instances their choice of employment is extremely limited. The entrepreneur's reward for undertaking risk is the profit generated by the enterprise, a reward shared to some extent by higher salaried management employees but not by the ordinary worker. Wages are compensation for work performed, not for assumption of risk. They are carried on the company's books as a cost item which the company has an obligation to pay whether or not it makes a profit. What our thesis asserts is that the company has certain unacknowledged structural costs consequent on the fact that it is operating the plant, over and above the operational obligation of wage payments.

Like the workers, the community is not a partner in the company's entrepreneurial risk, nor does it expect to share in the venture's profit. The company presumably pays its fair share of operational expenses through taxes (and perhaps to some extent through charitable contributions to civic causes). When the plant moves or shuts down, the community is left with significant structural changes brought about by company operations; it is the problem brought about by these changes which the company has a moral obligation to help solve.

One additional objection to the proposed thesis is that a company accepting it would be unable to compete with others which do not. The expense to the company, this argument holds, would make its costs higher than others producing the same product; others could then establish lower prices and gain a clear market advantage.

This is a powerful objection and gets to the heart of the question. Against it, one could urge that there are certain countervailing advantages in terms of worker morale, community cooperation and public relations; but in the end I would have to concede the economic soundness of the argument. What I would not concede is that the objection is a persuasive refutation of our thesis. To act in accordance with a moral obligation not infrequently en-

tails acceptance of personal disadvantage in terms of nonmoral goods. Personal and economic advantage or disadvantage doesn't count as an argument against the existence of a moral obligation.

The thesis asserts the existence of an obligation, on the part of a company, to give appropriate moral weight to the adverse consequences of its action in moving or discontinuing an operation and to take appropriate action to avoid those consequences even in the face of an economic disadvantage. If all companies similarly situated were to recognize this obligation, of course, the competitive disadvantage would disappear. Assuming the costs were internalized — anticipated and treated like other expense items — they would be reflected in the pricing mechanism and only market factors would determine the effect on profits.

But isn't this an unlikely outcome? Is it not more probable that those companies which recognize their moral obligations will suffer for it and lose the competitive edge to those which do not? If corporate management attempts to act morally in this regard and ends up with lower profits, will not stockholders replace them with less conscientious management or invest their money elsewhere? Will not consumers refuse to pay a price for a product which is higher simply because it reflects true costs previously borne by workers and the community?

An affirmative answer to those questions might well be appropriate in a purely descriptive account of the existing economic system. In considering the proposed thesis, however, we are concerned with normative rather than descriptive issues. The question is what should be done, not how does in fact the present system work. This thesis asserts a moral obligation to be concerned about certain human consequences of a company's action: it does not assert that other consequences should be disregarded. Certainly company management should consider what effect its decision will have on profits. Certainly stockholders will consider whether managers are acting in their best interest and whether their money could be invested more profitably elsewhere. Certainly consumers will express their preference in the market and decide whether the price asked for a product is a fair one which they are willing to pay. But the proposed thesis insists that there are moral questions which must be asked, along with economic questions; important as the economic issues may be, they should be considered relevant only within a context of morally permissible actions: the moral issues are overriding.

Notes

1. The author gratefully acknowledges support from the Rockefeller Foundation and the Center for the Study of Values, University of Delaware. These initial observations, as well as several others throughout the paper, are based on the author's direct involvement in plant relocation situations in the course of more than twenty-five years of work as a senior official in Michigan state government agencies concerned with economic development programs. . . .

2. For brevity's sake I will generally speak of "relocation," although I mean also to include discontinuation of operations in the community without removal to another location.

3. The question of whether a company, a corporation or any collective can be the subject of moral acts is much controverted, but it is not the point at issue here. For those who reject the collective responsibility position, substitute the phrase "those persons morally responsible for the actions of the company" for the "company." In support of collective responsibility, see Peter A. French, "The Corporation as a Moral Person," *American Philosophical Quarterly*, 16 (1979), p. 207.

4. See John M. Clark, *Economic Institutions and Human Welfare* (New York: Alfred A. Knopf, 1957), pp. 195–197, for an interesting discussion from an economist's viewpoint of social obligations of a company in a relocation situation.

5. One plan which has received considerable attention calls for the company to transfer ownership to former workers or the community or a joint community-employee corporation. This has worked well in particularly favorable circumstances but has failed in other cases. See Robert N. Stern, K. Haydn Wood, and Tove Helland Hammer, *Employee Ownership in Plant Shutdowns* (Kalamazoo, Michigan: The W. E. Upjohn Institute for Employment Research, 1979). A current (November, 1981) instance is a planned purchase of the New Departure-Hyatt Bearing Division of General Motors Corp. at Clark, N.J. by former employees after GM announced its intention to close the plant.

6. Externalities can be beneficial. A paper operation may require management of forest resources to assure an adequate supply of timber. This may open previously inaccessible land for recreational use. Although the company may only intend to improve its timber holdings, it may also enhance the wildlife capabilities of the forest. The paper plant itself may become a tourist attraction, providing an unintended benefit to the community.

7. See John Rawls, *A Theory of Justice* (Cambridge, Mass.: Harvard University Press, 1971), p. 343.

8. *1980 General Motors Public Interest Report*, p. 83.

9. Citing of General Motors' statement should not be interpreted as critical of that company; the Corporation has a policy of replacing obsolete plants with new facilities in the same area "whenever it is economically feasible" and also, under its union contracts and salaried worker policies, pays substantial compensation to laid-off employees. GM has currently committed $10 billion to the rehabilitation and replacement of production facilities in Michigan alone.

Review and Discussion Questions

1. How is the concept of "externalities" relevant to Kavanagh's argument?

2. What moral principle or principles underlie his argument? Practically speaking, how far do companies have to go to live up to the obligation that Kavanagh imposes upon them? Assess Kavanagh's argument from the different ethical perspectives discussed in Chapter 2 and Chapter 3.

3. What would Milton Friedman say in response to Kavanagh's position?

4. What is Kavanagh's reply to the argument that companies that accept his thesis will be at a competitive disadvantage?

5. Someone might point out that we all know that nothing lasts forever and that anyone who accepts a job knows, or should know, that there is a chance the firm might decide to relocate or close the plant down. Does this point pose a problem for Kavanagh's argument?

Ethical Dilemmas for Multinational Enterprise: A Philosophical Overview

Richard T. De George

Corporations today are increasingly multinational in their business activities. This fact has stirred up controversy about the effects of those activities on foreign countries and about what sort of moral responsibilities multinational corporations have. In this essay, Professor De George clarifies these issues by explaining and defending five basic theses, which provide a useful framework for discussing the moral dilemmas that multinationals can face. While De George defends multinationals against some of their critics, he maintains that there are definite moral standards to which they must adhere.

First World multinational corporations (MNCs) are both the hope of the Third World and the scourge of the Third World. The working out of this paradox poses moral dilemmas for many MNCs. I shall focus on some of the moral dilemmas that many American MNCs face.

Third World countries frequently seek to attract American multinationals for the jobs they provide and for the technological transfers they promise. Yet when American MNCs locate in Third World countries, many Americans condemn them for exploiting the resources and workers of the Third World. While MNCs are a means for improving the standard of living of the underdeveloped countries, MNCs are blamed for the poverty and starvation such countries suffer. Although MNCs provide jobs in the Third World, many criticize them for transferring these jobs from the United States. American MNCs usually pay at least as high wages as local industries, yet critics blame them for paying the workers in underdeveloped countries less than they pay American workers for comparable work. When American MNCs pay higher than local wages, local companies criticize them for skimming off all the best workers and for creating an internal brain-drain. Multinationals are presently the most effective vehicle available for the development of the Third World. At the same time, critics complain that the MNCs are destroying the local cultures and substituting for them the tinsel of American life and the worst aspects of its culture.

American MNCs seek to protect the interests of their shareholders by locating in an environment in which their enterprise will be safe from destruction by revolutions and confiscation by socialist regimes. When they do so, critics complain that the MNCs thrive in countries with strong, often right-wing, governments.[1]

The dilemmas the American MNCs face arise from conflicting demands made from opposing, often ideologically based, points of view. Not all of the demands that lead to these dilemmas are equally justifiable, nor are they all morally mandatory. We can separate the MNCs that behave immorally and reprehensibly from those that do not by clarifying the true moral responsibility of MNCs in the Third World. To help do so, I shall state and briefly defend five theses.

Thesis 1: Many of the moral dilemmas MNCs face are false dilemmas which arise from equating United States standards with morally necessary standards.

Many American critics argue that American multinationals should live up to and implement the same standards abroad that they do in the United States and that United States mandated norms should be followed.[2] This broad claim confuses morally necessary ways of conducting a firm with United States government regulations. The FDA sets high standards that may be admirable. But they are not necessarily morally required. OSHA specifies a large number of rules which in general have as their aim the protection of the worker. However, these should not be equated with morally mandatory rules. United States wages are the highest in the world. These also should not be thought to be the morally necessary norms for the whole world or for United States firms abroad. Morally mandatory standards that no corporation — United States or other — should violate, and moral minima below which no firm can morally go, should not be confused either with standards appropriate to the United States or with standards set by the United States government. Some of the dilemmas of United States multinationals come from critics making such false equations.

This is true with respect to drugs and FDA standards, with respect to hazardous occupations and OSHA standards, with respect to pay, with respect to internalizing the costs of externalities, and with respect to foreign corrupt practices. By using United States standards as moral standards, critics pose false dilemmas for American MNCs. These false dilemmas in turn obfuscate the real moral responsibilities of MNCs.

Thesis 2: Despite differences among nations in culture and values, which should be respected, there are moral norms that can be applied to multinationals.
I shall suggest seven moral guidelines that apply in general to any multinational operating in Third World countries and that can be used in morally evaluating the actions of MNCs. MNCs that respect these moral norms would escape the legitimate criticisms contained in the dilemmas they are said to face.

1. *MNCs should do no intentional direct harm.*
   This injunction is clearly not peculiar to multinational corporations. Yet it is a basic norm that can be usefully applied in evaluating the conduct of MNCs. Any company that does produce intentional direct harm clearly violates a basic moral norm.

2. *MNCs should produce more good than bad for the host country.*
   This is an implementation of a general utilitarian principle. But this norm restricts the extent of that principle by the corollary that, in general, more good will be done by helping those in most need, rather than by helping those in less need at the expense of those in greater need. Thus the utilitarian analysis in this case does not consider that more harm than good might justifiably be done to the host country if the harm is offset by greater benefits to others in developed countries. MNCs will do more good only if they help the host country more than they harm it.

3. *MNCs should contribute by their activities to the host country's development.*
   If the presence of an MNC does not help the host country's development, the MNC can be correctly charged with exploitation, or using the host country for its own purposes at the expense of the host country.

4. *MNCs should respect the human rights of its employees.*
   MNCs should do so whether or not local companies respect those rights. This injunction will preclude gross exploitation of workers, set minimum standards for pay, and prescribe minimum standards for health and safety measures.

5. *MNCs should pay their fair share of taxes.*
   Transfer pricing has as its aim taking advantage of different tax laws in different countries. To the extent that it involves deception, it is itself immoral. To the extent that it is engaged in to avoid legitimate taxes, it exploits the host country, and the MNC does not bear its fair share of the burden of operating in that country.

6. *To the extent that local culture does not violate moral norms, MNCs should respect the local culture and work with it, not against it.*
   MNCs cannot help but produce some changes in the cultures in which they operate. Yet, rather than simply transferring American ways into other lands, they can consider changes in operating procedures, plant planning, and the like, which take into account local needs and customs.

7. *MNCs should cooperate with the local government in the development and enforcement of just background institutions.*
   Instead of fighting a tax system that aims at appropriate redistribution of incomes, instead of preventing the organization of labor, and instead of resisting attempts at improving the health and safety standards of the host country, MNCs should be supportive of such measures.

Thesis 3: Wholesale attacks on multinationals are most often overgeneralizations. Valid moral evaluations can be best made by using the above moral criteria for context-and-corporation-specific studies and analysis.

Broadside claims, such that all multinationals exploit underdeveloped countries or destroy their culture, are too vague to determine their accuracy. United States multinationals have in the past engaged—and some continue to engage—in immoral practices. A case by case study is the fairest way to make moral assessments. Yet we can distinguish five types of business operations that raise very different sorts of moral issues: (1) banks and financial institutions; (2) agricultural enterprises; (3) drug companies and hazardous industries; (4) extractive industries; and (5) other manufacturing and service industries.

If we were to apply our seven general criteria in each type of case, we would see some of the differences among them. Financial institutions do not generally employ many people. Their function is to provide loans for various types of development. In the case of South Africa they do not do much—if anything—to undermine apartheid, and by lending to the government they usually strengthen the government's policy of apartheid. In this case, an argument can be made that they do more harm than good—an argument that several banks have seen to be valid, causing them to discontinue their South African operations even before it became financially dangerous to continue lending money to that government. Financial institutions can help and have helped development tremendously. Yet the servicing of debts that many Third World countries face condemns them to impoverishment for the foreseeable future. The role of financial institutions in this situation is crucial and raises special and difficult moral problems, if not dilemmas.

Agricultural enterprises face other demands. If agricultural multinationals buy the best lands and use them for export crops while insufficient arable land is left for the local population to grow enough to feed itself, then MNCs do more harm than good to the host country—a violation of one of the norms I suggested above.

Drug companies and dangerous industries pose different and special problems. I have suggested that FDA standards are not morally mandatory standards. This should not be taken to mean that drug companies are bound only to local laws, for the local laws may require less than morality requires in the way of supplying adequate information and of not producing intentional, direct harm.[3] The same type of observation applies to hazardous industries. While an asbestos company will probably not be morally required to take all the measures mandated by OSHA regulations, it cannot morally leave its workers completely unprotected.[4]

Extractive industries, such as mining, which remove minerals from a country, are correctly open to the charge of exploitation unless they can show that they do more good than harm to the host country and that they do not benefit only either themselves or a repressive elite in the host country.

Other manufacturing industries vary greatly, but as a group they have come in for sustained charges of exploitation of workers and the undermining of the host country's culture. The above guidelines can serve as a means of sifting the valid from the invalid charges.

Thesis 4: On the international level and on the national level in many Third World countries the lack of adequate just background institutions makes the use of clear moral norms all the more necessary.

American multinational corporations operating in Germany and Japan, and German and Japanese multinational corporations operating in the United States, pose no special moral problems. Nor do the operations of Brazilian multinational corporations in the United States or Germany. Yet First World multinationals operating in Third World countries have come in for serious and sustained moral criticism. Why?

A major reason is that in the Third World the First World's MNCs operate without the types of constraints and in societies that do not have the same kinds of redistributive mechanisms as in the developed countries. There is no special difficulty in United States multinationals operating in other First World countries because in general these countries *do* have appropriate background institutions.[5]

More and more Third World countries are developing controls on multinationals that insure the companies do more good for the country than harm.[6] Authoritarian regimes that care more for their own wealth than for the good of their people pose difficult moral conditions under which to operate. In such instances, the guidelines above may prove helpful.

Just as in the nations of the developed, industrial world the labor movement serves as a counter to the dominance of big business, consumerism serves as a watchdog on practices harmful to the consumer, and big government serves as a restraint on each of the vested interest groups, so international structures are necessary to provide the proper background constraints on international corporations.

The existence of MNCs is a step forward in the unification of mankind and in the formation of a global community. They provide the economic base and substructure on which true international cooperation can be built. Because of their special position and the special opportunities they enjoy, they have a special responsibility to promote the cooperation that only they are able to accomplish in the present world.

Just background institutions would preclude any company's gaining a competitive advantage by engaging in immoral practices. This suggests that MNCs have more to gain than to lose by helping formulate voluntary, UN (such as the code governing infant formulae),[7] and similar codes governing the conduct of all multinationals. A case can also be made that they have the moral obligation to do so.

Thesis 5: The moral burden of MNCs do not exonerate local governments from responsibility for what happens in and to their country. Since responsibility is linked to ownership, governments that insist on part or majority ownership incur part or majority responsibility.

The attempts by many underdeveloped countries to limit multinationals have shown that at least some governments have come to see that they can use multinationals to their own advantage. This may be done by restricting entry to those companies that produce only for local consumption, or that bring desired technology transfers with them. Some countries demand majority control and restrict the export of money from the country. Nonetheless, many MNCs have found it profitable to engage in production under the terms specified by the host country.

What host countries cannot expect is that they can demand control without accepting correlative responsibility. In general, majority control implies majority responsibility. An American MNC, such as Union Carbide, which had majority ownership of its Indian Bhopal plant, should have had primary control of the plant. Union Carbide, Inc. can be held liable for the damage the Bhopal plant caused because Union Carbide, Inc. did have majority ownership.[8] If Union Carbide did not have effective control, it is not relieved of its responsibility. If it could not exercise the control that its responsibility demanded, it should have withdrawn or sold off part of its holdings in that plant. If India had had majority ownership, then it would have had primary responsibility for the safe operation of the plant.

This is compatible with maintaining that if a company builds a hazardous plant, it has an obligation to make sure that the plant is safe and that those who run it are properly trained to run it safely. MNCs cannot simply transfer dangerous technologies without consideration of the people who will run them, the local culture, and similar factors. Unless MNCs can be reasonably sure that the plants they build will be run safely, they cannot morally build them. To do so would be to will intentional, direct harm.

The theses and guidelines that I have proposed are not a panacea. But they suggest how moral norms can be brought to bear on the dilemmas American multinationals face and they suggest ways out of apparent or false dilemmas. If MNCs observed those norms, they could properly avoid the moral sting of their critics' charges, even if their critics continued to level charges against them.

Notes

1. The literature attacking American MNCs is extensive. Many of the charges mentioned in this paper are found in Richard J. Barnet and Ronald E. Muller, *Global Reach: The Power of the Multinational Corporations*, New York: Simon & Schuster, 1974, and in Pierre Jalee, *The Pillage of the Third World*, translated from the French by Mary Klopper, New York and London: Modern Reader Paperbacks, 1968.

2. The position I advocate does not entail moral relativism, as my third thesis shows. The point is that although moral norms apply uniformly across cultures, U.S. standards are not the same as moral standards, should themselves be morally evaluated, and are relative to American conditions, standard of living, interests, and history.

3. For a fuller discussion of multinational drug companies see Richard T. De George, *Business Ethics*, 2nd ed., New York: Macmillan, 1986, pp. 363–367.

4. For a more detailed analysis of the morality of exporting hazardous industries, see my *Business Ethics*, 367–372.

5. This position is consistent with that developed by John Rawls in his *A Theory of Justice*, Cambridge, Mass.: Harvard University Press, 1971, even though Rawls does not extend his analysis to the international realm. The thesis does not deny that United States, German, or Japanese policies on trade restrictions, tariff levels, and the like can be morally evaluated.

6. See, for example, Theodore H. Moran, "Multinational Corporations: A Survey of Ten Years' Evidence," Georgetown School of Foreign Service, 1984.

7. For a general discussion of UN codes, see Wolfgang Fikentscher, "United Nations Codes of Conduct: New Paths in International Law," *The American Journal of Comparative Law*, 30 (1980), pp. 577–604.

8. The official Indian Government report on the Bhopal tragedy has not yet appeared. The Union Carbide report was partially reprinted in the *New York Times*, March 21, 1985, p. 48. The major *New York Times* reports appeared on December 9, 1984, January 28, 30, and 31, and February 3, 1985.

Review and Discussion Questions

1. Explain each of De George's five theses in your own words. Do you agree with them? Are any open to doubt or possible objection? Explain.

2. What do you see as the most important moral dilemmas that face American MNCs operating overseas? With regard to the five types of business operations distinguished by De George (in his discussion of Thesis 3), do you think that MNCs operating in Third World countries do more good than harm?

3. De George offers seven moral guidelines for multinationals operating in the Third World. Do you agree with them? What would a proponent of the narrow view of corporate responsibility say about them? Has De George overlooked any other responsibilities that multi-nationals have?

4. De George denies that American MNCs should live up to and implement the same standards abroad as they do at home. Do you agree? Does De George's position imply some kind of ethical relativism?

Business Ethics: On Getting to the Heart of the Matter

Paul F. Camenisch

It is common in discussions of business ethics to make one of two assumptions. The first is that business ethics is essentially the prevailing moral code of the society applied to business. The second is that business ethics is essentially applying to the corporate member of society some standards of social responsibility. Paul F. Camenisch argues in the following essay that neither approach gets to the heart of business ethics. To do this, we must inquire about the fundamental nature of business—what it is, what it claims to do, and what distinctive functions it performs.

Camenisch keys on two definite elements in business: profit and the provision of goods and services. We might call these elements dual ideals of business. By Milton Friedman's account, the profit ideal takes precedence over the other: If business makes a profit, it meets its responsibility to society.

Camenisch demurs; whereas profit may be an adequate criterion for assessing a business undertaking, he says it is an inadequate ethical ideal. Camenisch goes on to argue that the business activity itself must be scrutinized according to how it affects "human flourishing directly through the kind of products or services it provides, and through the responsible or irresponsible use of limited and often non-renewable resources."

Many current discussions of business ethics seem in the end to locate the ethical concern some distance from the central and essential activity of business. One way this is done is to assume that the content of business ethics is no more and no less

Paul F. Camenisch, "Business Ethics: On Getting to the Heart of the Matter," *Business and Professional Ethics Journal* 1 (Fall 1981): 59–69. Reprinted by permission of the author.

than the prevailing moral code of the society as applied to business activities. Business persons and institutions, like all other citizens, are expected to refrain from murder, from fraud, and from polluting the environment. But we cannot limit business ethics to such matters. In fact, perhaps we ought not even call this *business* ethics for the same reasons that we do not say that parental ethics prohibits my brutalizing my children. This is not parental ethics but just ethics plain and simple. This constraint arises from what it means to be a decent human being, not from what it means to be a parent. Similarly, the prohibition upon murdering to eliminate a business competitor is not part of a *business* ethic, for it does not arise from what it means to be engaged in business, nor does it apply to one simply because one is engaged in business. It too arises from what it means to be a decent, moral human being.

The second way of moving ethical issues to the edge of business's activities usually occurs under the rubric of "business's social responsibilities." The most remote of the issues raised here involve the question of whether corporations should devote any of their profits to philanthropic, educational and other sorts of humanitarian undertakings. This is a controversial issue which will not be easily resolved, but even if we concluded that this was a social responsibility of business, it would again fail to be business ethics in any specific and distinctive sense. It would simply be the application to this corporate member of a general societal expectation that members of a society existing in extensive interdependence with and benefitting from that society ought, if able, to contribute some portion of their wealth to such worthy causes. It should in passing be noted that there are persuasive grounds for rejecting this form of social responsibility for business.

Another class of social responsibilities urged upon business is somewhat closer to business activity as such since they can be fulfilled in the course of business's central activity of producing and marketing goods and services. These are the negative duties of neither creating nor aggravating social ills which might arise from business activity such as discriminatory employment, advancement and remuneration along racial, sexual, or other irrelevant lines, dangerous working conditions, and avoidable unemployment or worker dislocation.

Still we have not yet reached the heart of business ethics because we have said nothing of the ethics which come to bear on business *as business*, on business at its very heart and essence. But what is this "heart" of the business enterprise, and how and why are business ethics to be grounded in it?

Imagine a corporation which observes all the moral claims already noted—it does not commit fraud or murder, it freely contributes from its profits to various community "charities," its employment practices are above reproach, and it sells quality products at a fair and competitive price while securing for its investors a reasonable return on their investment. So far so good. Its moral record is impeccable. But imagine that the only conceivable use of its products is for human torture. Can we say that here there are no moral or ethical judgments to be made? That the kind of service or product which is at the heart of the enterprise is entirely inconsequential in any and all moral assessments of that enterprise? I do not see how morally sensitive persons or societies can set aside their moral perceptions at this point.

Of course one good reason for resisting this suggestion is the great difficulty in making such assessments of goods and services. *Whose* assessments will prevail? We might get general agreement on instruments of human torture—although even here I would not expect unanimity. But what of other goods such as napalm, Saturday-night specials, pornographic materials, junk foods, tobacco, liquors, etc., and services such as prostitution, the training of military mercenaries, or even the provision of such, or the training of the armed forces of repressive regimes, offensive-oriented "survival" courses, the construction of the usually redundant fast-food outlets along suburban slurp strips? In addition to these items in which virtually everyone should be able to see some detrimental elements, there is an additional class of items which some would list here because of their use of limited, even nonrenewable, resources for no purpose beyond momentarily satisfying the whimsey of the indiscriminate wealthy, the bored, the vain, or of increasing corporate profits. . . .

But how do we carry business ethics to the very heart of the business enterprise? I would argue that we can begin by asking the question of what the business sector is and claims to do, what its distinctive function is in the larger society of which it is a part. The norms, both moral and otherwise, for the conduct of an agent, whether individual or corporate,[1] can be determined only after we have established what that agent's relations are to other agents in the moral community, what role the agent plays in relation to them, what the agent's activities in the context of that community aim at. . . .

In looking for the essential or definitive element in business I would suggest that it is necessary and helpful to see business as one form of that activity by which humans have from the beginning sought to secure and/or produce the material means of sustaining and then of enhancing life. It is plausible to assume that in earlier times individuals and small groups did this for themselves in immediate and direct ways such as gathering, hunting and fishing, farming, producing simple tools and weapons, etc. With the passage of time developments such as co-operative efforts, barter and monetary exchange modified this simple and idyllic situation. Business, I would suggest, enters this picture as that form of such activities in which the exchanges engaged in are no longer motivated entirely by the intention of all participants to secure goods or services immediately needed to sustain and/or enhance their own lives, but by the design of at least some of the participants to make a profit, i.e., to obtain some value in excess of what they had before the exchange which is sufficiently flexible that it can be put to uses other than the immediate satisfaction of the recipient's own needs and desires. It should be noted that this last point is as much or more a matter of defining business, as it is of charting its historical emergence.

In the above statement I am suggesting that there are two essential elements in any adequate definition of business, the *provision of goods and services,* and the fact that this is done with the intention of making a *profit.* The first of these shows business's continuity with the various other human activities just noted by which life has been sustained and enhanced throughout the ages and enables us to understand business in relation to the larger society. The second is a more specific characteristic and sets business off from these other activities by revealing its distinctive internal dynamic. But this element does *not* sever business's connection with those predecessors. The crucial moral points to be made here are that moral/ethical issues arise around both of these elements and that

the most important ones concern the "goods and services" element, i.e., the connection between business and the larger society of which it is part.

This appears to put me in definite tension with Milton Friedman who attempts to ground business ethics, or at least that portion of it which he calls the social responsibility of business, in the profit element only: "In . . . [a free] economy, there is one and only one social responsibility of business — to use its resources and engage in activities designed to increase its profits so long as it stays within the rules of the game, which is to say, engages in open and free competition, without deception or fraud."[2]

Of course it is unfair to Friedman to say that for him the maximization of profit is business's only moral duty since he may assume that playing by the rules of the game and that even conducting oneself so as to make a profit in such a "game" would bring additional restraints to bear on business, restraints which many of us would consider to be *moral* restraints. Nevertheless, Friedman's statement does seem to put undue emphasis on business's profit-making function in answering the question of its social and/or moral responsibility.

But however one interprets Friedman's statement, we do here encounter a question fundamental to our present point. This is the question of whether, in defining business and understanding it as a moral reality, we should focus primarily on its goal of producing goods and services or of generating a profit. One can attempt to resolve this question in several ways. There is the rather common sense way of looking at the way most persons generally apply the label "business." A producer of goods and services intending to make a profit but failing to do so is still, by most accounts, engaged in business. Of course some might respond that the concept of profit is still crucial to this activity's being considered business even though here it is present in intention only. But consider the other side. What if profit is present but the provision of goods and services is entirely absent as in a bank robbery? Most, I take it, would deny that here we have just another instance of business, or even an instance of business of a rather unusual sort. Most would simply want to deny that the bank robber was engaged in business at all. Of course one might salvage the position that business is defined by profit-making and yet avoid having to consider the bank robber a businessman by arguing that profit is not just any kind of gain at all, but is a particular sort of gain or is gain realized only under certain circumstances. But even this move would tend to support my position that a single simple concept of profit is not by itself sufficient to define what we mean by business. Whether these additional defining characteristics are written into a more complex definition of profit or are seen as additional to profit is a matter of indifference in terms of the present argument.

Secondly, one could take a more reflective, analytical approach and ask what the relation between these two elements — providing goods and services and profit-making — is, to see if that relation grants a kind of priority to either of them. I would argue, consistent with the above scenario of the emergence of business, that business's primary function, like that of the activities it supplants, is the producing of goods and services to sustain and enhance human existence. Profit then, given the way business functions in the marketplace, becomes one of the necessary means by which business enables itself to continue supplying such goods and services. This would mean that the goods and services element must be given priority in our understanding of business as a social reality and in our moral/ethical response to it. For in the absence of goods and services which are really *goods* and *services*, the making of a profit is at best morally irrelevant. In the absence of the end sought, the means for achieving it are otiose. . . .

Finally, in trying to settle the question of the relation between profits on the one hand and goods and services on the other, one might look at business in terms of its social function and ask why societies have generated and now support and sustain business. Surely it is not for business's own sake, nor for the sake of the few who own and manage businesses so that they can make a profit. Society has no need for profit-making as such. But rather, societies generate, encourage and sustain business because societies need the available raw materials transformed into needed goods and services, and because business in its contemporary form has been conspicuously successful in doing just that. In fact, in the current setting it may be that only business has the resources and the know-how to do that job on the needed scale.

All three of these ways of addressing the relation between these two elements would seem to confirm my position that the provision of goods and services can, perhaps must, be given priority over the profit element in our understanding of business. The major implication of this position for the resulting business ethics would be that the assessment of business as such and of specific business enterprises would begin with the question of whether the goods and services produced thereby serve to enhance or detract from the human condition, whether they contribute to or obstruct human flouishing. Implicit here is the suggestion that businesses engaged in producing goods and services which do not contribute to human flourishing are engaged in a morally questionable enterprise, and those engaged in producing goods and services inimical to human flourishing are engaged in immoral activity. . . .

Of course this suggestion concerning the heart of business ethics is rife with problems. Chief among them is the question of how we define the human flouishing which business is to serve. While we cannot resolve this question here, raising it at least serves to demonstrate that business ethics, like any serious ethics, will need to develop a philosophical or theological anthropology, a view of humanity and what its proper pursuit, its appropriate fulfillment is.

Some, of course, will argue that the only proper answers to such questions are the ones given by consumers in the marketplace as they use their purchasing power to vote for or against the various answers business implicitly offers in the form of diverse goods and services. While this may be an acceptable answer when one focuses exclusively on the relation between the individual consumer and the marketplace, it is clearly inadequate when we focus on the marketplace in relation to the total society, its present condition and needs and its future prospects. And clearly it is unrealistic, even irresponsible, to attempt to view an enterprise as large and as extensively intertwined with the total fabric of the society as is business only in its relation to individual consumers and their choices. Furthermore, the "marketplace as voting booth" answer to these questions is a costly trial and error method. And given advertising and other forms of demand formation, the significance of consumer "votes" is very unclear. Yet to have such judgments made by any agency outside the marketplace has serious implications for citizen-consumer freedom and rights in a free society.

In light of these difficult problems it might be tempting to give up the search for criteria by which to assess the performance of business at the level of its central function. And yet there are at least three important reasons for attempting this assessment in spite of the obvious problems. As we become increasingly aware of the limits of the earth and its resources within which all of humanity both present and future must live, and of the fact that in our present setting only business has the means and the know-how to transform those resources on any significant scale into the needed goods and services, it becomes increasingly clear that the total society has a crucial stake in, and should therefore have a say about what business does with this our common legacy. As Keith Davis has suggested, ". . . business now has a new social role of . . . trustee for society's resources . . ."[3] The knowing use of non-renewable resources to make products of little or no human value and/or with short useful life solely for the sake of an immediate profit thus becomes a serious dis-service to the larger society. An ethic of the sort here proposed provides a framework within which we could raise the question of how this trusteeship can best be exercised.

Secondly, this enterprise of assessing business in terms of its contribution to human flourishing is called for and legitimated by the fact that business in its various activities is already propagating, whether consciously or not, a view of humanity and of what human flourishing consequently means, views which of course assign a major role to the consumption of the goods and services business produces.[4] Even if this view of humanity is only implicit or perhaps especially if it is implicit, its content and potential impact call for assessment by parties outside the business sector.

Finally, the difficult task of responding to business on these central issues is worth undertaking because of the role business plays in contemporary America and similar societies. In observing the role of business and related economic matters in contemporary America one might almost suggest that we have moved from a sacralized society dominated by religious concerns, through a secularized one in which various major sectors attained considerable autonomy in their own spheres, to a commercialized or an economized culture in which the common denominators which unify and dominate all areas of activity are business related or business

grounded considerations such as dollar-value, profitability, marketability, efficiency, contribution to the gross national product, etc. And as Thomas Donaldson and Patricia Werhane have written:

> There may be nothing inherently evil about the goals of economic growth, technological advance, and a higher material standard of living; but critics such as Galbraith have argued that when these become the primary goals of a nation there is a significant lowering in the quality of human life. Economic goals are able to distract attention from crucial human issues, and freedom, individuality, and creativity are lost in a society dominated by large corporations and economic goals.[5]

If the above is a plausible interpretation of the role of business, broadly understood, in contemporary America, and of some of its implications for human flourishing, then it should be obvious that we have need for an ethic which responds to the central activity of business, since the crucial human implications of such cultural domination by business arise from this central function and not from the less central concerns often raised in business ethics. . . .

But why should business submit to the scrutiny and recommendations of an ethic such as is proposed here? One answer would be because such an ethic is predicated on what business *is* — one important part of society's efforts to enable its members to flourish, specifically that part which deals with the provision of the material means for sustaining and enhancing life.

"Of course," the critic might respond, "this answer works *if* we agree on what you say business is. But if we maintain that business must be defined and understood in terms of its own internal dynamics and goals, e.g., profit-making, rather than in terms of society's needs and goals, then the answer falls apart." True enough. But given business's extensive interdependence with society — its reliance on society's educational system to provide educated workers, on society's maintenance of transportation systems, of a stable social and political setting in which to do business, of a legal system by which business can adjudicate its disputes with competitors and customers, of what E. F. Schumacher has called the "infrastructure"[6] — it is naive to suggest that business is a self-sufficient and self-contained entity which can define its own goals and functions entirely independently of the society's goals and needs. As Robert A. Dahl has written:

> Today it is absurd to regard the corporation simply as an enterprise established for the sole purpose of allowing profit making. We the citizens give them special rights, powers, and privileges, protection, and benefits on the understanding that their activities will fulfill purposes. Corporations exist only as they continue to benefit us . . . Every corporation should be thought of as a social enterprise whose existence and decisions can be justified only insofar as they serve public or social purposes.[7]

Furthermore, anyone who argues that business should be permitted to define its own goals and purposes and thus its own ethics independently of societal interests will have to explain why business should be granted latitude at this point that is denied to other major sectors of societal activity such as politics, education, or the traditional professions such as law and medicine. (This last of course is of special interest and relevance in light of the fact already noted that increasing numbers of business persons wish to be considered professionals.) And the questions raised here cannot be put to rest by facile references to the public vs. the private sector. First of all, much of education and certainly most of the legal and medical professions are not in the public sector. So that would not explain or justify different treatment for business at this point. But more fundamentally, such a response would miss the basic question being raised here, the question of whether in a society as complex and interdependent as ours there actually is a "private sector" in the simple, straightforward sense suggested by that response.

There are numerous varied matters which are legitimately included in any adequate definition of business ethics. In fact, in a nascent field such as this it is as yet impossible to say with any certainty what is within and what is without its borders. But it does seem clear that any business ethic that does not respond first and foremost to business's contribution to or detraction from human flourishing through its essential and definitive activity of generating life sustaining and enhancing goods and

services will have failed to lay a foundation from which to address all other questions for it will not yet have gotten to the heart of the matter.

Notes

1. I am not prepared to enter here into the current debate concerning the existence and/or nature of corporate moral agency. For my present point it is sufficient to note that the moral stances, decisions and actions of various persons engaged in business and working together as, or through a corporation, do have impacts on the life of society and of its members of the sort I here have in mind. Whether these impacts are to be credited to those individual persons or to the corporation seems to make little difference in the present analysis.

2. Milton Friedman, *Capitalism and Freedom* (Chicago: University of Chicago Press, 1962), 133.

3. Keith Davis, "Five Propositions for Social Responsibility," in Tom L. Beauchamp and Norman E. Bowie, eds., *Ethical Theory and Business* (Englewood Cliffs, N.J.: Prentice-Hall, 1979), 170.

4. For one interpretation of the understanding of human flourishing assumed and propagated by much of business in a consumer society, see Edward Stevens, *Business Ethics* (New York: Paulist Press, 1979), 205–211.

5. Thomas Donaldson and Patricia H. Werhane, eds., *Ethical Issues in Business* (Englewood Cliffs, N.J.: Prentice-Hall, 1979), 330.

6. E. F. Schumacher, *Small Is Beautiful* (New York: Harper & Row, 1975), 273–274.

7. Robert A. Dahl, "A Prelude to Corporate Reform," in Robert L. Heilbroner and Paul London, eds., *Corporate Social Policy* (Reading, MA: Addison-Wesley Publishing Company, 1975), 18–19, as cited in Norman E. Bowie, "Changing the Rules," in Tom L. Beauchamp and Norman E. Bowie, eds., *Ethical Theory and Business* (Englewood Cliffs, N.J.: Prentice-Hall, 1979), 148.

Review and Discussion Questions

1. Could a company that makes products for human torture be a "socially responsible" company? Explain your answer. What about companies that make cigarettes, cheap guns, pornographic movies, or junk food?

2. What are Camenisch's three reasons for maintaining that the business goal of providing goods and services takes priority over making a profit? Do you agree with them?

3. Camenisch argues that business should promote "human flourishing." What does that mean to you? Do you think that there is any means other than the marketplace itself to decide what goods and services promote human flourishing?

4. Why does Camenisch believe that it is justified and important to develop criteria for assessing business in terms of human flourishing?

5. Would you agree that Camenisch has taken us to the "heart" of business ethics? What practical implications does his approach have?

For Further Reading

Thomas Donaldson, *Corporations and Morality* (Englewood Cliffs, N.J.: Prentice-Hall, 1982) discusses the moral status of corporations, arguments for and against corporate social responsibility, and the idea of a social contract for business, among other issues.

Peter A. French, *Collective and Corporate Responsibility* (New York: Columbia University Press, 1984) analyzes the philosophical issues involved in assigning moral responsibility to corporations and other collectivities.

Elizabeth Gatewood and **Archie B. Carroll**, "The Anatomy of Corporate Social Response: The Rely, Firestone 500, and Pinto Cases," *Business Horizons* 24 (September–October 1981) analyzes different corporate responses in these three cases.

Saul W. Gellerman, "Why 'Good' Managers Make Bad Ethical Choices," *Harvard Business Review* 64 (July–August 1986) examines the rationalizations that lead to corporate misconduct.

Christopher McMahon, "Morality and the Invisible Hand," *Philosophy and Public Affairs* 10 (Summer 1981) is an insightful but advanced analysis of the relationship between common morality and the implicit morality of business.

Donald T. Risser, "Punishing Corporations: A Proposal," *Business and Professional Ethics Journal* 8 (Fall 1989) discusses the treatment of corporations found guilty of illegal conduct.

PART III

THE ORGANIZATION AND THE PEOPLE IN IT

CHAPTER 6

THE WORKPLACE (1): BASIC ISSUES

Scientists first described acquired immune deficiency syndrome, commonly known as AIDS, in 1981. Apparently the result of a new infection of human beings, AIDS probably stems originally from central Africa, possibly emerging as recently as the 1950s. Within three years scientists in the United States and France had isolated human T-lymphotropic virus III, now known as HIV, for "human immunodeficiency virus." HIV is the parent virus of AIDS and a couple of related diseases. To be infected with the virus is not automatically to have AIDS, but recent evidence suggests that most of those infected will go on to develop AIDS symptoms and die from them. After identifying the virus, scientists quickly developed blood tests for its presence. As of this writing, the scientific race to develop a vaccine is on. And the stakes are high. An estimated 2 million people in the United States alone are infected. Spread primarily by intimate contact, the virus has the potential to infect virtually all human beings.[1]

No one today can doubt the seriousness of AIDS. Media attention has ensured that the public is aware of this deadly disease and its threat of epidemic, and this is a good thing. But when fear of danger combines with ignorance about its nature and causes, panic is often the result. And this has sadly been the case with AIDS—not least in the workplace.

Take what is, unfortunately, a typical case. John L ———— is a white-collar employee, working in the downtown branch of a firm operating in a middle-sized West Coast city. He had been feeling generally run-down and complained of various small ailments to his physician. When a routine checkup didn't reveal anything specific, John's doctor encouraged him to undergo a blood test for AIDS. He tested positive, which means that the antibodies for HIV are present in his body. Their presence means that he is infected by the virus and that it is probable, given his symptoms, that he has AIDS.

A few of John's friends in the office know of his recent ill health, and gradually word of his test results has circulated. And now problems have begun—not just for John but also for his co-workers and for management. John's colleagues feel uneasy around him; they're not sure what to do or to say, and some of them are very worried about possible contagion. A few co-workers feel strongly that John should not be permitted to go on working there. The boss is concerned not just with the prospect of declining work performance from John but with the effects of his presence on office morale. She may herself also have doubts about the wisdom or even the safety of allowing John to continue to interact with the public, which is part of his job.

The myriad problems, doubts, tensions, possibly even mild hysteria that the mere presence of John L _____ can create in an organizational context are easy to imagine, but sorting out the morally relevant factors and deciding how the situation ought to be dealt with is less easy. What are John's rights and interests? How are these to be weighed against the interests and rights of both his co-workers and the organization itself? What responsibilities does an organization have to one of its members who may be facing a terminal illness? Given the size and organizational structure of John's workplace and the type of work in question, how — morally speaking — should management respond?

These are questions that more and more firms must answer. One-third of the companies responding to a recent survey by the American Society for Personnel Administration acknowledged having workers with AIDS, and three-quarters of U.S. organizations with more than 5,000 employees have had cases of AIDS among their employees or dependents.[2] For the foreseeable future, these figures can only continue to increase.

Traditionally, the obligations between a business organization and its employees could be boiled down to "A fair wage for an honest day's work." Business's primary, if not sole, obligation to its employees was to pay a decent wage. In return, employees were expected to work efficiently and to be loyal and obedient to their employer. This model of employer-employee relations is obviously too simple and fails to come to terms not just with the dilemmas facing John's office but also with many other major moral issues that arise in today's workplace. This chapter looks at some of these issues, in particular:

1. The state of civil liberties in the workplace

2. The efforts of some successful companies

to respect the rights and moral dignity of their employees

3. Moral issues that arise with respect to personnel matters — namely hiring, promotions, discipline and discharge, and wages

4. The role and history of unions in our economic system, their ideals and achievements, and the moral issues they raise

CIVIL LIBERTIES IN THE WORKPLACE

Employees have all sorts of job-related concerns. Generally speaking, they want to do well at their assignments, to get along with their colleagues, and to have their contributions to the organization recognized. Their job tasks, working conditions, wages, and the possibility of promotion are among the many things that occupy their day-to-day thoughts. Aside from the actual work that they are expected to perform, employees, being human, are naturally concerned about the way their organizations treat them. Frequently they find that treatment to be morally deficient and complain that the organizations for which they work violate their moral rights and civil liberties.

Consider the case of Louis V. MacIntire, who worked for the DuPont Company in Orange, Texas, for sixteen years. As a chemical engineer he was well paid, and during the course of his career at DuPont he received several promotions. MacIntire also had literary ambitions and wrote a novel, *Scientists and Engineers: The Professionals Who Are Not*. Several characters in the novel inveigh against various management abuses at the novel's fictional Logan Chemical Company and argue for a union for technical employees. Logan Chemical at least superficially resembles MacIntire's real-life employer, DuPont, and some of MacIntire's supervisors were unhappy with his thinly veiled criticisms. He was fired. MacIntire sued DuPont, claiming that his constitutional right of free speech had been violated. A Texas district judge threw that charge out of court.[3]

MacIntire's case illuminates what many see as the widespread absence of civil liberties in the workplace. David W. Ewing is one of those writers. He sees the corporate invasion of employees' civil liberties as rampant and attacks it in scathing terms:

> In most . . . [corporate] organizations, during working hours, civil liberties are a will-o'-the-wisp. The Constitutional rights that employees have grown accustomed to in family, school, and church life generally must be left outdoors, like cars in the parking lot. As in totalitarian countries, from time to time a benevolent chief executive or department head may encourage speech, conscience, and privacy, but these scarcely can be called rights, for management can take them away at will. . . . It is fair to say that an enormous corporate archipelago has grown which, in terms of civil liberties, is as different from the rest of America as day is from night. In this archipelago . . . the system comes first, the individual second.[4]

Two historical factors, in Ewing's view, lie behind the absence of civil liberties and the prevalence of authoritarianism in the workplace. One of these factors was the rise of professional management and personnel engineering at the turn of the century, following the emergence of large corporations. This shaped the attitudes of companies toward their employees in a way hardly conducive to respecting their rights. As Frederick Winslow Taylor, generally identified as the founder of "scientific management," bluntly put it, "In the past, the man has been first. In the future, the system must be first."[5]

The second historical factor is that the law has traditionally given the employer a free hand in hiring and firing employees. A century ago, a Tennessee court expressed this doctrine in memorable form. Employers, the court held, "may dismiss their employees at will . . . for good cause, for no cause, or even for cause morally wrong, without thereby being guilty of legal wrong." Similarly, a California court upheld this traditional rule shortly before World War I, observing that the "arbitrary right of the employer to employ or discharge labor, with or without regard to actuating motives" is a proposition "settled beyond peradventure." And in 1975 a U.S. district court in Missouri upheld the traditional position in ruling against a whistle-blowing engineer at General Motors.[6]

In addition, common law requires that an employee be loyal to an employer, acting solely for the employer's benefit in matters connected to work. The employee is also duty bound "not to act or speak disloyally," except in pursuit of his own interests outside work. It's no wonder, then, that traditional employer-employee law has hardly been supportive of the idea of freedom of speech and expression for employees. Against that background, DuPont's treatment of MacIntire and the court's refusal to see a First Amendment issue in his case are not surprising.

According to common law, then, unless there is an explicit contractual provision to the contrary, every employment is employment "at will," and either side is free to terminate it at any time without advance notice or reason. The common law, however, has been modified in important ways by congressional and state statutory provisions. The Wagner Act of 1935 was, in this respect, a watershed. It prohibited firing workers because of union membership or union activities. The Civil Rights Act of 1964 and subsequent legislation prohibit discrimination on the basis of race, creed, nationality, sex, or age. Federal and state laws also protect war veterans and public employees in civil service. And many workers are protected by their union contracts from unjust dismissals.

Thus, today working people have protection against some forms of unjust termination, and many of them enjoy the assurance that they can expect due process and that at least some of their civil liberties and other moral rights will be respected on the job.

"But," writes Clyde Summers in the *Harvard Business Review*, "random individuals who are unjustly terminated are isolated and without organizational or political voice. For them the harsh common law rule remains."[7]

Companies That Look Beyond the Bottom Line

The law is not static, however, and some courts have been willing in specific cases to break with tradition to protect employees' rights of speech, privacy, and conscience.[8] The Supreme Court, for instance, has ruled that a state cannot deny unemployment benefits to employees who are fired because they refuse to work on their Sabbath day, even if they aren't members of an organized religion.[9] And in 1987 Montana became the first state in the nation to enact legislation that workers cannot be fired without "good cause."[10] Even without explicit legislation, wrongfully dismissed employees frequently have legal recourse. Thus, for example, a federal jury held in 1990 that Mobil Chemical Company had wrongfully dismissed one of its top environmental officials after he refused to perform acts that would have violated federal and state environmental laws. The jury ordered Mobil to pay $375,000 in compensatory damages and $1 million in punitive damages. On the other hand, when Daniel Foley, district manager for Interactive Data Corporation, accurately reported to his employer that his new boss was under investigation by the FBI for embezzling funds on a former job, he was dismissed for "inadequate performance" three months later, despite a seven-year record of positive work reviews and a recent $6,700 bonus. He sued Interactive Data for wrongful termination, but in December 1988 the California Supreme Court decided that his dismissal did not violate the "public interest" and rejected his suit.

Thus, while the law seems to be gradually changing, leaving the common-law heritage of employer-employee doctrine behind, recent legal developments are complicated and not entirely consistent. The results depend not only on the details of each case but vary from jurisdiction to jurisdiction and from court to court. As argued in Chapter 1, however, our moral obligations extend beyond merely keeping within the law. Thus, it is particularly significant that more corporations are themselves coming to acknowledge, and to design institutional procedures that respect, the rights of their employees. Moreover, the firms taking the lead in this regard are often among the most successful companies in the country.

This fact cuts against the old argument that corporate efficiency requires employees to sacrifice their civil liberties and other rights between 9 and 5. Without strict discipline and the firm maintenance of management prerogatives, it has been claimed, our economic system would come apart at the seams. An increasing body of evidence, however, suggests just the opposite. As Ewing writes:

> Civil liberties are far less of a threat to the requirements of effective management than are collective bargaining, labor-management committees, job enrichment, work participation, and a number of other schemes that industry takes for granted. Moreover, the companies that lead in encouraging rights—organizations such as Polaroid, IBM, Donnelly Mirrors, and Delta Airlines—have healthier-looking bottom lines than the average corporation does.[11]

Although under no legal compulsion to do so, a small but growing number of companies encourage employee questions and criticisms about company policies affecting the welfare of employees and the community. Some companies foster open communication through regular, informal exchanges between management and other employees. Others, like Delta Airlines, have top officials answer questions submitted anonymously by employees—in the absence of supervisors. Still others, like General Electric and New England Telephone, have a hotline for questions, worries, and reports of wrongdoing. Finally, some, like Dow Chemical, open the pages of company publications to employee questions and criticisms.

Union contracts frequently require companies to set up grievance procedures and otherwise attempt to see that their members are guaranteed due process on the job. Some enlightened nonunionized companies have done the same. Polaroid, for instance, has a well-institutionalized committee whose job it is to represent an employee with a grievance. The committee members are elected from the ranks, and reportedly a fair number of management decisions are overruled in the hearings. If the decision goes against the aggrieved employee, he or she is entitled by company rules to submit the case to an outside arbitrator.

Some companies—like Johnson Wax, Procter & Gamble, and Aetna Life and Casualty—go further. As Tad Tuleja has shown, these companies have long followed no-layoff policies.[12] IBM is another example. Motivated by the personal philosophy of its founder, Thomas Watson, IBM promised in 1914 never to lay off an employee for purely economic reasons, a promise it has kept for over seventy-five years. Even during the Great Depression in the 1930s, IBM maintained a full payroll, despite a severely diminished market for its machines. In discussing this policy, Richard T. Liebhaber, IBM's director for business practices and development, states that IBM begins

with an unusual premise—the idea that the individual comes first. A lot of companies begin somewhere else—with profit or productivity or growth—and try to work the individual in. We start with respect for the person and hang everything else on that concept. When you come at business from that direction, decisions take on a very different tone, because the personal dimension is already built into your options.

Hewlett-Packard is another company with a firm commitment to full employment. During a recession in the early 1970s, orders had fallen so badly that management was considering a 10 percent cut in the work force. Since laying off people was anathema, HP went a different route. It set up a working schedule of nine days out of ten for everybody in the company, from the CEO on down. The program stayed in place for six months, when orders picked up, and the full ten-day schedule returned. "The net result of this program," says William Hewlett, "was that effectively all shared the burden of the recession, good people were not turned out on a very tough job market, and, I might observe, the company benefited by having in place a highly qualified work force when business returned."

Not only, then, is it a moral duty of companies to respect the rights and dignity of their employees, in particular by acknowledging their civil liberties and guaranteeing them due process, but doing so can also work to the company's benefit by enhancing employee morale and, thus, the company's competitive performance. Hence, there is little basis for the widespread belief that efficient management is incompatible with a fair workplace environment. Of course, a company that does not sincerely consider employee rights of inherent moral importance is not likely to reap the benefits of enhanced business performance. Employees can tell the difference between a company that has a genuine regard for their welfare and a company that only pretends to have moral concern.

An example is Pacific Bell, which has won high marks for its humane response to the AIDS problem. With its strong emphasis on two-way commitment and loyalty, Pacific Bell has never considered revoking the medical coverage of employees with AIDS, as some companies have done. (The lifetime cost of medical treatment for an AIDS victim can easily run to six digits.) Pacific Bell has committed itself to keeping employees with AIDS on the job. "They need to keep working," says Pacific

Bell's Tim O'Hara. "It gives them a reason to stay alive." And the company's executive director of human resources, Jim Henderson, says bluntly, "People with AIDS are sick. We don't fire sick people." The company has also been visible in various AIDS initiatives and innovative in its AIDS education efforts. And this from a company that had an antihomosexual policy as recently as 1976.[13]

So far this chapter has affirmed that the workplace should provide an environment in which employees are treated fairly and their inherent dignity respected, and it has argued that doing so can be perfectly compatible with a firm's business goals. Although important, these points are generalities. They do not provide much guidance for dealing with the specific moral issues and dilemmas that arise day in and day out on the job. The remainder of this chapter and the chapter that follows take a closer look at some of these issues.

PERSONNEL POLICIES AND PROCEDURES

People make up organizations, and how an organization impinges on the lives of its own members is a morally important matter. One obvious and very important way organizational conduct affects the welfare and rights of employees and potential employees is through personnel policies and procedures — that is, how the organization handles the hiring, firing, paying, and promoting of the people who work for it. These procedures and policies structure an organization's basic relationship with its employees. This section looks at some of the morally relevant concerns to which any organization must be sensitive.

Hiring

A basic task of the employer or personnel manager is hiring. Employers generally seek to hire people who will enhance efficiency or promote other goals of the organization. Fur-

thermore, the courts have used the principle of negligent hiring to broaden the liability of an employer for damage or injury caused by its employees — even after regular hours and away from the job site. For instance, Avis Rent-A-Car was required to pay $800,000 after a male employee raped a female employee; the jury found that the company had been negligent in hiring the man without thoroughly investigating his background.[14] In making hiring decisions, though, employers must be careful to treat job applicants fairly. As you might imagine, determining the fair thing to do is not always easy. One useful way to approach some of the moral aspects of hiring is to examine the principal steps involved in the process: screening, testing, and interviewing.

Screening. When firms recruit employees, they attempt to screen them — that is, to attract only those applicants who have a good chance of qualifying for the job. When done properly, screening ensures a pool of competent candidates and guarantees that everyone has been dealt with fairly. But when screening is done improperly, it undermines effective recruitment and invites injustices into the hiring process.

Screening begins with a job description and specification. A *job description* lists all pertinent details about a job, including its duties, responsibilities, working conditions, and physical requirements. A *job specification* describes the qualifications an employee needs, such as skills, educational experience, appearance, and physical attributes. Completeness is important. When either the job description or job specification is inadequate or unspecific, firms risk injuring candidates. Suppose, for example, candidate Rita Cox takes a day off from work and travels 200 miles at her own expense to be interviewed for a position as a computer programmer with Singleton Computer Company. During the interview, Cox discovers that Singleton needs someone with an IBM background, not the Sperry Rand background she has. Mention of that detail in the job specification could have prevented Cox's loss of time and money. But even when specifications don't directly injure candidates, as in this case, they can cause indirect injury by depriving candidates of information they need to make informed decisions about their job prospects.

Since Congress passed the Americans with Disabilities Act (ADA) in 1990, employers must be careful not to screen out disabled applicants who have the capacity to carry out the job. The ADA is intended, among other things, to protect the rights of people with disabilities to obtain gainful employment, and it forbids employers from discriminating against disabled employees or job applicants when making employment decisions. Employers must also make "reasonable accommodations" for an employee or job applicant with a disability as long as this doesn't inflict "undue hardship" on the business.

In addition, of course, the law has long forbidden discrimination against individuals on the basis of age, race, national origin, religion, or sex, and these are items that generally should never appear in job specifications or recruitment advertisements, nor should they figure in hiring. Consideration of such factors typically excludes job candidates on non-job-related grounds. Job specifications that are blatantly discriminatory—for instance, "help wanted: male" or "over 60"—are illegal. Firms must also be very careful about job specifications that more subtly discriminate—for example, "young person preferred" or "excellent opportunity for college student." Employers should eliminate such specifications from advertisements, not only because they are probably illegal, but also because they discourage qualified applicants from applying. Most organizations these days try to avoid gender-linked job terminology as well. The terms "salesperson," "mail carrier," and "bartender" are more inclusive than

"salesman," "mailman," and "barman." An alternative is to use terms denoting both sexes ("waiter/waitress").[15]

Bona fide occupational qualifications, or BFOQs, are job specifications to which the civil rights law does not apply. But BFOQs are very limited in scope. There are no BFOQs for race or color, and in the case of sex, BFOQs exist only to allow for authenticity (a male model) and modesty (a woman for a women's locker room attendant).[16] In validating job specifications, firms are not permitted to rely on the preferences of their customers as a reason for discriminatory employment practices. For example, the fact that for decades airline passengers were accustomed to being attended to by young female stewards and may even have preferred them could not legally justify excluding men from this occupation. Bilingual ability (English-Spanish, English-Vietnamese) may be a justifiable job specification in some areas of the country, where such skills can be essential for successful job performance. But employers need to be aware of the danger of creating unnecessary specifications for a position, especially if they unfairly discriminate on the basis of national origin.

The ability to communicate effectively in English is a common workplace requirement, but it can seriously impede the employment prospects of some workers—Hispanics, in particular. As a result, the Equal Employment Opportunity Commission (EEOC) is scrutinizing ever more closely employers' language requirements to see if there is a nondiscriminatory business reason for them. In addition, it has ruled in several cases that disqualifying a job applicant because the applicant has a pronounced foreign accent is unlawful national origin bias unless it can be proved that the accent would hinder the job seeker's ability to perform the job.[17] On the other hand, the U.S. Court of Appeals in San Francisco determined that a heavy Filipino accent was a legitimate basis for rejecting an applicant for a job at a state department of motor vehicles office that required dealing with the public, even though the plaintiff had scored higher than all other candidates on a written examination. And in a Texas case, a Vietnamese immigrant was lawfully rejected for the position of energy conservation inspector because of an inadequate oral command of English. The job involved explaining local law to building owners, evaluating their use of light, air, and water, and helping them devise an acceptable conservation plan. The position required constant dialogue with various people, many of whom, in the court's words, were "unaccustomed to the peculiarities of the plantiff's speech."[18]

Ill-considered educational requirements are also potentially objectionable. Requiring more formal education than a job demands is not fair to candidates or the firm. Yet increasingly employers are arbitrarily erecting an inflated educational barrier to employment. The thinking seems to be: "If I can get someone with at least two years of college (or a college degree, or postgraduate training), then why not?" An inflated educational requirement thins out the field of applicants, thereby reducing recruitment costs. But if the education requirement exceeds job demands, then can it be called relevant? Not only are candidates who don't meet the bogus requirement denied equal consideration, but one of them may be the best person for the job. Thus, the firm, as well as the "undereducated" applicant, stands to lose. Beyond this, companies may be inviting considerable frustration for themselves and the employee when the job does not challenge the worker's educational preparation.

The other side of the coin is to deny an applicant job consideration because he or she is "overqualified." Certainly, some candidates are by education or experience overqualified for jobs. To avoid the personal and organizational frustrations that often result from hiring overqualified people, companies are justified in raising the issue. But "raising the issue" is different from assuming that because on paper an applicant appears overqualified the applicant necessarily spells trouble for the company. The fact is that the employment ranks are filled with people successfully doing jobs for which they are technically overqualified.

One additional matter. As traditional gender roles change, more and more men are leaving the work world for personal reasons, such as to help raise children while their wives complete professional training. More often than not, when these men try to return to work they are thwarted. Employers assume that, since the man once quit work for personal reasons, he may very well do so again. Thus, discontinuity of employment is cutting some men off from job consideration, as it traditionally has for women.

"The hurdles men face returning to the job market are about three times greater" than those faced by women, says Charles Arons, president and chief executive officer for Casco Industries, a Los Angeles–based employment and recruiting firm. "There isn't a male I know of in an executive position who would accept raising kids as a legitimate excuse for not working for three years."[19]

Thomas Schumann, director of selection and placement for Dayton-based Mead Corporation, agrees. "If other qualified candidates are available," he says, "my guess is that a personnel manager would go with somebody who doesn't raise that question."[20]

Certainly, employers in highly technical, rapidly changing fields are warranted in suspecting that an individual's hiatus may have left him (or her) out of touch. But to automatically disqualify a candidate on the basis of deliberately chosen career interruption raises a question of fairness.

Tests.   Testing is an integral part of the hiring process, especially with large firms. Tests are generally designed to measure the applicant's verbal, quantitative, and logical skills. Aptitude tests help determine job suitability; skill tests measure the applicant's proficiency in specific areas, such as typing and shorthand; personality tests help determine the applicant's maturity and sociability. In addition, some firms engaged in the design and assembly of precision equipment administer dexterity tests to determine how nimbly applicants can use their hands and fingers.

To be successful, a test must be valid. *Validity* refers to the quality of measuring precisely what a test is designed to determine. Just as important, tests must be reliable. *Reliability* refers to the quality of exhibiting a reasonable consistency in results obtained. Clearly not all tests are both valid and reliable. Many tests are not able to measure desired qualities, and others exhibit a woefully low level of forecast accuracy. Some companies use tests that haven't been designed for the company's particular situation.

Legitimizing tests can be an expensive and time-consuming project. But if tests are used, the companies using them are obliged to ensure their validity and reliability. Otherwise, companies risk injuring applicants, stockholders, and even the general public. At the same time, companies must be cautious about the importance they place on such tests, because a test is only one measure in an overall evaluative process. Ignoring these things, firms can easily introduce injustices into the hiring process.

Even when tests are valid and reliable, they can be unfair. For example, people who have studied intelligence tests contend that they favor white, middle-class test takers, because the questions contain points of reference that this group relates to well as a result of their cultural and educational background. For ghetto-raised blacks, however, the tests can be as mystifying as if they were composed in a foreign language, because they don't relate to black culture. As a result, such tests can measure one's mastery of cultural assumptions more than one's intellectual capacity or potential. This was precisely the issue when, in July 1963, a young black man named Leon Myart applied for a job as an analyzer and phaser at Motorola's plant in Franklin Park, Illinois.

After Myart had filled out an application form, he was given General Ability Test No. 10, a test designed to measure candidates' abilities to acquire technical information by evaluating their verbal comprehension and simple reasoning skills. Myart scored four, two points below the minimum requirement. As a result, the personnel department gave Myart no further tests. He was briefly interviewed and dismissed, the entire process taking about fifteen minutes.

Myart, who had extensive background in electronics, sued Motorola, charging discrimination in its hiring practices. He claimed that Test No. 10 was discriminatory because it did not take trainability into account and because it tested for education and skills that were not actually needed on the job or that could easily be learned or conpensated for by other skills. On March 14, 1966, the Supreme Court of Illinois found Motorola innocent of discrimination in its hiring practices. But the court never decided whether Test No. 10 was biased.

In 1971, however, the United States Supreme Court took a decisive stand on testing in the case of *Griggs* v. *Duke Power Company*. The case involved thirteen black laborers who were denied promotions because they scored low on a company-sponsored intelligence test involving verbal and mathematical puzzles. In its decision, the Court found that the Civil Rights Act prohibits employers from requiring a high school education or the passing of a general intelligence test as a prerequisite for employment or promotion without demonstrable evidence that the associated skills relate directly to job performance. The *Griggs* decision makes it clear that, if an employment practice like testing has an adverse impact (or unequal effect) on groups protected by the Civil Rights Act, then the burden of proof is on the employer to show the job-relatedness or business necessity of the test or other procedure. Duke Power Company couldn't do this.

In the aftermath of *Griggs* and other cases, many American firms retreated from administering preemployment tests because of doubts about their legal validity. In recent years, though, testing has made a comeback in both the public and private sectors.[21] Extensive testing, for example, is standard procedure for Japanese employers operating in the United States, some of whom require job applicants to undergo as much as fourteen hours of testing, while others give probable hires forty hours of preemployment training without pay, which is a way of determining the ability of applicants to perform the job. Management, of course, is seeking through testing to gain a potentially more productive group of workers whose skills match more closely the requirements of their jobs. In addition, many applicants prefer the objectivity of tests to the subjectivity of job interviews. But most experts believe that even the best tests cannot be a substitute for face-to-face interviews.

Interviews.   When moral issues arise in interviewing, they almost always relate to the manner in which the interview was conducted. The literature of personnel management rightly cautions against rudeness, coarseness, hostility, and condescension in interviewing job applicants. In guarding against these qualities, personnel managers would do well to focus on the humanity of the individuals who sit across the desk from them, mindful of the very human need that has brought those people into the office. This is especially true when the interviewer might not otherwise identify closely with the person being interviewed because of cultural or other differences. Interviewers must exercise care to avoid thoughtless comments that may hurt or insult the person being interviewed — for instance, a passing remark about a person's physical disability or personal situation (a single parent, for instance). A comment that an unthinking interviewer might consider innocent or even friendly could be distressing to the person sitting across the table.

Interviewers risk treating applicants unfairly when they are unaware of, forget, or ignore their own personal biases and stereotypes. The human tendency in interviewing is to like and prefer persons we identify with. Thus, Greg Tremont feels especially sympathetic to George Horner because Horner has recently graduated from Tremont's alma mater. As a result of this bias, of which he may not be fully aware, Tremont treats Horner preferentially, thereby harming both other applicants and his firm.

Roland Wall, a job placement counselor for the disabled, describes taking a developmentally disabled client, with an I.Q. of about 70, for a job interview. The personnel manager emerged from the room in which Wall's client was taking an initial test along with several other job applicants. The personnel manager asked Wall where his client was and was amazed to learn that she had gone in along with the others for testing. "Really?" he said. "I didn't see one in there." This personnel manager is probably more sensitive about the disabled than many employers, given his willingness to interview Wall's client. Yet he assumed that because she was mentally retarded, the applicant would look a certain way — would look like "one."[22]

Although everyone suffers from conscious and unconscious biases and stereotypes, interviewers should strive to free themselves as much as possible from these "idols of the mind," as the English philosopher Francis Bacon (1561–1626) called them. As Bacon put it: "The human understanding is like a false mirror, which, receiving rays irregularly, distorts and discolors the nature of things by mingling its own nature with it."[23] In short, we view things, people included, through the lens of our own preconceptions. It's true that Bacon's remarks concerned scientific method, but his observations seem appropriate here as well. For failing to heed Bacon's "idols," interviewers can easily sacrifice the objectivity that both the nature of their jobs and fairness require of them.

Promotions

In theory, the same essential criterion that applies to hiring also applies to promotions: job qualifications. But like all generalizations about standards for decisions in the workplace, this one needs delimiting.

It's no secret that factors besides job qualifications often determine promotions. How long you've been with a firm, how well you're liked, whom you know, even when you were last promoted—all these influence promotions in the real business world. As with hiring, the key moral ideal here is fairness. Nobody would seriously argue that promoting the unqualified is fair or justifiable. It's a serious breach of duty to owners, employees, and ultimately the general public. But many reasonable people debate whether promoting by job qualification alone is the fairest thing to do. Are other criteria admissible? If so, when, and how much weight should those criteria carry? These are tough questions with no easy answers. To highlight the problem, consider seniority, inbreeding, and nepotism, three factors that sometimes serve as bases for promotions.

Seniority. *Seniority* refers to longevity on a job or with a firm. Frequently job transfers or promotions are made strictly on the basis of seniority; individuals with the most longevity automatically receive the promotions. But problems can occur with this promotion method.

Imagine that personnel manager Manuel Rodriguez needs to fill the job of quality-control supervisor. Carol Martin seems better qualified for the job than Jim Turner, except in one respect: Turner has been on the job for three years longer than Martin. Whom should Rodriguez promote to quality-control supervisor?

The answer isn't easy. Those who'd argue for Carol Martin—opponents of seniority—would undoubtedly claim that the firm has an obligation to fill the job with the most qualified person. In this way, the firm is served and the most qualified are rewarded. Those advancing Turner's promotion—proponents for seniority—would contend that the firm should be loyal to its senior employees, that it should reward them for faithful service. In this way, employees have an incentive to work hard and to remain with the firm.

When company policies indicate what part seniority should play in promotions and job transfers, the problem abates but does not vanish. We can still wonder about the morality of the policy itself. In cases where no clear policy exists, the problem begs for an answer.

The difficulty of the question is compounded by the fact that seniority in itself does not necessarily indicate competence or loyalty. Just because Jim Turner has been on the job three years longer than Carol Martin does not necessarily mean he is more competent or more loyal. Of course, in some instances seniority may be a real indicator of job qualifications. A pilot who has logged hundreds of hours of flying time with an airline is more qualified for captaincy than one who hasn't.

Then there's the question of employee expectations. If employees expect seniority to count substantially, management can injure morale and productivity by overlooking it. True, worker morale might suffer equally should seniority alone determine promotions. Ambitious and competent workers might see little point in refining skills and developing talents when positions are doled out strictly on a longevity basis.

It seems impossible, then, to say precisely what part, if any, seniority ought to play in promotions—all the more reason, therefore, for management to consider carefully its seniority policies. Of paramount importance in any decision is that management remember its twin responsibilities of promoting on the basis of qualifications and of recognizing prolonged and constructive contributions to the firm. A policy that provides for promotions strictly on the basis of qualifications seems heartless, whereas one that promotes by seniority alone seems mindless. The challenge for management is how to merge these dual responsibilities in a way that is beneficial to the firm and fair to all concerned.

Inbreeding.   All the cautions about seniority apply with equal force to *inbreeding*, the practice of promoting exclusively from within the firm. In theory, whenever managers must fill positions they should look only to competence. The most competent, whether within or without the firm, should receive the position. In this way responsibilities to owners are best served.

In practice, however, managers must seriously consider the impact of outside recruitment on in-house morale. Years of loyal service, often at great personal expense, invariably create a unique relationship between employer and employee and, with it, unique obligations of gratitude. The eighteen years that Becky Thompson has worked for National Textile creates a relationship between her and the firm that does not exist between the firm and an outsider it may wish to hire for the job Thompson seeks. Some would argue that management has a moral obligation to remember this loyalty when determining promotions, especially when outside recruitment departs from established policy.

Nepotism.   *Nepotism* is the practice of showing favoritism to relatives and close friends. Suppose a manager hired a relative strictly because of the relationship between them. Such an action would raise a number of moral concerns, chief among them disregard both of managerial responsibilities to the organization and of fairness to all other applicants.

Not all instances of nepotism raise serious moral concerns. For example, when a firm is strictly a family operation and has as its purpose providing work for family members, nepotistic practices are generally justified. Also, the fact that a person is a relative or friend of firm members should not automatically exclude him or her from job consideration. Nevertheless, even when such people are qualified for a position, responsible management must consider the impact of hiring relatives and friends of people inside the organization. Will the selection breed resentment and jealousy among other employees? Will it discourage qualified outsiders from seeking employment with the firm? Will it create problems in future placement, scheduling, or dismissal of the relative? Will it make the person an object of distrust and hostility within the organization?

It's worth noting that nepotism is by no means confined to business organizations. It can arise anywhere employers and employees come together. A few years ago, for example, a nationally syndicated columnist alleged widespread nepotism in hiring and promoting at the Los Alamos National Laboratory, the nuclear research facility in New Mexico. At about the same time, *U.S. News & World Report* ran an article on nepotism in the nation's labor unions. The article presented a compelling case for the claim that "some of the nation's largest and most powerful unions are run like family businesses, with relatives of high-ranking officers holding influential and often high-paying positions."[24]

Discipline and Discharge

For an organization to function in an orderly, efficient, and productive way, personnel departments establish guidelines for behavior based on such factors as appearance, punctuality, dependability, efficiency, and cooperation. This is not the place to examine the morality of specific rules and regulations, only the organization's treatment of employees when infractions occur.

At the outset, realize the managers are obliged to discipline workers who violate behavioral standards, because discipline is necessary for the good of the firm, other employees, and society at large. Most moral issues in this area relate to how the manager imposes the discipline. For example, it's one thing to speak with a person privately about some infraction and quite another to chastise or punish the person publicly. Also, trying to correct someone's behavior on a graduated basis, from verbal warning to dismissal, is different from firing someone for a first infraction. The point is that discipline, although desirable and necessary, raises concerns about fairness, noninjury, and respect for persons in the way it's administered. To create an atmosphere of fairness, one in which rules and standards are equally applied, the principles of just cause and due process must operate.

Just cause refers to reasons for discipline or discharge that deal directly with job performance. In general, whatever leads directly or indirectly to employee infractions of the job description may be considered a job-related reason. Thus, Charlie Whyte is justified in disciplining Phil Bruen for chronic tardiness but not for voting Republican.

Of course, the distinction between a job-related and nonrelated issue is not always so simple and can frequently be controversial. For example, if you are a pilot for American Airlines, you can have a protruding midsection, hefty thighs, sagging jowls, and a bulging bottom. It doesn't matter how you look, as long as you are in good health. But according to American's rule book, in order to have "an alert, efficient image," both male and female flight attendants must have "a firm, trim silhouette, free of bulges, rolls or paunches."[25]

In addition, how a person behaves outside work is often incompatible with the image a company wishes to project. Does the organization have a right to discipline its employees for off-the-job conduct? The answer depends largely on the legitimate extent of organizational influence over individual lives,

that is, on where precisely the company's legitimate interests stop and one's private life begins. Such concerns raise complex questions about privacy that are explored further in the next chapter.

The second principle related to fair worker discipline and discharge is *due process*, which refers to the fairness of the procedures an organization uses to impose sanctions on employees. Of particular importance is that the rules be clear and specific, that they be administered consistently and without discrimination or favoritism, and that workers who have violated them be given a fair and impartial hearing. Due process requires both the hearing of grievances and the setting up of a step-by-step procedure by which an employee can appeal a managerial decision. Where employees are unionized, such a procedure usually exists. Where no procedure exists, serious moral questions of fairness regarding employee discipline inevitably arise, because the worker has no way of appealing what may be unfair treatment.

All that has been said about discipline can also be applied to discharging employees. Four types of discharge can be distinguished. *Firing* is for-cause dismissal—the result of employee theft, gross insubordination, release of proprietary information, and so on. *Termination* results from an employee's poor performance—that is, from his or her failure to fulfill expectations. *Layoff* usually refers to hourly employees and implies that they are "subject to recall," while *position elimination* designates the permanent elimination of a job as a result of work-force reduction, plant closings, or departmental consolidation.[26]

Before dismissing an employee, it is important that management analyze carefully the reasons leading to this decision. The frequent success of wrongful termination suits highlights the need for a rational and unbiased decision-making process. The organization must ask itself if its treatment of the employee follows the appropriate procedures for that type of discharge, as those procedures are outlined in the employee handbook, collective bargaining agreement, or corporate policy statement. In addition, the company must guard against preferential treatment. Have there been employees who behaved in the same way but were not let go?

Even-handedness and strict compliance with established procedures may not guarantee fairness. For example, unless it is stated in the contract or employees have union representation, a company may not (depending on the type of case and where it occurs) be legally obligated to give reasons for firing an employee, and it may not be legally obligated to give advance notice. When employers terminate someone without notice or cause, they may have been strictly faithful to contractual agreement or customary policy, but have they been fair?

In answering this question, it's helpful to distinguish between two employer responsibilities. Employers bear the responsibility of terminating the employment of workers who don't discharge their contractual obligations, but they are also obliged to terminate these workers as painlessly as possible. In other words, although employers have the right to fire, this does not mean they have the right to fire however they choose. Because firing can be so materially and psychologically destructive to employees, management should take steps to ease its effects.

The literature on personnel management provides many suggestions for handling the discharge of employees more compassionately and humanely, ranging from the recommendation not to notify employees of termination on Fridays, birthdays, wedding anniversaries, or the day before a holiday to various steps to respect the terminated employee's privacy and dignity.[27] One obvious thing employers can do to ease the trauma of firing is to provide sufficient notice. Although a bill passed by Congress in 1988 requires companies to give sixty days' advance notice of plant closings, what constitutes sufficient

notice of termination or discharge still depends primarily on the nature of the job, the skill involved, the availability of similar jobs, and the longevity of employees. Where employers have reason to suspect that employees will react to notice of their terminations in a hostile, destructive way, "sufficient notice" might merely take the form of severance pay. Ideally, the length of notice should be spelled out in a work contract.

For most people who have to do it, firing a worker is painfully difficult, at times impossible. In part to help managers perform the dirty job of terminating, enlightened organizations are enlisting the services of displacement companies. For a fee, the displacement company sends in a counselor who assists the displaced employee to assess personal strengths and weaknesses, analyze the causes of the dismissal, and start planning a job search. This makes the distasteful task of firing a little more palatable than it would otherwise be. And to be sure, it protects the company from being sued by the seasoned, middle-aged executive who may feel trifled with. Self-serving interests notwithstanding, companies using displacement experts show more than imagination. They deserve recognition for their humanitarian attempt to ease the anguish of those who must fire and to help those terminated salvage both their interrupted careers and their self-respect.[28]

Today—with frequent plant shutdowns and relocations, sizable layoffs, and increasing automation—moral management requires careful study of responsibilities to workers in times of job elimination.[29] It is crucial to remember that termination of employment affects not only workers but their families and the larger community as well. It is impossible here to specify further what measures can or should be taken to ease the effects of displacement. Different circumstances suggest different approaches. In some instances, job retraining might be appropriate, together with adequate notice and sufficient severance pay.

Where mergers are involved, firms probably should notify workers well in advance and provide them with alternatives. Whatever the approach, the point remains that when firms terminate workers, serious moral questions regarding fair treatment arise.

Wages

Every employer faces the problem of setting wage rates and establishing salaries. From the moral point of view, it is very easy to say that firms should pay a fair and just wage, but what constitutes such a wage? So many variables are involved that no one can say with mathematical precision what a person should be paid for a job. The contribution to the firm, the market for labor and products, the competitive position of the company, the bargaining power of the firm and unions, seasonal fluctuations, and individual needs all conspire to make a simple answer impossible.

The impossibility of precisely determining a fair wage, however, does not mean that employers may pay workers anything they choose. In general, because work functions to fill human needs, employers should seek to pay a wage that significantly helps individuals satisfy their basic needs. Obviously, this directive is vague. A wage of significant help in one case may be rather meager in another. Moreover, various factors may impinge on the employer's ability to pay an ideal wage. But the issue of a fair wage is not as morally insoluble as it appears to be.

A number of factors bear on fairness, although none of them alone is enough to determine a fair wage. Indeed, all of them taken together can't guarantee it. But introducing these factors minimizes the chances of setting unfair wages and salaries and provides the well-intentioned business manager with some ethical guidelines.

1. *What is the law?* Federal law requires that businesses pay at least the minimum wage.

Even when a particular business is exempt from the law, this minimum can serve as a guide in setting wages. At the same time, of course, one can satisfy the minimum requirements of the law and still not act morally. Considering all factors involved, not just legislative guidelines, will help businesspeople set fair wages.

2. *What is the prevailing wage in the industry?* Although this factor is not foolproof, or even a moral barometer, the salaries given for similar positions in the industry can provide some direction for arriving at a fair wage.

3. *What is the community wage level?* This point recognizes that some communities have a higher cost of living than others. New York City, for example, is more expensive to live in than St. Louis. The cost of living relates to basic maintenance needs and must be considered very seriously in establishing a wage. To ignore the cost of living would be to seriously jeopardize worker welfare.

4. *What is the nature of the job itself?* Some jobs require more training, experience, and education than others. Some are physically or emotionally more demanding. Some jobs are downright dangerous, others socially undesirable. Risky or unskilled jobs often attract the least educated and the most desperate for work, thus occasioning worker exploitation. Although it is impossible to draw a precise correlation between the nature of the job and what someone should be paid, a relationship exists that must be taken into account.

5. *Is the job secure? What are its prospects?* Employment that promises little or no security fails to fulfill a basic need of employees. In such cases employers should seek to compensate workers for this deprivation through higher pay, better fringe benefits, or both. On the other hand, a secure

job with a guarantee of regular work and excellent retirement benefits (like a civil service position) may justify a more moderate wage. In addition, a relatively low salary may be acceptable for a job that is understood to be a stepping stone to better positions inside the organization.

6. *What are the employer's financial capabilities?* What can the organization afford to pay? A company's profit margin may be so narrow that it cannot afford to pay higher than a minimum wage. Another's may be so large that it can easily afford to pay more than it does.

7. *What are other employees inside the organization earning for comparable work?* In order to avoid discrimination and unfairness in setting wage rates, it is important to look at what the organization is already paying its present employees for work of a similar nature. Gross salary disparities that are not warranted by the nature of the work, the experience required, or other objective considerations can also hurt employee morale.

Guidelines 6 and 7 have recently come to the fore as more employees are scrutinizing the benefits and perks paid to top management, especially in lean times. Thus, when a cash-squeezed United Press International recently asked unionized workers for a 90-day, 35 percent wage reduction, union officials said they would comply only if an equal cut for managers were in place and no bonuses were awarded to executives. And employees joined shareholders in outrage when Commodore International's CEO, Irving Gold, received a 40 percent pay raise in 1989 while his company's profits plunged 97 percent. In fact, Gould's cash salary of $1,750,000 was higher than Commodore's net income for the year.[30]

Of equal importance with guidelines 1 through 7 is how the wage figure was arrived at. To a large extent, a fair wage presupposes a fair work contract, and the fairness of a work contract demands consideration of how the contract was wrought. Was it arbitrarily imposed? Did management unilaterally draw up a contract and present it to workers on a take-it-or-leave-it basis? Or was the contract arrived at through mutual consent of employer and employee? Answering these questions will help to determine the fairness of a contract and, by implication, the fairness of the wage.

Invariably the fairness of a work contract hinges on free and fair negotiations, which exhibit several characteristics. Fair negotiations must be representative of the interests of those persons directly concerned and sometimes of persons indirectly concerned. All parties should enjoy the freedom to express themselves openly without coercion or fear of reprisal. And they should operate in good faith, carefully avoiding the use of fraud, deceit, power, or institutional blackmail in effecting agreements.

In sum, a consideration of the factors upon which a wage is based and of the procedure that was followed in establishing the wage usually determines the fairness of the wage, which is the primary moral concern in discussions about wages. Establishing fair wages enhances the work environment by removing a potential cause of job dissatisfaction. Just as important, fair wages go a long way toward helping management discharge its responsibilities to employees.

UNIONS

This chapter and the next are concerned with a number of moral issues that arise in the context of employer-employee relations, but no discussion of the workplace should overlook one of the basic institutions structuring employer-employee relations, determining the terms and conditions of employment, and shaping the environment in which people work—namely, unions. Accordingly, this section briefly examines the history and

economic role of unions, the ideals that motivate them, and some of the moral dilemmas
they raise.

History of the Union Movement

Many economists and students of the
union movement give it primary credit for
raising the standard of living and increasing
the security of working people in this country.
They argue that almost all the benefits enjoyed by employees today, whether they happen to be in unions or not, can be traced back
to union victories or to union-backed legislation. At the same time, the higher wages, benefits, and increased security that unions have
brought have, in turn, contributed to social
stability in the country and, through enhanced demand, to economic growth itself.
Yet, as the history of the labor movement reveals, unionization and union demands have,
with few exceptions, been opposed at every
step of the way by employers—and often with
violence.

Just as the roots of capitalism can be
traced to the handicraft guilds, so the earliest
efforts of American unionism can be found in
the craft unions of the eighteenth century.[31]
At that time, groups of skilled artisans—car-
penters, shoemakers, tailors, and the like—
formed secret societies for two basic reasons:
to equalize their relationship with their employers and to "professionalize" their crafts.
They agreed on acceptable wages and working hours and pledged not to work for any
employer who didn't provide them, and they
set minimal admission standards for their
crafts. They also agreed to keep their allegiance secret—and for good reason. If found
out they would be fired, and if discovered trying to cause a strike they could be jailed.

Labor historians generally consider the
Knights of Labor (K of L), established in 1869,
the first truly national trade union. What distinguished the K of L from previous craft
unions was that it assembled in one labor or-

ganization both skilled and unskilled workers
from an industry. Although this arrangement
gave the organization the strength of numbers, it also created resentment among the
skilled workers, who viewed the unskilled as
inferior and therefore unworthy of their association. Friction and destructive rivalries also
broke out between the organization's more
radical national leadership and its more conservative local directors. Public sentiment,
although never wildly supportive, turned
sharply against unions in the wake of the
Chicago Haymarket Riot in 1886, in which a
bomb was lobbed into a group of police trying
to halt a labor rally. Compounding the fledg-
ling union's problems was a sour national
economy that left workers fearing for their
jobs and avoiding any entanglements that
might land them among the growing ranks of
the unemployed. In any event, between 1885
and 1890 K of L membership plummeted from
700,000 to 100,000.

But while the K of L was tottering, a new
union was being born. In 1886 the American
Federation of Labor (AFL) was founded. Within seven years, under the astute and temper-
ate leadership of Samuel Gompers, it built a
membership of 500,000, which increased to
about 2 million by 1917. Curiously, the survival and prosperity of the AFL must be attributed in no small measure to business itself.
Fearing the radical and revolutionary tendencies of the Industrial Workers of the World (the
"Wobblies"), business embraced Gompers's
union as the lesser of the evils.

The cause of unionism was significantly
advanced in 1935 with the passage of the National Labor Relations Act (also called the
Wagner Act). This legislation prohibited employers from interfering with employees trying to organize unions, from attempting to
gain control over labor unions, from treating
union workers differently from nonunion
workers, and from refusing to bargain with
union representatives. The act helped increase union membership to almost 12 million

by the end of World War II in 1945. Most of these members belonged to the Congress of Industrial Organizations (CIO), an offshoot of the AFL that brought together various workers—auto, sheet metal, steel, and so on—into industry-wide unions. The distinct advantage of the CIO over the AFL was that its unions could call a firm's entire work force out on strike, rather than just its skilled workers.

But increasing union strength also brought public suspicions and fears of union power. Many businesspeople and political critics encouraged these worries and quickly pointed to the wave of strikes after World War II as evidence of union abuse of power. In 1947 a newly elected Republican Congress passed the Taft-Hartley Act, which amended the National Labor Relations Act. The new act outlawed the closed shop (where a person must be a member of the union before being hired); Section 14(b) permitted individual states to outlaw union shops (where a person must join the union within a specified time after being hired). Today, some twenty-one states, mostly in the South and West, are so-called "right-to-work" states, with "open shop" laws on their books. These laws prohibit union contracts requiring all employees on a job site to pay union dues or their equivalent, once hired. The Taft-Hartley Act also prohibits various labor practices designated as "unfair," such as sympathy strikes and secondary boycotts.

Since the merging of the AFL and CIO in 1955, unions have attempted to increase membership by recruiting outside basic industry—for example, in education, government, white-collar professions, and service jobs. But they have been only moderately successful. Between 1968 and 1978, for instance, union membership increased by 2 million, while the work force itself swelled by 20 million. Since then, union membership has been falling, both absolutely and as a percentage of the work force. In 1979 unions could claim

20.9 million members and 24.1 percent of American employees; figures released in 1991 show 10.2 million union workers in private industry or 12.1 percent of the nongovernment work force (with an additional 6.5 million unionized government workers).[32] Thus, the present rate of union membership is a fraction of what it was in 1947, when the Taft-Hartley Act was passed. Union membership as a percentage of the work force is also substantially lower in the United States than it is in most Western nations—for instance, Australia, Belgium, France, Japan, the Netherlands, Germany, and the United Kingdom.

In recent years, unions have been more and more on the defensive, as the industries in which they have been traditionally based have declined. In 1990 the number of days lost to strikes, for instance, tied the record low set in 1988, and in the past decade many unions have been forced to go along with decreases in wages and benefits. Many corporate managements have become increasingly and aggressively anti-union. In 1983, for example, Frank Lorenzo's Continental Airlines voluntarily filed for bankruptcy, reneged on its labor contracts, sliced its pay scales in half, and then kept on flying.[33]

Or take the Pittston Company, the second-largest exporter of coal in the United States. In February 1988 it withdrew from the Bituminous Coal Operators' Association, which negotiates contracts with the United Mine Workers for the entire coal industry. The Pittston workers remained on their jobs even though they were without a contract and unable to get new contract talks going with the company. Pittston's production had gone up 72 percent in the preceding four years and the company had turned an overall profit of $48.6 million in 1988, but it was evidently determined to destroy the union. To do this, it first needed to provoke its workers into a strike. This it finally did in April 1989—in part, by cutting off at one stroke medical benefits for widows, retirees, and disabled miners.[34]

The general political and legal climate has been unfavorable to labor in recent years. President Reagan set the anti-union tone of the 1980s when he fired striking air traffic controllers in 1981 and broke their union. The union had been considered powerful, but it was soundly defeated. President Reagan prevailed because the controllers are federal employees and are forbidden by law from striking. More recently, however, the Supreme Court has allowed private employers to "replace permanently" workers who strike, despite the fact that the 1935 Wagner Act makes it illegal for employers to punish workers who go on strike by "firing" them.[35]

Whatever the terminology, if workers risk losing their jobs because of a strike, then the balance of power in collective bargaining is dramatically altered. Instead of negotiating in good faith, a company can now provoke a strike, hire new workers to replace the pickets, and cut costs. And management has done exactly this in recent strikes at Greyhound and at the *New York Daily News*. In the latter case, the Tribune Company, which then owned the *Daily News* and had broken three unions in a strike at the *Chicago Tribune* in 1986, spent a year preparing for a strike in New York. The company retained a Nashville law firm renowned for its union-busting activities, recruited and trained nonunion workers to produce a strike-breaking newspaper, and then in October 1990 forced the unions at the *Daily News* into calling a strike by locking out the paper's unionized delivery truck drivers.[36]

Richard Edwards and Michael Podgursky sum up labor's current situation this way:

> Bargaining structures built up over many years are crumbling and collapsing. . . . Rising product market competition, deregulation, and technological changes; adverse labor force dynamics; worsening public policy; and the legacy of the long stagnation have thrust the labor movement into a qualitatively new stage. This new period is characterized . . . by: (a) greater corporate mobility, power, and militancy; (b) ineffective labor law and a growing indifference, and in some cases, outright opposition of the government towards organized labor and collective bargaining; and (c) a waning belief in unions as the agents of working class interests. In these hostile circumstances, American unions face a difficult and troubling future.[37]

Union Ideals

From the beginning, unions have been driven by an attempt to protect workers from abuses of power at the hands of employers. This effort is based on the indisputable premise that employers have tremendous power over individual workers. They can hire and fire, relocate and reassign, set work hours and wages, create rules and work conditions. Acting individually, a worker rarely is an employer's equal in negotiating any of these items. The position of most workers acting independently is further weakened by their lack of capital, occupational limitations, and personal and family needs. Furthermore, while employers obviously need workers, they rarely need any particular worker. They can, generally speaking, select whomever they want, for whatever reasons they choose. In these respects, then, the employer-employee relationship is no more equal than the master-slave.

Interestingly, Adam Smith himself recognized this fundamental imbalance in his classic *The Wealth of Nations*. Regarding the respective bargaining power of workers and their "masters," or employers, he wrote that "upon all ordinary occasions" employers "have the advantage in the dispute, and force the other into a compliance with their terms."

> The masters, being fewer in number, can combine much more easily. . . . We have no acts of parliament against combining to lower the price of work; but many against combining to raise it. In all such

disputes the masters can hold out much longer. . . . Though they did not employ a single workman, [employers] could generally live a year or two upon the stocks which they have already acquired. Many workmen could not subsist a week, few could subsist a month, and scarce any a year without employment. In the long-run the workman may be as necessary to his master as his master is to him, but the necessity is not so immediate.[38]

In an attempt, then, to redress the balance of power in their dealings with employers, workers band together. In acting as a single body, a union, workers in effect make employers dependent on them in a way that no individual worker can. The result is partly based on mutual dependence. And this rough equality serves as a basis for collective bargaining — negotiations between the representatives of organized workers and their employers over things such as wages, hours, rules, work conditions, and, increasingly, participation in decisions affecting the workplace.

Certainly no one can object to unionism's initial and overriding impulse: to protect workers from abuse and give them a voice in matters that affect their lives. Indeed, these two purposes are specifications of two lofty moral ideals: noninjury and autonomy. Curiously, it is out of respect for these ideals that some individuals criticize modern unions.

The critics argue that union shops infringe on the autonomy and right of association of individual workers. Even if workers are not required to join the union, but only to pay some equivalent to union dues, the critics contend that this still infringes on their freedom. In addition, evidence suggests that companies in alliance with unions sometimes treat nonunion personnel less favorably than union members. Some workers have gone to court to argue that favoritism to union members is discriminatory and unlawful (see Case 6.4). Whether or not it is, it certainly raises a

moral question about the right to determine for oneself organizational membership and participation.

Taking the union's viewpoint reveals competing ideals and other consequences that must be considered. First, there is organized labor's ideal of solidarity, which is vital to collective bargaining and to winning worker equality. Union proponents point to the fact that per capita personal income is higher in states with free collective bargaining than in right-to-work states. In 1985, for example, of twenty right-to-work states, only Nevada and Virginia had personal incomes above the national average.

Second, there is a question of fairness. Is it fair for a nonunion member to enjoy the benefits often won by the union at great personal and organizational expense? This question arises most forcefully where unions are attempting to establish an "agency shop," in which all employees must pay union dues but are not required to join the union. The agency shop is designed to eliminate "free riders" while respecting the worker's freedom of choice. Opponents claim that an agency shop does not so much eliminate free riders as create "forced passengers."

Enforcement Tactics

The tactics unions employ to enforce their demands on management also raise moral issues.

Direct Strikes. The legal right to strike is labor's most potent tool in labor-management negotiations. A strike occurs when an organized body of workers withholds its labor to force the employer to comply with its demands. Since strikes can cause financial injuries to both employer and employee, inconvenience and perhaps worse to consumers, and economic dislocations in society, they always raise serious moral questions. On the other hand, sometimes workers cannot obtain justice and fair play in the workplace in any other way. Austin Fagothey and Milton A. Gonsalves suggest the following conditions of a justified strike:[39]

1. *Just cause.* "Just cause" refers to job-related matters. Certainly, inadequate pay, excessive hours, and dangerous and unhealthful working conditions are legitimate worker grievances and provide just cause for a strike. Revenge, personal ambition, petty jealousies, and the like do not constitute just cause and thus cannot justify a strike.

2. *Proper authorization.* For a strike to be justified it must spring from proper authorization. This means, first, that workers themselves must freely reach the decision without coercion and intimidation. Second, if the workers are organized, then the proposed strike must receive union backing (although this condition becomes difficult to apply when the local union chapter and the national organization don't see eye-to-eye).

3. *Last resort.* To be justified a strike must come as a last resort. This condition acknowledges the serious potential harm of strikes. A basic moral principle is that we should always use the least injurious means available to accomplish the good we desire. Since there is an array of collective-bargaining tactics that can and usually do achieve worker objectives, all these should be exhausted before a strike is called.

Simply because a strike is justified, however, does not mean that any manner of implementing it is morally justified. Peaceful picketing and an attempt by striking workers to publicize their cause and peacefully persuade others not to cross the picket line typically are considered moral means of striking. Physical violence, threats, intimidation, and sabotage are not. More controversially, Fagothey and Gonsalves argue that if workers have the right to withhold their labor and strike, then employers have a right to fill their jobs with other workers but not professional strikebreakers, whose presence incites violence and whose function extends beyond doing work to denying strikers justice and the right to organize.

The preceding observations deal with direct strikes — that is, cessation of work by employees with the same industrial grievance. There is, however, another kind of strike, far more controversial than the direct strike: the sympathetic strike.

Sympathetic Strikes. A sympathetic strike occurs when workers who have no particular grievance of their own and who may or may not have the same employer decide to strike in support of others. The bigger unions become and the more diverse the workers they count among their members, the more likely are sympathetic strikes aimed at different employers. Indeed, the sympathetic strike can take on global proportions, as when American dockside workers refused to unload Russian freighters to show support of the Solidarity movement in Poland.

Sometimes the sympathetic strike involves several groups of workers belonging to different unions but employed by the same individuals or company. Acting on a grievance, one group strikes. But because it is so small, it enlists the aid of the other groups; it asks them to engage in a sympathetic strike. Cases like these do not seem to differ in any morally significant way from direct strikes. Indeed, it could be argued that the affiliated groups have obligations of loyalty and beneficence to join the strike. It is true, of course, that the sympathetic strikers do not have personal grievances, but they do have the same unjust employer, and they are in a unique position to help remedy that injustice by withholding their labor.[40]

Sympathetic strikes involving groups of employees working for different employers differ in several morally significant ways from the direct strike or the sympathetic strike against the same employer. Many of the employers being struck out of sympathy may be perfectly innocent victims whose treatment of workers is beyond reproach. They have lived up to their end of the work contract, only to have their workers repudiate theirs.

On the other hand, such sympathetic strikes can be very effective. J.P. Stevens & Co., the second-largest company in the U.S. textile industry, fought unionization for decades. They engaged in a variety of flagrantly unfair labor practices and refused to recognize or bargain collectively with the union, despite various court orders to do so.[41] During the boycott of J.P. Stevens products, United Auto Workers members at a General Motors plant in Canada refused to install J.P. Stevens carpeting in the cars, thus shutting down the assembly line. In less than half a day, J.P. Stevens carpeting was gone from the plant. Had U.S. workers done something similar, both they and the textile workers union would have been subject to legal action, but J.P. Stevens would not have been able to refuse to bargain as long as it did.

Boycotts and "Corporate Campaigns."

Besides strikes, unions also employ boycotts to support their demands. A primary boycott occurs when union members and their supporters refuse to buy products from a company being struck. A secondary boycott occurs when people refuse to patronize companies that handle products of struck companies. Although the Taft-Hartley Act prohibits secondary boycotts, they still occur when unions urge shoppers not to buy from stores that purchase products from companies being struck.

The express purpose of any boycott is the same as a strike: to hurt the employer or company financially and thus enforce union demands. In general, a boycott is justifiable when it meets the same conditions as a strike. In the case of the secondary boycott, which is like a sympathetic strike, the damage is extended to those whose only offense may be that they are handling the products of the unjust employer—and perhaps they are handling them out of financial necessity. In such cases, Fagothey and Gonsalves reject secondary boycotts. But this assessment seems too automatic and doesn't allow us to weigh the likely harms and benefits in particular cases.[42]

A relatively new pressure tactic is the so-called "corporate campaign," in which unions enlist the cooperation of a company's creditors to pressure the company to unionize or comply with union demands. The tactic first gained national recognition in 1974 after it was successfully used to help the Amalgamated Clothing & Textile Workers Union win contracts with Farah Manufacturing Company, a Texas-based men's garment maker. Union representatives persuaded retailers in Birmingham, Alabama, to stop selling the slacks by threatening them with a consumer boycott and then persuaded Farah's major creditors to "help mediate" the dispute.

A corporation campaign was also used with effect against J.P. Stevens. The company ultimately abandoned its battle against unionization when the union pressured banks and insurance companies to intervene. Among other pressures, union officials told banks and insurance companies that if they didn't intervene on the union's behalf, the union would withdraw deposits and cancel insurance policies.

In September 1984, officials of the United Steelworkers of America threatened a corporate campaign against Phelps Dodge Corporation, the nation's second-largest copper producer. Union spokespersons said they intended to consult with high-level officials of all major creditors of Phelps Dodge to persuade them to pressure the copper company to comply with union demands. If the creditors rejected the union's plans, union officials said they would consider withdrawing more than $250 million in bank deposits and get other major unions to follow suit.[43]

At the heart of the corporate campaign is the issue of corporate governance. In pressuring financial institutions with mass withdrawals and cancellations of policies, unions and administrators of public-employee pension funds are trying to exert an influence over institutional policy. And when the financial institutions accede to union demands, they effectively dictate to the recalcitrant company its policy with respect to unions. The harshest critics of the corporate campaign call it corporate blackmail. Its most enthusiastic champions view it as an effective way to get financial institutions and companies to become good corporate citizens. Such tactics, they say, are necessary at a time when legal sentiment seems to be running against unions.

SUMMARY

Each one read

1. Writers like David Ewing believe that too many corporations routinely violate the civil liberties of their employees. Historically, this authoritarianism stems from (a) the rise of professional management and personnel engineering and (b) the common-law doctrine that employees can be discharged without cause.

2. Some very successful companies have taken the lead in respecting employees' rights and human dignity. Corporate profits and efficient management are compatible with a fair workplace environment.

3. Fairness in personnel matters requires, at least, that policies, standards, and decisions affecting workers are directly job-related and are applied equally.

4. Incomplete or unspecific job descriptions can injure candidates by denying them information they need to reach informed occupational decisions.

5. Ordinarily, questions of sex, age, race, national origin, and religion are non-job-related and thus should not enter into personnel decisions. Educational requirements may also be non-job-related or unfair, as when employers require more formal education than a job demands or summarily disqualify a candidate for being "overqualified." Discrimination against the disabled is now expressly forbidden by law.

6. A test is valid if it measures precisely what it is designed to determine and reliable when it provides reasonably consistent results. Tests that lack either validity or reliability are unfair. Tests may also be unfair if they are culturally biased or if the performance they measure does not relate directly to job performance.

7. Most moral concerns in interviewing relate to how the interview is conducted. Interviewers should focus on the humanity of the candidate and avoid allowing their personal biases to color their evaluations.

8. A key issue in promotions is whether job qualification alone should determine who gets promoted. Seniority, or longevity on the job, is not necessarily a measure of either competency or loyalty. The challenge for management is to accommodate its twin responsibilities of promoting on the basis of qualifications and recognizing long-term contributions to the company.

9. Inbreeding, or promoting exclusively within the organization, presents challenges similar to those presented by seniority. Nepotism, showing favoritism to relatives or close friends, is not always objectionable, but it may overlook managerial responsibilities to the organization and may result in unfair treatment of other employees.

10. Most moral issues in employee discipline and discharge concern how management carries out these unpleasant tasks. Due process and just cause must operate if treatment is to be fair. Due process re-

quires that there be procedures for workers to appeal discipline and discharge. To ease the trauma associated with discharge, employers should provide sufficient warning, severance pay, and perhaps displacement counseling.

11. The factors that bear on the fairness of wages include the law, the prevailing wage in the industry, the community wage level, the nature of the job, the security of the job, the company's financial capabilities, and the wages it is paying other employees for comparable work. Especially important is the manner in which the wage is established. Fairness requires a legitimate work contract, one arrived at through free and fair negotiation.

12. Unions attempt to protect workers from abuse and give them a voice in matters that affect their lives. Critics charge that forcing workers to join unions infringes on autonomy and the right of association. They allege that union workers receive discriminatory and unlawful favoritism.

13. A direct strike is justified, argue some moral theorists, when there is just cause and proper authorization and when it is called as a last resort.

14. Sympathetic strikes involve the cessation of work in support of other workers with a grievance. When the companies involved are different, questions arise concerning possible injury and injustice to innocent employers, consumers, and workers.

15. Primary boycotts—refusing to patronize companies being struck—seem morally comparable to direct strikes. Secondary boycotts—refusing to patronize companies handling products of struck companies—are morally analogous to sympathetic strikes. In corporate campaigns, unions enlist the cooperation of a company's creditors to pressure the company to permit unionization or to comply with union demands.

CASE 6.1
Burger Beefs

When seventeen-year-old Wendy Hamburger applied for a summer job at a Wendy's Old Fashioned Hamburgers outlet near her Barrington, Illinois, home, she hoped to earn some money for college. But after working there for only three months, she quit when a manager threatened to fire her if she refused to work an extra shift on a holiday.

Wendy wasn't too upset about losing her job. "It seemed like the job cost me more than I made," she says. She does concede, however, that Wendy's International did pay her a little attention during her brief connection with the company. It used her to get a lot of free publicity in Chicago-area newspapers, and its president and founder, R. David

Thomas, mailed her an autographed photograph of himself, which presumably she didn't have to return when she quit.[44]

Actually, there's nothing atypical about Wendy's experience. Rock-bottom pay, unpleasant working conditions, and bossy bosses—all are familiar to the millions of teenage employees in the fast-food industry. Little wonder the average teen-age worker quits in disgust within four months of being hired.

Such rapid turnover would disembowel most businesses. Not so for those that peddle billions of burgers, fries, and shakes a year. For them, frequent turnover is the rank fodder for their multimillion-dollar operations, at least according to critics.

"The whole system is designed to have turnover," says Robert Harbrant, secretary-treasurer for the AFL-CIO Food and Beverage Trades Department in Washington, D.C. That way the industry averts pay increases and thwarts union efforts to organize workers.

Industry executives deny such nefarious motives. They point out, correctly, that for most youngsters a fast-food job is their first work experience. Such unseasoned workers usually are undisciplined and unreliable. No sooner are they trained, say fast-food executives, than they up and leave.

Harlow E. White, president of Systems for Human Resources, Inc., thinks otherwise. He publicly wonders whether the 300 percent annual turnover of fast-food workers is the cause or effect of industry operations. He suspects that "the industry has managed to manufacture a self-fulfilling prophecy: 'We're going to have turnover. And by God, we do.'" White points out that an abrupt decline in employment turnover would turn the industry on its head. But there's little chance of that happening. A survey conducted by White finds that one-third of management employees and a whopping four-fifths of hourly employees in the fast-food industry plan to bolt at the first opportunity.

Nevertheless, while admitting that the teen-age part-timer is crucial to fast-food success, industry officials insist that they do not purposely encourage turnover. "Turnover costs us money," asserts a spokesperson for Burger King, even while conceding that it doesn't take more than a day or two to train a new worker. He profiles the typical worker as a teen-age student wanting temporary part-time or summer work to earn some spending money.

Despite industry's declared good intentions, the White survey turns up widespread discontent among fast-food workers. A teen-age waitress in an Atlanta Steak n' Shake complains that she is scheduled for a two-hour weekday, although it takes her that much time to make a round-trip from home to work.

(A company official says this is a management problem, that the policy of Steak n' Shake is to pay workers for a minimum of three hours.) A seventeen-year-old applicant in Westchester County, New York, recalled being kept waiting for weeks until Burger King informed him that he didn't get a job after all. The delay, he says, cost him a month of job hunting and $200 in forgone pay. (Burger King, says a spokesperson, deplores such delays, which it feels the installation of a new scheduling technique will prevent in the future.) A teen-age part-timer at a New York McDonald's shop says management there routinely has workers appear up to an hour ahead of work time and then "wait in the back room and punch in later when they need you."[45] (A McDonald's official insists that this is an isolated case, that McDonald's does not condone such a policy.)

Some believe company insistence that such problems lie with local management, not the home office, is buck passing. Richard Gilber, a compliance officer in the U.S. Labor Department's wage and hour division, places the blame squarely on the store-manager training programs conducted by the home offices. He says, "We find in many cases that the twenty-year-old managers are sales oriented and cleanliness oriented. But they aren't taught much about employee relations. And the Wage Hour Law is just another three pages in the operating manual."

Wendy Hamburger agrees. "I went through three managers in the short time I was at Wendy's," she recalls. "They needed managers so badly they hired anyone. They got a lot of young guys in there who think they're Mr. Macho and want to exercise their power. They don't know anything."

A Burger King official conceded that much of the criticism is warranted. The industry, he says, has put people in their early twenties in charge of a million-dollar restaurant and sometimes forty employees under age eighteen and expects them to function like professionals. The results are often less than ideal. "You can train someone to fix a piece of equipment a lot easier than you can to deal with people," he says. Burger King, for one, is trying to remedy the situation by including "people skills" as part of its ten-day training courses for managers at its $1.6 million Burger King University in Miami. Other fast-food companies are following suit.

White's survey indicates that low pay is workers' chronic complaint. Although most chains come under minimum-wage and over-time-pay laws, they don't always abide by them. Thus, a Kentucky Fried Chicken franchise had to make up $2,086 in overtime pay to each of 35 employees, and a federal court in Miami ordered some of Lum's and Ranch House's restaurants to pay $100,000 to 1,290 employees who weren't paid the required minimum and overtime wages. In New Jersey, the Department of Labor charged eighteen Burger King restaurants with systematically underpaying their workers and not keeping proper wage reports. Such cases can be multiplied across the country.

Hourly employees almost universally bristle at management policies and conduct, but the manager's job is no bowl of cherries either. Ask the young woman who is paid $12,000 a year to run a McDonald's outlet that grosses $750,000 annually. "They don't pay managers enough," she complains. "I'm on my feet from 6 A.M. to 6 P.M. Often I don't have time to eat all day. On days off I come in a couple of hours or call in to check on my assistant managers. And I have to take work home, like the weekly scheduling."

Discussion Questions

1. Do you think the fast-food industry dislikes turnover? Do you think it encourages turnover?

2. Are wages in the fast-food industry fair? Does the industry exploit teen-age workers?

3. How would you evaluate personnel procedures and working conditions in the fast-food industry? Are they reasonable? Could they be improved?

4. If you were an executive of a fast-food company like McDonald's or Burger King, what measures, if any, would you recommend to remedy the constant worker irritants that Mr. White's survey turned up?

5. Do you think companies have responsibilities for how licensees conduct their operations?

6. Discuss the merits and liabilities of unionizing fast-food workers.

7. Do you think conditions in the fast-food industry support or belie the laissez-faire assumption that the natural interplay between employer and employee will produce a fair wage and hospitable working conditions?

8. Rapid turnover in the fast-food industry, some would argue, just goes to show that young people today lack loyalty, industry, and perseverance — in short, that they really don't want to work. Would you agree?

CASE 6.2
Freedom to Fire

When can dancing get you fired? Apparently, when you're on a business trip, your partner is a co-worker, and your clothes are too tight. Ask Elizabeth Bellissimo.

Bellissimo, a twenty-six-year-old attorney for Westinghouse Electric Corporation, hap-

pily accepted a fellow worker's invitation to dance while they were on a business trip. Her supervisor didn't approve and told her so when she returned to the office. He accused the young attorney of "unprofessional behavior" and suggested that, rather than trotting out to the dance floor, she should have trotted out some excuse like a headache and returned to her room. He also chided Bellissimo for her fashion choices. Her clothes, he told her, were definitely too tight and the colors too flashy.

When Bellissimo threatened to report the reprimand to a company vice president, she was fired. Claiming sex discrimination, Bellissimo sued her supervisors and won $121,670 for lost pay and future wages.[46]

The court's ruling wasn't unusual. Federal and state laws have long prohibited companies from discriminating against workers on the basis of sex, race, national origin, and age. Many states also have laws prohibiting employers from discharging workers for filing a worker's compensation claim and from cheating them out of pensions or commissions. And several states have even passed legislation protecting whistle-blowers from organizational retaliation. The courts have thus made it clear that employers may not fire workers at will — that is, for any reason whatever or for no reason. Now, state court decisions in California, Michigan, and New York threaten to further restrict the employer's freedom to fire.

When American Airlines fired an agent with eighteen years of service, the agent sued in the California courts, claiming that he had not been given a hearing prescribed in the corporation's internal regulations. While admitting its corporation regulations make such a provision, American claimed it is under no contractual obligation to provide one. About the same time, the New York Court of Appeals heard a similar case involving a man let go after working for a company for eight years.

In both instances, the courts ruled in favor of the dismissed workers and thereby elevated to contractual status expressed or implied personnel policies contained in such corporate documents as job applications, handbooks, and stock option plans. The courts said, in effect, that discharge of an employee is a breach of contract where assurances are made in company handbooks that termina-

tion can be for just cause only, after all practical steps toward rehabilitation have been made. Employment manuals and related documents thus appear to constitute still another restriction on the employer's freedom to fire.

Experts think that those who stand to benefit the most from these rulings are lower- and middle-level professionals and managers not covered by collective bargaining agreements or personal contracts given to senior executives.[47] Already companies are beginning to shudder at the prospect of being held legally accountable for statements made in personnel handbooks. They're convinced it will make firing employees increasingly difficult and expensive. In the wake of the American Airlines decision, one of its executives had this caution for California corporations: "Companies that operate in California will have to be aware that when they fire managers and other unorganized employees, they had better document the reason pretty thoroughly because they might end up in court. And they had better be prepared to spend tens of thousands of dollars in attorney's fees."

Others maintain that there is an even more fundamental issue at stake: a company's right to manage its business as it sees fit.

McGraw-Hill, Inc., for example, believes that the court rulings are tantamount to abrogating company self-governance in matters of discharge. "Treatment of personnel handbooks as creating enforceable contract rights would . . . put upon the courts the burden of making, or at least second guessing, the myriad of personnel decisions which are currently made by the managers of business enterprises in the exercise of their business judgment," company officials claim.

Perhaps the courts ultimately will side with such arguments. In the meantime, legal consultants are advising corporate clients to protect themselves. Blue Cross & Blue Shield of Michigan, which lost in a precedent-setting decision by the Michigan Supreme Court that gave personnel policy statements the status of employee contractual rights, is taking the advice to heart. Karen S.Kienbaum, the insurer's assistant general counsel, explains: "We have changed our employee handbook so that it very explicitly states that you can be terminated at any time for any reason. It also says that it is not an employment contract."

Officials at McGraw-Hill predict that if other courts rule like California's and Michigan's, "employers would withdraw their personnel handbooks or plaster them with disclaimers."

Discussion Questions

1. Do you think Ms. Bellissimo's supervisor had just cause to fire her? Should he be required to have just cause?

2. Some would so apply the concept of property rights to a business that owners and their representatives should be allowed to terminate a worker for any reason whatever. Do you agree?

3. Do you agree with McGraw-Hill's position that the court ruling in effect undermines the company's self-governance in matters of discharge?

4. In your opinion, should statements that appear in job descriptions and employee handbooks have the status of contractual rights?

5. What do you think of the Blue Cross & Blue Shield of Michigan's employee handbook statement that an employee "can be terminated at any time for any reason just as you [the employee] can [quit] at any time for any reason"? Evaluate the insurer's policy from the perspectives of egoism, utilitarianism, and Kant's ethics.

CASE 6.3
Speak, If You Dare

Martin Davis, senior vice president for the National Power Company, wrote an article for a widely circulated magazine. It wasn't just any article. It questioned his company's social responsibility in planning to put a nuclear power plant near a small California town.

Davis not only raised serious doubts about the safety of nuclear power plants in general but also suggested that a plant in the proposed location would seriously undermine agricultural interests in that area by diverting much-needed water to the power plant. It was the kind of article that could only hurt National Power.

Some wholeheartedly supported Davis's position and told National so. But others didn't support Davis. They felt National had succumbed to political and social pressure to abort a project that would ease the country's energy burden and provide an alternative that might stabilize or even reduce the costs of soaring fuel bills. In addition, National received a large outpouring of local labor resentment. The company, according to charges, was preventing the creation of perhaps thousands of jobs in the area.

Needless to say, none of this criticism was lost on top management at National. They felt that, as vice president of the company, Davis had acted irresponsibly. They thought such a plant was not safe but absolutely vital to the national welfare. And yet Davis had entirely overlooked these points. He had even suggested awesome legal responsibilities National might incur should some remotely possible accident occur.

At the request of the board, National's chief operating officer instructed Davis never again to comment publicly without first clearing his remarks with the firm. Davis was outraged. He felt that National was "invading," as he termed it, his duties as a responsible citizen. In fact, Davis said that he intended to honor several speaking engagements to air further what he viewed as "a matter of conscience."

The chief operating officer relayed Davis's feelings to the board, which in turn issued Davis an ultimatum. Either he would conform with their order or submit his resignation immediately.

The chief operating officer delivered the message. "They expect your answer by the end of the week, Marty," he told the vice president.

Discussion Questions

1. What rival ideals and obligations are involved in this case?

2. Do you think National has a right to abridge Davis's freedom of expression on this issue? Do you think Davis acted irresponsibly, as the board charges?

3. Should there be any limits on an employee's freedom of expression? Under what circumstances is a company justified in restricting an employee's right to speak out? What policy would you recommend that companies follow?

4. What do you think Davis ought to do? Defend your answer by appeal to ethical principles.

CASE 6.4
Union Discrimination?

The National Right to Work Legal Defense Foundation is one of several anti-union organizations that have been active in recent years. The "right to work," in this context, means the alleged right of an individual to work without being obliged to join a union. To put it the other way around, it means that companies cannot sign contracts with unions agreeing to hire only workers who are willing to join the union.
advertisements, titled "Job Discrimination . . . It Still Exists":[48]

> Paul Robertson is not a member of a persecuted minority. But he has experienced blatant discrimination all the same because he has chosen not to join a union.
>
> Paul Robertson is a working man, a skilled licensed electrician with more than 20 years experience. He found out the hard way how a big company and a big union can discriminate on the job.
>
> Paul was hired by the Bechtel Power Corporation to work on their Jim Bridger Power Plant project in the Rock Springs, Wyoming, area. Only three months later, he was fired, supposedly because of a reduction in force.
>
> But during the week preceding his discharge, Bechtel hired at least 19 union electricians referred by the local union and retained at least 65 unlicensed electricians.
>
> A determined Paul Robertson filed unfair labor practice charges against the company and the union.
>
> An administrative law judge ruled and was upheld by the full National Labor Relations Board that the union and the employer had indeed discriminated. The judge ordered that Robertson and seven other electricians be given the back pay they would have earned if they had been treated fairly.
>
> The NLRB later reversed part of its decision, but Paul Robertson did not give

up. With the help of the National Right to Work Legal Defense Foundation, he appealed the Board's decision to the U.S. Court of Appeals, arguing that hiring hall favoritism is discriminatory and unlawful.

Paul Robertson was fortunate. He found experienced legal help—all important because the case dragged on for nearly four years in the courts and the union still refused to obey the NLRB's backpay order.

The National Right to Work Legal Defense Foundation is helping everyone it can—currently in more than 75 cases involving academic and political freedom, protection from union violence, and other fundamental rights. But it would like to do even more.

If you'd like to help workers like Paul Robertson write: The National Right to Work Legal Defense Foundation. . . .

Discussion Questions

1. Assuming the Foundation's description of the case is accurate, was Paul Robertson treated unfairly? Was this a case of discrimination?

2. Does it make a difference to your assessment of the case whether someone like Robertson knows, when he accepts a job, that he must join the union or that nonunion employees will be the first to be laid off?

3. If union employees negotiate a contract with management, part of which specifies that management will not hire nonunion employees, does this violate anyone's rights? Would a libertarian agree that the resulting union shop was perfectly acceptable?

4. Presumably Paul Robertson could have joined the union, but he chose not to. What principle, if any, do you think he was fighting for?

5. What do you see as the likely motivations of Bechtel Power and the union? How would they justify their conduct?

6. Why did the Foundation run this ad? Is the ad anti-union propaganda? Do you think the Foundation is sincerely interested in the rights of individual workers? Or is it simply interested in weakening unions vis-à-vis management?

7. Assess union shops and agency shops from the moral point of view. What conflicting rights, interests, and ideals are at stake? What are the positive and negative consequences of permitting union shops?

CASE 6.5
Rights Up in Smoke

The last thing Darlene Lambert felt like the first thing Monday morning was breathing in the smoke from Frank's and Alice's cigarettes. Darlene wasn't really crazy about breathing other people's smoke under the best of circumstances, especially after reading that nonsmokers like herself can get lung cancer and heart disease from doing so,* but today she

*Researchers in fact believe that passive smoking kills about 53,000 nonsmoking Americans annually, making it the third leading cause of preventable death. See "More Bad News on Passive Smoking," *San Francisco Chronicle*, January 10, 1991, A3.

was suffering from a mild cold and the prospect of those cigarette fumes made her feel slightly nauseated.

Darlene worked with one other person, a nonsmoker, in a small office of the personnel department at Redwood Associates, but her job required her to spend expended periods on and off throughout the day in the main files room where Frank and Alice worked and smoked. Darlene had told them that she didn't like breathing cigarette smoke. They were nice people and sympathetic to her feelings; they tried not to smoke too much when she was there. But, of course, the smell of cigarettes permeated the room whether they had a cigarette going or not. And as nice and friendly as they were, Frank and Alice nevertheless figured that since their desks were located in that room, they had a right to smoke there. Alice had as much as told Darlene that she thought Darlene was oversensitive to smoke, and Frank sometimes joked about smokers being persecuted these days for their habit.

At 9:05 A.M., Darlene marched into the office of her supervisor, Charles Renford, and told him that she couldn't work in the files room today because of the smoke. Renford was caught off guard and more than a little put out by Darlene's announcement because top management was suddenly requesting a report—"due yesterday"—and he needed Darlene to begin assembling the data in the files room. He reminded her that Redwood Associates made an effort to accommodate nonsmokers by guaranteeing that certain areas of the building be smoke free, but it wasn't prepared to ban smoking altogether. Not only do smokers have rights, Renford said, it would hurt productivity and morale to make employees leave the building to smoke. "They should quit smoking," Darlene rejoined. "It would be for their own good." "Maybe, it would," said Charles, "but the company shouldn't force them to quit. Besides, it is easy for you, who's never smoked,

to talk about quitting. I know, I used to smoke myself."

Renford brought the conversation back around to the required report and its importance. Darlene simply said, "I'm sorry Charles, but if it means going in that room—and it does—then I'm simply not going to do it." And then she got up and returned to her office, leaving Charles Renford trying to figure out what he was going to do.

Discussion Questions

1. Would Renford be within his rights to fire Darlene Lambert for insubordination? Can he order Frank and Alice not to smoke so that Darlene can work in the room? How would you deal with this situation if you were Renford?

2. Do employees like Frank and Alice have a right to smoke? Does Darlene have a right to a smoke-free workplace?

3. What policy on smoking would you recommend to Redwood Associates? Is it possible for employers to find some compromise between smokers and nonsmokers?

4. In 1914 Thomas Edison had a policy of employing "no person who smoked cigarettes." Is such a policy discriminatory? Is it reasonable?

NOTES

1. Robert C. Gallo, "The AIDS Virus," *Scientific American*, January 1987. See also *Scientific American's* special issue on AIDS, October 1988.
2. See David L. Kirp, "Uncommon Decency: Pacific Bell Responds to AIDS," *Harvard Business Review* 67 (May–June 1989): 142; and *Personnel*, March 1989, 11.
3. See David W. Ewing, "Civil Liberties in the Corporation," in Tom L. Beauchamp and Norman E. Bowie, eds., *Ethical Theory and Business*, 2nd ed. (Englewood Cliffs, N.J.: Prentice-Hall, 1983), 141.
4. Ibid., 139–140.

5. Ibid., 139.

6. Ibid., 140–141.

7. Clyde W. Summers, "Protesting All Employees Against Unjust Dismissal," *Harvard Business Review* 58 (January–February 1980); but see also "Business for Lawyers," *The Economist*, January 23, 1988.

8. See "Business for Lawyers," 61; Ewing, "Civil Liberties"; and Barbara A. Lee, "Something Akin to a Property Right," *Business and Professional Ethics Journal* 8 (Fall 1989).

9. Stephen Wermiel, "High Court Backs Refusal to Work on Sabbath Day," *Wall Street Journal*, March 30, 1989, B8.

10. *Wall Street Journal*, June 6, 1989, A1.

11. Ewing, "Civil Liberties," 148.

12. See Chapter 5 of Tuleja's *Beyond the Bottom Line* (New York: Penguin, 1987), from which this paragraph and the next are drawn.

13. See Kirp, "Uncommon Decency."

14. See Marian M. Extejt and William N. Bockanic, "Issues Surrounding the Theories of Negligent Hiring and Failure to Fire," *Business and Professional Ethics Journal* 8 (Winter 1989).

15. See John P. Kohl and David B. Stephens, "Wanted: Recruitment Advertising That Doesn't Discriminate," *Personnel*, February 1989.

16. Ibid., 23.

17. Eric Matusewitch, "Language Rules Can Violate Title VII," *Personnel Journal*, October 1990.

18. Ibid., 100.

19. Dean Rotbart, "Father Quit His Job For the Family's Sake; Now Hirers Shun Him," *Wall Street Journal*, April 13, 1981, 1.

20. Ibid.

21. See George Munchus, "Testing as a Selection Tool: Another Old and Sticky Managerial Human Rights Issue," *Journal of Business Ethics* 8 (October 1989).

22. Roland Wall, "Discovering Prejudice Against the Disabled," *ETC* 44 (Fall 1987): 236.

23. Francis Bacon, *The New Organon* (New York: Bobbs-Merrill, 1960), 48.

24. Jeffrey L. Sheller, "Nepotism: No Stranger to American Labor Unions," *U.S. News & World Report*, September 20, 1982, 40–41.

25. Mike Royko, "Lean, Trim Policy Covers a Big, Fat Lie," *San Francisco Chronicle*, April 12, 1990, A27.

26. Steven A. Jesseph, "Employee Termination, 2: Some Do's and Don'ts," *Personnel*, February 1989, 36–37.

27. Ibid.; also see Miriam Rothman, "Employee Termination, 1: A Four-Step Procedure," *Personnel*, February 1989.

28. For a personal reflection, see Ronald P. Quartararo, "The Human Side of Merger Mania," *Business and Society Review* 66 (Spring 1988).

29. In a wave of cost-cutting and restructuring, the *Fortune 500* companies alone slashed 2.8 million employees from their payrolls between 1977 and 1988. Millions more surrendered jobs or took pay cuts in the name of corporate streamlining. See "Management for the 1990s," *Newsweek* (international edition), April 25, 1988, 34.

30. Carol Hymowitz, "More Employees, Shareholders Demand That Sacrifices in Pay Begin at the Top," *Wall Street Journal*, November 8, 1990, B1.

31. The historical development of unions that is sketched here is based on the clear and succinct presentation in Robert B. Carson, *Business Issues Today: Alternative Perspectives* (New York: St. Martin's Press, 1984), 139–142.

32. *San Francisco Examiner*, September 3, 1989, A2; *San Francisco Chronicle*, February 11, 1991, D1.

33. Although the Supreme Court upheld this maneuver in a similar case in 1984, Congress has since revised the bankruptcy law.

34. Denise Giardina, "Solidarity in Appalachia," *The Nation*, July 3, 1989.

35. See Harry Bernstein, "Cards Stacked Against Strikers at Eastern," *Los Angeles Times*, March 7, 1989, IV-1; and Kenneth Eskey, "Labor's Main Tool Threatened," *San Francisco Examiner*, September 3, 1989, A2.

36. *San Francisco Chronicle*, March 2, 1991, A5; *The Economist*, November 3, 1990, 35; and "Union-busting Owners Force Strike on Daily News Workers," *Guardian* (New York), November 7, 1990.

37. "Labor Unions: Context and Crisis" in R. C. Edwards, M. Reich, and T. E. Weisskopf, eds., *The Capitalist System*, 3rd ed. (Englewood Cliffs, N.J.: Prentice-Hall, 1986), 165.

38. Adam Smith, *An Inquiry into the Nature and Causes of the Wealth of Nations* (New York: Modern Library, 1985), 68.

39. Austin Fagothey and Milton A. Gonsalves, *Right and Reason: Ethics in Theory and Practice* (St. Louis: Mosby, 1981), 428–429.

40. Ibid., 429.

41. See Chapter 4 of Mary Gibson, *Workers' Rights* (Totowa, N.J.: Rowman & Allanheld, 1983). The film *Norma Rae* portrays the dogged resistance of a company like J.P. Stevens to unionization.

42. Fagothey and Gonsalves, *Right and Reason*, 428–429.

43. See "Unions Pressure Phelps Dodge's Creditors Over 15-Month Copper Strike," *Los Angeles Times*, September 17, 1984, IV-1.

44. See Jim Montgomery, ''Burger Blues,'' *Wall Street Journal*, March 15, 1979, 1. The article is the source of the facts and quotations reported in this case. For an update on business's demand for teen-age employees, see Froma Joselow, ''Why Business Turns to Teen-Agers,'' *New York Times*, March 26, 1989, 3–1.

45. This and all other quotations in this case presentation are from Montgomery, ''Burger Blues,'' 33.

46. Cathy Trost, ''Labor Letter,'' *Wall Street Journal*, May 22, 1984, 1.

47. See ''A Fight Over the Freedom to Fire,'' *Business Week*, September 20, 1982, 116, from which the remaining quotations in this case presentation are taken.

48. Reprinted by permission of the National Right to Work Legal Defense Foundation, Inc., 8001 Braddock Road, Suite 600, Springfield, Virginia 22160.

An Employees' Bill of Rights

David W. Ewing

In this selection from his book Freedom Inside the Organization, *David Ewing presents a nine-point bill of rights for employees. Any bill of rights, Ewing suggests, should take the form of succinct, practical injunctions, injunctions that are negative in form (''Thou shalt not . . .'') and that can be readily understood by ordinary people. A bill of rights should also be enforceable, not just a statement of ideals. Ewing emphasizes that his bill of rights is a ''working proposal'' for further discussion.*

The bill of rights that follows is one person's proposal, a ''working paper'' for discussion, not a platform worked out in committee. . . .

1. *No organization or manager shall discharge, demote, or in other ways discriminate against any employee who criticizes, in speech or press, the ethics, legality, or social responsibility of management actions.*

Comment: This right is intended to extend the U.S. Supreme Court's approach in the *Pickering* case* to all employees in business, government, education, and public service organizations.

What this right does not say is as important as what it does say. Protection does not extend to employees who make nuisances of themselves or who balk, argue, or contest managerial decisions on normal operating and planning matters, such as the choice of inventory accounting method, whether to diversify the product line or concentrate it, whether to rotate workers on a certain job or specialize them, and so forth. ''Committing the truth,'' as Ernest Fitzgerald called it, is protected only for speaking out on issues where we consider an average citizen's judgment to be as valid as an expert's — truth in advertising, public safety standards, questions of fair disclosure, ethical practices, and so forth.

Nor does the protection extend to employees who malign the organization. We don't protect individuals who go around ruining other people's reputations, and neither should we protect those who vindictively impugn their employers.

Note, too, that this proposed right does not authorize an employee to disclose to outsiders information that is confidential.

This right puts publications of nonunionized employees on the same basis as union newspapers and journals, which are free to criticize an organization. Can a free press be justified for one group but not for the other? More to the point still, in a country that practices democratic rites, can the necessity of an ''underground press'' be justified in any socially important organization?

2. *No employee shall be penalized for engaging in outside activities of his or her choice after working hours, whether political, economic, civic, or cultural, nor for buying products and services of his or her choice for personal use, nor for expressing or encouraging views contrary to top management's on political, economic, and social issues.*

Comment: Many companies encourage employees to participate in outside activities, and some states have committed this right to legislation. Freedom of choice of products and services for personal use is also authorized in various state statutes as well as in arbitrators' decisions. The

*[eds.] In this important 1968 case, the Supreme Court found in favor of a public schoolteacher who had been fired for criticizing the policies of the school board in the local newspaper.

Reprinted by permission from David Ewing, *Freedom Inside the Organization* (New York: Dutton, 1977).

third part of the statement extends the protection of the First Amendment to the employee whose ideas about government, economic policy, religion, and society do not conform with the boss's. It would also protect the schoolteacher who allows the student newspaper to espouse a view on sex education that is rejected by the principal, the staff psychologist who endorses a book on a subject considered taboo in the board room, and other independent spirits.

Note that this provision does not authorize an employee to come to work "beat" in the morning because he or she has been moonlighting. Participation in outside activities should enrich employees' lives, not debilitate them; if on-the-job performance suffers, the usual penalties may have to be paid.

3. *No organization or manager shall penalize an employee for refusing to carry out a directive that violates common norms of morality.*

Comment: The purpose of this right is to . . . afford job security (not just unemployment compensation) to subordinates who cannot perform an action because they consider it unethical or illegal. It is important that the conscientious objector in such a case hold to a view that has some public acceptance. Fad moralities — messages from flying saucers, mores of occult religious sects, and so on — do not justify refusal to carry out an order. Nor in any case is the employee entitled to interfere with the boss's finding another person to do the job requested.

4. *No organization shall allow audio or visual recordings of an employee's conversation or actions to be made without his or her prior knowledge and consent. Nor may an organization require an employee or applicant to take personality tests, polygraph examinations, or other tests that constitute, in his opinion, an invasion of privacy.*

Comment: This right is based on policies that some leading organizations have already put into practice. If an employee doesn't want his working life monitored, that is his privilege so long as he demonstrates (or, if an applicant, is willing to demonstrate) competence to do a job well.

5. *No employee's desk, files, or locker may be examined in his or her absence by anyone but a senior manager who has sound reason to believe that the files contain information needed for a management decision that must be made in the employee's absence.*

Comment: The intent of this right is to grant people a privacy right as employees similar to that which they enjoy as political and social citizens under the "searches and seizures" guarantee of the Bill of Rights (Fourth Amendment to the Constitution). Many leading organizations in business and government have respected the principle of this rule for some time.

6. *No employer organization may collect and keep on file information about an employee that is not relevant and necessary for efficient management. Every employee shall have the right to inspect his or her personnel file and challenge the accuracy, relevance, or necessity of data in it, except for personal evaluations and comments by other employees which could not reasonably be obtained if confidentiality were not promised. Access to an employee's file by outside individuals and organizations shall be limited to inquiries about the essential facts of employment.*

Comment: This right is important if employees are to be masters of their employment track records instead of possible victims of them. It will help to eliminate surprises, secrets, and skeletons in the clerical closet.

7. *No manager may communicate to prospective employers of an employee who is about to be or has been discharged gratuitous opinions that might hamper the individual in obtaining a new position.*

Comment: The intent of this right is to stop blacklisting. The courts have already given some support for it.

8. *An employee who is discharged, demoted, or transferred to a less desirable job is entitled to a written statement from management of its reasons for the penalty.*

Comment: The aim of this provision is to encourage a manager to give the same reasons in a hearing, arbitration, or court trial that he or she gives the employee when the cutdown happens. The written statement need not be given unless requested; often it is so clear to all parties why an action is being taken that no document is necessary.

9. *Every employee who feels that he or she has been penalized for asserting any right described in this bill shall be entitled to a fair hearing before an impartial official, board, or arbitrator. The findings and conclusions of the hearing shall be delivered in writing to the employee and management.*

Comment: This very important right is the organizational equivalent of due process of law as we know it in political and community life. Without due process in a company or agency, the rights in this bill would all have to be enforced by outside courts and tribunals, which is expensive for society as well as time-consuming for the employees who are required to appear as complainants and witnesses. The nature of a "fair hearing" is purposely left undefined here so that different approaches can be tried, expanded, and adapted to changing needs and conditions.

Note that the findings of the investigating official or group are not binding on top management. This would put an unfair burden on an ombudsperson or "expedited arbitrator," if one of them is the investigator. Yet the employee is protected. If management rejects a finding of unfair treatment and then the employee goes to court, the investigator's statement will weigh against management in the trial. As a practical matter, therefore, employers will not want to buck the investigator-referee unless they fervently disagree with the findings.

In Sweden, perhaps the world's leading practitioner of due process in organizations, a law went into effect in January 1977 that goes a little farther than the right proposed here. The new Swedish law states that except in unusual circumstances a worker who disputes a dismissal notice can keep his or her job until the dispute has been decided by a court.

Every sizable organization, whether in business, government, health, or another field, should have a bill of rights for employees. Only small organizations need not have such a statement—personal contact and oral communications meet the need for them. However, companies and agencies need not have identical bills of rights. Industry custom, culture, past history with employee unions and associations, and other considerations can be taken into account in the wording and emphasis given to different provisions.

Review and Discussion Questions

1. What are the pros and cons of each of Ewing's nine points? Examine each point for any potential problems in enacting, interpreting, or enforcing it.

2. Are there any rights that you would add to Ewing's list? Are there any that you would delete?

3. Do you see any point in proposing and discussing a possible employees' bill of rights? Do you think employees would benefit from a bill of rights? Should each company adopt its own bill of rights or should a general bill of rights be enacted by law?

4. Some might argue that, instead of a bill of rights, it is up to individual employees, or their union, to negotiate their employment terms. Would you agree?

Employee and Employer Rights in an Institutional Context

Patricia H. Werhane

After examining possible justifications for the common law principle of "employment at will," Patricia Werhane rejects the principle, arguing that it conflicts with the very rights upon which it is supposed to be based. Although the principle can, when properly interpreted, be used to defend some employee rights, Werhane sees the moral rights of employees as fundamentally grounded in the reciprocal nature of employment relationships. That reciprocity involves role accountability and the obligation to treat employees fairly and with respect.

The common law principle of Employment at Will (EAW) states that in the absence of a specific contract or law, an employer may hire, fire, demote, or promote any employee (not covered by contract or law) when that employer wishes. The theory is that employers have rights—rights to control what happens in the workplace. These include decisions

This chapter, as abridged, appeared in Tom L. Beauchamp and Norman Bowie, eds., *Ethical Theory and Business*, 3rd ed. (Englewood Cliffs, N.J.: Prentice-Hall, 1988). The original version appeared in *Communicating Employee Responsibilities and Rights*, Chimezic A. B. Osigweh, ed. © 1978 by Chimezic A. B. Osigweh. Reprinted by permission of Greenwood Publishing Group, Inc.

concerning all business operations, extending of course to the hiring and placement of employees. Although EAW is a common-law doctrine, until recently it virtually dictated employment relationships.

What are the justifications for EAW? How would one define this idea? EAW is sometimes justified on the basis of property rights. It is contended that the rights to freedom and to property ownership are valid rights and that they include the right to use freely and to improve what one owns. According to this view, an employer has the right to dispose of her business and those who work for that business (and thus affect it) as she sees fit. Instituting employee rights such as due process or the protection of whistle blowers, for example, would restrict an employer's freedom to do what she wishes with her business, thus violating property rights.

In the twentieth century, employer property rights have changed. Businesses are mainly corporations owned by a large number of changing shareholders and managed by employees who usually own little or no stock in the company. The board of directors represents the owner-shareholder interests, but most business decisions are in the hands of managers. Despite this division of ownership from management, however, proprietory ownership rights of employers have translated themselves into management rights. Contemporary management sees itself as having the rights to control business and therefore to control employment. From a utilitarian perspective, control of a company by its managers is thought of as essential for maximum efficiency and productivity. To disrupt this would defeat the primary purpose of free enterprise organizations. Moreover, according to its proponents, EAW preserves the notion of "freedom of contract," the right of persons and organizations to enter freely into binding voluntary agreements (e.g., employment agreements) of their choice.

That managers see themselves in the role of proprietors is, of course, too simple a description. In complex organizations there is a hierarchy of *at-will* relationships. Each manager is an at-will employee, but sees himself as proprietor of certain responsibilities to the organization and as being in control of certain other employees whom the manager can dismiss at will, albeit within certain guidelines of legal restraint. That manager, in turn, reports to someone else who is herself an at-will employee responsible to another segment of the organization. These at-will relationships are thought to preserve equal employee and employer freedoms because, just as a manager can demote or fire an at-will employee at any time, so too an employee, any employee, can quit whenever he or she pleases for any reason whatsoever. Notice a strange anomaly here. Employees have responsibilities to their managers and are not free to make their own choices in the workplace. At the same time, employees are conceived of as autonomous persons who are at liberty to quit at any time.

Notice, too, that there is sometimes a sort of Social Darwinist theory of management functioning in many of these relationships. Managers are so-titled because it is felt that they are the most capable. By reason of education and experience and from the perspective of their position, they allegedly know what is best for the organization or the part of the organization they manage. This gives them the right to manage other employees. The employees they manage (who themselves may be managers of yet other employees) have roles within the organization to carry out the directives of their managers, and so on.

The employee-manager hierarchy of at-will employment relationships is both more complex and more simple in union-management relationships. It is more complex because often the relationship is specified or restricted by a number of well-defined rules for seniority, layoffs, dismissals, and so on. It is more simple because by and large union employees are *employees*, not managers. Their role responsibilities defined by hierarchical relationships are clear-cut, and those wishing to change or move up to management usually must give up union membership.

This oversimplified, crude, overstated, overview of hierarchical employment relationships in business may not currently exist in the ways I have described in any business. Yet such relationships are at least *implicit* in many businesses and perpetuated in the law by a continued management or employer-biased interpretation of the principle of EAW.

Despite the fact that the principle of EAW is defended on a number of grounds — including that it allegedly protects equal employee and manager freedoms, that it promotes efficiency, and that it preserves the notion of freedom of contract — EAW violates all of these for the following reasons. EAW does not preserve equal freedoms because in most employment relationships employer-managers are in positions of greater power than employees. This in itself does not undermine EAW, but the potential abuse of this power is what is at issue. Employees and managers allegedly have equal rights — rights to be fired or to quit at any time for any reason. But an at-will employee is seldom in a position within the law to inflict harm on an employer. Legally sanctioned at-will treatment by employers of employees can, however, harm employees. This is because when an employee is fired arbitrarily without some sort of grievance procedure, a hearing or an appeal, he cannot demonstrate that he was fired without good reason. Employees who have been fired have much more difficulty getting new jobs than those who have not been fired, even when that treatment was unjustified. Because arbitrarily fired employees are treated like those who deserve to lose their jobs, EAW puts such employees at an unfair disadvantage compared with other workers. The principle of EAW, then, does not preserve equal freedoms because it is to the advantage of the employer or manager and to the unfair disadvantage of the fired employee.

Worse, at-will practices violate the very right upon which EAW is allegedly based. Part of the appeal of EAW is that it protects the freedom of contract — the right to make employment agreements of one's choice. Abolishing EAW is coercive, according to its proponents, because this forces employers involuntarily to change their employment practices. But at-will employment practices too are or can be coercive. This is because when an employee is fired without sufficient reasons employers or managers place this person involuntarily in a personally harmful position unjustified by her behavior, a position that an employee would never choose. Thus the voluntary employment agreement according to which such practices are allowed is violated.

It is argued that EAW maximizes efficiency. But what is to prevent a manager from hiring a mentally retarded son-in-law or firing a good employee on personal grounds, actions that themselves damage efficiency? On a more serious level, if managers have prerogatives, these are based on a claim to the right to freedom — the freedom to conduct business as one pleases. But if this is a valid claim, then one must grant equal freedoms to everyone, including employees. Otherwise managers are saying that *they* have greater rights than other persons. This latter claim brings into question a crucial basis of democratic capitalism, namely that every person has *equal* rights, the most important of which is the equal right to freedom. The notion of equal rights does not necessarily imply that employees and managers have equal or identical prerogatives in business decision making or in managing a company. But what is implied is that the exercise of freedom requires a respect for the equal exercise of freedom by others, although the *kind* of exercises in each case may be different. EAW practices, then, are inconsistent practices because they do not preserve equal freedoms, they do not protect freedom of contract for both parties, and they do not guarantee efficiencies in the workplace. A number of thinkers contend that the principle should be abolished or disregarded in the law.

Interestingly, however, one can *defend* at least some employee rights from a consistent interpretation of the principle of EAW. This is because to be consistent the demands of EAW, principally the demand of management for the freedom to control business, require an equal respect for employee freedoms. In other words, EAW is to be justified on the basis of the right to freedom, it can only be justified for that reason if it respects everyone's freedoms equally. Otherwise, managers' alleged freedoms are merely unwarranted licenses to do anything they please, even abridging employee rights, and thus have no moral or constitutional basis. Such equal respect for employee rights cannot always be interpreted as equal participation in management decisions. Extending and respecting employee freedoms requires balancing equal but not necessarily identical liberties. The free exercise of management employment decisions, however, does seem to require that employees be given reasons, publicly stated and verifiable, for management decisions that affect employees, including hiring and firing. In this way voluntary choices in the job market are truly equal to management employment choices. Moreover, freedom of choice in management decision making requires allowing legitimate whistle blowing, conscientious objection, and even striking without employer retaliation when an employee is asked to perform illegal, immoral, and/or socially dangerous jobs, or when such practices occur in the workplace. I am suggesting that a proper interpretation of EAW is not inconsistent with granting some employee rights. It is the misinterpretation of EAW that has served as a basis for the exercise of management prerogatives at the expense of employee rights.

Employers and managers, of course, will not always be happy to grant these freedoms to employees, because such freedoms are often seen as giving employees too many rights. Other managers identify extending employee freedoms with participatory management programs that, they argue, would abridge management responsibilities. Neither of these consequences, however, necessarily follows from extending employee rights. On the other hand, continuing the present imbalance of freedoms in the workplace perpetuates injustices. Worse, from the perspective of management this is a highly risky policy in an age of employee enlightenment and a concern for employee rights. Many managers are sympathetic to arguments defending employee rights. However, they fear that instituting employee rights in the workplace entails government regulation of and intervention in the affairs of business, all of which is intrusive, expensive, and time-consuming. But there is no reason why businesses cannot voluntarily institute employment reforms, and in the climate of a surging interest in employee rights, such voluntary actions would help prevent government intervention and regulation.

Turning to a second moral justification for employee rights, balancing employee and employer freedoms in the workplace is also justified because of what I shall call the reciprocal nature of employment relationships. Employment relationships, which are by and large hierarchical role relationships tend to be destructive of employee rights, yet this need not be so, and in fact quite the contrary is required. The reasons for this are the following. In the workplace both management and employees have role responsibilities that are a source of job accountability. A person holding a job is held accountable for a certain performance; it is sometimes not considered unjust to dismiss someone for failure to perform his or her job even if the employer

pays poorly and sometimes even if the employer does not respect other employee rights. Employee job accountability in this context is usually described as first-party duties of the employee to a manager or to the organization for whom one works. However, this description is incomplete. There are, in addition, duties on the part of the manager or the institution to the employee who is held accountable. These obligations arise in part from the role responsibilities of the party to whom an employee is answerable and in part because of the nature of the relationship. These obligations, which are often neglected in an analysis of accountability, are reciprocal or correlative obligations implied by role responsibility to the employee in question. This notion of reciprocity, I shall argue, is crucial in employment relationships.

The notion of reciprocity in any social relationship is grounded on the basic fact that each party is a person or a group of persons. As the philosopher Carol Gould puts it,

> Reciprocity may be defined as a social relation among agents in which each recognizes the other as an agent, that is, as equally free, and each acts with respect to the other on the basis of a shared understanding and a free agreement to the effect that the actions of each with respect to the other are equivalent.[1]

This does not mean that each party must treat the other in the same way in every respect, but rather that each treats the other with equal respect and as equal possessors of rights and benefits. Because they are social relationships between persons or between persons and institutions developed by persons, accountability relationships entail this notion of reciprocity.

Reciprocity in accountability relationships operates in part, as follows. If I am accountable for my actions to a certain group or institution because of my role in that group or institution, this accountability implicitly assures a reciprocal accountability to me on the part of the institution to whom I am answerable. The obligations in each relationship are not necessarily contractual, but the strength of my role obligations depends at least in part on equally forceful, though obviously not identical, role obligations of the second party to me. And if no such reciprocal obligations exist, or if they are not respected, my accountability to that individual, group, or institution weakens.

What this brief analysis of role accountability suggests in the workplace is that when taking a job an employee has responsibilities connected with that job, responsibilities that are often only implicitly stated. At the same time, accountability does not consist merely of first-party duties of employees to employers or managers; it is also defined in reciprocal relationships with the party to whom one is accountable. The reason for this is that employee-employer relationships are both social and contractual arrangements. They are social because they are relationships entered into between persons or between persons and organizations created and run by persons. They are at least implicitly contractual ones voluntarily entered into and freely dissolvable by both parties. Therefore, if employees are accountable to managers or employers, managers or employers are also accountable for upholding their part of the agreement by being reciprocally accountable, albeit in different ways, to their employees.

The reciprocal nature of employee-employer relationships entails some important employee rights, in particular the rights to fair treatment and respect. What might constitute such fair treatment and respect? Obviously, fair pay or a living wage in exchange for work is an essential part of just treatment in the workplace. But if, in addition to working, employees are expected to respect and be fair to their employers, then employers have reciprocal obligations that go beyond merely offering fair pay. Employee respect demands from a manager a correlative respect for employee privacy, employee information, and for due process in the workplace, even for at-will employees.

Due process demands not that employees not be dismissed, but rather that any employer action meet impartial standards of reasonableness, the same sort of reasonableness expected of employees. Similarly, if an employee is to respect his or her employer and the decisions of that employer, the employer needs to honor the privacy of the employee as a human being, including protecting with confidentiality personnel information and respecting the privacy of employee activities outside the workplace. Respect for the employee also involves keeping the employee well-informed about his or her job, the quality of his or her work, and the stability of the company. This is a two-pronged responsibility. It entails not only the requirement that all employees are equally entitled to information, but the recognition that all employees actually in fact *have* such information. Employees have rights not merely to be informed but also to be communicated with in ways they understand.

The employee rights just enumerated—the rights to privacy, to employee information, and the right to due process—are moral rights that result from the nature of role accountability in the workplace. Like the right to freedom that is implied by a consistent interpretation of EAW, these rights are moral rather than legal rights, so employers need not respect them. But if the reciprocal requirements of employment accountability relationships are not met by employers or managers, those employers or managers undermine the basis for employee accountability in the workplace.

Note

1. Carol Gould, "Economic Justice, Self-Management and the Principle of Reciprocity," in *Economic Justice*, ed. Kenneth Kipnis and Diana T. Meyers (Totowa, N.J.: Rowman and Allanheld, 1985), pp. 213–214.

Review and Discussion Questions

1. How is the principle of employment at will usually defended? What are Werhane's reasons for rejecting it? Are you persuaded by her reasoning?

2. Even though Werhane rejects EAW, she argues that it is possible to defend certain employee rights based on it. Explain her argument. Would a proponent of EAW agree?

3. Explain what Werhane means by reciprocity and role accountability in the workplace. How do they provide a justification of employee rights?

The Public Worker's Right to Strike

Mary Gibson

Public employees have traditionally been denied the right to strike enjoyed by other workers. Gibson reviews and rejects the various rationales for this denial, including the claim that government services are too essential for strikes to be permitted. She argues that public employees have the same moral right to strike that private sector employees do, a right which should be protected by law. Even in the case of police and firefighters, Gibson maintains that compulsory binding arbitration is an unsatisfactory substitute for the right to strike.

Let us now consider the main arguments advanced against the right of public employees to strike. (In view of the clarification above, I should say that I shall understand arguments against the right to strike as supporting specific legislative prohibition, and arguments for the right as supporting specific legislative recognition.)

Perhaps the oldest argument—if it can be called an argument—is based on the doctrine of sovereignty. . . .

As originally conceived, this doctrine was appealed to as justification for denying public employees not only the right to strike, but the right to bargain as well:

> What this position comes down to is that governmental power includes the power, through law, to fix the terms and conditions of government employment, that this power cannot be given or taken away or shared and that any organized effort to interfere with this power through a process such as collective bargaining is irreconcilable with the idea of sovereignty and is hence unlawful. [Hanslowe, 1967, 14–15]

Another formulation of the view is provided by Neil W. Chamberlain:

> In Hobbesian terms, government is identified as the sole possessor of final power, since it is responsive to the interests of all its constituents. To concede to any *special* interest group a right to bargain for terms which sovereignty believes contravenes the *public* interest is to deny the government's single responsibility. The government must remain in possession of

the sole power to determine, on behalf of all, what shall be public policy. [Chamberlain, 1972, 13]

Applying the doctrine specifically to the right to strike, Herbert Hoover said in 1928 that "no government employee can strike against the government and thus against the whole people" (Aboud and Aboud, 1974, 3). And in 1947, Thomas Dewey stated that "a strike against government would be successful only if it could produce paralysis of government. This no people can permit and survive" (Aboud and Aboud, 1974, 3).

On the other side, Sterling Spero wrote in 1948:

> When the state denies its own employees the right to strike merely because they are its employees, it defines ordinary labor disputes as attacks upon public authority and makes the use of drastic remedies, and even armed forces the only method for handling what otherwise might be simple employment relations. [Spero, 1948, 16]

Even if one accepts the doctrine of sovereign authority, it has been argued, it does not follow that collective bargaining or striking by public employees must be prohibited. Legislatures have often waived sovereign immunity in other areas of law. In most jurisdictions, individuals are now able to sue public bodies for negligence, for example. And since sovereignty refers to the people's will as expressed in legislative action, the concept does not preclude—indeed, it seems to require—that the people may, through their representatives, enact legislation authorizing government to engage in collective bargaining and permitting public employees to strike. . . .

It has also been pointed out that the sovereignty argument as advanced by governmental units sounds suspiciously like the management prerogatives arguments private employers advanced against the rights of workers in the private sector to organize, bargain, and strike. If those arguments are properly rejected for the private sector, it is not clear why they should be accepted for the public sector. It is worth asking, moreover, what our reaction would be to the sovereignty argument if it were advanced by the government of another country as justification for prohibiting strikes by its citizen-employees. As the Executive Board of the Association of Federal, State, County, and Municipal Employees (AFSCME) has said, "Where one party at the bargaining table possesses all the power and authority, the bargaining process becomes no more than formalized petitioning" (Eisner and Sipser, 1970, 267).

A somewhat different version of the sovereignty argument relies on the claim that the public has rights, and these rights outweigh the right of public employees to strike. Hugh C. Hansen, for example, says:

> In a democracy, the people should decide
> what services the government will supply.
> The right to strike is a powerful weapon, sub-
> ject to abuse, which would indirectly give
> workers the power to make those decisions. A
> public employee strike is only successful if it
> hurts the public. . . . The public has rights; it
> should not be reluctant to assert them.
> [Hansen, 1980]

This sort of appeal to the rights of the public, however, is subject to what seems to me a decisive objection. As Ronald Dworkin has argued, it eliminates the protection which recognition of individual rights is supposed to provide:

> It is true that we speak of the 'right' of society
> to do what it wants, but this cannot be a 'com-
> peting right' of the sort that may justify the
> invasion of a right against the Government.
> The existence of rights against the Govern-
> ment would be jeopardized if the Government
> were able to defeat such a right by appealing
> to the right of a democratic majority to work
> its will. A right against the Government must
> be a right to do something even when the ma-
> jority thinks it would be wrong to do it, and
> even when the majority would be worse off
> for having it done. If we now say that society
> has a right to do whatever is in the general
> benefit, or the right to preserve whatever sort
> of environment the majority wishes to live in,
> and we mean that these are the sort of rights
> that provide justification for overruling any
> rights against the Government that may con-
> flict, then we have annihilated the latter
> rights. [R. Dworkin, 1978, 194]

Thus, if we take seriously the claim that workers in general have a right to strike, we cannot justify abrogating that right by appeal to a conflicting right of the public to decide what services government will supply. (Note that Dworkin is not here objecting to the idea of group rights in contrast to that of individual rights; it is only the idea of the rights of society as a whole, or of a democratic majority, as potentially competing with the rights of individuals, corporations, or other corporate-like entities within the society, that threatens to annihilate the latter rights.)

If we reject the argument from sovereignty, then, there are two further arguments against the right of public employees to strike that pick up different threads from the arguments discussed so far. One appeals to preservation of the normal American political process, and the other to the essentiality of government services. The former may be dealt with more quickly, so let us consider it first.

> What sovereignty should mean in this field is
> not the location of ultimate authority — on that
> the critics are dead right — but the right of
> government, through its laws, to ensure the
> survival of the "normal American political
> process." As hard as it may be for some to ac-
> cept, strikes by public employees may, as a
> long run proposition, threaten that process.
> [Wellington and Winter, 1969, 1125–26]

But what is this normal political process? "Is something abnormal because it does not operate in conjunction with the standard political process and procedures of a particular era? Does the normal political process automatically exclude any methods or goals which will disrupt existing power relations?" (Aboud and Aboud, 1974, 4). And if a group "distorts" the political process by having more power than the average interest group, are public sector unions the only, or even the most salient examples? (Note that, by Dworkin's argument above, the "right of government . . . to ensure the survival" of the normal political process cannot be understood simply as a right to prevent individuals or groups from affecting and influencing the political process through the exercise of their rights.) . . .

The claim that government services are essential may be thought to provide support for prohibition of strikes by public employees in one or more of at least three ways. First, it may be argued that, since these services are essential, it is intolerable that they be interrupted, even temporarily, as they would be by a strike. A second argument is that if essential services are interrupted, the public will put enormous pressure on government to restore them, and government will have little choice but to cave in to union demands, no matter what they are. Thus, if such strikes were permitted, public employee unions would be in an extraordinarily powerful position. Indeed, one opponent of the right to strike in the public sector likens public employee strikes to sieges or mass abductions because, in such a strike, an "indispensible element of the public welfare, be it general safety, health, economic survival, or a vital segment of cultural life such as public education, is made hostage by a numerically superior force and held, in effect, for ransom" (Saso, 1970, 37). A third argument is that, since government services are essential, the individual recipients of those services have a right to receive them. A strike that interrupted such services would, therefore, violate the rights of the would-be recipients, and, since the services are essential, the right to receive them must be an important right. These rights of individual recipients, then, may be said to compete with and outweigh any right of public employees to strike. (This appeal to the rights of individual members of the public does not run afoul of Dworkin's objection, above, which rejects only appeals to the rights of society, or the majority, as a whole.)

Clearly, however, not all government services are essential in the ways required for these arguments to be sound. In addition, somewhat different kinds and degrees of essentiality may be required by each of the three different arguments.

First, from the fact that a given service, such as public education, for example, is essential to society and its members over the long term, it by no means follows that any temporary interruption of such a service is intolerable. Public education is routinely interrupted for summer vacation, spring and fall breaks, holidays, and snow days. Time lost due to (legal or illegal) strikes by school employees can be, and is, made up by scheduling extra days and/or hours of classes. Are transportation services provided by municipal bus lines essential in ways that those provided by privately owned bus companies are not? If hospital workers in voluntary hospitals have the right to strike, why are public hospital employees different? Are their services any more essential? Upon reflection, it appears that

few, if any, public services are essential in the way required to make the first argument sound, i.e., that even temporary interruption of them would be intolerable. Many who reject the first argument as applied to most government services do, nonetheless, accept it for two specific categories of service, those provided by police and firefighters. We shall return to these possibly special cases below.

In response to the second argument, that enormous public pressure to end a strike and restore services would force government to yield even to unreasonable union demands, there are at least [two] things to be said. First, in the absence of the economic pressure that a strike in the private sector exerts on the employer, public pressure to restore services is the only real leverage public employees can bring to bear on management to come to terms. Striking workers, of course, forfeit wages and place their jobs on the line in the public sector just as in the private sector. So the pressure on workers to arrive at an agreement and end a strike is very strong indeed. In contrast, the public sector employer is likely to have tax revenues continue to accrue during a strike, while saving on the wage bill. Without public pressure for the restoration of services, management could comfortably wait out almost any strike, thus rendering the strike weapon totally ineffectual.

Second, the impact on tax rates of wage and benefit packages provides a strong incentive for public sector employers to bargain hard. "For the public employer, increases in the tax rate might mean political life or death; hence, unions are not likely to find him easy prey" (Aboud and Aboud, 1974, 6). And, as AFSCME's Victor Gotbaum points out:

> An automobile can increase in price 300 percent. Your food can go up 200 percent. If your taxes go up even less of a percentage, somehow the public is being raped by public employees. That is not so. In fact, our own studies show that the wage bill has not been going up that high since the arrival of unionism, taxes have not increased at a greater pace than costs in other areas, and yet we get this funny comparison that somehow when workers in the public sector strike, they get a helpless hopeless citizen. [Gotbaum, 1978, 161]

. . . Now let us consider the third argument, that the individual recipients of government services have rights to those services which would be violated if they were interrupted by a strike. First, from the fact that an individual has a right to a government service it does not follow that the right is violated if the service is temporarily interrupted. Even a very important right to a given service need not be violated by a temporary interruption, as it would be, let us suppose, by permanent cessation of the service. Moreover, from the fact that individuals have very important rights to certain services it does not follow that the onus is entirely upon government workers to provide those services without interruption under whatever conditions management chooses to impose. The right is against government or society as a whole, whose obligation it is to create and maintain conditions in which qualified workers are willing to work and provide those services.

It is worth noting, too, that in many instances the issues over which government employees are likely to strike are issues on which the interests of the recipients of government services coincide with those of the providers. Welfare workers demanding lighter case loads, teachers insisting on smaller classes, air traffic controllers complaining about obsolete equipment, understaffing, and compulsory overtime are all instances of government workers attempting to secure adequate conditions in which to do their jobs. The rights of the recipients of these services are not protected by prohibiting the providers from using what may be the only effective means of securing such conditions—quite the contrary. Even where this is not the case, there appear to be no grounds for a general claim that strikes by public employees would violate the rights of the recipients of governmental services. If such a case is to be made, it must be made in much more particular terms with respect to specific categories of service. . . .

We have been unable to find any justification for a general prohibition of strikes by public employees. I conclude that public employees generally, like workers in the private sector, have the moral right to strike, and the right ought to be recognized and protected by law, as it is for all other workers.

We must turn now to consider whether police and firefighters constitute a special case where prohibition of strikes may be justified, even though it is not justified for other public employees. We shall not be able to give this complex and admittedly difficult question adequate discussion here, but we can try at least to identify some of the relevant considerations.

Of the various arguments discussed above, only those appealing to essentiality of services may apply differently to police and firefighters than to other public employees, so those are the only arguments relevant here. As you may recall, there were three arguments from essentiality of services. First, it may be argued that police and firefighting services are essential in a way that makes it intolerable for them to be interrupted, even temporarily. The second argument claims that, if such services were interrupted by a strike, public pressure to have them restored would be so strong that even outrageous demands would be agreed to. Thus police and firefighters are in a position to "hold hostage" the public safety. And, third, individual members of the public may be said to have very important rights to protection of their lives, safety, and property that police and firefighters provide, rights that would be violated if those protections were suspended by a strike.

Concerning the second argument, the burden of proof must be on those who would deny an important right to show that there is more than a theoretical possibility that the right would be abused in seriously harmful ways. More than that, many of our important rights and freedoms are occasionally abused in ways that result in serious harm to others. In most cases, we reluctantly accept the risks in order to preserve the freedoms. Proponents of prohibition of strikes by police and firefighters must, then, provide convincing evidence that legal recognition of their right to strike would create a serious *practical* threat that is out of proportion to the other risks we endure out of respect for rights. I have so far seen no reason to believe that such evidence can be produced. Note, too, that the fact that the restriction in question applies to a minority of the members of society, in contrast to many other possible restrictions of rights that might be adopted, is a reason to be suspicious of it.

Let us grant, though, that one or more of these arguments may have some force in the case of police and firefighters. Is that force sufficient to justify flatly denying to these individuals an important right? The answer to this question seems to depend on what the available alternatives are. It may be that, with some constraints, the right to strike could be retained by these workers without serious threat to the rights or safety of the public. If so, outright prohibition of such strikes still would not be justified.

For example, provision might be made for partial work stoppages with emergency services continued for life-threatening situations. Police functions include many that could be interrupted with some inconvenience but little serious danger to the public; for example, traffic control, parking violations, paper work not immediately essential to protecting the rights either of victims of crime or of the accused. Firefighters might respond to alarms but limit their firefighting to those measures needed in order to carry out all possible rescue efforts.

Another possibility is to provide for a mandatory "cooling off" period of, say, thirty or sixty days. This could be either automatic or available to be invoked by the appropriate public official if he or she deemed it necessary. During this period, mediation could take place in an effort to help the parties reach voluntary agreement. (A mediator is a third party who attempts to help the disputants find a resolution they can agree upon. A mediator has no power to impose a settlement.) Also, during such a period, public officials would have the opportunity to make contingency plans for protecting the public in the event of a strike. It may be objected with some justification that such a "cooling off" period is, or should be, unnecessary. Mediation efforts could be undertaken before, rather than after, a contract runs out, and contingency plans could be made when officials see that negotiations are not going well and the contract is within a month or two of running out. Nevertheless, supposing that public officials sometimes lack wisdom and foresight, and that the public safety may be at stake as a result, there may be some grounds for such a provision.

I see no reason why some such constraints would not suffice to eliminate any serious special threat to the rights and safety of the public that the prospect of a strike by police or firefighters poses. But since some will no doubt remain unpersuaded, and since the precise nature and degree of constraints justifiable on these grounds will be controversial among those who are persuaded, it may be worthwhile to look briefly at what the alternative is if the right to strike is entirely denied. Some procedure must be provided for arriving at a settlement when contract negotions are at an impasse.

The principal alternative is compulsory binding arbitration. Arbitration differs from mediation in that an arbitrator investigates a dispute and issues a decision which is binding on both parties.

There are two sorts of labor disputes in which arbitration may be used. It is most commonly used as a final step for resolving individual grievances that arise under an existing contract. Frequently, the contract itself provides that grievances that are not resolved by the other measures provided in the grievance procedure will go to arbitration. The second kind of dispute is that in question here, where the parties are unable to reach agreement on a contract. We shall be discussing only arbitration of the latter sort.

In the most usual form of arbitration for settling the terms of a contract, the parties present and argue for their positions on the issues that are in dispute, and then the arbitrator draws up terms that he or she considers most fair. Thus the arbitrator may impose terms that were not proposed by either party. It has been objected against this sort of arbitration that, since arbitrators most often "split the difference" between the two sides, there is little incentive for the parties to bargain in good faith, since the more extreme the position they present to the arbitrator the more they are likely to get in the compromise. To avoid this problem, another form of arbitration has been proposed. It is called final-offer arbitration because the arbitrator is restricted to a choice between the final offers of the two parties on all unresolved issues. The arbitrator may not pick and choose among the offers of the parties on different issues — the choice is between one total package or the other. The purpose of this restriction is to provide a strong incentive for each party to make the most reasonable possible proposals — with the hope that, in so doing, they may even arrive at an agreement without going to arbitration. A serious problem with this procedure is that one or both of the final offers may contain some provisions which are eminently reasonable and others which are not. An employer's final offer, for example, might be very reasonable in terms of wages and benefits, but contain a change in the grievance procedure that would be disastrous for the union. In addition, an arbitrator, who is not familiar with the day-to-day operations and problems, may not be in a position accurately to assess which proposals — especially non-economic proposals — are reasonable.

This latter problem constitutes an objection against compulsory arbitration in any form. The parties themselves know best what the issues mean in terms of what it would be like to live and work under a given provision for the next year, two years, or three years, depending on the duration of the prospective contract. They know which issues are so important to them that they are worth risking a strike over, and which provisions they can live with. No third party can know these things as well as the disputants themselves. Thus, both practical considerations and appeal to the right of self-determination argue in favor of allowing the parties to settle their disputes themselves, even if that means strikes will sometimes occur.

Another potential problem with final-offer arbitration is that a different form of "splitting the difference" would tend to arise. Since both parties generally have the right to veto the appointment of an individual arbitrator—and surely they must have this right, since this individual will determine the terms and conditions that will govern their working lives for, typically, one to three years—there will be a strong tendency for arbitrators to decide half of their cases in favor of management and half in favor of unions. An arbitrator with a record of decisions going too often either way would soon be out of work. Now it may be thought that this pressure should be welcomed, since it amounts to a strong incentive for arbitrators to be evenhanded, and hence fair. But it must be noted that there is little reason to expect that, over any given period of time, for any particular arbitrator, management will have made the most reasonable offer in just 50 percent of the cases he or she hears, and the union in the other 50 percent. Yet the pressure is to build a record that appears to reflect just this situation.

Finally, whichever form of arbitration is used, some opponents of compulsory arbitration argue—with a good deal of plausibility, in my view—that arbitrators tend to have backgrounds, educations, life-styles, and social contacts that lead them, consciously or unconsciously, to identify more with supervisors, managers, and public officials than with workers. This identification cannot help but influence their sympathies, their assessment of the arguments put forth by the parties, and hence, ultimately, their decisions. Thus, a system of compulsory arbitration is, probably inevitably, biased in favor of management and against workers. Note that this objection is compatible with the previous one, although it may at first appear not to be. If unions are aware of the pro-management bias of arbitrators then they will risk going to arbitration only when their case is particularly strong. They

will settle voluntarily in many cases where they ought to win in arbitration but probably would not. In such a situation, unions would have a better case than management in significantly more than 50 percent of the cases that actually got to arbitration, so a fifty-fifty split of the decisions would reflect a promanagement bias.

For all of these reasons, then, compulsory binding arbitration is unsatisfactory as a substitute for the right to strike. As a matter of political reality, however, it may be that, given the kinds and degrees of constraint likely to be placed on their right to strike by legislators in a given jurisdiction, police and firefighters do better to accept a system of arbitration than to retain a right to strike that would be rendered utterly ineffectual.

To conclude this discussion of the right of public employees to strike, it must be emphasized that prohibition of strikes does not prevent strikes. Indeed, it can be argued that it is likely to have the opposite effect. New Jersey's Commissioner of Labor and Industry said in 1965 that "it may be more critical to have the strike weapon available to workers to alert management, government, the customers of the government, and the public that they must do something; they cannot go on ignoring the problem" (Male, 1965, 109). (As we noted above, New Jersey still has not recognized the right of public employees to strike.) Allan Weisenfeld develops the argument as follows:

> Strikes in the public sector will be no more frequent, probably less, than in the private sector and cause no greater inconvenience and dislocation. . . . It is the denial of the right to strike in the public sector . . . which invites strike threats. Anti-strike laws create a tendency on the part of public managers to rely on them to bail them out, and hence, they tend to contribute little to help solve the problems before the bargainers. [Weisenfeld, 1969, 139]

Prohibition of strikes may thus exacerbate the very problems it is intended to solve.

Review and Discussion Questions

1. What are the main arguments against granting public employees a right to strike? Which of

these arguments is the strongest? Do you find any of them convincing?

2. In your view, are there any important differences between public employees and workers in the private sector when it comes to the issue of strikes?

3. The claim that government services are essential has been used in three ways to support a prohibition on strikes by public employees. What are these three arguments and what are Gibson's responses to them? Do you agree with Gibson?

4. Should there be any limits on the right of firefighters and police to strike? Should such strikes be banned altogether? Do you agree with Gibson that compulsory binding arbitration is not a satisfactory substitute for the right to strike?

For Further Reading

Richard O. Boyer and **Herbert M. Morais**, *Labor's Untold Story*, 3rd ed. (New York: United Electrical, Radio, and Machine Workers of America, 1975) is a moving prolabor account of the history of the union movement in America.

Mary Gibson, *Workers' Rights* (Totowa, N.J.: Rowman & Allanheld, 1983) is rich in factual background and actual cases.

David R. Hiley, "Employee Rights and the Doctrine of At Will Employment," *Business and Professional Ethics Journal* 4 (Fall 1985) argues that employers do not have an unrestricted right to terminate employees at will.

Barbara Reisman and **Lance Compa**, "The Case for Adversarial Unions," *Harvard Business Review* 63 (May–June 1985); and Jack Barbash, "Do We Really Want Labor on the Ropes?" *Harvard Business Review* 63 (July–August 1985) are two interesting discussions of labor-management relations today.

Mary Strauss, "Sexist Speech in the Workplace," *Harvard Civil Rights–Civil Liberties Law Review* 25 (Winter 1990) discusses the problem of balancing freedom of expression and the protection of women from sexist speech at work.

Patricia Werhane, "Individual Rights in Business," in Tom Regan, ed., *Just Business. New Introductory Essays in Business Ethics* (New York: Random House, 1984) provides a useful overview of many basic moral issues in the workplace.

CHAPTER 7

THE WORKPLACE (2): TODAY'S CHALLENGES

October 29, 1987, was a routine business day for Eastern Airlines—until it received an anonymous tip that some of its baggage handlers at Miami International Airport used drugs. Eastern quickly sprang into action, ordering security guards to round up the ten employees then at work in the airport's plane-loading area. The employees were marched between two rows of guards and into waiting vans—"like terrorists," a lawsuit later claimed—all in full view of other employees and passengers. After questioning the workers, suspicious supervisors put them on board a bus, once again in front of onlookers, and took them to a hospital. There the employees were given an ultimatum: Either take a urine test or be fired on the spot.[1]

The baggage handlers were union members, but they caved in and took the test. All ten of them tested negative (that is, free of drugs), but they weren't happy about what they'd been through. Not long afterward, they filed suit against Eastern in federal court, seeking damages of $30,000 each on charges of invasion of privacy, defamation, and intentional infliction of emotional distress. Eastern won't discuss the incident, but whatever its ultimate legal resolution, the case represents in dramatic form one of the major issues dividing employers and employees today: privacy. Companies are delving further into employees' personal lives than ever before, claiming the need to probe deeper into their health and habits. Workers are resisting ever more adamantly, fighting back for the right to be left alone.

In 1928, U.S. Supreme Court Justice Louis D. Brandeis described the right to privacy, or "the right to be let alone," as "the right most valued by civilized men."[2] He was referring to the Fourth Amendment's guarantee that citizens are protected against illegal searches and seizures by government. Today many Americans are resisting invasions of their privacy not just by government agencies but also by intrusive employers. And not without reason: A recent survey shows that American bosses tend to be less respectful of employees' rights to privacy than their counterparts are in Europe and Canada.[3]

Businesses and other organizations frequently argue that they have a compelling need to know about the personal lives and conduct of their employees, while those employees firmly assert their right to a personal sphere, not subject to the needs, interests, or curiosity of their employers. "I don't think politicians and corporate executives realize how strongly Americans feel about it," says a San Francisco lawyer who specializes in employee lawsuits. "It's not a liberal or a conservative issue, and the fear of abuse doesn't emanate from personnel policies. It's coming out of the larger, impersonal notion that workers are fungible, expendable items."[4]

The previous chapter examined personnel policies and procedures, trade unions, the state of civil liberties on the job, and the efforts of some successful companies to respect the rights, dignity, and moral integrity of their workers. This chapter also focuses on moral issues that emerge in the workplace. It looks in detail at one crucial civil liberty—the right to privacy—and at the ethical choices it poses inside the organization. The remainder of the chapter examines several other topics that are stirring up controversy in today's workplace. More specifically, this chapter explores the following:

1. The nature of privacy and the problems of organizational influence over private decisions

2. The moral issues raised by the use of polygraph and personality tests, employee monitoring, and drug testing in the workplace

3. Working conditions — in particular, health and safety, styles of management, and provision of day-care facilities and maternity leave

4. Job satisfaction and dissatisfaction and the prospects for enhancing the quality of work life

ORGANIZATIONAL INFLUENCE IN PRIVATE LIVES

Privacy is widely acknowledged today to be a fundamental right. Yet corporate behavior and policies often threaten privacy, especially in the case of employees. One way this happens is through the release of personal information about employees. The data banks and personnel files of business and nonbusiness organizations contain an immense amount of private information, the disclosure of which can seriously violate employees' rights. Most firms guard their files closely and restrict the type of material that they can contain in the first place, but the potential for abuse is still great. Although a complicated set of laws and court rulings limits access to such information, a wide range of snoops still manage, legitimately or illegitimately, to get their hands on it.

As a related matter, more employees are successfully suing their former bosses for passing on damaging information to prospective employers. The courts have traditionally considered this sort of information exchange between employers to be "privileged," but

companies can lose this protection by giving information to too many people or by making false reports. Through fear of defamation suits, in fact, many organizations now refuse to reveal anything about former employees except their dates of employment. Such reticence obviously makes it harder for companies to screen job applicants.[5]

More significant are the threats to privacy that can arise on the job itself. For example, some bosses unhesitatingly rummage through the files of their workers, even when they are marked "private," and some companies routinely eavesdrop on their employees' phone calls. Equally important is the way organizations influence behavior that ought properly to be left to the discretion of their employees.

There is, however, no consensus among philosophers or lawyers about how to define privacy, how far the right to privacy extends, or how to balance a concern for privacy against other moral considerations. All of us would agree, nonetheless, that we have a clear right to keep private certain areas of our lives and that we need to have our privacy respected if we are to function as complete, self-governing entities. Particularly important is our right to make personal decisions autonomously, free from the illegitimate influence of our employers.

Even when a genuine privacy right is identified, the strength of that right depends on circumstances — in particular, on competing rights and interests. Privacy is not an absolute value. Corporations and other organizations often have legitimate interests that may conflict with the privacy concerns of employees. Determining when organizational infringement on a person's private sphere is morally justifiable is, of course, precisely the question at issue.

Consider the case of Virginia Rulon-Miller, a marketing manager in IBM's office product division. She made the mistake of falling in love. A week after receiving a 13.3 percent pay raise, she was called on the carpet for dating Matt Blum, a former IBM account manager who had gone to a competitor. She and Blum had begun dating when Blum was at IBM, and he still played on the IBM softball team. IBM told Rulon-Miller to give up Blum or be demoted. "I was so steeped in IBM culture," she says, "that I was going to break up with Matt." But the next day, before she had a chance to do anything, she was dismissed. Even though IBM's decision was based on written policy governing conflicts of interest, a California jury decided that Rulon-Miller's privacy had been invaded. It awarded her $300,000.

On the other hand, a year later the Oregon Supreme Court upheld J. C. Penney's firing of a merchandising manager for dating another employee. He claimed that his right to privacy had been violated. Although it may seem harsh to fire an employee on the basis of personal lifestyle, the court said, private firms aren't barred from discriminating against workers for their choice of mates. And a federal district court permitted the firing of a New Mexico employee with an excellent work record because she was married to a worker at a competing supermarket.[6]

As a general rule, whenever an organization infringes on what would normally be considered the personal sphere of an individual, it bears the burden of establishing the legitimacy of that infringement. The fact that a firm thinks an action or policy is justifiable does not, of course, prove that it is. The firm must establish both that it has some legitimate interest at stake and that the steps it is taking to protect that interest are reasonable and morally permissible. But what are the areas of legitimate organizational influence over the individual?

Legitimate and Illegitimate Influence

The work contract; the firm's responsibilities to owners, consumers, and society at large; and the purpose of the firm itself all support the proposition that the firm is legitimately interested in whatever significantly influences work performance. But no precise definition of a significant influence on work performance can be given, because the connection between an act or policy and the job is often fuzzy. Take, for example, the area of dress. Ace Construction seems to have a legitimate interest in the kind of shoes Doug Bell wears while framing its houses because the quality of the shoes could affect his safety and job performance as well as the firm's liability. On the other hand, whether American Airlines was legitimately pursuing a genuine corporate interest when it forbade a black employee from wearing her hair in corn rows, because the style clashed with the company's corporate image, is more debatable. Perhaps this was a legitimate demand in the name of good public relations, but maybe it was narrowminded, provincial, and idiosyncratic.[7]

An employer's concern with dress can interfere with an employee's personal choices in other ways. Consider the case of Margaret Hasselman, who worked as a lobby attendant in a New York City high-rise. Wearing the new uniform provided by her employer—a poncho with large openings under the arms, dancer's underpants, and white pumps—she repeatedly encountered sexual harassment. She complained about the outfit to her boss, but to no avail. When she eventually refused to wear it, Hasselman was fired. She filed suit, and the courts ruled that no employer has the right to force workers to wear revealing or sexually provocative clothing. On the other hand, in a later case the Equal Employment Opportunity Commission (EEOC) upheld an employer's firing of several female employees who refused to wear swimsuits as part of a swimsuit promotion. The EEOC agreed that the swimsuits were revealing but found no reason to expect that the women would encounter sexual harassment.[8]

The general proposition that a firm has a legitimate interest only in employee behavior that significantly influences work performance applies equally to off-the-job conduct. But determining when that conduct is significantly related to job performance can be difficult. For example, how would you decide the following case?

In an off-the-job fight, a plant guard drew his gun on his antagonist. Although no one was injured, the guard's employer viewed the incident as grounds for dismissal. The employer reasoned that such an action indicated a lack of judgment on the part of the guard. Do you think the employer had a right to fire the guard under these circumstances? The courts did.

By contrast, consider the employee who sold a small amount of marijuana to an undercover agent or the employee who made obscene phone calls to the teen-age daughter of a client. Their employers fired them, but the employees were reinstated by an arbitrator or the court.

Then there's the amorphous area of company image and the question of whether it can be affected by off-the-job conduct. For example, the political activities of a corporate executive could significantly affect the image a firm wishes to project. On the other hand, what an obscure worker on the firm's assembly line does politically might have a comparatively insignificant impact on the company's image.

Companies and other organizations have an interest in protecting their good names. The off-duty conduct of employees might damage an organization's reputation, but in practice damage is often hard to establish. For example, two IRS agents were suspended for "mooning" a group of women after leaving a bar. Would you agree with their suspension? An arbitrator didn't and revoked it. He couldn't see that their conduct damaged the IRS's reputation.[9]

Obviously we can't spell out exactly when off-duty conduct affects company image in some major way, any more than we can say precisely what constitutes a significant influence on job performance. But that doesn't prevent us from being able to judge that in many cases organizations step beyond legitimate boundaries and interfere with what should properly be personal decisions by their employees. This interference can take many forms, but three—one traditional, the other two modern—are worth discussing.

Involvement in Civic Activities. Business and other organizations have traditionally encouraged or pressured employees to participate in public-spirited activities off the job—presumably, in order to enhance the image of the company. Sometimes, for instance, organizations urge employees to participate in civic activities such as running for the local school board or heading up a commission on the arts. At other times business will encourage employees to join civic service organizations, such as Kiwanis, Lions, or Rotary. Still other times, firms may encourage and even compel employees to contribute to charities. Not too long ago a newspaper reported that an office worker was fired for not contributing more than $10 to the United Way. Such a "meager" contribution violated the firm's policy of requiring each employee to give the equivalent of an hour's pay each month. In this case the firm compelled workers to contribute; in other instances organizational "urgings" or "suggestions" have the impact of orders.

In 1979, members of the Army Band won a suit claiming that the posting of soldiers' names who had not contributed to the United Way constituted coercion. The federal judge who heard the case barred all federal departments from setting 100 percent participation goals, holding group meetings to raise money, or using supervisors as fund collectors. His ruling also prohibited making noncontributors return their payroll-deduction cards and restricted the cards of contributors to personnel use. So far, though, this ruling has not limited the scope of fund-raising practices in other organizations.

Attempts by companies to influence off-the-job behavior often constitute invasions of privacy, specifically the privacy of personal decisions. By explicitly or implicitly requiring employees to associate themselves with a particular activity, group, or cause, firms are telling workers what to believe, what values to hold, and what goals to seek outside work.

Health Programs. Sometimes organizations pressure employees in certain directions for "their own good." Consider the aggressive "wellness" programs that some companies are mounting to push employees toward healthier lifestyles. These programs are aimed at helping employees live longer and improve their health and productivity. The programs teach employees about nutrition, exercise, stress, and heart disease and encourage them to give up smoking, eat more healthfully, moderate their drinking, and work out in the company gym or join a company sports team after work. Wellness programs try to make fitness part of the corporate culture, and so far they seem innocent enough. But some worry that the next step is mandating off-the-job behavior. "I think employers are going to get deeper and deeper into the wellness business," says Professor Alan F. Westin of Columbia University. "This is going to throw up a series of profound ethical and legal dilemmas about how they should do it and what we don't want them to do."[10]

Intensive Group Experience. In recent years company interference has taken a more subtle form. Modern psychology has made us aware that most people never realize their potential for perceiving, thinking, feeling, creating, and experiencing. Attempts to enlarge the potential for personal growth have resulted in the human potential movement. The focus of this movement is on developing ways to help people lower their defenses, remove their masks, become more aware and open to experience, feel more deeply, express themselves more effectively, be more creative, and become everything they can be.[11]

Intensive group experience goes by various names, such as sensitivity training groups, encounter groups, T-groups, awareness groups, creativity groups, and workshops. Industry frequently employs a form of intensive group experience called team-building groups to facilitate the attainment of production and related goals as well as to provide opportunities for improved human relations and personal growth.[12] Whatever form it takes, the intensive group experience brings together people who through various exercises attempt to realize the goals of the human potential movement.

Although the potential benefits of such experiences in the workplace are exciting, especially in terms of filling higher-level needs, they nevertheless pose a threat to psychic privacy, especially when groups lay bare a participant's innermost feelings. Although this doesn't always occur, it can. When it does, privacy can be violated.

Obviously, as with most questions about organizational interference with individual privacy, the issue of voluntary participation arises. When employees are genuinely free to participate or not, then such group sessions are provided by management primarily as a means of job enrichment and function as legitimate vehicles to job satisfaction. But where coercion exists, infringement on personal decision making arises, and we must be morally concerned. The coercion may take an oppressive form, as when employers demand that employees participate in such group activities. At other times it can take a subtle form, as when participation in such groups becomes an unwritten prerequisite for job promotion. Sometimes the coercion can take an apparently munificent form, as when employers — rather than discharging workers for reprehensible behavior — order participation in an encounter group. Whatever the form, the presence of coercion raises moral concerns relative to privacy.

OBTAINING INFORMATION

It's no secret that firms frequently seek, store, and communicate information about employees without their consent. A firm may bug employee lounges, hoping to discover who's responsible for pilfering. Another firm may use a managerial grapevine, with supervisors meeting once a month to exchange anecdotal material about employees, some of it obtained in confidence, all of it gathered with the hope of anticipating potential troublemakers. Still another company may keep detailed files on the personal lives of its employees to ensure compatibility with organizational image and reputation.

Of special interest here are two common practices organizations engage in: subjecting employees to various tests and monitoring employees on the job to discover sundry information. Before beginning the discussion, however, a word is in order about the concept of "informed consent" and how it connects with these topics.

Informed Consent

Certainly no employee is ever "compelled" to take a lie-detector, personality, or other test in the sense that someone puts a loaded revolver to the person's head and says, "Take the test or else." But compulsion, like freedom, comes in degrees. Although an employee may not be compelled to take a test in the same way that a prisoner of war, for example, is compelled to cooperate with a captor, enough coercion may be present to significantly diminish the worker's capacity to consent freely to privacy-invading procedures.

Indeed, coercing someone to behave against the person's will is a grave violation of personal autonomy.

The critical issue is not whether workers agree or consent to participate. Obviously if workers sit for an honesty test, for example, they agree to do so. But was their consent valid and legitimate? That's the issue, and it is an altogether reasonable issue to raise, because information collected on workers is often intimately personal and private and, when used carelessly, can injure them.

Informed consent implies deliberation and free choice. Workers must understand what they are agreeing to, including its full ramifications, and must voluntarily choose it. Deliberation requires not only the availability of facts but also a full understanding of them. Workers must be allowed to deliberate on the basis of enough usable information, information that they can understand. Professor of politics Christopher Pyle insists that polygraphers, for example, be required to give subjects the following warning:

> Before you waive your rights, you should know that many decent people have come out of these interviews feeling demeaned.
>
> You should also know that your superior or personnel manager will receive my report and, if he is typical, will rarely risk his career by employing a person who has damaging information of any kind in his record. If you reveal embarrassing information, it may remain in somebody's file for years and you can never be sure who will see it or use it against you. And you should know that polygraphers have been known to wrongly accuse more than 10 percent of those they question.[13]

But usable information is not of itself enough to guarantee informed consent. Free choice is also important — the *consent* part is as significant as the *informed* part of informed consent.

Everyone agrees that for consent to be legitimate, it must be voluntary. Workers must willingly agree to the privacy-invading procedure. They must also be in a position to act voluntarily. One big factor that affects the voluntariness of consent is the pressures, expressed and implied, exerted on employees to conform to organizational policy. These pressures often elicit employee behavior based more on the worker's perception of organizational expectation than on personal preference. The structure and dynamics of the organization can function to exact conformity among its members. When these pressures to conform are reinforced with implicit reprisals, they can effectively undercut the voluntariness of consent. Thus, employers who ignore organizational pressures on workers to comply with privacy-invading procedures can misinterpret consent to a test as voluntary when it is not.

Polygraph Tests

When an individual is disturbed by a question, certain detectable physiological changes occur in the person. The person's heart may begin to race, blood pressure may rise, respiration may increase. The polygraph is an instrument that simultaneously records changes in these physiological processes and, thus, is often used in lie detection.

Businesses cite several reasons for using the polygraph to detect lying. First, the polygraph is a fast and economical way to verify the information provided by a job applicant. Lying on résumés is common, and as the nation's population becomes progressively more mobile, more individuals are seeking employment outside the areas where they grew up. Sometimes they haven't even lived in the community where they are seeking work long enough to establish verifiable records. For small businesses, the cost of running background checks on such applicants can be prohibitive. In contrast, for a mere $80 or $90, the polygraph supposedly can give employers all the answers they need about the applicant.

A second reason for using the polygraph in business concerns the staggering annual losses companies suffer through in-house theft. The polygraph, say its supporters, allows employers to identify dishonest employees or likely ones.

Third, companies argue that in certain decentralized retail operations, like small chain groceries, the use of polygraphs permits business to abolish audits and oppressive controls. They say the use of polygraphs actually increases workers' freedom.

Fourth, employers say the polygraph is a good way to screen candidates for employment. So used, it can help reveal personal philosophy, behavioral patterns, and character traits incompatible with the organization's purpose, function, and image.[14]

Relevant to the morality of polygraph use in the workplace are three major assumptions made by its supporters.[15] First, it's assumed that lying triggers an involuntary, distinctive response that truth telling does not. But this is not necessarily the case. What the polygraph can do is to record that the respondent was more disturbed by one question than by another. But it cannot determine why the person was disturbed. Perhaps the question made the person feel guilty or angry or frightened. But deception does not necessarily lurk behind the emotional response.

A classic case that makes the point involved Floyd Fay of Toledo, Ohio, who in 1978 was sentenced to life for murder, in part on the basis of having failed two polygraph tests. The tests included "control" questions, such as "Before the age of twenty-five, did you ever think of hurting someone for revenge?" Because Fay's heart beat harder and his palms perspired more when he was asked about the crime than when asked about the "control" questions, he was regarded as "deceptive." Fay spent two years in jail before the real killers confessed.

Second, it is assumed that polygraphs are extraordinarily accurate. Lynn March, president of the American Polygraph Association, says that "when administered correctly by qualified operators, the tests are accurate more than 90 percent of the time."[16] But David T. Lykken, a psychiatry professor, claims that these boasts are not borne out by three scientifically credible studies of the accuracy of polygraphs used on actual criminal suspects. The accuracies obtained by qualified operators in these experiments were 63 percent, 39 percent, and 55 percent.[17] Whether the polygraph is accurate 90 percent of the time or less, the conclusion is the same: It cannot reveal with certainty that a person is or is not telling the truth.

The third major assumption about polygraphs is that they cannot be beaten. Lykken, for one, suggests otherwise. The easiest way to beat the polygraph, the psychiatrist claims, is by "augmenting" your response to the control question by some form of covert self-stimulation, like biting your tongue. He says Fay taught some augmenting techniques to twenty-seven fellow inmates who were charged with smuggling drugs. Twenty-three of them subsequently beat the lie detector.

In addition to these considerations, polygraphs infringe on privacy. As professor of politics Christopher Pyle says, they violate "the privacy of beliefs and associations, the freedom from unreasonable searches, the privilege against self-accusation, and the presumption of innocence."[18] That is not to say employers never have the right to abridge privacy or employees never have an obligation to reveal themselves. In cases of excessive in-house theft, employers may be justified in using a polygraph as a last resort. But the threat to privacy remains, together with the other moral concerns that shroud polygraph use. And even if companies have moral justification for resorting to polygraphs, they must be judicious in how they administer them.

The use of polygraphs in business often creates the sinister impression among workers that they will be judged by a machine or that they are being presumed guilty until the machine proves them otherwise. Moreover, casually regarding the polygraph as just another screening device or inventory-control measure may invite employers to extend the sphere of questioning to non-job-related issues, such as marriage, sex, politics, religion, and so on.

The moral concerns embedded in the use of polygraphs suggest three points—in addition to the question of informed consent—to consider in evaluating their use in the workplace:

1. The information the organization seeks should be clearly and significantly related to the job. This caveat harkens back to a determination of the legitimate areas of organizational influence over the individual.

2. Because the polygraph intrudes on psychic freedom, those applying it should consider whether they have compelling job-related reasons for doing so. Some persons contend that among the reasons must be the fact that the polygraph is the only way the organization can get information about a significant job-related matter. They believe that a firm should not subject employees to polygraph tests without having first exhausted all other means of preventing pilferage.

3. We must be concerned with how the polygraph is being used, what information it's gathering, who has access to this information, and how it will be disposed of.

Responding to moral concerns about polygraphs as well as to their practical and statistical limitations, Congress passed the Employee Polygraph Protection Act in 1988. It prohibits most private employers from using lie detectors in "preemployment testing." Private security firms are exempted from the law, along with drug companies, contractors with certain government agencies, and selected others. The law permits the use of polygraphs in "ongoing investigations of economic loss or injury," but it provides a number of procedural safeguards. For instance, the employer must explain the test's purpose to the employee and the reason why he or she was selected to take it. The worker also has a right to consult with someone who will explain the workings and limitations of the machine. Ultimately, the worker retains the option not to submit to the test, and no one can be fired on the basis of a lie-detector test "without other supporting evidence."[19]

Personality Tests

Companies often wish to determine whether prospective employees are emotionally mature and sociable and whether they would fit in with the organization, so they sometimes administer personality tests. These tests can reveal highly personal information and invade privacy by collecting data about employees without their full consent. Consent is usually lacking because, like polygraphs, personality tests rarely are taken on a strictly voluntary basis. They generally function as part of a battery of tests that job applicants must take if they wish to be considered for a position.

Used properly, personality tests serve two purposes in the workplace. First, they help screen applicants for jobs by indicating areas of adequacy and inadequacy. Second, in theory they simplify the complexities of business life by reducing the amount of decision making involved in determining whether a person can relate to others. For example, if a firm knows that Frank Smith is an introvert, it would hardly place him in personnel or public relations.

But one key premise underlying the use of such tests is highly questionable. That premise is that all individuals can usefully and validly be placed into a relatively small number of categories in terms of personality types and character traits. In fact, people

rarely represent pure personality types, such as the classic introvert or extrovert. Nor is the possession of a character trait an all-or-nothing thing. Most of us possess a variety of personality traits in varying degrees, and social circumstances often influence the characteristics we display and the talents we develop. When organizations attempt to categorize employees, they oversimplify both human nature and their employees' potential and force people into artificial arrangements that may do justice neither to employees nor to the firms they work for.

Personality tests also screen for organizational compatibility, which has serious moral implications. From the firm's view, it is ironic that such a function can eliminate prospective employees whose creativity may be exactly what the firm needs. When used this way, personality tests raise a pressing moral issue in the employer–employee relationship: conformity of the individual to organizational ideals. Organizations by nature represent a danger to individual freedom and independence. When personality tests are used to screen for conformity to organizational values, goals, and philosophy, they can catalyze this natural tendency into a full-blown assault. For this reason the use of such tests always raises moral concerns.

Monitoring Employees on the Job

In the past decade, most major employers have gained the technical ability to monitor the performance of their employees through the computers and telephones they use. In service-oriented businesses like insurance and telecommunication, the practice is especially prevalent as a way of ensuring better and more efficient treatment of customers. And workers don't necessarily resent this monitoring, if it is in the open. "I don't think people mind having their work checked," says Morton Bahr, president of the Communications Workers of America. "It's the secretiveness of it." Legislation has been proposed in

Congress that would prohibit secret telephone monitoring and require regular beeps when a supervisor is listening to an employee's conversations.[20]

Employers sometimes monitor their employees for reasons other than checking on customer service. Where in-house theft, sabotage, or other threatening behavior occurs, organizations frequently install monitoring devices both to apprehend the employees who are responsible and to curtail the problem. These devices take the form of mirrors, cameras, and electronic devices. They can be used to monitor suspected trouble spots or private acts. As with personality and polygraph tests, monitoring can gather information about employees without their informed consent.

Organizations frequently confuse notification of such practices with employee consent, but notification does not constitute consent. When employee restrooms, dressing rooms, locker rooms, and other private places are being bugged, an obvious and serious threat to privacy exists—posted notices notwithstanding. It's true that in some cases surveillance devices may be the only way to apprehend the guilty. Nevertheless, they can do more harm than good by violating the privacy of the vast majority of innocent employees. Obviously, even more serious moral questions arise when monitoring devices are not used exclusively for the purposes intended but also for cajoling, harassing, or snooping on employees.

Drug Testing

Drug testing first became a live issue for some sports fans when in 1987 the National Collegiate Athletic Association (NCAA) banned, for the first time, some college football players from postseason bowl competition because of the results of steroid testing. But for some years now, political and legal battles have been raging in all states over the drug testing of employees—in part because the Bush administration, like its predecessor, has championed drug testing of federal workers for cocaine and other illicit drugs and encouraged private industry to do the same. Many companies have, in fact, embraced testing. Commonwealth Edison, for example, now routinely screens prospective employees for drug use. Its policy won support from a recent study published in the *Journal of the American Medical Association*, which showed that postal workers who tested positive for drug use in a preemployment urine test were at least 50 percent more likely to be fired, injured, disciplined, or absent than those who tested negative. Other companies, however, like Bank of America and American Telephone and Telegraph, remain skeptical of the benefits of testing either current employees or job applicants.[21]

In principle, testing employees to determine whether they are using illegal drugs raises the same questions that other tests raise: Is there "informed consent"? How reliable are the tests? Is testing really pertinent to the job in question? Are the interests of the firm significant enough to justify encroaching on the privacy of the individual? But rather than reiterate the above issues, all of which are important and relevant, this section limits itself to four additional remarks:

1. The issue of drug testing by corporations and other organizations arises in the broader context of the drug-abuse problem in America today (which includes the abuse not just of illegal "street drugs" but of alcohol and prescription medicines as well). To discuss this problem intelligently, one needs good information, reliable statistics, and sociological insight, yet these are notoriously hard to come by. Popular news magazines run frequent and alarming cover stories on drugs, particularly cocaine and crack, and hours of the nightly network news are given over to sensationalistic drug-related stories. Likewise, many politicians find it advantageous to

portray themselves as battling courageously against a rising flood of drugs. (Every president since John F. Kennedy has "declared war on drugs"—some more than once.) And our movies and television programs suggest a public fascination with the gangsterism that has come from outlawing these substances. Yet most of this media coverage and political hoopla is at best superficial, at worst misleading and even hysterical. For example, the public has yet to be presented with hard evidence that substance abuse is a greater problem today than it was ten years ago.

This is not to minimize the problems that drug abuse can pose for business and other organizations—some writers believe that 10 percent of the work force is addicted to alcohol or drugs[22]—but rather to observe that excessive media attention and political posturing can create a false sense of crisis, leading people perhaps to advocate unnecessarily extreme measures.

2. Drugs differ, so one must carefully consider both what drugs one is testing for and why. Steroids, for instance, are a problem for the NCAA but not for IBM. In addition, drug testing can only be defensible when it is really pertinent to employee performance and when there is a lot at stake. Testing airline pilots for alcohol consumption is one thing; testing the luggage crews is something else. To go on a "fishing trip" in search of possible employee drug abuse, when there is no evidence of a problem or of significant danger, seems unreasonable.

3. Drug abuse by an individual is a serious problem, calling for medical and psychological assistance rather than punitive action. The moral assessment of any program of drug testing must rest in part on the potential consequences for those taking the test: Will they face immediate dismissal and potential criminal proceedings or therapy and a chance to retain their positions? To put the issue another way, when an organization initiates a testing program, does it approach this as a kind of police function? Or is it responsive to the needs and problems of individual employees? Some business writers argue that voluntary, nonpunitive drug-assistance programs are far more cost-effective for companies, in any case, than testing initiatives.[23]

4. Any drug-testing program, assuming it is warranted, must be careful to respect the dignity and rights of the persons to be tested. "Due process" must also be followed, including advance notification of testing as well as procedures for retesting and appealing test results. All possible steps should be taken to ensure individual privacy.

WORKING CONDITIONS

In a broad sense, the conditions under which people work include personnel policies and procedures, as well as the extent to which an organization is committed to respecting the rights and privacy of its employees. This section, however, examines three other aspects of working conditions: health and safety on the job, styles of management, and the organization's maternity and day-care arrangements.

Health and Safety

In September 1989, ten miners died in a methane explosion at the Pyro Mining Company's William Station mine in Union County, Kentucky; the Labor Department subsequently found numerous electrical safety violations. In Galveston a few years before, a grain elevator exploded, injuring workers and leading to criminal indictment of the supervisors of the operation. These are dramatic episodes. By contrast, there was less publicity when

Dennis Claypool, 21, and Mark DeMoss, 18, suffocated as they cleaned a tanker trailer at a trucking company outside Chicago. The two didn't know that the tanker had recently been cleaned with nitrogen, which removes oxygen from the air. A freak accident? Experts say some 300 workers a year die in such "confined space" incidents.[24]

The electronics industry may look safe in comparison with occupations like mining, but behind its clean image lurk health hazards for workers.[25] Corrosive hydrochloric and hydrofluoric acids, poisons such as arsine gas and cyanide, known or suspected carcinogens like vinyl chloride and trichloroethylene, and other toxic chemicals are indispensable to the fabrication of computer chips. Industrial hygienists report that production workers in the San Francisco Bay area's Silicon Valley, a world center of the semiconductor industry, are increasingly suffering illnesses caused by chemical exposures. Many of these workers speak little English and may not even be aware that they are working with suspected carcinogens and toxic substances with possible long-range health and reproductive effects. Even if they could understand English well, it probably wouldn't help, for in 1981 the electronic lobby helped defeat a California Assembly bill that would have required companies to give workers written warnings on each chemical they handle.[26]

Employees in fact have a legal right to refuse work when it exposes them to imminent danger, and their employers are forbidden to reprimand or otherwise retaliate against them for doing so. The Supreme Court made this clear in 1980, when it upheld a lower court ruling in favor of two employees of the Whirlpool Corporation who had refused to follow their foreman's order to undertake maintenance activities they considered unsafe.[27] Although in 1991 California began requiring companies to inform workers in writing of any life-threatening hazards or face fines and prison terms,[28] employees across the nation are frequently unaware of the dangers they face in the workplace, some of which may be long term, rather than "imminent" hazards.

Despite legislation, the scope of occupational hazards remains awesome and generally unrecognized. A Mt. Sinai Hospital report, for example, estimates that occupational disease is the fourth-ranked cause of death in New York State, killing between 4,686 and 6,592 employees each year.[29] With 80 million workers nationwide, there are over 7 million annual work-related diseases and injuries, of which millions are disabling and many fatal. According to the National Institute of Occupational Safety and Health, an average of 32 workers are killed on the job each day of the year in the United States; another 5,500 suffer a disabling injury.[30] The financial cost is an estimated $48 billion a year in workers' compensation, plus billions more in Social Security and health payments, much of it reflected in higher prices for goods and services.[31]

Although the thrust of the 1970 Occupational Safety and Health Act is "to ensure so far as possible every working man and woman in the nation safe and healthful working conditions," implementation of the act has been spotty. Fewer than 100 qualified Occupational Safety and Health Administration (OSHA) industrial hygienists and approximately 500 OSHA inspectors oversee about 4 million workplaces. And OSHA has established only one permanent standard — for asbestos.

Compounding the problem is the cozy relationship between OSHA and industry that developed during the Reagan administration, which took measures that weakened the protective organization. For example, OSHA was required to target specific industries known to be especially hazardous. While economical, the move effectively relieved OSHA of one of its most potent weapons: the threat of an unannounced inspection. It also left unguarded millions of workers in "untargeted" industries. Despite the emphasis on specific industries, the percentage of inspections resulting in citations dropped substantially. The number of "Serious Citations" fell to about half of what it had been, and "Willful Citations" plunged even lower. Furthermore, regional OSHA offices were encouraged to reduce fines and the number of contested citations.

Consider the case of Stephen Golab, a fifty-nine-year-old immigrant from Poland who worked for a year stirring tanks of sodium cyanide at the Film Recovery Services plant in Elk Grove, Illinois. On February 10, 1983, he became dizzy from the cyanide fumes, went into convulsions, and died. OSHA then inspected the plant and fined Film Recovery Services $4,855 for twenty safety violations. Later OSHA cut the fine in half. In contrast, the state attorney general for Cook County filed criminal charges. Three company officials were convicted of murder and fourteen counts of reckless conduct. The company itself was also convicted of manslaughter and reckless conduct and was fined $24,000.

Ironically, employers staunchly opposed the creation of OSHA in the first place but are now trying to use the organization as a shield. They argue that the existence of OSHA legally preempts state criminal prosecutions in cases like the Golab case — that is, that it prevents states from imposing stronger civil or criminal penalties on companies for health and safety violations. This legal argument has met with success in some state courts.[32]

Recent evidence suggests that OSHA is beginning to recover from a long period of neglect and slashed budgets, but it will take some time to overcome its reputation for lax enforcement[33] One problem that OSHA will have to address in the future is "repetitive strain injury," or "cumulative trauma disorder," which results from the constant repetition of awkward hand and arm movements. Telephone operators, meat packers, court stenographers, supermarket check-out clerks, and many other workers are suffering from numb fingers, swollen knuckles, aching wrists, and other crippling injuries. These may sound like minor complaints, but they are anything but minor to those who suffer from them. Ask Janie Jue of San Francisco. For seventeen years she keyed in up to 48,000 strokes a day on an automatic letter-sorting machine for the post office. Today, just picking up a book or coffee pot sends bolts of pain tearing up her hand and arm. "I wish I could work," she says, "but it hurts from my elbow to my fingertips."[34]

The number of such cases reported by the Bureau of Labor Statistics has nearly tripled, but virtually all experts agree that the problem is vastly underreported. One expert calls it "the occupational epidemic of the 1990s." The breaking up of jobs into smaller and smaller units, with each worker performing fewer tasks but repeating them thousands of times a day, has contributed to the problem in manufacturing industries. Garment workers, meat packers, and others in hand-intensive jobs used to be able to recover at night from the cumulative stress on their bodies. But increased assembly-line speed and piecework rates now make it harder for their bodies to bounce back the next day. And to the dismay of many, repetitive stress injuries are spreading among white-collar office workers, who are supposedly in safe office jobs. Those who spend all day at the video display terminal risk developing tendonitis, carpal tunnel syndrome, and other hand ailments. This led San Francisco to become in 1991 the nation's first municipality to require employers to protect employees from the hazards of working at computers.[35]

The redesign of jobs, adjustable chairs, training in the proper use of video display terminals, and other preventive measures can often reduce the problem of repetitive strain injury. In the meantime, it is not only the employees who are suffering. Having a skilled worker go out on long-term disability and vocational rehabilitation can cost a company asmall fortune. Pacific Bell, for example, estimates that the direct cost to the company for the 140 repetitive-strain-injury complaints among its workers in a recent year was about $1.5 million. The United Auto Workers calculates that the costs are equivalent to adding 50 cents to the hourly wage of the average worker. And Roger Stephens of OSHA reckons that the total cost to industry of all types of repetitive strain injury could easily top $10 billion a year.

One aspect of work life over which OSHA exercises little direct control is the shifts people work. Yet a team of scientists from Harvard and Stanford universities believes that the health and productivity of 25 million Americans whose work hours change regularly can be measurably improved if employers schedule shift changes to conform with the body's natural and adjustable sleep cycles. The team reached this conclusion after studying workers at the Great Salt Lake Chemical and Minerals Corporation plant in Ogden, Utah. Corporate officials commissioned the study after workers repeatedly complained about insomnia, fatigue, digestive disorders, and falling asleep on the job. The workers had been changing shifts every week, usually to earlier rather than later starting times. The researchers discovered that moving workers to a later shift every three weeks enables them to adjust so they can sleep when they have to and be alert on the job.

We have only recently begun to appreciate fully another aspect of work life — the health implications of stress. Three-quarters of Americans say their jobs cause them stress; stress now accounts for 14 percent of workers' compensation claims and costs business an estimated $150 billion annually.[36] Revamping work environments that produce stress and helping employees learn to cope with stress are among the major health challenges facing us in the 1990s.

Management Styles

How managers conduct themselves on the job can do more to enhance or diminish the work environment than any other single facet of employer–employee relations. In survey after survey, employees rank honest company communications and respectful treatment as more important than good pay. James E. Challenger, president of the nation's oldest outplacement company, says personal recognition is the most important job consideration among the people he meets. It outweighs salary by a four-to-one margin.[37]

Mightily influencing management conduct are the general assumptions managers make about human beings and the subsequent leadership styles they adopt. The late Douglas McGregor observed that managers tend to hold one of two basic sets of culturally induced assumptions about human beings.[38] He called these Theories X and Y. According to McGregor, managers who espouse Theory X believe that workers essentially dislike work and will do everything they can to avoid it. Such managers insist that the average person wishes to avoid responsibility, lacks ambition, and values security over everything else. He or she must be coerced and bullied into conformity with organizational objectives.

In contrast, Theory Y managers believe workers basically like work and view it as something natural and potentially enjoyable. Workers are motivated as much by pride and a desire for self-fulfillment as by money and job security. They don't eschew responsibility but accept it and seek it out.

These basic assumptions about human nature can lead to contrasting styles of management. Theory X managers are likely to provide autocratic leadership. They closely shepherd workers by giving orders and directions. They rarely solicit ideas about how tasks should be performed but tell employees what to do and how to do it. They expect little more of employees than that they follow orders. Theory Y managers, on the other hand, are more likely to be democratic. While informing workers of the task to be performed, they also invite new ideas about how to do those tasks. They use this information to refine their own ideas about job performance. Theory Y managers can be virtually nondirective. Viewing themselves as resource persons, troubleshooters, and supporters rather than directors of the work force, they are inclined to leave decisions on work methods to the workers.

No set of assumptions about human nature is absolutely correct or incorrect, nor is there one perfectly right way to manage. But that's precisely the point. Moral problems inevitably arise when managers routinize their leadership style, regardless of the idiosyncrasies of their employees. Some employees, at whatever level, respond to and need little managerial orchestration; others need and want close supervision. When managers ignore these individual differences, they overlook people's needs and run risks of creating a work atmosphere that's not only distressing to workers but also less than optimally productive. If these problems are to be avoided, it seems that managers must carefully examine their preconceptions and choose a style of leadership suited to the needs, abilities, and predilections of those in their charge.

Increasingly, critics charge that American managerial style is too conservative, traditional, and inflexible and that many managers put their personal ambition ahead of everything else. One such critic is H. Ross Perot, a self-made billionaire. Perot became General Motors's largest shareholder and a member of its corporate board when he sold his computer services company, Electronic Data Systems Corporation, to GM in 1984 for $2.5 billion. Two years later GM ousted Perot from the board, buying back his GM stock for $700 million.

Why the buy-back? Observers agree that the fiery Perot was more than GM, widely considered one of the most tradition-bound corporations in America, could handle. Perot dared to question longstanding management practices; he talked to workers on the factory floor about new ideas; he shopped anonymously at GM dealerships, trying to evaluate customer service. All that was too much for GM. Under the buy-back agreement, Perot

isn't supposed to make negative comments about GM, but he does say the corporation is beset by power-hungry executives who spend all their time trying to move up the corporate ladder and care little about their product. "Corporate infighting," "management power struggles," "maneuvering and politics and power-grabbing," and "Machiavellian intrigues" are his phrases to describe the reality of corporate life today.[39]

We must be careful about generalizing from the experiences of one person in one company, but Perot's reports tally with too many others' to write him off as a crank. Managers who devote their energies to corporate infighting and personal advancement and corporations that are too tradition-bound to handle strong criticism, even inside the board room itself, are real problems. Dealing with them is part of the economic challenge facing America today, as discussed in Chapter 4. But problems of management style also affect unfavorably employees' working conditions.

Day Care and Maternity Leave

One often overlooked area in discussions of working conditions is the provision of maternity/paternity leave and child-care services for workers with children. The need for day-care services is clearly growing, yet the United States falls behind many industrialized nations in the provision of such services. The situation is even more striking with respect to maternity leave. At least 117 other countries provide paid maternity leave, but a California law requiring employers to provide unpaid leave and reinstatement of pregnant employees was fought all the way to the Supreme Court before finally being upheld in January 1987.[40] Four other states have joined California in guaranteeing pregnant workers leave and reinstatement in their previous jobs or equivalent positions.

Today women constitute about 45 percent of the paid labor force, a higher figure than at any time in history. In 1950 only 20 percent of the married women with children under the age of eighteen were in the paid labor force, but this number had grown to more than 50 percent by 1980. Today, two-thirds of all women with children under eighteen work, and only half of those with children under the age of one stay home.[41] The rise in the employment participation rates of women with small children is expected to continue.[42] Experts anticipate that two-thirds of all new workers through the year 2000 will be women.[43]

Given that women in our society continue to bear the primary responsibility for child rearing, their increasing participation in the paid work force represents a growing demand for reasonable maternity-leave policies and affordable child-care services. Nor is this demand likely to diminish. Many families are unable to make satisfactory child-care arrangements, either because the services are unavailable or for the simple reason that the parents cannot afford them.[44] An estimated 5 million children are thus left alone without any supervision while their parents work. The need for child-care services is particularly acute among single-parent families, 91 percent of which are headed by women. Single mothers have a higher rate of participation in the labor force than do married mothers. Nevertheless, many of them are poverty-stricken and hence unable to pay for satisfactory child-care services.[45]

Very few companies do much to help with employee child care. Campbell's Soup is one of the exceptions. It offers on-site day care, spending over $200,000 annually to subsidize 50 percent of tuition costs at the child-care center for the children of employees at corporate headquarters. Procter & Gamble holds priority rights for 75 percent of the spaces in two off-site centers near its Cincinnati headquarters. It also provides a day-care resource and referral service for the entire community. IBM provides a free nationwide referral system for its 237,000 employees and has helped to develop child-care services where they have been deficient or lacking. Polaroid Corporation provides assistance with child-care costs for permanent employees earning less than $30,000.[46] Because its employees work at all hours, America West airlines provides 24-hour child care with a sliding scale subsidy to make it affordable.[47] Despite these examples, the overall corporate record on child care is poor.

Employers are in a good position to assist in the provision of child-care services, especially in light of cutbacks in federal funding. Few if any employers, however, currently feel under an obligation to offer child-care services, primarily because initiating and maintaining such programs costs money. Yet viewed from a broader perspective, day-care arrangements set up by companies themselves or by several companies together in the same area are socially "cost-effective." With in-house day-care arrangements, parents do not have to make special trips to pick up and deposit their children. Since the parents are not far away, they can have more interaction with their children. Depending on the specific organization of work and the firm's flexibility, parents could share in the actual running of the child-care facility at assigned intervals during the course of their working day.

Some have argued, moreover, that offering child care as a fringe benefit may prove advantageous for most employers.[48] Such benefits can be cost-effective in the narrower sense by decreasing absenteeism, boosting morale and loyalty to the firm, and enhancing productivity. This is an important consideration.

Even more important are the underlying moral issues. First, women have a right to compete on an equal terrain with men. Firms that do not provide at least unpaid maternity leave and reinstatement clearly fail to respect this right. Those who oppose requirements like that of the California law mentioned previously could probably not sincerely universalize their position. Nor have they been able to point to any competing economic considerations strong enough to override women's right of equal opportunity. Whether firms should also provide paid maternity leave is more controversial, although one might argue that paid leave is necessary to give substance to this right. Or one might defend such a policy on the utilitarian ground that it would enhance total social welfare. In fact, many organizations find it in their self-interest to provide paid leave so they can attract better and more talented employees.

Second, from various ethical perspectives, the development of our potential capacities is a moral ideal—perhaps even a human right. For this reason, or from the point of view of promoting human well-being, many theorists would contend that women should not be forced to choose between childbearing and the successful pursuit of their careers. Nor should they be forced to reduce the quality of their commitment either to their children or to their careers. If circumstances of work force them to do so, and if those circumstances could reasonably be changed, then we have not lived up to the ideal of treating those women as persons whose goals are worthy of respect.

Third, although the last two decades have seen many criticisms of, and attempts to move beyond, the traditional male–female division of labor within the family, there can be little doubt that the world of work tends to reproduce those patterns. For instance, as mentioned in the previous chapter, men who leave work to help raise children often face enormous hurdles when returning to the job market. It seems clear that many fathers today feel hampered by work arrangements that pit meaningful career advancement against a fully developed family life. Enhanced opportunities for part-time employment and job sharing, along with generous parental leave arrangements and flexible, affordable, and accessible firm-sponsored child-care facilities could enable both fathers and mothers to achieve a more personally desirable balance between paid work and family relations.

The moral value here is not to promote any single vision of the good life but rather to permit individuals, couples, and families as much autonomy as possible, given other social goals. They should be able to define the good life for themselves and to seek the arrangement of work and personal relations that makes that life possible. Firm-affiliated child-care services and other institutional arrangements that accommodate parental needs can clearly play a key role in the overall redesigning of work to enhance workers' well-being.

REDESIGNING WORK

An earlier chapter looked at alienation under capitalism and changing attitudes toward work in America. And it remains true that many, perhaps even most, employees are dissatisfied with their jobs to some extent. Any investigation of the moral issues arising around the workplace and any discussion of the challenges facing business today must confront this basic problem and consider ways of improving the quality of work life.

Dissatisfaction on the Job

In the early 1970s the government conducted a study of work in America, whose basic findings are still relevant today.[49] The study identified three chief sources of worker dissatisfaction. The first concerned industry's preoccupation with quantity, not quality; the rigidity of rules and regulations; and the fracturing of work into the smallest possible tasks, together with the monotonous repetition of these tasks. The second source of dissatisfaction concerned the lack of opportunities to be one's own boss. The third source of dissatisfaction concerned "bigness": More people work for large corporations now than ever before. Other studies since then have cited workers' feelings of powerlessness, meaninglessness, isolation, and self-estrangement or depersonalization.

The *Work in America* survey reported similar feelings in the managerial ranks. One of three middle managers at that time was willing to join a union. A similar study by the American Management Association found that about half of the middle managers surveyed favored a change in the National Labor Relations Act to allow collective bargaining between middle and top management. Moreover, just as industrial workers voiced general complaints about work, so did middle managers. Some objected to the little influence they had in their organizations, and others objected to the organization's goals, policies, and ways of operating. Still other managers complained about tension, frustration, and infighting that intraorganizational competition can breed. Beyond these complaints, the *Work in America* survey reported that many managers felt like cogs in a machine, like parts that could and would be replaced when a better part came along.

Recent studies confirm that an increasing number of workers at all occupational levels express declining confidence and satisfaction with employer policies and practices and with the behavior of top management.[50] If industry is to improve productive capacity and be more competitive, it must seriously confront these attitudes and the sources of employee dissatisfaction. It must devise ways to make work more satisfying, thereby motivating workers to be more productive, and it must make certain work-practice reforms that will improve the quality of work life.

As early as the 1920s, researchers began to realize that workers would be more productive if management met those needs that money cannot buy. Managers at the Hawthorne factory of Western Electric Company were conducting experiments to determine the effect of the work environment on worker productivity. In the literature of work motivation, these studies have become known as the Hawthorne studies. What they discovered has been termed the "Hawthorne effect."

Researchers in the Hawthorne studies chose a few employees to work in an experimental area, apart from the thousands of employees in the rest of the factory. Every effort was made to improve working conditions, from painting walls a cheerful color to making lights brighter. Worker productivity increased with each improvement.

Then experimenters decided to reverse the process. For example, lights were made dimmer. To everyone's surprise, productivity continued to increase.

The conclusion researchers drew was that workers were producing more because they were receiving attention. Instead of feeling that they were cogs in the organizational wheel, they felt important and recognized. The attention had the effect of heightening their sense of personal identity and feeling of control over their work environment. Recognition of this effect can help management increase worker motivation and job satisfaction and also increase the organization's productivity.

More recent studies tend to corroborate and deepen the application of the Hawthorne effect. In an important study conducted to shed light on the problem of poor worker motivation, Frederick Herzberg discovered that factors producing job satisfaction differed from those producing job dissatisfaction. Herzberg found that job dissatisfaction frequently arises from extrinsic problems, such as pay, supervision, working conditions, and leadership styles. But resolving those extrinsic problems does not necessarily produce satisfied workers. They can still express little or no job satisfaction. The reason, Herzberg contends, is that worker satisfaction depends on such factors as a sense of accomplishment, responsibility, recognition, self-development, and self-expression.

Other surveys lend credence to Herzberg's findings. When 1,533 workers at all occupational levels were asked to rank in order of importance to them some twenty-five aspects of work, they listed interesting work; sufficient help, support, and information to accomplish the job; enough authority to carry out the work; good pay; the opportunity to develop special skills; job security; and a chance to see the results of their work.[51]

To dramatize the moral import of the work-design question, consider a study conducted by the Institute of Social Research. In studying a cross-section of American workers, the institute found numerous mental health problems directly attributable to lack of job satisfaction. These problems included psychosomatic diseases such as ulcers and hypertension, low self-esteem, anxiety, and impaired interpersonal relations.[52] Similarly, in an exhaustive study of industrial workers, A. W. Kornhauser found that about 40 percent of all auto workers exhibited some symptoms of mental health problems related to job satisfaction.[53] In general, studies indicate that greater mental health problems occur in low-status, boring, unchallenging jobs that offer little autonomy. These findings are of particular relevance to today's work force, in which many persons of relatively high educational achievement occupy comparatively low-status jobs.

One of the most intriguing studies not only suggests a correlation between longevity and job satisfaction but also contends that job satisfaction is the strongest predictor of longevity.[54] The second major factor for longevity is happiness. Both of these factors predict longevity better than either the physical health or genetic inheritance of individuals.

The moral thrust here is the idea that the design of work materially affects the total well-being of workers. This fact alone would make work content and job satisfaction paramount moral concerns. But of course there is the additional issue of worker productivity. If we assume that a happier, more contented worker is generally a more productive one, then it follows that business has an economic reason as well as a moral obligation to devise

ways, in concert with labor and perhaps even government, to improve the quality of work life (QWL).

Quality of Work Life (QWL)

This book isn't the place for determining precisely what QWL measures firms should take. For some firms QWL may mean providing workers with less supervision and more autonomy. For others it may mean providing work opportunities to develop and refine skills. Still other firms might try to provide workers with greater participation in the conception, design, and execution of their work—that is, with greater responsibility and a deeper sense of achievement. Perhaps all companies ought to examine the impact of technology on job satisfaction. While typically increasing the efficiency of operations and eliminating the physical drudgery that plagued yesterday's workers, today's technology sometimes results in repetitive and boring tasks that, in the long run, may diminish productivity and destroy job satisfaction.

One purpose of QWL programs is to thaw the antagonistic worker–boss climate that exists in many plants and hurts production. But the key purpose is to involve workers more fully in the production process by seeking their ideas. Accordingly, QWL programs go by various names: "worker participation," "labor–management teams," "industrial democracy," and so on. In the steel industry, to name one, labor–management participation teams have been used to deal with both quality and productivity challenges and with worker job satisfaction.

One very promising response to the need for QWL programs is quality-control circles, which two American personnel consultants introduced to Japanese industries more than thirty years ago. Now widely used in Japan, the "circles" are committees of workers and supervisors who meet to discuss quality improvement. Curiously, some U.S. companies are now rediscovering the concept. Westinghouse, for one, has established about 150 quality circles at fifty locations. By Westinghouse's account, these circles have suggested changes that have saved the company more than $1 million in two years.

But the only way management can implement such programs is with the full cooperation of workers and their representatives, and some union members are a little wary. "The largest loss is the union's autonomy," says one.[55] "We become one with the corporate agenda. It's an unnatural place for the union to be." Investigators believe that the success of QWL programs and other workplace reform efforts depends on the ability of the organization to reinforce high levels of trust. To the extent that it does so, organizational performance can improve.[56] But, warns William Cooke, professor at Wayne State University and author of a book on workplace reform, "if [workers] perceive management as doing this without due consideration for the welfare of employees . . . it will have the potential of destroying the efforts altogether."[57]

Granting workers new responsibilities and respect can benefit the entire organization. Randy Pennington, vice president of Performance Systems Corporation, tells of a friend who showed an ad for a new American car to a Japanese businessperson. The ad said that the car "set a new standard for quality because it was examined by 34 different quality inspectors." "Now, *this*," he said to his Japanese colleague, "is what we need to compete with you. Imagine: 34 quality inspectors!" The Japanese looked at the ad, smiled, and said, "You don't need 34 inspectors to get quality. You just need everyone who works on the car to be proud of the work. Then you'll need only one inspector."[58]

The case of GM's assembly plant at Tarrytown, New York, provides a classic example of how QWL programs and more collaborative labor relations can dramatically improve employee attendance, motivation, and performance. Back in the early 1970s, Tarrytown was in serious trouble. Rampant absenteeism, poor product quality, and strained labor–management relations all threatened to halt operations. As a result, United Auto Worker representatives and plant managers began to meet informally to solve labor problems. From these informal meetings emerged full-scale QWL programs throughout the plant.

The core of the Tarrytown program is a three-day orientation seminar for all plant workers. In these meetings, company and union goals are explained, workers are shown the interrelation of various assembly-line jobs, and they are introduced to workers in other departments. At a higher level, UAW local officials and plant managers meet regularly to anticipate problems before they become unwieldy. At Tarrytown worker input is invited, dress codes are relaxed, and socializing on the job is permitted. The UAW says it cooperates in the QWL programs because they make jobs more satisfying. For its part, management fosters the programs because they seem to improve productivity.

Today, closer union–management relations characterize many GM plants. Mike Spitzley, manager of GM's 5,300 worker car-truck plant in Janesville, Wisconsin, for example, says "most of the things we talk about, it's 'we.' It's not us versus them. We've pretty much realized that our goals are the same" as the union's. Mike O'Brien, president of the local chapter of the United Auto Workers, agrees. "There's something different going on," he says. "Years ago, it wasn't any of our business what went on in the business." The most striking example is GM's Saturn Corporation, where union and management share all big decisions, from choosing suppliers to picking the company's advertising agency.[59]

At GM, the ideals of improved job atmosphere, employee participation, and worker job security have meshed nicely with the goal of increased productivity. Recent studies provide evidence of this compatibility in many other cases, too. Not only is productivity 5 to 10 percent higher in companies with profit sharing, but productivity is also consistently higher in enterprises with an organized program of worker participation.[60]

Although a range of social and economic research supports this conclusion, there is no guarantee that worker participation and an improved quality of work life will always boost productivity; sometimes an apparent QWL improvement can lead to a decrease in productivity. For example, although diversifying tasks may make work more satisfying, it may hurt both productivity and quality. Japanese car makers, to cite one case, have effectively reduced the number of rejects on their assembly line, not by diversifying, but by standardizing the cars produced. Again, Volkswagen has found that its productivity and quality were higher when production consisted solely of the standard Rabbit than when other models were introduced. Job-enlargement programs, by definition, add to the variety of tasks the worker is assigned; job-enrichment programs add some planning, designing, and scheduling to the operative worker's tasks. Both programs can tax the abilities of workers and in some cases may slow output and bruise quality. Worker involvement in production management may not fit well, some argue, with the two other ingredients that managers and management consultants see as essential for manufacturing reform: a just-in-time approach to eliminating waste and rigorous statistical process control to improve quality.[61] The possibility of a conflict between the obligation to make work more satisfying and the goal of increasing productivity will likely be at the heart of moral decisions in this area for years to come. To resolve them will require a cooperative effort by labor and management, rooted in the recognition that trade-offs are inevitable.

SUMMARY

1. Individuals have a right to privacy, in particular a right to make personal decisions autonomously, free from illegitimate influence. Whenever an organization infringes on an individual's personal sphere, it must justify that infringement.

2. A firm is legitimately interested in whatever significantly influences job performance, but there is no precise definition of "significant influence." Organizations may be invading privacy when they coerce employees to contribute to charities or to participate in "wellness" programs or so-called intensive group experience.

3. Information-gathering on employees can be highly personal and subject to abuse. The critical issue here is informed consent, which implies deliberation and free choice. Deliberation requires that employees be provided all significant facts concerning the information-gathering procedure and understand their consequences. Free choice means that the decision to participate must be voluntary and uncoerced.

4. Polygraph tests, personality tests, drug tests, and the monitoring of employees on the job can intrude into employee privacy. The exact character of these devices, the rationale for using them to gather information in specific circumstances, and the moral costs of doing so must always be carefully evaluated.

5. Health and safety remain of foremost moral concern in the workplace. The scope of occupational hazards, including shift work and stress, and the number of employees harmed by work-related injuries and diseases are greater than many people think. Enforcement of existing regulations has too often been lax.

6. Management style greatly affects the work environment. Managers who operate with rigid assumptions about human nature or who devote themselves to infighting and political maneuvering damage employees' interests.

7. Day-care services and reasonable parental-leave policies also affect working conditions. Despite the genuine need for and the ethical importance of both day care and parental leave, only a handful of companies makes serious efforts to provide them.

8. Studies report extensive job dissatisfaction at all levels. Various factors influence satisfaction and dissatisfaction on the job. Redesigning the work process can enhance the quality of work life, the well-being of workers, and even productivity.

CASE 7.1
Unprofessional Conduct?

Teaching retarded elementary schoolchildren requires skill, patience, and devotion, and those who undertake this task are among the unsung heroes of our society. Their hard and challenging work rarely brings the prestige or financial rewards it deserves. Mrs. Pettit was one of those dedicated teachers. Licensed to teach in California since 1957, she had been working with retarded children for over thirteen years when her career came to an end in 1973. Throughout that career, her competence was never questioned, and the evaluations of her school principal were always positive.

Teaching was not Mrs. Pettit's only interest, however. She and her husband viewed with favor various "nonconventional sexual lifestyles," including "wife swapping," and in 1966 they had discussed their ideas on two local television shows. Although they wore disguises, at least one fellow teacher recognized them and discussed Mrs. Pettit's views with colleagues. A year later, in 1967, Pettit, then 48 years old, and her husband joined "The Swingers," a private club in Los Angeles that sponsored parties intended to promote diverse sexual activities among its members. An undercover police officer, Sergeant Berk, visited one of those parties at a private residence.

Amid a welter of sexual activity, he observed Mrs. Pettit commit three separate acts of oral copulation with three different men in a one hour period.

Pettit was arrested and charged with oral copulation. After a plea bargain was arranged, she pleaded guilty to the misdemeanor of outraging public decency and paid a fine. The school district renewed her teaching contract the next academic year, but in February 1970, disciplinary proceedings were initiated against her. The State Board of Education found no reason to complain about her services as a teacher, and it conceded that she was unlikely to repeat her sexual misconduct. But the Board revoked her elementary school life diploma — that is, her license to teach — on the ground that by engaging in immoral and unprofessional conduct at the party, she had demonstrated that she was unfit to teach.

Pettit fought the loss of her license all the way to the California Supreme Court, which in 1973 upheld the decision of the Board of Education.[62] In an earlier case, the court had reversed the firing of a public schoolteacher for unspecified homosexual conduct, concluding that a teacher's actions could not constitute "immoral or unprofessional conduct" or "moral turpitude" unless there was clear evidence of unfitness to teach. But Pettit's case was different, the court hastened to explain.

The conduct in the earlier case had not been criminal, oral copulation had not been involved, and it had been private. Further, in that case the Board had acted with insufficient evidence of unfitness to teach, while three school administrators had testified that in their opinion, Pettit's conduct proved her unfit to teach. These experts worried that she would inject her views of sexual morality into the classroom, and they doubted that she could act as a moral example to the children she taught. Yet teachers, the court reaffirmed, are supposed to serve as exemplars, and the Education Code makes it a statutory duty of teachers to "endeavor to impress upon the minds of the pupils the principles of morality . . . and to instruct them in manners and morals."

In a vigorous dissent, Justice Tobringer rejected the opinion of the majority, arguing that no evidence had established that Pettit was not fit to teach. The three experts didn't consider her record; they couldn't point to any past misconduct with students, nor did they suggest any reason to anticipate future problems. They simply assumed that the fact of her sexual acts at the "swingers" party itself demonstrated that she would be unable to set a proper example or to teach her pupils moral principles.

Such an attitude is unrealistic, Tobringer argued, when studies show that 75 to 80 percent of the women of Pettit's educational level and age range engage in oral copulation. The majority opinion, "is blind to the reality of sexual behavior" and unrealistically assumes that "teachers in their private lives should exemplify Victorian principles of sexual morality." Her actions were private and could not

have affected her teaching ability. Had there not been clandestine surveillance of the party, the whole issue would never have arisen.

Discussion Questions

1. In concerning itself with Mrs. Pettit's off-the-job conduct, did the Board of Education violate her right to privacy? Or was its concern with her lifestyle legitimate and employment related?

2. Was Mrs. Pettit's behavior "unprofessional"? What is "immoral"? Did it show a "lack of fitness" to teach? Explain how you understand the terms in quotation marks.

3. Was the Board of Education justified in firing Mrs. Pettit? Explain.

4. Was the court's verdict consistent with its earlier handling of the case of the homosexual teacher?

5. If teachers perform competently in the classroom, should they also be required to be positive "moral examples" in their private lives? Are employees in other occupations expected to provide a moral example — either on or off the job?

6. Which of the following would, in your view, show unprofessional conduct, immorality, or lack of fitness to teach: drunken driving, smoking marijuana, advocating the use of marijuana, forging a check, assaulting a police officer and resisting arrest, being discovered in a compromising position with a student, propositioning a student, cheating on income tax, leading an openly homosexual lifestyle?

7. Under what conditions do employers have a legitimate interest in their employees' off-the-job conduct?

CASE 7.2
Testing for Honesty

"Charity begins at home." If you don't think so, ask the Salvation Army, which has a severe problem with theft among its kettlers, the street people who collect money for the Army during the Christmas season. Some of the Army's kettlers—who are usually poor, unemployed individuals, paid minimum wage—were helping themselves to the Army's loot before the organization had a chance to dole it out. To put a stop to the problem, Army officials sought the assistance of Dr. John Jones, director of research of London House Management Consultants.

London House is one of several companies that market honesty tests for prospective employees. Some of these tests, like London House's Personnel Selection Inventory (PSI), also measure the applicant's tendency toward drug use and violence. All three categories—honesty, drugs, and violence—play a major part in company losses, according to the makers of these tests.

The company losses in question are astronomical. By some estimates, U.S. companies lose about $25 billion annually because of employee dishonesty, neglect, and disruption. The American Management Association estimates that as many as 20 percent of the businesses that fail do so because of employee crime. Bank losses alone, says the FBI, cost $250 million a year. Compounding the problem are losses due to employee drug use, which London House estimates at about $43 billion each year in absenteeism, lost initiative, inattentiveness, accidents, and diminished productivity.[63] Employee violence also costs companies millions of dollars in damages, lost productivity, and lawsuits.

Honesty test makers say that the only way to deal with these problems is before workers are hired, not after—by subjecting them to a preemployment psychological test that will identify the one-third of all prospective employees who will likely steal, the 15 percent who have a history of violence or emotional instability, the 25 percent who have a history of marijuana use, and the 10 percent who have used other illegal drugs on a regular basis.[64]

James Walls, one of the founders of Stanton Corporation, which has offered written honesty tests for twenty-five years, says that dishonest job applicants are clever at hoodwinking potential employers in a job interview. "They have a way of conducting themselves that is probably superior to the low-risk person. They have learned what it takes to be accepted and how to overcome the normal interview strategy," he says. "The high-risk person will get hired unless there is a way to screen him." For this reason, Walls maintains, written, objective tests are needed to weed out the crooks.[65]

So far, some 6 million written honesty tests have been given. Demand has been booming as a result of the congressional restrictions on polygraph testing, which went into effect at the end of 1988. The restrictions prohibit about 85 percent of applicant and employee polygraph testing in the United States. As a result, purveyors of written tests have also been in high demand: The British Maxwell Communication Corporation, for instance, spent $17.4 million to acquire London House; Business Risk International took over the Stanton Corporation; and Wackenhut Corporation of Coral Gables, Florida, acquired marketing rights to the Phase II Profile, a widely used honesty test.[66]

In addition to being legal, honesty tests are also more economical than polygraph tests. They cost between $7 and $14 per test, compared to $80 or so for a polygraph. Furthermore, the tests are easily administered at the workplace by a staff member to any category of worker, are easily and quickly evaluated by the test maker, and assess the applicant's overall answers rather than a few isolated responses. The tests are also nondiscriminatory. The Equal Employment Opportunity Commission's "Uniform Guidelines on Employee Selection Procedures" (1978) permits tests that measure psychological traits, because the race, gender, or ethnicity of applicants has no significant impact on scores.[67]

A typical test begins with some cautionary remarks. Test takers are told to be truthful because dishonesty can be detected, and they are warned that incomplete answers will be considered incorrect, as will any unanswered questions. Then applicants ordinarily sign a waiver permitting the results to be known to their prospective employer and authorizing the testing agency to check out their answers. Sometimes, however, prospective employees are not told that they are being tested for honesty, only that they are being asked questions about their background. James Walls justifies this less-than-frank explanation by saying that within a few questions it is obvious that the test deals with attitudes toward honesty. "The test is very transparent, it's not subtle."[68]

Next come the questions—and the source of growing controversy. Have you ever had an argument with someone and later wished you had said something else? If you were to answer no, you would be on your way to failing. Other questions that may face the test taker are: "How strong is your conscience?" "How often do you feel guilty?" "Do you always tell the truth?" "Do you occasionally have thoughts you wouldn't want made public?" "Does everyone steal a little?" "Do you enjoy stories of successful crimes?" "Have you ever been so intrigued by the cleverness of a thief that you hoped the person would escape detection?"

Once the tests are completed, they are evaluated by the test maker, who gives the applicant a "risk" rating of high, moderate, or low. The assessment is reported to the prospective employer, who can use it as part of the overall assessment of the applicant.

A big part of some tests is a behavioral history of the applicant. Applicants are asked to reveal the nature, frequency, and quantity of specific drug use, if any. They also must indicate if they have ever engaged in drunk driving, illegal gambling, selling or using pot, traffic violations, forgery, vandalism, and a host of other unseemly behaviors. They must also state their opinions about the social acceptability of drinking alcohol and using other drugs.

Some testing companies go further in this direction. Instead of honesty exams, they offer tests designed to draw a general psychological profile of the applicant, claiming that this sort of analysis can predict more accurately than either the polygraph or the typical honesty test how the person will perform on the job. Keith M. Halperin, a psychologist with Personnel Decision, Inc. (PDI), a company that offers such tests, complains that most paper-and-pencil honesty tests are simply written equivalents of the polygraph. They ask applicants whether they have stolen from their employers, how much they have taken, and other questions directly related to honesty. But why, asks Halperin, "would an applicant who is dishonest enough to steal from an employer be honest enough to admit it on a written test?" It is more difficult for applicants to fake their responses to PDI's tests, Halperin contends.[69]

Not everyone is persuaded. Phyllis Bassett, vice president of James Bassett Company of Cincinnati, believes tests developed by psychologists that do not ask directly about the applicant's past honesty are poor predictors of future trustworthiness. The questions on her company's Veracity Analysis Questionnaire were adapted from questions on polygraph tests.[70] In general, those who market honesty exams boast of their validity and reliability, as established by field studies. They insist that the tests do make a difference, that they enable employers to ferret out potential troublemakers—as in the Salvation Army case.

Dr. Jones administered London House's PSI to eighty kettler applicants, which happened to be the number that the particular theft-ridden center needed. The PSIs were not scored, and the eighty applicants were hired with no screening. Throughout the fund-raising month between Thanksgiving and Christmas, the center kept a record of each kettler's daily receipts. After the Christmas season, the tests were scored and divided into "recommended" and "not recommended" for employment. After accounting for the peculiarities of each collection neighborhood, Jones discovered that those kettlers the PSI had not recommended turned in on the average $17 per day less than those the PSI had recommended. Based on this analysis, he estimated the center's loss to employee theft during the fund drive at $20,000. In the future, the Salvation Army plans to identify high-risk applicants, which it intends to hire but keep out of money-handling positions.

The list of psychological-test enthusiasts is growing by leaps and bounds, but the tests have plenty of detractors. Many psychologists have voiced concern over the lack of standards governing the tests; the American Psychological Association favors the establishment of federal standards for written honesty exams. But the chief critics are the applicants who have taken them. They complain about having to reveal some of the most intimate details of their lives and opinions. In fact, some unions and lawyers brand the tests "confessional sheets," which ask many non-job-related questions that invade privacy. In California, the American Civil Liberties Union (ACLU) and the United Food and Commercial Workers Union unsuccessfully attempted to get legislation prohibiting such tests. They dismiss business's claim that no one's privacy is being invaded, since applicants can always refuse to take the test.

"Given the unequal bargaining power," says former ACLU official Kathleen Baily, "the ability to refuse to take a test is one of theory rather than choice—if one really wants a job."[71]

Discussion Questions

1. Describe how you'd feel having to take a psychological test as a precondition for employment. Under what conditions, if any, would you take such a test?

2. If you were an employer, would you require job applicants to pass an honestly exam? How useful do you think such tests are?

3. Do you think psychological tests invade privacy? Explain why or why not.

4. Assuming that psychological tests like those described are valid and reliable, do you think they are fair? Explain.

5. What do you think a business's reaction would be if the government required its executive officers to submit to a personality test as a precondition for the company's getting a government contract? The tests would probe attitudes about questionable business practices, such as bribery, product misrepresentation, unfair competition, and so forth. If, in your opinion, the business would object, does it have any moral grounds for subjecting workers to comparable tests?

6. Utilitarians would not find anything inherently objectionable about psychological tests so long as the interests of all parties are taken into account and given equal consideration before such tests are made a preemployment screen. Do you think this is generally the case?

7. What ideals, obligations, and effects must be considered in using psychological tests as preemployment screens? In your view, which is the most important consideration?

8. Should there be a law prohibiting or regulating psychological tests as a preemployment screen, or should the decision be left to the employer? Explain.

9. Do you think a decision to use these tests should be made jointly by management and labor, or is testing for employment an exclusive employer right?

CASE 7.3
She Snoops to Conquer

Jean Fanuchi, manager of a moderately large department store, was worried. Shrinkage in the costume jewelry department had continued to rise for the third consecutive month. In fact, this time it had wiped out the department's net profit in sales. Worse, it couldn't be attributed to damage or improper handling of markdowns or even to shoplifting. The only other possibility was in-house theft.

Fanuchi ordered chief of security Matt Katwalski to instruct his security people to keep a special eye on the jewelry department employees as they went about their business. She also instructed that packages, purses, and other containers employees carried with them be searched when workers left the store. When these measures failed to turn up any leads, Katwalski suggested they hire a couple of plainclothes officers to observe the store's guards. Fanuchi agreed. But still nothing turned up.

"We're going to have to install a hidden camera at the check-out station in the jewelry department," Katwalski informed the manager.

"I don't know," Fanuchi replied.

"Of course," said Katwalski, "it won't be cheap. But you don't want this problem spreading to other departments, do you?" Fanuchi didn't.

"One other thing," Katwalski said. "I think we should install some microphones in the restroom, stockroom, and employee lounge."

"You mean snoop on our own employees?" Fanuchi asked, surprised.

"We could pick up something that could crack this thing wide open," Katwalski explained.

"But what if our employees found out? How would they feel, being spied on? And then there's the public to consider. Who knows how they'd react? Why, they'd probably think that if we are spying on our own workers, we were surely spying on them. No, Matt," Fanuchi decided. "Frankly, this whole approach troubles me."

"Okay, Ms. Fanuchi, but if it was my store . . ."

Fanuchi cut in, "No."

"You're the boss," said Katwalski.

When the shrinkage continued, Fanuchi finally gave in. She ordered Katwalski to have the camera and microphones installed. Within ten days the camera had nabbed the culprit.

The microphones contributed nothing to the apprehension of the thief. But because of them Fanuchi and Katwalski learned that at least one store employee was selling marijuana and perhaps hard drugs, that one was planning to quit without notice, that three were taking food stamps fraudulently, and that one buyer was out to discredit Fanuchi. In solving their shrinkage problem, the pair had unwittingly raised another: What should they do with the information they had gathered while catching the thief?[72]

Discussion Questions

1. If you were Jean Fanuchi, how would you feel about your decision to order the installation of the viewing and listening devices? What other options did she have?

Did she overlook any moral considerations or possible consequences?

2. If you were an employee, would you think your privacy had been wrongfully invaded? How would you assess Fanuchi's actions if you were the owner of the store?

3. Do you think Jean Fanuchi acted immorally? Why or why not? Evaluate her action by appeal to ethical principles.

4. How should Fanuchi and Katwalski handle the information they've gathered about their employees? Explain by appealing to relevant ideals, obligations, and effects.

CASE 7.4
Protecting the Unborn at Work

The unobtrusive factory sits behind a hillside shopping center in the small college town of Bennington, Vermont. The workers there make lead automobile batteries for Sears, Goodyear, and other companies. Of the 280 workers employed there in 1990, only 12 were women, and none of them was able to have children. The company, Johnson Controls, Inc., refused to hire any who could.[73]

Why? Because tiny, toxic particles of lead and lead oxide fill the air inside the plant. According to the company, the levels of lead are low enough for adults, but too high for children and fetuses. Numerous scientific studies have shown that lead can damage the brain and central nervous system of a fetus. Moreover, lead lingers in the bloodstream, which means that fetuses can be affected by it even if a woman limits her exposure to lead once she learns she is pregnant. Because of this, Johnson Controls decided in 1982 that it would exclude women at all fourteen of its factories from jobs that entail high exposure to lead — unless they could prove that they couldn't become pregnant. The company made no exceptions for celibate women or women who used contraceptives. The company's position was simple: "The issue is protecting the health of unborn children."

Johnson Controls's stance was in line with the National Centers for Disease Control's 1985 recommendation that women of childbearing age be excluded from jobs involving significant lead exposure. Because by law its standards must be "feasible," Occupational Safety and Health Administration (OSHA) regulations permit chemicals in the workplace that are known to cause harm both to fetuses and to some adult employees. But OSHA holds that employers have a general duty to reduce the hazards of the workplace as far as possible. On this basis, employers like Olin Corporation, American Cyanamid, General Motors, Monsanto, Allied Chemical, Gulf Oil, and B. F. Goodrich also adopted policies excluding women from chemical plant jobs that were judged to be hazardous to their potential offspring.

Scientific studies of the effect of exposure to toxic manufacturing chemicals on workers' reproductive health are, unfortunately, few. Only a small percentage of the workplace chemicals with a potential for damaging reproduction have been evaluated, and each year many new chemicals are introduced into factories. Although employers are obviously dealing with many unknowns, no one doubts that they have a moral and legal obligation to control and limit these risks as best they can. Lawsuits and even criminal sanctions have battered companies that have managed hazardous chemicals irresponsibly. In 1988, for example, Monsanto Chemical Company agreed to pay $1.5 million to six employees because exposure to a chemical additive used for rubber production allegedly gave them bladder cancer. Fetal protection policies aren't just dictated by management, though. "Women who become pregnant," the *New York Times* reports, "are beginning to demand the right to transfer out of jobs they believe to be hazardous, even when there is only sketchy scientific evidence of any hazard."

But many women were unhappy about the decision of Johnson Controls. They worried that fetal protection policies would be used to exclude women from more and more workplaces on the grounds that different chemical substances or things like heavy lifting might be potential causes of miscarriage and fetal injury. In line with this, the United Automobile Workers, which represents many of the Johnson employees, sought to overturn a U.S. Court of Appeals decision that judged Johnson's policy "reasonably necessary to the industrial safety-based concern of protecting the unborn child from lead exposure." The union contends, to the contrary, that the policy discriminates against women, jeopardizing their hard-won gains in male-dominated industries.

Many women's advocates see the issue in slightly different terms. They believe policies like that of Johnson Controls not only challenge a woman's right to control her fetus, but to control her unfertilized eggs as well. In addition, such policies infringe on privacy: By taking a job at Johnson, a woman was in effect telling the world that she was sterile. And there is also the fundamental question of who knows what is best for a woman.

After bearing two children, Cheryl Chalifoux had a doctor block her Fallopian tubes so that she couldn't become pregnant again. Although career advancement wasn't the reason she made her decision, it did enable her to switch from a factory job paying $6.34 an hour to one at Johnson's Bennington plant paying $15 an hour. Still, she says that the policy was unfair and degrading. "Its your body," she complains. "They're implying they're doing it for your own good." Cheryl Cook, also a mother of two who had surgery for the same reasons, joined Chalifoux in leaving the other company to work for Johnson Controls. She says, "I work right in the lead. I make the oxide. But you should choose for yourself. Myself, I wouldn't go in there if I could get pregnant. But they don't trust you."

Isabelle Katz Pizler, director of women's rights at the American Civil Liberties Union, agrees. "Since time immemorial," she says, "the excuse for keeping women in their place has been because of their role in producing the next generation. The attitude of Johnson Controls is: 'We know better than you. We can't allow women to make this decision. We have to make it for them.'" And the ACLU has argued in court that "since no activity is risk-free, deference to an employer's analysis of fetal risk could limit women's participation in nearly every area of economic life."

To this the company responds that it has a moral obligation to the parties that cannot participate in the woman's decisions—namely, the unfertilized ovum and the fetus. In addition, the company has an obligation to stockholders, who would bear the brunt of lawsuits brought by employees' children born with retardation, nervous system disorders, or other disorders that lead can cause.

Joseph A. Kinney, executive director of the National Safe Workplace Institute in Chicago, sides with Johnson Controls, but only because he believes that letting women assume the burden of their safety undermines OSHA's responsibility to mandate workplace safety rules. "The discrimination side of the issue needs to be resolved," Kinney says. "But the ideal thing is to regulate lead out of the workplace and any other toxin that poses fetal damage."

In March 1991 the Supreme Court ruled unanimously that the fetal protection policy at Johnson Controls violated the Civil Rights Act of 1964, which prohibits sex discrimination in employment.[74] Pointing to evidence that lead affects sperm and can thus harm the offspring of men exposed to it at the time of conception, the Court stated:

Respondent does not seek to protect the unconceived children of all its employees. Despite evidence in the record about the debilitating effect of lead exposure on the male reproductive system, Johnson Controls is concerned only with the harms that may befall the unborn offspring of its female employees. . . . [The company's policy is] discriminatory because it requires only a female employee to produce proof that she is not capable of reproducing.

On the other hand, the Court was divided over whether fetal protection policies could ever be legally justified. Justice Harry A. Blackmun, writing for a majority of the Court, declared that they could not, that the Civil Rights Act prohibited all such policies:

Decisions about the welfare of future children must be left to the parents who conceive, bear, support and raise them rather than to the employers who hire those parents. Women as capable of doing their jobs as their male counterparts may not be forced to choose between having a child and having a job.

Referring to the Pregnancy Discrimination Act of 1978, which amended the 1964 Civil Rights Act and prohibits employment discrimination on the basis of pregnancy or potential pregnancy, Blackmun added:

Employment late in pregnancy often imposes risks on the unborn child, but Congress indicated that the employer may take into account only the woman's ability to get her job done.

A minority of the justices, however, were unwilling to go so far, and in a concurring opinion, Justice Byron R. White wrote that "common sense tells us that it is part of the normal operation of business concerns to avoid causing injury to third parties as well as to employees." But he added that, in his view,

a fetal protection policy would not be defensible unless an employer also addressed other known occupational health risks.

Discussion Questions

1. Do you agree that Johnson Controls's fetal protection policy discriminated against women? Do pregnant women have a moral—not just a legal— right to work with lead?

2. Suppose exposure to lead did not affect sperm or the male reproductive system. Would Johnson's policy still have been discriminatory? Would it hamper women's efforts to win equality in the workplace?

3. Can there be a nondiscriminatory fetal protection policy? Is Justice White correct in arguing that companies have an obligation to avoid causing injury to fetuses just as they do other "third parties"?

4. Suppose a company forbids any employee capable of reproducing from working with lead. Would such a policy wrongly interfere with employees' freedom of choice? Would it be an invasion of their privacy? Would it be fair to employees who are fertile but plan to have no children?

5. Evaluate fetal protection policies from the egoistic, utilitarian, and Kantian perspectives. What rights are involved? What are the likely benefits and harms of such policies?

6. Assuming they are fully informed, do employees with a certain medical condition have a right to work at jobs that can be hazardous to the health of people in their condition? Or can company policy or OSHA regulations justifiably prevent them from doing so for their own good?

7. Would you agree with Joseph Kinney that the real issue is to remove toxins from the workplace? Is this a realistic goal?

CASE 7.5
The "Mommy Track"

"The cost of employing women in management is greater than the cost of employing men. This is a jarring statement, partly because it is true, but mostly because it is something people are reluctant to talk about." So begins a recent article by Felice N. Schwartz.[75] Schwartz goes on to contend that the rate of turnover in management positions is two and a half times higher among top-performing women than it is among men. Moreover, one half of the women who take maternity leave return to their jobs late or not at all. "We know that women also have a greater tendency to plateau or to interrupt their careers," she writes. "But we have become so sensitive to charges of sexism and so afraid of confrontation, even litigation, that we rarely say what we know to be true."

Schwartz's article exploded like a bombshell. What really upsets her critics is the distinction Schwartz draws between two types of women: the career-primary woman and the career-and-family woman.[76] Those in the first category put their careers first. They remain single or childless, or if they do have children, they are satisfied to have others raise them. The automatic association of all women with babies is unfair to these women, according to Schwartz — after all, some 90 percent of executive men but only 35 percent of executive women have children by the age of forty. "The secret to dealing with such women," Schwartz writes, "is to recognize them early, accept them, and clear artificial barriers from their path to the top."

The majority of women fall into Schwartz's second category. They want to pursue genuine careers while participating actively in the rearing of their children. Most of them, Schwartz contends, are willing to trade some career growth and compensation for freedom from the constant pressure to work long hours and weekends. By forcing these women to choose between family and career, companies lose a valuable resource and a competitive advantage. Instead, firms must plan for and manage maternity, they must provide the flexibility to help career-and-family women be maximally productive, and they must take an active role in providing family support and in making high-quality, affordable child care available to all women.

Schwartz's various suggestions of ways for organizations to serve the needs of working mothers and benefit from their expertise seem humane and practical. But her feminist critics see her as distinguishing between the strivers and the breeders, between women who should be treated as honorary males and those who should be shunted onto a special lower-paid, low-pressure career track — the now-notorious "mommy track." Representative Patricia Schroeder of Colorado says that Schwartz actually "reinforces the idea that you can either have a family or a career, but not both, if you're a woman."[77] And other women worry that Schwartz's article will encourage corporations to reduce pay and withhold promotions in exchange for the parental leave, flextime, and child care that they will sooner or later have to provide as they become more and more dependent on female talent.[78]

Barbara Ehrenreich and Deidre English challenge Schwartz's data and call her article "a tortured muddle of feminist perceptions and sexist assumptions, good intentions and dangerous suggestions — unsupported by any acceptable evidence at all." What they resent is that Schwartz makes no mention of fathers or of shared parental responsibility for child-raising. Schwartz is also accused of assuming that mothers don't need top flight careers and of taking for granted the existing values, structures, and biases of a corporate world that is still male-dominated. "Bumping women—or just fertile women, or married women, or whomever—off the fast track may sound smart to cost-conscious CEOs," they write. "But eventually it is the corporate culture itself that needs to slow down to a human pace . . . [and end] work loads that are incompatible with family life."[79]

"What's so disturbing about Felice Schwartz's article," adds Fran Rodgers, president of Work-Family Directions, a Massachusetts research and referral group, "is that it is devoted to fitting women into the existing culture, instead of finding ways to change that culture." And Rodgers rejects the idea of "dividing women into two groups, but completely ignoring the diversity among men."[80]

Other observers fear that men will simply leave the mommy trackers in the dust. "In most organizations, the mommy track is a millstone around your neck," says Richard Belous, an economist at the National Planning Association. "CEOs and rainmakers don't come out of the mommy track," he warns. "If you go part-time, you're signaling to your employer you're on the B-team."[81] Traditionally, men who make it to the upper ranks have relied on their wives to raise the kids and to take full responsibility at home. A fast-track woman who wants children, however, gets caught in a time and energy squeeze, even if her husband is an equal partner at home. And while more men today are willing to share child-

raising responsibilities, most still seem hesitant about making significant career sacrifices for spouse and family. There's no analogous "daddy track," it seems.

Discussion Questions

1. Do you think Schwartz is correct to assert that the cost of employing women in management is greater than that of employing men? If you agree, what are the implications for corporate policy?

2. Can working women be divided into Schwartz's two categories? Is it desirable for companies to distinguish the different types of career paths followed by female employees?

3. Do you think there already is such a thing as a "mommy track"? Is the idea of a mommy track a good one? Is it somehow discriminatory against women? Against men?

4. Should special organizational arrangements be made for workers who wish to combine career and child-raising? Identify the steps that companies can take to accommodate parental needs more effectively.

5. Does a firm have an obligation to give employees the flexibility to work out the particular balance of career and family that is right for them? Or does this go beyond the social responsibilities of business?

CASE 7.6
Democracy at Harman

Harman Industries, on the edge of Bolivar, Tennessee (pop. 7,000), makes most of the rearview mirrors in the United States. Second only to the state mental hospital in the number of people it employs, Harman is a central force in Bolivar and surrounding Handeman

County. Although this alone may distinguish Harman in the minds of the local population, Harman has another, more important claim to fame: It is the site of the first and perhaps most important management-union experiment in worker participation in the United

States. Launched in 1972 by the United Auto Workers (UAW), Harman management, and consultants from the Harvard Project on Technology, Work, and Character, Harman's Work Improvement Program (WIP) has involved virtually every worker in the factory.

WIP was a response to the less-than-ideal work conditions that had soured the attitudes of Harman workers. Before WIP, the 1,000 or so Harman employees were housed in three huge Quonset huts, relics of World War II. When the project was just beginning, a consultant described the work atmosphere as dirty, noisy, and chaotic.[82] Beyond this, the economics of the auto parts industry, unblinking competition, uneven demand for cars, and price squeezing by customers all intensified the dehumanizing conditions of work that served to feed worker insecurity. In brief, workers viewed themselves as standardized, replaceable parts of the manufacturing process. This perception produced anger, hostility, and depression and blunted creativity. Clearly, something had to be done.

In the summer of 1973, management, the union, and a third-party team led by project director Michael Maccoby met to hammer out what would become WIP. The group decided to take a step at a time, ensuring a solid base before moving on to the next development. The first step consisted of gathering information about employee attitudes. The study, conducted with the help of the W. E. Upjohn Institute for Employment Research, was based on in-depth, four-hour interviews with 60 workers plus shorter interviews with about 300 more workers and 50 managers. The findings confirmed everyone's worst suspicions. Workers didn't trust the company, felt management was ignoring them, and were convinced that Harman cared more about profit than people. Indeed, the study discovered that workers at Harman were so hostile toward management that many admitted sabotaging plant operations by intentionally working badly, slowly, or incorrectly.

The next step in the experiment was to set up a management-union structure for the purpose of screening and approving all project developments. A top-level management union advisory committee was formed, consisting of the company executives, members of UAW International, and quality of work life (QWL) experts. Maccoby stressed that a key strategy of the project structure was never to bypass the conventional management-union structures but to strengthen them.

Management and union then agreed to pursue a common set of principles. Whereas many other work-participation projects in the United States have aimed at improving productivity or reducing absenteeism, turnover, or sabotage, the Harmon-UAW WIP program set out to reorganize the way the company itself operated. The Harvard Project declared pointedly: "The purpose is *not* to increase productivity" but "to make work better and more satisfying for all employees, salaried and hourly, while maintaining the necessary productivity for job security."[83] Specifically, management and union agreed that all workplace changes had to fulfill these four principles:

1. Security: creating conditions that free workers from fear of losing jobs and that maximize their financial earnings.

2. Equity: guaranteeing fairness in hiring, pay, and promotions; ending sexual and racial discrimination; and sharing profits with workers when productivity increases.

3. Individuation: understanding that each worker is different, and allowing each worker to satisfy his or her individual development.

4. Democracy: fostering free speech and due process, and permitting worker participation in decisions that directly affect them.

Having agreed on these basic principles, the participants then began to address specific problems at Harman. At first they focused on issues that workers had identified in survey interviews such as temperature extremes in the plant, the irritating air pollution, traffic jams in the parking lot, and management's policy of permitting bill collectors to track down debtors inside the factory.

Then experimental groups in three different departments were set up. One was in the assembly department, where the rearview mirrors were put together. Building on the principles of individuation and democracy, a steering committee, termed the Working Committee, had workers themselves analyze problems with their jobs and propose their own solutions.

Similarly, in the polish and buff department, workers were encouraged to decide their own work assignments as a team rather than merely to obey the directives of foremen. Also, individuals who finished their jobs early were urged to help out slower teammates; and the worker team was asked to keep its own records of parts, productivity, efficiency, and the number of "bonus" hours team members were accumulating as a result of achieving product quotas before quitting time on a given day. (Workers could use bonus hours to take time off in the future.) At the same time, workers in the preassembly department came up with eight goals, including helping each other achieve new production quotas, gaining free time to learn new skills or go home early, making the workplace more attractive, improving the quality of their work, reducing "downtime," and installing better tools and fixtures at their workstations.

But the heart of Harman's project was a network of thirty shop-floor committees, termed core groups, which consisted of management, local union, and employee representatives. Most suggestions for work changes originated in these core groups, whose meetings all workers were free to attend. When a core group approved an idea it was sent to the company's Working Committee for final approval or revision.

Beyond this, the Harman WIP attempted to bridge the gap between workers' work and private lives. The most unusual innovation in this regard was the in-plant school. Workers, their families, and even community residents were invited to attend a wide array of classes held before, after, or during a shift, or at lunch. Formed in 1975, the school today offers more than forty classes such as paint technology, die technology, computer language, leadership styles, hydraulics, introduction to data processing, metric measurement, square dancing, theatre group, ceramics, typing, car care for women, and even a class that earns for its students a high school diploma. Two of the most popular courses are first aid and art appreciation. Such courses are financed by the union-management project fund and by the county under its vocational education budget.

While the Harman WIP may seem an unqualified success, it has its critics. Some say that QWL changes have been few and that the program is, in fact, a management ruse to get more out of workers. Others charge that employees really have gained little power, that only company ideas get implemented. Part of the discontent seems to have resulted from the gap between worker expectations and the intent of the project. Some workers evidently expected the core groups and Working Committee to give employees sweeping decision-making powers. But, as Maccoby has stressed, the project intended nothing of the kind.

In late 1977, Sidney Harman sold the company to Beatrice Corporation, an international conglomerate. The Beatrice Corporation maintains that it supports WIP and encourages worker participation. For their part, workers say the program is in limbo: Core groups meet, classes are held, workers occasionally initiate change on the shop floor. But there have been no major new initiatives. Still, consultants say that workers have learned much about analyzing problems and proposing solutions on their own initiative. Perhaps most important, they have learned that change is possible. So has management.

cision making that can grow as participants develop greater understanding of the business? Can there be genuine democracy in the workplace if employees are not in some way owners of the enterprise?

Discussion Questions

1. What features of the workplace give rise to worker dissatisfaction and alienation? What are the most important steps that can be taken to enhance the quality of work life?

2. Is worker participation inherently valuable or is it valuable only as means to improving productivity or making workers content with their jobs?

3. To what extent should workplace democracy and improvements in work environment take precedence over profit and productivity?

4. Broadly speaking, could one say that concern for participation and the quality of work life take root in nonconsequentialist moral considerations? Explain.

5. Workers at Harman feared the effects of giving productivity top priority in any work improvement program. Why? What might some of these effects be?

6. Some writers argue that real democracy requires worker participation in decisions that directly affect them. Yet this principle is at odds with traditional prerogatives and rights of management (for example, appointing supervisors, deciding who will run the company, and setting prices). Do you think, then, that this makes democracy an unrealistic principle in the workplace? Or would you say that democracy remains a legitimate goal inasmuch as it can be used to carve out areas of worker participation in analysis and de-

NOTES

1. The facts reported here are from "Privacy," *Business Week*, March 28, 1988, 61–68.

2. Ibid.

3. "Don't Pry," *The Economist*, October 6, 1990, 18.

4. "Privacy," *Business Week*.

5. On the legal situation and its consequences, see Kenneth L. Sovereign, "Pitfalls of Withholding Reference Information," *Personnel Journal*, March 1990.

6. Larry Reibstein, "Firms Find It Tougher to Dismiss Employees for Off-Duty Conduct," *Wall Street Journal*, March 29, 1988, 31.

7. *Dollars & Sense*, April 1989, 4.

8. Ibid.

9. Terry L. Leap, "When Can You Fire for Off-Duty Conduct?" *Harvard Business Review* 66 (January–February 1988): 36.

10. "Privacy," 68.

11. See James C. Coleman and Constance L. Hammen, *Contemporary Psychology and Effective Behavior* (Glenview, Ill.: Scott, Foresman, 1974), 424.

12. Ibid., 425.

13. Christopher H. Pyle, "These Tests Are Meant to Scare People," *USA Today*, February 17, 1983, 10A.

14. See Keith Davis and Robert L. Blomstrom, *Business and Society* (New York: McGraw-Hill, 1975), 319.

15. See David T. Lykken, "Three Big Lies About the Polygraph," *USA Today*, February 17, 1983, 10A.

16. Lynn March, "Lie Detectors Are Accurate and Useful," *USA Today*, February 17, 1983, 10A.

17. Lykken, "Three Big Lies."

18. Pyle, "Tests Are Meant to Scare."

19. See William A. Nowlin and Robert Barbato, "The Truth About Lie Detectors," *Business and Society Review* 66 (Summer 1988).

20. "Privacy," *Business Week*, 68.

21. Ron Winslow, "Study May Spur Job-Applicant Drug Screening," *Wall Street Journal*, November 28, 1990, B1. See also *New York Times*, November 29, 1990, A17.

22. James T. Wrich, "Beyond Testing: Coping with Drugs at Work," *Harvard Business Review* 66 (January–February 1988).

23. Ibid.

24. William Serrin, "The Wages of Work," *The Nation*, January 28, 1991, 80–82, and Sue Shellenbarger, "Grain-Elevator Explosions Continue to Threaten Workers and Property," *Wall Street Journal*, July 21, 1981, 2–29.

25. See Joseph LaDoc, "The Not-So-Clean Business of Making Chips," *Technology Review* 87 (May–June 1984).

26. See Sue Martinez, "Workers Suffer as Industry Booms," *Bakersfield Californian*, March 19, 1981, C4.

27. *Whirlpool Corporation* v. *Ray Marshall*, 76–1970, BNA February 26, 1980, 48, 4189, and *Marshall* v. *Whirlpool*, 583 F2d 715 (1979).

28. "California Cracks Down on Crime in the Suites," *Wall Street Journal*, November 30, 1990, B1.

29. "Workers Are Dying to Make Jobsites Safe," *Guardian* (New York), April 15, 1987.

30. Dan Rodricks, "Book Pays Tribute to Workers Killed on the Job," *San Francisco Chronicle*, April 28, 1989, B5.

31. Serrin, "Wages of Work," 81.

32. "Getting Away With Murder," *Harvard Law Review* 101 (December 1987): 535. But see "Court Upholds Punishment of Employer," *Guardian* (New York), October 31, 1990, 5.

33. "OSHA Commended by Old Adversary," *San Francisco Chronicle*, September 5, 1989, C7; R. Henry Moore, "OSHA: What's Ahead for the 1990s," *Personnel*, June 1990.

34. David Tuller, "The '90s 'Occupational Epidemic,'" *San Francisco Chronicle*, June 12, 1989, C1. The next two paragraphs are also based on this article.

35. Charlotte-Anne Lucas, "Profiting from Pain," *San Francisco Examiner*, January 13, 1991, D1.

36. "Stress on the Job," *Newsweek* (international edition), April 25, 1988; see also "Stress: The Test Americans Are Failing," *Business Week*, April 18, 1988, and "Fear and Stress in Office Take Toll," *Wall Street Journal*, November 6, 1990, B1.

37. *Wall Street Journal*, June 6, 1989, A1; and "Love or Money?" *Personnel*, March 1989, 11.

38. Douglas McGregor, *The Human Side of Enterprise* (New York: McGraw-Hill, 1960).

39. James Risen, "For Ross Perot, GM Ouster Still Rankles," *International Herald Tribune*, November 19, 1987.

40. *California Federal Savings and Loan Association* v. *Guerra*, 93 L Ed 2d 613 (1987).

41. "Danger: Mother at Work," *The Economist*, April 16, 1988, 49; see also Janice Peterson, "The Feminization of Poverty," *Journal of Economic Issues* 21 (March 1987): 332.

42. JoAnne McCracken, "Child Care as an Employee Fringe Benefit: May an Employer Discriminate?" *Santa Clara Law Review* 26 (Summer–Fall 1986): 670.

43. *Business Week* (international edition), February 29, 1988, 58.

44. The average cost of day care is $3,000 per year, and licensed day-care centers have only 2.5 million places. See "Danger: Mother at Work," 49.

45. McCracken, "Child Care as an Employee Fringe Benefit," 671–672.

46. Rosalyn B. Will and Steven D. Lydenberg, "20 Corporations That Listen to Women," *Ms.*, November 1987, 49.

47. Karen Woodford, "Child Care Soars," *Personnel Journal*, December 1990.

48. McCracken, "Child Care as an Employee Fringe Benefit," 668.

49. *Work in America: Report of a Special Task Force to the Secretary of Health, Education, and Welfare* (Cambridge: MIT Press, 1972).

50. Thomas A. Kochan, Harry C. Katz, and Robert B. McKersie, *The Transformation of American Industrial Relations* (New York: Basic Books, 1986), 224.

51. Survey Research Center, *Survey of Working Conditions* (Ann Arbor: University of Michigan, 1970).

52. H. Sheppard and N. Herrick, *Where Have All The Robots Gone?* (New York: Free Press, 1972).

53. A. W. Kornhauser, *Mental Health of the Industrial Worker: A Detroit Study* (Huntington, N.Y.: Krieger, 1965).

54. E. Palmore, "Predicting Longevity: A Follow-Up Controlling for Age," *Gerontologist* 9 (1969): 247–250.

55. Sharon Cohen, "Management, Unions Join Forces," *San Francisco Examiner*, December 9, 1990, D3.

56. Kochan et al., *Transformation of American Industrial Relations*, 175–176.

57. Cohen, "Management, Unions."

58. Randy Pennington, "Collaborative Labor Relations: The First Line Is the Bottom Line," *Personnel*, March 1989, 78.

59. Cohen, "Management, Unions."

60. Alan S. Blinder, "Want to Boost Productivity? Try Giving Workers a Say," *Business Week*, April 17, 1989, 10.

61. On this problem, see Janice A. Klein, "The Human Costs of Manufacturing Reform," *Harvard Business Review* 67 (March–April 1989).

62. 10 C.3d 29a; 109 Cal. Rptr. 665.

63. "Are Your Employees Profit-Makers or Profit-Takers? Know Before You Hire," *Personnel Security Digest* 1 (Summer 1981): 8.

64. Ibid.

65. Judith Crossen, "Job Applicants Would Disappoint Diogenes," *San Francisco Examiner*, December 18, 1988, D15.

66. "Honest Answers—Postpolygraph," *Personnel*, April 1988, 8.

67. Susan Tempor, "More Employers Attempt to Catch a Thief by Giving Job Applicants 'Honesty' Exams," *Wall Street Journal*, August 3, 1981, 2–1.

68. Crosson, "Job Applicants."

69. "Honest Answers," *Personnel*, 10.

70. Ibid.

71. Tempor, "More Employers Attempt to Catch a Thief," 15.

72. This case study is based on a case reported in Thomas Garrett et al., *Cases in Business Ethics* (Englewood Cliffs, N.J.: Prentice-Hall, 1968), 9–10.

73. Peter T. Kilborn, "Who Decides Who Works at Jobs Imperiling Fetuses?" *New York Times*, September 2, 1990, 1, is the main source for this case study. See also John F. Quinn, "Business Ethics, Fetal Protection Policies, and Discrimination Against Women in the Workplace," *Business and Professional Ethics Journal* 7 (Fall–Winter 1988) and Christine Zielinksi, "The Toxic Trap," *Personnel Journal*, February 1990.

74. *New York Times*, March 21, 1991, A1. Excerpts from *Automobile Workers* v. *Johnson Controls* quoted below are from page A14.

75. Felice N. Schwartz, "Management Women and the New Facts of Life," *Harvard Business Review* 67 (January–February 1989): 65.

76. Ibid., 69.

77. Tamar Lewin, "New Look at Working Moms," *San Francisco Chronicle*, March 8, 1989, A1.

78. Barbara Ehrenreich and Deidre English, "Blowing the Whistle on the 'Mommy Track,'" *Ms.*, July–August 1989, 56.

79. Ibid., 58.

80. Lewin, "New Look at Working Moms."

81. "The Mommy Track," *Newsweek*, March 20, 1989, 132.

82. Daniel Zwerdling, "Democratizing the Workplace: A Case Study," in Mark Green and Robert Massie, Jr., eds. *The Big Business Reader* (New York: The Pilgrim Press, 1980), 106.

83. Ibid. 109.

Drug Testing in Employment

Joseph DesJardins and Ronald Duska

If drug testing of employees is not to violate privacy, the information it seeks must be relevant to the employment contract. DesJardins and Duska examine two arguments used to establish that knowledge of drug use is job-relevant information: first, that drug use adversely affects job performance and, second, that it can harm the employer, other employees, and the public. Although they reject the first argument, they grant that the second can, in certain limited circumstances, justify drug testing. But even in these cases, strict procedural limitations should be placed on drug testing—despite the fact that drug use itself is illegal. They conclude by raising the question of whether employee consent to drug testing is voluntary.

We take privacy to be an "employee right," by which we mean a presumptive moral entitlement to receive certain goods or be protected from certain harms in the workplace.[1] Such a right creates a prima facie obligation on the part of the employer to provide the relevant goods or, as in this case, refrain from the relevant harmful treatment. These rights prevent employees from being placed in the fundamentally coercive position where they must choose between their jobs and other basic human goods.

Further, we view the employer–employee relationship as essentially contractual. The employer–employee relationship is an economic one and, unlike relationships such as those between a gov-

Reprinted by permission from Joseph R. DesJardins and John J. McCall, eds., *Contemporary Issues in Business Ethics*, 2nd ed. (Belmont, Calif.: Wadsworth, 1990).

ernment and its citizens or a parent and a child, exists primarily as a means for satisfying the economic interests of the contracting parties. The obligations that each party incurs are only those that it voluntarily takes on. Given such a contractual relationship, certain areas of the employee's life remain his or her own private concern, and no employer has a right to invade them. On these presumptions we maintain that certain information about an employee is rightfully private, in other words, that the employee has a right to privacy.

The Right to Privacy

George Brenkert has described the right to privacy as involving a three-place relation between a person A, some information X, and another person B. The right to privacy is violated only when B deliberately comes to possess information X about A and no relationship between A and B exists that would justify B's coming to know X about A.[2] Thus, for example, the relationship one has with a mortgage company would justify that company's coming to know about one's salary, but the relationship one has with a neighbor does not justify the neighbor's coming to know that information.

Hence, an employee's right to privacy is violated whenever personal information is requested, collected, or used by an employer in a way or for any purpose that is *irrelevant to* or *in violation of* the contractual relationship that exists between employer and employee.

Since drug testing is a means for obtaining information, the information sought must be relevant to the contract if the drug testing is not to violate privacy. Hence, we must first decide whether knowledge of drug use obtained by drug testing is job relevant. In cases in which the knowledge of drug use is *not* relevant, there appears to be no justification for subjecting employees to drug tests. In cases in which information of drug use is job relevant, we need to consider if, when, and under what conditions using a means such as drug testing to obtain that knowledge is justified.

Is Knowledge of Drug Use Job-Relevant Information?

Two arguments are used to establish that knowledge of drug use is job-relevant information. The first argument claims that drug use adversely affects job performance, thereby leading to lower productivity, higher costs, and consequently lower profits. Drug testing is seen as a way of avoiding these adverse effects. According to some estimates $25 billion are lost each year in the United States through loss in productivity, theft, higher rates in health and liability insurance, and similar costs incurred because of drug use.[3] Since employers are contracting with an employee for the performance of specific tasks, employers seem to have a legitimate claim upon whatever personal information is relevant to an employee's ability to do the job.

The second argument claims that drug use has been and can be responsible for considerable harm to individual employees, to their fellow employees, and to the employer, and third parties, including consumers. In this case drug testing is defended because it is seen as a way of preventing possible harm. Further, since employers can be held liable for harms done to employees and customers, knowledge of employee drug use is needed so that employers can protect themselves from risks related to such liability. But how good are these arguments?

The First Argument: Job Performance and Knowledge of Drug Use

The first argument holds that drug use lowers productivity and that consequently, an awareness of drug use obtained through drug testing will allow an employer to maintain or increase productivity. It is generally assumed that the performance of people using certain drugs is detrimentally affected by such use, and any use of drugs that reduces productivity is consequently job relevant. If knowledge of such drug use allows the employer to eliminate production losses, such knowledge is job relevant.

On the surface this argument seems reasonable. Obviously some drug use, in lowering the level of performance, can decrease productivity. Since the employer is entitled to a certain level of performance and drug use adversely affects performance, knowledge of that use seems job-relevant.

But this formulation of the argument leaves an important question unanswered. To what level of performance are employers entitled? Optimal performance, or some lower level? If some lower level, what? Employers have a valid claim upon some *cer-*

tain level of performance, such that a failure to perform at this level would give the employer a justification for disciplining, firing, or at least finding fault with the employee. But that does not necessarily mean that the employer has a right to a maximum or optimal level of performance, a level above and beyond a certain level of acceptability. It might be nice if the employee gives an employer a maximum effort or optimal performance, but that is above and beyond the call of the employee's duty and the employer can hardly claim a right at all times to the highest level of performance of which an employee is capable. . . .

If the person is producing what is expected, knowledge of drug use on the grounds of production is irrelevant since, by this hypothesis, the production is satisfactory. If, on the other hand, the performance suffers, then to the extent that it slips below the level justifiably expected, the employer has preliminary grounds for warning, disciplining, or releasing the employee. But the justification for this action is the person's unsatisfactory performance, not the person's use of drugs. Accordingly, drug use information is either unnecessary or irrelevant and consequently there are not sufficient grounds to override the right of privacy. Thus, unless we can argue that an employer is entitled to optimal performance, the argument fails.

This counterargument should make it clear that the information that is job relevant, and consequently is not rightfully private, is information about an employee's level of performance and not information about the underlying causes of that level. The fallacy of the argument that promotes drug testing in the name of increased productivity is the assumption that each employee is obliged to perform at an optimal or at least quite high level. But this is required under few if any contracts. What is required contractually is meeting the normally expected levels of production or performing the tasks in the job description adequately (not optimally). If one can do that under the influence of drugs, then on the grounds of job-performance at least, drug use is rightfully private. An employee who cannot perform the task adequately is not fulfilling the contract, and knowledge of the cause of the failure to perform is irrelevant on the contractual model.

Of course, if the employer suspects drug use or abuse as the cause of the unsatisfactory performance, then she might choose to help the person with counseling or rehabilitation. However, this does not seem to be something morally required of the employer. Rather, in the case of unsatisfactory performance, the employer has a prima facie justification for dismissing or disciplining the employee. . . .

The Second Argument: Harm and the Knowledge of Drug Use to Prevent Harm

The performance argument is inadequate, but there is an argument that seems somewhat stronger. This is an argument that takes into account the fact that drug use often leads to harm. Using a variant of the Millian argument, which allows interference with a person's rights in order to prevent harm, we could argue that drug testing might be justified if such testing led to knowledge that would enable an employer to prevent harm.

Drug use certainly can lead to harming others. Consequently, if knowledge of such drug use can prevent harm, then knowing whether or not an employee uses drugs might be a legitimate concern of an employer in certain circumstances. This second argument claims that knowledge of the employee's drug use is job relevant because employees who are under the influence of drugs can pose a threat to the health and safety of themselves and others, and an employer who knows of that drug use and the harm it can cause has a responsibility to prevent it.

Employers have both a general duty to prevent harm and the specific responsibility for harms done by their employees. Such responsibilities are sufficient reason for any employer to claim that information about an employee's drug use is relevant if that knowledge can prevent harm by giving the employer grounds for dismissing the employee or not allowing him or her to perform potentially harmful tasks. Employers might even claim a right to reduce unreasonable risks, in this case the risks involving legal and economic liability for harms caused by employees under the influence of drugs, as further justification for knowing about employee drug use.

This second argument differs from the first, in which only a lowered job performance was relevant information. In this case, even to allow the performance is problematic, for the performance itself, more than being inadequate, can hurt people. We cannot be as sanguine about the prevention of harm as we can about inadequate production. Where drug use may cause serious harms, knowledge of that use becomes relevant if the knowledge of such use can lead to the prevention of harm and drug testing becomes justified as a means for obtaining that knowledge.

Jobs with Potential to Cause Harm

In the first place, it is not clear that every job has a potential to cause harm—at least, not a potential to cause harm sufficient to override a prima facie right to privacy. To say that employers can use drug testing where that can prevent harm is not to say that every employer has the right to know about the drug use of every employee. Not every job poses a threat serious enough to justify an employer coming to know this information.

In deciding which jobs pose serious-enough threats, certain guidelines should be followed. First the potential for harm should be *clear* and *present*. Perhaps all jobs in some extended way pose potential threats to human well-being. We suppose an accountant's error could pose a threat of harm to someone somewhere. But some jobs—like those of airline pilots, school bus drivers, public transit drivers, and surgeons—are jobs in which unsatisfactory performance poses a clear and present danger to others. It would be much harder to make an argument that job performances by auditors, secretaries, executive vice-presidents for public relations, college teachers, professional athletes, and the like could cause harm if those performances were carried on under the influence of drugs. They would cause harm only in exceptional cases.[4]

Not Every Person Is to Be Tested

But, even if we can make a case that a particular job involves a clear and present danger for causing harm if performed under the influence of drugs, it is not appropriate to treat everyone holding such a job the same. Not every jobholder is equally threatening. There is less reason to investigate an airline pilot for drug use if that pilot has a twenty-year record of exceptional service than there is to investigate a pilot whose behavior has become erratic and unreliable recently, or one who reports to work smelling of alcohol and slurring his words. Presuming that every airline pilot is equally threat-

ening is to deny individuals the respect that they deserve as autonomous, rational agents. It is to ignore their history and the significant differences between them. It is also probably inefficient and leads to the lowering of morale. It is the likelihood of causing harm, and not the fact of being an airline pilot per se, that is relevant in deciding which employees in critical jobs to test.

So, even if knowledge of drug use is justifiable to prevent harm, we must be careful to limit this justification to a range of jobs and people where the potential for harm is clear and present. The jobs must be jobs that clearly can cause harm, and the specific employee should not be someone who has a history of reliability. Finally, the drugs being tested should be those drugs that have genuine potential for harm if used in the jobs in question.

Limitations on Drug-Testing Policies

Even when we identify those situations in which knowledge of drug use would be job relevant, we still need to examine whether some procedural limitations should not be placed upon the employer's testing for drugs. We have said when a real threat of harm exists and when evidence exists suggesting that a particular employee poses such a threat, an employer could be justified in knowing about drug use in order to prevent the potential harm. But we need to recognize that so long as the employer has the discretion for deciding when the potential for harm is clear and present, and for deciding which employees pose the threat of harm, the possibility of abuse is great. Thus, some policy limiting the employer's power is called for.

Just as criminal law imposes numerous restrictions protecting individual dignity and liberty on the state's pursuit of its goals, so we should expect that some restrictions be placed on employers to protect innocent employees from harm (including loss of job and damage to one's personal and professional reputation). Thus, some system of checks upon an employer's discretion in these matters seems advisable.

A drug-testing policy that requires all employees to submit to a drug test or to jeopardize their jobs would seem coercive and therefore unacceptable. Being placed in such a fundamentally coercive position of having to choose between one's job and one's privacy does not provide the conditions for a truly free consent. Policies that are unilaterally established by employers would likewise be unacceptable. Working with employees to develop company policy seems the only way to ensure that the policy will be fair to both parties. Prior notice of testing would also be required in order to give employees the option of freely refraining from drug use. Preventing drug use is morally preferable to punishing users after the fact, because this approach treats employees as capable of making rational and informed decisions.

Further procedural limitations seem advisable as well. Employees should be notified of the results of the test, they should be entitled to appeal the results (perhaps through further tests by an independent laboratory), and the information obtained through tests ought to be kept confidential. In summary, limitations upon employer discretion for administering drug tests can be derived from the nature of the employment contract and from the recognition that drug testing is justified by the desire to prevent harm, not the desire to punish wrongdoing.

The Illegality Contention

At this point critics might note that the behavior which testing would try to deter is, after all, illegal. Surely this excuses any responsible employer from being overprotective of an employee's rights. The fact that an employee is doing something illegal should give the employer a right to that information about his or her private life. Thus it is not simply that drug use might pose a threat of harm to others, but that it is an *illegal* activity that threatens others. But again, we would argue that illegal activity itself is irrelevant to job performance. At best, *conviction* records might be relevant, but since drug tests are administered by private employers we are not only ignoring the question of conviction, we are also ignoring the fact that the employee has not even been arrested for the alleged illegal activity.

Further, even if the due process protections and the establishment of guilt are acknowledged, it still does not follow that employers have a claim to know about all illegal activity on the part of their employees.

Consider the following example: Suppose you were hiring an auditor whose job required certify-

ing the integrity of your firm's tax and financial records. Certainly, the personal integrity of this employee is vital to adequate job performance. Would we allow the employer to conduct, with or without the employee's consent, an audit of the employee's own personal tax return? Certainly if we discover that this person has cheated on a personal tax return we will have evidence of illegal activity that is relevant to this person's ability to do the job. Given one's own legal liability for filing falsified statements, the employee's illegal activity also poses a threat to others. But surely, allowing private individuals to audit an employee's tax returns is too intrusive a means for discovering information about that employee's integrity. The government certainly would never allow this violation of an employee's privacy. It ought not to allow drug testing on the same grounds. Why tax returns should be protected in ways that urine, for example, is not, raises interesting questions of fairness. Unfortunately, this question would take us beyond the scope of this paper.

Voluntariness

A final problem that we also leave undeveloped concerns the voluntariness of employee consent. For most employees, being given the choice between submitting to a drug test and risking one's job by refusing an employer's request is not much of a decision at all. We believe that such decisions are less than voluntary and thereby hold that employers cannot escape our criticisms simply by including within the employment contract a drug-testing clause.[5] Furthermore, there is reason to believe that those most in need of job security will be those most likely to be subjected to drug testing. Highly skilled, professional employees with high job mobility and security will be in a stronger position to resist such intrusions than will less skilled, easily replaced workers. This is why we should not anticipate surgeons and airline pilots being tested and should not be surprised when public transit and factory workers are. A serious question of fairness arises here as well.

Drug use and drug testing seem to be our most recent social "crisis." Politicians, the media, and employers expend a great deal of time and effort addressing this crisis. Yet, unquestionably, more lives, health, and money are lost each year to alcohol abuse than to marijuana, cocaine, and other controlled substances. We are well advised to be careful in considering issues that arise from such selective social concern. We will let other social commentators speculate on the reasons why drug use has received scrutiny while other white-collar crimes and alcohol abuse are ignored. Our only concern at this point is that such selective prosecution suggests an arbitrariness that should alert us to questions of fairness and justice.

In summary, then, we have seen that drug use is not always job relevant, and if drug use is not job relevant, information about it is certainly not job relevant. In the case of performance it may be a cause of some decreased performance, but it is the performance itself that is relevant to an employee's position, not what prohibits or enables that employee to do the job. In the case of potential harm being done by an employee under the influence of drugs, the drug use seems job relevant, and in this case drug testing to prevent harm might be legitimate. But how this is practicable is another question. It would seem that standard motor dexterity or mental dexterity tests given immediately prior to job performance are more effective in preventing harm, unless one concludes that drug use invariably and necessarily leads to harm. One must trust the individuals in any system for that system to work. One cannot police everything. Random testing might enable an employer to find drug users and to weed out the few to forestall possible future harm, but are the harms prevented sufficient to override the rights of privacy of the people who are innocent and to overcome the possible abuses we have mentioned? It seems not.

Clearly, a better method is to develop safety checks immediately prior to the performance of a job. Have a surgeon or a pilot or a bus driver pass a few reasoning and motor-skill tests before work. The cause of the lack of a skill, which lack might lead to harm, is really a secondary issue.

Notes

1. "A Defense of Employee Rights," Joseph DesJardins and John McCall, *Journal of Business Ethics* 4 (1985). We should emphasize that our concern is with the *moral* rights of privacy for employees and not with any specific or prospective *legal* rights. Readers interested in pursuing the legal aspects of employee drug testing should consult "Workplace Privacy Issues and Employer Screening Policies" by Richard Lehr and David Middlebrooks in *Employee Relations Law Journal*, vol. 11, no. 3, 407–421; and "Screening Workers for Drugs: A Legal and Ethical Framework," Mark Rothstein, in *Employee Relations Law Journal*, vol. 11, no. 3, 422–436.

2. "Privacy, Polygraphs, and Work," George Brenkert, *Journal of Business and Professional Ethics*, vol. 1, no. 1 (Fall 1981). For a more general discussion of privacy in the workplace see "Privacy in Employment" by Joseph DesJardins, in *Moral Rights in the Workplace*, edited by Gertrude Ezorsky (SUNY Press, 1987). A good resource for philosophical work on privacy can be found in "Recent Work on the Concept of Privacy" by W.A. Parent, in *American Philosophical Quarterly*, vol. 20 (Oct. 1983) 341–358.

3. *U.S. News and World Report*, 22 Aug. 1983; *Newsweek*, 6 May 1983.

4. Obviously we are speaking here of harms that go beyond the simple economic harm that results from unsatisfactory job performance. These economic harms are discussed in the first argument above. Further, we ignore such "harms" as providing bad role models for adolescents, harms often used to justify drug tests for professional athletes. We think it unreasonable to hold an individual responsible for the image he or she provides to others.

5. It might be argued that since we base our critique upon the contractual relationship between employers and employees, our entire position can be undermined by a clever employer who places within the contract a privacy waiver for drug tests. A full answer to this would require an account of the free and rational subject that the contract model presupposes. While acknowledging that we need such an account to prevent just any contract from being morally legitimate, we will have to leave this debate to another time. Interested readers might consult "The Moral Contract between Employers and Employees" by Norman Bowie in *The Work Ethic in Business*, edited by W. M. Hoffman and T. J. Wyly (Cambridge, MA: Oelgeschlager and Gunn, 1981) 195–202.

Review and Discussion Questions

1. DesJardins and Duska consider two arguments intended to show that knowledge of drug use is job-relevant information. What are their reasons for rejecting the first argument and what are the limitations of the second argument? Are you persuaded by their reasoning?

2. Do you agree that the crucial question regarding drug testing in employment is whether the information sought is job-relevant? Are there other reasons for drug testing that don't turn on this issue?

3. What, if any, procedural limitations should be placed on drug testing in those cases in which it is justified? Are DesJardins and Duska right to maintain that the illegality of drug use is irrelevant?

4. How voluntary do you think employee consent to drug testing really is?

5. What steps do you think employers should take to deal with the problem of employee drug use?

Work, Privacy, and Autonomy

Richard L. Lippke

Lippke argues that privacy is valuable because of its importance for human autonomy. Rejecting analyses of privacy in the workplace that focus on whether information is "job-relevant" as this is defined by the work contract, Lippke sets the question of workplace privacy in the broader context of the imbalance of power that actually exists between employers and employees. He contends that this power imbalance and the accompanying authoritarian organization of work already deprive employees of any significant input into the decisions that affect their working lives. As a result, information-gathering techniques like surveillance and drug testing are to be resisted as further eroding what little autonomy employees have left.

Employees today face what many believe are unjustified assaults on their privacy. At present, the most well-known and controversial such assault is the urine test. Estimates are that about 30% of the Fortune 500 companies in the United States require a urine test as part of the employment application process. Proponents of such testing warn of the dangers of rampant drug use and abuse in our society. They insist on the need to safeguard co-worker and consumer health and safety, and the need to maintain productivity. Opponents of testing conjure up images of Orwell's *1984* — of large and powerful institutions run amok, forcing innocent people to urinate while under the intense (and let us hope not prurient) supervision of official inspectors. Opponents lambast testing as an invasion of privacy and as a form of self-incrimination. Their most effective tactic has been to raise the specter of inaccurate tests; of persons unfairly scored with the scarlet letter of drug use.

Unfortunately, in the public debate over these issues there is little in the way of patient and careful analysis. . . . I will maintain that the philosophical defenses of employee privacy that have been offered are either incomplete or misguided. At times, they say too little about the value of privacy. Or, they offer suspect models of the employer/employee relationship. Or, they fail to convincingly show how we should deal with the conflict between privacy and other, competing values.

I will begin my analysis by arguing that privacy is valuable because of its relation to autonomy. For the purposes of this discussion, I will define autonomy as the capacity of persons to make rationally reflective choices about their ends and activities. All areas of persons' lives are assumed to be fit subjects for the exercise of their autonomy. Unless the relation between privacy and autonomy is kept clearly in view, we will not be able to establish the need for restrictions on the information employers may gather or on the means they may use. More importantly, I will argue that we must examine the privacy issue in the context of an understanding of how the contemporary organization of work in the United States affects the autonomy of workers. Simply put, workers in the U.S. face myriad assaults to their autonomy. I will show how failure to recognize this and to incorporate it into philosophical analyses of employee privacy inevitably weakens the case that can be made on behalf of employees. I will argue that when the reality of work is ignored, workers are more likely to be blamed for behavior that arguably stems (at least in part) from the system of private property rights in productive resources that deprives them of control over their working lives.

Though I will focus exclusively on the value of autonomy, I will not try to argue that it is the only value we should pay attention to in assessing the current organization of work in the U.S. I would contend that autonomy is an essential value, but I concede that other values are important as well. Others who have offered critiques of the current organization of work have tried to show that it undermines values like self-respect and welfare.[1] . . .

There are difficulties in defining what privacy is. However, I do not think we need to be detained by them.[2] Generally, there is a consensus that it involves two things: (1) control over some information about ourselves; and (2) some control over who can experience or observe us.[3] In the abstract, it is hard to further specify how much control privacy involves and over what types of information it ranges. This is because whether any given piece of information about me is private in relation to someone else depends on the type of relationship I have to that individual. What is private in relation to my spouse is very different from what is private in relation to an employer or working associate.

Joseph Kupfer has recently offered a compelling analysis of the value of privacy.[4] Two of the ways in which privacy is valuable are especially relevant to the employer/employee relationship, so I will concentrate on them. First, Kupfer argues that privacy plays an essential role in individuals coming to have an "autonomous self-concept," that is, a concept of themselves as in control of their own lives:

> An autonomous self-concept requires identifying with a particular body whose thoughts, purposes, and actions are subject to one's control . . . autonomy requires awareness of control over one's relation to others, including their access to us . . . privacy contributes to the formation and persistence of autonomous individuals by providing them with control over whether or not their physical and psychological existence becomes part of another's experience.[5]

Kupfer does not argue that privacy is intrinsically good. He argues that it is causally related to the formation and maintenance of an autonomous self-concept. An autonomous self-concept is, in turn, a necessary condition of the basic good of autonomy. In other words, unless individuals conceive of themselves as able to determine their own courses of action, their own life-plans, they cannot be autonomous. If individuals are to develop and main-

tain an autonomous self-concept, others must grant them control over information about themselves and control over who can experience them and when. Kupfer offers some empirical evidence to substantiate the claim that lack of privacy defeats the formation and maintenance of an autonomous self-concept.[6]

As Kupfer notes, the most autonomous person is one who evaluates his deepest convictions, or the most fundamental aspects of his life-plan. Privacy is essential to individuals having the concept that they can do this. It allows them to engage in this self-scrutiny without intrusion and distraction. When the most intimate aspects of their lives are up for scrutiny, individuals are vulnerable to ridicule or manipulation by others. It is vitally important for them to be able to remove themselves from observation and criticism by those they feel they cannot trust.

A second way in which privacy is valuable is that individuals subjected to invasions of their privacy seem less likely to conceive of themselves as *worthy* of autonomy:

> Privacy is a trusting way others treat us, resulting in a conception of ourselves as worth being trusted. In contrast, monitoring behavior or collecting data on us, projects a disvaluing of the self in question.[7]

Close, intrusive supervision and constant correction (or the threat of it) are inimical to individuals developing and maintaining a sense of themselves as worthy of autonomy. In contrast, social practices that respect privacy give the individual a chance to make mistakes or do wrong, and thus convey the message that the individual is worthy of acting autonomously. The sense that they are worthy of acting autonomously may, as Kupfer notes, increase the confidence of individuals in themselves, and so they may exercise their autonomy to an even greater extent. . . .

With this brief characterization of some of the ways in which privacy is valuable in hand, I turn first to consider the issues raised by the *content* of information that businesses might acquire about employees or prospective employees. Both George Brenkert and Joseph DesJardins offer arguments designed to restrict the types of information employers may justifiably gather about employees to information that is "job relevant." Both also construe the employer/employee relationship in contractual terms, relying, apparently, on the fact that the courts are increasingly viewing the relationship in that fashion.

DesJardins argues that the contractual model is a marked improvement over the old principal/agent model, where the moral and legal rights seemed to be largely on the side of the employer and the moral and legal duties on the side of the employee. The contractual model presumes the existence of a legal framework to enforce the contract. More importantly, "contracts also must be non-coercive, voluntary agreements between rational and free agents."[8] And, they must be free from fraud and deception.

DesJardins explores the implications of this model for the issue of privacy in the employment context. He argues that the employer is entitled to make sure that the contract is free from fraud and deception. The employer can legitimately acquire information about the prospective employee's job qualifications, work experience, educational background, and "other information relevant to the hiring decision."[9] Information is "relevant" if it has to do with determing whether or not the employee is capable of fulfilling her part of the contract. In a similar vein, Brenkert argues that the "job relevance" requirement limits the information sought "to that which is directly connected with the job description."[10] Brenkert admits that aspects of a person's social and moral character (for example, honesty, ability and willingness to cooperate with others) are job relevant. What both Brenkert and DesJardins want to rule out as job relevant is information about such things as a prospective employee's political or religious beliefs and practices, her sexual preferences, marital status, credit or other financial data, and the like. One of Brenkert's complaints about the use of polygraph tests is that they often involve asking employees for information that is *not* job relevant.

I am sympathetic with the idea of such content restrictions, but I believe the arguments of DesJardins and Brenkert are seriously flawed. In the first place, we should be wary of the contractual model of the employer/employee relationship. . . .

The danger in using this model is that it may lead us to ignore a crucial imbalance of power that exists in the marketplace. Individual employees rarely have bargaining power equal to that of their prospective employers. First, there are typically more potential employees available to firms than

there are job openings available. Many jobs require little training or pre-existing expertise, and so workers can often be easily replaced. The threat that "there is always someone to take your place" is not an idle one for most workers. Unemployment in the economy generally and the problems workers face in moving to areas where there are jobs contribute to this buyers' market that is to the advantage of firms. Second, firms seem able to absorb underemployment more easily than workers can absorb unemployment. While firms need employees, they rarely need them as desperately as workers need jobs. As a result of these two factors, individual workers are rarely in a position to bargain on anything like equal terms with their perspective employers.[11]

This imbalance of power renders most workers practically unable to resist the demands for information that precede and accompany employment offers, and makes all the more urgent the content restrictions DesJardins and Brenkert advocate. After all, what is the point of urging such restrictions if the wage-labor agreement is one between relative equals? Why not just leave the sorts of information to be exchanged up to the negotiations between employer and employee?

. . . My point is that the contractual model is very misleading if used as a way to conceive of the reality of work in the U.S. It suggests a type of equality that does not exist, and if its descriptive and normative functions are run together, it distorts our perception of where the balance of power lies in the relationship between workers and employers.

Leaving aside the problems with the contractual model, it does not seem that DesJardins and Brenkert help us to understand the moral basis for the content restrictions they advocate. The appeal to the notion of "job relevance" raises more questions than it answers. Lots of information both would prevent employers from obtaining is, arguably, job relevant. For instance, if all of my employees are politically and religiously conservative, knowing where prospective employees stand on these matters may very well be job relevant if my employees have to work closely together. After all, an atheist with socialist leanings may not get along at all with my employees and thereby disrupt productivity. Neither may a union supporter, a homosexual, or someone who is financially reckless or sexually promiscuous. I am not suggesting that we should cater to the prejudices of existing employees in making hiring decisions. What I am suggesting is that Brenkert's and DesJardins' arguments invoke a concept that is far from unproblematic.[12]

Even if the notion of "job relevance" was unproblematic, the argument would be incomplete. What we want is an argument that connects job relevance up with some moral value or values. In other words, why (morally speaking) limit employer access to only job relevant information? What is at stake in doing so?

If we turn back to the analysis of the value of privacy, the answer emerges. Suppose that employers are allowed to gather all of the sorts of information that the notion of "job relevance" is meant to exclude, and to use that information in making employment-related decisions. The result might be that business hiring and promotion decisions will wind up shaping peoples' lives in rather dramatic ways. Consider the likely chilling effects on employees. They may be reluctant to try out any new ideas or activities that may, at some future date, come back to haunt them. As we saw, privacy vitally contributes to our concept of ourselves as in control of our own lives. Part of this is that it protects our sense of self-determination by enabling us to enagage in a "no holds barred" examination of all aspects of our lives. It allows us to experiment with different courses of our lives, if only in thought. These different courses may not be popular, especially to employees who are very conscious of the bottom line.

There is also the very real danger that all sorts of mistaken inferences about employee behavior will be made from access to such information. For instance, suppose that a polygraph test uncovers the fact that a person sometimes fantasizes about theft. It seems clear that a person who fantasizes about theft may be a long way from behaving as a thief. We do not understand the connections between the "inner workings" of people's minds and their behavior anywhere near well enough to allow employers to make such predictions in an accurate fashion.[13]

In short, the content restrictions DesJardins and Brenkert favor are morally justified as ways of limiting the perceived power that businesses have over the lives of their employees. We should discourage invasions of privacy that will likely result in individuals narrowing the exploration and examination of their lives, or that will decrease their

sense that they control and are responsible for their lives. In a work environment without such restrictions, and where employers are already in a position to impose their wills on employees in other ways, it seems unlikely that employees will have as rich and lively a sense of their own autonomy. In turn, they will be less prone to exercise their autonomy.

It seems clear that many of the most controversial *means* of acquiring information about employees may provide employers with information that is, on any reasonable interpretation of the notion, job relevant. Surveillance to prevent theft or to maintain productivity provides such information. Urine tests will provide such information, though they will also provide information about off-the-job drug or alcohol use that is, less obviously, job relevant. Searches of employee desks or lockers, and even polygraph tests (where the questions are suitably restricted) will provide such information. Physical exams and skills tests will do so, though few have seen these as controversial.

Numerous writers have argued against the use of at least some of these means. One popular objection to some of these means is that they are so inaccurate. Polygraph tests, in particular, seem gravely defective in this way, and to a lesser extent, so do urine tests. The concern about accuracy is a concern about fairness, about the possibility of unfairly accusing individuals of actions they are innocent of. I think that the inaccuracy issue is a very serious one, but I do not believe we should base our case against such tests on it alone, or even primarily. The reason for this is simple: suppose through various technological developments such tests are made *very* accurate. Are we then to conclude that there is nothing objectionable about them? I think not. I will try to show that there are other objectionable features to such tests.

A second objection might be that such means of acquiring information are somehow too intrusive. It is important to ask what this means. Is it that such methods come too close to us, crossing some physical or psychological boundary that is morally significant? Administering the polygraph test does require that various devices be attached to our bodies, so maybe it is the actual physical contact that matters. It is hard to imagine anything more intrusive in this regard than a physical exam. Urine tests are not intrusive in this way, however, and neither are surveillance or forays through employee desks and lockers. Thus, physical contact does not seem to be a necessary condition of intrusiveness. It might be a sufficient condition, but we need to know precisely what is so objectionable about such contact. It does not seem objectionable in the same way that battery is, where the concern is with shielding individuals from physical harm. . . .

What all of these methods of acquiring information seem to have in common is that they are ways of checking on the things employees say about themselves or the ways employees present themselves. In this regard, I do not see how a urine test or surveillance is all that much different than the required disclosure of information about work experience or educational background. Perhaps some methods are more intrusive, as a matter of degree, than others. Employees are increasingly finding that not even their own bodies are safe havens, let alone their desks and lockers. At every turn, they are hounded by employee efforts to catch them speaking or acting in ways contrary to what are deemed the employer's interests.

The proliferation of these methods of acquiring contradicting information seems likely to have two sorts of effects on workers. First, all such methods implicitly remind the worker where the balance of power lies in the working world. Again, most workers are not in a position to refuse to cooperate with the use of such methods and workers are highly vulnerable to any negative employer reactions to the information so gleaned.[14] The more a worker is checked on, tested, spied upon, and so on, the less likely she is to feel that she controls her own life in the working world. The aggregate and cumulative effects of many (by themselves seemingly innocent) attempts to check on workers might be an increased sense on the part of workers that the workplace is an oppressive environment. It is distressing that so many employees apparently submit to polygraph or urine tests without any reluctance. Can this be because they have already internalized the message that in the workplace their lives are not their own?

Second, random or across-the-board drug testing, or surveillance without "reasonable cause" implicitly tells employees that they are not trustworthy. It is important to keep in mind that in spite of statistics on the use of drugs by workers (estimates as high as one in six use drugs either on or off the job), the vast majority of workers are probably "clean" and honest. However, instead of there be-

ing a presumption that employees will act responsibly, the presumption behind the use of these methods of gathering information is that they cannot be trusted to act responsibly. Individuals who find themselves with a presumption of doubt against them may simply react with resentment. That is bad enough and a potential cost to employers. What is worse is the tendency such methods might have to undermine the employees' sense of trustworthiness, and therefore their sense that they are worthy of acting autonomously. Again, one valuable thing about privacy is that it affirms an individual's sense that she is worthy of autonomy. The more she lacks that sense, the more she is prone to tolerate invasions of her privacy, with the resulting debilitating effects on her autonomy.

In the abstract, concerns about the effects of such methods on employee autonomy might appear legitimate, but not of a sufficiently compelling nature to convince us that their use is wholly objectionable. If they are employed in a work environment that is otherwise supportive of employee autonomy, they might be only minor threats. Therefore, in order to strengthen the case against the use of such methods, it will help here to focus attention on how the organization of work in the U.S. *already* undermines the autonomy of most workers to an extraordinary extent.

As numerous critics of the organization of work in the U.S. have pointed out, the majority of workers are routinely subjected to a hierarchical, authoritarian management structure that deprives them of any significant input into the economic decisions directly affecting their working lives. Most have very little input into decisions about the organization of work at even the shop-floor level, let alone at levels above it. As Adina Schwartz argues, most workers are subjected to a division of labor where they are confined to increasingly narrowly-defined tasks determined and supervised by others:

> These routine jobs provide people with almost no opportunities for formulating aims, for deciding on means for achieving their ends, or for adjusting their goals and methods in light of experience.[15]

Work technology is decided by others, as are productivity quotas, criteria for evaluation, discipline procedures, and plant closings or employee lay-offs. Even the attitudes with which work is to be done are prescribed and pressures are put on workers to "be a loyal member of the team" or to "please the customer at all costs." . . .

Thus, each concession made to management's desire to gather information using the methods we have been discussing adds to an already impressive arsenal of weapons at its disposal for the assault on employee autonomy. The question is *not* whether we should endorse the use of methods that undermine employee autonomy in a setting where that autonomy is otherwise affirmed and nurtured. The question is whether we should endorse the use of methods that might further erode employee autonomy. For instant, random or across-the-board urine tests do not send a message to workers that they are untrustworthy in a context where their trustworthiness is normally affirmed. Instead, it sends a message that is likely repeated to workers in a thousand different ways throughout their working lives. A verdict wholly in favor of employees on all of the privacy issues we have been considering will, by itself, come nowhere near establishing working conditions supportive of employee autonomy.

Another way to put the preceding point about the organization of work in the U.S. is to say that property rights, with their supporting political-social institutions and practices, give some individuals a considerable amount of *power* over the lives of others. It is with this in mind that we should consider attempts to override the privacy of employees by appeals to the property rights of the owners and stockholders.

Proponents of gathering information about employees may admit that privacy is a value and that it is threatened by the means employers want to use to gather information. But, they will argue, the property rights of the owners and stockholders are valuable as well. They will rightly demand to be shown that the privacy rights of workers ought to prevail over these property rights. . . .

What this plausible-sounding argument ignores is how property rights in productive resources differ from privacy rights. The right to privacy is such that respecting it provides individuals with an increased sense of control (a necessary condition of autonomy) over their own lives. Respecting it does *not* provide individuals with increased control over the lives of others. Property rights as they exist in the U.S. are, as we have seen, not like this. They do give some power over the lives of others. And, importantly, a verdict in favor of the

owners and stockholders will mean a further extension of that already considerable control.

Hence, the issue is not the rather abstract one of whether privacy rights are more or less important than property rights in relation to the autonomy of the bearers of those rights. Rather, since property rights as currently institutionalized give some power over the lives of others, the issue is whether to preserve or increase that power, *or* curtail it. Indeed, once the connection between property rights and power is revealed in this way, those rights become fit subjects for critical scrutiny. If we are concerned about the autonomy of workers, we can hardly ignore the existence of working conditions that systematically and pervasively undermine it.

A second reason for not allowing the issues to be framed simply in terms of conflicting rights is that this is likely to exonerate the existing organization of work from any blame for generating the employee behavior that is viewed as irresponsible. This irresponsible behavior is taken as a *given*, and various methods for collecting information about employees are proposed. The need to gather such information is implicitly attributed solely to defects in the character of employees. Those who seek to defend workers against invasions of their privacy are likely to be portrayed as condoning dishonesty, drug use, and the like. This portrayal is, of course, unfair, but it gains credence from the implicit assumption that such behaviors simply exist and must be countered. Thus, the debate about conflicting rights begins, and employers are all too easily depicted as the innocent victims of their unscrupulous, irresponsible, and ungrateful employees.

Many critics of the organization of work in the U.S. will argue that it is the character of that work itself which is a very significant factor in producing such "problem" behaviors. The research that exists in this area strongly suggests that this is a possibility we should not ignore.[16] It is surprising that in the popular and philosophical discussions of these issues, the following sorts of questions are so rarely asked: Why is it that employees show up drunk or drugged for work? Why is it that they shirk work and responsibility? Why is it that they lie about their credentials or exaggerate them? Why is it that they engage in theft or sabotage? When the question asked is whether the employee privacy that is violated in order to counter such behaviors outweighs or is outweighed by the right to property, the preceding sorts of questions are suppressed. Behaviors which may be symptomatic of a morally sick organization of work are viewed as the underlying cause of the conflict. Then, in a twist of bitter irony, the property rights in which that organization of work is anchored are brought in to beat back the challenge posed by the employees' privacy rights.

Appeals to co-worker health and safety, or to the health and safety of consumers and members of the general public, are also used to justify invasions of worker privacy. No one wants their airline pilot to be high on cocaine or their nuclear power plant operator to be blitzed on Jim Beam. Moreover, protecting people's health and safety does *not* ipso facto give them power over the lives of others. Health and safety are obviously essential conditions for the preservation and exercise of autonomy, perhaps more essential than privacy. So, it would seem that health and safety considerations ought to prevail over privacy considerations.

In response to this, I begin by noting that we should not isolate the issue of whether or not we can invade the privacy of workers to protect health and safety from the larger issue of the role of the current organization of work in generating dangerous behavior. The issue is not simply whether health and safety outweighs privacy, but also whether fundamental changes in the organization of work would lessen or eliminate the behavior that makes overriding privacy seem so reasonable. It is hard to say whether and to what extent the means many would now use to gather information about employees would be used in a more democratically and humanely organized economy. Such an economy would eliminate or at least lessen the specter of unemployment, and so the felt need to lie about or exaggerate credentials in order to obtain work might be eliminated. Such an economy would give workers more real control over their working lives, and would eliminate the division between those who make decisions at work and those who simply implement the decisions of others. Such an economy would give workers more control over the products of their labor, and give them the power to discipline other workers. How such changes would affect employee morale, productivity, and the sense of responsibility for work performed are things we can only speculate about.

It seems likely that such changes will *not* eliminate all dangerous or destructive behavior on the part of workers. I do not wish to rule out, once and for all, the use of means of acquiring information that encroach on privacy. What I do want to suggest, in closing, is that in a more democratically and humanely organized economy, decisions about what measures to use and when to use them would not be made unilaterally by some people and then simply imposed on others. If we are going to respect the autonomy of persons, then we must give them input into decisions like this that vitally affect their lives.

Notes

1. See, for instance, David Schweickart, *Capitalism or Worker Control? An Ethical and Economic Appraisal* (New York: Praeger Publishers, 1980); Gerald Doppelt, "Conflicting Social Paradigms of Human Freedom and the Problem of Justification," *Inquiry*, vol. 27 (1984), pp. 51–86.

2. For a useful discussion of the difficulties in defining privacy, see H. J. McCloskey, "Privacy and the Right to Privacy," *Philosophy*, vol. 55 (1980), pp. 17–38.

3. For instance, see Joseph Kupfer, "Privacy, Autonomy, and Self-Concept," *American Philosophical Quarterly*, vol. 24 (1987), pp. 81–89. Also, Richard Wasserstrom, "Privacy," in *Today's Moral Problems*, Richard Wasserstrom (ed.) (New York: Macmillan Publishing Co., 1979), pp. 392–408.

4. Kupfer, "Privacy, Autonomy, and Self-Concept," pp. 81–89. For a similar analysis, see Jeffrey H. Reiman, "Privacy, Intimacy, and Personhood," *Philosophy and Public Affairs*, vol. 6 (1976), pp. 26–44.

5. Kupfer, "Privacy, Autonomy, and Self-Concept," p. 82.

6. *Ibid.*, pp. 81–82.

7. *Ibid.*, p. 85.

8. Joseph R. DesJardins, "Privacy in Employment," in *Moral Rights in the Workplace*, Gertrude Ezorsky (ed.) (Albany, NY: State University of New York Press, 1987), pp. 127–139, 131.

9. *Ibid.*, p. 132.

10. George G. Brenkert, "Privacy, Polygraphs, and Work," in *Contemporary Issues in Business Ethics*, Joseph R. DesJardins and John J. McCall (eds.) (Belmont, CA: Wadsworth, 1985), pp. 227–237, 231.

11. For those who might say that labor unions provide workers with such equality, I point out that, at present, less than 15% of U.S. workers are represented by labor unions.

12. Brenkert, "Privacy, Polygraphs, and Work," p. 231. Brenkert admits that the criterion of job relevance is "rather vague," yet proceeds to use it.

13. One of the most frightening prospects employees face is the availability of so-called "genetic marker" tests. These tests will allow employers to tell which individuals have genetic *tendencies* for such things as alcoholism, heart attacks, and cancer. Suppose businesses decide to gather and use such information in making employment-related decisions. Though there are things individuals can do to counteract their tendencies, they might find themselves labeled due to their genetic tendencies, and so denied jobs or promotions. This threatens their abilities to determine how their lives will go *in spite of* their genetic tendencies.

14. In light of this vulnerability, I think we can better understand the vocal opposition to polygraphs and drug tests based on their inaccuracy. Most workers who are victims of inaccurate tests cannot simply fall back on adequate unemployment compensation or secure comparable employment.

15. Adina Schwartz, "Meaningful Work," *Ethics*, vol. 92 (1982), pp. 634–646, 634. Cf. also Edward Sankowski, "Freedom, Work, and the Scope of Democracy," *Ethics*, vol. 91 (1981), pp. 228–242.

16. See, for instance, *Work in America: Report of a Special Task Force to the Secretary of Health, Education, and Welfare* (Cambridge, MA: MIT Press, 1973); Harry Braverman, *Labor and Monopoly Capital: The Degradation of Work in the Twentieth Century* (New York: Monthly Review Press, 1974).

Review and Discussion Questions

1. Lippke maintains that privacy is valuable because of its relation to autonomy and (following Joseph Kupfer) highlights two ways in which privacy contributes to autonomy. Explain the connections between privacy and autonomy. Do you agree that autonomy is the reason privacy is valuable?

2. Relying on a contractual model of employer-employee relations, some writers use the concept of "job-relevant" to restrict the types of information employers may justifiably gather about employees. What are Lippke's reasons for rejecting this approach? Are you persuaded by his arguments?

3. By contrast with the contractual model, what are Lippke's reasons both for opposing employers acquiring certain sorts of information and for objecting to certain methods of gathering it?

4. Do you agree with Lippke that there is a grave imbalance in power between employers and employees and that the workplace is characterized by authoritarian management structures that deprive employees of much of their autonomy? What are the implications of viewing privacy rights in this context?

5. How does Lippke respond to the argument that the property rights of owners and stockholders should take precedence over the privacy rights of employees? Do you agree that the existing organization of work contributes significantly to problems like drug use and dishonesty?

Participation in Employment _____

John J. McCall

After distinguishing different types of worker participation, John McCall presents five moral reasons that argue in favor of strong worker participation in the codetermination of policy. All of these reasons derive from a need to protect centrally important human goods. McCall contends that, in practice, protection for these goods is most effective when there are strong forms of employee participation. McCall also considers some traditional arguments against participation, none of which, he concludes, are of sufficient weight for rejecting it.

Reprinted by permission from Joseph R. DesJardins and John J. McCall, eds., *Contemporary Issues in Business Ethics*, 2nd ed. (Belmont, Calif.: Wadsworth, 1990).

Until recently, worker participation in corporate decision making was a topic largely ignored in American management training and practice. Even in recent years, the attention usually given to worker participation by management theory has been confined to small-scale experiments aimed at increasing labor productivity. Little, if any, attention has been given to the possibility that there is a moral basis for extending a right to participation to all workers.

Numerous explanations for this lack of attention are possible. One is that management sees worker participation as a threat to its power and status. Another explanation may be found in a pervasive ideology underlying our patterns of industrial organization. The ruling theory of corporate property distinguishes sharply between the decision-making rights of ownership and its management representatives on the one hand, and employee duties of loyalty and obedience on the other. The justification for that distinction lies partly in a view of the rights of property owners to control their goods and partly in a perception that non-management employees are technically unequipped to make intelligent policy decisions. The perceived threat to power and this dominant ideology of employment provide for strong resistance even to a discussion of broad worker participation in corporate decisions. But perhaps as strong a source of this resistance comes from a confusion about the possible meanings of and moral justifications for worker participation. The primary aim of this essay is to clarify those meanings and justifications. If the essay is successful, it might also suggest that the above sources of resistance to participation should be abandoned.

What people refer to when they use the term "participation" varies widely. We can get a better grasp of that variation in meaning if we recognize that it is a function of variety in both the potential issues available for participatory decisions and the potential mechanisms for that decision making. The potential issues for participation can be divided into three broad and not perfectly distinct categories. First, employees could participate in decisions involving shop-floor operations. Characteristic shop-floor issues are the schedule of employee work hours, assembly line speed, and the distribution of work assignments. Second, employees could participate in decisions that have

been the traditional prerogative of middle management. Issues here are hiring or discharge decisions, grievance procedures, evaluations of workers or supervisors, the distribution of merit wage increases, etc. Finally, employees might participate in traditional board-level decisions about investment, product diversification, pricing or output levels, and the like. Simply put, employee participation might refer to participation in decision making over issues that arise at any or all levels of corporate policy.

The mechanisms for participation vary as widely as do the potential issues. These participatory mechanisms vary both in terms of their location within or outside the corporation and in terms of the actual power they possess. For instance, some see employees participating in the shaping of corporate policy by individual acceptance or rejection of employment offers and by collective bargaining through union membership. These mechanisms are essentially external to the particular business institution. Internal mechanisms for participation in corporate policy making include employee stock ownership plans, "quality circle" consulting groups, and bodies that extend employees partial or total effective control of the enterprise. Employee participation through stock ownership might exist either through union pension fund holdings or through individual employee profit sharing plans.

Internal participation can also exist in ways more directly related to the day-to-day functioning of the corporation. For example, quality circle participation is a recent adaptation of some Japanese approaches to the management of human resources. Employees in these quality circles are invited to participate in round-table discussions of corporate concerns such as improving productivity. It is important to note that these quality circle groups are advisory only; their function within the corporation is consultative and they have no actual authority to implement decisions.

Distinct from these advisory bodies are those mechanisms by which employees share in the actual power to make corporate policy. Among the mechanisms for such partial effective control are worker committees with authority to govern selected aspects of the work environment or worker representatives on the traditional organs of authority. An example of the former would be an employee-run grievance board; an example of the latter received significant notice in the United States when United Auto Workers' President Douglas Fraser assumed a seat on Chrysler's Board of Directors. Either of these mechanisms provides for only partial control, since one has a highly defined area of responsibility and the other provides employees with only one voice among many.

A final form of participation provides employees with full control of the operations of the corporation. Examples of this extensive participation are rare in North America, although some midwest farm and northwest lumber cooperatives are organized in this way.

Note that these varied mechanisms combine with the potential issues for participation in numerous ways. We might see union collective bargaining influence merit wage increases or working schedules; worker committee mechanisms of participation might deal with flexible work assignments or with evaluation of supervisors. This brief survey should indicate that discussions of employee participation must be pursued with care, since arguments criticizing or supporting participation might be sufficient grounds for drawing conclusions about one form of participation but not sufficient grounds for conclusions about other forms. That caution brings us to the second major aim of this essay—the clarification of moral arguments in favor of broad extensions of worker rights to participate in corporate decisions. Five justifications, or arguments, for participation will be sketched. Comments about the issues of mechanisms required by each justification will follow each argument sketch.

Argument 1

The first . . . justification for employee participation . . . takes it cue from the fundamental objective of any morality—the impartial promotion of human welfare. That requirement of impartiality can be understood as a requirement that we try to guarantee a fair hearing for the interests of every person in decisions concerning policies that centrally affect their lives. Certainly, many decisions at work can have a great impact on the lives of employees. For instance, an employee's privacy and health, both mental and physical, can easily be threatened in his or her working life. Morality, then, requires that there be some attempt to guar-

antee fair treatment for workers and their interests. We might attempt to institutionalize that guarantee through government regulation of business practices. However, regulation, while helpful to some degree, is often an insufficient guarantee of fair treatment. It is insufficient for the following reasons:

1. Regulation, when it does represent the interests of workers, often does so imprecisely because it is by nature indirect and paternalistic.

2. Business can frequently circumvent the intent of regulations by accepting fines for violations or by judicious use of regulatory appeal mechanisms.

3. Perhaps most importantly, corporate interests can emasculate the content of proposed legislation or regulation through powerful lobbying efforts.

So it seems that an effective guarantee that worker interests are represented fairly requires at least some mechanisms additional to regulation.

We might avoid many of the difficulties of legislation and regulation if workers were allowed to represent their interests more directly whenever crucial corporate decisions are made. Thus, a fair hearing for workers' interests might have a more effective institutional guarantee where workers have available some mechanisms for participation in those decisions. In practice, then, morality's demand for impartiality presumptively may require worker input in the shaping of corporate policies. . . .

Clearly, if worker interests are to be guaranteed as much fair treatment as possible, the participatory mechanisms must have actual power to influence corporate decisions. For while workers might receive fair treatment even where they lack such power, possession of real power more effectively institutionalizes a *guarantee* of fairness. Thus, internal participatory mechanisms that serve in a purely advisory capacity (e.g., quality circle groups) are obviously insufficient vehicles for meeting the fairness demands of morality.

Less obvious are the weaknesses of individual contract negotiations, union membership, and stock ownership as devices for guaranteeing fairness. None of these devices, in practice, can provide enough power to protect fair treatment for workers. Individual contract decisions often find the prospective employee in a very poor bargaining position. The amount of effective power possessed through union membership varies with the changing state of the economy and with changes in particular industrial technologies. In addition, the majority of workers are not unionized; the declining proportion of union membership in the total workforce now stands at about one-fifth. Stock ownership plans provide employees very little leverage on corporate decisions because, commonly, only small percentages of stock are held by workers. Moreover, all three of these participation mechanisms most often have little direct power over the important operating decisions which affect worker interests. Those decisions are usually made and implemented for long periods before contract negotiations, union bargaining or stockholder meetings could have any chance at altering corporate policy.

Thus, a serious moral concern for fairness, a concern central to any moral perspective, presumptively requires that mechanisms for employee participation provide workers with at least partial effective control of the enterprise. And since decisions that have important consequences for the welfare of workers are made at every level of the corporation, employees ought to participate on issues from the shop floor to the board room. Moreover, since a balanced and impartial consideration of all interests is more probable when opposing parties have roughly equal institutional power, employees deserve more than token representation in the firm's decision-making structure. Rather, they should possess an amount of authority that realistically enables them to resist policies that unfairly damage their interests. This first moral argument, then, provides strong presumptive support for the right of employees to co-determine corporate policy.

Argument 2

The second moral argument . . . derives from points that . . . are similar to those of the preceding argument. Any acceptable moral theory must recognize the inherent value and dignity of the human person. One traditional basis for that belief in the dignity of the person derives from the fact that persons are agents capable of free and rational deliberation. We move towards respect for the dignity of the person when we protect individuals from humanly alterable interferences that jeopardize important human goods and when we allow them, equally, as much freedom from other interferences

as possible. Persons with this freedom from interference are able to direct the courses of their own lives without threat of external control or coercion. (Such a view of persons provides for the moral superiority of self-determining, democratic systems of government over oppressive or totalitarian regimes.)

This moral commitment to the dignity of persons as autonomous agents has significant implications for corporate organization. Most of our adult lives are spent at our places of employment. If we possess no real control over that portion of our lives because we are denied the power to participate in forming corporate policy, then at work we are not autonomous agents. Instead we are merely anonymous and replaceable elements in the production process, elements with a moral standing little different from that of the inanimate machinery we operate. This remains true of our lives *at* work even if we have the opportunity to change employers. (Many workers do not have even that opportunity, and if they did it would be of little consequence for this issue, since most workplaces are similarly organized.) The moral importance of autonomy in respecting the dignity of persons should make us critical of these traditional patterns of work and should move us in the direction of more employee participation. However, since autonomy is understood as an ability to control one's activities, the preferred mechanisms of participation should allow employees real control at work. Thus, a commitment to the autonomy and the dignity of persons, just as a commitment to fairness, appears to require that workers have the ability to co-determine policy that directs important corporate activity.

Argument 3

These first two arguments for broad worker participation rights have ended in an explicit requirement that workers have real and actual power over corporate policy. The final three arguments focus not on actual power but on the worker's *perception* of his or her ability to influence policy. All of these last arguments concern the potential for negative consequences created when workers see themselves as having little control over their working lives.

The third argument warns that workers who believe themselves powerless will lose the important psychological good of self-respect.[1] Moral philosophers have contended that since all persons should be treated with dignity, all persons consequently deserve the conditions that generally contribute to a sense of their own dignity or self-worth. Psychologists tell us that a person's sense of self is to a large degree conditioned by the institutional relationships she has and the responses from others that she receives in those relationships. A person will have a stronger sense of her own worth and will develop a deeper sense of self-respect when her social interactions allow her to exercise her capacities in complex and interesting activities and when they reflect her status as an autonomous human being. Of course, in contemporary America the development of the division of labor and of hierarchical authority structures leaves little room for the recognition of the worker's autonomy or for the ordinary worker to exercise capacities in complex ways. The consequence of such work organization is the well-documented worker burnout and alienation; workers disassociate themselves from a major portion of their lives, often with the psychological consequence of a sense of their own unimportance. Contemporary American patterns of work, then, often fail to provide individuals with those conditions that foster a strong sense of self-respect; instead, they more often undermine self-respect. Numerous studies have indicated that a reversal of these trends is possible where workers are provided greater opportunities for exercising judgment and for influencing workplace activities.

If we take seriously a demand for the universal provision of the conditions of self-respect, we ought to increase opportunities for satisfying work by allowing workers to participate in corporate policy decisions. It would seem, however, that this argument for worker participation need not conclude that workers be given actual power. All that the argument requires is that a worker's *sense* of self-respect be strengthened, and that is at least a possible consequence of participation in an advisory capacity. In fact, worker satisfaction has been shown to increase somewhat when employees are involved in Japanese-style quality circles that offer suggestions for improving production. Nor does it appear that the self-respect argument requires that workers be able to influence all aspects of corporate activity, since an increased sense of one's own significance could be had through participation only on immediate shop-floor issues.

However, we must be careful to estimate the long-range effects on worker alienation and self-respect of these less extensive forms of participation. Some evidence indicates that, over time, workers can grow more dissatisfied and alienated than ever if they perceive the participatory program as without real power or as simply a management attempt to manipulate workers for increased productivity.[2] We should consider, then, that a concern for long-run and substantial increases in self-respect might require workers to exercise some actual authority, of a more than token amount, over the workplace.

Argument 4

The fourth argument supporting participation also takes its cue from the studies that show repetitive work without control over one's activities causes worker alienation. The specific consequence that this argument focuses on, however, is not a lessening of self-respect but a potential threat to the mental and physical health of workers. Certainly, everyone is now aware that alienated individuals suffer from more mental disturbances and more stress-related physical illnesses. Workers who are satisfied because they feel able to contribute to corporate policy are held to suffer from less alienation. Since mental and physical health are undoubtedly very central human goods, there seems strong presumptive moral reason for minimizing any negative effects on them that institutional organizations might have. Since broader powers apparently help to minimize such effects, we again have an argument for an expansion of worker rights to participate in corporate decisions.

As with the self-respect argument, however, the issues and mechanisms of participation that this requires are unclear. It could be that negative health effects are minimized in the short run through advisory bodies of participation. On the other hand, minimizing threats to mental or physical well-being in the long run might require more actual authority. Which sorts of mechanisms help most is a question only further empirical research can answer. However, since we have already seen presumptive reasons for actual power to codetermine policy from the first two arguments and since that power can have positive effects on self-respect and health, we perhaps have reasons for preferring the stronger forms of participation if we are presented with a choice between alternatives.

Argument 5

The fifth argument for worker participation also derives from the purported negative consequences of hierarchical and authoritarian organizations of work. This argument, however, focuses on broader social consequences — the danger to our democratic political structures if workers are not allowed to participate in corporate decisions.[3]

Many political theorists are alarmed by contemporary voter apathy. They worry that with that apathy the political process will be democratic in name only, and that the actual business of government will be controlled by powerful and private economic interests. To reverse this trend that threatens democratic government demands that individual citizens become more involved in the political process. However, increased individual involvement is seen as unlikely unless citizens believe themselves to have political power. But an initial increased sense of one's own political power does not seem possible from involvement in the large macroscopic political institutions of contemporary government. Rather, involvement in smaller, more local and immediate social activities will nurture a sense of political efficacy. Since so much time and attention is devoted to one's work life, the place of employment appears a prime candidate for that training in democracy necessary for development of civic involvement. In fact, powerless and alienated workers can bring their sense of powerlessness home and offer their children lessons in the futility of involvement. Allowing those lessons to continue would only exacerbate the threat to vital democratic institutions. This fifth argument, then, sees participation at work as a necessary condition for the existence of a healthy and lasting system of democracy where citizens have the confidence to engage in self-determining political activities.

Again, since this argument focuses on the worker's perception of his or her own power, it provides presumptive support for those mechanisms that would increase both that sense of power and the tendency for political activity. Just what mechanisms these are can be open to argument. However, as before, if workers feel that their participatory mechanisms lack power, there is the danger that they will become even more cynical about their ability to influence political decisions. And since we have already seen arguments supporting participation with actual power to co-determine policy, there should be a presumption in favor of using mechanisms with real power.

Sources of Resistance

We have, then, five significant reasons for extending to workers a broad right to co-determine corporate policy. Now, in order to determine whether the presumption in favor of worker participation can be overridden, we need only to consider some of the common reasons for resisting this employee right to participate. Common sources of resistance to worker participation are that managers perceive it as a threat to their own status or power, that owners feel entitled to the sole control of their property, and that ordinary employees are believed incompetent to make corporate decisions. We shall consider briefly each of these sources of resistance in turn. Our evaluation of these claims will show them to be unacceptable sources of resistance when measured against the above moral reasons in favor of broad participation.

First, in order for management's perception that participation threatens its power to count as an acceptable moral reason for resistance, management power must have some moral basis of its own. According to even traditional conservative theories of corporate property, management has no basic moral right of its own to control the corporation. Rather, management's authority stems from its position as an agent of the economic interests of shareholders, who are seen as the ultimate bearers of a right to use, control, or dispose of property. On the traditional theory, then, management can find a legitimate moral reason for resisting participation only if it can show that schemes of employee participation are real threats to the economic interests of shareholders. Presently, we shall refer to evidence that this case against participation cannot be supported by the available data.

(Management, of course, might still resist even without a moral reason. However, such resistance can have no claim to our support; it is merely an obstacle to be overcome if there are moral reasons to support participation.)

Does participation damage the interests of ownership in a morally unacceptable way? To answer this question, we need to consider what interests ownership has and to what benefits property ownership should entitle one. In the process of confronting these issues, we will also see reasons for suspicion about claims that workers are not capable of participating in the intelligent setting of corporate policy.

In legally incorporated businesses, shareholders commonly have a monetary return on their investment as their principal desire.[4] Moreover, corporate property owners generally have surrendered their interest in day-to-day control of the corporation.[5] The usual owner interest, then, concerns the profitability of the business. Worker participation does not pose a serious threat to this interest in monetary return. Evidence shows that worker participation schemes often improve the economic condition of the business by increasing the interest, motivation, and productivity of employees.[6] In addition, corporations seeking qualified and motivated workers in the future might, out of self-interest, have to construct mechanisms for participation to satisfy the demands of a more slowly growing but more highly educated entry-level labor force.[7] And even in those cases where experiments at worker participation have not succeeded, the failures can often be explained by shortcomings of the particular program that are not generic to all forms of participation. In fact, some of those with experience in constructing participatory work schemes believe that employees can be trained to operate most efficiently with expanded responsibilities.[8] When programs are designed carefully and when time is invested in training both former managers and employees, the competence of workers has not been seen as a crucial reason behind examples of participation's lack of success. Thus, in light of both the marked economic successes of broader worker participation programs and the apparent absence of any *generic* threats to profitability (such as employee incompetence), the economic interests of owners do not appear to provide a substantial basis for a justified resistance to an employee right to participate in corporate decision making.

Some might object, however, that corporate property owners have other interests at stake.

Many see a right to control one's goods as fundamental to the concept of property ownership, for example. Thus, they might claim that shareholders have, because of their property ownership, rights to retain control of the business enterprise even if they fail to exercise those rights on a day-to-day basis. This right to control one's property would effectively eliminate the possibility of an employee right to co-determine policy.

There are two reasons, however, to question whether a right to control property can provide a moral basis for denying workers a right to participate in corporate decisions. First, corporate property owners have been granted by society a limit on their legal liability for their property. If a legally incorporated business is sued, owners stand to lose only the value of their investment; an owner of an unincorporated business can lose personal property beyond the value of the business. Part of the motivation behind making this legal limit on liability available was that society would thereby encourage investment activity that would increase the welfare of its members.[9] It is not unreasonable to suggest that this justification for the special legal privilege requires that corporations concern themselves with the welfare of persons within the society in exchange for limited liability. Society, then, places limits on the extent to which owners can direct the use of their corporate property. For example, society can require that corporations concern themselves with the environmental health effects of their waste disposal policies. Failure to require such concern is tantamount to allowing some to profit from harms to others while preventing those others from obtaining reasonable compensation for grievous harms. However, if the legal limitation on liability requires corporations to have some moral concern for the welfare of others, it can also require corporations to protect the welfare of its employees. We have already seen, though, that morally serious goods are at stake when employees are unable to participate significantly in corporate decisions. Thus, if in exchange for limited liability the control of the corporation is to be limited by a concern for others, then the shareholders' interest in controlling corporate property could be limited to allow for an employee right to participate.

A second reason for rejecting the claim that an ownership right to control prohibits employee participation looks not on the legal privileges associated with corporate property but on the very concept of property itself. This argument makes points similar to ones made in the preceding paragraph, but the points apply to property whether it is incorporated or not. It is certainly true that property ownership is meaningless without some rights to control the goods owned. It is equally true, however, that no morally acceptable system of property rights can allow unlimited rights to control the goods owned. You, for example, are not allowed to do just anything you please with your car; you cannot have a right to drive it through my front porch. We accept similar restrictions on the control of business property; we prohibit people from selling untested and potentially dangerous drugs that they produce. The point of these examples is to illustrate that control of property, corporate or not, has to be limited by weighing the constraints on owners against the significance of the human goods that would be jeopardized in the absence of the constraints. Acceptable institutions of property rights, then, must mesh with a society's moral concern for protecting the fundamental human goods of all its members.

We have seen in the first part of this essay that there are significant reasons for thinking that important moral values are linked to a worker's ability to participate in corporate decision making. If control of property, personal or corporate, is to override these moral concerns, we need to be presented with an argument showing what more central goods would be jeopardized if employees were granted strong participation rights. The burden of proof, then, is on those who want to deny an employee right to co-determine corporate policy. They must show that an owner's interest in broad control of corporate policy can stand as an interest worthy of protection as a moral right even when such protection would threaten the dignity, fair treatment, self-respect, and health of workers, as well as the continued viability of a democratic polity with an actively self-determining citizenship.

Summary

To summarize: We have seen that there are various understandings of worker participation. The difference between these various understandings is a function of the workplace issues addressed and the participatory mechanisms that address them. We have also seen sketches of five arguments that

purport to show a moral presumption in favor of strong worker participation in the form of an ability to actually co-determine policy. We have seen, further, that some traditional sources of resistance to worker participation (a threat to management or owner prerogatives of control, a belief in the incompetence of workers, a fear that profits will suffer) are either not supported by the evidence or are incapable of sustaining a moral basis for rejecting participation. The provisional conclusion we should draw, then, is that our society ought to move vigorously in the direction of a broader authority for all workers in their places of employment.

Notes

1. This argument has been made by Joe Grčić in "Rawls and Socialism," *Philosophy and Social Criticism* 8:1 (1980), and in "Rawls' Difference Principle, Marx's Alienation and the Japanese Economy," a paper presented at the Ninth Plenary Session of Amintaphil, 1983. It is also suggested by John Cotter in "Ethics and Justice in the World of Work: Improving the Quality of Working Life," *Review of Social Economy* 40:3 (1982).

2. Cf. Daniel Zwerdling, *Workplace Democracy* (New York: Harper and Row, 1980).

3. This argument is made forcefully by Carole Pateman, *Participation and Democratic Theory* (Cambridge: Cambridge University Press, 1970).

4. Of course, the matter is more complex than this simple statement indicates. Some investors might even have interests in losing money if they are attempting to avoid taxes. Others might want to guarantee that their company does not produce immoral goods (as some Dow Chemical investors claimed was the case with Dow's napalm production). Still, in most cases the primary motivation for investment is a monetary return.

5. It is, of course, not always true that shareholders surrender their interest in day-to-day control, since some corporations are headed by their principal stockholders.

6. Additional evidence is found in the experiences of the small but highly publicized Volvo experiments and of Donnelly Mirrors, Inc. Interviews with heads of both Volvo and Donnelly can be found in *Harvard Business Review*, 55:4 (1977) and 55:1 (1977), respectively. In West Germany, co-determination is mandated by law in some major industries that have been highly competitive with their American counterparts.

7. John Cotter, *op cit.*

8. The Donnelly interview, *op cit.*, and Nancy Foy and Herman Gadon, "Worker Participation: Contrasts in Three Countries," *Harvard Business Review*, v. 54, no. 3 (1976).

9. Cf. W. Michael Hoffman and James Fisher, "Corporate Responsibility: Property and Liability," in *Ethical Theory and Business*, 1st ed., T. Beauchamp and N. Bowie, eds. (Englewood Cliffs, N.J.: Prentice-Hall, 1979), pp. 187–196.

Review and Discussion Questions

1. What are the different forms that employee participation can take? Which do you see as the most valuable forms? In your experience, how extensive is employee participation today?

2. McCall argues for participation in terms of the values of fair treatment, human dignity, self-respect, physical and mental health, and the promotion of a democratic society. Explain how each of these values, according to him, supports the case for participation. Are you persuaded by his reasoning?

3. On what grounds does management typically resist worker participation? How sound are its reasons for doing so? Does participation violate the rights of the owners of corporate property?

4. Is worker participation compatible with the efficient functioning of a free-enterprise system?

5. Do you think that more extensive worker participation would make companies more socially responsible? Do you agree with McCall's conclusion "that our society ought to move vigorously in the direction of a broader authority for all workers in their places of employment"?

For Further Reading

Gertrude Ezorsky, ed., *Moral Rights in the Workplace* (Albany: State University of New York Press, 1987) is a good collection of articles on the right to meaningful work, occupational health and safety, employee privacy, unions, industrial flight, and related topics.

Berth Jönsson, "The Quality of Work Life—The Volvo Experience," *Journal of Business Ethics* 1 (May 1982) discusses the innovative changes in production technology and work organization made by Volvo in Sweden.

Benjamin Kleinmuntz, "Lie Detectors Fail the Truth Test," *Harvard Business Review* 63 (July–August 1985) is a critique of reliance on polygraph tests.

Richard M. Pfeffer, *Working for Capitalism* (New York: Columbia University Press, 1979) describes the author's experience of factory work today.

Ralph Stayer, "How I Learned to Let My Workers Lead," *Harvard Business Review* 68 (November–December 1990) tells how the workers at Johnsonville Sausage have learned to run the company.

Daniel Zwerdling, *Workplace Democracy* (New York: Harper & Row, 1980) contains a wealth of detailed information about efforts at worker self-management.

(Consult also the readings suggested at the end of Chapter 6.)

CHAPTER 8

MORAL CHOICES
FACING EMPLOYEES

George Spanton was a sixty-two-year-old federal auditor when he blew the whistle on "irregularities" in Department of Defense contract spending at a jet-engine testing plant. That one toot launched a federal grand jury inquiry into spending by Pratt & Whitney Aircraft Group, a division of United Technologies Corporation. It also meant personal trouble for Spanton, who was due to retire after eighteen years with the agency. When he sought a routine ten-month extension as resident auditor at Pratt & Whitney, Charles O. Starrett, director of the Defense Contract Auditing Agency (DCAA), wrote Spanton that he had to accept a transfer or be fired.

K. William O'Connor, special counsel to the Merit System Protection Board, questioned the propriety of certain actions by DCAA.[1] He said, "I now have reasonable grounds on the basis of the investigation to date to believe that DCAA denied Spanton's request for waiver and is now rotating him out of the Atlanta region because he provided nonclassified information to the press."

For his part, Spanton promised to fight the transfer. "I will take whatever legal action is necessary to prevent them from moving me," he said. "Furthermore, I will continue to expose improper action on the part of the contractor and the agency."[2]

For someone in a situation like George Spanton's, two general issues come up. First is a question of where an employee's overall moral duty lies. For a professional auditor to decide to report "irregularities" may be a more straightforward moral decision than that faced by an employee who suspects wrong-

doing in an area unrelated to his or her own job. In that case, the employee may well have conflicting moral obligations. Even the auditor, having reported irregularities to the appropriate authority, must decide whether he is morally obligated to pursue the matter further. Again, other moral considerations come into play.

Second, having decided that one ought to blow the whistle, an employee must face the possible negative consequences. Spanton was close to retirement and in that respect had less to risk than many potential whistle blowers stretched by financial obligations and with their full careers in front of them. Nor is this simply a tug-of-war between moral duty and self-interest. Some moral theorists would argue that certain personal sacrifices are so great that we cannot reasonably be morally obliged to make them.

These two themes—determining one's moral responsibility amid a welter of conflicting demands and paying the personal costs that can be involved in living up to one's obligations—recur throughout this chapter. In particular, this chapter looks at the following topics:

1. Obligations employees have to the firm and the problem of conflicts of interest

2. The illegitimate use of one's official position for private gain, through insider trading or access to proprietary data

3. Domestic and foreign bribery and the factors to consider in determining the morality of giving and receiving gifts in a business context

4. The obligations employees have to third parties and the considerations they should weigh in cases of conflicting moral duties or divided loyalties

5. What whistle blowing is and the factors relevant to evaluating it morally

6. The problem of how considerations of self-interest are to be weighed by an employee facing a tough moral choice

OBLIGATIONS TO THE FIRM AND CONFLICTS OF INTEREST

You don't have to work for an organization very long, at a management or nonmanagement level, to realize that your interests often collide with those of the organization. You want to dress one way, the organization wants you to dress another way; you'd prefer to show up for work at noon, the organization expects you to be present at 8 A.M.; you'd like to receive $50,000 a year for your labor, the organization gives you a fraction of that figure. Whatever the value in question, attitudes can differ. The reward, autonomy, and self-fulfillment that workers seek aren't always compatible with the worker productivity that the organization desires.

Sometimes this clash of perspectives or goals can take a serious form: a *conflict of interest*. In an organization, a conflict of interest arises when employees at any level have a private interest in a transaction substantial enough that it does or reasonably might affect their independent judgment.[3] Looked at another way, the organization has the right to expect employees to use independent judgment on its behalf. Conflicts of interest arise when employees jeopardize their independence of judgment.

The work contract is the primary source of the organization's right to expect independent judgment on its behalf and the concomitant employee responsibility to exercise such judg-

ment in carrying out the job. When a person is hired, he or she agrees to discharge contractual obligations in exchange for pay. Thus, the employee does specified work, puts in prescribed hours, and expends energy in return for remuneration, usually in the form of money. In general, if the contents of the work agreement are legal and workers freely consent to them, then they place themselves under an obligation to fulfill the terms of the agreement.

Implicit in any work contract is the idea that employees will not use the firm for personal advantage. Of course, individuals may seek to benefit from being employed with a firm, but in discharging their contractual obligations employees should not subordinate the welfare of the firm to personal gain.

Conflicts of interest may be either actual or potential. An *actual conflict of interest* arises when employees allow their interest in a transaction to cloud the independence of judgment that they are supposed to exercise on behalf of the firm. For example, Bart Williams, sales manager for Leisure Sports World, gives all his firm's promotional work to Impact Advertising because its chief officer is Bart's brother-in-law. The transaction costs Leisure World about 15 percent more in advertising costs than would comparable work with another agency. The conflict here is actual: Bart has allowed his judgment on behalf of Leisure Sports World to be influenced by his own interest in Impact. Note that Williams's interest is not a financial one. This fact underscores the point that a conflict of interest can take various forms. The issue is always whether the transaction functions to hamper one's independent judgment on behalf of the firm.

Even if Bart Williams does not actually compromise himself in this way, he still faces a potential conflict of interest just by being in a position where he might be tempted to compromise the interest of the firm. A *potential conflict of interest* arises when an employee's ability to exercise independent judgment on behalf of the organization is likely to be in jeopardy. Williams could easily throw some business his brother-in-law's way at the expense of Leisure Sports World.

Some would point to the Bert Lance affair as one of the more celebrated examples of a conflict of interest. Lance was the amiable Georgian who directed the Office of Management and Budget — but not for long. Less than a year after being appointed by President Jimmy Carter, Lance resigned under fire.

The several factors that led to Lance's departure can be summed up with the phrase "highly dubious banking practices." Before assuming his government post, Lance was president of the Calhoun First National Bank in Georgia. During that time, Lance apparently drew large personal loans from banks with which his own bank had established correspondent relationships. In a "correspondent relationship," large banks perform various services for smaller banks in return for balances that the small banks keep with them. One such large bank was Georgia's Fulton National Bank.

Over a period of twelve years, Lance and his wife LaBelle apparently received nearly twenty loans from Fulton National, totaling close to $4 million. In documents related to these loans, the Fulton bank noted that "satisfactory balances are maintained by Calhoun National Bank," thus implying a direct connection between the loans and the interest-free deposits that Lance's bank had placed with Fulton to establish the correspondent relationship.[4] In his report, Comptroller of the Currency John Heimann concluded that Lance may not have received the loans had it not been for the correspondent accounts. Heimann further indicated that Lance had established a similar pattern of personal loans with two smaller Georgia banks in which he had an interest.

Investigators also discovered that Lance might have profited from selling a Beechcraft

airplane that the Calhoun National Bank had purchased while Lance was its president. The bank subsequently sold the plane to Lancelot Company, whose owners were Bert and LaBelle. When Lance later became president of the National Bank of Georgia, that bank purchased the Beechcraft from Lancelot.

Apparently Lance also used the Calhoun National Bank to help finance and promote his bid for governor. His campaign accounts at the bank, which he then headed, were at one point overdrawn by $99,529. Further investigation indicated that the bank may have paid for entertainment, supplied computers for sending out campaign literature, and provided time to help with Lance's campaign. Evidently Calhoun National also paid many of Lance's campaign bills but listed them as business expenses. Lance later reimbursed the bank.

Lance and his family also ran up personal overdrafts at the Calhoun National Bank while he was its president. Comptroller Heimann reported that Lance's account was overdrawn by about $50,000 at least twenty-five times. Furthermore, LaBelle Lance overdrew her account one year by nearly $110,000. And during just one eight-month period, nine Lance relatives were overdrawn by $450,000.

It's easy to become disoriented by the dizzying effect of the figures and financial razzle-dazzle in the Lance case. Yet most people in and out of the banking profession would agree that, judging from the evidence, Bert Lance used his professional banking status to advance his own interests. In other words, he seems to have engaged in practices that many bankers would consider irregular and not in the best interests of one's bank — thus, a conflict of interest.

Conflict of interest can arise in all sorts of ways and take many forms. Its most common expressions, however, involve actions related to financial investments, the use of official position (especially with regard to insider trading and proprietary data), bribery, kickbacks, gifts, and entertainment. Although these phenomena do not necessarily involve conflicts of interests, they often do; and they always raise moral questions about what employees owe organizations.

Financial Investments

Conflicts of interest may exist when employees have financial investments in suppliers, customers, or distributors with whom their organizations do business. For example, Fred Walters, purchasing agent for Trans-Con Trucking, owns a substantial amount of stock with Timberline Paper. When ordering office supplies, Fred buys exclusively through a Timberline affiliate, even though he could get the identical supplies cheaper from another supplier. This is an actual conflict of interest. But even if Fred never advantages himself this way, he is potentially conflicted because of his interest in Timberline.

It's impossible to say how much of a financial investment compromises one's independent judgment in acts for the organization or to specify the exact point at which a potential conflict of interest is serious enough to be morally troubling. Ordinarily it is acceptable to hold a small percentage of stock in a publicly owned supplier that is listed on a public stock exchange. Some organizations state what percentage of outstanding stock their members may own—usually from 1 to 10 percent. Companies may also restrict the percentage of the employee's total investment funds that are involved in an investment. Some corporations even require key officers to make a full disclosure of all outside interests or of other relationships that could cloud their judgment on behalf of the organization. Quite obviously, then, organizational policy may go a long way toward determining the morally permissible limits of outside investments and potential conflicts of interest, since organizational policy reflects the specific needs and interests of a firm. It's worth noting, however, that since

such a policy can affect the financial well-being of those who fall under it, it should be subjected to the same kind of free and open negotiations that any form of compensation is.

Use of Official Position

A serious area of conflict of interest involves the use of one's official position for personal gain. Cases in this area range from using subordinates for nonorganization-related work to using an important position within an organization to enhance one's own financial leverage and holdings. This latter form of conflict of interest was evident in the Lance case. Lance apparently used his bank's correspondent account to float personal loans upward of $4 million. Also, he seems to have used his position to overdraw his Calhoun National Bank account by about $100,000 while financing his gubernatorial campaign. And Lance's relatives appear to have benefited directly from Lance's position.

Insider Trading.   Although not present in the Lance case, many abuses of official position arise from insider trading. *Insider trading* refers to the use of significant facts that have not yet been made public and will likely affect stock prices. For example, a few years ago the Justice Department was looking into the possibility that some Social Security officials, anticipating that the government was about to award Paradyne Corporation a computer contract, bought Paradyne common stock and sold short shares in one or more of the five companies that lost out to Paradyne. (In a short sale, investors sell borrowed stock, hoping to make a profit by buying back an equal number of shares at a lower price.) If the employees did do that, they engaged in insider trading. But you don't have to profit yourself in order to cross the line. For example, in 1990 the wife of the president and chief executive of Genentech was charged with insider trading for providing confidential information to her brother. Before the biotechnology firm was partly acquired by another company, she told her brother that "some good things were about to happen" to the company and suggested that he buy a few thousand dollars worth of stock, even if he had to borrow the funds. She also advised him to keep the purchase secret and make it in the name of a "trustworthy" friend.[5]

Increasingly in the world of big business, the pervasive desire to make "a fast buck" takes the form of illegally profiting from inside information. Currently, business is brisk for the Securities and Exchange Commission (SEC), which is charged with policing the stock market for insider-trading violations. Not only has the SEC been filing dozens of cases annually, but it also sent a seismic tremor through Wall Street in late 1986 by arresting the financial giant Ivan Boesky for insider trading and other securities infractions. Boesky's fall, however, does not seem to have reduced greatly the number of individuals trying to trade inside information for fast and sometimes big profits.

Inside traders ordinarily defend their actions by claiming they didn't injure anyone. It's true that trading by insiders on the basis of nonpublic information seldom directly injures anyone. But moral concerns arise from indirect injury, as well as from direct. As one author puts it, "What causes injury or loss to outsiders is not what the insiders knew or did; rather it is what [the outsiders] themselves did not know. It is their own lack of knowledge which exposes them to risk of loss or denies them an opportunity to make a profit."[6] Case in point: the Texas Gulf Sulphur stock case.

In 1963 test drilling by Texas Gulf indicated a rich ore body near Timins, Ontario. In a press release of April 12, 1964, some officials at Texas Gulf attempted to play down the potential worth of the Timins property by describing it as a prospect. But on April 16 a second press release termed the Timins property a major discovery. In the interim, inside investors made a handsome personal profit through stock purchases. At the same time, stockholders who unloaded stock based on the first press release lost money. Others who might have bought the stock lost out on a chance to make a profit.

In 1965 the SEC charged that a group of insiders—including Texas Gulf directors, officers, and employees—violated the disclosure section of the Securities and Exchange Act of 1934 by purchasing stock in the company while withholding information about the rich ore strike the company had made. The courts upheld the charge, finding that the first press release was "misleading to the reasonable investor using due care."[7] As a result, the courts not only ordered the insiders to pay into a special court-administered account all profits they made but also ordered them to repay profits made by outsiders whom they had tipped. The courts then used this account to compensate persons who had lost money by selling their Texas Gulf Sulphur stock on the basis of the first press release. This incident illustrates how indirect injury can result from insider dealings and the legal risks that insiders run in trading on inside information.

To be sure, insider dealings raise moral questions not easily resolved. When can employees buy and sell securities in their own companies? How much information must they disclose to stockholders about the firm's plans, outlooks, and prospects? When must this information be disclosed? Also, if people in business are to operate from a cultivated sense of moral accountability, it's important for them to understand who is considered to be an insider. In general, an *insider* could be anyone with access to inside information. In practice, determining precisely who this is isn't always easy. On the one hand, corporate executives, directors, officers, and other key employees surely are insiders. But what about outsiders whom a company temporarily employs, such as accountants, lawyers, and contractors?

The SEC's insider-trading rule is intended to equalize opportunity in the marketplace, and "insider" was originally taken in the broadest sense to mean anyone who gains an advantage by using inside information. But that changed in 1980 with the case of Vincent Chiarella, a financial printer who traded on information he culled from documents passing through his shop. The Supreme Court ruled that Chiarella was not an insider and thus didn't fall under the SEC insider-trading rule.

In *SEC* v. *Dirks* (1983), the Supreme Court further narrowed the scope of insiders. The case involved Raymond L. Dirks, a securities analyst, who recommended which stocks to buy. Just before he blew the whistle on a huge fraud at Equity Funding Corporation of America, Dirks advised several of his clients to dump their shares in Equity. Sure enough, when the scandal broke the company's stock plunged, and Dirks's clients avoided huge losses. The SEC charged Dirks with insider trading, but the Supreme Court reversed the decision. In ruling that Dirks was not an insider, the Court established that there is nothing improper about an outsider using information, as long as the information is not obtained from an insider who seeks personal gain, such as profit or showing favor to friends.

The SEC thinks the Court erred in narrowing the range of "insider." And Congress has agreed. In 1984 it broadened the definition of "insiders" to encompass accountants, lawyers, consultants, and other outsiders.

John M. Fedders, the enforcement director of the SEC, welcomes the help from Capitol Hill. He likens insider trading to white-collar crime. "It is the rawest kind of misconduct without broken windows [from looting]," he says. "Simply put, it's stealing by people in white shirts and suspenders."

Law professor Henry Manne disagrees. He thinks the SEC should stay totally out of the insider-trading field. "The use of insider information should be governed by private contractual relationships," he believes, such as those between corporations and their personnel.[8]

At the base of this disagreement are two opposed philosophies about what makes the market work. Fedders and like-minded analysts contend that the marketplace can work only if it is perceived as being honest and offering equal investment opportunity. Insider trading, they argue, makes that impossible. But those who think like Manne believe that permitting insiders to trade accelerates the information flow to the rest of the shareholders and investors. As a result, information is more quickly reflected in share value, which is healthy for the market.[9]

The information that employees garner within the company is not always the kind that they can use to affect stock prices. Sometimes the information concerns highly sensitive data concerning company research, technology, product development, and so on. How employees use such secret or classified data can also raise important moral concerns.

Proprietary Data.   Companies guard information that can affect their competitive standing with all the zealousness of a bulldog guarding a ham bone. Take Procter & Gamble, for example. Having patented the baking technique of its Duncan Hines brand of homemade-style chocolate chip cookies a few years ago, it then sued three rival food chains, charging them with using the patented process to make "infringing cookies." P & G further claimed that these companies had spied at a sales presentation and at cookie plants. One company allegedly even flew a spy plane over a P & G plant under construction. One of the defendants, Frito-Lay, admitted to sending a worker to photograph the outside of a Duncan Hines bakery. But it denied telling the man's college-age son to walk into the plant and ask for some unbaked cookie dough—

which the enterprising youth did, and got. Frito-Lay insisted that it destroyed both the pictures and the dough without scrutinizing either and formally apologized to P & G. It also countersued P & G for trying to eliminate competition.[10]

When information is patented or copyrighted, it is legally protected but not secret. Others may have access to the information, but they are forbidden to use it (without permission) for the life of the patent or copyright. When a company patents a process, as Kleenex did with pop-up tissues, for example, the company has a monopoly on that process. No other firm may compete in the production of pop-up facial tissues. Although on the face of it this rule violates the ideal of a free market and would appear to slow the spread of new processes and technology, patents and copyrights are generally defended on the ground that without them technological innovation would be hampered. Individuals and companies would not be willing to invest in the development of a new process if other firms could then immediately exploit any new invention without having themselves invested in developing it.[11]

Although patent law is complicated and patents are not easy to acquire, what it means for something to be patented is well defined legally. By contrast, the concept of a "trade secret" is broad and imprecise. The standard legal definition says that a trade secret is "any formula, pattern, device, or compilation of information which is used in one's business and which gives him an opportunity to obtain an advantage over competitors who do not know or use it."[12] Virtually any information that is not generally known (or whose utility is not recognized) is eligible for classification as a trade secret, as long as such information is valuable to its possessor and is treated confidentially. On the other hand, although a growing number of states now punish theft of trade secrets, trade secrets do not enjoy the same protection as patented information. The formula for Coca-Cola, for instance, is secret but not patented. No competitor has yet succeeded in figuring it out by "reverse engineering," but if your company managed to do so, then it would be entitled to use the formula itself.

One of an organization's biggest challenges is to protect trade secrets and proprietary data from being misused by its own employees. This is an especially troublesome problem in high-tech firms when employees who are privy to sensitive information leave the organization. And the problem is compounded by at least two factors: first, the individual's right to seek new employment and, second, the difficulty of separating "trade secrets" from the technical knowledge, experience, and skill that are part of the employee's own intellect and talents.

A classic case involved Donald Wohlgemuth, who worked in the spacesuit department of B. F. Goodrich in Akron, Ohio.[13] Eventually Wohlgemuth became general manager of the spacesuit division and learned Goodrich's highly classified spacesuit technology for the Apollo flights. Shortly thereafter, Wohlgemuth, desiring a higher salary, joined Goodrich's competitor, International Latex Corporation in Dover, Delaware. His new position was manager of engineering for the industrial area that included making spacesuits in competition with Goodrich. Goodrich protested by seeking an order restraining Wohlgemuth from working for Latex or for any other company in the space field. The Court of Appeals of Ohio denied Goodrich's request for an injunction, respecting Wohlgemuth's right to choose his employer. But it did provide an injunction restraining Wohlgemuth from revealing Goodrich's trade secrets.

Cases like Wohlgemuth's are fundamentally different from those involving insider trading, for they pit a firm's right to protect its secrets against an employee's right to seek employment wherever he or she chooses. As a result, the moral dilemmas that arise in proprietary-data cases are not easily resolved. For one thing, the trade secrets that companies seek to protect have often become an integral part of the departing employee's total capabilities. They may, for instance, manifest themselves simply in a subconscious or intuitive sense of what will or will not work in the laboratory. Wohlgemuth's total intellectual capacity included the information, experience, and technical skills acquired at his former workplace. Goodrich might with justification claim much of Wohlgemuth's intellectual capacity as its corporate property, but it is hard to see how he could divest himself of it.

One can also ask whether Wohlgemuth acted morally in leaving Goodrich for a competitor, the legality of his action notwithstanding. Such a question seems especially appropriate when one learns that Wohlgemuth, when asked by Goodrich management whether he thought his action was moral, replied, "Loyalty and ethics have their price and International Latex has paid the price."

Bribes and Kickbacks

Bribery involves an obvious conflict of interest. A *bribe* is a remuneration for the performance of an act that's inconsistent with the work contract or the nature of the work one has been hired to perform. The remuneration can be money, gifts, entertainment, or preferential treatment.

A typical but blatant case was that of Norman Rothberg, an accountant working at ZZZZ Best Carpet Cleaning Company in the Los Angeles area. When he learned that ZZZZ Best had falsified accounts on insurance restoration jobs, he gave the information to the accounting firm of Ernst & Whinney, which was overseeing ZZZZ Best's planned multimillion-dollar acquisition of another carpet-cleaning chain. When an investigation began, Rothberg accepted $17,000 from

ZZZZ Best officials to backtrack from his initial reports.[14]

Bribery can, of course, occur in somewhat more subtle forms. For instance, in exchange for a "sympathetic reading of the books," a company gives a state auditor a trip to Hawaii. Or a sporting goods company provides the child of one of its retailers with free summer camp in exchange for preferred display, location, and space for its products. In both instances, individuals have received payments inconsistent with the work contract or the nature of the work they contracted to perform.

Bribery sometimes takes the form of *kickbacks*, a practice that involves a percentage payment to a person able to influence or control a source of income. Thus, Alice Farnsworth, sales representative for Sisyphus Books, offers a book-selection committee member a percentage of the handsome commission she stands to make if a Sisyphus civics text is adopted. The money the committee member receives for the preferred consideration is a kickback.

Bribery is generally illegal in the United States, but U.S. companies have a history of paying off foreign officials for business favors. Such acts were declared illegal in the Foreign Corrupt Practices Act (FCPA) of 1977, which was passed in the wake of the discovery that nearly 400 American companies had made such payments over several years amounting to about $300 million. Egregious within the sordid pattern of international bribery is Lockheed Aircraft Corporation's $22 million in secret payoffs to foreign politicians to get aircraft contracts. Lest one understate the effects of such bribery, it is worth dwelling on the fact that revelations of Lockheed bribes in Japan caused a government crisis there, and in Holland Prince Bernhardt was forced to resign his government duties after admitting that he took a $1 million payoff from Lockheed. Gulf also admitted to making secret payments of $4 million to the ruling political party in South Korea to firm up its investments there. Exxon

Corporation said it paid $59 million to Italian politicians to promote its business objectives in that country. And only after the suicide of United Brands chairman Eli Black did an SEC investigation reveal that United Brands had paid a $1.25 million bribe to a Honduran official to win a reduction in that country's business export tax.

In 1986 Ashland Oil was caught violating the FCPA. Under its then CEO Orin Atkins, Ashland had agreed to pay an entity controlled by an Omani government official approximately $29 million for a majority interest in Midlands Chrome, Inc., a price far higher than it was worth, for the purpose of obtaining crude oil at a highly favorable price. When Atkins proposed the acquisition of Midlands Chrome to his board of directors, he told it that while the acquisition was a high risk project, it "had the potential for being more than offset by a potential crude oil contract." Midlands Chrome did not in fact prove profitable, but the Omani government awarded Ashland a contract for 20,000 barrels a day for one year at a $3 per barrel discount from the regular selling price—a discount that was worth $40 million.[15]

Another example is Harris Corporation, a major telecommunications firm. Charged with trying to bribe Colombian officials to gain multimillion-dollar contracts, two of the company's executives were tried in 1991 on five counts of conspiring to violate the FCPA. In this case, though, the company had a prior history of corrupt behavior back at home. In 1987 Harris had been convicted of violating federal pricing laws, and in 1989 it had pleaded no contest to charges of making kickbacks in Virginia.[16]

The Foreign Corrupt Practices Act provides stiff fines and prison sentences for corporate officials engaging in bribery overseas and requires corporations to establish strict accounting and auditing controls to guard against the creation of slush funds from which bribes can be paid. The FCPA does not,

however, prohibit "grease payments" to the employees of foreign governments who have primarily clerical or ministerial responsibilities. These payments are sometimes necessary to ensure that the recipients carry out their normal job duties. On the other hand, the FCPA makes no distinction between bribery and extortion. A company is extorted by a foreign official, for instance, if the official threatens to violate the company's rights, perhaps by closing down a plant on some legal pretext, unless the official is paid off.

Since passage of the FCPA, many corporations have lobbied for changes that would extract some of the teeth from the law. They claim that the law has put American corporations at a competitive disadvantage in relation to foreign competitors whose governments permit them to bribe. Some corporations further assert that the law has resulted in lost exports for the United States. They have pushed for easing of accounting requirements and eliminating the responsibility of U.S. companies for actions of their foreign agents.

Before accepting such arguments, one should note that competition is not always a factor in foreign bribes, as illustrated in the United Brands case. Moreover, an investigation of corporate bribery overseas conducted during the Ford administration belies the foreign-competition defense. In 1976 Elliot Richardson, then Commerce Secretary, reported to Congress that "in a multitude of cases—especially those involving the sale of military and commercial aircraft—payments have been made not to outcompete foreign competitors, but rather to gain a competitive edge over other U.S. manufacturers."[17] Furthermore, there's no compelling evidence that U.S. companies have lost exports as a result of the Foreign Corrupt Practices Act. But even if it is true that the United States is losing exports and that U.S. companies are at a competitive disadvantage because of the 1977 law, such considerations must be carefully weighed against the ample documentary evidence of the serious harm done to individuals, companies, and governments as a result of systematic bribery overseas.

A frequently heard argument against the FCPA is that the law imposes American standards on foreign countries and that bribery and payoffs are common business practices in other nations. But this argument is too glib, especially when it comes from those who don't really have a working knowledge of another culture. In some other nations, to be sure, bribery does seem more widespread than it is here. But that doesn't imply that bribery is considered morally acceptable even in those nations. (Drug dealing is not morally acceptable here, even though it is, unfortunately, widespread.) If other countries really did consider bribery and related practices to be morally acceptable, then the people engaging in them would not mind this fact being publicized. But it is hard to find a real-life example of foreign officials willing to let the public know they accept bribes.

Certainly the FCPA reflects our own moral standards, but those standards are not simply matters of taste (like clothing styles) or completely arbitrary (like our decision to drive on the right, while the British drive on the left). Good, objective arguments can be given against bribery and related corrupt practices, whether overseas or at home. First, even an occasional corporate bribe overseas can foster bribery and kickbacks at home and lead employees to subordinate the interest of the organization to their own private gain. Corruption is hard to cordon off. Once a company engages in it, corruption can easily spread throughout the organization.

Bribery is intended to induce people inside a business or other organization to make a decision that they would not be justified in making according to normal business or other criteria. For example, by encouraging on nonmarket grounds the purchase of inferior goods or the payment of an exorbitant price, bribery can clearly injure a variety of legitimate interests—from stockholders to consumers, from taxpayers to other businesses. It subverts market competition by giving advantage in a way that is not directly or indirectly product related. There is nothing "relative" about the damage that such corruption can do to a society. If we were to permit U.S. companies to engage in bribery overseas, we would be encouraging in other countries practices that we consider too harmful to tolerate at home.

The multiple impacts of bribery can be succinctly drawn out in one final case, which involved Bethlehem Steel Corporation, the nation's second-largest steel company. In 1980, Bethlehem was fined $325,000 by a federal judge for bribery and other corrupt practices stretching over four years. Bethlehem admitted to paying more than $400,000 in bribes to shipowners' representatives, including officers of the Colombian Navy. The bribes were paid to ensure that ships needing repairs would be steered into Bethlehem's eight shipyards. Thus, competitive bidding for the contracts was effectively eliminated, various members of the Colombian Navy were corrupted, and the Colombian government may have ended up paying more for the repair work than it had to. Beyond this, Bethlehem generated more than $1.7 million for the payoffs by padding bills and skimming profits from legitimate shipyard repair work. Thus, unsuspecting clients of Bethlehem were made to pay the bill for Bethlehem's bribery.

Gifts and Entertainment

Business gifts and entertainment of clients and business associates are a familiar part of the business world. But both practices can raise conflict-of-interest problems, and knowing where to draw the line is not always easy. One thing is clear: Those who cross that line, wittingly or not, can end up in big trouble.

Ask the former General Services Administration (GSA) official who pleaded guilty in 1989 to a criminal charge of accepting free lunches from a subsidiary of the BellSouth Corporation, which was seeking a telephone contract with the GSA.[18]

The federal government, in fact, now provides its procurement officers with two days' worth of lectures and case-study discussions on the ethics of government contracting. Procurement officers, for example, are taught that they may accept an invitation to speak before a trade association consisting of the contractors they buy from. But they must decline the $50 honorarium, whatever the topic of their talk. They must also refuse a ticket for their transportation to the meeting, although they may be permitted to accept lunch as a guest seated at the head of the table, if this is compatible with the policy of their particular agency.[19]

For people in the business world, the rules are not so cut-and-dried, but a number of considerations can help one determine the morality of giving and receiving gifts in a business situation.

1. *What is the value of the gift?* Is the gift of nominal value, or is it substantial enough to influence a business decision? Undoubtedly, definitions of "nominal" and "substantial" are open to interpretation and are often influenced by situational and cultural variables. Nevertheless, many organizations consider a gift worth $20 or less given infrequently — perhaps once a year — a nominal gift. Anything larger or more frequent would constitute a substantial gift. Although this standard may be arbitrary and inappropriate in some cases, it does indicate that a rather inexpensive gift might be construed as substantial.

2. *What is the purpose of the gift?* Dick Randall, a department store manager, accepts small gifts like pocket calculators from an electronics firm. He insists that the transactions are harmless and that he doesn't intend to give the firm any preferential treatment in terms of advertising displays in the store. As long as the gift is not intended or received as a bribe and remains nominal, there doesn't appear to be any material conflict of interest in such cases. But it would be important to ascertain the electronics firm's intention in giving the gift. Is it to influence how Randall lays out displays? Does Randall himself expect it as a palm-greasing device before he'll ensure that the firm receives equal promotional treatment? If so, extortion may be involved. Important to this question of purpose is a consideration of whether the gift is directly tied to an accepted business practice. For example, appointment books, calendars, or pens and pencils with the donor's name clearly imprinted on them serve to advertise a firm. Trips to Hawaii rarely serve this purpose.

3. *What are the circumstances under which the gift was given or received?* A gift given during the holiday season, for a store opening, or to signal other special events is circumstantially different from one unattached to any special event. Whether the gift was given openly or secretly should also be considered. A gift with the donor's name embossed on it usually constitutes an open gift, whereas one known only to the donor and recipient would not.

4. *What is the position and sensitivity to influence of the person receiving the gift?* Is the person in a position to affect materially a business decision on behalf of the gift giver? In other words, could the recipient's opinion, influence, or decision of itself result in preferential treatment for the donor? Another important point is whether the recipients have made it abundantly clear to the donors that they don't intend

to allow the gift to influence their action one way or the other.

5. *What is the accepted business practice in the area?* Is this the customary way of conducting this kind of business? Monetary gifts and tips are standard practice in numerous service industries. Their purpose is not only to reward good service but to ensure it again. But it's not customary to tip the head of the produce department in a supermarket so the person will put aside the best of the crop for you. Where gratuities are an integral part of customary business practice they are far less likely to pose conflict-of-interest questions.

6. *What is the company's policy?* Many firms explicitly forbid the practice of giving and receiving gifts to minimize even the suspicion that a conflict may exist. Where such a policy exists, the giving or receiving of a gift would normally be wrong.

7. *What is the law?* This consideration is implicit in all facets of conflicts of interest. Some laws, for example, forbid all gift giving and receiving among employees and firms connected with government contracts. Where gift transactions violate the law, they are clearly unacceptable.

Related to gift giving is the practice of entertaining. In general, entertainment should be interpreted more sympathetically than gifts because it usually occurs within the context of doing business in a social situation. Some companies distinguish entertainment from gifts as follows: If you can eat or drink it on the spot, it's entertainment.

Ordinarily the morality of entertainment may be evaluated on the same basis as gifts — that is, with respect to value, purpose, circumstances, position and sensitivity to influence of recipient, accepted business practices, company policy, and law. In each case the ultimate moral judgment hinges largely on a decision as to whether an objective party could reasonably suspect that the gift or entertainment was aimed at blurring the recipient's independent judgment.

OBLIGATIONS TO THIRD PARTIES

A worker knows that a fellow worker occasionally snorts cocaine on the job. Should she inform the boss?

A chef knows that his restaurant typically reheats three- or four-day-old food and serves it as fresh. When he informs the manager, he is told to forget it. What should the chef do?

A consulting engineer discovers a defect in a structure that is about to be sold. If the owner will not disclose the defect to the potential purchaser, should the engineer do so?

An accountant learns of the illegal activities of a client, including deliberate violations of building codes. What should she do about it?

On a regular basis, a secretary is asked by her boss to lie to his wife about his whereabouts. "If my wife calls," the boss tells her, "don't forget that 'I'm calling on a client.'" In fact, as the secretary well knows, the boss is having an affair with another woman. What should the secretary do?

Such cases are not unusual, but they are different from the ones considered until now in this chapter because they involve workers caught in the cross fire of conflicting obligations. On the one hand, workers have obligations to the employer or organization; on the other, they have obligations to third parties: to fellow employees, to customers and other outside individuals affected by the organization, to government, and to society generally.

Conflicts between a worker's obligation to the firm and to others are at the heart of many moral decisions. A way to resolve these conflicts is needed, but that in turn requires identifying what obligations workers have to third parties.

Employees have three basic obligations to third parties as a matter of ordinary morality: truthfulness, noninjury, and fairness. In some instances, the application of these obligations to outside parties is relatively straightforward. For example, in engineering, obligations to third parties are fundamental, and the obligation of noninjury predominates because almost all architectural and engineering projects have a potential for injuring people. Whether the design is of an automobile, airplane, building, bridge, electric power system, sewer system, or nuclear power plant, a faulty design clearly can result in injury to others.

Similarly, those commercially serving alcoholic beverages have a noninjury obligation to monitor the amount of alcohol they serve customers — despite the U.S. Supreme Court's 1979 ruling ending liability for overserving intoxicated customers. (People who commercially serve alcohol still can be cited for a misdemeanor if they overserve an intoxicated person, and the establishment can lose its license.)

For accountants, it is not so much the obligation of noninjury that dominates the relationship to third parties but the obligations of truthfulness and justice. Most of the injury that accountants cause others results from deceit or unfairness. Accordingly, auditors certify that financial statements present data fairly, as determined by generally accepted accounting principles. An untruthful audit can cause others to make unwise investments. Likewise, failure to be truthful and fair in preparing an income-tax statement cheats government and society generally.

Truthfulness, noninjury, and fairness are the ordinary categories of obligations that employees have to third parties, but how are workers to reconcile obligations to employer or organization and others? Should the employee ensure the welfare of the organization by reporting the fellow worker using drugs, or should she be loyal to the fellow worker and say nothing? Should the secretary carry out her boss's instructions, or should she tell his wife the truth? Should the accountant say nothing about the building-code violations, or should she inform authorities? In each case the employee experiences divided loyalties. Resolving such conflicts is never easy, and much hangs on the specific details of the situation. How an employee resolves the moral conflict also depends on the moral principles to which the employee subscribes and the values that are important in his or her life.

According to the procedure recommended in Chapter 2, any moral decision should take account of the relevant obligations, ideals, and effects. The three ordinary obligations of truthfulness, noninjury, and fairness have already been mentioned. And as indicated, the specific responsibilities that one assumes in a given business or professional role affect the strength of one's obligations to third parties. When an engineer or an accounting auditor, for example, suspects some "irregularity," he or she may have a stronger obligation to get to the bottom of the matter than would an ordinary employee who has a hunch that something is not in order in another department. And now a further question: While we all have the three general obligations mentioned above, how far must we go to uncover or remedy possible violations of those obligations by others? It is unlikely that any moral theory can give a general answer to this question, applicable to all cases.

So far the talk of obligations of employees to third parties has been a little abstract, but remember that these third parties are not just the "public" at large, but often our friends, co-workers, and family members — real, flesh-and-blood people with whom our lives are interwoven. Our ongoing relationships with them may give rise to moral obligations based on those relationships, above and beyond any moral obligations we have to third parties in general. Sometimes these obligations have to be balanced against obligations to the firm and obligations arising from the business, professional, or organizational roles we have assumed.

The impact of our action on significant moral ideals is the second consideration to be weighed. Moral decisions must take account, not only of distinct ethical obligations, but also of the various ideals advanced or respected, ignored or hindered, by the alternative actions open to us. In addition, our moral choices are often influenced strongly by the personal weight we place on the different values that may be at stake in a specific situation. Sometimes these values can point in different directions, as when our simultaneous commitment to professional excellence, personal integrity, and loyalty to friends pulls us in three different ways.

Third, but not least, we must examine the effects of the different courses of action. Even staunch nonconsequentialists acknowledge that the likely results of our actions are relevant to their moral assessment and that we have a duty to promote human well-being. In addition, considerations of consequences can help us determine the exact strength of our different obligations in a given situation.

As discussed in Chapter 2, we must first identify the relevant obligations, ideals, and effects and then try to decide where the emphasis should lie. There is nothing mechanical about this process, but when we as employees weigh moral decisions, two simple things can help keep our deliberations free from the various rationalizations to which we are all prone. First, we can ask ourselves whether we would be willing to read an account of our actions in the newspaper. That is, when we have made our decisions, are the contemplated actions ones that we would be willing to defend publicly? Second, discussing a moral dilemma or ethical problem with a friend can often help us avoid bias and gain a better perspective. People by themselves, and especially when emotionally involved in a situation, sometimes focus unduly on one or two points, ignoring other relevant factors. Input from others can keep us from overlooking pertinent considerations, thus helping us make a better, more objective moral judgment.

As the preceding discussion mentioned, employees frequently know about the illegal or immoral actions of a supervisor or firm. When an employee tries to correct the situation within institutional channels and is thwarted, a central moral question emerges: Should the employee go public with the information? Should a worker who is ordered to do something illegal or immoral, or who knows of the illegal or immoral behavior of a supervisor or organization, inform the public?

Whistle Blowing

On October 11, 1979, Morris H. Baslow, a forty-seven-year-old biologist and father of three, dropped an envelope in the mail to Thomas B. Yost, an administrative law judge with the Environmental Protection Agency (EPA). Later that day, Baslow was fired from his job with Lawler, Matusky & Skelly, an engineering consulting firm that had been hired by Consolidated Edison of New York to help it blunt EPA demands. The EPA was insisting that the power company's generating plants on the Hudson River had to have cooling towers to protect fish from excessively warm water that it was discharging into the river.

Baslow claims that the documents he sent showed that Con Ed and Lawler, Matusky & Skelly had knowingly submitted to the EPA invalid and misleading data, giving the false impression that the long-term effects of the utility's effluent on fish was negligible. On the basis of his own research, Baslow believed that the fish could be significantly harmed by the warm-water discharge. He says that for two years he tried to get his employers to listen to him, but they wouldn't.

Shortly after being fired, Baslow sent seventy-one company documents supporting his allegation to the EPA, the Federal Energy Regulatory Commission, and the Justice Department. In the month following these disclosures, Baslow's employers accused him of stealing the documents and sued him for defamation. Baslow countersued, citing the Clean Water Act, which protects consultants from reprisals for reporting findings prejudicial to their employers and clients.

A year later, Lawler, Matusky & Skelly dropped all legal action against Baslow and gave him a cash settlement, reportedly of around $100,000. In return, Baslow wrote to the EPA and other government agencies, withdrawing his complaint of wrongdoing and perjury on the part of the defendants but not recanting his own scientific conclusions. Asked why he finally accepted the cash payment, the unemployed Baslow said, "I've had to bear the brunt of this financially by myself . . . I just wish somebody had listened to me six months ago."[20]

The Baslow case and scores more like it illustrate the ethical problem and personal risks that employees face who blow the whistle on what they perceive as organizational misconduct.

Whistle blowing refers to an employee act of informing the public about the illegal or immoral behavior of an employer or organization. Professor of philosophy Norman Bowie provides the following detailed definition:

> A whistle blower is an employee or officer of any institution, profit or nonprofit, private or public, who believes either that he/she has been ordered to perform some act or he/she has obtained knowledge that the institution is engaged in activities which (a) are believed to cause unnecessary harm to third parties, (b) are in violation of human rights, or (c) run counter to the defined purpose of the institution and who informs the public of this fact.[21]

This definition limits the class of moral infractions that an employee should make public. Accordingly, a worker who publicizes in-house indiscretions is not a whistle blower but a gossip monger. Such persons not only exhibit character flaws but also an ignorance of their basic obligation of loyalty and confidentiality to the firm. By contrast, "whistle blowing" is reserved conceptually only for activities that are harmful to third parties, violations of human rights, or contrary to the public purpose and legitimate goals of the organization. Also, this definition limits the scope of one's responsibility to informing the public. Responsibility does not extend to taking retaliatory action against the employer or firm, such as sabotaging operations.

Bowie correctly points out that a discussion of whistle blowing in the 1990s parallels the discussion of civil disobedience in the 1960s. Just as civil disobedients of that time felt their duty to obey the law was overridden by other moral obligations, so the whistle blower overrides loyalty to colleagues and to the organization in order to serve the public interest. But whistle blowing presents dangers, as Professor Sissela Bok reminds us.[22] The whistle can be blown in error or malice, privacy invaded, and trust undermined. Not least, publicly accusing others of wrongdoing can be very destructive and brings with it an obligation to be fair to the persons accused. In addition, internal prying and mutual suspicion make it hard for any organization to function.

In developing his analogy with civil disobedience, Professor Bowie proposes several conditions that must be met for an act of whistle blowing to be morally justified. These conditions may not be the last word on this controversial subject, but they do provide a good starting point for further debate over the morality of whistle blowing. According to Bowie, whistle blowing is morally justified only if

1. *It is done from the appropriate moral motive — namely, as provided in the definition of whistle blowing.* This criterion focuses on the crucial question of motive. For an act of whistle blowing to be justified, it must be motivated by a desire to expose unnecessary harm, violation of human rights, or con-

duct counter to the defined purpose of the organization. Desire for attention or profit or the exercise of one's general tendency toward "wave making" is not a justification for whistle blowing.

Although the question of motive is an important one in Kantian ethics, as Chapter 2 explained, not all moral theorists would agree with Bowie's first condition. Might not an employee be justified in blowing the whistle on serious wrongdoing by the employer, even if the employee's real motivation was the desire for revenge? Granted that the motivation was ignoble, the action itself may nonetheless be the morally right one. An action can still be morally justified, say some theorists, even when it is done for the wrong reason.

2. *The whistle blower, except in special circumstances, has exhausted all internal channels for dissent before going public.* The duty of loyalty to the firm obligates workers to seek an internal remedy before informing the public of a misdeed. This is an important consideration, but in some cases the attempt to exhaust internal channels may result in dangerous delays or expose the would-be whistle blower to retaliation.

3. *The whistle blower has compelling evidence that the inappropriate actions have been ordered or have occurred.* While it is impossible to say how much or what kind of evidence constitutes "compelling evidence," employees can ask themselves whether the evidence is so strong that any reasonable person in a similar situation would be convinced that the activity is illegal or immoral. Although this is not a decisive guideline, the standard of what a reasonable person would believe is commonly invoked in other cases, such as deceptive advertising and negligence lawsuits.

4. *The whistle blower has acted after careful analysis of the danger: How serious is the moral violation? How immediate is the moral viola-*

tion? Is the moral violation one that can be specified? These criteria focus on the nature of the wrongdoing. Owing loyalty to employers, employees should blow the whistle only for grave legal or moral matters. Additionally, they should consider the time factor. The greater the time before the violation is to occur, the more likely the firm's own internal mechanisms will prevent it; and the more immediate a violation, the more justified the whistle blowing. Finally, violations must be specific. General allegations, such as that a company is "not operating in the best interests of the public" or is "systematically sabotaging the competition," won't do. Concrete examples are needed that can pass the other justificatory tests.

5. *The whistle blowing has some chance of success.* This criterion recognizes that the chances of remedying an immoral or illegal action are an important consideration. Sometimes the chances are good; other times they're slim. Probably most cases fall somewhere between these extremes. In general, whistle blowing that stands no chance of success is less justified than that with some chance of success. Even so, one may sometimes be justified in blowing the whistle when there is no chance of success. Sometimes merely drawing attention to an objectional practice, although it may fail to improve the specific situation, encourages government and society to be more watchful of certain behavior. Still, given the potential harmful effects of whistle blowing, it seems fair to say that justification for whistle blowing increases with the chances of success.

THE QUESTION OF SELF-INTEREST

Conspicuously absent so far in the discussion of obligations to third parties and the special problem of whistle blowing has been any mention of the worker's own interests. And yet for many workers, protecting themselves or safeguarding their jobs is the primary factor in deciding whether to put third-party interests above those of the firm.

Concern with self-interest in cases that pit loyalty to the firm against obligations to third parties is altogether understandable and even warranted. After all, workers who subordinate the organization's interests to an outside party's expose themselves to charges of disloyalty, disciplinary action, "freezes" in job status, forced relocations, and even dismissal. Furthermore, even when an employee successfully blows the whistle, he or she can be blacklisted in an industry. Given the potential harm to self and family that employees risk in honoring third-party obligations, it is perfectly legitimate to inquire about the weight considerations of self-interest should be given in resolving cases of conflicting obligations.

Sadly, there is no clear, unequivocal answer to this question. Moral theorists and society as a whole do distinguish between prudential reasons and moral reasons. "Prudential" (from the word "prudence") refers here to considerations of self-interest; "moral" refers here to considerations of the interests of others and the demands of morality. Chapter 1 explained that it is possible for prudential and moral considerations to pull us in different directions. One way of looking at their relationship is this: If prudential concerns outweigh moral ones, then employees may do what is in their own best interest. If moral reasons override prudential ones, then workers should honor their obligations to others.

Consider the case of a cashier at a truck stop who is asked to write up phony chits so the truckers can get a larger expense reimbursement from their employers than they really deserve. The cashier doesn't think this is right, so she complains to the manager. The manager explains that the restaurant is largely dependent on trucker business and that this is a good way to ensure it. The cashier is ordered to do the truckers' bidding and is thus being

told to violate the three basic moral obligations to an outside party (the trucking firms): truth, noninjury, and fairness. Given these moral considerations, the cashier ought to refuse, and perhaps she should even report the conduct to the trucking companies.

But let's suppose that the cashier happens to be a recent divorcee with no formal education. She lacks occupational skills and stands little chance of getting another job in an economy that happens to be depressed — for months she was unemployed before landing her present job. With no other means of support, the consequences of job loss for her would be serious indeed. Now, given this scenario and given that the wrongdoing at issue is relatively minor, prudential concerns would probably take legitimate precedence over moral ones. In other words, the cashier would be justified in "going along," at least on a temporary basis.

Some moral theorists would agree with this conclusion but analyze the case somewhat differently. They think it is incorrect to say that in some circumstances we may permit prudential considerations to outweigh moral considerations. There is no neutral perspective outside both morality and self-interest from which one can make such a judgment. Furthermore, they would say that, by definition, nothing can outweigh the demands of morality.

Does that mean the cashier should refuse to do what her manager wants and, thus, lose her job? Not necessarily. Morality does not, these theorists contend, require us to make large sacrifices to right small wrongs. Writing up phony chits does violate some basic moral principles, and the cashier has some moral obligation not to go along with it. But morality does not, all things considered, require her — under the present circumstances — to take a course of action that would spell job loss. She should, however, take less drastic steps to end the practice (like continuing to talk to her boss and the truckers about it) and perhaps eventually find other work. Thus, in this view, she is not sacrificing morality to self-interest in "going along" for a while. The idea is that morality does not impose obligations on us without regard to their cost; it does not, under the present circumstances, demand an immediate resignation by the cashier.

Whichever way one looks at it, the question of balancing our moral obligations, consideration of the rights and interests of others, and our own self-interest is particularly relevant to whistle blowing. In situations where whistle blowing threatens one's livelihood and career, prudential concerns may properly be taken into account in deciding what one should do, all things considered. This doesn't mean that, if the worker blows the whistle despite compelling prudential reasons not to, he or she is not moral. On the contrary, such an action could be highly moral. (As Chapter 2 explained, ethicists term such actions "superogatory," meaning that they are, so to speak, above and beyond the call of duty.) On the other hand, when the moral concerns are great (for example, when the lives of others are at stake), elementary morality and personal integrity can require people to make substantial sacrifices.

A couple of further observations are in order here. First, an evaluation of prudential reasons obviously is colored by one's temperament and perceptions of self-interest. Each of us has a tendency to magnify potential threats to our livelihood or career. Exaggerating the costs to ourselves of acting otherwise makes it easier to rationalize away the damage we are doing to others. In the business world, for instance, people talk about the "survival" of the firm as if it were literally a matter of "life and death." Going out of business is the worst thing that can happen to a firm, but the people who make it up will live on and get other jobs. Keeping the company "alive" (let alone "competitive" or "profitable") cannot justify seriously injuring innocent people.

Not only do we tend to exaggerate the importance of self-interested considerations, but most of us also typically have been socialized to heed authority, sometimes to the extent of causing others great personal harm. As a result, we are disinclined to question the orders of someone "above" us, especially when the authority is an employer or supervisor with power to influence our lives for better or worse. It's easy for us to assume that any "boat rocking" will be very harmful, even self-destructive.

It follows, then, that each of us has an obligation to perform a kind of character or personality audit. Do we follow authority blindly? Do we suffer from moral tunnel vision on the job? Do we mindlessly do what is demanded of us, oblivious to the impact of our cooperation and actions on outside parties? Have we given enough attention to our possible roles as accomplices in the immoral undoing of other individuals, businesses, and social institutions? Do we have a balanced view of our own interests versus those of others? Do we have substantial evidence for believing that our livelihoods are really threatened, or is that belief based more on an exaggeration of the facts? Have we been imaginative in trying to balance prudential and moral concerns? Have we sought to find some middle ground, or have we set up a false self-other dilemma in which our own interests and those of others are erroneously viewed as incompatible? These are just some of the questions that a personal inventory should include if we are to combat the all-too-human tendency to stack the deck in favor of prudential reasons whenever they are pitted against moral ones.

A second observation about the relationship between prudential and moral considerations concerns the welfare of society. In some cases, as we have seen, considerations of self-interest may mean one does not have an overriding moral obligation to blow the whistle; when that occurs, how can society be protected from wrongdoing? Is the welfare of society to be left to those few heroic souls willing to perform superogatory actions? Perhaps the only reasonable solution is to restructure business and social institutions so such acts no longer carry such severe penalties. Just as laws currently exist to protect whistle blowers in the public sector from reprisals, so comparable legislation is probably needed in the private sector.

A good example of such legislation is Michigan's Whistle Blowers Protection Act, the first law of its kind to cover corporate employees. Under this act, any employee in private industry fired or disciplined for reporting alleged violations of federal, state, or local law to public authorities can now bring an action in state court for unjust reprisal. If the employer cannot show that treatment of the employee was based on proper personnel standards or valid business reasons, the court can award back pay, reinstatement of job, costs of litigation, and attorneys' fees and also fine the employer. Every employer in Michigan must now post a notice of this new law in the workplace. Commenting on the impact of this legislation, professor of public law and government Alan F. Westin predicts that it will prod large firms to draft fair and effective procedures to deal with alleged company violations of public-protection laws. Doing so may entail experimenting with new mechanisms: "company ombudsmen; inspector-general systems; special regulatory-compliance review committees, such as Allied Chemical recently created; or the kind of worldwide Ethical Practices Complaint Committee at corporate headquarters that Citicorp instituted."[23] The Michigan law may help convince leading managements that creating the climate and procedures to encourage employees to blow the whistle is an important corporate priority for the 1990s.

SUMMARY

1. Conflicts of interest arise when one has a personal interest in a transaction substantial enough that it does (actual conflict) or might reasonably be expected to (potential conflict) affect one's judgment when one is acting on behalf of the organization.

2. When employees have financial investments in suppliers, customers, or distributors with whom the organization does business, conflicts of interest can arise. Company policy usually determines the permissible limits of such financial interests.

3. *Insider trading* refers to the use of significant facts that have not yet been made public and will likely affect stock prices. Insider trading seems unfair and can injure other investors. In practice, determining what counts as insider information is not easy, and the meaning of "insider" is currently under debate. Some writers defend insider trading as performing a necessary and desirable economic function.

4. *Proprietary data* refers to an organization's classified or secret information. Increasingly, problems arise as employees in high-tech occupations with access to sensitive information and trade secrets quit and take jobs with competitors. Proprietary-data issues pose a conflict between two legitimate rights: the right of employers to keep certain information secret and the right of individuals to work where they choose.

5. A *bribe* is payment in some form for an act that runs counter to the work contract or the nature of the work one has been hired to perform. The Foreign Corrupt Practices Act prohibits corporations from engaging in bribery overseas. Bribery generally involves injury to individuals, competitors, or political institutions and damage to the free-market system.

6. The following considerations are relevant in determining the moral acceptability of gift giving and receiving: the value of the gift, its purpose, the circumstances under which it is given, the position and sensitivity to influence of the person receiving the gift, accepted business practice, company policy, and what the law says.

7. Workers have three ordinary moral obligations to third parties: truthfulness, non-injury, and fairness. In addition, one's professional or business role may affect the nature and strength of one's obligations to third parties.

8. Balancing these obligations against obligations to employer or organization, friends, and co-workers can create conflicts and divided loyalties. In resolving such moral conflicts, we must identify the relevant obligations, ideals, and effects and decide where the emphasis among them should lie.

9. *Whistle blowing* refers to an employee informing the public about the illegal or immoral behavior of an employer or organization.

10. An act of whistle blowing can be presumed to be morally justified if it is done from the appropriate moral motive; if the whistle blower, except in special circumstances, has exhausted internal channels before going public; if the whistle blower has compelling evidence; if the whistle blower has carefully analyzed the dangers; and if the whistle blowing has some chance of success.

11. Prudential considerations based on self-interest can conflict with moral considerations, which take account of the interests of others. Some sacrifices of self-interest would be so great that moral considerations must give way to prudential ones. But employees must avoid the temptation to exaggerate prudential concerns, thereby rationalizing away any individual moral responsibility to third parties. Legislation can protect whistle blowing so that it involves less personal sacrifice.

CASE 8.1

Profiting on Columns Prior to Publication

In April 1984, R. Foster Winans, who wrote *The Wall Street Journal's* highly influential stock-market column, "Heard on the Street," was fired from the paper after admitting to federal investigators that he had improperly taken advantage of his position. The thirty-six-year-old business analyst confirmed that he had leaked information about upcoming columns to associates who were able to profit from the information by buying or selling stock.

On May 17, the Securities and Exchange Commission charged Winans with violating federal law by failing to disclose to readers that he had financial interests in the securities he wrote about. Winans, whose tips about columns prior to publication helped two stockbrokers net about half a million dollars, also was charged with personally profiting from the material.

The basis of the charges was an SEC rule that prohibits anyone from omitting to state a material fact regarding the purchase or sale of securities. But applicability of the SEC rule to Winans's case is unclear. Professor of journalism Gilbert Cranberg phrases the ambiguity this way: "Is the ownership by a reporter of stock in a company about which he writes a 'material fact' to readers sufficient to require disclosure, or must the reporter also intend to profit from the story?"[24] Ambiguous or not, the SEC's action has convinced some legal scholars that the media must disclose the financial holdings of their financial analysts.

Even before the Winans case, some publications had formulated explicit policies designed to leave no doubt in reporters' minds about the impropriety of trading on knowledge of stories. For example, the *Washington*

Post requires that all its financial and business reporters submit to their editors a confidential statement outlining their stock holdings. *Post* policy prohibits writers from either writing about companies in which they have an interest or buying stock in companies they have written about. *The New York Times* has a similar policy, and *Forbes* magazine and the *Chicago Tribune* require editorial employees to divulge their corporate investments. Ralph Schulz, senior vice president at McGraw-Hill's publication unit, says his company has a conflict-of-interest policy based on the premise that "nobody who writes about a company ought to own stock in it."[25] And *The Wall Street Journal's* three-and-a-half-page conflict-of-interest policy warns employees against trading in companies immediately before or after a *Journal* piece on that company. The policy reads in part:

> It is not enough to be incorruptible and act with honest motives. It is equally important to use good judgment and conduct one's outside activities so that no one — management, our editors, an SEC investigator with power of subpoena, or a political critic of the company — has any grounds for even raising the suspicion that an employee misused a position with the company.[26]

But such written policies remain the exception, as shown by an informal survey of the country's media conducted by *The Wall Street Journal*. Although many newspapers have formal dress codes, few have formal rules about stock trading. Moreover, few news executives show any concern about insider trading by noneditorial employees, although sensitive investigative reports generally are accessible to any employee in the newsroom.

The Wall Street Journal survey also reveals general indifference among media executives to stock trading by subjects of interviews, as in the case of G. D. Searle & Co. Early in 1984, the SEC began investigating unusual activity in options on that company's stock just before the mid-January "CBS Evening News" report that raised questions about NutraSweet, Searle's new low-calorie sweetener. The SEC charged that an Arizona scientist interviewed by CBS for the report bought "put" options in Searle's NutraSweet before the story aired, convinced that the stock would tumble as a result of negative comments by himself and others. "I honestly believe I had a right to do it," says the Arizona scientist. He adds, "I don't think it's unethical. It's the American way."[27] The scientist's lawyer and some CBS employees also were targets of the SEC investigation.

Syndicated financial columnist Dan Dorman admits that his stories may affect the price of stocks, and by implication, shrewd subjects of interviews could stand to benefit on the stories. But he doesn't think there's anything he can do about that. "It's not my job to police," Dorman says. "My job is to get information."[28]

John G. Craig, Jr., editor of the *Pittsburg Post Gazette*, agrees. In his view, preventing sources from trading on an article "is an ethical responsibility a newspaper can't assume."[29]

And yet James Michaels, the editor of *Forbes*, recalls once holding out a story when he learned that one of the sources had sold stock short, betting the article would have a negative impact. And *The Wall Street Journal* admits to killing stories upon learning that investors were using their knowledge of it to wheel and deal on Wall Street.

In the meantime, the government pressed its case against R. Foster Winans. In September 1984, the Justice Department brought a sixty-one-count indictment for fraud and conspiracy against him and two alleged collaborators. Among other things, the indictment charged that, in the first half of 1983, Winans and his roommate speculated on stocks about to be mentioned in forthcoming columns. They made about a $3,000 profit on a $3,000 investment.[30] Although Winans describes his role in these deals as "stupid" and "wrong," he denies he broke any law. After a long and technical legal battle, the Supreme Court in November 1987 upheld the Justice Department's contention that what he did was not just imprudent but criminal.

Professor Cranberg fears that the Winans case may ultimately make bad law. Although he thinks that the time has come for reporters and editors to report outside compensation and financial interests, he worries that the SEC and the courts may equate business-news reporters with investment advisers and, as a result, wield undue influence on the press.

Cranberg fears that such a development not only threatens freedom of the press but would have a chilling effect on press coverage of corporate America. "Not every problem has, or should have, a legal solution," Cranberg points out. "Most problems involving the press are best handled by voluntary measures. The way for the press to show that it can keep its house in order is to do it. More actions and less self-satisfied ridicule of concern about conflicts of interest would be signs that the press can and will."[31]

Michael Missal, a lawyer for the SEC, thinks such fears are unfounded. "We don't expect every journalist to disclose all financial relationships," he says. Instead, the government wishes to prevent profiteering on advance knowledge of stories. That, Missal says, is what the Winans case is all about.[32]

Discussion Questions

1. In your opinion, did Winans engage in insider trading? Did he do something wrong?

2. Do you believe that media financial analysts should disclose to their audience any financial interests they have in the securities they write about? Do you think they should be required to make such disclosures? If so, should the requirement take the form of an institutional policy, law, or both?

3. Would you say that, as long as reporters do not intend to profit from their stories, they cannot and should not be held guilty of insider trading? Or do you think that a reporter can engage in insider trading even if he or she does not intend to profit personally?

4. Do you think that McGraw-Hill's policy — that "nobody who writes about a company ought to own stock in it" — is fair? Or do you think it is an unreasonable encroachment on the employee's right to profit through investments?

5. Do you agree that the Arizona scientist had a "right" to trade on the information before it was broadcast?

6. What obligations, ideals, and effects do you think Winans should have considered before acting as he did?

7. What do you think Kant's position on insider trading would be?

8. As a rule utilitarian, formulate a rule for insider trading. Do you think the rule is a good one?

9. Under what circumstances does a company have a right to know about the financial investments of its employees?

CASE 8.2

The Tavoulareas Affair: Nepotism at Mobil?

In 1979, the *Washington Post* alleged that William Tavoulareas had used his position as Mobil Corporation's president to help his son Peter's London-based shipping firm, Atlas Maritime, get a $100,000-per-year contract to manage ships in which Mobile had a 30 percent interest. In November 1980, the Tavoulareas sued the *Post* for libel and won —

well, partly. A jury unanimously found that the *Post* had libeled the older Tavoulareas but not the younger and awarded the senior Tavoulareas $2.1 million in damages. But a year later, Judge Oliver Gasch, who presided over the original trial, ruled that there was insufficient evidence to support the jury's finding and threw out the libel judgment. Although that may prove the end of the Tavoulareases' suit against the *Post*, it certainly hasn't ended the younger Tavoulareas's dealings with Mobil.[33]

The business relationship between Mobil and Peter Tavoulareas began in 1974 when Peter, a twenty-four-year-old MBA from Columbia University and previously a $14,000-a-year shipping clerk at Mobil, became junior partner in Atlas. (The *Post* article claimed he was set up by his father.) One of Atlas's main functions was to manage a fleet of ships owned by Saudi Maritime Co. (Samarco), in which Mobil had a 30 percent interest. The majority interest in Samarco was held by prominent Saudis, such as Prince Mohamed Bin Fahd. In 1976 Mobil and the prince set up a similar company, Arabian International Maritime Co. (Aimco), whose fleet Atlas also manages.

During the mid-1970s, Atlas expanded its operations to include investing in vessels, among other things. Capitalizing on the shipping boom of 1979, Peter Tavoulareas, who had by then become the majority owner of Atlas, ordered six 39,600-ton chemical-carrying transports for launch in 1981, 1982, and 1983; he signed contracts for three more in 1981. But the bright future for this type of ship had begun to dim by 1981. Industry analysts and trade journals warned of surplus capacity in the category of chemical-transport vessels. They suspected that the only way such vessels could remain afloat financially was for them to carry petroleum products, which Atlas's ships were capable of doing.

During the first half of 1981, shortly before the first of the nine Atlas vessels was to be delivered, Mobil officials recommended that Aimco invest in some of Atlas's chemical ships. Internal memos predicted low risk on limited cost outlays and high rates of return. As a result, in the second half of 1981 Atlas sold Aimco 50 percent interests in three vessels, based on valuations millions of dollars above their initial construction price. In 1982 Mobil bought out Atlas's interest in a fourth and fifth of the unbuilt vessels.

Peter Tavoulareas claims that Mobil took over control "on terms which gave no financial benefit to Atlas, and I believe were generous to Mobil." Mobil officials agree. Herbert Schmertz, vice president of Mobil, describes the transaction as simply a matter of Atlas's offering a deal to a company whose fleet it was managing, Aimco. He says that "Atlas would have and could have taken the deals elsewhere because of their attractiveness."

One of the ships was valued at $36 million, which was $20 million above construction costs but consistent with market values in mid-1981. For its 50 percent share, then, Aimco paid $18 million, financed through relatively low-cost sources, such as new shipyard mortgages. Although the costs may appear high to the untutored eye, one Aimco member described it as "realistic and attractive . . . in terms of current market prices and new building costs for similar vessels." Apparently one big factor in Aimco's decision was the belief that the ships it was buying would prove profitable. As it turned out, rather than yielding an expected $14 per deadweight ton a month, by 1983 the ships were earning between $7 and $8—enough, by some estimates, to cover their operating costs and about half of their interest costs. Industry analysts pegged the market value of the ships that year at between $20 and $25 million.

During the 1980 *Post* libel trial, the senior Tavoulareas was asked why he had no reservations about such a business relationship with his son. "It wasn't a question of what I could do for my son," he testified. "It was a question of would I stand in the way of my son." According to testimony, Tavoulareas informed Mobil of the situation, and an internal memo was circulated emphasizing that dealings with Atlas were to be businesslike, without any regard to the family connection. Tavoulareas testified further that he had sought assurance from Mobil's outside accountants that all such dealings with Atlas were commercially sound. He said he even told his subordinates that all decisions regarding Atlas be sent not to him but to his superior, Mobil chairman and chief executive Rawleigh Warner, Jr. Tavoulareas did admit, however, that consistent with Mobil's internal procedures, he was permitted to and sometimes did participate in discussions concerning Atlas.

Vice president Schmertz asserts not only that Mobil's executive committee approved of these transactions but also that committee member William Tavoulareas didn't even vote when the approval was made. Some of Mobil's outside directors confirm that they were fully informed of the transactions. Says Samuel C. Johnson, a Mobil director: "The transactions were in the normal course of business and arm's length." Another Mobile director, Lewis M. Branscomb, praised the Mobil-Atlas relationship: "I was very impressed with the amount of care that Tav took to see that he notified the company and the board and removed himself from areas of decision making."

But some students of corporate ethics have been less impressed. Richard West, dean of business administration at Dartmouth College and director of several companies, thinks that businesses simply should not deal with relatives unless the relatives are the sole source of a product or unless there is competitive bidding. Kenneth Goodpaster of Harvard Business School believes it's naive to think it sufficient merely to tell employees to ignore the fact that they're dealing with the boss's son. It's "like telling them not to think about an elephant," he says. And shortly after the *Post* story in 1979, George McGhee, who was then a Mobil director, sent a memo to the board in which he wrote: "The present arrangement is in my view a case of nepotism which is intrinsically bad policy both from the standpoint of

the company and the corporate system generally." He characterized the Mobil-Atlas relationship as "setting a bad precedent within the company. It could have a negative effect on employee morale and respect for the company. It's unfair for those in the company who must deal with Atlas."

William Tavoulareas scoffs at such criticism. "If anything, when my son's involved, [Mobile employees] bend over backwards the other way around, and don't even do things for him they'd do for an outsider." As for the suggestion that company policy should prohibit dealings with relatives, Mobil's president wonders where the line should be drawn: "Friends, schoolmates, cousins, sisters-in-law? Where do we stop this?"

Discussion Questions

1. As the case is described, did William Tavoulareas have an actual or potential conflict of interest? Explain. Was this a case of nepotism?

2. Do we have an obligation to help close relatives, if possible, in business transactions? How far is an employee permitted to go in helping a relative with whom the employee's firm has business dealings?

3. Compare former Mobile director George McGhee's characterization of the Mobil-Atlas relationship with that of Mobil director Lewis M. Branscomb. With whom do you agree?

4. If you were a stockholder of Mobil, would you be satisfied with William Tavoulareas's conduct? If not, explain why not. If you think his conduct was acceptable, do you think that he should have gone further to avoid any possible suggestion of impropriety?

5. How are the ethics of the transaction affected by the question of whether Mobil lost money in its dealings with Atlas?

6. Do you agree with Richard West's belief that companies should have strict policies prohibiting doing business with relatives except when relatives are the sole source of a product or unless there is competitive bidding?

CASE 8.3
Storms Make Waves for Navy

Zeke Storms, a fifty-two-year-old retired Navy chief, began his career as a whistle blower in March 1983, when he wrote to protest Congressman Charles Pashayan's support of President Ronald Reagan's budget cuts.[34] Storms had been employed as a civilian repairing flight simulators at the Lemoore Naval Air Base station near Fresno, California, since his retirement in 1973. Now he was suggesting that, instead of supporting Reagan's proposed reductions in the Civil Service pay scale, Pashayan ought to take a closer look at Navy procurement practices. Enclosed in the letter was a list of spare parts showing that defense contractors were charging $435 for ordinary claw hammers and $100 or more for such electronic spare parts as diodes, transistors, and semiconductors, which cost less than $1 each. He also charged that the Navy purchased transistors at $100 each, which it could have obtained through the federal supply system for five cents apiece.

Storms's letter prompted Pashayan to query the Defense Department, which in turn kicked off an interservice investigation of military procurement practices. In May 1983, the Defense Department inspector general's office reported that the Navy had indeed failed to determine the most economical manner to acquire the spare parts Zeke Storms had listed. It also suggested that the spare-parts-overcharge problem was more widespread than at first thought. The investigative body left no doubt that the Navy was wasting millions of dollars annually and that, on first look, such waste was occurring outside the Navy as well.

As a result, the inspector general's office said it planned to do an interservice audit.

In the wake of this report, Defense Secretary Caspar Weinberger ordered a tightening of procurement procedures to ensure the lowest price for spare parts. Meanwhile, Navy Secretary John Lehman ordered contractors at Lemoore to refund $160,000 in overcharges. He also gave Storms a $4,000 award.

But Storms wasn't about to lay down his muckrake. He suggested that Defense Department auditors review overpayment for jet-aircraft support equipment in the base shops. The auditors did and discovered overpayment of $482,000, most of it spent on four spectrum analyzers. Had the items been bought through the federal supply system, they would have cost $47,500.

Storms then discovered that the Navy had engaged private contractors to operate its flight simulators for a new aircraft. "I got mad," he says. "[The Navy] had spent $1 million training their own people to do the work, then they just scrapped that and turned the maintenance over to the contractor." The contractor in question apparently was demanding $785,000 to maintain the simulators, which worked out to about $100,000 per person per year. "I showed them that we [a team of Navy and Civil Service technicians] could do it for one-fourth that cost, so the contract was dropped to $411,000," says Storms.

That $411,000 was still higher than Storms believed the Navy had to pay, especially since the Navy had been maintaining its own trainers for two decades. So he took his case directly to

Lehman, arguing that the Office of Management and Budget (OMB) regulations required the Navy to do comparative cost studies to ensure the most cost-effective means. Lehman balked at Storms's proposal, saying that such studies would cost $45,000 each. That was too high a price to pay "to indulge Mr. Storms's eccentricities," the Secretary said in a letter to Congressman Pashayan. Lehman also pointed out that OMB Director David Stockman personally had rejected the need for cost studies.

Evidently deciding it was time to quiet the querulous Storms, Lehman then sent nine Navy brass to Lemoore in February 1984. In the two-hour session that ensued, Storms did most of the talking. In the end, a commodore, four captains, two commanders, and two lieutenant commanders could do nothing to divert Storms from his course.

It was shortly thereafter that the ex-Navy chief did the "unpardonable." He accused Secretary Lehman and "his admirals" of lying. He said he had turned over to OMB officials Navy documents showing that in 1982 Navy admirals willfully ignored requirements to do cost studies for private maintenance work. One of the documents, dated March 1982, included a message from Vice Admiral Robert F. Schoultz, the commander of naval forces in the Pacific. Addressing Admiral James D. Watkins, then commander of the Pacific Fleet, Schoultz wrote: "It is our intention to contract out all major training device maintenance. . . . [However] under the [contract] program our objective is hindered with cost studies that would yield inappropriate results." Schoultz's "inappropriate results" apparently was an allusion to the January 1982 report by the fleet's top training officer, who estimated that the Navy's own people could do for $7 million the same work for which private contractors would charge $28 million. In mid-1984, OMB announced it was reviewing the matter but opined that the Navy was probably in compliance with regulations.

In a letter dated June 4, 1984, N. R. Lessard, officer in charge of the flight training group that Storms was working for, informed the ten-year Lemoore veteran that "your recent comments concerning senior Navy officials . . . constitute unacceptable employee conduct."

To which Storms replied in a way most befitting a tobacco-chewing old salt: "[The Navy is] covering up, goddammit. I've got the facts, and they know it."

Discussion Questions

1. Do you think Storms qualifies as a whistle blower? What do you think his motives were?

2. Examine Storms's actions from the perspective of Bowie's criteria for justified whistle blowing. Are those criteria satisfied in Storms's case? Are Bowie's criteria themselves satisfactory?

3. What obligations, ideals, and effects do you think Storms should have considered before becoming a whistle blower? In this case, which of these considerations is the most important? Why?

4. Based on the details provided, would you consider Storms's whistle blowing morally justified? Explain.

5. If you believe Storms's whistle blowing was permissible, do you also believe that it was morally required of him? Would someone in Storms's position have been justified in subordinating moral reasons to prudential concerns and thus in remaining silent? Explain.

6. Should whistle blowers be protected by law? How feasible would such a law be? Identify the advantages and disadvantages of such a law.

7. The Federal False Claims Act awards whistle blowers a portion of any money recov-

ered by the government as a result of legal action against companies that overcharge it. Will such a law have good results, or will it encourage irresponsible whistle blowing?

NOTES

1. "Transfer or Be Fired, Whistle Blower Told," *Bakersfield Californian*, March 18, 1983.

2. See Ronald B. Taylor, "Making Waves: Whistle-Blower Keeps Heat on Navy in Revealing Waste of Millions of Dollars," *Los Angeles Times*, June 26, 1984.

3. Keith Davis and Robert L. Blomstrom, *Business and Society* (New York: McGraw-Hill, 1975), 182. See also Manuel G. Velasquez, *Business Ethics*, 2nd ed. (Englewood Cliffs, N.J.: Prentice-Hall, 1988), 358.

4. "Lance: Going, Going . . . " *Newsweek*, September 19, 1977, 7. The details reported here can be found in this article.

5. Douglas Frantz, "Genentech Chief's Wife Settles SEC's Insider Trading Charges," *Los Angeles Times*, November 21, 1990, D1.

6. John A. C. Hetherington, "Corporate Social Responsibility, Stockholders, and the Law," *Journal of Contemporary Business* (Winter 1973): 51.

7. "Texas Gulf Ruled to Lack Diligence in Minerals Case," *Wall Street Journal* (Midwest Edition), February 9, 1970, 1.

8. "SEC, Professor Split on Insider Trades," *Wall Street Journal*, March 2, 1984, 8.

9. Ibid. See also Bill Shaw, "Should Insider Trading Be Outside the Law?" *Business and Society Review* 66 (Summer 1988).

10. See "Cookie Cloak and Dagger," *Time*, September 10, 1984, 44.

11. On recent legal developments, see "The Battle Raging Over 'Intellectual Property,'" *Business Week*, May 22, 1989.

12. Sissela Bok, *Secrets* (New York: Vintage, 1983), 136.

13. See Michael S. Baram, "Trade Secrets: What Price Loyalty?" reprinted below.

14. Kim Murphy, "Accountant for ZZZZ Best Convicted of Fraud," *Los Angeles Times*, December 20, 1988, II-1.

15. Bill Shaw, "Foreign Corrupt Practices Act: A Legal and Moral Analysis," *Journal of Business Ethics* 7 (October 1988): 789–790.

16. *San Francisco Chronicle*, March 4, 1991, A7.

17. Normal C. Miller, "U.S. Business Overseas: Back to Bribery?" *Wall Street Journal*, April 30, 1981, 22.

18. Calvin Sims, "Ex-U.S. Official Admits Guilt on Phone Contract," *New York Times*, May 24, 1989, C2.

19. David Johnston, "Boning Up on New Ethics of Procurement," *New York Times*, May 24, 1989, A16.

20. Andy Pasztor, "Speaking Up Gets Biologist into Big Fight," *Wall Street Journal*, November 26, 1980, sec. 2, 25.

21. Norman Bowie, *Business Ethics* (Englewood Cliffs, N.J.: Prentice-Hall, 1982), 142.

22. Bok, *Secrets*, Chapter 14.

23. Alan F. Westin, "Michigan's Law to Protect the Whistle Blowers," *Wall Street Journal*, April 13, 1981, 18.

24. Gilbert Cranberg, "*Wall Street Journal* Case Could Bring Overreaction," *Los Angeles Times*, June 4, 1984, II-5.

25. See "Media Policies Vary on Preventing Employees and Others from Profiting on Knowledge of Future Business Stories," *Wall Street Journal*, March 2, 1984, 8.

26. Ibid.

27. "Market Leaks: Illegal Insider Trading Seems to Be on Rise," *Wall Street Journal*, March 2, 1984, 8.

28. "Media Policies . . . ," *Wall Street Journal*, 8.

29. Ibid.

30. See William A. Henry, III, "Impropriety or Criminality?" *Time*, September 10, 1984, 45.

31. Cranberg, "Case Could Bring Overreaction," 5.

32. Henry, "Impropriety or Criminality?" 43.

33. See Paul Blustein, "Mobil President's Son Sold Tankers to Mobil in an Uncertain Market," *Wall Street Journal*, April 6, 1983, 1. This article served as the primary source of the material reported in this case, and all quotations in this case presentation are from this article.

34. The facts and quotations in this case are drawn from Ronald B. Taylor, "Making Waves: Whistle Blower Keeps Heat on Navy in Revealing Waste of Millions of Dollars," *Los Angeles Times*, June 26, 1984.

What Is Really Unethical about Insider Trading?

Jennifer Moore

In this article Jennifer Moore examines the principal ethical arguments against insider trading: the claim that the practice is unfair, the claim that it involves a "misappropriation" of information, and the claim that it harms ordinary investors. She concludes that each of these arguments has serious deficiencies and that none of them suffices to outlaw insider trading. Instead, she argues that the real reason for prohibiting insider trading is that it undermines the fiduciary relationship that lies at the heart of American business.

This paper is divided into two parts. In the first part, I examine critically the principal ethical arguments against insider trading. The arguments fall into three main classes: arguments based on fairness, arguments based on property rights in information, and arguments based on harm to ordinary investors or the market as a whole. Each of these arguments, I contend, has some serious deficiencies. No one of them by itself provides a sufficient reason for outlawing insider trading. This does not mean, however, that there are no reasons for prohibiting the practice. Once we have cleared away the inadequate arguments, other, more cogent reasons for outlawing insider trading come to light. In the second part of the paper, I set out what I take to be the real reasons for laws against insider trading.

The term "insider trading" needs some preliminary clarification. Both the SEC and the courts have strongly resisted pressure to define the notion clearly. In 1961, the SEC stated that corporate insiders—such as officers or directors—in possession of material, non-public information were required to disclose that information or to refrain from trading.[1] But this "disclose or refrain" rule has since been extended to persons other than corporate insiders. People who get information from insiders ("tippees") and those who become "temporary insiders" in the course of some work they perform for the company, can acquire the duty of insiders in some cases.[2] Financial printers and newspaper columnists, not "insiders' in the technical sense, have also been found guilty of insider trading.[3] Increasingly, the term "insider" has come to refer to the kind of information a person possesses rather than to the status of the person who trades on that information. My use of the term will reflect this ambiguity. In this paper, an "insider trader" is someone who trades in material, non-public information—not necessarily a corporate insider.

I. Ethical Arguments Against Insider Trading

Fairness

Probably the most common reason given for thinking that insider trading is unethical is that it is "unfair." For proponents of the fairness argument, the key feature of insider trading is the disparity of information between the two parties to the transaction. Trading should take place on a "level playing field," they argue, and disparities in information tilt the field toward one player and away from the other. There are two versions of the fairness argument: the first argues that insider trading is unfair because the two parties do not have *equal* information; the second argues that insider trading is unfair because the two parties do not have equal *access* to information. Let us look at the two versions one at a time.

According to the equal information argument, insider trading is unfair because one party to the transaction lacks information the other party has, and is thus at a disadvantage. Although this is a very strict notion of fairness, it has its proponents,[4] and hints of this view appear in some of the judicial opinions.[5] One proponent of the equal information argument is Saul Levmore, who claims that "fairness is achieved when insiders and outsiders are in equal positions. That is, a system is fair if we would not expect one group to envy the position of the other." As thus defined, Levmore claims, fairness "reflects the 'golden rule' of impersonal behavior—treating others as we would ourselves."[6] If

Journal of Business Ethics 9 (March 1990). Copyright ©1990 by D. Reidel Publishing Co. Reprinted by permission of Kluwer Academic Publishers.

Levmore is correct, then not just insider trading, but *all* transactions in which there is a disparity of information are unfair, and thus unethical. But this claim seems overly broad. An example will help to illustrate some of the problems with it.

Suppose I am touring Vermont and come across an antique blanket chest in the barn of a farmer, a chest I know will bring $2,500 back in the city. I offer to buy it for $75, and the farmer agrees. If he had known how much I could get for it back home, he probably would have asked a higher price—but I failed to disclose this information. I have profited from an informational advantage. Have I been unethical? My suspicion is that most people would say I have not. While knowing how much I could sell the chest for in the city is in the interest of the farmer, I am not morally obligated to reveal it. I am not morally obligated to tell those who deal with me *everything* that it would be in their interest to know. . . .

In general, it is only when I owe a *duty* to the other party that I am legally required to reveal all information that is in his interest. In such a situation, the other party believes that I am looking out for his interests, and I deceive him if I do not do so. Failure to disclose is deceptive in this instance because of the relationship of trust and dependence between the parties. But this suggests that trading on inside information is wrong, *not* because it violates a general notion of fairness, but because a breach of fiduciary duty is involved. Cases of insider trading in which no fiduciary duty of this kind is breached would not be unethical. . . .

The "equal information" version of the fairness argument seems to me to fail. However, it could be argued that insider trading is unfair because the insider has information that is not *accessible* to the ordinary investor. For proponents of this second type of fairness argument, it is not the insider's information advantage that counts, but the fact that this advantage is "unerodable," one that cannot be overcome by the hard work and ingenuity of the ordinary investor. No matter how hard the latter works, he is unable to acquire non-public information, because this information is protected by law.[7]

This type of fairness argument seems more promising, since it allows people to profit from informational advantages of their own making, but not from advantages that are built into the system. Proponents of this "equal access" argument would probably find my deal with the Vermont farmer unobjectionable, because information about antiques is not in principle unavailable to the farmer. The problem with the argument is that the notion of "equal access" is not very clear. What does it mean for two people to have equal access to information?

Suppose my pipes are leaking and I call a plumber to fix them. He charges me for the job, and benefits by the informational advantage he has over me. Most of us would not find this transaction unethical. True, I don't have "equal access" to the information needed to fix my pipes in any real sense, but I could have had this information had I chosen to become a plumber. The disparity of information in this case is simply something that is built into the fact that people choose to specialize in different areas. But just as I could have chosen to become a plumber, I could have chosen to become a corporate insider with access to legally protected information. . . .

One might argue that I have easier access to a plumber's information than I do to an insider trader's, since there are lots of plumbers from whom I can buy the information I seek.[8] The fact that insiders have a strong incentive to keep their information to themselves is a serious objection to insider trading. But if insider trading were made legal, insiders could profit not only from trading on their information, but also on selling it to willing buyers. Proponents of the practice argue that a brisk market in information would soon develop—indeed, it might be argued that such a market already exists, though in illegal and clandestine form.[9] . . .

The most interesting thing about the fairness argument is not that it provides a compelling reason to outlaw insider trading, but that it leads to issues we cannot settle on the basis of an abstract concept of fairness alone. The claim that parties to a transaction should have equal information, or equal access to information, inevitably raises questions about how informational advantages are (or should be) acquired, and when people are entitled to use them for profit. . . .

Property Rights in Information

As economists and legal scholars have recognized, information is a valuable thing, and it is possible to view it as a type of property. We already treat certain types of information as property: trade secrets, inventions, and so on—and protect them by law. Proponents of the property rights argument claim that material, non-public information is also a kind of property, and that insider trading is wrong because it involves a violation of property rights.

If inside information is a kind of property, whose property is it? How does information come to belong to one person rather than another? This is a very complex question, because information differs in many ways from other, more tangible sorts of property. But one influential argument is that information belongs to the people who discover, originate or "create" it. As Bill Shaw put it in a recent article, "the originator of the information (the individual or corporation that spent hard-earned bucks producing it) owns and controls this asset just as it does other proprietary goods."[10] Thus if a firm agrees to a deal, invents a new product, or discovers new natural resources, it has a property right in that information and is entitled to exclusive use of it for its own profit.

It is important to note that it is the firm itself (and/or its shareholders), and not the individual employees of the firm, who have property rights in the information. To be sure, it is always certain individuals in the firm who put together the deal, invent the product, or discover the resources. But they are able to do this only because they are backed by the power and authority of the firm. The employees of the firm—managers, officers, directors—are not entitled to the information any more than they are entitled to corporate trade secrets or patents on products that they develop for the firm.[11] It is the firm that makes it possible to create the information and that makes the information valuable once it has been created. As Victor Brudney puts it,

> The insiders have acquired the information at the expense of the enterprise, and for the purpose of conducting the business for the collective good of all the stockholders, entirely apart from personal benefits from trading in its securities. There is no reason for them to be entitled to trade for their own benefit on the basis of such information. . . . [12]

If this analysis is correct, then it suggests that insider trading is wrong because it is a form of theft. It is not exactly like theft, because the person who uses inside information does not deprive the company of the use of the information. But he does deprive the company of the *sole* use of the information, which is itself an asset. The insider trader "misappropriates," as the laws puts it, information that belongs to the company and uses it in a way in which it was not intended—for personal profit. It is not surprising that this "misappropriation theory" has begun to take hold in the courts, and has become one of the predominant rationales in prosecuting insider trading cases. In *U.S. v. Newman*, a case involving investment bankers and securities traders, for example, the court stated:

> In *US* v. *Chiarella*, Chief Justice Burger . . . said that the defendant "misappropriated"—stole to put it bluntly—"valuable nonpublic information entrusted to him in the utmost confidence." That characterization aptly describes the conduct of the connivers in the instant case. . . . By sullying the reputations of [their] employers as safe repositories of client confidences, appellee and his cohorts defrauded those employers as surely as if they took their money.[13]

The misappropriation theory also played a major role in the prosecution of R. Foster Winans, a *Wall Street Journal* reporter who traded on and leaked to others the contents of his "Heard in the Street" column.[14]

This theory is quite persuasive, as far as it goes. But it is not enough to show that insider trading is always unethical or that it should be illegal. If insider information is really the property of the firm that produces it, then using that property is wrong *only when the firm prohibits it*. If the firm does not prohibit insider trading, it seems perfectly acceptable.[15] Most companies do in fact forbid insider trading. But it is not clear whether they do so because they don't want their employees using corporate property for profit or simply because it is illegal. Proponents of insider trading point out that most corporations did not prohibit insider trading until recently, when it became a prime concern of enforcement agencies. . . . [16]

A crucial factor here would be the shareholders' agreement to allow insider information. Shareholders may not wish to allow trading on inside information because they may wish the employees of the company to be devoted simply to advancing shareholder interests. We will return to this point below. But if shareholders did allow it, it would seem to be permissible. Still others argue that shareholders would not need to "agree" in any way other than to be told this information when they were buying the stock. If they did not want to hold stock in a company whose employees were permitted to trade in inside information, they would not buy that stock. Hence they could be said to have "agreed."

Manne and other proponents of insider trading have suggested a number of reasons why "shareholders would voluntarily enter into contractual arrangements with insiders giving them property rights in valuable information."[17] Their principal argument is that permitting insider trading would serve as an incentive to create more information — put together more deals, invent more new products, or make more discoveries. Such an incentive, they argue, would create more profit for shareholders in the long run. Assigning employees the right to trade on inside information could take the place of more traditional (and expensive) elements in the employee's compensation package. Rather than giving out end of the year bonuses, for example, firms could allow employees to put together their own bonuses by cashing in on inside information, thus saving the company money. In addition, proponents argue, insider trading would improve the efficiency of the market. We will return to these claims below.

If inside information really is a form of corporate property, firms may assign employees the right to trade on it if they choose to do so. The only reason for not permitting firms to allow employees to trade on their information would be that doing so causes harm to other investors or to society at large. Although our society values property rights very highly, they are not absolute. We do not hesitate to restrict property rights if their exercise causes significant harm to others. The permissibility of insider trading, then, ultimately seems to depend on whether the practice is harmful.

Harm

There are two principal harm-based arguments against insider trading. The first claims that the practice is harmful to ordinary investors who engage in trades with insiders; the second claims that insider trading erodes investors' confidence in the market, causing them to pull out of the market and harming the market as a whole. I will address the two arguments in turn.

Although proponents of insider trading often refer to it as a "victimless crime," implying that no one is harmed by it, it is not difficult to think of examples of transactions with insiders in which ordinary investors are made worse off. Suppose I have placed an order with my broker to sell my shares in Megalith Co., currently trading at $50 a share, at $60 or above. An insider knows that Behemoth Inc. is going to announce a tender offer for Megalith shares in two days, and has begun to buy large amounts of stock in anticipation of the gains. Because of his market activity, Megalith stock rises to $65 a share and my order is triggered. If he had refrained from trading, the price would have risen steeply two days later, and I would have been able to sell my shares for $80. Because the insider traded, I failed to realize the gains that I otherwise would have made.

But there are other examples of transactions in which ordinary investors *benefit* from insider trading. Suppose I tell my broker to sell my shares in Acme Corp., currently trading at $45, if the price drops to $40 or lower. An insider knows of an enormous class action suit to be brought against Acme in two days. He sells his shares, lowering the price to $38 and triggering my sale. When the suit is made public two days later, the share price plunges to $25. If the insider had abstained from trading, I would have lost far more than I did. Here, the insider has protected me from loss. . . .

The truth about an ordinary investor's gains and losses from trading with insiders seems to be not that insider trading is never harmful, but that it is not systematically or consistently harmful. Insider trading is not a "victimless crime," as its proponents claim, but it is often difficult to tell exactly who the victims are and to what extent they have been victimized. The stipulation of the law to "disclose *or* abstain" from trading makes determining victims even more complex. While some investors are harmed by the insider's trade, to others the insider's actions make no difference at all; what harms them is simply *not having complete information* about the stock in question. Forbidding insider trading will not prevent these harms. Investors who neither buy nor sell, or who buy or sell for reasons independent of share price, fall into this category.

Permitting insider trading would undoubtedly make the securities market *riskier* for ordinary investors. Even proponents of the practice seem to agree with this claim. But if insider trading were permitted openly, they argue, investors would compensate for the extra riskiness by demanding a discount in share price:

> In modern finance theory, shareholders are seen as investors seeking a return proportionate with that degree of systematic or market-related risk which they have chosen to incur. . . . [The individual investor] is "protected" by the price established by the market mechanism, not by his personal bargaining power or position. . . . To return to the gambling analogy, if I know you are using percentage dice, I won't play without an appropriate adjustment of the odds; the game is, after all, voluntary.[18]

If insider trading were permitted, in short, we could expect a general drop in share prices, but no net harm to investors would result. Moreover, improved efficiency would result in a bigger pie for everyone. These are empirical claims, and I am not equipped to determine if they are true. If they are, however, they would defuse one of the most important objections to insider trading, and provide a powerful argument for leaving the control of inside information up to individual corporations.

The second harm-based argument claims that permitting insider trading would cause ordinary investors to lose confidence in the market and cease to invest there, thus harming the market as a whole. As former SEC Chairman John Shad puts it, "if people get the impression that they're playing against a marked deck, they're simply not going to be willing to invest."[19] Since capital markets play a crucial role in allocating resources in our economy, this objection is a very serious one.

The weakness of the argument is that it turns almost exclusively on the *feelings* or *perceptions* of ordinary investors, and does not address the question of whether these perceptions are justified. If permitting insider trading really does harm ordinary investors, then this "loss of confidence" argument becomes a compelling reason for outlawing insider trading. But if, as many claim, the practice does not harm ordinary investors, then the sensible course of action is to educate the investors, not to outlaw insider trading. It is irrational to cater to the feelings of ordinary investors if those feelings are not justified. We ought not to outlaw perfectly permissible actions just because some people feel (un-

justifiably) disadvantaged by them. More research is needed to determine the actual impact of insider trading on the ordinary investor.[20]

II. Is There Anything Wrong with Insider Trading?

My contention has been that the principal ethical arguments against insider trading do not, by themselves, suffice to show that the practice is unethical and should be illegal. The strongest arguments are those that turn on the notion of a fiduciary duty to act in the interest of shareholders, or on the idea of inside information as company "property." But in both arguments, the impermissibility of insider trading depends on a contractual understanding among the company, its shareholders and its employees. In both cases, a modification of this understanding could change the moral status of insider trading.

Does this mean that there is nothing wrong with insider trading? No. If insider trading is unethical, it is so *in the context* of the relationship among the firm, its shareholders and its employees. It is possible to change this context in a way that makes the practice permissible. But *should* the context be changed? I will argue that it should not. Because it threatens the fiduciary relationship that is central to business management, I believe, permitting insider trading is in the interest neither of the firm, its shareholders, nor society at large.

Fiduciary relationships are relationships of trust and dependence in which one party acts in the interest of another. They appear in many contexts, but are absolutely essential to conducting business in a complex society. Fiduciary relationships allow parties with different resources, skills and information to cooperate in productive activity. Shareholders who wish to invest in a business, for example, but who cannot or do not wish to run it themselves, hire others to manage it for them. Managers, directors, and to some extent, other employees, become fiduciaries for the firms they manage and for the shareholders of those firms.

The fiduciary relationship is one of moral and legal obligation. Fiduciaries, that is, are bound to act in the interests of those who depend on them even if these interests do not coincide with their own. Typically, however, fiduciary relationships are constructed as far as possible so that the interests of the fiduciaries and the parties for whom they act *do* coincide. Where the interests of the two parties compete or conflict, the fiduciary relationship is threatened. In corporations, the attempt to discourage divergences of interest is exemplified in rules against bribery, usurping corporate opportunities, and so forth. In the past few years, an entire discipline, "agency theory," has developed to deal with such questions. Agency theorists seek ways to align the interests of agents or fiduciaries with the interests of those on behalf of whom they act.

Significantly, proponents of insider trading do not dispute the importance of the fiduciary relationship. Rather, they argue that permitting insider trading would *increase* the likelihood that employees will act in the interest of shareholders and their firms.[21] We have already touched on the main argument for this claim. Manne and others contend that assigning employees the right to trade on inside information would provide a powerful incentive for creative and entrepreneurial activity. It would encourage new inventions, creative deals, and efficient new management practices, thus increasing the profits, strength, and overall competitiveness of the firm. Manne goes so far as to argue that permission to trade on insider information is the only appropriate way to compensate entrepreneurial activity, and warns: "[I]f no way to reward the entrepreneur within a corporation exists, he will tend to disappear from the corporate scene."[22] The entrepreneur makes an invaluable contribution to the firm and its shareholders, and his disappearance would no doubt cause serious harm.

If permitting insider trading is to work in the way proponents suggest, however, there must be a direct and consistent link between the profits reaped by insider traders and the performance that benefits the firm. It is not at all clear that this is the case—indeed, there is evidence that the opposite is true. There appear to be many ways to profit from inside information that do not benefit the firm at all. I mention four possibilities below. Two of these (2 and 3) are simply ways in which insider traders can profit without benefiting the firm, suggesting that permitting insider trading is a poor incentive for performance and fails firmly to link the interests of managers, directors and employees to those of the corporation as a whole. The others (1 and 4) are

actually harmful to the corporation, setting up conflicts of interest and actively undermining the fiduciary relationship.[23]

(1) Proponents of insider trading tend to speak as if all information were positive. "Information," in the proponents' lexicon, always concerns a creative new deal, a new, efficient way of conducting business, or a new product. If this were true, allowing trades on inside information might provide an incentive to work ever harder for the good of the company. But information can also concern *bad* news—a large lawsuit, an unsafe or poor quality product, or lower-than-expected performance. Such negative information can be just as valuable to the insider trader as positive information. If the freedom to trade on positive information encourages acts that are beneficial to the firm, then by the same reasoning the freedom to trade on negative information would encourage harmful acts. At the very least, permitting employees to profit from harms to the company decreases the incentive to avoid such harms. Permission to trade on negative inside information gives rise to inevitable conflicts of interest. Proponents of insider trading have not satisfactorily answered this objection.[24]

(2) Proponents of insider trading also assume that the easiest way to profit on inside information is to "create" it. But it is not at all clear that this is true. Putting together a deal, inventing a new product, and other productive activities that add value to the firm usually require a significant investment of time and energy. For the well-placed employee, it would be far easier to start a rumor that the company has a new product or is about to announce a deal than to sit down and produce either one—and it would be just as profitable for the employee. If permitting insider trading provides an incentive for the productive "creation" of information, it seems to provide an even greater incentive for the nonproductive "invention" of information, or stock manipulation. The invention of information is in the interest neither of the firm nor of society at large.

(3) Even if negative or false information did not pose problems, the incentive argument for insider trading overlooks the difficulties posed by "free riders"—those who do not actually contribute to the creation of the information, but who are nevertheless aware of it and can profit by trading on it. . . . Unless those who do not contribute can be ex-

cluded from trading on it, there will be no incentive to produce the desired information; it will not get created at all.

(4) Finally, allowing trading on inside information would tend to deflect employees' attention from the day-to-day business of running the company and focus it on major changes, positive or negative, that lead to large insider trading profits. This might not be true if one could profit by inside information about the day-to-day efficiency of the operation, a continuous tradition of product quality, or a consistently lean operating budget. But these things do not generate the kind of information on which insider traders can reap large profits. Insider profits come from dramatic changes, from "news" — not from steady, long-term performance. If the firm and its shareholders have a genuine interest in such performance, then permitting insider trading creates a conflict of interest for insiders. The ability to trade on inside information is also likely to influence the types of information officers announce to the public, and the timing of such announcements, making it less likely that the information and its timing is optimal for the firm. And the problems of false or negative information remain.[25]

If the arguments given above are correct, permitting insider trading does not increase the likelihood that insiders will act in the interest of the firm and its shareholders. In some cases, it actually causes conflicts of interest, undermining the fiduciary relationship essential to managing the corporation. This claim, in turn, gives corporations good reason to prohibit the practice. But insider trading remains primarily a private matter among corporations, shareholders, and employees. It is appropriate to ask why, given this fact about insider trading, the practice should be *illegal*. If it is primarily corporate and shareholder interests that are threatened by insider trading, why not let corporations themselves bear the burden of enforcement? Why involve the SEC? There are two possible reasons for continuing to support laws against insider trading. The first is that even if they wish to prohibit insider trading, individual corporations do not have the resources to do so effectively. The second is that society itself has a stake in the fiduciary relationship. . . .

The notion of the fiduciary duty owed by managers and other employees to the firm and its shareholders has a long and venerable history in our society. Nearly all of our important activities require some sort of cooperation, trust, or reliance on others, and the ability of one person to act in the interest of another — as a fiduciary — is central to this cooperation. The role of managers as fiduciaries for firms and shareholders is grounded in the property rights of shareholders. They are the owners of the firm, and bear the residual risks, and hence have a right to have it managed in their interest. The fiduciary relationship also contributes to efficiency, since it encourages those who are willing to take risks to place their resources in the hands of those who have the expertise to maximize their usefulness. While this "shareholder theory" of the firm has often been challenged in recent years, this has been primarily by people who argue that the fiduciary concept should be widened to include other "stakeholders" in the firm.[26] I have heard no one argue that the notion of managers' fiduciary duties should be eliminated entirely, and that managers should begin working primarily for themselves.

III. Conclusion

I have argued that the real reason for prohibiting insider trading is that it erodes the fiduciary relationship that lies at the heart of our business organizations. The more frequently heard moral arguments based on fairness, property rights in information, and harm to ordinary investors, are not compelling. Of these, the fairness arguments seem to me the least persuasive. The claim that a trader must reveal everything that it is in the interest of another party to know, seems to hold up only when the other is someone to whom he owes a fiduciary duty. But this is not really a "fairness" argument at all. Similarly, the "misappropriation" theory is only persuasive if we can offer reasons for corporations not to assign the right to trade on inside information to their employees. I have found these in the fact that permitting insider trading threatens the fiduciary relationship. I do believe that lifting the ban against insider trading would cause harms to shareholders, corporations, and society at large. But again, these harms stem primarily from the cracks in the fiduciary relationship caused by permitting insider trading, rather than from actual trades with insiders. Violation of fiduciary duty, in short, is at the center of insider trading offenses . . .

Notes

1. *In re Cady, Roberts,* 40 SEC 907 (1961).

2. On tippees, see *Dirks v. SEC,* 463 US 646 (1983) at 659; on "temporary insiders," see *Dirks v. SEC,* 103 S. Ct. 3255 (1983) at 3261 n. 14, and *SEC v. Musella* 578 F. Supp. 425.

3. See *Materia v. SEC,* 725 F. 2d 197, involving a financial printer and the Winans case, involving the author of the *Wall Street Journal*'s "Heard on the Street" column, *Carpenter v. US,* 56 LW 4007; *U.S. v. Winans,* 612 F. Supp. 827. It should be noted that the Supreme Court has not wholeheartedly endorsed these further extensions of the rule against insider trading.

4. See Kaplan, "*Wolf v. Weinstein:* Another Chapter on Insider Trading," 1963 *Supreme Court Review* 273. For numerous other references, see Brudney, "Insiders, Outsiders and Informational Advantages Under the Federal Securities Laws," 93 *Harvard Law Review* 339, n. 63.

5. See *Mitchell v. Texas Gulf Sulphur Co.,* 446 F. 2d. 90 (1968) at 101; *SEC v. Great American Industries,* 407 F. 2d. 453 (1968) at 462; *Birdman v. Electro-Catheter Corp.,* 352 F. Supp. 1271 (1973) at 1274.

6. Saul Levmore, "Securities and Secrets: Insider Trading and the Law of Contracts," 68 *Virginia Law Review* 117.

7. The equal access argument is perhaps best stated by Victor Brudney in his influential article, "Insiders, Outsiders and Informational Advantages Under the Federal Securities Laws," 93 *Harvard Law Review* 322.

8. Robert Frederick brought this point to my attention.

9. Manne, *Insider Trading and the Stock Market* (Free Press, New York, 1966), p. 75.

10. Bill Shaw, "Should Insider Trading Be Outside The Law?" *Business and Society Review* 66, p. 34. See also Macey, "From Fairness to Contract: The New Direction of the Rules Against Insider Trading," 13 *Hofstra Law Review* 9 (1984).

11. Easterbrook points out the striking similarity between insider trading cases and cases involving trade secrets, and cites *Perrin v. US,* 444 US 37 (1979), in which the court held that it was a federal crime to sell confidential corporate information.

12. Brudney, "Insiders, Outsiders, and Informational Advantages," 344.

13. *U.S. v. Newman,* 664 F. 2d 17.

14. *U.S. v. Winans,* 612 F. Supp. 827. The Supreme Court upheld Winans' conviction, but was evenly split on the misappropriation theory. As a consequence, the Supreme Court has still not truly endorsed the theory, although several lower court decisions have been based on it. *Carpenter v. U.S.,* 56 LW 4007.

15. Unless there is some other reason for forbidding it, such as that it harms others. See p. 395 below.

16. Easterbrook, "Insider Trading as an Agency Problem," *Principals and Agents: The Structure of Business* (Harvard University Press, Cambridge, MA, 1985).

17. Carlton and Fischel, "The Regulation of Insider Trading," 35 *Stanford Law Review* 857. See also Manne, *Insider Trading and the Stock Market.*

18. Kenneth Scott, "Insider Trading: Rule 10b–5, Disclosure and Corporate Privacy," 9 *Journal of Legal Studies* 808.

19. "Disputes Arise Over Value of Laws on Insider Trading," *The Wall Street Journal,* November 17, 1986, p. 28.

20. One area that needs more attention is the impact of insider trading on the markets (and ordinary investors) of countries that permit the practice. Proponents of insider trading are fond of pointing out that insider trading has been legal in many overseas markets for years, without the dire effects predicted by opponents of the practice. Proponents reply that these markets are not as fair or efficient as U.S. markets, or that they do not play as important a role in the allocation of capital.

21. See Frank Easterbrook, "Insider Trading as an Agency Problem." I speak here as if the interests of the firm and its shareholders are identical, even though this is sometimes not the case.

22. Manne, *Insider Trading and the Stock Market,* p. 129.

23. For a more detailed discussion of the ineffectiveness of permitting insider trading as an incentive, see Roy Schotland, "Unsafe at any Price: A Reply to Manne, *Insider Trading and the Stock Market,*" 53 *Virginia Law Review* 1425.

24. Manne is aware of the "bad news" objection, but he glosses over it by claiming that bad news is not as likely as good news to provide large gains for insider traders. *Insider Trading and the Stock Market,* p. 102.

25. There are ways to avoid many of these objections. For example, Manne has suggested "isolating" non-contributors so that they cannot trade on the information produced by others. Companies could also forbid trading on "negative" information. The

problem is that these piecemeal restrictions seem very costly — more costly than simply prohibiting insider trading as we do now. In addition, each restriction brings us farther and farther away from what proponents of the practice actually want: unrestricted insider trading.

26. See Freeman and Gilbert, *Corporate Strategy and the Search for Ethics* (Prentice-Hall, Englewood Cliffs, NJ, 1988).

Review and Discussion Questions

1. Do you agree with Moore's criticism of the fairness argument, or is there something unethical about transactions between parties that lack equal information or equal access to information?

2. If insider trading were not illegal, would it be in the interest of firms to prohibit it?

3. Critics of insider trading argue that permitting it would cause ordinary investors to lose confidence in the market. Is Moore right to reject this argument so quickly?

4. What are fiduciary relationships, and what is their role in business? Would insider trading undermine such relationships, as Moore argues? Is this a sufficient reason for outlawing insider trading?

5. Are there any arguments against or for insider trading that Moore has overlooked or paid insufficient attention to?

Trade Secrets: What Price Loyalty?

Michael S. Baram

The problem of employees leaving firms and taking with them proprietary data raises a number of operational and moral concerns, especially in the research and development (R&D) sector of the economy. As Michael S. Baram, attorney and executive officer of the graduate school of the Massachusetts Institute of Technology, points out in the following article, employee mobility and high personnel turnover in R&D threaten industrial reliance on trade secrets for the protection of certain forms of intellectual property. There's no question that safeguarding the right of the corporation to its trade secrets while upholding the right of employees to depart for more favorable job opportunities poses difficult legal, practical, and ethical questions. Baram examines these seemingly irreconcilable interests and presents a five-step management approach to meet the challenge.

In 1963, the Court of Appeals of Ohio heard an appeal of a lower court decision from the B. F. Goodrich Company. The lower court had denied Goodrich's request for an injunction, or court order, to restrain a former employee, Donald Wohlgemuth, from disclosing its trade secrets and from working in the space suit field for any other company.

This case, as it was presented in the Court of Appeals, is a fascinating display of management issues, legal concepts, and ethical dilemmas of concern to research and development organizations and their scientist and engineer employees. The case also represents an employer-employee crisis of increasing incidence in the young and vigorous R&D sector of U.S. industry. Tales of departing employees and threatened losses of trade secrets or proprietary information are now common.

Such crises are not surprising when one considers the causes of mobility. The highly educated employees of R&D organizations place primary emphasis on their own development, interests, and satisfaction. Graduates of major scientific and technological institutions readily admit that they accept their first jobs primarily for money and for the early and brief experience they feel is a prerequisite for seeking more satisfying futures with smaller companies which are often their own. Employee mobility and high personnel turnover rates are also due to the placement of new large federal contracts and the termination of others. One need only look to the Sunday newspaper employment advertisements for evidence as to the manner in which such programs are used to attract highly educated R&D personnel.

This phenomenon of the mobile employee seeking fulfillment reflects a sudden change in societal and personal values. It also threatens industrial reliance on trade secrets for the protection of certain forms of intellectual property. There are no union solutions, and the legal framework in which it occurs is an ancient structure representing values of an earlier America. The formulation of management responses—with cognizance of legal, practical, and ethical considerations—is admittedly a difficult task, but one which must be undertaken.

In this article I shall examine the basic question of industrial loyalty regarding trade secrets, using the Goodrich-Wohlgemuth case as the focal point of the challenge to the preservation of certain forms of intellectual property posed by the mobile employee, and then offer some suggestions for the development of sound management policies.

The Appeals Case

Donald Wohlgemuth joined the B. F. Goodrich Company as a chemical engineer in 1954, following his graduation from the University of Michigan, and by 1962 he had become manager of the space suit division. As the repository of Goodrich know-how and secret data in space suit technology, he was indeed a key man in a rapidly developing technology of interest to several government agencies. Nevertheless, he was dissatisfied with his salary ($10,644) and the denial of his requests for certain additional facilities for his department

A Goodrich rival, International Latex, had recently been awarded the major space suit subcontract for the Apollo program. Following up a contact from an employment agency hired by Latex, Wohlgemuth negotiated a position with Latex, at a substantial salary increase. In his new assignment he would be manager of engineering for industrial products, which included space suits. He then notified Goodrich of his resignation, and was met with a reaction he apparently did not expect. Goodrich management raised the moral and ethical aspects of his decision, since the company executives felt his resignation would result in the transfer of Goodrich trade secrets to Latex.

After several heated exchanges, Wohlgemuth stated that "loyalty and ethics have their price and International Latex has paid the price. . . ." Even though Goodrich threatened legal action, Wohlgemuth left Goodrich for Latex. Goodrich thereupon requested a restraining order in the Ohio courts.

At the appeals court level, the Goodrich brief sought an injunction that would prevent Wohlgemuth from working in the space field for *any* other company, prevent his disclosure of *any* information or space suit technology to *anyone*, prevent his consulting or conferring with *anyone* on Goodrich trade secrets, and finally, prevent *any* future contact he might seek with Goodrich employees.

These four broad measures were rejected by the Ohio Court of Appeals. All were too wide in scope, and all would have protected much more than Goodrich's legitimate concern of safeguarding its trade secrets. In addition, the measures were speculative, since no clear danger seemed imminent. In sum, they represented a form of "overkill" that would have placed undue restraints on Wohlgemuth.

The court did provide an injunction restraining Wohlgemuth from disclosure of Goodrich trade secrets. In passing, the court noted that in the absence of any Goodrich employment contract restraining his employment with a competitor, Wohlgemuth could commence work with Latex. With ample legal precedent, the court therefore came down on both sides of the fence. Following the decision, Wohlgemuth commenced his career with Latex and is now manager of the company's Research and Engineering Department.

Common-Law Concepts

The two basic issues in crises such as the Goodrich-Wohlgemuth case appear irreconcilable: (1) the right of the corporation to its intellectual property—its proprietary data or trade secrets; and (2) the right of the individual to seek gainful employment and utilize his abilities—to be free from a master-servant relationship.

There are no federal and but a few state statutes dealing with employment restraints and trade secrets. The U.S. courts, when faced with such issues, have sought to apply the various common-law doctrines of trade secrets and unfair competition at hand to attain an equitable solution. Many of these common-law doctrines were born in pre-industrial England and later adopted by English and U.S. courts to meet employment crises of this nature through ensuing centuries of changing industrial and social patterns. In fact, some of the early cases of blacksmiths and barbers seeking to restrain departing apprentices are still cited today.

To the courts, the common legal solution, as in *Goodrich* v. *Wohlgemuth*, is pleasing because it theoretically preserves the rights of both parties. However, it is sadly lacking in practicality, since neither secrets nor individual liberty are truly preserved.

The trade secrets which companies seek to protect have usually become an integral portion of the departing employee's total capabilities. He cannot divest himself of his intellectual capacity, which is a compound of information acquired from his employer, his co-workers, and his own self-generated experiential information. Nevertheless, all such information, if kept secret by the company from its competition, may legitimately be claimed as corporate property. This is because the employer-employee relationship embodied in the normal employment contract or other terms of employment provides for corporate ownership of all employee-generated data, including inventions. As a result, a departing employee's intellectual capacity may be, in large measure, corporate property.

Once the new position with a competitor has been taken, the trade secrets embodied in the departing employee may manifest themselves quite clearly and consciously. This is what court injunctions seek to prohibit. But, far more likely, the trade secrets will manifest themselves subconsciously and in various forms—for example, as in the daily decisions by the employee at his new post, or in the many small contributions he makes to a large team effort—often in the form of an intuitive sense of what or what not to do, as he seeks to utilize his overall intellectual capacity. Theoretically, a legal injunction also serves to prohibit such "leakage." However, the former employer faces the practical problem of securing evidence of such leakage, for little will be apparent from the public activities and goods of the new employer. And if the new employer's public activities or goods appear suspicious, there is also the further problem of distinguishing one's trade secrets from what may be legitimately asserted as the self-generated technological skills or state of the art of the new employer and competitor which were utilized.

This is a major stumbling block in the attempt to protect one's trade secrets, since the possessor has no recourse against others who independently generate the same information. It is therefore unlikely that an injunction against disclosure of trade secrets to future employers prevents any "unintentional" transfer (or even intentional transfer) of information, except for the passage of documents and other physical embodiments of the secrets. In fact, only a lobotomy, as yet not requested nor likely to be sanctioned by the courts, would afford security against the transfer of most trade secrets.

Conversely, the departing employee bears the terrible burden of sensitivity. At his new post, subconscious disclosure and mental and physical utilization of what he feels to be no more than his own intellectual capacity may result in heated exchanges between companies, adverse publicity, and litigation. He is marked, insecure, and unlikely to contribute effectively in his new position. In fact, new co-workers may consider him to be a man with a price, and thus without integrity. Frequently, caution on the part of his new employer will result in transfer to a nonsensitive post where he is unlikely to contribute his full skills, unless he has overall capability and adaptability.

The fact that neither secrets nor individual liberty will be truly preserved rarely influences the course of litigation. Similarly, these practical considerations are usually negligible factors in the out-of-court settlements which frequently terminate such litigation, because the settlements primarily reflect the relative bargaining strengths of disputing parties.

Finally, there is the full cost of litigation to be considered. In addition to the obvious court costs and attorney's fees, there is the potentially great cost to the company's image. Although the drama enacted in court reflects legitimate corporate concerns, the public may easily fail to see more than an unequal struggle between the powerful corporate machine and a lonely individual harassed beyond his employment tenure. Prospective employees, particularly new and recent graduates whose early positions are stepping stones, may be reluctant to accept employment with what appears to be a vindictive and authoritarian organization.

Practical and Legal Aspects

Trade secrets are, of course, a common form of intellectual property. Secrecy is the most natural and the earliest known method of protecting the fruits of one's intellectual labors. Rulers of antiquity frequently had architects and engineers murdered, after completion of their work, to maintain secrecy and security. The medieval guilds and later the craftsmen of pre-industrial Europe and America imposed severe restraints on apprentices and their future activities.

Recognition and acceptance of the practice of protecting intellectual property by secrecy is found throughout Anglo-American common or judge-made law, but statutory protection has not been legislated. Perhaps the failure to do so is because of the recognition by the elected officials of industrial societies that secrecy is not in the public interest and that the widest dissemination of new works and advances in technology and culture is necessary for optical public welfare. . . .

To summarize this common law briefly, virtually all information—ranging from full descriptions of inventions to plant layouts, shop know-how, methods of quality control, customer and source lists, and marketing data—is eligible for protection as trade secrets. No standards of invention or originality are required. If such information is not known to the public or to the trade (or it is known but its utility is not recognized), and if such information is of value to its possessor, it is eligible for protection by the courts.

Further, and of greatest importance in terms of favorably impressing the courts, there must be evidence that the possessor recognized the value of his information and treated it accordingly. In the context of confidential relationships, "treatment" normally means that the possessor provided for limited or no disclosure of trade secrets. This means many things: for example, total prohibition of disclosure except to key company people on a need-to-know basis; provision of the information to licensees, joint ventures, or employees having contractual restraints against their unauthorized disclosure or use; division of employee responsibilities so that no employee is aware of more than a small segment of a particular process; and use in labs of unmarked chemicals and materials.

There must also be evidence that particular efforts were expended for the purpose of preserving secrecy for the specific data claimed as trade secrets. General company policies indiscriminately applied to data and employees or licensees will not suffice in the legal sense to convince the courts of the presence of trade secrets.

When the possessor and his information do fulfill such criteria, court recognition and the award of compensation to damaged parties, or injunctive restraints to protect parties in danger of imminent or further damage, will follow. If there is evidence of (a) breach of confidential relationships (contracts or licenses) which were established to preserve the secrecy of company information, (b) unauthorized copying and sale of secrets, or (c) conspiracy to damage the possessor, the courts will act with greater certitude. But in many cases, such as in the Goodrich-Wohlgemuth litigation, no such evidence is present.

Finally, the courts will not move to protect trade secrets when an action is brought by one party against another who independently generated similar information, or who "reverse-engineered" the publicly sold products of the party petitioning the court, unless there is some contractual, fiduciary, or other relationship based on trust connecting the parties in court.

Other Considerations

In addition to the foregoing practical and legal aspects, basic questions of industrial ethics and the equitable allocation of rights and risks should be examined to provide management with intelligent and humane responses to employer-employee crises that involved intellectual property. The patent and copyright systems for the stimulation and protection of such property are premised on dissemination of information and subsequent public welfare. These systems reflect public concern with the proper use of intellectual property, which the common law of trade secrets lacks.

Will the courts continue to utilize common-law concepts for the protection of trade secrets, when such concepts are based solely on the rights of the possessors of secret information, and when the application of such concepts has a detrimental effect on both the rights of employees and the public welfare? Since current court practice places the burden of industrial loyalty solely on the employee, the skilled individual has to pay the price. In other words, the law restricts the fullest utilization of his abilities. And the detrimental effect on public welfare can be inferred from recent federal studies of technology transfer, which indicate that employee mobility and the promotion of entrepreneurial activities are primary factors in the transfer of technology and the growth of new industries.

The continuation of trade secret concepts for the preservation of property rights in secret information at the expense of certain basic individual freedoms is unlikely. The law eventually reflects changing societal values, and the mobile R&D employee who seeks career fulfillment through a succession of jobs, frequently in sensitive trade secret areas, is now a reality — one not likely to disappear. Thus it is probable that the courts will eventually adopt the position that those who rely on trade secrets assume the realities or risks in the present context of public concern with technological progress and its relationship to the public good, and with the rights of the individual. Resulting unintentional leakage of secret information through the memory of a departing employee is now generally accepted as a reasonable price to pay for the preservation of these societal values. However, the courts will never condone the theft or other physical appropriation of secret information, nor are the courts likely to condone fraud, conspiracy, and other inequitable practices resulting in some form of unfair competition.

The failings of the statutory systems serve not as justification for the inequitable application of medieval trade secret concepts, but as the basis for legislative reform. Injunctive restraints against the unintentional leakage of secrets and the harassment of departing employees through litigation should not be part of our legal system. This is especially true when there is a growing body of evidence that management can respond, and has intelligently done so, to such crises without detriment to the individual employee, the public good, or the company itself.

Management Response

How then shall managers of research and development organizations respond to the reality of the mobile employee and his potential for damage to corporate trade secrets?

Contractual Restraints

Initial response is invariably consideration of the use of relevant contractual prohibitions on employees with such potential. For a minority of companies, this means the institution of employment contracts or other agreements concerning terms of employment. For most, a review of existing company contracts, which at a minimum provide for employee disclosure of inventions and company

ownership of subsequent patents, will be called for to determine the need for relevant restraints.

Contractual prohibitions vary somewhat, but they are clearly of two general types: (1) restraints against unauthorized disclosure and use of company trade secrets or proprietary information by employees during their employment tenure or at any time thereafter; (2) restraints against certain future activities of employees following their employment tenure.

A restraint against unauthorized disclosure or use is normally upheld in the courts, provided it is limited to a legitimate company concern — trade secrets. But it is usually ineffective, due to the unintentional leakage and subconscious utilization of trade secrets, and the difficulties of "policing" and proving violation, as discussed earlier. In fact, several authorities feel that this type of restraint is ineffective unless coupled with a valid restraint against future employment with competitors. . . .

Courts have been naturally reluctant to extend protection to trade secrets when the freedom of an individual to use his overall capability is at stake. In addition, the former employer faces the practical difficulty of convincing almost any court that a prohibition of future employment is necessary, since the court will look for clear and convincing evidence that the ex-employee has, or inevitably will, exercise more than the ordinary skill a man of his competence possesses. A few states — such as California by statute and others by consistent court action — now prohibit future employment restraints.

It therefore appears that a contractual prohibition of future employment in a broad area, which prevents an ex-employee from using his overall capability is invalid in most states. And a request for an injunction to prohibit such employment, without a prior contractual provision, stands an even poorer chance of success, as Goodrich learned when it sought to prevent Wohlgemuth from working in the space suit field for any other company. . . .

Internal Policies

Another response of R&D management to the mobile employee and his potential for damage to corporate trade secrets is the formulation of internal company policies for the handling of intellectual property of trade secret potential. Such policies may call for the prior review of publications and addresses of key employees, prohibition of consulting and other "moonlighting," dissemination of trade secrets on a strict "need to know" basis to designated employees, and prohibitions on the copying of trade secret data. More "physical" policies may restrict research and other operational areas to access for designated or "badge" employees only and divide up operations to prevent the accumulation of extensive knowledge by any individual—including safety and other general plant personnel. Several companies I know of distribute unmarked materials—particularly chemicals—to employees.

Although internal policies do not necessarily prevent future employment with competitors, they can serve to prevent undue disclosures and lessen the criticality of the departure of key personnel. All must be exercised with a sophisticated regard for employee motivation, however, because the cumulative effect may result in a police state atmosphere that inhibits creativity and repels prospective employees.

Several farsighted R&D organizations are currently experimenting with plans which essentially delegate the responsibility for nondisclosure and nonuse of their trade secrets to the key employees themselves. These plans include pension and consulting programs operative for a specified post-employment period. In one company, for example, the pension plan provides that the corporate monies which are contributed to the employee pension fund in direct ratio to the employee's own contributions will remain in his pension package following his term of employment, provided he does not work for a competing firm for a specified number of years. In another company, the consulting plan provides that certain departing employees are eligible to receive an annual consulting fee for a given number of years following employment if they do not work for a competitor. The consulting fee is a preestablished percentage of the employee's annual salary at the time of his departure.

Obviously, such corporate plans are subject to employee abuse, but if limited to truly key employees, they may succeed without abuse in most cases. They not only have the merit of providing the employee with a choice, an equitable feature likely to incur employee loyalty, but they also have no apparent legal defects.

Another valid internal practice is the debriefing of departing employees. The debriefing session, carried out in a low-key atmosphere, affords management an excellent opportunity to retrieve company materials and information in physical form, to impart to the employee a sense of responsibility regarding trade secrets and sensitive areas, and to discuss mutual anxieties in full.

External Procedures

Several management responses relating to external company policies are worth noting, as they also serve to protect trade secrets in cases involving employee departures. Among several industries, such as in the chemical field, it is common to find gentlemen's agreements which provide mutuality in the nonhiring of competitors' key employees, following notice. Employees who have encountered this practice have not found the experience a pleasant one. This same practice is also found in other areas, such as the industrial machinery industry, that are in need of innovation; and it appears that the presence of such agreements helps to depict these industries in an unappealing fashion to the types of employees they need.

Another external response for management consideration is company reliance on trademarks. Given a good mark and subsequent public identification of the product with the mark, a company may be able to maintain market despite the fact that its intellectual property is no longer a trade secret. Competitors may be hesitant about utilizing the former trade secrets of any company whose products are strongly identified with trademarks and with the company itself.

Some trade secrets are patentable, and management faced with the potential loss of such secrets should consider filing for patent protection. The application is treated confidentially by the U.S. Patent Office and some foreign patent offices up to the time of award. Moreover, if the application is rejected, the secrecy of the information is not legally diminished. In any case, the subject matter of the application remains secret throughout the two- to three-year period of time normally involved in U.S. Patent Office review.

Conclusion

A major concern of our society is progress through the promotion and utilization of new technology. To sustain and enhance this form of progress, it is necessary to optimize the flow of information and innovation all the way from conception to public use. This effort is now a tripartite affair involving federal agencies, industry, and universities. A unique feature of this tripartite relationship is the mobility of R&D managers, scientists, and engineers who follow contract funding and projects in accordance with their special competence. Neither the federal agencies nor the universities rely on trade secret concepts for the protection of their intellectual property. However, industry still does, despite the fact that trade secret concepts bear the potential ancillary effect of interfering with employee mobility.

It is becoming increasingly clear that new societal values associated with the tripartite approach to new technology are now evolving, and that the common law dispensed by the courts has begun to reflect these values. A victim of sorts is trade secret law, which has not only never been clearly defined, but which has indeed been sustained by court concepts of unfair competition, equity, and confidence derived from other fields of law. The day when courts restrict employee mobility to preserve industrial trade secrets appears to have passed, except— as we noted earlier—in cases involving highly charged factors such as conspiracy, fraud, or theft.

In short, it is now unwise for management to rely on trade secret law and derivative employee contractual restraints to preserve trade secrets. Companies must now carefully weigh the nature and value of their intellectual property, present and potential employees, competition, and applicable laws in order to formulate sound management policies.

Programmed Approach

Regarding the challenge to the preservation of trade secrets posed by the mobile employee, sophisticated management will place its primary reliance on the inculcation of company loyalty in key employees, and on the continual satisfaction of such key employees. For example, management might consider adopting the following five-step basis for developing an overall approach to the challenge:

1. Devise a program for recognition of employee achievement in the trade secret area. At present, this form of recognition is even more neglected than is adequate recognition of employee inventions.

2. Make an appraisal of trade secret activities. This should result in a limitation of (a) personnel with access to trade secrets, (b) the extent of trade secrets available to such personnel, and (c) information which truly deserves the label of trade secret.

3. Review in-house procedures and the use of physical safeguards, such as restrictions on access to certain specified areas and on employee writings for outside publication. Restrictions may tend to stifle creativity by inhibiting communication and interaction conducive to innovation. Striking the balance between too few and too many safeguards is a delicate process and depends on employee awareness of what is being sought and how it will benefit them.

4. Appraise the legal systems available for the protection of intellectual property. Utility and design patents may be advisable in some cases. The copyright system now offers some protection to certain types of industrial designs and computer software. Trademarks may be adroitly used to maintain markets.

5. Recognize that all efforts may fail to persuade a key employee from leaving. To cope with this contingency, the "gentle persuasion" of a pension or consulting plan in the post-employment period has proved effective and legally sound. A thorough debriefing is a further safeguard. Other cases wherein employee mobility is accompanied by fraud, unfair competition, or theft will be adequately dealt with by the courts.

The problem of the departing employee and the threatened loss of trade secrets is not solved by exhortations that scientists and engineers need courses in professional ethics. Management itself should display the standards of conduct expected of its employees and of other companies.

Finally, let me stress again that success probably lies in the inculcation of company loyalty in key employees, not in the enforcement of company desires or in misplaced reliance on the law to subsidize cursory management. Better employee relations—in fact, a total sensitivity to the needs and aspirations of highly educated employees—requires constant management concern. In the long run, total sensitivity will prove less costly and more effective than litigation and the use of questionable contractual restraints.

Review and Discussion Questions

1. What was at stake in the Wohlgemuth case? Do you think that Wohlgemuth behaved unethically? Should he have been more loyal to Goodrich? Did Goodrich overreact?

2. Explain why Baram is critical of the court's decision.

3. If an employee invents a new process for a company, who owns that knowledge? Does it make a difference to your assessment whether or not the skills that made the invention possible were acquired by the employee on the job?

4. What makes something a "trade secret"? Give examples both of information that would constitute a trade secret and of information that would not. In your opinion, how important are trade secrets in business today?

5. What problems face a company trying to protect its intellectual property? What steps would you recommend that it take? Why does Baram think that it is unwise for a company to rely on the trade-secrets law or on contractual restraints?

6. Baram emphasizes the importance of inculcating company loyalty in key employees. What does "company loyalty" mean to you? What, specifically, do employees owe the company in terms of loyalty?

A Business Traveler's Guide to Gifts and Bribes

Jeffrey A. Fadiman

Americans who travel on business to other lands frequently find themselves trying to do business against a backdrop of cultural patterns and expectations that they do not fully understand. This naturally causes uncertainty, especially when the situation involves what appears to be begging, bribery, or blackmail. How should businesspeople deal with customs that conflict with both their sense of ethics and our nation's laws? In discussing this, professor of international marketing Jeffrey A. Fadiman analyzes three important non-Western traditions which American businesspeople need to understand and goes on to provide specific suggestions on how they can respond to approaches for payoffs in foreign countries.

"What do I say if he asks for a bribe?" I asked myself while enduring the all-night flight to Asia. Uncertain, I shared my concern with the man sitting beside me, a CEO en route to Singapore. Intrigued, he passed it on to his partners next to him. No one seemed sure.

Among American executives doing business overseas, this uncertainty is widespread. Consider, for example, each of the following situations:

You are invited to the home of your foreign colleague. You learn he lives in a palatial villa. What gift might both please your host and ease business relations? What if he considers it to be a bribe? What if he *expects* it to be a bribe? Why do you feel uneasy?

Your company's product lies on the dock of a foreign port. To avoid spoilage, you must swiftly transport it inland. What "gift," if any, would both please authorities and facilitate your business? What if they ask for "gifts" of $50? $50,000? $500,000? When does a gift become a bribe? When do you stop feeling comfortable?

Negotiations are complete. The agreement is signed. One week later, a minister asks your company for $1 million—"for a hospital"—simultaneously suggesting that "other valuable considerations" might come your way as the result of future favors on both sides. What response, if any, would please him, satisfy you, and help execute the signed agreement?

You have been asked to testify before the Securities and Exchange Commission regarding alleged violations of the Foreign Corrupt Practices Act. How would you explain the way you handled the examples above? Would your explanations both satisfy those in authority and ensure the continued overseas operation of your company?

Much of the discomfort Americans feel when faced with problems of this nature is due to U.S. law. Since 1977, congressional passage of the Foreign Corrupt Practices Act has transformed hypothetical problems into practical dilemmas and has created considerable anxiety among Americans who deal with foreign governments and companies. The problem is particularly difficult for those conducting business in the developing nations, where the rules that govern payoffs may differ sharply from our own. In such instances, U.S. executives may face not only legal but also ethical and cultural dilemmas: How do businesspeople comply with customs that conflict with both their sense of ethics and this nation's law?

One way to approach the problem is to devise appropriate corporate responses to payoff requests. The suggestions that follow apply to those developing Asian, African, and Middle Eastern nations, still in transition toward industrial societies, that have retained aspects of their communal traditions. These approaches do not assume that those who adhere to these ideals exist in selfless bliss, requesting private payments only for communal ends, with little thought of self-enrichment. Nor do these suggestions apply to situations of overt extortion, where U.S. companies are forced to provide funds. Instead they explore a middle way in which non-Western colleagues may have several motives when requesting a payoff, thereby providing U.S. managers with several options.

Decisions & Dilemmas

My own first experience with Third World bribery may illustrate the inner conflict Americans can feel when asked to break the rules. It occurred in East Africa and began with this request: "Oh, and Bwana, I would like 1,000 shillings as Zawadi, my gift. And, as we are now friends, for Chai, my tea, an eight-band radio, to bring to my home when you visit."

Both *Chai* and *Zawadi* can be Swahili terms for "bribe." He delivered these requests in respectful tones. They came almost as an afterthought, at the conclusion of negotiations in which we had settled the details of a projected business venture. I had looked forward to buying my counterpart a final drink to complete the deal symbolically in the American fashion. Instead, after we had settled every contractual aspect, he expected money.

The amount he suggested, although insignificant by modern standards, seemed large at the time. Nonetheless, it was the radio that got to me. Somehow it added insult to injury. Outwardly, I kept smiling. Inside, my stomach boiled. My own world view equates bribery with sin. I expect monetary issues to be settled before contracts are signed. Instead, although the negotiations were complete, he expected me to pay out once more. Once? How often? Where would it stop? My reaction took only moments to formulate. "I'm American," I declared. "I don't pay bribes." Then I walked away. That walk was not the longest in my life. It was, however, one of the least commercially productive.

As it turned out, I had misunderstood him — in more ways than one. By misinterpreting both his language and his culture, I lost an opportunity for a business deal and a personal relationship that would have paid enormous dividends without violating either the law or my own sense of ethics.

Go back through the episode — but view it this time with an East African perspective. First, my colleague's language should have given me an important clue as to how he saw our transaction. Although his limited command of English caused him to frame his request as a command — a phrasing I instinctively found offensive — his tone was courteous. Moreover, if I had listened more carefully, I would have noted that he had addressed me as a superior: he used the honorific *Bwana*, meaning "sir," rather than *Rafiki* (or friend), used between equals. From his perspective, the language was appropriate; it reflected the differences in our personal wealth and in the power of the institutions we each represented.

Having assigned me the role of the superior figure in the economic transaction, he then suggested how I should use my position in accord with his culture's traditions — logically assuming that I would benefit by his prompting. In this case, he suggested that money and a radio would be appropriate gifts. What he did not tell me was that his culture's traditions required him to use the money to provide a feast — in my honor — to which he would invite everyone in his social and commercial circle whom he felt I should meet. The radio would simply create a festive atmosphere at the party. This was to mark the beginning of an ongoing relationship with reciprocal benefits.

He told me none of this. Since I was willing to do business in local fashion, I was supposed to know. In fact, I had not merely been invited to a dwelling but through a gateway into the maze of gifts and formal visiting that linked him to his kin. He hoped that I would respond in local fashion. Instead, I responded according to my cultural norms and walked out both on the chance to do business and on the opportunity to make friends.

The Legal Side

Perhaps from a strictly legal perspective my American reaction was warranted. In the late 1970s, as part of the national reaction to Watergate, the SEC sued several large U.S. companies for alleged instances of bribery overseas. One company reportedly authorized $59 million in contributions to political parties in Italy, including the Communist party. A second allegedly paid $4 million to a political party in South Korea. A third reportedly provided $450,000 in "gifts" to Saudi generals. A fourth may have diverted $377,000 to fly planeloads of voters to the Cook Islands to rig elections there.

The sheer size of the payments and the ways they had been used staggered the public. A U.S. senate committee reported "corrupt" foreign payments involving hundreds of millions of dollars by more than 400 U.S. corporations, including 117 of the *Fortune* "500." The SEC described the problem as a national crisis.

In response, Congress passed the Foreign Corrupt Practices Act in 1977. The law prohibits U.S. corporations from providing or even offering payments to foreign political parties, candidates, or officials with discretionary authority under circumstances that might induce recipients to misuse their positions to assist the company to obtain, maintain, or retain business.

The FCPA does not forbid payments to lesser figures, however. On the contrary, it explicitly allows facilitating payments ("grease") to persuade foreign officials to perform their normal duties, at both the clerical and ministerial levels. The law establishes no monetary guidelines but requires companies to keep reasonably detailed records that accurately and fairly reflect the transactions.

The act also prohibits indirect forms of payment. Companies cannot make payments of this nature while "knowing or having reason to know" that any portion of the funds will be transferred to a forbidden recipient to be used for corrupt purposes as previously defined. Corporations face fines of up to $1 million. Individuals can be fined $10,000 —

which the corporation is forbidden to indemnify — and sentenced to a maximum of five years in prison. In short, private payments by Americans abroad can mean violation of U.S. law, a consideration that deeply influences U.S. corporate thinking.

The Ethical Side

For most U.S. executives, however, the problem goes beyond the law. Most Americans share an aversion to payoffs. In parts of Asia, Africa, and the Middle East, however, certain types of bribery form an accepted element of their commercial traditions. Of course, nepotism, shakedown, and similar practices do occur in U.S. business; these practices, however, are both forbidden by law and universally disapproved.

Americans abroad reflect these sentiments. Most see themselves as personally honest and professionally ethical. More important, they see themselves as preferring to conduct business accordingly to the law, both American and foreign. They also know that virtually all foreign governments — including those notorious for corruption — have rigorously enforced statutes against most forms of private payoff. In general, there is popular support for these anticorruption measures. In Malaysia, bribery is publicly frowned on and punishable by long imprisonment. In the Soviet Union, Soviet officials who solicit bribes can be executed.

Reflecting this awareness, most U.S. businesspeople prefer to play by local rules, competing in the open market according to the quality, price, and services provided by their product. Few, if any, want to make illegal payments of any kind to anybody. Most prefer to obey both local laws and their own ethical convictions while remaining able to do business.

The Cultural Side

Yet, as my African experience suggests, indigenous traditions often override the law. In some developing nations, payoffs have become a norm. The problem is compounded when local payoff practices are rooted in a "communal heritage," ideals inherited from a preindustrial past where a community leader's wealth — however acquired — was shared throughout the community. Those who hoarded were scorned as antisocial. Those who shared won status and authority. Contact with Western commerce has blurred the ideal, but even the most individualistic businesspeople remember their communal obligations.

Contemporary business practices in those regions often reflect these earlier ideals. Certain forms of private payoff have endured for centuries. The Nigerian practice of *dash* (private payments for private services), for example, goes back to fifteenth century contacts with the Portuguese, in which Africans solicited "gifts" (trade goods) in exchange for labor. Such solicitation can pose a cultural dilemma to Americans who may be unfamiliar with the communal nuances of non-Western commercial conduct. To cope, they may denigrate these traditions, perceiving colleagues who solicit payments as unethical and their culture as corrupt. . . .

My experience suggests that most non-Westerners are neither excessively corrupt nor completely communal. Rather, they are simultaneously drawn to both indigenous and Western ideals. Many have internalized the Western norms of personal enrichment along with those of modern commerce, while simultaneously adhering to indigenous traditions by fulfilling communal obligations. Requests for payoffs may spring from both these ideals. Corporate responses must therefore be designed to satisfy them both.

Background for Payoffs

Throughout non-Western cultures, three traditions form the background for discussing payoffs: the inner circle, future favors, and the gift exchange. Though centuries old, each has evolved into a modern business concept. Americans who work in the Third World need to learn about them so they can work within them.

The Inner Circle

Most individuals in developing nations classify others into some form of "ins" and "outs." Members of more communal societies, influenced by the need to strive for group prosperity, divide humanity into those with whom they have relationships and those with whom they have none. Many Africans, for instance, view people as either "brothers" or "strangers." Relationships with brothers may be real—kin, however distant—or fictional, extending to comrades or "mates." Comrades, however, may both speak and act like kin, address one another as family, and assume obliga-

tions of protection and assistance that Americans reserve for nuclear families.

Together, kin and comrades form an inner circle, a fictional "family," devoted to mutual protection and prosperity. Like the "old boy networks" that operate in the United States, no single rule defines membership in the inner circle. . . . Beyond this magic circle live the "outs": strangers, aliens, individuals with no relationship to those within. . . .

Not every U.S. manager is aware of this division. Those who investigate often assume that their nationality, ethnic background, and alien culture automatically classify them as "outs." Non-Western colleagues, however, may regard specific Westerners as useful contacts, particularly if they seem willing to do business in local fashion. They may, therefore, consider bringing certain individuals into their inner circles in such a manner as to benefit both sides.

Overseas executives, if asked to work within such circles, should find their business prospects much enhanced. These understandings often lead to implicit quid pro quos. For example, one side might agree to hire workers from only one clan; in return the other side would guarantee devoted labor. As social and commercial trust grows, the Westerners may be regarded less and less as aliens or predators and more and more as comrades or kin. Obviously, this is a desirable transition, and executives assigned to work within this type of culture may wish to consider whether these inner circles exist, and if so, whether working within them will enhance business prospects.

The Future Favor

A second non-Western concept that relates to payoffs is a system of future favors. Relationships within the inner circles of non-Western nations function through such favors. . . . All systems of this type assume that any individual under obligation to another has entered a relationship in which the first favor must be repaid in the future, when convenient to all sides.

Neither side defines the manner of repayment. Rather, both understand that some form of gift or service will repay the earlier debt with interest. This repayment places the originator under obligation. The process then begins again, creating a lifelong cycle. The relationship that springs from meeting lifelong obligations builds the trust that forms a basis for conducting business.

My own introduction to the future favors system may illustrate the process. While conducting business on Mt. Kenya in the 1970s, I visited a notable local dignitary. On completing our agenda, he stopped my rush to leave by presenting me a live and angry hen. Surprised, I stammered shaky "thank-yous," then walked down the mountain with my kicking, struggling bird. Having discharged my obligation—at least in Western terms—by thanking him, I cooked the hen, completed my business, eventually left Kenya, and forgot the incident.

Years later, I returned on different business. It was a revelation. People up and down the mountain called out to one another that I had come back to "return the dignitary's hen." To them, the relationship that had sprung up between us had remained unchanged throughout the years. Having received a favor, I had now come back to renew the relationship by returning it.

I had, of course, no such intention. Having forgotten the hen incident, I was also unaware of its importance to others. Embarrassed, I slipped into a market and bought a larger hen, then climbed to his homestead to present it. Again I erred, deciding to apologize in Western fashion for delaying my return. "How can a hen be late?" he replied. "Due to the bird, we have *uthoni* [obligations, thus a relationship]. That is what sweetens life. What else was the hen for but to bring you here again?"

These sentiments can also operate within non-Western commercial circles, where business favors can replace hens, but *uthoni* are what sweetens corporate life. Western interest lies in doing business; non-Western, in forming bonds so that business can begin. Westerners seek to discharge obligations; non-Westerners, to create them. Our focus is on producing short-term profit; theirs, on generating future favors. The success of an overseas venture may depend on an executive's awareness of these differences.

The Gift Exchange

One final non-Western concept that can relate to payoffs is a continuous exchange of gifts. In some developing nations, gifts form the catalysts that trigger future favors. U.S. executives often wish to present gifts appropriate to cultures where they are assigned, to the point where at least one corporation has commissioned a special study of the subject. They may be less aware, however, of the long-range implications of gift giving within these cultures. Two of these may be particularly relevant to CEOs concerned with payoffs.

In many non-Western commercial circles, the tradition of gift giving has evolved into a modern business tool intended to create obligation as well as affection. Recipients may be gratified by what they receive, but they also incur an obligation that they must some day repay. Gift giving in these cultures may therefore operate in two dimensions: one meant to provide short-term pleasure; the other, long-range bonds.

This strategy is common in Moslem areas of Africa and Asia. Within these cultures, I have watched export merchants change Western clientele from browsers to buyers by inviting them to tea. Seated, the customers sip at leisure, while merchandise is brought before them piece by piece. The seller thus achieves three goals. His clients have been honored, immobilized, and placed under obligation.

In consequence, the customers often feel the need to repay in kind. Lacking suitable material gifts, they frequently respond as the merchant intends: with decisions to buy—not because they need the merchandise but to return the seller's gift of hospitality. The buyers, considering their obligation discharged, leave the premises believing relations have ended. The sellers, however, hope they have just begun. Their intent is to create relationships that will cause clients to return. A second visit would mean presentation of another gift, perhaps of greater value. That, in turn, might mean a second purchase, leading to further visits, continued gifts, and a gradual deepening of personal and commercial relations intended to enrich both sides.

The point of the process, obviously, is not the exchanges themselves but the relationships they engender. The gifts are simply catalysts. Under ideal circumstances the process should be unending, with visits, gifts, gestures, and services flowing back and forth among participants throughout their lives. The universally understood purpose is to create reciprocal good feelings and commercial prosperity among all concerned.

Gift giving has also evolved as a commercial "signal." In America, gifts exchanged by business colleagues may signal gratitude, camaraderie, or perhaps the discharge of minor obligations. Among non-Westerners, gifts may signal the desire to begin both social and commercial relationships with members of an inner circle. That signal may also apply to gifts exchanged with Westerners. If frequently repeated, such exchanges may be signals of intent. For Americans, the signal may suggest a willingness to work within a circle of local business colleagues, to assume appropriate obligations, and to conduct business in local ways. For non-Western colleagues, gifts may imply a wish to invite selected individuals into their commercial interactions.

Approaches to Payoffs

While U.S. corporations may benefit from adapting to local business concepts, many indigenous business traditions, especially in developing regions, are alien to the American experience and therefore difficult to implement by U.S. field personnel—as every executive who has tried to sit cross-legged for several hours with Third World counterparts will attest.

Conversely, many non-Western administrators are particularly well informed about U.S. business practices, thus permitting U.S. field representatives to function on familiar ground. Nonetheless, those willing to adapt indigenous commercial concepts to U.S. corporate needs may find that their companies can benefit in several ways. Through working with a circle of non-Western business colleagues, and participating fully in the traditional exchange of gifts and favors, U.S. executives may find that their companies increase the chance of preferential treatment; use local methods and local contacts to gain market share; develop trust to reinforce contractual obligations; and minimize current risk, while maximizing future opportunities by developing local expertise.

Corporations that adapt to local business concepts may also develop methods to cope with local forms of payoff. Current approaches vary from culture to culture, yet patterns do appear. Three frequently recur in dealings between Americans and non-Westerners: gifts, bribes, and other considerations.

Gifts: The Direct Request

This form of payoff may occur when key foreign businesspeople approach their U.S. colleagues to solicit "gifts." Solicitations of this type have no place in U.S. business circles where they could be construed as exploitation. Obviously, the

same may hold true overseas, particularly in areas where shakedown, bribery, and extortion may be prevalent. There is, however, an alternative to consider. To non-Western colleagues, such requests may simply be a normal business strategy, designed to build long-term relationships.

To U.S. businesspeople, every venture is based on the bottom line. To non-Western colleagues, a venture is based on the human relationships that form around it. Yet, when dealing with us they often grow uncertain as to how to form these relationships. How can social ties be created with Americans who speak only of business, even when at leisure? How can traditions of gift giving be initiated with people unaware of the traditions? Without the exchange of gifts, how can obligations be created? Without obligations, how can there be trust?

Faced with such questions, non-Western colleagues may understandably decide to initiate gift-giving relationships on their own. If powerful, prominent, or wealthy, they may simply begin by taking on the role of giver. If less powerful or affluent, some may begin by suggesting they become recipients. There need be no dishonor in such action, since petitioners know they will repay with future favors whatever inner debt they incur.

The hosts may also realize that, as strangers, Americans may be unaware of local forms of gift giving as well as their relationship to business norms. Or they may be cognizant of such relationships but may have no idea of how to enter into them. In such instances, simple courtesy may cause the hosts to indicate—perhaps obliquely—how proper entry into the local system should be made. Such was the unfortunate case with my East African colleague's request for the eight-band radio.

Cultural barriers can be difficult to cross. Most Americans give generously, but rarely on request. When solicited, we feel exploited. Solicitations may seem more relevant, however, if examined from the perspective of the non-Western peoples with whom we are concerned.

Often, in societies marked by enormous gaps between the rich and the poor, acts of generosity display high status. To withhold gifts is to deny the affluence one has achieved. Non-Western counterparts often use lavish hospitality both to reflect and to display their wealth and status within local society. When Americans within these regions both represent great wealth through association with their corporations and seek high status as a tool to conduct business, it may prove more profitable for the corporation to give than to receive.

In short, when asked for "gifts" by foreign personnel, managers may consider two options. The first option is to regard each query as extortion and every petitioner as a potential thief. The second is to consider the request within its local context. In nations where gifts generate a sense of obligation, it may prove best to give them, thereby creating inner debts among key foreign colleagues in the belief that they will repay them over time. If such requests indeed reflect a local way of doing business, they may be gateways into the workings of its commercial world. One U.S. option, therefore, is to consider the effect of providing "gifts" — even on direct request — in terms of the relationships required to implement the corporation's long-range plans.

Bribes: The Indirect Request

A second approach to payoffs, recurrent in non-Western business circles, is the indirect request. Most Third World people prefer the carrot to the stick. To avoid unpleasant confrontation, they designate third parties to suggest that "gifts" of specified amounts be made to those in local power circles. In explanation they cite the probability of future favors in return. No line exists, of course, dividing gifts from bribes. It seems that direct solicitation involves smaller amounts, while larger ones require go-betweens. On occasion, however, the sums requested can be staggering: in 1976, for example, U.S. executives in Qatar were asked for a $1.5 million "gift" for that nation's minister of oil.

U.S. responses to such queries must preserve both corporate funds and executive relationships with those in power. While smaller gifts may signal a desire to work with the local business circles, a company that supplies larger sums could violate both local antipayoff statutes and the FCPA. Conversely, outright rejection of such requests may cause both the go-betweens and those they represent to lose prestige and thus possibly prompt retaliation.

In such instances, the FCPA may actually provide beleaguered corporate executives with a highly convenient excuse. Since direct compliance with requests for private funds exposes every U.S. company to threats of negative publicity, blackmail, le-

gal action, financial loss, and damage to corporate image, it may prove easy for Americans to say no — while at the same time offering nonmonetary benefits to satisfy both sides.

U.S. competitors may, in fact, be in a better situation than those companies from Europe and Japan that play by different rules. Since the principle of payoffs is either accepted or encouraged by many of their governments, the companies must find it difficult to refuse payment of whatever sums are asked.

Nor should the "right to bribe" be automatically considered an advantage. Ignoring every other factor, this argument assumes contracts are awarded solely on the basis of the largest private payoff. At the most obvious level, it ignores the possibility that products also compete on the basis of quality, price, promotion, and service — factors often crucial to American success abroad. U.S. field representatives are often first to recognize that payoffs may be only one of many factors in awarding contracts. In analyzing U.S. competition in the Middle East, for instance, one executive of an American aircraft company noted: "The French have savoir faire in giving bribes discreetly and well, but they're still not . . . backing up their sales with technical expertise." The overseas executive should consider to what degree the right to bribe may be offset by turning the attention of the payoff seekers to other valuable considerations.

Other Considerations:
The Suggested Service

A third approach, often used by members of a non-Western elite, is to request that U.S. companies contribute cash to public service projects, often administered by the petitioners themselves. Most proposals of this type require money. Yet if American executives focus too sharply on the financial aspects, they may neglect the chance to work other nonmonetary considerations into their response. In many developing nations, nonmonetary considerations may weigh heavily on foreign colleagues.

Many elite non-Westerners, for example, are intensely nationalistic. They love their country keenly, deplore its relative poverty, and yearn to help it rise. They may, therefore, phrase their requests for payoffs in terms of a suggested service to the nation. In Kenya, for example, ministerial requests to U.S. companies during the 1970s suggested a contribution toward the construction of a hospital. In Indonesia, in the mid-1970s, a top executive of Pertamina, that nation's government-sponsored oil company, requested contributions to an Indonesian restaurant in New York City as a service to the homeland. In his solicitation letter, the executive wrote that the restaurant was in fact intended to "enhance the Indonesian image in the U.S.A., . . . promote tourism, . . . and attract the interest of the U.S. businessmen to investments in Indonesia."

Westerners may regard such claims with cynicism. Non-Westerners may not. They recognize that, even if the notables involved become wealthy, some portion of the wealth, which only they can attract from abroad, will still be shared by other members of their homeland.

That belief is worth consideration, for many elite non-Westerners share a second concern: the desire to meet communal obligations by sharing wealth with members of their inner circle. Modern business leaders in communal cultures rarely simply hoard their wealth. To do so would invite social condemnation. Rather, they provide gifts, funds, and favors to those in their communal settings, receiving deference, authority, and prestige in return.

This does not mean that funds transferred by Western corporations to a single foreign colleague will be parceled out among a circle of cronies. Rather, money passes through one pair of hands, over time, flowing slowly in the form of gifts and favors to friends and kin. The funds may even flow beyond this inner circle to their children, most often to ensure their continued education. Such generosity, of course, places both adult recipients and children under a long-term obligation, thereby providing donors both with current status and with assurance of obtaining future favors.

In short, non-Western colleagues who seek payoffs may have concerns beyond their personal enrichment. If motivated by both national and communal idealism, they may feel that these requests are not only for themselves but also a means to aid much larger groups and ultimately their nation.

A Donation Strategy

Requests for payoffs give executives little choice. Rejection generates resentment, while

agreement may lead to prosecution. Perhaps appeals to both communal and national idealism can open up a third alternative. Consider, for example, the possibility of deflecting such requests by transforming private payoffs into public services. One approach would be to respond to requests for private payment with well-publicized, carefully tailored "donations" — an approach that offers both idealistic and practical appeal.

This type of donation could take several forms. The most obvious, monetary contribution, could be roughly identical to the amount requested in private funds. Donating it publicly, however, would pay off important foreign colleagues in nonmonetary ways.

At the national level, for instance, the most appropriate and satisfying corporate response to ministerial requests for "contributions" toward the construction of a hospital, such as occurred in Kenya, might be actually to provide one, down to the final door and stethoscope, while simultaneously insisting that monetary payments of any kind are proscribed by U.S. law. . . .

Yet donations alone seem insufficient. To serve as an alternative to payoffs, the concept should have practical appeal. Consider, for example, the story of a Western company in Zaire. During the 1970s, Zaire's economy decayed so badly that even ranking civil servants went unpaid. As a result, key Zairian district officials approached officers of the Western company, requesting private funds for future favors. Instead, the company responded with expressions of deference and "donations" of surplus supplies, including goods that could be sold on the black market. The resulting cash flow enabled the officials to continue in their posts. This in turn allowed them to render reciprocal services, both to their district and to the company. By tailoring their contribution to local conditions, the company avoided draining its funds, while providing benefits to both sides.

There are many ways to tailor donations. At the most obvious level, funds can support social projects in the home areas of important local colleagues. Funds or even whole facilities can be given in their names. Production centers can be staffed by members of their ethnic group. Educational, medical, and other social services can be made available to key segments of a target population based on the advice of influential foreign counterparts. Given the opportunity, many non-Westerners would direct the contributions toward members of their inner circles profiting from local forms of recognition and prestige. These practices, often used in one form or another in the United States, can provide non-Western counterparts with local recognition and authority and supply a legal, ethical, and culturally acceptable alternative to a payoff.

Donating Services

U.S. companies may also deflect payoff proposals by donating services, gratifying important foreign colleagues in nonmonetary fashion, and thus facilitating the flow of future business. In 1983, for example, a British military unit, part of the Royal Electrical and Mechanical Engineers, planned an African overland vehicle expedition across the Sahara to Tanzania. On arrival, they were "expected" to make a sizable cash donation to that nation to be used in support of its wildlife.

Usually this meant meeting a minister, handing over a check, and taking a picture of the transfer. Instead, the British assembled thousands of dollars worth of tools and vehicle parts, all needed in Tanzanian wildlife areas for trucks on antipoaching patrols. Tanzania's weakened economy no longer permitted the import of enough good tools or parts, which left the wildlife authorities with few working vehicles. As a result, wild-game management had nearly halted. By transporting the vital parts across half of Africa, then working alongside local mechanics until every vehicle was on the road, the British reaped far more goodwill than private payments or even cash donations would have gained. More important, they paved the way for future transactions by providing services meant to benefit both sides.

Donating Jobs

A third alternative to private payoffs may be to donate jobs, particularly on projects meant to build goodwill among a host nation's elite. In the 1970s, for example, Coca-Cola was the object of a Middle Eastern boycott by members of the Arab League. Conceivably, Coca-Cola could have sought to win favor with important individuals through gifts or bribes. Instead, the company hired hundreds of Egyptians to plant thousands of acres of orange trees. Eventually the company carpeted a considerable stretch of desert and thereby created both employment and goodwill.

More recently, Mexico refused to let IBM become the first wholly owned foreign company to make personal computers within its borders. Like Coca-Cola in Egypt, IBM employed a strategy of national development: it offered a revised proposal, creating both direct and indirect employment for Mexican nationals, in numbers high enough to satisfy that nation's elite. Such projects do more than generate goodwill. Those able to involve key foreign colleagues in ways that lend prestige on local terms may find they serve as viable alternatives to bribery.

Good Ethics, Good Business

Three strategies do not exhaust the list. U.S. executives in foreign countries should be able to devise their own variants based on local conditions. . . .

Non-Western business practices may be difficult to comprehend, especially when they involve violations of U.S. legal, commercial, or social norms. Nonetheless, U.S. business options are limited only by our business attitudes. If these can be expanded through selective research into those local concepts that relate to payoffs, responses may emerge to satisfy both congressional and indigenous demands. What may initially appear as begging, bribery, or blackmail may be revealed as local tradition, cross-cultural courtesy, or attempts to make friends. More important, when examined from a non-American perspective, mention of "gifts," "bribes," and "other valuable considerations" may signal a wish to do business.

Review and Discussion Questions

1. In Fadiman's first encounter with Third World bribery, what did he fail to understand about the situation? How would you have acted in his place?

2. Explain the three non-Western cultural traditions that Fadiman identifies as forming the context of payoffs.

3. Critics of the FCPA claim that the act ties the hands of American corporations by forbidding them to bribe foreign officials. Fadiman appears skeptical of this argument. Why? Do you think the FCPA is a good law?

4. Americans view bribery as immoral. But if bribery is an accepted practice in a foreign country,

is it still immoral? Explain your answer. Why do we consider bribery wrong in the first place?

5. Describe the donation strategy that Fadiman recommends. Does it solve the problem of respecting local customs while remaining true to our own legal and ethical standards? Do you see any problems with the strategy?

In Defense of Whistle Blowing

Gene G. James

Professor of philosophy Gene G. James begins his examination of whistle blowing with some pertinent definitions and an overview of the current legal status of the phenomenon. He then challenges Professor De George's analysis of whistle blowing. Among other things, James argues, counter to De George, that workers have an obligation to warn the public of dangers, even if they believe that the public will ignore the warnings. He also rejects De George's claim that engineers are not obligated to blow the whistle when, by so doing, they will likely lose their jobs. In James's view that kind of risk-running is part and parcel of the engineer's professional obligations. James also questions De George's insistence that one must exhaust all internal channels before blowing the whistle. It all depends, says James, on the nature of the wrongdoing, the kind of organization involved, and the likelihood of retaliation. James then sketches the factors that whistle blowers should consider "if they are to act prudently and morally." He concludes with a brief discussion of the need for protective legislation for whistle blowers and changes within organizations to prevent the need for whistle blowing.

Whistle blowing may be defined as the attempt by an employee or former employee of an organization to disclose what he or she believes to be wrongdoings in or by the organization. Like blowing a whistle to call attention to a thief, whistle blowing is an effort to make others aware of practices one considers illegal, unjust, or harmful. Whenever someone goes over the head of immediate supervisors to inform higher management of wrongdoing, the whistle blowing is *internal* to the organization. Whenever someone discloses wrongdoing to outside individuals or groups such as reporters, public interest groups, or regulatory agencies, the whistle blowing is *external*.

Most whistle blowing is done by people presently employed by the organization. However, people who have left the organization may also blow the whistle. The former may be referred to as *current* whistle blowers; the latter as *alumni* whistle blowers. If the whistle blower discloses his or her identity, the whistle blowing may be said to be *open*; if the person's identity is not disclosed, the whistle blowing is *anonymous*.

Whistle blowers differ from muckrakers because the latter do not have any ties to the organizations whose wrongdoing they seek to disclose. They differ from informers and stool pigeons because the latter usually have self-interested reasons for their disclosures, such as obtaining prosecutorial immunity. The term *whistle blower*, on the other hand, usually refers to people who disclose wrongdoing for moral reasons. However, unless whistle blowing is *defined* as disclosing wrongdoing for moral reasons, the distinction between whistle blowing and informing cannot be a sharp one. Thus, although most whistle blowers do it for moral reasons, one cannot take for granted that their motives are praiseworthy.

Whistle blowers almost always experience retaliation. If they work for private industry, they are likely to be fired. They also receive damaging letters of recommendation and may be blacklisted so they cannot find work in their profession. If they are not fired, or work for government agencies, they are still likely to be transferred, demoted, given less interesting work, and denied salary increases and promotions. Their professional competence is usually attacked. They are said to be unqualified to judge, misinformed, and so forth. Since their actions seem to threaten both the organization and their fellow employees, attacks on their personal lives are also frequent. They are called traitors, rat finks, and other names. They are also said to be disgruntled, known troublemakers, people who make an issue out of nothing, self-serving, and publicity-seekers. Their life-styles, sex lives, and mental stability may be questioned. Physical assaults, abuse of their families, and even murder are not unknown as retaliation to whistle blowing.

Whistle Blowing and the Law[1]

The law does not at present offer whistle blowers very much protection. Agency law, the area of common law which governs relations between employees and employers, imposes a duty on employees to keep confidential any information learned through their employment which might be detrimental to their employers. However, this duty does not hold if the employee has knowledge that the employer either has committed or is about to commit a felony. In this case the employee has a positive obligation to report the offense. Failure to do so is known as misprision and makes one subject to criminal penalties.

The problem with agency law is that it is based on the assumption that unless there are statutes or agreements to the contrary, contracts between employees and employers can be terminated at will by either party. It therefore grants employers the right to discharge employees at any time for any reason or even for no reason at all. The result is that most employees who blow the whistle on their employers, even those who report felonies, are fired or suffer other retaliation. One employee of thirty years was even fired the day before his pension became effective for testifying under subpoena against his employer, without the courts doing anything to aid him.

This situation has begun to change somewhat in recent years. In *Pickering* v. *Board of Education* in 1968 the Supreme Court ruled that government employees have the right to speak out on policy issues affecting their agencies provided doing so does not seriously disrupt the agency. A number of similar decisions have followed and the right of government employees to speak out on policy issues now seems firmly established. But employees in private industry do not have the right to speak out on company policies without being fired. In one case involving both a union and a company doing a substantial portion of its business with the federal government, federal courts did award back pay to an employee fired for criticizing the union and the company, but did not reinstate him or award him punitive damages.

A few state courts have begun to modify the right of employers to dismiss employees at will. Courts in Oregon and Pennsylvania have awarded damages to employees fired for serving on juries. A New Hampshire court granted damages to a woman fired for refusing to date her foreman. A West Virginia court reinstated a bank employee who reported illegal interest rates. The Illinois Supreme Court upheld the right of an employee to sue when fired for reporting and testifying about criminal activities of a fellow employee. However, a majority of states still uphold the right of employers to fire employees at will unless there are statutes or agreements to the contrary. Only one state, Michigan, has passed a law prohibiting employers from retaliating against employees who report violations of local, state, or federal laws.

A number of federal statutes contain provisions intended to protect whistle blowers. The National Labor Relations Act, Fair Labor Standards Act, Title VII of the 1964 Civil Rights Act, Age Discrimination Act, and Occupation Safety and Health Act all have sections prohibiting employers from taking retaliatory actions against employees who report or testify about violations of the acts.

Although these laws seem to encourage and protect whistle blowers, to be effective they must be enforced. A 1976 study[2] of the Occupational Safety and Health Act showed that only about 20 percent of the 2300 complaints filed in fiscal years 1975 and 1976 were judged valid by OSHA investigators. About half of these were settled out of court. Of the sixty cases taken to court at the time of the study in November 1976, one had been won, eight were lost, and the others were still pending. A more recent study[3] showed that of the 3100 violations reported in 1979, only 270 were settled out of court and only sixteen litigated.

Since the National Labor Relations Act guarantees the right of workers to organize and bargain collectively and most collective bargaining agreements contain a clause requiring employers to have just cause for discharging employees, these agreements would seem to offer some protection for whistle blowers. In fact, however, arbitrators have tended to agree with employers that whistle blowing is an act of disloyalty which disrupts business and injures the employer's reputation. Their attitude seems to be summed up in a 1972 case in which the arbitrator stated that one should not "bite the hand that feeds you and insist on staying for future banquets."[4] One reason for this, pointed out by David Ewing, is that unions are frequently as corrupt as the organizations on which the whistle is being blown. Such unions, he says, "are not likely to feed a hawk that comes to prey in their own barnyard."[5] The record of professional societies is not any better. They generally have failed to come to the defense of members who have attempted to live up to their professional codes of ethics by blowing the whistle on corrupt practices.

The Moral Justification of Whistle Blowing

Under what conditions, if any, is whistle blowing morally justified? Some people have argued that it is always justified because it is an exercise of free speech. But the right to free speech, like most other rights, is not absolute. Thus, even if whistle blowing is a form of free speech, that does not mean it is justified in every case. Others have argued that whistle blowing is never justified because employees have obligations of absolute loyalty and confidentiality to the organization for which they work. However, because the actions of organizations often harm or violate the rights of others, and one has an obligation to prevent harmful actions if one can, a universal prohibition against whistle blowing is not justifiable.

Assuming that we reject such extreme views, what conditions must be satisfied for whistle blowing to be morally justified? Richard De George believes that whistle blowing is morally permissible if it meets the following three conditions:

1. The company must be engaged in a practice or about to release a product which does *serious* harm to individuals or to society in general. The more serious the harm, the more serious the obligation.

2. The employee should report his concern or complaint to his immediate superior.

3. If no appropriate action is taken the employee should take the matter up the managerial line. Before he or she is obliged to go public, the resources for remedy within the company should be exhausted.[6]

For whistle blowing to be morally obligatory De George thinks two other conditions must be satisfied:

4. The employee should have documentation of the practice or defect. . . . Without adequate evidence his chances of being successful . . . are slim.

5. The employee must have good reason to believe that by going public he will be able to bring about the necessary changes.[7]

De George believes that because of the almost certain retaliation whistle blowers experience, whistle blowing is frequently morally permissible but not morally obligatory. He holds that this is true even when the person involved is a professional whose code of ethics requires him or her to put the public good ahead of personal good. He argues, for example:

> The myth that ethics has no place in engineering has . . . at least in some corners of the engineering profession . . . been put to rest. Another myth, however, is emerging to take its place—the myth of the engineer as moral hero. . . . The zeal . . . however, has gone too far, piling moral responsibility upon moral responsibility on the shoulders of the engineer. This emphasis . . . is misplaced. Though engineers are members of a profession that holds public safety paramount, we cannot reasonably expect engineers to be willing to sacrifice their jobs each day for principle and to have a whistle ever at their sides. . . .[8]

He contends that engineers only have an obligation to do their jobs as best they can. This includes reporting observations about safety to management. But engineers do not have an "obligation to insist that their perceptions or their standards be accepted. They are not paid to do that, they are not expected to do that, and they have no moral or ethical obligation to do that."[9]

There are a number of problems with this analysis of whistle blowing.

The first condition is far too strong because it requires de facto wrongdoing instead of extremely probable evidence of wrongdoing before whistle blowing is morally justified. All that should be required of whistle blowers in this regard is that they be diligent in gathering evidence and act on the basis of the best evidence available to them. They should not be held to a more rigid standard than is usually applied to moral actions.

What constitutes serious and considerable harm? Must the harm be physical? Since De George was writing on business ethics, it is understandable that he only discussed whistle blowing involving corporations. But businesses, like governments, can be guilty of wrongs other than physically harming people. Should one, for example, never blow the whistle on such things as invasions of privacy?

If the harm is physical, how many people's health or safety must be endangered before the harm can be said to be considerable? And do professionals not have an obligation to inform the public of dangerous products and practices even if they will lose their jobs? Even though some Ford engineers had serious misgivings about the safety of Pinto gas tanks and several people were killed when tanks exploded after rear-end crashes, De George says that Ford engineers did not have an obligation to make their misgivings public. He maintains that although engineers are better qualified than other people to calculate cost versus safety, decisions about acceptable risk are not primarily engineering but managerial decisions. He believes that under ideal conditions the public itself would make this kind of decision. "A panel of informed people, not necessarily engineers, should decide . . . acceptable risk and minimum standards."[10] This information should then be relayed to car buyers who, he believes, are entitled to it.

One of the reasons it is difficult to decide when employees have an obligation to blow the whistle is that this is part of the larger problem of the extent to which people are responsible for actions by organizations of which they are members. The problem arises because it is extremely difficult to determine when a given individual in an organization is responsible for a particular decision or policy. Decisions are often the product of committees rather than single individuals. Since committee members usually serve temporary terms, none of the members who helped make a particular decision may be on the committee when it is implemented. Implementation is also likely to be the responsibility of others. Since committee membership is temporary, decisions are often made that contradict previous decisions. Even when decisions are made by individuals, these individuals seldom have control over the outcome of the decisions.

The result is that no one feels responsible for the consequences of organizational decisions. Top management does not because it only formulates policy; it does not implement it. Those in the mid-dle and at the bottom of the chain of authority do not, because they simply carry out policy. If challenged to assume moral responsibility for their actions, they reply "I'm not responsible, I was simply carrying out orders" or "I was just doing my job." But, as De George points out, absence of a feeling of obligation does not mean absence of obligation.

Whenever one acts in such a way as to harm or violate the rights of others, one is justly held accountable for those actions. This is true regardless of one's occupation or role in society. Acting as a member of an institution or corporation does not relieve a person of moral obligations. To the contrary. Because most of the actions we undertake in such settings have more far-reaching consequences than those we undertake in our personal lives, our moral obligation is *increased*. The amount of responsibility one bears for organizational actions is dependent on the extent to which (a) one could foresee the consequences of the organizational action, and (b) one's own acts or failures to act are a cause of those consequences. It is important to include failures to act here because frequently it is easier to determine what will happen if we don't act than if we do and because we are morally responsible for not preventing evil as well as for causing it.

Although the foregoing discussion is brief and the ideas not fully worked out, if the criteria which are presented are applied to the engineers in the Pinto case, I think one must conclude that they had an obligation to blow the whistle. They knew the gas tanks were likely to explode, injuring or killing people, if Pintos were struck from behind by cars traveling thirty miles per hour. They knew that if they did not blow the whistle, Ford would market the cars. They were also members of a profession that, because of its special knowledge and skills, has a particular obligation to be concerned about public safety.

De George thinks that the Ford engineers would have had an obligation to blow the whistle only if they had also known that doing so would have been likely to prevent the deaths. But we have an obligation to warn others of danger even if we believe they will ignore our warnings. This is especially true if the danger will come about partly because we did not speak out. De George admits that the public has a right to know about dangerous products. If that is true, it would seem that those who have knowledge about such products have an obligation to inform the public. This is not usurping the public's right to decide acceptable risk; it is supplying it with the information necessary to exercise the right.

De George also believes we are not justified in asking engineers to blow the whistle if it would threaten their jobs. It is true that we would not be justified in demanding that they blow the whistle if that would place their or their families' lives in danger. But this is not true if only their jobs are at stake. Engineers are recognized as professionals and accorded respect and high salaries, not only because of their specialized knowledge and skills, but also because of the special responsibilities we entrust to them. All people have a prima facie obligation to blow the whistle on practices that are illegal, unjust, or harmful to others. But engineers who have special knowledge about, and are partially responsible for, dangerous practices or products have an especially strong obligation to blow the whistle if they are unsuccessful in getting the practices or products modified. Indeed, if they do not have an obligation to blow the whistle in such situations, no one ever has such an obligation.

A number of people have argued that for external whistle blowing to be justified the whistle blower must first make his or her concern known within the organization. "Surely," says Arthur S. Miller, "an employee owes his employer enough loyalty to try to work, first of all, within the organization to attempt to effect change."[11] De George even states that for whistle blowing to be morally justified one must first have informed one's immediate supervisor and exhausted all possible avenues of change within the organization. The problems with this kind of advice are: (1) It may be one's immediate supervisor who is responsible for the wrongdoing. (2) Organizations differ considerably in both their mechanisms for reporting and how they respond to wrongdoing. (3) Not all wrongdoing is of the same type. If the wrongdoing is one which threatens people's health or safety, exhausting all channels of protest within the organization could result in unjustified delay in correcting the problem. Exhausting internal channels of protest can also give people time to destroy evidence needed to substantiate one's allegations. Finally, it may expose the employee to possible retaliation that he or she would have some protection against if the wrongdoing were reported to an external agency.

It has also been argued that anonymous whistle blowing is never justified. It is said, for example, that anonymous whistle blowing violates the right of people to face their accusers. The fact that the whistle blower's identity is unknown also raises questions about his or her motives. But, as Frederick Elliston points out, anonymous whistle blowing can both protect whistle blowers from unjust retaliation and prevent those on whom the whistle is blown from engaging in an ad hominem attack to draw attention away from their wrongdoing. As he also points out, people should be protected from false accusations, but it is not necessary for the identity of whistle blowers to be known to accomplish this. "It is only necessary that accusations be properly investigated, proven true or false, and the results widely disseminated."[12] Discovering the whistle blower's motive is also irrelevant as far as immediate public policy is concerned. All that matters is whether wrongdoing has taken place and, if so, what should be done about it.

It has also been argued that anonymous whistle blowing should be avoided because it is ineffective. In fact, if anonymous whistle blowing is ineffective, it is more likely to be a function of lack of documentation and follow-up testimony than of its anonymity. Moreover, anonymity is a matter of degree. For whistle blowing to be anonymous, the whistle blower's identity does not have to be unknown to everyone, only to those on whom the whistle is blown and the general public. A few key investigators may know his or her identity. It should also not be forgotten that one of the most dramatic and important whistle-blowing incidents in recent years, Deep Throat's disclosure of Richard Nixon's betrayal of the American people, was an instance of anonymous whistle blowing.

Factors to Consider in Whistle Blowing

I have argued that because we have a duty to prevent harm and injustice to others, which holds even though we are members of organizations, we have a prima facie obligation to disclose organizational wrongdoing we are unable to prevent. The degree of the obligation depends on the extent to which we are capable of foreseeing the consequences of organizational actions and our own acts or failures to act are causes of those consequences. It also depends on the kind and extent of the wrongdoing. Even a part-time or temporary employee has an obligation to report serious or extensive wrongdoing. But, in general, professionals who occupy positions of trust and special responsibilities have a stronger obligation to blow the whistle than ordinary workers.

Although we have an obligation to document wrongdoing as thoroughly as possible, we can only act on the basis of probability, so it is possible for the whistle blower to be in error about the wrongdoing and the whistle blowing still be justified. Whether we have an obligation to express our concern within the organization before going outside depends on the nature of the wrongdoing, the kind of organization involved, and the likelihood of retaliation. Whether we have an obligation to blow the whistle openly rather than anonymously depends on the extent to which it helps us avoid unfair retaliation and is effective in exposing the wrongdoing. The same is true of alumni as opposed to current whistle blowing.

Since whistle blowing usually involves conflicting obligations and a wide range of variables and has far-reaching consequences for all people involved, decisions to blow the whistle are not easily made. Like all complicated moral actions, whistle blowing cannot be reduced to a how-to-do list. However, some of the factors whistle blowers should take into consideration, if they are to act prudently and morally, can be stated. The following is an attempt to do this.

- *Make sure the situation is one that warrants whistle blowing.* Make sure the situation involves illegal actions, harm to others, or violation of people's rights, and is not one in which you would be disclosing personal matters, trade secrets, customer lists, or similar material. If disclosure of the wrongdoing would involve that latter, make sure that the harm to be avoided is great enough to offset the harm from the latter.

- *Examine your motives.* Although it is not necessary for the whistle blower's motive to be praiseworthy for the action to be justified in terms of the public interest, examination of your motives will help in deciding whether the situation warrants whistle blowing.

- *Verify and document your information.* If at all possible, try to obtain evidence that would stand up in court or regulatory hearings. If the danger to others is so great that you believe you are justified in obtaining evidence by surreptitious methods such as eavesdropping or recording telephone calls, examine your motives thoroughly, weigh carefully the risks you are taking, and try to find alternative and independent sources for any evidence you uncover. In general, it is advisable to avoid surreptitious methods.

- *Determine the type of wrongdoing you are reporting and to whom it should be reported.* Determining the exact nature of the wrongdoing can help you decide both what kind of evidence to obtain and to whom it should be reported. For example, if the wrongdoing consists of illegal actions such as the submission of false test reports to government agencies, bribery of public officials, racial or sexual discrimination, or violation of safety, health, or pollution laws, then determining the nature of the laws being violated will also indicate which agencies have authority to enforce those laws. If, on the other hand, the wrongdoing consists of actions which are legal but contrary to the public interest, determining this will help you decide whether you have an obligation to publicize the actions and, if so, in what way. The best place to report this type of wrongdoing is usually a public interest group. Such an organization is more likely than the press to: (1) be concerned about and advise the whistle blower regarding retaliation, (2) maintain confidentiality, (3) investigate the whistle blower's allegations to try to substantiate them rather than sensationalize them by turning the issue into a "personality dispute." If releasing information to the press is the best way to remedy the situation, the public interest group can help with or do this.

- *State your allegations in an appropriate way.* Be as specific as possible without being unintelligible. If you are reporting violation of a law to a government agency and it is possible for you to do so, include information and technical data necessary for experts to verify the wrongdoing. If you are disclosing wrongdoing which does not require technical information to substantiate it, still be as specific as possible in stating the type of illegal or immoral action involved, who is being injured, and in what ways.

- *Stick to the facts.* Avoid name calling, slander, and being drawn into a mud-slinging contest. As Peter Raven-Hansen wisely points out: "One of the most important points . . . is to focus on the disclosure. . . . This rule applies even when the whistle blower believes that certain individuals are responsible. . . . The disclosure itself usually leaves a trail for others to follow to the miscreants."[13] Sticking to the facts also helps the whistle blower minimize retaliation.

- *Decide whether the whistle blowing should be internal or external.* Familiarize yourself with all available internal channels for reporting wrongdoing and obtain as many data as you can both on how people who have used these channels were treated by the organization and on what was done about the problems they reported. If you are considering blowing the whistle on an immediate supervisor, find out what has happened in the past in this kind of situation. If people who report wrongdoing have been treated fairly and problems corrected, use internal channels to report the wrongdoing. If not, decide to what external agencies you should report the wrongdoing.

- *Decide whether the whistle blowing should be open or anonymous.* If you intend to remain anonymous, decide whether partial or total anonymity is required. Also, make sure your documentation is as thorough as possible. Finally, since anonymity may be difficulty to preserve, anticipate what you will do if your identity becomes known.

- *Decide whether current or alumni whistle blowing is required.* Sometimes it is advisable to resign your present position and obtain another before blowing the whistle. This protects you from being fired, receiving damaging letters of recommendation, or even being blacklisted from your profession. Alumni whistle blowing may also be advisable if you are anticipating writing a book about the wrongdoing. Since this can be profitable, anyone planning to take this step has a particularly strong obligation to examine his or her motives to make sure they are morally praiseworthy.

- *Find out how much protection is available for whistle blowers in your industry, state, or federal agency.* Follow any guidelines that have been established and make sure you meet all qualifications, deadlines, and so on for filing reports.

- *Anticipate and document retaliation.* Although it is not as certain as Newton's law of motion that for every action there is an equal reaction, whistle blowers whose identities are known can expect retaliation. Thus whether you decide to work within the organization or go outside, document every step with letters, records, tape recordings of meetings, and so forth. Unless you do this, you may find that regulatory agencies and the courts are of no help.

- *Consult a lawyer.* Lawyers are advisable at almost every stage of whistle blowing. They can help you determine if the wrongdoing violates the law, aid you in documenting information about it, inform you of any laws you might be breaking in documenting it, assist you in deciding to whom to report it, make sure reports are filed on time, and help you protect yourself against retaliation. However, since lawyers tend to view problems within a narrow legal framework and decisions to blow the whistle are moral decisions, in the final analysis you must rely on your conscience.

Beyond Whistle Blowing

What can be done to eliminate the wrongdoing which gives rise to whistle blowing? One solution would be to give whistle blowers greater legal protection. Another would be to try to change the nature of organizations so as to diminish the need for whistle blowing. These solutions of course are not mutually exclusive.

Many people are opposed to legislation protecting whistle blowers because they think it is unwarranted interference with the right to freedom of contract. However, if the right to freedom of contract is to be consistent with the public interest, it cannot serve as a shield for wrongdoing. It does this when threat of dismissal prevents people from blowing the whistle. The right of employers to dismiss at will has been restricted previously by labor laws which prevent employers from dismissing employees for union activities. It is ironic that we have restricted the right of employers to fire employees who are pursuing their economic self-interest, but allowed employers to fire employees acting in behalf of the public interest. The right of employers to dismiss employees in the interest of efficiency should be balanced against the right of the public to know about illegal, dangerous, and unjust practices of organizations. The most effective way to achieve the latter goal would be to pass a federal law protecting whistle blowers.

Laws protecting whistle blowers have also been opposed on the grounds that (1) employees would use them as an excuse to mask poor performance, (2) they would create an "informer ethos" within organizations, and (3) they would take away the autonomy of business, strangling it in red tape.

The first objection is illegitimate because only those employees who could show that an act of whistle blowing preceded their being dismissed or penalized and that their employment records were adequate up to the time of the whistle blowing could seek relief under the law.

The second objection is more formidable. A society that encourages snooping, suspicion, and mistrust is not most people's idea of the good society. Laws which encourage whistle blowing for self-interested reasons, such as the federal tax law, which pays informers part of any money that is collected, could help bring about such a society. However, laws protecting whistle blowers from being penalized or dismissed are quiet different. They do not reward the whistle blower; they merely protect him or her from unjust retaliation. It is unlikely that federal or state laws of this sort would promote an informer society.

The third objection is also unfounded. Laws protecting whistle blowers would not require any positive duties on the part of organizations — only the negative duty of not retaliating against employees who speak out in the public interest. However, not every act of apparent whistle blowing should be protected. Only people who can show they had probable reasons for believing wrongdoing existed should be protected. Furthermore, the burden of proof should be on the individual. People who cannot show they had good cause to suspect wrongdoing may justly be penalized or dismissed. If the damage to the organization is serious, it should also be allowed to sue. Since these conditions would impose some risks on potential whistle blowers, they would reduce the possibility of frivolous action.

If, on the other hand, someone who has probable reasons for believing wrongdoing exists blows the whistle and is fired, the burden of proof should be on the organization to show that he or she was not fired for blowing the whistle. If the whistle blowing is found to be the reason for the dismissal, the whistle blower should be reinstated and awarded damages. If there is further retaliation after reinstatement, additional damages should be awarded.

What changes could be made in organizations to prevent the need for whistle blowing? Some of the suggestions which have been made are that organizations develop effective internal channels for reporting wrongdoing, reward people with salary increases and promotions for using these channels, and appoint senior executives, board members, ombudspersons, and so on whose primary obligations would be to investigate and eliminate organizational wrongdoing. These changes could be undertaken by organizations on their own or mandated by law. Other changes which might be mandated are requiring that certain kinds of records be kept, assessing larger fines for illegal actions, and making executives and other professionals personally liable for filing false reports, knowingly marketing dangerous products, failing to monitor how policies are being implemented, and so forth. Although these reforms could do much to reduce the need for whistle blowing, given human nature it is highly unlikely that this need can ever be totally eliminated. Therefore, it is important to have laws which protect whistle blowers and for us to state as clearly as we can both the practical problems and moral issues pertaining to whistle blowing.

Notes

1. For discussion of the legal aspects of whistle blowing see Lawrence E. Blades, "Employment at Will vs. Individual Freedom: On Limiting the Abusive Exercise of Employer Power," *Columbia Law Review*, vol. 67 (1967); Philip Blumberg, "Corporate Responsibility and the Employee's Duty of Loyalty

and Obedience: A Preliminary Inquiry," *Oklahoma Law Review*, vol. 24 (1971); Clyde W. Summers, "Individual Protection Against Unjust Dismissal: Time for a Statute," *Virginia Law Review*, vol. 62 (1976); Arthur S. Miller, "Whistle Blowing and the Law," in Ralph Nader, Peter J. Petkas, and Kate Blackwell, *Whistle Blowing*, New York: Grossman Publishers, 1972; Alan F. Westin, *Whistle Blowing!*, New York: McGraw-Hill, 1981; Martin H. Marlin, "Current Status of Legal Protection for Whistleblowers," paper delivered at the Second Annual Conference on Ethics in Engineering, Illinois Institute of Technology, 1982. See also Gene G. James, "Whistle Blowing: Its Nature and Justification," *Philosophy in Context*, vol. 10 (1980).

2. For a discussion of this study which was by Morton Corn see Frank von Hipple, "Professional Freedom and Responsibility: The Role of the Professional Society," *Newsletter on Science, Technology and Human Values*, vol. 22, January 1978.

3. See Westin, op. cit.

4. See Marlin, op. cit.

5. David W. Ewing, *Freedom Inside the Organization*, New York: E. P. Dutton, 1977, pp. 165–166.

6. Richard T. De George, *Business Ethics*, New York: Macmillan, 1982, p. 161. See also De George, "Ethical Responsibilities of Engineers in Large Organizations," *Business and Professional Ethics Journal*, vol. 1, no. 1, Fall 1981, pp. 1–14. He formulates the first criterion in a slightly different way in the last work, saying that the harm must be both serious and considerable before whistle blowing is justified.

7. Ibid.

8. De George, "Ethical Responsibilities of Engineers in Large Organizations," op. cit., p. 1.

9. Ibid., p. 5.

10. Ibid., p. 7.

11. Miller, op. cit., p. 30.

12. Frederick A. Elliston, "Anonymous Whistleblowing," *Business and Professional Ethics Journal*, vol. 1, no. 2, Winter 1982.

13. Peter Raven-Hansen, "Dos and Don'ts for Whistleblowers: Planning for Trouble," *Technology Review*, May 1980, p. 30. My discussion in the present section is heavily indebted to this article.

Review and Discussion Questions

1. James and De George differ over what the engineers at Ford were morally required to do. With whom do you side and why?

2. Writers like De George and Bowie maintain that potential whistle blowers should first exhaust internal channels. Other authors maintain that whistle blowing should not be anonymous. James rejects both claims. Do you agree?

3. How important are the motives of a whistle blower? How important is the likelihood that blowing the whistle will bring results?

4. Do you think that laws protecting whistle blowers are a good idea? Do such laws reward disloyalty? Can internal organizational changes prevent the need for whistle blowing?

5. Compare the approaches of Bowie, De George, and James to whistle blowing. Whose analysis is the most persuasive?

For Further Reading

Sissela Bok, *Secrets* (New York: Vintage, 1983) writes insightfully on trade secrets and patents in Chapter 10 and on whistle blowing in Chapter 14.

Richard T. De George, "Ethical Responsibilities of Engineers in Large Organizations," *Business and Professional Ethics Journal* 1 (Fall 1981) discusses whistle blowing in the context of the Ford Pinto case.

Mark Pastin and **Michael Hooker**, "Ethics and the Foreign Corrupt Practices Act," *Business Horizons* 23 (December 1980) criticize the Foreign Corrupt Practices Act.

Martin Snoeyenbos, Robert Almeder, and **James Humber**, eds., *Business Ethics* (Buffalo: Prometheus, 1983), Part 3, provides essays and cases on conflict of interest, gifts and payoffs, patents, and trade secrets.

CHAPTER 9

JOB DISCRIMINATION

"Sick humor and racist clichés" abound at the White House. So says Terrel H. Bell, President Reagan's first Secretary of Education.[1] When the Reagan-Bush administration was vigorously fighting passage of the bill to establish Martin Luther King, Jr.'s birthday as a national holiday, "mid-level" staffers referred to Dr. King as "Martin Lucifer Coon." Over at the Attorney General's office, the section of the Civil Rights Act that safeguards women against discrimination was nicknamed "the lesbian's bill of rights." Staffers at the State Department, when discussing the Middle East, quipped that Arabs are just "sand niggers." And women will have a hard time forgetting Chief of Staff Don Regan's widely published denigrations. After the first Reagan-Gorbachev summit meeting, he stated that women are more interested in fashion than arms control. On another occasion he claimed they care more about their diamonds (many of which come from South Africa) than they do about apartheid.

If the attitudes these remarks display are prevalent in the highest reaches of government, it is hard to believe that they are not also to be found in the board rooms and executive suits of many American corporations. Many people would of course reject such racist and sexist jokes as at best crude and unseemly, at worst immoral. But explicit prejudice is just part of the problem. Even open-minded people may operate on implicit assumptions that work to the disadvantage of women, and many who believe themselves to be unprejudiced harbor unconscious racist attitudes.

Stanford law professor Charles R. Lawrence III, for instance, recalls his college days as a token black presence in a white world.

Companions would say to him, "I don't think of you as a Negro." Their conscious intent was benign and complimentary. The speaker was saying, "I think of you as a normal human being, just like me."

> But he was not conscious of the underlying implications of his words. What did this mean about most Negroes? Were they not normal human beings? . . . To say that one does not think of a Negro as a Negro is to say that one thinks of him as something else. The statement is made in the context of the real world, and implicit in it is a comparison to some norm. In this case the norm is whiteness. The white liberal's unconscious thought . . . is, "I think of you as different from other Negroes, as more like white people."[2]

In other cases unconscious racist stereotypes, which are normally repressed, slip out, as when sportscaster Howard Cosell, carried away by the excitement of the game, referred to a black football player as a "little monkey" or when Nancy Reagan told a public gathering that she wished her husband could be there to "see all these beautiful white people."[3]

Slavery in our country resulted in a long legacy of legally institutionalized racism and socioeconomic subordination of blacks and other minorities. That history, and centuries of discrimination against women, lie behind the racially and sexually prejudiced attitudes so prevalent in the United States. We must bear that history and those attitudes in mind as we explore the area of job discrimination. In particular, this chapter examines the following topics:

1. The meaning of job discrimination and its different forms

2. The statistical and attitudinal evidence of discrimination

3. The historical and legal context of affirmative action

4. The moral arguments for and against affirmative action

5. The doctrine of comparable worth and the controversy over it

6. The problem of sexual harassment in employment—what it is, what forms it takes, what the law says about it, and why it's wrong

THE MEANING OF JOB DISCRIMINATION

According to Professor Manuel G. Velasquez, to discriminate in employment is to make an adverse decision against employees based on their membership in a certain class.[4] Determining whether discrimination occurs in employment depends on three basic facts: (1) whether the decision is a function of an employee's or prospective employee's membership in a certain group, rather than individual merit; (2) whether the decision is based on the assumption that the group is in some way inferior and thus deserving of unequal treatment; and (3) whether the decision in some way harms those it's aimed at. Since most discrimination in the American workplace has traditionally been aimed at women and at such minorities as blacks and Hispanics, the following discussion focuses on these groups.

Job discrimination can take different forms. Individuals can intentionally discriminate out of personal prejudice or on the basis of stereotypes. For example, a member of a company's personnel department might routinely downgrade applications from women who want to work in the company's production plant because he believes, and knowingly acts on the belief, that "ladies don't understand machines." On the other hand, individuals may discriminate because they unthinkingly or unconsciously adopt traditional practices and stereotypes. For example, if the man in the preceding case acted without being aware of the bias underlying his decisions, his action would fall into this category.

Institutions can also discriminate. Sometimes this form of discrimination can be explicit and intentional. An example is when company policy dictates that women not be placed in supervisory positions because "the boys in the company don't like to take orders from females." Or consider the employment agencies recently charged with screening out blacks, Latinos, older workers, and others at the request of their corporate clients.[5] On the other hand, the routine operating procedures of a company may reflect stereotypes and prejudiced practices that it is not fully aware of. For example, the FBI routinely transfers its Hispanic agents around the country on temporary, low-level assignments where a knowledge of Spanish is needed; the Hispanic agents function as little more than assistants to non-Hispanic colleagues. Hispanic agents dub this the "taco circuit" and claim that it adversely affects their opportunities for promotion. A federal court has now agreed with them that the practice is indeed discriminatory.[6]

In addition, institutional practices that appear neutral and nondiscriminatory may harm members of groups that are traditionally discriminated against. When membership in an all-white craft union, for instance, requires nomination by those who are already members, racial exclusion is likely to result even if the motivation of those who do the nominating is purely nepotistic and results from no racially motivated ill will or stereotyping. Institutional procedures like this may not involve job discrimination in the narrow sense, but they clearly work to the disadvantage of women and minority groups, denying them full equality of opportunity.

From a variety of moral perspectives there are compelling moral arguments against job discrimination on racial or sexual grounds. Discrimination involves false assumptions about the inferiority of a certain group and harms individual members of that group, so utilitarians would reject it because of its ill effects on total human welfare. Kantians would clearly repudiate it as failing to respect people as ends in themselves. Universalizing the maxim underlying discriminatory practices is virtually impossible. No people who now discriminate would be willing to accept such treatment themselves. Discrimination on grounds of sex or race also violates people's basic moral rights and mocks the ideal of human moral equality. Furthermore, such discrimination is unjust. To use Rawls's theory as an illustration, parties in the original position would clearly choose for themselves the principle of equal opportunity.

On the other hand, there are no respectable arguments in favor of racial and sexual discrimination. Whatever racist or sexist attitudes people might actually have, no one today is prepared to defend job discrimination publicly, any more than someone would publicly defend slavery or repeal of the Nineteenth Amendment (which gave women the right to vote). This attitude toward job discrimination is reflected in legal and political efforts to develop programs to root out job discrimination and ameliorate the results of past discrimination.

Before looking at the relevant legal history and the controversies surrounding various antidiscrimination measures, this chapter examines the relative positions of whites and minorities and of males and females in the American workplace to see if they say anything about ongoing discrimination.

EVIDENCE OF DISCRIMINATION

Determining the presence of discrimination isn't easy, because many factors could account for the relative positions of various groups in the work world. But generally speaking, an institution would seem to be practicing discrimination (intentional or unintentional) when (1) statistics indicate that members of a group are being treated unequally in comparison with other groups and (2) endemic attitudes, practices, and policies are biased in ways that seem to account for the skewed statistics.

Statistical Evidence

As noted in a previous chapter, racial minorities bear the brunt of poverty in our nation. Blacks are about three times more likely to be poor than whites. Although one out of every nine white Americans is poor, one out of every three blacks and Native Americans is poor and more than one out of every four Hispanics is poor. Today a black child has nearly one chance in two of being born into poverty.[7]

Overall black family income is only 55 percent of white family income, down from 62 percent in 1975; many fear that the gap will further widen. William F. Buckley notes that, if we put the income of the average American at 100, then Native Americans are at 60, blacks at 62, Puerto Ricans at 63, and Mexican-Americans at 76.[8] In the 1980s the salary gap between whites and blacks increased.[9] According to a 1991 Census Bureau report, the median wealth of white households is ten times that of black households—$43,280 versus $4,170. And 29 percent of black households, but only 9 percent of all white households, are reported as having no wealth at all, meaning that they own no assets or that their liabilities exceed their assets.[10]

Unemployment hits racial minorities hard, because they are often last hired and first fired. Unemployment among blacks is in general twice as high as that of whites. Of every three minority workers, one is employed irregularly or has given up looking for work, and one in three is engaged primarily in a job that pays less than a living wage. Official unemployment figures for inner-city black youths exceed 40 percent, but the actual figures are thought to be much higher.

Black and other minority workers are overwhelmingly clustered in low-paying, low-prestige, dead-end work. U.S. government statistics reveal clearly the extent to which the most desirable occupations (in management and administration, professional and technical jobs, sales, and crafts) are dominated by whites; blacks, Hispanics, and other ethnic minorities are relegated to less desirable jobs (in manual labor, service, and farm work).[11] As Gertrude Ezorsky remarks, today every other person involved by occupation with dirt or garbage is black.[12] Of roughly 2 million engineers in America, about 2 percent are blacks and 2 percent Hispanics. Of approximately 225,000 physical scientists, 3 percent are blacks and less than 2 percent Hispanics.[13] The *National Law Journal* reports that blacks make up about 1.5 percent of the lawyers in the nation's hundred largest law firms. The percentage of Hispanic lawyers in these firms is even smaller: 0.65 percent.[14] And only 440 of the 23,195 partners of the nation's 250 largest law firms are members of minorities.[15] Education does not account for this disparity in pay and position. In 1982, a white head of household with a high school degree earned more than a black male with a college degree.[16]

Women, too, are clustered in poorer-paying jobs—the so-called "pink-collar" occupations. They tend to work as librarians, nurses, elementary school teachers, sales clerks, secretaries, bank tellers, and waitresses. The top-paying occupations have been, and to a large extent continue to be, almost exclusively male preserves. For example, 99 percent of dental hygienists, but only 6.2 percent of dentists, are women. Nor is the problem simply that men monopolize the very top positions. Figures from the Bureau of Labor Statistics show that traditionally "female occupations" pay less than traditionally "male occupations,"

like plumber, pharmacist, mail carrier, and shipping clerk. Sixty percent of all women work in only ten occupations, and most new jobs for women are in areas with low pay and limited chances of advancement.[17] A Cornell study found that a quarter of the 1,315 working women it polled earn a poverty-level income (which varies according to the number of children in the household). The situation is even worse for black women.[18]

Education does not explain the differences in position and pay. On average, men consistently earn more than women with higher levels of education. In occupation after occupation, women make less money than men—even for the same work—despite legislation forbidding discrimination on the basis of sex and requiring equal pay for equal jobs. According to a Rand Corporation study released in October 1984, however, the wage gap between men and women is closing.[19] The study concluded that the average hourly wage for working women will rise from 64 percent to 75 percent of the average for working men by the year 2000. In fact, the male-female wage differential has increased slightly since 1984, but even if the study's long-term prediction is correct, a 25 percent average wage difference is far from parity. Moreover, the 64 percent figure, although up from 1979 when women's earnings were 58.9 percent of men's, is no more than it was in 1955. The fact is that, although recent years have seen women enter the work force in greater numbers and in more diverse fields than ever before, men remain ahead in pay.[20]

Women and minorities have made inroads into white-collar and professional ranks, but few have made it to the top of their professions. For example, only 5 percent of law partnerships are held by women. About 40 percent of working blacks hold white-collar jobs, up from 11 percent in 1960, although they are still 14 percent behind whites. Surveys of *Fortune 1000* companies reveal that there is little penetration of the top rungs of America's largest corporations. A 1979 survey of 1,708 senior executives discovered only three blacks, two Asians, two Hispanics, and eight women. A 1985 survey of 1,362 senior executives found little improvement: four blacks, six Asians, three Hispanics, and twenty-nine women.[21] In 1988 *Fortune* magazine found one black CEO among its top 1,000 corporations and one black among its top 500 industrials; *Business Week's* 1990 directory of the CEOs of the top 1,000 publicly held companies lists two women and one black.[22]

Attitudinal Evidence

Although some would disagree, statistics alone do not conclusively establish discrimination because one can always argue that other things account for the disparities in income and position between men and women and between whites and other races. The Supreme Court, in fact, has recently argued that "no matter how stark the numerical disparity of the employer's workforce," statistical evidence by itself does not prove discrimination.[23] But when widespread attitudes and institutional practices and policies are taken into account, they point to discrimination as the cause of the statistical disparities.

Consider the case of Elizabeth Hishon, who went to work for King & Spaulding, a big Atlanta law firm, in 1972. Customarily, associates like Hishon are given a period of time to either make partner or seek another job. So when Hishon had not attained partner status by 1979, she was terminated. Hishon, however, claimed that her failure to become a partner was due to the law firm's sexism, and she filed a suit seeking monetary damages under Title VII of the Civil Rights Act of 1964, which prohibits sexual and racial discrimination at work. A federal district court held that the rights guaranteed by Title VII do not apply to the selection of partners in a law firm, but the Supreme Court overturned that ruling in a unanimous 1984 decision that held that

women can bring sex-discrimination suits against law firms that unfairly deny them promotions to partner. In the meantime, however, Elizabeth Hishon, had settled out of court with King & Spaulding, and the case never went to trial.

In November 1990 Nancy O'Mara Ezold became the first woman to win a sex-discrimination trial against a law firm in a partnership decision. And a few days later, in a case in which the Supreme Court had already found sex discrimination, a federal appeals judge ruled that Price Waterhouse, the accounting firm, must give a partnership and back pay to Ann Hopkins, against whom it had discriminated. These decisions are having a significant impact on the one million partnership concerns nationwide. Promotional practices are being reevaluated, not only in law and accounting firms, but also in advertising agencies, brokerage houses, architectural concerns, and engineering firms.

Of particular interest here are the discriminatory attitudes and policies revealed by these cases. In the Ezold case, the judge found that the prominent Philadelphia law firm for which she had worked had applied tougher standards to women seeking partnerships than to men. And Ezold herself said, "It wasn't just that similarly situated men were treated better than me, which is the double-standard idea. Another thing that came out of the trial was that in the year preceding the partnership decision, [the firm] assigned me to less complex cases and to fewer partners than it did men, so that I was denied the exposure that was critical to the partnership decision."[24]

In Ann Hopkins's case, sex stereotyping was at the root of the discrimination. Though she was considered an outstanding worker, Price Waterhouse denied her the position because she was allegedly an abrasive and overbearing manager. Co-workers referred to her as "macho," advised her to go to charm school, and intimated that she was overcompensating for being a woman. One partner in the firm even told her that she should "walk more femininely, talk more femininely, dress more femininely, wear make-up, have her hair styled, and wear jewelry." Hopkins argued, and the court agreed, that comments like these revealed an underlying sexism at the firm and that her strident manner and occasional cursing would have been overlooked if she had been a man.[25]

As for the earlier Hishon decision, the case is noteworthy because the defendants expressed no specific complaints about Hishon's work. They apparently denied her a partnership based on a general feeling that "she just didn't fit in." In the words of another woman who had been an associate at King & Spaulding, "If you can't discuss the Virginia–North Carolina basketball game, you're an outcast."[26] Her pithy comment speaks volumes about how deep-seated attitudes operate against women and minorities in the workplace.

Surveys further support the evidence of these cases, suggesting that sex stereotyping and sexist assumptions are widespread in the world of business. For example, in a questionnaire submitted to 5,000 of its subscribers, the *Harvard Business Review* found a double standard in managers' expectations of men and women. In sum, managers expect male employees to put job before family when conflicting obligations arise, but they expect female employees to sacrifice career to family responsibilities. Also, when personal conduct threatens an employee's job, managers go to greater lengths to retain a valuable male employee than an equally qualified female. The survey also turned up antifemale bias: In employee selection and promotion and in career-development decisions, managers clearly favor men.[27] Over the years, various reports have indicated that myths, stereotypes, and false preconceptions victimize women and minorities. For example, studies of MBA students over the years show male students re-

maining consistently negative in their attitudes toward women as executives.[28]

When women and minorities enter male-dominated areas, they frequently are assumed incompetent until they prove otherwise. A good example is scientific fields. "Employers make certain assumptions about what the best look like," says Shirley Malcolm, head of the office of opportunities in science of the American Association for the Advancement of Science.[29] Betty Vetter, executive director of the Scientific Manpower Commission in Washington, elaborates: "When men come in as new engineers into a job, they are assumed to be competent until proved otherwise. . . . When women come in, they are assumed to be incompetent until they have proved over and over and over again that indeed they are not."[30]

Moreover, a woman entering "male turf" can find herself uncomfortably measured according to the predominant male value system. Here's how Florence Blair, a twenty-five-year-old black civil engineer, describes working as a civil engineer at Corning Glass Works:

> As a minority woman, you are just so different from everyone else you encounter. . . . I went through a long period of isolation. . . . When I came here, I didn't have a lot in common with the white males I was working with. I didn't play golf, I didn't drink beer, I didn't hunt. All these things I had no frame of reference to.
>
> You need to do your job on a certain technical level, but a lot of things you do on the job come down to socializing and how well you mesh with people. Sometimes I look at my role as making people feel comfortable with me.
>
> Sometimes it's disheartening. You think why do I have to spend all of my time and my energy making them feel comfortable with me when they're not reciprocating?[31]

Blair also says she experienced a double standard. Soon after she started work, with an engineering degree from Purdue, she was told by her supervisor that her drafting skills were not up to par and that she should take a remedial drafting course at a local community college. In contrast, when young white men showed less than adequate drafting skills, supervisors told them, "We know that your skills are rusty, but we'll work with you a little bit, and through practice you will improve." This worker's experience may not be typical, but it does point up how ill-considered assumptions and stereotypes in the workplace, which admittedly can sometimes victimize all of us, are a special problem that women and minorities face.

For example, a recent survey shows that three out of four whites believe that blacks and Hispanics are more likely than whites to prefer living on welfare, and a majority of whites also believe that blacks and Hispanics are more likely to be lazy, unpatriotic, and prone to violence.[32] Another survey, this time of Ivy League graduates, class of 1957, also illustrates the prevalence of racial stereotypes and assumptions. For these men, "dumb" came to mind when they thought of blacks. Only 36 percent of the Princeton class, 47 percent of the Yale class, and 55 percent of the Harvard men agreed with the statement "Blacks are as intelligent as whites." These are graduates of three leading universities who are now in their fifties, the age of promotion into senior corporate positions. In discussing this survey, Edward W. Jones, Jr., writes:

> All people possess stereotypes, which act like shorthand to avoid mental overload. . . . Most of the time stereotypes are mere shadow images rooted in one's history and deep in the subconscious. But they are very powerful. For example, in controlled experiments the mere insertion of the word black into a sentence has resulted in people changing their responses to a statement.
>
> One reason for the power of stereotypes is their circularity. People seek to confirm their expectations and resist contradictory evidence, so we cling to beliefs and stereotypes that become self-fulfilling. If, for example, a white administrator makes a mistake, his boss is likely to tell him, "That's OK. Everybody's entitled to one goof." If, however, a black counterpart commits the same error, the boss thinks, "I knew he couldn't do it. The guy is incompetent." The stereotype reinforces itself.[33]

Taken together, the statistics and the personal and institutional attitudes, assumptions and practices provide powerful evidence of intractable discrimination against women and minorities in the American workplace. Recognizing the existence of such discrimination and believing for a variety of reasons that it is wrong, we have as a nation passed laws to provide equality of opportunity to women and minorities. They expressly forbid discrimination in recruitment, screening, promotion, compensation, and firing. But antidiscrimination laws do not address the present-day effects of past discrimination. To remedy the effects of past discrimination and counteract visceral racism and sexism, some companies and institutions have adopted stronger and more controversial affirmative action measures.

AFFIRMATIVE ACTION: THE LEGAL CONTEXT

In 1954 the Supreme Court decided in the case of *Brown* v. *Board of Education* that racially segregated schooling is unconstitutional. In doing so, the Court conclusively rejected the older doctrine that "separate but equal" facilities are legally permissible. Not only were segregated facilities in the South unequal, the Court found, but the very ideal of separation of the races, based as it was on a belief in black racial inferiority, inherently led to unequal treatment. That famous decision helped to launch the civil rights movement in this country. One fruit of that movement was a series of federal laws and orders that attempt to implement the right of each person to equal treatment in employment.

The changes began in 1961, when President John F. Kennedy signed Executive Order 10925, which decreed that federal contractors should "take affirmative action to ensure that applicants are employed without regard to their race, creed, color, or national origin." In 1963 the Equal Pay Act was passed by Congress. Aimed especially at wage discrimination against women, it guaranteed the right to equal pay for equal work. That was followed by the Civil Rights Act of 1964 (which was later amended by the Equal Employment Opportunity Act of 1972). It prohibits all forms of discrimination based on race, color, sex, religion, or national origin. Title VII, the most important section of the act, prohibits discrimination in employment. It says:

> It shall be an unlawful employment practice for an employer (1) to fail or refuse to hire or to discharge any individual, or otherwise discriminate against any individual with respect to his compensation, terms, conditions, or privileges of employment, because of such individual's race, color, religion, sex, or national origin; or (2) to limit, segregate, or classify his employees or applicants for employment in any way that would deprive or tend to deprive any individual of employment opportunities or otherwise adversely affect his status as an employee, because of such individual's race, color, religion, sex, or national origin.

The Civil Rights Act of 1964 applies to all employers, both public and private, with fifteen or more employees. In 1967 the Age Discrimination in Employment Act was passed (amended in 1978). In addition, several acts and executive orders regulate government contractors and subcontractors and require equal opportunities for the handicapped and for veterans. All of these acts are enforced through the Equal Employment Opportunity Commission (EEOC).[34]

By the late 1960s and early 1970s, companies contracting with the federal government (first in construction and then generally) were required to develop *affirmative action programs*, designed to correct imbalances in employment that exist directly as a result of past discrimination. These programs corresponded with the courts' recognition that job discrimination can exist even in the absence of conscious intent to discriminate.[35] Affirmative action riders were added, with varying degrees of specificity, into a larger number of federal programs. Many state and local bodies adopted comparable requirements.[36]

What do affirmative action programs involve? The EEOC lists general guidelines as steps to affirmative action. Under these steps, firms must issue a written equal-employment policy and an affirmative action commitment. They must appoint a top official with responsibility and authority to direct and implement their program and to publicize their policy and affirmative action commitment. In addition, firms must survey current female and minority employment by department and job classification. Where underrepresentation of these groups is evident, firms must develop goals and timetables to improve in each area of underrepresentation. They then must develop specific programs to achieve these goals, establish an internal audit system to monitor them, and evaluate progress in each aspect of the program. Finally, companies must develop supportive in-house and community programs to combat discrimination.

Critics of affirmative action charge that it means, in practice, illegal quotas, preferential treatment of blacks and women, and even "reverse discrimination" against white men. In the 1960s and early 1970s, however, federal courts dismissed legal challenges to affirmative action, and in 1972 Congress gave it increased legislative validity by passing the Equal Employment Opportunity Act. Eventually, however, the Supreme Court had to address the question. Although its decisions determine the law of the land with regard to affirmative action, the Court's rulings have not always been as simple and straightforward as one might wish.

The Supreme Court's Position

The Supreme Court's first major ruling on affirmative action was in 1978, in the case of *Bakke* v. *Regents of the University of California.* Allan Bakke is a white man who applied for admission to the medical school at the University of California at Davis. Only a tiny percentage of doctors are not white. To help remedy this situation, Davis's affirmative action program set aside for minority students sixteen out of its hundred entrance places. If qualified minority students could not be found, those places were not to be filled. In addition to the special admissions process, minority students were free to compete through the regular admissions process for one of the unrestricted eighty-four positions. Bakke was refused admission, but he sued the University of California, contending that it had discriminated against him in violation of both the 1964 Civil Rights Act and the Constitution. He argued that he would have won admission if those sixteen places had not been withdrawn from open competition and reserved for minority students. Bakke's grades, placement-test scores, and so on were higher than several minority students who were admitted. The University did not deny this but defended its program as legally permissible and socially necessary affirmative action.

Bakke won his case, although it was a close, five-to-four decision. Four justices sided with the University of California at Davis; four found that Davis's program was illegal in light of the 1964 Civil Rights Act; and one justice (Powell) held that, while the program did not violate that act, it was invalid on constitutional grounds. In announcing the judgment of the Court, Powell's opinion rejected explicit racial criteria setting rigid quotas and excluding nonpreferred groups from competition. At the same time he held that the selection process can take race and ethnic origin into account as one factor and pointed to Harvard's admission program as a model. In such a program, "race or ethnic background may be deemed a 'plus' in a particular applicant's file, yet it does not insulate the individual from comparison with all other candidates for the available seats." Powell also granted that numerical goals may be permissible when the institution in question has illegally discriminated in the past.

A year later, in *United Steelworkers of America* v. *Weber*, the Supreme Court took up the issue again—but in a different situation and with a different verdict. Brian Weber worked at Kaiser Aluminum's Gramercy, Louisiana, plant. The steelworkers' union had been pressing Kaiser to train its own workers for better-paying skilled craft positions instead of hiring craft workers from outside the company. Kaiser was also under pressure from various federal agencies to employ more black workers in skilled positions. At the Gramercy plant, for example, only 5 out of 273 skilled craft workers were black, although the local work force was 39 percent black. Kaiser therefore entered into a collective-bargaining agreement with the United Steelworkers that contained a plan "to eliminate conspicuous racial imbalances" in Kaiser's skilled craft positions. Kaiser agreed to set up a training program to qualify its own workers for craft positions and to choose trainees from the existing work force on the basis of seniority, except that 50 percent of the positions would be reserved for blacks until the percentage of blacks in these jobs approximated the percentage of blacks in the local work force.

Weber, a young semiskilled worker, was one of several whites who had failed to gain admission to the training program for skilled craft positions, despite having more seniority than the most senior black trainee. Weber sued, arguing that he had been discriminated against on the basis of his race. This time the Supreme Court upheld the affirmative action program in a five-to-two decision. In delivering the Court's opinion, Justice Brennan made clear that legal prohibition of racial discrimination does not prevent "private, voluntary, race-conscious affirmative action plans." He wrote:

> We need not today define in detail the line of demarcation between permissible and impermissible affirmative action plans. It suffices to hold that the challenged Kaiser-USWA affirmative action plan falls on the permissible side of the line. The purposes of the plan mirror those of the [Civil Rights] statute. Both were designed to break down old patterns of racial segregation and hierarchy. Both were structured to "open employment opportunities for Negroes in occupations which have been traditionally closed to them" . . .
>
> At the same time, the plan does not unnecessarily trammel the interest of the white employees. . . . Moreover, the plan is a temporary measure . . . simply to eliminate a manifest racial imbalance.

In 1984, however, the Supreme Court upheld seniority over affirmative action in *Memphis Firefighters* v. *Stotts*. The city of Memphis, Tennessee, hired its first black firefighter in 1955 and its second in 1964. Between 1950 and 1976, the fire department hired 1,683 whites but only 94 blacks. A class-action suit was filed in 1977, charging the city with racial discrimination in hiring and promoting firefighters, and in 1980 the city signed a consent decree with the Justice Department. While not admitting it had engaged in racial discrimination, the city agreed to attempt to give 50 percent of new jobs and 20 percent of promotions to blacks. Under the plan the percentage of black firefighters rose from 4 to 11.5 percent.

When financial difficulties forced the city to lay off firefighters, it followed the seniority rules negotiated with the union. Last hired were to be let go first. Fearing that the progress black firefighters had made would be quickly lost, Carl Stotts, who had brought the original suit, asked a federal district court to protect blacks from layoffs. It did, and seventy-two whites, but only eight blacks, were laid off or demoted. The city of Memphis and the union appealed the ruling and, after losing before a federal appeals court, took their cause to the Supreme Court. In the meantime, additional funds had been found to rehire the laid-off workers, but the Supreme Court agreed to hear the case anyway.

The Supreme Court reversed the district court's ruling, holding that seniority systems are racially neutral and that the city may not lay off white workers to save the jobs of black workers with less seniority. Speaking for the majority, Justice White wrote, "It is inappropriate to deny an innocent employee the benefits of his seniority . . . to provide a remedy in a [case] such as this." A court can award competitive seniority to an individual black only when he or she has been the actual victim of illegal discrimination. He continued:

> Mere membership in the disadvantaged class is insufficient to warrant a seniority award. . . . Even when an individual shows that the discriminatory practice has had an impact on him, he is not automatically entitled to have a non-minority employee laid off to make room for him. He may have to wait until a vacancy occurs.

The principle of affirmative action was, however, upheld again in 1987, this time in a case concerning women. In *Johnson* v. *Transportation Agency*, the Supreme Court affirmed that considerations of sex were permissible as one factor in promoting Diane Joyce, a female county employee, to the position of road dispatcher over an equally qualified male employee, Paul Johnson. In summing up the Court's position, Justice Brennan stated that the promotion of Joyce "was made pursuant to an affirmative action plan that represents a moderate, flexible, case-by-case approach to effecting a gradual improvement in the representation of minorities and women in the Agency's work force."

These cases illustrate well the Supreme Court's cautious approach to alleged abuses of affirmative action. Instead of trying to establish at one blow a hard and fast "line of demarcation between permissible and impermissible affirmative action plans," the Court has been developing its position gradually, based on the relatively specific details of the individual cases it examines. Despite variations in the cases just described and despite dissenting opinions, a solid majority of the Supreme Court has continued to uphold the general principle of affirmative action.

Or at least it continued to do so until 1989, when the legal situation became less stable. In that year the Supreme Court, led by its Reagan-era appointees, began handing down a series of legal rulings generally antagonistic to affirmative action. Among other decisions, the Court invalidated a Richmond, Virginia, law that channeled 30 percent of public-works funds to minority-owned construction companies. It reversed an eighteen-year-old precedent and put the burden of proof on plaintiffs, not employers, to prove whether a job requirement that is shown statistically to screen out minorities or women is a "business necessity." And it has made it easier for white men to challenge court-approved "consent de-

crees," in which employers undertake programs to hire and promote blacks, even when the plan was approved years earlier.[37]*

The upshot of these recent developments is not clear, tangled up as they are in legal technicalities, case details, and split opinions. Although the future is hard to predict, the Supreme Court is not likely to reverse itself directly and outlaw "moderate" and "flexible" affirmative action programs across the board. But it is increasingly hostile to job-discrimination suits and more clearly attuned than ever to what it perceives to be excesses in the cause of affirmative action.

AFFIRMATIVE ACTION: THE MORAL ISSUES

Understanding the Supreme Court's evolving position on affirmative action is important, because the Court sets the legal context in which business acts and lets employers know what they are and are not legally permitted to do. But legal decisions by themselves do not exhaust the relevant moral issues. Employers — as well as women, minorities, and white men — want to know whether affirmative action programs are morally right. Indeed, it is a safe bet that the Supreme Court's own decisions are influenced not just by technical legal questions but also by how the justices answer this moral question.

Before evaluating arguments for and against affirmative action, one needs to know what is being debated. "Affirmative action"

---

* Ironically, on the same day the Court permitted white firefighters to challenge an eight-year-old, court-approved affirmative action settlement, it told the women who had been demoted by AT&T under an allegedly discriminatory seniority system that they had waited too long to challenge the AT&T system. They sued immediately after their demotions but had not challenged the program when the company originally adopted it a few years earlier.

here means programs taking the race or sex of employees or job candidates into account as part of an effort to correct imbalances in employment that exist as a result of past discrimination, either in the company itself or in the larger society. To keep the discussion relevant, it is limited to affirmative action programs that might reasonably be expected to be upheld by the Supreme Court. Excluded are programs that establish rigid, permanent quotas or that hire and promote unqualified persons. Included are programs that hire or promote a woman or black who might not otherwise, according to established but fair criteria, be the best-qualified candidate.

A word about terminology: Critics of affirmative action often label it "reverse discrimination," but this term is misleading. According to the definition offered earlier, job discrimination involves the assumption that a certain group is inferior and deserves unequal treatment. No such assumption is at work in the affirmative action cases already discussed. Those who designed the programs that worked to the disadvantage of Allan Bakke, Brian Weber, and Paul Johnson did not do so because they believed white men are inferior and deserving of less respect than other human beings. Those who designed the programs in question were themselves white men.

Arguments for Affirmative Action

1. *Compensatory justice demands affirmative action programs.*

POINT: "As groups, women and minorities have historically been discriminated against, often viciously. As individuals and as a nation, we can't ignore the sins of our fathers and mothers. In fact, we have an obligation to do something to help repair the wrongs of the past. Affirmative action in employment is one sound way to do this."

COUNTERPOINT: "People today can't be expected to atone for the sins of the past. We're not responsible for them, and in any case, we wouldn't be compensating those who rightly deserve it. Young blacks and women coming for their first job have never suffered employment discrimination. Their parents and grandparents may deserve compensation, but why should today's candidates receive any special consideration? No one should discriminate against them, of course, but they should have to compete openly and on their merits, just like everybody else."

2. *Affirmative action is necessary to permit fairer competition.*

POINT: "Even if young blacks and young women today have not themselves suffered job discrimination, blacks in particular have suffered all the disadvantages of growing up in families that have been affected by discrimination. In our racist society, they have suffered from inferior schools and poor environment. In addition, as victims of society's prejudiced attitudes, young blacks and young women have been hampered by a lack of self-confidence and self-respect. Taking race and sex into account makes job competition fairer by keeping white men from having a competitive edge that they don't really deserve."

COUNTERPOINT: "Your point is better when applied to blacks than to women, it seems to me, but I'm still not persuaded. You overlook the fact that there are a lot of disadvantaged whites out there, too. Is an employer going to have to investigate everyone's life history to see who had to overcome the most obstacles? I think an employer has a right to seek the best-qualified candidate, without trying to make life fair for everybody. And isn't the best-qualified person entitled to get the job or the promotion?"

3. *Affirmative action is necessary to break the cycle that keeps minorities and women locked into low-paying, low-prestige jobs.*

POINT: "You advocate neutral, nondiscriminatory employment practices, as if we could just ignore our whole history of racial and sexual discrimination. Statistics show that blacks in particular have been trapped in a socioeconomically subordinate position. If we want to break that pattern and eventually heal the racial rifts in our country, we've got to adopt vigorous affirmative action programs that push more blacks into middle-class jobs. Even assuming racism were dead in our society, with mere nondiscrimination alone it would take a hundred years or more for blacks to equalize their position."

COUNTERPOINT: "You ignore the fact that affirmative action has its costs, too. You talk about healing the racial rifts in our country, but affirmative action programs make everybody more racially conscious. They also cause resentment and frustration among white men. Many blacks and women also resent being advanced on grounds other than merit. Finally, if you hire and promote people faster and further than they merit, you're only asking for problems."

Arguments Against Affirmative Action

1. *Affirmative action injures white men and violates their rights.*

POINT: "Even moderate affirmative action programs injure the white men who are made to bear their brunt. Other people design the programs, but it is Allan Bakke, Brian Weber, Paul Johnson, and others like them who find their career opportunities hampered. Moreover, such programs violate the right of white men to be treated as individuals and to have racial or sexual considerations not affect employment decisions."

COUNTERPOINT: "I'm not sure Bakke, Weber, and Johnson have the rights you are talking about. Racial and sexual considerations are of-

ten relevant to employment decisions. Jobs and medical school places are scarce resources, and society may distribute these in a way that furthers its legitimate ends — like breaking the cycle of poverty for minorities. I admit that with affirmative action programs white men do not have as many advantages as they did before, and I'm against extreme programs that disregard their interests altogether. But their interests have to be balanced against society's interest in promoting these programs."

2. *Affirmative action itself violates the principle of equality.*

POINT: "Affirmative action programs are intended to enhance racial and sexual equality, but you can't do that by treating people unequally. If equality is the goal, it must be the means too. With the affirmative action programs, you use racial and sexual considerations — but that is the very thing that has caused so much harm in the past and that affirmative action itself is hoping to get rid of."

COUNTERPOINT: "I admit that it is distasteful to have to take racial and sexual considerations into account when dealing with individuals in employment situations. I wish we didn't have to. But the unfortunate reality is that in the real world racial and sexual factors go a long way toward determining what life prospects an individual has. We can't wish that reality away by pretending the world is colorblind when it is not. Formal, colorblind equality has to be infringed now if we are ever to achieve real, meaningful racial and sexual equality."

3. *Nondiscrimination will achieve our social goals; stronger affirmative action is unnecessary.*

POINT: "The 1964 Civil Rights Act unequivocally outlaws job discrimination, and numerous employees and job candidates have won discrimination cases before the EEOC or in court. We need to insist on rigorous enforcement of the law. Also, employers should continue to recruit in a way that attracts minority applicants and to make sure that their screening and review practices do not involve any implicit racist or sexist assumptions. And they should monitor their internal procedures and the behavior of their white male employees to root out any discriminatory behavior. Stronger affirmative action measures, in particular taking race or sex into account in employment matters, are unnecessary. They only bring undesirable results.''

COUNTERPOINT: ''Without affirmative action, progress often stops. The percentage of minorities and women employed by those subject to federal affirmative action requirements has risen much higher than it has elsewhere. Or take the example of Alabama. In the late 1960s, a federal court found that only 27 out of the state's 3,000 clerical and managerial employees were black. Federal Judge Frank Johnson ordered extensive recruiting of blacks, as well as the hiring of the few specifically identified blacks who could prove they were victims of discrimination. Nothing happened. Another suit was filed, this time just against the state police, and this time a 50 percent hiring quota was imposed, until blacks reached 25 percent of the force. Today Alabama has the most thoroughly integrated state police force in the country.''[38]

The debate over affirmative action is not the only controversy connected with job discrimination. Two other issues, both primarily concerning women, have been at the center of recent moral, legal, and political debate: the issue of comparable worth and the problem of sexual harassment on the job.

COMPARABLE WORTH

In 1983 Louise Peterson was a licensed practical nurse at Western State Hospital in Tacoma, Washington. That year she received $1,462 a month for supervising the daily care of sixty men convicted of sex crimes, which was $192 a month less than the hospital's grounds-keepers earned and $700 a month less than men doing work similar to hers at Washington state prisons. Convinced of the inequity in the state's pay scale, Peterson filed a suit claiming that she and other women were being discriminated against because men of similar skills and training and with similar responsibilities were being paid significantly more. A federal judge found Washington guilty of sex discrimination and ordered the state to reimburse its female employees a whopping $838 million in back pay.

Prodded by this and by its biggest public employee union, in 1986 the state of Washington began a program intended to raise the pay for government jobs typically considered ''women's work.'' While the program has flaws,[39] it has helped raise to national prominence the doctrine of comparable worth and signaled a dramatic escalation in women's fight for equal employment rights.

In essence, the doctrine of *comparable worth* holds that women and men should be paid on the same scale, not just for doing the same or equivalent jobs, but for doing different jobs of equal skill, effort, and responsibility. One legal-affairs correspondent rightly says, ''The issue pits against each other two cherished American values: the ethic of nondiscrimination versus the free enterprise system.''[40]

Advocates of comparable worth point to the substantial statistical evidence demonstrating that women are in more low-paying jobs than men. They also note the consistent relationship between the percentage of women in an occupation and the salary of that occupation: The more women dominate an occupation, the less it pays.[41] Comparable-worth advocates contend that women have been shunted into a small number of ''pink-collar'' occupations and that a biased and discriminatory wage system has kept their pay below that of male occupations requiring a comparable degree of skill, education, responsibility, and so on. For example, studies have shown that legal secretaries and instrument-repair technicians hold jobs with the same relative value for a company in terms of accountability, know-how, and problem-solving skill. Yet legal secretaries, who are almost all women, earn an average of $9,432 less than instrument-repair technicians, who are generally men.[42]

As comparable-worth advocates see it, justice demands that women receive equal pay for doing work of comparable value. Jobs should be objectively evaluated in terms of the education, skills, and experience required and in terms of responsibilities, working conditions, and other relevant factors. Equivalent jobs should receive equivalent salaries, even if discriminatory job markets would otherwise put them on different pay scales. Some comparable-worth advocates further argue that, in cases where women have not received equivalent pay for jobs of comparable worth, justice requires that employers pay them reparation damages for the money they have been forced to forgo. While the cost of retroactive wage adjustments would be very high indeed, all comparable-worth programs envision adjusting the salary schedules of women upward rather than the pay of men downward. That would also be expensive.

Opponents of comparable worth insist that women, desiring flexible schedules and less taxing jobs, have freely chosen lower-paying occupations and thus are not entitled to any readjustment in pay scales. Phyllis Schlafly, for one, calls comparable worth "basically a conspiracy theory of jobs. . . . It asserts that, first, a massive societal male conspiracy has segregated or ghetto-ized women into particular occupations by excluding them from others; and then, second, devalued the women's job by paying them lower wages than other occupations held primarily by men." She adds: "Not a shred of evidence has been produced to prove those assumptions. For two decades at least women have been free to go into any occupation. . . . But most women continue to choose traditional, rather than nontraditional jobs. This is their own free choice. Nobody makes them do it."[43]

Others who are sympathetic to the concept of comparable worth worry about its implementation. How are different jobs to be evaluated and compared, they wonder. "How do you determine the intrinsic value of one job and then compare it to another?" asks Linda Chavez, staff director of the Commission on Civil Rights. She points out that "for 200 years, this has been done by the free marketplace. It's as good an alternative as those being suggested by comparable-worth advocates. I'm not sure the legislative bodies or courts can do any better."[44] Even if judgments of comparability are possible, opponents worry about the cost: A revision of federal workers' salaries alone could run as high as $1.8 billion in annual pay increases and extra pension costs.

Advocates of comparable worth respond to these criticisms by pointing not only to statistical evidence demonstrating the inequity of pay scales but also to massive research documenting the reality of visceral discrimination in the workplace and to the hundreds of legal cases involving workplace discrimination. They argue that it is not by accident or free choice that women find themselves in jobs paying less than men doing similar work. They have been victimized by a combination of institutional discrimination and a socialization process that has directed them to "female jobs." Moreover, they reject the argument that implementing comparable worth would be prohibitively expensive. They point to Minnesota, for example, which is phasing in a comparable-worth program over several years so the state incurs an expense of about 1 percent a year. But the core of their arguments remains an appeal to fairness and equity, which, they insist, cannot be sacrificed on the altar of economy.

The comparable-worth issue continues to engender legal controversy. The federal courts have not explicitly accepted the doctrine of comparable worth, even when they've rendered legal decisions that seem to support it. One form of job discrimination against women that the courts agree about, however, is sexual harassment.

SEXUAL HARASSMENT

Many men find the term "sexual harassment" amusing and have a hard time taking it seriously. "It wouldn't bother me," they feel certain. "In fact," they chuckle, "I wouldn't mind being harassed a little more often." Others shrug it off, saying, "What's the big deal? You know what the world is like. Men and women, love and sex, they make it go 'round. Only uptight women are going to complain about sexual advances." But for millions of working women, the reality of sexual harassment is not something to be shrugged off. For them it is no laughing matter.

The courts agree. Sexual-harassment claims have emerged in the past decade as a potent force in the effort to eliminate sex discrimination. These claims fall primarily under Title VII of the Civil Rights Act, which in certain circumstances imposes liability on employers for the discriminatory acts of their employees—including sexual harassment. The Supreme Court has now joined a number of federal district and appeals courts in holding that sexual harassment is an objectionable act that violates the Civil Rights Act because it is based on the sex of the individual.[45] In short, sexual harassment is illegal.

It is also expensive and—unfortunately—widespread. A survey by *Working Woman* magazine reveals that 90 percent of the companies that make up the *Fortune 500* have received complaints of sexual harassment,[46] and another study estimates that the annual average cost of sexual harassment to these firms is $6,719,593.[47] One-third of them have been sued on grounds of sexual harassment,

but the above figure doesn't include the cost of litigation. Rather, it calculates only the costs incurred when employees quit their jobs because of harassment, stay at their jobs but become less productive, take leaves of absence, or seek assistance either within or outside the company.

Men, as well as women, can be victims of sexual harassment. The focus here is on women, however, because they are the ones who suffer most from it. The U.S. Merit Systems Protection Board found that 42 percent of all female employees of the federal government have been sexually harassed; a study of private employers found that 62 percent of the women surveyed had been harassed in the office. And nine-tenths of the 9,000 women who responded to a questionnaire in *Redbook* magazine reported sexual harassment on the job.[48]

We are all familiar with the stereotype of construction workers who whistle and make lewd comments about women who walk by. But the truth is that all types of men in all sorts of occupations have been reported as harassers. Survey after survey, for example, reveals that high percentages of female professors and female students have encountered some form of sexual harassment from a person in authority at least once while they were in the university.

Critics may find it odd that sexual harassment is viewed by the courts as a kind of sex discrimination. If an infatuated supervisor harasses only the female employee who is the object of his desire, is his misconduct really best understood as discrimination against women? He does not bother women in general, just this particular individual. In viewing sexual harassment as a violation of the 1964 Civil Rights Act, however, the courts are rightly acknowledging that such behavior, and the larger social patterns that reinforce it, rest on male attitudes and assumptions that work against women.

Accepting this viewpoint still leaves puzzles, however. Assume the infatuated supervisor is a woman and the employee a man.

Are we to interpret this situation as sex discrimination, considering that it does not take place against a social backdrop of exploitation and discrimination against men? Or imagine a bisexual employer who sexually harasses both male and female employees. Since he discriminates against neither sex, is there no sexual harassment?

These conceptual puzzles have to do with the law's interpretation of sexual harassment as a kind of sex discrimination. Practically speaking, this interpretation has benefited women and brought them better and fairer treatment on the job, but it clearly has its limits. Legally speaking, the most important aspect of sexual harassment may be that it represents discrimination. But it is doubtful that discrimination is morally the worst aspect of sexual harassment. Morally, there is much more to be said about the wrongness of sexual harassment.*

What exactly is sexual harassment? The Equal Employment Opportunity Commission says that it is "unwelcome sexual advances, requests for sexual favors, and other verbal or physical conduct of a sexual nature." Catherine A. MacKinnon, author of *Sexual Harassment of Working Women*, describes sexual harassment as "sexual attention imposed on someone who is not in a position to refuse it." And Alan K. Campbell, director of the Federal Office of Personnel Management, defines it as "deliberate or repeated unsolicited verbal comments, gestures, or physical contact of a sexual nature which are unwelcome."[49] Here is one useful legal definition of sexual harassment, which reflects the way most courts understand it:

Unwelcome sexual advances, requests for sexual favors, and other verbal or

---

* By analogy, compare the fact that often the only grounds on which the federal government can put a murderer on trial is on the charge of having violated the civil rights of his or her victim. The charge of violating the victim's civil rights doesn't get to the heart of the murderer's wrongdoing, even if it is the only legally relevant issue.

physical conduct of a sexual nature constitute sexual harassment when (1) submission to such conduct is made either explicitly or implicitly a term or condition of an individual's employment, (2) submission to or rejection of such conduct by an individual is used as the basis for employment decisions affecting such individual, or (3) such conduct has the purpose or effect of substantially interfering with an individual's work performance or creating an intimidating, hostile, or offensive working environment.[50]

This definition helps us to distinguish three different types of sexual harassment.

Sexual threats are the first type — in its crudest form, "You'd better agree to sleep with me if you want to keep your job." The immorality of such threats seems clear. In threatening harm, they are coercive and violate the rights of the person threatened, certainly depriving him or her of equal treatment on the job. Obviously such threats can be seriously psychologically damaging and are hence wrong.

Sexual offers are the second type: "If you sleep with me, I'm sure I can help you advance more quickly in the firm." Often such offers harbor an implied threat, and unlike genuine offers, the employee may risk something by turning them down. Larry May and John Hughes have argued that such offers by a male employer to a female employee put her in a worse position than she was before and, hence, are coercive. Even sexual offers without hint of retaliation, they suggest, change the female employee's working environment in an undesirable way.[51] In the case of both threats and offers, the employer is attempting to exploit the power imbalance between him and the employee.

The third category is the broadest, but in some ways it is the most important because it is so pervasive. Sexual harassment includes behavior of a sexual nature that is distressing to women and interferes with their ability to perform on the job, even when the behavior is not an attempt to pressure the woman for sexual favors. Sexual innuendos; leering or ogling at a woman; sexist remarks about women's bodies, clothing, or sexual activities; the posting of pictures of nude women; and unnecessary touching, patting, or other physical conduct can all constitute sexual harassment. Such behavior is humiliating and degrading to its victim. It interferes with her peace of mind and undermines her work performance.

Neither the wrongness nor the illegality of sexual harassment requires that the harassing conduct be by the employee's supervisor. This is particularly relevant in the third category, where the harassment a woman endures may come from co-workers. Firms, however, are responsible for providing a work environment in which an employee is free from harassment, and they can be sued for damages if they fail to do so. Different courts have reached different decisions on the question of whether supervisory personnel must be notified or made aware of sexual harassment by employees before the firm can be found legally liable.[52] One can nevertheless safely say that, morally speaking, a company needs to be alert to the possibility of sexual harassment by its employees and take reasonable steps to guard against it.

An isolated or occasional sexist remark or innuendo, although it might be morally objectionable, does not constitute harassment. Harassment of the third type requires that the objectionable behavior be persistent. The same holds for racial slurs and epithets. An ethnic joke by itself does not constitute discriminatory harassment, but a concerted pattern of "excessive and opprobrious" racially derogatory remarks and related abuse does violate the law.[53]

Human beings are sexual creatures, and wherever men and women work together, there are bound to be sexual undertones to their interactions. Women as well as men can appreciate, with the right persons and at the appropriate times, sexual references, sex-related humor, and physical contact with members of the opposite sex. Flirting, too, is often appreciated by both parties. It is not necessary that a serious and professional work environment be entirely free from sexuality, nor is this an achievable goal.

When, then, is behavior objectionable or offensive enough to constitute harassment? What one person views as innocent fun or a friendly overture may be seen as objectionable and degrading by another. Comments that one woman appreciates or enjoys may be distressing to another. Who can decide what is right? In the case of sexual harassment, who determines what is objectionable or offensive?

The answer is very simple: Harassment lies in the eyes of the receiver. There is no need for a theory of what is objectively insulting or inappropriate. Even if such a theory were possible, it would be irrelevant. The moral point is to respect a person's choices and wishes. Even if the other women in the office like it when the boss gives them a little hug, it would still be wrong to hug the one woman who is made uncomfortable. If the behavior is unwanted—that is, if the woman doesn't like it—then persisting in it is wrong. The fact that objectionable behavior must be persistent and repeated to be sexual harassment allows for the possibility that people can honestly misread co-workers' signals or misjudge their likely response to a sexual innuendo, a joke, or a friendly pat. That may be excusable; what is not excusable is persisting in the behavior once you know it is unwelcome.

Practically speaking, what should a female employee do if she encounters sexual harassment? First, she must make it clear that the behavior is unwanted. This may be harder to do than it sounds, because most of us like to please others and do not want to be thought to be prudes or to lack a sense of humor. The employee may wish to be tactful and even pleasant in rejecting behavior she finds inappropriate, especially if she thinks the offending party is well intentioned. But in any case, she has to make her feelings known clearly and unequivocally. Second, if the behavior persists, she should try to document it by keeping a record of what has occurred, who was involved, and when it happened. If others have witnessed some of the incidents, then that will help her document her case.

The third thing the female employee must do when faced with sexual harassment is to complain to the appropriate supervisor, sticking to the facts and presenting her allegations as objectively as possible. She should do this immediately in the case of sexual threats or offers by supervisors; in the case of inappropriate behavior by co-workers, she should generally wait to see if it persists despite telling the offending party that she objects. If complaining to her immediate supervisor does not bring quick action, then she must try whatever other channel is available to her in the organization—the grievance committee, for example, or the chief executive's office.

Fourth, if internal complaints do not bring results, then the employee should seriously consider seeing a lawyer and learning in detail what legal options are available. Many women try to ignore sexual harassment, but the evidence suggests that in most cases it continues or grows worse. When sexual threats or offers are involved, a significant number of victims are subject to unwarranted reprimands, increased work loads, or other reprisals. The employee must remember, too, that she has both a moral and a legal right to work in an environment free from sexual harassment.

SUMMARY

1. Discrimination in employment involves adverse decisions against employees based on their membership in a group that is viewed as inferior or deserving of unequal treatment. Discrimination can be intentional or unintentional, institutional or individual.

2. Statistics, together with evidence of deep-seated attitudes and institutional practices and policies, point to racial and sexual discrimination in the workplace.

3. The Civil Rights Act of 1964 forbids discrimination in employment on the basis of race, color, sex, religion, and national origin. In the late 1960s and early 1970s, many companies developed affirmative action programs to correct racial imbalances existing as a result of past discrimination. Critics charge that in practice affirmative action has often meant preferential treatment of women and minorities and even "reverse discrimination" against white men.

4. The Supreme Court has adopted a moderate, case-by-case approach to affirmative action. Although recent decisions make the legal future less certain, in a series of rulings over the years, a majority of the Court has upheld the general principle of affirmative action, as long as such programs are moderate and flexible. Race can legitimately be taken into account in employment-related decisions, but only as one among several factors. Affirmative action programs that rely on rigid and unreasonable quotas or that impose excessive hardship on present employees are illegal.

5. The moral issues surrounding affirmative action are controversial. Its defenders argue that compensatory justice demands affirmative action programs; affirmative action is necessary to permit fairer competition; and affirmative action is necessary to break the cycle that keeps minorities and women locked into poor-paying, low-prestige jobs.

6. Critics of affirmative action argue that affirmative action injures white men and violates their rights; affirmative action itself violates the principle of equality; and nondiscrimination (without affirmative action) will suffice to achieve our social goals.

7. The doctrine of comparable worth holds that women and men should be paid on the same scale for doing different jobs of equal skill, effort, and responsibility.

8. Advocates of comparable worth say that women have been forced into more lower-paying jobs than men and justice requires that women receive equal pay for doing jobs of equal worth. Some contend further that monetary reparations are due to women who in the past have not received equal pay for doing jobs of equal value.

9. Opponents of comparable worth claim that women have freely chosen their occupations and are not entitled to compensation. They contend that only the market can and should determine the value of different jobs. Revising pay scales would also be prohibitively expensive.

10. Sexual harassment is widespread. It includes unwelcome sexual advances and other conduct of a sexual nature where submission to such conduct is a basis for employment decisions or such conduct substantially interferes with an individual's work performance. Sexual harassment is a kind of discrimination and is illegal.

11. Employees encountering sexually harassing behavior from co-workers should make it clear that the behavior is unwanted. If it persists, harassed employees should document the behavior and report it to the appropriate person or office in the organization. In the case of sexual threats or offers from supervisors, they should do this immediately. If internal channels are ineffective, employees should seek legal advice.

CASE 9.1
Minority Set-Asides

Richmond, Virginia, is the former capital of the Confederacy. It's not the sort of place one would normally associate with controversial efforts at affirmative action. But aware of its legacy of racial discrimination and wanting to do something about it, the Richmond City Council adopted on April 11, 1983, what it called the Minority Business Utilization Plan—a plan that eventually brought it before the Supreme Court.

The plan, which the Council adopted by a five to two vote after a public hearing, required contractors to whom the city awarded construction contracts to subcontract at least 30 percent of the dollar amount of their contracts to Minority Business Enterprises (MBEs). A business was defined as an MBE if minority group members controlled at least 51 percent of it. There was no geographical limit, however; a minority-owned business from anywhere in the United States could qualify as an MBE subcontractor. (The 30 percent set-aside did not apply to construction contracts that were awarded to minority contractors in the first place.)

Proponents of the set-aside provision relied on a study that indicated that, while the general population of Richmond was 50 percent black, only 0.67 percent of the city's construction contracts had been awarded to minority businesses. Councilperson Marsh, a proponent of the ordinance, made the following statement:

> I have been practicing law in this community since 1961, and I am familiar with the practices in the construction industry in this area, in the state, and around the nation. And I can say without equivocation, that the general conduct of the construction industry . . . is one in which race discrimination and exclusion on the basis of race is widespread.

Opponents, on the other hand, questioned both the wisdom and the legality of the ordinance. They argued that the disparity between minorities in the population of Richmond and the low number of contracts awarded to MBEs did not prove racial discrimination in the construction industry. They also questioned whether there were enough MBEs in the Richmond area to satisfy the 30 percent requirement.

The city's plan was in effect for five years until it expired on June 30, 1988. During that time, though, the plan was challenged in the courts. A federal district court upheld the set-aside ordinance, stating that the city council's "findings [were] sufficient to ensure that, in adopting the Plan, it was remedying the present effects of past discrimination in the construction industry." However, the case was appealed to the Supreme Court, which in 1989 ruled in *City of Richmond* v. *Croson* that the Richmond plan was in violation of the equal protection clause of the Fourteenth Amendment.[54] In delivering the opinion of the majority of the Court, Justice O'Connor argued that Richmond had not supported its plan with sufficient evidence of past discrimination in the city's construction industry:

> A generalized assertion that there has been past discrimination in an entire industry provides no guidance for a legislative body to determine the precise scope of the injury it seeks to remedy. It "has no logical stopping point." . . . "Relief" for such an ill-defined wrong could extend until the percentage of public contracts awarded to MBEs in Richmond mirrored the percentage of minorities in the population as a whole.
>
> [The City of Richmond] argues that it is attempting to remedy various forms of past discrimination that are alleged to be responsible for the small number of minority businesses in the local contracting industry. . . . While there is no doubt that the sorry history of both private and public discrimination in this country has

contributed to a lack of opportunities for black entrepreneurs, this observation, standing alone, cannot justify a rigid quota in the awarding of public contracts in Richmond, Virginia. Like the claim that discrimination in primary and secondary schooling justifies a rigid racial preference in medical school admissions, an amorphous claim that there has been past discrimination cannot justify the use of an unyielding racial quota.

It is sheer speculation how many minority firms there would be in Richmond absent past societal discrimination, just as it was sheer speculation how many minority medical students would have been admitted to the medical school at Davis absent past discrimination in educational opportunities. Defining these sorts of injuries as "identified discrimination" would give local governments license to create a patchwork of racial preferences based on statistical generalizations about any particular field of endeavor.

These defects are readily apparent in this case. The 30% quota cannot in any realistic sense be tied to any injury suffered by anyone . . .

In sum, none of the evidence presented by the city points to any identified discrimination in the Richmond construction industry. We, therefore, hold that the city has failed to demonstrate a compelling interest in apportioning public contracting opportunities on the basis of race. To accept Richmond's claim that past societal discrimination alone can serve as the basis for rigid racial preference would be to open the door to competing claims for "remedial relief" for every disadvantaged group. The dream of a Nation of equal citizens in a society where race is irrelevant to personal opportunity and achievement would be lost in a mosaic of shifting preferences based on inherently unmeasurable claims of past wrongs. . . . We think such a result would be contrary to both the letter and spirit of a constitutional provision whose central command is equality.

But the Court's decision was not unanimous, and Justice Marshall was joined by Justices Brennan and Blackmun in dissenting vigorously to the opinion of the majority. Justice Marhsall wrote:

> The essence of the majority's position is that Richmond has failed to . . . prove that past discrimination has impeded minorities from joining or participating fully in Richmond's construction contracting industry. I find deep irony in second-guessing Richmond's judgment on this point. As much as any municipality in the United States, Richmond knows what racial discrimination is; a century of decisions by this and other federal courts has richly documented the city's disgraceful history of public and private racial discrimination. In any event, the Richmond City Council *has* supported its determination that minorities have been wrongly excluded from local construction contracting. Its proof includes statistics showing that minority-owned businesses have received virtually no city contracting dollars . . .; testimony by municipal officials that discrimination has been widespread in the local construction industry; and . . . federal studies . . . which showed that pervasive discrimination in the Nation's tight-knit construction industry had operated to exclude minorities from public contracting. These are precisely the types of statistical and testimonial evidence which, until today, this Court has credited in cases approving of race-conscious measures designed to remedy past discrimination.

Discussion Questions

1. What was the Richmond City Council trying to accomplish with its Minority Business Utilization Plan? If you had been a member of the council, would you have voted for the plan?

2. What are the pros and cons of a minority set-aside plan like Richmond's? Will it have good consequences? Does it infringe on anyone's rights? What conflicting moral principles, ideals, and values are at stake?

3. Do you believe that there was sufficient evidence of racial discrimination to justify the city's plan? Who is right about this—Justice O'Connor or Justice Marshall?

4. Justice O'Connor and the majority of the Court seem to believe that there must be some specific, identifiable individuals who have been discriminated against before race-conscious measures can be adopted to remedy past discrimination. Do you agree that affirmative action measures must meet this standard?

5. In light of the fact that no federal statute specifically bars racial discrimination in private domestic commercial transactions between two business firms and given the evidence that racism is an obstacle to black business success,[55] what obligation, if any, does state, local, or federal government have to assist minority-owned companies?

6. What measures could Richmond have taken that would have increased opportunities for minority business but would not have involved racial quotas? Would such measures be as effective as the original plan?

CASE 9.2
Warning: Pregnancy May Be Hazardous to Your Job

Not too long ago, a working woman who found herself pregnant could expect to find herself jobless. Very few employers offered disability benefits for childbirth, and many did not grant pregnancy leaves. In the 1970s, as more women began to enter the work force, it became increasingly difficult for employers to discharge pregnant women or deny them disability benefits. Still, employers insisted that the uniqueness of pregnancy and childbirth placed it outside the realm of illness benefits. And they received support from the Supreme Court, which in 1976 ruled that, despite Title VII's prohibition against sex discrimination, it was legal for General Electric to grant its workers disability benefits for every non-job-related disability except pregnancy.[56] In other words, General Electric — or any company, for that matter — could compensate men recovering from male medical problems — for example, prostate operations — and still deny benefits to women recovering from childbirth.

Reacting to widespread criticism of the Court's decision, Congress passed legislation in 1978 requiring employers to treat pregnancy and childbirth like any other nonoccupational illness or injury. The Pregnancy Discrimination Act did not require that pregnant women receive disability leave or benefits — only that whatever the employer's disability program, it should apply equally to pregnancy and childbirth. What at the time was celebrated in many quarters, especially among feminists and others battling for female equality in the workplace, soon turned into a rat's nest of legal confusion. Ask Lillian Garland.[57]

About the same time the Supreme Court was ruling in the General Electric case, Garland was being hired by California Federal Savings and Loan Association (Cal Fed) as a receptionist in the bank's commercial loans department. She immediately took a liking to her job and over the next five years competently did her work, which included answering telephones and attending to customers. What promised to be a long and fruitful association with Cal Fed ended abruptly with Garland's pregnancy in 1981.

Garland trained a woman to do her job during her absence with every expectation of returning to the position after the birth of her child. But when she returned to the bank on April 20, 1982, two months after a Cesarean section, she was informed that there was no receptionist or similar position open at the time. It was only then she realized that having a baby had cost her her job.

"I mean, I felt cold all over," Garland recalls. "I stood there and said, 'What do you mean, you don't have a position available for me? What about my job?' They said, 'Well, we have hired somebody in your place.' And I said, 'Who?' And it was the person I trained. And I said, 'What do I do now?' And they said, 'We'll call you, as soon as a position becomes available.'"

In November Cal Fed offered Garland a position as a receptionist in accounting, and she took it. In the seven-month interim, Cal Fed had also offered her several typing jobs, which she felt unqualified to accept, and jobs at other branches, which she refused because she had no car. She had also sought but failed to get jobs as a barmaid, waitress, and salesperson.

Although Garland was relieved to have a job again with Cal Fed, she filed a complaint with the California Department of Fair Employment and Housing. The basis of her action was a California state law that requires employers not only to allow pregnant workers a disability leave but to return them to their jobs or comparable jobs, regardless of what they offer other employees. In other words, no matter what a company's disability policies are, it owes every pregnant woman a job-secure leave of up to four months for the time she is incapacitated by pregnancy and childbirth.

Cal Fed contended that its action was perfectly consistent with the federal law that requires employers to treat pregnancy and childbirth exactly as it does any other disability. Since under the bank's disability policy no employee is guaranteed a job immediately upon returning to work, Cal Fed claimed that Garland should not have expected nor have received special treatment.

U.S. District Judge Manuel L. Real agreed with the bank's position. Acting on a motion by Cal Fed and two major state employers' organizations, the judge ruled that the California law constituted "preferential treatment of females disabled by pregnancy, childbirth, or related medical conditions." In the judge's opinion, then, the California law is discriminatory because it violates the prohibition against sex discrimination in Title VII of the 1964 Civil Rights Act.

Eventually the case reached the Supreme Court. Ironically, the National Organization for Women (NOW) sided with Cal Fed, arguing that special treatment of pregnant employees reinforces gender-based stereotypes traditionally used to exclude women. The Court's 1987 decision, however, backed Garland.[58] Writing for the majority, Justice Marshall ruled that the California statute does not unlawfully discriminate against men by providing women with some benefit not provided to other disabled workers. Rather, the statute is within the meaning and the intention of the Civil Rights Act, as amended by the Pregnancy Discrimination Act. It fairly and legally promotes equality of employment for women.

Marshall added another subtle argument. He reasoned that, even if one falsely assumes that federal law prohibits employers from providing pregnant women with benefits not provided to other disabled employees, the California statute would still be acceptable. In requiring leave for pregnant workers, the statute does not compel employers to treat them better than other employees. Employers are still free to guarantee their other disabled workers leave and reinstatement! That was definitely a conclusion Cal Fed didn't like hearing.

Discussion Questions

1. The California law provides certain protections just for pregnant employees. Is there anything wrong about the state treating pregnant workers differently from other disabled employees or from other employees in general? What do you think of NOW's argument?

2. The courts continually discuss pregnancy as a medical disability, analogous with medical disabilities men might suffer. Is this a good analogy? Is pregnancy best understood as a "disability"?

3. Only women can become pregnant. Does that mean the California statute is giving special privileges to women?

4. Does the statute discriminate against men? Is there anything morally objectionable about the California law?

5. Does not providing women with unpaid maternity leave and reinstatement constitute discrimination against women?

6. Suggest possible arguments for and against paid maternity leave.

CASE 9.3
Raising the Ante

Having spearheaded the women's cause on behalf of equal pay for jobs of equal value, Phyllis Warren was elated when the board decided to readjust salaries. Its decision meant Phyllis and the other women employed by the crafts firm would receive pay equivalent to men doing comparable jobs. But in a larger sense it constituted an admission of guilt on the part of the board, acknowledgment of a history blemished with sexual discrimination.

In the euphoria that followed the board's decision, neither Phyllis nor any of the other activists thought much about the implied admission of female exploitation. But some weeks later, Herm Leggett, a sales dispatcher, half-jokingly suggested to Phyllis over lunch that she shouldn't stop with equal pay now. Phyllis asked Herm what he meant.

"Back pay," Herm said without hesitation. "If they're readjusting salaries for women," he explained, "they obviously know that salaries are out of line and have been for some time." Then he asked her pointedly, "How long you been here, Phyl?" Eleven years, she told him. "If those statistics you folks were passing around last month are accurate," Herm said, "then I'd say you've been losing about $500 a year, or $5,500 over eleven years." Then he added with a laugh, "Not counting interest, of course."

"Why not?" Phyllis thought. Why shouldn't she and other women who'd suffered past inequities be reimbursed?

That night Phyllis called a few of the other women and suggested that they press the board for back pay. Some said they were satisfied and didn't think they should force the issue. Others thought the firm had been fair in readjusting the salary schedule, and they were willing to let bygones be bygones. Still others thought that any further efforts might, in fact, roll back the board's favorable decision.

Yet a nucleus agreed that workers who had been unfairly treated in the past ought to receive compensation. They decided, however, that since their ranks were divided, they shouldn't wage as intense an in-house campaign as previously but instead take the issue directly to the board, while it might still be inhaling deeply the fresh air of social responsibility.

The following Wednesday, Phyllis and four other women presented their case to the board, intentionally giving the impression that they enjoyed as much support from other workers as they had the last time they appeared before it. Although this wasn't true, Phyllis suggested it as an effective strategic ploy.

Phyllis's presentation had hardly ended when board members began making their feelings known. One called her proposal "industrial blackmail." "No sooner do we try to right an injustice," he said testily, "than you take our good faith and threaten to beat us over the head with it unless we comply with your request."

Another member just as vigorously argued that the current board couldn't be held accountable for the actions, policies, and decisions of previous boards. "Sure," he said, "we're empowered to alter policies as we see fit, as new conditions chart new directions. And we've done that. But to expect us to bear the full financial liability of decisions we never made is totally unrealistic—and unfair."

Still another member wondered where it would all end. "If we agree," he asked, "will you then suggest we should track down all those women who ever worked for us and provide them compensation?" Phyllis said no, but the board should readjust retirement benefits for those affected.

At this point the board asked Phyllis if she had any idea what her proposal would cost the firm. "Whatever it is, it's a small price to pay for righting wrong," she said firmly.

"But is it a small price to pay for severely damaging our profit picture?" one of the members asked. Then he added, "I needn't remind you that our profit outlook directly affects what we can offer our current employees in terms of salary and fringe benefits. It directly affects our ability to revise our salary schedule." Finally, he asked Phyllis whether she'd accept the board reducing everyone's current compensation to meet what Phyllis termed the board's "obligation to the past."

Despite its decided opposition to Phyllis's proposal, the board agreed to consider it and render a decision at its next meeting. As a final broadside, Phyllis hinted that, if the board didn't comply with the committee's request, the committee was prepared to submit its demand to litigation.

Discussion Questions

1. If you were a board member, how would you vote? Why?

2. What moral values are involved in this case?

3. Do you think Phyllis Warren was unfair in taking advantage of the board's implied admission of salary discrimination on the basis of sex? Why?

4. Do you think Phyllis was wrong in giving the board the impression that her proposal enjoyed broad support? Why?

5. If the board rejects the committee's request, do you think the committee ought to sue? Give reasons.

CASE 9.4
Mandatory Retirement

Congress acted in 1978 to include age among the categories of discrimination prohibited by the Civil Rights Act. The year before, the Congressional Select Committee on Aging heard arguments for and against mandatory retirement—from large and small corporations, interest groups, labor unions, scholars, legal experts, and economists. The committee summed up their arguments this way:[59]

A. For Mandatory Retirement

1. Older persons as a group may be less well-suited for some jobs than younger workers because:
   a. Declining physical and mental capacity are found in greater proportion among older persons.
   b. Generally older persons do not learn new skills as easily as younger persons.

   c. Older workers have more inflexibility with regard to work due to work rules, seniority systems and pay scales.
   d. Older workers typically have less education than younger workers.

2. Medical science is not capable of making accurate individual assessments of physical and psychological competencies of employees which would presumably be required if there was no standard mandatory retirement age; or substantial time and money may be required to make such individual determinations of fitness. Also, it is difficult to administer any such individual test of fitness fairly.

3. Mandatory retirement saves face for the older workers no longer capable of performing his or her job adequately, who would otherwise be singled out for forced retirement.

4. Mandatory retirement provides a predictable situation allowing both management and employees to plan ahead.

5. It is sometimes more costly for employers to have an older work force in terms of maintaining various pension, health and life insurance plans.   *

6. By forcing retirement at an earlier age than a person might otherwise choose, there are more opportunities for younger workers. This may aid in recruiting additions and replacements to the work force and allow infusion of new ideas.

7. Older workers can often retire to social security or other retirement income, making jobs available to younger unemployed workers who do not have other income potential.

B. Against Mandatory Retirement

1. Mandatory retirement based on age alone is discriminatory against workers. It is contrary to equal employment opportunity. Mandatory retirement laws have been challenged as unconstitutional because of denying individuals equal protection of the law.

2. Chronological age alone is a poor indicator of ability to perform a job. Mandatory retirement at a certain age does not take into consideration actual, differing abilities and capacities. Studies demonstrate that many workers can continue to work effectively beyond age 65, and may be better employees than younger workers because of experience and job commitment.

3. Mandatory retirement can cause hardships for older persons. For example:
   a. Mandatory retirement often results in loss of role and income for individuals.
   b. Mandatory retirement at a certain age may very well result in a lower retirement benefit under social security if the last years the employee would have worked would have brought higher earnings than earlier years.
   c. Mandatory retirement is especially disadvantageous to some women who do not start work until after the children are grown or after being widowed or divorced. Forced retirement limits the work life of these women and reduces their ability to build up significant benefits.
   d. Mandatory retirement can cause great economic hardship on a growing number of older workers who have many financial obligations usually considered the province of younger persons, e.g., home mortgages, installment payments on cars, etc. In addition, a rapidly increasing number of older persons ages 60–65 are experiencing the financial responsibility for aged parents or other relatives.
   e. Mandatory retirement on the basis of age may well impair the health of many individuals whose job represents a major source of status, creative satisfaction, social relationships, or self-respect.

4. Mandatory retirement causes loss of skills and experience from the work force, resulting in reduced national output (GNP).

5. Forced retirement causes an increased expense to government income maintenance programs such as social security and supplemental security income, as well as to social service programs.

6. The declining birth rate will mean a proportionately smaller labor force supporting a larger retiree population early in the next century. The economics of this situation could be eased by later retirement or elimination of mandatory retirement at any set age.

Discussion Questions

1. Is mandatory retirement a form of job discrimination? Explain. What other consid-

erations of justice and rights are involved in the debate over mandatory retirement?

2. Evaluate both the pro and the con arguments carefully from the utilitarian perspective.

3. In your view, is mandatory retirement morally required; wise and morally permissible (but not required); morally permissible but misguided; morally suspect or questionable; or flatly immoral?

4. Should corporate retirement policies be regulated by law? If so, how? If not, why not?

5. If you were hired as a company consultant on this issue, what would you recommend as a good, nondiscriminatory retirement policy?

CASE 9.5
Consenting to Sexual Harassment

In the recent case of *Vinson* v. *Taylor*, heard before the federal district court for the District of Columbia, Mechelle Vinson alleged that Sidney Taylor, her supervisor at Capital City Federal Savings and Loan, sexually harassed her.[60] But the facts of the case are contested. In court Vinson testified that, about a year after she began working at the bank, Taylor asked her to have sexual relations with him. She claimed that Taylor said she "owed" him because he had obtained the job for her.

Although she turned down Taylor at first, she eventually became involved with him. She and Taylor engaged in sexual relations, both during and after business hours, in the remaining three years she worked at the bank. The encounters included intercourse in a bank vault and in a storage area in the bank basement. Vinson also testified that Taylor often actually "assaulted or raped" her. She contended that she was forced to submit to Taylor or jeopardize her employment.

Taylor, for his part, denied the allegations. He testified that he had never had sex with Vinson. On the contrary, he alleged that Vinson had made advances toward him and that he had declined them. He contended that Vinson had brought the charges against him to "get even" because of a work-related dispute.

In its ruling on the case, the court held that, if Vinson and Taylor engaged in a sexual relationship, that relationship was voluntary on the part of Vinson and was not employment-related. The court also held that Capital City Federal Savings and Loan did not have "notice" of the alleged harassment and was therefore not liable. Although Taylor was Vinson's supervisor, the court reasoned that notice to him was not notice to the bank.

Vinson appealed the case, and the Court of Appeals held that the district court had erred in three ways. First, the district court had overlooked the fact that there are two possible kinds of sexual harassment. Writing for the majority, Chief Judge Robinson distinguished cases where the victim's continued employment or promotion is conditioned on giving in to sexual demands and those cases in which the victim must tolerate a "substantially discriminatory work environment." The lower court had failed to consider Vinson's case as possible harassment of the second kind.

Second, the higher court also overruled the district court's finding that, because Vinson voluntarily engaged in a sexual relationship with Taylor, she was not a victim of sexual harassment. Voluntariness on Vinson's part had "no bearing," the judge wrote, on "whether Taylor made Vinson's toleration of sexual harassment a condition of her employment." Third, the court of appeals held that any discriminatory activity by a supervisor is attributable to the employer, regardless of whether the employer had specific notice.

In his dissent to the decision by the Court of Appeals, Judge Bork rejected the majority's claim that "voluntariness" did not automatically rule out harassment. He argued that this position would have the result of depriving the accused person of any defense, since he could no longer establish that the supposed victim was really "a willing participant." Judge Bork contended further that an employer should not be held vicariously liable for a supervisor's acts that it didn't know about.

In 1986 the Supreme Court upheld the majority verdict of the Court of Appeals, stating that:

> [T]he fact that sex-related conduct was "voluntary," in the sense that the complainant was not forced to participate against her will, is not a defense to a sexual harassment suit brought under Title VII. The gravamen of any sexual harassment claim is that the alleged sexual advances were "unwelcome." . . . The correct inquiry is whether respondent by her conduct indicated that the alleged sexual advances were unwelcome, not whether her actual participation in sexual intercourse was voluntary.

The Court, however, declined to provide a definite ruling on employer liability for sexual harassment. It did, however, reject the Court of Appeals's position that employers are strictly liable for the acts of their supervisors, regardless of the particular circumstances.[61]

Discussion Questions

1. According to her own testimony, Vinson acquiesced to Taylor's sexual demands. In this sense her behavior was "voluntary." Does the voluntariness of her behavior mean that she had "consented" to Taylor's advances? Does it mean that they were "welcome"? Do you agree that Vinson's acquiescence shows there was no sexual harassment? Which court was right about this? Defend your position.

2. In your opinion, under what circumstances would acquiescence be a defense to charges of sexual harassment? When would it not be a defense? Can you formulate a general rule for deciding such cases?

3. Assuming the truth of Vinson's version of the case, should her employer, Capital City Federal Savings and Loan, be held liable for sexual harassment it was not aware of? Should the employer have been aware of it? Does the fact that Taylor was a supervisor make a difference? In general, when should an employer be liable for harassment?

4. What steps do you think Vinson should have taken when Taylor first pressed her for sex? Should she be blamed for having given in to him? Assuming that there was sexual harassment despite her acquiescence, does her going along with Taylor make her partly responsible or mitigate Taylor's wrongdoing?

5. In court, Vinson's allegations were countered by Taylor's version of the facts. Will there always be a "your word against mine" problem in sexual harassment cases? What could Vinson have done to strengthen her case?

NOTES

1. "So Who's Laughing?" *Guardian* (New York), November 4, 1987.
2. Charles R. Lawrence III, "The Id, the Ego, and Equal Protection: Reckoning with Unconscious Racism," *Stanford Law Review* 39 (January 1987): 318, 340.
3. Ibid., 339–340.

4. Manuel G. Velasquez, *Business Ethics*, 2nd ed. (Englewood Cliffs, N.J.: Prentice-Hall, 1988), 311–312.

5. David Tuller, "Screening Out Minority Workers," *San Francisco Chronicle*, December 5, 1990, A1.

6. Philip Shenon, "Judge Finds F.B.I. Is Discriminatory," *New York Times*, October 1, 1988, 1.

7. See Michael Parenti, *Democracy for the Few*, 5th ed. (New York: St. Martin's, 1988), 30; and the National Conference of Catholic Bishops, *Economic Justice for All* (Washington: U.S. Catholic Conference, 1986), 89–90.

8. On his television show "Firing Line", a transcript of which appears in John Arthur, ed., *Morality and Moral Controversies*, 2nd ed. (Englewood Cliffs, N.J.: Prentice-Hall, 1986), Buckley goes on to argue somewhat implausibly that differences in median age account for this income disparity among ethnic groups.

9. *Newsweek* (international edition), March 8, 1988, 36.

10. Robert Pear, "Rich Got Richer in 80s; Others Held Even," *New York Times*, January 11, 1991, A1.

11. Velasquez, *Business Ethics*, 320–321.

12. "Individual Candidate Remedies: Why They Won't Work," in Gertrude Ezorsky, ed., *Moral Rights in the Workplace* (Albany: State University of New York Press, 1987), 260.

13. Lee Dembart, "Science: Still Few Chances for Women," *Los Angeles Times*, March 7, 1984.

14. Reported in "Women Lawyers Gain, Blacks Lose, Survey Finds," *USA Today*, May 17, 1984.

15. Steven A. Chin, "Minority Lawyers Quitting in Droves," *San Francisco Examiner*, September 30, 1990, A1.

16. U.S. Bureau of the Census, *Money Income of Households, Families, and Persons in the United States: 1982* (Washington, D.C.: U.S. Government Printing Office, 1984).

17. National Conference of Catholic Bishops, *Economic Justice for All*, 88; and Doug Grider and Mike Shurden, "The Gathering Storm of Comparable Worth," *Business Horizons* 30 (July–August 1987): 61. See also Robert Lewis, "When It Comes to Pay, It's a Man's World," *San Francisco Examiner*, April 16, 1989, A7.

18. See "Women Finding Jobs, Less Money," *Santa Barbara News Press*, October 3, 1984.

19. Allan Parachini, "Male-Female Wage Gap Closing," *Los Angeles Times*, October 31, 1984, I-3.

20. See the comparisons reported in *USA Today*, May 29, 1984, 4D.

21. Edward W. Jones, Jr., "Black Managers: The Dream Deferred," *Harvard Business Review* 64 (May–June 1986): 84; and Colin Leinster, "Black Executives: How They're Doing," *Fortune*, January 18, 1988, 110.

22. *Fortune*, January 18, 1988, 109; *Business Week*, October 19, 1990.

23. *Wards Cove Packing Co., Inc.* v. *Atonio*, 109 S. Ct. 2115 (1989).

24. Tamar Lewin, "Sex Bias Found in Awarding of Partnerships at Law Firm," *New York Times*, November 30, 1990, B14.

25. "Judge Orders Partnership in a Bias Case," *Wall Street Journal*, December 5, 1990, B6, and *Price Waterhouse* v. *Hopkins*, 109 S. Ct. 1775 (1989).

26. Ellen Goodman, "Women Gain a Better Shot at Top Rungs," *Los Angeles Times*, May 29, 1984, II-45.

27. Benson Rosen and Thomas H. Jerdee, "Sex Stereotyping in the Executive Suite," *Harvard Business Review* 52 (May–June 1974): 45–58.

28. Peter Dubno, "Is Corporate Sexism Passé?" *Business and Society Review* 53 (Spring 1985).

29. Lee Dembart, "Science: Still Few Chances for Women," *Los Angeles Times*, March 7, 1984, 1.

30. Ibid.

31. Ibid., 3. For an update on Corning Glass Works's effort to overcome ingrained biases, see Carol Hymowitz, "One Firm's Bid to Keep Blacks, Women," *Wall Street Journal*, February 16, 1989, B1.

32. "Racial Stereotypes Still Persist Among Whites, Survey Finds," *San Francisco Chronicle*, January 9, 1991, A10.

33. Jones, "Black Managers," 88.

34. Richard T. De George, *Business Ethics*, 2nd ed. (New York: Macmillan, 1986), 247–248.

35. See *Griggs* v. *Duke Power Co.*, 401 U.S. 424 (1971) and *Wards Cove Packing* v. *Atonio*, 109 S. Ct. 2115 (1989) at 2115, where the Court reiterates that Title VII can be violated by "not only overt discrimination but also practices that are fair in form but discriminatory in practice."

36. James E. Jones, "Reverse Discrimination in Employment," in Joseph R. DesJardins and John J. McCall, eds., *Contemporary Issues in Business Ethics* (Belmont, Calif.: Wadsworth, 1985), 431–432.

37. *Richmond* v. *Croson*; *Wards Cove Packing Co.* v. *Atonio*; and *Martin* v. *Wilks*.

38. Herman Schwartz, "Affirmative Action," in Gertrude Ezorsky, ed., *Moral Rights in the Workplace*, 276.

39. Peter Kilborn, "Comparable-Worth Pay Plan Creates Unseen Woe for State," *Denver Post*, June 3, 1990, 3A.

40. Nina Totenberg, "Why Women Earn Less," *Parade Magazine*, June 10, 1984, 5.

41. Velasquez, *Business Ethics*, 322.

42. Ibid., 340.

43. Caroline E. Mayer, "The Comparable Pay Debate," *Washington Post National Weekly Edition*, August 6, 1984, 9.

44. Ibid.

45. Mary Jo Shaney, "Perceptions of Harm: The Consent Defense in Sexual Harassment Cases," *Iowa Law Review* 71 (May 1986): 1109; and *Meritor Savings Bank FSB* v. *Vinson*, 106 S. Ct. 2399 (1986).

46. Ronni Sandroff, "Sexual Harassment in the *Fortune* 500," *Working Woman*, December 1988, 69.

47. Norma R. Fritz, "In Focus," *Personnel*, February 1989, 4.

48. Shaney, "Perceptions of Harm," 1112n; and "Is Sexual Harassment Still on the Job?" *Business and Society Review* 67 (Fall 1988): 5, 8.

49. Shaney, 1109.

50. Ibid.

51. Larry May and John C. Hughes, "Sexual Harassment," in Ezorsky, ed., *Moral Rights*.

52. Shaney, 1110n.

53. Terry L. Leap and Larry R. Smeltzer, "Racial Remarks in the Workplace: Humor or Harassment?" *Harvard Business Review* 62 (November–December 1984).

54. *City of Richmond* v. *J.A. Croson Co.*, 109 S. Ct. 706 (1989).

55. Robert E. Suggs, "Rethinking Minority Business Development Strategies," *Harvard Civil Rights–Civil Liberties Law Review* 25 (Winter 1990) and Brent Bowers, "Black Owners Fight Obstacles to Get Orders," *Wall Street Journal*, November 16, 1990, B1.

56. *General Electric Co.* v. *Gilbert*, 429 U.S. 125 (1976).

57. See Cynthia Gorney, "The Law's the Same for a Man: Have a Baby, Lose Your Job," *Washington Post National Weekly Edition*, April 23, 1984, 6. The quotations reported here are from this source.

58. *California Federal Savings and Loan Assoc.* v. *Guerra*, 93 L. Ed. 2d 613 (1987).

59. From the Report by the Select Committee on Aging, *The Social and Human Cost of Enforced Idleness* (Washington, D.C.: U.S. Government Printing Office, 1977); reprinted in David Braybrooke, *Ethics in the World of Business* (Totowa, N.J.: Rowman and Allanheld, 1983).

60. See Mary Jo Shaney, "Perceptions of Harm: The Consent Defense in Sexual Harassment Cases," *Iowa Law Review* 71 (May 1986) for the relevant legal citations and a presentation of the facts of this case.

61. *Meritor Savings Bank* v. *Vinson*, 106 S. Ct. 2399 (1986). On subsequent legal developments, see Clifford M. Koen, Jr., "Sexual Harassment Claims Stem from a Hostile Work Environment," *Personnel Journal*, August 1990.

A Defense of Programs of Preferential Treatment

Richard Wasserstrom

Many critics of programs of preferential treatment for women and minorities argue that, even if such programs are effective, they are unfair or unjust. One common objection to them is that if it was wrong to take race or sex into account in the past when blacks and women were excluded, then it is wrong to take race or sex into account now. A second objection is that preferential treatment programs are wrong because they do not base hiring or other decisions on an individual's qualifications. In this essay, Professor Richard Wasserstrom responds to these two criticisms of preferential treatment programs, arguing that such programs are not unjust or objectionable in the way that the discrimination they seek to remedy is.

Many justifications of programs of preferential treatment depend upon the claim that in one respect or another such programs have good consequences or that they are effective means by which to bring about some desirable end, e.g., an integrated, equalitarian society. I mean by "programs of preferential treatment" to refer to programs such as those at issue in the *Bakke* case—programs which set aside a certain number of places (for example, in a law school) as to which members of minority groups (for example, persons who are nonwhite or female) who possess certain minimum qualifications (in terms of grades and test scores) may be preferred for admission to those places over some members of the majority group who possess higher qualifications (in terms of grades and test scores).

Many criticisms of programs of preferential treatment claim that such programs, even if effec-

Reprinted with permission from *National Forum: The Phi Kappa Phi Journal*, Volume LVIII, Number 1 (Winter 1978).

tive, are unjustifiable because they are in some important sense unfair or unjust. In this paper I present a limited defense of such programs by showing that two of the chief arguments offered for the unfairness or injustice of these programs do not work in the way or to the degree supposed by critics of these programs.

The first argument is this. Opponents of preferential treatment programs sometimes assert that proponents of these programs are guilty of intellectual inconsistency, if not racism or sexism. For, as is now readily acknowledged, at times past employers, universities, and many other social institutions did have racial or sexual quotas (when they did not practice overt racial or sexual exclusion), and many of those who were most concerned to bring about the eradication of those racial quotas are now untroubled by the new programs which reinstitute them. And this, it is claimed, is inconsistent. If it was wrong to take race or sex into account when blacks and women were the objects of racial and sexual policies and practices of exclusion, then it is wrong to take race or sex into account when the objects of the policies have their race or sex reversed. Simple considerations of intellectual consistency — of what it means to give racism or sexism as a reason for condemning these social policies and practices — require that what was a good reason then is still a good reason now.

The problem with this argument is that despite appearances, there is no inconsistency involved in holding both views. Even if contemporary preferential treatment programs which contain quotas are wrong, they are not wrong for the reasons that made quotas against blacks and women pernicious. The reason why is that the social realities do make an enormous difference. The fundamental evil of programs that discriminated against blacks or women was that these programs were a part of a larger social universe which systematically maintained a network of institutions which unjustifiably concentrated power, authority, and goods in the hands of white male individuals, and which systematically consigned blacks and women to subordinate positions in the society.

Whatever may be wrong with today's affirmative action programs and quota systems, it should be clear that the evil, if any, is just not the same. Racial and sexual minorities do not constitute the dominant social group. Nor is the conception of who is a fully developed member of the moral and social community one of an individual who is either female or black. Quotas which prefer women or blacks do not add to an already relatively overabundant supply of resources and opportunities at the disposal of members of these groups in the way in which the quotas of the past did maintain and augment the overabundant supply of resources and opportunities already available to white males.

The same point can be made in a somewhat different way. Sometimes people say that what was wrong, for example, with the system of racial discrimination in the South was that it took an irrelevant characteristic, namely race, and used it systematically to allocate social benefits and burdens of various sorts. The defect was the irrelevance of the characteristic used — race — for that meant that individuals ended up being treated in a manner that was arbitrary and capricious.

I do not think that was the central flaw at all. Take, for instance, the most hideous of the practices, human slavery. The primary thing that was wrong with the institution was not that the particular individuals who were assigned the place of slaves were assigned there arbitrarily because the assignment was made in virtue of an irrelevant characteristic, their race. Rather, it seems to me that the primary thing that was and is wrong with slavery is the practice itself — the fact of some individuals being able to own other individuals and all that goes with that practice. It would not matter by what criterion individuals were assigned; human slavery would still be wrong. And the same can be said for most if not all of the other discrete practices and institutions which comprised the system of racial discrimination even after human slavery was abolished. The practices were unjustifiable — they were oppressive — and they would have been so no matter how the assignment of victims had been made. What made it worse, still, was that the institutions and the supporting ideology all interlocked to create a system of human oppression whose effects on those living under it were as devastating as they were unjustifiable.

Again, if there is anything wrong with the programs of preferential treatment that have begun to flourish within the past ten years, it should be evident that the social realities in respect to the distribution of resources and opportunities make the difference. Apart from everything else, there is simply no way in which all of these programs taken together could plausibly be viewed as capable of relegating white males to the kind of genuinely oppressive status characteristically bestowed upon women and blacks by the dominant social institutions and ideology.

The second objection is that preferential treatment programs are wrong because they take race or sex into account rather than the only thing that does matter — that is, an individual's qualifications. What all such programs have in common and what makes them all objectionable, so this argument goes, is that they ignore the persons who are more qualified by bestowing a preference on those who are less qualified in virtue of their being either black or female.

There are, I think, a number of things wrong with this objection based on qualifications, and not the least of them is that we do not live in a society in which there is even the serious pretense of a qualification requirement for many jobs of substantial power and authority. Would anyone claim, for example, that the persons who comprise the judiciary are there because they are the most qualified lawyers or the most qualified persons to be judges? Would anyone claim that Henry Ford II is the head of the Ford Motor Company because he is the most qualified person for the job? Part of what is wrong with even talking about qualifications and merit is that the argument derives some of its force from the erroneous notion that we would have a meritocracy were it not for programs of preferential treatment. In fact, the higher one goes in terms of prestige, power and the like, the less qualifications seem ever to be decisive. It is only for certain jobs and certain places that qualifications are used to do more than establish the possession of certain minimum competencies.

But difficulties such as these to one side, there are theoretical difficulties as well which cut much more deeply into the argument about qualifications. To begin with, it is important to see that there is a serious inconsistency present if the person who favors "pure qualifications" does so on the ground that the most qualified ought to be selected because this promotes maximum efficiency. Let us suppose that the argument is that if we have the most qualified performing the relevant tasks we will get those tasks done in the most economical and efficient manner. There is nothing wrong in principle with arguments based upon the good consequences that will flow from maintaining a social practice in a certain way. But it is inconsistent for the opponent of preferential treatment to attach much weight to qualifications on this ground, because it was an analogous appeal to the good consequences that the opponent of preferential treatment thought was wrong in the first place. That is to say, if the chief thing to be said in favor of strict qualifications and preferring the most qualified is that it is the most efficient way of getting things done, then we are right back to an assessment of the different consequences that will flow from different programs, and we are far removed from the considerations of justice or fairness that were thought to weigh so heavily against these programs.

It is important to note, too, that qualifications — at least in the educational context — are often not connected at all closely with any plausible conception of social effectiveness. To admit the most qualified students to law school, for example — given the way qualifications are now determined — is primarily to admit those who have the greatest chance of scoring the highest grades at law school. This says little about efficiency except perhaps that these students are the easiest for the faculty to teach. However, since we know so little about what constitutes being a good, or even successful lawyer, and even less about the correlation between being a very good law student and being a very good lawyer, we can hardly claim very confidently that the legal system will operate most effectively if we admit only the most qualified students to law school.

To be at all decisive, the argument for qualifications must be that those who are the most qualified deserve to receive the benefits (the job, the place in law school, etc.) because they are the most qualified. The introduction of the concept of desert now makes it an objection as to justice or fairness of the sort promised by the original criticism of the programs. But now the problem is that there is no reason to think that there is any strong sense of "desert" in which it is correct that the most qualified deserve anything.

Let us consider more closely one case, that of preferential treatment in respect to admission to college or graduate school. There is a logical gap in the inference from the claim that a person is most qualified to perform a task, e.g., to be a good student, to the conclusion that he or she deserves to be admitted as a student. Of course, those who deserve to be admitted should be admitted. But why do the most qualified deserve anything? There is simply no necessary connection between academic merit (in the sense of being the most qualified) and deserving to be a member of a student body. Suppose, for instance, there is only one tennis court in the community. Is it clear that the two best tennis players ought to be the ones permitted to use it? Why not those who were there first? Or those who will enjoy playing the most? Or those who are the worst and, therefore, need the greatest opportunity to practice? Or those who have the chance to play least frequently?

We might, of course, have a rule that says that the best tennis players get to use the court before the others. Under such a rule the best players would deserve the court more than the poorer ones. But that is just to push the inquiry back one stage. Is there any reason to think that we ought to have a rule giving good tennis players such a preference? Indeed, the arguments that might be given for or against such a rule are many and varied. And few if any of the arguments that might support the rule would depend upon a connection between ability and desert.

Someone might reply, however, that the most able students deserve to be admitted to the university because all of their earlier schooling was a kind of competition, with university admission being the prize awarded to the winners. They deserve to be admitted because that is what the rule of the competition provides. In addition, it might be argued, it would be unfair now to exclude them in favor of others, given the reasonable expectations they developed about the way in which their industry and performance would be rewarded. Minority-admission programs, which inevitably prefer some who are less qualified over some who are more qualified, all possess this flaw.

There are several problems with this argument. The most substantial of them is that it is an empirically implausible picture of our social world. Most of what are regarded as the decisive characteristics for higher education have a great deal to do with things over which the individual has neither control nor responsibility: such things as home environment, socioeconomic class of parents, and, of course, the quality of the primary and secondary schools attended. Since individuals do not deserve having had any of these things vis-à-vis other individuals, they do not, for the most part, deserve their qualifications. And since they do not deserve

their abilities they do not in any strong sense deserve to be admitted because of their abilities.

To be sure, if there has been a rule which connects, say, performance at high school with admission to college, then there is a weak sense in which those who do well at high school deserve, for that reason alone, to be admitted to college. In addition, if persons have built up or relied upon their reasonable expectations concerning performance and admission, they have a claim to be admitted on this ground as well. But it is certainly not obvious that these claims of desert are any stronger or more compelling than the competing claims based upon the needs or advantages to women or blacks from programs of preferential treatment. And as I have indicated, all rule-based claims of desert are very weak unless and until the rule which creates the claim is itself shown to be a justified one. Unless one has a strong preference for the status quo, and unless one can defend that preference, the practice within a system of allocating places in a certain way does not go very far at all in showing that that is the right or the just way to allocate those places in the future.

A proponent of programs of preferential treatment is not at all committed to the view that qualifications ought to be wholly irrelevant. He or she can agree that, given the existing structure of any institution, there is probably some minimal set of qualifications without which one cannot participate meaningfully within the institution. In addition, it can be granted that the qualifications of those involved will affect the way the institution works and the way it affects others in the society. And the consequences will vary depending upon the particular institution. But all of this only establishes that qualifications, in this sense, are relevant, not that they are decisive. This is wholly consistent with the claim that race or sex should today also be relevant when it comes to matters such as admission to college or law school. And that is all that any preferential treatment program—even one with the kind of quota used in the *Bakke* case—has ever tried to do.

I have not attempted to establish that programs of preferential treatment are right and desirable. There are empirical issues concerning the consequences of these programs that I have not discussed, and certainly not settled. Nor, for that matter, have I considered the argument that justice may permit, if not require, these programs as a way to provide compensation or reparation for injuries suffered in the recent as well as distant past, or as a way to remove benefits that are undeservedly enjoyed by those of the dominant group. What I have tried to do is show that it is wrong to think that programs of preferential treatment are objectionable in the centrally important sense in which many past and present discriminatory features of our society have been and are racist and sexist. The social realities as to power and opportunity do make a fundamental difference. It is also wrong to think that programs of preferential treatment are in any strong sense either unjust or unprincipled. The case for programs of preferential treatment could, therefore, plausibly rest both on the view that such programs are not unfair to white males (except in the weak, rule-dependent sense described above) and on the view that it is unfair to continue the present set of unjust — often racist and sexist — institutions that comprise the social reality. And the case for these programs could rest as well on the proposition that, given the distribution of power and influence in the United States today, such programs may reasonably be viewed as potentially valuable, effective means by which to achieve admirable and significant social ideals of equality and integration.

Review and Discussion Questions

1. Do you agree with Wasserstrom that there is nothing inconsistent about programs of preferential treatment?

2. How does Wasserstrom respond to the argument that such programs are to be rejected because they ignore an individual's qualifications? What about the related argument that the most able candidates deserve to be admitted? Are you persuaded by his reasoning?

3. Are there any important arguments against preferential treatment programs that Wasserstrom has neglected?

4. What goals do such programs seek to achieve and how effective are they in achieving them? Do preferential treatment programs have any negative consequences?

5. Assuming that Wasserstrom is right that preferential treatment programs are not unjust, does justice require us to adopt such programs?

Debate over Comparable Worth: Facts and Rhetoric

Judith Olans Brown, Phyllis Tropper Baumann, and Elaine Millar Melnick

Recent court decisions concerning job discrimination against women have given support to the principle of "equal pay for work of comparable value." After defining "comparable worth," the authors contend that the necessity for job comparison and evaluation poses no real problem. They then examine and rebut three common arguments against comparable worth: first, that the male-female wage gap is not due to discrimination; second, that it is an attempt to compare "apples and oranges"; and third, that comparable worth schemes would cripple the free market.

A. Definitions: The Heart of the Debate

"Comparable worth" means that workers, regardless of their sex, should earn equal pay for work of comparable value to their common employer. Imprecise use of the phrase hinders meaningful discussion. Comparable worth is equated indiscriminately with comparable work, work of equal worth, work of equal value, or pay equity; however, these terms are not synonymous. Comparable worth theory addresses wage inequities that are associated with job segregation. The basic premise of comparable worth theory is that women should be able to substantiate a claim for equal wages by showing that their jobs and those of male workers are of equal value to their common employer. The doctrine allows comparison of jobs which are different but which require comparable skills, effort and responsibility.[1] In other words, this doctrine permits comparison of jobs which do not come within the ambit of the Equal Pay Act requirement of equal pay for jobs which are "substantially equal."

Opponents of comparable worth, however, focus on jobs that are not demonstrably equivalent and where a comparable worth claim is thus not present. Their rhetoric too often sacrifices accuracy to ideology.[2] In a popular but mistaken example, comparable worth opponents ask why such unrelated workers as nurses (not generally unionized) and truck drivers (highly unionized) should receive the same wages.[3] Opponents also ask why nurses and teamsters, who do not even work for the same employer, should receive the same pay. The response must emphasize that comparable worth cases always involve the same employer. The cases also always involve occupations which, according to a rational standard, are of comparable value to that employer.

The nurse/truck driver example implies that comparable worth requires equal pay for randomly selected job categories simply because the jobs being compared are ordinarily performed by members of one sex. What is really at issue, however, is equal pay for demonstrably equivalent jobs, as measured by either job content or a standard of experience, skill, or responsibility. An appropriate index against which to measure nurses' salaries might be the salaries of hospital sanitarians. Similarly, the appropriate comparable job for a truck driver is one which, although perhaps different in job content, is rated as equivalent in a job evaluation study, or which is capable of being so rated.[4]

Comparable worth doctrine differs from the Equal Pay Act formula in that it permits comparison of jobs which are not substantially similar in content. The Equal Pay Act of 1963 requires equal pay for work of equal skill, effort and responsibility performed under similar working conditions. But the statute requires pay equality only for jobs which are *substantially equal*. If the jobs are relatively equivalent yet not sufficiently similar to meet that standard, no Equal Pay Act violation exists.

[In 1981 the Supreme Court] eliminated the requirement that Title VII plaintiffs prove the substantial equality of the jobs being compared.[5] . . . All Title VII plaintiffs alleging gender-based discrimination are comparing jobs which may have dissimilar functions but are of comparable value to the common employer.

The question for Title VII plaintiffs invoking comparable worth theory then becomes how to demonstrate that their jobs and those of male workers are of equal value to their common employer. [After the Court's 1981 decision] plaintiffs need not demonstrate job equivalency. Nor does a successful comparable worth claim require proof of undervaluation due to historical discrimination.[6] Instead, comparable worth requires proof that the employer's male and female workers perform work of comparable value and that the female workers are paid less. Such a demonstration necessarily depends upon the evaluation of jobs which are different in content.

B. Job Evaluation: The Red Herring of the Comparable Worth Debate

Job evaluation techniques provide a method for comparing jobs which are dissimilar in content. Job evaluation is a formal procedure which classifies a set of jobs on the basis of their relative value to the employer. Although the courts are uncomfortable with the concept of comparable worth, the technique of job evaluation has been familiar to American industry for decades.[7] Contrary to the claims of comparable worth critics, job evaluation does not require governmental participation . Evaluation merely eliminates resort to guesswork or unsubstantiated assertions of comparability. It provides a way of identifying situations in which wages remain artificially low because of sex, but where men and women are not performing identical or nearly identical operations.

Formal job evaluation originated in the late nineteenth century as part of a generalized expansion of organizational techniques and a restructuring of workplace control systems. Indeed, job evaluation was such a familiar method for comparing jobs that it provided the theoretical underpinning for the Equal Pay Act of 1963.[8] The various evaluation techniques all use similar methods to inject objectivity and equality into pay structures. The first stage requires a formal description of the duties, requirements and working conditions of each job within the unit being evaluated. Next, jobs are evaluated in terms of "worth" to the organization.

The outcome of these two processes is a ranking of all jobs in the evaluation unit. The third stage involves setting wage rates for each job in accordance with the evaluation—the higher the ranking, the higher the wages. The job itself, not the worker performing it, is the subject of evaluation.

Any attempt to raise wages on the basis of comparable worth turns on effective use of wage rate, job classification, promotion policy and contractual data. Job evaluations assemble the relevant information in a form useful to employers, employees, and courts. Firmly grounded in existing industrial relations practice, job evaluation itself is hardly controversial. What is new is the use of this practice to address sex discrimination in wages.

Women in diverse occupations have begun to use job evaluation to demonstrate the discriminatory nature of their employers' male/female pay discrepancies.[9] The public rhetoric that characterizes job evaluation as an impossible task of comparing "apples and oranges" merely ignores the factual basis of the technique. The employer has already fashioned a wholly rational hierarchy of "apples and oranges" on the basis of relative worth to the employer. Unfortunately, the mistaken but popular notion of job evaluation has nonetheless prejudiced the courts against evaluation techniques that are essential to plaintiffs' cases.

C. Arguments Against Comparable Worth: The Crux of the Rhetoric

Intense hostility has surrounded the idea of comparable worth. In order to understand this hostility, it is necessary to examine the arguments used by opponents of comparable worth. These arguments involve three related contentions: the male/female earnings gap results, at least in large part, from factors unrelated to discrimination by particular employers; comparable worth analysis is logistically impossible since there is no objective basis for establishing comparisons between different jobs; and, third, pay equity based on comparable worth would cripple the so-called free market.

1. The Non-Discriminatory Nature of the Wage Gap

The argument that the wage gap between men and women results from non-discriminatory fac-

tors is clearly expressed in a report by the U.S. Civil Rights Commission. In its findings, the Civil Rights Commission states that:

> The wage gap between female and male earnings in America results, at least in significant part from a variety of things having nothing to do with discrimination by employers, including job expectations resulting from socialization beginning in the home; educational choices of women who anticipate performing child-bearing and child-rearing functions in the family and who wish to prepare for participation in the labor force in a manner which accommodates the performance of those functions, like the desire of women to work in the kinds of jobs which accommodate their family roles and the intermittency of women's labor force participation.

Essentially, one can reduce the Commission's argument to three basic propositions: women choose low-paying jobs because of their sociological predisposition; women make educational choices which lead to low-paying jobs; and the interrupted participation of women in the labor force leads to lower pay.

The first contention is misguided; comparable worth does not raise job *access* issues. Instead, it addresses situations where women who are already employed are paid less for jobs demonstrably similar to those of male co-workers. In comparable worth cases, women are not socialized to hold "easier" jobs: they are paid less for work of equivalent value. While the effect of socialization on job expectations is relevant to a woman's choice to become a nurse rather than a doctor, it does not address why female nurses are paid less than male orderlies or sanitarians at the same hospital. Comparable worth theory addresses inequities subsequent to access. The Commission simply misses the point in arguing that disadvantage results from the victim's choice, based on her own lower expectations.

The second and third contentions reflect the analytical framework used by human capital theorists to account for employment discrimination.[10] The touchstone of human capital theory as an explanation of wage differentials is productivity. Wages are viewed as a return on investments in human capital. The argument proceeds from the premise that individuals make investments in their productive capacity through education and training. These investments have costs, but they also produce returns in the form of higher wages. The male/female wage differential, therefore, merely reflects the different investments that men and women make.

Mincer and Polachek provide the classic formulation of the theory that women's lower wages merely reflect lower investments in human capital.[11] Productivity of men and women arguably differs . . . [due to] differences in education, training, or length of experience. [However] comparable worth theory does not rely on generalized statistical assertions; it requires a demonstration that in a particular case no other factor appears capable of explaining a proven disparity.

2. Comparing "Apples and Oranges"

The second major argument espoused by opponents of comparable worth is that no objective technique exists for comparing jobs that are not identical in content. The Civil Rights Commission contends that in comparable worth litigation job evaluations are inherently subjective and cannot establish jobs' intrinsic worth. Instead, the Commission claims that such studies function only "to establish rational pay-setting policies within an organization, satisfactory to the organization's employees and management."

This objection, though partially valid, goes too far. Although job evaluation is not absolutely objective, it is a well-established technique in American industry for determining relative wage levels. Representatives of business interests successfully sought to incorporate the concepts of job evaluation into the definition of equality in the Equal Pay Act of 1963. They argued that such a course was necessary because the use of job evaluation techniques was so widespread in industry. For example, E. G. Hester, the director of industrial relations research for Corning Glass, told the Senate Committee on Labor and Public Welfare of his company's concern over the proposed equality criteria. According to Mr. Hester, the proposed criteria would require equal pay "for equal work on jobs the performance of which requires equal skills." He asserted that his approach:

> . . . could give a great deal of difficulty to that large part of American industry and business which has relied upon systematic methods of job evaluation for establishment of equitable rate relationships. Such job evaluation plans depend for their reliability upon other factors than skill alone.

Mr. Hester's statement to the Committee included evidence of the extent to which job evaluation was used. He argued that:

> With this general acceptance of job evaluation throughout industry on the part of both management and labor, we feel it most desirable that legislation related to the equal-pay principle incorporate in its language, recognition of job evaluation (or job classification) principles that have been developed, accepted, and are in general use.

In arguing for the incorporation of job evaluation principles, Mr. Hester conceded that job evaluation was "not a precise science governed by natural laws" but still lauded it as "a systematic approach to establish relative job order. . . . " He pointed out that industries using job evaluation principles had customarily constructed the hierarchy on the basis of "effort, skill, responsibility, and working conditions." The Equal Pay Act incorporates these same four factors.

Even a cursory examination of industrial relations practices demonstrates that business and industry have long used specific techniques to determine the relative wage rates of jobs which are dissimilar in content. While evaluation techniques are not absolutely objective, they are a logical starting point in any meaningful wage determination process. Comparable worth cases do not require an abstract showing of intrinsic value. Instead, plaintiffs' cases turn on proof that the employer's job worth determinations are gender-based. Since comparable worth cases always address alleged discrimination of a particular employer, they compare "pay-setting policies within an organization." The Commission itself admits that this use of job evaluation is "rational."

3. Laissez-Faire Economics and Antidiscrimination Law

The third argument commonly raised against comparable worth is that it requires an unwarranted intrusion into the market. Again, the Civil Rights Commission report provides an example. The Commission notes that: "The setting of wages is not and cannot be divorced from the forces of labor supply and demand. These factors heavily influence the setting of pay in many jobs and play an important role in setting wages for virtually all other jobs." The Commission then argues that there is nothing in the language or legislative history of Title VII to indicate that Congress intended to prevent employers from relying on the operation of the market in setting wages.

Courts have also made this assertion. However, any statute governing the employment relationship must by its very nature interfere with an employer's absolute freedom to determine wages by reference to the market. The enactment of Title VII indicates congressional intent to intervene in the market to further significant policy interests.

Those who argue that comparable worth is an unwarranted interference insist that supply and demand curves create the wage disparity at issue. Thus, comparable worth theory is not a legitimate response to discrimination but rather a specious definition of discrimination. If there is no impermissible discrimination, they argue, there is no social justification for judicial interference with market forces. A recent article called equal pay for work of comparable worth "a fallacious notion that apples are equal to oranges and that prices for both should be the same, even if that means overriding the law of supply and demand."[12] Market forces are the only relevant measure of value.

The argument's proponents would cloak impermissible sex-based discrimination in the putative legality of "market operation." Yet the argument sidesteps the contention of comparable worth proponents that, despite a pay differential, the jobs are equivalent according to a rational standard. Extolling the overriding authority of supply and demand is to ignore the possibility that that "law" conflicts with Title VII, which like other regulatory legislation necessarily interferes with a laissez-faire economy. The market-based argument against comparable worth is nonetheless instructive since it links criticisms of the allegedly spurious nature of comparable worth with antipathy to the remedy — interference with the market — that comparable worth purportedly implies. It is this connection which is critical to an understanding of judicial opinions in the comparable worth area, since judges often defer to the operation of the market.

Notes

1. See, e.g., Newman and Wilson, "Comparable Worth: A Job Inequity By Any Other Name," in *Manual On Pay Equity: Raising Wages for Women's Work* 54 (J. Grune ed. undated) (on file with Harv. C.R.-C.L. L. Rev.).

2. President Reagan even dismissed comparable worth as a "cockamamie idea." Connant & Paine, "A Loss for Comparable Worth," *Newsweek*, Sept. 16, 1985, 36.

3. See, e.g., Krucoff, "Money: The Question of Men, Women, and 'Comparable Worth,'" *Wash. Post*, Nov. 13, 1979, B5, col. 1.

4. The point is not to assert that equal pay *must* be based on similarity of job content, although it may be so based. Jobs which are quite different in content may properly be the basis for an equal pay claim if it can be demonstrated that they are of equal worth. A case brought under the British Equal Pay Act of 1970 provides an illustration. In *Hayward v. Cammell Laird Shipbuilders Ltd.*, IRLR 463 (1984), ICR 71 (1985), a female cook employed in the works cafeteria at the employer's shipyard sought equal pay with men employed as painters, thermal insulation engineers and joiners. An independent expert appointed by the industrial tribunal assessed the various jobs under five factors: physical demands, environmental demands, planning and decisionmaking, skill and knowledge required, and responsibility involved. On the basis of this evaluation he found the jobs to be of equal value.

5. "Respondent's claims of discriminatory undercompensation are not barred by § 703(h) of Title VII merely because respondents do not perform work equal to that of male jail guards." *Gunther*, 452 U.S. at 181.

6. For a discussion of the historic undervaluation of women's jobs, see Blumrosen, "Wage Discrimination, Job Segregation, and Title VII of the Civil Rights Act of 1964," 12 *U. Mich. J.L. Ref.* 397 (1979).

7. See, e.g., *Laffey v. Northwest Airlines*, 567 F.2d 429 (D.C. Cir. 1976), vacating and remanding in part, aff'g in pertinent part, 366 F. Supp. 763 (D.D.C. 1973), cert. denied, 434 U.S. 1080 (1978) (Court of Appeals agreeing with District Court judge who found, after testimony from expert witnesses on job evaluation presented by both plaintiff and defendant, that "pursers" and "stewardesses" performed substantially equal work even though jobs had different titles, descriptions and responsibilities).

8. The "effort, skill, responsibility and working conditions" criteria which the Equal Pay Act uses to determine whether jobs are equal were derived from then-current job evaluation systems.

9. See American Federation of State, County, and Municipal Employees, AFL-CIO (AFSCME), *Guide to Comparable Worth, in Pay Equity: A Union Issue for the 1980's* 11–12 (1980). Unions representing women workers have begun to use evaluation techniques

to demonstrate the extent to which women's work is undervalued and underpaid. AFSCME bargained for job evaluation studies in San Jose, California, Lane County, Oregon, and statewide in Minnesota, Wisconsin, and Michigan. *Manual on Pay Equity: Raising Wages for Women's Work* 152–53 (J. Grune ed. undated) (on file with Harv. C.R.-C.L. L. Rev.). The trend has been especially pronounced in the public sector where 100 municipalities are now re-evaluating their job classification systems. See Noble, "Comparable Worth: How It's Figured," *New York Times*, Feb. 27, 1985, p. C7, col. 1.

10. See Amsden, "Introduction," in *The Economics of Women and Work* 13–18 (A. Amsden ed. 1980).

11. See Mincer & Polachek, "Family Investments in Human Capital: Earnings of Women," 82 *J. Pol. Econ.* 76 (1974) (supp.).

12. Smith, "The EEOC's Bold Foray into Job Evaluation," *Fortune*, Sept. 11, 1978, 58. The author goes on to talk of the "enormous inflationary effect" of comparable worth, which "at the extreme [would] raise the aggregate pay of the county's 27.3 million full-time working women high enough . . . [to] add a staggering $150 billion a year to civilian payrolls." *Id.* at 59. The statement is typical of the hyperbole on which comparable worth arguments often are

based. The author fails to acknowledge that no comparable worth advocate has suggested that all American working women will benefit from the implementation of the doctrine—only those doing work of demonstrably comparable value to that of a male worker of the same employer.

Review and Discussion Questions

1. How does comparable worth doctrine differ from what is required by the Equal Pay Act?

2. Can job evaluation techniques provide a satisfactory method for comparing jobs that are dissimilar in content? Are such methods better than the market?

3. Assess Brown, Baumann, and Melnick's critique of the three common arguments against comparable worth. Do you find them convincing?

4. Are there other arguments against comparable worth that Brown, Baumann, and Melnick have overlooked?

5. In your view, how strong is the overall case for comparable worth?

Sexual Harassment

Susan M. Dodds, Lucy Frost, Robert Pargetter, and Elizabeth W. Prior

Many cases of sexual harassment are obvious, but explaining what makes something sexual harassment is not easy. Dodds, Frost, Pargetter, and Prior argue that sexual harassment need not entail sexual discrimination and that it need not always have negative consequences for the person harassed. Nor does misuse of power itself constitute sexual harassment. Rather, the authors offer a "behavioral account" which, they contend, succeeds in showing the connection between harassment in general and sexual harassment, in distinguishing between sexual harassment and legitimate sexual interaction, and in providing a useful basis for public policy.

Mary has a problem. Her boss, Bill, gives her a bad time. He is constantly making sexual innuendoes and seems always to be blocking her way and brushing against her. He leers at her, and on occasions has made it explicitly clear that it would be in her own best interests to go to bed with him. She is

the one woman in the office now singled out for this sort of treatment, although she hears that virtually all other attractive women who have in the past worked for Bill have had similar experiences. On no occasion has Mary encouraged Bill. His attentions have all been unwanted. She has found them threatening, unpleasant and objectionable. When on some occasions she has made these reactions too explicit, she has been subjected to unambiguously detrimental treatment. Bill has no genuinely personal feelings for Mary, is neither truly affectionate nor loving: his motivation is purely sexual.

Surely this is a paradigmatic case of sexual harassment. Bill discriminates against Mary, and it seems that he would also discriminate against any

Reprinted by permission from *Social Theory and Practice* 14 (Summer 1988).

other attractive woman who worked for him. He misuses his power as an employer when he threatens Mary with sex she does not want. His actions are clearly against her interests. He victimizes her at present and will probably force her to leave the office, whatever the consequences to her future employment.

Not all cases of sexual harassment are so clear. Indeed, each salient characteristic of the paradigmatic case may be missing and yet sexual harassment still occur. Even if all the features are missing, it could still be a case of sexual harassment.

We aim to explicate the notion of sexual harassment. We note that our aim is not to provide an analysis of the ordinary language concept of sexual harassment. Rather we aim to provide a theoretical rationale for a more behavioral stipulative definition of sexual harassment. For it is an account of this kind which proves to be clearly superior for policy purposes. It provides the basis for a clear, just and enforceable policy, suitable for the workplace and for society at large. Of course ordinary language intuitions provide important touchstones. What else could we use to broadly determine the relevant kind of behavior? But this does not mean that all ordinary language considerations are to be treated as sacrosanct. Sexual harassment is a concept with roots in ordinary language, but we seek to develop the concept as one suitable for more theoretical purposes, particularly those associated with the purposes of adequate policy development.

In brief we aim to provide an account which satisfies three desiderata. The account should:

a. show the connection between harassment in general and sexual harassment
b. distinguish between sexual harassment and legitimate sexual interaction
c. be useful for policy purposes.

1. Sexual Harassment and Sexual Discrimination

It seems plausible that minimally harassment involves discrimination, and more particularly, sexual harassment involves sexism. Sexual discrimination was clearly part of the harassment in the case of Mary and Bill.

The pull towards viewing sexual harassment as tied to sexual discrimination is strengthened by consideration of the status of most harassers and most harassees. In general, harassers are men in a position of power over female harassees. The roles of these men and women are reinforced by historical and cultural features of systematic sexual discrimination against women. Generally, men have control of greater wealth and power in our society, while women are economically dependent on men. Men are viewed as having the (positive) quality of aggression in sexual and social relations, while women are viewed as (appropriately) passive. These entrenched attitudes reflect an even deeper view of women as fundamentally unequal, that is in some sense, less fully persons than men. Sexual harassment, then, seems to be just one more ugly manifestation of the sexism and sexual inequality which is rampant in public life.

MacKinnon sees this connection as sufficient to justify treating cases of sexual harassment as cases of sexual discrimination.[1] Sexual discrimination, for MacKinnon, can be understood through two approaches. The first is the "difference approach," under which a "differentiation is based on sex when it can be shown that a person of the opposite sex in the same position is not treated the same." The other is the "inequality approach," which "requires no compatibility of situation, only that a rule or practice disproportionately burden one sex because of sex."[2] Thus, even when no comparison can be made between the situation of male and female employees (for example, if the typing pool is composed entirely of women, then the treatment a woman in the pool receives cannot be compared with the treatment of a man in the same situation), if a rule or practice disproportionately burdens women, because they are women, that rule or practice is sexually discriminatory. For MacKinnon all cases of sexual harassment will be cases of sexual discrimination on one or other of these approaches.

Closer consideration reveals, however, that while discrimination may be present in cases of harassment, it need not be. More specifically, while sexual discrimination may be (and often is) present in cases of sexual harassment, it is not a necessary feature of sexual harassment.

The fact that in most cases women are (statistically, though not necessarily) the objects of sexual harassment, is an important feature of the issue of sexual harassment, and it means that in many cases where women are harassed, the harassment will involve sexual discrimination. However, sexual harassment need not entail sexual discrimination.

Consider the case of Mary A and Bill A, a case very similar to that of Mary and Bill. The only relevant difference is that Bill A is bisexual and is sexually attracted to virtually everyone regardless of sex, appearance, age or attitude. Perhaps all that matters is that he feels that he has power over them (which is the case no matter who occupies the position now occupied by Mary A). Mary A or anyone who filled her place would be subjected to sexual harassment.

The point of this variant case is that there appears to be no discrimination, even though there clearly is harassment. Even if it is argued that there is discrimination against the class of those over whom Bill A has power, we can still describe a case where no one is safe. Bill A could sexually harass anyone. This particular case clearly defeats both of MacKinnon's conceptual approaches to sexual discrimination; it is neither the case that Bill A treats a man in Mary A's position differently from the way in which he treats Mary A, nor is it the case that (in Bill A's office) the burden of Bill A's advances is placed disproportionately on one sex. . . .[3]

A different point, but one worth making here, is that there is a difference between sexual harassment and sexist harassment. A female academic whose male colleagues continually ridicule her ideas and opinions may be the object of sexist harassment, and this sexist harassment will necessarily involve sexual discrimination. But she is not, on this basis, the object of sexual harassment.

2. Negative Consequences and Interests

Perhaps sexual harassment always involves action by the harasser which is against the interests of the harassee, or has overall negative consequences for the harassee.

However consider Mary B who is sexually harassed by Bill B. Mary B gives in, but as luck would have it, things turn out extremely well; Mary B is promoted by Bill B to another department. The long term consequences are excellent, so clearly it has been in Mary B's best interests to be the object of Bill B's attentions. One could also imagine a case

where Mary B rejects Bill B, with the (perhaps unintentional) affect that the overall consequences for Mary B are very good. . . .

In general, harassment need not be against the interests of the harassee. You can be harassed to stop smoking, and harassed to give up drugs. In these cases the consequences may well be good, and the interests of the harassee adequately considered and served, yet it is still harassment. This general feature seems equally applicable to sexual harassment.

3. Misuse of Power

Bill has power over Mary and it is the misuse of this power which plays an important role in making his treatment of Mary particularly immoral. For, on almost any normative theory, to misuse power is immoral. But is this misuse of power what makes this action one of sexual harassment?

If it is, then it must not be restricted to the formal power of the kind which Bill has over Mary — the power to dismiss her, demote her, withhold benefits from her, and so on. We also usually think of this sort of formal power in cases of police harassment. But consider the harassment of women at an abortion clinic by Right-To-Lifers. They cannot prevent the women having abortions and indeed lack any formal power over them. Nonetheless, they do possess important powers — to dissuade the faint-hearted (or even the over-sensitive), and to increase the unpleasantness of the experience of women attending the clinic.

Now consider the case of Mary C. Bill C and Mary C are coworkers in the office, and Bill C lacks formal power over Mary C. He sexually harasses her — with sexual innuendoes, touches, leers, jokes, suggestions, and unwanted invitations. To many women Bill C's actions would be unpleasant. But Mary C is a veteran — this has happened to her so many times before that she no longer responds. It is not that she desires or wants the treatment, but it no longer produces the unpleasant mental attitudes it used to produce — it just rolls off her. She gives the negative responses automatically, and goes on as though nothing had happened.

It would still seem to us that Mary C has been sexually harassed. But what power has Bill C misused against Mary C? He has not used even some informal power which has caused her some significantly unpleasant experience. . . . Misuse of power cannot in itself therefore constitute sexual harassment.

4. Attitudes, Intentions and Experiences

In our discussions so far, it seems that we have not taken into account, to any significant extent, how Mary and Bill feel about things. It may be argued that what defines or characterizes sexual harassment is the mental state of the harasser, or harassee, or both.

Bill wanted to have sex with Mary. He perceived her as a sex object. He failed to have regard for her as a person. He failed to have regard for how she might feel about things. And his actions gave him egotistical pleasure. These attitudes, intentions and experiences may help constitute Bill's action as a case of sexual harassment.

Mary also had very specific kinds of mental states. She found Bill's actions unpleasant, and unwanted. She wished Bill would not act in that way towards her, and she disliked him for it. She was angry that someone would treat her in that way, and she resented being forced to cope with the situation. So again we have attributed attitudes and mental experiences to Mary in describing this case as one of sexual harassment.

We do not want to have to label as sexual harassment all sexual actions or approaches between people in formally structured relationships. Cases of sexual harassment and non-harassing sexual interaction may appear very similar (at least over short time intervals). It seems that in the two kinds of cases only the mental features differ. That is, we refer to attitudes, intentions or experiences in explaining the difference between the two cases. But attention to this feature of sexual harassment is not enough in itself to identify sexual harassment.

We will now consider one of the more salient features of the mental attitudes of Bill and Mary, and show that sexual harassment is not dependent on these or similar features. Then we shall describe a case where the mental experiences are very different, but where sexual harassment does, in fact, still occur.

Consider the claim that Bill uses (or tries to use) Mary as a sex object. The notion of sex object is somewhat vague and ill-defined, but we accept that it is to view her as merely an entity for sexual activity or satisfaction, with no interest in her attributes as a person and without any intention of developing any personal relationship with her.

This will not do as a sufficient condition for sexual harassment. We normally do not think of a client sexually harassing a prostitute. And surely there can be a relationship between two people where each sees the other merely as a sex object without there being harassment. Nor is viewing her merely as a sex object a necessary condition.[4] For surely Bill could love Mary deeply, and yet by pursuing her against her wishes, still harass her.

Now consider the claim that what is essential is that Mary not want the attentions of Bill. This is not a sufficient condition — often the most acceptable of sexual approaches is not wanted. Also a woman may not want certain attentions, and even feel sexually harassed, in situations which we would not want to accept as ones of sexual harassment.

Imagine that Mary D is an abnormally sensitive person. She feels harassed when Bill D comments that the color she is wearing suits her very well, or even that it is a cold day. Bill D is not in the habit of making such comments, nor is he in the habit of harassing anyone. He is just making conversation and noting something (seemingly innocuous) that has caught his attention. Mary D feels harassed even though she is not being harassed.

Perhaps this condition is a necessary one. But this too seems implausible. Remember Mary C, the veteran. She is now so immune to Bill C that she has no reaction at all to his approaches. He does not cause unpleasantness for her; she does not care what he does. Yet nonetheless Bill C is harassing Mary C.

Mary E and Bill E interact in a way which shows that sexual harassment is not simply a matter of actual attitudes, intentions or experiences. Bill E is infatuated with Mary E and wants to have sex with her. In addition to this, he genuinely loves her and generally takes an interest in her as a person. But he is hopeless on technique. He simply copies the brash actions of those around him and emulates to perfection the actions of the sexual harasser. Most women who were the object of his infatuation (for instance, someone like our original Mary) would feel harassed and have all the usual emotions and opinions concerning the harasser.

But Mary E is different. Outwardly, to all who observe the public interactions between them, she seems the typical harassee — doing her best to politely put off Bill E, seeming not to want his attentions, looking as though she is far form enjoying it. That is how Bill E sees it too, but he thinks that that is the way women are.

Inwardly Mary E's mental state is quite different. Mary E is indifferent about Bill E personally, and is a veteran like Mary C in that she is not distressed by his actions. But she decides to take advantage of the situation and make use of Bill E's attentions. By manipulating the harassing pressures and invitations, she believes she can obtain certain benefits that she wants and can gain certain advantages over others. The attention from Bill E is thus not unwanted, nor is the experience for her unpleasant. In this case neither the harasser nor the harassee have mental states in any way typical of harassers and harassees, yet it is a case of sexual harassment.

Such a case, as hypothetical and unlikely as it is, demonstrates that the actual mental states of the people involved cannot be what is definitive of sexual harassment. They are not even necessary for sexual harassment.

5. A Behavioral Account of Sexual Harassment

The case of Mary E and Bill E persuades us that we require a behavioral account of sexual harassment. For a harasser to sexually harass a harassee is for the harasser to behave in a certain way towards the harassee. The causes of that behavior are not important, and what that behavior in turn causes is not important. The behavior itself constitutes the harassment.

But how then are we to specify the behavior that is to count as sexual harassment? . . .

Consider the behavior which is typically associated with a mental state representing an attitude which seeks sexual ends without any concern for the person from whom those ends are sought, and which typically produces an unwanted and unpleasant response in the person who is the object of the behavior. Such behavior we suggest is what constitutes sexual harassment even if the mental states of the harasser or harassee (or both) are different from those typically associated with such behavior. The behavior constitutes a necessary and sufficient condition for sexual harassment.

According to this view, the earlier suggestion that attitudes, intentions and experience are essential to an adequate characterization of sexual harassment is correct. It is correct to the extent that we need to look at the mental states typical of the harasser, rather than those present in each actual harasser, and at those typical of the harassee, rather than those present in each actual harassee. The empirical claim is that connecting these typical mental states is a kind of behavior — behavior not incredibly different from instance to instance, but with a certain sameness to it. Thus it is a behavior of a definite characteristic *type*. This type of behavior is sexual harassment.

This proffered account may at first appear surprising. But let us look at some of its features to alleviate the surprise, and at the same time increase the plausibility of the account.

Most importantly, the account satisfies our three desiderata: to show the connection between harassment in general and sexual harassment, to distinguish between sexual harassment and legitimate sexual interaction, and to assist in guiding policy on sexual harassment.

The relationship between harassment and sexual harassment is to be accounted for in terms of a behavioral similarity. This at first may seem to be a sweeping suggestion, since *prima facie*, there need be no descriptive similarity between sexual harassment, harassment by police, harassment of homosexuals, harassment of Jews, and so on. But the behavioral elements on which each kind of harassment supervenes will have enough in common to explain our linking them all as harassment, while at the same time being sufficiently different to allow for their differentiation into various kinds of harassment. The most plausible similarity, as we shall argue later, will be in the presence of certain behavioral dispositions, though the bases for these dispositions may differ.

Our approach allows for an adequate distinction between sexual harassment and legitimate sexual approaches and interactions. The approach requires that this be a behavioral difference. There is something intrinsically different about the two kinds of activity. Given that the typical causal origin of each of the kinds of behavior is different and so too is the typical reaction it in turn produces, it is to be expected that there would be a difference in the behavior itself. It is important to note that the constitutive behavior will be within a particular context, in particular circumstances. (The importance of this is well illustrated in cases such as a student and her lecturer at a university.[5]) Further it will include both overt and covert behavior (subtle differences count). In many cases it will also be behavior over a time interval, not just behavior at a time.

From the policy guiding perspective the account is very attractive. It is far easier to stipulate a workable, practical, defensible, and legally viable policy on harassment if it is totally definable in behavioral terms. Definition in terms of mental experiences, intentions and attitudes spells nothing but trouble for a viable social policy on sexual harassment.

The analysis we have offered entails that if there were no such characteristic kind of behavior there would be no sexual harassment. This seems to be right. In this case no legislation to ground a social policy would be possible. We would instead condemn individual actions on other moral grounds — causing pain and distress, acting against someone's best interests, misusing power, and so on.

In addition to satisfying these three desiderata, our account has numerous other positive features. First our account is culturally relative. It is highly likely that the kind of behavior constitutive of sexual harassment will vary from culture to culture, society to society. That is, it will be a culture-relative kind of behavior that determines sexual harassment. In any culture our reference to the typical mental states of the harasser and harassee will identify a kind of behavior that is constitutive of sexual harassment in that culture. This kind of behavior matches well with the empirical observations. There is so much variation in human behavior across cultures that behavior which may be sexual harassment in one need not be in another. The same is true of other kinds of human behavior. In the middle east, belching indicates appreciation of a meal. In western society, it is considered bad manners. The practice of haggling over the price of a purchase is acceptable (indeed expected) in some societies, and unacceptable in others. But in almost any culture, some kind of behavior may reasonably be judged to be sexual harassment.

Second, while we have cast our examples in terms of a male harasser and female harassee, there is nothing in the account which necessitates any gender restriction on sexual harassment. All that is required is that the behavior is sexual in nature and has other behavioral features which make it an instance of sexual harassment. The participants could be of either sex in either role, or of the same sex.

We acknowledge that we use the notion of an action being sexual in nature without attempting any explication of that notion. Such an explication is a separate task, but we believe that for our purposes there is no problem in taking it as primitive.

Third, the account allows for the possibility of sexual harassment without the presence of the mental states typical of the harasser or the harassee. There is an important connection between these typical mental states and sexual harassment, but it does not restrict instances of sexual harassment to instances where we have these typical mental states.

Further as the account focuses on behavior, rather than mental states, it explains why we feel so skeptical about someone who behaves as Bill behaves, yet pleads innocence and claims he had no bad intentions. The intentions are not essential for the harassment, and such a person has an obligation to monitor the responses of the other person so that he has an accurate picture of what is going on. Moreover, he has an obligation to be aware of the character of his own behavior. . . .

We acknowledge that it will be difficult in many situations to obtain sufficient evidence that a proposed act will not be one of sexual harassment. This will be true especially in cases where the potential harassee may believe that any outward indication of her displeasure would have bad consequences for her. The awareness of this difficulty is probably what has led others to promote the policy of a total ban on sexual relationships at the office or work place. While we acknowledge the problem, we feel that such a policy is both unrealistic and overrestrictive.

Fourth, the account allows an interesting stance on the connection between sexual harassment and morality. For consequentialist theories of morality, it is possible (though unlikely) that an act of sexual harassment may be, objectively, morally right. This would be the case if the long term good consequences outweighed the bad effects (including those on the harassee at the time of the harassment). For other moral theories it is not clear that this is a possibility, except where there are sufficiently strong overriding considerations present, such as to make the sexual harassment morally permissible. From the agent's point of view, it would seem that the probable consequences of sexual harassment (given the typical attitude of the typical harasser and the typical effects on the typical harassee) will be bad. Hence it is very likely, on any moral theory, that the agent evaluation for a harasser will be negative. The possible exceptions are where the harasser's actual mental state is not typical of a harasser, or the harassee's is not typical of a harassee.

Further, on this account many of the salient features of the case of Mary and Bill—such as misuse of power, discrimination, unfair distribution of favors, and so on—are not essential features of sexual harassment. They are usually immoral in their own right, and their immorality is not explained by their being part of the harassment. But the behavior characteristic of sexual harassment will be constituted by features which we commonly find in particular instances of sexual harassment. For sexual harassment must supervene on the behavioral features which constitute its instances, but there is a range of such behavior, no one element of which need be present on any particular occasion. Similarly the morality of an instance of sexual harassment (at least for the consequentialist) will supervene on the morality of those same features of behavior.

6. Objections to the Behavioral Account

. . . [One] objection to our behavioral account focuses on our use of the mental state *typical* of harassers and harassees. We have noted that it is possible that some instances of harassment will involve a harasser or harassee with mental states significantly different from those of the typical harasser or harassee. So it is possible that the harassee is not even offended or made to feel uncomfortable, and it is possible that the harasser did not have intentions involving misuse of power against, and disregard for the interests of, the harassee. It is even possible that one or both of the harasser and harassee could know about the atypical mental states of the other. Why, at least in this last case, insist that the behavior is sufficient for sexual harassment?

From our concern to provide an account of sexual harassment adequate for policy purposes, we would be inclined to resist this kind of objection, given the clear advantage in policy matters of a behavioral account. But there is more to say in reply to this objection. Policy is directed at the action of agents, and in all cases except where at least one of the agents involved has justified beliefs about the atypical actual mental states of the agents involved, it is clearly appropriate to stipulate behavior associated with the states of mind typical of harassers and harassees as sexual harassment. For agents ought to be guided by what it is reasonable to predict, and rational prediction as to the mental states of those involved in some kind of behavior will be determined by the mental states typically associated with that behavior. So only in cases where we have reliable and justified knowledge of atypical mental states does the objection have any substance at all.

But even in these cases it seems the behavior should not be regarded as innocuous. Instances of behavior all form parts of behavioral patterns. People are disposed to behave similarly in similar circumstances. Hence we ought not to overlook instances of behavior which would typically be instances of sexual harassment. Agents ought not be involved in such patterns of behavior. It is for similar reasons that while we allow for cultural relativity in the behavior constitutive of sexual harassment, this relativity should not be taken to legitimate patterns of behavior which do constitute sexual harassment but which are taken as the standard mode of behavior by a culture.[6] . . .

Notes

1. Catherine MacKinnon, *Sexual Harassment of Working Women*, (London: Yale University Press, 1979), Ch. 6.

2. MacKinnon, p. 225.

3. Given that sexual harassment is possible between men, by a woman harassing a man, among co-workers, and so on, MacKinnon's view of sexual harassment as nothing but one form of sexual discrimination is even less persuasive. It is also interesting that the problems which MacKinnon recognizes in trying to characterize the "offence" of sexual harassment (p. 162 ff.), indicate a need for a behavioral analysis of sexual harassment, like the one we offer.

4. If it is, it needs to be connected to a general view that women are sex objects, for pornographic pinups and sexist jokes and language may harass a woman without anyone viewing *that* woman as a sex object. (See Nathalie Hadjifotiou, *Women and Harassment at Work*, (London: Pluto Press, 1983), p. 14.) Note that we have urged that sexual harassment should be a special case of harassment. But what is the general form of the sex object account? It seems implausible that for each form of harassment there is something corresponding to the notion of sex object.

5. See, for example, Billie Wright Dzeich and Linda Weiner, *The Lecherous Professor: Sexual Harassment on Campus*, (Boston: Beacon Press, 1984).

6. What will be culturally relative are types of behavior incidental to their being viewed as constituting sexual harassment in a particular culture. Acceptable standards concerning modes of address, physical proximity, touching, and so forth will vary among cultures, so the behavior patterns which will constitute sexual harassment will also vary. Of course we must be careful not to confuse socially accepted behavior with behavior which is not sexually harassing, especially in cultures where men have much greater power to determine what is to count as socially acceptable behavior. However, so long as there are typical mental states of harassers and harassees, the behavior which constitutes sexual harassment will be identifiable in each culture.

Review and Discussion Questions

1. According to the authors, why is sexual harassment not the same as sexual discrimination? What do you see as the relation between harassment and discrimination? How does sexual harassment differ from sexist harassment? Do you agree with the authors that sexual harassment is not necessarily against the interests of the woman being harassed?

2. Many writers on the subject contend that sexual harassment is more about power than about sex; others see it as one aspect of a social system based on male domination of women. Yet the authors maintain that sexual harassment cannot be defined as misuse of power. What, if any, connection do you see between sexual harassment and male power?

3. Explain the author's behavioral account of sexual harassment. How does it compare with the definitions of sexual harassment presented in the text? Does their account accomplish what they want it to? Do you have any criticisms of it? Is a person guilty of sexual harassment if he or she engages in what looks like harassing behavior but where this is unintentional and he or she does not have the mentality of the typical sexual harasser?

4. The authors believe that the kind of behavior that constitutes sexual harassment will vary from culture to culture, yet they conclude by saying that this does not "legitimate patterns of sexual behavior which do constitute sexual harassment but which are taken as the standard mode of behavior by a culture." Is their position consistent?

Facial Discrimination: Employment Discrimination on the Basis of Physical Appearance

Editors, Harvard Law Review

Unattractive people regularly face severe discrimination in employment decisions. This essay from the Harvard Law Review *argues that appearance is almost always an illegitimate employment criterion and that decisions based on appearance frequently rest on personal dislike or prejudice rather than merit. The authors maintain that existing legislation barring discrimination against the handicapped should be interpreted to protect people against employment discrimination on the basis of immutable aspects of their physical appearance, like shortness, obesity, and unattractive facial characteristics.*

> "He had but one eye, and the popular prejudice runs in favour of two."
> —Charles Dickens, *Nicholas Nickleby*

The most physically unattractive members of our society face severe discrimination. People who are regarded as unattractive are, for example, perhaps the only noncriminal, noncontagious group in America ever to have been barred by law from appearing in public.[1] The unattractive are poorly treated in such diverse contexts as employment decisions, criminal sentencing, and apartment renting. Although appearance discrimination can have a devastating economic, psychological, and social impact on individuals, its victims have not yet found a legal recourse.

This Note will argue that appearance, like race and gender, is almost always an illegitimate employment criterion, and that it is frequently used to make decisions based on personal dislike or prejudicial assumptions rather than actual merit. It will suggest that existing legislation — in particular, the Rehabilitation Act of 1973, prohibiting discrimination on the basis of physical handicaps — should be construed to protect people against employment discrimination on the basis of largely immutable aspects of bodily and facial appearance. Thus, mutable aspects of personal grooming such as hair length, cleanliness or nontraditional dress are outside of the discussion of this Note, whereas shortness, obesity, and unattractive facial characteristics are the sort of criteria considered.[2] Rather than attempting to delineate specific categories of physical appearance to be protected, this Note proposes that administrative agencies and courts accord handicap status to appearance discrimination victims using the same case-by-case analysis of the individual's impairment and employment situation that is generally used in handicap law.

Part I of the Note describes the problem of appearance discrimination in a number of contexts, with particular reference to employment. . . . Part II explores how the employment process can be restructured to alleviate appearance discrimination.

I. The Phenomenon of Appearance Discrimination

To be human is to discriminate. Humans constantly evaluate people, places, and things and choose some over others. The premise of antidiscrimination law is that in some areas, such as employment and housing, certain criteria are not permissible bases of selection. Antidiscrimination law has yet to state a general model of discrimination that describes precisely which criteria are "illegitimate." Despite the difficulty of developing such criteria, some inner and outer bounds are clear. In the domain of employment, for example, members of racial and religious minority groups are legally protected from discrimination. Those who score poorly on employment aptitude tests found to bear a legitimate relation to the job generally are not.

One approach to antidiscrimination law would protect any member of a minority group who faces discrimination because of membership in that group. This approach is consistent with Louis Wirth's influential definition of a minority: "a group of people who, because of their physical or cultural characteristics, are singled out from the others in the society in which they live for differential and unequal treatment and who therefore regard themselves as objects of collective discrimination." Physically unattractive people do not fall precisely within Wirth's formulation. First, the physically unattractive do not constitute a cohesive group; a thin person with an unattractive face, for example, may feel little kinship with an obese person. In addition, physical attractiveness is a continuum, and neat determinations of who is "unattractive" are impossible. Nevertheless, the physically unattractive share many of the burdens of Wirth's minority groups. Although our society professes a commitment to judge people by their inner worth, physically unattractive people often face differential and unequal treatment in situations in which their appearance is unrelated to their qualifications or abilities. In the employment context, appearance often functions as an illegitimate basis on which to deny people jobs for which they are otherwise qualified.

A. Appearance Discrimination Generally

People in our society often have a visceral dislike for individuals whom they find unattractive. The bias is so strong that it is not deemed inappropriate to express this dislike; the physically unattractive are a frequent subject of derisive humor. People frequently believe, either consciously or unconsciously, that people with unattractive exteriors were either born with equally unattractive interiors or gradually developed them. By contrast, people tend to think, often with very little basis, that people they find physically attractive are generally worthy and appealing or that, as the title of one study has it, "What Is Beautiful Is Good."

Social science studies have shown that people attribute a wide range of positive characteristics to those whom they find physically attractive. These studies also indicate that when less attractive people are compared to more attractive people, the less attractive men and women are accorded worse treatment simply because of their appearance. This less-favored treatment apparently begins as early as the first few months of life. Throughout childhood, unattractive children face parents who have lower expectations for their success than for more attractive children, teachers who have lower expectations for their academic success, and contemporaries who prefer more attractive children as friends. This less generous treatment of unattractive people continues through adulthood. For example, studies of "helping behavior"—the willingness of subjects to do small favors for a stranger—show that such behavior varies directly with the stranger's attractiveness. Likewise, simulation studies of court proceedings have found that unattractive people receive higher sentences in criminal cases and lower damage awards in civil lawsuits.

Physical appearance can also warp the functioning of ordinarily "objective" evaluations of individuals' work. This distortion has been shown in studies in which subjects were asked to evaluate a written essay that was accompanied by a photograph of the purported author. When copies of the same essay were evaluated with a photograph of an attractive or an unattractive person attached, the essays with the more attractive purported author were judged to have better ideas, better style, and more creativity. Moreover, studies have shown that in general, attractive people are disproportionately likely to receive credit for good outcomes, whereas the good outcomes of unattractive people are more likely to be attributed to external factors, such as luck. Such biases might easily lead an employer to underrate the talents of an unattractive job applicant.

Empirical research on the real-world effects of appearance discrimination supports the results of these simulation exercises. Considerable empirical research has been done in the area of obesity. One study showed that obese high school students were significantly less likely than non-obese students to be admitted to selective colleges, when academic achievement, motivation, and economic class were held constant; another found that obese adults were discriminated against in the renting of apartments.

Appearance discrimination thus seems to occur in a wide variety of situations. Clearly, the law cannot intervene directly to prevent all such discrimination; no law, for example, can itself make a teacher have more faith in an unattractive child's academic success. The law can, however, address discrimination in discrete areas. One such area is employment selection, in which appearance discrimination is widespread.

B. Appearance Discrimination in Employee Selection

Physical appearance is a significant factor in employee selection, regardless of the nature of the job or the relevance of appearance to the task at hand. One of the primary methods of assessing applicants for all levels of jobs is the personal interview, in which the applicant's appearance is a central criterion. One survey found that appearance was the single most important factor in determining candidate acceptability for a wide variety of jobs, regardless of the level of training of the interviewers. Another study asked 2804 employment interviewers throughout the United States to give "favorability" scores to a variety of characteristics of applicants for various positions. Interviewers considered as important positive characteristics such factors as "Has a good complexion" and rated as important negative characteristics factors such as "Is markedly overweight," and, for men, "Physique appears feminine." Interview manuals written for employers make clear the importance of physical appearance in the selection process. One general employment handbook places "Appearance" first on its list of "hire appeal" factors.

Research in specific areas of physical difference reinforces the claim that appearance discrimination pervades the job market. The National Association to Aid Fat Americans found that fifty-one percent of its members who responded to a survey reported instances of employment discrimination. A report of the State of Maryland's Commission on Human Relations concluded that it may well be easier to place a thin black person on a job than a fat white person. Extremely short people also experience severe employment discrimination.

There have as yet been no direct challenges to appearance discrimination, although appearance issues have been raised in other lawsuits. Hiring practice based on explicit evaluations of applicants' physical appearance were challenged in the courts for the first time in the 1960s and early 1970s in lawsuits charging airlines with sex and race discrimination in the hiring of flight attendants. One Equal Employment Opportunity Commission hearing of a race discrimination claim revealed that an interview form contained the written comment that a black applicant had "unattractive, large lips." The Commission found that this negative evaluation of a race-related aspect of the applicant's appearance provided reasonable cause to believe that unlawful racial discrimination had taken place. More recently, a computer programmer successfully sued under New York State law a company that failed to hire her because she was obese. The challenge alleged, however, that obesity was a medical handicap, and did not raise the broader issue of appearance discrimination. . . .

C. Deciding Which Jobs Are Covered

Even if physical unattractiveness can at times be a handicap, difficult questions emerge concerning which jobs should be covered under the Act. In many cases, employers will likely argue that an attractive appearance is "necessary" for a job. Courts will have to decide when, if ever, an employer should be permitted to reject an applicant on the basis of appearance.

Under the Act, the question would be phrased in terms of when an applicant is "otherwise qualified" for the job at issue. Courts have been unclear in their interpretations of this concept. It may be argued that certain jobs—for example, modeling and acting—require people who look a certain way. Nevertheless, courts have defined job "requirements" narrowly. "The test," said the Fifth Circuit in *Prewett v. United States Postal Service*, "is whether a handicapped individual who meets all employment criteria except for the challenged discriminatory criterion 'can perform the essential functions of the position in question without endangering the health and safety of the individuals or others.'"

No doubt employers would urge exceptions to appearance discrimination rules not only for persons, such as models and actors, who perform clearly appearance-related work, but also for receptionists, flight attendants, salespeople, and many other jobs in which physical attractiveness might be an important asset. Courts should grant such exceptions sparingly. If they follow the lead of *Prewett*, they will take a narrow view of the "essence" of a job and will in most cases decide that appearance is not relevant. The flight attendant litigation under title VII of the Civil Rights Act of 1964 provides a good model for courts in defining jobs narrowly. Those cases held that appearance was not part of the essence of the job of flight attendant. As the Fifth Circuit stated in holding that men were just as capable as women of being flight attendants, "[w]hile a pleasant environment, enhanced by the obvious cosmetic effect that female stewardesses provide . . . [may] be important, [it is] tangential to the essence of the business involved." By similar logic, it should be determined that physical attractiveness is not essential to most jobs. . . .

II. Reforming Employment Selection to Prevent Appearance Discrimination

In addition to the deterrent effect of individual complaints, restructuring the employment selection process can also prevent appearance discrimination. Employers may be reluctant at first to embark on new approaches to selecting employees. But the Rehabilitation Act and its accompanying regulations are written in aspirational terms. The regulations state that "[t]he Federal Government shall become a model employer of handicapped individuals." This Part will suggest several ways to restructure the system to make the federal government and its contractors such a model. In addition, it will discuss some of the tensions and broader issues raised by efforts to minimize appearance discrimination.

A. Restructuring Employment Selection to Reduce Appearance Discrimination

Even if employers agreed in principle that considerations of physical appearance should ideally be eliminated from the hiring process, this ideal would be difficult to achieve in practice. As long as hiring is based on face-to-face interviews, physical appearance will inevitably have an impact on impressions. This problem can be avoided, however, by restructuring the hiring process to eliminate or reduce information about applicants' appearance when applicants are evaluated and hiring decisions are made.

The regulations promulgated by the HHS bar "preemployment inquiries" concerning a job applicant's handicapped status, unless the inquiries specifically concern the applicant's ability to do the job. To meet this requirement, employers could publicly announce a policy of not soliciting information about an applicant's appearance, other than grooming and neatness, and of not considering appearance as a factor in employee selection. The standard face-to-face interview, in which the applicant's appearance is highly salient, in many ways resembles just such a statutorily forbidden preemployment inquiry into appearance handicaps. To conform with the ban on preemployment inquiries, employers should reevaluate their commitment to the standard employment interview.

To be sure, interviews undoubtedly have some informational value beyond permitting illegitimate appearance evaluations. An employer may justifiably be concerned, for example, with an applicant's interpersonal skills. But this information can be obtained in ways that avoid the prejudicial process of face-to-face interviews. One possible method is the expanded use of telephone interviews. Another possibility, which could work well for many kinds of jobs, is the adoption of the practice used by virtually every American symphony orchestra to avoid discrimination and favoritism in hiring: auditions conducted behind screens. Such an interview process would provide employers with useful information about an applicant, revealing factors such as a "pleasant personality," without prejudicing the selection process by injecting appearance into the calculus.

Employers could also reduce or eliminate appearance discrimination through less dramatic modifications in the selection process. They could, for example, set a rigid dividing line between the person who meets and interviews job applicants and the person who makes the decision about whom to hire. The interviewer could pass along a form to the decisionmaker that includes only job-related information and impressions. Although the applicant's appearance might still influence the interviewer's perceptions of other subjective qualities, it would nevertheless be a considerable reform.

Objections that employment decisions will be difficult or "random" under such a new regime are misplaced. Workable selection procedures and criteria can be maintained without permitting appearance discrimination. Employers could continue to use the battery of legitimate, work-related criteria: they could ask about education, prior work experience, and success in school and at previous jobs. And they could administer bona fide, work-related, nondiscriminatory tests. Indeed, to the extent that these reforms eliminate irrelevant criteria, they should lead to a greater weighting of job-relevant criteria and hence a fairer overall process.

B. Moving From "Efficiency" to Equality

Efforts to eliminate appearance discrimination would significantly restructure employment practices. Inevitably, such proposed reforms raise questions about the sort of criteria on which our society should permit employment decisions to be based. One objection to eliminating physical appearance as a criterion for hiring is an argument about economic efficiency. If an employer can show that an applicant's appearance makes him or her more profitable, why should this not be a valid criterion for employment? The response to this objection is that "efficiency" is not always an acceptable basis on which to make distinctions in the employment process.

In fact, many sorts of discrimination may be "economically efficient." For example, a restaurant owner in a racist neighborhood might enlarge his or her clientele — and thus increase profits — by refusing to hire black waiters and waitresses. Yet in all forms of antidiscrimination law we proclaim that our society has some principles of equality that it holds more dear than efficiency.

Notes

1. Until recently, a number of major American cities had so-called "ugly laws," generally part of their vagrancy laws, which imposed fines on "unsightly" people who were seen in public places. . . . For an example of such a statute, see *Chicago, Ill., Mun. Code* § 36–34 (1966) (repealed 1974) (imposing fines on persons who appear in public who are "diseased, maimed, mutilated or in any way deformed so as to be an unsightly or disgusting object"). . . . As recently as 1974, the city of Omaha, Nebraska arrested a man under a similar city ordinance.

2. Some argue that appearance is under the control of the individual, and that individuals who do not present a more appealing physical appearance are themselves at fault. This argument is frequently made in the case of the obese. . . . In many instances, however, this simply is not true. Recent evidence suggests that many obese people are overweight for biological reasons largely beyond their own control. See Brody, *Research Lifts Blame from Many Obese, New York Times*, Mar. 24, 1987, C1, col. 3 (stating that "[o]ne by one, obesity experts are concluding that many, if not most, people with serious weight problems can hardly be blamed for their rotund shape"). Furthermore, many other aspects of physical appearance are immutable characteristics that "good grooming" would not affect. See G. Patzer, *The Physical Attractiveness Phenomena* 154 (1985) (listing some immutable aspects of a person's face that have been found to be important components of physical attractiveness).

Review and Discussion Questions

1. How frequently are people discriminated against on the basis of their looks? Is it a serious problem in job situations?

2. Some might argue that there is nothing wrong with "facial discrimination" — it simply reflects the fact that human beings are naturally attracted to, or repelled by, other human beings on the basis of their physical characteristics. How would you respond to this argument?

3. Under what circumstances is physical attractiveness a legitimate job-related employment criterion? Is it relevant to being a salesperson, a flight steward, or a receptionist?

4. What steps can be taken to prevent appearance discrimination in the workplace?

For Further Reading

Affirmative Action

Marshall Cohen, Thomas Nagel, and **Thomas Scanlon,** eds., *Equality and Preferential Treatment* (Princeton, N.J.: Princeton University Press, 1976); *Social Philosophy and Policy* 5 (Autumn 1987); and Richard Wasserstrom, ed., *Today's Moral Problems*, 3rd ed. (New York: Macmillan, 1985) provide a selection of philosophical essays both for and against affirmative action.

Jere W. Morehead and **Peter J. Shedd**, "Civil Rights and Affirmative Action: Revolution or Fine-Tuning?" *Business Horizons*, September–October 1990, reviews recent legal developments.

Comparable Worth

June O'Neill, "An Argument Against Comparable Worth" and **Ray Marshall** and **Beth Pauline**, "The Comparable Worth Debate," in **Joseph R. DesJardins** and **John J. McCall**, eds., *Contemporary Issues in Business Ethics*, 2nd ed. (Belmont, Calif.: Wadsworth, 1990) provide a clear and thorough introduction to the comparable worth debate.

Laurie Shrage, "Some Implications of Comparable Worth," *Social Theory and Practice* 13 (Spring 1987) discusses some of the philosophical issues surrounding comparable worth.

Sexual Harassment

"Is Sexual Harassment Still on the Job?" *Business and Society Review* 67 (Fall 1988) presents the views of some top female managers on sexual harassment.

Thought & Action 5 (Spring 1989) contains a thoughtful symposium on sexual harassment in the university.

PART IV

BUSINESS AND SOCIETY

CHAPTER 10

CONSUMERS

The "Marlboro man" has long mesmerized people around the world, and few can deny the glamour of the ruggedly good-looking Marlboro cowboy, with boots, hat, chaps — and, of course, a cigarette in his mouth. Product of one of the most successful advertising campaigns in history, the Marlboro man revolutionized the image of Marlboro cigarettes, making it a top-selling brand year in, year out. Few people remember, however, that the actor who originally portrayed the Marlboro man died of lung cancer as a result of smoking.

Everybody, of course, knows that smoking is hazardous to one's health — everyone, that is, but the tobacco industry. It continues to assert that "there is no proof that a cause-and-effect relationship exists between smoking and any disease." Yet a smoker has ten times the chance of getting lung cancer and twice the chance of getting heart disease that a nonsmoker has. According to figures released by the federal Centers for Disease Control, smoking remains the leading cause of preventable deaths and is responsible for 16 percent of deaths overall. Although the percentage of Americans who smoke is dropping, the absolute number of smokers — and smoking's death toll — remains as high as ever. Hardly any consumer good compares to cigarettes in terms of individual injury and social costs.[1]

The American Medical Association has posed that the federal government ban all promotion and advertising of cigarettes. Meanwhile, waves of lawsuits continue to crash against the tobacco industry. Cigarette smokers are going to court and suing tobacco companies for injuries allegedly caused by their deadly habit. Despite the warning labels that have been required since 1966, many smokers — or their estates — contend that they were addicted and couldn't stop. They have also produced evidence that the tobacco companies suppressed research results showing that cigarette smoke contains carcinogens. If the smokers win, cigarette manufacturers may be held accountable for an estimated $80 billion a year in losses related to smoking. And cigarette prices may jump to three dollars a pack — thus reducing the numbers of smokers and saving millions from premature death.[2]

Cigarettes are an especially dangerous product, and their manufacture, marketing, advertising, and sale raise in acute form a number of questions relevant to the consumer issues of this chapter. For instance, what responsibility to consumers do companies have that sell potentially or (in the case of cigarettes) inherently harmful products? To what extent do manufacturers abuse advertising? How should we decide what is or is not deceptive advertising? Can advertisements create or at least stimulate desires for products that consumers would not otherwise want or would not otherwise want as much? How, if at all, should advertising be restricted?

What about possibly deceptive labeling and packaging? Are consumers sufficiently well informed about the products they buy? How far should we go in monitoring the claims of advertisers, in regulating product packaging and labels, and in upholding set standards of reliability and safety? In a market-oriented economic system, how do we balance the interests of business with the rights of consumers? How do we promote social well-being while still respecting the choices of individuals?

These are among the issues probed in this chapter — in particular:

1. Product safety — the legal and moral responsibilities of manufacturers and the pros and cons of government regulations designed to protect us

2. The responsibilities of business to consumers in the areas of product quality, prices, labeling, and packaging

3. Deceptive and morally questionable techniques used in advertising

4. The choice between the "reasonable" consumer and "ignorant" consumer standards as the basis for identifying deceptive advertisements

5. Advertising and children

6. The social desirability of advertising in general — is it a positive feature of our economic system? Does it manipulate, or merely respond to, consumer needs?

PRODUCT SAFETY

Business's responsibility for understanding and providing for consumer needs derives from the fact that citizen-consumers are completely dependent on business to satisfy their needs. This dependence is particularly true in our highly technological society, characterized as it is by a complex economy, intense specialization, and urban concentration. These conditions contrast with those prevailing in the United States when the country was primarily agrarian, composed of people who could satisfy most of their own needs. Today, however, we rely more and more on others to provide the wherewithal for our survival and prosperity. We now rarely make our own clothing, supply our own fuel, manufacture our own tools, or construct our own homes. Food travels an average of 1,200 miles before we eat it.

The increasing complexity of today's economy and the growing dependence of consumers on business for their survival and enrichment have heightened business's responsibilities to consumers — particularly in the area of product safety. From toys to tools, consumers use products believing that they won't be harmed or injured by them. Since consumers are not in a position of technical expertise to judge the sophisticated products that are necessary for contemporary life, they must rely primarily on the conscientious efforts of business to ensure consumer safety.

Unfortunately, statistics indicate that the faith consumers must place in manufacturers is often misplaced. Over 20 million Americans per year require medical treatment from product-related accidents. Of these persons, 110,000 are permanently disabled and 30,000 die.[3]

The Legal Liability of Manufacturers

If you are injured by a defective product, you can sue the manufacturer of that product. We take this legal fact for granted, but it wasn't always true. Before the famous case of *MacPherson* v. *Buick Motor Car* in 1916, injured consumers could only recover damages from the retailer of the defective product — that is, from the party with whom they had actually done business. That made sense in an older day of small-scale, local capitalism. If the shoes you bought from the local shoemaker were defective, then your complaint was against him. By contrast, when a wheel fell off MacPherson's Buick, the firm he had bought the Buick from hadn't actually made it.

Legal policy before *MacPherson* was to base a manufacturer's liability on the contractual relationship between the producer and the purchaser. Their contractual relationship is simply the sale — that is, the exchange of money for a commodity of a certain description. But that contractual relationship is an important source of moral and legal responsibilities for the producer. It obligates business firms to provide customers with a product that lives up to the claims the firm makes about the product. Those claims shape customers' expectations about what they are buying and lead them to enter into the contract in the first place. The question in *MacPherson*, however, was whether a manufacturer's liability for defective products was limited to those with whom it had a direct contractual relationship.

The New York Court of Appeals's *MacPherson* decision recognized the twentieth-century economic reality of large manufacturing concerns and national systems of product distribution. Among other things, local retailers are not as likely as large manufacturers to be able to bear financial responsibility for defective products that injure others. One can also see the court moving in *MacPherson* to a "due care" theory of the manufacturer's duties to consumers. *Due care* is the idea that consumers and sellers do not meet as equals and that the consumer's interests are particularly vulnerable to being harmed by the manufacturer, who has knowledge and expertise the consumer does not have.[4] MacPherson, for instance, was in no position to have discovered the defective wheel before the Buick was purchased. According to the due-care view, then, manufacturers have an obligation, above and beyond any contract, to ex-

ercise due care to prevent the consumer from being injured by defective products.

As the concept of due care spread, legal policy moved decisively beyond the old doctrine of *caveat emptor*, which was seldom the guiding principle by the time of *MacPherson* anyway. *Caveat emptor* means "let the buyer beware," and today we associate it with an era of patent medicines and outrageously false product claims. Although legally the doctrine of "let the buyer beware" was never upheld across the board, it still symbolizes a period in which consumers themselves had a greater legal responsibility to accept the consequences of their product choices.

Consumers at that time were held to the ideal of being knowledgeable, shrewd, and skeptical. It was their free choice whether to buy a certain product. Accordingly, they were expected to take the claims of manufacturers and salespersons with a grain of salt, to inspect any potential purchase carefully, to rely on their own judgment, and to accept any ill results of their decision to use a given product. In the first part of the twentieth century, however, the courts repudiated this doctrine, largely on grounds of its unrealistic assumptions about consumer knowledge, competence, and behavior.

Despite *MacPherson*'s support for the due-care theory and for a broader view of manufacturer's liability, the case still left the burden on the injured consumer to prove that the manufacturer had been negligent. Not only might such an assertion be hard to prove, but also a product might be dangerously defective despite the manufacturer having taken reasonable steps to avoid such a defect.

Two important cases changed this situation. In the 1960 New Jersey case *Henningsen* v. *Bloomfield Motors* and in the 1963 California case *Greenman* v. *Yuba Power Products*, injured consumers were awarded damages without having to prove that the manufacturers of the defective products were negligent. Consumers, the courts ruled, have a right to expect that the products they purchase are reasonably safe when used in the intended way. On the basis of these cases and hundreds of subsequent cases, the "strict liability" approach to product safety has come to dominate legal thinking.

Strict product liability is the doctrine that the seller of a product has legal responsibilities to compensate the user of that product for injuries suffered due to a defective aspect of the product, even though the seller has not been negligent in permitting that defect to occur.[5] Under this doctrine a judgment for the recovery of damages could conceivably be won even if the manufacturer adhered to strict quality-control procedures.[6] Strict liability, however, is not absolute liability. The manufacturer is not responsible for any injury whatsoever that might befall the consumer. The product must be defective, and the consumer always has the responsibility to exercise care.

Strict product liability is not without its critics, however. They contend that the doctrine is unfair. If a firm has exercised due care and taken reasonable precautions to avoid or eliminate foreseeable dangerous defects, they argue, then it should not be held liable for defects that are not its "fault" — that is, for defects that happen despite its best efforts to guard against them. To hold the firm liable anyway seems unjust.

The argument for strict liability is basically utilitarian. Its advocates contend, first, that only such a policy leads firms to bend over backward to guarantee product safety. Since they know that they will be held liable for injurious defects no matter what, they make every effort to enhance safety. Second, proponents of strict liability contend that the manufacturer is best able to bear the cost of injuries due to defects. Naturally, firms raise the price of their products to cover their legal costs (or pay for liability insurance). Defenders of strict liability do not disapprove of this. They see it as a perfectly reasonable way of spreading the cost of injuries among all consumers of the product, rather than letting it fall on a single individual — a kind of insurance scheme.

Protecting the Public

These developments in product liability law set the general framework within which manufacturers must operate today. In addition, a number of government agencies have become involved in regulating product safety. Congress created one of the most important of these agencies in 1972 when it passed the Consumer Product Safety Act. This act empowers the Consumer Product Safety Commission to "protect the public against unreasonable risks of injury associated with consumer products." The five-member commission sets standards for products, bans products presenting undue risk of injury, and in general polices the entire consumer-product marketing process from manufacture to final sale.[7]

In undertaking its policing function, the commission aids consumers in evaluating product safety, develops uniform standards, gathers data, conducts research, and coordinates local, state, and federal product safety laws and enforcement. The commission's jurisdiction extends to more than 10,000 products, and it has the power to require recalls, public warnings, and refunds. Exceptionally risky products can be seized and condemned by court order. Rather than stressing punitive action, however, the commission emphasizes developing new standards and redesigning products to accommodate possible consumer misuse.[8] It is less concerned with assigning liability than with avoiding injuries in the first place.

Despite the obvious public benefits of safety regulations, critics worry about the economic costs. New safety standards add millions of dollars to the cumulative price tag of goods like power lawn mowers. Recalls, too, are expensive. General Motors had to spend

$3.5 million for postage alone to notify by certified mail, as required by law, the 6.5 million owners of cars with questionable engine mounts. The cost to Panasonic to recall and repair 280,000 television sets, as ordered by the commission because of harmful radiation emission, was probably equal to the company's profits in the United States for several years.[9]

In addition, consumers sometimes reject mandated safety technology. In 1974, for example, Congress legislated an interlock system that would require drivers to fasten their seat belts before their cars could move. A public outcry forced lawmakers to rescind the law.

Safety regulations may also prevent individuals from choosing to purchase a riskier, though less expensive, product. Take the notorious Ford Pinto with its unsafe gas tank, for example. In 1978, after all the negative publicity, scores of lawsuits, and the trial of Ford Motor Company for reckless homicide, the sale of Pintos fell dramatically. Consumers preferred a safer car for comparable money. The state of Oregon took all the Pintos out of its fleet and sold them. At least one dealer selling turned-in Pintos, however, reported brisk sales at their low, second-hand price.[10] Some consumers were willing to accept the risks of a Pinto at the right price.

Economists worry about the inefficiencies of preventing individuals from balancing safety against price. Philosophers worry about interfering with people's freedom of choice. Take automobile safety again. Small cars are more dangerous than large cars because people in small cars are less likely to survive accidents. Bigger, safer cars are more expensive, however, and many would prefer to spend less on their cars despite the increased risk. If we only allowed cars to be sold that were as safe as, say, a Mercedes, then there would be fewer deaths on the highways. There would also be fewer people who could afford cars.

This example touches on the larger controversy over *legal paternalism*, which is the

doctrine that the law may justifiably be used to restrict the freedom of individuals for their own good. No one doubts that laws justifiably restrict people from harming other people, but a sizable number of moral theorists deny that laws should attempt to prevent people from running risks that affect only themselves. Requiring your car to have brakes protects others; without brakes, you are more likely to run over a pedestrian. On the other hand, requiring you to wear a seat belt when you drive affects only you. Antipaternalists would protest that your being forced to wear a seat belt despite your wishes fails to respect your moral autonomy. Nonetheless, the twentieth century has seen a growing number of paternalistic laws.

Paternalism is a large issue that can't be done justice here. But in regard to safety regulations, three comments are in order. First, the safety of some products or some features of products (like a car's brakes) affects not just the consumer who purchases the product but third parties as well. Regulating these products or product features can be defended on nonpaternalistic grounds. Second, antipaternalism gains plausibility from the view that individuals know their own interests better than anyone else and that they are fully informed and able to advance those interests. But in the increasingly complex consumer world, this assumption is often doubtful. Where citizens lack knowledge and are unable to make intelligent comparisons and safety judgments, they may find it in their collective self-interest to set minimal safety standards. Such standards are particularly justifiable where few, if any, reasonable persons would want a product that did not satisfy those standards.

Finally, the controversy over legal paternalism pits the values of individual freedom and autonomy against social welfare. Requiring people to wear seat belts may infringe the former but saves thousands of lives each year.

We may simply have to acknowledge that clash of values and be willing to make trade-offs. This doesn't imply a defense of paternalism across the board. Arguably, some paternalistic regulations infringe autonomy more than laws about seat belts do but bring less gain in social welfare. In the end, one may have to examine paternalistic product-safety legislation case by case and try to weigh the conflicting values and likely results.

How Effective Is Regulation?

There is no doubt that in some cases regulation does interfere with rather than safeguard consumer interests. Take, for example, the area of drug regulation. In the late 1960s the Food and Drug Administration (FDA), with considerable fanfare, banned the sweetener cyclamate. Several years later scientific bodies around the world determined that cyclamate was safe, and Abbott Laboratories, makers of cyclamate, asked the FDA to rescind the ban. The FDA refused, so Abbott petitioned the court to take jurisdiction over cyclamate proceedings, enjoin the FDA from further administrative action, and given the evidence, override the agency and approve the sale of cyclamate. The court ruled that Abbott could proceed with what in law is called "discovery."

Emboldened with subpoena power, Abbott discovered compelling evidence of the FDA's abuse of both regulatory process and scientific method, as well as a massive attempt at a cover-up. In particular, Abbott put into the record damning affidavits from a meeting between the FDA commissioner and corporate executives: The commissioner conceded that cyclamate was safe but would remain banned for political reasons. Abbott also forced the agency to turn over internal memos and other documents in which qualified FDA staffers admitted without reservation that cyclamate was safe and that superiors merely saw no point in permitting it back on the market.

In this instance, the interests of the consuming public do not seem to have been served. But regulations often do prod business to recognize and act on their responsibilities to consumers. Sometimes even without applying the force of law, agencies can effectively safeguard the health and safety of consumers. A good example concerns the connection between certain kinds of tampons and the sometimes fatal disease called toxic shock syndrome.

In May 1980 the federal Centers for Disease Control (CDC) published the first report indicating many new cases of toxic shock affecting menstruating women. In June the CDC asked tampon makers for market information, partly because a reporter in Los Angeles had suggested that tampons might be involved. A subsequent CDC study confirmed a correlation between toxic shock and tampon use but termed the rate of incidence too low to recommend that women stop using tampons. But in studying cases of toxic shock contracted in July and August, the CDC found that women with toxic shock were more than twice as likely as a similar group of healthy women to have used Procter & Gamble's Rely, which had garnered about one-quarter of the tampon market.

From the moment that the CDC's second report became public, Procter & Gamble tried to shore up its defense of Rely. Despite many denials about its product's complicity in toxic shock, it couldn't stem the flood of bad publicity. Knowing that Procter & Gamble was sensitive to bad publicity and aware of its own charge to protect the public health, the FDA, the regulatory agency charged with acting on CDC findings, deliberately used the media as a weapon to drive Rely off the market. In the words of Wayne L. Pines, associate FDA commissioner for public affairs: "Throughout the series of events, we made sure the press was notified so as to keep the story alive. We wanted to saturate the market with information on Rely. We deliberately delayed issuing press releases for a day to maximize the media impact. There was quite a concerted and deliberate effort to keep a steady flow of information before the public."[11] The upshot: On September 23, 1980, Procter & Gamble voluntarily agreed to withdraw Rely from the market.

Because Procter & Gamble remained convinced that Rely was a safe product, it's fair to surmise that it would not have withdrawn the product without agency pressure. After all, there was no laboratory evidence implicating highly absorbent tampons in the incidence of toxic shock until over a year later. Had the FDA not acted as it did and had Procter & Gamble continued to sell the product, many women undoubtedly would have suffered and even died between September 1980 and December 1981, when incontrovertible clinical evidence became available.

Do regulations, then, help business meet its responsibility to consumers? Judging from these cases, the answer is generally yes but sometimes no. Nonetheless, the prevailing view today among businesspeople favors self-regulation. Such a view certainly is in keeping with the tenets of classical capitalism and is arguably an attractive ideal. However, self-regulation can easily become an instrument for subordinating consumer interests to profit making when the two goals clash. Under the guise of self-regulation, businesses may end up ignoring or minimizing responsibility to consumers.

Consider the auto industry. For more than twenty-five years it has been fighting a battle against safety and pollution regulations for cars. Jolted a few years ago by the industry's staggering losses and mounting layoffs, Washington started going easier on Detroit. Sensing an opportunity, industry officials embarked on a major effort to rid themselves of many regulations they considered unnecessary and too costly. Automakers began circulating thick books detailing how dozens of revisions to existing laws would save themselves and car buyers vast sums of money. In particular, auto officials wanted to roll back car and truck pollution rules, completely revamp emissions enforcement, scrap a requirement for automatic crash-protection devices for passengers, and dilute existing standards for bumpers. As a result, the Reagan-Bush administration targeted some three dozen safety and pollution rules for delay, revision, or cancellation. Such steps may have saved the industry billions in capital outlays. Whether U.S. carmakers have been made more competitive as a result is open to debate. But at least some of these deregulations jeopardize the safety of drivers and add to already soaring public health costs.

To illustrate, the federal government delayed the requirement to equip cars with air bags or automatic seat belts. Each year of the delay saved the industry $30 million. But according to Joan Clayburn, former safety-agency chief of the U.S. Department of Transportation (DOT), passive restraints reduce highway deaths by 9,000 a year and injuries by tens of thousands. DOT's own analysis conceded that each year of postponement meant an additional 600 motor vehicle deaths and 4,300 serious injuries. Using DOT's figures, the American Academy of Pediatricians estimated that, although further delay would have saved the auto industry about $70 million in manufacturing and purchase costs, it would have ended up costing $457,693,000 in health-care costs, not to mention the tragedy of numerous deaths and injuries.[12]

When the law finally required new cars to come equipped with some form of passive restraint system, Chrysler Motors became (in 1989) the first American auto manufacturer to install driver-side air bags in all its new models. Only five years earlier, Chrysler chairman Lee Iacocca had boasted in his autobiography of fighting against air bags since their invention in the mid-1960s. In 1971, he and Henry Ford II (then the top executives at Ford) met secretly with President Richard Nixon to persuade him to kill a pending DOT regulation requiring air bags in every new car sold in the

United States. As car buyers have indicated an increasing concern with safety, however, Iacocca finally seems to have abandoned his old bromide, "Safety doesn't sell."[13]

The Responsibilities of Business

Simply obeying regulations and laws does not exhaust the moral responsibilities of business in the area of consumer safety. The exact nature of those responsibilities is hard to specify in general, since much depends on the particular product or service being provided. But abiding by the following steps would do much to help business behave morally with respect to consumer safety:

1. *Business can give safety the priority warranted by the product.* This is an important factor because businesses often base safety considerations strictly on cost. If the margin of safety can be increased without significantly insulting budgetary considerations, fine. If not, then safety questions are shelved. Moreover, businesses frequently allow the law to determine the extent to which they'll ensure safety.

Although both cost and the law are factors in safety control, two other considerations seem of more moral importance. One is the seriousness of the injury the product can cause. The automobile, for example, can cause severe injury or death and is thus an item of the highest priority. Other products that can cause serious injury— such as power tools, pesticides, and chemicals—also deserve high priority. The second factor to consider is the frequency of occurrence. How often is a particular product involved in an accident? Car crashes, for instance, are the leading killer of Americans under thirty-five. When a product scores high on both the seriousness and frequency tests, it warrants the highest priority as a potential safety hazard.

2. *Business should abandon the misconception that accidents occur exclusively as a result of product misuse and that it is thereby absolved of all responsibility.* At one time such a belief may have been valid. But in using today's highly sophisticated products, numerous people have followed product instructions explicitly and have still been injured. In any case, the point is that the company shares responsibility for product safety with the consumer. Rather than insisting that consumers' abuse of product leads to most accidents and injuries, firms would probably accomplish more by carefully pointing out how their products can be used safely.

A Pennsylvania court recently endorsed this perspective. It awarded $11.3 million in damages to a twenty-year-old Philadelphia woman who was accidentally shot in the head when a handgun owned by her neighbor went off. The court decided the shop that had sold the weapon should pay 30 percent of the damages, because it had provided the buyer with no demonstration or written instructions for safe use of the gun.[14]

Both manufacturers and retailers have an obligation to try to anticipate and minimize the ways their products can cause harm, whether or not those products are "misused." For example, a four-year-old girl stood on an open oven door to peak into a pot on top of the stove. She was seriously injured when her weight caused the stove to tip over. A manufacturer can reasonably foresee that a cook might place a heavy roasting pan on the oven door. If doing so caused the stove to tip over, a court would probably find the stove's design defective. But should the manufacturer have foreseen the use of the door not as a shelf but as a stepstool? The courts ruled that it should have.

If a product poses a potential, serious threat, a company may need to take extraordinary measures to ensure continued safe use of it. Determining the extent to which the company must go, however, isn't an easy task. Sometimes a firm's moral responsibility for ensuring safety doesn't reach much beyond the sale of the product. Other times it may extend well beyond that. Consider, for example, the case of a company producing heavy machinery. Workers using its products could easily fall into bad habits. Some would argue, therefore, that the company has an obligation to follow up the sale of such a product, perhaps by visiting firms using its machinery to see if they've developed dangerous shortcuts.

3. *Business must monitor the manufacturing process itself.* Frequently firms fail to control key variables during the manufacturing process, resulting in product defects. Companies should periodically review working conditions and the competence of key personnel. At the design stage of the process, they need to predict ways the product might fail and the consequences of this failure. For production, companies ordinarily can select materials that have been pretested or certified as flawless. If a company fails to do this, then we must question the priority it gives safety. Similar questions arise when companies do not make use of research available about product safety. When none is available, a company really interested in safety can generate its own. However, independent research groups ensure impartial and disinterested analysis and are usually more reliable than in-house studies.

Testing should be rigorous and simulate the toughest conditions. Tests shouldn't assume that the product will be used in just the way the manufacturer intends it to be used. Even established products should be tested. The courts have repeatedly held that a trouble-free history does not justify the assumption that the product is free of defects.[15]

When a product moves into production, it is often changed in a variety of ways. These changes should be documented and referred to some appropriate party, like the safety engineer, for analysis. The firm must be scrupulous about coordinating department activities so manufacturing specifications are not changed without determining any potential dangers related to these changes.

4. *When a product is ready to be marketed, companies should have their product-safety staff review advertising for safety-related content.* This step not only ensures accuracy and completeness but also provides consumers with vital information. A corollary to this rule would be to inform salespeople about the product's hazardous aspects.

5. *When a product reaches the marketplace, firms should make available to consumers written information about the product's performance.* This information should include operating instructions, the product's safety features, conditions that will cause it to fail, a complete list of the ways the product can be used, and a cautionary list of the ways it should not be used. Warnings must be specific.

6. *Companies should investigate consumer complaints.* This process encourages firms to deal fairly with consumers and to use the most effective source of product improvement: the opinions of those who use it.

Even if firms seriously attended to these safety considerations, they couldn't guarantee an absolutely safe product. Some hazards invariably attach to certain products, heroic efforts notwithstanding. But business must acknowledge and discharge its responsibilities in this area. Morally speaking, no one's asking for an accident- and injury-proof product—only that a manufacturer do everything reasonable to approach that ideal.

Cigarette fires illustrate the shortcomings of the tobacco industry in this respect. According to government estimates, about 1,500 Americans are killed each year in cigarette fires, making cigarettes the country's leading cause of fatal fires. Cigarette fires are responsible for 7,000 serious injuries per year and for property damage of $400 million annually. Research shows, however, that small design changes in cigarettes would make them less likely to ignite furniture and bedding, and lawmakers in a number of states have called for legislation to set a fire-resistance standard for cigarettes. But cigarette manufacturers have launched a sophisticated campaign to defuse the issue, and no laws have been passed.[16]

Unfortunately, there are numerous examples of companies and entire industries that play fast and loose with safety, resisting product improvements and dodging responsibility for consumer injury. But many companies do respond quickly to perceived or suspected hazards. Consider two examples of successful companies that place a premium on product safety.[17]

Burning Radios.   Back in the early 1960s, a few of the radios sold by J.C. Penney were reported to have caught fire in customers' homes. J.C. Penney tested the radios and discovered a defective resistor in a few of them — less than 1 percent. Nonetheless, J.C. Penney informed the manufacturer, withdrew the entire line of radios, ran national ads informing the public of the danger, and offered immediate refunds. "This was before the Consumer Product Safety Commission even existed," says J.C. Penney vice chairman Robert Gill. "I guess some people might have thought we were crazy, and said that liability insurance was specifically designed to take care of such problems. But we felt we just could not sell that kind of product."

Fluorocarbons.   In the mid-1970s, environmentalists were seriously alarmed at the possibility that fluorocarbons released from aerosol cans were depleting the earth's thin and fragile ozone layer. The media rapidly picked up the story, but virtually all manufacturers of aerosol cans denounced the scientific findings and stood by their products. The exception was Johnson Wax. The company acknowledged that the scientific questions were difficult to resolve, but it took seriously consumer concern about the ozone. Years before the FDA ban, Johnson Wax withdrew all its fluorocarbon products worldwide. "We picked up a lot of flak from other manufacturers," recalls company chairman Samuel Johnson, "and we lost business in some areas, but I don't have any question we were right. . . . Our belief is that as long as you can make do without a potentially hazardous material, why not do without it?"

OTHER AREAS OF BUSINESS RESPONSIBILITY

Product safety is naturally a dominant concern of consumers. No one wants to be injured by the products he or she uses. But safety is far from the only interest of consumers. The last twenty-five years have seen a general increase in consumer awareness and an ever stronger consumer advocacy movement. One chief consumer issue has been advertising and its possible abuse, which will be discussed in later sections. Three other areas of business responsibility — product quality, pricing, and packaging and labeling — are equally important and are taken equally seriously by the consumer movement.

Product Quality

The demand for high-quality products is closely related to a number of themes mentioned in the discussion of safety. Most would agree that business bears a general responsibility to ensure that the quality of a product measures up to the claims made about it and to reasonable consumer expectations. They would undoubtedly see this responsibility as deriving primarily from the consumer's basic right to get what he or she pays for. But product quality is also in the interest of business. Just as the burden of guaranteeing product safety has shifted to the producer, so has the burden of guaranteeing product performance. As a result, product-quality laws have toughened and judicial resistance to consumer complaints has softened. In increasing numbers, consumers are going to court when products don't perform. What's more, the courts often uphold their complaints.

One way that business assumes responsibilities to consumers is through *warranties,* which are obligations that sellers assume to purchasers. People generally speak of two kinds of warranties, express and implied. *Express warranties* are the claims that sellers explicitly state. They include assertions about the product's characteristics, assurances of product durability, and other statements on warranty cards, labels, wrappers, and packages or in the advertising of the product. The moral concern here is that the manufacturer ensure a product living up to its billing. Just as important, however, is the question of reparation. When a product fails to perform as promoted, whether and how the manufacturer rectifies the consumer's loss raises moral concerns. In some cases, the manufacturer may issue a refund or a new product; in others, greater reparation may be required.

Implied warranties include the implicit claim that a particular product is fit for the ordinary use for which it is likely to be employed. Again, the failure of a product to perform as it should raises serious moral and legal questions. Suppose, for example, that Eleanor Solano buys a used automobile. After she drives the car around for a few days under normal conditions, its steering mechanism fails. In such a case, the used car company may bear both a moral and a legal responsibility, even if on purchase Solano received a disclaimer stating that the company had no responsibility for defective parts.

Advertising can result in implied warranties, even when its claims are not very specific. For example, in one case a man named Inglis bought a Rambler, relying on an American Motors advertising claim that a Rambler would be trouble-free, economical to run, and superior in quality. Sadly, Inglis's expectations proved unrealistic. Not only was his Rambler's trunk out of line, but it couldn't even be opened. The door handles were loose; the steering gear was improperly set; the oil

pump was defective; the brakes squeaked and grated; the engine leaked oil; and loose parts inside the car occasionally fell on the floor. If not a lemon, certainly Inglis's car was of the citrus variety. Unable to get satisfaction from his dealer, Inglis went to court. The court ruled that in cases where there is a difference between advertising claims and a product's actual performance, there is no sound reason that consumers shouldn't be permitted to recoup their losses.[18]

Prices

Have you ever wondered why a product is priced at $9.88 rather than $9.99 or simply $10.00? Or why a product that retails for $3.80 on Monday is selling for $4.10 on Friday? The answers may have nothing to do with inflation, production costs, overhead expenses, labor demands, or the more conventional influences on product prices.

It is true that prices do reflect the costs of material, labor, and operating expenses. In many cases, other factors help shape the price, including a shop's location and the volume of merchandise bought and paid for at one time. But, more and more frequently, purely psychological factors enter into the price-setting equation.

For example, one manufacturer prices jeans at $9.88 instead of $9.99. Why? "When people see $9.99, they say, 'That's $10,'" explains the company's general sales manager. "But $9.88 isn't $10. It's just psychological."[19]

For many consumers, higher prices mean better products. So manufacturers arbitrarily raise the price of a product to give the impression of superior quality or exclusivity. But as often as not, the price is higher than the product's extra quality. For example, a few years ago Proctor-Silex's most expensive fabric iron sold for $54.95, five dollars above the company's next most expensive. Its wholesale price was $26.98 against $24.20, a difference of

$2.78. Moreover, the extra cost of producing the top model was less than one dollar for a light that signaled when the iron was ready.[20]

Manufacturers trade on human psychology when they sell substantially identical products at different prices. For example, Heublein, Inc., raised the price of its Popov brand vodka from about $3.80 to $4.10 a fifth without altering the vodka that went into the fifth. Why the price increase? Heublein sales representatives believed that consumers wanted a variety of vodka prices to choose from. Apparently they were right: While Popov lost 1 percent of its market share, it increased its profits by 30 percent. Applying its theory further, Heublein offers vodka drinkers an even more expensive vodka, Smirnoff. Analysts insist that there is no qualitative difference among vodkas made in the United States.[21]

In this case, the use of psychological pricing is closely related to the problem of pricing branded products higher than generic products that are otherwise indistinguishable. Consumers pay more assuming that the brand name or the higher price implies a better product. Another ethically dubious practice is printing a suggested retail price on packages that is substantially higher than what retailers are known to charge. When retailers mark a new price over the "suggested price," customers receive the false impression that the item is selling below its customary price. Retailers themselves are on questionable ethical ground when they use special pricing codes or fail to post a price on or near products, thus hindering consumers from easily comparing prices.[22]

Many practical consumers tend to think of these pricing practices as more of a nuisance or irritant they must live with than as something morally objectionable. But these practices do raise moral questions — not least about business's view of itself and its role in the community — that businesspeople and ethical theorists are now beginning to take seriously.

Much more attention has been devoted to price fixing, which despite its prevalence is widely recognized as a violation of the "rules of the game" in a market system whose ideal is open and fair price competition. An example is a 1989 legal settlement with New York State in which the Panasonic Company agreed to pay between $8.5 million and $16 million in rebates to purchasers of videocassette recorders, telephone answering machines, video cameras, cordless telephones, and stereo components sold under the brand names Panasonic and Technics. The reason? Panasonic had pressured major retailers and chains like Circuit City, K mart, and Montgomery Ward into selling its products at the company's suggested retail price and not at a discount. Although manufacturers often suggest prices to their retailers, the retailers are supposed to be free to set their own prices, depending on the profit they foresee in the market. Any agreement between a manufacturer and a retailer to fix a price is illegal. Panasonic sales executives, however, badgered stores that did not honor the manufacturer's minimum prices and threatened to stop doing business with retailers that didn't comply. Until one large New York retailer finally complained to the New York State Attorney General's office, not only did the stores and chains go along, but they also reported uncooperative competitors to Panasonic.[23]

When a few companies gain control of a market, they are often in a position to force consumers to pay artificially high prices. To take a notorious example, in 1960 General Electric, Westinghouse, and twenty-seven other companies producing electrical equipment were found guilty of fixing prices in that billion-dollar industry. The companies were made to pay about $2 million in fines and many more millions to their corporate victims.[24] Given the oligopolistic nature of the electrical equipment market, consumers could not reasonably be said to have had the option to take their business elsewhere and thus drive down prices. (In fact, until it was exposed, they had no reason to believe they were being victimized by price fixing.)

Of course, controlling prices need not be done so blatantly. Firms in an oligopoly can tacitly agree to remain uncompetitive with one another, thereby avoiding losses that might result from price-cutting competition. They can then play "follow the leader": Let the lead firm in the market raise its prices, and then the rest follow suit. The result is a laundered form of price fixing.

Even without tacit price fixing, the firms that dominate a field often implicitly agree not to compete in terms of price. Nobody, they say to themselves, wants a "price war," as if price competition were a threat to a market system rather than its lifeblood. Familiar rivals like Pepsi and Coca-Cola or McDonald's and Burger King generally choose to compete in terms of image and jingles rather than price. In the 1980s deregulation and People Express did much to encourage price competition among airlines, but many carriers, judging from their advertisements, still prefer to compete on the basis of meals and the uniforms of flight attendants rather than the cost of their tickets.

From the moral point of view, prices, like wages, should be just. What is a just price? It's not enough to say that a just price exists when a merchant makes a "fair profit" after expenses, for we can still ask what a fair profit is. In the end, the question "What is a just price?" probably defies a precise answer. Still, merchants cannot morally charge whatever they want or whatever the market will bear any more than employers can pay workers whatever they (the employers) want simply because it is impossible to be precise about a "fair wage."

Just as in the case of wages, one can approach an answer to the just-price question by assessing the factors the price is based on and the process used to determine it. Certainly factors such as costs of material and production, operating and marketing expenses, and profit are relevant to price setting. In addition,

consumer choice in the marketplace does, and should, affect prices. Product price, in other words, reflects in part the considered beliefs and judgments of the consuming public regarding the relative value of the article. In a capitalist economy, these beliefs are formed and judgments made in the open market in a free interplay between sellers and buyers.

For this process to function satisfactorily, however, buyers must be in a position to exercise informed consent. Informed consent, as noted in Chapter 7, calls for deliberation and free choice. Deliberation requires that buyers understand all significant facts about the goods and services they are purchasing and then voluntarily purchase them. But clearly consumers are at least sometimes, perhaps often, denied informed consent. They do not always receive the clear, accurate, and complete information about product quality and price that they need to make prudent choices.

Labeling and Packaging

Business's general responsibility to provide clear, accurate, and adequate information undoubtedly applies to product labeling and packaging. The reason is that, despite the billions of dollars spent annually on advertising, a product's label and package remain the consumer's primary source of product information. Yet labels are often hard to understand or even misleading, and what they omit to say may be more important than what they do say. For example, nothing is more misleading than the terms "low in cholesterol" and "cholesterol-free." Cholesterol is contained only in animal products and by-products. Yet, not only do many vegetable and grain products, like cooking oils, proudly declare on their labels that they are cholesterol-free, they are also often replete with saturated vegetable fats and hydrogenated oils, which your body converts into cholesterol.

A particularly blatant example of label abuse is Sebastiani Vineyards' new wine product, Domaine Chardonnay. "Chardonnay" has a high level of name recognition and a positive reputation among wine consumers. Unfortunately for them, however, there isn't a drop of chardonnay in Domaine Chardonnay, which is a blend of chenin blanc, sauvignon blanc, French colombard, riesling, and other grapes. After a public outcry when the wine was introduced in 1989, the Bureau of Alcohol, Tobacco, and Firearms required the company to redesign its label, which now has a large "DC" and a small "Domaine Chardonnay" at the bottom. Many people, however, continue to feel that letting Sebastiani use the name of a grape varietal as a brand name is a travesty of labeling law—even if Sebastiani decides in the future to include a little chardonnay in the wine mixture.

In addition to misleading labels, package shape that exploits certain optical illusions can trick consumers. Tall and narrow cereal boxes look larger than short, squat ones that actually contain more cereal; shampoo bottles often have pinched waists to give the illusion of quantity; fruits are packed in large quantities of syrup; and dry foods often come in tins or cartons stuffed with cardboard.[25]

Consider a representative study made of five randomly selected housewife-shoppers.[26] Each shopper had a college education and extensive family marketing experience. The five women were taken to a supermarket, where they were each given a set amount of money and asked to purchase any fourteen items, the average number of purchases that shoppers make. When they finished, their selections were compared with the merchandise available in the supermarket. Of the seventy items chosen, only thirty-six were "best buys"— that is, the most economical selections available of products of comparable quality. Even granting that the sample was too small to draw firm conclusions, the results suggest that some shoppers are fooled by labeling and packaging.

Language abuse partly accounts for consumer bewilderment in the marketplace. Frequently shoppers are mystified by such terms as "large," "extra large," and "economy size"; by the net quantities of the contents (ounces, pints, quarts, liters, grams); as well as by special terms, such as "prime," "choice," "graded," and "ungraded," which are applied to meat. Without a pocket computer, consumers find it difficult in many stores to calculate the relative prices of items. They can fall victim to terms and numbers, even though unit pricing is doing much to alleviate the problem.

What's more, although the Truth in Packaging Act (Fair Packaging and Labeling Act, 1966) empowers representative agencies to rank and list all ingredients in the order of decreasing percentage of total contents, wily marketers can sometimes circumvent this at the consumer's expense. For example, because sugar is the predominant ingredient in Shazam! breakfast cereal, it must be listed first. But by breaking down sugar into its various forms—sucrose, glucose, fructose, lactose—the manufacturer of Shazam! can minimize the appearance of sugar in the product. Indeed, it can avoid the word "sugar" entirely.

As with product information in advertising, the moral issues involved in packaging and labeling relate primarily to truth telling and consumer exploitation. Sound moral conduct in this area must rest on a strong desire to provide consumers with clear and usable information about the price, quality, and quantity of a product so they can make intelligent choices. When marketers are interested primarily in selling a product and only secondarily in providing relevant information, then morally questionable practices are bound to follow. Those responsible for labeling and packaging would be well advised to consider at least the following questions, a negative answer to any of which could signal a moral problem: Is there anything about the packaging that is likely to mislead consumers? Have we clearly and specifically identified the exact nature of the product in an appropriate part of the label? Is the net quantity prominently located? Is it readily understandable to those wishing to compare prices? If a term such as "serving" is used, as in soups or puddings, is the net quantity of the serving stipulated? Are ingredients listed so they can be readily recognized and understood? Have we indicated and represented the percentage of the contents that is filler, such as the bone in a piece of meat?

These questions represent only some that a morally responsible businessperson might ask. In addition, we must not forget people whose health necessitates certain dietary restrictions. They often have great difficulty determining what products they can safely purchase.

DECEPTION AND UNFAIRNESS IN ADVERTISING

We tend to take advertising for granted, yet sociologically and economically it is enormously important. Ads dominate our environment. Famous ones become part of our culture; their jingles dance in our heads, and their images haunt our dreams and shape our tastes. Advertising is also big business. In a recent year, for instance, Sears spent $887 million for advertising space and time in the mass media, McDonald's $649 million, and PepsiCo $704 million. Philip Morris and Procter & Gamble topped the list of big advertisers at $1,558 million and $1,387 million, respectively.[27] In 1988 advertisers in the United States spent a total of $118 billion on all forms of media advertising. That works out to nearly $5,000 for every person in the country.[28]

When people are asked what advertising does, their first thought is often that it provides consumers with information about goods and services. In fact, advertising conveys very little information. Nor are most ads intended to do so. Except for classified ads (by amateurs!) and newspaper ads reporting supermarket prices, very few advertisements offer any information of genuine use to the consumer. (If you want useful product information, you have to go to a magazine like *Consumer Reports*, which publishes objective and comparative studies of various products.) In-

stead, advertisements offer us jingles, rhymes, and attractive images.

The goal of advertising, of course, is to persuade us to buy the products that are being touted. Providing objective and comparative product information may be one way to do this. But it is not the only way, and judging from ads these days—which frequently say nothing at all about the product's qualities—it is not a very common way. The similarity among many competing products may be the explanation. One writer identifies the effort to distinguish among basically identical products as the "ethical, as well as economic, crux of the [advertising] industry"; another refers to it as the "persistent, underlying bad faith" of much American advertising.[29]

Deceptive Techniques

Since advertisers are trying to persuade people to buy their products and since straight product information is not necessarily the best way to do this, there is a natural temptation to obfuscate, misrepresent, or even lie. In an attempt to persuade, advertisers are prone to exploit ambiguity, conceal facts, exaggerate, and employ psychological appeals.

Ambiguity.   When ads are ambiguous, they can be deceiving. For example, the Continental Baking Company was charged with such ambiguity by the Federal Trade Commission (FTC). In advertising Profile bread, Continental implied that eating the bread would lead to weight loss. The fact was that Profile had about the same number of calories per ounce as other breads; each slice contained seven fewer calories but only because it was sliced thinner than most breads. Continental issued a corrective advertisement.

In all aspects of advertising, much potential moral danger lies in the interpretation. The Profile ad is a good example. A large number of people interpreted that ad to mean that eating Profile bread would lead to a weight loss.[30] Likewise, for years consumers have inferred from its advertisements that Listerine mouthwash effectively fights bacteria and sore throats. Not so; accordingly, the FTC ordered Listerine to run a multimillion-dollar disclaimer. And when Sara Lee began promoting its Light Classics desserts, the natural implication was that "light" meant the products contained fewer calories than other Sara Lee desserts. When pressed by investigators to support this implied claim, Sara Lee contended that "light" referred only to the texture of the product.[31]

In cases like these, advertisers and manufacturers invariably deny that they intended consumers to draw false inferences. But sometimes the ambiguity is such that a reasonable person wouldn't infer anything else. When a cold tablet advertisement says, "At the first sign of a cold or flu—Coricidin," what is the consumer likely to think? The fact is that neither Coricidin nor any other cold remedy can cure the common cold. At best it can only provide temporary symptomatic relief. But a consumer is left to draw his or her own conclusion, and it's likely to be the wrong one.

Aiding and abetting ambiguity is the use of "weasel" words, words used to evade or retreat from a direct or forthright statement. Consider the weasel word "help." "Help" means "aid" or "assist" and nothing else. Yet as one author has observed, " 'help' is the one single word which, in all the annals of advertising, has done the most to say something that couldn't be said."[32] Because the word "help" is used to qualify, almost anything can be said after it. Thus we're exposed to ads for products that "help us keep young," "help prevent cavities," "help keep our houses germ-free." Consider for a moment how many times a day you hear or read phrases like these: "helps stop," "helps prevent," "helps fight," "helps overcome," "helps you feel," "helps you look." And, of course, "help" is hardly the only weasel word. "Like," "virtual" or "virtually," "can be," "up to" (as in "provides relief up to eight hours"), "as much as" (as in "saves as much as one gallon of gas"), and numerous other weasel words are used to imply what can't be said.

The fact that ads are open to interpretation doesn't exonerate advertisers from the obligation to provide clear information. Indeed, this fact intensifies their responsibility, because the danger of misleading through ambiguity increases as the ad is subject to interpretation. At stake are not only people's money but also their health, loyalties, and expectations. The potential harm a misleading ad can cause is great, not to mention its cavalier treatment of the truth. For these reasons ambiguity in ads is of serious moral concern.

Concealed Facts.   When advertisers conceal facts, they suppress information that is unflattering to their products. Put another way, a fact is concealed when its availability would probably make the product less desirable. Shell, for example, used to advertise that its gasoline had "platformate" but neglected to mention that all other brands did too. Subway ads for the Bowery Bank in New York use former baseball star Joe DiMaggio to tout the fact that it is "federally insured," but then so is almost every bank in the country. Kraft advertises its Philadelphia Cream Cheese as having "half the calories of butter," but doesn't tell consumers that it is also high in fat. Similarly, Weight Watchers tells consumers that its frozen meals are without butter, chicken fat, or tropical oils but not that they are high in salt.

Advertisements for painkillers routinely conceal relevant information. For years, Bayer aspirin advertised that it contained "the ingredient that doctors recommend most." What is that ingredient? Aspirin. The advertising claim that "last year hospitals dispensed ten times as much Tylenol as the next four brands combined" does not disclose the fact that Johnson & Johnson supplies hospitals with Tylenol at a cost well below what consumers pay. Interestingly, American Home Products sued Johnson & Johnson on the grounds that the Tylenol ad falsely implies that it is more effective than competing products. But at the same time, American Home Products was advertising its Anacin-3 by claiming that "hospitals recommended acetaminophen, the aspirin-free pain reliever in Anacin-3, more than any other pain reliever" — without telling consumers that the acetaminophen hospitals recommend is, in fact, Tylenol.

Concealment of relevant facts and information can exploit people by misleading them; it also undermines truth telling. Unfortunately, truth rarely seems foremost in the minds of advertisers. As Samm Sinclair Baker writes: "Inside the agency the basic approach is hardly conducive to truth telling. The usual thinking in forming a campaign is first what can we say, true or not, that will sell the product best? The second consideration is, how can we say it effectively and get away with it so that (1) people who buy won't feel let down by too big a promise that doesn't come true, and (2) the ads will avoid quick and certain censure by the FTC."[33] This observation shows one businessperson's tendency to equate what's legal with what's moral. It's precisely this outlook that leads to advertising behavior of dubious morality.

Examples of ads that conceal important facts are legion. An old Colgate-Palmolive ad for its Rapid Shave Cream used sandpaper to demonstrate the cream's effect on tough beards. Colgate concealed the fact that the "sandpaper" in the ad was actually Plexiglas and that actual sandpaper had to be soaked in Rapid Shave for about eighty minutes before it came off in a stroke. A few years ago, Campbell vegetable soup ads showed pictures of a thick, rich brew calculated to whet even a gourmet's appetite. What the ads didn't show were clear glass marbles deposited in that bowl to give the soup the appearance of solidity. More recently, a television ad for Volvo showed a row of cars being crushed by a big-wheel truck, with only a Volvo remaining intact. What the ad neglected to say was that the Volvo had been reinforced and the other cars weakened.

Then there's the whole area of feminine deodorant sprays (FDS), currently an industry in excess of $55 million. FDS ads not only fail to mention that such products in most cases are unnecessary but that they frequently produce unwanted side effects: itching, burning, blistering, and urinary infections. A Food and Drug Administration (FDA) "caution" now appears on these products.

If business has obligations to provide clear, accurate, and adequate information, we must wonder if it meets this charge when it hides facts relevant to the consumer's purchase of a product. Concealing information raises serious moral concerns relative to truth telling and consumer exploitation. When consumers are deprived of comprehensive knowledge about a product, their choices are constricted and distorted.

If pushed farther, the moral demand for full information challenges almost all advertising. Even the best advertisements never point out the negative features of their products or that there is no substantive difference between the product being advertised and its competitors, as is often the case. In this sense, they could be accused of concealing relevant information. Most advertisers would be shocked at the suggestion that honesty requires an objective presentation of the pros and cons of their products, and in fact consumers don't expect advertisers or salespersons to be impartial. Nevertheless, it is not clear why this moral value should not be relevant to assessing advertising. And it can be noted that retail salespersons, despite a sometimes negative reputation, often do approach this level of candor — at least when they are fortunate enough to sell a genuinely good and competitive product or when they do not work on commission.

Exaggeration.   Advertisers can mislead through exaggeration — that is, by making claims unsupported by evidence. For example, claims that a pain reliever provides "extra pain relief" or is "50 percent stronger than aspirin," that it "upsets the stomach less frequently" or is "superior to any other nonprescription painkiller on the market" contradict evidence that all analgesics are effective to the same degree.[34]

Nabisco's advertising of its 100-percent bran cereal as being "flavored with two naturally sweet fruit juices" is typical of exaggerated product claims. Although fig juice and prune juice have indeed been added to the product, they are its least significant ingredients in terms of weight; the primary sweetener is sugar.[35] As in this case, exaggeration often goes hand in hand with concealed information. Trident chewing gum has long advertised that it helps fight cavities, but its ads (which describe Trident as a "dental instrument") clearly exaggerate the benefits of chewing Trident. Chewing gum can indeed help to dislodge debris on the enamel of your teeth, but so can eating an apple or rinsing your mouth with water. And the sugar substitute used by Trident (sorbitol) can indirectly promote tooth decay: It nurtures the normally harmless bacteria that sugar activates into decay microrganisms.[36]

"Antiaging" skin-care products are one of the fastest-growing segments of the cosmetic industry, partly because the baby boom generation is getting older. The FDA, however, is upset about cosmetic firms' claims about their antiaging skin treatments. Companies portray their products as "repairing cells" or skin layers below the surface rather than having only an external effect. The FDA says that, if the companies want to keep making these claims, they have to seek new-drug status for their treatments. And the FDA says it is prepared to take "appropriate regulatory sanctions, such as seizure or injunction," if they don't.

Part of the labeling for Avon's Bioadvance Beauty Recovery System, for example, claims that it "actually helps reverse many signs of facial aging in just six weeks . . . helps revitalize and invigorate your skin's regenerative system." Christiaan Barnard, the first heart-transplant surgeon, endorses the antiaging skin cream made by Alfin Fragrances. The product's distinctive ingredient, Glycosphingolipid — said by critics to be only a natural body fat with a fancy name — is claimed to make skin "function as if it were young again."[37]

Clearly the line between deliberate deception and what advertising mogul David Ogilvy has termed "puffery" is not always clear. By "puffery" Ogilvy means the use of "harmless" superlatives. Thus advertisers frequently boast of the merits of their products by using words such as "best," "finest," or "most," or phrases like "king of beers" or "breakfast of champions." In many instances the use of such puffery is indeed harmless, as in the claim that a soap is the "best loved in America." Other times, however, it's downright misleading, as in the Dial soap ad that claimed Dial was "the most effective deodorant soap you can buy." When asked to substantiate that claim, Armour-Dial Company insisted that it was not claiming product superiority; all it meant was that Dial soap was as effective as any other soap.

Of moral importance in determining the line between puffery and deliberate deception would seem to be the advertiser's intention and the likely interpretation of the ad. Are the claims intended as no more than verbal posturing, or are they intended to sell through deceptive exaggeration? Are advertisers primarily interested in saying as much as they can without drawing legal sanction or in providing consumers with accurate information? But even when the intention is harmless, advertisers must consider how the ad is likely to be interpreted. What conclusion is the general consuming public likely to draw about the product? Is that conclusion contrary to likely performance? Without raising questions like these about their ads, advertisers and manufacturers risk warping the truth and injuring consumers, two significant moral concerns.

Psychological Appeals.   A psychological appeal is one that aims to persuade by appealing primarily to human emotional needs and not to reason. This is potentially the area of greatest moral concern in advertising. An automobile ad that presents the product in an elitist atmosphere peopled by members of the "in" set appeals to our need and desire for status. A life insurance ad that portrays a destitute family woefully struggling in the aftermath of a provider's death tries to persuade through pity and fear. Reliance on such devices, although not unethical per se, raises moral concerns because rarely do such ads fully deliver what they promise.

Ads that rely extensively on pitches to power, prestige, sex, masculinity, femininity, acceptance, approval, and the like aim to sell more than a product. They are peddling psychological satisfaction. Perhaps the best example is the increasingly explicit and pervasive use of sexual pitches in ads:

Scene:	An artist's skylit studio. A young man lies nude, the bedsheets in disarray. He awakens to find a tender note on his pillow. The phone rings and he gets up to answer it.
Woman's Voice:	"You snore."
Artist (smiling):	"And you always steal the covers."

More cozy patter between the two. Then a husky-voiced announcer intones: "Paco Rabanne. A cologne for men. What is remembered is up to you."[38]

Although sex has always been used to sell products, it has never before been used as explicitly in advertising as it is today. And the sexual pitches are by no means confined to products like cologne. The California Avocado Commission supplements its "Love Food from California" recipe ads with a campaign featuring leggy actress Angie Dickinson, who is sprawled across two pages of some eighteen national magazines to promote the avocado's nutritional value. The copy line

reads: "Would this body lie to you?" Similarly, Dannon yogurt recently ran an ad featuring a bikini-clad beauty and this message: "More nonsense is written on dieting than any other subject—except possibly sex."

Some students of marketing claim that ads like these appeal to the subconscious mind of both marketer and consumer. Purdue University psychologist and marketing consultant Jacob Jacoby contends that marketers, like everyone else, carry around sexual symbols in their subconscious that, intentionally or not, they use in ads. A case in point: the widely circulated Newport cigarette "Alive with Pleasure" campaign. One campaign ad featured a woman riding the handlebars of a bicycle driven by a man. The main strut of the bike wheel stands vertically beneath her body. In Jacoby's view, such symbolism needs no interpretation.

Author Wilson Bryan Key, who has extensively researched the topic of subconscious marketing appeals, claims that many ads take a subliminal form. *Subliminal advertising* is advertising that communicates at a level beneath our conscious awareness, where some psychologists claim that the vast reservoir of human motivation primarily resides. Most marketing people would likely deny that such advertising occurs. Key disagrees. Indeed, he goes so far as to claim: "It is virtually impossible to pick up a newspaper or magazine, turn on a radio or television set, read a promotional pamphlet or the telephone book, or shop through a supermarket without having your subconscious purposely massaged by some monstrously clever artist, photographer, writer, or technician."[39]

Concern with the serious nature of psychological appeals is what the California Wine Institute seemed to have in mind when it adopted an advertising code of standards. The following restrictions are included:

No wine ad shall present persons engaged in activities with appeal particularly to minors. Among those excluded:

amateur or professional sports figures, celebrities, or cowboys; rock stars, race car drivers.

No wine ad shall exploit the human form or "feature provocative or enticing poses or be demeaning to any individual."

No wine ad shall portray wine in a setting where food is not presented.

No wine ad shall present wine in "quantities inappropriate to the situation."

No wine ad shall portray wine as similar to another type of beverage or product such as milk, soda, or candy.

No wine ad shall associate wine with personal performance, social attainment, achievement, wealth, or the attainment of adulthood.

No wine ad shall show automobiles in a way that one could construe their conjunction.

As suggested, the code seems particularly sensitive to the subtle implications and psychological nuances of ads. In adopting such a rigorous code of advertising ethics, the California Wine Institute recognizes the inextricable connection between what is communicated and how it is communicated. In other words, as media expert Marshall McLuhan always insisted, content cannot be distinguished from form, nor form from content. Sensitivity to this proposition would go far toward raising the moral recognition level in advertising and toward alerting businesspeople to the moral overtones of psychological appeals.

The Federal Trade Commission

The Federal Trade Commission (FTC) was established more than seventy-five years ago to protect consumers against deceptive advertising. Although the FTC is not the only regulatory body monitoring advertisements, it is mainly thanks to the FTC that today we are spared the most blatant abuses of advertising.

During the Reagan-Bush administration, however, there were complaints that the FTC wasn't doing as much as it should. As a result, consumer groups and rival manufacturers started going directly to court to challenge dubious advertising claims. Ironically, the laissez-faire approach of the conservative Reagan FTC can be said to have backfired, because advertisers found the courts less cooperative and more expensive than the FTC was even in its more vigorous days. A district court, for example, fined Jartran $20 million in punitive damages—something the FTC can't do—on top of the $20 million awarded to U-Haul to compensate it for Jartran's advertising claim that it had newer, easier-to-drive trucks than U-Haul.[40]

One important question running through the FTC's history is relevant to all efforts to prohibit deceptive advertising: whether the FTC (or any other regulatory body) is obligated to protect only reasonable, intelligent consumers who conduct themselves sensibly in the marketplace. Or should it also protect ignorant consumers who are careless or gullible in their purchases?[41] If the FTC uses the reasonable-consumer standard, then it should prohibit only advertising claims that would deceive reasonable people. People who are more gullible or less bright than average and are taken in as a result would be unprotected. On the other hand, if the FTC uses the ignorant-consumer standard and prohibits an advertisement that misleads anyone, no matter how ill informed and naive, then it will handle a lot more cases and restrict advertising much more. But in spending its time and resources on such cases, it is not clear that the FTC will be proceeding in response to a substantial public interest, as it is legally charged with doing.[42]

The reasonable-person standard was traditional in a variety of areas of the law long before the FTC was established. If you are sued for negligence, you can successfully defend yourself if you can establish that you behaved as a hypothetical reasonable person would have behaved under like circumstances. On the other hand, in the law of misrepresentation, when you as a deceived consumer sue a seller on grounds that you were misled, then—assuming the deception is not proved to be intentional—you must establish that you were acting reasonably in relying on the false representation. If a reasonable person would not have been misled in like circumstances, then you will not win your case. Ads that make physically impossible or obviously exaggerated claims would thus escape legal liability under the reasonable-person standard.[43]

One decisive case in the legal transition away from the reasonable-person standard in matters of advertising, sales, and marketing was *FTC* v. *Standard Education* in 1937.[44] In this case an encyclopedia company was charged by the FTC with a number of deceptive and misleading practices. Potential customers were told by the company's agents that their names had been specially selected and that the encyclopedia they were being offered was being given away free as part of an advertising plan in return for use of their name for advertising purposes and as a reference. The customer was only required to pay $69.50 for a loose-leaf extension service. Potential buyers were not told that both books and supplements regularly sold for $69.50.

In deciding the case, the Supreme Court noted the view of the appellate court, which had earlier dismissed the FTC's case. Writing for the appellate court, Judge Learned Hand had declared that the FTC was occupying itself with "trivial niceties" that only "divert attention from substantial evils." "We cannot take seriously the suggestion," he wrote, "that a man who is buying a set of books and a ten years' 'extension service,' will be fatuous enough to be misled by the mere statement that the first are given away, and that he is paying only for the second." The Supreme Court itself, however, looked at the matter in a different light and held for the FTC and against Standard Education.

First, it noted that the practice had successfully deceived numerous victims, apparently including teachers, doctors, and college professors. But instead of resting its decision on the claim that a reasonable person might have been deceived, it advocated a change of standard to something like the ignorant-consumer standard:

> The fact that a false statement may be obviously false to those who are trained and experienced does not change its character, nor take away its power to deceive others less experienced. There is no duty resting upon a citizen to suspect the honesty of those with whom he transacts business. Laws are made to protect the trusting as well as the suspicious. The best element of business has long since decided that honesty should govern competitive enterprises, and that the rule of *caveat emptor* should not be relied upon to reward fraud and deception.

The decision in *FTC* v. *Standard Education*, as Ivan L. Preston notes, led the FTC to apply the ignorant-man standard liberally, even in cases where there was no intent to deceive. In the 1940s the FTC challenged ads in some cases where it is hard to believe that anyone could possibly have been deceived. For example, it issued a complaint against Bristol-Myers's Ipana toothpaste on the grounds that its "smile of beauty" slogan would lead some to believe that Ipana toothpaste would straighten their teeth. Eventually, however, the FTC abandoned the ignorant-consumer standard in its extreme form and stopped trying to protect everybody from everything that might possibly deceive them. It now follows the "modified" ignorant-consumer standard and protects only those cases of foolishness that are committed by significant numbers of people.[45]

Still, deciding what is likely to be misleading to a significant number of consumers is not necessarily easy. Consider these advertising claims, which are contested by some as deceptive: that Kraft Cheez Whiz is real cheese; that Chicken McNuggets are made from "whole breasts and thighs" (when they allegedly contain processed chicken skin as well and are fried in highly saturated beef fat); that ibuprofen causes stomach irritation (as Tylenol's ads seem to imply). Was it deceptive of Diet Coke to proclaim that it was sweetened "now with NutraSweet," even though the product also contained saccharin? Under legal pressure, Diet Coke changed its ads to read "NutraSweet blend." Is that free of any misleading implications?[46]

Children

The FTC has always looked after one special group of consumers without regard to how reasonable they are: children. Still, several consumer groups think the FTC has not done enough, and they advocate even stricter controls over advertisements that reach children.

Advertising to children is big business. Children under twelve have nearly $9 billion of their own money and spend approximately $6.2 billion of it annually (up from $4.2 billion in 1984) to buy such items as snacks, candy, and toys. And this figure doesn't begin to take into account the billions of adult purchases for gifts, clothes, and groceries that are influenced by children.[47] In 1990, advance sales of ad time for children's television hit a record $450 million.[48] The text of an ad in *Broadcast* magazine, directed at potential television sponsors, underscores the lucrativeness of advertising to children:

> If you're selling, Charlie's Mom is buying. But you've got to sell Charlie first.
>
> His allowance is only 50¢ a week but his buying power is an American phenomenon. He's not only tight with his Mom, but he has a way with his Dad, his Grandma, and Aunt Harriet, too.
>
> When Charlie sees something he likes, he usually gets it.[49]

Not only are advertisers selling products to children today, but they are also trying to create customers for the future. As Jackie Pate of Delta Air Lines puts it, "By building brand loyalty in children today, they'll be the adult passengers of tomorrow." And Ann Moore, publisher of *Sports Illustrated for Kids*, says, "We believe children make brand decisions very early that will carry into their adult lives."[50]

Television and advertising play a large role in most children's lives. The person or character with the highest level of recognition among young children is not the president, not Mickey Mouse, not even Santa Claus, but—Ronald McDonald. Children, particularly young children, are naive and gullible and thus particularly vulnerable to advertisers' enticements. Consider, for example, General Foods Corporation's advertisements for its Honeycomb cereal, in which children are shown, after eating the cereal, to have enough power to lift large playhouses.[51] No adult would be misled by that ad, but children lack experience and independent, critical judgment. This provides at least a *prima facie* case for protecting them.

Advertisers, however, argue that parents still have ultimate control over what gets purchased and what doesn't. But is the strategy of selling to parents by convincing the children a fair one? The president of Kellogg Foods, William La Mothe, puts the case for the advertisers this way: "Once we start deciding which group can be advertised to and which group cannot, advertising as an efficient and economic method will be on its way to oblivion."[52]

Consumer advocate Peggy Charren of Action for Children's Television challenges that attitude. She attacks the products that are being sold to children:

> The two things sold to children most on TV are toys and food, and we've found that 98 percent of the food advertising is for products children don't have to eat, nonnutritive things. Now in fact they're designing foods that would never be on the market if it weren't for television and its ability to sell them. They actually de-

sign junk cereals like Frankenberry and Cocoa Pebbles and Cookie Crisps because they can push them to kids on television.[53]

Advertising to children obviously raises the question of children's special susceptibilities and how far we need to go to protect them from possible manipulation. It also leads to the larger question of the nature and desirability of advertising's role in today's media-dominated society, which is our next topic.

THE DEBATE OVER ADVERTISING

The controversy over advertising does not end with the issue of deceptive techniques and unfair advertising practices. Advertising provides little usable information to consumers. Advertisements almost always conceal relevant negative facts about their products, and they are frequently based on subtle appeals to psychological needs, which the products they peddle are unlikely to satisfy. These realities are the basis for some critics' wholesale repudiation of advertising on moral grounds. They also desire a less commercially polluted environment, one that does not continually reinforce materialistic values.

Consumer Needs

Some defenders of advertising take the above points in stride. They concede that images of glamour, sex, or adventure sell products, but they argue that these images are what we, the consumers, want. We don't just want blue jeans; we want romance or sophistication or status with our blue jeans. By connecting products with important emotions and feelings, advertisements can also satisfy our deeper needs and wants. As one advertising executive puts it:

> Advertising can show a consumer how a baby powder helps affirm her role as a nurturing mother—Johnson & Johnson's

"The Language of Love." Or it can show a teenager how a soft drink helps assert his or her emerging independence—Pepsi's "The Choice of a New Generation."[54]

Harvard business professor Theodore Levitt has drawn an analogy between advertising and art. Both take liberties with reality, both deal in symbolic communication, and neither is interested in literal truth or in pure functionality. Rather, both art and advertising help us repackage the otherwise crude, drab, and generally oppressive reality that surrounds us. They create "illusions, symbols, and implications that promise more." They help us modify, transform, embellish, enrich, and reconstruct the world around us. "Without distortion, embellishment, and elaboration," Levitt writes, "life would be drab, dull, anguished, and at its existential worst." Advertising helps satisfy this legitimate human need. Its handsome packages and imaginative promises produce that "elevation of the spirit" that we want and need. Embellishment and distortion are therefore among advertising's socially desirable purposes. To criticize advertising on these counts, Levitt argues, is to overlook the real needs and values of human beings.[55]

Levitt's critics contend that, even if advertising appeals to the same deep needs that art does, advertising promises satisfaction of those needs in the products it sells, and that promise is rarely kept. At the end of the day, blue jeans are still just blue jeans, and your love life will be unaffected by which soap you shower with. The imaginative, symbolic, and artistic content of advertising, which Levitt sees as answering real human needs, is viewed by critics as manipulating, distorting, and even creating those needs.

In his influential books *The Affluent Society* and *The New Industrial State*, John Kenneth Galbraith has criticized advertising on just this point. Galbraith argues that the process of production today, with its expensive marketing campaigns, subtle advertising techniques, and sophisticated sales strategies, creates the very wants it then satisfies. Producers, that is, create both the goods and the demand for those goods. If a new breakfast cereal or detergent were so much wanted, Galbraith reasons, why must so much money be spent trying to get the consumer to buy it? He thinks it is obvious that "wants can be synthesized by advertising, catalyzed by salesmanship, and shaped by" discreet manipulations.

Accordingly, Galbraith rejects the traditional economist's belief in "consumer sovereignty": the idea that consumers should and do control the market through their purchases. Rather than independent consumer demand shaping production, as classical economic theory says it does, nowadays it is the other way around. Galbraith dubs this the "dependence effect": "As a society becomes increasingly affluent, wants are increasingly created by the process by which they are satisfied."[56]

One consequence, Galbraith thinks, is that our system of production cannot be defended on the ground that it is satisfying urgent or important wants. We can't defend production as satisfying wants if the production process itself creates those wants. "In the absence of the massive and artful persuasion that accompanies the management of demand," Galbraith argues,

> increasing abundance might well have reduced the interest of people in acquiring more goods. They would not have felt the need for multiplying the artifacts — autos, appliances, detergents, cosmetics — by which they were surrounded.[57]

Another consequence is our general preoccupation with material consumption. In particular, Galbraith claims, our pursuit of private goods, continually reinforced by advertising, leads us to neglect public goods and services. We need better schools, parks, artistic and recreational facilities; safer and cleaner cities and air; more efficient, less crowded transportation systems. We are rich in the private production and use of goods, Galbraith thinks, and starved in public services. Our preoccupation with private consumption leads us to overlook opportunities for enjoyment that could be provided more efficiently by public production.

Galbraith's critics have concentrated their fire on a couple of points. First, Galbraith never shows that advertising has the power he attributes to it. Despite heavy advertising, most new products fail to win a permanent place in the hearts of consumers. Advertising campaigns like that for Listerine in the 1920s, which successfully created the problem of "halitosis" in order to sell the new idea of "mouthwash," are rare.* Although it is true that we are inundated with ads, experiments suggest we no longer care much about them. Each of us sees an average of 1,600 advertisements a day, notices around 1,200 of them, and responds favorably or unfavorably to only about 12. We also appear to pay more attention to ads for products that we already have.[58]

Second, critics have attacked Galbraith's belief that the needs supposedly created by advertisers and producers are, as a result, "false" or "artificial" needs and therefore less worthy of satisfaction. Human needs, they stress, are always socially influenced and are never static. How are we to distinguish between "genuine" and "artificial" wants, and why should the latter be thought less important? Ads might produce a want that we would not otherwise have had — say, for guaranteed overnight mail delivery — without that want being in any way objectionable.

Although conclusive evidence is unavailable, critics of advertising continue to worry about its power to influence our lives and shape our culture and civilization. Even if producers cannot create wants out of whole cloth,

---

* Since the saliva in one's mouth is completely replenished every fifteen minutes or so anyway, no mouthwash can have an effect longer than that.

many worry that advertising can manipulate our existing desires—that it can stimulate certain desires, both at the expense of other, nonconsumer-oriented desires and out of proportion to the likely satisfaction that fulfillment of those desires will bring.

Market Economics

Defenders of advertising are largely untroubled by these worries. They see advertising as an aspect of free competition in a competitive market, which ultimately works to the benefit of all. But this simple free-market defense of advertising has weaknesses. First, advertising doesn't fit too well into the economist's model of the free market. Economists can prove, if we grant them enough assumptions, that free-market buying and selling lead to optimal results.* One of these assumptions is that everyone has full and complete information, on the basis of which they then buy and sell. But if this were so, advertising would be pointless.

One might argue that advertising moves us closer to the ideal of full information, but there is good reason to doubt this. Even if we put aside the question of whether ads can create, shape, or manipulate wants, they do seem to enhance brand loyalty, which generally works to thwart price competition. A true brand-name consumer is willing to pay more for a product that is otherwise indistinguishable from its competitors. He or she buys a certain beer despite being unable to taste the difference between it and other beers.

More generally, critics of advertising stand the "invisible hand" argument on its head. The goal of advertisers is to sell you products and to make money, not to maximize your well-being. Rational demonstration of how a product will in fact enhance your

well-being is not the only way advertisers can successfully persuade you to buy their products. Indeed, it is far from the most common technique. Critics charge, accordingly, that there is no reason to think that advertising even tends to maximize the well-being of consumers.

Defenders of advertising may claim that, nonetheless, advertising is necessary for economic growth, which benefits us all. The truth of this claim, however, is open to debate. Critics maintain that advertising is a waste of resources and only serves to raise the price of advertised goods. Like Galbraith, they may also contend that advertising in general reinforces mindless consumerism. It corrupts our civilization and misdirects our society's economic effort toward private consumption and away from the public realm. The never-ending pursuit of material goods may also divert us as a society from the pursuit of a substantially shorter workday.†

Free Speech and the Media

Two final issues should be briefly noted. Defenders of advertising claim that, despite criticisms, advertising enjoys protection under the First Amendment as a form of speech. Legally this claim probably requires qualification, especially in regard to radio and television, where one must have a license to broadcast. Banning cigarette advertisements from television, for instance, did not run contrary to the Constitution. More important, even if we concede advertisers the legal right to free speech, not every exercise of that legal right is morally justifiable. If advertisements in general or of a certain type or for a certain product were shown to have undesirable social consequences, or if certain sorts of ads relied on objectionable or nonrational persuasive tech-

---

* Technically, they lead to *Pareto optimality*, which means that no one person can be made better off without making someone else worse off.

† For a development of this argument, see G. A. Cohen's "A Distinctive Contradiction of Advanced Capitalism," reprinted beginning on page 529.

niques, then there would be a strong moral argument against such advertisements regardless of their legal status.

Advertising subsidizes the media, and that is a positive but far from conclusive consideration in its favor. This is not the place to launch a discussion of the defects of American television. But the very fact that it is free results in far more consumption than would otherwise be the case and probably, as many think, far more than is good for us. Nor is the mediocrity of much American television fare accidental. The networks need large audiences. Obviously they can't run everyone's favorite type of program, because people's tastes differ, so they seek to reach a common denominator. If viewers instead of advertisers paid for each show they watched, things would be different.[59]

SUMMARY

1. The complexity of today's economy and the dependence of consumers on business increase business's responsibility for product safety.

2. The legal liability of manufacturers for injuries caused by defective products has evolved over the years. Today the courts have moved to the doctrine of strict liability, which holds the manufacturer of a product responsible for any injuries suffered as a result of defects in the product, regardless of whether the manufacturer was negligent.

3. Government agencies, like the Consumer Product Safety Commission, have broad powers to regulate product safety. Critics contend that these regulations are costly and that they prevent individuals from choosing to purchase a riskier but less expensive product. This argument touches on the controversy over legal paternalism, the doctrine that the law may justifiably be used to restrict the freedom of individuals for their own good.

4. Although there are exceptions, regulations generally help ensure that business meets its responsibilities to consumers. Businesspeople, however, tend to favor self-regulation and government deregulation.

5. To increase safety, companies need to give safety the priority necessitated by the product, abandon the misconception that accidents are solely the result of consumer misuse, monitor closely the manufacturing process, review the safety content of their advertising, provide consumers with full information about product performance, and investigate consumer complaints. Some successful companies already put a premium on safety.

6. Business also has other obligations to consumers: Product quality must live up to express and implied warranties; prices should be just, and business should refrain from manipulative pricing and the use of price fixing to avoid competition; and product labeling and packaging should provide clear, accurate, and adequate information.

7. Advertising tries to persuade people to buy products. Ambiguity, the concealment of relevant facts, exaggeration, and psychological appeals are among the morally dubious techniques that advertisers use.

8. The Federal Trade Commission protects us from blatantly deceptive advertising. But it is debatable whether the FTC should ban only advertising that is likely to deceive reasonable people or whether it should protect careless or gullible consumers as well. The FTC now seeks to prohibit advertising that misleads a significant number of consumers, regardless of whether it was reasonable for them to have been misled.

9. Advertising to children is big business, but children are particularly susceptible to the blandishments of advertising. Advertisers contend that parents still control

what gets purchased and what doesn't. But critics doubt the fairness of selling to parents by appealing to children.

10. Defenders of advertising view its imaginative, symbolic, and artistic content as answering real human needs. Critics maintain that advertising manipulates those needs or even creates artificial ones. John Kenneth Galbraith contends that today the same process that produces products also produces the demand for those products (the dependence effect). Galbraith argues, controversially, that advertising encourages a preoccupation with material goods and leads us to favor private consumption at the expense of public goods.

11. Defenders of advertising see it as a necessary and desirable aspect of competition in a free-market system, a protected form of free speech, and a useful sponsor of the media, in particular television. Critics challenge all three claims.

CASE 10.1

Aspartame: Miracle Sweetener or Dangerous Substance?

Diet Coke stands alone as the greatest overnight success in the marketplace. But when you quaff a Diet Coke on a hot summer's day, you may be doing more than quenching your thirst. You could be inviting a headache, depression, seizure, aggressive behavior, visual impairment, or menstrual disturbances. You might even be loading your tissues with a carcinogen. The reason, say most nutritionists and medical scientists, is that soft drinks like Diet Coke—and a host of other products—contain the low-calorie sweetener aspartame, which goes by the name NutraSweet.

In 1983 the Reagan administration's commissioner of the Food and Drug Administration, Dr. Arthur Hull Hayes, Jr., approved the use of aspartame in carbonated beverages. In one stroke, he seemed to end the prolonged controversy over the safety of the artificial sweetener. That controversy erupted in 1974, when the FDA first approved aspartame as a food additive.

No sooner had aspartame's manufacturer, G. D. Searle & Co., begun to celebrate the FDA's initial approval of its profits-promising sweetener than things turned sour. Largely as a result of the rancorous protests of lawyer James Turner, author of a book about food additives, the FDA suspended its approval. Armed with the results of animal experiments conducted at Washington University, Turner insisted that aspartame could damage the brain, especially in infants and children. Searle pooh-poohed the charges, citing experiments of its own that, it said, established the safety of its chemical sweetener. Unconvinced, Dr. Alexander M. Schmidt, then FDA commissioner, appointed a task force of six scientists to examine Searle's experiments.

The task force's findings did not corroborate Searle's rosy assurances of safety. In fact, it concluded that Searle had distorted the safety data to win FDA approval of aspartame. According to the task force's 1976 report, "Searle made a number of deliberate decisions which seemingly were calculated to minimize the chances of discovering toxicity and/or to allay FDA concern."[60] Schmidt not only endorsed the task force's findings but told Congress in April 1976 that he saw in Searle's experiments "a pattern of conduct which compromises the scientific integrity of the studies." He added: "At the heart of the FDA's regulatory process is the ability to rely upon the integrity of the basic safety data submitted by the sponsors of regulated products.

Our investigation clearly demonstrates that, in the G. D. Searle Co., we have no basis for such reliance now." Specifically addressing the tests of aspartame, the commissioner and other FDA officials reported such irregularities as test animals recorded as dead on one date and alive on another and autopsies on rats conducted a year after the rodents had died during a feeding experiment. Schmidt further branded Searle's animal studies as "poorly conceived, carelessly executed, or inaccurately analyzed or reported."

Understandably, Searle wasn't about to allow these broadsides to pass unanswered. In a May 1976 letter to Schmidt, the firm's executive vice president, James Buzard, asserted that the FDA task force investigators "totally failed to find fraud, totally failed to find concrete evidence of an intent to deceive or mislead the agency or any advisory committee, or a failure to make any required report."

Sticking to his opinions, Schmidt asked the Justice Department to investigate the possibility that Searle had deliberately misled the FDA. After looking into the matter, a grand jury brought no indictment against the company. Nevertheless, under FDA pressure Searle enlisted the services of Universities Associated for Research and Education in Pathology (UAREP), a private group of fifteen universities that work under contracts and grants for paying clients. UAREP was to scrutinize eight of the fifteen as yet unreviewed aspartame studies to check Searle's conclusions. Under the terms of its agreement with Searle, UAREP would submit its findings to the company before submitting them to the FDA. Searle said that procedure was necessary to ensure accuracy. But Adrian Gross, a task force member and senior FDA scientist, expressed misgivings about the arrangement to his superiors. The report that UAREP submitted, Gross argued, "may well be interpreted as nothing short of an improper whitewash."

Despite Gross's concern, the UAREP body proceeded, focusing solely on the microscopic slides produced by Searle in its animal experiments. In the end, the consortium could find nothing improper in Searle's interpretation of the slides. But James Turner complained that the review was unacceptably narrow and incomplete because it had failed to consider either the design or execution of Searle's experiments. He was assured in writing that these and other relevant matters would be taken up by a public board of inquiry.

That board, made up of three independent scientists, had plenty to do. By January 1980, when the panel convened, the FDA had amassed 140 volumes of data on aspartame. Unable to deal with the mountain of information, the board concentrated on the same studies UAREP had examined. On September 30, 1980, the panel recommended that the FDA withdraw approval of aspartame. In making its recommendation, the board said it couldn't exclude the possibility that aspartame causes cancer in rats.

It thus appeared that the FDA would keep aspartame off the market for good. But in November 1980 the country elected a new president, and within a few short months, the chemical would be sweetening a multitude of products and making millions of dollars for its manufacturer.

The day after Ronald Reagan was inaugurated president of the United States, Searle repetitioned the FDA to approve the sale of aspartame. It based its appeal on the same data it had previously submitted. Six months later, on July 24, 1981, the new FDA commissioner, Dr. Hayes, approved the sale of aspartame as a "tabletop sweetener and ingredient of dry foods."

In approving the product for sale, Hayes discounted the possible cancer connection. He cited a study done in 1981 by Ajinomoto, a Japanese chemical firm. Its study found that, while rats fed with aspartame did develop more brain tumors than untreated rats, the increase was not statistically significant. The commissioner took the results as breaking the tie between two similar experiments conducted earlier by Searle, which had produced differing results.

Some scientists immediately discredited the Ajinomoto experiments, claiming that they used a strain of rat different from the one used in earlier Searle studies. In reply, Searle insisted that all three rat studies demonstrated that aspartame was noncarcinogenic.

In 1983 Searle successfully petitioned the FDA to permit aspartame to be used in carbonated beverages. Hayes gave FDA approval on July 8, 1983. Worldwide sales of aspartame the next year were estimated at $600 million.

One month after granting Searle permission to use aspartame in soft drinks, Dr. Hayes resigned from the FDA to become dean of New York Medical College. Three months later, in November 1983, he also took a job as senior scientific consultant to Burson-Marsteller, the public relations firm that has Searle's account for aspartame.

Discussion Questions

1. Does the aspartame controversy tend to support or belie the assumption that regulatory agencies are sufficient to ensure consumer safety?

2. Do you think the evidence supports a conclusion that Searle allowed pursuit of self-interest to bias a scientifically objective assessment of the safety of aspartame?

3. Who do you think should have primary responsibility for ensuring product safety — manufacturer or government agency?

4. Does requiring a label warning consumers that a food or beverage contains carcinogenic chemicals sufficiently discharge a government agency's obligation to protect the public? Or should such products be banned? What if the product contains a substance that is only possibly carcinogenic?

5. If you were a Searle shareholder, would you think the company acted responsibly? Would you want it to have acted other than it did?

6. On safety matters, should the FDA or any regulatory agency err on the side of overprotection rather than underprotection?

7. Did Dr. Hayes act responsibly in his role as FDA commissioner?

8. Some would argue that chemical sweeteners give the weight-conscious and diabetics a needed alternative to sugar. In short, the availability of products containing saccharin or aspartame enlarges consumer freedom of choice. Thus, consumers and only consumers should decide whether they want to run the health risks associated with these chemicals. Would you agree?

CASE 10.2
FTC v. Colgate-Palmolive Company

Colgate-Palmolive Company was as proud as a new papa. The baby in this case was not the cuddly cute kind found snoozing and squalling in a maternity ward, but a shaving cream, which, Palmolive boasted, outshaved them all. Rapid Shave was its name.

To inform consumers of this blessed commercial event, Colgate enlisted the service of Ted Bates & Company, Inc., an advertising agency. Bates prepared three one-minute commercials designed to show that Rapid Shave could soften even the toughness of sandpaper. Each of the commercials contained the same "sandpaper test." "To prove Rapid Shave's super-moisturizing power," the announcer proclaimed, "we put it right from the can onto this tough, dry sandpaper. It was apply . . . soak . . . off in a stroke." The accompanying visual showed Rapid Shave being applied to what looked like sandpaper and immediately thereafter a razor shaving the substance clean. To any man who ever scraped his way awake in the morning, the ad bordered on the irresistible — well, almost.

Federal Trade Commission (FTC) officials found the commercials less than compelling. In fact, the Commission charged Colgate and Bates with false and deceptive advertising. It based the charge on evidence disclosing that sandpaper of the type depicted in the commercial could not be shaved immediately after the application of Rapid Shave. Indeed, it required about eighty minutes of soaking. What's more, the sandpaper substance of the commercials was actually a simulated prop, a plexiglass mock-up to which sand had been applied. The FTC did concede that Rapid Shave could shave sandpaper, though not in the time depicted, and that real sandpaper is not very telegenic — it photographs like plain, colored paper.

The Court of Appeals backed up the FTC's claim that it was misleading of Colgate and Bates not to inform viewers that eighty minutes were required before one could shave sandpaper with Rapid Shave. But it did not agree with the Commission that the undisclosed use of plexiglass was a second, additional misrepresentation. This aspect of the case was appealed to the Supreme Court.

The Supreme Court accepted the Commission's determination that the commercials contained three representations to the public: (1) that Rapid Shave could shave sandpaper; (2) that an experiment had been conducted which verified this claim; and (3) that TV viewers were seeing the experiment for themselves. Putting aside the question of time, the first two representations are true, but the third is false. The question, then, is: Does this constitute a "material" or significant deception?

In a 7 to 2 ruling, the majority of the Court answered yes. They decided that television commercials that depict an experiment with undisclosed simulated props are deceptive. Speaking for the Majority, Chief Justice Warren stated:

> Respondents . . . insist that the present case . . . is . . . like a case in which a celebrity or independent testing agency has in fact submitted a written verification of an experiment actually observed, but, because of the inability of the camera to transmit accurately an impression of the paper on which the testimonial is written, the seller reproduces it on another substance so that it can be seen by the viewing audience. This analogy ignored the finding of the Commission that in the present case the seller misrepresented to the public that it was being given objective proof of a product claim. In respondents' hypothetical the objective proof of the product claim that is offered, the word of the celebrity or agency that the experiment was actually conducted, does exist; while in the case before us the objective proof offered, the viewer's own perception of an actual experiment, does not exist . . .
>
> The Court of Appeals has criticized the reference in the Commission's order to "test, experiment or demonstration" as not being capable of practical interpretation. It could find no difference between the Rapid Shave commercials and a commercial which extolled the goodness of ice cream while giving viewers a picture of a scoop of mashed potatoes appearing to be ice cream. We do not understand this difficulty. In the ice cream case the mashed potato prop is not being used for traditional proof of the product claim, while the purpose of the Rapid

Shave commercial is to give the reviewer objective proof of the claims made. If in the ice cream hypothetical the focus of the commercial becomes the undisclosed potato prop and the viewer is invited, explicitly or by implication, to see for himself the truth of the claims about the ice cream's rich texture and full color, and perhaps compare it to a "rival product," then the commercial has become similar to the one now before us. Clearly, however, a commercial which depicts happy actors delightedly eating ice cream that is in fact mashed potatoes . . . is not covered by the present order.

Justice Harlan wrote the dissenting opinion in favor of Colgate and Bates:

The only question here is what techniques the advertiser may use to convey essential truth to the television viewer. If the claim is true and valid, then the technique for projecting that claim, within broad boundaries, falls purely within the advertiser's art. The warrant to the Federal Trade Commission is to police the verity of the claim itself . . .

I do not see how such a commercial can be said to be "deceptive" in any legally acceptable use of that term. The Court attempts to distinguish the case where a "celebrity" has written a testimonial endorsing some product, but the original testimonial cannot be seen over television and a copy is shown over the air by the manufacturer . . . But in both cases the viewer is told to "see for himself," in the one case that the celebrity has endorsed the product; in the other, that the product can shave sandpaper; in neither case is the viewer actually seeing the proof; and in both cases the objective proof does exist, be it in the original testimonial or the sandpaper test actually conducted by the manufacturer. In neither case, however, is there a material misrepresentation, because what the viewer sees *is* an accurate image of the objective proof . . .

It is commonly known that television presents certain distortions in transmission for which the broadcasting industry must compensate. Thus, a white towel will look a dingy gray over television, but a blue towel will look sparkling white. On the Court's analysis, an advertiser must achieve accuracy in the studio even though it results in an inaccurate image being projected on the home screen . . . Would it be proper for respondent Colgate, in advertising a laundry detergent, to "demonstrate" the effectiveness of a major competitor's detergent in washing white sheets; and then "before the viewer's eyes," to wash a white (not blue) sheet with the competitor's detergent? The studio test would accurately show the quality of the product, but the image on the screen would look as though the sheet had been washed with an ineffective detergent. All that has happened here is the converse: a demonstration has been altered in the studio to compensate for the distortions of the television medium, but in this instance in order to present an accurate picture to the television viewers.[61]

Discussion Questions

1. In what ways, if any, were television viewers misled by the Rapid Shave advertisement?

2. Do you agree with the Federal Trade Commission and with Chief Justice Warren that the Rapid Shave commercial led the public to believe that it was seeing an objective proof of Rapid Shave's claim to shave sandpaper? Do you think that viewers suffered a "material" deception by not being told about the plexiglass prop?

3. Compare the use of a sandpaper prop in this case with the examples involving a celebrity's testimonial, mashed potatoes, and white sheets. Under what circum-

stances is it permissible for television commercials to use props? Must viewers always be informed of this fact?

4. Would the hypothetical "reasonable consumer" have been deceived by this commercial? Is this the appropriate standard to use in assessing the deceptiveness of commercials? Do you think the FTC was right to have concerned itself with this case?

5. Do you think that the advertising agency, Ted Bates and Company, acted responsibly in designing this ad? Did Colgate-Palmolive behave in a morally justifiable way in agreeing to run it?

CASE 10.3

Warning: The Following Ad May Contain a Subliminal Embed

There's nothing like the smell of a new car, right? Well, now there is—a product called Velvet Touch, which is an aerosol fountain of youth for any moribund old clunker. With a blast or two of this vehicular elixir, you can instantly give an auto that smells like a stockyard a "new car scent."

Marvin Ivy, president of the National Independent Auto Dealers Association, disapproves of using such products to sell used cars. "I think you'll deceive the public," he says. "That car could have 60,000 miles on it and smell like hell."[62]

Joseph Eikenberg, owner of Aero Motors, doesn't know what hell smells like, but his nose knows the lingering fetor left in cars by dogs and smokers. And the Baltimore car dealer thinks it's okay to use the artificial odor to combat them.

Synthetic scents are by no means confined to the used-car business. Have you ever been strolling through a shopping mall and been seduced by the mouthwatering aroma of a freshly baked chocolate chip cookie? If so, the source of your temptation may not have been a cookie at all but one of the many scents made and packaged by International Flavors & Fragrances. IF&F infuses into aerosol cans the palate-pleasing scents of such foods as fresh pizza, hot apple pie, nongreasy french fries, and to be sure, the once inimitable choc-

olate chip cookie. Sniffing profits in the scents wafting from IF&F's olfactory factory, many merchants are time-releasing the odors into the walkways of shopping malls. They hope shoppers will find the aromas so tempting that they will succumb to their urge to splurge.

IF&F's success comes as no surprise to Minnesota Mining and Manufacturing (3M), which provides most of the music we hear in commercial buildings. "We have been told [by retailers] that it will increase impulse purchases," says Donald Conlin, project manager at 3M.[63] The specially arranged music is also supposed to reduce absenteeism, worker turnover, and customer complaints as well as increase sales volume and profit.

Hal C. Becker, president of Behavioral Engineering Corporation, claims that what people don't consciously hear can be as influential as what they do. He has developed a subliminal message machine being marketed as "Dr. Becker's Black Box." (It sells for $9,180 or leases for $4,800 a year.) The messages and recipients vary. A Louisiana supermarket beams to workers and shoppers the inaudible message, "I will not steal. If I steal I go to jail." The owner of the supermarket is thrilled with the results. Before buying the device, he claims, pilferage used to run about $4,500 over six months and cashier shortages about $125 a month. Now the pilferage is down to $1,300 and the shortages to less than $10. In a Buffalo, New York, real estate management concern, salespeople hear tapes saying, "I love my job" and "I am the greatest salesman." According to the company's president, revenue has risen 35 percent despite a drop in advertising.[64]

Many of Becker's customers don't want to be identified for fear that the American Civil Liberties Union (ACLU) will sue them. Apparently their fears have some merit.

"The potential for abuse is enormous," says Barbara Shack, executive director of the New York branch of the ACLU. "If it is a distortion of sound and camouflaged so the receiver isn't aware and can influence his behavior, it's tantamount to brainwashing and ought to be prohibited by legislation." Adds Jack Novik, the ACLU's national staff counsel: "We are very skeptical and suspicious of anything that imposes outside control on behavior."[65]

Some academicians consider the "black box" no more than a money machine for Becker. Professor of business Jay Russo points to the inconclusiveness of studies in subliminal suggestions. "It's an open issue," he says. "It won't die, but every time you do research it disappears like sand through your hands."[66]

Don't tell that to Wilson Key, though. He has worked in the media and advertising for thirty years. Since *Subliminal Seduction*, his first book, in 1973, Key has been the center of the controversy over alleged widespread use of subliminals in advertising. He has been both praised as a trenchant critic of the mass media and criticized as a "kook" and "paranoid" for suggesting that ads are glutted with subliminally suggestive graphics. Although invisible to anyone not looking for them, such graphics can manipulate the beholder. Key has compiled a massive collection of ads that he claims present shockingly erotic images disguised as something innocuous.

"The strange-but-true part is that messages might actually affect us under certain conditions," says professor of communications Phillip Bozek. "Research suggests that our minds can register and begin to process information we didn't clearly hear or see, and that subliminal techniques can suggest to us images or phrases which we may later think we conceived ourselves, and which we are therefore less likely to resist. A subliminal message could urge a consumer to go ahead and buy something after all, and he or she might never suspect the subtle prodding."[67] Bozek sees ample evidence of the commercial use of subliminals.

So does one California legislator, who has sponsored a bill that would require broadcasters to warn the public of subliminally embedded communications. Assemblyman Phillip Wyman's bill would not outlaw subliminal communications but would require consumer warnings when "sounds" and "visual images" are "conveyed to people" but are "not immediately and consequently perceptible" to normal seeing and hearing faculties.

Discussion Questions

1. How effective do you think subliminal communication is? What examples of subliminal communication have you encountered?

2. What moral issues are raised by the use of subliminal communication? What rights, if any, are at stake? What moral factors must be taken into account by a company considering using subliminal communication?

3. How would a utilitarian assess the use of subliminals in advertising?

4. Do you think the end or purpose for which a subliminal message is used affects its morality? For example, would there be a significant moral difference between the Surgeon General's use of subliminals on television to get people to stop smoking and cigarette manufacturers' use of them to get people to buy and smoke a particular cigarette?

5. Professor Bozek, for one, draws a distinction between electronic and printed subliminals. You need special equipment to pick out electronic subliminals, but you can see printed subliminals unassisted if you know how to look for them. This distinction leads Bozek to conclude that government should regulate electronically transmitted subliminals, whereas education should inform us about print subliminals. Do you agree? Or do you think both should be regulated? Or neither?

CASE 10.4
Closing the Deal

Now that she had to, Jean McGuire wasn't sure she could. Not that she didn't understand what to do. Wright Boazman, sales director for Sunrise Land Developers, had made the step clear enough when he described a variety of effective "deal-closing techniques."

As Wright explained it, very often people actually want to buy a lot but suffer at the last minute from self-doubt and uncertainty. The inexperienced salesperson can misinterpret this hesitation as a lack of interest in a property. "But," as Wright pointed out, "in most cases it's just an expression of the normal reservations everyone shows when the time comes to sign our names on the dotted line."

In Wright's view, the job of a land salesperson was "to help the prospect make the decision to buy." He didn't mean to suggest that salespeople should misrepresent a piece of property or in any way mislead people about what they were purchasing. "Law prohibits this," he pointed out, "and personally I find such behavior repugnant. What I'm talking about is helping them buy a lot that they genuinely want and that you're convinced will be compatible with their needs and interests." For Wright Boazman, salespeople should serve as motivators, people who could provide whatever impulse was needed for prospects to close the deal.

In Wright's experience, one of the most effective closing techniques was what he termed "the other party." It went something like this.

Suppose someone like Jean McGuire had a "hot" prospect, someone who was exhibiting real interest in a lot but who was having trouble deciding. To motivate the prospect into buying, Jean ought to tell the person that she wasn't even sure the lot was still available, since there were a number of other salespeople showing the same lot, and they could already have closed a deal on it. As Wright put it, "This first ploy generally has the effect of increasing the prospect's interest in the property, and more important to us, in closing the deal pronto."

Next Jean should say something like, "Why don't we go back to the office, and I'll call headquarters to find out the status of the lot?" Wright indicated that such a suggestion ordinarily "whets their appetite" even more. In addition, it turns prospects away from wondering whether they should purchase the land and toward hoping that it's still available.

When they return to the office, Jean should make a call in the presence of the prospect. The call, of course, would not be to "headquarters" but to a private office only yards from where she and the prospect sit. Wright or someone else would receive the call, and Jean should fake a conversation about the property's availability, punctuating her comments with contagious excitement about its desirability. When she hangs up, she should breathe a sigh of relief that the lot's still available—but barely. At any minute, Jean should explain anxiously, the lot could be "green-tagged," meaning that headquarters is expecting a call from another salesperson who's about to close a deal and will remove the lot from open stock. (An effective variation of this, Wright pointed out, would have Jean abruptly excuse herself on hanging up and dart over to another sales representative with whom she'd engage in a heated, although staged, debate about the availability of the property—loud enough, of course, for the prospect to hear. The intended effect, according to Wright, would place the prospect in the "now or never" frame of mind.)

When Jean first heard about this and other closing techniques, she felt uneasy. Even though the property was everything it was represented to be and the law allowed purchasers ten days to change their minds after closing a deal, she instinctively objected to the use of psychological manipulation. Nevertheless, Jean never expressed her reservations to anyone, primarily because she didn't want to endanger her job. She desperately needed it owing to the recent and unexpected death of her husband, which left her as the sole support of herself and three young children. Besides, Jean had convinced herself that she could deal with closures more respectably than Wright and other salespeople might. But the truth was that, after six months of selling land for Sunrise, Jean's sales lagged far behind those of the other sales representatives. Whether she liked it or not, Jean had to admit she was losing a considerable number of sales because she couldn't close. And she couldn't close because, in Wright Boazman's words, she lacked technique. She wasn't employing the psychological closing devices that he and others had found so successful.

Now as she drove back to the office with two "hot prospects" in hand, she wondered what to do.

Discussion Questions

1. Do you disapprove of this sales tactic, or is it a legitimate business technique? How might it be morally defended?

2. Suppose you knew either that the person would eventually decide to buy the property anyway or that it would genuinely be in the person's interest to buy it. Would that affect your moral assessment of this closing technique? Do customers have any grounds for complaining about this closing technique if the law allows them ten days to change their minds?

3. What ideals, obligations, and effects must Jean consider? What interests and rights of the customer are at stake?

4. What weight should Jean give to self-interest in her deliberations? What do you think she should do? What would you do?

5. What rule, if any, would a rule utilitarian encourage realtors in this situation to follow? What should the realtors' professional code of ethics say about closing techniques?

CASE 10.5

The Ad Too Hot to Touch

Jack Saroyan, vice president in charge of advertising for *American Companion*, a family magazine with a multimillion circulation, had heard of Car/Puter, but he never imagined that it would pitch him into a dilemma that could cost him his job.

Saroyan knew that Car/Puter International Corporation was a firm based in Brooklyn, New York, that for twenty dollars would provide any person interested in buying a specific car with a computer printout of the list prices and the dealer's cost for the car and any accessories or options available. For another twenty dollars it would order the car from one of 900 participating dealers at $160 above the dealer's cost, far below the usual markup.

Although Saroyan realized that many people had learned of this unique service through news articles, he also knew that rarely had Car/Puter ads appeared in the print media. Not that Car/Puter hadn't tried to place ads, but dozens of newspapers and periodicals had refused to run them.

To Saroyan's knowledge, no periodical had ever said why it wouldn't sell Car/Puter some advertising space, but he could figure out the reason. Car/Puter's services directly competed with automotive dealers. If a newspaper or magazine were to advertise a service that car dealers disapproved of, automobile manufacturers would be highly reluctant to continue advertising in it. The result would be a tremendous loss of advertising revenue.

Most magazines simply couldn't risk losing such a considerable source of profit. For example, Saroyan's *American Companion* attributed more than half its annual advertising revenue to ads placed by Ford, General Motors, Chrysler, and American Motors. Saroyan was no fool. To jeopardize this income by running ads for Car/Puter struck him as the height of economic folly. What's more, if he lost even a fraction of these revenues by approving Car/Puter ads, Saroyan would be held personally accountable. He didn't wish to dwell on the career implications of that.

Unfortunately, Jack Saroyan had never been one to see things entirely in economic or self-interested terms. In this instance, for example, he felt sensitive to the significant social service he would perform by running Car/Puter ads. The ads would help consumers avail themselves of information they needed to make wise and prudent decisions about a car purchase. It also offered a service calculated to help them save hundreds of millions of dollars annually. Besides, Saroyan was keenly aware of the economic disadvantage that Car/Puter suffered by being denied advertising space in the print media, by being denied its general right to make its service known to the public through advertising.

Saroyan viewed his decision as a choice between rendering the public at large and Car/Puter in particular a service or doing what he thought to be in the best interests of *American Companion*. As hard as he tried, he didn't see these values as compatible.

Discussion Questions

1. What should Saroyan do? Explain by appeal to ethical principles.

2. What conflicting values and ideals are at stake for a magazine like *American Companion*?

3. Do you think the media ought to grant advertising space to all who desire it and can pay for it? If not, what limitations would you impose, and why?

4. Does it violate some right of a company like Car/Puter for a magazine to refuse to accept its advertisements?

CASE 10.6
The Skateboard Scare

Colin Brewster, owner of Brewster's Bicycle Shop, had to admit that skateboard sales had salvaged his business now that interest in the bicycle seemed to have peaked. In fact, skateboard business was so brisk that Brewster could hardly keep them in stock. But the picture was far from rosy.

Just last week a concerned consumer group visited his shop. They informed Brewster that they had ample evidence to prove that skateboards present a real and immediate hazard to consumer safety. Brewster conceded that the group surely provided enough statistical support; the number of broken bones and concussions that had resulted directly and indirectly from accidents involving skateboards was shocking. But he thought the group's position was fundamentally unsound because, as he told them, "It's not the skateboards that are unsafe but how people use them."

Committee members weren't impressed with Brewster's distinction. They likened it to saying automobile manufacturers shouldn't be conscious of consumer safety because it's not the automobiles that are unsafe but how we drive them. Brewster objected that automobiles present an entirely different problem, because a number of things could be done to ensure their safe use. "But what can you do about a skateboard?" he asked them. "Besides, I don't manufacture them, I just sell them."

The committee pointed out that other groups were attacking the problem on the manufacturing level. What they expected of Brewster was some responsible management of the problem at the local retail level. They pointed out that recently Brewster had run a series of local television ads portraying young but accomplished skateboarders performing fancy flips and turns. The ad implied that anyone could easily accomplish such feats. Only yesterday one parent had told the committee of her child's breaking an arm attempting such gymnastics after having purchased a Brewster skateboard. "Obviously," Brewster countered, "the woman has an irresponsible kid whose activities she should monitor, not me." He pointed out that his ad was not intended to imply anyone could or should do those tricks, no more than an ad showing a car traveling at high speeds while doing stunt tricks implies that you should drive that way.

The committee disagreed. They said Brewster not only should discontinue such misleading advertising but also should actively publicize the potential dangers of skateboarding. Specifically, the committee wanted him to display prominently beside his skateboard stock the statistical data testifying to its hazards. Furthermore, he should make sure anyone buying a skateboard reads this material before purchase.

Brewster argued that the committee's demands were unreasonable. "Do you have any idea what effect that would have on sales?" he asked them.

Committee members readily admitted that they were less interested in his sales than in their children's safety. Brewster told them that in this matter their children's safety was their responsibility, not his. But the committee was adamant. Members told Brewster that they'd be back in a week to find out what positive steps, if any, he'd taken to correct the problem. In the event he'd done nothing, they indicated they were prepared to picket his shop.

Discussion Questions

1. With whom do you agree—Brewster or the committee? Why?

2. Would you criticize Brewster's advertisements? Do you think the demand that he publicize the dangers of skateboarding is reasonable?

3. What responsibilities, if any, do retailers have to ensure consumer safety? Compare the responsibilities of manufacturers, skateboarders, and parents.

4. What steps could Brewster take to promote skateboard safety?

5. Identify the ideals, obligations, and effects that Brewster should consider in reaching his decision. Which of the considerations do you think is most important?

NOTES

1. *Business and Society Review* 69 (Spring 1989): 67; "Tobacco's Toll," *Newsweek* (international edition), November 9, 1979; and James Shriver, "Sharp Drop in Cigaret Smokers," *San Francisco Chronicle*, May 31, 1989, A4.

2. Lawrence H. Tribe, "Federalism with Smoke and Mirrors," *The Nation*, June 7, 1986; "Taking on Big Tobacco in Dixie," *U.S. News and World Report*, February 8, 1988; and "Of Mice and Men," *The Economist*, April 16, 1988. On recent legal developments, see John Crudele, "Profit and Loss," *San Francisco Examiner*, November 6, 1988, D2.

3. Fred Luthans and Richard M. Hodgetts, *Social Issues in Business* (New York: Macmillan, 1976), 362.

4. Manuel G. Velasquez, *Business Ethics* (Englewood Cliffs, N.J.: Prentice-Hall, 1982), 235.

5. George G. Brenkert, "Strict Products Liability and Compensatory Justice," in W. Michael Hoffman and Jennifer Mills Moore, eds., *Business Ethics: Readings and Cases in Corporate Morality* (New York: McGraw-Hill, 1984).

6. Joseph R. DesJardins and John J. McCall, eds., *Contemporary Issues in Business Ethics* (Belmont, Calif.: Wadsworth, 1985), 51.

7. Murray Weidenbaum, "Consumer Product Regulation," in DesJardins and McCall, *Contemporary Issues in Business Ethics*, 79.

8. Ibid., 79–80.

9. Ibid., 83.

10. Richard T. De George, "Ethical Responsibilities of Engineers in Large Organizations," *Business and Professional Ethics Journal* 1 (Fall 1981).

11. Dean Rothbart and John A. Prestbo, "Taking Rely Off Market Cost Procter & Gamble a Week of Agonizing," *Wall Street Journal*, November 3, 1980, 1.

12. See Allan Parachini, "Pediatricians Raise Issue in Auto Safety Debate," *Los Angeles Times*, April 3, 1981.

13. Dan Oldenburg, "Chrysler's Reversal in Airbag Debate," *San Francisco Chronicle* ("Business Briefing"), August 23, 1989, 9.

14. Milo Geyelin, "Gun Dealer Is Held Liable in Accident for Not Teaching Customer Safe Use," *Wall Street Journal*, June 6, 1989, B10.

15. Marisa Manley, "Products Liability: You're More Exposed Than You Think," *Harvard Business Review* 65 (September–October 1987): 28–29.

16. Myron Levin, "Fighting Fire with P.R.," *The Nation*, July 10, 1989.

17. These are taken from Tad Tuleja, *Beyond the Bottom Line* (New York: Penguin, 1987), 77–78.

18. David L. Rados, "Product Liability: Tougher Ground Rules," *Harvard Business Review* 47 (July–August 1969): 148.

19. Jeffrey H. Birnbaum, "Pricing of Product Is Still an Art, Often Having Little Link to Costs," *Wall Street Journal*, November 25, 1981, 2–29.

20. Ibid.

21. Ibid.

22. See William J. Kehoe, "Ethics, Price Fixing, and the Management of Price Strategy," in Gene R. Laczniak and Patrick E. Murphy, eds., *Marketing Ethics* (Lexington, Mass.: Lexington Books, 1985) for a discussion of ethical issues in pricing.

23. Constance L. Hays, "Panasonic to Return $16 Million to Consumers," *New York Times*, January 19, 1989, A1.

24. For a thorough look at this case, see M. David Ermann and Richard J. Lundman, *Corporate Deviance* (New York: Holt, Rinehart & Winston, 1982), Chapter 5.

25. Burton Leiser, "Deceptive Practices in Advertising," in Tom L. Beauchamp and Norman E. Bowie, eds., *Ethical Theory and Business*, 2nd ed. (Englewood Cliffs, N.J.: Prentice-Hall, 1983), 337.

26. E. B. Weiss, "Marketers Fiddle While Consumers Burn," *Harvard Business Review* 46 (July–August 1968): 48.

27. *Business and Society Review* 69 (Spring 1989): 50.

28. Paul Farhi, "Madison Avenue Adrift in Advertising Doldrums," *San Francisco Chronicle*, May 9, 1989, C5.

29. Roger Draper, "The Faithless Shepherd," *New York Review of Books*, June 26, 1986, 17.

30. See "Mea Culpa, Sort Of," *Newsweek*, September 27, 1971, 98.

31. *Business and Society Review* 67 (Fall 1988): 27.

32. Paul Stevens, "Weasel Words: God's Little Helpers," in Paul A. Eschhol, Alfred A. Rosa, and Virginia P. Clark, eds., *Language Awareness* (New York: St. Martin's Press, 1974), 156.

33. Samm Sinclair Baker, *The Permissible Lie* (New York: World Publishing, 1968), 16.

34. *Consumer Reports: The Medicine Show* (Mt. Vernon, N.Y.: Consumers Union, 1972), 14.

35. *Business and Society Review* 67 (Fall 1988): 27.

36. J. L. English, "Those Devious TV Ads," *The Sun* (Santa Cruz, Calif.), August 11, 1988, 16.

37. Ann Hagedorn, "FDA Cracks Down on Cosmetic Firms' Age-Treatment Drugs," *Wall Street Journal*, April 27, 1987.

38. Gail Bronson, "Sexual Pitches in Ads Become More Explicit and Pervasive," *Wall Street Journal*, November 18, 1980, 1.

39. Wilson Bryan Key, *Subliminal Seduction* (New York: New American Library, 1973), 11.

40. "Deceptive Ads: The FTC's Laissez-Faire Approach Is Backfiring," *Business Week*, December 2, 1985.

41. See Ivan L. Preston, "Reasonable Consumer or Ignorant Consumer? How the FTC Decides," in Tom L. Beauchamp and Norman E. Bowie, eds., *Ethical Theory and Business*, 2nd ed. (Englewood Cliffs, N.J.: Prentice-Hall, 1983).

42. Ibid., 348.

43. Ibid.

44. 302 U.S. 112.

45. Preston, "Reasonable Consumer," 352–355.

46. "Deceptive Ads," *Business Week*.

47. Patricia Sellers, "The ABC's of Marketing to Kids," *Fortune*, May 8, 1989, 115; Lisa J. Moore, "The Littlest Consumers," *San Francisco Chronicle*, January 13, 1991, "This World," 8.

48. Moore, "Littlest Consumers," 8.

49. Quoted in John Culkin, "Selling to Children: Fair Play in TV Commercials," in DesJardins and McCall, 193.

50. Moore, "Littlest Consumers."

51. "Deceptive Ads," *Business Week*.

52. Culkin, 194.

53. Ibid.

54. Randall Rothenberg, "Executives Defending Their Craft," *New York Times*, May 22, 1989, C7.

55. Theodore Levitt, "The Morality (?) of Advertising," *Harvard Business Review* 48 (July–August 1970): 84–92.

56. John Kenneth Galbraith, *The Affluent Society*, 3rd ed. (New York: Houghton Mifflin, 1976), 131.

57. John Kenneth Galbraith, *The New Industrial State* (New York: Signet, 1967), 219.

58. Draper, "The Faithless Shepherd," 16.

59. For a discussion of this, see "All by the Numbers," *The Economist*, December 20, 1986.

60. Judith Randal, "Is Aspartame Really Safe? The Fight over the Miracle Sweetener Hasn't Ended Yet," *Washington Post National Weekly Edition*, May 28, 1984, 7–8. This article is the source of the case presented and of all the quotations that appear in the remainder of the case.

61. *Federal Trade Commission v. Colgate-Palmolive Co. et al.*, 380 U.S. 374, 85 S. Ct. 1035, 13 L. Ed. 2d 904 (1965).

62. Bernard Wysocki, Jr., "Sight, Smell, Sound: They're All Arms in Retailers' Arsenal," *Wall Street Journal*, April 17, 1979, 27.

63. Neil Maxwell, "Words Whispered to Subconscious Supposedly Deter Theft, Fainting," *Wall Street Journal*, November 25, 1980, 26.

64. Ibid.

65. Wysocki, "Retailers' Arsenal," 1.

66. Ibid., 1, 27.

67. "Letters to Editor," *Bakersfield Californian*, June 3, 1983, 5.

A Moral Evaluation of Sales Practices

David M. Holley

How can we determine when a sales practice is morally acceptable and when it is not? Anchoring his analysis in the context of the market system, David Holley argues that sales personnel have a moral obligation to respect the three conditions that are necessary for an exchange to be voluntary and mutually beneficial: knowledge, noncompulsion, and rationality. He then uses these three conditions to provide a framework for evaluating a number of different types of sales practices, including deception, witholding information, restricting customers' choices, and making emotional appeals.

In this paper I will attempt to develop a framework for evaluating the morality of various sales practices. Although I recognize that much of the salesforce in companies is occupied exclusively or primarily with sales to other businesses, my discussion will focus on sales to the individual consumer. Most of what I say should apply to any type of sales activity, but the moral issues arise most clearly in cases in which a consumer may or may not be very sophisticated in evaluating and responding to a sales presentation.

My approach will be to consider first the context of sales activities, a market system of production and distribution. Since such a system is generally justified on teleological grounds, I describe several conditions for its successful achievement of key goals. Immoral sales practices are analyzed as attempts to undermine these conditions.

I

The primary justification for a market system is that it provides an efficient procedure for meeting people's needs and desires for goods and services.[1] This appeal to economic benefits can be elaborated in great detail, but at root it involves the claim that people will efficiently serve each other's needs if they are allowed to engage in voluntary exchanges.

A crucial feature of this argument is the condition that the exchange be voluntary. Assuming that individuals know best how to benefit themselves and that they will act to achieve such benefits, voluntary exchange can be expected to serve both parties. On the other hand, if the exchanges are not made voluntarily, we have no basis for expecting mutually beneficial results. To the extent that mutual benefit does not occur, the system will lack efficiency as a means for the satisfaction of needs and desires. Hence, this justification presupposes that conditions necessary for the occurrence of voluntary exchange are ordinarily met.

What are these conditions? For simplicity's sake, let us deal only with the kind of exchange involving a payment of money for some product or service. We can call the person providing the product the *seller* and the person making the monetary payment the *buyer*. I suggest that voluntary exchange occurs only if the following conditions are met:

1. Both buyer and seller understand what they are giving up and what they are receiving in return.

2. Neither buyer nor seller is compelled to enter into the exchange as a result of coercion, severely restricted alternatives, or other constraints on the ability to choose.

3. Both buyer and seller are able at the time of the exchange to make rational judgments about its cost and benefits.

I will refer to these three conditions as the knowledge, noncompulsion, and rationality conditions, respectively.[2] If the parties are uninformed, it is possible that an exchange might accidentally turn out to benefit them. But given the lack of information, they would not be in a position to make a rational judgment about their benefit, and we cannot reasonably expect beneficial results as a matter

of course in such circumstances. Similarly, if the exchange is made under compulsion, then the judgment of personal benefit is not the basis of the exchange. It is possible for someone to be forced or manipulated into an arrangement that is in fact beneficial. But there is little reason to think that typical or likely.[3]

It should be clear that all three conditions are subject to degrees of fulfillment. For example, the parties may understand certain things about the exchange but not others. Let us posit a theoretical situation in which both parties are fully informed, fully rational, and enter into the exchange entirely of their own volition. I will call this an *ideal exchange*. In actual practice there is virtually always some divergence from the ideal. Knowledge can be more or less adequate. Individuals can be subject to various irrational influences. There can be borderline cases of external constraints. Nevertheless, we can often judge when a particular exchange was adequately informed, rational, and free from compulsion. Even when conditions are not ideal, we may still have an *acceptable exchange*.

With these concepts in mind, let us consider the obligations of sales personnel. I suggest that the primary duty of salespeople to customers is to avoid undermining the conditions of acceptable exchange. It is possible by act or omission to create a situation in which the customer is not sufficiently knowledgeable about what the exchange involves. It is also possible to influence the customer in ways that short-circuit the rational decision-making process. To behave in such ways is to undermine the conditions that are presupposed in teleological justifications of the market system. Of course, an isolated act is not sufficient to destroy the benefits of the system. But the moral acceptability of the system may become questionable if the conditions of acceptable exchange are widely abused. The individual who attempts to gain personally by undermining these conditions does that which, if commonly practiced, would produce a very different system from the one that supposedly provides moral legitimacy to that individual's activities.

II

If a mutually beneficial exchange is to be expected, the parties involved must be adequately informed about what they are giving up and what they are receiving. In most cases this should create no great problem for the seller,[4] but what about the buyer? How is she to obtain the information needed? One answer is that the buyer is responsible for doing whatever investigation is necessary to acquire the information. The medieval principle of *caveat emptor* encouraged buyers to take responsibility for examining a purchase thoroughly to determine whether it had any hidden flaws. If the buyer failed to find defects, that meant that due caution had not been exercised.

If it were always relatively easy to discover defects by examination, then this principle might be an efficient method of guaranteeing mutual satisfaction. Sometimes, however, even lengthy investigation would not disclose what the buyer wants to know. With products of great complexity, the expertise needed for an adequate examination may be beyond what could reasonably be expected of most consumers. Even relatively simple products can have hidden flaws that most people would not discover until after the purchase, and to have the responsibility for closely examining every purchase would involve a considerable amount of a highly treasured modern commodity, the buyer's time. Furthermore, many exchange situations in our context involve products that cannot be examined in this way — goods that will be delivered at a later time or sent through the mail, for example. Finally, even if we assume that most buyers, by exercising enough caution, can protect their interests, the system of *caveat emptor* would take advantage of those least able to watch out for themselves. It would in effect justify mistreatment of a few for a rather questionable benefit.

In practice the buyer almost always relies on the seller for some information, and if mutually beneficial exchanges are to be expected, the information needs to meet certain standards of both quality and quantity. With regard to quality, the information provided should not be deceptive. This would include not only direct lies but also truths that are intended to mislead the buyer. Consider the following examples:

1. An aluminum siding salesperson tells customers that they will receive "bargain factory prices" for letting their homes be used as models in a new advertising campaign. Prospective customers will be brought to view the houses, and a commission of $100 will be paid for each sale that results. In fact, the price paid is well above market rates, the workmanship and materials are substandard, and no one is ever brought by to see the houses.[5]

2. A used car salesperson turns back the odometer reading on automobiles by an average of 25,000 to 30,000 miles per car. If customers ask whether the reading is correct, the salesperson replies that it is illegal to alter odometer readings.

3. A salesperson at a piano store tells an interested customer that the "special sale" will be good only through that evening. She neglects to mention that another "special sale" will begin the next day.

4. A telephone salesperson tells people who answer the phone that they have been selected to receive a free gift, a brand new freezer. All they have to do is buy a year's subscription to a food plan.

5. A salesperson for a diet system proclaims that under this revolutionary new plan the pounds will melt right off. The system is described as a scientific advance that makes dieting easy. In fact, the system is a low-calorie diet composed of foods and liquids that are packaged under the company name but are no different from standard grocery store items.

The possibilities are endless, and whether or not a lie is involved, each case illustrates a salesperson's attempt to get a customer to believe something that is false in order to make the sale. It might be pointed out that these kinds of practices would not deceive a sophisticated consumer. Perhaps so, but whether they are always successful deceptions is not the issue. They are attempts to mislead the customer, and given that the consumer must often rely on information furnished by the salesperson, they are attempts to subvert the conditions under which mutually beneficial exchange can be expected. The salesperson attempts to use misinformation as a basis for customer judgment rather than allowing that judgment to be based on accurate beliefs. Furthermore, if these kinds of practices were not successful fairly often, they would probably not be used. . . .

Only a few people would defend the moral justifiability of deceptive sales practices. However, there may be room for much more disagreement with regard to how much information a salesperson is obligated to provide. In rejecting the principle of *caveat emptor*, I have suggested that there are pragmatic reasons for expecting the seller to communicate some information about the product. But how much? When is it morally culpable to withhold information? Consider the following cases:

1. An automobile dealer has bought a number of cars from another state. Although they appear to be new or slightly used, these cars have been involved in a major flood and were sold by the previous dealer at a discount rate. The salesperson knows the history of the cars and does not mention it to customers.

2. A salesperson for an encyclopedia company never mentions the total price of a set unless he has to. Instead he emphasizes the low monthly payment involved.

3. A real estate agent knows that one reason the couple selling a house with her company want to move is that the neighbors often have loud parties and neighborhood children have committed minor acts of vandalism. The agent makes no mention of this to prospective customers.

4. An admissions officer for a private college speaks enthusiastically about the advantages of the school. He does not mention the fact that the school is not accredited.

5. A prospective retirement home resident is under the impression that a particular retirement home is affiliated with a certain church. He makes it known that this is one of the features he finds attractive about the home. Though the belief is false, the recruiters for the home make no attempt to correct the misunderstanding.

In all these cases the prospective buyer lacks some piece of knowledge that might be relevant to the decision to buy. The conditions for ideal exchange are not met. Perhaps, however, there can be an acceptable exchange. Whether or not this is the case depends on whether the buyer has adequate information to decide if the purchase would be beneficial. In the case of the flood-damaged autos, there is information relevant to evaluating the worth of the car that the customer could not be expected to know unless informed by the seller. If this

information is not revealed, the buyer will not have adequate knowledge to make a reasonable judgment. Determining exactly how much information needs to be provided is not always clear-cut. We must in general rely on our assessments of what a reasonable person would want to know. As a practical guide, a salesperson might consider, "What would I want to know if I were considering buying this product?"

Surely a reasonable person would want to know the total price of a product. Hence the encyclopedia salesperson who omits this total is not providing adequate information. The salesperson may object that this information could be inferred from other information about the monthly payment, length of term, and interest rate. But if the intention is not to have the customer act without knowing the full price, then why shouldn't it be provided directly? The admissions officer's failure to mention that the school is unaccredited also seems unacceptable when we consider what a reasonable person would want to know. There are some people who would consider this a plus, since they are suspicious about accrediting agencies imposing some alien standards (e.g., standards that conflict with religious views). But regardless of how one evaluates the fact, most people would judge it to be important for making a decision.

The real estate case is more puzzling. Most real estate agents would not reveal the kind of information described, and would not feel they had violated any moral duties in failing to do so. Clearly, many prospective customers would want to be informed about such problems. However, in most cases failing to know these facts would not be of crucial importance. We have a case of borderline information. It would be known by all parties to an ideal exchange, but we can have an acceptable exchange even if the buyer is unaware of it. Failure to inform the customer of these facts is not like failing to inform the customer that the house is on the sight of a hazardous waste dump or that a major freeway will soon be adjacent to the property.

It is possible to alter the case in such a way that the information should be revealed or at least the buyer should be directed another way. Suppose the buyer makes it clear that his primary goal is to live in a quiet neighborhood where he will be undisturbed. The "borderline" information now becomes more central to the customer's decision. Notice that thinking in these terms moves us away from the general standard of what a reasonable person would want to know to the more specific standard of what is relevant given the criteria of this individual. In most cases, however, I think that a salesperson would be justified in operating under general "reasonable person" standards until particular deviations become apparent.[6]

The case of the prospective retirement home resident is a good example of how the particular criteria of the customer might assume great importance. If the recruiters, knowing what they know about this man's religious preferences, allow him to make his decision on the basis of a false assumption, they will have failed to support the conditions of acceptable exchange. It doesn't really matter that the misunderstanding was not caused by the salespeople. Their allowing it to be part of the basis for a decision borders on deception. If the misunderstanding was not on a matter of central importance to the individual's evaluation, they might have had no obligation to correct it. But the case described is not of that sort.

Besides providing nondeceptive and relatively complete information, salespeople may be obligated to make sure that their communications are understandable. Sales presentations containing technical information that is likely to be misunderstood are morally questionable. However, it would be unrealistic to expect all presentations to be immune to misunderstanding. The salesperson is probably justified in developing presentations that would be intelligible to the average consumer of the product he or she is selling and making adjustments in cases where it is clear that misunderstanding has occurred.

III

The condition of uncompelled exchange distinguishes business dealings from other kinds of exchanges. In the standard business arrangement, neither party is forced to enter the negotiations. A threat of harm would transform the situation to something other than a purely business arrangement. Coercion is not the only kind of compulsion, however. Suppose I have access to only one producer of food. I arrange to buy food from this producer, but given my great need for food and the absence of alternatives, the seller is able to dictate the terms. In one sense I choose to make the deal,

but the voluntariness of my choice is limited by the absence of alternatives.

Ordinarily, the individual salesperson will not have the power to take away the buyer's alternatives. However, a clever salesperson can sometimes make it seem as if options are very limited and can use the customer's ignorance to produce the same effect. For example, imagine an individual who begins to look for a particular item at a local store. The salesperson extols the line carried by his store, warns of the deficiencies of alternative brands, and warns about the dishonesty of competitors, in contrast to his store's reliability. With a convincing presentation, a customer might easily perceive the options to be very limited. Whether or not the technique is questionable may depend on the accuracy of the perception. If the salesperson is attempting to take away a legitimate alternative, that is an attempt to undermine the customer's voluntary choice.

Another way the condition of uncompelled choice might be subverted is by involving a customer in a purchase without allowing her to notice what is happening. This would include opening techniques that disguise the purpose of the encounter so there can be no immediate refusal. The customer is led to believe that the interview is about a contest or a survey or an opportunity to make money. Not until the end does it become apparent that this is an attempt to sell something, and occasionally if the presentation is smooth enough, some buyers can be virtually unaware that they have bought anything. Obviously, there can be degrees of revelation, and not every approach that involves initial disguise of certain elements that might provoke an immediate rejection is morally questionable. But there are enough clear cases in which the intention is to get around, as much as possible, the voluntary choice of the customer. Consider the following examples:

1. A seller of children's books gains entrance to houses by claiming to be conducting an educational survey. He does indeed ask several "survey" questions, but he uses these to qualify potential customers for his product.

2. A salesperson alludes to recent accidents involving explosions of furnaces and, leaving the impression of having some official government status, offers to do a free safety inspection. She almost always discovers a "major

problem'' and offers to sell a replacement furnace.

3. A man receives a number of unsolicited books and magazines through the mail. Then he is sent a bill and later letters warning of damage to his credit rating if he does not pay.

These are examples of the many variations on attempts to involve customers in exchanges without letting them know what is happening. The first two cases involve deceptions about the purpose of the encounter. Though they resemble cases discussed earlier that involved deception about the nature or price of a product, here the salesperson uses misinformation as a means of limiting the customer's range of choice. The customer does not consciously choose to listen to a sales presentation but finds that this is what is happening. Some psychological research suggests that when people do something that appears to commit them to a course of action, even without consciously choosing to do so, they will tend to act as if such a choice has been made in order to minimize cognitive dissonance. Hence, if a salesperson successfully involves the customer in considering a purchase, the customer may feel committed to give serious thought to the matter. The third case is an attempt to get the customer to believe that an obligation has been incurred. In variations on this technique, merchandise is mailed to a deceased person to make relatives believe that some payment is owed. In each case, an effort is made to force the consumer to choose from an excessively limited range of options.

IV

How can a salesperson subvert the rationality condition? Perhaps the most common way is to appeal to emotional reactions that cloud an individual's perception of relevant considerations. Consider the following cases:

1. A man's wife has recently died in a tragic accident. The funeral director plays upon the husband's love for his wife and to some extent his guilt about her death to get him to purchase a very expensive funeral.

2. A socially insecure young woman has bought a series of dance lessons from a local studio. During the lessons, an attractive male instructor constantly compliments her on her poise and natural ability and tries to persuade her to sign up for more lessons.[7]

3. A life insurance salesperson emphasizes to a prospect the importance of providing for his family in the event of his death. The salesperson tells several stories about people who put off this kind of preparation.

4. A dress salesperson typically tells customers how fashionable they look in a certain dress. Her stock comments also include pointing out that a dress is slimming or sexy or "looks great on you."

5. A furniture salesperson regularly tells customers that a piece of furniture is the last one in stock and that another customer recently showed great interest in it. He sometimes adds that it may not be possible to get any more like it from the factory.

These cases remind us that emotions can be important motivators. It is not surprising that salespeople appeal to them in attempting to get the customer to make a purchase. In certain cases the appeal seems perfectly legitimate. When the life insurance salesperson tries to arouse the customer's fear and urges preparation, it may be a legitimate way to get the customer to consider something that is worth considering. Of course, the fact that the fear is aroused by one who sells life insurance may obscure to the customer the range of alternative possibilities in preparing financially for the future. But the fact that an emotion is aroused need not make the appeal morally objectionable.

If the appeal of the dress salesperson seems more questionable, this is probably because we are not as convinced of the objective importance of appearing fashionable, or perhaps because repeated observations of this kind are often insincere. But if we assume that the salesperson is giving an honest opinion about how the dress looks on a customer, it may provide some input for the individual who has a desire to achieve a particular effect. The fact that such remarks appeal to one's vanity or ambition does not in itself make the appeal unacceptable.

The furniture salesperson's warnings are clearly calculated to create some anxiety about the prospect of losing the chance to buy a particular item unless immediate action is taken. If the warnings are factually based, they would not be irrelevant to the decision to buy. Clearly, one might act impulsively or hastily when under the spell of such thoughts, but the salesperson cannot be faulted for pointing out relevant considerations.

The case of the funeral director is somewhat different. Here there is a real question of what benefit is to be gained by choosing a more expensive funeral package. For most people, minimizing what is spent on the funeral would be a rational choice, but at a time of emotional vulnerability it can be made to look as if this means depriving the loved one or the family of some great benefit. Even if the funeral director makes nothing but true statements, they can be put into a form designed to arouse emotions that will lessen the possibility of a rational decision being reached.

The dance studio case is similar in that a weakness is being played upon. The woman's insecurity makes her vulnerable to flattery and attention, and this creates the kind of situation in which others can take advantage of her. Perhaps the dance lessons fulfill some need, but the appeal to her vanity easily becomes a tool to manipulate her into doing what the instructor wants.

The key to distinguishing between legitimate and illegitimate emotional appeals lies in whether the appeal clouds one's ability to make a decision based on genuine satisfaction of needs and desires. Our judgment about whether this happens in a particular case will depend in part on whether we think the purchase likely to benefit the customer. The more questionable the benefits, the more an emotional appeal looks like manipulation rather than persuasion. When questionable benefits are combined with some special vulnerability on the part of the consumer, the use of the emotional appeal appears even more suspect. . . .

V

I have attempted to provide a framework for evaluating the morality of a number of different types of sales practices. The framework is based on conditions for mutually beneficial exchange and ultimately for an efficient satisfaction of economic needs and desires. An inevitable question is whether this kind of evaluation is of any practical importance.

If we set before ourselves the ideal of a knowledgeable, unforced, and rational decision on the part of a customer, it is not difficult to see how some types of practices would interfere with this process. We must, of course, be careful not to set the standards too high. A customer may be partially but adequately informed to judge a purchase's potential benefits. A decision may be affected by nonrational and even irrational factors and yet still be rational enough in terms of being plausibly related to the individual's desires and needs. There may be borderline cases in which it is not clear whether acting in a particular way would be morally required or simply overscrupulous, but that is not an objection to this approach, only a recognition of a feature of morality itself.

Notes

1. The classic statement of the argument from economic benefits is found in Adam Smith, *The Wealth of Nations* (1776) (London: Methusen and Co. Ltd., 1930). Modern proponents of this argument include Ludwig von Mises, Friedrich von Hayek, and Milton Friedman.

2. One very clear analysis of voluntariness making use of these conditions may be found in John Hospers' *Human Conduct: Problems of Ethics*, 2nd ed. (New York: Harcourt Brace Jovanovich, 1982), pp. 385–388.

3. I will refer to the three conditions indifferently as conditions for voluntary exchange or conditions for mutually beneficial exchange. By the latter designation I do not mean to suggest that they are either necessary or sufficient conditions for the occurrence of mutual benefit, but that they are conditions for the reasonable expectation of mutual benefit.

4. There are cases, however, in which the buyer knows more about a product than the seller. For example, suppose Cornell has found out that land Fredonia owns contains minerals that make it twice as valuable as Fredonia thinks. The symmetry of my conditions would lead me to conclude that Cornell should give Fredonia the relevant information unless perhaps Fredonia's failure to know was the result of some culpable negligence.

5. This case is described in Warren Magnuson and Jean Carper, *The Dark Side of the Market-Place* (Englewood Cliffs, N.J.: Prentice-Hall, 1968), pp. 3–4.

6. My reference to a reasonable person standard should not be confused with the issue facing the FTC of whether to evaluate advertising by the reasonable consumer or ignorant consumer standard as described in Ivan Preston, "Reasonable Consumer or Ignorant Consumer: How the FTC Decides," *Journal of Consumer Affairs* 8 (Winter 1974):

131–143. There the primary issue is with regard to whom the government should protect from claims that might be misunderstood. My concern here is with determining what amount of information is necessary for informed judgment. In general I suggest that a salesperson should begin with the assumption that information a reasonable consumer would regard as important needs to be revealed and that when special interests and concerns of the consumer come to light they may make further revelations necessary. This approach parallels the one taken by Tom Beauchamp and James Childress regarding the information that a physician needs to provide to obtain informed consent. See their *Principles of Biomedical Ethics*, 2nd ed. (New York: Oxford University Press, 1983), pp. 74–79.

7. This is adapted from a court case quoted in Braybrooke, pp. 68–70.

Review and Discussion Questions

1. Are Holley's three conditions necessary for a market system to be efficient and mutually beneficial? What are the consequences of these conditions being abused?

2. Do you agree that salespeople have a moral duty to avoid undermining these conditions? Why? How far do they have to go to fulfill this duty? Do they have any other obligations that might conflict with this duty?

3. How much information about a product or service is a salesperson obligated to provide? Formulate a rule or set of rules that salespeople should follow.

4. Successful selling frequently involves emotional and psychological appeals to the potential customer. What are the moral limits on such appeals?

5. Some would argue that the ideal of "salesmanship," or being a successful salesperson, is inevitably in conflict with a salesperson's moral obligations. Assess this argument. To what extent does selling require one to look at buyers as means and not ends?

Advertising and Behavior Control

Robert L. Arrington

After defining and illustrating the meaning of "puffery" in advertising, professor of philosophy Robert L. Arrington turns to the central question of his article: "Do the advertising techniques we have discussed involve a violation of human autonomy and a manipulation and control of consumer behavior, or do they simply provide an efficient and effective means of giving the consumer information on the basis of which he or she makes a free choice?" Or more briefly: "Is advertising information, or creation of desire?"

In answering the question, Arrington examines the notions of autonomous desire, rational desire and choice, free choice, and control or manipulation. He concedes that advertising may in some individual cases control behavior, produce compulsive behavior, or create irrational wants or wants not truly those of the consumer. But he does not believe that advertising does this in most cases or that there is anything about the nature of advertising that necessarily leads to violations of autonomy.

Consider the following advertisements:

1. "A woman in *Distinction Foundations* is so beautiful that all other women want to kill her."

2. Pongo Peach color from Revlon comes "from east of the sun . . . west of the moon where each tomorrow dawns." It is "succulent on your lips" and "sizzling on your finger tips (And on your toes, goodness knows)." Let it be your "adventure in paradise."

3. "Increase the value of your holdings. Old Charter Bourbon Whiskey—The Final Set Up."

4. Last Call Smirnoff Style: "They'd never really miss us, and it's kind of late already, and it's quite a long way, and I could build a fire, and you're looking very beautiful, and we could have another martini, and it's awfully nice just being home . . . you think?"

5. A Christmas Prayer. "Let us pray that the blessings of peace be ours—the peace to build and grow, to live in harmony and sympathy with others, and to plan for the future with confidence." New York Life Insurance Company.

Excerpted from "Advertising and Behavior Control," published in *Journal of Business Ethics* 1 (February 1982): 3–12. Copyright © 1982 by D. Reidel Publishing Company, Dordrecht, Holland.

These are instances of what is called puffery—the practice by a seller of making exaggerated, highly fanciful or suggestive claims about a product or service. Puffery, within ill-defined limits, is legal. It is considered a legitimate, necessary, and very successful tool of the advertising industry. Puffery is not just bragging; it is bragging carefully designed to achieve a very definite effect. Using the techniques of so-called motivational research, advertising firms first identify our often hidden needs (for security, conformity, oral stimulation) and our desires (for power, sexual dominance and dalliance, adventure) and then they design ads which respond to these needs and desires. By associating a product, for which we may have little or no direct need or desire, with symbols reflecting the fulfillment of these other, often subterranean interests, the advertisement can quickly generate large numbers of consumers eager to purchase the product advertised. What woman in the sexual race of life could resist a foundation which would turn other women envious to the point of homicide? Who can turn down an adventure in paradise, east of the sun where tomorrow dawns? Be at the pinnacle of success—drink Old Charter. Or stay at home and dally a bit—with Smirnoff. And let us pray for a secure and predictable future, provided for by New York Life, God willing. It doesn't take very much motivational research to see the point of these sales pitches. Others are perhaps a little less obvious. The need to feel secure in one's home at night can be used to sell window air conditioners, which drown out small noises and provide a friendly, dependable companion. The fact that baking a cake is symbolic of giving birth to a baby used to prompt advertisements for cake mixes which glamorized the 'creative' housewife. And other strategies, for example involving cigar symbolism, are a bit too crude to mention, but are nevertheless very effective.

Don't such uses of puffery amount to manipulation, exploitation, or downright control? In his very popular book *The Hidden Persuaders*, Vance Packard points out that a number of people in the advertising world have frankly admitted as much:

> As early as 1941 Dr. Dichter (an influential advertising consultant) was exhorting ad agencies to recognize themselves for what they actually were—"one of the most advanced laboratories in psychology". He said the successful ad agency "manipulates human motivations and desires and develops a need for

goods with which the public has at one time been unfamiliar—perhaps even undesirous of purchasing". The following year *Advertising Agency* carried an ad man's statement that psychology not only holds promise for understanding people but "ultimately for controlling their behavior."[1]

Such statements lead Packard to remark: "With all this interest in manipulating the customer's subconscious, the old slogan 'let the buyer beware' began taking on a new and more profound meaning."[2]

B. F. Skinner, the high priest of behaviorism, has expressed a similar assessment of advertising and related marketing techniques. Why, he asks, do we buy a certain kind of car?

> Perhaps our favorite TV program is sponsored by the manufacturer of that car. Perhaps we have seen pictures of many beautiful or prestigeful persons driving it—in pleasant or glamorous places. Perhaps the car has been designed with respect to our motivational patterns: the device on the hood is a phallic symbol; or the horsepower has been stepped up to please our competitive spirit in enabling us to pass other cars swiftly (or, as the advertisements say, 'safely'). The concept of freedom that has emerged as part of the cultural practice of our group makes little or no provision for recognizing or dealing with these kinds of control.[3]

In purchasing a car we may think we are free, Skinner is claiming, when in fact our act is completely controlled by factors in our environment and in our history of reinforcement. Advertising is one such factor.

A look at some other advertising techniques may reinforce the suspicion that Madison Avenue controls us like so many puppets. T.V. watchers surely have noticed that some of the more repugnant ads are shown over and over again, *ad nauseum*. My favorite, or most hated, is the one about A-1 Steak Sauce which goes something like this: Now, ladies and gentlemen, what *is* hamburger? It has succeeded in destroying my taste for hamburger, but it has surely drilled the name of A-1 Sauce into my head. And that is the point of it. Its very repetitiousness has generated what ad theorists call *information*. In this case it is indirect information, information derived not from the content of what is said but from the fact that it is said so often and so vividly that it sticks in one's mind — i.e., the information yield has increased. And not only do I always remember A-1 Sauce when I go to the grocers, I tend to assume that any product advertised so often has to be good — and so I usually buy a bottle of the stuff. . . .

Are these techniques of manipulation and control whose success shows that many of us have forfeited our autonomy and become a community, or herd, of packaged souls?[4] The business world and the advertising industry certainly reject this interpretation of their efforts. *Business Week*, for example, dismissed the charge that the science of behavior, as utilized by advertising, is engaged in human engineering and manipulation. It editorialized to the effect that "it is hard to find anything very sinister about a science whose principle conclusion is that you get along with people by giving them what they want."[5] The theme is familiar: businesses just give the consumer what he/she wants; if they didn't they wouldn't stay in business very long. Proof that the consumer wants the products advertised is given by the fact that he buys them, and indeed often returns to buy them again and again.

The techniques of advertising we are discussing have had their more intellectual defenders as well. For example, Theodore Levitt, Professor of Business Administration at the Harvard Business School, has defended the practice of puffery and the use of techniques dependent on motivational research.[6] What would be the consequences, he asks us, of deleting all exaggerated claims and fanciful associations from advertisements? We would be left with literal descriptions of the empirical characteristics of products and their functions. Cosmetics would be presented as facial and bodily lotions and powders which produce certain odor and color changes; they would no longer offer hope or adventure. In addition to the fact that these products would not then sell as well, they would not, according to Levitt, please us as much either. For it is hope and adventure we want when we buy them. We want automobiles not just for transportation, but for the feelings of power and status they give us. Quoting T. S. Eliot to the effect that "Human kind cannot bear very much reality," Levitt argues that advertising is an effort to "transcend nature in the raw," to "augment what nature has so crudely fashioned." He maintains that "everybody everywhere wants to modify, transform, embel-

lish, enrich and reconstruct the world around him." Commerce takes the same liberty with reality as the artist and the priest — in all three instances the purpose is "to influence the audience by creating illusions, symbols, and implications that promise more than pure functionality." . . . A poem, a temple, a Cadillac — they all elevate our spirits, offering imaginative promises and symbolic interpretations of our mundane activities. Seen in this light, Levitt claims, "Embellishment and distortion are among advertising's legitimate and socially desirable purposes." To reject these techniques of advertising would be "to deny man's honest needs and values."

Phillip Nelson, a Professor of Economics at SUNY-Binghampton, has developed an interesting defense of indirect information advertising.[7] He argues that even when the message (the direct information) is not credible, the fact that the brand is advertised, and advertised frequently, is valuable indirect information for the consumer. The reason for this is that the brands advertised most are more likely to be better buys — losers won't be advertised a lot, for it simply wouldn't pay to do so. Thus even if the advertising claims made for a widely advertised product are empty, the consumer reaps the benefit of the indirect information which shows the product to be a good buy. . . .

The defense of advertising which suggests that advertising simply is information which allows us to purchase what we want, has in turn been challenged. Does business, largely through its advertising efforts, really make available to the consumer what he/she desires and demands? John Kenneth Galbraith has denied that the matter is as straightforward as this.[8] In his opinion the desires to which business is supposed to respond, far from being original to the consumer, are often themselves created by business. The producers make both the product and the desire for it, and the "central function" of advertising is "to create desires." Galbraith coins the term 'The Dependence Effect' to designate the way wants depend on the same process by which they are satisfied.

David Braybrooke has argued in similar and related ways.[9] Even though the consumer is, in a sense, the final authority concerning what he wants, he may come to see, according to Braybrooke, that he was mistaken in wanting what he did. The statement 'I want x,' he tells us, is not incorrigible but is "ripe for revision." If the consumer had more objective information than he is provided by product puffing, if his values had not been mixed up by motivational research strategies (e.g., the confusion of sexual and automotive values), and if he had an expanded set of choices instead of the limited set offered by profit-hungry corporations, then he might want something quite different from what he presently wants. This shows, Braybrooke thinks, the extent to which the consumer's wants are a function of advertising and not necessarily representative of his real or true wants.

The central issue which emerges between the above critics and defenders of advertising is this: do the advertising techniques we have discussed involve a violation of human autonomy and a manipulation and control of consumer behavior, or do they simply provide an efficient and cost-effective means of giving the consumer information on the basis of which he or she makes a free choice? Is advertising information, or creation of desire?

To answer this question we need a better conceptual grasp of what is involved in the notion of autonomy. This is a complex, multifaceted concept, and we need to approach it through the more determinate notions of (a) autonomous desire, (b) rational desire and choice, (c) free choice, and (d) control or manipulation. In what follows I shall offer some tentative and very incomplete analyses of these concepts and apply the results to the case of advertising.

(a) Autonomous Desire

Imagine that I am watching T.V. and see an ad for Grecian Formula 16. The thought occurs to me that if I purchase some and apply it to my beard, I will soon look younger — in fact I might even be myself again. Suddenly I want to be myself! I want to be young again! So I rush out and buy a bottle. This is our question: was the desire to be younger manufactured by the commercial, or was it 'original to me' and truly mine? Was it autonomous or not?

F. A. von Hayek has argued plausibly that we should not equate nonautonomous desires, desires which are not original to me or truly mine, with those which are culturally induced.[10] If we did equate the two, he points out, then the desires for music, art, and knowledge could not properly be attributed to a person as original to him, for these are surely induced culturally. The only desires a person would really have as his own in this case would be the purely physical ones for food, shelter, sex, etc. But if we reject the equation of the nonautonomous and the culturally induced, as von Hayek would have us do, then the mere fact that my desire to be young again is caused by the T.V. commercial — surely an instrument of popular culture transmission — does not in and of itself show that this is not my own, autonomous desire. Moreover, even if I never before felt the need to look young, it doesn't follow that this new desire is any less mine. I haven't always liked 1969 Aloxe Corton Burgundy or the music of Satie, but when the desires for these things first hit me, they were truly mine.

This shows that there is something wrong in setting up the issue over advertising and behavior control as a question whether our desires are truly ours *or* are created in us by advertisements. Induced and autonomous desires do not separate into two mutually exclusive classes. To obtain a better understanding of autonomous and non-autonomous desires, let us consider some cases of a desire which a person does not *acknowledge* to be his own even though he *feels* it. The kleptomaniac has a desire to steal which in many instances he repudiates, seeking by treatment to rid himself of it. And if I were suddenly overtaken by a desire to attend to an REO concert, I would immediately disown this desire, claiming possession or momentary madness. These are examples of desires which one might have but with which one would not identify. They are experienced as foreign to one's character or personality. Often a person will have what Harry Frankfurt calls a second-order desire, that is to say, a desire *not* to have another desire.[11] In such cases, the first-order desire is thought of as being nonautonomous, imposed on one. When on the contrary a person has a second-order desire to maintain and fulfill a first-order desire, then the first-order desire is truly his own, autonomous, original to him. So there is in fact a distinction between desires which are the agent's own and those which are not, but this is not the same as the distinction between desires which are innate to the agent and those which are externally induced.

If we apply the autonomous/nonautonomous distinction derived from Frankfurt to the desires brought about by advertising, does this show that advertising is responsible for creating desires which are not truly the agent's own? Not necessarily, and indeed not often. There may be some desires I feel which I have picked up from advertising and which I disown—for instance, my desire for A-1 Steak Sauce. If I act on these desires it can be said that I have been led by advertising to act in a way foreign to my nature. In these cases my autonomy has been violated. But most of the desires induced by advertising I fully accept, and hence most of these desires are autonomous. The most vivid demonstration of this is that I often return to purchase the same product over and over again, without regret or remorse. And when I don't, it is more likely that the desire has just faded than that I have repudiated it. Hence, while advertising may violate my autonomy by leading me to act on desires which are not truly mine, this seems to be the exceptional case. . . .

What are we to say in response to Braybrooke's argument that insofar as we might choose differently if advertisers gave us better information and more options, it follows that the desires we have are to be attributed more to advertising than to our own real inclinations? This claim seems empty. It amounts to saying that if the world we lived in, and we ourselves, were different, then we would want different things. This is surely true, but it is equally true of our desire for shelter as of our desire for Grecian Formula 16. If we lived in a tropical paradise we would not need or desire shelter. If we were immortal, we would not desire youth. What is true of all desires can hardly be used as a basis for criticizing some desires by claiming that they are nonautonomous.

(b) Rational Desire and Choice

Braybrooke might be interpreted as claiming that the desires induced by advertising are often irrational ones in the sense that they are not expressed by an agent who is in full possession of the facts about the products advertised or about the alternative products which might be offered him. Following this line of thought, a possible criticism of advertising is that it leads us to act on irrational desires or to make irrational choices. It might be said that our autonomy has been violated by the fact that we are prevented from following our rational wills or that we have been denied the 'positive freedom' to develop our true, rational selves. It might be claimed that the desires induced in us by

advertising are false desires in that they do not reflect our essential, i.e., rational, essence.

The problem faced by this line of criticism is that of determining what is to count as rational desire or rational choice. If we require that the desire or choice be the product of an awareness of *all* the facts about the product, then surely every one of us is always moved by irrational choices. How could we know all the facts about a product? If it be required only that we possess all of the *available* knowledge about the product advertised, then we still have to face the problem that not all available knowledge is *relevant* to a rational choice. If I am purchasing a car, certain engineering features will be, and others won't be, relevant, *given what I want in a car*. My prior desires determine the relevance of information. Normally a rational desire or choice is thought to be one based upon relevant information, and information is relevant if it shows how other, prior desires may be satisfied. It can plausibly be claimed that it is such prior desires that advertising agencies acknowledge, and that the agencies often provide the type of information that is relevant in light of these desires. To the extent that this is true, advertising does not inhibit our rational wills or our autonomy as rational creatures.

(c) Free Choice

It might be said that some desires are so strong or so covert that a person cannot resist them, and that when he acts on such desires he is not acting freely or voluntarily but is rather the victim of an irresistible impulse or an unconscious drive. Perhaps those who condemn advertising feel that it produces this kind of desire in us and consequently reduces our autonomy.

This raises a very difficult issue. How do we distinguish between an impulse we *do* not resist and one we *could* not resist, between freely giving in to a desire and succumbing to one? A person acts or chooses freely if he does so for a reason, that is, if he can adduce considerations which justify in his mind the act in question. Many of our actions are in fact free because this condition frequently holds. Often, however, a person will act from habit, or whim, or impulse, and on these occasions he does not have a reason in mind. Nevertheless he often acts voluntarily in these instances, i.e., he could have acted otherwise. And this is because if there *had been* a reason for acting otherwise of which he was aware, he would in fact have done so. Thus acting from habit or impulse is not necessarily to act in an involuntary manner. If, however, a person is aware of a good reason to do x and still follows his impulse to do y, then he can be said to be impelled by irresistible impulse and hence to act involuntarily. Many kleptomaniacs can be said to act involuntarily, for in spite of their knowledge that they likely will be caught and their awareness that the goods they steal have little utilitarian value to them, they nevertheless steal. Here their 'out of character' desires have the upper hand, and we have a case of compulsive behavior.

Applying these notions of voluntary and compulsive behavior to the case of behavior prompted by advertising, can we say that consumers influenced by advertising act compulsively? The unexciting answer is: sometimes they do, sometimes no. I may have an overwhelming, T.V. induced urge to own a Mazda Rx-7 and all the while realize that I can't afford one without severely reducing my family's caloric intake to a dangerous level. If, aware of this good reason not to purchase the car, I nevertheless do so, this shows that I have been the victim of T.V. compulsion. But if I have the urge, as I assure you I do, and don't act on it, or if in some other possible world I could afford an Rx-7, then I have not been the subject of undue influence by Mazda advertising. Some Mazda Rx-7 purchasers act compulsively; others do not. The Mazda advertising effort *in general* cannot be condemned, then, for impairing its customers' autonomy in the sense of limiting free or voluntary choice. Of course the question remains what should be done about the fact that advertising may and does *occasionally* limit free choice.

(d) Control or Manipulation

Briefly let us consider the matter of control and manipulation. Under what conditions do these activities occur? . . .

A person C controls the behavior of another person P if

1. C intends P to act in a certain way A;

2. C's intention is causally effective in bringing about A; and

3. C intends to ensure that all of the necessary conditions of A are satisfied.

These criteria may be elaborated as follows. To control another person it is not enough that one's actions produce certain behavior on the part of that person; additionally one must intend that this happen. Hence control is the intentional production of behavior. Moreover, it is not enough just to have the intention; the intention must give rise to the conditions which bring about the intended effect. Finally, the controller must intend to establish by his actions any otherwise unsatisfied necessary conditions for the production of the intended effect. The controller is not just influencing the outcome, not just having input; he is as it were guaranteeing that the sufficient conditions for the intended effect are satisfied.

Let us apply these criteria of control to the case of advertising and see what happens. Conditions 1 and 3 are crucial. Does the Mazda manufacturing company or its advertising agency intend that I buy an Rx-7? Do they intend that a certain number of people buy the car? *Prima facie* it seems more appropriate to say that they *hope* a certain number of people will buy it, and hoping and intending are not the same. . . .

Let us turn to the third condition of control, the requirement that the controller intend to activate or bring about any otherwise unsatisfied necessary conditions for the production of the intended effect. It is in terms of this condition that we are able to distinguish brainwashing from liberal education. The brainwasher arranges all of the necessary conditions for belief. On the other hand, teachers (at least those of liberal persuasion) seek only to influence their students — to provide them with information and enlightenment which they may absorb *if they wish*. We do not normally think of teachers as controlling their students, for the students' performances depend as well on their own interests and inclinations.

Now the advertiser — does he control, or merely influence, his audience? Does he intend to ensure that all of the necessary conditions for purchasing behavior are met, or does he offer information and symbols which are intended to have an effect only *if* the potential purchaser has certain desires? Undeniably advertising induces some desires, and it does this intentionally, but more often than not it intends to induce a desire for a particular object, *given* that the purchaser already has other desires. Given a desire for youth, or power, or adventure, or ravishing beauty, we are led to desire Grecian

Formula 16, Mazda Rx-7's, Pongo Peach, and Distinctive Foundations. In this light, the advertiser is influencing us by appealing to independent desires we already have. He is not creating those basic desires. Hence it seems appropriate to deny that he intends to produce all of the necessary conditions for our purchases, and appropriate to deny that he controls us.

Let me summarize my argument. The critics of advertising see it as having a pernicious effect on the autonomy of consumers, as controlling their lives and manufacturing their very souls. The defense claims that advertising only offers information and in effect allows industry to provide consumers with what they want. After developing some of the philosophical dimensions of this dispute, I have come down tentatively in favor of the advertisers. Advertising may, but certainly does not always or even frequently, control behavior, produce compulsive behavior, or create wants which are not rational or are not truly those of the consumer. Admittedly it may in individual cases do all of these things, but it is innocent of the charge of intrinsically or necessarily doing them or even, I think, of often doing so. This limited potentiality, to be sure, leads to the question whether advertising should be abolished or severely curtailed or regulated because of its potential to harm a few poor souls in the above ways. This is a very difficult question, and I do not pretend to have the answer. I only hope that the above discussion, in showing some of the kinds of harm that can be done by advertising and by indicating the likely limits of this harm, will put us in a better position to grapple with the question.

Notes

1. Vance Packard, *The Hidden Persuaders* (Pocket Books, New York, 1958), pp. 20–21.

2. Ibid., p. 21.

3. B. F. Skinner, "Some Issues Concerning the Control of Human Behavior: A Symposium," in Karlins and Andres (eds.), *Man Controlled* (The Free Press, New York, 1972).

4. I would like to emphasize that in what follows I am discussing these techniques of advertising from the standpoint of the issue of control and not from that of deception. For a good and recent discussion of the many dimensions of possible deception in advertising, see Alex C. Michalos, "Advertising: Its Logic, Ethics, and Economics," in J. A. Blair and R. H. Johnson (eds.), *Informal Logic: The First International Symposium* (Edgepress, Pt. Reyes, Calif., 1980).

5. Quoted by Packard, *op. cit.*, p. 220.

6. Theodore Levitt, "The Morality (?) of Advertising," *Harvard Business Review* 48 (1970): 84–92.

7. Phillip Nelson, "Advertising and Ethics," in Richard T. De George and Joseph A. Pichler (eds.), *Ethics, Free Enterprise, and Public Policy* (Oxford University Press, New York, 1978), pp. 187–198.

8. John Kenneth Galbraith, *The Affluent Society*; reprinted in Tom L. Beauchamp and Norman E. Bowie (eds.), *Ethical Theory and Business* (Prentice-Hall, Englewood Cliffs, N.J., 1979), pp. 496–501.

9. David Braybrooke, "Skepticism of Wants, and Certain Subversive Effects of Corporations on American Values," in Sidney Hook (ed.), *Human Values and Economic Policy* (New York University Press, 1967); reprinted in Beauchamp and Bowie (eds.), *op. cit.*, pp. 502–508.

10. F. A. von Hayek, "The *Non Sequitur* of the 'Dependence Effect,'" *Southern Economic Journal* (1961); reprinted in Beauchamp and Bowie (eds.), *op. cit.*, pp. 508–512.

11. Harry Frankfurt, "Freedom of the Will and the Concept of a Person," *Journal of Philosophy* LXVIII (1971), 5–20.

Review and Discussion Questions

1. Give your own examples of advertisements that associate products for which we have little or no direct need or desire with symbols reflecting other, hidden needs or desires.

2. What does Arrington see as the central issue between critics and defenders of advertising?

3. Explain how Arrington defines "autonomous desire," "rational desire or choice," "free choice," and "control."

4. Explain the relevance of Arrington's analysis of each of these terms to the central issue between critics and defenders of advertising.

5. Does advertising manipulate us even if, as Arrington argues, it does not control us, destroy our autonomy, or make our choices involuntary?

6. Although Arrington is skeptical of the extreme claims made by advertising's critics, he does concede that in some cases "advertising may . . . control behavior, produce compulsive behavior, or create wants which are not rational or are not truly those of the consumer." Do you think that this provides a sufficient basis for abolishing or severely regulating advertising?

A Distinctive Contradiction of Advanced Capitalism

G. A. Cohen

Capitalism has produced unprecedented technological progress. Oxford University professor G. A. Cohen argues, however, that the system is biased in favor of expanding output rather than reducing the amount of time worked and that at a certain stage of affluence this becomes irrational. Advertising encourages us to acquiesce in this systemic bias. No ads stress leisure, rather than consumption. Advertising increases our desire for consumption goods without increasing the satisfaction which that consumption brings.

Capitalist society is responsible for technological power on an unprecedented scale, progressing at an unprecedented rate. This is because the competitive position of its industrial decision-makers compels them to increase the productivity of production processes. The compulsion does not lapse when capitalism reaches its misnamed 'monopoly stage,' for competition persists in pertinent respects. Since total consumer spending power is finite, heterogeneous products of monopolized industries compete against one another for buyers. There is also competition for shareholders, for skilled labour, etc.

Improvement in productivity is a condition of persistence and success in the multidimensional competition which characterizes capitalism in *all* of its stages. 'It is therefore the economic tendency of capital which teaches humanity to husband its strength and to achieve its productive aim with the least possible expenditure of means.'[1]

Now improvements in productivity, whether labour-saving or capital-saving, are open to two uses. One way of exploiting enhanced productivity is to reduce toil and extend leisure, while maintaining output constant. Alternatively, output may be increased, while labour stays the same. It is also possible to achieve a measure of both *desiderata*.

'Leisure' is used broadly here, in rough synonymy with 'freedom from unappealing activity,' and 'toil' refers to activity in so far as it is unappealing. One is leisured to the extent that his time and energy is *not* spent in the service of goals he would prefer fulfilled without such expenditure. One toils to the extent that the motivation of his activity is remuneration or other external reward. It follows that leisure time can be filled strenuously. It also follows that amelioration of working conditions counts as expanding leisure.

The economic distinction between job time and time off coincides imperfectly with the distinction here envisaged between toil and freedom from it. Some 'gainful employment' is enjoyable, and some time off is spent toilsomely. But the distinctions are sufficiently coextensive for the purposes of our argument. What particularly matters is that, as things are, for most people most of the time earning a living is not a joy. Most people are so situated that they would benefit not only from more goods and services but also from reduced working hours and/or enhanced working conditions. It is clear that advances in productivity enable gains in either direction, typically at the expense of gains in the other direction.

Now capitalism inherently tends to promote just one of the options, output expansion, since the other, toil reduction, threatens a sacrifice of the profit associated with increased output and sales, and hence a loss of competitive strength.[2] When the efficiency of a firm's production improves, it does not simply reduce the working day of its employees and produce the same amount as before. It produces more of the goods in question, or, if that course is, because of the structure of the market, not optimal, it adopts another non-labour-reducing strategy, to be described shortly.

But first let us note that there has indeed been a titanic growth of output and a comparatively small reduction of labour expenditure since the inception of capitalism (date that where you will). That the reduction in the working day has been small by comparison with the volume of output expansion is beyond controversy. But it is arguable that it has also been fairly small in absolute terms, if sophisticated but defensible criteria of the amount of time people spend supporting themselves are used. Meriting consideration here are such activities as travelling to work, shopping in so far as it is felt to be a nuisance, and any activity in itself unattractive but performed as a means to fulfilling consumption purposes.[3] In sheer hours of work per year (admittedly, not the only relevant index), the modern American worker is not obviously better off than the European peasant of the Middle Ages, many of whose days were made idle by the weather and by observance of the Christian calendar.[4] Nor has there been stunning progress since, say, 1920, if everything pertinent, notably overtime, is taken into account. There has of course been an impressive decline in labour time since the earlier part of the nineteenth century, but the capitalist system need not be thanked for effecting it, since it was capitalism which stretched the working day in the first place. In any case, even that decline loses force in comparison with the accompanying increase in output, and the bias here attributed to capitalism is sufficiently evidenced by the relative position.

Output expansion takes different forms. If the market for the good whose production has improved is expansible, output expansion may take the immediate form of more products of the same kind. Otherwise, and especially if the market in question is more or less saturated, output expands elsewhere, as newly available funds (generated by reductions in the wages bill) flow into another line of production. This does not always occur promptly or smoothly, but eventually it occurs. Jobs are generally destroyed and created in the process.

As long as production remains subject to the capitalist principle, the output-increasing option will tend to be selected, and implemented in one way or another. Whether or not they have capitalist mentalities, it is imperative for capitalists to continue accumulating exchange-value, and thus to expand output. But it is unlikely that the principle should prevail while the mentality is wholly absent, and the mentality fortifies and augments the output-favouring effect of the purely objective constraint of competition.

Now the consequence of the increasing output which capitalism necessarily favours is increasing consumption. Hence the boundless pursuit of consumption goods is a result of a productive process oriented to exchange-values rather than consumption-values. It is the Rockefellers who ensure that the Smiths need to keep up with the Jones's. . . .

To recapitulate. The argument is that even if and when it becomes possible and desirable to reduce or transform unwanted activity, capitalism continues to promote consumption instead, and therefore functions irrationally, in the sense that the structure of the economy militates against optimal use of its productive capacity. It is undeniable that capitalist relations of production possess an output-expanding bias. So the only way of denying that they are potentially irrational in the stated respect is to assert that labour is so enjoyable (or not so unenjoyable) and resources are so plentiful and the satisfaction to be had from goods and services is so limitless that no matter how much is being consumed it remains desirable to consume more, instead of expanding freedom from labour: a rather large assertion. . . .

For a long time the benefits of this tilted decision-making perhaps outweigh the sacrifice exacted in labour. But when output is of a very high order and it remains true that most people devote most of their substance to doing what they would rather not do, then to persist in favour of further output at the expense of relief from undesired work is irrational. . . .

An Objection

Here is one way of developing the objection mentioned [earlier]: 'You have proved at most that capitalism *tends* to select output expansion. It does not follow that if it actually expands output, then this is adequately explained by the bias you identified. There are other tendencies attributable to capitalism on similar grounds—the need to accumulate capital—which are completely unfulfilled. One is the tendency of firms not to raise their workers' wages. The tendency is there, but its effect is neutralized by countervailing trade union power. Why does that same power not check the propensity towards output? Why do unions generally press for more income rather than less labour? If the system's bias harms their members' interests, why do they co-operate with it? When the contradiction looms, why does union policy not change? If the United States has crossed the border into contradiction, why is union policy what is it?'

Note the nature of the objection. It is *not*: output expansion is favoured not by the system but only by the aims the population wants the system to accomplish. That claim cannot stand, since the system demonstrably possesses an output-expanding bias. But the presence of that tendency does not show that it explains the realization of what it is a tendency to. That lesser claim is the basis of the objection.

We shall meet the objection by exploiting quite uncontroversial premises. It is easily met on the radical premiss that much of what is consumed gives no real satisfaction, but people cherish it because they are dupes of advertising and ideology. Later, a reduced version of that thesis will be defended, but first let us magnanimously assume that by and large the given consumer goods are desirable, that desire for them is in some relevant sense awakened, not contrived, by advertising and affiliated processes, and that the satisfaction they afford is genuine.

On the other side, the opponent must concede that plenty of labour is not desired. If God gave workers *gratis* the pay they now get, and granted them freedom to choose whether or not to work at their jobs, for as long as they pleased, without remuneration, then there would result a very substantial decline in labouring activity. Superficial observation suggests that people enjoy what they consume, but it also reveals that they do not enjoy much of what they must do to be able to consume it.

Then what advertising (etc.) may be said to do, on the most generous account, is to draw attention to and emphasize (what we have supposed are) the independently desirable qualities of the products it displays. This is balanced by no similar campaign stressing the goods of leisure. No ads say: WHEN *YOUR* UNION NEGOTIATES, MAKE IT GO FOR SHORTER HOURS, NOT MORE PAY. ELECTRIC CARVING KNIVES ARE FINE, BUT NOTHING BEATS FREEDOM. There are no 'leisure ads' because firms have no interest in financing them, nor

in paying for public reminders of the unpleasant side of the labour which buys the goods.

There is, of course, promotion of so-called 'leisure products,' but rising income is required to procure them, and the advertisements do not mention the sacrifice of leisure needed to sustain that income. One can imagine someone saying, in an extreme case: 'I am taking a week-end job to maintain the payments on the snowmobile I use at week-ends.'

Thus labour acquiescence in the bias is itself traceable to the bias: workers are influenced by its operation in the emphases promoted by the media.[5]

The foregoing scepticism about the process of desire formation in capitalist society does not rest on a theory disclosing the optimal desire structure for human beings: that would be difficult to supply. It would, more particularly, be hazardous to attempt a realistic general statement of the relative merits of increments of consumption and leisure at varying levels of each. Such doctrine being foresworn, what are the principles behind the critique that was given?

A distinction obtains between what a man is disposed to seek, and what would in fact afford him satisfaction. We can, on that basis, distinguish, more elaborately, between two schedules pertinently descriptive of a person's make-up and circumstances: his *pursuit* schedule and his *satisfaction* schedule. Each orders objects of his desire, but from different points of view. The pursuit schedule orders them by reference to the relative strengths of his dispositions to seek them. The satisfaction schedule orders them according to the amounts of satisfaction he would obtain from possessing them. (We ignore (a) satisfactions he would obtain from objects he does not pursue, and (b) probabilities of attaining pursued objects: suppose that whatever is pursued is attained.) These schedules are, of course, constantly changing with changes in information, taste, and external conditions, but we can say that a person's situation at a given time is likely to be unfortunate to the extent that objects are differently ordered in his two schedules. If the ordering in his satisfaction schedule differs from the ordering in his pursuit schedule, he is unlikely to be making optimal use of the resources available to him.

Now if an agency increases a man's pursuit of an object, without commensurately increasing the satisfaction he would get from possessing it, then it probably produces the unwanted misalignment of schedules, and therefore has a negative effect on his welfare, *unless* his pursuit of the object increases because the agency supplies a more accurate account than he had before of the satisfaction it would give him (in which case, an — in that respect — improved alignment results). But the agencies in capitalist society which promote a preference for output over leisure cannot be credited with a comparable tendency to increase the satisfaction to be had from output as opposed to leisure, nor may they be said to provide a more accurate account than might otherwise be available of the relative values of the two. There is therefore a case for saying that they corrupt the individual's preference structure, a claim we can make without describing the content of an uncorrupted preference structure.

We criticize capitalism not because it causes desires which might otherwise not have arisen, but because it causes desires the fulfilment of which does not afford an appropriate degree of satisfaction. The system requires the pursuit of consumption goods: it is indifferent to the quality of satisfaction which lies at the end of it, except in so far as high satisfaction might reinforce the pursuit. But it is naive to think that a particularly effective way of sustaining the commitment to consumption is to make consumption rewarding. On the contrary, there is reason to suppose — and here we approach the 'radical premiss' not used in our reply to the objection — that the pursuit of goods will, in important ranges, be stronger to the extent that their power to satisfy the pursuer is limited. The system cannot abide consumers who are content with what they already have. As Baker says:

> . . . while trying to increase sales and profits, a business enterprise will want to create tastes that are (1) cheapest to develop or stimulate and (2) for which palliatives can be produced but (3) which are never completely satisfied and do not cause other desires to be satiated.[6]

Business wants contented customers, but they must not be too contented. Otherwise they will buy less and work less, and business will dwindle.

Finally, a reply to those who use their leisure time arguing that if people had lots of it they would not know how to use it. No well-confirmed propositions about human beings support this arrogant pessimism. It is, moreover predictable that a society rigged up to maximize output will fail to develop the theory and practice of leisure.[7] And this further manifestation of the output bias adds to the explanation of general acquiescence in it. Free time looks empty when the salient available ways of filling it are inane.

Notes

1. Karl Marx, *Theories of Surplus Value*, ii. 548.
2. See *Grundrisse*, pp. 701, 707–12; *Theories of Surplus Value*, i. 223, 226–8, ii. 468. . . .
3. Also needing attention, in more than just a footnote, is the complicated effect of capitalism on the amount of labour performed by women. In *some* respects their leisure can increase since the output bias leads to a proliferation of devices which reduce domestic labour. But the same devices enable women to join the remunerated labour force, so their total effect is not easy to judge.

   According to Galbraith, the net result of the increasing flow of goods into the home is to make housewives hard-pressed managers of consumption, so that 'the menial role of the woman becomes more arduous the higher the family income.' Galbraith is evidently no connoisseur of low-income family life, but there may be a grain of truth in what he says. See *Economics and the Public Purpose*, p. 32.
4. For further discussion, see Parker, *The Sociology of Leisure*, p. 24, the references he cites, and those cited by Howard and King, *The Political Economy of Marx*, p. 124, n. 7.
5. We have dealt only with the most manifest messages in favour of goods projected by capitalist society. To show how much else in its culture has the same end is more than can be done here. Advertising is no doubt a relatively secondary influence, reinforcing much deeper sources of commitment to consumption.
6. 'The Ideology of the Economic Analysis of Law,' p. 38.
7. ' . . . we are now at a point at which sociologists are discussing the "problem" of leisure. And a part of the problem is: how did it come to be a problem?' Thompson, 'Time, Work-Discipline, and Industrial Capitalism,' p. 67.

Review and Discussion Questions

1. Explain what Cohen sees as "a distinctive contradiction of advanced capitalism."

2. Do you agree that capitalism gives rise to this contradiction? Is Cohen correct in thinking that it is "distinctive" of capitalism?

3. What objection to his thesis does Cohen discuss, and what is his reply to it?

4. What is the relevance of the distinction between "pursuit schedule" and "satisfaction schedule" for Cohen's argument?

For Further Reading

Joseph R. DesJardins and **John J. McCall,** eds., *Contemporary Issues in Business Ethics*, 2nd ed. (Belmont, Calif.: Wadsworth, 1990), contains important and useful essays on product lia- bility, consumer regulation, advertising and free speech, subliminal advertising, and advertising to children, among other issues.

Roger Draper, "The Faithless Shepherd," *New York Review of Books*, June 26, 1986 is a good, intelligent review of recent books on advertising.

A. Pablo Iannone, ed., *Contemporary Moral Controversies in Business* (New York: Oxford University Press, 1989), Part IV, has some good articles and legal cases on moral issues in marketing and advertising.

Manuel G. Velasquez, *Business Ethics*, 2nd ed. (Englewood Cliffs, N.J.: Prentice-Hall, 1988), Chapter 6, provides a good discussion of consumer issues.

CHAPTER 11

THE ENVIRONMENT

No one can deny that, in manufacturing products and consuming the fruits of their labors, human beings have scarred the globe and contaminated the natural environment. The effects of our environmental recklessness are now coming home, threatening the integrity of the biosphere and possibly life itself. The planet appears to be warming, its protective ozone layer thinning, its lush forests disappearing. Our rivers and lakes are dirty; our air is unclean. Pollution besets us.

In his book on the subject, professor of philosophy Tom Regan begins by saying: "The concerns of environmental ethics might begin with the food on our plate."[1] Food is of concern because agriculture increasingly uses hundreds of chemicals in crop production, including fertilizers, herbicides, and pesticides. Although chemically intensive agriculture has yielded many benefits, it also raises worries about harmful chemical residue left in food.

A public health disaster in Puerto Rico is but one dramatic and tragic example. An estimated 3,000 youngsters under ten years of age — some as young as seventeen months — began suffering from abnormal sexual development, including menstruation and fully developed breasts. Authorities suspect an environmental contaminant, probably the steroid hormone estrogen, in the food chain. One possible source of the estrogen is growth stimulant for cattle and chickens. Although estrogen is restricted, some experts believe its use is common in Puerto Rico.[2] That claim raises the specter of government agencies that, while setting standards regarding food contaminants, are unwilling or powerless to enforce them. This conclusion approximates the one drawn by Lewis Regenstein in his book *America the Poisoned*. Regenstein says that:

> A review of the government's policy in setting and enforcing tolerance levels of toxic pesticides leads to the inescapable conclusion that the program exists primarily to insure the public that it is being protected from harmful chemical residues. In fact, the program, as currently administered, does little to minimize or even monitor the amount of poisons in our food, and serves the interests of the users and producers of pesticides rather than those of the public.[3]

In 1972 the brand-new Environmental Protection Agency was given the job of regulating new pesticides and of reevaluating the old ones using modern standards. The old pesticides, with about 600 active ingredients, constitute the bulk of those in use, but the agency has only evaluated a handful of them. "It is almost as if the 1972 law had never been passed," the *Washington Post* has commented, calling pesticides our most serious environmental problem and the one we are doing the least about.[4]

The contaminants that infiltrate the food chain can also spread into our water. The toxic chemicals used in farming can and do run off into underground reservoirs, which are a major source of our water. "The drinking water of every major American city," claims Regenstein, "contains dozens of cancer-causing chemicals and other toxins," many of which can be traced to chemicals used in agriculture.[5]

In 1972 Congress passed the Clean Water Act, which proclaimed the goal of eliminating all water pollution by 1985. Since Congress acted, over $250 billion has been spent on pollution control. Some streams and lakes have improved; others have gotten worse. On average, though, according to government figures, water quality hasn't changed much.[6]

Pollutants also contaminate the air we breathe, despoiling vegetation and crops, corroding construction materials, and threatening our lives and health. In 1989 the House Energy and Commerce subcommittee on health and the environment released the first national survey of toxic air pollution; it showed that the level of dangerous substances discharged by industrial plants into the atmosphere is far greater than previously estimated. Although Congress authorized controls on hazardous pollutants in 1970, the Environmental Protection Agency (EPA) has issued regulations for only 7 of the 329 substances considered toxic. The subcommittee's report revealed that 2.4 billion pounds of those hazardous pollutants, including tons of toxic chemicals that cause cancer and damage the nervous system, are emitted each year. "The magnitude of the problem exceeds our worst fears," says the chairman of the subcommittee, Representative Henry Waxman of California.[7]

The subcommittee's figures don't include emissions of nontoxic substances like sulfur and nitrogen oxides (emitted by electric power plants) that are a major source of acid rain. Nor do they include the volatile chemicals from gasoline vapor and various industrial and commercial sources that react with sunlight to create ozone, a chief ingredient of the smog that blankets so many American cities.

Thanks to the ground-breaking Clean Air Act of 1970, our air is better than it would otherwise have been, and by some measures it is better than it was ten years ago. In particular, by banning lead as a fuel additive, the act has reduced its presence in the air by nearly 90 percent. And the Clean Air Act Amendments of 1990 require new measures to be taken to fight smog, acid rain, and toxic emissions. But the fact remains: More than twenty years after Congress first set a strict deadline for reducing air pollution to safe levels, the air in more than fifty U.S. cities remains a health risk. What is at stake, says S. William Becker, executive director of the State and Territorial Air Pollution Administrators, "is the health of over 135 million people in this country who live in areas that have not attained the ozone standard" along with "over 2,500 excess cancers alone just from routine day-to-day exposure to toxic air pollution." Also at stake, he adds, "is the deterioration of thousands of miles of streams, thousands of miles of lakes" from acid rain.[8]

The National Academy of Science estimates that 15,000 deaths a year and 7 million sick days are traceable to air pollution. And according to EPA figures, about $9 billion a year is spent on health costs incurred for air-related ailments, such as lung cancer and emphysema. The EPA also estimates that air pollution causes $8 billion a year in property losses and $7.6 billion in destruction of vegetation.[9] In addition, some scientists believe that the release of chlorofluorocarbons is leading to the destruction of the atmosphere's ozone layer, which partially screens ultraviolet light rays from the earth's surface. (Chlorofluorocarbons are widely used in refrigeration, air-conditioning, aerosol cans, and the manufacture of plastics, computer chips, and numerous other products.) Other scientists have linked the release of carbon dioxide and heat into the atmosphere to a "greenhouse effect," which is leading to a gradual and potentially dangerous increase in the earth's temperature.[10]

When the pollution of the land and water is taken into account alongside air pollution, EPA figures show that industry dumps a combined annual total of 22.5 billion pounds of toxic substances into our environment. The 3,849 chemical-manufacturing plants nationwide are responsible for about 56 percent of this total.[11] Current figures do not, of course, include the millions of tons of toxic chemicals that have already been dumped. The EPA estimates that toxic chemicals have been dumped at up to 50,000 sites nationwide, at least 2,500 of which pose serious health hazards. The Office of Technology Assessment places the number of priority waste sites at 10,000.[12]

We are just beginning to recognize the illnesses and health risks due to toxic chemicals — lung cancer from asbestos, leukemia from benzene, cancer of the liver from vinyl chloride, sterility from Kepone — because the symptoms of such diseases often do not show up for years. Some health experts suspect that a substantial proportion of all cancers may be environmentally induced — from exposure in the workplace, from toxic dumps, from chemicals that seep into water supplies, and from food additives and other sources.[13]

Nuclear wastes are in a class by themselves. Significant danger arises from even the small amounts that are released into the atmosphere during normal operation of a nuclear power plant or in mining, processing, or transporting nuclear fuels. By government estimates, at least 1,000 people will die between the years 1975 and 2000 as a result of cancer caused by exposure to these routine emissions.[14] A nuclear-plant accident, of course, could sizably increase the casualty rate, as the 1986 disaster at the Soviet city of Chernobyl brought vividly home to the world. And the disposal of nuclear wastes has to worry anyone who is sensitive to the legacy we leave future generations. Will the nuclear toxins we bury today return to haunt us tomorrow?

It is little wonder, then, that considerable attention has focused on business's and industry's responsibility for preserving the integrity of our physical environment. This chapter deals with some of the moral dilemmas posed for business by our environmental relationships — not just the problem of pollution but also the ethical issues posed by the depletion of natural resources and by our treatment of animals. The chapter's purpose is not to argue that the environmental problems facing us are serious and that industry has greatly contributed to them. Few people today doubt this. Rather, this chapter is largely concerned with a more practical question: Given the problems of environmental degradation, of resource depletion, and of the abuse of animals for commercial purposes, what are business's responsibilities? Specifically, this chapter examines:

1. The meaning and significance of "ecology"

2. The traditional business attitudes toward the environment that have encouraged environmental degradation and resource depletion

3. The moral problems underlying business abuse of the environment — in particular, the question of externalities, the problem of free riders, and the right to a livable environment

4. The costs of environmental protection and the question of who should pay them

5. Three methods — regulations, incentives, and pricing mechanisms — for allocating the costs of environmental protection

6. Some of the deeper and not fully resolved questions of environmental ethics: What obligations do we have to future generations? Does nature have value in itself? Is our commercial exploitation of animals immoral?

BUSINESS AND ECOLOGY

To deal intelligently with the question of business's responsibilities for the environment, one must realize that business functions within an ecological system. *Ecology* refers to the science of the interrelationships among organisms and their environments. The operative term is "interrelationships," implying that an interdependence exists among all entities in the environment.

In speaking about ecological matters, ecologists frequently use the term *ecosystem*, which refers to a total ecological community, both living and nonliving. An ordinary example of an ecosystem is a pond. It consists of a complex web of animal and vegetable life. Suppose the area where the pond is located experiences a prolonged period of drought or someone begins to fish in the pond regularly or, during a period of excessive rainfall, plant pesticides begin to spill into it. Under any of these circumstances, changes will occur in the relationships among the pond's constituent members. Damage to a particular form of plant life may mean that fewer fish can live in the pond; a particular species might even disappear. A change in the pond's ecosystem may also affect other ecosystems. Because of water contamination, for example, a herd of deer that live nearby may have to go elsewhere for water; their presence there may reduce the berry crop which had previously supported other animals. The point is that in considering any ecosystem, one must remember its complex and interrelated nature and the intricate network of interdependencies that bind it to other ecosystems.

Every living organism affects its environment, yet the species *Homo sapiens* possesses the power to upset dramatically the stability of natural ecosystems. The problem to be considered is that many human commercial activities (for example, using pesticides and establishing oil fields) can have unpredictable and disruptive consequences for the ecosystem.

Tampering with ecosystems does not always have injurious effects, however. On the contrary, sometimes unforeseen benefits result, as was true of the expansive oil and gas drilling activity in the Gulf of Mexico. Much to everyone's surprise, the operational docks, pipes, and platforms provided a more beneficient place to which lower forms of life could attach themselves than the silt-laden sea ever did. As a result, oil drilling in the Gulf of Mexico has greatly increased the commercial fish catch in the area.

But even in fortuitous instances like this, environmental intrusions affect the integrity of ecosystems. And that's the point. Because an ecosystem represents a delicate balance of interrelated entities and because ecosystems are interlocked, an intrusion into one will affect its integrity and the integrity of others. And we are not usually so lucky in the results. Dr. Paul Ehrlich, one of the best-known exponents of ecological awareness, has put the matter succinctly. "There are a number of ecological rules it would be wise for people to remember," Ehrlich has written. "One of them is that there is no such thing as a free lunch. Another is that when we change something into something else, the new thing is usually more dangerous than what we had originally."[15]

In its role as the major instrument of production in our society, business must intrude into ecosystems. Yet not all intrusions or all kinds of intrusions are thereby justifiable. In fact, precisely because of the interrelated nature of ecosystems and because intrusions generally produce serious unfavorable effects, business must scrupulously avoid actions, practices, and policies that have an undue impact on the physical environment. There's ample documentation to show that business traditionally has been remiss in both recognizing and adequately discharging its obligations in this area. We needn't spend time retelling the sorry tale. But it does seem worthwhile to isolate some business attitudes that historically have supported this indifference.

Business's Traditional Attitudes Toward the Environment

Several related attitudes, prevalent in our society in general and in business in particular, have led to or increased our environmental problems. One of these is the tendency to view the natural world as a "free and unlimited good"—that is, as something we can squander without regard to the future. Writer John Steinbeck once reflected on this attitude:

> I have often wondered at the savagery and thoughtlessness with which our early settlers approached this rich continent. They came at it as though it were an enemy, which of course it was. They burned the forests and changed the rainfall; they swept the buffalo from the plains, blasted the streams, set fire to the grass, ran a reckless scythe through the virgin and noble timber. Perhaps they felt that it was limitless and could never be exhausted and that a man could move on to new wonders endlessly. Certainly there are many examples to the contrary, but to a large extent the early people pillaged the country as though they hated it, as though they held it temporarily and might be driven off at any time.
>
> This tendency toward irresponsibility persists in very many of us today; our rivers are poisoned by reckless dumping of sewage and toxic industrial wastes, the air of our cities is filthy and dangerous to breathe from belching or uncontrolled products from combustion of coal, coke, oil, and gasoline. Our towns are girdled with wreckage and debris of our toys—our automobiles and our packaged pleasures. Through uninhibited spraying against one enemy, we have destroyed the natural balances our survival requires. All these evils can and must be overcome if America and Americans are to survive; but many of us conduct ourselves as our ancestors did, stealing from the future for our clear and present profit.[16]

Traditionally, business has considered the environment to be a free, virtually limitless good. In other words, air, water, land, and other natural resources from coal to beavers (trapped almost to extinction for their pelts in the last century) were seen as available for business to use as it saw fit. In this context, pollution and the depletion of natural re-

sources are two aspects of the same problem: Both involve using up natural resources that are limited. Pollution uses up clean air and water, just as extraction uses up the minerals or oil in the ground. The belief that both sorts of resources are unlimited and free promotes wasteful consumption of them.

Garrett Hardin describes the consequences of this attitude in his modern parable, "The Tragedy of the Commons." Hardin asks us to imagine peasants who allow their animals to graze in the commons, the collectively shared village pasture. It is in the interest of each to permit his or her animals to graze without limit on the public land. But the result of each doing so is that the commons is soon overgrazed, making it of no further grazing value to anyone.[17]

This story can be generalized. When it comes to "the commons"—that is, to public or communal goods like air, water, and unowned wilderness—problems arise as the result of individuals and companies following their own self-interest. Each believes that his or her own use of the commons has a negligible effect, but the cumulative result can be the gradual destruction of the public domain, which makes everyone worse off. In the "tragedy of the commons" we have the reverse of Adam Smith's "invisible hand": Each person's pursuit of self-interest makes everyone worse off.

The "tragedy of the commons" also illustrates the more general point that there can be a difference between the private costs and the social costs of a business activity. Chapter 5 discussed this issue when it described what economists call "externalities," but it is worth reviewing the point in the present context.

Suppose a paper mill only partially treats the chemical wastes it emits into a lake that's used for fishing and recreational activities, thus saving on production costs. If the amount of effluent is great enough to reduce the fishing productivity of the lake, then while the mill's customers pay a lower price for its paper than they otherwise would, other people end up paying a higher price for fish. Moreover, the pollution may make the lake unfit for such recreational activities as swimming and boating or for use as a source of fresh water. The result is that other people and the public generally pay the cost of the mill's inadequate water-treatment system. Economists term this disparity between private industrial costs and public social costs a *spillover* or *externality*. In viewing things strictly in terms of private industrial costs, business overlooks spillover. This is an economic problem because the price of the paper does not reflect the true cost of producing it. Paper is underpriced and overproduced, thus leading to a misallocation of resources. This is also a moral problem because the purchasers of paper are not paying its full cost. Instead, part of the cost of producing paper is being unfairly imposed on other people.

In sum, then, spillovers or externalities, pursuit of private interest at the expense of the commons, and a view of the environment as a free good that can be consumed without limit have combined with an ignorance of ecology and of the often fragile interconnections and interdependencies of the natural world to create the serious environmental problems facing us today.

THE ETHICS OF ENVIRONMENTAL PROTECTION

Much of what we do to reduce, eliminate, or avoid pollution and the depletion of scarce natural resources is in our collective self-interest. Accordingly, many measures that we take — for example, recycling our cans or putting catalytic converters on our cars — are steps that benefit all of us, collectively and individually: Our air is more breathable and our landscapes less cluttered with garbage. But even if such measures benefit each and every one of us, there will still be a temptation to shirk individual responsibilities and be a "free rider." The individual person or company

may rationalize that the little bit it adds to the total pollution problem won't make any difference. The firm benefits from the efforts of others to avoid pollution but "rides for free" by not making the same effort itself.

The unfairness here is obvious. Likewise, as explained in the previous section, the failure of companies to "internalize" their environmental "externalities" spells unfairness. Others are forced to pick up the tab when companies do not pay all the environmental costs involved in producing their own products. As mentioned in Chapter 5, those who adopt the broader view of corporate social responsibility emphasize that business and the rest of society have an implicit social contract. This contract reflects what society hopes to achieve by allowing business to operate; it sets the "rules of the game" governing business activity. Companies that try to be "free riders" in environmental matters or who refuse to address the spillover or external costs of their business activity violate this contract.

So far this chapter has emphasized that we need to view the environment differently if we are to improve our quality of life and even to continue to exist. And it has just stressed how the failure of an individual or business to play its part is unfair. Some moral theorists, like William T. Blackstone, have gone further to argue that each of us has a human right to a livable environment. "Each person," Blackstone argues, "has this right *qua* being human and because a livable environment is essential for one to fulfill his human capacities."[18] This right has emerged, he contends, as a result of changing environmental conditions, which impact on the very possibility of human life as well as on the possibility of realizing other human rights.

Recognition of a right to a livable environment would strengthen further the ethical reasons for business to respect the integrity of the natural world. In addition, recognition of this moral right could, Blackstone suggests, form a sound basis for establishing a legal right to a livable environment through legislation and even, perhaps, through a constitutional amendment or an environmental bill of rights. An official recognition of such rights would enhance our ability to go after polluters and other abusers of the natural environment.

Acknowledging a human right to a livable environment, however, does not solve many of the hard problems facing us. In the effort to conserve irreplaceable resources, to protect the environment from degradation, and to restore it to where it was before being injured, we are still faced with difficult choices. And each choice has its economic and moral costs. The next section focuses on pollution control, but most of the points apply equally to other problems of environmental protection, as well as to the conservation of scarce resources.

The Costs of Pollution Control

It is easy to say that we should do whatever is necessary to improve the environment. Before this answer has any operational worth, however, we must consider a number of things. One is the quality of environment that we want. This can vary from an environment restored to its pristine state to one minimally improved over the current state. Then there's the question of precisely what is necessary to effect the kind of environment we want. In some cases we may not have the technological capacity to improve the environment. But an important concern in any determination of what should be done to improve the environment is a calculation of what it will cost.

To draw out this point, we must consider a technique that plays a major role in determining the total costs of environmental improvement. Cost-benefit analysis is a device used to determine whether it's worthwhile to incur a particular cost—for instance, the cost of employing a particular pollution-control device. The general approach is to evaluate a project's direct and indirect costs and benefits, the difference being the net result for so-

ciety. Suppose that the estimated environmental damage of operating a particular plant is $1,000 per year, that closing the plant would have dire economic consequences for the community, and that the only technique that would permit the plant to operate in an environmentally nondamaging way would cost $6,000 per year. In this case, cost-benefit analysis would rule against requiring the plant to introduce the new technique.* If the cost of the technique had been only $800, however, cost-benefit analysis would have favored it.

Cost-benefit analysis can quickly get very complicated. For example, in determining whether it would be worthwhile to initiate more stringent air-pollution standards for a particular industry, a multitude of cost-benefit factors must be considered. Possible costs might include lower corporate profits, higher prices for consumers, unfavorable effects on employment, and adverse consequences for the nation's balance of payments. On the side of anticipated benefits, a reduction in airborne particulates over urban areas would reduce illness and premature death from bronchitis, lung cancer, and other respiratory diseases by some determinate percentage. The effect on life expectancy would have to be estimated along with projected savings in medical costs and productivity. In addition, diminished industrial discharges would mean reduced property and crop damage from air pollution, and that would save more money.

This example suggests the extreme difficulty of making reliable estimates of actual costs and benefits, of putting price tags on the different effects of the policy being considered. Any empirical prediction in a case like this is bound to be controversial. This problem is compounded by the fact that the decision maker is unlikely to know for certain all future results of the policy being studied. Not

---

* Cost-benefit analysis would not, however, prevent other strategies for getting the plant to internalize this externality. It could be taxed $1,000 or be required to reimburse those who suffer the $1,000 loss.

only is estimating the likelihood of its various possible effects difficult, but some future effects may be entirely unanticipated. Even if these problems are put aside, a cost-effectiveness analysis still involves value judgments about nonmonetary costs and benefits. Costs relative to time, effort, and discomfort can and must be introduced. Benefits can take even more numerous forms: health, convenience, comfort, enjoyment, leisure, self-fulfillment, freedom from odor, visibility, and so on. Benefits are especially difficult to calculate in environmental matters because they often take an aesthetic form. Some environmentalists, for example, may campaign for the preservation of a remote forest visited annually by only a handful of stalwart backpackers, while developers wish to convert it into a more accessible and frequented ski resort. Should the forest be preserved or should it be converted into a ski resort? Conflicting value judgments are at stake.

Not only is an evaluation of costs and benefits wed to values, assessments of worth, and an ordering of those values, but also the values at stake are themselves affected by changes in the environment. Thus, the high value that some environmentalists might attach to the forest is directly related to the fact that such wilderness areas are becoming rarer. As a result, they might now see the cost of obliterating the forest as prohibitive, whereas in former times they might not have. Although a cost-effectiveness analysis may be necessary for determining the soundness of an environmental-preservation measure or a pollution-control project, it seems inevitable that an assessment of costs and benefits will be subject to various factual uncertainties and significantly influenced by the values one holds.

Who Should Pay the Costs?

One aspect of the environmental dilemma that raises questions of social justice is determining who should pay the costs of environ-

mental protections and restorations. Two popular answers to this question currently circulate: that those responsible for causing the pollution ought to pay and that those who stand to benefit from protection and restoration should pick up the tab.

Those Responsible. The claim that those responsible for causing the pollution ought to pay the costs of pollution control seems eminently fair until one asks a simple question. Just who is responsible for the pollution? Who are the polluters? Proponents of this claim observe that individuals and institutions with large incomes generally produce disproportionately more pollution than those with low incomes. Thus, big business is the chief polluter, and this alone, according to the argument, is enough to justify the claim that business ought to bear the lion's share of pollution control. But there's another reason. Shifting environment-improvement costs to society or customers would only increase the economic disparity that already exists between polluters and those damaged by pollution. In effect, a policy of making polluters pick up the tab for environmental restoration would probably have the desirable social effect of shifting income from the richer to the poorer and thus providing for a more equitable distribution of wealth. In the minds of some persons, the question of who should pay the bill is connected with the fair and just distribution of wealth.

Although it's true that business probably has benefited financially more than any other group as a result of treating the environment as a free good, not all of a firm's wealth or even most of it has resulted directly from doing so. Moreover, consumers themselves have benefited enormously by not having to pay higher costs for products.

In fact, some would argue that consumers are primarily to blame for pollution and therefore should pay the bill for its control. Because customers create the demand for the products whose production eventually impairs the environment, then customers ought to pay for the spillover. In this way, the argument goes, social costs are not unfairly passed on to those who have not incurred them. In sum, let those who want the products pay a price for them that includes all the costs of production without degrading the environment. But questions still remain.

Consider this case, for example. The citizens of Massachusetts, wanting cleaner air, vote to pay higher prices for their electricity. It appears that they will pay the entire economic costs of the environmental improvement. But some of the costs of the cleaner air in Massachusetts may be borne by miners of high-sulfur coal in Pennsylvania, who lose their jobs because this coal will no longer be used in Massachusetts. These miners neither caused the pollution nor benefit from controlling it. At the same time, miners of low-sulfur coal in, say, some western state stand to reap a windfall benefit, along with the railroad that hauls the coal.[19] This one example is enough to show that assigning pollution-control costs to customers can affect an intricate network of economic interdependence in ways that raise questions of social justice.

The fact is that those arguing either version of the polluter-should-pay-the-bill thesis, attributing primary responsibility for pollution to big business or to customers, largely ignore the manifold, deep-rooted causes of environmental degradation.

Two important causes of pollution have been a growing population and its increasing concentration in urban areas. In 1900, Americans numbered 76.2 million; by 1990 our population had more than tripled, to approximately 250 million. And we have become an increasingly urbanized nation. Between 1950 and 1990, for instance, the increase in our urban population has been nearly 75 percent.[20] We are a long way from being the rural, agriculturally oriented society we once were. To-

day, for example, the number of college students is nearly three times the entire American farm population. More than 70 million Americans live in our ten largest metropolitan areas, and nearly half the country lives in metropolitan areas with populations of a million or more. This tremendous population growth and equally staggering level of urbanization have brought with them an ever-increasing demand for goods and services, natural resources, energy, and industrial production. And these in turn have increased air, water, space, and noise pollution.

Another root cause of environmental problems is rising affluence. As people get more money to spend, they buy and consume more tangible goods, discard them more quickly, and produce more waste, all of which hasten degradation of the environment. There are, for example, over 180 million registered cars and trucks in the United States — far and away the world record — which only makes the problem of reducing air pollution less tractable.[21] Add to these causes our general tendency to value quantity over quality, our government's failure to demand an accounting of the social costs of environmental pollution, and our ignorance of the interrelated nature of the global ecosystem. Thus, the enemy in the war against environmental decadence turns out to be all of us. No solution to the question of who should pay the costs of pollution control can ignore this fact.

Those Who Would Benefit.   A second popular reply to the payment problem is that those who will benefit from environmental improvement should pay the costs.

The trouble with this argument is that every individual, rich or poor, and every institution, large or small, stands to profit from environmental improvement, albeit not to the same degree. As a result, the claim that those who will benefit should pay the costs is not satisfactory, because everyone is touched by pollution. If, on the other hand, this position means that individuals and groups should pay to the degree that they will benefit, then one must wonder how this could possibly be determined. But perhaps the most serious objection to this thesis is that it seems to leave out responsibility as a legitimate criterion.

Any equitable solution to the problem of who should pay the bill of environmental cleanup should take into account responsibility as well as benefit. The preceding analysis suggests that we all share the blame for pollution and collectively stand to benefit from environmental improvement. This doesn't mean, however, that individual entities cannot be isolated as chronic and flagrant polluters or that certain individuals will not benefit more than others, as residents of the Los Angeles basin might benefit more from stringently enforced federal auto-emission-control standards than those living in a remote corner of Wyoming. The point is that a fair and just program for assigning costs begins with a recognition that we all bear responsibility for environmental problems and that we all stand to benefit from correcting them.

But even if we agree it is only fair that everyone share the cost of environmental improvement, we can still wonder about how the bill ought to be paid. What would be the fairest way of handling those costs?

COST ALLOCATION

Most would probably agree that environmental pollution cannot be stopped without business and government working together. The main proposals for revitalizing the environment conceptualize government as initiating programs that will prod business into responsible action. The moral question that concerns us, then, is the fairest way of allocating costs for environmental revitalization.

Three approaches have gained the most attention: the use of regulations, incentives, and pricing mechanisms. Although similar in some respects, they carry different assumptions about the roles of government and business, as well as about what's fair and just. Each approach has distinct advantages and weaknesses; each raises some questions of social justice.

Regulations

The regulatory approach makes use of direct public regulation and control in determining how the pollution bill is paid. This approach can take the form of establishing environmental standards through legislation, which are then applied by administrative agencies and courts. An effluent standard, for example, would prohibit industries from releasing more than a certain percentage of fly ash from a smokestack. Thus, a plant would be required to install a fly-ash control device to comply with the standard.

A clear advantage to such a regulatory approach is that standards would be legally enforceable. Firms not meeting them could be fined or even shut down. Also, from the view of morality, such standards would be fair in that they would be applied to all industries in the same way. There are, however, distinct disadvantages in this approach.

First, pollution statutes basically require polluters to use the strongest feasible means of pollution control. But that requires the EPA or some other regulatory body to investigate pollution-control technologies and economic conditions in each industry to find the best technology that companies can afford. Such studies may require tens of thousands of pages of documentation, and legal proceedings may even be necessary before the courts give final approval to the regulation. Moreover, in expecting the EPA to master the economics and technology of dozens of industries, from petrochemicals to steel to electric utilities, we may be unreasonable. It is bound to make mistakes, asking more from some companies than they can ultimately achieve while letting others off too lightly.[22]

Second, there's the question of both the equity and the economic sense of requiring compliance with universal standards, without regard for the idiosyncratic nature of each industry or the particular circumstances of individual firms. Is it reasonable to force two companies that cause very different amounts of environmental damage to spend the same amount on pollution abatement? In one case, the courts required two paper mills on the West Coast to install expensive pollution-control equipment, even though their emissions were harmlessly diluted by the Pacific Ocean. It took a special act of Congress to rescue the mills.[23]

Although universal environmental standards are fair in the sense that they apply to all in the same way, this very fact raises questions about their effectiveness. In attempting to legislate realistic and reliable standards for all, will government so dilute the standards that they become ineffectual? Or consider areas where the environment is cleaner than government standards. In such cases, should an industry be allowed to pollute up to the maximum of the standard? The Supreme Court thinks not. In a case brought before it by the Sierra Club, the Court ruled that states with relatively clean air must prohibit industries from producing significant air pollution even when Environmental Protection Agency (EPA) standards are not violated. In this case a firm is being forced to pay the costs of meeting an environmental standard that, in one sense, is sterner than the one competitors must meet elsewhere.

Regulation can also take away an industry's incentive to do more than the minimum required by law. No polluter has any incentive to discharge less muck than regulations allow. No entrepreneur has an incentive to devise technology that will bring pollution levels below the registered maximum. Moreover, firms have an incentive not to let the EPA know

they can pollute less. And in the regulatory approach, an agency may have the desire to regulate pollution but lack the information to do it efficiently. The position of industry is reversed: It may have the information and the technology but no desire to use it.[24]

Finally, there's the problem of displacement costs resulting from industrial relocation or shutdown due to environmental regulations. For example, Youngstown Sheet and Tube Company moved its corporate headquarters and some production lines to the Chicago area, thus eliminating 500 jobs in Youngstown and causing serious economic problems in nearby communities. One of the reasons for the transfer was the need to implement water-pollution controls, which depleted vital capital. Consider also the marginal firms that would fail while attempting to meet the costs of such standards. When air-pollution regulations were applied to a sixty-year-old cement plant in San Juan Bautista, California, the plant had to close because it was too obsolete to meet the standard economically. The shutdown seriously injured the economy of the town, which had been primarily supported by the cement plant.[25]

On the other hand, if regulations are tougher for new entrants to an industry than for existing firms, as they often are, then new investment may be discouraged—even if newer plants would be cleaner than older ones. Clearly, then, a regulatory approach to environmental improvement, while having advantages, also raises serious questions.

Incentives

A widely supported approach to the problem of cost allocation for environmental improvement is government investment, subsidy, and general economic incentive.

The government might give a firm a tax incentive for the purchase and use of pollution equipment, or it might offer matching grants to companies that install such devices. The advantage of this approach is that it minimizes government interference in business and encourages voluntary action rather than coercing compliance, as in the case of regulation. By allowing firms to move at their own pace, it avoids the evident unfairness to firms that cannot meet regulatory standards and must either relocate or fail. In addition, whereas regulated standards can encourage minimum legal compliance, an incentive approach provides an economic reason for going beyond minimal compliance. Firms have a financial inducement to do more than just meet EPA standards.

But incentives are not without disadvantages that bear moral overtones. First, as an essentially voluntary device, an incentive program is likely to be slow. Environmental problems that cry out for a solution may continue to fester. Incentive programs may allow urgently needed action to be postponed. In addition, any kind of government incentive program amounts to a subsidy for polluters. Polluting firms are being paid not to pollute. Although this approach may sometimes address the economics of pollution more effectively than the regulatory approach, it nonetheless raises questions about the justice of benefiting not the victims of pollution but some of the egregious polluters. This problem grows darker when one realizes that, as indirect government expenditures, incentives rarely involve close government scrutiny. Thus, a firm already guilty of pollution can rather easily bury or manipulate the total costs of antipollution equipment within a nest of other business expenditures reported in tax returns. Not only is the government thereby defrauded, but it is also left without any realistic way of determining the cost-effectiveness payoff of its incentive program.[26]

Pricing Mechanisms

A third approach to the cost-allocation problem involves programs designed to charge firms for the amount of pollution they produce. This could take the form of pricing mechanisms, or effluent charges, which spell out the cost for a specific kind of pollution in a specific area at a specific time. The prices would vary from place to place and from time to time and would be tied to the amount of damage caused. For example, during the summer months in the Los Angeles basin, a firm might pay much higher charges for fly ash emitted into the environment than it would during the winter months. Whatever the set of prices, they would apply equally to every producer of a given type of pollution at the same time and place. The more a firm pollutes, the more it pays.

One advantage in this approach is that it places the cost of pollution control on the polluters. Pricing mechanisms or effluent charges would penalize, not compensate, industrial polluters. For many persons this is inherently more fair than a program that compensates polluters.

Also, because costs are internalized, firms would be encouraged to do more than meet the minimal requirements established under a strict regulatory policy. Under this approach a firm, in theory, could be charged for any amount of pollution and not just incur legal penalties whenever it exceeded an EPA standard. In effect, pollution costs become production costs.

Pollution Permits. Instead of imposing a tax or a fee on the pollutants released into the environment, the government could charge companies for pollution permits. Or it could auction off a limited number of permits. An even more market-oriented approach is to give companies permits to discharge a limited amount of pollution and then to allow them to buy and sell the right to emit pollutants. Companies with low pollution levels can make money by selling their pollution rights to companies with poorer controls. Thus, each firm can estimate the relative costs of continuing to pollute as opposed to investing in cleaner procedures. The government can also set the precise amount of pollution it is prepared to allow and, by lowering the amount permitted over time, can reduce or even eliminate it.[27]

The EPA successfully experimented with this strategy back in the 1970s. It gave oil refineries two years to reduce the allowable lead content in gasoline. Refineries received quotas on lead, which they could then trade with one another. Half the refineries took part in the trading. As a result, they were allowed to phase in the cut at their own pace. But three special features helped the scheme work. First, the amount of lead in gasoline is easy to monitor; second, only a small number of firms were involved; and third, the environmental goals of the program were clear and widely accepted. Attempts by the EPA since then to allow companies to trade air-pollution permits have been less successful.[28]

Although economists generally favor pricing mechanisms and pollution permits, environmentalists and others are troubled by them. For one thing, the pollution costs seem arbitrary. How will effluent charges or permit prices be set? What is a fair price? Any decision seems bound to reflect debatable economic and value judgments. Others worry that companies located in areas with strict environmental controls and expensive pricing plans would operate at a competitive disadvantage. Also, under any pollution pricing or permit scheme, some companies still might fail or be forced to relocate as a result of the new system.

Finally, environmentalists dislike the underlying principle of pricing mechanisms and pollution permits and view with suspicion anything that sounds like a license to pollute. They resent the implication that companies have a right to pollute and reject the notion that companies should be able to make money by selling this right to other firms.

In sum, although each of the approaches to cost allocation has decided advantages, none is without its weak points. Because there appears to be no single, ideal approach to all our environmental problems, a combination of regulation, incentive, effluent charges, and permits is probably called for. Any such combination must take into account not only effectiveness but also fairness to those who will have to foot the bill. Fairness in turn calls for input from all sectors of society, a deliberate commitment on the part of all parties to work in concert, a sizable measure of good faith, and perhaps above all else a heightened sense of social justice. This is no mean challenge.

DEEPER INTO ENVIRONMENTAL ETHICS

So far the discussion of environmental ethics has focused on business's obligation to understand its environmental responsibilities, to acknowledge and internalize it externalities (or spillovers), and to avoid free riding. It has stressed the extent to which environmental protection is in our collective self-interest, and it has looked at the operational and moral dilemmas involved in dealing with the costs of pollution.

The subject of environmental ethics can be pursued deeper than this, and many moral theorists would advocate doing so. In particular, they would insist that we also consider our obligations to those who live outside our society. The United States has 6 percent of the world's population but uses 30 percent of the world's refined oil. Similar figures hold for other irreplaceable natural resources. Moreover, the United States must depend on foreign nations to supply its needs.

The average amount of energy consumed per year by a person in the United States is equivalent to forty-five barrels of oil. By contrast, the average person in China consumes three barrels, in India one barrel, and in Kenya only one-half barrel. The birth of a baby in the United States imposes more than a hundred times the stress on the world's resources as a birth in, say, Bangladesh. Babies from Bangladesh do not grow up to own automobiles and air conditioners or to eat huge quantities of grain-fed beef. Their lifestyles do not require large inputs of minerals and energy, and they do not undermine the planet's life-support capacity.[29]

Tropical rain forests are of special concern. They are the earth's richest, oldest, and most complex ecosystems. Tropical forests are major reservoirs of biodiversity, home to 40 to 50 percent of all types of living things—as many as 5 million species of plants, animals, and insects. At least 50 million acres of tropical rain forest are destroyed each year, or 100 acres every minute. And already half the globe's original rain forest has disappeared.[30] Tropical forests are often cleared in an attempt to provide farms for growing populations of poor people. But the affluence of people in rich nations like the United States is responsible for much forest destruction. Central American forests are cleared in part for pasture land to make pet food and convenience food slightly cheaper in the United States. In Papua, New Guinea, forests are destroyed to supply cardboard packaging for Japanese electronic products. Thus, an American living thousands of miles away can cause more tropical forest destruction than a poor person living within the forest itself.[31]

Our bloated levels of consumption, our dependence on foreign resources to satisfy our needs, and the impact of both on the economies and environments of other nations raise a variety of moral and political issues. This section considers briefly just two of those problems.

First is the question of how the continued availability of foreign resources is to be secured. Will our need for resources outside our territory lead us to dominate other lands, politically and economically, particularly in the Middle East, Asia, and Latin America? To do so is morally risky, because political and economic domination almost always involves violations of the rights and interests of the dom-

inated population, as well as of our own moral ideals and values.

Second is the question of whether any nation has a right to consume the world's irreplaceable resources at a rate so grossly out of proportion to the size of its population. Of course, we pay to consume resources like oil that other nations own, but in the view of many the fact that other nations acquiesce in our disproportionate consumption of resources does not resolve the moral problem of our doing so. Are we respecting the needs and interests of both our present co-inhabitants on this planet and the future generations who will live on earth?

Obligations to Future Generations

Almost everybody feels intuitively that it would be wrong to empty the globe of resources and to contaminate the environment that we pass on to future generations. Certainly there is a strong danger that we will do both of these things. But the question of what moral obligations we have to future generations is surprisingly difficult, and discussion among philosophers has not resolved all the important theoretical issues.

While most of us agree that it would be immoral to make the world uninhabitable for future people, can we talk meaningfully of those future generations having a right that we not do this? After all, our remote descendants are not yet alive and thus cannot claim a right to a livable environment. In fact, since these generations do not yet exist, they cannot at present, it seems, be said to have any interests at all. How can they then have rights?

Professor of philosophy Joel Feinberg argues, however, that whatever future human beings turn out to be like, they will have interests that we can affect, for better or worse, right now. Even though we do not know who the future people will be, we do know that they will have interests and what the general nature of those interests will be. This is enough, he contends, both to talk coherently about their having rights and to impose a duty on us not to leave ecological time bombs for them.

Feinberg concedes that it doesn't make sense to talk about future people having a right to be born. The child that you could conceive tonight, if you felt like it, cannot intelligibly be said to have a right to be born. Thus, the rights of future generations are "contingent," says Feinberg, on those future people coming into existence. But this qualification does not affect his main contention: "The interests that [future people] are sure to have when they come into being . . . cry out for protection from invasions that can take place now."[32]

Even if we are persuaded that future generations have rights, we still do not know exactly what those rights are or how they are to be balanced against the interests and rights of present people. If we substantially injure future generations to gain some small benefit for ourselves, we are being as selfish and short-sighted as we would be by hurting other people today for some slight advantage for ourselves. Normally, however, if the benefits of some environmental policy outweigh the costs, then a strong case can be made for adopting the policy. But what if it is the present generation that receives the benefits and the future generation that pays the costs? Would it be unfair of us to adopt such a policy? Would doing so violate the rights of future people?

An additional puzzle is raised by the fact that policies we adopt will affect who is born in the future. Imagine that we must choose between two environmental policies, one of which would cause a slightly higher standard of living over the next century. Given the effects of those policies on the details of our lives, over time it would increasingly be true that people would marry different people under one policy than they would under the other. And even within the same marriages,

children would increasingly be conceived at different times:

> Some of the people who are later born would owe their existence to our choice of one of the two policies. If we had chosen the other policy, these particular people would never have existed. And the proportion of those later born who owe their existence to our choice would, like ripples in a pool, steadily grow. We can plausibly assume that, after three centuries, there would be no one living in our community who would have been born whichever policy we chose.*

This reasoning suggests that later generations cannot complain about an environmental policy choice we make today that causes them to have fewer opportunities and a lower standard of living. If we had made a different choice, then those people would not have existed at all. On the other hand, it can be claimed that we act immorally in causing people to exist whose rights to equal opportunity and an equally high standard of living cannot be fulfilled. But if those future people knew the facts, would they regret that we acted as we did?[33]

Perhaps it is mistaken to focus on the rights and interests of future people as individuals. Annette Baier argues that the important thing is to "recognize our obligations to consider the good of the continuing human community."[34] This stance suggests adopting a utilitarian perspective and seeking to maximize total human happiness through time. But a utilitarian approach is also not without problems. If our concern is with total happiness, we may be required to increase greatly the earth's population. Even if individuals on an overcrowded earth do not have much happiness, there may still be more total happi-

---

*Derek Parfit, *Reasons and Persons* (New York: Oxford University Press, 1986), 361. Parfit adds: "It may help to think about this question: how many of us could truly claim, 'Even if railways and motor cars had never been invented, I would still have been born'?"

ness than there would be if we followed a population-control policy that resulted in fewer, but better-off, people. This distasteful conclusion has led some utilitarians to modify their theory and maintain that with regard to population policy we should aim for the highest average happiness rather than the highest total happiness.

John Rawls has suggested another approach to the question of our obligations to future generations, an approach that reflects his general theory of justice (which was discussed in Chapter 3). He suggests that the members of each generation put themselves in the "original position." Then, without knowing what generation they belong to, they could decide what would be a just way of distributing resources between adjacent generations. They would have to balance how much they are willing to sacrifice for their descendants against how much they wish to inherit from their predecessors. In other words, the device of the original position and veil of ignorance might be used to determine our obligations to future generations—in particular, how much each generation should save for use by those who inherit the earth from it.[35]

The Value of Nature

A more radical approach to environmental ethics goes beyond the question of our obligations to future generations. It challenges the human-centered approach adopted so far. Implicit in the discussion has been the assumption that preservation of the environment is good solely because it is good for human beings. This reflects a characteristic human attitude that nature has no intrinsic value. It only has value because people value it. If human nature were different and none of us cared about the beauty of, say, the Grand Canyon, then it would be without value.

Many writers on environmental issues do not recognize their anthropocentric, or human-oriented, bias. William F. Baxter is one who

does. In discussing his approach to the pollution problem, Baxter mentions the fact that the use of DDT in food production is causing damage to the penguin population. He writes:

> My criteria are oriented to people, not penguins. Damage to penguins, or sugar pines, or geological marvels is, without more, simply irrelevant. . . . Penguins are important because people enjoy seeing them walk about rocks. . . . In short, my observations about environmental problems will be people-oriented. . . . I have no interest in preserving penguins for their own sake. . . .
>
> I reject the proposition that we *ought* to respect the "balance of nature" or to "preserve the environment" unless the reason for doing so, express or implied, is the benefit of man.[36]

Contrast Baxter's position with what Holmes Rolston III calls the "naturalistic ethic." Advocates of a naturalistic ethic contend, contrary to Baxter's view, "that some natural objects, such as whooping cranes, are morally considerable in their own right, apart from human interests, or that some ecosystems, perhaps the Great Smokies, have intrinsic values, such as aesthetic beauty, from which we derive a duty to respect these landscapes."[37] Human beings may value a mountain for a variety of reasons—because they can hike it, build ski lifts on it, mine the ore deep inside it—or simply because they like looking at it. According to a naturalistic ethic, however, the value of the mountain is not simply a function of these human interests. Nature can have value in and of itself, apart from human beings.

Some defenders of a naturalistic ethic contend that we have a particularly strong obligation to preserve species from extinction. This attitude, shared by many, was one of the factors behind the controversial legal efforts to prevent construction of the Tellico Dam on the Little Tennessee River in order to save the only known population of snail darters. But do species really have value above and beyond the individuals that make them up? Scientists have formally identified 1.4 million species (including, for example, 6,700 kinds of starfish and 12,000 species of earthworms), and recent studies suggest that the number of species inhabiting the planet may be much, much higher—with perhaps as many as 30 million kinds of insects alone. Species are always coming into and going out of existence. How valuable is this diversity of species, and how far are we morally required to go in maintaining it?

Adopting a naturalistic ethic would definitely alter our way of looking at nature and our understanding of our moral obligations to preserve and respect the natural environment. Many philosophers doubt, however, that nature has intrinsic value or that we can be said to have moral duties to nature. Having interests is a precondition, they would contend, of something's having rights or of our having moral duties to that thing. Natural objects, however, have no interests. Can a rock meaningfully be said to have an interest in not being eroded or in not being smashed into smaller pieces?

Plants and trees are different from rocks and streams. They are alive, and we can talk intelligibly about what is good or bad for a tree, plant, or vegetable. They can flourish or do poorly. Nonetheless, philosophers who discuss moral rights generally hold that this is not enough for plants to be said to have rights. To have rights a thing must have genuine interests, and to have interests, most theorists contend, a thing must have beliefs and desires. Vegetative life, however, lacks any cognitive awareness. Claims to the contrary are biologically unsupportable.

Even if the plant world lacks rights, can it still have intrinsic value? Can we still have a moral obligation to respect that world and not abuse it? Or are the only morally relevant values the various interests of human beings

and other sentient creatures? These are hard questions. Among philosophers there is no consensus on how to answer them.

Animals

Above a certain level of complexity, animals do have at least rudimentary cognitive awareness. No owner of a cat or dog doubts that his pet has beliefs and desires. Accordingly, a number of philosophers have recently defended the claim that animals can have rights. Because they have genuine interests, animals can have genuine moral rights—despite the fact that they cannot claim their rights, that they cannot speak, that we cannot reason with them, and that they themselves lack a moral sense. Animals, it is more and more widely contended, do not have to be equal to human beings to have certain moral rights that we must respect.

Rather than talking about animals' rights, utilitarians would stress that higher animals are sentient—that is, that they are capable of feeling pain. Accordingly, there can be no justifiable reason for excluding their pleasures and pains from the overall utilitarian calculus. As Jeremy Bentham, one of the founders of utilitarianism, put it: "The question is not, Can they *reason*? nor, Can they *talk*? but, Can they *suffer*?" Our actions have effects on animals, and these consequences cannot be ignored. When one is deciding, then, what the morally right course of action is, the pleasures and pains of animals must be taken into account too.

Business affects the welfare of animals very substantially. One way is through experimentation and the testing of products on animals. Critics like Peter Singer contend that the vast majority of experimentation and testing cannot be justified on moral grounds. Consider the "LD 50" test, which until very recently was the standard method of testing new foodstuffs. The object of the test is to find the dosage level at which 50 percent of the test animals die. Nearly all test animals become very sick before finally succumbing or surviving. When the substance is harmless, huge doses must be forced down the animals, until in some cases the sheer volume kills them.[38]

In principle, utilitarians are willing to permit testing and experimentation on animals, provided the overall results justify their pain and suffering. Not only is this proviso frequently ignored, but human beings typically disregard altogether the price the animals must pay. Consider the pharmaceutical firm Merck Sharp and Dohme, which sought to import chimpanzees to test a vaccine for hepatitis B. Chimps are an endangered species and highly intelligent. Capturing juvenile chimps requires shooting the mother. One analyst assessed the situation this way:

> The world has a growing population of 4 billion people and a dwindling population of some 50,000 chimpanzees. Since the vaccine seems unusually innocuous, and since the disease is only rarely fatal, it would perhaps be more just if the larger population could find some way of solving its problem that was not to the detriment of the smaller.[39]

Business's largest and most devastating impact on animals, however, is through the production of animal-related products—in particular, meat. Many of us still think of our chicken and beef as coming from something like the idyllic farms pictured in storybooks, where the animals roam contentedly and play with the farmer's children. But meat and egg production is big business, and today most of the animal products we eat are from factory farms. In 1921 the largest commercial egg farm had a flock of 2,000 hens that ran loose in a large pasture. Today the largest commercial flock contains 2.5 million birds, and 80 percent of the 440 million laying hens are housed in 3

percent of the known chicken farms. These birds live in small multitiered wire cages.[40]

Laying hens that are stuffed into tiny cages with several other chickens now produce over 95 percent of our eggs. In these cages, hens are unable to satisfy such fundamental behavioral needs as stretching their wings, perching, walking, scratching, and nest building. Unsuited for wire cages, they suffer foot damage, feather loss, and other injuries. Birds are "debeaked" to prevent pecking injuries and cannibalism from overcrowding.[41]

Of the 95 million hogs born each year in the United States, 80 percent spend their lives in intensive confinement. Piglets are weaned after only three weeks and placed in bare wire cages or tiny cement pens. Once they reach 50 pounds, they are moved into bare 6-foot stalls with concrete-slatted floors. Veal calves have even worse lives. To produce gourmet "milk-fed" veal, newborn calves are taken from their mothers and chained in crates measuring only 22 inches by 54 inches. Here they spend their entire lives. To prevent muscle development and speed weight gain, the calves are allowed absolutely no exercise; they are unable even to turn around or lie down. Their special diet of growth stimulators and antibiotics causes chronic diarrhea, and the withholding of iron to make their meat light-colored makes them anemic. The calves are kept in total darkness to reduce restlessness.[42]

The individuals involved in the meat and animal-products industries are not brutal, but the desire to cut business costs and to economize routinely leads to treatment of animals that can only be described as cruel. Philosopher and animal-rights advocate Tom Regan describes their treatment this way:

> In increasing numbers, animals are being brought in off the land and raised indoors, in unnatural, crowded conditions—raised "intensively," to use the jargon of the animal industry . . . . The inhabitants of these "farms" are kept in

cages, or stalls, or pens . . . living out their abbreviated lives in a technologically created and sustained environment: automated feeding, automated watering, automated light cycles, automated waste removal, automated what-not. And the crowding: as many as 9 hens in cages that measure 18 by 24 inches; veal calves confined to 22 inch wide stalls; hogs similarly confined, sometimes in tiers of cages, two, three, four rows high. Could any impartial, morally sensitive person view what goes on in a factory farm with benign approval?[43]

When it comes to the protection of animals, England has stricter laws than the United States. Consider, then, the following proposals for protecting commercially farmed animals, which were turned down by the British government as being too idealistic and unrealistic: (1) Any animal should have room to turn around. (2) A dry bed should be provided for all stock. (3) Palatable roughage must be readily available to all calves after one week of age. (4) Cages for poultry should be large enough for a bird to be able to stretch one wing at a time.[44]

Moral vegetarians are people who reject the eating of meat on moral grounds. Their argument is simple and powerful: The raising of animals for meat, especially with modern factory farming, sacrifices the most important and basic interests of animals simply to satisfy human tastes. Americans eat, per capita, a phenomenal amount of meat, by some estimates twice as much as we ate in 1950. Many people eat meat three times a day. Our preference for a Big Mac over a soybean burger, however, is only a matter of taste and culture, and the extra pleasure we believe we get from eating the hamburger cannot justify the price the animal must pay.

Would it be wrong to eat animals that were raised humanely, like those who run around freely and happily in children's picture books of farms? Unlike the lives of animals that we do in fact eat, the lives of such humanely raised animals, before being abruptly terminated, are not painful ones. Some philosophers would contend that it is permissible to raise animals for food if their lives are, on balance, positive. Other moral theorists challenge this view, contending that at least higher animals have a right to life and should not be killed.

This debate raises important philosophical issues; but it is also rather hypothetical. Given economic reality, mass production of meat at affordable prices dictates factory farming. The important moral issue, then, is the real suffering and unhappy lives that billions of creatures experience on the way to our dinner tables. This aspect of environmental ethics is often overlooked, but it raises profound and challenging questions for both business and consumers.

SUMMARY

1. Business functions within a global ecological system. Because of the interrelated nature of ecosystems, and because intrusion into ecosystems frequently creates unfavorable effects, business must be sensitive to its impact on the physical environment.

2. Traditionally, business has regarded the natural world as a free and unlimited good. Pollution and resource depletion are examples of situations in which each person's pursuit of self-interest can make everyone worse off (the "tragedy of the commons"). Business must be sensitive to possible disparities between its private economic costs and the social costs of its activities (the problems of "externalities" or spillovers).

3. Companies that attempt to be "free riders" in environmental matters or that refuse to address the external costs of their business activities behave unfairly. Some philoso-

phers maintain, further, that each person has a human right to a livable environment.

4. Pollution control has a price, and trade-offs have to be made. But weighing costs and benefits involves controversial factual assessments and value judgments. Any equitable solution to the problem of who should pay must recognize that all of us in some way contribute to the problem and benefit from correcting it.

5. Cost allocation requires a combination of regulations, incentives, and charges or permits for polluting. Such an approach must not only consider what is effective but must also seek a fair assignment of costs.

6. A broader view of environmental ethics considers our obligations to those in other societies and to future generations. Some philosophers argue that we must respect the right of future generations to inherit an environment that is not seriously damaged, but talk of the rights of future people raises puzzles.

7. Philosophers disagree about whether nature has intrinsic value. Some, adopting a human-oriented point of view, contend that the environment is valuable only because human beings value it. Those adopting a naturalistic ethic believe that the value of nature is not simply a function of human interests.

8. Through experimentation, testing, and the production of animal products, business has a very substantial impact on the welfare of animals. The meat and animal-products industries rely on factory-farming techniques, which many describe as cruel and horrible. Because of these conditions, moral vegetarians argue that meat eating is wrong.

CASE 11.1
BKK: The Story of a Waste Site

On an otherwise uneventful Tuesday night in July 1984, police ordered nineteen families out of their homes in West Covina, one of the many cities in the megalopolis of Los Angeles. They were told that their health was jeopardized by high levels of methane and vinyl chloride gases, which had been escaping from the nearby BKK landfill into their homes.

When a plastics company makes a plastic razor or ballpoint pen, it must dispose of vinyl chloride, which tends to cause cancer when inhaled above acceptable levels. Until 1980, vinyl chloride was discarded at the BKK landfill — that is, in the middle of a city of more than 80,000 people. When authorities roused families out of their quarters that quiet summer evening, they did so because fumes of the deadly chemical were seeping into nearby homes at a rate ninety-nine times the acceptable standard.

Local officials quickly began urging the Environmental Protection Agency (EPA) to do something and do it fast. But amidst the urgent pleas could be heard skeptical voices doubting that the EPA would take quick and decisive action.

The skeptics had some basis for doubting the EPA's resolve. One California Representative, Vic Fazio, asserted that the EPA "omitted and ignored" 120 sites in its survey of waste dumps at federal installations and laboratories. He pointed to a study done by the General Accounting Office indicating that some of the federal government's own facilities might be more threatening to health than private-sector waste sites like BKK. Fazio charged that the EPA simply had not been aggressive enough in dealing with federal waste sites, and he wanted legislation forcing the agency to set up strict rules and schedules for waste cleanup at federal installations.[45]

Fueling the case made by Fazio and other EPA critics was a nineteen-state survey conducted by an environmental coalition group, the National Campaign Against Toxic Hazards. The survey, said its sponsors, found that nearly 60 percent of toxic-waste dumps marked for cleanup since 1983 under the federal "Superfund" program remained basically untouched. But EPA official Russell A. Dawson said the survey masked "substantial work" that would soon double at targeted Superfund sites.[46] Environmentalists treated Dawson's assurance as so much eyewash. But they hoped that the toxic-hazards report would pressure Congress into expanding the scope and activities of Superfund.

"These sites are not like fine wine," said John O'Connor, director of the Toxic Hazards Campaign. "They get worse with age, and they get more difficult and costly to clean up."[47]

Meanwhile, Representative Esteban E. Torres, whose district included the BKK landfill, was calling on the EPA to shut down the dump immediately. Federal law, Torres pointed out, allows the EPA head to close a landfill when, in the administrator's view, it "may present an imminent and substantial endangerment to health or the environment." "All he [the EPA head] has to prove is that the BKK landfill is a public nuisance," said Torres. He added, "I am sure he can prove it, but he refuses to exercise his discretion at this time."[48]

Reacting to the pressures, federal and state officials urged the BKK Corporation, operators of the landfill, to close the site. On September 26, 1984, BKK officials announced that as of November 30 it would stop receiving liquid and solid hazardous wastes. But Kenneth Kazarian, vice president of BKK, wanted to make it clear that BKK was not being forced into the decision. The company, he said, was simply withdrawing its request to be granted a permanent federal permit to operate a hazardous landfill.

An official from the Health Services Department welcomed the BKK decision. "That will put them out of the hazardous waste business entirely," he said. Meanwhile, state and federal officials were assuring West Covina residents that the landfill presented "no imminent danger to public health." They added that after November 30 as many as forty trucks a day carrying toxic waste to BKK would be rerouted to landfills in other California counties.[49]

But not everyone received news of the dump shutdown with enthusiasm. One California Assemblyman, whose district includes BKK, immediately called for a hearing to determine whether the landfill is safe. "If this is the great solution we've been hearing about . . . I'm very disappointed," he said.[50]

And grumbles of protest reverberated within the counties earmarked for the diverted toxic wastes. One of the most emphatic cries of outrage came from Santa Barbara County, where former President Reagan has his ranch. Just a few months earlier, a truck carrying toxic waste had overturned and jackknifed while passing through the city of Santa Barbara en route to a nearby dump site. The toxins discarded in the accident caused officials to shut down the highway for several hours and evacuate people from nearby homes and businesses.

Moreover, word of the BKK closure did nothing to deter Representative Torres from seeking support for a bill he was sponsoring in the House of Representatives. The bill would require hazardous-waste landfill operators to conduct health-effects studies for areas around their facilities. The legislation would make it possible for people living near a toxic waste site to make an informed judgment about possible hazards to their health.

Discussion Questions

1. Identify the values and describe the attitudes that have contributed to the problems associated with toxic waste sites.

2. What would your reaction be if you were a citizen of a county to which toxic wastes were being diverted? How should we handle the problem of toxic-waste disposal?

3. Who do you think should pay the costs of cleaning up a site like BKK?

4. What obligations do we have to future generations in the disposal of our toxic wastes?

5. Do you think the EPA should have shut down BKK? Why?

6. Do you think the BKK Corporation had a moral obligation to shut down the landfill, even if it was not legally forced to? Explain by appeal to ethical principles.

CASE 11.2
The Valley of Death

It is called Brazil's "valley of death," and it may be the most polluted place on the earth. It lies about an hour's drive south of São Paulo, where the land suddenly drops 2,000 feet to a coastal plane. More than 100,000 people live in the valley, along with a variety of industrial plants that discharge thousands of tons of pollutants into the air every day. A reporter for *National Geographic* recalls that, within an hour of his arrival in the valley, his chest began aching as the polluted air inflamed his bronchial tubes and restricted his breathing.[51]

The air in the valley is rich with toxins — among them benzene, a known carcinogen. One in ten of the area's factory workers has a low white-blood-cell count, a possible precursor to leukemia. Infant mortality is 10 percent higher here than in the state as a whole. Out of 40,000 urban residents in the valley municipality of Cubatão, nearly 13,000 cases of respiratory disease were reported in a recent year.

Few of the local inhabitants complain, however. For them, the fumes smell of jobs. They also distrust bids to buy their property by local industry, which wants to expand, as well as government efforts to relocate them to free homesites on a landfill. One young mother says, "Yes, the children are often ill and sometimes can barely breathe. We want to live in another place, but we cannot afford to."

A university professor of public health, Dr. Oswaldo Campos views the dirty air in Cubatão simply as the result of economic priorities. "Some say it is the price of progress," Campos comments, "but is it? Look who pays the price — the poor."

Discussion Questions

1. What attitudes and values on the part of business and others lead to the creation of areas like the "valley of death"?

2. Some say "pollution is the price of progress." Is this slogan correct? What is meant by "progress"? Who does pay the price? Explain both the economic and the moral issues raised by the slogan.

3. It might be argued that, if the people of the valley don't complain and don't wish to move, then they accept the risks of living there and the polluters are not violating their rights. Assess this argument.

CASE 11.3
Sharing the Blame

SCENE: The office of the director of a midwestern advertising agency
CHARACTERS: Donna Ellis, assistant director of advertising; Bryan Lavelle, director
SITUATION: Donna Ellis is vehemently protesting the agency's complicity in an ad campaign commissioned by Mid-Valley Gas and Electric, a utility firm with pronounced antienvironmental tendencies. Mid-Valley has consistently propagandized for increased electric power use. Its latest campaign solicits public support to build more power plants. Some persons doubt whether such plants are needed. Vigorously promoting less power use might accomplish what additional plants would be intended to do. Ellis is particularly incensed about a leaflet her agency has worked up to accompany the bills consumers will receive in the months ahead. The content of the leaflet is captured in the bold-print headline on the first page. It reads: "Balance Ecology with Power."

Ellis: The point is that ecology is not a thing to be balanced against anything else.

Lavelle: What do you mean?

Ellis: I mean this ad is tremendously misleading. It misses the whole concept of ecology, its essential meaning. "Ecology" refers to a science of the interrelatedness of everything. To speak of balancing it with anything else is just plain dumb. In fact, it's downright distorting. It gives the impression that somehow we must be just as concerned with energy as we are with ecology.

Lavelle: But isn't that true?

Ellis: It's not so much a question of truth as one of emphasis and impact within an advertising gestalt.

Lavelle: Gestalt?

Ellis: That's right. Look, we both know that for years now Mid-Valley has been trying to get people to use more power. Now with the energy crunch on, they're obviously concerned with maintaining their mind-boggling profits while not appearing to be callously indifferent to environmental concerns. The result is this ad. Taken within the total framework of where Mid-Valley's coming from, it amounts to a not-so-subtle pitch calculated to marshal public support for building additional power plants, which they've already begun to lobby for in Washington and in the state capital.

Lavelle: But you can't expect them not to. I mean, calling for power conservation and a moratorium on plant construction just isn't in their best business interests.

Ellis: Obviously. But that doesn't mean we should assist them in furthering what may be of highly questionable social value.

Lavelle: But Donna, that's totally unrealistic. You're asking us to sit in judgment of the moral worth of our clients' interests.

Ellis: I'm suggesting that on matters as serious as a firm's environmental responsibilities, we must act in a socially responsible way.

Lavelle: You realize, of course, that we already devote 20 percent of our advertising time to what we consider sound social causes? Nobody can accuse this agency of being socially indifferent.

Ellis: But that's a cop-out. Remember, only a small fraction of that time is earmarked for environmental matters. What's worse, it seems to me we're undoing what little good we may be achieving when we run ads like this. It talks about the research necessary to deal with environmental pollution, but we both know Mid-Valley has done no research at all.

Lavelle: But it's not our job to sit in judgment of our clients' interests. That's the job of government.

Ellis: But certainly we should sit in judgment of our own activities, shouldn't we?

Lavelle: Okay, let's do that, let's really do it. Do you think we'd be doing the right thing if we jeopardized Mid-Valley's three-million-dollar annual account with us by imposing our own environmental philosophy on their ads or telling them to peddle their propaganda elsewhere? What about our stockholders? Our own employees? Our other accounts? We've got obligations to them as well, you know.

Ellis: Sure we do, but that shouldn't blind us to our social obligations. Simply because we function in this society as information communicators, we're not relieved of the obligation to examine the likely impact of that information, the impressions it gives, the opinions it helps form, the attitudes it molds. That we ourselves don't operate belching smokestacks or discharge waste into rivers doesn't mean we have no business responsibilities to the environment. The fact is that on environmental questions our role is a pivotal one. We control what the most obvious vested interests can say to generate public opinion. If Mid-Valley persists in behaving in an environmentally irresponsible way, we share the blame.

Lavelle: Donna, I hear what you're saying and appreciate your concerns, but this is a decision I'm going to have to mull over. I may even have to go to the board.

Ellis: I think you should.

Discussion Questions

1. Is Donna Ellis right in speaking out? Would you, too, be critical of Mid-Valley's campaign?

2. What should Lavelle do? If he takes the matter to the board, what do you think the board should do?

3. With respect to the environment, do you think advertising agencies have any general responsibilities?

4. If the board chooses to take no action, what should Donna Ellis do?

CASE 11.4
Rewrapping the Big Mac

Consumers don't much like campaigns that promote corporate donations to environmental groups and causes. In the spring of 1990 Minute Maid started running advertisements urging consumers to send in 75 cents and a proof-of-purchase seal, after which the company would "help keep America growing and beautiful" by matching each donation with equal money and a planted redwood seedling. When only 8,500 donations came in, Minute Maid's redwood campaign sputtered embarrassingly to a halt. Worse yet from the company's point of view, it was soon caught up in a flap with environmentalists who publicly pointed out that Minute Maid's juice cartons were not recyclable.

A recent study, in fact, establishes the not-so-surprising fact that Americans quite sensibly prefer companies to clean up their own environmental problems before trying to hitch their names and products to the green bandwagon.[52] Perhaps an appreciation of this fact was behind McDonald's decision in November of that year to do away with its fa-"clamshell"-style, polystyrene foam hamburger box and switch to paper packaging. This decision came as an abrupt one because only a week before the company had been preparing to respond to public pressure for a cleaner environment by announcing that it would extend its limited plastics-recycling program to all of its 8,500 restaurants.

The company continues to insist that its foam packaging was environmentally sound. But "our customers just don't feel good about it," said Edward H. Rensi, the president of McDonald's U.S.A. "So we're changing." McDonald's, which has gone beyond selling hamburgers to become a kind of national institution, knew that the last thing it needed was to have schoolchildren told that its products were damaging society. As one commentator put it, "If it appeared to be putting profit over the environment by stubbornly staying with a material widely regarded as detrimental to the environment, the company risked alienating many of the same younger customers who avoided buying tuna caught by methods that kill dolphins." "Customer demands are changing," adds a design firm executive. "In the past, convenience was the most important attribute of a package. Now there is a new need: to be sensitive to the environment."

One person who helped drive this message home to President Rensi was Frederic D. Krupp, executive director of the Environmental Defense Fund. When he learned that McDonald's had decided to stick with recycling, he called Rensi personally to air his objections. Krupp let McDonald's know that the Environmental Defense Fund was prepared to oppose publicly the recycling program if the company went ahead with it. Krupp and the Fund are not against recycling, but they felt that the benefit of a switch in materials was greater. "The hierarchy is this: reduce, reuse, and recycle," Krupp says, adding that "the new packaging has 90 percent less bulk than foam." Krupp also argued that switching to paper would save McDonald's money, something Rensi now says the company already knew.

In any case, Krupp's intervention prompted a top-level management review and, after years of defending the use of foam, a swift reversal of policy. So swift in fact that Allen Hershkowitz, a senior scientist with the Natural Resources Defense Council, says, "This is a case for the business schools. The decision was made in the last 72 hours. You get the impression they do something and then try to figure out what it means."

While some applaud the plastic-to-paper decision as proof that corporations and environmentalists can work together, others, especially those in the polystyrene packaging industry, resent what they see as McDonald's caving in to the ill-considered demands of the environmental lobby. "This came as a shock to us," reports R. Jerry Johnson, president of the polystyrene packagers' trade association. "We have been working for ten years with these guys on recycling." Joseph W. Bow, president of the Foodservice and Packaging Institute, adds, "This is a big deal to us because of the fact that McDonald's bowed to public pressure. We want to see a free economy where materials are used based on their advantages, not on the wishes of powerful groups."

In terms of design, there's no question that the old foam carton was a packaging success. Not only did it protect the hamburger, but its revolutionary design allowed it to latch itself; all an employee had to do was shove it shut. And it was ideal for maintaining the hamburger at an appropriate temperature; even McDonald's concedes that their new containers will not be as good as foam at retaining heat. The company's critics see the pressure on McDonald's simply as an environmentalist attack on a major symbol of the throwaway, fast-food lifestyle. "This is not about polystyrene," says John Giroux, president of the Amoco subsidiary that supplied foam packaging to McDonald's, noting that the material is widely used throughout the food industry — for example, in egg cartons, which have not come under attack. Other commentators join him, seeing the pressure on McDonald's as one more ill-informed, middle-class enthusiasm of the environmental movement. And some environmentalists agree.

"Using a lot more paper means a lot more pollution," points out Jan Beyea, a scientist at the National Audubon Society. "It is a mistake to make plastic the great satan and paper the great saint." For one thing, polystyrene can be recycled, while McDonald's new paper packaging cannot because of its multi-layered construction. Furthermore, the production of paper packaging requires significantly more energy than polystyrene manufacture, and it produces more atmospheric emissions and waterborne wastes.

Ironically, McDonald's introduced its clamshell foam box in 1975, replacing its earlier paper packaging, in part because of environmental concerns. At the time, an independent study by the Stanford Research Institute had reported: "There appears to be no supportable basis for any claim that paper-related products are superior from an environmental standpoint to plastic-related ones, including polystyrene. The weight of existing evidence indicates that the favorable true environmental balance, if any, would be in the direction of the plastic-related product." Chuck Ebeling, director of communications for McDonald's, acknowledges that the foam boxes were considered environmentally innovative. "There was a lot of concern about paper [then]," he says. "Getting out of paper was considered a real progressive move."

Discussion Questions

1. Describe the factors that prompted McDonald's decision. Why do you think it reversed its long-standing policy so quickly? To what extent was the company motivated by a genuine concern for the environment and to what extent by self-interest?

2. Do you agree with the decision? Was it an environmentally sound one? Should the issue have been studied further?

3. What were McDonald's moral obligations in this case? How should we address the problem of fast-food packaging, waste, and recycling?

4. Was the pressure applied by the Environmental Defense Fund and other environmentalists a good thing, or was it, as Johnson and Bow intimate, an illegitimate intrusion into a business decision? Does such pressure cause the environmental issues to be oversimplified, or is it necessary to ensure that companies behave responsibly toward the environment?

5. Critics of the decision claim that environmentalists focused on McDonald's because the company symbolizes a throwaway, fast-food culture that they don't like, and not because its cartons were particularly damaging to the environment. Do you agree?

NOTES

1. Tom Regan, ed., *Earthbound: Introductory Essays in Environmental Ethics* (New York: Random House, 1984), 3.

2. Margaret Engel, "A Mystery in Puerto Rico: Why Babies Menstruate," *Washington Post National Weekly Edition*, October 1, 1984, 7.

3. Lewis Regenstein, *America the Poisoned* (Washington, D.C.: Acropolis Books, 1982), 861. Quoted in Regan, *Earthbound*, 4.

4. "Tolerating Pesticides," reprinted in the *International Herald Tribune*, November 18, 1987.

5. Regenstein, 182. Quoted in Regan, 4.

6. "Grime and Punishment," *The New Republic*, February 20, 1989, 7.

7. "U.S. Reveals How Much Industry Pollutes the Air," *San Francisco Chronicle*, March 23, 1989, A1.

8. Philip Shabecoff, "In Search of a Better Law to Clear the Air," *New York Times*, May 14, 1989, 4–1.

9. Lewis Lipsitz and David M. Speak, *American Democracy*, 2nd ed. (New York: St. Martin's Press, 1989), 569.

10. In 1991 meteorologists reported that 1990 had been the hottest year since records began and that six of the seven warmest years in a century have occurred since 1980. For more on global warming, see Bill McKibben, "Is the World Getting Hotter?" *New York Review of Books*, December 8, 1988, 7.

11. "Toxic Waste Data Made Public," *San Francisco Chronicle*, June 20, 1989, A8.

12. Lipsitz and Speak, *American Democracy*, 574.

13. Ibid., 575.

14. Manuel G. Velasquez, *Business Ethics: Concepts and Cases* (Englewood Cliffs, N.J.: Prentice-Hall, 1982), 183.

15. "*Playboy* Interview: Dr. Paul Ehrlich," *Playboy*, August 1970, 56.

16. John Steinbeck, *America and Americans* (New York: Viking Press, 1966), 127.

17. Garrett Hardin, "The Tragedy of the Commons," *Science* 162 (December 13, 1968): 1243–1248.

18. William T. Blackstone, "Ethics and Ecology," in William T. Blackstone, ed., *Philosophy and Environmental Crisis* (Athens: University of Georgia Press, 1974).

19. Keith Davis and Robert L. Blomstrom, *Business and Society* (New York: McGraw-Hill, 1975), 439.

20. This figure is from Paul R. Ehrlich and Anne H. Ehrlich, "Population, Plenty, and Poverty," *National Geographic*, December 1988, 935. Other figures in this paragraph are derived from *The World Almanac, 1989* (New York: Pharos Books, 1988).

21. Ehrlich and Ehrlich, "Population, Plenty, and Poverty," 938.

22. "Grime and Punishment," *The New Republic*, 7.

23. Ibid.

24. Ibid., 8.

25. Davis and Blomstrom, *Business and Society*, 440.

26. See George Steiner, *Business and Society* (New York: Random House, 1973), 247.

27. "A Survey of the Environment," *The Economist*, September 2, 1989, 7; "Grime and Punishment," 8. See also James Marks, "Meet the Master of Smokestack Magic," *Business Month*, June 1990.

28. "Survey of the Environment," *The Economist*, 8.

29. Ehrlich and Ehrlich, "Population, Plenty, and Poverty," 917.

30. Catherine Caufield, "Paradise Lost," *San Francisco Chronicle* ("This World"), October 1, 1989, 19.

31. Ehrlich and Ehrlich, "Population, Plenty, and Poverty," 917.

32. Joel Feinberg, "The Rights of Animals and Unborn Generations," in Tom L. Beauchamp and Norman E. Bowie, eds., *Ethical Theory and Business*, 2nd ed. (Englewood Cliffs, N.J.: Prentice-Hall, 1983), 435.

33. Derek Parfit, *Reasons and Persons* (New York: Oxford University Press, 1986), 365.

34. Annette Baier, "The Rights of Past and Future Persons," in Joseph R. DesJardins and John J. McCall, eds., *Contemporary Issues in Business Ethics* (Belmont, Calif.: Wadsworth, 1985), 501.

35. See John Rawls, *A Theory of Justice* (Cambridge, Mass.: Harvard University Press, 1971), 284–293.

36. William F. Baxter, "People or Penguins," in Donald VanDeVeer and Christine Pierce, eds., *People, Penguins, and Plastic Trees* (Belmont, Calif.: Wadsworth, 1986), 215–216.

37. Holmes Rolston III, "Just Environmental Business," in Tom Regan, ed., *Just Business: New Introductory Essays in Business Ethics* (New York: Random House, 1984), 325.

38. Peter Singer, "Animal Liberation," *New York Review of Books*, April 5, 1973.

39. Quoted by Rolston, "Just Environmental Business," 340.

40. Tom L. Beauchamp, *Case Studies in Business, Society, and Ethics* (Englewood Cliffs, N.J.: Prentice-Hall, 1983), 118–119.

41. Bradley S. Miller, "The Dangers of Factory Farming," *Business and Society Review* 65 (Spring 1988): 44.

42. Ibid., 43, 44.

43. Tom Regan, "Ethical Vegetarianism and Commercial Animal Farming," in Richard A. Wasserstrom, ed., *Today's Moral Problems*, 3rd ed. (New York: Macmillan, 1985), 463–464.

44. Singer, "Animal Liberation."

45. Roberta A. Rosenblatt, "Toxic Flow From Acid Pits Creates Water Basin Peril," *Los Angeles Times*, August 7, 1984, II-2.

46. See Michael Wines, "Waste Dumps Untouched, Survey Says," *Los Angeles Times*, September 7, 1984, I-5.

47. Ibid.

48. Esteban E. Torres, "Solution to BKK's Hazards Starts with Closing It Now," *Los Angeles Times*, August 6, 1984, II-5.

49. Mark Gladstone, "BKK Landfill to Cease All Hazardous Waste Dumping," *Los Angeles Times*, September 27, 1984, II-1.

50. Ibid.

51. See Noel Grove, "Air: An Atmosphere of Uncertainty," *National Geographic* 171 (April 1987), from which this case study and the quotations below are drawn.

52. Joann S. Lublin, "'Green' Ads Can Make Consumer See Red," *Wall Street Journal*, December 5, 1990, B4. The rest of this case study is based on John Holusha, "Packaging and Public Image: McDonald's Fills a Big Order" and Patricia Leigh Brown, "A Symbol of America's Fast-Food Culture," *New York Times*, November 2, 1990, and Warren T. Brookes, "How McDonald's Caved in to Environmental Yuppies," *San Francisco Chronicle*, December 11, 1990, C3. See also Charles Petit, "Plastic Finds Friend in Canadian Chemist," *San Francisco Chronicle*, February 2, 1991, A6.

The Environmental Crisis and the Quality of Life

Nicholas Rescher

While agreeing that attempts to clean up the environment are noble, Professor Rescher believes that they are too little, too late. In Rescher's view, society simply must learn to live with scarce environmental goods and scale down its expectations for the quality of life accordingly. Our ideas about material progress, our faith in the power of technology, and our hope for a perfect future will all have to give way, Rescher argues, as a result of the environmental crisis.

Introduction

Most of us tend to think of the environmental crisis as resulting from "too much" — too much pollution, wastage, pesticide, and so forth. But from the economists' angle the problem is one of *scarcity*: too little clean air, pure water, recreationally usable land, safe fruit. The answer traditional among welfare economists to problems of scarcity is based singlemindedly on the leading idea of *production*. But alas the things which the environmental crisis leaves in too short supply — fresh air, clean rivers, unpolluted beaches, and the like are not things to which the standard, traditional concept of the production of goods and services — or anything like it — will be applicable. The project of *producing* another planet earth to live on after we have used this one up is unfortunately unfeasible.

For reasons such as this, various economists — Kenneth Boulding most prominent among them — have urged a broadening of economic horizons and redeployment of concern. Economics is to deal not just narrowly with the production and consumption of goods and services but broadly with the maintenance of a quality of life. Such a reorientation of welfare economics has profound consequences. It once again renders relevant to economics the traditional concerns of the philosopher with matters of norms and values, of ideology and the rational structure of social appraisal.

It is from this philosophical vantage point — not ignoring the concerns of the economist and sociologist and social psychologist but seeking to transcend the bounds of their disciplinary bailiwicks — that I should like to consider the impact of the environmental crisis.

Most of the discussions of the environmental crisis in which I have been a participant or witness are basically exercises in social uplift. The lesson is driven home that if only we are good and behave ourselves everything will come out just fine. To adopt more stringent legislation of control, to subject grasping enterprise to social pressure, to adopt better social values and attitudes, to espouse the program and ideology of planned parenthood or women's lib, to hand the control of affairs over to those who are younger and purer of heart . . . so runs the gamut of remedies which their respective advocates would have us adopt and which, once adopted, will—so we are told—put everything to rights. Throughout this stance there runs the fundamentally activistic optimism of the American experience: virtue will be rewarded; and by the end of the sixth reel, the good guys will be riding off into the glorious sunset.

My aim is to dash some cold water on all this. I want to propose the deeply pessimistic suggestion that, crudely speaking, the environment has had it and that we simply cannot "go home again" to "the good old days" of environmental purity. We all know of the futile laments caused by the demise of the feudal order by such thinkers as Thomas More or the ruralistic yearnings voiced by the romantics in the early days of the Industrial Revolution. Historical retrospect may well cast the present spate of hand-wringing over environmental deterioration as an essentially analogous—right-minded but utterly futile—penchant for the easier, simpler ways of bygone days. Actually even to think of the problem as an environmental crisis is tendentious. Crises are by definition transitory phenomena: they point toward a moment of decision for life or death, not toward a stable condition of things. The very terminology indicates an unwillingness to face the prospect of a serious environmental degradation as a permanent reality, an ongoing "fact of life."

To take this view goes deep against the grain, and I have little hope of persuading many people of its correctness. I certainly do not like it myself. But perhaps it could be granted—at least for the sake of discussion—that the view might be correct. Granting this hypothesis, let us explore its implications.

First let me be clearer about the hypothesis itself. I am not saying that environmental activism is futile—that man cannot by dint of energy and effort manage to clean up this or that environmental mess. What I am saying is that we may simply be unable to solve the environmental crisis as a whole: that once this or that form of noxiousness is expelled from one door some other equally bad version comes in by another. My hypothesis in short is that the environmental crisis may well be incurable. It just may be something that we cannot solve but have to learn to live with.

This hypothesis is surely not altogether unrealistic and fanciful. Basically the environmental mess is a product of the conspiration of three forces: (1) high population densities, (2) high levels of personal consumption, and (3) a messy technology of production. Can one even realistically expect that any of these can really be eliminated? Not the population crunch surely. As the character remarked in a recent "Peanuts" cartoon: "Everybody says there are too many of us, but nobody wants to leave." So much for population. Moreover, lots of people everywhere in the world are clamoring for affluence and a place on the high-consumption bandwagon, and pitifully few are jumping off. . . .

The Escalation of Expectations

The concept of social *progress* is deeply, almost irremovably, impressed on the American consciousness. And this is so not just in the remote past but very much in our own day. Take just the most recent period since World War II. Consider the marked signs of progress:

1. The increase of life expectancy (at birth) from sixty-three years in 1940 to seventy years in 1965.

2. The rise of per capita personal income from $1,810 in 1950 to $2,542 in 1965 (in constant [1958] dollars).

3. The increase in education represented by a rise in school enrollments from 44 percent of the five-to-thirty-four-year-old group in 1950 to 60 percent in 1965.

4. The growth of social welfare expenditures from $88 per capita in 1945 to $360 per capita in 1965 (in constant [1958] dollars).

Taken together, these statistics bring into focus the steady and significant improvement in the provisions for individual comfort and social welfare that has taken place in the United States since World War II. If the progress-oriented thesis that increased physical well-being brings increased happiness were correct, one would certainly expect Americans to be substantially happier today than ever before. This expectation is not realized. In fact, the available evidence all points the reverse way.

. . . We are facing . . . an escalation of expectations, a raising of the levels of expectations with corresponding increased aspirations in the demands people make upon the circumstances and conditions of their lives. With respect to the requisites of happiness, we are in the midst of a revolution of rising expectations, a revolution that affects not only the man at the bottom, but operates throughout, to the very top of the heap.

This supposition of an escalation of expectations regarding the quality of life, and correspondingly of aspirations regarding the requisites of happiness, finds striking confirmation in the fact that despite the impressive signs that people think of themselves as less happy than their predecessors of a generation or so ago, they would be unwilling to contemplate a return to what we hear spoken of (usually cynically) as the good old days.

. . . This sort of perception of unhappiness has a surprising twist to it. It indicates a deep faith in progress—a progression of steady improvement in the circumstances of life, however little we may actually savor this improvement in terms of increased happiness.

Some Ideological Victims

Let us now return in the light of these considerations to my initial hypothesis. If in the continued unfolding an ongoing environmental crisis occurs, various conceptions integral to the American social ideology will have to go by the board: in particular the conceptions of material progress, of technological omnipotence, and of millennial orientation.

Material Progress

. . . A parting of the ways with the concept of progress will not come easy to us. It's going to take a lot of doing to accustom us to the idea that things are on balance to get worse or at any rate no better as concerns the quality of life in this nation. (And once we are persuaded of this, there may be vast social and political repercussions in terms of personal frustration and social unrest.) The conception of a deescalation of expectations, of settling for less

than we've been accustomed to, is something Americans are not prepared for. We have had little preparatory background for accepting the realization that in some key aspects in the quality of life the best days may be behind us. I myself very much doubt that we are going to take kindly to the idea. The British have made a pretty good show of having to haul down the flag of empire. You will, I hope, forgive me for evincing skepticism about our ability to show equally good grace when the time comes to run down our banner emblazoned with "Standard of Living."

Technological Omnipotence

The conception of get-it-done confidence, virtually of technological omnipotence, runs deep in the American character. We incline to the idea that, as a people, we can do anything we set our mind to. In a frontier nation there was little tendency toward a serious recognition of limits of any sort. The concept of finite resources, the reality of opportunity costs, the necessity for *choice* in the allocation of effort and the inescapable prospect of unpleasant consequences of choices (negative externalities) are newcomers to American thinking. This era of economic awareness and recognition of the realities of cost-benefit analysis is so recent it has hardly trickled down to the popular level.

The course of our historical experience has not really prepared us to face the realities of finiteness and incapacity. We expect government to "handle things"—not only the foreign wars, economic crises, and social disorders of historical experience, but now the environmental crises as well. The idea that our scientific technology and the social technology of our political institutions may be utterly inadequate to the task does not really dawn on us. If and when it finally does, you may be sure that the fur will fly.

Millennial Hankerings

Americans have manifested more millennial hankerings than perhaps any other people since the days when apocalyptic thinking was in fashion. The idea that a solution to our problems lies somehow just around the corner is deeply ingrained in our consciousness. Nobody knows the themes to which people resonate better than politicians. And from Woodrow Wilson's Fourteen Points to Franklin Roosevelt's New Deal to the quality-of-life rhetoric of Lyndon Johnson's campaign the fundamentally millennial nature of our political rhetoric is clear. "Buy our program, accept our policies, and everything in the country will be just about perfect." That is how the politicians talk, and they do so because that is what people yearn to hear. We can accept deprivation now as long as we feel assured that prosperity lies just around the corner. No political campaign is complete without substantial pandering to our millennial yearnings through assurances that if only we put the right set of men in office all our troubles will vanish and we can all live happily ever after. We as a nation have yet to learn the unpleasant lesson that such pie-in-the-sky thinking is a luxury we can no longer afford.

The ideological consequences of the demise of a faith in progress, technological omnipotence, and the millennial orientation will clearly be profound. The result cannot but be a radically altered ideology, a wholly new American outlook. What will this be? All too temptingly it may be a leap to the opposite extreme: to hopelessness, despondency, discouragement—the sense of impotence and *après nous le déluge*. I am afraid that such an era of disillusionment may well be the natural consequence of the presently popular rhetoric of the environmental crisis. And the American people do not have a particularly good record for sensible action in a time of disappointed expectations. Our basic weakness is a rather nonstandard problem of morale: a failure not of nerve but of patience.

Yet such a result—despair and disillusionment—seems to me wholly unwarranted. It is realism not hopelessness that provides the proper remedy for overconfidence. Let us by all means carry on the struggle to "save the environment" by all feasible steps. But let us not entertain misguided expectations about the prospects of success—expectations whose probable disappointment cannot but result in despondency, recrimination, and the tempting resort to the dire political measures that are natural to gravely disillusioned people.

The stance I see as necessary is not one of fatalistic resignation but of carrying on the good fight to save the environment—but doing so in fully realistic awareness that we are carrying on a limited war in which an actual victory may well lie beyond our grasp. It has taken an extraordinarily difficult struggle for us to arrive at a limited war perspective in international relations under the inexorable pressure of the political and technological facts of our times. And we have not even begun to move toward the corresponding mentality in the sphere of social problems and domestic difficulties. Yet just this—as I see it—is one of the crucial sociotechnological imperatives of our day.

Conclusion

The time has come for summing up. The conception that the quality of life—currently under threat by the environmental crisis—represents simply another one of those binds for which the welfare economists' classic prescription of "producing oneself out of it" seems to me profoundly misguided. In my discussion I have set before you the hypothesis of the environmental crisis as not really a crisis at all, but the inauguration of a permanent condition of things.

I have tried to argue that one of the main implications of this is a reversal of the ongoing escalation of expectations that is and long has been rife among Americans. In various crucial respects regarding the quality of life we just may have to settle for less. I have maintained that this development will exact from Americans a great price in terms of ideological revisionism. In particular, it will demand as victims our inclination to progressivism, our Promethean faith in man's technological omnipotence, and our penchant for millennial thinking. What is needed in the face of the environmental crisis at this point, as I see it, may well be not a magisterial confidence that things can be put right, but a large dose of cool realism tempered with stoic resignation. We had better get used to the idea that we may have to scale down our expectations and learn to settle for less in point of standard of living and quality of life.

This conclusion will very likely strike many as a repulsive instance of "gloom and doom" thinking. This would be quite wrong. The moral, as I see it, is at worst one of gloom without doom. Man is a being of enormous adaptability, resiliency, and power. He has learned to survive and make the best of it under some extremely difficult and unpleasant conditions. By all means, let us do everything we can to save the environment. But if we do not do a very good job of it—and I for one do not think we will—it is not necessarily the end of the world. Let us not sell man short. We have been in some unpleasant circumstances before and have managed to cope.

Review and Discussion Questions

1. Why does Rescher think that the environmental "crisis" is not really a crisis at all but a permanent condition? Do you agree? With regard to the quality of life, is it true that "we just may have to settle for less"?

2. Has Rescher correctly identified three main features of "American social ideology"? Would accepting his point of view require us to modify our ideology, as he maintains?

3. Is Rescher pessimistic or just "realistic"? Are Americans likely to adopt his perspective on the environmental crisis? What would be the results if they did?

The Place of Nonhumans in Environmental Issues

Peter Singer

Professor of philosophy Peter Singer argues that the effects of our environmental actions on nonhumans should figure directly in our deliberations about what we ought to do. Because animals can feel pleasure and pain and have the capacity for subjective experience, they can therefore be said to have interests, interests we must not ignore. Singer contends that we must extend the moral principle of "equal consideration of interests" to include the interests of nonhumans, and he sketches the implications of our doing so—including the necessity of abandoning our present practice of rearing and killing other animals for food.

I. Humans and Nonhumans

When we humans change the environment in which we live, we often harm ourselves. If we discharge cadmium into a bay and eat shellfish from that bay, we become ill and may die. When our industries and automobiles pour noxious fumes into the atmosphere, we find a displeasing smell in the air, the long-term results of which may be every bit as deadly as cadmium poisoning. The harm that humans do the environment, however, does not rebound solely, or even chiefly, on humans. It is nonhumans who bear the most direct burden of human interference with nature.

By "nonhumans" I mean to refer to all living things other than human beings, though for reasons to be given later, it is with nonhuman animals, rather than plants, that I am chiefly concerned. It is also important, in the context of environmental issues, to note that living things may be regarded either collectively or as individuals. In debates about the environment the most important way of regarding living things collectively has been to regard them as species. Thus, when environmentalists worry about the future of the blue whale, they usually are thinking of the blue whale as a species, rather than of individual blue whales. But this is not, of course, the only way in which one can think of blue whales, or other animals, and one of the topics I shall discuss is whether we should be concerned about what we are doing to the environment primarily insofar as it threatens entire species of nonhumans, or primarily insofar as it affects individual nonhuman animals.

The general question, then, is how the effects of our actions on the environment of nonhuman beings should figure in our deliberations about what we ought to do. There is an unlimited variety of contexts in which this issue could arise. To take just one: Suppose that it is considered necessary to build a new power station, and there are two sites, A and B, under consideration. In most respects the sites are equally suitable, but building the power station on site A would be more expensive because the greater depth of shifting soil at that site will require deeper foundations; on the other hand to build on site B will destroy a favored breeding ground for thousands of wildfowl. Should the presence of the wildfowl enter into the decision as to where to build? And if so, in what manner should it enter, and how heavily should it weigh?

From K. E. Goodpaster and K. M Sayre, eds., *Ethics and Problems of the 21st Century* (Notre Dame, Ind.: University of Notre Dame Press, 1979). Reprinted by permission. (Section headings have been added.)

In a case like this the effects of our actions on nonhuman animals could be taken into account in two quite different ways: directly, giving the lives and welfare of nonhuman animals an intrinsic significance which must count in any moral calculation; or indirectly, so that the effects of our actions on nonhumans are morally significant only if they have consequences for humans. . . .

II. Speciesism

The view that the effects of our actions on other animals has no direct moral significance is not as likely to be openly advocated today as it was in the past; yet it is likely to be accepted implicitly and acted upon. When planners perform cost-benefit studies on new projects, the costs and benefits are costs and benefits for human beings only. This does not mean that the impact of the power station or highway on wildlife is ignored altogether, but it is included only indirectly. That a new reservoir would drown a valley teeming with wildlife is taken into account only under some such heading as the value of the facilities for recreation that the valley affords. In calculating this value, the cost-benefit study will be neutral between forms of recreation like hunting and shooting and those like bird watching and bush walking—in fact hunting and shooting are likely to contribute more to the benefit side of the calculations because larger sums of money are spent on them, and they therefore benefit manufacturers and retailers of firearms as well as the hunters and shooters themselves. The suffering experienced by the animals whose habitat is flooded is not reckoned into the costs of the operation; nor is the recreational value obtained by the hunters and shooters offset by the cost to the animals that their recreation involves.

Despite its venerable origin, the view that the effects of our actions on nonhuman animals have no intrinsic moral significance can be shown to be arbitrary and morally indefensible. If a being suffers, the fact that it is not a member of our own species cannot be a moral reason for failing to take its suffering into account. This becomes obvious if we consider the analogous attempt by white slave-owners to deny consideration to the interests of blacks. These white racists limited their moral concern to their own race, so the suffering of a black did not have the same moral significance as the suffering of a white. We now recognize that in doing so they were making an arbitrary distinction, and that the existence of suffering, rather than the race of the sufferer, is what is really morally significant. The point remains true if "species" is substituted for "race." The logic of racism and the logic of the position we have been discussing, which I have elsewhere referred to as "speciesism," are indistinguishable; and if we reject the former then consistency demands that we reject the latter too.[1]

It should be clearly understood that the rejection of speciesism does not imply that the different species are in fact equal in respect of such characteristics as intelligence, physical strength, ability to communicate, capacity to suffer, ability to damage the environment, or anything else. After all, the moral principle of human equality cannot be taken as implying that all humans are equal in these respect either—if it did, we would have to give up the idea of human equality. That one being is more intelligent than another does not entitle him to enslave, exploit, or disregard the interests of the less intelligent being. The moral basis of equality among humans is not equality in fact, but the principle of equal consideration of interests, and it is this principle that, in consistency, must be extended to any nonhumans who have interests.

III. Nonhumans Have Interests

There may be some doubt about whether any nonhuman beings have interests. This doubt may arise because of uncertainty about what it is to have an interest, or because of uncertainty about the nature of some nonhuman beings. So far as the concept of "interest" is the cause of doubt, I take the view that only a being with subjective experiences, such as the experience of pleasure or the experience of pain, can have interests in the full sense of the term; and that any being with such experiences does have at least one interest, namely, the interest in experiencing pleasure and avoiding pain. Thus consciousness, or the capacity for subjective experience, is both a necessary and a sufficient condition for having an interest. While there may be a loose sense of the term in which we can say that it is in the interests of a tree to be watered, this attenuated sense of the term is not the sense covered by the principle of equal consideration of interests. All we mean when we say that it is in the interests of a tree to be watered is that the tree needs water if it is to continue to live and grow normally; if we regard this as evidence that the tree has interests, we might almost as well say that it is in the interests of a car to be lubricated regularly because the car needs lubrication if it is to run properly. In neither case can we really mean (unless we impute consciousness to trees or cars) that the tree or car has any preference about the matter.

The remaining doubt about whether nonhuman beings have interests is, then, a doubt about whether nonhuman beings have subjective experiences like the experience of pain. I have argued elsewhere that the commonsense view that birds and mammals feel pain is well founded,[2] but more serious doubts arise as we move down the evolutionary scale. Vertebrate animals have nervous systems broadly similar to our own and behave in ways that resemble our own pain behavior when subjected to stimuli that we would find painful; so the inference that vertebrates are capable of feeling pain is a reasonable one, though not as strong as it is if limited to mammals and birds. When we go beyond vertebrates to insects, crustaceans, mollusks and so on, the existence of subjective states becomes more dubious, and with very simple organisms it is difficult to believe that they could be conscious. As for plants, though there have been sensational claims that plants are not only conscious, but even psychic, there is no hard evidence that supports even the more modest claim.[3]

The boundary of beings who may be taken as having interests is therefore not an abrupt boundary, but a broad range in which the assumption that the being has interests shifts from being so strong as to be virtually certain to being so weak as to be highly improbable. The principle of equal consideration of interests must be applied with this in mind, so that where there is a clash between a virtually certain interest and highly doubtful one, it is the virtually certain interest that ought to prevail.

In this manner our moral concern ought to extend to all beings who have interests. . . .

IV. Equal Consideration of Interests

Giving equal consideration to the interests of two different beings does not mean treating them alike or holding their lives to be of equal value. We may recognize that the interests of one being are greater than those of another, and equal consideration will then lead us to sacrifice the being with lesser interests, if one or the other must be sacrificed. For instance, if for some reason a choice has to be made between saving the life of a normal human being and that of a dog, we might well decide to save the human because he, with his greater awareness of what is going to happen, will suffer more before he dies; we may also take into account the likelihood that it is the family and friends of the human who will suffer more; and finally, it would be the human who had the greater potential for future happiness. This decision would be in accordance with the principle of equal consideration of interests, for the interests of the dog get the same consideration as those of the human, and the loss to the dog is not discounted because the dog is not a member of our species. The outcome is as it is because the balance of interests favors the human. In a different situation—say, if the human were grossly mentally defective and without family or anyone else who would grieve for it—the balance of interests might favor the nonhuman.[4]

The more positive side of the principle of equal consideration is this: where interests are equal, they must be given equal weight. So where human and nonhuman animals share an interest—as in the case of the interest in avoiding physical pain—we must give as much weight to violations of the interest of the nonhumans as we do to similar violations of the human's interest. This does not mean, of course, that it is as bad to hit a horse with a stick as it is to hit a human being, for the same blow would cause less pain to the animal with the tougher skin. The principle holds between similar amounts of felt pain, and what this is will vary from case to case.

It may be objected that we cannot tell exactly how much pain another animal is suffering, and that therefore the principle is impossible to apply. While I do not deny the difficulty and even, so far as precise measurement is concerned, the impossibility of comparing the subjective experiences of members of different species, I do not think that the problem is different in kind from the problem of comparing the subjective experiences of two members of our own species. Yet this is something we do all the time, for instance when we judge that a wealthy person will suffer less by being taxed at a higher rate than a poor person will gain from the welfare benefits paid for by the tax; or when we decide to take our two children to the beach instead of to a fair, because although the older one would prefer the fair, the younger one has stronger preference the other way. These comparisons may be very rough, but since there is nothing better, we must use them; it would be irrational to refuse to do so simply because they are rough. Moreover, rough as they are, there are many situations in which we can be reasonably sure which way the balance of interests lies. While a difference of species may make comparisons rougher still, the basic problem is the same, and the comparisons are still often good enough to use, in the absence of anything more precise. . . .

The difficulty of making the required comparison will mean that the application of this conclusion is controversial in many cases, but there will be some situations in which it is clear enough. Take, for instance, the wholesale poisoning of animals that is euphemistically known as "pest control." The authorities who conduct these campaigns give no consideration to the suffering they inflict on the "pests," and invariably use the method of slaughter they believe to be cheapest and most effective. The result is that hundreds of millions of rabbits have died agonizing deaths from the artificially introduced disease, myxomatosis, or from poisons like "ten-eighty"; coyotes and other wild dogs have died painfully from cyanide poisoning; and all manner of wild animals have endured days of thirst, hunger, and fear with a mangled limb caught in a leg-hold trap.[5] Granting, for the sake of argument, the necessity for pest control—though this has rightly been questioned—the fact remains that no serious attempts have been made to introduce alternative means of control and thereby reduce the incalculable amount of suffering caused by present methods. It would not, presumably, be beyond modern science to produce a substance which, when eaten by rabbits or coyotes, produced sterility instead of a drawn-out death. Such methods might be more expensive, but can anyone doubt that if a similar amount of human suffering were at stake, the expense would be borne?

Another clear instance in which the principle of equal consideration of interests would indicate methods different from those presently used is in the timber industry. There are two basic methods of obtaining timber from forests. One is to cut only selected mature or dead trees, leaving the forest substantially intact. The other, known as clear-cutting, involves chopping down everything that grows in a given area, and then reseeding. Obviously when a large area is clear-cut, wild animals find their whole living area destroyed in a few days, whereas selected felling makes a relatively minor disturbance. But clear-cutting is cheaper, and timber companies therefore use this method and will continue to do so unless forced to do otherwise.[6] . . .

V. The Meat Industry

It is not merely the act of killing that indicates what we are ready to do to other species in order to gratify our tastes. The suffering we inflict on the animals while they are alive is perhaps an even clearer indication of our speciesism than the fact that we are prepared to kill them.[7] In order to have meat on the table at a price that people can afford, our society tolerates methods of meat production that confine sentient animals in cramped, unsuitable conditions for the entire durations of their lives. Animals are treated like machines that convert fodder into flesh, and any innovation that results in a higher "conversion ratio" is liable to be adopted. As one authority on the subject has said, "cruelty is acknowledged only when profitability ceases."[8] So hens are crowded four or five to a cage with a floor area of twenty inches by eighteen inches, or around the size of a single page of the *New York Times*. The cages have wire floors, since this reduces cleaning costs, though wire is unsuitable for the hens feet; the floors slope, since this makes the eggs roll down for easy collection, although this makes it difficult for the hens to rest comfortably. In these conditions all the birds' natural instincts are thwarted: They cannot stretch their wings fully, walk freely, dust-bathe, scratch the ground, or build a nest. Although they have never known other conditions, observers have noticed that the birds vainly try to perform these actions. Frustrated at their inability to do so, they often develop what farmers call "vices," and peck each other to death. To prevent this, the beaks of young birds are often cut off.

This kind of treatment is not limited to poultry. Pigs are now also being reared in cages inside sheds. These animals are comparable to dogs in intelligence, and need a varied, stimulating environment if they are not to suffer from stress and boredom. Anyone who kept a dog in the way in which pigs are frequently kept would be liable to prosecution, in England at least, but because our interest in exploiting pigs is greater than our interest in exploiting dogs, we object to cruelty to dogs while consuming the produce of cruelty to pigs. Of the other animals, the condition of veal calves is perhaps worst of all, since these animals are so closely confined that they cannot even turn around or get up and lie down freely. In this way they do not develop unpalatable muscle. They are also made anaemic and kept short of roughage, to keep their flesh pale, since white veal fetches a higher price; as a result they develop a craving for iron and roughage, and have been observed to gnaw wood off the sides of their stalls, and lick greedily at any rusty hinge that is within reach.

Since, as I have said, none of these practices cater to anything more than our pleasures of taste, our practice of rearing and killing other animals in order to eat them is a clear instance of the sacrifice of the most important interests of other beings in order to satisfy trivial interests of our own. To avoid speciesism we must stop this practice, and each of us has a moral obligation to cease supporting the practice. Our custom is all the support that the meat industry needs. The decision to cease giving it that support may be difficult, but it is no more difficult than it would have been for a white Southerner to go against the traditions of his society and free his slaves; if we do not change our dietary habits, how can we censure those slaveholders who would not change their own way of living?

Notes

1. For a fuller statement of this argument, see my *Animal Liberation* (New York: A New York Review Book, 1975), especially ch. 1.
2. *Ibid.*
3. See, for instance, the comments by Arthur Galston in *National History*, 83, no. 3 (March 1974): 18, on the "evidence" cited in such books as *The Secret Life of Plants*.
4. Singer, *Animal Liberation*, pp. 20–23.
5. See J. Olsen, *Slaughter the Animals, Poison the Earth* (New York: Simon and Schuster, 1971), especially pp. 153–164.
6. See R. and V. Routley, *The Fight for the Forests* (Canberra: Australian National University Press, 1974); for a thoroughly documented indictment of clearcutting in America, see *Time*, May 17, 1976.
7. Although one might think that killing a being is obviously the ultimate wrong one can do to it, I think that the infliction of suffering is a clearer indication of speciesism because it might be argued that at least part of what is wrong with killing a human is that most humans are conscious of their existence over time, and have desires and purposes that extend into the future — see, for instance, M. Tooley, "Abortion and Infanticide," *Philosophy and Public Affairs*, vol. 2, no. 1 (1972). Of course, if one took this view one would have to hold — as Tooley does — that killing a human infant or mental defective is not in itself wrong, and is less serious than killing certain higher mammals that probably do have a sense of their own existence over time.
8. Ruth Harrison, *Animal Machines* (Stuart, London, 1964). This book provides an eye-opening account of intensive farming methods for those unfamiliar with the subject.

Review and Discussion Questions

1. Describe the human practices that most clearly demonstrate speciesism.
2. What does the principle of "equal consideration of interests" imply for our treatment of animals? What does it not imply?
3. Give examples of how adherence to the principle of equal consideration would change our conduct. What are the principle's implications for business?
4. Singer rejects "our practice of rearing and killing other animals in order to eat them." Explain why. How might a critic respond to his argument? Can meat eating be morally justified?

Should Trees Have Standing? — Toward Legal Rights for Natural Objects

Christopher D. Stone

Professor of law Christopher D. Stone argues that we should extend legal rights to forests, oceans, rivers, and other natural objects. Although the proposal may sound absurd, so did earlier proposals to extend rights, for example, to blacks and women. Stone discusses what it means to be a holder of legal rights and how extending rights to natural objects would change dramatically our approach to environmental protection. Stone's proposal is in part pragmatic—a legal move to enable environmentalists to better protect the environment. But it also reflects the view that nature deserves to be protected for its own sake.

Throughout legal history, each successive extension of rights to some new entity has been, theretofore, a bit unthinkable. We are inclined to suppose the rightlessness of rightless "things" to be a decree of Nature, not a legal convention acting in support of some status quo. It is thus that we defer considering the choices involved in all their moral, social, and economic dimensions. And so the United States Supreme Court could straightfacedly tell us in *Dred Scott* that Blacks had been denied the rights of citizenship "as a subordinate and inferior class of beings, who had been subjugated by the dominant race. . . ."[1] In the nineteenth century, the highest court in California explained that Chinese had not the right to testify against white men in criminal matters because they were "a race of people whom nature has marked as inferior, and who are incapable of progress or intellectual development beyond a certain point . . . between whom and ourselves nature has placed an impassable difference."[2] The popular conception of the Jew in the 13th Century contributed to a law which treated them as "men *ferae naturae*, protected by a quasi-forest law. Like the roe and the deer, they form an order apart."[3] Recall, too, that it was not so long ago that the foetus was "like the roe and the deer." In an early suit attempting to establish a wrongful death action on behalf of a negligently killed foetus (now widely accepted practice), Holmes, then on the Massachusetts Supreme Court, seems to have

thought it simply inconceivable "that a man might owe a civil duty and incur a conditional prospective liability in tort to one not yet in being."[4] The first woman in Wisconsin who thought she might have a right to practice law was told that she did not, in the following terms:

> The law of nature destines and qualifies the female sex for the bearing and nurture of the children of our race and for the custody of the homes of the world. . . . [A]ll life-long callings of women, inconsistent with these radical and sacred duties of their sex, as is the profession of the law, are departures from the order of nature; and when voluntary, treason against it. . . . The peculiar qualities of womanhood, its gentle graces, its quick sensibility, its tender susceptibility, its purity, its delicacy, its emotional impulses, its subordination of hard reason to sympathetic feeling, are surely not qualifications for forensic strife. Nature has tempered woman as little for the juridical conflicts of the court room, as for the physical conflicts of the battle field. . . .[5]

The fact is, that each time there is a movement to confer rights onto some new "entity," the proposal is bound to sound odd or frightening or laughable. This is partly because until the rightless thing receives its rights, we cannot see it as anything but a *thing* for the use of "us" — those who are holding rights at the time. In this vein, what is striking about the Wisconsin case above is that the court, for all its talk about women, so clearly was never able to see women as they are (and might become). All it could see was the popular "idealized" version of *an object it needed*. Such is the way the slave South looked upon the Black. There is something of a seamless web involved: there will be resistance to giving the thing "rights" until it can be seen and valued for itself; yet, it is hard to see it and value it for itself until we can bring ourselves

Christopher D. Stone, "Should Trees Have Standing?—Toward Legal Rights for Natural Objects," *Southern California Law Review* 45 (1972). Reprinted with the permission of the *Southern California Law Review*.

to give it "rights" — which is almost inevitably going to sound inconceivable to a large group of people.

The reason for this little discourse on the unthinkable, the reader must know by now, if only from the title of the paper. I am quite seriously proposing that we give legal rights to forests, oceans, rivers and other so-called "natural objects" in the environment — indeed, to the natural environment as a whole. . . .

Toward Rights for the Environment

Now, to say that the natural environment should have rights is not to say anything as silly as that no one should be allowed to cut down a tree. We say human beings have rights, but — at least as of the time of this writing — they can be executed. Corporations have rights, but they cannot plead the fifth amendment; *In re Gault* gave 15-year-olds certain rights in juvenile proceedings, but it did not give them the right to vote. Thus, to say that the environment should have rights is not to say that it should have every right we can imagine, or even the same body of rights as human beings have. Nor is it to say that everything in the environment should have the same rights as every other thing in the environment. . . .

For a thing to be *a holder of legal rights* something more is needed than that some authoritative body will review the actions and processes of those who threaten it. As I shall use the term, "holder of legal rights," each of three additional criteria must be satisfied. All three, one will observe, go towards making a thing *count* jurally — to have a legally recognized worth and dignity in its own right, and not merely to serve as a means to benefit "us" (whoever the contemporary group of rights-holders may be). They are, first, that the thing can institute legal actions *at its behest*; second, that in determining the granting of legal relief, the court must take *injury to it* into account; and, third, that relief must run to the *benefit of it*. . . .

The Rightlessness of Natural Objects at Common Law

Consider, for example the common law's posture toward the pollution of a stream. True, courts have always been able, in some circumstances, to issue orders that will stop the pollution. . . . But the stream itself is fundamentally rightless, with implications that deserve careful reconsideration.

The first sense in which the stream is not a rights-holder has to do with standing. The stream itself has none. So far as the common law is concerned, there is in general no way to challenge the polluter's actions save at the behest of a lower riparian — another human being — able to show an invasion of *his* rights. . . .

The second sense in which the common law denies "rights" to natural objects has to do with the way in which the merits are decided in those cases in which someone is competent and willing to establish standing. At its more primitive levels, the system protected the "rights" of the property owning human with minimal weighting of any values. . . . Today we have come more and more to make balances — but only such as will adjust the economic best interests of identifiable humans. . . .

Thus, we find the highest court of Pennsylvania refusing to stop a coal company from discharging polluted mine water into a tributary of the Lackawana River because a plaintiff's "grievance is for a mere personal inconvenience; and . . . mere private personal inconveniences . . . must yield to the necessities of a great public industry, which although in the hands of a private corporation, subserves a great public interest."[6] The stream itself is lost sight of in "a quantitative compromise between *two* conflicting interests."[7]

The third way in which the common law makes natural objects rightless has to do with who is regarded as the beneficiary of a favorable judgment. Here, too, it makes a considerable difference that it is not the natural object that counts in its own right. To illustrate this point let me begin by observing that it makes perfectly good sense to speak of, and ascertain, the legal damage to a natural object, if only in the sense of "making it whole" with respect to the most obvious factors. The costs of making a forest whole, for example, would include the costs of reseeding, repairing watersheds, restocking wildlife — the sorts of costs the Forest Service undergoes after a fire. Making a polluted stream whole would include the costs of restocking with fish, water-fowl, and other animal and vegetable life, dredging, washing out impurities, establishing natural and/or artificial aerating agents, and so forth. Now, what is important to note is that, under our present system, even if a plaintiff riparian wins a water pollution suit for damages, no money goes to the benefit of the stream itself to repair *its* damages. . . .

None of the natural objects, whether held in common or situated on private land, has any of the three criteria of a rights-holder. They have no standing in their own right; their unique damages do not count in determining outcome; and they are not the beneficiaries of awards. In such fashion, these objects have traditionally been regarded by the common law, and even by all but the most recent legislation, as objects for man to conquer and master and use—in such a way as the law once looked upon "man's" relationships to African Negroes. Even where special measures have been taken to conserve them, as by seasons on game and limits on timber cutting, the dominant motive has been to conserve them *for us*—for the greatest good of the greatest number of human beings. Conservationists, so far as I am aware, are generally reluctant to maintain otherwise. As the name implies, they want to conserve and guarantee *our* consumption and *our* enjoyment of these other living things. In their own right, natural objects have counted for little, in law as in popular movements.

As I mentioned at the outset, however, the rightlessness of the natural environment can and should change; it already shows some signs of doing so.

Toward Having Standing in Its Own Right

It is not inevitable, nor is it wise, that natural objects should have no rights to seek redress in their own behalf. It is no answer to say that streams and forests cannot have standing because streams and forests cannot speak. Corporations cannot speak either; nor can states, estates, infants, incompetents, municipalities or universities. Lawyers speak for them, as they customarily do for the ordinary citizen with legal problems. One ought, I think, to handle the legal problems of natural objects as one does the problems of legal incompetents—human beings who have become vegetable. If a human being shows signs of becoming senile and has affairs that he is de jure incompetent to manage, those concerned with his well being make such a showing to the court, and someone is designated by the court with the authority to manage the incompetent's affairs. . . .

On a parity of reasoning we should have a system in which, when a friend of a natural object perceives it to be endangered, he can apply to a court for the creation of a guardianship. . . .

The potential "friends" that such a statutory scheme would require will hardly be lacking. The Sierra Club, Environmental Defense Fund, Friends of the Earth, Natural Resources Defense Counsel, and the Izaak Walton League are just some of the many groups which have manifested unflagging dedication to the environment and which are becoming increasingly capable of marshalling the requisite technical experts and lawyers. If, for example, the Environmental Defense Fund should have reason to believe that some company's strip mining operations might be irreparably destroying the ecological balance of large tracts of land, it could, under this procedure, apply to the court in which the lands were situated to be appointed guardian. As guardian, it might be given rights of inspection (or visitation) to determine and bring to the court's attention a fuller finding on the land's condition. If there were indications that under the substantive law some redress might be available on the land's behalf, then the guardian would be entitled to raise the land's rights in the land's name, *i.e.*, without having to make the roundabout and often unavailing demonstration . . . that the "rights" of the club's members were being invaded. . . .

One reason for making the environment itself the beneficiary of a judgment is to prevent it from being "sold out" in a negotiation among private litigants who agree not to enforce rights that have been established among themselves. Protection from this will be advanced by making the natural object a party to an injunctive settlement. Even more importantly, we should make it a beneficiary of money awards. . . .

The idea of assessing damages as best we can and placing them in a trust fund is far more realistic than a hope that a total "freeze" can be put on the environmental status quo. Nature is a continuous theatre in which things and species (eventually man) are destined to enter and exit. In the meantime, co-existence of man and his environment means that *each* is going to have to compromise for the better of both. Some pollution of streams, for example, will probably be inevitable for some time. Instead of setting an unrealizable goal of enjoining absolutely the discharge of all such pollutants, the trust fund concept would (a) help assure that pollution would occur only in those instances where the social need for the pollutant's product (via his present method of production) was so high as to enable the polluter to cover *all* homocentric costs, plus some estimated costs to the environment *per se* and (b) would be a corpus for preserving monies, if necessary, while the technology developed to a point where repairing the damaged portion of the environment was feasible. Such a fund might even finance the requisite research and development. . . .

A radical new conception of man's relationship to the rest of nature would not only be a step towards solving the material planetary problems; there are strong reasons for such a changed consciousness from the point of making us far better humans. If we only stop for a moment and look at the underlying human qualities that our present attitudes toward property and nature draw upon and reinforce, we have to be struck by how stultifying of our own personal growth and satisfaction they can become when they take rein of us. Hegel, in "justifying" private property, unwittingly reflects the tone and quality of some of the needs that are played upon:

> A person has as his substantive end the right of putting his will into any and every thing and thereby making it his, because it has no such end in itself and derives its destiny and soul from his will. This is the absolute right of appropriation which man has over all "things."[8]

What is it within us that gives us this need not just to satisfy basic biological wants, but to extend our wills over things, to object-ify them, to make them ours, to manipulate them, to keep them at a psychic distance? Can it all be explained on "rational" bases? Should we not be suspect of such needs within us, cautious as to why we wish to gratify them? When I first read that passage of Hegel, I immediately thought not only of the emotional contrast with Spinoza, but of the passage in Carson McCullers' *A Tree, A Rock, A Cloud*, in which an old derelict has collared a twelve year old boy in a streetcar cafe. The old man asks whether the boy knows "how love should be begun?"

> The old man leaned closer and whispered:
> "A tree. A rock. A cloud."
> "The weather was like this in Portland, he said. "At the time my science was begun. I meditated and I started very cautious. I would

pick up something from the street and take it home with me. I bought a goldfish and I concentrated on the goldfish and I loved it. I graduated from one thing to another. Day by day I was getting this technique. . . .
> . . . "For six years now I have gone around by myself and built up my science. And now I am a master. Son. I can love anything. No longer do I have to think about it even. I see a street full of people and a beautiful light comes in me. I watch a bird in the sky. Or I meet a traveler on the road. Everything, Son. And anybody. All stranger and all loved! Do you realize what a science like mine can mean?"[9]

To be able to get away from the view that Nature is a collection of useful senseless objects is, as McCullers' "madman" suggests, deeply involved in the development of our abilities to love — or, if that is putting it too strongly, to be able to reach a heightened awareness of our own, and others' capacities in their mutual interplay. To do so, we have to give up some psychic investment in our sense of separateness and specialness in the universe. And this, in turn, is hard giving indeed, because it involves us in a fight backwards, into earlier stages of civilization and childhood in which we had to trust (and perhaps fear) our environment, for we had not then the power to master it. Yet, in doing so, we — as persons — gradually free ourselves of needs for supportive illusions. Is not this one of the triumphs for "us" of our giving legal rights to (or acknowledging the legal rights of) the Blacks and women? . . .

The time may be on hand when these sentiments, and the early stirrings of the law can be coalesced into a radical new theory of myth — felt as well as intellectualized — of man's relationships to the rest of nature. I do not mean "myth" in a demeaning sense of the term, but in the sense in which, at different times in history, our social "facts" and relationships have been comprehended and integrated by reference to the "myths" that we are co-signers of a social contract, that the Pope is God's agent, and that all men are created equal. Pantheism, Shinto and Tao all have myths to offer. But they are all, each in its own fashion, quaint, primitive and archaic. What is needed is a myth that can fit our growing body of knowledge of geophysics, biology and the cosmos. In this vein, I do not think it too remote that we may come to regard the Earth, as some have suggested, as one organism, of which Mankind is a functional part — the mind, perhaps: different from the rest of nature, but different as a man's brain is from his lungs. . . .

Notes

1. *Dred Scott v. Sanford*, 60 U.S. (19 How.) 396, 404–05 (1856).
2. *People v. Hall*, 4 Cal. 399, 405 (1854).
3. Schechter, "The Rightlessness of Mediaeval English Jewry," 45 *Jewish Q. Rev.* 121, 135 (1954) quoting from M. Bateson, *Medieval England* 139 (1904).
4. *Dietrich v. Inhabitants of Northampton*, 138 Mass. 14, 16 (1884).
5. *In re Goddell*, 39 Wisc. 232, 245 (1875).
6. *Pennsylvania Coal Co. v. Sanderson*, 113 Pa. 126, 149, 6 A. 453, 459 (1886).
7. Hand, J. in *Smith v. Staso Milling Co.*, 18 F.2d 736, 738 (2d Cir. 1927) (emphasis added).
8. G. Hegel, *Hegel's Philosophy of Right*, 41 (T. Knox transl. 1945).
9. C. McCullers, *The Ballad of the Sad Cafe and Other Stories*, 150–51 (1958).

Review and Discussion Questions

1. What does it mean to be a "holder of legal rights"?
2. Do you think the idea of granting legal rights to natural objects is workable? What would be the practical results of doing so?
3. Singer states that "consciousness, or the capacity for subjective experience, is both a necessary and a sufficient condition for having an interest." This suggests that he would disagree with Stone's talk of protecting the "interests" of nature. Whose point of view is more plausible? Can something without conscious awareness have rights?
4. Does our conception of our relationship to nature need to be radically changed, as Stone suggests?

For Further Reading

Robin Attfield, *The Ethics of Environmental Concern* (New York: Columbia University Press, 1983) is a solid introduction to environmental ethics.

R. G. Frey, *Rights, Killing and Suffering* (Oxford: Basil Blackwell, 1983) defends meat eating.

Lisa H. Newton, "The Chainsaws of Greed: The Case of Pacific Lumber," *Business and Professionals Ethics Journal* 8 (Fall 1989) explores the issues of environmental and business ethics that engulf the logging industry.

Derek Parfit, *Reasons and Persons* (Oxford: Oxford University Press, 1984), part 4, is a philosophically challenging exploration of some puzzling aspects of our obligations to future generations.

Tom Regan, ed., *Earthbound: Introductory Essays in Environmental Ethics* (New York: Random House, 1984) and **Donald VanDeVeer** and **Christine Pierce,** eds., *People, Penguins, and Plastic Trees* (Belmont, Calif.: Wadsworth, 1986) are very useful collections of writings on various topics in environmental ethics.

Mark Sagoff, "Process or Product? Ethical Priorities in Environmental Management," *Environmental Ethics* 8 (Summer 1986) discusses two conflicting approaches to environmental regulation.

Peter Singer, *Animal Liberation* (New York: New York Review Book [distributed by Random House], 1975) is a seminal work advocating a radical change in our treatment of animals.

Peter Singer and **Tom Regan,** eds., *Animal Rights and Human Obligations* (Englewood Cliffs, N.J.: Prentice-Hall, 1976) contains good, generally pro-animal-rights essays.

Jang B. Singh and **V. C. Lakhan,** "Business Ethics and the International Trade in Hazardous Wastes," *Journal of Business Ethics* 8 (November 1989) analyzes the international aspects of a growing problem.

INDEX